PSYCHOLOGY

THE PEARSON CUSTOM LIBRARY

Portland State University
Introductory Psychology
PSYCHOLOGY: 200 and 204

PEARSON   ISBN 10: 1-269-28016-3
ISBN 13: 978-1-269-28016-7

Table of Contents

Psychology and Scientific Thinking

Psychology and Scientific Thinking

A FRAMEWORK FOR EVERYDAY LIFE

Think About It

Is psychology mostly just common sense?

Should we trust most self-help books?

Is psychology really a science?

Are claims that can't be proven wrong scientific?

Are all clinical psychologists psychotherapists?

Watch in **MyPsychLab** the **Video:**
Thinking Like a Psychologist: Debunking Myths

Each of these panels from everyday life poses a different psychological question: (1) Why do we fall in love? (2) Why do some of us become depressed for no apparent reason? (3) What makes us angry? Although the science of psychology doesn't provide easy answers to any of these questions, it does offer valuable insights into them.

Psychology and Scientific Thinking

Listen in **MyPsychLab** to chapter audio

Test of Popular Psychology Knowledge

1. Most people use only about 10 percent of their brain capacity.   **True / False**

2. Newborn babies are virtually blind and deaf.   **True / False**

3. Hypnosis enhances the accuracy of our memories.   **True / False**

4. All people with dyslexia see words backward (like *tac* instead of *cat*).   **True / False**

5. In general, it's better to express anger than to hold it in.   **True / False**

6. The lie-detector (polygraph) test is 90–95 percent accurate at detecting falsehoods.   **True / False**

7. People tend to be romantically attracted to individuals who are opposite them in personality and attitudes.   **True / False**

8. The more people present at an emergency, the more likely it is that at least one of them will help.   **True / False**

9. People with schizophrenia have more than one personality.   **True / False**

10. All effective psychotherapies require clients to get to the root of their problems in childhood.   **True / False**

For many of you reading this text, it's may be your first psychology course. If you're like most people, much of what you've learned about psychology comes from watching television programs and movies, listening to radio call-in shows, reading self-help books and popular magazines, surfing the Internet, and talking to friends. In short, most of your psychology knowledge probably derives from the popular psychology industry: a sprawling network of everyday sources of information about human behavior.

Take a moment to review the preceding ten questions. Beginning psychology students typically assume that they know the answers to most of them. That's hardly surprising, as these assertions have become part of popular psychology lore. Yet most students are surprised to learn that *all* ten of these statements are false! This little exercise illustrates a take-home message: *Although common sense can be enormously useful for some purposes, it's sometimes completely wrong* (Chabris & Simons, 2010). This can be especially true in psychology, a field that strikes many of us as self-evident, even obvious. In a sense, we're *all* psychologists, because we deal with psychological phenomena like love, friendship, anger, stress, happiness, sleep, memory, and language in our daily lives (Lilienfeld et al., 2009). Everyday experience can often be helpful in allowing us to navigate the psychological world, but it doesn't necessarily make us an expert (Kahneman & Klein, 2009).

What Is Psychology? Science Versus Intuition

1   Explain why psychology is more than just common sense.

2   Explain the importance of science as a set of safeguards against biases.

William James (1842–1910), often regarded as the founder of American psychology, once described psychology as a "nasty little subject." As James noted, psychology is difficult to study, and simple explanations of behavior are few and far between. Your study of psychology won't give you black-and-white answers to psychological questions, but you will acquire more insight into the hows and whys of human behavior.

Psychology and Levels of Analysis

The first question often posed in introductory psychology textbooks could hardly seem simpler: "what is psychology?" Although psychologists disagree about many things, they agree on one thing: psychology isn't easy to define (Henriques, 2004; Lilienfeld, 2004). For our purposes, though, we'll simply refer to **psychology** as the scientific study of the mind, brain, and behavior.

Psychology is a discipline that spans multiple **levels of analysis**. We can think of levels of analysis as rungs on a ladder, with the lower rungs tied most closely to biological influences and the higher rungs tied most closely to social influences (Ilardi & Feldman, 2001; Kendler, 2005). The levels of analysis in psychology stretch all the way from molecules to brain structures on the low rungs to thoughts, feelings, and emotions and to social and cultural influences on the high rungs, with many levels in between (Cacioppo et al., 2000; Satel & Lilienfeld, 2013) (see **FIGURE 1**). The lower rungs are more closely tied to what we traditionally call "the brain"; the higher rungs to what we traditionally call "the mind." But it's crucial to understand that "brain" and "mind" are just different ways of describing the same material "stuff" at different levels of analysis: the "mind" is really just the brain in action. Although psychologists may differ in which rungs they choose to investigate, they're united by a shared commitment to understanding the causes of human and animal behavior.

In our study of psychology, we need to keep one crucial guideline in mind: *to fully understand psychology, we must consider multiple levels of analysis*. That's because each level tells us something different, and we gain new knowledge from each vantage point. Some psychologists believe that biological factors—like the actions of the brain and its billions of nerve cells—are most critical for understanding the causes of behavior. Others believe that social factors—like parenting practices, peer influences, and culture—are most critical for understanding the causes of behavior (Meehl, 1972). We'll steer away from these two extremes, because both biological and social factors are essential for a complete understanding of psychology (Kendler, 2005).

What Makes Psychology Distinctive—and Fascinating

We can approach psychological questions scientifically, and in much the same way as we can approach questions in biology, chemistry, and physics. Yet in some ways, psychology is distinctive, if not unique, from other sciences. A host of challenges make the study of mind, brain, and behavior especially complex; yet it's precisely these challenges that also make psychology fascinating, because they contribute to scientific mysteries that psychologists have yet to solve. Here, we'll touch briefly on five especially intriguing challenges.

First, human behavior is difficult to predict, in part because almost all actions are **multiply determined**, that is, produced by many factors. That's why we need to be skeptical of *single-variable explanations* of behavior, which are widespread in popular psychology. Although it's tempting to explain complex human behaviors like violence in terms of a single causal factor like poverty, bad upbringing, or genes, such behaviors are almost surely due to the interplay of an enormous array of factors (Stern, 2002).

FIGURE 1 Levels of Analysis in Depression. We can view psychological phenomena, in this case the disorder of depression, at multiple levels of analysis, with lower levels being more biological and higher levels being more social. Each level provides unique information and offers a distinctive view of the phenomenon at hand. (Based on data from Ilardi, Rand, & Karwoski, 2007)

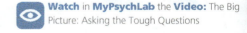

Watch in **MyPsychLab** the **Video:** The Big Picture: Asking the Tough Questions

psychology
the scientific study of the mind, brain, and behavior

levels of analysis
rungs on a ladder of analysis, with lower levels tied most closely to biological influences and higher levels tied most closely to social influences

multiply determined
caused by many factors

Psychology may not be one of the traditional hard sciences like chemistry, but many of its fundamental questions are even more difficult to answer.

In the museum of everyday life, causation isn't a one-way street. In conversations, one person influences a second person, who in turn influences the first person, who in turn influences the second person, and so on. This principle, called *reciprocal determinism*, makes it challenging to pinpoint the causes of behavior.

In a study by Chua, Boland, and Nisbett (2005), European Americans tend to focus more on the central details of photographs, like the tiger itself (top), whereas Asian Americans tend to focus more on the peripheral details, like the rocks and leaves surrounding the tiger (bottom).

individual differences
variations among people in their thinking, emotion, personality, and behavior

Second, psychological influences are rarely independent of each other, making it difficult to pin down which cause or causes are operating. Imagine yourself a scientist attempting to explain why some women develop *anorexia nervosa*, a severe eating disorder. You could start by identifying several factors that might contribute to anorexia nervosa, like anxiety-proneness, compulsive exercise, perfectionism, excessive concern with body image, and exposure to television programs that feature thin models. Let's say that you want to focus on just one of these potential influences, like perfectionism. Here's the problem: women who are perfectionists also tend to be anxious, to exercise a lot, to be overly concerned with their body image, to watch television programs that feature thin models, and so on (Egan et al., 2013). The fact that all of these factors tend to be interrelated makes it tricky to pinpoint which one actually contributes to anorexia nervosa. The odds are high that they all play at least some role.

Third, people differ from each other in thinking, emotion, personality, and behavior. These **individual differences** help to explain why we each person responds in different ways to the same objective situation, such as an insulting comment from a boss (Harkness & Lilienfeld, 1997). Entire fields of psychology, such as the study of intelligence, interests, personality, and mental illness, focus on individual differences (Lubinski, 2000). Individual differences make psychology challenging because they make it difficult to come up with explanations of behavior that apply to everyone; at the same time, they make psychology exciting, because people we might assume we understand well often surprise us in their reactions to life events.

Fourth, people often influence each other, often making it difficult to pin down what causes what (Wachtel, 1973). For example, if you're an extraverted person, you're likely to make the people around you more outgoing. In turn, their outgoing behavior may "feed back" to make you even more extraverted, and so on. This is an example of what Albert Bandura (1973) called *reciprocal determinism*—the fact that we mutually influence each other's behavior. Reciprocal determinism can make it challenging to isolate the causes of human behavior.

Fifth, people's behavior is often shaped by culture. Cultural differences, like individual differences, place limits on the generalizations that psychologists can draw about human nature (Henrich, Heine, & Norenzayan, 2010). To take one example, Richard Nisbett and his colleagues found that European-American and Chinese participants often attend to strikingly different things in pictures (Chua, Boland, & Nisbett, 2005). In one case, the researchers showed people a photograph of a tiger walking on rocks next to a river. Using eye-tracking technology, which allows researchers to determine where people are moving their eyes, they found that European Americans tend to look mostly at the tiger, whereas Chinese tend to look mostly at the plants and rocks surrounding it. This finding dovetails with evidence that European Americans tend to focus on central details, whereas Asian Americans tend to focus on peripheral or incidental details (Nisbett, 2003; Nisbett et al., 2001).

All five of these challenges are worth bearing in mind. The good news is that psychologists have made substantial progress toward solving all of them and that a deeper and richer appreciation of these challenges helps us to better predict—and in some cases understand—behavior.

Why We Can't Always Trust Our Common Sense

To understand why others act as they do, most of us trust our common sense—our gut intuitions about how the social world works. Yet, as we've already discovered, our intuitive understanding of ourselves and the world is frequently mistaken (Cacioppo, 2004; Van Hecke, 2007). As the quiz at the start of this chapter showed us, sometimes our commonsensical understanding of psychology isn't merely incorrect but entirely backward. For example, although many people believe the old adage "There's safety in numbers," psychological research actually shows that the more people present at an emergency, the *less* likely at least one of them will help (Darley & Latané, 1968a; Fischer et al., 2011; Latané & Nida, 1981).

Here's another illustration of why we can't always trust our common sense. Read the following well-known proverbs, most of which deal with human behavior, and ask yourself whether you agree with them:

1. Birds of a feather flock together.
2. Absence makes the heart grow fonder.
3. Better safe than sorry.
4. Two heads are better than one.
5. Actions speak louder than words.
6. Opposites attract.
7. Out of sight, out of mind.
8. Nothing ventured, nothing gained.
9. Too many cooks spoil the broth.
10. The pen is mightier than the sword.

To most of us, these proverbs all ring true. Yet in fact, each proverb contradicts the proverb across from it. So our common sense can lead us to believe two things that can't both be true simultaneously—or at least that are largely at odds with each other. Strangely enough, in most cases, we never notice the contradictions until other people, like the authors of an introductory psychology textbook, point them out to us. This example reminds us of why scientific psychology doesn't rely exclusively on intuition, speculation, or common sense.

NAIVE REALISM: IS SEEING BELIEVING? We trust our common sense largely because we're prone to **naive realism**: the belief that we see the world precisely as it is (Lilienfeld, Lohr, & Olatanji, 2008; Ross & Ward, 1996). We assume that "seeing is believing" and trust our intuitive perceptions of the world and ourselves. In daily life, naive realism often serves us well. If we're driving down a one-lane road and see a tractor trailer barreling toward us at 85 miles per hour, it's a good idea to get out of the way. Much of the time, we *should* trust our perceptions.

Yet appearances can sometimes be deceiving. The earth *seems* flat. The sun *seems* to revolve around the earth (see **FIGURE 2** for another example of deceptive appearances). Yet in both cases, our intuitions are wrong. Similarly, naive realism can trip us up when it comes to evaluating ourselves and others. Our common sense assures us that people who don't share our political views are biased but that we're objective. Yet psychological research demonstrates that just about all of us tend to evaluate political issues in a biased fashion (Pronin, Gilovich, & Ross, 2004). So our tendencies toward naive realism can lead us to draw incorrect conclusions about human nature. In many cases, "believing is seeing" rather than the reverse: our beliefs shape our perceptions of the world, often in ways we don't realize (Gilovich, 1991).

WHEN OUR COMMON SENSE IS RIGHT. That's not to say that our common sense is always wrong. Our intuition comes in handy in many situations and sometimes guides us to the truth (Gigerenzer, 2007; Gladwell, 2005; Myers, 2002). For example, our snap (five-second) judgments about whether someone we've just watched on video is trustworthy or untrustworthy tend to be right more often than we'd expect by chance (Fowler, Lilienfeld, & Patrick, 2009). Common sense can also be a helpful guide for generating hypotheses that scientists can later test in rigorous investigations (Redding, 1998). Moreover, some everyday psychological notions are indeed correct. For example, most people believe that happy employees tend to be more productive on the job compared with unhappy employees, and research shows that they're right (Kluger & Tikochinsky, 2001).

But to think scientifically, we must learn when—and when not—to trust our common sense. Doing so will help us to become more informed consumers of popular psychology and make better real-world decisions. You will need a framework of scientific thinking tools for making this crucial distinction. This thinking framework can help you to better evaluate psychological claims in everyday life.

? Why are marriages like that of Mary Matalin, a prominent conservative political strategist, and James Carville, a prominent liberal political strategist, rare?

FIGURE 2 Naive Realism Can Fool Us. Even though our perceptions are often accurate, we can't always trust them to provide us with an error-free picture of the world. In this case, take a look at *Shepard's tables,* courtesy of psychologist Roger Shepard (1990). Believe it or not, the tops of these tables are identical in size: One can be directly superimposed on top of the other (get out a ruler if you don't believe us!).

naive realism
belief that we see the world precisely as it is

Answer: Despite the commonsense belief that opposites attract, psychological research shows that people are generally drawn to others who are similar to them in beliefs and values.

Psychology as a Science

A few years ago, one of our academic colleagues was advising a psychology major about his career plans. Out of curiosity, he asked the student, "So why did you decide to go into psychology?" The student responded, "Well, I took a lot of science courses and realized I didn't like science, so I picked psychology instead."

We're going to try to persuade you that the student was wrong—not about selecting a psychology major, that is, but about psychology not being a science. Modern psychology, or at least a hefty chunk of it, is scientific. But what does the word *science* really mean, anyway?

We might assume that *science* is just a word for all of that really complicated stuff people learn in their biology, chemistry, and physics classes. But science isn't a body of knowledge. Instead, it's a systematic *approach* to evidence (Bunge, 1998). Specifically, science consists of a set of attitudes and skills designed to prevent us from fooling ourselves. Science begins with *empiricism*, the premise that knowledge should initially be acquired through observation. Yet such observation is only a rough starting point for obtaining psychological knowledge. As the phenomenon of naive realism reminds us, it isn't sufficient by itself, because our observations can fool us. So science refines our initial observations, subjecting them to stringent tests to determine whether they are accurate. The observations that stand up to rigorous examination are retained; those that don't are revised or discarded.

Survey data show that a large percentage, and perhaps even a majority, of the general public doubts that psychology is truly scientific (Janda et al., 1998; Lilienfeld, 2012). Some of this skepticism probably reflects the fact that when psychologists appear on the news or other popular media outlets, they're rarely scientists. So it's not entirely surprising that in a recent poll of the American public, only 30 percent agreed that "psychology attempts to understand the way people behave through scientific research"; in contrast, 52 percent believed that "psychology attempts to understand the way people behave by talking to them and asking them why they do what they do" (Penn & Schoen and Berland Associates, 2008, p. 29). In fact, scientific psychologists almost always rely on systematic research methods, of which talking to people is only one component. Another reason many people question psychology's scientific status is that psychology is intimately familiar to all of us; memory, learning, love, sleep and dreams, personality, and the like are part and parcel of everyday lives. Because psychology is so familiar to all of us, we may assume that it's easy (Lilienfeld, 2012). Indeed, children and adults alike tend to regard psychology as simpler and more self-evident than physics, chemistry, and biology (Keil, Lockhart, & Schlegel, 2010), which probably helps to explain why these other fields are often called the hard sciences. Yet there are many ways in which psychology is even "harder" than physics, because behavior—especially human behavior—is often challenging to predict (Meehl, 1978).

Here's another case in which our naive realism can trick us. Take a look at these two upside-down photos. They look quite similar, if not identical. Now turn your text upside down.

Watch in **MyPsychLab** the **Video:** John Cacioppo: Can you explain psychology as a hub science?

scientific theory
explanation for a large number of findings in the natural world

hypothesis
testable prediction derived from a scientific theory

WHAT IS A SCIENTIFIC THEORY? Few terms in science have generated more confusion than the deceptively simple term *theory*. Some of this confusion has contributed to serious misunderstandings about how science works. We'll first examine what a scientific theory is and then address two misconceptions about what a scientific theory *isn't*.

A **scientific theory** is an explanation for a large number of findings in the natural world, including the psychological world. A scientific theory offers an account that ties multiple findings together into one pretty package.

But good scientific theories do more than account for existing data. They generate predictions regarding new data we haven't yet observed. For a theory to be scientific, it must generate novel predictions that researchers can test. Scientists call a testable prediction a **hypothesis**. In other words, theories are general explanations, whereas hypotheses are specific predictions derived from those explanations (Bolles, 1962; Meehl, 1967). Based on their tests of hypotheses, scientists can provisionally accept the theory that generated these hypotheses, reject this theory outright, or revise it (Proctor & Capaldi, 2006).

Misconception 1: *A theory explains one specific event.* The first misunderstanding is that a theory is a specific explanation for an event. The popular media get this distinction wrong much of the time. We often hear television reporters say something like, "The most likely theory for the robbery at the downtown bank is that it was committed by two former bank employees who dressed up as armed guards." But this isn't a "theory" of the robbery. For one thing, it attempts to explain only one event rather than a variety of diverse observations. It also doesn't generate testable predictions.

Misconception 2: *A theory is just an educated guess.* A second myth is that a scientific theory is merely a guess about how the world works. People often dismiss a theoretical explanation on these grounds, arguing that it's "just a theory."

In fact, *all* general scientific explanations about how the world works are theories. A few theories are extremely well supported by multiple lines of evidence; for example, the Big Bang theory, which proposes that the universe began in a gigantic explosion about 14 billion years ago, helps scientists to explain a diverse array of observations. They include the findings that (1) galaxies are rushing away from each other at remarkable speeds; (2) the universe exhibits a background radiation suggestive of the remnants of a tremendous explosion; and (3) powerful telescopes reveal that the oldest galaxies originated about 14 billion years ago, right around the time predicted by the Big Bang theory. Like all scientific theories, the Big Bang theory can never be "proved" because it's always conceivable that a better explanation might come along one day. Nevertheless, because this theory is consistent with many differing lines of evidence, the overwhelming majority of scientists accept it as a good explanation. Darwinian evolution, the Big Bang, and other well-established theories aren't guesses about how the world works, because they've been substantiated over and over again by independent investigators. In contrast, many other scientific theories are only moderately well supported, and still others are questionable or entirely discredited. Not all theories are created equal.

So when we hear that a scientific explanation is "just a theory," we should remember that theories aren't just guesses. Some theories have survived repeated efforts to refute them and are well-confirmed models of how the world works (Kitcher, 2009).

SCIENCE AS A SAFEGUARD AGAINST BIAS: PROTECTING US FROM OURSELVES. Some people assume that scientists are objective and free of biases. Yet scientists are human and have their biases, too (Mahoney & DeMonbreun, 1977). The best scientists are aware of their biases and try to find ways of compensating for them. This principle applies to all scientists, including psychological scientists—those who study mind, brain, and behavior. In particular, the best scientists realize that they *want* their pet theories to turn out to be correct. After all, they've invested months or even years in designing and running a study to test a theory, sometimes a theory they've developed. If the results of the study are negative, they'll often be bitterly disappointed. They also know that because of this deep personal investment, they may bias the results unintentionally to make them turn out the way they want (Greenwald et al., 1986). Scientists are prone to self-deception, just like the rest of us. There are several traps into which scientists can fall unless they're careful. We'll discuss two of the most crucial next.

Confirmation Bias. To protect themselves against bias, good scientists adopt procedural safeguards against errors, especially errors that could work in their favor. In other words, scientific methods are tools for overcoming **confirmation bias**: the tendency to seek out evidence that supports our beliefs and deny, dismiss, or distort evidence that contradicts them (Nickerson, 1998; Risen & Gilovich, 2007). We can sum up confirmation bias in five words: *seek and ye shall find.*

Because of confirmation bias, our preconceptions often lead us to focus on evidence that supports our beliefs, resulting in psychological tunnel vision (Wagenmakers et al., 2012). One of the simplest demonstrations of confirmation bias comes from research on the *Wason selection task* (Wason, 1966), an example of which we can find in **FIGURE 3**. There, you'll see four cards, each of which has a number on one side and a letter on the other side. Your task

This textbook contains material on evolution. Evolution is a theory, not a fact, regarding the origin of living things. This material should be approached with an open mind, studied carefully, and critically considered.

Approved by
Cobb County Board of Education
Thursday, March 28, 2002

Some creationists have argued that evolution is "just a theory." Cobb County, Georgia, briefly required high school biology textbooks to carry this sticker (Pinker, 2002).

Here are four cards. Each of them has a letter on one side and a number on the other side. Two of these cards are shown with the letter side up, and two with the number side up.

Indicate which of these cards you have to turn over in order to determine whether the following claim is true:

If a card has a vowel on one side, then it has an odd number on the other side.

FIGURE 3 Diagram of Wason Selection Task. In the Wason selection task, you must pick two cards to test the hypothesis that all cards that have a vowel on one side have an odd number on the other. Which two will you select?

confirmation bias
tendency to seek out evidence that supports our hypotheses and deny, dismiss, or distort evidence that contradicts them

is to determine whether the following hypothesis is correct: *all cards that have a vowel on one side have an odd number on the other side*. To test this hypothesis, you need to select *two* cards to turn over. Which two will you pick? Decide on your two cards before reading on.

Most people pick the cards showing *E* and 5. If you selected *E*, you were right, so give yourself one point there. But if you selected 5, you've fallen prey to confirmation bias, although you'd be in good company because most people make this mistake. Although 5 *seems* to be a correct choice, it can only confirm the hypothesis, not disconfirm it. Think of it this way: If there's a vowel on the other side of the 5 card, that doesn't rule out the possibility that the 4 card also has a vowel on the other side, which would disconfirm the hypothesis. So the 4 card is actually the other card to turn over, as that's the only other card that could demonstrate that the hypothesis is wrong.

Confirmation bias wouldn't be especially interesting if it were limited to cards. What makes confirmation bias so important is that it extends to many areas of daily life, including friendship, romance, and politics (Nickerson, 1998; Rassin, Eerland, & Kuijpers, 2010). For example, research shows that confirmation bias affects how we evaluate candidates for political office—including those on both the left and right sides of the political spectrum. Research shows that if we agree with a candidate's political views, we quickly forgive the candidate for contradicting herself or herself, but if we disagree with a candidate's views, we criticize him or her as a "flip-flopper" (Tavris & Aronson, 2007; Westen et al., 2006). Similarly, in a classic study of a hotly contested football game, Dartmouth fans saw Princeton players as "dirty" and as committing many penalties, while Princeton fans saw Dartmouth players in exactly the same light (Hastorf & Cantril, 1954). When it comes to judging right and wrong, our side almost always seems to be in the right; the other side, in the wrong.

Although you are likely to encounter a variety of biases, you can think of confirmation bias as the "mother of all biases." That's because it's the bias that can most easily fool you into seeing what you want to see. For that reason, it's the most crucial bias that psychologists need to counteract. What distinguishes psychological scientists from nonscientists is that the former adopt systematic safeguards to protect against confirmation bias, whereas the latter don't (Lilienfeld, Ammirati, & Landfield, 2009).

Belief Perseverance. Confirmation bias predisposes us to another shortcoming to which we're all prone: **belief perseverance**. Belief perseverance refers to the tendency to stick to our initial beliefs even when evidence contradicts them (Nestler, 2010). In everyday language, belief perseverance is the "don't confuse me with the facts" effect. Because none of us wants to think we're wrong, we're usually reluctant to give up our cherished notions. In a striking demonstration of belief perseverance, Lee Ross and his colleagues asked students to inspect 50 suicide notes and determine which were real and which were fake (in reality, half were real and half were fake). They then gave students feedback on how well they did—they told some students they were usually right; others, they were usually wrong. Unbeknownst to the students, this feedback was unrelated to their actual performance. Yet even after the researchers informed the students that the feedback was bogus, students based their estimates of ability on the feedback they'd received. Students who were told they were good at detecting real suicide notes were convinced that they were better at it than students who were told they were bad at it (Ross, Lepper, & Hubbard, 1975).

Beliefs endure. Even when informed that we're wrong, we don't completely wipe our mental slates clean and start from scratch.

Explore in **MyPsychLab** the **Concept:** Confirmation Bias

Metaphysical Claims: The Boundaries of Science

It's essential to distinguish scientific claims from **metaphysical claims**: assertions about the world that we can't test (Popper, 1965). Metaphysical claims include assertions about the existence of God, the soul, and the afterlife. These claims differ from scientific claims in that we could never test them using scientific methods. (How could we design a scientific test to conclusively disprove the existence of God?)

belief perseverance
tendency to stick to our initial beliefs even when evidence contradicts them

metaphysical claim
assertion about the world that is not testable

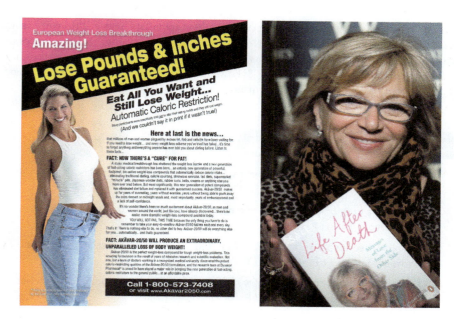

? Which of these claims is metaphysical, and which is probably pseudoscientific? (See answer upside down on bottom of page.)

This point doesn't mean that metaphysical claims are wrong, let alone unimportant. To the contrary, some scholars would contend that questions concerning the existence of God are even more significant and profound than scientific questions are. Moreover, regardless of our beliefs about religion, we need to treat these questions with respect. But it's crucial to understand that there are certain questions about the world that science can—and can't—answer (Gould, 1997; Novella, 2013). Science has its limits. So it needs to respect the boundaries of religion and other metaphysical domains. Testable claims fall within the province of science; untestable claims don't (see **FIGURE 4**). Moreover, according to many (although admittedly not all) scholars, there's no inherent conflict between science and the vast majority of religious claims (Dean, 2005). One can quite comfortably adhere to one's religious views while embracing psychology's scientific tools and findings.

FIGURE 4 Nonoverlapping Realms. Scientist Stephen Jay Gould (1997) argued that science and religion are entirely different and nonoverlapping realms of understanding the world. Science deals with testable claims about the natural world that can be answered with data, whereas religion deals with untestable claims about moral values that can't be answered with data. Not all scientists and theologians accept Gould's model. (*Source:* Gould, 1997)

Recognizing That We Might Be Wrong

Good scientists are keenly aware that they might be mistaken (Sagan, 1995). In fact, initial scientific conclusions are often wrong or at least partly off base. Medical findings are prime examples. Eating a lot of chocolate reduces your risk for heart disease; oops, no, it doesn't (I bet you were disappointed to learn that). Drinking a little red wine now and then is good for you; no, actually, it's bad for you. And on and on it goes. It's no wonder that many people just throw up their hands and give up reading medical reports altogether. One researcher (Ioannidis, 2005) found that about a third of findings from published medical studies don't hold up in later studies (of course, we have to wonder: do we know that the results of *this* analysis will hold up?). But the beauty of this messy process is that scientific knowledge is almost always tentative and potentially open to revision. The fact that science is a process of continually revising and updating findings lends it strength as a method of inquiry. It does mean, though, that we usually acquire knowledge slowly and in small bits and pieces.

One way of characterizing this process is to describe science, including psychological science, as a *prescription for humility* (McFall, 1997). Good scientists never claim to "prove" their theories and try to avoid committing to definitive conclusions unless the evidence supports them overwhelmingly. Such terms and phrases as *suggests*, *appears*, and *raises the possibility that* are widespread in scientific writing and allow scientists to remain tentative in their interpretations of findings. Many beginning students understandably find this hemming and hawing frustrating.

Answer: Image on the left is probably pseudoscientific because it makes extreme claims that aren't supported by evidence. Image on right is metaphysical because it makes a claim that science cannot test.

Yet as Carl Sagan (1995) observed, the best scientists hear a little voice in their heads that keeps repeating the same words: "but I might be wrong." Science forces us to question our findings and conclusions and encourages us to ferret out mistakes in our belief systems (O'Donohue, Lilienfeld, & Fowler, 2007). Science also forces us to attend to data that aren't to our liking, whether or not we want to—and often we don't.

✔ **Study** and **Review** in **MyPsychLab**

Assess Your Knowledge   FACT or FICTION?

1. Psychology involves studying the mind at one specific level of explanation.
   True / False

2. Science is a body of knowledge consisting of all of the findings that scientists have discovered. **True / False**

3. Scientific theories are general explanations, and hypotheses are specific predictions derived from these explanations. **True / False**

4. Good scientists are confident they're right, so they don't need to protect themselves against confirmation bias. **True / False**

5. Metaphysical claims are not testable. **True / False**

Answers: 1. F; 2. F; 3. T; 4. F; 5. T

Psychological Pseudoscience: Imposters of Science

3   Describe psychological pseudoscience and distinguish it from psychological science.

4   Identify reasons we are drawn to pseudoscience.

Of course, you might be interested in learning how to understand yourself, your friends, or a boyfriend or girlfriend. If so, you might well be thinking, "But I don't want to become a scientist. In fact, I'm not even interested in research. I just want to understand people."

Actually, we're not trying to persuade you to become a scientist. Instead, our goal is to persuade you to *think scientifically:* to become aware of your biases and to take advantage of the tools of the scientific method to try to overcome them. By acquiring these skills, you'll make better educated choices in your everyday life, such as what weight loss plan to choose, what psychotherapy to recommend to a friend, and maybe even what potential romantic partner to pursue. You'll also learn how to avoid being tricked by bogus claims. Not everyone needs to become a scientist, but just about everyone can learn to think like one.

The Amazing Growth of Popular Psychology

Distinguishing real from bogus claims is crucial, because the popular psychology industry is huge and growing rapidly. On the positive side, this fact means that the American public has unprecedented access to psychological knowledge. On the negative side, the remarkable growth of popular psychology has led not only to an information explosion, but also to a *misinformation explosion* because there's scant quality control over what this industry produces.

For example, about 3,500 self-help books are published every year (Arkowitz & Lilienfeld, 2006). Some of these books are effective for treating depression, anxiety, and other psychological problems, but about 95 percent of all self-help books are untested (Gould & Clum, 1993; Gregory et al., 2004; Rosen, 1993) and recent evidence suggests that a few may even make people worse (Haeffel, 2010; Rosen, 1993; Salerno, 2005).

Coinciding with the rapid expansion of the popular psychology industry is the enormous growth of treatments and products that claim to cure almost every imaginable psychological ailment. There are well over 500 "brands" of psychotherapy (Eisner, 2000), with new ones being added every year. Fortunately, research shows that some of these treatments are helpful for numerous psychological problems.

Subliminal self-help tapes supposedly influence behavior by means of messages delivered to the unconscious. But do they really work?

Yet the substantial majority of psychotherapies remain untested, so we don't know whether they help (Baker, McFall, & Shoham, 2009). Some may even be harmful (Lilienfeld, 2007).

Some self-help books base their recommendations on solid research about psychological problems and their treatment. We can often find excellent articles in the *New York Times, Scientific American Mind,* and *Discover* magazines and other media outlets that present high-quality information regarding scientific psychology. In addition, hundreds of websites provide helpful information and advice concerning numerous psychological topics like memory, personality testing, and psychological disorders and their treatment. The websites of such organizations as the Association for Psychological Science (www.psychologicalscience.org), American Psychological Association (www.apa.org), Canadian Psychological Association (www.cpa.ca), and National Institute of Mental Health (www.nimh.nih.gov/index.shtml) are good starting points for obtaining accurate information regarding human behavior. In contrast, many other websites contain misleading or erroneous information, so we need to be armed with accurate knowledge to evaluate them.

What Is Pseudoscience?

These facts highlight a crucial point: we need to distinguish claims that are genuinely scientific from those that are merely imposters of science. An imposter of science is **pseudoscience**: a set of claims that *seems* scientific but isn't. In particular, *pseudoscience lacks the safeguards against confirmation bias and belief perseverance that characterize science.* We must be careful to distinguish pseudoscientific claims from metaphysical claims, which, as we've seen, are untestable and therefore lie outside the realm of science. In principle, at least, we can test pseudoscientific claims.

Pseudoscientific and other questionable beliefs are widespread. A recent survey of the U.S. public shows that 41 percent of us believe in extrasensory perception (ESP); over 30 percent of us in haunted houses, ghosts, and telepathy; and 25 percent of us in astrology (Musella, 2005). The fact that many Americans *entertain* the possibility of such beliefs isn't by itself worrisome, because a certain amount of open-mindedness is essential for scientific thinking. Instead, what's troubling is that many Americans appear convinced that such claims are correct even though the scientific evidence for them is weak, as in the case of ESP, or essentially nonexistent, as in the case of astrology. Moreover, it's troubling that many poorly supported beliefs are more popular, or at least more widespread, than well-supported beliefs. To take merely one example, there are about 20 times as many astrologers as astronomers in the United States (Gilovich, 1991); as a consequence, the general public may often have a difficult time distinguishing accurate from inaccurate claims regarding astronomy. The same principle may hold for other sciences, including psychology.

WARNING SIGNS OF PSEUDOSCIENCE. Numerous warning signs can help us distinguish science from pseudoscience; we've listed some of the most useful ones in **TABLE 1**. They're extremely helpful rules of thumb. We can—and should— use them in everyday life. None of these signs is by itself proof positive that a set of claims is pseudoscientific. Nevertheless, the more of these signs we see, the more skeptical of these claims we should become.

Here, we'll discuss three of the most crucial of these warning signs.

Overuse of ad hoc immunizing hypotheses: yes, we know this one is a mouthful. But it's actually not as complicated as it appears, because an **ad hoc immunizing hypothesis** is just an escape hatch or loophole that defenders of a theory use to protect this theory from being disproven. For example, some psychics have claimed to perform remarkable feats of ESP in the real world, like reading others' minds or forecasting the future. But when brought into the laboratory and tested under tightly controlled conditions, most have bombed, performing no better than chance. Some of these psychics and their proponents have invoked an ad hoc immunizing

Simulate in **MyPsychLab** the **Experiment:** The Pseudoscience of Astrology

Pseudoscientific and otherwise questionable claims have increasingly altered the landscape of modern life.

pseudoscience
set of claims that seems scientific but isn't

ad hoc immunizing hypothesis
escape hatch or loophole that defenders of a theory use to protect their theory from falsification

Psychology and Scientific Thinking

TABLE 1 Some Warning Signs That Can Help Us Recognize Pseudoscience.

SIGN OF PSEUDOSCIENCE	EXAMPLE
Overuse of ad hoc immunizing hypotheses	The psychic who claimed to predict the future failed all controlled tests in the lab, but that's because the experimenters inhibited his extrasensory powers.
Exaggerated claims	Three simple steps will change your love life forever!
Overreliance on anecdotes	This woman practiced yoga daily for three weeks and hasn't had a day of depression since.
Absence of connectivity to other research	Amazing new innovations in research have shown that eye massage results in reading speeds 10 times faster than average!
Lack of review by other scholars (called *peer review*) or replication by independent labs	Fifty studies conducted by the company all show overwhelming success!
Lack of self-correction when contrary evidence is published	Although some scientists say that we use almost all our brains, we've found a way to harness additional brain power previously undiscovered.
Meaningless "psychobabble" that uses fancy scientific-sounding terms that don't make sense	Sine-wave filtered auditory stimulation is carefully designed to encourage maximal orbitofrontal dendritic development.
Talk of "proof" instead of "evidence"	Our new program is proven to reduce social anxiety by at least 50 percent!

hypothesis to explain away these failures: the skeptical "vibes" of the experimenters are somehow interfering with psychic powers (Carroll, 2003; Lilienfeld, 1999c). Although this hypothesis isn't necessarily wrong, it makes the psychics' claims essentially impossible to test.

Lack of self-correction: as we've learned, many scientific claims turn out to be wrong. That may seem like a weakness of science, but it's actually a strength. That's because in science, wrong claims tend to be weeded out eventually, even though it often takes a while. In contrast, in most pseudosciences, wrong claims never seem to go away, because their proponents fall prey to belief perseverance, clinging to them stubbornly despite contrary evidence. Moreover, pseudoscientific claims are rarely updated in light of new data. Most forms of astrology have remained almost identical for about 4,000 years (Hines, 2003) despite the discovery of outer planets in the solar system (Uranus and Neptune) that were unknown in ancient times.

Overreliance on anecdotes: there's an old saying that "the plural of anecdote isn't fact" (Park, 2003). A mountain of numerous anecdotes may seem impressive, but it shouldn't persuade us to put much stock in others' claims. Most anecdotes are *I know a person who* assertions (Nisbett & Ross, 1980; Stanovich, 2009). This kind of secondhand evidence— "I know a person who says his self-esteem skyrocketed after receiving hypnosis" —is commonplace in everyday life. So is firsthand evidence—"I felt less depressed after taking this herbal remedy"—that's based on subjective impressions.

Pseudosciences tend to rely heavily on anecdotal evidence. In many cases, they base claims on the dramatic reports of one or two individuals: "I lost 85 pounds in three weeks on the Matzo Ball Soup Weight Loss Program." Compelling as this anecdote may appear, it doesn't constitute good scientific evidence (Davison & Lazarus, 2007; Loftus & Guyer, 2002). For one thing, anecdotes don't tell us anything about cause and effect. Maybe the Matzo Ball Soup Weight Loss Program caused the person to lose 85 pounds, but maybe other factors were responsible. Perhaps he went on an additional diet or started to exercise frantically during that time. Or perhaps he underwent drastic weight loss surgery during this time but didn't bother to mention it. Anecdotes also don't tell us anything about how representative the cases are. Perhaps most people who went on the Matzo Ball Soup Weight Loss Program gained weight, but we never heard from them. Finally, anecdotes are often difficult to verify. Do we really know for sure that he lost 85 pounds? We're taking his word for it, which is a risky idea.

Simply put, most anecdotes are extremely difficult to interpret as evidence. As clinical psychologist Paul Meehl (1995) put it, "The clear message of history is that the anecdotal method delivers both wheat and chaff, but it does not enable us to tell which is which" (p. 1019).

WHY ARE WE DRAWN TO PSEUDOSCIENCE? There are a host of reasons why so many of us are drawn to pseudoscientific beliefs.

Perhaps the central reason stems from the way our brains work. *Our brains are predisposed to make order out of disorder and find sense in nonsense.* This tendency is generally adaptive, as it helps us to simplify the often bewildering world in which we live (Alcock, 1995; Pinker, 1997; Shermer, 2011). Without it, we'd be constantly overwhelmed by endless streams of information we don't have the time or ability to process. Yet this adaptive tendency can sometimes lead us astray because it can cause us to perceive meaningful patterns even when they're not there (Carroll, 2003; Davis, 2009).

---

from inquiry to understanding

WHY DO WE PERCEIVE PATTERNS EVEN WHEN THEY DON'T EXIST?

Our tendency to see patterns in meaningless data is so profound that one science writer, Michael Shermer (2008), gave it a name: **patternicity**. Although patternicity can lead to errors, it probably stems from an evolutionarily adaptive tendency (Reich, 2010). If we eat a specific food, say a bacon cheeseburger, for lunch tomorrow and become violently ill soon afterward, we'll tend to avoid bacon cheeseburgers for a while. We'll do so even though there's a very good chance that the link between the cheeseburger and our becoming ill was purely coincidental. No matter—our brains tend to seek out patterns and connections among events, because of a basic evolutionary principle: "better safe than sorry." All things being equal, it's usually better to assume that a connection between two events exists than to assume that it doesn't, especially when one of the events is physically dangerous.

We all fall prey to patternicity from time to time. If we think of a friend with whom we haven't spoken in a few months and immediately afterward receive a phone call from him or her, we may jump to the conclusion that this striking co-occurrence stems from ESP. Well, it *might*.

But it's also entirely possible, if not likely, that these two events happened at about the same time by chance alone. For a moment, think of the number of times one of your old friends comes to mind and then think of the number of phone calls you receive each month. You'll realize that the laws of probability make it likely that at least once over the next few years, you'll be thinking of an old friend at about the same time he or she calls.

Another manifestation of patternicity is our tendency to detect eerie coincidences among persons or events. To take one example, read through each of the uncanny similarities between Abraham Lincoln and John F. Kennedy, two American presidents who were the victims of assassination, listed in **TABLE 2**.

Conspiracy theories are manifestations of patternicity. Believers in conspiracies often claim to detect hidden interconnections among powerful people and institutions.

Pretty amazing stuff, isn't it? So extraordinary, in fact, that some writers have argued that Lincoln and Kennedy are somehow linked by supernatural forces (Leavy, 1992). In actuality, though, coincidences are everywhere. They're surprisingly easy to detect if we make the effort to look for them. Because of patternicity, we may attribute paranormal significance to coincidences that are due to chance. (The term *paranormal* describes phenomena like ESP that fall outside the boundaries of traditional science.) Moreover, we often fall victim to confirmation bias and neglect to consider evidence that *doesn't* support our hypothesis. Because we typically find coincidences to be far more interesting than noncoincidences, we tend to forget that Lincoln was a Republican whereas Kennedy was a Democrat; that Lincoln was shot in Washington, D.C., whereas Kennedy was shot in Dallas; that Lincoln had a beard, but Kennedy didn't; and on and on. Recall that scientific thinking is designed to counteract confirmation bias. To do so, we must

patternicity
the tendency to detect meaningful patterns in random stimuli

seek out evidence that contradicts our ideas. In extreme forms, patternicity leads us to embrace conspiracy theories, in which individuals detect supposedly hidden connections among numerous largely or entirely unrelated events (Douglas & Sutton, 2011).

TABLE 2 Some Eerie Commonalities Between Abraham Lincoln and John F. Kennedy.

ABRAHAM LINCOLN	JOHN F. KENNEDY
Was elected to Congress in 1846	Was elected to Congress in 1946
Was elected President in 1860	Was elected President in 1960
The name "Lincoln" contains seven letters	The name "Kennedy" contains seven letters
Was assassinated on a Friday	Was assassinated on a Friday
Lincoln's secretary, named Kennedy, warned him not to go to the theater, where he was shot	Kennedy's secretary, named Lincoln, warned him not to go to Dallas, where he was shot
Lincoln's wife was sitting beside him when he was shot	Kennedy's wife was sitting beside him when he was shot
John Wilkes Booth (Lincoln's assassin) was born in 1839	Lee Harvey Oswald (Kennedy's assassin) was born in 1939
Was succeeded by a president named Johnson	Was succeeded by a president named Johnson
Andrew Johnson, who succeeded Lincoln, was born in 1808	Lyndon Johnson, who succeeded Kennedy, was born in 1908
Booth fled from a theater to a warehouse	Oswald fled from a warehouse to a theater
Booth was killed before his trial	Oswald was killed before his trial

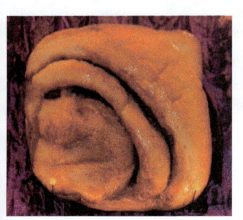

Patternicity can lead us to perceive meaningful people or objects in largely random stimuli. The "nun bun," a cinnamon roll resembling the face of nun Mother Teresa, was discovered in 1996 in a Nashville, Tennessee, coffee shop.

A final reflection of patternicity is our tendency to see meaningful images in meaningless visual stimuli. Any of us who's looked at a cloud and perceived the vague shape of an animal has experienced this version of patternicity, as has any of us who's seen the oddly misshapen face of a "man" in the moon. A more stunning example comes from the photograph in **FIGURE 5a**. In 1976, the *Mars Viking Orbiter* snapped an image of a set of features on the Martian surface. As we can see, these features bear an eerie resemblance to a human face. So eerie, in fact, that some individuals maintained that the "Face on Mars" offered conclusive proof of intelligent life on the Red Planet (Hoagland, 1987). In 2001, during a mission of a different spacecraft, the *Mars Global Surveyor,* the National Aeronautics and Space Administration (NASA) decided to adopt a scientific approach to the face on Mars. NASA was open-minded but demanded evidence. It swooped down much closer to the face and pointed the *Surveyor*'s cameras directly at it. If we look at **FIGURE 5b**, we'll see what NASA found: absolutely nothing. The patternicity in this instance was a consequence of a peculiar configuration of rocks and shadows present at the angle at which the photographs were taken in 1976, a camera artifact in the original photograph that just happened to place a black dot where a nostril should be, and perhaps most important, our innate tendency to perceive meaningful faces in what are basically random visual stimuli.

psychomythology

THE HOT HAND: REALITY OR ILLUSION?

Because we're meaning-seeking organisms, we find it almost impossible *not* to detect patterns in random data. If we flip a coin four times and it comes up heads all four times, we may begin to think we're on a streak. Instead, we're probably just being fooled by randomness (Mlodinow, 2008; Taleb, 2004). The same phenomenon extends to sports.

Basketball players, coaches, and fans are fond of talking about the "hot hand." Once a player has made three or four shots in a row, he or she is "hot," "in the zone," and "on a roll." One television basketball announcer, former star center Bill Walton, once criticized a team's players for not getting the ball to a fellow player who'd just made several consecutive baskets ("He's got the hot hand—get him the ball!"). It certainly *seems* as though basketball players go on streaks. Do they?

To find out, Thomas Gilovich and his colleagues got hold of the shooting records of the 1980–1981 Philadelphia 76ers, then the only basketball team to keep precise records of which player made which shot in which order (Gilovich, Vallone, & Tversky, 1985). Let's look at **TABLE 3**, which displays the results of two representative players on the 76ers (you basketball fans out there may recognize "Erving" as the famous "Dr. J," widely regarded as one of the greatest players of all time). There we can see six rows, with *h* standing for a hit, that is, a successful shot, and *m* standing for a miss, that is, an unsuccessful shot. As we move from top to bottom, we see six different probabilities (abbreviated with *P*), starting with the probability of a successful shot (a hit) following three misses, then the probability of a successful shot following two misses, all the way (in the sixth and final row) to the probability of a successful shot following three successful shots.

If the hot hand is real, we should see the probabilities of a successful shot increasing from top to bottom. Once a player has made a few shots in a row, he should be more likely to make another. But as we can see from the data on these two players, *there's no evidence for the hot hand*. The proportions don't go up and, in fact, go down slightly (perhaps we should call this the "cool hand"?). Gilovich and his colleagues found the same pattern for all the other 76ers players.

Perhaps the absence of a hot hand is due to the fact that once a player has made several shots in a row, the defensive team makes adjustments, making it tougher for him to make another shot. To rule out this possibility, Gilovich and his colleagues examined foul shots, which are immune from this problem because players attempt these shots without any interference from the defensive team. Once again, they found no hint of "streaky" shooting.

Later researchers have similarly found little or no evidence for "streaky performance" in a host of other sports and games, including golf, pool, and baseball (Avugos et al., 2012; Bar-Eli, Avugos, & Raab, 2006; Clark, 2005; Mlodinow, 2008). Still, belief perseverance makes it unlikely that these findings will shake the convictions of dyed-in-the-wool hot-hand believers. When told about the results of the Gilovich hot-hand study, late Hall of Fame basketball coach Red Auerbach replied, "Who is this guy? So he makes a study. I couldn't care less." The hot hand may be an illusion, but it's a remarkably stubborn one.

FIGURE 5 Face on Mars. At the top (a) is the remarkable "Face on Mars" photo taken by the *Mars Viking Orbiter* in 1976. Some argued that this face provided conclusive proof of intelligent life on other planets. Below (b) is a more detailed photograph of the Face on Mars taken in 2001, which revealed that this "face" was just an illusion.

TABLE 3 Is the Hot Hand a Reality or an Illusion? Let's look at the data from these two players on the Philadelphia 76ers to help us find out.

	ERVING	TONEY
P(h/mmm)	0.52	0.52
P(h/mm)	0.51	0.53
P(h/m)	0.51	0.51
P(h/h)	0.53	0.43
P(h/hh)	0.52	0.40
P(h/hhh)	0.48	0.32

(*Source:* Based on data from Gilovich, 1991)

Finding Comfort in Our Beliefs. Another reason for the popularity of pseudoscience is motivational: we believe in part because we want to believe. As the old saying goes, "hope springs eternal": Many pseudoscientific claims, such as astrology, may give us comfort because they seem to offer us a sense of control over an often unpredictable world (Shermer, 2002). Research suggests that we're especially prone to patternicity when we experience a loss of control over our surroundings. Jennifer Whitson and Adam Galinsky (2008) deprived some participants of a sense of control—for example, by having them try to solve an unsolvable puzzle or recall a life experience in which they lacked control—and found that they were more likely than other participants to perceive conspiracies, embrace superstitious beliefs, and detect patterns in meaningless visual stimuli (see **FIGURE 6**). These results may help to explain why so many of us believe in astrology, ESP, and other belief systems that claim to foretell the future: they lend us a sense of control over the uncontrollable (Wang, Whitson, & Menon, 2012).

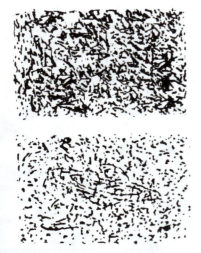

FIGURE 6 Regaining Control. Do you see an image in either of these pictures? Participants in Whitson and Galinsky's (2008) study who were deprived of a sense of control were more likely than other participants to see images in both pictures, even though only the picture on the bottom contains an image (a faint drawing of the planet Saturn).

Factoid

"Streaks" of several consecutive heads (H) or tails (T) in a row when flipping a coin, like HTTHTTTTTHHHTHHTTHH, are more common than we believe. Moreover, they're inevitable in long random sequences. Indeed, the sequence above is almost perfectly random (Gilovich, 1991). Because we tend to underestimate the probability of consecutive sequences, we're prone to attributing more significance to these sequences than they deserve ("Wow . . . I'm on a winning streak!").

According to terror management theory, reminders of our death can lead us to adopt comforting worldviews—in some cases, beliefs in the paranormal.

According to **terror management theory**, our awareness of our own inevitable death leaves many of us with an underlying sense of fear (Solomon, Greenberg, & Pyszczynski, 2000; Vail et al., 2012). We cope with these feelings of terror, advocates of this theory propose, by adopting cultural worldviews that reassure us that our lives possess a broader meaning and purpose—one that extends well beyond our vanishingly brief existence on this planet.

Can terror management theory help to explain the popularity of certain paranormal beliefs, such as astrology, ESP, and communication with the dead? Perhaps. Our society's widespread beliefs in life after death and reincarnation may stem in part from the terror that stems from knowing we'll eventually die (Lindeman, 1998; Norenzayan & Hansen, 2006). Two researchers (Morier & Podlipentseva, 1997) found that compared with other participants, participants who were asked to contemplate death reported higher levels of beliefs in the paranormal, such as ESP, ghosts, reincarnation, and astrology, than did other participants. It's likely that such beliefs are comforting to many of us, especially when confronted with reminders of our demise, because they imply the existence of a dimension beyond our own.

Terror management theory doesn't demonstrate that paranormal claims are false; we still need to evaluate these claims on their own merits. Instead, this theory suggests that we're likely to hold many paranormal beliefs regardless of whether they're correct.

THINKING CLEARLY: AN ANTIDOTE AGAINST PSEUDOSCIENCE. To avoid being seduced by the charms of pseudoscience, we must learn to avoid commonplace pitfalls in reasoning. Students new to psychology commonly fall prey to *logical fallacies*: traps in thinking that can lead to mistaken conclusions. It's easy for us to make these errors, because they seem to make intuitive sense. We should remember that scientific thinking often requires us to cast aside our beloved intuitions, although doing so can be extremely difficult.

Here we'll examine three especially important logical fallacies that are essential to bear in mind when evaluating psychological claims; we can find other useful fallacies in **TABLE 4**. All of them can help us separate science from pseudoscience.

Emotional Reasoning Fallacy. "The idea that day care might have negative emotional effects on children gets me really upset, so I refuse to believe it."

The *emotional reasoning fallacy* is the error of using our emotions as guides for evaluating the validity of a claim (some psychologists also refer to this error as the *affect heuristic*; Kahneman, 2011; Slovic & Peters, 2006). If we're honest with ourselves, we'll realize that findings that challenge our preexisting beliefs often make us angry, whereas findings that confirm these beliefs often make us happy or at least relieved. We shouldn't make the mistake of assuming that because a scientific claim makes us feel uncomfortable or indignant, it must be wrong. In the case of scientific questions concerning the psychological effects of day care, which are scientifically controversial (Belsky, 1988; Hunt, 1999), we need to keep an open mind to the data, regardless of whether they confirm or disconfirm our preconceptions.

Bandwagon Fallacy. "A lot of people I know believe in astrology, so there's got to be something to it."

The *bandwagon fallacy* is the error of assuming that a claim is correct just because many people believe it. It's an error because popular opinion isn't a dependable guide to the accuracy of an assertion. Prior to 1500, almost everyone believed the sun revolved around the earth, rather than vice versa, but they were woefully mistaken.

Not Me Fallacy. "My psychology professor keeps talking about how the scientific method is important for overcoming biases. But these biases don't apply to me, because *I'm* objective."

The *not me fallacy* is the error of believing that we're immune from errors in thinking that afflict other people. This fallacy can get us into deep trouble, because it can lead us to conclude mistakenly that we don't require the safeguards of the scientific method. Many pseudoscientists fall into this trap: they're so certain their claims are right—and uncontaminated by mistakes in their thinking—that they don't bother to conduct scientific studies to test these claims.

TABLE 4 Logical Fallacies to Avoid When Evaluating Psychological Claims.

LOGICAL FALLACY	EXAMPLE OF THE FALLACY
Error of using our emotions as guides for evaluating the validity of a claim (*emotional reasoning fallacy*)	"The idea that day care might have negative emotional effects on children gets me really upset, so I refuse to believe it."
Error of assuming that a claim is correct just because many people believe it (*bandwagon fallacy*)	"A lot of people I know believe in astrology, so there's got to be something to it."
Error of framing a question as though we can only answer it in one of two extreme ways (*either-or fallacy*)	"I just read in my psychology textbook that some people with schizophrenia were treated extremely well by their parents when they were growing up. This means that schizophrenia can't be due to environmental factors and therefore must be completely genetic."
Error of believing we're immune from errors in thinking that afflict other people (*not me fallacy*)	"My psychology professor keeps talking about how the scientific method is important for overcoming biases. But these biases don't apply to me, because *I'm* objective."
Error of accepting a claim merely because an authority figure endorses it (*appeal to authority fallacy*)	"My professor says that psychotherapy is worthless; because I trust my professor, she must be right."
Error of confusing the correctness of a belief with its origins or genesis (*genetic fallacy*)	"Freud's views about personality development can't be right, because Freud's thinking was shaped by sexist views popular at the time."
Error of assuming that a belief must be valid just because it's been around for a long time (*argument from antiquity fallacy*)	"There must be something to the Rorschach Inkblot Test, because psychologists have been using it for decades."
Error of confusing the validity of an idea with its potential real-world consequences (*argument from adverse consequences fallacy*)	"IQ can't be influenced by genetic factors, because if that were true, it would give the government an excuse to prevent low-IQ individuals from reproducing."
Error of assuming that a claim must be true because no one has shown it to be false (*appeal to ignorance fallacy*)	"No scientist has been able to explain away every reported case of ESP, so ESP probably exists."
Error of inferring a moral judgment from a scientific fact (*naturalistic fallacy*)	"Evolutionary psychologists say that sexual infidelity is a product of natural selection. Therefore, sexual infidelity is ethically justifiable."
Error of drawing a conclusion on the basis of insufficient evidence (*hasty generalization fallacy*)	"All three people I know who are severely depressed had strict fathers, so severe depression is clearly associated with having a strict father."
Error of basing a claim on the same claim reworded in slightly different terms (*circular reasoning fallacy*)	"Dr. Smith's theory of personality is the best, because it seems to have the most evidence supporting it."

Social psychologists have recently uncovered a fascinating phenomenon called *bias blind spot*, which means that most people are unaware of their biases but keenly aware of them in others (Pronin, Gilovich, & Ross, 2004). None of us believes that we have an accent because we live with our accents all of the time. Similarly, few of us believe that we have biases, because we've grown accustomed to seeing the world through our own psychological lenses. To see the not me fallacy at work, watch a debate between two intelligent people who hold extremely polarized views on a political issue. More likely than not, you'll see that the debate participants are quite adept at pointing out biases in their opponents, but entirely oblivious of their own equally glaring biases. People who are highly intelligent are just as prone to bias blind spot as are other people (West, Meserve, & Stanovich, 2012), so we shouldn't assume that more knowledge, education, or sophistication make us immune to this error. Bias blind spot reminds us yet again that we all need to be humble and that science can assist us in this regard.

The Dangers of Pseudoscience: Why Should We Care?

Up to this point, we've been making a big deal about pseudoscience. But why should we care about it? After all, isn't a great deal of pseudoscience, like astrology, pretty harmless? In fact, pseudoscience can be dangerous, even deadly. This point applies to a variety of questionable claims that we encounter in everyday life. There are three major reasons we should all be concerned about pseudoscience.

- **Opportunity Cost: What We Give Up**. Pseudoscientific treatments for mental disorders can lead people to forgo opportunities to seek effective treatments (Lazar, 2010; Lilienfeld, Lynn, & Lohr, 2003). As a consequence, even treatments

The bandwagon fallacy reminds us that the number of people who hold a belief isn't a dependable barometer of its accuracy.

terror management theory
theory proposing that our awareness of our death leaves us with an underlying sense of terror with which we cope by adopting reassuring cultural worldviews

19

Candace Newmaker was a tragic victim of a pseudoscientific treatment called rebirthing therapy. She died of suffocation at age 10 after her therapists wrapped her in a flannel blanket and squeezed her to simulate birth contractions.

Stem cell research is controversial on both scientific and ethical grounds. To evaluate this and other controversies properly, we need to be able to think critically about the potential costs and benefits of such research.

that are themselves harmless can cause harm indirectly by causing people to forfeit the chance to obtain a treatment that works. For example, a major community survey (Kessler et al., 2001) revealed that Americans with severe depression or anxiety attacks more often received scientifically unsupported treatments than scientifically supported treatments like cognitive-behavioral therapy. The unsupported treatments included acupuncture, which hasn't been shown to work for depression despite a few scattered positive findings; laughter therapy, which is based on the untested notion that laughing can cure depression; and energy therapy, which is based on the untestable notion that all people possess invisible energy fields that influence their moods. Although some future research might reveal some of these treatments to be helpful in certain cases, consumers who seek them out are rolling the dice with their mental health.

- **Direct Harm.** Pseudoscientific treatments sometimes do dreadful harm to those who receive them, causing psychological or physical damage—on rare occasions, even death (Barlow, 2010; Lilienfeld, 2007). The tragic case of Candace Newmaker, a 10-year-old child who received treatment for her behavioral problems in Evergreen, Colorado, in 2000, illustrates this point (Mercer, Sarner, & Rosa, 2003). Candace received a treatment called *rebirthing therapy*, which is premised on the scientifically doubtful notion that children's behavioral problems are attributable to difficulties in forming attachments to their parents that stem from birth—in some cases, even before birth. During rebirthing, children or adolescents reenact the trauma of birth with the "assistance" of one or more therapists (Mercer, 2002). During Candace's rebirthing session, two therapists wrapped her in a flannel blanket, sat on her, and squeezed her repeatedly in an effort to simulate birth contractions. During the 40-minute session, Candace vomited several times and begged the therapists for air, complaining desperately that she couldn't breathe and felt as though she was going to die. When Candace was unwrapped from her symbolic "birth canal," she was dead (Mercer, Sarner, & Rosa, 2003).
- **An Inability to Think Scientifically as Citizens.** Scientific thinking skills aren't just important for evaluating psychological claims—we can apply them to all aspects of our lives. In our increasingly complex scientific and technological society, we need scientific thinking skills to reach educated decisions about global warming, genetic engineering, stem cell research, novel medical treatments, and parenting and teaching practices, among dozens of other claims (Mooney & Kirshenbaum, 2010).

The take-home message is that pseudoscience matters. That's what makes scientific thinking essential: although far from foolproof, it's our best safeguard against errors to which we're all prone.

Assess Your Knowledge   FACT or FICTION?

1. Most self-help books and psychotherapies have been tested.   True / False

2. Humans' tendency to see patterns in random data is entirely maladaptive.
   True / False

3. According to terror management theory, our fears of death are an important reason for pseudoscientific beliefs.   True / False

4. The fact that many people believe in a claim is a good indicator of its validity.
   True / False

5. Pseudoscientific treatments can cause both direct and indirect harm.   True / False

Answers: 1.F 2.F 3.T 4.F 5.T

Scientific Thinking: Distinguishing Fact From Fiction

5 Identify the key features of scientific skepticism.

6 Identify and explain the text's six principles of scientific thinking.

Given that the world of popular psychology is chock-full of remarkable claims, how can we distinguish psychological fact—that is, the body of psychological findings that are so dependable we can safely regard them as true—from psychological fiction?

Scientific Skepticism

The approach we'll emphasize throughout this text is **scientific skepticism**. To many people, *skepticism* implies closed-mindedness, but nothing could be further from the truth. The term *skepticism* derives from the Greek word *skeptikos,* meaning "to consider carefully" (Shermer, 2002). The scientific skeptic evaluates all claims with an open mind but insists on persuasive evidence before accepting them.

As astronomer Carl Sagan (1995) noted, to be a scientific skeptic, we must adopt two attitudes that may seem contradictory but aren't: (1) a willingness to keep an open mind to all claims and (2) a willingness to accept claims only after researchers have subjected them to careful scientific tests. Scientific skeptics are willing to change their minds when confronted with evidence that challenges their preconceptions. At the same time, they change their minds only when this evidence is persuasive. The motto of the scientific skeptic is the Missouri principle, which we'll find on many Missouri license plates: "Show me" (Dawes, 1994).

Another feature of scientific skepticism is an unwillingness to accept claims on the basis of authority alone. Scientific skeptics evaluate claims on their own merits and refuse to accept them until they meet a high standard of evidence. Of course, in everyday life we're often forced to accept the word of authorities simply because we don't possess the expertise, time, or resources to evaluate every claim on our own. Most of us are willing to accept the claim that our local government keeps our drinking water safe without conducting our own chemical test. While reading this chapter, you're also placing trust in us—the authors, that is—to provide you with accurate information about psychology. Still, this doesn't mean you should blindly accept everything we've written hook, line, and sinker. Consider what we've written with an open mind, but evaluate it skeptically. If you disagree with something we've written, get a second opinion by asking your instructor.

A Basic Framework for Scientific Thinking

The hallmark of scientific skepticism is **critical thinking**. Many students misunderstand the word *critical* in *critical thinking,* assuming incorrectly that it entails a tendency to attack all claims. In fact, critical thinking is a set of skills for evaluating all claims in an open-minded and careful fashion. We can also think of critical thinking in psychology as *scientific thinking,* as it's the form of thinking that allows us to evaluate scientific claims not only in the laboratory, but also in everyday life (Willingham, 2007).

Just as important, scientific thinking is a set of skills for overcoming our own biases, especially confirmation bias, which, as we've learned, can blind us to evidence we'd prefer to ignore (Alcock, 1995). We should keep the principles of scientific thinking in mind when evaluating all psychological claims, including claims in the media, in self-help books, on the Internet, and in an introductory psychology course.

These six scientific thinking principles are so crucial that we'll indicate each of them with a different-colored arrow you'll see throughout the text.

This welcome sign for the state of Missouri captures the central motto of scientific skepticism.

"…and, as you go out into the world, I predict that you will, gradually and imperceptibly, forget all you ever learned at this university."

You'll probably forget many of the things you learn in college. But you'll be able to use the approach of scientific skepticism throughout your life to evaluate claims. (© Science CartoonsPlus.com)

scientific skepticism
approach of evaluating all claims with an open mind but insisting on persuasive evidence before accepting them

critical thinking
set of skills for evaluating all claims in an open-minded and careful fashion

 Scientific thinking involves ruling out rival hypotheses. In this case, do we know that this woman's weight loss was due to a specific diet plan? **What might be some alternative explanations for her weight loss?** (See answer upside down at bottom of page.)

Answer: During this time, she might have exercised or used another diet plan. Or perhaps the larger pants she's holding up were never hers to begin with.

THE FAMILY CIRCUS.   By Bil Keane

"I wish they didn't turn on that seatbelt sign so much! Every time they do, it gets bumpy."

Correlation isn't always causation. (Family Circus © Bil Keane, Inc. King Features Syndicate)

Whenever one of these principles arises in our discussion, we'll display that arrow in the margin to remind you of the principle that goes along with it (see **FIGURE 7**).

SCIENTIFIC THINKING PRINCIPLE #1: *RULING OUT RIVAL HYPOTHESES.* Most psychological findings we'll hear about on television or read about online lend themselves to multiple explanations. Yet more often than not, the media report only one explanation. We shouldn't automatically assume it's correct. Instead, we should ask ourselves: is this the only good explanation for this finding? Have we ruled out other important competing explanations (Huck & Sandler, 1979; Platt, 1964)?

Let's take a popular treatment for anxiety disorders: eye movement desensitization and reprocessing (EMDR). Introduced by Francine Shapiro (1989), EMDR asks clients to track the therapist's back-and-forth finger movements with their eyes while imagining distressing memories that are the source of their anxiety, such as the recollection of seeing someone being killed. Proponents of EMDR have consistently maintained that it's far more effective and efficient than other treatments for anxiety disorders. Some have claimed that these eye movements somehow synchronize the brain's two hemispheres or stimulate brain mechanisms that speed up the processing of emotional memories.

Here's the problem: almost all well-controlled studies show that the eye movements of EMDR don't contribute to its effectiveness. EMDR works just as well when people stare straight ahead at an immobile dot while thinking about the source of their anxiety (Davidson & Parker, 2001; Lohr, Tolin, & Lilienfeld, 1998). Most EMDR advocates neglected to consider a rival explanation for EMDR's success: EMDR asks patients to expose themselves to anxiety-provoking imagery. Researchers and therapists alike have long known that prolonged exposure itself can be therapeutic (Bisson et al., 2007; Lohr et al., 2003). By not excluding the rival hypothesis that EMDR's effectiveness stemmed from exposure rather than eye movements, EMDR advocates made claims that ran well ahead of the data.

The bottom line: whenever we evaluate a psychological claim, we should ask ourselves whether we've excluded other plausible explanations for it.

SCIENTIFIC THINKING PRINCIPLE #2: *CORRELATION ISN'T CAUSATION.* Perhaps the most common mistake psychology students make when interpreting studies is to conclude that when two things are associated with each other—or what psychologists call "correlated" with each other—one thing must cause the other. This point leads us to a crucial principle (get your highlighters out for this one): *correlational designs don't permit causal inferences,* or, putting it less formally, *correlation isn't causation.* When we conclude that a correlation means causation, we've committed the **correlation–causation fallacy.** This conclusion is a fallacy because the fact that two variables are correlated doesn't necessarily mean that one causes the other. Incidentally, a **variable** is anything that can *vary,* such as height, IQ, or extraversion. Let's see why correlation isn't causation.

If we start with two variables, A and B, that are correlated, there are three major explanations for this correlation.

1. A $\rightarrow$ B. It's possible that variable A causes variable B.

2. B $\rightarrow$ A. It's possible that variable B causes variable A.

   So far, so good. But many people forget that there's also a third possibility, namely, that

3. $C \nearrow^{A}_{\searrow B}$

In this third scenario, there's a third variable, C, that causes *both* A and B. This scenario is known as the *third variable problem.* It's a problem because it can lead us to conclude mistakenly that A and B are causally related to each other when they're not. For example, researchers found that teenagers who listen to music with a lot of sexual lyrics have sexual intercourse more often than teenagers who listen to music with tamer lyrics

correlation–causation fallacy
error of assuming that because one thing is associated with another, it must cause the other

variable
anything that can vary

What Scientific Thinking Principle Should We Use?	When Might We Use It?	How Do We Use It?
RULING OUT RIVAL HYPOTHESES ▶ HAVE IMPORTANT ALTERNATIVE EXPLANATIONS FOR THE FINDINGS BEEN EXCLUDED?	You're reading the newspaper and come across the headline: "Study shows depressed people who receive a new medication improve more than equally depressed people who receive nothing."	The results of the study could be due to the fact that people who received the medication expected to improve.
CORRELATION VS. CAUSATION ▶ CAN WE BE SURE THAT A CAUSES B?	A researcher finds that people eat more ice cream on days when crimes are committed than when they aren't, and concludes that eating ice cream causes crime.	Eating ice cream (A) might not cause crime (B). Both could be due to a third factor (C), such as higher temperatures.
FALSIFIABILITY ▶ CAN THE CLAIM BE DISPROVED?	A self-help book claims that all human beings have an invisible energy field surrounding them that influences their moods and well-being.	We can't design a study to disprove this claim.
REPLICABILITY ▶ CAN THE RESULTS BE DUPLICATED IN OTHER STUDIES?	A magazine article highlights a study that shows people who practice meditation score 50 points higher on an intelligence test than those who don't.	We should be skeptical if no other scientific studies have reported the same findings.
EXTRAORDINARY CLAIMS ▶ IS THE EVIDENCE AS STRONG AS THE CLAIM?	You come across a website that claims that a monster, like Bigfoot, has been living in the American Northwest for decades without being discovered by researchers.	This extraordinary claim requires more rigorous evidence than a less remarkable claim, such as the assertion that people remember more words from the beginning than from the end of a list.
OCCAM'S RAZOR ▶ DOES A SIMPLER EXPLANATION FIT THE DATA JUST AS WELL?	Your friend, who has poor vision, claims that he spotted a UFO while attending a Frisbee tournament.	Is it more likely that your friend's report is due to a simpler explanation—his mistaking a Frisbee for a UFO—than to alien visitation?

FIGURE 7 This figure was intentionally excluded from this edition.

(Martino et al., 2006). So listening to sexual lyrics is *correlated* with sexual behavior. One newspaper summarized the findings of this study with an attention-grabbing headline: "Sexual lyrics prompt teens to have sex" (Tanner, 2006). Like many headlines, this one went well beyond the data. It's possible that music with sexual lyrics (A) causes sexual behavior (B). But it's also possible that sexual behavior (B) causes teens to listen to music with sexual lyrics (A) or that a third variable, like impulsivity (C), causes teens to listen to music with sexual lyrics *and* to engage in sexual behavior. Given the data reported by the authors, there's no way to know. *Correlation isn't causation.*

The bottom line: we should remember that a correlation between two things doesn't demonstrate a causal connection between them.

SCIENTIFIC THINKING PRINCIPLE #3: *FALSIFIABILITY*. Philosopher of science Sir Karl Popper (1965) observed that for a claim to be meaningful, it must be **falsifiable**, that is, capable of being disproved. If a theory isn't falsifiable, we can't test it. Some students misunderstand this point, confusing the question of whether a theory is *falsifiable* with whether it's *false*. The principle of falsifiability doesn't mean that a theory must be false to be meaningful. Instead, it means that for a theory to be meaningful, it *could* be proven wrong if there were certain types of evidence against it. For a claim to be falsifiable, its proponent must state clearly *in advance,* not after the fact, which findings would count as evidence for and against the claim (Dienes, 2008; Proctor & Capaldi, 2006).

A key implication of the falsifiability principle is that a theory that explains everything—a theory that can account for every conceivable outcome—in effect explains nothing. That's because a good scientific theory must predict only certain outcomes, but not others. If a friend told you he was a master "psychic sports forecaster" and predicted with great confidence that "Tomorrow, all of the major league baseball teams that are playing a game will either win or lose," you'd probably start giggling. By predicting every potential outcome, your friend hasn't really predicted anything.

If your friend instead forecasted "The New York Yankees and New York Mets will both win tomorrow by three runs, but the Boston Red Sox and Los Angeles Dodgers will lose by one run," this prediction could be either correct or incorrect. There's a possibility he'll be wrong—the prediction is falsifiable. If he's right, it wouldn't prove he's psychic, of course, but it might make you wonder whether he has some special predictive abilities.

The bottom line: whenever we evaluate a psychological claim, we should ask ourselves whether one could, in principle, disprove it or whether it's consistent with any conceivable body of evidence.

SCIENTIFIC THINKING PRINCIPLE #4: *REPLICABILITY*. Barely a week goes by that we don't hear about another stunning psychological finding on the evening news: "Researchers at Cupcake State University detect a new gene linked to excessive shopping"; "Investigators at the University of Antarctica at Igloo report that alcoholism is associated with a heightened risk of murdering one's spouse"; "Nobel Prize–winning professor at Cucumber State College isolates brain area responsible for the enjoyment of popcorn." One problem with these conclusions, in addition to the fact that the news media often tell us nothing about the design of the studies on which they're based, is that the findings often haven't been replicated. **Replicability** means that a study's findings can be duplicated consistently. If they can't be duplicated, it increases the odds that the original findings were due to chance. *We shouldn't place too much stock in a psychological finding until it's been replicated.*

Indeed, over the past decade, psychological scientists have become increasingly aware of the importance of replication (Asendorpf et al., 2013; Nosek, Spies, & Moytl, 2012). Some of this heightened awareness stems from difficulties in replicating certain well-established findings in psychology (Pashler & Wagenmakers, 2012), and some of it stems from a phenomenon known as the **decline effect**—the fact that the size of certain psychological findings appears to be shrinking over time (Schooler, 2011). For example, early studies of the effectiveness of newly developed medications for schizophrenia showed larger effects than did more recent studies (Leucht et al., 2009). The same decline in effectiveness over time may hold for parenting interventions for autism spectrum disorder (Ozonoff, 2011)

ESP researchers often ask participants to predict the outcomes of random events. Yet ESP findings have proven difficult to replicate.

falsifiable
capable of being disproved

replicability
when a study's findings are able to be duplicated, ideally by independent investigators

decline effect
fact that the size of certain psychological findings appears to be shrinking over time

as well as numerous other psychological phenomena. Although psychologists aren't sure how widespread a problem the decline effect is, virtually all agree that it sometimes exists. In 2012, University of Virginia psychologist Brian Nosek and his collaborators launched the "Reproducibility Project," a coordinated effort by more than 100 psychologists to try to replicate widely cited studies in psychology (Carpenter, 2012).

Most replications aren't exact duplications of the original researchers' methods. Most involve introducing minor variations in the original design or extending this design to different participants, including those in various cultures, races, and geographical locations. In general, the more we can replicate our findings using different participants in different settings, the more confidence we can place in those findings (Schmidt, 2009; Shadish, Cook, & Campbell, 2002).

We should bear in mind that the media are far more likely to report initial positive findings than failures to replicate. The initial findings may be especially fascinating or sensational, whereas replication failures are often disappointing: they don't make for juicy news stories. It's especially crucial that investigators other than the original researchers replicate the results because this increases our confidence in them. If I tell you that I've created a recipe for the world's most delicious veal parmigiana, but it turns out that every other chef who follows my recipe ends up with a meal that tastes like an old piece of cardboard smothered in rotten cheese and six-month-old tomato sauce, you'd be justifiably skeptical. Maybe I flat-out lied about my recipe. Or perhaps I wasn't following the recipe very closely and was instead tossing in ingredients that weren't even in the recipe. Or perhaps I'm such an extraordinary chef that nobody else can come close to replicating my miraculous culinary feats. In any case, you'd have every right to doubt my recipe until someone else replicated it. The same goes for psychological research.

The literature on ESP offers an excellent example of why replicability is so essential. Every once in a blue moon, a researcher reports a striking new finding that seemingly confirms the existence of ESP (Bem, 2011). Yet time and again, independent researchers haven't been able to replicate these tantalizing results (Galak et al., 2012; Ritchie, Wiseman, & French, 2012; Hyman, 1989; Lilienfeld, 1999c), which might lead a skeptical observer to wonder whether many of the initial positive findings were due to chance.

The bottom line: whenever we evaluate a psychological claim, we should ask ourselves whether independent investigators have replicated the findings that support this claim; otherwise, the findings might be a one-time-only fluke.

SCIENTIFIC THINKING PRINCIPLE #5: *EXTRAORDINARY CLAIMS REQUIRE EXTRAORDINARY EVIDENCE.* This principle was proposed in slightly different terms by eighteenth-century Scottish philosopher David Hume (Sagan, 1995; Truzzi, 1978). According to Hume, the more a claim contradicts what we already know, the more persuasive the evidence for this claim must be before we accept it.

A handful of researchers believe that every night, hundreds and even thousands of Americans are being lifted magically out of their beds, taken aboard flying saucers, and experimented on by aliens, only to be returned safely to their beds hours later (Clancy, 2005). According to some alien abduction advocates, aliens are extracting semen from human males to impregnate female aliens in an effort to create a race of alien–human hybrids.

Of course, alien abduction proponents *might* be right, and we shouldn't dismiss their claims out of hand. But their claims are pretty darned extraordinary, especially because they imply that tens of thousands of invading flying saucers from other solar systems have inexplicably managed to escape detection by hundreds of astronomers, not to mention air traffic controllers and radar operators. Alien abduction proponents have been unable to provide even a shred of concrete evidence that supposed abductees have actually encountered extraterrestrials—say, a convincing photograph of an alien, a tiny piece of a metal probe inserted by an alien, or even a strand of hair or shred of skin from an alien. Thus far, all that alien abduction proponents have to show for their claims are the self-reports of supposed abductees. Extraordinary claims, but decidedly ordinary evidence.

According to a few researchers, tens of thousands of Americans have been abducted by aliens and brought aboard spaceships to be experimented on. Could it really be happening, and how would we know?

MEN'S TOILETRIES

Too complicated

NEW QUADRUPLE BLADE

TBX TECHNOLOGY

TITANIUM ADVANCED SWIVEL HEAD

SUPER FLEXI-GRIP

www.chrismadden.co.uk

Occam chooses a razor

The bottom line: whenever we evaluate a psychological claim, we should ask ourselves whether this claim runs counter to many things we know already and, if it does, whether the evidence is as extraordinary as the claim.

SCIENTIFIC THINKING PRINCIPLE #6: *OCCAM'S RAZOR.* Occam's Razor, named after fourteenth-century British philosopher and monk Sir William of Occam, is also called the "principle of parsimony" (*parsimony* means logical simplicity). According to Occam's Razor, if two explanations account equally well for a phenomenon, we should generally select the more parsimonious one. Good researchers use Occam's Razor to "shave off" needlessly complicated explanations to arrive at the simplest explanation that does a good job of accounting for the evidence. Scientists of a romantic persuasion refer to Occam's Razor as the principle of KISS: keep it simple, stupid. Occam's Razor is only a guideline, not a hard-and-fast rule (Uttal, 2003). Every once in a while the best explanation for a phenomenon is the most complex, not the simplest. But Occam's Razor is a helpful rule of thumb, as it's right far more often than it's wrong.

During the late 1970s and 1980s, hundreds of mysterious designs, called crop circles, began appearing in wheat fields in England. Most of these designs were remarkably intricate. How on Earth (pun intended) can we explain these designs? Many believers in the paranormal concluded that these designs originated not on Earth, but on distant planets. The crop circles, they concluded, are proof positive of alien visitations to our world.

The crop circle excitement came crashing down in 1991, when two British men, David Bower and Doug Chorley, confessed to creating the crop circles as a barroom prank intended to poke fun at uncritical believers in extraterrestrials. They even demonstrated on camera how they used wooden planks and rope to stomp through tall fields of wheat and craft the complex designs. Occam's Razor reminds us that when confronted with two explanations that fit the evidence equally well, we should generally select the simpler one—in this case, human pranksters.

The bottom line: whenever we evaluate a psychological claim, we should ask ourselves whether the explanation offered is the simplest explanation that accounts for the data or whether simpler explanations can account for the data equally well.

Simulate in **MyPsychLab** the **Experiment:** Critical Thinking

Answers are located at the end of the text.

HEALTH BENEFITS OF FRUITS AND VEGETABLES   evaluating **CLAIMS**

We all know the importance of eating a balanced diet with plenty of fruits and vegetables. Yet many popular media sources exaggerate the health benefits of fruits and vegetables and even make dangerous claims about their ability to cure serious illnesses like diabetes or cancer. Let's evaluate some of these claims, which are modeled after actual advertisements.

"*Studies show* that eating walnuts *may* reduce your risk and delay the onset of Alzheimer's."

The use of the qualifying word *may* renders the claim difficult or impossible to falsify. What would we need to know about how these studies were conducted to validate the claim?

"Eating peaches gives you energy and makes you feel *light and fresh* throughout the year."

This claim is vague and difficult to falsify. How would you define or measure "light and fresh"?

"Avoid drugs or surgery and find a *completely natural* cure for your disease."

The phrase *completely natural* implies that the cure is safer than drugs or surgery. Can you think of any natural substances (including fruits and vegetables) that are dangerous or even fatal?

"These natural cures come from *ancient cultures* and have been handed down for thousands of years."

Does the fact that something has been around for a long time mean it is trustworthy? What logical fallacy does this ad commit?

26

Assess Your Knowledge — FACT or FICTION?

1. Scientific skepticism requires a willingness to keep an open mind to all claims. **True / False**

2. When evaluating a psychological claim, we should consider other plausible explanations for it. **True / False**

3. The fact that two things are related doesn't mean that one directly influences the other. **True / False**

4. Falsifiability means that a theory must be false to be meaningful. **True / False**

5. When psychological findings are replicated, it's especially important that the replications be conducted by the same team of investigators. **True / False**

Answers: 1. F; 2. T; 3. T; 4. F; 5. F

Psychology's Past and Present: What a Long, Strange Trip It's Been

7 Identify the major theoretical frameworks of psychology.

8 Describe different types of psychologists and identify what each of them does.

9 Describe the two great debates that have shaped the field of psychology.

10 Describe how psychological research affects our daily lives.

How did psychology emerge as a discipline, and has it always been plagued by pseudoscience? The scientific approach to the study of the mind, brain, and behavior emerged slowly, and the field's initial attempts displayed many of the weaknesses that pseudoscientific approaches possess today. Informal attempts to study and explain how our minds work have been with us for thousands of years. But psychology as a science has existed for only about 130 years, and many of those years were spent refining techniques to develop research methods that were free from bias (Coon, 1992). Throughout its history, psychology has struggled with many of the same challenges that we confront today when reasoning about psychological research. So it's important to understand how psychology evolved as a scientific discipline— that is, a discipline that relies on systematic research methods to avoid being fooled.

Psychology's Early History

We'll start our journey with a capsule summary of psychology's bumpy road from non-science to science (a timeline of significant events in the evolution of scientific psychology can be seen in **FIGURE 8**).

For many centuries, the field of psychology was difficult to distinguish from philosophy. Most academic psychologists held positions in departments of philosophy (psychology departments didn't even exist back then) and didn't conduct experimental research. Instead, they mostly sat and contemplated the human mind from the armchair. In essence, they relied on common sense.

Yet beginning in the late 1800s, the landscape of psychology changed dramatically. In 1879, Wilhelm Wundt (1832–1920) developed the first full-fledged psychological laboratory in Leipzig, Germany. Most of Wundt's investigations and those of his students focused on basic questions concerning our mental experiences: How different must two colors be for us to tell them apart? How long does it take us to react to a sound? What thoughts come to mind when we solve a math problem? Wundt used a combination of experimental methods, including reaction time procedures, and a technique called **introspection**, which required trained observers to carefully reflect and report on their mental experiences. Introspectionists might ask participants to look at an object, say an apple, and carefully report everything they saw. In many respects, the pioneering work of Wundt marked the beginnings of psychology as a science. Soon, psychologists elsewhere around the world followed Wundt's bold lead and opened laboratories in departments of psychology.

Study and **Review** in **MyPsychLab**

There are two explanations for crop circles, one supernatural and the other natural. Which should we believe?

Wilhelm Wundt (*right*) in the world's first psychology laboratory. Wundt is generally credited with launching psychology as a laboratory science in 1879.

introspection
method by which trained observers carefully reflect and report on their mental experiences

Psychology and Scientific Thinking

1649: René Descartes writes about the mind–body problem

Late 1700s: Frans Anton Mesmer discovers principles of hypnosis

Early 1800s: Due to efforts of Franz Joseph Gall and Joseph Spurzheim, phrenology becomes immensely popular in Europe and the United States

1850: Gustav Fechner experiences crucial insight linking physical changes in the external world to subjective changes in perception; leads to establishment of psychophysics

1859: Charles Darwin writes *Origin of Species*

1875: William James creates small psychological laboratory at Harvard University

1879: Wilhelm Wundt creates world's first formal psychological laboratory, launching psychology as an experimental science

1881: Wundt establishes first psychology journal

1883: J. Stanley Hall, one of Wundt's students, opens first major psychology laboratory in the United States, at Johns Hopkins University

1888: James McKeen Cattell becomes first professor of psychology in the United States

1889: Sir Francis Galton introduces concept of correlation, allowing psychologists to quantify associations among variables

1890: William James writes *Principles of Psychology*

1892: American Psychological Association (APA) founded

1896: Lightmer Witmer creates first psychological clinic at the University of Pennsylvania, launching field of clinical psychology

1900: Sigmund Freud writes *The Interpretation of Dreams*, landmark book in the history of psychoanalysis

1904: Mary Calkins is first woman elected president of the American Psychological Association

---

1967: Ulric Neisser writes *Cognitive Psychology*; helps to launch field of cognitive psychology

1963: Stanley Milgram publishes classic laboratory studies of obedience

1958: Joseph Wolpe writes *Psychotherapy by Reciprocal Inhibition*, helping to launch field of behavioral therapy

1954: Paul Meehl writes *Clinical versus Statistical Prediction*, first major book to describe both the strengths and weaknesses of clinical judgment

1953: Rapid eye movement (REM) sleep discovered

1953: Francis Crick and James Watson discover structure of DNA, launching genetic revolution

1952: Antipsychotic drug Thorazine tested in France, launching modern era of psychopharmacology

1949: Conference held at University of Colorado at Boulder to outline principles of scientific clinical psychology; founding of the "Boulder" (scientist-practitioner) model of clinical training

1938: B. F. Skinner writes *The Behavior of Organisms*

1935: Kurt Koffka writes *Principles of Gestalt Psychology*

1920s: Gordon Allport helps to initiate field of personality trait psychology

1920: Jean Piaget writes *The Child's Conception of the World*

1913: John B. Watson writes *Psychology as Behavior*, launching field of behaviorism

1911: E. L. Thorndike discovers instrumental (later called operant) conditioning

1910: Ivan Pavlov discovers classical conditioning

1907: Oscar Pfungst demonstrates that the amazing counting horse, Clever Hans, responds to cues from observers; demonstrates power of expectancies

1905: Alfred Binet and Henri Simon develop first intelligence test

---

1974: Positron emission tomography (PET) scanning introduced, launching field of functional brain imaging

1974: Elizabeth Loftus and Robert Palmer publish paper showing that memory is more reconstructive than previously believed

1976: Founding of Committee for the Scientific Investigation of Claims of the Paranormal, first major organization to apply scientific skepticism to paranormal claims

1977: First use of statistical technique of meta-analysis, which allows researchers to systematically combine results of multiple studies; demonstrated that psychotherapy is effective

1980: *Diagnostic and Statistical Manual of Mental Disorders,* Third Edition (*DSM-III*) published; helps standardize the diagnosis of mental disorders

1980s: Recovered memory craze sweeps across America; pits academic researchers against many clinicians

1988: Many scientifically oriented psychologists break off from APA to found American Psychological Society (APS)

1990: Thomas Bouchard and colleagues publish major results of Minnesota Study of Twins Reared Apart, demonstrating substantial genetic bases for intelligence, personality, and other individual differences

1995: Task force of Division 12 (Society of Clinical Psychology) of American Psychological Association publishes list of, and criteria for, empirically supported psychotherapies

2000: Human genome sequenced

2002: Daniel Kahneman becomes first Ph.D. psychologist to win Nobel Prize; honored for his pioneering work (with the late Amos Tversky) on biases and heuristics

2004: APS members vote to change name to Association for Psychological Science

2009: New graduate accreditation system proposed to place psychotherapy training on a firmer scientific footing.

2012: Reproducibility Project launched to find out how many psychological findings can be replicated.

2013: Diagnostic and Statistical Manual of Mental Disorders, Fifth Edition (DSM-5) published.

FIGURE 8 Timeline of Major Events in Scientific Psychology.

Before becoming a science, psychology also needed to break free from another influence: spiritualism. The term *psychology* literally means the study of the "psyche," that is, spirit or soul. In the mid and late 1800s, Americans became fascinated with spirit mediums, people who claimed to contact the dead, often during séances (Blum, 2006). These were group sessions that took place in darkened rooms, in which mediums attempted to "channel" the spirits of deceased individuals. Americans were equally enchanted with psychics, individuals who claimed to possess powers of mind reading and other extrasensory abilities. Many famous psychologists of the day invested a great deal of time and effort in the search for these paranormal capacities (Benjamin & Baker, 2004; Blum, 2006).

They ultimately failed, and psychology eventually developed a respectful distance from spiritualism. It did so largely by creating a new field: the psychology of human error and self-deception. Rather than asking whether extrasensory powers exist, a growing number of psychologists in the late 1800s began to ask the equally fascinating question of how people can fool themselves into believing things that aren't supported by evidence (Coon, 1992).

The Great Theoretical Frameworks of Psychology

Almost since its inception, psychological science has confronted a thorny question: what unifying theoretical perspective best explains behavior?

Five major theoretical perspectives—structuralism, functionalism, behaviorism, cognitivism, and psychoanalysis—have played pivotal roles in shaping contemporary psychological thought. Many beginning psychology students understandably ask, "Which of these perspectives is the right one?" As it turns out, the answer isn't entirely clear. Each theoretical viewpoint has something valuable to contribute to scientific psychology, but each has its limitations (see **TABLE 5**). In some cases, these different viewpoints may not be contradictory, as

Factoid

One of William James' Ph.D. students was Mary Whiton Calkins (1863–1930), who became the first female president of the American Psychological Association in 1905. Despite being an outstanding student at Harvard University, the faculty denied her tenure because of her gender—and in spite of James's recommendation of her. Calkins made significant contributions to the study of memory, sensation, and self-concept.

TABLE 5 The Theoretical Perspectives That Shaped Psychology.

PERSPECTIVE		LEADING FIGURES	SCIENTIFIC GOAL	LASTING SCIENTIFIC INFLUENCE
Structuralism ◀ E. B. Titchener		E.B. Titchener	Uses introspection to identify basic elements or "structures" of experience	Emphasis on the importance of systematic observation to the study of conscious experience
Functionalism ◀ William James		William James; influenced by Charles Darwin	To understand the functions or adaptive purposes of our thoughts, feelings, and behaviors	Has been absorbed into psychology and continues to influence it indirectly in many ways
Behaviorism ◀ B. F. Skinner		Ivan Pavlov; John B. Watson; B. F. Skinner	To uncover the general principles of learning that explain all behaviors; focus is largely on observable behavior	Influential in models of human and animal learning and among the first to focus on need for objective research
Cognitivism ◀ Jean Piaget		Jean Piaget; Ulric Neisser	To examine the role of mental processes on behavior	Influential in many areas, such as language, problem solving, concept formation, intelligence, memory, and psychotherapy
Psychoanalysis ◀ Sigmund Freud		Sigmund Freud	To uncover the role of unconscious psychological processes and early life experiences in behavior	Understanding that much of our mental processing goes on outside of conscious awareness

Charles Darwin's theory of evolution by natural selection was a significant influence on functionalism, which strove to understand the adaptive purposes of psychological characteristics.

John B. Watson, one of the founders of behaviorism. Watson's stubborn insistence on scientific rigor made him a hero to some and an enemy to others.

structuralism
school of psychology that aimed to identify the basic elements of psychological experience

functionalism
school of psychology that aimed to understand the adaptive purposes of psychological characteristics

natural selection
principle that organisms that possess adaptations survive and reproduce at a higher rate than do other organisms

behaviorism
school of psychology that focuses on uncovering the general laws of learning by looking at observable behavior

they may be explaining behavior at different levels of analysis. As we wind our way through these five frameworks, we'll discover that psychology's view of what constitutes a scientific approach to behavior has changed over time. Indeed, it continues to evolve even today.

STRUCTURALISM: THE ELEMENTS OF THE MIND. Edward Bradford Titchener (1867–1927), a British student of Wundt who emigrated to the United States, founded the field of structuralism. **Structuralism** aimed to identify the basic elements, or "structures," of psychological experience. Adopting Wundt's method of introspection, structuralists dreamed of creating a comprehensive "map" of the elements of consciousness—which they believed consisted of sensations, images, and feelings—much like the periodic table of the elements we can find in every chemistry classroom (Evans, 1972).

Structuralism eventually ran out of steam. At least two major problems eventually did it in. First, even highly trained introspectionists often disagreed on their subjective reports. Second, German psychologist Oswald Kulpe (1862–1915) showed that participants asked to solve certain mental problems engage in *imageless thought:* thinking unaccompanied by conscious experience. If we ask an introspecting participant to add 10 and 5, he or she will quickly respond "15," but usually be unable to report what came to mind when performing this calculation (Hergenhahn, 2000). The phenomenon of imageless thought dealt a serious body blow to structuralism because it demonstrated that some important aspects of human psychology lie outside conscious awareness.

Structuralism correctly emphasized the importance of *systematic observation* to the study of conscious experience. Nevertheless, structuralists went astray by assuming that a single, imperfect method—introspection—could provide all of the information needed for a complete science of psychology. In the time since introspectionism came and went, psychologists have learned that multiple methods are almost always needed to understand complex psychological phenomena (Cook, 1985; Figueredo, 1993).

FUNCTIONALISM: PSYCHOLOGY MEETS DARWIN. Proponents of **functionalism** strove to understand the adaptive purposes, or functions, of psychological characteristics, such as thoughts, feelings, and behaviors (Hunt, 1993). Whereas structuralists asked "what" questions, such as "What is conscious thought like?" functionalists asked "why" questions, such as "Why do we sometimes forget things?" The founder of functionalism, William James, rejected structuralists' approach and methods, arguing that careful introspection doesn't yield a fixed number of static elements of consciousness but rather an ever-changing "stream of consciousness," a famous phrase he coined. James is also famous for writing the influential text *Principles of Psychology* (1890), which introduced the science of psychology to the general public.

The functionalists of the late 1800s were influenced substantially by biologist Charles Darwin's (1809–1882) still-young theory of **natural selection**, which emphasized that physical and behavioral characteristics evolved because they increased the chances of their survival and reproduction. The functionalists believed that Darwin's theory applied to psychological characteristics, too. Just as the trunk of an elephant serves useful survival functions such as snaring distant water and food, the human memory system, for example, must similarly serve a purpose. It's the job of psychologists, functionalists maintained, to act as "detectives," figuring out the evolved functions that psychological characteristics serve for organisms.

Like structuralism, functionalism doesn't exist in its original form today. Instead, functionalism was gradually absorbed into mainstream scientific psychology and continues to influence it indirectly in many ways.

BEHAVIORISM: THE LAWS OF LEARNING. By the early twentieth century, many American psychologists were growing impatient with the touchy-feely nature of their discipline. In particular, they believed that Titchener and other introspectionists were leading psychology down a misguided path. For these critics, the study of consciousness was a waste of time because researchers could never verify conclusively the existence of the basic elements of mental experience. Psychological science, they contended, must be objective, not subjective.

Foremost among these critics was a flamboyant American psychologist, John B. Watson (1878–1958). Watson was a founder of the still-influential school of **behaviorism**, which focuses on uncovering the general principles of learning underlying human and animal behavior. For Watson (1913), the proper subject matter of psychology was observable behavior, plain and simple. Subjective reports of conscious experience should play no part in psychology. If it followed his brave lead, Watson proclaimed, psychology could become just as scientific as physics, chemistry, and other hard sciences.

Watson, like his follower Burrhus Frederic (B.F.) Skinner (1904–1990), insisted that psychology should aspire to uncover the general laws of learning that explain all behaviors, whether they be riding a bicycle, eating a sandwich, or becoming depressed. All of these behaviors, they proposed, are products of a handful of basic learning principles. Moreover, according to Watson and Skinner, we don't need to peer "inside" the organism to grasp these principles. We can comprehend human behavior exclusively by looking *outside* the organism, to rewards and punishments delivered by the environment. For traditional behaviorists, the human mind is a black box: we know what goes in it and what comes out of it, but we needn't worry about what happens between the inputs and the outputs. For this reason, psychologists sometimes call behaviorism *black box psychology*.

Behaviorism has left a stamp on scientific psychology that continues to be felt today. By identifying the fundamental laws of learning that help to explain human and animal behavior, behaviorists placed psychology on firmer scientific footing. Although early behaviorists' deep mistrust of subjective observations of conscious experience probably went too far, these psychologists properly warned us of the hazards of relying too heavily on reports that we can't verify objectively.

COGNITIVISM: OPENING THE BLACK BOX. Beginning in the 1950s and 1960s, growing numbers of psychologists grew disillusioned with behaviorists' neglect of *cognition,* the term psychologists use to describe the mental processes involved in different aspects of thinking. Although some behaviorists acknowledged that humans and even many intelligent animals do think, they viewed thinking as merely another form of behavior. Proponents of **cognitive psychology**, in contrast, argued that our thinking affects our behavior in powerful ways. For example, Swiss psychologist Jean Piaget (1896–1980) argued compellingly that children conceptualize the world in markedly different ways than do adults. Later, led by Ulric Neisser (1928–2012), cognitivists argued that thinking is so central to psychology that it merits a separate discipline in its own right (Neisser, 1967).

According to cognitivists, a psychology based solely on rewards and punishments will never be adequate because our *interpretation* of rewards and punishments is a crucial determinant of our behavior. Take a student who receives a B+ on his first psychology exam. A student accustomed to getting Fs on his tests might regard this grade as a reward, whereas a student accustomed to A's might view it as a punishment. Without understanding how people evaluate information, cognitivists maintain, we'll never fully grasp the causes of their behavior. Moreover, according to cognitivists, we often learn not merely by rewards and punishments but by *insight,* that is, by grasping the underlying nature of problems.

Cognitive psychology is a thriving approach today, and its tentacles have spread to such diverse domains as language, problem solving, concept formation, intelligence, memory, and even psychotherapy. By focusing not merely on rewards and punishments but on organisms' interpretation of them, cognitivism has encouraged psychologists to peek inside the black box to examine the connections between inputs and outputs. Moreover, cognitivism has increasingly established strong linkages to the study of brain functioning, allowing psychologists to better understand the physiological bases of thinking, memory, and other mental functions (Ilardi & Feldman, 2001). A burgeoning field, **cognitive neuroscience**, which examines the relation between brain functioning and thinking, has come to the fore over the past decade or so (Gazzaniga, Ivry, & Mangun, 2002). Cognitive neuroscience and the allied field of affective neuroscience (Panksepp, 2004), which examines the relation between brain functioning and emotion, hold out the promise of allowing us to better understand the biological processes associated with thinking and feeling.

PSYCHOANALYSIS: THE DEPTHS OF THE UNCONSCIOUS. Around the time that behaviorism was becoming dominant in the United States, a parallel movement was gathering momentum in Europe. This field, psychoanalysis, was founded by Viennese neurologist Sigmund Freud (1856–1939). In sharp contrast to behaviorism, **psychoanalysis** focused

Two students may react to the same grade on a test—say a B+—in markedly different ways. One may be pleased, the other, disappointed. Cognitive psychologists would say that these different reactions stem from the students' different interpretations of what these grades mean to them.

The couch that Sigmund Freud used to psychoanalyze his patients, now located in the Freud museum in London, England. Contrary to popular conception, most psychologists aren't psychotherapists, and most psychotherapists aren't even psychoanalysts. Nor do most modern therapists ask patients to recline on couches.

cognitive psychology
school of psychology that proposes that thinking is central to understanding behavior

cognitive neuroscience
relatively new field of psychology that examines the relation between brain functioning and thinking

psychoanalysis
school of psychology, founded by Sigmund Freud, that focuses on internal psychological processes of which we're unaware

on internal psychological processes, especially impulses, thoughts, and memories of which we're unaware. According to Freud (1900) and other psychoanalysts, the primary influences on behavior aren't forces outside the organism, like rewards and punishments, but rather unconscious drives, especially sexuality and aggression.

Psychoanalysts maintain that much of our everyday psychological life is filled with symbols—things that represent other things (Loevinger, 1987; Moore & Fine, 1995). For example, if you refer accidentally to one of your female professors as "Mom," Freudians would be unlikely to treat this embarrassing blooper as an isolated mistake. Instead, they'd quickly suggest that your professor probably reminds you of your mother, which may be a good reason to transfer to a different course. The goal of the psychoanalyst is to decode the symbolic meaning of our slips of the tongue (or *Freudian slips,* as they're often called), dreams, and psychological symptoms. By doing so, psychoanalysts contend, they can get to the roots of our deep-seated psychological conflicts. Psychoanalysts also place considerably more emphasis than do other schools of thought on the role of infant and childhood experience. For Freud and others, the core of our personality is molded in the first few years of life.

The influence of Freud and psychoanalysis on scientific psychology is controversial. On the one hand, some critics insist that psychoanalysis retarded the progress of scientific psychology because it focused heavily on unconscious processes that are difficult or impossible to falsify. These critics probably have a point (Crews, 2005; Esterson, 1993). On the other hand, at least some psychoanalytic claims, such as the assertion that a great deal of important mental processing goes on outside conscious awareness, have held up well in scientific research (Westen, 1998; Wilson, 2002). It's not clear, however, whether the Freudian view of the unconscious bears anything more than a superficial resemblance to more contemporary views of unconscious processing (Kihlstrom, 1987).

The Multifaceted World of Modern Psychology

Psychology isn't just one discipline, but rather an assortment of many subdisciplines. These subdisciplines differ widely in their preferred level of analysis, ranging all the way from biological to cultural. In most major psychology departments, we can find researchers examining areas as varied as the neurological bases of visual perception, the mechanisms of memory, the causes of prejudice, and the treatment of depression.

THE GROWTH OF A FIELD. Today, there are about 500,000 psychologists worldwide (Kassin, 2004), with more than 100,000 in the United States alone (McFall, 2006). The American Psychological Association (APA), founded in 1892 and now the world's largest association of psychologists, consists of more than 150,000 members. (To give us a sense of how much the field has grown, there were only 150 APA members in 1900.) A more research-oriented organization, the Association for Psychological Science, which began in 1988, has over 23,000 members. The percentage of women and minorities within the APA has grown steadily, too. These members' interests span such topics as addiction; art psychology; clinical psychology; hypnosis; law and psychology; media psychology; mental retardation; neuroscience; psychology and religion; sports psychology; the psychology of women; and gay, lesbian, bisexual, and transgendered issues.

TYPES OF PSYCHOLOGISTS: FICTION AND FACT. FIGURE 9 shows a breakdown of the settings in which psychologists work. As we can see, some work primarily in research settings; others, primarily in practice settings. **TABLE 6** describes a few of the most important types of psychologists. It also dispels common misconceptions about what each type of psychologist does, pairing each misconception with accurate information (Rosenthal et al., 2004).

As we can see, the field of psychology is remarkably diverse, as are the types of careers psychology majors pursue. Moreover, the face of psychology is changing, with more women and minorities entering many of its subfields (see **FIGURE 10**). Despite their differences in content, all of these areas of psychology have one thing in common: most of the psychologists who specialize in them rely on scientific methods. Specifically, they

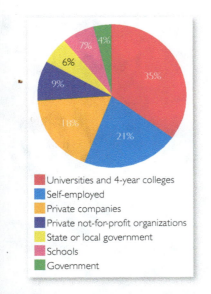

FIGURE 9 Approximate Distribution of Psychologists in Different Settings. Psychologists are employed in a diverse array of settings. (Based on data from the National Science Foundation, 2003)

- Universities and 4-year colleges
- Self-employed
- Private companies
- Private not-for-profit organizations
- State or local government
- Schools
- Government

 Explore in **MyPsychLab** the **Concept:** Early Schools of Thoughts

Psychologists Elizabeth Loftus (a) and Paul Meehl (b) are far less well known to the general public than are psychologists Dr. Phil (c) and John Gray (d), but they've had a much greater impact on how we think about ourselves and the world.

 Explore in **MyPsychLab** the **Concept:** Psychologists at Work

TABLE 6 Types of Psychologists, What They Do, and What They Don't Do.

TYPE OF PSYCHOLOGIST	WHAT DO THEY DO?	FREQUENT MISCONCEPTION AND TRUTH
Clinical Psychologist	• Perform assessment, diagnosis, and treatment of mental disorders • Conduct research on people with mental disorders • Work in colleges and universities, mental health centers, and private practice	*Misconception: You need a Ph.D. to become a therapist.* • **Truth:** Most clinical psychology Ph.D. programs are highly research-oriented. Other options for therapists are a Psy.D. (doctor of psychology), which focuses on training therapists rather than researchers, and an M.S.W., a master's degree in social work, which also focuses on training therapists.
Counseling Psychologist	• Work with people experiencing temporary or relatively self-contained life problems, like marital conflict, sexual difficulties, occupational stressors, or career uncertainty • Work in counseling centers, hospitals, and private practice (although some work in academic and research settings)	*Misconception: Counseling psychology is pretty much the same as clinical psychology.* • **Truth:** Whereas clinical psychologists work with people with serious mental disorders like severe depression, most counseling psychologists don't.
School Psychologist	• Work with teachers, parents, and children to remedy students' behavioral, emotional, and learning difficulties	*Misconception: School psychology is another term for educational psychology.* • **Truth:** Educational psychology is a substantially different discipline that focuses on helping instructors identify better methods for teaching and evaluating learning.
Developmental Psychologist	• Study how and why people change over time • Conduct research on infants', children's, and sometimes adults' and elderly people's emotional, physiological, and cognitive processes and how these change with age	*Misconception: Developmental psychologists spend most of their time on their hands and knees playing with children.* • **Truth:** Most spend their time in the laboratory, collecting and analyzing data.
Experimental Psychologist	• Use research methods to study memory, language, thinking, and social behaviors of humans • Work primarily in research settings	*Misconception: Experimental psychologists do all of their work in psychological laboratories.* • **Truth:** Many conduct research in real-world settings, examining how people acquire language, remember events, apply mental concepts, and the like, in everyday life.
Biological Psychologist	• Examine the physiological bases of behavior in animals and humans • Most work in research settings	*Misconception: All biological psychologists use invasive methods in their research.* • **Truth:** Although many biological psychologists create brain lesions in animals to examine their effects on behavior, others use brain imaging methods that don't require investigators to damage organisms' nervous systems.
Forensic Psychologist	• Work in prisons, jails, and other settings to assess and diagnose inmates and assist with their rehabilitation and treatment • Others conduct research on eyewitness testimony or jury decision making • Typically hold degrees in clinical or counseling psychology	*Misconception: Most forensic psychologists are criminal profilers, like those employed by the FBI.* • **Truth:** Criminal profiling is a small and controversial subspecialty within forensic psychology.
Industrial-Organizational Psychologists	• Work in companies and businesses to help select productive employees, evaluate performance, examine the effects of different working and living conditions on people's behavior (called *environmental psychologists*) • Design equipment to maximize employee performance and minimize accidents (called *human factors* or *engineering psychologists*)	*Misconception: Most industrial/organizational psychologists work on a one-to-one basis with employees to increase their motivation and productivity.* • **Truth:** Most spend their time constructing tests and selection procedures or implementing organizational changes to improve worker productivity and satisfaction.

use scientific methods to generate new findings about human or animal behavior or use existing findings to enhance human welfare. But as we've discussed, many pseudoscientists try to lead us to believe that they're using a genuinely scientific approach.

The Great Debates of Psychology

Now that we've learned a bit about the past and present of psychology, we need to set the stage for things to come. Two great debates have shaped the field of psychology since its inception and seem likely to continue to shape it in the future.

THE NATURE–NURTURE DEBATE. The nature–nurture debate poses the following question: *are our behaviors attributable mostly to our genes (nature) or to our rearing environments (nurture)?*

The nature–nurture debate has proven especially controversial in the domains of intelligence, personality, and psychopathology (mental illness). Many early thinkers, such as British philosopher John Locke (1632–1704), likened the human mind at birth to white paper that hadn't been written on. Others after him referred to the mind as a *tabula rasa* ("blank slate"). For Locke and his followers, we enter the world with no genetic preconceptions or preconceived ideas: we're shaped exclusively by our environments (Pinker, 2002). For much of the twentieth century, most psychologists assumed that virtually all human behavior was exclusively a product of learning. But research conducted by *behavior geneticists,* who use sophisticated designs such as twin and adoption studies, shows that most important psychological traits, including intelligence, interests, personality, and many mental illnesses, are influenced substantially by genes. Increasingly, modern psychologists have come to recognize that human behavior is attributable not only to our environment, but also to our genes (Bouchard, 2004; Harris, 2002).

Because just about everyone now agrees that both genes and environment play crucial roles in most human behaviors, some people have declared the nature–nurture debate dead (Ferris, 1996). Yet we still have a great deal to learn about how much nature or nurture contributes to different behaviors and how nature and nurture work together. Indeed, the old dichotomy between nature and nurture is far less clear-cut—and far more interesting—than once believed. Nature and nurture sometimes intersect in complex and surprising ways.

One domain of psychology that's shed light on the nature–nurture debate is **evolutionary psychology**, which applies Darwin's theory of natural selection to human and animal behavior (Barkow, Cosmides, & Tooby, 1992; Dennett, 1995; Tooby & Cosmides, 1989). It begins with the assumption, shared by William James and other functionalists, that many human psychological systems, like memory, emotion, and personality, serve key adaptive functions: They help organisms survive and reproduce. Darwin and his followers suggested that natural selection favored certain kinds of mental traits, just as it did physical ones, like our hands, livers, and hearts.

Biologists refer to *fitness* as the extent to which a trait increases the chances that organisms that possess this trait will survive and reproduce at a higher rate than competitors who lack it. Fitness has nothing to do, by the way, with how strong or powerful an organism is. By surviving and reproducing at higher rates than other organisms, more fit organisms pass on their genes more successfully to later generations. For example, humans who have at least some degree of anxiety probably survived at higher rates than humans who lacked it, because anxiety serves an essential function: it warns us of impending danger (Barlow, 2000; Damasio & Carvalho, 2013).

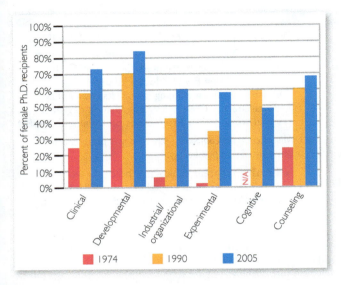

FIGURE 10 The Face of Psychology Has Changed Dramatically over the Past Three Decades. Across most areas, the percentage of women earning doctoral degrees has increased. In clinical and developmental psychology, women comprise three-fourths to four-fifths of those attaining Ph.D.s. (Based on data from APA, 2007)

"The title of my science project is 'My Little Brother: Nature or Nurture.'"

evolutionary psychology
discipline that applies Darwin's theory of natural selection to human and animal behavior

Still, evolutionary psychology has received more than its share of criticism (Kitcher, 1985; Panksepp & Panksepp, 2000). Many of its predictions are extremely difficult to falsify. In part, that's because behavior, unlike the bones of dinosaurs, early humans, and other animals, doesn't leave fossils. As a consequence, it's far more challenging to determine the evolutionary functions of anxiety or depression than the functions of birds' wings. For example, two researchers speculated that male baldness serves an evolutionary function, because women supposedly perceive a receding hairline as a sign of maturity (Muscarella & Cunningham, 1996). But if it turned out that women preferred men with a lot of hair to bald men, it would be easy to cook up an explanation for that finding ("Women perceive men with a full head of hair as stronger and more athletic"). Evolutionary explanations could account for either outcome. Evolutionary psychology has the potential to be an important unifying framework for psychology (Buss, 1995; Confer et al., 2010), but we should beware of evolutionary explanations that can fit almost any piece of evidence after the fact (de Waal, 2002).

THE FREE WILL–DETERMINISM DEBATE. The free will–determinism debate poses the following question: *to what extent are our behaviors freely selected rather than caused by factors outside our control?*

Most of us like to believe that we're free to do what we want whenever we want. You may believe that at this very moment, you can decide to continue reading to the end of the chapter or take a well-deserved break to watch TV. Indeed, our legal system is premised on the concept of free will. We punish criminals because they're supposedly free to abide by the law but choose otherwise. One major exception, of course, is the insanity defense, in which the legal system assumes that severe mental illness can interfere with people's free will (Hoffman & Morse, 2006; Stone, 1982). Some prominent psychologists agree that we all possess free will (Baumeister, 2008).

Yet many others maintain that free will is actually an illusion (Bargh, 2008; Sappington, 1990; Wegner, 2002). Behaviorist B. F. Skinner (1971) argued that our sense of free will stems from the fact that we aren't consciously aware of the thousands of subtle environmental influences impinging on our behavior at any given moment. Much like puppets in a play who don't realize that actors are pulling their strings, we conclude mistakenly that we're free simply because we don't realize all of the influences acting on our behavior. For Skinner and others, our behaviors are completely determined.

Some psychologists argue that most or even all of our behaviors are generated *automatically*—that is, without conscious awareness (Bargh, 2011; Kirsch & Lynn, 1999; Libet, 1985). We may even come to believe that something or someone else is producing behaviors we ourselves are generating. For example, people who engage in *automatic writing*—writing sentences while seemingly in a trance—typically insist they're being compelled to do so by some outside force. But there's strong evidence that they're generating this behavior themselves, although unconsciously (Wegner, 2002). According to many determinists, our everyday behaviors are produced in the same way—triggered automatically by influences of which we're unaware (Bargh & Chartrand, 1999). Still, other psychologists aren't convinced; they believe that we maintain a great deal of conscious control over our behavior (Newell & Shanks, 2013).

How Psychology Affects Our Lives

Psychological science and scientific thinking offer important applications for a variety of aspects of everyday life. Psychological scientists often distinguish basic from applied research. **Basic research** examines how the mind works, whereas **applied research** examines how we can use basic research to solve real-world problems (Nickerson, 1999). Within most large psychology departments, we find a healthy mix of people conducting basic research, such as investigators who study the laws of learning, and applied research, such as investigators who study how to help people cope with the psychological burden of cancer.

The fact that American men spend billions of dollars per year on hair replacement treatments is difficult to square with evolutionary hypotheses suggesting that women prefer bald men. The bottom line: beware of unfalsifiable evolutionary stories.

Watch in **MyPsychLab** the **Video:** Thinking Like a Psychologist: Evolutionary Psychology

Factoid

Inducing students to believe in determinism—by having them read a scientific passage suggesting that free will is an illusion—makes them more likely to cheat on a test in the laboratory (Vohs & Schooler, 2008). So regardless of whether free will exists, belief in it may serve a useful function—inhibiting unethical behavior.

basic research
research examining how the mind works

applied research
research examining how we can use basic research to solve real-world problems

APPLICATIONS OF PSYCHOLOGICAL RESEARCH. Surveys show few people are aware of the substantial impact of psychology on their everyday lives (Lilienfeld, 2012; Wood, Jones, & Benjamin, 1986). Indeed, psychological science has found its way into far more aspects of contemporary society than most of us realize (Salzinger, 2002; Zimbardo, 2004a). Let's look at a sampling of these applications; we can discover more about these and other examples on a free pamphlet produced by the American Psychological Association: www.decadeofbehavior.org/BehaviorMattersBooklet.pdf.

Increasingly, today's fire trucks are lime-yellow rather than red. That's because psychological research has demonstrated that lime-yellow objects are easier to spot in the dark than are red objects.

Thanks to psychological research, advertisers know that placing a model's face on the left and written text on the right of an advertisement best captures readers' attention.

A classic simultaneous eyewitness lineup. Although police commonly use such lineups, most research suggests that they're more prone to error than are sequential lineups.

- If you live in or near a big city, you may have noticed a gradual change in the color of fire engines. Although old fire engines were bright red, most new ones are lime-yellow. That's because psychological researchers who study perception found that lime-yellow objects are easier to detect in the dark. Indeed, lime-yellow fire trucks are only about half as likely to be involved in traffic accidents as are red fire trucks (American Psychological Association, 2003; Solomon & King, 1995).

- As a car driver, have you ever had to slam on your brakes to avoid hitting a driver directly in front of you who stopped short suddenly? If so, and if you managed to avoid a bad accident, you may have John Voevodsky to thank. For decades, cars had only two brake lights. In the early 1970s, Voevodsky hit on the bright (pun intended) idea of placing a third brake light at the base of cars' back windshields. He reasoned that this additional visual information would decrease the risk of rear-end collisions. He conducted a ten-month study of taxis with and without the new brake lights and found a 61 percent lower rate of rear-end accidents in the first group (Voevodsky, 1974). As a result of his research, all new American cars have three brake lights.

- If you're anything like the average American, you see more than 100 commercial messages every day. The chances are that psychologists had a hand in crafting many of them. The founder of behaviorism, John B. Watson, pioneered the application of psychology to advertising in the 1920s and 1930s. Today, psychological researchers still contribute to the marketing success of companies. For instance, psychologists who study magazine advertisements have discovered that human faces better capture readers' attention on the left side rather than the right side of pages. Written text, in contrast, better captures readers' attention on the right side rather than the left side of pages (Clay, 2002).

- To get into college, you probably had to take one or more tests, like the SAT or ACT. If so, you can thank—or blame—psychologists with expertise in measuring academic achievement and knowledge, who were primarily responsible for developing these measures (Zimbardo, 2004a). Although these tests are far from perfect predictors of academic performance, they do significantly better than chance in forecasting how students perform in college (Geiser & Studley, 2002; Sackett, Borneman, & Connelly, 2008).

- Police officers often ask victims of violent crimes to select a suspect from a lineup. When doing so, they've traditionally used *simultaneous lineups,* in which one or more suspects and several decoys (people who aren't really suspects) are lined up in a row, often of five to eight individuals. These are the kinds of lineups we've most often seen on television crime shows. Yet psychological research shows that *sequential lineups*—those in which victims view each person individually and then decide whether he or she was the perpetrator of the crime—are generally more accurate than simultaneous lineups (Cutler & Wells, 2009; Steblay et al., 2003; Wells, Memon, & Penrod, 2006). As a result of this research, police departments around the United States are increasingly using sequential rather than simultaneous lineups (Lilienfeld & Byron, 2013).

- For many years, many American public schools were legally required to be racially segregated. Before 1954, the law of the land in the United States was that "separate but equal" facilities were sufficient to guarantee racial equality.

But based in part on the pioneering research of psychologists Kenneth and Mamie Clark (1950), who demonstrated that African-American children preferred white to African-American dolls, the U.S. Supreme Court decided—in the landmark 1954 case of *Brown v. Board of Education of Topeka, Kansas*—that school segregation exerted a negative impact on the self-esteem of African-American children.

So, far more than most of us realize, the fruits of psychological research are all around us. Psychology has dramatically altered the landscape of everyday life, in most cases for the better.

THINKING SCIENTIFICALLY: IT'S A WAY OF LIFE. learning to think scientifically will help you make better decisions not only in psychology courses, but also in everyday life. Each day, the news and entertainment media bombard us with confusing and contradictory claims about a host of topics: herbal remedies, weight loss plans, parenting methods, insomnia treatments, speed-reading courses, urban legends, political conspiracy theories, unidentified flying objects, and "overnight cures" for mental disorders, to name only a few. Some of these claims are partly true, whereas others are entirely bogus. Yet the media typically offer little guidance for sorting out which claims are scientific, pseudoscientific, or a bit of both. It's scarcely any wonder that we're often tempted to throw up our hands in despair and ask, "What I am supposed to believe?"

Fortunately, the scientific thinking skills can assist you in successfully navigating the bewildering world of popular psychology and popular culture. The trick is to bear three words in mind: *Insist on evidence.* By recognizing that common sense can take us only so far in evaluating claims, we can come to appreciate the need for scientific evidence to avoid being fooled—and to avoid fooling ourselves.

The classic doll studies of Kenneth and Mamie Clark paved the way for the 1954 Supreme Court decision of *Brown v. Board of Education,* which mandated racial integration of public schools.

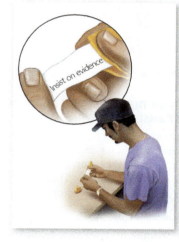

When it comes to evaluating psychological claims in the news or entertainment media, there's a simple bottom-line message: we should always insist on rigorous research evidence.

Study and **Review** in **MyPsychLab**

Assess Your Knowledge
FACT or FICTION?

1. Behaviorism focuses on uncovering the general laws of learning in animals, but not humans.   True / False

2. Cognitive psychologists argue that we need to understand how organisms interpret rewards and punishments.   True / False

3. Advocates of determinism believe that free will is an illusion.   True / False

4. Studying color discrimination in the lab is basic research, whereas testing which color fire trucks are painted results in the fewest traffic accidents is applied research.   True / False

5. Achievement tests such as the SAT do no better than chance at predicting how students will perform in college.   True / False

Answers: 1. F; 2. T; 3. T; 4. T; 5. F

Your Complete Review System

 Study and **Review** in **MyPsychLab**

((· **Listen** in **MyPsychLab** to chapter audio

What Is Psychology? Science Versus Intuition

1 EXPLAIN WHY PSYCHOLOGY IS MORE THAN JUST COMMON SENSE.

Psychology is the scientific study of the mind, brain, and behavior. Although we often rely on our common sense to understand the psychological world, our intuitive understanding of ourselves and others is often mistaken. Naive realism is the error of believing that we see the world precisely as it is. It can lead us to false beliefs about ourselves and our world, such as believing that our perceptions and memories are always accurate.

1. Which would be a better description of naive realism, "seeing is believing" or "believing is seeing"?

2. What does Shepard's table illusion tell us about our ability to trust our own intuitions and experiences?

3. Our common sense (is/isn't) always wrong.

2 EXPLAIN THE IMPORTANCE OF SCIENCE AS A SET OF SAFEGUARDS AGAINST BIASES.

Confirmation bias is the tendency to seek out evidence that supports our hypotheses and deny, dismiss, or distort evidence that doesn't. Belief perseverance is the tendency to cling to our beliefs despite contrary evidence. The scientific method is a set of safeguards against these two errors.

4. Science is a(n) _____ to evidence.

5. A scientific model like the Big Bang theory, which provides an explanation for a large number of findings in the natural world, is known as a _____ _____.

6. In scientific research, _____ are general explanations, whereas _____ are specific predictions derived from those explanations.

7. Review each of the statements in the table and identify whether each is a theory (T) or hypothesis (H).

T OR H	EXPLANATION
1. _____	Sarah's motivation for cheating on the test was fear of failure.
2. _____	Darwin's evolutionary model explains the changes in species over time.
3. _____	The universe began in a gigantic explosion about 14 billion years ago.
4. _____	Our motivation to help a stranger in need is influenced by the number of people present.
5. _____	Crime rates in Nashville increase as the temperature rises.

8. When presented with both contradictory and supportive evidence regarding a hypothesis we are researching, our tendency to disregard the contradictory evidence is our _____ _____.

9. Our _____ _____ kicks in when we refuse to admit our beliefs are incorrect in the face of evidence that contradicts them.

10. Metaphysical claims such as the existence of God, the soul, or the afterlife differ from pseudoscientific claims in that they aren't _____.

Psychological Pseudoscience: Imposters of Science

3 DESCRIBE PSYCHOLOGICAL PSEUDOSCIENCE AND DISTINGUISH IT FROM PSYCHOLOGICAL SCIENCE.

Pseudoscientific claims appear scientific but don't play by the rules of science. In particular, pseudoscience lacks the safeguards against confirmation bias and belief perseverance that characterize science.

11. The growth of popular psychology has led to a(n) _____ explosion.

12. About _____ percent of self-help books are untested.

13. There are over 500 "brands" of _____, with new ones being added every year.

14. A recent survey of the American public shows that pseudoscientific and other questionable beliefs are (rare/widespread).

15. Match the warning signs of pseudoscience with the examples shown.

EXAMPLE	SIGN OF PSEUDOSCIENCE
1. _____ Three simple steps will change your love life forever!	a. Meaningless "psychobabble" that uses fancy scientific-sounding terms that don't make sense
2. _____ This woman practiced yoga daily for three weeks and hasn't had a day of depression since.	b. Exaggerated claims
3. _____ Amazing new innovations in research have shown that eye massage results in reading speeds 10 times faster than average!	c. Overreliance on anecdotes
4. _____ Fifty studies conducted by the company all show overwhelming success!	d. Lack of self-correction when contrary evidence is published
5. _____ Although some scientists say that we use almost all of our brain, we've found a way to harness additional brain power previously undiscovered.	e. Absence of connectivity to other research
6. _____ Sine-wave filtered auditory stimulation is carefully designed to encourage maximal orbitofrontal dendritic development.	f. Talk of "proof" instead of "evidence"
7. _____ Our new program is proven to reduce social anxiety by at least 50 percent!	g. Overuse of ad hoc immunizing tactics.
8. _____ A self-proclaimed "psychic" who fails controlled tests in the laboratory claims that the skeptical experimenters are interfering with his psychic powers.	h. Lack of review by other scholars (called *peer review*) or replication by independent labs

4 IDENTIFY REASONS WE ARE DRAWN TO PSEUDOSCIENCE.

We are drawn to pseudoscientific beliefs because the human mind tends to perceive sense in nonsense and order in disorder. Although generally adaptive, this tendency can lead us to see patterns when they don't exist. Pseudoscientific claims can result in opportunity costs and direct harm due to dangerous treatments. They can also lead us to think less scientifically about other important domains of modern life.

16. Although the tendency to make order out of disorder is generally _____, it can lead us astray into pseudoscientific thinking.

17. Patternicity is the tendency for us to make meaningful connections among (related/unrelated) phenomena.

18. We may attribute paranormal significance to coincidences that are probably due to _____.

19. The _____ _____, otherwise known as streak shooting, appears to be an illusion that results from our tendency to perceive patterns in their absence.

20. According to _____ _____ theory, our awareness of our own inevitable death leaves many of us with an underlying sense of fear, which leads to us adopt reassuring world views.

Scientific Thinking: Distinguishing Fact From Fiction

5 IDENTIFY THE KEY FEATURES OF SCIENTIFIC SKEPTICISM.

Scientific skepticism requires us to evaluate all claims with an open mind but to insist on compelling evidence before accepting them. Scientific skeptics evaluate claims on their own merits and are unwilling to accept them on the basis of authority alone.

21. Being open-minded but conservative about accepting claims without evidence is _____ _____.

6 IDENTIFY AND EXPLAIN THE TEXT'S SIX PRINCIPLES OF SCIENTIFIC THINKING.

Six key scientific thinking principles are ruling out rival hypotheses, correlation versus causation, falsifiability, replicability, extraordinary claims, and Occam's Razor.

22. The skill set for evaluating all claims in an open-minded and careful manner, both inside and outside the classroom or laboratory, is called _____ _____.

23. Scientific thinking (can/can't) be applied to claims in the media, on the Internet, in self-help books, and from any other information outlet outside the psychology laboratory.

24. When evaluating a claim, we should ask ourselves whether we've excluded other plausible _____ for it.

25. The assumption that because one thing is associated with another, it must cause the other is the definition of the _____ _____.

26. A claim is considered _____ if it could in principle be disproved.

27. The ability of others to consistently duplicate a study's findings is called _____.

28. Occam's Razor is also called the principle of _____.

29. How would you use Occam's Razor to select among different explanations for crop circles like this one?

30. Match the scientific thinking principle (left) with the accurate description (right).

NAME OF SCIENTIFIC THINKING PRINCIPLE	EXPLANATION OF SCIENTIFIC THINKING PRINCIPLE
1. _____ Ruling Out Rival Hypotheses	a. Claims must be capable of being disproved.
2. _____ Correlation versus Causation	b. If two hypotheses explain a phenomenon equally well, we should generally select the simpler one.
3. _____ Falsifiability	c. The fact that two things are associated with each other doesn't mean that one causes the other.
4. _____ Replicability	d. The more a claim contradicts what we already know, the more persuasive the evidence for this claim must be before we accept it.
5. _____ Extraordinary Claims	e. A finding must be capable of being duplicated by independent researchers following the same "recipe."
6. _____ Occam's Razor	f. Findings consistent with several hypotheses require additional research to eliminate these hypotheses.

Psychology's Past and Present: What a Long, Strange Trip It's Been

7 IDENTIFY THE MAJOR THEORETICAL FRAMEWORKS OF PSYCHOLOGY.

Five major theoretical orientations have played key roles in shaping the field. Structuralism aimed to identify the basic elements of experience through the method of introspection. Functionalism hoped to understand the adaptive purposes of behavior. Behaviorism grew out of the belief that psychological science must be completely objective and derived from laws of learning. The cognitive view emphasized the importance of mental processes in understanding behavior. Psychoanalysis focused on unconscious processes and urges as causes of behavior.

31. Structuralism aimed to identify the basic elements of thought through _____.

32. For traditional behaviorists, the human mind is a(n) _____ _____: we know what goes into it and what comes out of it, but we needn't worry about what happens between inputs and outputs.

33. Cognitivists believe our _____ of rewards and punishments is a crucial determinant of our behavior.

8 DESCRIBE DIFFERENT TYPES OF PSYCHOLOGISTS AND IDENTIFY WHAT EACH OF THEM DOES.

There are many types of psychologists. Clinical and counseling psychologists often conduct therapy. School psychologists develop intervention programs for children in school settings. Industrial/organizational psychologists often work in companies and business and are involved in maximizing employee performance. Many forensic psychologists work in prisons or court settings. Many other psychologists conduct research. For example, developmental psychologists study systematic change in individuals over time. Experimental psychologists study learning and thinking, and biological psychologists study the biological basis of behavior.

34. You (need/don't need) a Ph.D. to become a therapist.

35. How do developmental psychologists spend the bulk of their time?

Developmental Psychologist

9 DESCRIBE THE TWO GREAT DEBATES THAT HAVE SHAPED THE FIELD OF PSYCHOLOGY.

The two great debates are the nature–nurture debate, which asks whether our behaviors are attributable mostly to our genes (nature) or our rearing environments (nurture), and the free will–determinism debate, which asks to what extent our behaviors are freely selected rather than caused by factors outside our control. Both debates continue to shape the field of psychology.

36. _____ _____, a discipline that applies Darwin's theory of natural selection to human and animal behavior, has shed light on the nature–nurture debate.

37. Many psychologists, such as B. F. Skinner, believe that free will is a(n) _____.

10 DESCRIBE HOW PSYCHOLOGICAL RESEARCH AFFECTS OUR DAILY LIVES.

Psychological research has shown how psychology can be applied to such diverse fields as advertising, public safety, the criminal justice system, and education.

38. _____ research examines how the mind works, whereas _____ research examines how we use research to solve real-world problems.

39. What have psychologists who study magazine advertisements learned about how best to capture readers' attention?

40. Psychologists with expertise in measuring academic achievement and knowledge were primarily responsible for developing the _____ and _____ tests.

Apply Your Scientific Thinking Skills

Use your scientific thinking skills to answer the following questions, referencing specific scientific thinking principles and common errors in reasoning whenever possible.

1. Psychology is a discipline that spans many levels of analysis, yet the popular media often assigns only a single cause to a complex issue. Locate three media articles on an issue such as homelessness or terrorism and compare the views on the root causes and possible solutions to this issue. How many levels of analysis does each article consider?

2. How can our scientific thinking skills help us to evaluate the seemingly conflicting news we hear about nutrition and exercise? Choose a health topic to investigate further (for example, how much exercise we need each day, whether drinking red wine every day is healthy, or whether we should limit our intake of carbohydrates) and locate three articles with conflicting views on the topic. What errors or logical fallacies do the articles commit? How can you evaluate the accuracy of the articles and the advice they provide?

3. Confirmation bias is widespread in everyday life, especially in the world of politics. Choose a political issue that's been controversial in recent months (such as health care, our nation's approach to terrorism, or abortion) and locate two opinion pieces that adopt opposing stances on this issue. Did each author attempt to avoid confirmation bias—for example, by acknowledging and thoughtfully discussing arguments that might challenge his or her position—or instead fall victim to confirmation bias? Did each author try to interpret contrary evidence in a fair or in a biased fashion? Explain your answer with reference to one or more specific examples in each case.

Further Your Understanding

EXTEND YOUR KNOWLEDGE WITH THE MYPSYCHLAB VIDEO SERIES

Watch these videos in MyPsychLab. Follow the "Video Series" link.

👁 **The Big Picture: Asking the Tough Questions** Learn why the study of psychology is so valuable to society and how it is improving daily life. Take a look at the broad spectrum of professions and specializations in the field.

👁 **The Basics: Diverse Perspectives** See how research psychologists help us better understand the brain, behavior, and the mind using different perspectives and treatments.

👁 **Thinking Like a Psychologist: Debunking Myths** Discover how scientific research and myths in popular culture influence our opinions and beliefs as information consumers.

APPLY YOUR CRITICAL THINKING SKILLS WITH MYPSYCHLAB WRITING ASSESSMENTS

Complete these writing assignments in MyPsychLab.

Jake has become very anxious since he started taking harder classes in his major. The university's counselor diagnosed him with an anxiety disorder. Compare and contrast how the behavioral, humanistic, and cognitive approaches would view the origins and treatment of Jake's anxiety. Then, describe how each of the three approaches is viewed by psychologists today.

Answer Key

WHAT IS PSYCHOLOGY? SCIENCE VERSUS INTUITION?

1. seeing is believing
2. These tables are identical in size—one can be directly superimposed on top of the other. Even though our perceptions are often accurate, we can't always trust them to provide us with an error-free picture of the world.
3. isn't
4. approach
5. scientific theory
6. theories; hypotheses
7. 1: H; 2: T; 3: T; 4: H; 5: H
8. confirmation bias
9. belief perseverance
10. testable

PSYCHOLOGICAL PSEUDOSCIENCE: IMPOSTERS OF SCIENCE

11. misinformation
12. 95
13. psychotherapy
14. widespread
15. 1b; 2c; 3e; 4h; 5d; 6a; 7f; 8g
16. adaptive
17. unrelated
18. chance
19. "hot hand"
20. terror management

SCIENTIFIC THINKING: DISTINGUISHING FACT FROM FICTION

21. scientific skepticism
22. critical (or scientific) thinking
23. can

24. explanations
25. correlation–causation fallacy
26. falsifiable
27. replicability
28. parsimony
29. There are two explanations for crop circles—one supernatural and the other natural. According to Occam's Razor, we should generally select the simplest explanation.
30. 1f; 2c; 3a; 4e; 5d; 6b

PSYCHOLOGY'S PAST AND PRESENT: WHAT A LONG, STRANGE TRIP IT'S BEEN

31. introspection
32. black box
33. interpretation
34. don't need
35. Developmental psychologists spend most of their time in the lab, collecting and analyzing data on children's behavior.
36. Evolutionary psychology
37. illusion
38. Basic; applied
39. Human faces better capture readers' attention on the left rather than the right side of pages. Written text, in contrast, better captures readers' attention on the right side.
40. SAT; ACT

References

Alcock, J. E. (1995). The belief engine. *Skeptical Inquirer, 19*(3), 14–18.

Alvarez, L. W. (1965). A pseudo experience in parapsychology. *Science, 148*(3677), 1541.

American Psychological Association. (2003). Fire trucks are supposed to be red, right? Not if you want to reduce accidents. Retrieved from http://www.apa.org/research/action

Arkowitz, H., & Lilienfeld, S. O. (2006). Psychotherapy on trial. *Scientific American Mind, 3*, 42–49.

Asendorpf, J. B., Conner, M., De Fruyt, F., De Houwer, J., Denissen, J. J. A., Fiedler, K., . . . Wicherts, J. M. (2013). Replication is more than hitting the lottery twice *European Journal of Personality*.

Avugos, S., Köppen, J., Czienskowski, U., Raab, M., & Bar-Eli, M. (2012). The "hot hand" reconsidered: A meta-analytic approach. *Psychology of Sport and Exercise, 24*, 21–27.

Baker, T. B., McFall, R. M., & Shoham, V. (2009). Current status and future prospects of clinical psychology toward a scientifically principled approach to mental and behavioral health care. *Perspectives on Psychological Science, 9*, 67–103.

Bandura, A. (1973). *Aggression: A social learning analysis.* Oxford, England: Prentice Hall.

Bar-Eli, M., Avugos, S., & Raab, M. (2006). Twenty years of "hot hand" research: Review and critique. *Psychology of Sport and Exercise, 7*, 525–553.

Bargh, J. (2008). Free will is unnatural. In J. Baer, J. Kaufmann, and R. Baumeister (Eds), *Are we free: Psychology and free will* (pp. 128–154). New York, NY: Oxford University Press.

Bargh, J. A. (2011). Unconscious thought theory and its discontents: A critique of the critiques. *Social Cognition, 29*, 629–647.

Bargh, J. A., & Chartrand, T. L. (1999). The unbearable automaticity of being. *American Psychologist, 54*, 462–479.

Barkow, J. H., Cosmides, L., & Tooby, J. (1992). *The adapted mind: Evolutionary psychology and the generation of culture.* New York, NY: Oxford University Press.

Barlow, D. H. (2000). Unraveling the mysteries of anxiety and its disorders from the perspective of emotion theory. *American Psychologist, 55*, 1247–1263.

Barlow, D. H. (2010). Negative effects from psychological treatment: A perspective. *American Psychologist, 65*, 13–20.

Baumeister R. F. (2008). Free will in scientific psychology. *Perspectives on Psychological Science, 3*, 14–19.

Belsky, J. (1988). The "effects" of infant day care reconsidered. *Early Childhood Research Quarterly, 3*, 235–272.

Bem, D. J. (2011). Feeling the future: Experimental evidence for anomalous retroactive influences on cognition and affect. *Journal of Personality and Social Psychology, 100*, 407–425.

Benjamin, L. T., & Baker, D. B. (2004). From séance to science: A history of the profession of psychology in America. Belmont, CA: Wadsworth.

Bisson, J. I. (2007). Post-traumatic stress disorder. *Occupational Medicine, 57*(6), 399–403. http://dx.doi.org/10.1093/occmed/kqm069

Blum, D. (2006). *Ghost hunters: William James and the search for scientific proof of life after death.* New York, NY: Penguin Press.

Bolles, R. C. (1962). The difference between statistical hypotheses and scientific hypotheses. *Psychological Reports, 11*, 639–645.

Bouchard, T. J., Jr. (2004). Genetic influence on human psychological traits. *Current Directions in Psychological Science, 4*, 148–151.

Bunge, M. (1998). *Philosophy of science: From problem to theory* (Vol. 1). Piscataway, NJ: Transaction.

Buss, D. M. (1995). Evolutionary psychology: A new paradigm for psychological science. *Psychological Inquiry, 6*, 1–30.

Cacioppo, J. T. (2004). Common sense, intuition, and theory in personality and social psychology. *Personality and Social Psychology Review, 8*, 114–122.

Cacioppo, J. T., Berntson, G. G., Sheridan, J. F., & McClintock, M. K. (2000). Multi-level integrative analyses of human behavior: Social neuroscience and the complementing nature of social and biological approaches. *Psychological Bulletin, 126*, 829–843.

Carpenter, S. (2012). Psychology's bold initiative. *Science, 335*, 1558–1561.

Carroll, R. T. (2003). *The skeptic's dictionary: A collection of strange beliefs, amusing deceptions, and dangerous delusions.* New York, NY: Wiley.

Chabris, C., & Simons, D. (2010). *The invisible gorilla and other ways our intuitions deceive us.* New York, NY: Crown.

Chua, H. F., Boland, J. E., & Nisbett, R. E. (2005). Cultural variation in eye movements during scene perception. *Proceedings of the National Academy of Sciences, 102*, 12629–12633.

Clancy, S. A. (2005). *Abducted: How people come to believe they were kidnapped by aliens.* Cambridge, MA: Harvard University Press.

Clark, K. B., & Clark, M. P. (1950) Emotional factors in racial identification and preference in Negro children. *Journal of Negro Education, 19*, 506–513.

Clark, R. D. (2005). An examination of the "hot hand" in professional golfers. *Perceptual and Motor Skills, 101*, 365–372.

Clay, R. A. (2002). Advertising as science. *American Psychological Association Monitor, 33*, 38.

Confer, J. C., Easton, J. A., Fleischman, D. S., Goetz, C. D., Lewis, D. M., Perilloux, C., & Buss, D. M. (2010). Evolutionary psychology: Controversies, questions, prospects, and limitations. *American Psychologist, 65*, 110–126.

Cook, T. D. (1985). Post-positivist critical multiplism. In R. L. Shotland & M. M. Mark (Eds.), *Social science and social policy* (pp. 21–62). Beverly Hills, CA: Sage.

Coon, D. J. (1992). Testing the limits of sense and science: American experimental psychologists combat spiritualism: 1880–1920. *American Psychologist, 47*, 143–151.

Crews, F. (2005). Response to Holland. *Scientific Review of Alternative Medicine, 10*, 24–28.

Cutler, B. L., & Wells, G. L. (2009). Expert testimony regarding eyewitness identification. In J. L. Skeem, K. S. Douglas, & S. O. Lilienfeld (Eds.), *Psychological science in the courtroom: Consensus and controversy* (pp. 100–123). New York, NY: Guilford Press.

Damasio, A., & Carvalho, G. B. (2013). The nature of feelings: Evolutionary and neurobiological origins. *Nature Reviews Neuroscience, 14*, 143–152.

Darley, J. M., & Latané, B. (1968a). Bystander intervention in emergencies: Diffusion of responsibility. *Journal of Personality and Social Psychology, 8*, 377–383.

Davidson, P. R., & Parker, K. C. (2001). Eye movement desensitization and reprocessing (EMDR): A meta-analysis. *Journal of Consulting and Clinical Psychology, 69*, 305–316.

Davis, H. (2009). *Caveman logic: The persistence of primitive thinking in a modern world.* Amherst, New York, NY: Prometheus.

Davison, G. C., & Lazarus, A. A. (2007). Clinical case studies are important in the science and practice of psychotherapy. In S. O. Lilienfeld & W. T. O'Donohue (Eds.), *The great ideas of clinical science: 17 principles that every mental health professional should understand* (pp. 149–162). New York, NY: Routledge.

Answer Key

WHAT IS PSYCHOLOGY? SCIENCE VERSUS INTUITION?

1. seeing is believing
2. These tables are identical in size—one can be directly super-imposed on top of the other. Even though our perceptions are often accurate, we can't always trust them to provide us with an error-free picture of the world.
3. isn't
4. approach
5. scientific theory
6. theories; hypotheses
7. 1: H; 2: T; 3: T; 4: H; 5: H
8. confirmation bias
9. belief perseverance
10. testable

PSYCHOLOGICAL PSEUDOSCIENCE: IMPOSTERS OF SCIENCE

11. misinformation
12. 95
13. psychotherapy
14. widespread
15. 1b; 2c; 3e; 4h; 5d; 6a; 7f; 8g
16. adaptive
17. unrelated
18. chance
19. "hot hand"
20. terror management

SCIENTIFIC THINKING: DISTINGUISHING FACT FROM FICTION

21. scientific skepticism
22. critical (or scientific) thinking
23. can

24. explanations
25. correlation–causation fallacy
26. falsifiable
27. replicability
28. parsimony
29. There are two explanations for crop circles—one supernatural and the other natural. According to Occam's Razor, we should generally select the simplest explanation.
30. 1f; 2c; 3a; 4e; 5d; 6b

PSYCHOLOGY'S PAST AND PRESENT: WHAT A LONG, STRANGE TRIP IT'S BEEN

31. introspection
32. black box
33. interpretation
34. don't need

35. Developmental psychologists spend most of their time in the lab, collecting and analyzing data on children's behavior.
36. Evolutionary psychology
37. illusion
38. Basic; applied
39. Human faces better capture readers' attention on the left rather than the right side of pages. Written text, in contrast, better captures readers' attention on the right side.
40. SAT; ACT

References

Alcock, J. E. (1995). The belief engine. *Skeptical Inquirer, 19*(3), 14–18.

Alvarez, L. W. (1965). A pseudo experience in parapsychology. *Science, 148*(3677), 1541.

American Psychological Association. (2003). Fire trucks are supposed to be red, right? Not if you want to reduce accidents. Retrieved from http://www.apa.org/research/action

Arkowitz, H., & Lilienfeld, S. O. (2006). Psychotherapy on trial. *Scientific American Mind, 3*, 42–49.

Asendorpf, J. B., Conner, M., De Fruyt, F., De Houwer, J., Denissen, J. J. A., Fiedler, K., . . . Wicherts, J. M. (2013). Replication is more than hitting the lottery twice *European Journal of Personality.*

Avugos, S., Köppen, J., Czienskowski, U., Raab, M., & Bar-Eli, M. (2012). The "hot hand" reconsidered: A meta-analytic approach. *Psychology of Sport and Exercise, 24*, 21–27.

Baker, T. B., McFall, R. M., & Shoham, V. (2009). Current status and future prospects of clinical psychology toward a scientifically principled approach to mental and behavioral health care. *Perspectives on Psychological Science, 9*, 67–103.

Bandura, A. (1973). *Aggression: A social learning analysis.* Oxford, England: Prentice Hall.

Bar-Eli, M., Avugos, S., & Raab, M. (2006). Twenty years of "hot hand" research: Review and critique. *Psychology of Sport and Exercise, 7*, 525–553.

Bargh, J. (2008). Free will is unnatural. In J. Baer, J. Kaufmann, and R. Baumeister (Eds), *Are we free: Psychology and free will* (pp. 128–154). New York, NY: Oxford University Press.

Bargh, J. A. (2011). Unconscious thought theory and its discontents: A critique of the critiques. *Social Cognition, 29*, 629–647.

Bargh, J. A., & Chartrand, T. L. (1999). The unbearable automaticity of being. *American Psychologist, 54*, 462–479.

Barkow, J. H., Cosmides, L., & Tooby, J. (1992). *The adapted mind: Evolutionary psychology and the generation of culture.* New York, NY: Oxford University Press.

Barlow, D. H. (2000). Unraveling the mysteries of anxiety and its disorders from the perspective of emotion theory. *American Psychologist, 55*, 1247–1263.

Barlow, D. H. (2010). Negative effects from psychological treatment: A perspective. *American Psychologist, 65*, 13–20.

Baumeister R. F. (2008). Free will in scientific psychology. *Perspectives on Psychological Science, 3*, 14–19.

Belsky, J. (1988). The "effects" of infant day care reconsidered. *Early Childhood Research Quarterly, 3*, 235–272.

Bem, D. J. (2011). Feeling the future: Experimental evidence for anomalous retroactive influences on cognition and affect. *Journal of Personality and Social Psychology, 100*, 407–425.

Benjamin, L. T., & Baker, D. B. (2004). From séance to science: A history of the profession of psychology in America. Belmont, CA: Wadsworth.

Bisson, J. I. (2007). Post-traumatic stress disorder. *Occupational Medicine, 57*(6), 399–403. http://dx.doi.org/10.1093/occmed/kqm069

Blum, D. (2006). *Ghost hunters: William James and the search for scientific proof of life after death.* New York, NY: Penguin Press.

Bolles, R. C. (1962). The difference between statistical hypotheses and scientific hypotheses. *Psychological Reports, 11*, 639–645.

Bouchard, T. J., Jr. (2004). Genetic influence on human psychological traits. *Current Directions in Psychological Science, 4*, 148–151.

Bunge, M. (1998). *Philosophy of science: From problem to theory* (Vol. 1). Piscataway, NJ: Transaction.

Buss, D. M. (1995). Evolutionary psychology: A new paradigm for psychological science. *Psychological Inquiry, 6*, 1–30.

Cacioppo, J. T. (2004). Common sense, intuition, and theory in personality and social psychology. *Personality and Social Psychology Review, 8*, 114–122.

Cacioppo, J. T., Berntson, G. G., Sheridan, J. F., & McClintock, M. K. (2000). Multi-level integrative analyses of human behavior: Social neuroscience and the complementing nature of social and biological approaches. *Psychological Bulletin, 126*, 829–843.

Carpenter, S. (2012). Psychology's bold initiative. *Science, 335*, 1558–1561.

Carroll, R. T. (2003). *The skeptic's dictionary: A collection of strange beliefs, amusing deceptions, and dangerous delusions.* New York, NY: Wiley.

Chabris, C., & Simons, D. (2010). *The invisible gorilla and other ways our intuitions deceive us.* New York, NY: Crown.

Chua, H. F., Boland, J. E., & Nisbett, R. E. (2005). Cultural variation in eye movements during scene perception. *Proceedings of the National Academy of Sciences, 102*, 12629–12633.

Clancy, S. A. (2005). *Abducted: How people come to believe they were kidnapped by aliens.* Cambridge, MA: Harvard University Press.

Clark, K. B., & Clark, M. P. (1950) Emotional factors in racial identification and preference in Negro children. *Journal of Negro Education, 19*, 506–513.

Clark, R. D. (2005). An examination of the "hot hand" in professional golfers. *Perceptual and Motor Skills, 101*, 365–372.

Clay, R. A. (2002). Advertising as science. *American Psychological Association Monitor, 33*, 38.

Confer, J. C., Easton, J. A., Fleischman, D. S., Goetz, C. D., Lewis, D. M., Perilloux, C., & Buss, D. M. (2010). Evolutionary psychology: Controversies, questions, prospects, and limitations. *American Psychologist, 65*, 110–126.

Cook, T. D. (1985). Post-positivist critical multiplism. In R. L. Shotland & M. M. Mark (Eds.), *Social science and social policy* (pp. 21–62). Beverly Hills, CA: Sage.

Coon, D. J. (1992). Testing the limits of sense and science: American experimental psychologists combat spiritualism: 1880–1920. *American Psychologist, 47*, 143–151.

Crews, F. (2005). Response to Holland. *Scientific Review of Alternative Medicine, 10*, 24–28.

Cutler, B. L., & Wells, G. L. (2009). Expert testimony regarding eyewitness identification. In J. L. Skeem, K. S. Douglas, & S. O. Lilienfeld (Eds.), *Psychological science in the courtroom: Consensus and controversy* (pp. 100–123). New York, NY: Guilford Press.

Damasio, A., & Carvalho, G. B. (2013). The nature of feelings: Evolutionary and neurobiological origins. *Nature Reviews Neuroscience, 14*, 143–152.

Darley, J. M., & Latané, B. (1968a). Bystander intervention in emergencies: Diffusion of responsibility. *Journal of Personality and Social Psychology, 8*, 377–383.

Davidson, P. R., & Parker, K. C. (2001). Eye movement desensitization and reprocessing (EMDR): A meta-analysis. *Journal of Consulting and Clinical Psychology, 69*, 305–316.

Davis, H. (2009). *Caveman logic: The persistence of primitive thinking in a modern world.* Amherst, New York, NY: Prometheus.

Davison, G. C., & Lazarus, A. A. (2007). Clinical case studies are important in the science and practice of psychotherapy. In S. O. Lilienfeld & W. T. O'Donohue (Eds.), *The great ideas of clinical science: 17 principles that every mental health professional should understand* (pp. 149–162). New York, NY: Routledge.

Dawes, R. M. (1994). *House of cards: Psychology and psychotherapy built on myth.* New York, NY: Free Press.

Dean, C. (2005, August 23). Scientists speak up on mix of God and science. *New York Times.* Retrieved from http://personal.bgsu.edu/~edwards/NYTimesCSL.pdf

Dennett, D. C. (1995). *Darwin's dangerous idea: Evolution and the meanings of life.* New York, NY: Simon & Schuster.

de Waal, F. B. M. (2002). Evolutionary psychology: The wheat and the chaff. *Current Directions in Psychological Science, 11,* 187–191.

Dienes, Z. (2008). *Understanding psychology as a science: An introduction to scientific and statistical inference.* New York, NY: Palgrave Macmillan.

Douglas, K. M., & Sutton, R. M. (2011). Does it take one to know one? Endorsement of conspiracy theories is influenced by personal willingness to conspire. *British Journal of Social Psychology, 50,* 544–552.

Egan, S. J., Watson, H. J., Kane, R. T., McEvoy, P., Fursland, A., & Nathan, P. R. (2013). Anxiety as a mediator between perfectionism and eating disorders. *Cognitive Therapy and Research, 37,* 1–9.

Eisner, D. A. (2000). *The death of psychotherapy: From Freud to alien abductions.* Westport, CT: Praeger.

Esterson, A. (1993). *Seductive mirage: An exploration of the work of Sigmund Freud.* Chicago, IL: Open Court.

Evans, R. B. (1972). Titchener and his lost system. *Journal of the History of the Behavioral Sciences, 8,* 168–180.

Ferris, C. F. (1996). The rage of innocents. *The Sciences, 36,* 22–26.

Figueredo, A. J. (1993). Critical multiplism, meta-analysis, and generalization: An integrative commentary. *New Directions for Program Evaluation, 60,* 3–12.

Fischer P., Krueger, J. I., Greitemeyer, T., Vogrincic, C., Kastenm, I. A., . . . Kainbacher, M. (2011). The bystander-effect: A meta-analytic review on bystander intervention in dangerous and non-dangerous emergencies, *Psychological Bulletin, 137,* 517–537.

Fowler, K. A., Lilienfeld, S. O., & Patrick, C. P. (2009). Detecting psychopathy from thin slices of behavior. *Psychological Assessment, 21,* 68–78.

Freud, S. (1900). *The interpretation of dreams* (J. Crick, Trans.). London, England: Oxford University Press.

Galak, J., LeBoeuf, R. A., Nelson, L. D., & Simmons, J. P. (2012). Correcting the past: Failures to replicate psi. *Journal of Personality and Social Psychology, 103,* 933–948.

Gazzaniga, M. S., Ivry, R., & Mangun, G. R. (2002). *Fundamentals of cognitive neuroscience* (2nd ed.). New York, NY: Norton.

Geiser, S., & Studley, R. (2002). UC and the SAT: Predictive validity and differential impact of the SAT I and SAT II at the University of California. *Educational Assessment, 8,* 1–26.

Gigerenzer, G. (2007). *Gut feelings: The intelligence of the unconscious.* New York, NY: Viking Press.

Gilovich, T. (1991). *How we know what isn't so: The fallibility of human reason in everyday life.* New York, NY: Free Press.

Gilovich, T., Vallone, R., & Tversky, A. (1985). The hot hand in basketball—On the misperception of random sequences. *Cognitive Psychology, 17,* 295–314.

Gladwell, M. (2005). *Blink: The power of thinking without thinking.* Boston, MA: Little, Brown.

Gould, R. A., & Clum, G. A. (1993). A meta-analysis of self-help treatment approaches. *Clinical Psychology Review, 13,* 169–186.

Gould, S. J. (1997). Nonoverlapping magisteria. *Natural History, 106,* 16–22.

Greenwald, A. G., Leippe, M. R., Pratkanis, A. R., & Baumgardner, M. H. (1986). Under what conditions does theory obstruct research progress? *Psychological Review, 93,* 216–229.

Gregory, R. J., Canning, S. S., Lee, T. W., & Wise, J. (2004). Cognitive bibliotherapy for depression: A meta-analysis. *Professional Psychology: Research and Practice, 35,* 275–280.

Haeffel, G. (2010). When self-help is no help: Traditional cognitive skills training does not prevent depressive symptoms in people who ruminate. *Behaviour Research and Therapy, 48,* 152–157.

Harkness, A. R., & Lilienfeld, S. O. (1997). Individual differences science for treatment planning: Personality traits. *Psychological Assessment, 9,* 349–360. http://dx.doi.org/10.1037/1040-3590.9.4.349

Harris, J. R. (2002). *The nurture assumption: Why children turn out the way they do* (2nd ed). New York, NY: Free Press.

Hastorf, A. H., & Cantril, A. H. (1954). They saw a game: A case study. *Journal of Abnormal and Social Psychology, 49,* 129–134.

Henrich, J., Heine, S., & Norenzayan, A. (2010). The weirdest people in the world? *Behavioral and Brain Sciences, 33*(2-3), 61–83.

Henriques, G. (2004). Psychology defined. *Journal of Clinical Psychology, 60,* 1207–1221.

Hergenhahn, B. R. (2000). *An introduction to the history of psychology* (4th ed.). Pacific Grove, CA: Wadsworth.

Hines, T. (2003). *Pseudoscience and the paranormal: A critical examination of the evidence* (2nd ed.). Buffalo, NY: Prometheus.

Hoagland, R. C. (1987). *The monuments of Mars: A city on the edge of forever.* Berkeley, CA: North Atlantic.

Hoffman, M. B., & Morse, S. J. (2006, July 30). The insanity defense goes back on trial. *New York Times.* Retrieved from http://www.nytimes.com/2006/07/30/opinion/30hoffman.html?_r=1&oref=slogin

Huck, S. W., & Sandler, H. M. (1979). *Rival hypotheses: Alternative interpretation of data based conclusions.* New York, NY: Harper & Row.

Hunt, E. (1999). Intelligence and human resources: Past, present, and future. In P. L. Ackerman, P. C. Kyllonen, & R. D. Roberts (Eds.), *Learning and individual differences: Process, trait, and content determinants* (pp. 3–30). Washington, DC: American Psychological Association.

Hunt, M. (1993). *The story of psychology.* New York, NY: Doubleday.

Hyman, R. (1989). *The elusive quarry: A scientific appraisal of psychical research.* Buffalo, NY: Prometheus.

Ilardi, S. S., & Feldman, D. (2001). The cognitive neuroscience paradigm: A unifying meta-theoretical framework for the science and practice of clinical psychology. *Journal of Clinical Psychology, 57,* 1067–1088.

Ilardi, S. S., Rand, K., & Karwoski, L. (2007). The cognitive neuroscience perspective allows us to understand abnormal behavior at multiple levels of complexity. In S. O. Lilienfeld & W. O. O'Donohue (Eds.), *The great ideas of clinical science: 17 principles that all mental health professionals should understand* (pp. 291–309). New York, NY: Routledge.

Ioannidis, J. P. A. (2005). Contradicted and initially stronger effects in highly cited clinical research. *Journal of the American Medical Association, 294,* 218–228.

Janda, L. H., England, K., Lovejoy, D., & Drury, K. (1998). Attitudes toward psychology relative to other disciplines. *Professional Psychology: Research and Practice, 29,* 140–143.

Kahneman, D. (2011). *Thinking, fast and slow.* New York, NY: Farrar, Straus & Giroux.

Kahneman, D., & Klein, G. (2009). Conditions for intuitive expertise: A failure to disagree. *American Psychologist, 64,* 515–526.

Kassin, S. (2004). *Psychology* (4th ed.). Upper Saddle River, NJ: Prentice Hall.

Keil, F. C., Lockhart, K. L., & Schlegel, E. (2010). A bump on a bump?: Emerging intuitions concerning the relative difficulty of the sciences. *Journal of Experimental Psychology: General, 139,* 1–15.

Kendler, K. S. (2005). Toward a philosophical structure for psychiatry. *American Journal of Psychiatry, 162,* 433–440.

Kessler, R. C., Soukup, J., Davis, R. B., Foster, D. F., Wilkey, S. A., van Rompay, M. I., & Eisenberg, D. M. (2001). The use of complementary and alternative therapies to treat anxiety and depression in the United States. *American Journal of Psychiatry, 158,* 289–294.

Kihlstrom, J. F. (1987). The cognitive unconscious. *Science, 237,* 1445–1452.

Kirsch, I., & Lynn, S. J. (1999). Automaticity in clinical psychology. *American Psychologist, 54,* 504–515.

Kitcher, P. (1985). *Vaulting ambition: Sociobiology and the quest for human nature.* Cambridge, MA: MIT Press.

Kitcher, P. (2009, October 25). The fact of evolution. *New York Times Book Review,* 6.

Kluger, A. N., & Tikochinsky, J. (2001). The error of accepting the "theoretical" null hypothesis: The rise, fall and resurrection of common sense hypotheses in psychology. *Psychological Bulletin, 127,* 408–423.

Latané, B., & Nida, S. (1981). Ten years of research on group size and helping. *Psychological Bulletin, 89,* 308–324.

Lazar, S. G. (Ed.). (2010). *Psychotherapy is worth it: A comprehensive review of its cost-effectiveness.* Washington, DC: American Psychiatric.

Leavy, J. (1992). Spooky presidential coincidences contest. *Skeptical Inquirer, 16,* 316–320.

Leucht, S., Corves, C., Arbter, D., Engel, R. R., Li, C., & Davis, J. M. (2009). Second-generation versus first-generation antipsychotic drugs for schizophrenia: A meta-analysis. *The Lancet, 373,* 31–41.

Libet, B. (1985). Unconscious cerebral initiative and the role of conscious will in voluntary action. *Behavioral and Brain Sciences, 8,* 529–566.

Lilienfeld, S. O. (1999c, November/December). New analyses raise doubts about replicability of ESP findings. *Skeptical Inquirer, 24,* 9–10.

Lilienfeld, S. O. (2004). Defining psychology: Is it worth the trouble? *Journal of Clinical Psychology, 60,* 1249–1253.

Lilienfeld, S. O. (2007). Psychological treatments that cause harm. *Perspectives on Psychological Science, 2*(1), 53–70. http://dx.doi.org/10.1111/j.1745-6916.2007.00029.x

Lilienfeld, S. O. (2012). Public skepticism of psychology: Why many people perceive the study of human behavior as unscientific. *American Psychologist, 67,* 111–129.

Lilienfeld, S. O., Ammirati, R., & Landfield, K. (2009). Giving debiasing away: Can psychological research on correcting cognitive errors improve human welfare? *Perspectives on Psychological Science, 4,* 390–398.

Lilienfeld, S. O., & Byron, R. (2013) Your brain on trial. *Scientific American Mind, 23,* 44–53.

Lilienfeld, S. O., Lohr, J. M., & Olatunji, B. O. (2008). Overcoming naive realism: Encouraging students to think critically about psychotherapy. In D. S. Dunn (Ed.), *Teaching critical thinking in psychology: A handbook of best practices* (pp. 267–271). Malden, MA: Blackwell.

Lilienfeld, S. O., Lynn, S. J., & Lohr, J. M. (2003). *Science and pseudoscience in clinical psychology.* New York, NY: Guilford Press.

Lindeman, M. (1998). Motivation, cognition and pseudoscience. *Scandinavian Journal of Psychology, 39,* 257–265.

Loevinger, J. (1987). *Paradigms of personality.* New York, NY: W. H. Freeman.

Loftus, E. F., & Guyer, M. (2002). Who abused Jane Doe? The hazards of the single case history: Part I and Part II. *Skeptical Inquirer, 26,* 24–32.

Lohr, J. M., Hooke, W., Gist, R., & Tolin, D. F. (2003). Novel and controversial treatments for trauma-related disorders. In S. O. Lilienfeld, S. J. Lynn, & J. M. Lohr (Eds.), *Science and pseudoscience in clinical psychology* (pp. 243–272). New York, NY: Guilford Press.

Lohr, J. M., Tolin, D. F., & Lilienfeld, S. O. (1998). Efficacy of eye movement desensitization and reprocessing. *Behavior Therapy, 29*, 123–156.

Lubinski, D. (2000). Scientific and social significance of assessing individual differences: Sinking shafts at a few critical points. In S. T. Fiske (Ed.), *Annual Review of Psychology, 51*, 404–444.

Mahoney, M. J., & DeMonbreun, B. G. (1977). Confirmatory bias in scientists and non-scientists. *Cognitive Therapy and Research, 1*, 176–180.

Martino, S. C., Collins, R. L., Elliott, M. C., Strachman, A., Kanouse, D. E., & Berry, S. H. (2006). Exposure to degrading versus nondegrading music lyrics and sexual behavior among youth. *Pediatrics, 118*, 430–441.

McFall, R. M. (1997). Making psychology incorruptible. *Applied and Preventive Psychology, 5*, 9–15.

McFall, R. M. (2006). Doctoral training in clinical psychology. *Annual Review of Clinical Psychology, 2*, 21–49.

Meehl, P. E. (1967). Theory-testing in psychology and physics: A methodological paradox. *Philosophy of Science, 34*, 103–115.

Meehl, P. E. (1972). Reactions, reflections, projections. In J. N. Butcher (Ed.), *Objective personality assessment: Changing perspectives* (pp. 131–189). New York, NY: Academic Press.

Meehl, P. E. (1978). Theoretical risks and tabular asterisks: Sir Karl, Sir Ronald, and the slow progress of soft psychology. *Journal of Consulting and Clinical Psychology, 46*, 806–834. http://dx.doi.org/10.1037/0022-006X.46.4.806

Meehl, P. E. (1995). Psychoanalysis is not yet a science: Comment on Shevrin. *Journal of the American Psychoanalytic Association, 43*, 1015–1023.

Mercer, J. (2002). Attachment therapy: A treatment without empirical support. *Scientific Review of Mental Health Practice, 1*, 9–16.

Mercer, J., Sarner, L., & Rosa, L. (2003). *Attachment therapy on trial: The torture and death of Candace Newmaker.* Westport, CT: Praeger.

Mlodinow, L. (2008). *The drunkard's walk: How randomness rules our lives.* New York, NY: Vintage Books.

Mooney, C., & Kirshenbaum, S. (2010). *Unscientific America: How scientific illiteracy threatens our future.* New York, NY: Basic Books.

Moore, B., & Fine, B. (Eds.). (1995). *Psychoanalysis: The major concepts.* New Haven, CT: Yale University Press.

Morier, D., & Podlipentseva, J. (1997, April). Mortality salience effects on paranormal beliefs and essay ratings. Paper presented at the 77th Annual Meeting of the Western Psychological Association, Seattle, WA.

Muscarella, F., & Cunningham, M. R. (1996). The evolutionary significance and social perception of male pattern baldness and facial hair. *Ethology and Sociobiology, 17*, 99–117.

Musella, D. P. (2005, September/October). Gallup poll shows that Americans' belief in the paranormal persists. *Skeptical Inquirer, 29*, 5.

Myers, D. G. (2002). *Intuition: Its powers and perils.* New Haven, CT: Yale University Press.

National Science Foundation. (2003). Table C-2: Employed U.S. scientists and engineers, by level and field of highest degree attained, sex, and employment sector: 1999. Retrieved from http://www.nsf.gov/statistics/us-workforce/1999/dst1999.htm

Neisser, U. (1967). *Cognitive psychology.* New York, NY: Appleton-Century-Crofts.

Nestler, S. (2010). Belief perseverance. *Social Psychology, 41*, 35–41.

Newell, B. R., & Shanks, D. R. (2013). Unconscious influences on decision making: A critical review. *Behavioral and Brain Sciences*, awaiting volume and page numbers.

Nickerson, R. S. (1998). Confirmation bias: A ubiquitous phenomenon in many guises. *Review of General Psychology, 2*, 175–220.

Nickerson, R. S. (1999). Basic versus applied research. In R. J. Sternberg (Ed.), *The nature of cognition* (pp. 409–444). Cambridge, MA: MIT Press.

Nisbett, R. E. (2003). *The geography of thought: How Asians and Westerners think differently . . . and why.* New York, NY: Free Press.

Nisbett, R. E., Peng, K. P., Choi, I., & Norenzayan, A. (2001). Culture and systems of thought: Holistic versus analytic cognition. *Psychological Review, 108*, 291–310.

Nisbett, R. E., & Ross, L. D. (1980). *Human Inference: Strategies and shortcomings of social judgment.* Englewood Cliffs, NJ: Prentice Hall.

Norenzayan, A., & Hansen, I. G. (2006). Belief in supernatural agents in the face of death. *Personality and Social Psychology Bulletin, 32*, 174–187.

Nosek, B., Spies, J., & Motyl, M. (2012). Scientific utopia: II-Restructuring incentives and practices to promote truth over publishability. *Perspectives on Psychological Science, 7*, 615–631.

Novella, S. (2013). Bigfoot skeptics, New Atheists, politics and religion. *Neurologica Blog.* Retrieved from http://theness.com/neurologicablog/index.php/bigfoot-skeptics-new-atheists-politics-and-religion

O'Donohue, W. T., Lilienfeld, S. O., & Fowler, K. A. (2007). Science is an essential safeguard against human error. In S. O. Lilienfeld & W. T. O'Donohue (Eds.), *The great ideas of clinical science: 17 principles that every mental health professional should understand* (pp. 3–27). New York, NY: Routledge.

Ozonoff S. (2011). Editorial: The first cut is the deepest: Why do the reported effects of treatments decline over trials? *Journal of Child Psychology and Psychiatry, 52*, 729–730.

Panksepp, J. (2004). Free will and the varieties of affective and conative selves. *Behavioral and Brain Sciences, 27*(5), 671–672. Retrieved from http://search.proquest.com/docview/620720288?accountid=14168

Panksepp, J., & Panksepp, J. B. (2000). The seven sins of evolutionary psychology. *Evolution and Cognition, 6*, 108–131.

Park, R. L. (2003, January 21). The seven warning signs of bogus science. *Chronicle Review.* Retrived from http://chronicle.com/article/The-Seven-Warning-Signs-of/13674

Pashler, H., & Wagenmakers, E. J. (2012). Editors' introduction to the special section on replicability in Psychological Science: A crisis of confidence? *Perspectives on Psychological Science, 7*, 528–530.

Penn & Schoen and Berland Associates. (2008). *American Psychological Association benchmark study.* New York, NY: Author.

Pinker, S. (1997). *How the mind works.* New York, NY: Norton.

Pinker, S. (2002). *The blank slate: The modern denial of human nature.* New York, NY: Penguin Press.

Platt, J. R. (1964). Strong inference. *Science, 146*, 347–353.

Popper, K. R. (1965). *The logic of scientific discovery.* New York, NY: Harper & Row.

Proctor, R. W., & Capaldi, E. J. (2006). *Why science matters: Understanding the methods of psychological research.* Malden, MA: Blackwell.

Pronin, E., Gilovich, T., & Ross, L. (2004). Objectivity in the eye of the beholder: Divergent perceptions of bias in self versus others. *Psychological Review, 3*, 781–799.

Rassin, E., Eerland, A., & Kuijpers, I. (2010). Let's find the evidence: An analogue study of confirmation bias in criminal investigations. *Journal of Investigative Psychology and Offender Profiling, 7*, 231–246.

Redding, R. E. (1998). How common-sense psychology can inform law and psycholegal research. *University of Chicago Law School Roundtable, 5*, 107–142.

Reich, K. H. (2010). Shortcomings of the human brain and remedial action by religion. *Cultural Studies of Science Education, 5*, 157–162.

Risen, J., & Gilovich, T. (2007). Informal logical fallacies. In R. J. Sternberg, H. L. Roediger, & D. F. Halpern (Eds.), *Critical thinking in psychology* (pp. 110–130). New York, NY: Cambridge University Press.

Ritchie, S. J., Wiseman, R., & French, C. C. (2012). Failing the future: Three unsuccessful attempts to replicate Bem's "Retroactive Facilitation of Recall" Effect. *PLoS One, 7*(3), e33423.

Rosen, G. M. (1993). Self-help or hype? Comments on psychology's failure to advance self-care. *Professional Psychology: Research and Practice, 24*, 340–345.

Rosenthal, G. T., Soper, B., Rachal, C., McKnight, R. R., & Price, A. W. (2004). The Profession of Psychology Scale: Sophisticated and naive students' responses. *Journal of Instructional Psychology, 31*, 202–205.

Ross, L., Lepper, M. R., & Hubbard, M. (1975). Perseverance in self-perception and social perception: Biased attributional processes in the debriefing paradigm. *Journal of Personality and Social Psychology, 32*, 880–892.

Ross, L., & Ward, A. (1996). Naive realism: Implications for social conflict and misunderstanding. In T. Brown, E. Reed, & E. Turiel (Eds.), *Values and knowledge* (pp. 103–135). Hillsdale, NJ: Erlbaum.

Sackett, P. R., Borneman, M. J., & Connelly, B. S. (2008). High stakes testing in higher education and employment: Appraising the evidence for validity and fairness. *American Psychologist, 63*(4), 215–227. http://dx.doi.org/10.1037/0003-066X.63.4.215

Sagan, C. (1995). *The demon-haunted world: Science as a candle in the dark.* New York, NY: Random House.

Salerno, S. (2005). *SHAM: How the self-help movement made America helpless.* New York, NY: Crown Books.

Salzinger, K. (2002). *Gugelhupf.* Retrieved from http://www.apa.org/monitor/jun02/sd.html

Sappington, A. A. (1990). Recent psychological approaches to the free will versus determinism controversy. *Psychological Bulletin, 108*, 19–29.

Satel, S., & Lilienfeld, S.O. (2013). *Brainwashed: How we are seduced by mindless neuroscience.* New York, NY: Basic Books.

Schmidt, S. (2009). Shall we really do it again? The powerful concept of replication is neglected in the social sciences. *Review of General Psychology, 13*, 90–100.

Schooler, J. (2011). Unpublished results hide the decline effect. *Nature, 470*, 437.

Shadish, W. R., Cook, T. D., & Campbell, D. T. (2002). *Experimental and quasi-experimental designs for generalized causal inference.* Boston, MA: Houghton Mifflin.

Shapiro, F. (1989). Eye movement desensitization: A new treatment for post-traumatic stress disorder. *Journal of Behavior Therapy and Experimental Psychiatry, 20*, 211–217.

Shepard, R. N. (1990). *Mind sights: Original visual illusions, ambiguities, and other anomalies.* New York, NY: W. H. Freeman.

Shermer, M. (2002). *Why people believe weird things: Pseudoscience, superstition, and other confusions of our time* (2nd ed.). New York, NY: W. H. Freeman.

Shermer, M. (2008, October). Five ways brains scans mislead. *Scientific American.* http://www.scientificamerican.com/article.cfm?id=five-ways-brain-scans-mislead-us

Shermer, M. (2011). *The believing brain: From ghosts to Gods to politics and conspiracies—How we construct beliefs and reinforce them as truths.* New York, NY: Times Books.

Skinner, B. F. (1971). *Beyond freedom and dignity.* New York, NY: Knopf.

Slovic, P., & Peters, E. (2006). Risk perception and affect. *Current Directions in Psychological Science, 15,* 322–325.

Solomon, S., Greenberg, J., & Pyszczynski, T. (2000). Pride and prejudice: Fear of death and social behavior. *Current Directions in Psychological Science, 6,* 200–204.

Solomon, S. S., & King, J. G. (1995). Influence of color on fire vehicle accidents. *Journal of Safety Research, 26,* 41–48.

Stanovich, K. E. (2009). *Decision making and rationality in the modern world.* New York, NY: Oxford University Press.

Steblay, N. M., Dysart, J. E., Fulero, S., & Lindsay, R. C. L. (2003). Eyewitness accuracy rates in police showup and lineup presentations: A meta-analytic comparison. *Law and Human Behavior, 27,* 523–540.

Stern, P. C. (2002). New environmental theories: Toward a coherent theory of environmentally significant behavior. *Journal of Social Issues, 56,* 407–424.

Stone, A. A. (1982). The insanity defense on trial. *Hospital and Community Psychiatry, 33,* 636–640.

Taleb, N. N. (2004). *Fooled by randomness: The hidden role of chances in the markets and life.* New York, NY: Texere.

Tanner, L. (2006, August 6). Sexual lyrics prompt teens to have sex. *Associated Press.* Retrieved from http://forum.psychlinks.ca/psychology-psychiatry-and-mental-health/4913-sexual-lyrics-prompt-teens-to-have-sex-or-just-bad-research.html

Tavris, C., & Aronson, E. (2007). *Mistakes were made (but not by me): How we justify foolish beliefs, bad decisions, and hurtful acts.* New York, NY: Harcourt.

Tooby, J., & Cosmides, L. (1989). Evolutionary psychology and the generation of culture: I. Theoretical considerations. *Ethology & Sociobiology, 10,* 29–49.

Truzzi, M. (1978). On the extraordinary: An attempt at clarification. *Zetetic Scholar, 1,* 11–22.

Uttal, W. R. (2003). *Psychomythics: Sources of artifacts and misconceptions in scientific psychology.* Mahwah, NJ: Lawrence Erlbaum.

Vail, K. E., Rothschild, Z. K., Weise, D. R., Solomon, S., Pyszczynski, T., & Greenberg, J. (2010). A terror management analysis of the psychological functions of religion. *Personality and Social Psychology Review, 14,* 84–94.

Van Hecke, M. L. (2007). *Blind spots: Why smart people do dumb things.* Amherst, NY: Prometheus.

Voevodsky, J. (1974). Evaluation of a deceleration warning light for reducing rear-end automobile collisions. *Journal of Applied Psychology, 59,* 270–273.

Vohs, K. D., & Schooler, J. W. (2008). The value of believing in free will: Encouraging a belief in determinism increases cheating. *Psychological Science, 19,* 49–54.

Wachtel, P. L. (1973). Psychodynamics, behavior therapy, and the implacable experimenter: An inquiry into the consistency of personality. *Journal of Abnormal Psychology, 82,* 324–334.

Wagenmakers, E.-J., Wetzels, R., Borsboom, D., van der Maas, H. L., & Kievit, R. A. (2012). An agenda for purely confirmatory research. *Perspectives on Psychological Science, 7,* 632–638.

Wagner, M. W., & Monnet, M. (1979). Attitudes of college professors toward extra-sensory perception. *Zetetic Scholar, 5,* 7–16.

Wang, C. S., Whitson, J. A., & Menon, T. (2012). Culture, control, and illusory pattern perception. *Social Psychological and Personality Science, 3,* 630–638.

Wason, P. C. (1966). Reasoning. In B. M. Foss (Ed.), *New horizons in psychology* (pp. 135–151). Harmondsworth, England: Penguin.

Watson, J. B. (1913). Psychology as the behaviorist views it. *Psychological Review, 20,* 158–177.

Wegner, D. M. (2002). *The illusion of conscious will.* Cambridge, MA: MIT Press.

Wells, G. L., Memon, A., & Penrod, S. D. (2006). Eyewitness evidence: Improving its probative value. *Psychological Science in the Public Interest, 7,* 45–75.

West, R. F., Meserve, R. J., & Stanovich, K. E. (2012). Cognitive sophistication does not attenuate the bias blind spot. *Journal of Personality and Social Psychology, 103,* 506–519.

Westen, D. (1998). The scientific legacy of Sigmund Freud: Toward a psychodynamically informed psychological science. *Psychological Bulletin, 124,* 333–371.

Westen, D., Kilts, C., Blagov, P., Harenski, K., & Hamann, S. (2006). The neural basis of motivated reasoning: An fMRI study of emotional constraints on political judgment during the U.S. presidential election of 2004. *Journal of Cognitive Neuroscience, 18,* 1947–1958.

Whitson, J. A., & Galinsky, A. D. (2008). Lacking control increases illusory pattern perception. *Science, 322,* 115–117.

Willingham, D. T. (2007, Summer). Why is critical thinking so hard to teach? *American Educator, 31*(2), 8–19.

Wilson, T. D. (2002). *Strangers to ourselves: Discovering the adaptive unconscious.* Cambridge, MA: Harvard University Press.

Wood, M. J., Douglas, K. M., & Sutton, R. M. (2012). Dead and alive: Beliefs in contradictory conspiracy theories. *Social Psychological and Personality Science,* awaiting page numbers.

Wood, W., Jones, M., & Benjamin, L. T. (1986). Surveying psychological public image. *American Psychologist, 41,* 947–953.

Zimbardo, P. G. (2004a). Does psychology make a significant difference in our lives? *American Psychologist, 59,* 339–351.

Credits

Credits listed in order of appearance.

Figure 1: Based on data from Bbllardi, Rand, & Karwoski, 2007. **Figure 4:** Gould, 1997. **Text:** Penn, Schoen and Berland Associates. (2008). American Psychological Association benchmark study. New York, NY: Author. **Text:** Red Auerbach. **Table 3:** Based on data from Gilovich, 1991. **Text:** Tanner, 2006. **Figure 9:** Based on data from the National Science Foundation, 2003. **Figure 10:** Based on data from APA, 2007.

Photo Credits

Photo Credits listed in order of appearance.

Image Source/Getty Images; Lourens Smak/Alamy; **(bottom left):** Auremar/Fotolia; **(bottom center):** Vita Khorzhevska/Shutterstock; **(bottom right):** Aaron Amat/Shutterstock; **(top center):** Picture Partners/Alamy; **(center left):** Henry Westheim Photography/Alamy; **(bottom left):** Hannah Faye Chua/Courtesy of Hannah Faye Chua; **(top right):** Stuart Ramson/AP Images; **(left):** Warren Goldswain/Shutterstock; **(top left):** PR Newswire/AP Images; **(top center):** PRNewsFoto/Dynakor Pharmacal/AP Images; **(center right):** Dave Ellison/Alamy; **(top center):** Library of Congress Prints and Photographs Division [LC-DIG-ppmsca-19305]; **(top right):** World History Archive/Alamy; **(bottom left):** Nashville Tennesean, Bill Steber/AP Images; **(top right):** NASA Jet Propulsion Laboratory; **(bottom left):** Robert McGouey/Landscape/Alamy; **(center right):** The Olmpian/Steve Bloom/AP Images; **(bottom right):** The Olmpian/Steve Bloom/AP Images; **(top left):** AP Images; **(center left):** John Bazemore/AP Images; **(top right):** Don Smetzer/PhotoEdit; **(center right):** ScienceCartoonsPlus.com; **(bottom center):** John Stillwell/PA Photos/Landov; **(top left):** Bil Kean/King Features Syndicate;

(center left): Darren Greenwood/Design Pics Inc./Alamy; **(bottom right):** Mary Evans Picture Library/The Image Works; **(top left):** Chris Madden; **(bottom center):** Viktor1/Shutterstock; **(top right):** Marcel Jancovic/Shutterstock; **(center right):** Archives of the History of American Psychology - The University of Akron; **(top left):** Archives of the History of American Psychology - The University of Akron; **(top left):** Picture History/Newscom; **(center):** Omikron/Science Source/Photo Researchers; **(bottom left):** Bettmann/Corbis; **(bottom left):** Library of Congress; **(top left):** Spl/Science Source/Photo Researchers; **(center left):** Archives of the History of American Psychology - The University of Akron; **(center right):** Peter Aprahamian/Encyclopedia/Corbis; **(top right):** OJO Images/SuperStock; **(center left):** Dr. Elizabeth Loftus; **(center):** Leslie J. Yonce; **(bottom left):** Zuma Wire Service/Alamy; **(bottom center):** Rose Hartman/Time Life Pictures/Getty Images; **(bottom left):** Cartoonbank; **(top left):** Clayton Sharrard/PhotoEdit; **(center left):** Illene MacDonald/PhotoEdit; **(bottom left):** Fat Chance Productions/Flirt/Corbis; **(top right):** Conde Nast Archive/Corbis; **(top right):** AP Images; **(center right):** Robert McGouey/Landscape/Alamy; **(center left):** Marcel Jancovic/Shutterstock; **(top right):** Illene MacDonald/PhotoEdit.

Research Methods

From Chapter 2 of *Psychology: From Inquiry to Understanding,* Third Edition. Scott O. Lilienfeld, Steven Jay Lynn, Laura L. Namy, Nancy J. Woolf. Copyright © 2014 by Pearson Education, Inc. All rights reserved.

Research Methods

SAFEGUARDS AGAINST ERROR

Think About It

Do we really need research designs to figure out the answers to psychological questions?

How do our intuitions sometimes deceive us?

Can we perceive statistical associations even when they don't exist?

What's an "experiment," and is it just like any other psychological study?

How can we be fooled by statistics?

Facilitated communication in action. The rationale is that, because of a severe motor impairment, some children with autism are unable to speak or type on their own. Therefore, with the help of a facilitator, they can supposedly type out complete sentences on a keyboard or letter pad. Is it too good to be true?

EXTRAORDINARY CLAIMS ▶
Is the evidence as strong as the claim?

Research Methods

((•)) **Listen** in **MyPsychLab** to chapter audio

Jenny Storch was 14 years old, but she was no ordinary teenager. She was mute. Like all people with infantile autism, a severe psychological disorder that begins in early childhood, Jenny's language and ability to bond with others were severely impaired. Like three-fourths of individuals with infantile autism (American Psychiatric Association, 2013), Jenny had mental retardation. And, like all parents of children with infantile autism, Mark and Laura Storch were desperate to find some means of connecting emotionally with their child.

In the fall of 1991, Mark and Laura Storch enrolled Jenny in the Devereux School in Red Hook, New York. Only a year before, Douglas Biklen, a professor of education at Syracuse University, had published an article announcing the development of a technique called *facilitated communication*. Developed in Australia, facilitated communication was a stunning breakthrough in the treatment of infantile autism—or so it seemed.

Facilitated communication possessed a charming simplicity that somehow rang true. A "facilitator" sits next to the child with autism, who in turn sits in front of a computer keyboard or letter pad. According to Biklen, the facilitator must be present because infantile autism is actually a motor (movement) disorder, not a mental disorder as scientists had long assumed. Boldly challenging conventional wisdom, Biklen (1990) proclaimed that children with autism are just as intelligent as other children. But they suffer from a severe motor disorder that prevents them from talking or typing on their own. By holding the child's hands ever so gently and steadying them as they approach the intended letter keys, the facilitator supposedly permits the child to communicate by typing out words. Not just isolated words, like *Mommy,* but complete sentences like, *Mommy, I want you to know that I love you even though I can't speak.* Using facilitated communication, one child with autism even asked his mother to change his medication after reading an article in a medical journal (Mann, 2005). Facilitated communication was the long-sought-after bridge between the hopelessly isolated world of children with autism and the adult world of social interaction.

The psychiatric aides at the Devereux School had heard about facilitated communication, which was beginning to spread like wildfire throughout the autism treatment community. Thousands of mental health and education professionals across America were using it with apparently astonishing effects. Almost immediately after trying facilitated communication with Jenny, the Devereux aides similarly reported amazing results. For the first time, Jenny produced eloquent statements describing her innermost thoughts and feelings, including her deep love for her parents. The emotional bond that Mark and Laura Storch had dreamt of having with Jenny for 14 years was at last a reality.

Yet the Storchs' joy proved to be short-lived. In November 1991, Mark Storch received a startling piece of news that was to forever change his life. With the aid of a facilitator, Jenny had begun to type out allegations of brutal sexual abuse against him. When all was said and done, Jenny had typed out 200 gruesome accusations of rape, all supposedly perpetrated by her father. A second facilitator, who'd heard about these accusations, reported similar findings while assisting Jenny at the keyboard.

Although there was no physical evidence against Mark Storch, the Department of Social Services in Ulster County, New York, restricted contact between Jenny and her parents and removed Jenny from the Storch home. Jenny was eventually returned to her parents following a legal challenge, but not before Mark Storch's reputation had been stained. History repeated itself in a Detroit suburb in 2007, when Aislinn Wendrow, a 14-year-old nonverbal girl with autism who was using facilitated communication, accused her father Julian of sexual abuse. Following this allegation, a judge placed him in solitary confinement in a jail for 80 days. Again, there was not a shred of evidence against Julian Wendrow other than the facilitated claim of abuse.

What had once seemed like a miracle cure to the Storches and Wendrows had turned into a nightmare. What was the truth? The claims of facilitated communication proponents seemed extraordinary. Was the evidence for these claims equally extraordinary?

Since Douglas Biklen introduced facilitated communication to the United States, dozens of investigators have examined this procedure under tightly controlled laboratory conditions. In a typical study, the facilitator and child are seated in adjoining cubicles.

A wall separates them, but an opening between them permits hand-to-hand contact on a keyboard (see **FIGURE 1**). Then, researchers flash two different pictures on adjacent screens, one of which is seen only by the facilitator and the other of which is seen only by the child. The facilitator might view a photograph of a dog, the child a photograph of a cat. The crucial question is this: Will the word typed out by the child be the picture shown to the facilitator—*dog*—or the picture shown to the child—*cat*?

The results of these studies were as stunning as they were unanimous. In virtually 100 percent of trials, the typed word corresponded to the picture flashed to the facilitator, not the child (Jacobson, Mulick, & Schwartz, 1995; Romancyzk et al., 2003). Unbelievable as it seems, facilitated communication originates entirely from the minds of facilitators (Todd, 2012). *Unbeknownst to facilitators, their hands are effortlessly guiding the fingers of children toward the keyboard, and the resulting words are coming from their minds, not the children's.* Scientists had known for decades that our thoughts can control our movements without our knowledge (Wegner, 2002) You might have discovered this phenomenon while typing on a computer keyboard or texting a friend, when you found yourself intending to write one sentence (like "See you later at the movie"), but instead wrote a different sentence containing a word about which you were preoccupied ("See you later at the test"). The facilitated communication keyboard is no different. It turns out to be little more than a modern version of the Ouija board, a popular device used by spiritualists to try to communicate with the dead. Just like facilitators, players in the game of Ouija are controlling the movements of the little pointer without even realizing it. Regrettably, proponents of facilitated communication neglected to consider this rival hypothesis for its apparent effects.

FIGURE 1 Putting Facilitated Communication to the Test. By placing a child with autism and the facilitator in adjoining cubicles and flashing different pictures to each of them on some trials, researchers demonstrated that the "facilitated communications" emanated from the mind of the facilitator, not the child.

◄ **RULING OUT RIVAL HYPOTHESES**
Have important alternative explanations for the findings been excluded?

The Beauty and Necessity of Good Research Design

| Identify two modes of thinking and their application to scientific reasoning.

The facilitated communication story imparts an invaluable lesson: *Research design matters.* For two reasons, this story is also a powerful illustration of the triumph of science over pseudoscience. First, science has helped practitioners who work with individuals with autism to avoid wasting valuable time on facilitated communication and other interventions that are ineffective or harmful. Second, science has allowed practitioners to develop and test treatments for autism that work. Rigorous research by psychologists has helped them to design and evaluate interventions that genuinely permit individuals with autism to communicate more effectively, as well as to improve their social and problem-solving skills. Unlike facilitated communication, these techniques aren't magical quick fixes, but they offer real hope—not false hope—to afflicted individuals and their loved ones.

Why We Need Research Designs

Many beginning psychology students understandably wonder, "Why do I need to learn about research design? I took this course to learn about people, not numbers." Some of you may be puzzling over the same question. The facilitated communication story gives us the answer. Without research designs, even intelligent and well-trained people can be fooled. After all, the aides who worked with Jenny Storch and Aislinn Wendrow were sure that facilitated communication worked: Their naïve realism led them to see these children's abuse allegations "with their own eyes," and their confirmation bias created a self-fulfilling prophecy, making them see what they wanted to see. But like many advocates of pseudoscientific techniques, they were the victims of a cruel illusion. If the proponents of other facilitated communication had only made use of some of the research designs we'll discuss in this text, they wouldn't have been fooled. In this text, we'll learn what

FIGURE 2 The Prefrontal Lobotomy. In a prefrontal lobotomy, the surgeon severs the fibers connecting the brain's frontal lobes from the underlying thalamus.

prefrontal lobotomy
surgical procedure that severs fibers connecting the frontal lobes of the brain from the underlying thalamus

these research designs are. We'll also discover how they can help us to avoid being deceived and to better evaluate claims, both in psychology courses and in everyday life.

Let's look at another tragic example. For several decades of the early twentieth century, mental health professionals were convinced that the technique of **prefrontal lobotomy** (referred to in popular lingo as a "lobotomy") was an effective treatment for schizophrenia, as well as other severe mental disorders . Surgeons who used this technique severed the neural fibers that connect the brain's frontal lobes to the underlying thalamus (**FIGURE 2**).

The scientific world was so certain that prefrontal lobotomy was a remarkable breakthrough that they awarded its developer, Portuguese neurosurgeon Egas Moniz, the Nobel Prize in 1949. As in the case of facilitated communication, stunning reports of the effectiveness of prefrontal lobotomy were based almost exclusively on subjective clinical reports. One physician who performed lobotomies proclaimed, "I am a sensitive observer, and my conclusion is that a vast majority of my patients get better as opposed to worse after my treatment" (see Dawes, 1994, p. 48).

Like proponents of facilitated communication, believers in prefrontal lobotomy didn't conduct systematic research. They assumed that their clinical observations—"I can see that it works"—were sufficient evidence for this treatment's effectiveness for schizophrenia. They were mistaken. When scientists finally performed controlled studies on the effectiveness of prefrontal lobotomy, they found it to be essentially useless. The operation certainly produced radical changes in behavior, but it didn't target the specific behaviors associated with schizophrenia, such as hearing voices and holding persecutory beliefs. Moreover, lobotomies created a host of other problems, including extreme apathy (Valenstein, 1986). Again, the believers had been deceived by naïve realism and confirmation bias. Nowadays, prefrontal lobotomy is little more than a relic of an earlier pseudoscientific era of mental health treatment. What's more, prefrontal lobotomy has since been replaced by medications and other interventions that have a much firmer grounding in science. Although these treatments aren't cures for schizophrenia, they are often quite helpful, and they've allowed hundreds of thousands of individuals with serious mental illnesses to attain a semblance of normal everyday functioning (Lieberman et al., 2005). Research design matters.

How We Can Be Fooled: Two Modes of Thinking

At this point, you might be feeling just a bit defensive. At first glance, the authors of your text may seem to be implying that many people, perhaps you included, are foolish. But we shouldn't take any of this personally, because one of our central themes is that we can *all* be fooled, and that includes your text's authors.

How can we all be fooled so easily? A key finding emerging from the past few decades of research is that *the same psychological processes that serve us well in most situations also predispose us to errors in thinking.* That is, most mistaken thinking is cut from the same cloth as useful thinking (Ariely, 2008; Lehrer, 2009; Pinker, 1997).

To understand how and why we can all be fooled, it's helpful to introduce the distinction between two modes of thinking (Kahneman, 2011; Stanovich & West, 2000). The first was popularized by journalist Malcolm Gladwell in his 2005 book, *Blink*, which pointed out that our first impressions are at times surprisingly accurate. This type of thinking is quick and reflexive, and its output consists mostly of "gut hunches." This mode of thinking also doesn't require much mental effort. Nobel Prize winner Daniel Kahneman (2011) refers to this type of thinking as System 1 thinking, but we'll call it "intuitive" thinking (Hammond, 1996). When we're in intuitive thinking mode, our brains are largely on autopilot. We engage in intuitive thinking when we meet someone new and form an immediate first impression of him or her, or see an oncoming car rushing toward us as we're crossing the street and decide that we need to get out of the way. Without intuitive thinking, we'd all be in serious trouble, because much of everyday life requires snap decisions.

But there's a second mode of thinking. Kahneman (2011) calls it System 2 thinking, but we'll call it "analytical" thinking (Hammond, 1996). In contrast to intuitive thinking, analytical thinking is slow and reflective. It takes mental effort. We engage in analytical thinking whenever we're trying to reason through a problem, or figure out a complicated concept in an introductory psychology textbook (you're performing analytical thinking right now as you read this sentence). In some cases, analytic thinking allows us to override intuitive thinking (Gilbert, 1991; Herbert, 2010) and reject our gut hunches when they seem to be wrong. You've engaged in this process when you've met someone at a party you initially disliked because of a negative expression on his face, only to change your mind after talking to him and realizing that he's not such a bad person after all.

Our intuitive mode of thinking works well most of the time (Gigerenzer, 2007; Krueger & Funder, 2005; Shepperd & Koch, 2005). Here's an example drawn from actual research. Imagine that we ask a group of Americans the following question: "Which city is larger, San Diego or San Antonio?" and then ask a group of Germans the same question. Which group do you think would be more likely to the correct answer (Gigerenzer & Gaissmaier, 2011)?

If you're like most people, you might be surprised to learn that Germans are more likely to get the right answer than are Americans. That's because most Germans haven't heard of San Antonio. So they default to their intuitive (System 1) thinking, Specifically, they probably relied on what psychologists term a **heuristic,** a mental short-cut or rule of thumb. In this case, the heuristic they probably used was "When I've heard of a city, I'll assume it's larger in population than a city I've never heard of." More often than not, this heuristic, like most mental shortcuts, works just fine. In contrast, the Americans had heard of both cities and probably became confused, so many got the question wrong.

But intuitive thinking which often relies on heuristics, occasionally leads us to make mistakes, because our gut hunches and snap judgments aren't always right (Myers, 2004). To understand what we mean, try your hand at the following question. *Imagine that you are in Reno, Nevada. If you wanted to get to San Diego, California, what compass direction would you take? Close your eyes for a moment and picture how you'd get there* (Piatelli-Palmarini, 1994).

Well, we'd of course need to go southwest to get to San Diego from Reno, because California is west of Nevada, right? Wrong. Actually, to get from Reno to San Diego, we'd go *southeast*, not southwest. If you don't believe us, look at **FIGURE 3**.

If you got this one wrong (and, if you did, don't feel bad, because your book's authors did, too), you almost certainly relied on intuitive thinking. Specifically, the heuristic you probably used in this case was: *California is west of Nevada, and San Diego is at the bottom of California, whereas Reno has a lot more land south of it before you hit Mexico.* What you either forgot or didn't know is that a large chunk of California (the bottom third or so) is actually *east* of much of Nevada. Of course, for most geographical questions (such as, "Is St. Louis east or west of Los Angeles?") these kinds of mental shortcuts work just fine. But in this case the heuristic tripped us up. The people who assumed that facilitated communication and prefrontal lobotomy was beneficial also relied on intuitive thinking, relying largely on heuristics (like "This person seems to be improving, so I guess the treatment worked") to infer whether a treatment is effective.

The good news is that research designs can help us avoid the pitfalls that can result from an overreliance on intuitive thinking and an uncritical use of heuristics. We can think of research designs as systematic techniques developed by scientists in psychology and other fields to harness the power of other type of thinking—analytical thinking. That's because research designs force us to consider alternative explanations for findings that our intuitive thinking overlooks. In everyday life, research designs

We use both intuitive and analytical thinking in our everyday life. With intuitive thinking we make snap judgments such as swerving to avoid a pot hole (*top*). Analytical thinking is slow and reflective, as when we solve a math problem (*bottom*).

heuristic
mental shortcut or rule of thumb that helps us to streamline our thinking and make sense of our world

◀ **RULING OUT RIVAL HYPOTHESES**
Have important alternative explanations for the findings been excluded?

can be our best friends, protecting us against misguided snap judgments that would otherwise lead us astray.

Study and Review in MyPsychLab

FIGURE 3 In Which Compass Direction Would You Travel to Get from Reno, Nevada, to San Diego, California? If you didn't guess southeast (which is the correct answer), you're not alone. By relying on a heuristic—that is, a mental shortcut—we can sometimes be fooled.

Assess Your Knowledge — FACT or FICTION?

1. Psychological research suggests that we're all capable of being fooled.   **True / False**

2. Analytic thinking tends to be rapid and intuitive.   **True / False**

3. The psychological processes that give rise to heuristics are generally maladaptive.   **True / False**

4. Research methods help us to get around some of the problems produced by uncritical use of intuitive thinking.   **True / False**

Answers: 1. T; 2. F; 3. F; 4. T.

The Scientific Method: Toolbox of Skills

2 Describe the advantages and disadvantages of using naturalistic observation, case studies, self-report measures, and surveys.

3 Describe the role of correlational designs and distinguish correlation from causation.

4 Identify the components of an experiment, the potential pitfalls that can lead to faulty conclusions, and how psychologists control for these pitfalls.

In actuality, the heading of this section is a bit of a fib, because there's no *single* scientific method. "The" scientific method is a myth, because the techniques that psychologists use are very different from those that their colleagues in chemistry, physics, and biology use (Bauer, 1992).

The scientific method is a toolbox of skills designed to counteract our tendency to fool ourselves. Using the language we've learned in this text, we might say that it consists of safeguards against the dangers of putting too much stock in our intuitive thinking. All of the tools we'll describe have one major thing in common: They permit us to test *hypotheses,* which are predictions often derived from broader theories. If these hypotheses are confirmed by research, we're justified in having more confidence in our theory, although we should recall that this theory is never really "proven." If these hypotheses are disconfirmed, scientists often revise this theory or abandon it altogether. This toolbox of the scientific method isn't perfect by any means, but it's the best set of safeguards we have against bias and other errors in intuitive thinking. Let's now open up this toolbox and peek at what's inside (see **TABLE 1**).

TABLE 1 Advantages and Disadvantages of Research Designs.

	ADVANTAGES	DISADVANTAGES
Naturalistic Observation	High in external validity	Low in internal validity Doesn't allow us to infer causation
Case Studies	Can provide existence proofs Allow us to study rare or unusual phenomena Can offer insights for later systematic testing	Are typically anecdotal Don't allow us to infer causation
Correlational Designs	Can help us to predict behavior	Don't allow us to infer causation
Experimental Designs	Allow us to infer causation High in internal validity	Can sometimes be low in external validity

Naturalistic Observation: Studying Humans "In the Wild"

Let's say we wanted to conduct a study to find out about laughter. How often do people laugh in the real world? When are people most likely to laugh? We could try to answer these questions by bringing people into our laboratory and observing their laughter across various situations. But it's unlikely we'd be able to re-create the full range of settings that trigger laughter. Moreover, even if we observed participants without their knowing it, their laughter could still have been influenced by the fact that they were in a laboratory. Among other things, they may have been more nervous or less spontaneous than in the real world.

One way of getting around these problems is **naturalistic observation:** watching participants' behavior in real-world settings without trying to manipulate their actions. With this technique, we watch behavior unfold "naturally" without intervening in it. We can perform naturalistic observation using a video camera or tape recorder or, if we're willing to go low-tech, only a paper and pencil. Many psychologists who study animals, such as chimpanzees, in their natural habitats use naturalistic observation, although psychologists who study humans sometimes use it, too. By doing so, we can better understand the range of behaviors displayed by individuals in the "real world," as well as the situations in which they occur.

Robert Provine (1996, 2000) relied on naturalistic observation in an investigation of human laughter. He eavesdropped on 1,200 instances of laughter in social situations—shopping malls, restaurants, and street corners—and recorded the gender of the laugher and "laughee," the remarks that preceded laughter, and others' reactions to laughter. He found that women laugh much more than men in social situations. Surprisingly, he discovered that less than 20 percent of laughing incidents are preceded by statements that could remotely be described as humorous. Instead, most cases of laughter are preceded by decidedly unfunny comments (like "It was nice meeting you, too."). Provine also found that speakers laugh considerably more than listeners, a finding painfully familiar to any of us who've had the experience of laughing out loud at one of our jokes while our friends looked back at us with a blank stare. Provine's work, which would have been difficult to pull off in a laboratory, sheds new light on the interpersonal triggers and consequences of laughter.

The major advantage of naturalistic designs is that they're often high in **external validity:** the extent that our findings generalize to real-world settings (Neisser & Hyman, 1999). Because psychologists apply these designs to organisms as they go about their daily business, their findings are frequently relevant to the real world. Some psychologists contend that naturalistic designs almost always have higher external validity than laboratory experiments, although there's actually not much research support for this claim (Mook, 1983).

Still, no research design is perfect, and naturalistic designs have their disadvantages too. In particular, they tend to be low in **internal validity:** the extent to which we can draw cause-and-effect inferences. As we'll soon learn, well-conducted laboratory experiments are high in internal validity, because we can manipulate the key variables ourselves. In contrast, in naturalistic designs we have no control over these variables and need to wait for behavior to unfold before our eyes. Naturalistic designs can also be problematic if people know they're being observed, as this awareness can affect their behavior.

Case Study Designs: Getting to Know You

One of the simplest designs in the psychologist's investigative toolbox is the case study. In a **case study,** researchers examine one person or a small number of people, often over an extended period of time (Davison & Lazarus, 2007). An investigator could spend 10 or even 20 years studying one person with schizophrenia, carefully documenting his childhood experiences, job performance, family life, friendships, and the ups and downs of his mental problems. There's no single "recipe" for a case study. Some researchers might simply observe a person over time, others might administer questionnaires, and still others might conduct repeated interviews.

Case studies can be helpful in providing **existence proofs:** demonstrations that a given psychological phenomenon can occur. For example, the existence of "recovered memories" of child abuse is one of the most heated controversies in psychology.

Researcher Jane Goodall has spent much of her career using techniques of naturalistic observation with chimpanzees in Gombe, Kenya. Her work strongly suggests that warfare is not unique to humans.

naturalistic observation
watching behavior in real-world settings without trying to manipulate the situation

external validity
extent to which we can generalize findings to real-world settings

internal validity
extent to which we can draw cause-and-effect inferences from a study

case study
research design that examines one person or a small number of people in depth, often over an extended time period

existence proof
demonstration that a given psychological phenomenon can occur

Case studies can sometimes provide access to the rare or unusual. For example, people with the condition of Capgras' syndrome believe that their relatives or loved ones have been replaced by identical-looking doubles. The study of this condition has shed light on neurological and psychological processes involved in identifying other people.

RULING OUT RIVAL HYPOTHESES ▶
Have important alternative explanations for the findings been excluded?

Experts disagree about whether individuals can completely forget episodes of childhood sexual abuse for years or even decades, only to remember them, often with the aid of a psychotherapist, in perfectly accurate form in adulthood. To demonstrate the presence of recovered memories, all we'd need is *one* clear-cut case of a person who'd forgotten an abuse memory for decades and then recalled it suddenly. Although there have been several suggestive existence proofs of recovered memories (Duggal & Sroufe, 1998; Schooler, 1997), none has been entirely convincing (McHugh, 2008; McNally, 2003).

Case studies also provide a valuable opportunity to study rare or unusual phenomena that are difficult or impossible to re-create in the laboratory, such as people with atypical symptoms or rare types of brain damage. Richard McNally and Brian Lukach (1991) reported a case history of a man who exposed himself sexually to large dogs, and obtained sexual gratification from doing so, a condition known as "zoophilic exhibitionism." To treat this man's condition, they developed a 6-month program that incorporated techniques designed to enhance his sexual arousal in response to women and snuff out his sexual response to dogs. Researchers might wait around for decades in the laboratory before accumulating a sample of 50 or even 5 individuals with this bizarre condition. McNally and Lukach's case study provided helpful insights into the treatment of this condition that laboratory research couldn't.

Finally, case studies can offer useful insights that researchers can follow up on and test in systematic investigations (Davison & Lazarus, 2007). In this respect, they can be enormously helpful for generating hypotheses. For example, in the 1960s, psychiatrist Aaron Beck was conducting psychotherapy with a female client who appeared anxious during the session (Smith, 2009). When Beck asked her why she was nervous, she reluctantly admitted she was afraid she was boring him. Beck probed in more depth, discovering that she harbored the irrational idea that just about everyone found her boring. From these and other informal observations, Beck pieced together a new and influential form of therapy based on the premise that people's emotional distress stems from their deep-seated irrational beliefs.

Nevertheless, if we're not careful, case studies can lead to misleading, even disastrously wrong, conclusions. The *plural of anecdote isn't fact*. Hundreds of observations purporting to show that facilitated communication is effective for autism or that prefrontal lobotomy is effective for schizophrenia aren't sufficient to conclude that these techniques are effective, because carefully controlled studies have pinpointed alternative explanations for their effects. As a consequence, case studies almost never lend themselves to systematic tests of hypotheses about *why* a given phenomenon occurred. So even though case studies can be helpful for generating hypotheses, they tend to be quite limited for testing them.

Self-Report Measures and Surveys: Asking People about Themselves and Others

If we want to find out about someone's personality and attitudes, a good place to start is to ask them directly. Psychologists frequently use *self-report measures*, often called questionnaires, to assess a variety of characteristics, such as personality traits, mental illnesses, and interests. Closely related to self-report measures are *surveys*, which psychologists typically use to measure people's opinions and attitudes. Questionnaires and surveys can be tricky to interpret, as we'll see, but we can also learn a great deal from them if we design and administer them well.

RANDOM SELECTION: THE KEY TO GENERALIZABILITY. Imagine being hired by a research firm to gauge people's attitudes toward a new brand of toothpaste, Brightooth, which supposedly prevents 99.99 percent of cavities. How should we do it? We could stop people we see on the street, pay them money to brush their teeth with Brightooth, and measure their reactions to Brightooth on a survey. Is this a good approach?

No, because the people on your local street probably aren't typical of people in the broader population. Moreover, some people will almost surely refuse to participate, and they may differ from those who agreed to participate. For example, people with especially bad teeth might refuse to try Brightooth, and they may be the very people to whom Brightooth executives would most want to market their product.

Here's a better approach that modern psychologists would use: Identify a representative sample of the population, and administer our survey to people drawn from that sample. For example, we could look at U.S. population census data, scramble all of the names, and try to contact every 10,000th person listed. This approach, often used in survey research, is called **random selection.** In random selection, every person in the population has an equal chance of being chosen to participate. Random selection is crucial if we want to generalize our results to the broader population. Political pollsters keep themselves awake at night worrying about random selection. If their selection of survey respondents from the population is nonrandom, their election forecasts may well be skewed and wildly inaccurate as a result.

Obtaining a random sample is usually more important than obtaining a large sample if we want to generalize our results to most people. If we want to find out how the average American feels about singer Taylor Swift, it's actually better to ask 100 randomly sampled Americans than to ask 100,000 people in the city in Nashville, Tennessee, which is one of the world's centers for country music. The second sample is likely to be hopelessly skewed and atypical of the average person in the United States. When it comes to surveys, bigger isn't always better.

So, nonrandom selection can lead to wildly misleading conclusions. Take the infamous *Hite Report on Love, Passion and Emotional Violence* (1987). In the mid-1980s, researcher Shere Hite sent out 100,000 surveys to American women inquiring about their relationships with men. She'd identified potential survey respondents from lists of subscribers to women's magazines. Hite's findings were so startling that *Time* magazine and other prominent publications featured them as their cover story. Here's a sampling of Hite's findings:

- 70 percent of women married 5 or more years say they've had extramarital affairs.

- 87 percent of married women say their closest emotional relationship is with someone other than their husband.

- 95 percent of women say they're "emotionally and psychologically harassed" by their love partner.

- 98 percent of women say they're generally unsatisfied with their present love relationship.

That's all pretty depressing news, to put it mildly. Yet lost in the furor over Hite's findings was one crucial point: Only 4.5 percent of her sample had responded to her survey. What's more, Hite had no way of knowing whether this 4.5 percent was representative of her full sample. Interestingly, a poll conducted by the Harris organization at around the same time used random selection and reported results virtually opposite to Hite's. In their better-conducted survey, 89 percent of women said they were generally satisfied with their current relationship, and only a small minority reported extramarital affairs. More likely than not, Hite's high percentages resulted from nonrandom selection: The 4.5 percent of participants who responded to her survey were probably the very women experiencing the most relationship problems to begin with. Therefore they were the most motivated to participate in the survey.

EVALUATING MEASURES. When evaluating the results from any dependent variable or measure, we need to ask two crucial questions: Is our measure reliable? Is it valid?

Reliability refers to consistency of measurement (Haynes, Smith, & Hunsley, 2011). A reliable questionnaire, for example, yields similar scores over time. This type of reliability is called *test–retest reliability*. To assess test–retest reliability, we could

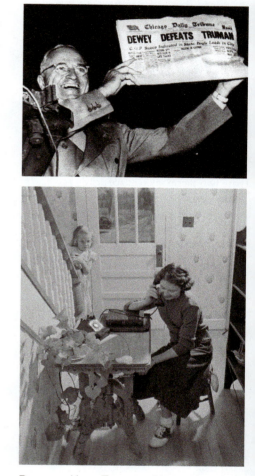

Democrat Harry Truman at his presidential victory rally (*top*), famously holding up an early edition of the *Chicago Daily Tribune* incorrectly proclaiming Republican Thomas Dewey the winner of the 1948 presidential election. In fact, Truman won by nearly 5 percentage points. The pollsters got it wrong largely because they based their survey results on people with telephones. Back in 1948, considerably more Republicans (who tended to be richer) owned telephones than Democrats, resulting in a skewed preelection prediction.

random selection
procedure that ensures every person in a population has an equal chance of being chosen to participate

reliability
consistency of measurement

These two thermometers are providing different readings for the temperature in an almost identical location. Psychologists might say that these thermometers display less-than-perfect interrater reliability.

CON NEWS VIEWER POLL

Do you believe that UFOs are flying saucers from other planets?

Yes 56%
No 33%
Undecided 11%

Total votes: 19,726

Warning: This is not a scientific poll.

? Frequently, one will see polls in the news that carry the disclaimer "This is not a scientific poll" (Of course, one then has to wonder: Why report the results?) **Why is this online poll not scientific?** (See answer upside down on bottom of page.)

administer a personality questionnaire to a large group of people today and readminister it in 2 months. If the measure is reasonably reliable, participants' scores should be similar at both times. Reliability also applies to interviews and observational data. *Interrater reliability* is the extent to which different people who conduct an interview, or make behavioral observations, agree on the characteristics they're measuring. If two psychologists who interview patients in a psychiatric hospital unit disagree on most of their diagnoses—if one psychologist diagnoses most of the patients as having schizophrenia and the other diagnoses most of the patients as having depression—then their interrater reliability will be low.

Validity is the extent to which a measure assesses what it purports (claims) to measure (Borsboom, 2005; Haynes et al., 2011). We can think of validity as "truth in advertising." If we went to a computer store, purchased a fancy package labeled "iPhone" and on opening it discovered a wristwatch, we'd demand our money back. Similarly, if a questionnaire we're administering purports to be a valid measure of introversion, but studies show it's really measuring anxiety, then this measure isn't valid. As users of the test, we should similarly demand our money back.

Reliability and validity are different concepts, although people routinely confuse them. In courts of law, we'll frequently hear debates about whether the polygraph (or so-called lie-detector) test is scientifically "reliable." But the central question concerning the polygraph isn't its reliability, because it typically yields fairly consistent scores over time. Instead, the central question is its validity, because many critics maintain that the polygraph actually detects emotional arousal, not lying (Grubin, 2010; Lykken, 1998; Ruscio, 2005).

Reliability is necessary for validity, because we need to measure something consistently before we can measure it well. Imagine trying to measure the floors and walls of an apartment using a ruler made of Silly Putty, that is, a ruler whose length changes each time we pick it up. Our efforts at accurate measurement would be doomed. Nevertheless, reliability doesn't guarantee validity. Although a test must be reliable to be valid, a reliable test can be completely invalid. Imagine we've developed a new measure of intelligence, the "Distance Index-Middle Width Intelligence Test" (DIMWIT), which subtracts the width of our index finger from that of our middle finger. The DIMWIT would be a highly reliable measure of intelligence, because the widths of our fingers are

validity
extent to which a measure assesses what it purports to measure

Answer: The poll isn't scientific because it's based on people who logged onto the website, who are probably not a representative sample of all people who watch Con News—and almost certainly not of all Americans.

unlikely to change much over time (high test-retest reliability) and are likely to be measured similarly by different raters (high interrater reliability). But the DIMWIT would be a completely invalid measure of intelligence, because finger width has nothing to do with intelligence.

When interpreting the results of self-report measures and surveys, we should bear in mind that we can obtain quite different answers depending on how we phrase the questions (Schwarz, 1999; Smith, Schwarz, & Roberts, 2006). One researcher administered surveys to 300 women homemakers. In some surveys, women answered the question "Would you like to have a job, if this were possible?," whereas others answered the question "Would you prefer to have a job, or do you prefer to do just your housework?" These two questions seem remarkably similar. Yet although 81 percent of those who were asked the first question said they'd like to have a job, only 32 percent who were asked the second question said they'd like to have a job (Noelle-Neumann, 1970; Walonick, 1994). Moreover, we shouldn't assume that people who respond to survey questions even understand the answers they're giving. In one study, researchers asked people about their views of the "Agricultural Trade Act of 1978." About 30 percent of participants expressed an opinion about this act, even though no such act exists (Bishop, Oldendick, & Tuchfarber, 1986; Schwarz, 1999).

A widely publicized 1992 poll by the Roper organization asked Americans the following confusing question, which contained two negatives: "Does it seem possible or does it seem impossible to you that the Nazi extermination of the Jews never happened?" A shocking 22 percent of respondents replied that the Holocaust may not have happened. Yet when a later poll asked the question more clearly, this number dropped to only 1 percent. Survey wording counts.

ADVANTAGES AND DISADVANTAGES OF SELF-REPORT MEASURES. Self-report measures have an important advantage: They're easy to administer. All we need are a pencil, paper, and a willing participant, and we're off and running. Moreover, if we have a question about someone, it's often a good idea to first ask that person directly. That person frequently has access to subtle information regarding his or her emotional states, like anxiety or guilt, about which outside observers aren't aware (Grove & Tellegen, 1991; Lilienfeld & Fowler, 2006).

Self-report measures of personality traits and behaviors often work reasonably well. For example, people's reports of how outgoing or shy they are tend to be moderately associated with the reports of people who have spent a lot of time with them. These associations are somewhat higher for more observable traits, like extraversion, than for less observable traits, like anxiety (Gosling, Rentfrow, & Swann, 2003; Kenrick & Funder, 1988).

Yet self-report measures have their disadvantages, too. First, they typically assume that respondents possess enough insight into their personality characteristics to report on them accurately (Nisbett & Wilson, 1977; Oltmanns & Turkheimer, 2009). This assumption is questionable for certain groups of people. For example, people with high levels of narcissistic personality traits, like self-centeredness and excessive self-confidence, view themselves more positively than others do (Campbell & Miller, 2011; John & Robins, 1994). (The word *narcissistic* derives from the Greek mythological character Narcissus, who fell in love with his reflection in the water.) Narcissistic people tend to perceive themselves through rose-colored glasses.

Second, self-report questionnaires typically assume that participants are honest in their responses. Imagine that a company required you to take a personality test for a job you really wanted. Would you be completely frank in your evaluation of yourself, or would you minimize your personality quirks? Not surprisingly, some respondents engage in **response sets**—tendencies to distort their answers to questions, often in a way that paints them in a positive light (Edens, Buffington, & Tomicic, 2001; Paulhus, 1991).

One response set is the tendency to answer questions in a socially desirable direction, that is, to make ourselves look better than we are (Paunonen & LeBel, 2012; Ray et al., 2012). We're especially likely to engage in this response set when applying for an important job. This response set can make it difficult to trust people's reports of their abilities and achievements. For example, college students overstate their SAT scores by an average of 17 points (Hagen, 2001). Fortunately, psychologists have devised clever ways to measure this response set and thereby compensate for it in clinical practice and research

response set
tendency of research participants to distort their responses to questionnaire items

(van de Mortel, 2008). For example, within their measures they might embed several questions that measure respondents' tendency to make themselves seem perfect (like "I never get upset at other people."). Positive responses to several of these items alert researchers to the possibility that people are responding to questionnaires in a socially desirable fashion.

A nearly opposite response set is *malingering,* the tendency to make ourselves appear psychologically disturbed with the aim of achieving a clear-cut personal goal (Rogers, 2008). We're especially likely to observe this response set among people who are trying to obtain financial compensation for an injury or mistreatment on the job, or among people trying to escape military duty—in the last case, perhaps by faking insanity. Just as with socially desirable responding, psychologists have developed methods to detect malingering on self-report measures, often by inserting items that assess nonexistent or extremely implausible symptoms of mental illness (like "I often hear barking sounds coming from the upper left corner of my computer screen.").

RATING DATA: HOW DO THEY RATE? An alternative to asking people about themselves is asking others who know them well to provide ratings on them. In many job settings, employers rate their employees' work productivity and cooperativeness in routine evaluations. Rating data can circumvent some of the problems with self-report data, because observers may not have the same "blind spots" as the people they're rating (who are often called the "targets" of the rating). Imagine asking your introductory psychology instructor, "How good a job do you think you did in teaching this course?" It's unlikely she'd say "Just awful." In fact, there's good evidence that observers' ratings of personality traits, like conscientiousness, are often more valid than self-reports of these traits for predicting students' academic achievement and employers' work performance (Connelly & Ones, 2010).

Nevertheless, like self-report measures, rating data have their drawbacks; one such shortcoming is the *halo effect.* This is the tendency of ratings of one positive characteristic to "spill over" to influence the ratings of other positive characteristics (Guilford, 1954; Moore, Filippou, & Perrett, 2011). Raters who fall victim to the halo effect seem almost to regard the targets as "angels"—hence the halo—who can do no wrong. If we find an employee physically attractive, we may unknowingly allow this perception to influence our ratings of his or her other features, such as conscientiousness and productivity. Indeed, people perceive physically attractive people as more successful, confident, assertive, and intelligent than other people even though these differences often don't reflect objective reality (Dion, Berscheid, & Walster, 1972; Eagly et al., 1991).

Student course evaluations of teaching are especially vulnerable to halo effects, because if you like a teacher personally you're likely to give him "a break" on the quality of his teaching. In one study, Richard Nisbett and Timothy Wilson (1977) placed participants into one of two conditions. Some participants watched a videotape of a college professor with a foreign accent who acted friendly to his students; others watched a videotape of the same professor (speaking with the same accent) who acted unfriendly to his students. Participants watching the videotapes not only liked the friendly professor better, but rated his physical appearance, mannerisms, and accent more positively. Students who like their professors also tend to give them high ratings on characteristics that are largely irrelevant to teaching effectiveness, like the quality of the classroom audiovisual equipment and the readability of their handwriting (Greenwald & Gillmore, 1997; Williams & Ceci, 1997).

Correlational Designs

Does being an outgoing person go along with being less honest? Are people with higher IQs snobbier than other people? These are the kinds of questions addressed by another essential research method in the psychologist's toolbox, the correlational design. When using a **correlational design,** psychologists examine the extent to which two variables are associated. A *variable* is anything that can vary across individuals, like impulsivity, creativity, or religiosity. When we think of the word

People often perceive highly attractive individuals as possessing many other desirable attributes. This phenomenon is one illustration of the halo effect.

Factoid

The converse of the halo effect is called the *horns effect*—picture a devil's horns—or pitchfork effect. In this effect, the ratings of one negative trait, such as arrogance, spill over to influence the ratings of other negative traits (Corsini, 1999).

correlational design
research design that examines the extent to which two variables are associated

correlate, we should decompose it into its two parts: *co-* and *relate.* If two things are correlated, they relate to each other—not interpersonally, that is, but statistically.

Whereas naturalistic observation and case studies allow us to describe the state of the psychological world, correlational designs allow us to generate predictions about the future. If SAT scores are correlated with college grades, then knowing people's SAT scores allows us to forecast—although by no means perfectly—what their grades will be. Conclusions from correlational research are limited, however, because we can't be sure *why* these predicted relationships exist.

IDENTIFYING CORRELATIONAL DESIGNS. Identifying a correlational design can be trickier than it seems, because investigators who use this design—and news reporters who describe it—don't always use the word *correlated* in their description of findings. Instead, they'll often use terms like *associated, related, linked,* or *went together.* Whenever researchers conduct a study of the extent to which two variables "travel together," their design is correlational even if they don't describe it that way.

CORRELATIONS: A BEGINNER'S GUIDE. Before we go any further, let's lay some groundwork by examining two basic facts about correlations:

1. Correlations can be *positive, zero,* or *negative.* A positive correlation means that as the value of one variable changes, the other goes in the same direction: If one goes up, the other goes up, and if one goes down, the other goes down. If the number of college students' Facebook friends is positively correlated with how outgoing these students are, this means that more outgoing students have more Facebook friends and less outgoing students have fewer Facebook friends. A zero correlation means that the variables don't go together at all. If math ability has a zero correlation with singing ability, then knowing that someone is good at math tells us nothing about his singing ability. A negative correlation means that as the value of one variable changes, the other goes in the opposite direction: If one goes up, the other goes down, and vice versa. If social anxiety is negatively correlated with perceived physical attractiveness, then more socially anxious people would be rated as less attractive, and less socially anxious people as more attractive.

2. Correlation coefficients (the statistics that psychologists use to measure correlations), at least the ones we'll be discussing in this textbook, range in value from -1.0 to 1.0. A correlation coefficient of -1.0 is a perfect negative correlation, whereas a correlation coefficient of $+1.0$ is a perfect positive correlation. We won't talk about how to calculate correlation coefficients, because the mathematics of doing so gets pretty technical (those of you who are really ambitious can check out www.easycalculation.com/statistics/correlation.php to learn how to calculate a correlation coefficient). Values lower than 1.0 (either positive or negative values), such as .23 or .69, indicate a less-than-perfect correlation coefficient. To find how strong a correlation coefficient is, we need to look at its *absolute value,* that is, the size of the coefficient without the plus or minus sign in front of it. The absolute value of a correlation coefficient of $+.27$ is .27, and the absolute value of a correlation coefficient of $-.27$ is also .27. Both correlation coefficients are equally large in size—and equally informative—but they're going in opposite directions.

THE SCATTERPLOT. FIGURE 4 shows three panels depicting three types of correlations. Each panel shows a **scatterplot:** a grouping of points on a two-dimensional graph. Each dot on the scatterplot depicts a person. As we can see, each person differs from other persons in his or her scores on one or both variables.

The panel on the left displays a fictional scatterplot of a moderate ($r = -.5$) negative correlation, in this case, the association between the average number of beers that students drink the night before their first psychology exam and their scores on that exam. We can tell

Watch in **MyPsychLab** the **Video:** Research Methods

scatterplot
grouping of points on a two-dimensional graph in which each dot represents a single person's data

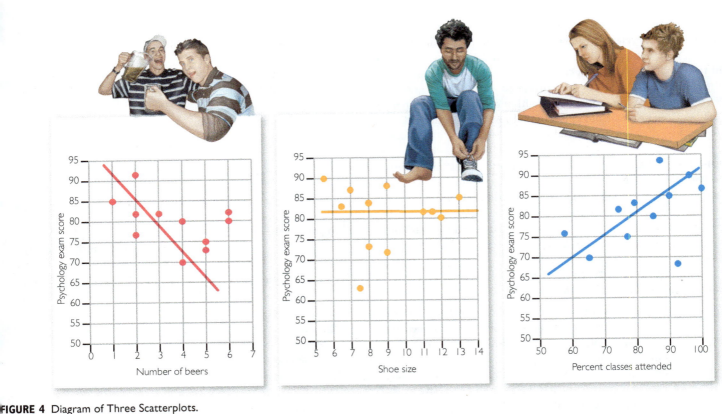

FIGURE 4 Diagram of Three Scatterplots. Scatterplot (*left*) depicts a moderate negative correlation (*r* = −.5); scatterplot (*middle*) depicts a zero correlation; and scatterplot (*right*) depicts a moderate positive correlation (*r* = .5).

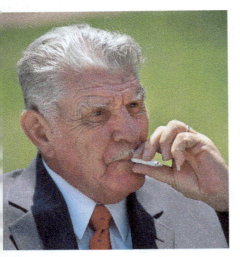

Just because we know one person who was a lifelong smoker and lived to a ripe old age doesn't mean there's no correlation between smoking and serious illnesses, like lung cancer and heart disease. Exceptions don't invalidate the existence of correlations.

that this correlation coefficient is negative because the clump of dots goes from higher on the left of the graph to lower on the right of the graph. Because this correlation is negative, it means that the more beers students drink, the worse they tend to do on their first psychology exam. Note that this negative correlation isn't perfect (it's not *r* = −1.0). That means that some students drink a lot of beer and still do well on their first psychology exam and that some students drink almost no beer and do poorly on their first psychology exam.

The middle panel shows a fictional scatterplot of a zero (*r* = 0) correlation coefficient, in this case the association between the students' shoe sizes and scores on their first psychology exam. The easiest way to identify a zero correlation is that the scatterplot looks like a blob of dots that's pointing neither upward nor downward. This zero correlation means there's no association whatsoever between students' shoe sizes and how well they do on their first psychology exam. Knowing one variable tells us absolutely nothing about the other. If we tried to guess people's exam grades from their shoe sizes, we'd do no better in our predictions than flipping pennies.

The panel on the right shows a fictional scatterplot of a moderate (*r* = .5) positive correlation, in this case, the association between students' attendance in their psychology course and their scores on their first psychology exam. Here, the clump of dots goes from lower on the left of the graph to higher on the right of the graph. This positive correlation means that the more psychology classes students attend, the better they tend to do on their first psychology exam. Because the correlation isn't perfect (it's not *r* = 1.0), there will always be the inevitable annoying students who don't attend any classes yet do well on their exams, and the incredibly frustrated souls who attend all of their classes and still do poorly.

Remember that unless a correlation coefficient is perfect, that is, 1.0 or −1.0, there will always be exceptions to the general trend. Because virtually all correlations in psychology have an absolute value of less than one, *psychology is a science of exceptions*. To argue against the existence of a correlation, it's tempting to resort to "I know a person who . . ." reasoning. So if we're trying to refute the overwhelming scientific evidence that cigarette smoking is correlated with lung cancer, we might insist, "But I know a person who smoked five packs of cigarettes a day for 40 years and never got lung cancer." But this anecdote doesn't refute the existence of the correlation, because the correlation between cigarette smoking and lung cancer isn't perfect. Because the correlation is less than 1.0, such exceptions are to be completely expected—in fact, they're required mathematically.

ILLUSORY CORRELATION. Why do we need to calculate correlations? Can't we just use our eyeballs to estimate how well two variables go together?

No, because psychological research demonstrates that we're all poor at estimating the sizes of correlations. In fact, we're often prone to an extraordinary phenomenon termed **illusory correlation**: the perception of a statistical association between two variables where none exists (Chapman & Chapman, 1967, 1969; Dawes, 2006). An illusory correlation is a statistical mirage. Here are two striking examples:

1. Many people are convinced of a strong statistical association between the full moon and a variety of strange occurrences, like violent crimes, suicides, psychiatric hospital admissions, and births—the so-called lunar lunacy effect (the word *lunatic* derives from *Luna,* the Roman goddess of the moon). Some police departments even put more cops on the beat on nights when there's a full moon, and many emergency room nurses insist that more babies are born during full moons (Hines, 2003). Yet a mountain of data shows that the full moon isn't correlated with any of these events: that is, the correlation is almost exactly $r = 0$ (Plait, 2002; Rotton & Kelly, 1985).

2. Many individuals with arthritis are convinced their joint pain increases during rainy weather, yet carefully conducted studies show no association between joint pain and rainy weather (Quick, 1999).

Illusory Correlation and Superstition. Illusory correlations form the basis of many superstitions (Vyse, 2000). Take the case of Wade Boggs, Hall of Fame baseball player and one of the game's greatest hitters. For 20 years, Boggs ate chicken before every game, believing this peculiar habit was correlated with successful performance in the batter's box. Boggs eventually became so skilled at cooking chicken that he even wrote a cookbook called *Fowl Tips.* It's unlikely that eating chicken and belting 95-mile-an-hour fastballs into the outfield have much to do with each other, but Boggs perceived such an association. Countless other superstitions, like keeping a rabbit's foot for good luck and not walking under ladders to avoid bad luck, probably also stem in part from illusory correlation .

Why We Fall Prey to Illusory Correlation. So you may be wondering: How on earth could so many people be so wrong? Indeed, we're all susceptible to illusory correlation, so this phenomenon is an inescapable fact of daily life. To understand why, we can think of much of everyday life in terms of a table of four probabilities, like that shown in **TABLE 2**. As you can see, we call this table "The Great Fourfold Table of Life."

Let's return to the lunar lunacy effect. As we can see from the Great Fourfold Table of Life, there are four possible relations between the phase of the moon and whether a crime is committed. The upper left-hand (A) cell of the table consists of cases in which there was a full moon and a crime occurred. The upper right-hand (B) cell consists of cases in which there was a full moon and no crime occurred. The bottom left-hand (C) cell

Although legend has it that animals and humans behave strangely during full moons, research evidence demonstrates that this supposed correlation is an illusion.

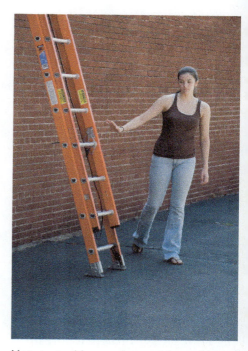

Many superstitions, such as avoiding walking under ladders, probably stem in part from illusory correlation.

TABLE 2 The Great Fourfold Table of Life.

		DID A CRIME OCCUR?	
		YES	NO
Did a Full Moon Occur?	**Yes**	(A) Full moon + crime	(B) Full moon + no crime
	No	(C) No full moon + crime	(D) No full moon + no crime

illusory correlation
perception of a statistical association between two variables where none exists

consists of cases in which there was no full moon and a crime occurred. Finally, the bottom right-hand (D) cell consists of cases in which there was no full moon and no crime.

Decades of psychological research lead to one inescapable conclusion: We tend to pay too much attention to the *upper left-hand (A) cell* of the fourfold table (Eder, Fielder, & Hamm-Eder, 2011; Lilienfeld et al., 2010). This cell is especially interesting to us, because it typically fits what we expect to see, causing our confirmation bias to kick in. In the case of the lunar lunacy effect, instances in which there was both a full moon and a crime are especially memorable ("See, just like I've always said, weird things happen during full moons."). Moreover, when we think about what occurs during full moons, we tend to remember instances that are the most dramatic, and that therefore come most easily to mind. In this case, these instances are usually those that grab our attention, namely, those that fall into the (A) cell (Gilovich, 1991).

Unfortunately, our minds aren't good at detecting and remembering *nonevents*, that is, things that don't happen. It's unlikely we're going to rush home excitedly to tell our friend, "Wow, you're not going to believe this. There was a full moon tonight, and nothing happened!" Our uneven attention to the different cells in the table leads us to perceive illusory correlations.

How can we minimize our tendencies toward illusory correlation? One way is to force ourselves to keep track of disconfirming instances—to give the other three cells of the fourfold table a little more of our time and attention. When James Alcock and his students asked a group of participants who claimed they could predict the future from their dreams—so-called prophetic dreamers—to keep careful track of their dreams by using a diary, their beliefs that they were prophetic dreamers vanished (Hines, 2003). By encouraging participants to record all of their dreams, Alcock forced them to attend to the (B) cell, the cell consisting of cases that disconfirm prophetic dreams.

The phenomenon of illusory correlation explains why we can't rely on our subjective impressions to tell us whether two variables are associated—and why we need correlational designs. Our intuitions often mislead us, especially when we've learned to expect two things to go together (Myers, 2002). Indeed, adults may be more prone to illusory correlation than children, because they've built up expectations about whether certain events—like full moons and odd behavior—go together (Kuhn, 2007). Fortunately, correlational designs help us to control for the problem of illusory correlation, because they force us to weigh all cells in the table equally.

CORRELATION VERSUS CAUSATION: JUMPING THE GUN. As we've seen, correlational designs can be extremely useful for determining whether two (or more) variables are related. As a result, they can allow us to predict behavior. For example, they can help us discover which variables—like personality traits or history of crimes—predict which inmates will reoffend after being released from prison, or what life habits—like heavy drinking or cigarette smoking—predict heart disease. Nevertheless, there are important limitations to the conclusions we can draw from correlational designs. The most common mistake we can make when interpreting these designs is to jump the gun and draw *causal* conclusions from them: Correlation doesn't necessarily mean causation. Although a correlation *sometimes* results from a causal relationship, we can't tell from a correlational study alone whether the relationship is causal.

Incidentally, we shouldn't confuse the correlation versus causation fallacy—the error of equating correlation with causation—with illusory correlation. Illusory correlation refers to perceiving a correlation where none exists. In the case of the correlation versus causation fallacy, a correlation exists, but we mistakenly interpret it as implying a causal association. Let's look at two examples of illusory correlation.

1. A statistician with too much time on his hands once uncovered a substantial negative correlation between the number of Ph.D. degrees awarded in a state within the United States and the number of mules in that state (Lilienfeld, 1995). Yes, *mules*. Does this negative correlation imply that the number of Ph.D. degrees (A) influences the number of mules (B)? It's possible—perhaps people

CORRELATION VS. CAUSATION ▶
Can we be sure that A causes B?

✳ **Explore** in **MyPsychLab** the **Concept:**
Correlations Do Not Show Causation

with Ph.D.s have something against mules and campaign vigorously to have them relocated to neighboring states. But this scenario seems rather unlikely. Or does this negative correlation instead imply that mules (*B*) cause people with Ph.D. degrees (*A*) to flee the state? Maybe, but don't bet on it. Before reading the next paragraph, ask yourself whether there's a third explanation.

Indeed there is. Although we don't know for sure, the most likely explanation is that a third variable, *C*, is correlated with both *A* and *B*. In this case, the most probable culprit for this third variable is *rural versus urban status*. States with large rural areas, like Wyoming, contain many mules and few universities. In contrast, states with many urban (big city) areas, like New York, contain few mules and many universities. So in this case, the correlation between variables *A* and *B* is almost certainly due to a third variable, *C*.

2. One team of researchers found a positive correlation over time between the number of babies born in Berlin, Germany (*A*), and the number of storks in nearby areas (*B*) (Hofer, Przyrembel, & Verleger, 2004). Specifically, over a 30-year period, more births were consistently accompanied by more storks. As the authors themselves noted, this correlation doesn't demonstrate that storks deliver babies. Instead, a more likely explanation is a third variable, population size (*C*): Highly populated city areas are characterized by large numbers of both births, because big cities have lots of hospitals, and storks, which tend to be attracted to inner-city areas.

We shouldn't rely on the news media to help us distinguish correlation from causation, because they frequently fall prey to the correlation versus causation fallacy (see some examples of misleading headlines in **FIGURE 5**).

Take, for example, the headline "Low Self-Esteem Shrinks Brain." The article's title implies a correlation, in this case a positive one, between self-esteem and brain size (it's positive because it claims that low self-esteem goes along with small brains, and vice-versa for people with high self-esteem). Yet the article's title implies a *causal* association between low self-esteem and brain size. Although it's possible that low self-esteem "shrinks" people's brains, it's also possible that shrinking brains lower people's self-esteem. Alternatively, an undetected third variable, such as alcohol use, might contribute to both low self-esteem and smaller brains (people who drink heavily may both think more poorly of themselves and suffer long-term brain damage). *The bottom line:* We should be on the lookout for headlines or news stories that proclaim a causal association between two variables. If the study is based on correlational data alone, we know they're almost always taking their conclusions too far.

Low Self-Esteem "Shrinks Brain"

A Surprising Secret to a Long Life: Stay in School

Housework Cuts Breast Cancer Risk

Fear of hell makes us richer, Fed says

Wearing a helmet puts cyclists at risk, suggests research

Winning World Cup lowers heart attack deaths

Eating fish prevents crime

? There's a positive correlation between the amount of ice cream consumed and the number of violent crimes committed on that same day, but that doesn't mean that eating ice cream causes crime. **Can you think of a third variable that might explain this correlation?** (See answer upside down on bottom of page.)

FIGURE 5 Examples of Newspaper Headlines That Confuse Correlation with Causation. Here are some actual newspaper headlines that suggest a causal association between two variables. Can you think of alternative explanations for the findings reported in each headline? (See http://jonathan.mueller.faculty. noctrl.edu/100/correlation_or_causation. htm for a good source of other newspaper headlines incorrectly suggesting causation from correlational findings.)

Experimental Designs

If observational designs, case studies, and correlational designs don't allow us to draw cause-and-effect conclusions, what kinds of designs do? The answer: Experimental designs, often known simply as "experiments." These designs differ from other designs in one crucial way: When performed correctly, *they permit cause-and-effect inferences*. To see why, we need to understand that in correlational designs researchers are measuring preexisting differences in participants, like age, gender, IQ, and extraversion. These are differences over

Answer: On hotter days, people both commit more crimes (in part because they go outside more often, and in part because they're more irritable) and eat more ice cream.

which investigators have no control. In contrast, in experimental designs researchers *manipulate* variables to see whether these manipulations produce differences in participants' behavior. Putting it another way, in correlational designs the differences among participants are *measured*, but in experimental designs they're *created*.

WHAT MAKES A STUDY AN EXPERIMENT: TWO COMPONENTS. Although news reporters frequently use the term *experiment* rather loosely to refer to any kind of research study, this term actually carries a specific meaning in psychology. To be precise, an **experiment** consists of *two* ingredients:

1. Random assignment of participants to conditions
2. Manipulation of an independent variable

Both of these ingredients are necessary for the recipe; if a study doesn't contain both of them, it's *not* an experiment. Let's look at each one in turn.

Random Assignment. By **random assignment,** we mean that the experimenter randomly sorts participants into one of two groups. By doing so, we tend to cancel out preexisting differences between the two groups, such as differences in their gender, race, or personality traits. One of these two groups is the **experimental group:** This group receives the manipulation. The other is the **control group:** This group doesn't receive the manipulation. Scientific thinking doesn't come naturally to the human species. When viewed through this lens, it's perhaps not surprising that the concept of the control group didn't clearly emerge in psychology until the turn of the twentieth century (Coover & Angell, 1907; Dehue, 2005). Before then, many psychologists thought that they could find out whether a treatment worked without using control groups. Yet as the prefrontal lobotomy example taught us, they were wrong.

To take an example of random assignment, let's imagine we wanted to find out whether a new drug, Miraculin, is effective for treating depression. We'd start with a large sample of individuals with depression. We'd then randomly assign (say, by flipping a coin) half of the participants to an experimental group, which receives Miraculin, and the other half to a control group, which doesn't receive Miraculin.

Incidentally, we shouldn't confuse random assignment with *random selection*, which, as we discussed earlier, is a procedure that allows every person an equal chance to participate. Random selection deals with how we initially choose our participants, whereas random assignment deals with how we assign our participants *after we've already chosen them.*

Manipulation of an Independent Variable. The second ingredient of an experiment is manipulation of an independent variable. An **independent variable** is the variable the experimenter manipulates. The **dependent variable** is the variable that the experimenter measures to see whether this manipulation has had an effect. To understand this distinction, remember that the dependent variable is "dependent on" the level of the independent variable. In the experiment using Miraculin as a treatment for depression, the independent variable is the presence versus absence of Miraculin. In contrast, the dependent variable is the level of participants' depression following the experimental manipulation.

When we define our independent and dependent variables for the purposes of a study, we're providing what some psychologists call an **operational definition**—a working definition of what they're measuring. For example, an investigator who wants to measure the effects of a novel psychotherapy on chronic worrying could operationally define her dependent measure as "Worrying more than 2 hours per day for 4 consecutive weeks." It's important to specify how we're measuring our variables because different researchers may define the same variables in different ways and end up with different conclusions as a result. Imagine that two researchers used two different doses of Miraculin and measured depression using two different scales, one that operationally defines depression as extremely sad mood lasting 2 weeks or more and another that operationally defines depression as moderately or extremely sad mood lasting 5 days or more.

MCHUMOR.com by T. McCracken

McWIT LABS

CONTROL GROUP

OUT OF CONTROL GROUP

© T. McCracken
www.mchumor.com

The control group is an essential part of the "recipe" for a psychological experiment.

experiment
research design characterized by random assignment of participants to conditions and manipulation of an independent variable

random assignment
randomly sorting participants into two groups

experimental group
in an experiment, the group of participants that receives the manipulation

control group
in an experiment, the group of participants that doesn't receive the manipulation

independent variable
variable that an experimenter manipulates

dependent variable
variable that an experimenter measures to see whether the manipulation has an effect

operational definition
a working definition of what a researcher is measuring

The investigators might well end up drawing drastically different conclusions about Miraculin's effectiveness because their measures told different stories. Still, operational definitions aren't like "dictionary" definitions of a word, in which just about all dictionaries agree on the "right" definition (Green, 1992). Different researchers can adopt different operational definitions for their own purposes.

CONFOUNDS: A SOURCE OF FALSE CONCLUSIONS. For an experiment to possess adequate internal validity—the ability to draw cause-and-effect conclusions—the level of the independent variable must be the *only* difference between the experimental and control groups. If there's some other difference between these groups, there's no way of knowing whether the independent variable itself exerted an effect on the dependent variable. Psychologists use the term *confounding variable,* or confound, to refer to any variable that differs between the experimental and control groups other than the independent variable. In our depression treatment example, let's imagine that the patients who received Miraculin, not those in the control group, also received a few sessions of psychotherapy. This extra treatment would be a confounding variable, because it's a variable other than the independent variable that differed between the experimental and control groups. Because of this confounding variable, there's no way to know whether the differences between groups on the dependent variable (level of depression) were due to Miraculin, psychotherapy, or both.

CAUSE AND EFFECT: PERMISSION TO INFER. These two major features of an experiment—random assignment to conditions and manipulation of an independent variable—permit us to infer cause-and-effect relations if we've done the study right. To decide whether to infer cause-and-effect relations from a study, here's a tip that will work 100 percent of the time. *First,* using the criteria we've outlined, ask yourself whether a study is an experiment. *Second,* if it isn't an experiment, don't draw causal conclusions from it, no matter how tempting it might be.

Before going further, let's make sure the major points concerning experimental designs are clear. Read this description of a study, and answer the four questions below it.

Acupuncture Study: Assess Your Knowledge. A researcher hypothesizes that acupuncture, an ancient Chinese medical practice that involves inserting thin needles into specific places on the body, can allow stressed-out psychology students to decrease their anxiety. She randomly assigns half of her participants to undergo acupuncture and half to receive no treatment. Two months later, she measures their anxiety levels and finds that people who received acupuncture are less stressed out than participants who received no treatment.

1. Is this a correlational or an experimental design?
2. What are the independent and dependent variables?
3. Is there a confound in this design? If so, what is it?
4. Can we infer cause and effect from this study? Why or why not?

PITFALLS IN EXPERIMENTAL DESIGN. Like correlational designs, experimental designs can be tricky to interpret, because there are numerous pitfalls to beware of when evaluating them. We'll focus on the most important traps here, and explain how psychological scientists control for them.

The Placebo Effect. To understand the first major pitfall in experiments, imagine we've developed what we believe to be a new wonder drug that treats attention-deficit/hyperactivity disorder (ADHD) in children. We randomly assign half of our participants with this condition to receive the drug and the other half to receive no treatment. At the conclusion of our study, we find that children who received the drug are much less

Does yoga help people to lower their blood pressure and relieve stress? Only an experiment, with random assignment to conditions and manipulation of an independent variable, gives us permission to infer a cause-and-effect relationship.

"FIND OUT WHO SET UP THIS EXPERIMENT. IT SEEMS THAT HALF OF THE PATIENTS WERE GIVEN A PLACEBO, AND THE OTHER HALF WERE GIVEN A DIFFERENT PLACEBO."

(© ScienceCartoonsPlus.com)

This joke advertisement reminds us that the effects of placebos can sometimes be just as powerful as those of real medications.

placebo effect
improvement resulting from the mere expectation of improvement

blind
unaware of whether one is in the experimental or control group

inattentive and hyperactive than children who received nothing. That's good news, to be sure, but does it mean we can now break out the champagne and celebrate the news that the drug is effective? Before reading the next paragraph, try to answer this question yourself.

If you answered no, you were right. The reason we can't celebrate just yet is that we haven't controlled for the placebo effect. The term *placebo* derives from the Latin for "I will please." The **placebo effect** is improvement resulting from the mere expectation of improvement (Kaptchuk, 2002; Kirsch, 2010). Participants who received the drug may have improved merely because they knew they were receiving treatment. This knowledge could have instilled confidence and hope, or exerted a calming influence. The placebo effect is a powerful reminder that expectations can create reality.

In medication research, researchers typically control for the placebo effect by administering a sugar pill (sometimes referred to as a "dummy pill," although this term isn't meant as an insult to either the researchers or patients), which is itself often called a *placebo*, to members of the control group. In this way, patients in both the experimental and control groups don't know whether they're taking the actual medication or a placebo, so they're roughly equated in their expectations of improvement. In the Miraculin study, a placebo effect might have been operating, because participants in the control group didn't receive a placebo—they received nothing. So participants in the experimental group might have improved more than those in the control group because they were aware they were getting treatment.

To avoid placebo effects, it's critical that patients not know whether they're receiving the real medication or a placebo. That is, patients must remain **blind** to the condition to which they've been assigned, namely, experimental or control. If patients aren't blind to their condition, then the experiment is essentially ruined, because the patients may differ in their expectations of improvement.

Two different things can happen if the "blind is broken," which is psychological lingo for what happens when patients find out which group (experimental or control) they're in. First, patients in the experimental group (the ones receiving the drug) might improve more than patients in the control group (the ones receiving the placebo) because they know their treatment is real rather than fake. Second, patients in the control group might become resentful that they're receiving a placebo and try to "beat out" the patients in the experimental group ("Hey, we're going to show those experimenters what we're really made of.").

People sometimes think of placebo effects as being all in people's heads. Yet placebo effects are just as real as those of actual drugs (Mayberg et al., 2002) and worthy of psychological investigation in their own right. Placebos show many of the same characteristics as do real drugs, such as having a more powerful effect at higher doses (Buckalew & Ross, 1981; Rickels et al., 1970). Placebos injected through a needle (researchers usually use a salt and water solution for this purpose) tend to show more rapid and powerful effects than placebos that are swallowed (Buckalew & Ross, 1981), probably because people assume that injectable placebos enter the bloodstream more quickly than pill placebos. Some patients even become addicted to placebo pills (Mintz, 1977). And placebos we believe to be more expensive tend to work better than placebos we believe to be cheaper (Ariely, 2008), probably because we assume that if something costs more, it's probably more effective. As the old saying goes, "you get what you pay for."

Moreover, some researchers maintain that up to 80 percent of the effectiveness of antidepressants is attributable to placebo effects (Kirsch, 2010; Kirsch & Saperstein, 1998), although others suspect the true percentage is somewhat lower (Dawes, 1998; Klein, 1998). There's growing evidence that placebos are equivalent to antidepressant medication in all but severe cases of depression, in which antidepressants have a clear edge over placebos (Fournier et al., 2010; Kirsch, Deacon, & Huedo-Medina, 2008). Placebo effects also aren't equally powerful for all conditions. They generally exert their strongest effects on subjective reports of depression and pain, but their effects on objective measures of physical illnesses, such as cancer and heart disease, are weaker (Hröbjartsson & Götzsche, 2001). Also, the effects of placebos may be more short-lived than those of actual medications (Rothschild & Quitkin, 1992).

from inquiry to understanding

HOW DO PLACEBOS WORK?

As we've seen, our expectations can sometimes exert a powerful influence over our health. There've been cases in which a patient's health improves based on the mere expectation of a treatment or cure. But how do placebos actually work?

In our attempt to answer this question, we travel back in time to the mid-eighteenth century, when physician Frans Anton Mesmer was all the rage in Paris. Mesmer, who lent his name to the term "mesmerism" (a synonym for hypnosis), claimed to cure people of all manner of physical and psychological ailments. Mesmer believed that an invisible magnetic fluid filled the universe and triggered emotional illnesses when it became imbalanced in people's bodies. Dressed in a flowing cape, the flamboyant Mesmer merely needed to touch his patients with a magnetic wand to cause them to shriek, laugh, and enter a stupor, followed by the abrupt disappearance of their symptoms. Mesmer became so much in demand that he took to magnetizing trees for the masses, which supposedly afforded the same cures but in far less time.

But the French government was skeptical of Mesmer's extraordinary claims, wondering whether they were supported by evidence. So they appointed a commission, headed up by none other than Benjamin Franklin, who was U.S. Ambassador to France at the time, to investigate Mesmer's assertions. Franklin set up a series of clever tests to find out whether Mesmer's techniques were as magical as they seemed (Kihlstrom, 2002; Lynn & Lilienfeld, 2002). For example, in some cases, the members of Franklin's commission magnetized a tree but told people that it wasn't magnetized; in other cases, they didn't magnetize a tree but told people it was. People experienced fainting spells only when they *believed* the trees had been magnetized, even if they hadn't been.

Franklin had pulled off two impressive scientific feats. First, he was among the first persons to stumble on what eventually came to be known as the placebo effect. Second and just as important, he had found an ingenious way to isolate this effect. Here's the formula: Present participants with a manipulation in which only some are exposed to the supposed treatment (in this case, a magnetized tree), but others to a control treatment (a nonmagnetized tree), while ensuring that all participants are "blind" to the treatment they're receiving. This is the essence of the same research approach that psychological scientists use in controlled studies today.

Scientists today don't know for sure how the placebo effect works, but one tantalizing clue comes from research on the effects of surgery on patients with Parkinson's disease, a condition marked by severe movement problems, including tremors. Parkinson's disease is caused by a deterioration in brain areas rich in the chemical messenger dopamine, which plays a vital role in both movement and the anticipation of reward. In a study that would have made Benjamin Franklin proud, researchers attempted to treat Parkinson's disease patients by implanting fetal cells containing dopamine into their brains. To control for the placebo effect, the investigators randomly assigned other Parkinson's patients to a condition in which they received surgery but no injection of fetal cells (patients were blind to which condition they were in). As expected, patients who received the fetal cell implants improved in their movement and quality of life (McRae et al., 2004). Yet remarkably, patients assigned to the placebo control condition did too. Later research showed that this effect was generated by a burst of dopamine in control participants' brains. The prospect of improvement had boosted their brain's reward systems, as well as eased their movement abnormalities, both of which are controlled partly by dopamine.

These findings suggest that at least some placebos work in part by jacking up the activity of dopamine, although other neural processes are almost certainly involved too (Lidstone et al., 2010). By enhancing hope, the placebo effect may often capitalize on our brain's natural reward system.

The Nocebo Effect. The placebo effect has an "evil twin" of sorts: the nocebo effect (Benedetti, Lanotte, & Lopiano, 2007; Häuser, Hansen, & Enck, 2012). The *nocebo effect* is harm resulting from the mere expectation of harm (*nocebo* comes from the Latin phrase meaning "to harm"). The ancient African, and later Caribbean, practice of voodoo

◄ **EXTRAORDINARY CLAIMS**
Is the evidence as strong as the claim?

Although Mesmer believed he was curing people using his remarkable magnetic powers, he probably was just harnessing the power of the placebo effect.

Answers to questions on bottom:
1. This study is experimental because there's random assignment to groups and the experimenter manipulated whether or not participants received treatment.
2. The independent variable is the presence versus absence of acupuncture treatment. The dependent variable is the anxiety level of participants.
3. There is a potential confound in that those who received acupuncture knew they were receiving treatment. Their lower anxiety may have been the result of expectations that they'd be feeling better following treatment.
4. Yes. Because of the confound, we don't know why the experimental group was less anxious. But we can conclude that something about the treatment reduced anxiety.

People who believe in the power of voodoo, a supernatural practice popular in Haiti, West Africa, and some regions of the U.S. state of Louisiana, may experience pain when one of their enemies inserts a pin into a doll intended to symbolize them. **What psychological effect does this phenomenon demonstrate, and why?** (See answer upside down at bottom of page.)

"IT WAS MORE OF A 'TRIPLE-BLIND' TEST. THE PATIENTS DIDN'T KNOW WHICH ONES WERE GETTING THE REAL DRUG, THE DOCTORS DIDN'T KNOW, AND, I'M AFRAID, NOBODY KNEW."

(© ScienceCartoonsPlus.com)

experimenter expectancy effect
phenomenon in which researchers' hypotheses lead them to unintentionally bias the outcome of a study

double-blind
when neither researchers nor participants are aware of who's in the experimental or control group

Answer: Nocebo effect—the expectation of pain can itself create pain.

presumably capitalizes on the nocebo effect: People who believe that others are sticking them with pins sometimes experience pain themselves. In one study, individuals who were allergic to roses sneezed when presented with fake roses (Reid, 2002). In another case, researchers deceived a group of college students into believing that an electric current being passed into their heads could produce a headache. More than two-thirds of the students reported headaches, even though the current was imaginary (Morse, 1999). One patient even experienced serious physical symptoms, like extremely low blood pressure, after overdosing on fake pills that he thought were antidepressants (Enck, 2012).

The Experimenter Expectancy Effect. Including a control condition that provides a placebo treatment is extremely important, as is keeping participants blind to their condition assignment. Still, there's one more potential concern with experimental designs. In some cases, the participant doesn't know the condition assignment, but the experimenter does.

When this happens, a nasty problem can arise: The **experimenter expectancy effect** or *Rosenthal effect*. It occurs when researchers' hypotheses lead them to unintentionally bias a study's outcome. It may be worth underlining the word *unintentionally* in the previous sentence, because this effect doesn't refer to deliberate "fudging" or making up of data, which fortunately happens only rarely in science. Instead, in the experimenter expectancy effect, researchers' biases affect the results in subtle ways, almost always outside of their knowledge. In some cases, these researchers may end falling prey to confirmation bias, seeming to find evidence for their hypotheses even when these hypotheses are wrong.

Because of this effect, psychological investigators now always try to conduct their experiments in a **double-blind** fashion. By double-blind, we mean that neither researchers nor participants know who's in the experimental or control group. By voluntarily shielding themselves from the knowledge of which subjects are in which group, researchers are guarding themselves against confirmation bias. Double-blind designs represent science at its best, because they show how good scientists take special precautions to avoid fooling themselves and others.

One of the oldest and best-known examples of the experimenter expectancy effect is the infamous tale of German teacher Wilhelm von Osten and his horse (Fernald, 1984). In 1900, von Osten had purchased a handsome Arabian stallion, known in the psychological literature as Clever Hans, who seemingly displayed astonishing mathematical abilities. By tapping with his hooves, Clever Hans responded correctly to mathematical questions from von Osten (such as, "How much is 8 plus 3?"). He calculated square roots, added and subtracted fractions, and could tell the time of day. He could even give accurate answers to more specific questions, like the number of men in front of him who were wearing black hats. Understandably, von Osten was so proud of Clever Hans that he began showing him off in public for large throngs of amazed spectators.

You might be wondering whether Clever Hans's feats were the result of trickery. A panel of 13 psychologists who investigated Clever Hans witnessed no evidence of fraud on von Osten's part, and concluded that Clever Hans possessed the arithmetic abilities of a 14-year-old human. Moreover, Clever Hans seemed to be a true-blue math whiz, because he could add and subtract even when von Osten wasn't posing the questions.

Nevertheless, psychologist Oscar Pfungst was skeptical of just how clever Clever Hans really was, and in 1904 he launched a series of careful observations. In this case, Pfungst did something that previous psychologists didn't think to do: He focused not on the horse, but on the people asking him questions. When he did, he discovered that von Osten and others were cuing the horse *unintentionally* to produce correct answers. Pfungst found that Clever Hans's questioners almost invariably tightened their muscles immediately before the correct answer. When Pfungst prevented Clever Hans from seeing the questioner or anyone else who knew the correct answer, the celebrated horse did no better than chance, and no better than any ordinary horse. The puzzle was solved: Clever Hans was cleverly detecting subtle physical cues emitted by questioners.

The Clever Hans story showed that people can—even without their knowledge—give off cues that affect a subject's behavior, even when that subject is a horse. This story also reminds us that an extraordinary claim, in this case that a horse can perform arithmetic, requires extraordinary evidence. Von Osten's claims were remarkable, but his evidence wasn't. Interestingly, in a play on words, some authors have referred to facilitated communication, which we encountered at the beginning of this text, as the "phenomenon of Clever Hands" (Wegner, Fuller, & Sparrow, 2003), because it too appeared to be the result of an experimenter expectancy effect.

We mentioned that the experimenter expectancy effect is also called the Rosenthal effect. That's because in the 1960s psychologist Robert Rosenthal conducted an elegant series of experiments that persuaded the psychological community that experimenter expectancy effects were genuine. In one of them, Rosenthal and Kermit Fode (1963) randomly assigned some psychology students a group of five so-called maze bright rats— rats bred over many generations to run mazes quickly—and other students a group of five so-called maze dull rats—rats bred over many generations to run mazes slowly. Note that this is an experiment, because Rosenthal and Fode randomly assigned students to groups and manipulated which type of rat the students supposedly received. They then asked students to run the rats in mazes and to record each rat's completion time. But there was a catch: Rosenthal and Fode had actually randomly assigned rats to the students rather than the other way around. The story about the "maze bright" and "maze dull" rats was all cooked up. Yet when Rosenthal and Fode tabulated their results, they found that students assigned the "maze bright" rats reported 29 percent faster maze running times than did students assigned the "maze dull" rats. In some unknown fashion, the students had influenced their rats' running times. That's why experimenters need to be kept blind to which condition is which; by shielding them from this knowledge, they can't unintentionally influence the results of the study.

Demand Characteristics. A final potential pitfall of psychological research can be difficult to eliminate. Research participants can pick up cues, known as **demand characteristics,** from an experiment that allow them to generate guesses regarding the researcher's hypotheses (Orne, 1962; Rosnow, 2002). In some cases, participants' guesses about what the experimenter is up to may be correct; in other cases, they may not. The problem is that when participants think they know how the experimenter wants them to act, they may alter their behavior accordingly. So whether they've guessed right or wrong, their beliefs can prevent researchers from getting an unbiased view of participants' thoughts and behaviors.

To combat demand characteristics, researchers may disguise the purpose of the study, perhaps by providing participants with a plausible "cover story" that differs from the investigation's actual purpose. Alternatively, they may include "distractor" tasks or "filler" items—measures unrelated to the question of interest. These items help to prevent participants from altering their responses in ways they think the experimenters are looking for.

◄ **EXTRAORDINARY CLAIMS**
Is the evidence as strong as the claim?

Clever Hans performing in public. If one can observe powerful experimenter (in this case, owner) expectancy effects even in animals, how powerful might such effects be in humans?

psycho**mythology**

LABORATORY RESEARCH DOESN'T APPLY TO THE REAL WORLD, RIGHT?

Beginning psychology students often assume that most laboratory research doesn't generalize to the real world. This assumption seems reasonable at first blush, because behavior that emerges in the artificial confines of the laboratory doesn't always mirror behavior in natural settings. Moreover, psychologists conduct a great deal of their research on college students, who tend to be more intelligent, more self-absorbed, less certain of their identities, and more reliant on

demand characteristics
cues that participants pick up from a study that allow them to generate guesses regarding the researcher's hypotheses

Research Methods

social approval than non-college participants. Indeed, about 75 percent of published studies of interpersonal interactions are conducted on undergraduates (Sears, 1986). It's not always clear how generalizable these findings are to the rest of humanity (Henrich, Heine, & Norenzayan, 2010; Peterson, 2000).

But is the "truism" that laboratory research is low in external validity—generalizability to the real world—true? As Douglas Mook (1983) noted, high internal validity can often lead to high external validity. That's because carefully controlled experiments generate conclusions that are more trustworthy than are loosely controlled studies. In addition, the results of carefully controlled experiments are more likely to replicate than the results of loosely controlled studies (Ioannidis, 2005).

REPLICABILITY ▶

Can the results be duplicated in other studies?

Craig Anderson, James Lindsay, and Brad Bushman (1999) took a systematic look at this issue. They examined the correspondence between laboratory studies of various psychological phenomena—including aggression, helping, leadership, interpersonal perception, performance on exams, and the causes of depressed mood—as measured in the laboratory and real world. Anderson and his colleagues computed how large the effects were in laboratory and real-world studies and correlated these effects. For example, in studies of the relation between watching violent television and aggressive behavior, they examined the correspondence between findings from controlled laboratory studies—in which investigators randomly assign participants to watch either violent television or nonviolent television, and then measure their aggression—and real-world studies—in which investigators observe people's television viewing habits and aggression in daily life.

Contrary to what many psychologists have assumed, Anderson and his collaborators found the correlation between the sizes of the effects in laboratory and real-world studies to be $r = .73$, which is a high association. Laboratory research often generalizes surprisingly well to the real world.

Even so, we shouldn't assume that a laboratory study always possesses high external validity. A more recent analysis revealed that although Anderson and colleagues were mostly right, there were exceptions (Mitchell, 2012). In particular, laboratory studies in social psychology, which examine the effects of situations on people's behavior tend to generalize less well to real world settings ($r = .51$) than do studies in industrial-organizational psychology ($r = .89$), which examine predictors of people's work performance and satisfaction or in personality psychology ($r = .83$), which examine how people's enduring traits predict their behavior. Investigations that yielded weak effects within the laboratory were especially unlikely to be mirrored in behavior outside the laboratory, raising the possibility that these effects weren't replicable in the first place.

REPLICABILITY ▶

Can the results be duplicated in other studies?

So the safest approach is to examine both well-controlled laboratory experiments and studies using naturalistic observation to see whether results from both research designs converge. If they do, that should make us more confident in our conclusions (Shadish, Cook, & Campbell, 2002). If they don't, that should make us scratch our heads and try to figure out what's accounting for the difference.

✔ **Study** and **Review** in **MyPsychLab**

Assess Your Knowledge   FACT or FICTION?

1. Case studies can sometimes provide existence proofs of psychological phenomena.   **True** / **False**

2. Rating data can be biased because some respondents allow their ratings of one positive characteristic to spill over to other positive characteristics.   **True** / **False**

3. A correlation of −.8 is just as large in magnitude as a correlation of +.8.   **True** / **False**

4. Experiments are characterized by two, and only two, features.   **True** / **False**

5. To control for experimenter expectancy effects, only participants need to be blind to who's in the experimental and control groups.   **True** / **False**

Answers: 1. T; 2. T; 3. T; 4. T; 5. F

Ethical Issues in Research Design

5 Explain the ethical obligations of researchers toward their research participants.

6 Describe both sides of the debate on the use of animals as research subjects.

When designing and conducting research studies, psychologists need to worry about more than their scientific value. The ethics of these studies also matter. Although psychology adheres to the same basic scientific principles as other sciences, let's face it: A chemist needn't worry about hurting his mineral's feelings, and a physicist needn't be concerned about the long-term emotional well-being of a neutron. The scientific study of people and their behavior raises unique concerns.

Many philosophers believe—and the authors of this text agree—that science itself is value-neutral. Because science is a search for the truth, it's neither inherently good nor bad. This fact doesn't imply, though, that scientific *research* is value-neutral, as there are both ethical and unethical ways of searching for the truth. Moreover, we may not all agree on which ways of searching for the truth are ethical. We'd probably all agree that it's acceptable to learn about brain damage by studying the behavior of people with brain damage on laboratory tasks of learning, just so long as these tasks aren't overly stressful. We'd also all agree (we hope!) that it's unacceptable for us to learn about brain damage by hitting people over the head with baseball bats and then testing their motor coordination by measuring how often they fall down a flight of stairs. Nevertheless, we might not all agree on whether it's ethically acceptable to learn about brain damage by creating severe lesions (wounds) in the brains of cats and examining their effects on cats' responses to fear-provoking stimuli (like scary dogs). In many cases, the question of whether research is ethical isn't clear-cut, and reasonable people will sometimes disagree on the answer.

Tuskegee: A Shameful Moral Tale

Scientists have learned the hard way that their thirst for knowledge can blind them to crucial ethical considerations. One deeply troubling example comes from the Tuskegee study performed by the United States Public Health Service, an agency of the United States Government, from 1932 to 1972 (Jones, 1993). During this time, a number of researchers wanted to learn more about the natural course of syphilis, a sexually transmitted disease. What happens, they wondered, to syphilis over time if it is left untreated?

Historical photo of the Tuskegee study. This study demonstrates the tragic consequences of ignoring crucial ethical considerations in research.

The "subjects" in this study were 399 African American men living in the poorest rural areas of Alabama who'd been diagnosed with syphilis. Remarkably, the researchers never informed these men that they had syphilis, nor that an effective treatment for syphilis, namely, antibiotics, had become available. Indeed, the subjects didn't even know they were subjects, as researchers hadn't informed them of that crucial piece of information. Instead, the researchers merely tracked the subjects' progress over time, withholding all important medical information and all available treatments. By the end of the study, 28 men had died of syphilis, 100 had died of syphilis-related complications, 40 of the men's wives had been infected with syphilis, and 19 children had been born with syphilis. In 1997—25 years after the termination of this study—then-President Bill Clinton, on behalf of the United States government, offered a formal apology for the Tuskegee study to the study's eight remaining survivors.

Ethical Guidelines for Human Research

If any good at all came out of the horrific Tuskegee study and other ethical catastrophes in scientific research, it was a heightened appreciation for protecting the rights of human subjects. Fortunately, researchers could never perform the Tuskegee study today, at least not in the United States. That's because every major American research college and university has at least one *institutional review board* (IRB), which reviews all research carefully with an eye toward protecting participants against abuses. IRBs typically consist of faculty members drawn from various departments within a college or university, as well as one or more outside members, such as a person drawn from the nearby community.

INFORMED CONSENT. IRBs insist on a procedure called **informed consent**: Researchers must tell subjects what they're getting into before asking them to participate. During the informed consent process, participants can ask questions about the study and learn more about what will be involved. The Tuskegee subjects never received informed consent, and we can be certain they wouldn't have agreed to participate had they known they wouldn't be receiving treatment for a potentially fatal illness.

Nevertheless, IRBs may occasionally allow researchers to forgo certain elements of informed consent, but only when doing so is deemed to be essential. In particular, some psychological research entails *deception*. When researchers use deception, they deliberately mislead participants about the study's design or purpose. In one of the most controversial studies in the history of psychology, Stanley Milgram (1963), then at Yale University, invited volunteers to participate in a study of the "effects of punishment on learning." The experimenter deceived participants into believing they were administering painful electric shocks to another participant, who made repeated errors on a learning task. In reality, the other "participant" never received any shocks. He was actually a *confederate* of the experimenter, that is, a research assistant who played the part of a participant. Moreover, Milgram had no interest in the effects of punishment on learning; he was interested in the influence of authority figures on obedience. Many of the true participants experienced considerable distress during the procedure, and some were understandably troubled by the fact that they delivered what they believed to be extremely painful—even potentially fatal—electric shocks to an innocent person.

Was Milgram's elaborate deception justified? Milgram (1964) argued that the hoax was required to pull off the study, because informing subjects of its true purpose would have generated obvious demand characteristics. He further noted that he went out of his way to later explain the study's true purpose to participants and assure them that their obedience wasn't a sign of cruelty or psychological disturbance. In addition, he sent a questionnaire to all subjects after the studies were completed and found that only 1.3 percent reported any negative emotional aftereffects. In contrast, Diana Baumrind (1964) argued that Milgram's study wasn't worth the knowledge or psychological distress it generated. Milgram's failure to provide subjects with full informed consent, she maintained, was ethically indefensible. Simply put, Milgram's subjects didn't know what they were getting into when they volunteered.

The debate concerning the ethics of Milgram's study continues to this day (Blass, 2004). Although we won't try to resolve this controversy here, we'll point out that the ethical standards of the American Psychological Association (2002) affirm that deception is justified only when (a) researchers couldn't have performed the study without the deception and (b) the scientific knowledge to be gained from the study outweighs its costs (see **TABLE 3**). Needless to say, evaluating (b) isn't easy, and it's up to researchers—and ultimately, the IRB—to decide whether the potential scientific benefits of a study are sufficient to justify deception. Over the years, IRBs—which didn't exist in Milgram's day—have become more stringent about the need for informed consent.

DEBRIEFING: EDUCATING PARTICIPANTS. IRBs may also request that a full debriefing be performed at the conclusion of the research session. *Debriefing* is a process whereby researchers inform participants what the study was about. In some cases, researchers use debriefings to explain their hypotheses in nontechnical language. By administering a debriefing, the study becomes a learning experience for not only the investigator, but also the subject.

Ethical Issues in Animal Research

Few topics generate as much anger and discomfort as animal research. This is especially true of *invasive* research, in which investigators cause physical harm to animals. In psychology departments, invasive research most often takes the form of producing lesions in animals' brains, usually by means of surgery, and observing their effects on animals' behavior. About 7 to 8 percent of published research in

Simulate in **MyPsychLab** the **Experiment:** Ethics in Psychological Research

informed consent
informing research participants of what is involved in a study before asking them to participate

TABLE 3 APA Ethical Principles for Human Research. Psychological researchers must carefully weigh the potential scientific benefits of their research against the potential danger to participants. In 2002, the American Psychological Association (APA) published a code of ethics to govern all research with human participants. The following is a summary of the key ethical principles.

Informed Consent

- Research participants should be fully informed of the purpose of the research, its expected duration, and any potential risks, discomfort, or adverse effects associated with it.
- Participants should enter the study voluntarily and be informed of their right to withdraw from it at any time.
- A contact who can answer questions about the research and the participant's rights should be provided.

Protection from Harm and Discomfort

- Psychologists must take reasonable steps to avoid harm to research participants.

Deception and Debriefing

- When deceptive techniques are used in research, the participants should be informed of the deception as soon as possible after the deception takes place.
- Participants should not be deceived about research procedures that may cause the participants physical pain or emotional distress.
- Once the research study has concluded, participants should not only be informed of the deception but fully debriefed about the true nature of the research and its results.

psychology relies on animals (American Psychological Association, 2008) with the overwhelming majority of studies conducted on rodents (especially rats and mice) and birds. The goal of such research is to generate ideas about how the brain relates to behavior in animals—and how these findings generalize to humans—without inflicting harm on people.

Many animal rights activists have raised useful concerns regarding the ethical treatment of animals and have underscored the need for adequate housing and feeding conditions (Marino, 2009; Ott, 1995). In contrast, others have gone to extremes that could themselves be considered unethical, such as ransacking laboratories and liberating animals. In 1999, the Animal Liberation Front attacked several psychology laboratories at the University of Minnesota, releasing rats and pigeons and inflicting about $2 million worth of damage (Azar, 1999; Hunt, 1999). Incidentally, most individuals on both sides of the animal rights debate agree that liberating animals is a dreadful idea, because many or most animals die shortly after being released.

These excessive tactics aside, the ethical issues here aren't easily resolved. Some commentators maintain that the deaths of approximately 20 million laboratory animals every year (Cunningham, 1993) aren't worth the cost. For many critics, the knowledge gleaned from animal research on aggression, fear, learning, memory, and related topics is of such doubtful external validity to humans as to be virtually useless (Ulrich, 1991).

This position has some merit but may be too extreme. Some animal research has led to direct benefits to humans, as well as immensely useful knowledge in its own right. Many psychological treatments, especially those based on principles of learning, derived from animal research. Without animal research, we'd know relatively little about the physiology of the brain (Domjan & Purdy, 1995). Moreover, to answer many critical psychological questions, there are simply no good alternatives to using animals (Gallup & Suarez, 1985). For example, without animals we'd be unable to test the safety and effectiveness of many medications.

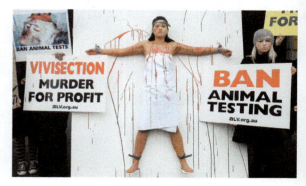

A great deal of animal research remains intensely controversial. It will probably always remain this way given the complex ethical questions involved.

None of this tells us when we should and shouldn't use animals in research. Nevertheless, it's clear that animal research has yielded enormously important insights about the brain and behavior and that psychologists are likely to rely on such research for some time to come. It's also clear that animal researchers must weigh carefully the potential scientific gains of their inquiries against the costs in death and suffering they produce. Because reasonable people will inevitably disagree about how to weigh these pros and cons, the intense controversy surrounding animal research is unlikely to subside anytime soon.

✔ **Study** and **Review** in **MyPsychLab**

Assess Your Knowledge   FACT or FICTION?

1. The Tuskegee study violated the principles of informed consent.   **True / False**

2. Milgram's study would be considered unethical today because the shock could have caused injury or death.   **True / False**

3. In debriefing, the researcher informs participants of what will happen in the procedure before asking them to participate.   **True / False**

4. Before conducting invasive research on animals, investigators must weigh carefully the potential scientific benefits of this research against the costs of animal death and suffering.   **True / False**

Answers: 1. T; 2. F; 3. F; 4. T

(© ScienceCartoonsPlus.com)

Statistics: The Language of Psychological Research

7 Identify uses of various measures of central tendency and variability.

8 Explain how inferential statistics can help us to determine whether we can generalize from our sample to the full population.

9 Show how statistics can be misused for purposes of persuasion.

Up to this point, we've mostly spared you the gory mathematical details of psychological research. Aside from correlation coefficients, we haven't said much about how psychologists analyze their findings. Still, to understand psychological research and how to interpret it, we need to know a bit about **statistics:** the application of mathematics to describing and analyzing data. For you math phobics (or "arithmophobics," if you want to impress your friends with a technical term) out there, there's no cause for alarm. We promise to keep things simple.

Descriptive Statistics: What's What?

Psychologists use two kinds of statistics. The first are **descriptive statistics.** They do exactly what the name implies: describe data. Using descriptive statistics on a sample of 100 men and 100 hundred women whose levels of extraversion we assess using a self-report measure, we could ask the following questions:

- What's the average level of extraversion in this sample?
- What's the average level of extraversion among men, and what's the average level of extraversion among women?
- How much do all of our participants, as well as men and women separately, vary in how extraverted they are?

To maintain our promise of keeping things simple, we'll discuss only two major types of descriptive statistics. The first is the **central tendency,** which gives us a sense of the "central" score in our data set or where the group tends to cluster. In turn, there are

statistics
application of mathematics to describing and analyzing data

descriptive statistics
numerical characterizations that describe data

central tendency
measure of the "central" scores in a data set, or where the group tends to cluster

three measures of central tendency: mean, median, and mode (known as the "three Ms"). Follow along in **TABLE 4a** (the left half of the table below) as we calculate each.

The **mean,** also known as the average, is just the total score divided by the number of people. If our sample consists of five people as shown in the table, the mean IQ is simply the total of the five scores divided by five, which happens to be 102.

The **median** is the middle score in our data set. We obtain the median by lining up our scores in order and finding the middle one. So in this case, we'd line up the five IQ scores in order from lowest to highest, and find that 100 is the median because it's the score smack in the middle of the distribution.

The **mode** is the most frequent score in our data set. In this case, the mode is 120, because two people in our sample received scores of 120 on the IQ test and one person each received other scores.

As we can see, the three Ms sometimes tell us rather different things. In this case, the mean and median were close to each other, but the mode was much higher than both. The mean is generally the best statistic to report when our data form a bell-shaped or "normal" distribution, as we can see in the top panel of **FIGURE 6**. But what happens when our distribution is "skewed," that is, tilted sharply to one side or the other, as in the bottom panels? Here the mean provides a misleading picture of the central tendency, so it's better to use the median or mode instead, as these statistics are less affected by extreme scores at either the low or high end.

To hammer this point home, let's look at **TABLE 4b** to see what happens to our measures of central tendency. The mean of this distribution is 116, but four of the scores are much below 116, and the only reason the mean is this high is the presence of one person who scored 220 (who in technical terms is an *outlier,* because his or her score lies way outside the other scores). In contrast, both the median and mode are 95, which capture the central tendency of the distribution much better.

The second type of descriptive statistic is **variability** (sometimes called dispersion), which gives us a sense of how loosely or tightly bunched the scores are. Consider the following two sets of IQ scores from five people:

- 80, 85, 85, 90, 95
- 25, 65, 70, 125, 150

In both groups of scores, the mean is 87. But the second set of scores is much more spread out than the first. So we need some means of describing the differences in variability in these two data sets.

The simplest measure of variability is the **range.** The range is the difference between the highest and lowest scores. In the first set of IQ scores, the range is only 15, whereas in the second set the range is 125. So the range tells us that although the two sets of scores have a similar central tendency, their variability is wildly different (as in **FIGURE 7a**). Although the range is the easiest measure of variability to calculate, it can be deceptive because, as shown in **FIGURE 7b**, two data sets with the same range can display a very different distribution of scores across that range. To compensate for this problem,

Simulate in **MyPsychLab** the **Experiment:** Doing Simple Statistics

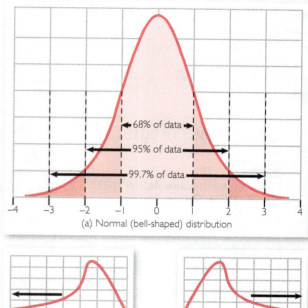

(a) Normal (bell-shaped) distribution

(b) Negative skew
Elongated tail at the **left**
More data in the tail than would be expected in a normal distribution

(c) Positive skew
Elongated tail at the **right**
More data in the tail than would be expected in a normal distribution

FIGURE 6 Distribution Curves. (a) a normal (bell-shaped) distribution, (b) a markedly negative skewed distribution, and (c) a markedly positive skewed distribution.

TABLE 4 The Three Ms: Mean, Median, and Mode.

(a)	(b)
Sample IQ scores: 100, 90, 80, 120, 120 **Mean:** (100 + 90 + 80 + 120 + 120)/5 = 102 **Median:** order scores from lowest to highest: 80, 90, 100, 120, 120; middle score is 100 **Mode:** only 120 appears twice in the data set, so it's the most common score.	**Sample IQ scores:** 80, 85, 95, 95, 220 **Mean:** (80 + 85 + 95 + 95 + 220)/5 = 116 **Median:** 95 **Mode:** 95 **Note:** Mean is affected by one extreme score, but median and mode aren't.

mean
average; a measure of central tendency

median
middle score in a data set; a measure of central tendency

mode
most frequent score in a data set; a measure of central tendency

variability
measure of how loosely or tightly bunched scores are

range
difference between the highest and lowest scores; a measure of variability

psychologists often use another measure called the **standard deviation** to depict variability (this index is a bit complicated to calculate, so we'll spare you the trouble of that here). This measure is less likely to be deceptive than the range because it takes into account how far *each* data point is from the mean, rather than simply how widely scattered the most extreme scores are.

FIGURE 7 The Range versus the Standard Deviation. These two number lines display data sets with the same *range* but different *standard deviations*. The variability is more tightly clustered in (a) than in (b), so the standard deviation in (a) will be smaller.

Inferential Statistics: Testing Hypotheses

In addition to descriptive statistics, psychologists use **inferential statistics,** which allow us to determine how much we can generalize findings from our sample to the full population. When using inferential statistics, we're asking whether we can draw "inferences" (conclusions) regarding whether the differences we've observed in our sample apply to similar samples. Earlier, we mentioned a study of 100 men and 100 women who took a self-report measure of extraversion. In this study, inferential statistics allow us to find out whether the differences we've observed in extraversion between men and women are believable, or if they're just a fluke occurrence in our sample. Let's imagine we calculated the means for men and women (we first verified that the distribution of scores in both men and women approximated a bell curve). After doing so, we found that men scored 10.4 on our extraversion scale (the scores range from 0 to 15) and that women scored 9.9. So, *in our sample,* men are more extraverted, or at least say they are, than women. Can we now conclude that men are more extraverted than women in general? How can we rule out the possibility that this small sex difference in our sample is due to chance? That's where inferential statistics enter the picture.

What's wrong with this (fake) newspaper headline?

STATISTICAL SIGNIFICANCE. To figure out whether the difference we've observed in our sample is a believable (real) one, we need to conduct statistical tests to determine whether we can generalize our findings to the broader population. To do so, we can use a variety of statistics depending on the research design. But regardless of which test we use, we generally use a .05 level of confidence when deciding whether a finding is trustworthy. This minimum level—5 in 100—is taken as the probability that the finding occurred by chance. When the finding would have occurred by chance less than 5 in 100 times, we say that it's *statistically significant.* A statistically significant result is believable; it's probably a real difference in our sample. In psychology journals, we'll often see the expression "$p < .05$," meaning that the probability (the lowercase p stands for probability) that our finding would have occurred by chance alone is less than five in 100, or one in 20.

A large sample size can yield a statistically significant result, but this result may have little or no practical significance.

PRACTICAL SIGNIFICANCE. Writer Gertrude Stein said that "a difference is a difference that makes a difference." Stein's quotation reminds us not to confuse statistical significance with *practical significance,* that is, real-world importance. A finding can be statistically significant yet not make much, if any, difference in the real world. To understand this point, we need to understand that a major determinant of statistical significance is sample size. The larger the sample size, the greater the odds (all else being equal) that a result will be statistically significant (Meehl, 1978; Schmidt, 1992). With huge sample sizes, virtually all findings—even tiny ones—will become statistically significant.

If we were to find a correlation of $r = .06$ between IQ and nose length in a sample of 500,000 people, this correlation would be statistically significant at the $p < .05$ level. Yet it's so miniscule in magnitude that it would be essentially useless for predicting anything.

How People Lie with Statistics

Humorist Mark Twain is often credited with writing that there are three kinds of untruths: "lies, damned lies, and statistics." Because many people's eyes glaze over when they see lots of numbers, it's easy to fool them with statistical sleight of hand. Here, we'll provide three examples of how people can misuse statistics and, just as important, how people can use them correctly. Our goal, of course, isn't to encourage you to lie with statistics, but to equip you with scientific thinking skills for spotting statistical abuses (Huck, 2008; Huff, 1954).

standard deviation
measure of variability that takes into account how far each data point is from the mean

inferential statistics
mathematical methods that allow us to determine whether we can generalize findings from our sample to the full population

EXAMPLE 1

Your Congressional Representative, Ms. Dee Section, is running for reelection. As part of her platform, she's proposed a new tax plan for everyone in your state. According to the "fine print" in Ms. Section's plan, 99 percent of people in your state will receive a $100 tax cut this year. The remaining 1 percent, who make over $3 million per year, will receive a tax cut of $500,000 (according to Ms. Section, this large tax cut for the richest people is necessary because she gets her biggest campaign contributions from them).

Based on this plan, Ms. Dee Section announces at a press conference, "If I'm elected and my tax plan goes through, the average person in our state will receive a tax cut of $5,099." Watching this press conference on television, you think, "Wow … what a deal! I'm definitely going to vote for Dee Section. If she wins, I'll have over 5,000 extra bucks in my bank account."

Question: *Why should you be skeptical of Dee Section's claim?*

Answer: Ms. Dee Section has engaged in a not-especially-subtle deception, suggesting that she's aptly named. She assures us that under her plan the "average person" in her state will receive a tax cut of $5,099. In one respect she's right, because the *mean* tax cut is indeed $5,099. But in this case, the mean is highly misleading, because under Section's plan virtually everyone in her state will receive only a $100 tax cut. Only the richest of the rich will receive a tax cut of $500,000, making the mean highly unrepresentative of the central tendency. Dee Section should have instead reported the median or mode, which are both only $100, as measures of central tendency. As we learned earlier, the median and mode are less affected by extreme scores than the mean.

"There are lies, damn lies, and statistics. We'r looking for someone who can make all three of these work for us."

(© www.CartoonStock.com)

EXAMPLE 2

A researcher, Dr. Faulty Conclusion, conducts a study to demonstrate that transcendental meditation (TM), a form of relaxation that originated in East Asian cultures, reduces crime rates. According to Dr. Conclusion, towns whose citizens are taught to practice TM will experience a dramatic drop in arrests. He finds a small town, Pancake, Iowa (population 300), and teaches all citizens of Pancake to practice TM. For his control group, he identifies a small neighboring town in Iowa, called Waffle (population also 300), and doesn't introduce them to TM. According to Dr. Conclusion, Waffle is a good control group for Pancake, because it has the same population, ethnic makeup, income, and initial arrest rates.

Two months after the introduction of TM to Pancake, Dr. Conclusion measures the arrest rates in Pancake and Waffle. At a major conference, he proudly announces that although the arrest rates in Waffle stayed exactly the same, the arrest rates in Pancake experienced a spectacular plunge. To demonstrate this astonishing effect, he directs the audience to a graph (see **FIGURE 8**). As he does, the audience gasps in astonishment. "As you can see from this graph," Conclusion proclaims, "the arrest rates in Pancake were initially very high. But after I taught Pancake's citizens TM, their arrest rates two months later were much, much lower." Dr. Conclusion concludes triumphantly, "Our findings show beyond a shadow of a doubt that TM reduces crime rates."

Question: *What's wrong with Dr. Conclusion's conclusion?*

Answer: Dr. Conclusion's graph in Figure 8 sure looks impressive, doesn't it? The arrest rates have indeed gone down from the beginning to the end of the study. But let's take a good close look at the *y* axis (that's the vertical axis) of the graph. Can we see anything suspicious about it?

Dr. Conclusion has tricked us, or perhaps he's tricked himself. The *y* axis starts at 15.5 arrests per month and goes up to 16 arrests per month. In fact, Dr. Conclusion has demonstrated only that the arrest rate in Pancake declined from 15.9 arrests per month to 15.6 arrests per month—a grand total of less than one-third of an arrest per month! That's hardly worth writing home about, let alone mastering TM for.

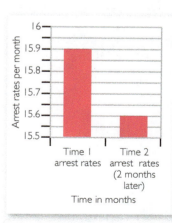

FIGURE 8 Arrest Rates Before and After Transcendental Meditation. Arrest rates per month in Pancake before (*left*) and after (*right*) introduction of transcendental meditation.

Dr. Conclusion used what's termed a "truncated line graph." That kind of graph is a real "no-no" in statistics, although many researchers still use it (Huff, 1954; Smith, 2001). In this kind of graph, the y axis starts not at the lowest possible score, where it should start (in this case, it should start at zero, because that's the lowest possible number of arrests per month), but somewhere close to the highest possible score. By using a truncated line graph, Dr. Conclusion made the apparent effects of TM appear huge when in fact they were pitifully small. Next time, he'd be better off using the full range of possible scores on his graph.

EXAMPLE 3

Ms. Representation conducts a study to determine the association between nationality and drinking patterns. According to Professor Representation's new "Grand Unified Theory of Drinking Behavior," people of German descent are at higher risk for alcoholism than people of Norwegian descent. To test this hypothesis, she begins with a randomly selected sample of 10,000 people from the city of Inebriated, Indiana. She administers a survey to all participants inquiring about their drinking habits and national background. When she analyzes her data, she finds that 1,200 citizens of Inebriated meet official diagnostic criteria for alcoholism. Of these 1,200 individuals, 450 are of German descent, whereas only 30 are of Norwegian descent—a 15-fold difference! She conducts a statistical test (we won't trouble you with the precise mathematics) and determines that this amazingly large difference is statistically significant at $p < .05$. At the annual convention of the International Society of Really, Really Smart Alcoholism Researchers, Ms. Representation asserts, "My bold hypothesis has been confirmed. I can conclude confidently that Germans are at higher risk for alcoholism than Norwegians."

Question: *Why are Ms. Representation's conclusions about drinking all washed up?*

Answer: Remember the *base rate fallacy* we introduced in this chapter? When interpreting findings, it's easy to forget about base rates. That's because base rates often "lurk in the distance" of our minds and aren't especially vivid. In this case, Ms. Representation forgot to take a crucial fact into account: In Inebriated, Indiana, the base rate of people of German descent is 25 times higher than the base rate of people of Norwegian descent. As a result, the fact that there are 15 times more German than Norwegian alcoholics in Inebriated doesn't support her hypothesis. In fact, given there are 25 times more Germans than Norwegians in Inebriated, the data actually run *opposite* to Ms. Representation's hypothesis: The percentage of alcoholic Norwegians is higher than the percentage of alcoholic Germans!

The bottom line: *Don't trust all of the statistics you read in a newspaper.*

Bear in mind that we've focused here on misuses and abuses of statistics. That's because we want to immunize you against statistical errors you're likely to encounter in the newspaper as well as on TV and the Internet. But you shouldn't conclude from our examples that we can *never* trust statistics. As we'll learn throughout this text, statistics are a wonderful set of tools that can help us to understand behavior. When evaluating statistics, it's best to steer a middle course between dismissing them out of hand and accepting them uncritically. As is so often the case in psychology, remember that we should keep our minds open, but not so open that our brains fall out.

To evaluate claims about statistics on the Internet, we must equip ourselves with tools that protect us against errors in reasoning.

Assess Your Knowledge   FACT or FICTION?

1. The mean is not always the best measure of central tendency.   True / False

2. The mode and standard deviation are both measures of variability.   True / False

3. All statistically significant findings are important and large in size.   True / False

4. Researchers can easily manipulate statistics to make it appear that their hypotheses are confirmed even when they're not.   True / False

Answers: 1. T; 2. F; 3. F; 4. T

Evaluating Psychological Research

10 Identify flaws in research designs and how to correct them.

11 Identify skills for evaluating psychological claims in the popular media.

Every day, the Internet, newspapers, and television stations bombard us with the results of psychological and medical studies. Some of these studies are trustworthy, yet many others aren't. How can we sort out which are which?

Becoming a Peer Reviewer

Nearly all psychological journals send submitted articles to outside reviewers, who screen the articles carefully for quality control. As we'll recall, this often ego-bruising process is called *peer review*. One crucial task of peer reviewers is to identify flaws that could undermine a study's findings and conclusions, as well as to tell researchers how to do the study better next time. Now that we've learned the key ingredients of a psychological experiment and the pitfalls that can lead experiments to go wrong, let's try our hands at becoming peer reviewers. Doing so will allow us to become better consumers of real-world research.

We'll present descriptions of two studies, modeled after actual published investigations, both of which contain at least one hidden flaw. Read each study and try to figure out what's wrong with it. Once you have, try to suggest a way of fixing the flaw. Then, read the paragraph below it to see how close you came.

Ready? Here goes.

STUDY 1

An investigator, Dr. Sudo Sigh-Ents, sets out to test the hypothesis that subliminal self-help tapes increase self-esteem. She randomly selects 50 college freshmen from the subject pool to receive a commercially available subliminal self-help tape, which contains the words "You will feel better about yourself." She asks them to play the tape for two months each night for one hour before going to sleep (which is consistent with the standard instructions on the tape). Dr. Sigh-Ents measures participants' self-esteem at the start of the study and again after two months. She finds that their self-esteem has increased significantly over these two months, and concludes that "subliminal self-help tapes increase self-esteem."

Question: *What's wrong with this experiment and how would you fix it?*

Answer: What's wrong with this "experiment" is that it's not even an experiment. There's no random assignment of participants to experimental and control groups; in fact, there's no control group at all. There's also no manipulation of an independent variable. Remember that a variable is something that varies. In this case, there's no independent variable because all participants received the same manipulation, namely, playing the subliminal self-help tape every night. As a result, we can't know whether the increase in self-esteem was really due to the tape. It could have been due to any number of other factors, such as placebo effects or increases in self-esteem that might often occur over the course of one's freshman year.

Next time, Dr. Sigh-Ents would be better off randomly assigning some participants to receive the subliminal self-help tape designed to increase self-esteem and other participants to receive a different subliminal self-help tape, maybe one with neutral instructions (like "You will feel the same about yourself").

STUDY 2

A researcher, Dr. Art E. Fact, is interested in determining whether a new treatment, Anger Expression Therapy, is effective in treating anxiety. He randomly assigns 100 individuals with anxiety disorders to two groups. The experimental group receives Anger Expression Therapy (which is administered by Dr. Fact himself), whereas the control group is placed on a waiting list and receives no treatment. At the conclusion of six months, Dr. Fact interviews his patients and finds that the rate of anxiety disorders is significantly lower in the experimental group than in the control group. He concludes, "Anger Expression Therapy is helpful in the treatment of anxiety disorders."

"THAT'S IT? THAT'S PEER REVIEW?"

(© ScienceCartoonsPlus.com)

? In an experiment on marital therapy for anger problems, a researcher could examine whether individuals who receive a specific treatment show less anger than people who don't receive this treatment. **In such a study, what's the independent variable?** What's the dependent variable? (See the answers upside down at the bottom of this page.)

◄ **RULING OUT RIVAL HYPOTHESES**
Have important alternative explanations for the findings been excluded?

Question: *What's wrong with this experiment and how would you fix it?*

Answer: On its surface, this experiment looks okay. There's random assignment of participants to experimental and control groups, and manipulation of an independent variable, namely, the presence versus absence of Anger Expression Therapy. But Dr. Fact hasn't controlled for two crucial pitfalls. First, he hasn't controlled for the placebo effect, because people receiving Anger Expression Therapy know they're receiving a treatment, and people in the control group know they're not.

To control for this problem, Dr. Fact should probably have built in an *attention-placebo control condition*: A condition in which a counselor provides attention, but no formal psychotherapy, to patients (Baskin et al., 2003). For example, the counselor might chat with her patients once a week for the same length of time as the patients who receive Anger Expression Therapy.

Second, Dr. Fact hasn't controlled for the experimenter expectancy effect. He knows which patients are in which group and could subtly influence patients who are receiving Anger Expression Therapy to improve or report better results. To control for this effect and minimize conformation bias, it might be better to ask the same therapist—someone other than Dr. Fact—to administer both the treatment and control conditions, and to keep Dr. Fact blind to the group assignment when he interviews the patients at the conclusion of the study.

Most Reporters Aren't Scientists: Evaluating Psychology in the Media

Few major American newspapers hire reporters with any formal psychological training—the *New York Times* is a notable exception—so we shouldn't assume that people who write news stories about psychology are trained to distinguish psychological fact from fiction (Stanovich, 2009). Most aren't. This means that news stories are prone to faulty conclusions because reporters rely on the same heuristics and biases that we all do.

When evaluating the accuracy of psychological reports in the media, it's worth keeping a few tips in mind. First, we should *consider the source* (Gilovich, 1991). We should generally place more confidence in a finding reported in a reputable science magazine (like *Scientific American Mind* or *Discover*) than in a supermarket tabloid (like the *National Enquirer*) or a popular magazine (like *People* or *Us*). This "consider the source" principle also applies to websites. Moreover, we should place more trust in findings from primary sources, such as the original journal articles themselves (if we can look them up in the library or on the Internet) than from secondary sources, such as newspapers, magazines, or websites that merely report findings from primary sources.

Second, we need to be on the lookout for excessive *sharpening* and *leveling* (Gilovich, 1991). *Sharpening* refers to the tendency to exaggerate the gist, or central message, of a study, whereas *leveling* refers to the tendency to minimize the less central details of a study. Sharpening and leveling often result in a "good story," because they end up bringing the most important facts of a study into sharper focus. Of course, secondary sources in the news media need to engage in a certain amount of sharpening and leveling when reporting studies, because they can't possibly describe every minor detail of an investigation. Still, too much sharpening and leveling can result in a misleading picture. If an investigator discovers that a new medication is effective for 35 percent of people with anxiety disorders, but that a placebo is effective for 33 percent of people with anxiety disorders, the newspaper editor may lead off the story with this eye-popping headline: "Breakthrough: New Medication Outperforms Other Pills in Treating Anxiety." This headline isn't literally wrong, but it oversimplifies greatly what the researcher found.

Third, we can easily be misled by seemingly "balanced" coverage of a story. There's a crucial difference between genuine scientific controversy and the kind of balanced coverage that news reporters create by ensuring that representatives from both sides of the story receive equal air time. When covering a story relating to psychology, the news media usually try to include comments from "experts" (we place this term in quotation marks, because they're not always genuine experts) on opposing sides of an issue to make the story appear more balanced.

When evaluating media claims, we often need to consider the source.

The problem is that "balanced coverage" sometimes creates *pseudosymmetry* (Park, 2002): the appearance of a scientific controversy where none exists. A newspaper might feature a story about a study that provides scientific evidence against extrasensory perception (ESP). They might devote the first four paragraphs to a description of the study but the last four paragraphs to impassioned critiques of the study from ESP advocates. This coverage may create the impression that the scientific evidence for ESP is split right down the middle, with about half of the research supporting it and about half disputing it. It's easy to overlook the fact that there was no scientific evidence in the last four paragraphs, only criticisms of the evidence against ESP. Moreover, the article might fail to note that the scientific evidence regarding ESP is largely negative (Hines, 2003; Wagenmakers et al., 2011).

One reason why most of us find it difficult to think scientifically about research evidence is that we're continually bombarded with media reports that (unintentionally) provide us with poor role models for interpreting research (Lilienfeld, Ruscio, & Lynn, 2008; Stanovich, 2009). Bearing these tips in mind should help us become better consumers of psychological science in everyday life and to make better real-world decisions.

Answers are located at the end of the text.

HAIR-LOSS REMEDIES   evaluating **CLAIMS**

"Grow back a full head of hair in only three weeks!" Sounds great (for those of us who've experienced hair loss), but is it too good to be true? Let's evaluate some of these claims, which are modeled after actual ads for hair-loss remedies.

"Call us now to learn more about the *advantages and highlights* of our product."

Beware of ads that only focus on the advantages of their products. What questions would you have about potential disadvantages or side effects?

"Thousands of others have seen results—read their *testimonials.*"

Can we rely on testimonial or anecdotal evidence alone? Why or why not?

"Use our supplements and grow back your hair *without the use of chemicals* or surgery."

Why is the claim that this supplement doesn't contain chemicals implausible?

"Our hair-loss cure is *doctor approved* and recommended."

Does the fact that doctors approve this cure make it more legitimate in your eyes? What questions would you ask about the number and type of doctors who approve of this product?

Assess Your Knowledge   FACT or FICTION?

 Study and **Review** in **MyPsychLab**

1. Few psychological journals use a peer-review process. **True / False**

2. When evaluating the quality of a study, we must be on the lookout for potential confounds, expectancy effects, and nonrandom assignment to experimental and control groups. **True / False**

3. Most newspaper reporters who write stories about psychology have advanced degrees in psychology. **True / False**

4. "Balanced" coverage of a psychology story is sometimes inaccurate. **True / False**

Answers: 1. F; 2. T; 3. F; 4. T

Your Complete Review System

(((**Listen** in **MyPsychLab** to chapter audio

The Beauty and Necessity of Good Research Design

1 IDENTIFY TWO MODES OF THINKING AND THEIR APPLICATION TO SCIENTIFIC REASONING.

Increasing evidence suggests that there are two major modes of thinking. System 1 thinking, or "intuitive thinking," tends to be rapid and to rely on gut hunches, whereas System 2 thinking, or "analytical thinking," tends to be slow and to rely on a thoughtful examination of issues. Research designs make use of analytical thinking, because scientific reasoning often requires us to question and at times override our intuitions about the world.

1. The same processes that serve us well can also predispose us to _____ in thinking.

2. Our first impressions can be surprisingly _____.

3. System 1, or "intuitive," thinking (does/doesn't) require much mental effort.

4. Jumping out of the street to avoid an oncoming car involves _____ thinking.

5. Our _____ thinking allows us to override our _____ thinking.

6. Which mode of thinking does this image best represent?

7. How can we explain why most people say they'd have to travel southwest to get from Reno to San Diego?

8. A _____ is a mental short-cut or rule of thumb.

9. People who believed that facilitated communication was beneficial likely relied on _____ thinking.

10. Research designs allow us to harness _____ thinking

The Scientific Method: Toolbox of Skills

2 DESCRIBE THE ADVANTAGES AND DISADVANTAGES OF USING NATURALISTIC OBSERVATION, CASE STUDIES, SELF-REPORT MEASURES, AND SURVEYS.

Naturalistic observation, case studies, self-report measures, and surveys are all important research designs. Naturalistic observation involves recording behaviors in real-world settings, but is often not carefully controlled. Case studies involve examining one or a few individuals over long periods of time; these designs are often useful in generating hypotheses but are typically limited in testing them rigorously. Self-report measures and surveys ask people about themselves; they can provide a wealth of useful information, but have certain disadvantages, especially response sets.

11. Although the major advantage of naturalistic designs is that they are often high in _____ _____, or the extent to which we can generalize our findings to real-world settings, they also tend to be low in _____ _____, or the extent to which we can draw cause-and-effect inferences.

12. Using your knowledge of random selection, explain what pollsters did wrong in reporting the 1948 presidential election results.

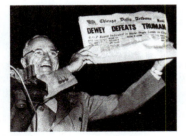

13. When evaluating results, we need to be able to evaluate the consistency of the measurement, or _____, and the extent to which a measure assesses what it claims to measure, or _____.

14. In using _____ _____, psychologists need to evaluate whether questionnaire respondents distorted their responses by engaging in _____ _____.

3 DESCRIBE THE ROLE OF CORRELATIONAL DESIGNS AND DISTINGUISH CORRELATION FROM CAUSATION.

Correlational studies allow us to establish the relations among two or more measures, but do not allow causal conclusions.

15. A positive correlation means that as the value of one variable changes, the other goes in (the same/a different) direction.

4 IDENTIFY THE COMPONENTS OF AN EXPERIMENT, THE POTENTIAL PITFALLS THAT CAN LEAD TO FAULTY CONCLUSIONS, AND HOW PSYCHOLOGISTS CONTROL FOR THESE PITFALLS.

Experimental designs involve random assignment of participants to conditions and manipulation of an independent variable, and when conducted properly, permit us to draw conclusions about the causes of a psychological intervention. Placebo effects and experimenter expectancy effects are examples of pitfalls in experimental designs that can lead us to draw false conclusions.

16. If a study is a properly conducted experiment we (can/can't) infer cause and effect, but if the study is correlational we (can/can't).

17. A(n) _____ is a research design that consists of two components: 1) a random assignment of participants to conditions, and 2) manipulation of an independent variable.

18. The group of participants in a study that doesn't receive the manipulation is the _____ group.

19. To avoid the _____ effect during medication research, it's crucial that the subject remain _____ to whether he/she has been assigned to the experimental group.

20. How does this photo illustrate the nocebo effect?

Ethical Issues in Research Design

5 **EXPLAIN THE ETHICAL OBLIGATIONS OF RESEARCHERS TOWARD THEIR RESEARCH PARTICIPANTS.**

Concerns about ethical treatment of research participants have led research facilities, such as colleges and universities, to establish institutional review boards that review all research involving human participants and require informed consent by participants. In some cases, they may also require a full debriefing at the conclusion of the research session.

21. In the Tuskegee study performed by the U.S. government starting in 1932, the researchers never informed the subjects that they had _____, nor did they inform them that _____ were available to treat the disease.

22. What important changes have been made to research procedures in the United States to ensure that an ethical catastrophe like the Tuskegee study doesn't happen again?

23. The process in which researchers tell potential participants what's involved in a study is called _____ _____.

24. Milgram's controversial study relied on _____ because he deliberately misled the participants about the study's purpose.

25. _____ is a process whereby researchers inform participants what the study was about.

26. The _____ _____ _____ published a code of ethics to govern all research with human participants.

6 **DESCRIBE BOTH SIDES OF THE DEBATE ON THE USE OF ANIMALS AS RESEARCH SUBJECTS.**

Animal research has led to clear benefits in our understanding of human learning, brain physiology, and psychological treatment, to mention only a few advances. To answer many critical psychological questions, there are simply no good alternatives to using animals. Nevertheless, many critics have raised useful questions about the treatment of laboratory animals and emphasized the need for adequate housing and feeding conditions. Many protest the large number of laboratory animals killed each year and question whether animal research offers sufficient external validity to justify its use.

27. The goal of a(n) _____ research study on animals is to learn how the brain relates to behavior in humans without having to inflict harm on people.

28. About _____ percent of published psychology research relies on animals.

29. What are some of the arguments for and against the ethics of animal testing?

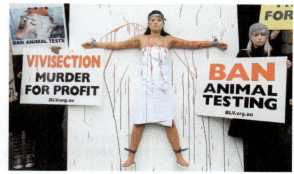

30. Animal researchers must carefully weigh the potential _____ _____ against the costs in death and suffering they produce.

Statistics: The Language of Psychological Research

7 **IDENTIFY USES OF VARIOUS MEASURES OF CENTRAL TENDENCY AND VARIABILITY.**

Three measures of central tendency are the mean, median, and mode. The mean is the average of all scores. The median is the middle score. The mode is the most frequent score. The mean is the most widely used measure but is the most sensitive to extreme scores. Two measures of variability are the range and standard deviation. The range is a more intuitive measure of variability, but can yield a deceptive picture of how spread out individual

Answers are located at the end of the text.

scores are. The standard deviation is a better measure of variability, although it's more difficult to calculate.

31. In _____ statistics, the _____ _____ provides a sense of the "central" score in a data set, or where the group tends to cluster.

32. Match up the measure to the definition

_____	Mode	1. Middle score in a data set
_____	Mean	2. Most frequent score in a data set
_____	Median	3. Average score in a data set

33. The best measure of central tendency to report when the data form a "bell-shaped" or normal distribution is the _____.

34. Using your knowledge of distribution curves, label these two different types of skews.

(a) Elongated tail at the **left**
More data in the tail than would be expected in a normal distribution

(b) Elongated tail at the **right**
More data in the tail than would be expected in a normal distribution

35. Another type of descriptive statistic is _____, which gives a sense of how loosely or tightly bunched the data are.

36. The difference between the highest and lowest scores is the _____.

37. The _____ _____ takes into account how far each data point is from the mean.

8 EXPLAIN HOW INFERENTIAL STATISTICS CAN HELP US TO DETERMINE WHETHER WE CAN GENERALIZE FROM OUR SAMPLE TO THE FULL POPULATION.

Inferential statistics allow us to determine how much we can generalize findings from our sample to the full population. Not all statistically significant findings are large enough in magnitude to make a real-world difference, so we must also consider practical significance when evaluating the implications of our results.

38. When using inferential statistics, we're asking whether we can draw "inferences" (or _____) regarding whether the differences we've observed in our sample apply to other samples drawn from the same population.

39. The larger the sample size, the (greater/lesser) the odds that a result will be statistically significant.

9 SHOW HOW STATISTICS CAN BE MISUSED FOR PURPOSES OF PERSUASION.

Reporting measures of central tendency that are nonrepresentative of most participants, creating visual representations that exaggerate effects, and failing to take base rates into account are all frequent methods of manipulating statistics for the purposes of persuasion.

40. In a _____ _____ _____, the y axis starts somewhere close to the highest possible score, instead of at the lowest score, where it should start.

Evaluating Psychological Research

10 IDENTIFY FLAWS IN RESEARCH DESIGNS AND HOW TO CORRECT THEM.

Good experimental design requires not only random assignment and manipulation of an independent variable, but also inclusion of an appropriate control condition to rule out placebo effects. Most important, it requires careful attention to the possibility of alternative explanations of observed effects.

41. The crucial task of a _____ _____ is to identify flaws that could undermine a study's findings.

42. By definition, an experiment is flawed if it doesn't include a manipulation of a(n) _____ _____.

43. In Study 1, the researcher puts all the subjects in a single group and is therefore lacking a necessary _____ group.

44. In Study 1, there's no _____ variable because all participants played the self-help tape every night.

45. In Study 2, the researcher hasn't controlled for the _____ effect because participants are aware of whether or not they are receiving treatment.

46. In Study 2, the researcher knows which participants are in which groups, so he has created an opportunity for the _____ _____ effect.

11 IDENTIFY SKILLS FOR EVALUATING PSYCHOLOGICAL CLAIMS IN THE POPULAR MEDIA.

To evaluate psychological claims in the news and elsewhere in the popular media, we should bear in mind that few reporters have formal psychological training. When considering media claims, we should consider the source, beware of excessive sharpening and leveling, and be on the lookout for pseudosymmetry.

47. News stories about psychology (are/are not) typically written by people who have formal training in psychology.

48. When evaluating the legitimacy of psychological reports in the media, one should consider the _____.

49. _____ refers to the tendency to exaggerate the central message of a study, whereas _____ refers to the tendency to minimize the less central details of a study.

50. When a news story mistakenly suggests that experts are equally divided over a topic, it creates _____.

Apply Your Scientific Thinking Skills

Use your scientific thinking skills to answer the following questions, referencing specific scientific thinking principles and common errors reasoning whenever possible.

1. Many media sources report findings showing an association between violent video games or violent song lyrics, on one hand, and violent behavior, on the other. Locate two examples of such media reports (check websites, newspapers, and magazines) and use your scientific thinking skills to determine whether the sources properly interpreted the original study's findings. If the study was correlational, did the reporters infer a causal relationship between the variables?

2. As we've learned, the results of a poll can vary based on the sample, as well as on the wording of the questions. Pick a current social or political issue (such as abortion or global warming) and identify three polls on that issue (such as Gallup or cable news polls). How does the wording vary? How were individuals sampled? To what extent might these differences have contributed to differences in results across the polls?

3. Most of us have heard the statistic that half of all marriages end in divorce. Is this claim really true? Research different statistics concerning marriage and divorce rates in the United States and explain how they support or refute this claim.

Further Your Understanding

EXTEND YOUR KNOWLEDGE WITH THE MYPSYCHLAB VIDEO SERIES

Watch these videos in MyPsychLab. Follow the "Video Series" link.

The Big Picture: How to Answer Psychological Questions See how psychology is based on scientific inquiry and look at the basic scientific methods used to study the brain, the mind, and behavior.

The Basics: Scientific Research Methods Learn how experiments are designed and conducted, and understand the importance of independent and dependent variables, and control and experimental groups.

Special Topics: Ethics and Psychological Research Learn about ethical concerns related to scientific research, and the regulations that researchers follow to keep their subjects healthy.

Thinking Like a Psychologist: Thinking Critically Watch how psychologists use critical thinking to sharpen the focus and results of their experiments and make better decisions.

EXPERIENCE PSYCHOLOGICAL RESEARCH WITH MYPSYCHLAB SIMULATIONS

Access these simulations in MyPsychLab. Follow the "Simulations" link.

Participating in a Research Survey Participate in a survey to learn about your attitudes towards and experiences with participating in psychological research.

APPLY YOUR CRITICAL THINKING SKILLS WITH MYPSYCHLAB WRITING ASSESSMENTS

Complete these writing assignments in MyPsychLab.

Imagine you have been asked to create an experimental design to test the hypothesis that talking on a cell phone impairs driving skills. Explain why a control condition would be important to include in testing this hypothesis. How should subjects be assigned to conditions? How can the researchers design the experiment so that the only difference between both conditions is the use of a cell phone?

Answer Key

THE BEAUTY AND NECESSITY OF GOOD RESEARCH DESIGN

1. errors
2. accurate
3. doesn't
4. intuitive
5. analytical; intuitive
6. analytical
7. By relying on a mental shortcut or a heuristic based on the knowledge that California is on the West Coast, most people forget or don't know that a large chunk of California is east of Nevada.
8. heuristic
9. intuitive
10. analytical

THE SCIENTIFIC METHOD: TOOLBOX OF SKILLS

11. external validity; internal validity
12. The pollsters got it wrong largely because they based their results on telephone surveys. Back in 1948, considerably more Republicans (who tended to be richer) owned telephones than Democrats, resulting in a biased sampling and a skewed pre-election prediction.
13. reliability; validity
14. self-report measures; response sets
15. the same
16. can; can't
17. experiment
18. control
19. placebo; blind
20. The nocebo effect is harm resulting from the mere expectation of harm. People who believe in voodoo may experience pain when one of their enemies inserts a pin into a doll symbolizing them.

ETHICAL ISSUES IN RESEARCH DESIGN

21. syphilis; antibiotics
22. All research with human participants requires approval from an IRB before it can be conducted. IRBs evaluate the ethics of the study and require a procedure called informed consent: researchers must tell participants what they're getting into before asking them to participate.
23. informed consent
24. deception
25. Debriefing
26. American Psychological Association
27. invasive
28. 7–8
29. Arguments for: some animal research has led to direct benefits to humans as well as immensely useful knowledge in its own right; many psychological treatments were derived from animal research that could not have been developed using human participants. Arguments against: the deaths of approximately 20 million lab animals a year aren't worth the benefits; many critics argue that the knowledge gleaned from animal research is of such doubtful external validity to humans as to be virtually useless.
30. scientific gains

STATISTICS: THE LANGUAGE OF PSYCHOLOGICAL RESEARCH

31. descriptive; central tendency
32. Mode: 2; Mean: 3; Median: 1
33. mean
34. a) negative skew; b) positive skew
35. variability
36. range
37. standard deviation
38. conclusions
39. greater
40. truncated line graph

EVALUATING PSYCHOLOGICAL RESEARCH

41. peer reviewer
42. independent variable
43. control
44. independent
45. placebo
46. experimenter expectancy
47. are not
48. source
49. Sharpening; leveling
50. pseudosymmetry

References

American Psychiatric Association. (2000). *Diagnostic and statistical manual of mental disorders: DSM-IV-TR* (4th ed.). Washington, DC: Author.

American Psychological Association (2002). Ethical principles of psychologists and code of conduct. *American Psychologist, 57*, 1060–1073.

American Psychological Association. (2008). *Research animals in psychology.* http://www.apa.org/research/responsible/research-animals.pdf

Anderson, C. A., Lindsay, J. J., & Bushman, B. J. (1999). Research in the psychological laboratory: Truth or triviality? *Current Directions in Psychological Science, 8*, 3–9.

Ariely, D. (2008). *Predictably irrational: The hidden forces that shape our decisions.* New York, NY: HarperCollins.

Azar, B. (1999, July/August). Destructive lab attack sends a wake-up call. *APA Monitor, 30* (7), 16.

Baskin T. W., Tierney S. C., Minami T., & Wampold B. E. (2003). Establishing specificity in psychotherapy: A meta-analysis of structural equivalence of placebo controls. *Journal of Clinical Psychology, 71*, 973–979.

Bauer, H. (1992). *Scientific literacy and the myth of the scientific method.* Urbana, IL: University of Illinois Press.

Baumrind, D. (1964). Some thoughts on ethics of research: After reading Milgram's "Behavioral study of obedience." *American Psychologist, 19*, 421–423.

Benedetti, F., Lanotte, M., Lopiano, L., & Colloca, L. (2007). When words are painful: Unraveling the mechanisms of the nocebo effect. *Neuroscience, 147*, 260–271.

Bishop, G. F., Oldendick, R. W., & Tuchfarber, A. J. (1986). Opinions on fictitious issues: The pressure to answer survey questions. *Public Opinion Quarterly, 50*, 240–250.

Blass, T. (2004). *The man who shocked the world: The life and legacy of Stanley Milgram.* New York, NY: Perseus.

Boese, A. (2007, November 3). The whacko files. *New Scientist, 196*, 49–55.

Borsboom, D. (2005). *Measuring the mind: Conceptual issues in contemporary psychometrics.* Cambridge University Press.

Buckalew, L. W., & Ross, S. (1981). Relationship of perceptual characteristics to efficacy of placebos. *Psychological Reports, 49*, 955–961.

Campbell, W. K., & Miller, J. D. (2011). *The handbook of narcissism and narcissistic personality disorder.* New York, NY: Wiley.

Ceci, S. J., & Williams, W. M. (1997). Schooling, intelligence, and income. *American Psychologist, 52*, 1051–1058.

Chapman, L. J., & Chapman, J. P. (1969). Illusory correlation as an obstacle to the use of valid psychodiagnostic signs. *Journal of Abnormal Psychology, 74*, 271–280.

Connelly, B. S., & Ones, D. S. (2010). Another perspective on personality: Meta-analytic integration of observers' accuracy and predictive validity. *Psychological Bulletin, 136*(6), 1092.

Coover, J. E., & Angell, F. (1907). General practice effect of special exercise. *American Journal of Psychology, 18*, 328–340.

Corsini, R. J. (1999). *Dictionary of psychology.* Philadelphia, PA: Brunner/Mazel.

Cunningham, P. F. (1993, October). *Can the use of animals in neuropsychological and psychopharmacological experiments continue to be justified?* Paper presented at the New England Psychological Association 33rd Annual Meeting, Goffstown, NH.

Dawes, R. M. (1998, June). "Listening to Prozac but hearing placebo": Commentary on Kirsch and Sapirstein. *Prevention & Treatment, 1*(2).

Dawes, R. M. (2006). Experience and validity of clinical judgement: The illusory correlation. *Behavioral Sciences and the Law, 7*, 457–467.

Dehue, T. (2005). History of the control group. In B. Everitt & D. Howell (Eds.), *Encyclopedia of Statistics in Behavioral Science* (pp. 829–836). Chichester, England: Wiley.

Dion, K., Berscheid, E., & Walster, E. (1972). What is beautiful is good. *Journal of Personality and Social Psychology, 24*, 285–290.

Domjan, M., & Purdy, J. E. (1995). Animal research in psychology. *American Psychologist, 50*, 496–503.

Duggal S., & Sroufe L. A. (1998). Recovered memory of childhood sexual trauma: A documented case from a longitudinal study. *Journal of Traumatic Stress, 11*, 301–321.

Eagly, A. H., Ashmore, R. D., Makhijani, M. G., & Longo, L. C. (1991). What is beautiful is good, but . . .: A meta-analytic review of research on the physical attractiveness stereotype. *Psychological Bulletin, 110*, 109–128.

Edens, J. F., Buffington, J. K., Tomicic, T. L., & Riley, B. D. (2001). Effects of positive impression management on the Psychopathic Personality Inventory. *Law and Human Behavior, 25*, 235–256.

Eder, A. B., Fiedler, K., & Hamm-Eder, S. (2011). Illusory correlations revisited: The role of pseudocontingencies and working-memory capacity. *The Quarterly Journal of Experimental Psychology, 64*, 517–532. http://dx.doi.org/10.1080/17470218.2010.509917

Enck, P., & Hauser, W. (2012, August 10). Beware the nocebo effect. *New York Times.* Retrieved from http://www.nytimes.com/2012/08/12/opinion/sunday/beware-the-nocebo-effect.html?_r=0

Fernald, L. D. (1984). *The Hans legacy: A story of science.* Hillsdale, NJ: Erlbaum.

Fournier, J. C., DeRubeis, R. J., Hollon, S. D., Dimidjian, S., Amsterdam, J. D., Shelton, R. C., & Fawcett, J. (2010). Antidepressant drug effects and depression severity. *Journal of the American Medical Association, 303*, 47–53.

Gallup, G. G., Jr., & Suarez, S. D. (1985). Alternatives to the use of animals in psychological research. *American Psychologist, 40*, 1104–1111.

Gigerenzer, G., & Gaissmaier, W. (2011). Heuristic decision making. *Annual Review of Psychology, 62*, 451–482.

Gilbert, D. T. (1991). How mental systems believe. *American Psychologist, 46* (2), 107.

Gosling, S. D., Rentfrow, P. J., & Swann, W. B. (2003). A very brief measure of the Big-Five personality domains. *Journal of Research in Personality, 36,* 504–528.

Green, C. D. (1992). Is unified positivism the answer to psychology's disunity? *American Psychologist, 48,* 1057–1058.

Grove, W. M., & Tellegen, A. (1991). Problems in the classification of personality disorders. *Journal of Personality Disorders, 5,* 31–41.

Grubin, D. (2010). The polygraph and forensic psychiatry. *Journal of the American Academy of Psychiatry and the Law Online, 38*(4), 446–451.

Guilford, J. P. (1954). *Psychometric methods* (2nd ed.). New York, NY: McGraw-Hill.

Hagen, M. (2001). Damaged goods? What, if anything, does science tell us about the long-term effects of childhood sexual abuse? *Skeptical Inquirer, 24*(1), 54–59.

Hammond, K. R. (1996). *Human judgment and social policy: Irreducible uncertainty, inevitable error, unavoidable justice.* New York, NY: Oxford University Press.

Häuser, W., Hansen, E., & Enck, P. (2012). Nocebo phenomena in medicine: Their relevance in everyday clinical practice. *Deutsches Ärzteblatt International, 109*(26), 459.

Haynes, S. N., Smith, G. T., & Hunsley, J. D. (2011). *Scientific foundations of clinical assessment.* New York, NY: Routledge/Taylor & Francis Group.

Herbert, W. (2010). *On second thought: Outsmarting your mind's hard-wired habits.* New York, NY: Crown.

Hofer, T., Przyrembel, H., & Verleger, S. (2004). New evidence for the theory of the stork. *Paediatric and Perinatal Epidemiology, 18,* 88–92.

Hróbjartsson, A., & Gøtzsche, P. C. (2001). Is the placebo powerless? An analysis of clinical trials comparing placebo with no treatment. *New England Journal of Medicine, 344,* 1594–1602.

Huck, S. W. (2008). *Statistical misconceptions.* New York, NY: Routledge.

Huff, D. (1954). *How to lie with statistics.* New York, NY: Norton.

Jacobson, J., Mulick, J., & Schwartz, A. (1995). A history of facilitated communication. *American Psychologist, 50,* 750–765.

John, O. P., & Robins, R. W. (1994). Accuracy and bias in self-perception: Individual differences in self-enhancement and the role of narcissism. *Journal of Personality and Social Psychology, 66,* 206–219.

Jones, J. H. (1993). *Bad blood: The Tuskegee syphilis experiment* (2nd ed.). New York, NY: Free Press.

Kaptchuk, T. J. (2002). The placebo effect in alternative medicine: Can the performance of a healing ritual have clinical significance? *Annals of Internal Medicine, 136,* 817–825.

Kihlstrom, J. F. (2002). Mesmer, the Franklin Commission, and hypnosis: A counterfactual essay. *International Journal of Clinical and Experimental Hypnosis, 50*(4), 407–419.

Kirsch, I. (2010). *The emperor's new drugs.* New York, NY: Basic Books.

Kirsch, I., Deacon, B. J., Huedo-Medina, T. B., Scoboria, A. Moore, T. J., & Johnson, B. T. (2008). Initial severity and antidepressant benefits: A meta-analysis of data submitted to the food and drug administration. *PLoS Medicine, 5*(2), e45. http://dx.doi.org/10.1371/journal.pmed.0050045

Kirsch, I., & Lynn, S. J. (1998). Dissociation theories of hypnosis. *Psychological Bulletin, 123,* 100–115.

Klein, D. F. (1998). Listening to meta-analysis but hearing bias. *Prevention & Treatment, 1,* art. 0006c. Retrieved from http://psycnet.apa.org/index. cfm?fa=buy.optionToBuy&id=1999-11094-005

Krueger, J. I., & Funder, D. C. (2004). Towards a balanced social psychology: Causes, consequences, and cures for the problem-seeking approach to social behavior and cognition. *Behavioral and Brain Sciences, 27,* 313–327.

Kuhn, D. (2007). Jumping to conclusions. *Scientific American Mind, 18*(1), 44–51.

Lehrer, J. (2009). *How we decide.* Boston, MA: Houghton-Mifflin.

Lidstone, S. C., Schulzer, M., Dinelle, K., Mak, E., Sossi, V., Ruth, T. J., . . . Stoessl, A. J. (2010). Effects of expectation on placebo-induced dopamine release in Parkinson disease. *Archives of General Psychiatry, 67*(8), 857.

Lieberman, J. A., Stroup, T. S., McEvoy, J. P., Swartz, M. S., Rosenheck, R. A., Perkins, D. O., . . . Hsiao, J. K. (2005). Effectiveness of antipsychotic drugs in patients with chronic schizophrenia. *New England Journal of Medicine, 353*(12), 1209–1223.

Lilienfeld, S. O. (1995). *Seeing both sides: Classic controversies in abnormal psychology.* Pacific Grove, CA: Brooks/Cole.

Lilienfeld, S. O., & Fowler, K. A. (2006). The self-report assessment of psychopathy: Problems, pitfalls, and promises. In C. J. Patrick (Ed.), *Handbook of psychopathy* (pp. 107–132). New York, NY: Guilford Press.

Lilienfeld, S. O., Lynn, S. J., Ruscio, J., & Beyerstein, B. L. (2010). *50 great myths of popular psychology: Shattering widespread misconceptions about human behavior.* Malden, MA: Wiley-Blackwell.

Lilienfeld, S. O, Ruscio, J., & Lynn, S. J. (2008). *Navigating the mindfield: A guide to separating science from pseudoscience in mental health.* Buffalo, NY: Prometheus Books.

Lykken, D. T. (1998). *A tremor in the blood: Uses and abuses of the lie detector* (2nd ed.). Reading, MA: Perseus.

Lynn, S. J., & Lilienfeld, S. (2002). A critique of the Franklin Commission report: Hypnosis, belief and suggestion. *International Journal of Clinical and Experimental Hypnosis, 50*(4), 369–386.

Mann, L. B, (2005, February 22). Oscar nominee: Fact or fiction? *Washington Post,* HE01

Marino, L. (2009, March 20). Another kind of scientist activism. *Chronicle of Higher Education,* Retrieved from http://chronicle.com/article/Another-Kind-of-Scientist/24559

Mayberg, H. S., Silva, J. A., Brannan, S. K., Tekell, J. L., Mahurin, R. K., McGinnis, S., Jerabek, P. A. (2002). The functional neuroanatomy of the placebo effect. *American Journal of Psychiatry, 159,* 728–737.

McHugh P. R. (2008). *Try to remember: Psychiatry's clash over meaning, memory, and mind.* New York, NY: Dana Press.

McNally, R. J. (2003). *Remembering trauma.* Cambridge, MA: Belknap Press.

McNally, R. J., & Lukach, B. M. (1991). Behavioral treatment of zoophilic exhibitionism. *Journal of Behavioral Research and Experimental Psychiatry, 22,* 281–284.

McRae, C., Cherin, E., Yamazaki, G., Diem, G., Vo, A. H., Russell, D., . . . Freed, C. R. (2004). Effects of perceived treatment on quality of life and medical outcomes in a double-blind placebo surgery trial. *Archives of General Psychiatry, 61,* 412–420.

Milgram, S. (1963). Behavioral study of obedience. *Journal of Abnormal and Social Psychology, 67,* 371–378.

Milgram, S. (1964). Issues in the study of obedience: A reply to Baumrind. *American Psychologist, 19,* 848–852.

Mintz, I. (1977). A note on the addictive personality: Addiction to placebos. *American Journal of Psychiatry, 134,* 3–27.

Mitchell, G. (2012). Revisiting truth or triviality: The external validity of research in the psychological laboratory. *Perspectives on Psychological Science, 7*(2), 109–117.

Mook, D. (1983). In defense of external invalidity. *American Psychologist, 38,* 379–387.

Moore, F. R., Filippou, D., & Perrett, D. I. (2011). Intelligence and attractiveness in the face: Beyond the attractiveness halo effect. *Journal of Evolutionary Psychology, 9*(3), 205–217.

Morse, G. (1999, November). The nocebo effect: Scattered findings suggest that negative thinking can harm patients' health. *Hippocrates, 13,* 10.

Myers, D. G. (2004). *Intuition: Its powers and perils.* New Haven, CT: Yale University Press.

Nisbett, R. E., & Wilson, T. D. (1977). Telling more than we can know: Verbal reports on mental processes. *Psychological Review, 84,* 231–259.

Noelle-Neumann, E. (1970). Wanted: Rules for wording structured questionnaires. *Public Opinion Quarterly, 34,* 191–201.

Oltmanns, T. F., & Turkheimer, E. (2009). Person perception and personality pathology. *Current Directions in Psychological Science, 18,* 32–36.

Orne, M. T. (1962). On the social psychology of the psychological experiment: With particular reference to demand characteristics and their implications. *American Psychologist, 17,* 776–783.

Ott, R. (1995). The natural wrongs about animal rights and animal liberation. *Journal of the American Veterinary Medical Association, 207,* 1023–1030.

Park, R. (2002). *Voodoo science: The road from foolishness to fraud.* New York, NY: Oxford University Press.

Paulhus, D. L. (1991). Measurement and control of response bias. In J. P. Robinson & P. R. Shaver (Eds.), *Measures of personality and social psychological attitudes* (pp. 17–59). San Diego, CA: Academic Press.

Paunonen, S. V., & LeBel, E. P. (2012). Socially desirable responding and its elusive effects on the validity of personality assessments. *Journal of Personality and Social Psychology, 103*(1), 158.

Peterson, C. (2000). The future of optimism. *American Psychologist, 55,* 44–55.

Piatelli-Palmarini, M. (1994). *Inevitable illusions: How mistakes of reason rule our minds.* New York, NY: Wiley.

Plait, P. C. (2002). *Bad astronomy: Misconceptions and misuses revealed from astrology to the moon landing "hoax."* New York, NY: Wiley.

Provine, R. R. (1996). Laughter. *American Scientist, 84,* 38–45.

Quick, D. C. (1999, March/April). Joint pain and weather. *Skeptical Inquirer, 23,* 49–51.

Ray, J. V., Hall, J., Rivera-Hudson, N., Poythress, N. G., Lilienfeld, S. O., & Morano, M. (2012). The relation between self-reported psychopathic traits and distorted response styles: A meta-analytic review. *Personality Disorders: Theory, Research, and Treatment.* Retrieved from http://psycnet.apa.org/psycinfo/2012-01747-001

Reid, B. (2002, April 30). The nocebo effect: Placebo's evil twin. *Washington Post,* HE01.

Rickels, K., Hesbacher, P. T., Weise, C. C., Gray, B., & Feldman, H. S. (1970). Pills and improvement: A study of placebo response in psychoneurotic outpatients. *Psychopharmacologia, 16*(4), 318–328.

Rogers, R. (2008). *Clinical assessment of malingering and deception.* New York, NY: Guilford Press.

Romanczyk, R. G., Arnstein, L., Soorya, L. V., & Gillis, J. (2003). The myriad of controversial treatments for autism: A critical evaluation of efficacy. In S. O. Lilienfeld, S. J. Lynn, & J. M. Lohr (Eds.), *Science and pseudoscience in clinical psychology* (pp. 363–395). New York, NY: Guilford Press.

Rosenthal, R., & Fode, K. L. (1963). Psychology of the scientist: V. Three experiments in experimenter bias. *Psychological Reports, 12,* 491–511.

Rosnow, R. L. (2002). The nature and role of demand characteristics in scientific inquiry. *Prevention and Treatment, 5*(1). Retrieved from http://psycnet.apa.org/index.cfm?fa=buy.optionToBuy&id=2003-04137-004

Rothschild, R., & Quitkin, F. M. (1992). Review of the use of pattern analysis to differentiate true drug and placebo responses. *Psychotherapy and Psychosomatics, 58,* 170–177.

Rotton, J., & Kelly, I. W. (1985). Much ado about the full moon: A meta-analysis of lunar-lunacy research. *Psychological Bulletin, 97,* 286–306.

Ruscio, J. (2005). Exploring controversies in the art and science of polygraph testing. *Skeptical Inquirer, 29,* 34–39.

Schmidt, F. L. (1992). What do data really mean? Research findings, meta-analysis, and cumulative knowledge in psychology. *American Psychologist, 47,* 1173–1181.

Schooler, J. W. (1997). Reflections on a memory discovery. *Child Maltreatment, 2,* 126–133.

Schwarz, N. (1999). Self-reports: How the questions shape the answers. *American Psychologist, 54,* 93–105.

Sears, D. O. (1986). College sophomores in the laboratory: Influences of a narrow data base on social-psychology's view of human nature. *Journal of Personality and Social Psychology, 51,* 515–530.

Smith, D. M., Schwarz, N., Roberts, T. R., & Ubel, P. A. (2006). Why are you calling me? How study introductions change response patterns. *Quality of Life Research, 15,* 621–630.

Smith, J. (2009). Pseudoscience and extraordinary claims of the paranormal. New York, NY: Wiley.

Smith, R. A. (2001). *Challenging your preconceptions: Thinking critically about psychology.* Pacific Grove, CA: Wadsworth.

Stanovich, K. E. (2009). *What intelligence tests miss: The psychology of rational thought.* New Haven, CT: Yale University Press.

Stanovich, K. E., & West, R. F. (2000). Advancing the rationality debate. *Behavioral and Brain Sciences, 23,* 701–726.

Todd, J. T. (2012). The moral obligation to be empirical: Comments on Boynton's "Facilitated communication—What harm it can do: Confessions of a former facilitator." *Evidence-Based Communication Assessment and Intervention, 6*(1), 36–57.

Ulrich, R. E. (1991). Animal rights, animal wrongs and the question of balance. *Psychological Science, 2,* 197–201.

Valenstein, E. S. (1986). *Great and desperate cures: The rise and decline of psychosurgery and other radical treatments for mental illness.* New York, NY: Basic Books.

van de Mortel, T. F. (2008). Faking it: Social desirability response bias in self-report research. *Australian Journal of Advanced Nursing, 25*(4), 40.

Vyse, S. A. (2000). *Believing in magic: The psychology of superstition.* New York, NY: Oxford University Press.

Wagenmakers, E.-J., Wetzels, R., Borsboom, D., & van der Maas, H. L. J. (2011). Why psychologists must change the way they analyze their data: The case of psi: Comment on Bem (2011). *Journal of Personality and Social Psychology, 100,* 426–432.

Walonick, D. S. (1994). *Do researchers influence survey results with their question wording choices?* Retrieved from http://www.statpac.com/research-papers/researcher-bias.doc

Wegner, D. M., Fuller, V. A., & Sparrow, B. (2003). Clever hands: Uncontrolled intelligence in facilitated communication. *Journal of Personality and Social Psychology, 85,* 5–19.

Williams, W. M., & Ceci, S. J. (1997, September/October). "How'm I doing?" *Change, 29*(5), 13–23.

Credits

Credits listed in order of appearance.

Text: http://www.easycalculation.com/statistics/correlation.php. **Figure 5:** Used with permission of Jon Mueller. **Text:** Popularized by Mark Twain.

Photo Credits

Photo Credits listed in order of appearance.

Masterfile; Ann Rayworth/Alamy; **(center):** Alan Carey/The Image Works; **(top right):** Mark Lees/Alamy; **(center left):** Szasz-Fabian Erika/Fotolia; **(top right):** Penelope Breese/Liaison/Getty Images; **(top):** Brand New Images/Stone/Getty Images; **(top right):** Underwood Archives/Alamy; **(top center):** Charles E. Rotkin/Corbis; **(top):** MPVHistory/Alamy; **(center):** Marcus Lund/Alamy; **(bottom):** Sonda Dawes/The Image Works; **(top right):** Photosani/Fotolia; **(bottom right):** John Morrison/PhotoEdit; **(top right):** Fbhenrg/Fotolia; **(center right):** Topham/The Image Works; **(top):** Theresa McCracken; **(center left):** James Kent; **(top left):** Sidney Harris; **(center):** Roger-Viollet/The Image Works; **(top left):** Fer Gregory/Shutterstock; **(center left):** Sidney Harris; **(top):** Topham/The Image Works; **(center):** National Archives and Records Administration; **(bottom right):** William West/AFP/Getty Images; **(bottom):** Sidney Harris; **(center left):** Moodboard/Alamy; **(top):** CartoonStock; **(center):** Ocean/Corbis; **(top right):** Sidney Harris; **(center right):** Lisa F. Young/Shutterstock; **(bottom):** Grizelda/CSL, CartoonStock; **(center):** Lyndsay Russell/Alamy; **(center left):** Szasz-Fabian Erika/Fotolia; **(center right):** Underwood Archives/Alamy; **(top left):** Fer Gregory/Shutterstock; **(bottom left):** National Archives and Records Administration; **(center right):** William West/AFP/Getty Images; **(center right):** Lisa F. Young/Shutterstock; **(top):** Grizelda/CSL, CartoonStock.

Biological Psychology

From Chapter 3 of *Psychology: From Inquiry to Understanding,* Third Edition. Scott O. Lilienfeld, Steven Jay Lynn, Laura L. Namy, Nancy J. Woolf. Copyright © 2014 by Pearson Education, Inc. All rights reserved.

Biological Psychology

BRIDGING THE LEVELS OF ANALYSIS

Think About It

Do specific regions on the brain's surface correspond to different personality traits?

Do we use only about 10 percent of our brain's capacity?

Can we trace complex psychological functions, like religious belief, to specific brain regions?

Are there left- and right-brained people?

Is the heritability of a trait fixed within populations, or can it change from one year to another?

Biological Psychology

Listen in **MyPsychLab** to chapter audio

July 31, 2001 started normally for Howard Engel, a well-known Canadian author of detective novels. As he did every other morning, Engel made himself breakfast and opened his front door to grab his newspaper. When he did, he noticed something exceedingly odd (Sacks, 2010).

Engel could see the newspaper just fine, and he could tell that it contained words. Yet the words that he had read effortlessly for most of the 70 years of his life suddenly looked like gibberish. They seemed to be written in a bizarre language, much like Egyptian hieroglyphics. He initially wondered whether this was all a prank pulled on newspaper readers by the editors, but when he looked at one of the books in his collection, he found to his horror that the words were written in the same nonsensical language.

Engel soon learned that he had experienced a serious stroke. A stroke is in essence a "brain attack," a loss of neural tissue stemming from a sudden cut-off of blood supply to the brain. Engel's stroke, it turns out, damaged the area of his brain that allows us to read by sight, producing a rare condition called "word blindness."

Yet over time, Engel learned to compensate for the deficits caused by his stroke, and regained his ability to read. Remarkably, he found that he could trace the shape of words using his tongue. By quickly tracing the shapes of letters with his tongue and transferring these shapes to his front teeth, Engel discovered a different way to read. Moreover, his brain had learned to reorganize itself, delegating the functions that allow us to read from its visual areas to its touch areas.

Today, none of us is surprised to learn that Howard Engel's striking deficits stemmed from damage to his brain. In the early twenty-first century, we take for granted the fact that the brain is the seat of psychological activity, including reading, memorizing, and thinking. When we struggle with a difficult homework problem, we say that "our brains hurt"; when we consult friends for advice about a complicated question, we "pick their brains"; and when we compliment others' intelligence, we call them "brainiacs." Yet throughout much of human history, it seemed self-evident that the brain *wasn't* the prime location for our memories, thoughts, and emotions.

For example, the ancient Egyptians believed that the heart was the seat of the human soul and the brain was irrelevant to mental life (Finger, 2000; Raulin, 2003). Egyptians often prepared corpses for mummification by scooping their brains out through the nostrils using an iron hook (you'll be pleased to know that no drawings of this practice survive today) (Leek, 1969). Although some ancient Greeks correctly pinpointed the brain as the source of the psyche, others, like the great philosopher Aristotle, were convinced that the brain functions merely as a radiator, cooling the heart when it becomes overheated. Even today, we can find holdovers of this way of thinking in our everyday language. When we memorize something, we come to know it "by heart" (Finger, 2000), and when we're devastated by the loss of a romantic relationship, we feel "heartbroken."

CORRELATION VS. CAUSATION ▶
Can we be sure that A causes B?

Why were so many of the ancients certain that the heart, not the brain, was the source of mental activity? It's probably because they trusted their "common sense," which as we've learned is often a poor signpost of scientific truth. They noticed that when people become excited, angry, scared, or passionate, their hearts pound quickly, whereas their brains seem to be doing little or nothing. Therefore, they reasoned, the heart must be causing these emotional reactions. By confusing correlation with causation, the ancients' intuitions probably misled them.

Today, we recognize that the mushy pinkish organ lying between our two ears is by far the most complicated structure in the known universe. Our brain has the consistency of gelatin, and it weighs a mere 3 pounds. Despite its rather unimpressive appearance, it's capable of astonishing feats. As poet Robert Frost wrote, "The brain is a wonderful organ. It starts working the moment you get up in the morning and does not stop until you get into the office."

In recent decades, scientists have made huge technological strides that have taught us a great deal about how our brains work and helped them to correct age-old misconceptions (Aamodt & Wang, 2008). Researchers who study the relationship between the nervous system—a vast communication network consisting of nerve cells, both inside and outside of the brain and spinal cord—and behavior go by the names of *biological psychologists* or *neuroscientists.* By linking brain to behavior, these scientists often bridge multiple levels of analysis within psychology. The history of our evolving understanding of the brain provides a wonderful example of the self-correcting nature of science.

Nerve Cells: Communication Portals

1 Distinguish the parts of neurons and what they do.
2 Describe electrical responses of neurons and what makes them possible.
3 Explain how neurons use neurotransmitters to communicate with each other.
4 Describe how the brain changes as a result of development, learning, and injury.

If we wanted to understand how a car works, we'd open it up and identify its parts, like its engine, carburetor, and transmission, and figure out how they operate in tandem. Similarly, to understand how our brain works, we first need to get a handle on its key components and find out how they cooperate. To do so, we'll start with the brain's most basic unit of communication: its cells, and then examine how they work in concert to generate our thoughts, feelings, and behaviors.

Neurons: The Brain's Communicators

The functioning of our brain depends on cross-talk among **neurons**—nerve cells specialized for communication with each other (see **FIGURE 1**). Our brains contain about 85 billion neurons. To give you a sense of how enormous this number is, there are more than 10 times as many neurons in each of our brains as there are people on Earth. If we lined up all the neurons in our brain side to side, they would reach back and forth from New York to California five times. In turn, neurons make tens of thousands of connections with other neurons, permitting a staggering amount of inter-cellular communication. In total, there are probably about 160 *trillion* connections in the human brain, a number too large for any of us to grasp (Tang et al., 2001). Moreover, although our brains are much slower than our desktop computers or iPhones, they are still unmatched in many crucial psychological abilities. For example, no computer comes close to the human brain in its capacities for face or voice recognition (Li & Jain, 2011). You've probably discovered this if you've ever tried speaking to a computerized voice recognition system over the telephone and discovered that it couldn't understand what you were saying.

Although many cells have simple and regular shapes, neurons are markedly different. They have long extensions that help them respond to stimulation from other neurons and communicate with them. To understand how the neuron works, let's first look at the components that make it up.

THE CELL BODY. The *cell body*, also called the soma, is the central region of the neuron. It manufactures new cell components, which consist of small and large molecules (refer to Figure 1). Because the cell body contains the nucleus, where proteins are manufactured, damage to this part of the neuron is fatal. The cell body also provides continual renewal of cell components.

DENDRITES. Neurons contain multiple branchlike extensions for receiving information from other neurons. Like the receivers on our cell phones, these numerous **dendrites** spread out to "listen in" on conversations from neighboring neurons and pass them on to the cell body (refer to Figure 1).

AXONS AND AXON TERMINALS. If dendrites are like cell phone receivers, **axons** are the transmitters. They're specialized for sending messages to other neurons. These long tail-like extensions are usually very thin near the cell body. This narrowness creates an area that's easily activated by incoming signals. Tiny spheres called **synaptic vesicles** travel the length

Factoid

Despite what many people believe, alcohol doesn't actually kill brain cells. But that doesn't mean it's a safe to drink heavily, because alcohol may damage or destroy some of the dendrites of nerve cells (Aamodt & Wang, 2007; O'Connor, 2007). This finding may explain the origin of this false belief, because prolonged heavy drinking does shrink brain volume.

Explore in **MyPsychLab** the **Concept:** the Structure of a Neuron

Neurons and their dendrites (shown stained blue) with their nuclei (shown stained pink).

neuron
nerve cell specialized for communication

dendrite
portion of neuron that receives signals

axon
portion of neuron that sends signals

synaptic vesicle
spherical sac containing neurotransmitters

Dendrite
Projection that picks up impulses from other neurons

Synapse
Terminal point of axon branch, which releases neurotransmitters

Node
Gap in the myelin sheath of an axon, which helps the conduction of nerve impulses

Action potential

Neuron

Action potential

Synapse

Nucleus

Axon terminal
(Synaptic knob)

Axon
Nerve fiber projecting from the cell body that carries nerve impulses

Myelin sheath
Fatty coat that insulates the axons of some nerve cells, speeding transmission of impulses

Cell body
Materials needed by the neuron are made here

FIGURE 1 A Neuron with a Myelin Sheath. Neurons receive chemical messages from other neurons by way of synaptic contacts with dendrites. Next, neurons send action potentials down along their axons, some of which are coated with myelin to make the electrical signal travel faster. (*Source:* Modified from Dorling Kindersley)

of the axon on their way to a knoblike structure at its far end called the *axon terminal* (see **FIGURE 2**). When the synaptic vesicle reaches the end of its little journey at the axon terminal, it bursts, releasing **neurotransmitters,** chemical messengers that neurons use to communicate with each other. We can think of the synaptic vesicles as similar to gel capsules filled with cold medicine. When we swallow a capsule, its exterior dissolves and the medicine inside it moves down our digestive tracts.

SYNAPSES. Once released from the synaptic vesicle, neurotransmitters enter the **synapse,** a tiny fluid-filled space between neurons through which neurotransmitters travel. The synapse consists of a **synaptic cleft,** a gap into which neurotransmitters are released from the axon terminal. This gap is surrounded by small patches of membrane on each side,

neurotransmitter
chemical messenger specialized for communication from neuron to neuron

synapse
space between two connecting neurons through which messages are transmitted chemically

synaptic cleft
a gap into which neurotransmitters are released from the axon terminal

one on the sending axon of the first neuron and the other on the receiving dendrite of the second neuron. As neurotransmitters are released from the axon of a cell into the synapse, they're picked up quickly by the dendrites of nearby neurons, just as cell phone receivers quickly pick up signals from other cell phones.

Glial Cells

Neurons aren't the only players in our nervous systems: **Glial cells** ("glial" means glue) are also remarkably plentiful. Although researchers once thought that glial cells greatly outnumbered neurons, by as much as 10:1, recent research suggests that the ratio is much lower, and closer to 1:1 (Azevedo et al., 2009). Glial cells perform a variety of functions. Scientists once regarded them as nothing more than a sort of protective scaffolding for the neurons held by synapses. Nevertheless, over the past 20 years or so, researchers have realized that glial cells do much more (Fields, 2009).

The most abundant of glial cells are *astrocytes*. A single astrocyte interacts with as many as 300,000–1,000,000 neurons. Astrocytes communicate closely with neurons, increase the reliability of their transmission, control blood flow in the brain, and play a vital role in the development of the embryo (Metea & Newman, 2006). Astrocytes, in concert with other glial cells, are intimately involved in thought, memory, and the immune system (Gibbs & Bowser, 2009; Koob, 2009).

We can find astrocytes in abundant supply in the *blood–brain barrier*, a protective shield that insulates the brain from infection by bacteria and other intruders. Tiny blood vessels are wrapped with a fatty coating, blocking large molecules, highly charged particles, and molecules that dissolve in water but not fat from entering the brain.

Another type of glial cell, an *oligodendrocyte*, promotes new connections among nerve cells and releases chemicals to aid in healing. In addition, this cell produces an insulating wrapper around axons called the **myelin sheath.** This sheath contains numerous gaps all the way along the axon called *nodes*, which help the neuron conduct electricity more efficiently (refer again to Figure 1). Much like a person playing hopscotch, the neural signal jumps from node to node, speeding up its transmission. The importance of the myelin sheath is illustrated in sufferers of multiple sclerosis. In this autoimmune disease, the myelin sheaths surrounding neurons are progressively "eaten away," resulting in a loss of insulation of neural messages. As a consequence, these messages become hopelessly scrambled, resulting in a wide variety of physical and emotional symptoms.

Glial cells also clear away debris, acting as the brain's cellular garbage disposals. Treatments that target glial cells may one day assist in treating a variety of conditions related to the number and activity of these cells, including depression and schizophrenia (Cotter, Pariant, & Everall, 2001; Schroeter et al., 2009), as well as inflammation, chronic pain, and Alzheimer's disease (Suter et al., 2007).

Electrifying Thought

Neurons respond to neurotransmitters by generating electrical activity (see **FIGURE 3**). We know this to be true because scientists have recorded electrical activity from neurons using *electrodes*, small devices made from wire or fine glass tubes. These electrodes allow researchers to measure the *potential difference* in electrical charge inside versus outside the neuron. The basis of all electrical responses in neurons depends on an uneven distribution of charged particles across the membrane surrounding the neuron (see Figure 3). Some particles are positively charged, others negatively charged. When there are no neurotransmitters acting on the neuron, the membrane is at the **resting potential.** In this baseline state, when the neuron isn't doing much of anything, there are more negative particles inside than outside the neuron. In some large neurons, the voltage of the resting potential is about one-twentieth that of a flashlight battery, or about −60 millivolts (the negative sign means the inside charge is more negative than outside). While at rest,

FIGURE 2 The Axon Terminal. The axon terminal contains synaptic vesicles filled with neurotransmitter molecules.

Factoid

Recent research reveals that Albert Einstein's brain contained twice as many glial cells as do typical brains (Fields, 2009). We must be cautious in drawing conclusions from case study evidence, this intriguing finding may fit with evidence that glial cells play key roles in neural transmission.

glial cell
cell in nervous system that plays a role in the formation of myelin and the blood–brain barrier, responds to injury, removes debris, and enhances learning and memory

myelin sheath
glial cells wrapped around axons that act as insulators of the neuron's signal

resting potential
electrical charge difference (−60 millivolts) across the neuronal membrane, when the neuron is not being stimulated or inhibited

FIGURE 3 The Action Potential. When a neuron is at rest there are positive and negative ions on both sides of the membrane. During an action potential, positive ions rush in and then out of the axon. This process recurs along the axon until the axon terminal releases neurotransmitters.

At rest.

During an action potential, positive particles rapidly flow into the axon.

When the inside of the axon accumulates maximal levels of positive charge, positive particles begin to flow back out of the axon.

Neurotransmitter release

Direction of action potential

When the action potential reaches the axon terminal, it triggers release of neurotransmitters.

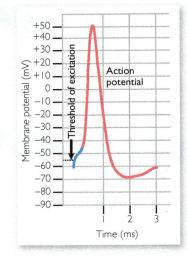

FIGURE 4 Voltage across the Membrane during the Action Potential. The membrane potential needed to trigger an action potential is called the *threshold*. Many neurons have a threshold of −55 mV. That means only 5 mV of current above resting (at −60 mV) is needed to trigger an action potential.

Factoid

The neurons of the largest animal on earth, the blue whale, contain axons that reach up to 60 feet.

threshold
membrane potential necessary to trigger an action potential

action potential
electrical impulse that travels down the axon triggering the release of neurotransmitters

absolute refractory period
time during which another action potential is impossible; limits maximal firing rate

receptor site
location that uniquely recognizes a neurotransmitter

particles of both types are flowing in and out of the membrane. When the electrical charge inside the neuron reaches a high enough level relative to the outside, called the **threshold,** an electrical impulse called an action potential is triggered.

ACTION POTENTIALS. Action potentials are the language of neurons; they're what they use to communicate. These potentials are abrupt waves of electric discharge triggered by a change in charge inside the axon. When this change occurs, we can describe the neuron as "firing," similar to the firing of a gun. Much like a gun, neurons obey the "all or none" law: They either fire or they don't. Action potentials originate in the trigger zone near the cell body and continue all the way down the axon to the axon terminal. During an action potential, positively charged particles flow rapidly into the axon and then flow out just as rapidly, causing a spike in positive charge followed by a sudden decrease in charge, with the inside charge ending up at a slightly more negative level than its original resting value (see **FIGURES 3** and **4**). These sudden shifts in charge produce a release of electricity. When the electrical charge reaches the axon terminal, it triggers the release of neurotransmitters—chemical messengers—into the synapse.

THE ABSOLUTE REFRACTORY PERIOD. Neurons can fire extremely rapidly, up to 100 to 1,000 times per second. At this very moment, energy is traveling down tens of millions of your axons at breakneck speeds of about 220 miles per hour. Pause to think about that fact for a moment; it's remarkable. Each action potential is followed by an **absolute refractory period,** a brief interval during which another action potential can't occur. This period limits the fastest rate at which a neuron can fire, much as it takes us a while to reload some guns after firing them. The rate at which action potentials travel becomes a limiting factor in very long axons, such as the sciatic nerve, which runs from the spinal cord down the leg. In humans, this axon extends a whopping 3 feet on average.

Chemical Communication: Neurotransmission

Whereas electrical events transmit information *within* neurons, chemical events triggered by neurotransmitters orchestrate communication *among* neurons. After neurotransmitters are released into the synapse, they bind with **receptor sites** along the dendrites of neighboring neurons. Much as a lock works for only one key, different receptor sites recognize different types of neurotransmitters (see **FIGURE 5**). We can think of each neurotransmitter as a key that unlocks only its own type of receptor.

Neurotransmission can be halted by **reuptake** of the neurotransmitter back into the axon terminal—a continually occurring process by which the synaptic vesicle reabsorbs the neurotransmitter. We can think of release and reuptake of the neurotransmitter as analogous to letting some liquid drip out of the bottom of a straw (release) and then sucking it back up again (reuptake). Reuptake is one of nature's recycling mechanisms.

NEUROTRANSMITTERS. Different neurotransmitters communicate different messages. Some *excite* the nervous system, increasing its activity, whereas others *inhibit* the nervous system, decreasing its activity. Some play a role in movement, others in pain perception, and still others in thinking and emotion. Let's now meet a few of the more prominent members of the neurotransmitter family (see **TABLE I**).

Glutamate and GABA. *Glutamate* and gamma-aminobutyric acid (*GABA*) are the most common neurotransmitters in the central nervous system (CNS), which as we'll later learn, consists of the brain and spinal cord. Neurons in virtually every brain area

FIGURE 5 The Lock-and-Key Model of Neurotransmitter Binding to Receptor Sites. Receptor sites are specialized to receive only certain types of neurotransmitters.

TABLE I Neurotransmitters and Their Major Functional Roles.

NEUROTRANSMITTER	SELECTED ROLES	DRUGS THAT INTERACT WITH THE NEUROTRANSMITTER SYSTEM
Glutamate	Main excitatory neurotransmitter in the nervous system; participates in relay of sensory information and learning	*Alcohol* and *memory enhancers* interact with N-methyl-D-aspartate (NMDA) receptors, a specific type of glutamate receptor.
Gamma-aminobutyric acid (GABA)	Main inhibitory neurotransmitter in the nervous system	*Alcohol* and *antianxiety drugs* increase GABA activity.
Acetylcholine (ACh)	Muscle contraction (PNS) Cortical arousal (CNS)	*Nicotine* stimulates ACh receptors. *Memory enhancers* increase ACh. *Insecticides* block the breakdown of ACh. *Botox* causes paralysis by blocking ACh.
Norepinephrine (NE)	Brain arousal and other functions like mood, hunger, and sleep	*Amphetamine* and *methamphetamine* increase NE.
Dopamine	Motor function and reward	*L-Dopa*, which increases dopamine, is used to treat *Parkinson's* disease. *Antipsychotic drugs*, which block dopamine action, are used to treat schizophrenia.
Serotonin	Mood and temperature regulation, aggression, and sleep cycles	*Serotonin-selective reuptake inhibitor (SSRI) antidepressants* are used to treat depression.
Anandamide	Pain reduction, increase in appetite	*Tetrahydrocannabinol (THC)*— found in marijuana—produces euphoria.
Endorphins	Pain reduction	*Narcotic drugs*—codeine, morphine, and heroin—reduce pain and produce euphoria.

reuptake
means of recycling neurotransmitters

use these two chemical messengers to communicate with each other (Cai et al., 2012; Fagg & Foster, 1983). Glutamate rapidly excites neurons, increasing the odds that they'll talk with other neurons. The release of glutamate is associated with enhanced learning and memory. When abnormally elevated, though, glutamate may contribute to schizophrenia and other mental disorders, because in high doses it can be toxic, damaging neural receptors by overstimulating them (Goff & Coyle, 2001; Karlsson et al., 2008).

GABA, in contrast, inhibits neurons, thereby dampening neural activity. That's why most anti-anxiety drugs bind to GABA receptors; they tend to suppress overactive brain areas linked to worry. GABA is a workhorse in our nervous systems, playing critical roles in learning, memory, and sleep (Gottesman, 2002; Jacobson et al., 2007; Wang & Kriegstein, 2009). Scientists are intrigued by the promise of drugs that target GABA to one day treat a variety of conditions, including anxiety disorders, insomnia, depression, and epilepsy (Gerard & Aybala, 2007; Mann & Mody, 2008; Winkelman et al., 2008).

Acetylcholine. Acetylcholine plays roles in arousal, selective attention, sleep, and memory (McKinney & Jacksonville, 2005; Woolf, 1991). In Alzheimer's disease, neurons containing acetylcholine (and several other neurotransmitters) are gradually destroyed, leading to severe memory loss. Medications that alleviate some of the memory-related symptoms of Alzheimer's, like Aricept (its generic name is Donezepil), boost acetylcholine levels in the brain. Neurons that connect directly to muscle cells also release acetylcholine, allowing them to trigger movement. That's how most insecticides work; they limit the breakdown of acetylcholine (allowing more acetylcholine to stick around the synapse), causing insects to engage in violent, uncontrolled movements that that kill them.

Monoamines. *Norepinephrine, dopamine*, and *serotonin* are the monoamine neurotransmitters (they're called "monoamines" because they contain only one amino acid, the building block of proteins). Dopamine plays a critical role in the rewarding experiences that occur when we seek out or anticipate goals, whether they be sex, a fine meal, or a gambling jackpot (Schultz, 2012). Research even shows that brain areas rich in dopamine become active when we hear a funny joke (Mobbs et al., 2003). Norepinephrine and serotonin activate or deactivate various parts of the brain, influencing arousal and our readiness to respond to stimuli (Jones, 2003).

Anandamide. We knew about marijuana and its active ingredient, *tetrahydrocannabinol* (THC), long before we understood how they worked. The neurotransmitter anandamide helped scientists to solve this mystery. Cells in our bodies, like neurons, make anandamide, which binds to the same receptors as THC. Anandamide plays roles in eating, motivation, memory, and sleep, which may explain why marijuana often gives people "the munchies," not to mention makes them sleepy.

Neuropeptides. Neuropeptides are short strings of amino acids (the building blocks of proteins) in the nervous system. They act somewhat like neurotransmitters, but they tend to be more narrowly targeted in their jobs. **Endorphins** are a type of neuropeptide that play a specialized role in pain reduction (Holden, Jeong, & Forrest, 2005). They were discovered in the early 1970s by neuroscientists Candace Pert and Solomon Snyder, who were trying to pinpoint the physiological mechanisms of opioids, drugs such as morphine and codeine that produce pain relief and euphoria. Remarkably, they discovered that our brains contain their own receptors for endogenous, or naturally occurring, opioids—endorphins (Pert, Pasternak, & Snyder, 1973). So human-made opioids, like morphine, exert their effects by "hijacking" the endorphin system, binding to endorphin receptors and mimicking their effects. Our brains contain a host of other neuropeptides; some regulate hunger and satiety (fullness), and others learning and memory.

NEUROTRANSMITTERS AND PSYCHOACTIVE DRUGS. Scientists have developed specific medications to target the production or inhibition of certain neurotransmitters (refer again to Table 1). Drugs that interact with neurotransmitter systems are called *psychoactive*, meaning they affect mood, arousal, or behavior.

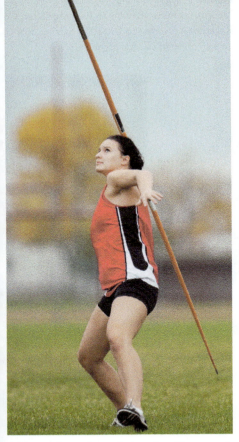

Athletes often rely on their endorphins to push them through intense pain.

endorphin
chemical in the brain that plays a specialized role in pain reduction

Knowing how psychoactive drugs interact with neurotransmitter systems often allows us to predict how they'll affect us psychologically. Opiates, such as codeine and morphine, function as *agonists*, meaning they increase receptor site activity. They reduce our emotional response to painful stimuli by binding with opioid receptors (the receptors discovered by Pert and Snyder) and mimicking endorphins (Evans, 2004). Tranquilizers, like Xanax (whose generic name is Alprazolam), diminish anxiety by stimulating GABA receptor sites, thereby driving down neuronal activity (Roy-Byrne, 2005). As we've already seen with insecticides, still other drugs block the reuptake of neurotransmitters. Many antidepressants, like Prozac (whose generic name is Fluoxetine) and Paxil (whose generic name is Paroxetine), inhibit the reuptake of certain neurotransmitters, especially serotonin, from the synapse (Schatzberg, 1998). By allowing these neurotransmitters to remain in the synapse longer than usual, they enhance these neurotransmitters' effects on receptor sites—much as we can heighten the pleasurable sensations of a delicious food by keeping it in our mouths a bit longer than usual.

Some drugs work in the opposite way, functioning as *antagonists*, meaning they decrease receptor site activity (think of the word "antagonistic"). Most medications used to treat schizophrenia block dopamine receptors by binding to them, thereby blocking dopamine from binding to the receptors themselves (Bennett, 1998; Compton & Broussard, 2009). In essence, they act as "fake neurotransmitters," fooling receptors into thinking they are dopamine without exerting the effects of this neurotransmitter.

Neural Plasticity: How and When the Brain Changes

We'll conclude our guided tour of neurons by looking at the ability of the nervous system to change. Nature—our genetic makeup—influences what kind of changes are possible and when they'll occur during the long and winding road from birth to old age. Nurture, consisting of learning, life events, injuries, and illnesses, affects our genetically influenced course. Scientists use the term **plasticity** to describe the nervous system's ability to change. We can talk about brain circuits being "hardwired" when they don't change much, if at all.

But despite what the popular media often implies, few human behaviors are "hardwired." The nervous system is continually changing, by leaps and bounds, as in early development, or more subtly, as with learning. Unfortunately, the nervous system often doesn't change enough following injury or stroke, which can lead to permanent paralysis and disability.

NEURAL PLASTICITY OVER DEVELOPMENT. Typically, our brain is most flexible during early development, when much of our nervous system has yet to be set in stone. Our brains don't mature fully until late adolescence or early adulthood. Some brain structures mature more rapidly than others. So some parts of the brain are quite plastic throughout childhood, but others lose their extreme plasticity in infancy. Yet as the remarkable case of George Engel we encountered at the outset of the text illustrates, our brains are capable of plasticity even in our later years.

The network of neurons in the brain changes over the course of development in four primary ways:

1. *growth* of dendrites and axons;

2. *synaptogenesis*, the formation of new synapses;

3. *pruning*, consisting of the death of certain neurons and the retraction of axons to remove connections that aren't useful; and

4. *myelination*, the insulation of axons with a myelin sheath.

Of these four steps, pruning is probably the most surprising. During pruning, as many as 70 percent of all neurons die off. This process is helpful, though, because it streamlines neural organization, thereby enhancing communication among brain structures (Oppenheim, 1991).

Watch in **MyPsychLab** the **Video:** Brain Building

plasticity
ability of the nervous system to change

In a real sense, less is more, because our brains can often process information more efficiently with fewer neurons. One theory of infantile autism suggests that this disorder is caused by inadequate pruning (Hill & Frith, 2003), which may explain why individuals with autism tend to have unusually large brains (Herbert, 2005).

NEURAL PLASTICITY AND LEARNING. Our brains change as we learn. These changes can result from the formation of new synapses, generating increased connections and communication among neurons. They can also result from the strengthening of existing synaptic connections, so that the neurotransmitters released into synapses produce a stronger and more prolonged response from neighboring neurons. Researchers call this second phenomenon potentiation.

Many scientists believe that structural plasticity, that is, change in the shape of neurons, is also critical for learning (Woolf, 2006). In one study, researchers trained rats to swim to a platform hidden in a tub of milky water. By the time the rats became adept at doing so, axons entering a part of their brains relevant to spatial ability had expanded (Holahan et al., 2006). Exposure to enriched environments also results in structural enhancements to dendrites. For example, rats exposed to an enriched environment—such as large cages with multiple animals, toys, and running wheels—develop more elaborate dendrites with more branches than do rats exposed to a standard environment of a cage with only two animals and no objects (Freire & Cheng, 2004; Leggio et al., 2005; see **FIGURE 6**).

FIGURE 6 Neurons in Standard and Enriched Conditions. Neurons of rats reared in enriched conditions (*bottom*) show more branching and extensions of dendrites than do neurons of rats reared in standard conditions (*top*).

NEURAL PLASTICITY FOLLOWING INJURY AND DEGENERATION. The human brain and spinal cord display only limited regeneration following injury or serious illness. Yet as probably occurred with George Engel, certain brain regions can sometimes take over the functions previously performed by others. For example, in blind people, the capacity to read Braille (a system of raised dots that correspond to letters in the alphabet) with the fingers is taken over by brain regions associated with vision in sighted people (Hamilton & Pascual-Leone, 1998).

Scientists are trying to find ways to enhance the brain and spinal cord's abilities to repair themselves following injury (Maier & Schwab, 2006). Because degenerative disorders, such as Alzheimer's disease and Parkinson's disease, pose enormous challenges to society, scientists are actively investigating ways of preventing damage or enabling the brain to heal itself.

Adult Neurogenesis. Neurogenesis is the creation of new neurons in the adult brain. Fewer than 20 years ago, most scientists were sure that we're born with all the neurons we'll ever have. Then, Fred Gage (interestingly, a descendant of Phineas Gage, whom we'll meet later in the text), Elizabeth Gould, and their colleagues discovered that in adult monkeys, neurogenesis occurs in certain brain areas (Gage, 2002; Gould & Gross, 2002). The odds are high that neurogenesis occurs in adult human brains, too. By triggering neurogenesis, scientists may one day be able to induce the adult nervous system to heal itself (Kozorovitskiy & Gould, 2003; Lie et al., 2004). Neurogenesis may also play a useful role in learning (Aimone, Wiles, & Gage, 2006).

Senile plaques (large yellow/black splotch on lower left) and neurofibrillary tangles (smaller yellow spots) in the brain of a patient with Alzheimer's disease. The degeneration in several brain regions may contribute to the memory loss and intellectual decline associated with this disorder.

Stem Cells. Many of us have heard or read about research on stem cells, especially embryonic stem cells, in the news. One reason they've garnered so much attention is **stem cells** haven't yet committed themselves to a specific function, so they have the potential to become a wide variety of specialized cells (see **FIGURE 7**). This is akin to being a first-year undergraduate who has yet to declare a major: He or she might become nearly anything. Once the cell begins to specialize, though, the cell type becomes more permanently cast, much like an undergraduate who's spent 3 years taking pre-med courses. Stem cells offer several ways of treating diseases marked by neural degeneration (Fukuda & Takahashi, 2005; Miller, 2006; Muller, Snyder, & Loring, 2006). For example, researchers can implant stem cells directly into the host's nervous system and induce them to grow and replace damaged cells. In addition, researchers can genetically engineer stem cells to provide gene therapy—that is, provide the patient with replacement genes.

neurogenesis
creation of new neurons in the adult brain

stem cell
a cell, often originating in embryos, having the capacity to differentiate into a more specialized cell

Yet stem cell research is exceedingly controversial for ethical reasons. Although its advocates champion its potential for treating serious diseases, including Alzheimer's, diabetes, and some cancers, its opponents point out that such research requires investigators to create and then extract lab-created balls of cells that are 4 or 5 days old (which at that stage are smaller than the period at the end of this sentence). For opponents of stem cell research, these cells are an early form of human life. Certain profoundly important questions are metaphysical and therefore lie outside the boundaries of science: Science deals only with testable claims within the realm of the natural world (Gould, 1997). The question of whether stem cell research may one day cure diseases falls within the scope of science, but the question of whether such research is ethical doesn't. Nor, in all likelihood, can science ever resolve definitively the question of when human life begins (Buckle, Dawson, & Singer, 1989). As a consequence, reasonable people will continue to disagree on whether stem cell research should be performed.

Stem cells yield different cell types with different growth factors

Muscle

Blood

Neurons

FIGURE 7 Stem Cells and Growth Factors. Stem cells have the capacity to become many different cell types depending on the growth factors to which they're exposed.

Study and **Review** in **MyPsychLab**

Assess Your Knowledge — FACT or FICTION?

1. Dendrites are the sending portions of neurons.   **True / False**
2. Positive particles flowing into the neuron inhibit its action.   **True / False**
3. Neurotransmitters send messages between neurons.   **True / False**
4. Some antidepressants block the reuptake of serotonin from the synapse.   **True / False**
5. Neurogenesis is equivalent to pruning.   **True / False**

Answers: 1. F; 2. F; 3. T; 4. T; 5. F

The Brain–Behavior Network

5 Identify what roles different parts of the central nervous system play in behavior.

6 Clarify how the somatic and autonomic nervous systems work in emergency and everyday situations.

The connections among neurons provide the physiological bases of our thoughts, emotions, and behaviors. But how do we get from electrical charges and the release of neurotransmitters to complex behaviors, like writing a term paper or asking someone out for a date? Let's say we decide to walk to a vending machine to buy a can of soda. How does our brain, this motley collection of tens of billions of neurons, accomplish this feat? First, our brain decides to do so—or so it seems. Second, our nervous system propels our body into action. Third, we need to locate and operate the vending machine. We must accurately identify the machine based on how it looks and feels, insert the right amount of money, and retrieve our soda to take a well-deserved sip. Communication among neurons in the vast network of connections we call our nervous system allows us to take these complex actions for granted.

We can think of our nervous system as a superhighway with a two-way flow of traffic. Sensory information comes into—and decisions to act come out of—the **central nervous system (CNS)**. The CNS is composed of the brain and spinal cord, whereas the **peripheral nervous system (PNS)** (see **FIGURE 8**) is composed of all the nerves that extend outside of the CNS. The PNS is further divided into the somatic nervous system, which controls voluntary behavior, and the autonomic nervous system, which controls nonvoluntary functions of the body. When you see the word "autonomic" prior to nervous system, think of the similar word "automatic," because the autonomic nervous system controls behaviors that occur automatically, that is, outside of our conscious awareness.

Factoid

Years of professional football may be bad for our brain's health. A study of over 3,400 individuals who had played in the National Football League for five or more seasons from 1959 to 1988 revealed that they were more than three times more likely to die from degenerative brain illnesses, such as Alzheimer's disease and amyotrophic lateral sclerosis (also known as Lou Gehrig's disease, after the baseball player who died of it), than individuals in the general population. The risk was especially high for players in high-speed positions, like receivers and running backs, probably because they sustain especially severe injuries (Lehman et al., 2012).

central nervous system (CNS)
part of nervous system containing brain and spinal cord that controls the mind and behavior

peripheral nervous system (PNS)
nerves in the body that extend outside the central nervous system (CNS)

FIGURE 8 The Nervous System Exerts Control over the Body. *(Source: Modified from Dorling Kindersley)*

Cerebral cortex

Cerebellum

Nerve that allows the facial muscles to move

Nerve that allows toes to flex and curve

Nerve that controls the muscles that lift the foot

Nerve that serves the hip joint and hamstring

Spinal cord
Nerve cable that emerges from the base of the brain and extends down about two-thirds of the length of the vertebral column

Nerve that conveys sensation from the forearm and controls the muscles that straighten the elbow and fingers

Nerves emerging from the lumbar region of the spine join in a group that supplies the lower back and parts of the thighs and legs

Nerve that controls the muscles that straighten the knee

The Central Nervous System: The Command Center

Scientists divide the CNS into six distinct sections or systems (see **TABLE 2**). The brain and spinal cord are protected by *meninges*, three thin layers of membranes. Further protection is afforded by the **cerebral ventricles**, fluid-filled pockets that extend throughout the entire

TABLE 2 The Organization of the Central Nervous System.

Central Nervous System	
Cortex	**FrontalLobe:** performs executive functions that coordinate other brain areas, motor planning, language, and memory
	ParietalLobe: processes touch information, integrates vision and touch
	Temporal Lobe: processes auditory information, language, and autobiographical memory
	Occipital Lobe: processes visual information
Basal Ganglia	control movement and motor planning
Limbic system	**Thalamus:** conveys sensory information to cortex
	Hypothalamus: oversees endocrine and autonomic nervous system
	Amygdala: regulates arousal and fear
	Hippocampus: processes memory for spatial locations
Cerebellum	controls balance and coordinated movement
Brain Stem	**Midbrain:** tracks visual stimuli and reflexes triggered by sound
	Pons: conveys information between the cortex and cerebellum
	Medulla: regulates breathing and heartbeats
Spinal Cord	conveys information between the brain and the rest of the body

cerebral ventricles
pockets in the brain that contain cerebrospinal fluid (CSF), which provide the brain with nutrients and cushion against injury

FIGURE 9 The Human Brain: A Simple Map.
(Source: Modified from Dorling Kindersley)

Forebrain (including cerebral cortex) The site of most of the brain's conscious functions

Corpus callosum Bundle of nerve fibers connecting the cerebrum's two hemispheres

Hypothalamus Partly controls the body's endocrine, or hormone-producing, system

Thalamus Area that relays nerve signals to the cerebral cortex

Cerebellum Regulates balance and body control

Brain stem Regulates control of involuntary functions such as breathing and heart rate

Left cerebral hemisphere

Right cerebral hemisphere

Corpus callosum

FIGURE 10 The Cerebral Hemispheres and the Corpus Callosum. The corpus callosum connects the two cerebral hemispheres.

brain and spinal cord. A clear liquid, called *cerebrospinal fluid* (CSF), runs through these ventricles and bathes our brain and spinal cord, providing nutrients and cushioning us against injury. This fluid is the CNS's shock absorber, allowing us to move our heads rapidly in everyday life without sustaining brain damage.

As we review different brain regions, bear in mind that although they serve different functions, they cooperate seamlessly to generate our thoughts, feelings, and behaviors (see **FIGURE 9**). We'll begin our guided tour of the brain with the part of the brain studied most extensively by psychologists.

Central sulcus

Frontal lobe

Parietal lobe

Occipital lobe

Temporal lobe

FIGURE 11 The Four Lobes of the Cerebral Cortex. The cerebral cortex consists of four interacting lobes: frontal, parietal, temporal, and occipital.

THE CEREBRAL CORTEX. The **cerebral cortex** analyzes sensory information, helping us to perform complex brain functions, including reasoning and language. It's the largest component of the *cerebrum* or **forebrain,** the most highly developed area of the human brain, containing some 12 to 20 billion neurons, and accounting for about 40% of its volume. The cerebrum gives us our advanced intellectual abilities—which explains why it's of such keen interest to psychologists. The cerebrum consists of two **cerebral hemispheres** (see **FIGURE 10**). These hemispheres look alike but serve somewhat different functions. Nevertheless, like two figure skaters in a pairs competition, they communicate and cooperate continually. A huge band of fibers called the **corpus callosum,** meaning "colossal body" in Latin, connects the two hemispheres and permits them to communicate (see Figure 10).

The cerebral cortex is the outermost part of the cerebrum. It's aptly named, because *cortex* means "bark," as the cortex surrounds the hemispheres much like bark on a tree. In turn, the cortex contains four regions called *lobes,* each associated with somewhat different functions (see **FIGURE 11**). Each of our hemispheres contains the same four lobes; they are the next stops in our tour.

cerebral cortex
outermost part of forebrain, responsible for analyzing sensory processing and higher brain functions

forebrain (cerebrum)
forward part of the brain that allows advanced intellectual abilities

cerebral hemispheres
two halves of the cerebral cortex, each of which serve distinct yet highly integrated functions

corpus callosum
large band of fibers connecting the two cerebral hemispheres

FIGURE 12 Representation of the Body Mapped onto the Motor and Sensory Areas of the Cerebral Cortex. The brain networks with the body in a systematic way, with specific regions of both the motor and primary sensory cortex mapping onto specific regions of the body.

FIGURE 13 Selected Areas of the Cerebral Cortex. The prefrontal cortex controls various aspects of behavior and personality. Broca's area is vital for the formation of speech, and Wernicke's area interprets spoken and written language. Other cortical areas include the motor cortex, primary sensory areas, and association areas.

frontal lobe
forward part of cerebral cortex responsible for motor function, language, memory, and planning

motor cortex
part of frontal lobe responsible for body movement

prefrontal cortex
part of frontal lobe responsible for thinking, planning, and language

Broca's area
language area in the prefrontal cortex that helps to control speech production

REPLICABILITY ▶
Can the results be duplicated in other studies?

Frontal Lobes. The **frontal lobes** lie in the forward part of the cerebral cortex. If you touch your forehead right now, your fingers are less than an inch away from your frontal lobes. The frontal lobes assist us in motor function (movement), language, and memory. They also oversee and organize most other brain functions, a process called *executive functioning.* Just as the U.S. president exerts control over the members of his (and surely one day, her) Cabinet, the brain's executive function provides a kind of top-level governance over other cognitive functions.

In most people's brains, a deep groove, called the *central sulcus,* separates the frontal lobe from the rest of the cortex. The **motor cortex** is the part of the frontal lobe that lies next to the central sulcus. Each part of the motor cortex controls a specific part of the body, with regions requiring more precise motor control, like our fingers, consuming more cortical space (see **FIGURE 12**).

In front of the motor cortex lies a vast expanse of the frontal lobe called the **prefrontal cortex,** which is responsible for thinking, planning, and language (see **FIGURE 13**). One region of the prefrontal cortex, **Broca's area,** is named after French surgeon Paul Broca, who discovered that it plays a key role in language production (Broca, 1861). Broca found that this site was damaged in many patients who were having trouble generating speech. His first patient with this strange condition, known by the name of "Tan," responded only with the word "Tan" when asked questions. Broca soon recognized that brain damage in Tan and other patients with this speech disorder was almost always confined to the left cerebral hemisphere, a finding replicated by many researchers.

The prefrontal cortex, which receives information from many other regions of the cerebral cortex, also contributes to mood, personality, and self-awareness (Chayer & Freedman, 2001; Fuster, 2000). The tragic story of Phineas Gage demonstrates how crucial the prefrontal cortex can be to personality.

Gage was a railroad foreman who experienced a horrific accident in 1848. His job was to build railroad tracks running through rural Vermont. Gage was performing his usual task of filling holes with gunpowder to break up stubborn rock formations. He was pressing gunpowder into one hole with a tamping iron when an explosion suddenly propelled the iron with great velocity through his head. The iron pierced Gage's face under his cheekbone and destroyed much of his prefrontal cortex. Remarkably, Gage survived but he was never the same. His physician, J. M. Harlow (1848), described Gage's personality after the accident as

> fitful, irreverent, indulging at times in the grossest profanity (which was not previously his custom) . . . his mind was radically changed, so decidedly that his friends and acquaintances said he was "no longer Gage."

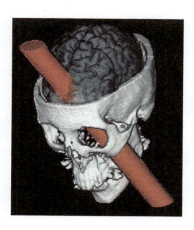

A computer-generated image showing the tamping iron that pierced through the skull and frontal lobes of Phineas Gage.

Admittedly, we don't know exactly what Gage was like before the accident, and some scholars have contended that his personality didn't change as much as is often claimed (Macmillan, 2000). We do know more about the exact location of Gage's brain damage, however. Hanna Damasio and her colleagues (1994) examined the skull of Phineas Gage with brain imaging techniques and confirmed that both the right and left sides of his prefrontal cortex were seriously damaged. History tragically repeated itself in August of 2012, when the frontal lobe of an Argentinian construction worker named Eduardo Leite was impaled by a 6-foot pole. Amazingly, Leite survived and appears to be doing well, but it's too early to tell whether he will emerge free of personality difficulties (MacKinnon, 2012).

Parietal Lobe. The **parietal lobe** is the upper middle part of the cerebral cortex lying behind the frontal lobe (refer to Figure 11). The back region of the parietal lobe, lying just behind the motor cortex, is the primary sensory cortex, which is sensitive to touch, including pressure and pain, and temperature (Figure 12). The parietal lobe helps us track objects' locations (Nachev & Husain, 2006; Shomstein & Yantis, 2006), shapes, and orientations. It also helps us process others' actions and represent numbers (Gobel & Rushworth, 2004). The parietal lobe relays visual and touch information to the motor cortex every time we reach, grasp, and move our eyes (Culham & Valyear, 2006). If you close your eyes right now and try to imagine how the pillow on your bed feels, you can conjure up a mental image of that soft, fluffy, sensation. That's your parietal lobe at work.

In 2009, this photograph of a man believed by historians to be Phineas Gage surfaced (Wilgus & Wilgus, 2009). One can clearly see (a) Gage holding the huge tamping rod that passed through his frontal lobes, (b) his missing left eye, which was destroyed by the rod, and (c) a tuft of hair on the left side of his head, presumably covering the region of his scalp from which the rod exited.

Because of the role of the parietal lobe in spatial perception, patients with parietal damage often have a hard time making sense of their immediate surroundings, even their own bodies. One frequent consequence of parietal lobe damage is a neglect of the opposite side of the body from where the damage happened (the neglect occurs on the opposite side because brain pathways cross over to the other side of the body; Mattingly, 1999). One patient, Mrs. S., who experienced a serious stroke in her right parietal lobe, routinely put make-up only on the right side of her face and ignored the left half of her body. She often went hungry because she noticed food only on the left side of plates, even though it was technically within her field of vision. Fortunately, she was able to solve this problem by shifting her wheelchair slightly to the right after eating her food so that she attended to the remainder of her plate (Gautier, 2011).

Temporal Lobe. The **temporal lobe** is the prime site of hearing, understanding language, and storing memories of our past (look again at Figure 11). This lobe is separated from the rest of the cortex by a horizontal groove called the *lateral fissure.*

parietal lobe
upper middle part of the cerebral cortex lying behind the frontal lobe that is specialized for touch and perception

temporal lobe
lower part of cerebral cortex that plays roles in hearing, understanding language, and memory

The top of the temporal lobe contains the *auditory cortex*, the part of the cortex devoted to hearing. The language area in the temporal lobe is called **Wernicke's area**, although this area also includes the lower parietal lobe (look again at Figure 13). It's located slightly above and behind your left ear (unless you're a lefty, in which case it might be above your right ear). Damage to Wernicke's area results in severe difficulties with understanding speech. Moreover, patients with damage to this area tend to speak mostly in gibberish, probably because they don't realize that the words coming out of their mouths don't make sense. When asked what the saying "Strike while the iron is hot" means, one patient with damage to this area responded in part that: "Ambition is very very and determined. Better to be good and to Post Office and Pillar Box and to distribution and to mail and survey and headmaster" (Kinsbourne & Warrington, 1963, p. 29).

from inquiry to understanding

HOW DO WE RECOGNIZE FACES?

Imagine what it would be like to pass your best friend on the street and not recognize her, or to mistake your date for a complete stranger—or vice-versa! Face recognition is vital to our ability to navigate our social worlds, not to mention follow the plot of a movie containing a slew of characters (Russell et al., 2009). It's a remarkable capacity that we typically take for granted. How can psychological science help to explain our ability to recognize faces?

In an effort to explain how facial recognition works, it is helpful to look at cases of people who are unable to recognize faces. Most of us recognize familiar faces effortlessly in a tiny fraction of a second (Bruce & Young, 1986). Yet for some individuals, face recognition is by no means a "given." Although once assumed to be extremely rare, a condition called prosopagnosia—face blindness—may at least partially afflict as many as two percent of people. Prosopagnosics need to depend on nonfacial cues, like freckles, weight, eyeglasses, and clothing, to recognize familiar people (Nakayama, 2006). In some cases, they can't even recognize parents and spouses from their facial features (Duchaine & Nakayama, 2006). Their profound impairment in recognition can be present at birth, but it's more often due to brain trauma, stroke, or neurological disease. In addition, it's typically restricted to the face, rather than to stimuli or objects in general (Busigny et al., 2010).

Many psychologists believe that holistic processing—the ability to visualize a face as a whole, rather than the sum of its parts—is crucial to face recognition. People who are especially good at recognizing faces are also better at processing faces as a whole (Wang et al., 2012), although all of us may also process facial features, like a large nose or widely spaced eyes, to improve our recognition of people (Rothshtein et al., 2007). The fact that many people with prosopagnosia lack the ability to process facial features holistically implies that this type of processing explains both impaired and normal face recognition (Busigny et al., 2010; Duchaine et al., 2006).

Researchers have recently uncovered important clues regarding the biological bases of face recognition. Although much still needs to be learned, we now know that a region of the temporal lobe called the fusiform gyrus plays a central role in this capacity; when it's damaged, prosopagnosia can result (Ramon et al., 2010). In people who suffer prosopagnosia from birth, the connections and number of fibers of white matter, which link diverse areas of the brain associated with facial recognition, are compromised. When this problem occurs, neural communication is disrupted, interfering with face processing even as these infants grow into adults (Cibu, et al., 2009; Garrido et al., 2009). Prosopagnosia is an excellent example of the limits of plasticity. Facial recognition impairments persist over a lifetime despite countless opportunities to learn to recognize the faces of friends and loved ones dearest to our hearts.

This photo captures the way in which most people with prosopagnosia process faces – in bits and pieces rather than as integrated wholes.

Wernicke's area
part of the temporal lobe involved in understanding speech

The lower part of the temporal lobe is critical to storing memories of autobiographical events. Penfield (1958) discovered that stimulating this region with electrical probes elicited memories, like vivid recollections of "a certain song" or "the view from

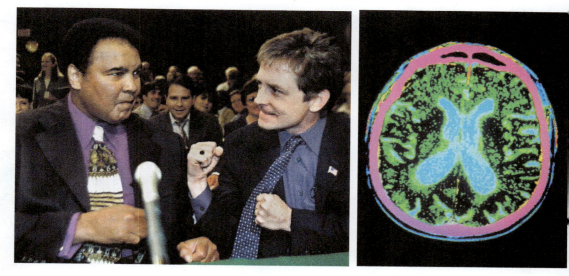

Boxer Muhammad Ali (*left*) and actor Michael J. Fox (*right*) both live with Parkinson's disease. Damage to the basal ganglia contributes to the disease, resulting in a lack of motor control. The computed tomography scan on the right shows the dramatic loss of dopamine neurons, which naturally contain a dark pigment, in a brain affected by Parkinson's disease. The ventricles, shown in blue in the middle of the brain, are abnormally large due to the death of surrounding brain tissue.

a childhood window." Yet many psychologists today suspect that stimulating the brain is eliciting false memories or altered perceptions rather than genuine memories of past events (Schacter, 1996). Indeed, this alternative hypothesis is difficult to rule out.

Occipital Lobe. At the back of our brain lies the **occipital lobe,** containing the *visual cortex*, dedicated to seeing. Compared with most animals, we human beings are highly dependent on our visual systems—we've even been called the "visual primate" (Angier, 2009)—so it stands to reason that we have an awful lot of cortical real estate devoted to seeing. Still, we're by no means the only highly visual creatures. For each species, the amount of sensory cortex of each type is roughly proportional to the degree to which it relies on that sense. Ghost bats depend highly on sound cues and have proportionally more auditory cortex; platypuses rely heavily on touch cues and have proportionally more touch cortex; and squirrels, like humans, rely strongly on visual inputs and have proportionally more visual cortex (Krubitzer & Kaas, 2005).

Cortical Hierarchies. When information from the outside world is transmitted by a specific sense (like sight, hearing, or touch), it reaches the **primary sensory cortex** specific to that sense (look at Figure 13 again). After the eye, ear, or skin transmits sense information to the primary sensory cortex, it's passed on to another area for that sense called the **association cortex,** which is spread throughout all four of the brain's lobes. In fact, most of the cerebrum—about three-fourths of it—consists of association cortex, suggesting that much of what makes us smart relies on integrating (or "associating") information across different brain areas. The association cortex synthesizes information to perform more complex functions, such as pulling together size, shape, color, and location information to identify an object. The overall organization of the cortex is "hierarchical" because processing becomes increasingly complex as information is passed up the network. People with significant damage to the association cortex in the temporal lobes may experience difficulties recognizing previously familiar faces or answering questions about people just by looking at their faces, a condition called prosopagnosia (see *From Inquiry to Understanding* feature).

THE BASAL GANGLIA. The **basal ganglia** are structures buried deep inside the cortex that help to control movement. Damage to the basal ganglia contributes to Parkinson's disease, resulting in a lack of control over movement and uncontrollable tremors. Tourette's disorder, a condition characterized by both motor tics (like shrugging our shoulders) and vocal tics (like grunting, and in rarer cases, cursing), appears to be associated with abnormalities in the basal ganglia (Peterson et al., 2003). After sensory information reaches primary and association areas, it's transmitted to the basal ganglia, which calculate a course of action and transmit it to the motor cortex.

◀ **RULING OUT RIVAL HYPOTHESES**
Have important alternative explanations for the findings been excluded?

occipital lobe
back part of cerebral cortex specialized for vision

primary sensory cortex
regions of the cerebral cortex that initially process information from the senses

association cortex
regions of the cerebral cortex that integrate simpler functions to perform more complex functions

basal ganglia
structures in the forebrain that help to control movement

FIGURE 14 The Limbic System. The limbic system consists mainly of the thalamus, hypothalamus, amygdala, and hippocampus.

- Cingulate cortex
- Corpus callosum
- Thalamus
- Hypothalamus
- Hippocampus
- Amygdala

The basal ganglia also allow us to perform movements to obtain rewards (Graybiel et al., 1994; Seger & Spiering, 2011). When we anticipate a pleasurable outcome, such as a tasty sandwich or hot date, we depend on activity in our basal ganglia.

THE LIMBIC SYSTEM. The diverse parts of the brain dedicated to emotion are housed within the **limbic system** (Lambert, 2003; McClean, 1990), a set of highly interconnected brain regions. In contrast to the cortex, which processes information about external stimuli, the limbic system processes information about our internal states, such as blood pressure, heart rate, respiration, and perspiration, as well as our emotions.

We can think of the limbic system as the brain's emotional center. Limbic system structures also play roles in smell, motivation, and memory, all of which contribute to and shape our emotions. The limbic system evolved out of the primitive olfactory system (dedicated to smell), which controlled various survival behaviors in early mammals. As anyone who's walked a dog knows, smell remains vitally important to many animals in helping them understand their worlds.

We'll explore four areas of the limbic system: the thalamus, the hypothalamus, the amygdala, and the hippocampus (see **FIGURE 14**). The **thalamus** contains many areas, each of which connects to a specific region of the cerebral cortex. We can think of the thalamus as a sensory relay station. The vast majority of sensory information first passes through its doors, undergoing some initial processing, before traveling on to the cortex (refer again to Figure 14).

The **hypothalamus** (meaning "below the thalamus"), located on the floor of the brain, regulates and maintains constant internal bodily states. Different areas of the hypothalamus play various roles in emotion and motivation. Some help to regulate hunger, thirst, sexual motivation, or other emotional behaviors. The hypothalamus also assists with controlling our body temperature, acting much like a thermostat that adjusts our home's temperature in response to indoor changes in temperature.

The **amygdala** is responsible for excitement, arousal, and especially fear. In studies of teenagers, the amygdala kicks into high gear when people play violent video games (Mathews et al., 2006), or when we view fearful faces (Killgore & Yergelun-Todd, 2005). It also plays a key role in fear conditioning, a process by which animals, including humans, learn to predict when something scary is about to happen (Davis & Shi, 2000; LeDoux, 2000). Ralph Adolphs and colleagues verified the role of the amygdala in fear in a 30-year-old woman whose left and right amygdalas were almost entirely destroyed by disease. Although she had no difficulty identifying faces, she was markedly impaired in detecting

Explore in **MyPsychLab** the **Concept:** the Limbic System

limbic system
emotional center of brain that also plays roles in smell, motivation, and memory

thalamus
gateway from the sense organs to the primary sensory cortex

hypothalamus
part of the brain responsible for maintaining a constant internal state

amygdala
part of limbic system that plays key roles in fear, excitement, and arousal

hippocampus
part of the brain that plays a role in spatial memory

cerebellum
brain structure responsible for our sense of balance

fear in these faces (Adolphs et al., 1994). In addition, she displayed no fear when asked to handle a snake in a pet store and was not at all frightened during horror movies, like *The Blair Witch Project* (Feinstein et al., 2011). Still, we need to take isolated case studies with a grain of salt, so replication of these findings in other individuals with amygdala damage will be important.

The **hippocampus** plays crucial roles in memory, especially spatial memory—the memory of the physical layout of things in our environment. When we make a mental map of how to get from one place to another, we're in part using our hippocampus. This may explain why a portion of the hippocampus is larger in London taxi drivers than in non–taxi drivers and is especially large in experienced taxi drivers (Maguire et al., 2000). This correlation could mean either that people with greater amounts of experience navigating complex environments develop larger hippocampi or that people with larger hippocampi seek out occupations, like taxi driving, which rely on spatial navigation. One study that could help us figure out what's causing what would be to examine whether cab drivers' hippocampi become larger as they acquire more driving experience. Although researchers haven't yet conducted this study, they've looked at this issue in people who've recently learned to juggle. Sure enough, they've found evidence for short-term increases in the size of the hippocampus, suggesting that this brain area can change in size following learning (Boyke et al., 2008).

Damage to the hippocampus causes problems with forming new memories, but leaves old memories intact. One hypothesis is that the hippocampus stores memories temporarily before transferring them to other sites, such as the cortex, for permanent storage (Sanchez-Andres, Olds, & Alkon, 1993). The multiple trace theory is a rival hypothesis of memory storage in the hippocampus (Moscovitch et al., 2005). According to this theory, memories are initially stored at multiple sites. Over time, storage becomes stronger at some sites but weaker at others. The multiple trace theory implies that memories aren't transferred from the hippocampus to the cortex. Instead, memories are already stored in the cortex and merely strengthen over time.

THE CEREBELLUM. The **cerebellum** is Latin for "little brain," and in many respects it's a miniature version of the cortex. Part of the hindbrain, the cerebellum plays a predominant role in our sense of balance and enables us to coordinate movement and learn motor skills. Among other things, it helps prevent us from falling down. But in recent years, scientists have come to realize that the cerebellum does much more: It also contributes to executive, memory, spatial, and linguistic abilities (Schmahmann, 2004; Swain, Kerr, & Thompson, 2011). When humans experience damage to the cerebellum, they frequently suffer from serious balance problems (Fredericks, 1996).

THE BRAIN STEM. The **brain stem,** housed inside the cortex and located at the very back of our brains, contains the *midbrain, pons,* and the *medulla* (see **FIGURE 15**). The brain stem performs some of the basic bodily functions that keep us alive. The **midbrain,** in turn, plays an important role in movement. It also controls the tracking of visual stimuli and reflexes triggered by sound, like jumping after we're startled by a car backfiring.

Reticular Activating System. The **reticular activating system (RAS)** connects with the forebrain and cerebral cortex; this system plays a key role in arousal. Damage to the RAS can result in a coma. Some scientists even believe that many knockdowns in boxing result from a temporary compression of the RAS following a powerful punch (Weisberg, Garcia, & Strub, 1996).

The pathways emanating from the RAS activate the cortex by jacking up the *signal-to-noise ratio* among neurons in the brain (Gu, 2002). When it's working well, a cell phone produces sound with a high signal-to-noise ratio so that each caller can understand the other's messages. But when there's a great deal of background static—resulting in a low signal-to-noise ratio—callers find it difficult to understand each other.

◄ **REPLICABILITY**
Can the results be duplicated in other studies?

◄ **CORRELATION VS. CAUSATION**
Can we be sure that A causes B?

The hippocampi of taxi drivers seem to be especially large, although the causal direction of this finding is unclear.

◄ **RULING OUT RIVAL HYPOTHESES**
Have important alternative explanations for the findings been excluded?

Cortex
Midbrain
Cerebellum
Pons
Medulla
Spinal cord

FIGURE 15 The Brain Stem. The brain stem is located at the top of the spinal cord, below the cortex.

brain stem
part of the brain between the spinal cord and cerebral cortex that contains the midbrain, pons, and medulla

midbrain
part of the brain stem that contributes to movement, tracking of visual stimuli, and reflexes triggered by sound

reticular activating system (RAS)
brain area that plays a key role in arousal

We may see this problem in action in attention-deficit/hyperactivity disorder (ADHD), a disorder originating in childhood. ADHD is marked by inattention, overactivity, and impulsivity. Stimulant drugs used to treat ADHD, such as methylphenidate (often marketed under the brand names Ritalin or, in extended release form, Concerta) appear to increase the signal-to-noise ratio in the prefrontal cortex (Devilbiss & Berridge, 2006). One hypothesis is that these drugs mimic activity in the RAS and neighboring brain regions, but other explanations are possible. For example, methylphenidate boosts levels of the neurotransmitter dopamine, which may be help to explain why it improves attention and impulse control (Volkow et al., 2005).

The Pons and Medulla. The *pons* and *medulla* lie below the midbrain in the region of the brain called the **hindbrain.** The **pons,** which plays a crucial role in triggering dreams, connects the cortex to the cerebellum.

The **medulla** regulates breathing, heartbeat, and other vital functions. Interestingly, it also controls nausea and vomiting (Hesketh, 2008), which explains why you may have had the unpleasant experience of wanting to throw up if you've experienced a hard hit to the back of your head. Serious damage to the medulla can cause *brain death*, which scientists define as irreversible coma. People who are brain dead are totally unaware of their surroundings and unresponsive, even to ordinarily very painful stimuli. They show no signs of spontaneous movement, respiration, or reflex activity.

People often confuse a *persistent vegetative state*, or cortical death, with brain death, but the two differ. Terri Schiavo made headlines in 2005 as the woman who had lain in a persistent vegetative state for 15 years. Schiavo collapsed in her Florida home in 1990 following temporary cardiac arrest, depriving her brain of oxygen and resulting in severe brain damage. The deep structures in her brain stem that control breathing, heart rate, digestion, and certain reflexive responses were still operating, so Schiavo wasn't brain dead, as much of the news media reported incorrectly. Nevertheless, her higher cerebral structures, necessary for awareness of herself and her environment, were damaged permanently. Her doctors knew that much of her cortex had withered away, and an autopsy later showed that she'd lost about half of her brain.

Those who believe that death of the higher brain centers essential for consciousness is equivalent to actual death felt that Schiavo had, in fact, died 15 years earlier. Nevertheless, her death raises difficult questions that science can't fully resolve: Should brain death be the true criterion for death, or should this criterion instead be the permanent loss of consciousness?

THE SPINAL CORD. The **spinal cord** extends from our brain stem and runs down the middle of our backs, conveying information between the brain and the rest of the body. *Nerves* extend from neurons to the body, traveling in two directions much like the traffic on a two-lane highway. Sensory information is carried from the body to the brain by way of *sensory nerves*; motor commands are carried from the brain to the body by way of *motor nerves*. The spinal cord also contains sensory neurons that contact **interneurons,** neurons that send messages to other neurons located nearby. Interneurons connect sensory nerves with motor nerves within the spinal cord without having to report back to the brain. Interneurons explain how **reflexes,** automatic motor responses to sensory stimuli, can occur.

Consider an automatic behavior called the stretch reflex, which relies only on the spinal cord. We're carrying our textbooks in our arms on our way to class, but over time our grasp releases ever so slightly without our even noticing. Our sensory nerves detect the muscle stretch and relay this information to the spinal cord. Interneurons intervene and motor neurons automatically send messages that cause our arm muscles to contract. Without our ever knowing it, a simple reflex causes our arm muscles to tighten, preventing us from dropping our books (see **FIGURE 16**).

The Peripheral Nervous System

Thus far, we've explored the inner workings of the CNS—the central nervous system. Now let's peer into the peripheral nervous system (PNS), the part of the nervous system consisting of the nerves that extend outside of the CNS. The PNS itself contains two branches, somatic and autonomic.

RULING OUT RIVAL HYPOTHESES ▶
Have important alternative explanations for the findings been excluded?

FIGURE 16 The Spinal Reflex. We detect even small amounts of muscle stretch and compensate by contraction. In this way we can maintain balance or keep from losing our grip.

Spinal cord — Interneuron
Sensory neuron
Motor neuron
Muscle
Skin receptors

hindbrain
region below the midbrain that contains the cerebellum, pons, and medulla

pons
part of the brain stem that connects the cortex with the cerebellum

medulla
part of brain stem involved in basic functions, such as heartbeat and breathing

spinal cord
thick bundle of nerves that conveys signals between the brain and the body

interneuron
neuron that sends messages to other neurons nearby

reflex
an automatic motor response to a sensory stimulus

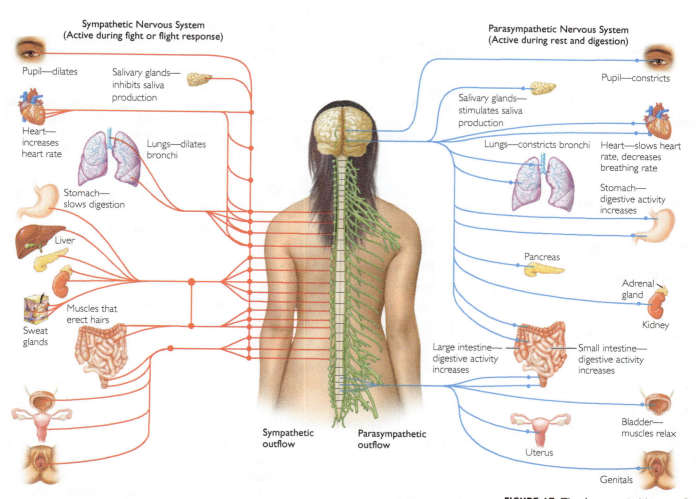

Sympathetic Nervous System
(Active during fight or flight response)

Pupil—dilates

Salivary glands—
inhibits saliva
production

Heart—
increases
heart rate

Lungs—dilates
bronchi

Stomach—
slows digestion

Liver

Muscles that
erect hairs

Sweat
glands

Sympathetic
outflow

Parasympathetic Nervous System
(Active during rest and digestion)

Pupil—constricts

Salivary glands—
stimulates saliva
production

Lungs—constricts bronchi

Heart—slows heart
rate, decreases
breathing rate

Stomach—
digestive activity
increases

Pancreas

Adrenal
gland

Kidney

Large intestine—
digestive activity
increases

Small intestine—
digestive activity
increases

Bladder—
muscles relax

Uterus

Genitals

Parasympathetic
outflow

FIGURE 17 The Autonomic Nervous System
(Female Shown). The sympathetic and
parasympathetic divisions of the autonomic
nervous system control the internal organs
and glands.

THE SOMATIC NERVOUS SYSTEM. The **somatic nervous system** carries messages from the CNS to muscles throughout the body, controlling movement (look back to Figure 8). Whenever we stabilize or move our many joints, the CNS cooperates with the somatic nervous system to regulate our posture and bodily movement.

Let's review what happens when we decide to stroll over to the vending machine to purchase a can of soda. Sensory inputs of all types reach the cortex. Then all parts of the cortex send information to the basal ganglia. The basal ganglia contribute to our decision about what to do and relay that information to the motor cortex. Next up, the motor cortex sends commands to the spinal cord, activating motor neurons. These motor neurons send messages through nerves that reach muscles throughout the body and trigger muscle contractions. We walk, reach, touch, and grasp. Our brain triggers all of these movements, but our somatic nervous system carries them out. After we finish our drink, our somatic nervous system keeps working, enabling us to walk away—ideally, to the nearest recycling container.

THE AUTONOMIC NERVOUS SYSTEM. The brain and spinal cord interact with our somatic nervous system to bring about sensation and behavior. In much the same way, the brain, especially the limbic system, interacts with the **autonomic nervous system** to control emotion and internal physical states. The autonomic nervous system is the part of the nervous system that controls the involuntary actions of our organs and glands; along with the limbic system, it regulates our emotions.

The autonomic nervous system, in turn, consists of two divisions: sympathetic and parasympathetic (see **FIGURE 17**). These two divisions work in opposing directions, so that when one is active, the other is passive. The **sympathetic nervous system,** so called because its neurons tend to fire together ("in sympathy"), is active during emotional arousal,

somatic nervous system
part of the nervous system that conveys
information between the CNS and the
body, controlling and coordinating voluntary
movement

autonomic nervous system
part of the nervous system controlling the
involuntary actions of our internal organs and
glands, which (along with the limbic system)
participates in emotion regulation

sympathetic nervous system
division of the autonomic nervous system
engaged during a crisis or after actions
requiring fight or flight

especially during crises. This system mobilizes the *fight-or-flight response*, described by Walter Cannon in 1929. Cannon noticed that when we encounter threats, like the sight of a huge predator charging toward us, our sympathetic nervous system becomes aroused and prepares us for fighting or fleeing. Sympathetic activation triggers a variety of physical responses helpful for reacting in a crisis, including increased heart rate (allowing more blood to flow into our extremities, thereby preparing us to fight or flee), respiration, and perspiration. The **parasympathetic nervous system,** in contrast, is active during rest and digestion. This system kicks into gear when there's no threat on our mental radar screens.

> **parasympathetic nervous system**
> division of autonomic nervous system that controls rest and digestion

✓ **Study** and **Review** in **MyPsychLab**

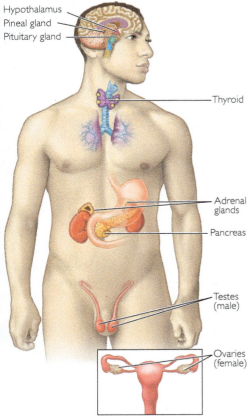

FIGURE 18 The Major Endocrine Glands of the Body. Endocrine glands throughout the body play specialized roles.

> **endocrine system**
> system of glands and hormones that controls secretion of blood-borne chemical messengers
>
> **hormone**
> chemical released into the bloodstream that influences particular organs and glands
>
> **pituitary gland**
> master gland that, under the control of the hypothalamus, directs the other glands of the body

Hypothalamus
Pineal gland
Pituitary gland
Thyroid
Adrenal glands
Pancreas
Testes (male)
Ovaries (female)

Assess Your Knowledge   FACT or FICTION?

1. The cortex is divided into the frontal, parietal, temporal, and hippocampal lobes.
    True / False

2. The basal ganglia control sensation.   **True / False**

3. The amygdala plays a key role in fear.   **True / False**

4. The cerebellum regulates only our sense of balance.   **True / False**

5. There are two divisions of the autonomic nervous system.   **True / False**

Answers: 1. F, 2. F, 3. T, 4. F, 5. T

The Endocrine System

7   Describe what hormones are and how they affect behavior.

The nervous system interfaces with the **endocrine system,** a network of glands that release **hormones** into the bloodstream (see **FIGURE 18**). Hormones are molecules that influence particular organs. They differ from neurotransmitters in that they're carried through our blood vessels rather than our nerves, so they're much slower in their actions. We can think of hormonal messages as a bit like regular mail and neurotransmitter messages as a bit like e-mail. But hormones tend to outlast neurotransmitters in their effects, so their impact tends to be more enduring.

The Pituitary Gland and Pituitary Hormones

The **pituitary gland** controls the other glands in the body. For this reason, it was once called the "master gland," although scientists now realize that it depends heavily on the actions of other glands, too. It, in turn, is controlled by the hypothalamus. The pituitary gland releases a variety of hormones that serve numerous functions, ranging all the way from regulating physical growth, controlling blood pressure, and determining how much water we retain in our kidneys.

One pituitary hormone, *oxytocin,* has received substantial attention in recent years. It's responsible for a several reproductive functions, including stretching the cervix and vagina during birth and aiding milk flow in nursing mothers. Oxytocin also plays essential roles in maternal and romantic love (Esch & Stefano, 2005), so much so that it's even been called the "love molecule" (Zak, 2012). Scientists have identified two closely related species of voles (a type of rodent) that differ in their pair bonding: The males of one species are promiscuous, flitting from one attractive partner to another, whereas the males of the other remain faithfully devoted to one partner for life. Only in the brains of the loyal voles are oxytocin receptors linked to the dopamine system, which as we've learned influences the expectation of reward (Young & Wang, 2004). For male voles, at least, remaining faithful isn't a chore: It's literally a labor of love.

Although these two vole species (the prairie vole on the left and the montane vole on the right) look quite similar, they differ in their "personalities," at least when it comes to romance. The male prairie vole stays loyal to one partner, but the male montane vole doesn't. The difference lies in their oxytocin systems.

Oxytocin also seems to influence how much we trust others. In one study, men exposed to a nasal spray containing oxytocin were more likely than men to exposed to a placebo spray to hand over money to their team partners in a risky investment game (Kosfeld et al., 2005; Rilling, King-Cassas, & Sanfey, 2008). At the same time, the effects of oxytocin on trust and attachment aren't simple, suggesting that the phrase "love molecule" is oversimplified. For example, although oxytocin makes us treat people within our favored groups better, it makes us treat outsiders worse (De Drue et al, 2011).

The Adrenal Glands and Adrenaline

Psychologists sometimes call the **adrenal glands** the emergency centers of the body. Located atop of the kidneys, they manufacture the hormones *adrenaline* and *cortisol*. Adrenaline boosts energy production in muscle cells, thrusting them into action, while conserving as much energy as possible. Nerves of the sympathetic nervous system signal the adrenal glands to release adrenaline. Adrenaline triggers many actions, including (1) contraction of our heart muscle and constriction of our blood vessels to provide more blood to the body, (2) opening the bronchioles (tiny airways) of the lungs to allow inhalation of more air, (3) breakdown of fat into fatty acids, providing us with more fuel, (4) breakdown of glycogen (a carbohydrate) into glucose (a sugar) to energize our muscles, and (5) opening the pupils of our eyes to enable better sight during emergencies. Adrenaline also inhibits gastrointestinal secretions, explaining why we often lose our appetites or experience dry mouths when we feel nervous, as when anticipating a big job interview or final exam.

Adrenaline allows people to perform amazing feats in crisis situations, although these acts are constrained by people's physical limitations. One desperate mother was energized to lift a heavy automobile to save her trapped infant (Solomon, 2002). She probably had evolution to thank, as natural selection has almost surely predisposed the sympathetic nervous system to react to dangerous stimuli to prepare us for counter-attack (fight) or escape (flight). But adrenaline isn't activated only during threatening

adrenal gland
tissue located on top of the kidneys that releases adrenaline and cortisol during states of emotional arousal

Explore in **MyPsychLab** the **Concept:** the Endocrine System

 If this rhinoceros suddenly charged at the three people on this African safari, which branch of their autonomic nervous systems would (we hope!) become activated? (See answer upside down at bottom of page.)

Answer: Sympathetic.

115

The thrill of watching others win can increase testosterone in sports fans. Males watching World Cup soccer matches showed increased testosterone levels in their saliva if their favorite team won, but decreased testosterone levels if their favorite team lost (Bernhardt et al., 1998).

situations. Pleasurable and exciting activities, like race car driving and skydiving, can also produce adrenaline rushes.

Like adrenaline, cortisol increases in response to physical and psychological stressors. Individuals with some anxiety disorders tend to have elevated levels of cortisol (Mantello et al., 2008), and children with conduct problems, like lying, cheating, and stealing, tend to have low levels of cortisol (Oosterlaan et al., 2005), perhaps suggesting that they aren't anxious enough. Cortisol regulates blood pressure and cardiovascular function, as well as the body's use of proteins, carbohydrates, and fats. The way in which cortisol regulates nutrients has led some researchers to suggest that it regulates body weight. Elevated cortisol produced by stress may contribute to weight gain (Talbott, 2002).

Sexual Reproductive Glands and Sex Hormones

The sexual reproductive glands are the testes in males and ovaries in females (refer back to Figure 18). Most of us think of *sex hormones* as either male or female. After all, the testes make the male sex hormone, called *testosterone*, and the ovaries make the female sex hormone, called *estrogen*. Although males and females do have more of their own type of sex hormone, both sexes manufacture some amount of the sex hormone associated with the opposite sex. Women's bodies produce about one-twentieth the amount of testosterone as those of males. That's because the ovaries also make testosterone, and the adrenal gland makes low amounts of testosterone in both sexes. Conversely, the testes manufacture estrogen, but in low levels (Hess, 2003).

Scientists have long debated the relationship between sex hormones and sex drive (Bancroft, 2005). Most scientists believe that testosterone, which increases sex drive in men, increases it in women as well, but to a lesser degree. Australian researchers conducted a survey of 18- to 75-year-old women regarding their sexual arousal and frequency of orgasm (Davis et al., 2005). They found no correlation between the levels of male sex hormone in a woman's blood and her sex drive. However, the study relied exclusively on self-reports and contained no controls for demand characteristics. Most researchers still accept the hypothesis that testosterone influences female sex drive, but additional research from multiple laboratories is needed before we can draw firm conclusions.

REPLICABILITY ▶
Can the results be duplicated in other studies?

Study and **Review** in **MyPsychLab**

Assess Your Knowledge   FACT or FICTION?

1. Hormones are more rapid in their actions than neurotransmitters.   **True / False**

2. Adrenaline sometimes allows people to perform amazing physical feats.   **True / False**

3. Cortisol tends to increase in response to stressors.   **True / False**

4. Most women have no testosterone.   **True / False**

Answers: 1. F; 2. T; 3. T; 4. F

Mapping the Mind: The Brain in Action

8   Identify different brain-stimulating, -recording, and -imaging techniques.

9   Evaluate results demonstrating the brain's localization of function.

Although many questions about the brain remain unanswered, we know far, far more about it today than we did 200, or even 20, years ago. For this, we owe a major debt of gratitude to psychologists and related scientists who've developed a host of methods to explore the brain and its functioning.

Listen in **MyPsychLab** to the **Podcast:** Brain Mapping

A Tour of Brain-Mapping Methods

Many advances over the past two centuries have enabled scientists to measure brain activity, resulting in a better understanding of how the most complicated organ in the known universe works. But brain research tools weren't always grounded in solid science. Some of the earliest methods were fundamentally flawed, but they paved the way for the newer and improved methods used today.

PHRENOLOGY: AN INCORRECT MAP OF THE MIND. Phrenology, a wildly popular theory in the 1800s, was one of the first attempts to map mind onto brain. Phrenologists assessed bumps on the head and attributed various personality and intellectual characteristics to those who sought their "expertise." Phrenologists assumed that enlargements of the skull corresponded to brain enlargements, and that these brain enlargements were linked directly to psychological capacities. From the 1820s through the 1840s, thousands of phrenology shops popped up in Europe and North America. Anyone could go to a phrenology parlor to discover his or her psychological makeup. This popular practice was the origin of the familiar expression "having one's head examined."

The founder of phrenology, Viennese physician Franz Joseph Gall (1758–1828), based his hypotheses about the supposed associations between brain areas and personality traits almost entirely on anecdotal observations, which are often subject to a host of errors. Still, phrenology had one virtue: It was falsifiable. Ironically, this lone asset proved to be its undoing. Eventually, researchers discovered that patients with damage to specific brain areas didn't experience the kinds of psychological deficits the phrenologists had predicted. Even more critically, because the shape of the outer surface of the skull doesn't closely match that of the underlying brain, phrenologists weren't even measuring bumps on the brain, as they'd believed. These discoveries ultimately led to phrenology's demise.

BRAIN DAMAGE: UNDERSTANDING HOW THE BRAIN WORKS BY SEEING HOW IT DOESN'T. New methods quickly arose to fill the void left by phrenology. Foremost among them were methods of studying psychological functioning following damage to specific brain regions. Many contemporary neuroscientists create lesions, that is, areas of damage, in experimental animals using stereotaxic methods, techniques that permit them to pinpoint the location of specific brain areas using coordinates, much like those that navigators use on a map. Today, *neuropsychologists* rely on sophisticated psychological tests, like measures of reasoning, attention, and verbal and spatial ability, to infer the location of brain dysfunction in human patients. Neuropsychological tests, which require specialized training to administer, score, and interpret, include laboratory, computerized, and paper-and-pencil measures designed to assess patients' cognitive strengths and weaknesses (Lezak et al., 2012).

ELECTRICAL STIMULATION AND RECORDING OF NERVOUS SYSTEM ACTIVITY. Although early studies of function following brain damage provided valuable insights, a host of questions remained. Researchers soon discovered that stimulating parts of the human motor cortex in patients undergoing brain surgery produced extremely specific movements (Penfield, 1958). This finding, among others, led to the hypothesis that neurons use electrical activity to send information. But to test that hypothesis, scientists needed to record electrical activity from the nervous system.

To that end, Hans Berger (1929) developed the **electroencephalograph (EEG)**, a device—still widely used today—that measures electrical activity generated by the brain (see **FIGURE 19**). Patterns and sequences in the EEG allow scientists to infer whether a person is awake or asleep, dreaming or not, and to tell which regions of the brain are active during specific tasks. To obtain an EEG record, researchers record electrical activity from multiple electrodes placed on the scalp's surface.

Because the EEG is noninvasive (that is, it doesn't require us to penetrate bodily tissue), scientists frequently use it in both animal and human studies. EEGs can detect very rapid changes in the electrical activity of the brain occurring in the range of milliseconds (one-thousandths of seconds). Even today, researchers use EEGs to study brain activity in

A phrenologist's chart showing where certain psychological traits are supposedly associated with bumps on the skull.

◀ **FALSIFIABILITY**
Can the claim be disproved?

Factoid

Mark Twain (1835–1910), often considered America's greatest humorist, once underwent a phrenology reading from Lorenzo Fowler, probably the foremost U.S. proponent of phrenology. Fowler, who was then ignorant of Twain's identity, informed Twain that the pattern of bumps on his skull indicated that he had an entirely unremarkable personality with one exception: He lacked a sense of humor. When Twain returned 3 months later and identified himself, Fowler "discovered" a large skull bump corresponding to humor (Lopez, 2002).

electroencephalograph (EEG)
recording of brain's electrical activity at the surface of the skull

FIGURE 19 Electroencephalograph (EEG). An EEG reading during wakefulness.

Magnetic resonance imaging (MRI) is a noninvasive procedure that reveals high-resolution images of soft tissue, such as the brain.

the brains of individuals with schizophrenia, epilepsy, and other psychiatric and neurological disorders as well as those without disorders. But EEGs have a few disadvantages. Because they show averaged neural activity that reaches the surface of the scalp, they tell us little, if anything, about what's happening inside of neurons. EEGs also aren't especially good for determining exactly where in the brain the activity is occurring.

BRAIN SCANS AND OTHER IMAGING TECHNIQUES. Although electrical recording and stimulation provided the initial routes for mapping mind functions onto brain areas, a virtual revolution in brain research occurred with the advent of brain scans, or *neuroimaging*. These imaging methods enable us to peer inside the brain's structure (that is, its appearance), its function (that is, its activity), and sometimes both.

CT Scans and MRI Images. In the mid-1970s, independent teams of researchers developed **computed tomography (CT)** and **magnetic resonance imaging (MRI)**, both of which allow us to visualize the brain's structure (Hounsfield, 1973; Lauterbur, 1973). The CT scan is a three-dimensional reconstruction of multiple X-rays taken through a part of the body, such as the brain. As a result, it displays far more detail than an individual X-ray. The MRI shows structural detail using a different principle. The MRI scanner measures the release of energy from water in biological tissues following exposure to a magnetic field. MRI images are superior to CT scans for detecting soft tissues, such as brain tumors.

PET. CT and MRI scans show only the brain's structure, not its activity. Therefore, neuroscientists interested in thought and emotion typically turn to *functional imaging* techniques like **positron emission tomography (PET)**, which measures changes in the brain's activity in response to stimuli. PET relies on a basic principle: Neurons, like other cells, increase their intake of glucose (a sugar) when they're active. We can think of glucose as the brain's gasoline. PET requires the injection of radioactive glucose-like molecules into patients. Although they're radioactive, they're short-lived, so they do little or no harm. The scanner measures where in the brain most of these glucose-like molecules are gobbled up, allowing neuroscientists to figure out which brain regions are most active at any given time. Because PET is invasive, researchers continued to work to develop functional imaging methods that wouldn't require injections of radioactive molecules.

fMRI. In 1990, researchers discovered that as neural activity quickens, there's an increase in oxygenated blood in response to heightened demand by neurons (Ogawa et al., 1990). Like athletes who require more fluids as they exert themselves, brain cells require more oxygen to do their work when busy. The discovery of this response enabled the development of the **functional MRI (fMRI)**. Because fMRI measures the change in blood oxygen level, it's an indirect indicator of neural activity. Neuroscientists frequently use fMRI to image brain activity in response to specific tasks, like looking at emotional faces or solving math problems (Marsh et al., 2008). The fMRI relies on magnetic fields, as does MRI. fMRI's strength, especially compared with PET, is its ability to provide detailed images of activity in small brain regions and over brief time intervals. But in contrast to PET and some other imaging techniques, fMRI is extremely sensitive to motion, so researchers often have to toss out fMRI data if participants move too much.

MAGNETIC STIMULATION AND RECORDING. Transcranial magnetic stimulation (TMS) applies strong and quickly changing magnetic fields to the skull to create electric fields in the brain. Depending on the level of stimulation, TMS can either enhance or interrupt brain function in a specific region. TMS offers useful insights regarding which brain areas are involved in different psychological processes. For example, if TMS interrupts functioning in the temporal lobe and the subject displays (temporary!) language impairment as a result, we can tentatively conclude that this lobe plays a role in language processing. Because it allows us to manipulate brain areas directly, TMS is the only noninvasive brain imaging technique that allows us to infer causation—all other techniques can only *correlate* brain activation with psychological processing. Some reports suggest that TMS provides relief for depression and may decrease auditory hallucinations, that is, the hearing of sounds, typically voices (Saba, Schurhoff, & Leboyer, 2006). *Repetitive TMS* (rTMS) also shows promise as a treatment for depression (Lee et al., 2012).

A final imaging technique is **magnetoencephalography (MEG),** which detects electrical activity in the brain by measuring tiny magnetic fields (Hari & Salmelin, 2011; Vrba & Robinson, 2001). In this way, MEG reveals patterns of magnetic fields on the skull's surface, thereby revealing which brain areas are becoming active in response to stimuli. MEG's strength is its ability to track brain changes over extremely small time intervals. In contrast to PET and fMRI scans, which measure activity changes second by second, MEG measures activity changes millisecond by millisecond.

How to Interpret—and Misinterpret—Brain Scans. PET, fMRI, and other functional brain imaging techniques have taught us a great deal about how the brain's activity changes in response to different stimuli. They've also helped scientists to uncover deficits in the brain functioning of people with certain psychiatric disorders. For example, they've revealed that schizophrenia, a severe disorder of thought and emotion marked by a loss of contact with reality, is often associated with underactivity of the frontal lobes (Andreasen et al., 1997).

Yet it's extremely easy to misinterpret brain scans, largely because many laypersons and even newspaper reporters hold misunderstandings of how they work (Poldrack, 2011; Racine, BarIlan, & Illes, 2006). For one thing, many people assume that functional brain images, like the multicolor images generated by PET and fMRI scans, are like photographs of the brain in action (Roskies, 2007; Satel & Lilienfeld, 2013). They aren't. In most cases, these images are produced by subtracting brain activity on a "control" task from brain activity on an "experimental" task, which is of primary interest to the researchers. For example, if researchers wanted to find out how people with clinical depression process sad faces, they could subtract the brain's activity following neutral faces from

An fMRI of the brain showing areas that were active when subjects remembered something they saw (*green*), something they heard (*red*), or both (*yellow*). (*Source:* M. Kirschen/Stanford University)

its activity following sad faces. So although we're seeing one image, it's actually one image subtracted from another. Moreover, the pretty colors in these images are arbitrary and superimposed by researchers. They don't correspond directly to the brain's activity (Shermer, 2008). Making matters more complicated, when a brain area "lights up" on a brain scan, we know only that neurons in that region are becoming more active. They might actually be *inhibiting* other neurons rather than exciting them.

Another complexity is introduced by the fact that when researchers conduct the calculations that go into brain scans, they're typically comparing the activity of hundreds of brain areas across neutral versus experimental tasks (Vul et al., 2009). As a result, there's a risk of chance findings—those that won't replicate in later studies.

To make this point, one mischievous team of researchers (Bennett et al., 2009) placed a dead salmon in a brain scanner, flashed it photographs of people in social situations, and asked the salmon to guess which emotions the people were experiencing (no, we're not making this up). Remarkably, the investigators "found" an area in the salmon's brain that became active in response to the task. In reality, of course, this activation was just a statistical artifact, a result of the fact that they'd computed so many analyses that a few were likely to be statistically significant by chance. This finding is a needed

◀ **CORRELATION VS. CAUSATION**
Can we be sure that A causes B?

PET scans show more regions displaying low activity (blue and black areas) in an Alzheimer's disease brain (*right*) than a control brain (*left*), whereas the control brain displays more areas showing high activity (red and yellow).

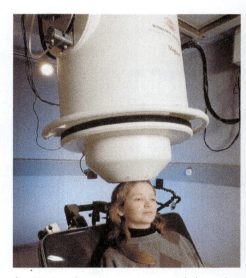

A patient undergoing magnetoencephalography (MEG), a technique that measures the presence of magnetic fields on the surface of the cerebral cortex.

◀ **REPLICABILITY**
Can the results be duplicated in other studies?

magnetoencephalography (MEG)
technique that measures brain activity by detecting tiny magnetic fields generated by the brain

A "Fishy" Result? Researchers (Bennett et al., 2009) showed that even a dead salmon can seem to be responding to stimuli—see the red regions of "brain activation"—if we're not careful to control for chance findings in brain imaging research.

Factoid

Because brain imaging research seems scientific, we can be more persuaded by it than we should be. Some studies show that non-experts may be especially likely to accept bogus claims when they're accompanied by brain imaging findings (McCabe & Castel, 2008; Weisberg et al., 2008). We must be cautious about the dangers of "neuro-seduction" (Satel & Lilienfeld, 2013)—placing unwarranted confidence in evidence derived from brain imaging studies.

Contrary to popular psychology claims that we use only 10% of our brain, we use most or even all of our brain capacity virtually all of the time.

reminder that we should view many brain imaging findings with a bit of caution until other investigators have replicated them.

How Much of Our Brain Do We Use?

Despite having so much information available at their fingertips, many people understandably hold misconceptions regarding the relationship between brain and behavior, because the media often doesn't get things quite right. The good news is that these myths have been debunked by solid scientific research. One widely held misunderstanding is that most of us use only 10 percent of our brains (Beyerstein, 1999). What could we do if we could access the other 90 percent? Would we find the cure for cancer, acquire great wealth, or write our own psychology textbook?

The 10-percent myth gained its toehold at around the same time as phrenology, in the late 1800s. William James (1842–1910), one of the fathers of psychology, wrote that most people fulfill only a small percent of their intellectual potential. Some people misconstrued James to mean that we only use about 10 percent of our brain. As the 10-percent myth was repeated, it acquired the status of an urban legend.

Early difficulties in identifying which brain regions controlled which functions probably fueled the misconception. In 1929, Karl Lashley showed that there was no single memory area in the brain. He made multiple knife cuts in the brains of rats and tested them on mazes, finding that no specific cortical area was more critical to maze learning than any other. Lashley's results were ripe for misinterpretation as evidence for "silent" areas in the cerebral cortex—those that presumably did nothing. In fact, we know today that these supposedly silent areas comprise much of the association cortex, which as we've already learned serves invaluable functions. Given the immense appeal of the idea of tapping into our full potential, it's no wonder that scores of pop psychology writers and self-improvement experts have assured us they know how to harness our brain's full potential. Some authors of self-help books who were particularly fond of the 10-percent myth liberally misquoted scientists as saying that 90 percent of the brain isn't doing anything. Believers in psychic phenomena have even spun the fanciful story that because scientists don't know what 90 percent of the brain is doing, it must be serving a psychic purpose, like extrasensory perception (ESP) (Clark, 1997). The 2010 science fiction film *Inception* presented a variation on this theme, informing viewers that we use only a small fraction of our brain capacity, and the 2011 science fiction film *Limitless* doubled the traditional estimate, saying that we use only 20% of our brains.

Today, we know enough to safely conclude that these claims indeed belong best in science fiction movies. Specialists in clinical neurology and neuropsychology, who deal with the effects of brain damage, have shown that losses of even small areas of certain parts of the brain can cause devastating, often permanent, losses of function (Sacks, 1985). If 90 percent of our brains served no function, that wouldn't be the case. Even when brain damage doesn't cause severe deficits, it produces some change in behavior, even if it's subtle.

The fatal blow against the 10-percent myth, however, came from neuroimaging and brain stimulation studies. No investigator using these techniques has ever uncovered any perpetually silent areas, nor found that 90 percent of the brain produces no psychological changes when stimulated. The bottom line: All brain areas become active on brain scans at one time or another as we think, feel, and perceive, so the 10 percent claim is indeed a myth (Beyerstein, 1999).

Which Parts of Our Brain Do We Use for What?

Scientists refer to *localization of function* when they identify brain areas that are active during a specific psychological task over and above a baseline rate of activity. We should be careful not to overemphasize localization of function, though, and we need to be especially cautious in our interpretations of neuroimaging results. William Uttal (2001) warned that researchers are too quick to assign narrowly defined functions to specific brain regions. He pointed out that we can't always dissect higher brain functions into narrower components, because most brain regions work in concert.

Regrettably, much of the popular media oversimplifies matters, often linking complex psychological functions to one and only one brain area (Miller, 2010). On a virtually weekly basis, we'll encounter news headlines like "Alcoholism Center in Brain Located" or "Brain Basis of Jealousy Found" (Cacioppo et al., 2003). To take another example, in the late 1990s and as recently as 2009, some newspapers announced the discovery of a "God spot" in the brain when scientists found that certain areas of the frontal lobes become active when individuals think of God. Yet most brain imaging research shows that religious experiences activate a wide variety of brain areas, not just one (Beauregard & Paquette, 2006). Just as multiple brain regions contribute to each psychological function, individual brain areas contribute to multiple psychological functions. Broca's area, which plays a role in speech production, also becomes active when we notice that a musical note is off key (Limb, 2006). There's enhanced activity in the amygdala and other limbic regions when we listen to inspiring music, even though these regions aren't traditionally known as "musical areas" (Blood & Zatorre, 2001). The rule of thumb is that each brain region participates in many functions, so coordination across multiple brain regions is the rule. When interpreting brain imaging studies, we should beware of the error of isolating psychological functions to a single region of the brain.

Some news sources refer to the possibility of a God spot in the brain as identified by imaging research. Yet most scientists, like Dr. Andrew Newberg (shown here), argue that the localization of religion and other complex cognitive capacities to one or two brain regions is extremely unlikely.

 Simulate in **MyPsychLab** the **Experiment:** the Hemispheric Experiment

Which Side of Our Brain Do We Use for What?

As we've learned, the cerebral cortex consists of two hemispheres, which are connected largely by the corpus callosum. Although they work together closely to coordinate functions, each hemisphere serves somewhat different functions. Many capacities rely on one cerebral hemisphere more than the other, a phenomenon called **lateralization** (see **TABLE 3**). Many lateralized functions concern specific language and verbal skills.

Roger Sperry (1974) won the Nobel Prize for showing that the two hemispheres serve different functions, such as different levels of language ability. His remarkable studies examined epilepsy patients who underwent **split-brain surgery,** an exceedingly rare operation once performed to alleviate seizures, during which neurosurgeons separate a patient's hemispheres by severing the corpus callosum.

Carefully designed studies reveal surprising deficits in split brain patients. Specifically, they experience a bizarre fragmenting of mental functions that most of us normally experience as integrated (Gazzaniga, 2000; Zaidel, 1994).

Sperry and his colleagues presented stimuli, such as written words, to either patients' right or left *visual field*. The right visual field is the right half of information entering each eye, and the left visual field is the left half of information entering each eye. In normal brains most visual information from either the left or right visual field ends up on the opposite side of the visual cortex. The brain's anatomy also produces a crossing over for movement: The left hemisphere controls the right hand; the right hemisphere controls the left hand.

Because the corpus callosum transfers information between the two hemispheres, cutting it prevents most visual information in each of the right or left visual field from reaching the visual cortex on the same side. That's because when the corpus callosum is slashed, information originating in the left visual field, which initially goes to the right hemisphere, is blocked from crossing over to the left hemisphere (and vice-versa for information

lateralization
cognitive function that relies more on one side of the brain than the other

split-brain surgery
procedure that involves severing the corpus callosum to reduce the spread of epileptic seizures

121

TABLE 3 Lateralized Functions.

LEFT HEMISPHERE
Fine-tuned language skills
• Speech comprehension
• Speech production
• Phonology
• Syntax
• Reading
• Writing
Actions
• Making facial expressions
• Motion detection
RIGHT HEMISPHERE
Coarse language skills
• Simple speech
• Simple writing
• Tone of voice
Visuospatial skills
• Perceptual grouping
• Face perception

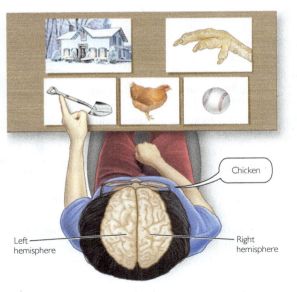

FIGURE 20 Split-Brain Subject. This woman's right hemisphere recognizes the snow scene and leads her to point to the shovel, but her left hemisphere recognizes the claw and indicates verbally that the chicken is the matching object.

This man has suffered a stroke that affected the left side of his face. On what side of his brain did his stroke probably occur, and why? (See answer upside down on bottom of page.)

originating in the right visual field). As a consequence of this disruption in information transfer across hemispheres, we often see a stunning separation of functions. In one extreme case, a split-brain subject complained that his left hand wouldn't cooperate with his right hand. His left hand misbehaved frequently; it turned off TV shows while he was in the middle of watching them and frequently hit family members against his will (Joseph, 1988).

Split-brain subjects often experience difficulties integrating information presented to separate hemispheres, but find a way to explain away or make sense of their bewildering behaviors. In one study, researchers flashed a chicken claw to a split-brain patient's left hemisphere and a snow scene to his right hemisphere (see **FIGURE 20**). When asked to match what he saw with a set of choices, he pointed to a shovel with his left hand (controlled by his right hemisphere) but said "chicken" (because speech is controlled by his left hemisphere). When asked to explain these actions, he said, "I saw a claw and I picked the chicken, and you have to clean out the chicken shed with a shovel."

Still, we should guard against taking lateralization of function to an extreme. Remarkably, it's possible to live with only half a brain, that is, only one hemisphere. Indeed, a number of people have survived operations to remove one hemisphere to spare the brain from serious disease. Their outlook is best when surgeons perform this operation in childhood, which gives the remaining hemisphere a fighting chance to assume the functions of the missing hemisphere (Kenneally, 2006). The fact that many children who undergo this procedure develop almost normally suggests that functional localization isn't a foregone conclusion.

psychomythology

ARE SOME PEOPLE LEFT-BRAINED AND OTHERS RIGHT-BRAINED?

Despite the great scientific contribution of split-brain studies, the popular notion that people are either "left-brained" or "right-brained" is a misconception (Lilienfeld et al., 2010). According to this myth, left-brained people are scholarly, logical, and analytical, and right-brained people are artistic, creative, and emotional. One Internet blogger tried to explain the differences between people's political beliefs in terms of the left–right brain distinction; conservatives, he claimed, tend to be left-brained and liberals right-brained (Block, 2006). Yet these claims are vast oversimplifications of a small nugget of truth, because research demonstrates that we use both sides of our brain in a complementary way (Corballis, 1999; Hines, 1987). Furthermore, the corpus callosum and other interconnections ensure that both hemispheres are in continual communication.

Answer: Right side, because nerves cross over from one side of the brain to the other side of the body.

We can trace the myth of exaggerated left-brain versus right-brain differences to misinterpretations of accurate science. Self-help books incorporating the topic have flourished. Robert E. Ornstein was among those to promote the idea of using different ways to tap into our creative right brains versus our intellectual left brains in his 1997 book *The Right Mind: Making Sense of the Hemispheres*. Right brain–oriented educational programs for children sprang up that deemphasized getting the correct answers on tests in favor of developing creative ability. Such programs as the "Applied Creative Thinking Workshop" trained business managers to use their right brain (Herrmann, 1996). For a mere $195, "whole brain learning" supposedly expanded the mind in new ways using "megasubliminal messages," heard only by the left or the right brain (Corballis, 1999). Although there's nothing wrong with trying to be more creative by using our minds in different ways, using both hemispheres in tandem works far better.

Supposedly, we can also use left-brain, right-brain differences to treat mood disorders or anger. There are even sunglasses with flip-up side panels designed to selectively increase light to either the left or right hemisphere. Nevertheless, there's little or no scientific support for "goggle therapy" (Lilienfeld, 1999a). The magazine *Consumer Reports* (2006) couldn't confirm the claim that the sunglasses reduced anger or other negative feelings, with seven out of 12 subjects reporting no change. Surely, more evidence is required before we can accept an extraordinary claim of this kind.

Left-side, right-side flip-up sunglasses designed to improve mental state.

◄ **EXTRAORDINARY CLAIMS**
Is the evidence as strong as the claim?

Answers are located at the end of the text.

DIAGNOSING YOUR BRAIN ORIENTATION

evaluating **CLAIMS**

Many online quizzes claim to identify you as either "left-brained" or "right-brained" based on which direction you see an image move, whether you can find an image hidden in an ambiguous photo, or your answers to a series of multiple-choice questions. Other websites and books claim to help you improve your brain's nondominant side. Let's evaluate some of these claims, which are modeled after actual tests and products related to brain lateralization.

"*Left-brained people* are more likely to focus on details and logic and to follow rules and schedules. They do well in math and science. *Right-brained people* are more likely to be deep thinkers or dreamers, and to act more spontaneously. They excel in the social sciences and the arts."

The ad implies incorrectly that some people are left-brained and others right-brained, when in fact the left and right hemispheres differ only in emphasis.

"Use these exercises to improve the information flow between your left and right brain and *improve your performance* on spelling tests and listening comprehension."

There's no research to support the claim that these exercises will improve your academic performance.

"This *quick test* can help you determine your dominant side in just a few seconds."

This extraordinary claim isn't supported by extraordinary evidence. Furthermore, what would we need to know about this test to determine if it's valid?

Study and Review in MyPsychLab

"Roger doesn't use the left side of his brain or the right side. He just uses the middle."

(© ScienceCartoonsPlus.com)

Assess Your Knowledge — FACT or FICTION?

1. PET scans detect changes in cerebral blood flow that tend to accompany neural activity.   **True / False**

2. Most people use only about 10 percent of their brain.   **True / False**

3. Psychological functions are strictly localized to specific areas of the cerebral cortex.   **True / False**

4. Split-brain subjects are impaired at integrating information from both visual fields.   **True / False**

Answers: 1. F; 2. F; 3. F; 4. T

FIGURE 21 Human Chromosomes. Humans have 46 chromosomes. Males have an XY pair and females have an XX pair. The other 22 pairs of chromosomes aren't sex linked.

chromosome
slender thread inside a cell's nucleus that carries genes

gene
genetic material, composed of deoxyribonucleic acid (DNA)

genotype
our genetic makeup

phenotype
our observable traits

Nature and Nurture: Did Your Genes—or Parents—Make You Do It?

10 Describe genes and how they influence psychological traits.

11 Explain the concept of heritability and the misconceptions surrounding it.

Up to this point in the text, we've said relatively little about what influences shape the development of our brains. Our nervous system is shaped by both our genes (nature) and our environments (nurture)—everything that affects us after fertilization. But how do nature and nurture shape our physiological, and ultimately our psychological, makeup?

How We Come to Be Who We Are

As little as 150 years ago, even the smartest of scientists knew almost nothing about how we humans came to be. Today, the average educated person knows more about the origins of human life and the human brain than did Charles Darwin. We're remarkably fortunate to be armed with scientific principles concerning heredity, adaptation, and evolution that enable us to understand the origins of many of our psychological characteristics.

THE BIOLOGICAL MATERIAL OF HEREDITY. In 1866, a monk named Gregor Mendel published a classic treatise on inheritance based on his research on pea plants, but Mendel didn't understand how the height, shape, and color of these plants are transmitted across generations. We now know that plants and animals possess **chromosomes** (see **FIGURE 21**), slender threads inside the cell's nucleus that carry **genes,** the genetic material (we humans have 46 chromosomes). Genes, in turn, are composed of deoxyribonucleic acid (DNA); a remarkable substance shaped like a double helix that stores everything cells need to replicate (reproduce) themselves (see **FIGURE 22**). The monumental *Human Genome Project*, which characterized all human genes, was completed in 2001. This project has garnered enormous attention and stirred great hopes, as it holds out the promise of treating—and perhaps one day curing—many human disorders, including mental disorders influenced by genes (Plomin & Crabbe, 2000).

GENOTYPE VERSUS PHENOTYPE. Our genetic makeup, the set of genes transmitted from our parents to us, is our **genotype.** In contrast, our **phenotype** is our set of observable traits. We can't easily infer people's genotypes by observing their phenotypes in part because our phenotypes are shaped by environmental influences, such as parenting

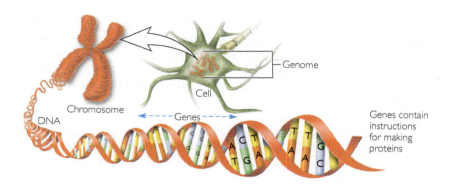

Chromosome

DNA

Cell

Genes

Genome

Genes contain instructions for making proteins

FIGURE 22 Genetic Expression. The nucleus of the neuron houses chromosomes, which contain strands of DNA. They store codes for constructing proteins needed by the cell.

and life stressors in the case of our personality traits. Genotypes and phenotypes also differ because some genes are **dominant,** meaning they mask other genes' effects. In contrast, other genes are **recessive,** meaning they're expressed only in the absence of a dominant gene.

Eye, hair, and even skin color are influenced by combinations of recessive and dominant genes. For example, two brown-eyed parents could have a blue-eyed child because the child inherited recessive genes for blue eyes from both parents.

BEHAVIORAL ADAPTATION. Charles Darwin's classic book *On the Origin of Species* (1859) introduced the broad brushstrokes of his theory of evolution by natural selection. Darwin hypothesized that populations of organisms change gradually over time. Some organisms, he argued, possess *adaptations* that make them better suited to their environments. They survive and reproduce at higher rates than other organisms. We now understand that these organisms are more likely than others to pass on their genes to subsequent generations. Many adaptations are physical changes that enable organisms to better adjust to or manipulate their environments. An opposable thumb—one that can be moved away from the other fingers—for example, greatly enhanced our hand function. Compared with other organisms, those with successful adaptations have heightened levels of **fitness,** meaning they have a better chance of passing on their genes to later generations.

Other adaptations are behavioral. Indeed, the field of evolutionary psychology examines the potential adaptive functions of psychological traits (Buss, 1995; Kenrick & Butner, 2003). According to most evolutionary psychologists, aggressive behavior is an adaptation, because it enables organisms to obtain more resources and perhaps fight off potential rivals to one's favored mate. Too much aggression, however, is usually maladaptive, meaning it often decreases organisms' chances of survival or reproduction, perhaps because they're likely to be killed in fights or because their aggression scares off potential mates. But evolutionary psychology is controversial, largely because it's difficult to know whether a psychological trait is a direct product of natural selection (Buller, 2009; Kitcher, 1985; Panksepp & Panksepp, 2000). In contrast to bones and some other physical characteristics, psychological traits don't leave fossils, so we need to make educated guesses about these traits' past adaptive functions. For example, is religion an evolutionary adaptation, perhaps because it helps us to cement social ties? It's difficult to know (Boyer, 2003). Or what about morality, jealousy, artistic ability, and scores of other psychological traits? In all of these cases, we may never know whether they're direct products of natural selection as opposed to indirect byproducts of other traits that have been selected. Nevertheless, it's likely that some psychological characteristics, like anxiety, disgust, happiness, and other emotions are adaptations that prepare organisms to react to certain stimuli (Nesse & Elsworth, 2009). Anxiety, for example, predisposes us to attend to potential threats, like predators.

 Explore in **MyPsychLab** the **Concept:** Dominant and Recessive Traits

dominant gene
gene that masks other genes' effects

recessive gene
gene that is expressed only in the absence of a dominant gene

fitness
organisms' capacity to pass on their genes

The brain of a human (*top*) and that of a chimpanzee (*bottom*). The human brain is about three times larger, even though humans are only about two times as large overall.

? The distinction of the largest brain in the animal kingdom—between 15 and 20 pounds—goes to the sperm whale. **Does this mean that sperm whales are the most intelligent creatures? Why or why not?** (See answer upside down on bottom of page.)

heritability
percentage of the variability in a trait across individuals that is due to genes

Answer: No, this fact doesn't make the sperm whale the "brainiest" creature on the planet because we must correct for its huge body size when determining its relative brain size.

HUMAN BRAIN EVOLUTION. The relationship between the human nervous system and behavior has been finely tuned over millions of years of evolution (Cartwright, 2000). Brain regions with complicated functions, such as the cortex, have evolved the most (Karlen & Krubitzer, 2006). As a result, our behaviors are more complex and flexible than those of other animals, allowing us to respond in many more ways to a given situation.

What makes us so distinctive in the animal kingdom? Fossil and genetic evidence suggests that somewhere between 6 and 7 million years ago, humans and apes split off from a shared ancestor. After that critical fork in the evolutionary road, we went our separate ways. The human line eventually resulted in our species, *Homo sapiens*, whereas the ape line resulted in the great apes: chimpanzees, bonobos (once called "pygmy chimpanzees"), gorillas, and orangutans. Putting this timeline in perspective, *Homo sapiens* has been around for only about 1 percent of the total time period of the human race (Calvin, 2004).

Around the time of our divergence from apes, our brains weren't that much larger than theirs. Then, around 3 to 4 million years ago, something dramatic happened, although we don't know why. We do know that within a span of only a few million years—a mere blink of an eye in the earth's 4.5-billion-year history—one tiny area of the human genome changed about 70 times more rapidly than other areas, resulting in significant changes in the cortex (Pollard et al., 2006). The human brain mushroomed in size, more than tripling from less than 400 grams—a bit less than a pound—to its present hefty weight of 1,300 grams—about 3 pounds (Holloway, 1983). The brains of modern great apes weigh between 300 and 500 grams, even though their overall body size doesn't differ that much from humans' (Bradbury, 2005).

Relative to our body size, we're proportionally the biggest-brained animals (we need to correct for body size, because large animals, like whales and elephants, have huge brains in part because their bodies are also huge). Second in line are dolphins (Marino, McShea, & Uhen, 2004), followed by chimpanzees and other great apes. Research suggests that across species, relative brain size—brain size corrected for body size—is associated with behaviors we typically regard as intelligent (Jerison, 1983). For example, big-brained animals tend to have especially large and complex social networks (Dunbar, 2003).

Behavioral Genetics: How We Study Heritability

Scientists use *behavioral genetics* to examine the influence of nature and nurture on psychological traits, such as intelligence. In reality, behavioral genetic designs are misnamed, because they permit us to look at the roles of both genes *and* environment in behavior (Waldman, 2007).

Behavioral genetic designs also allow us to estimate the **heritability** of traits and diseases. By heritability, we mean the extent to which genes contribute to differences in a trait *among individuals*. Typically, we express heritability as a percentage. So, if the heritability of a trait is 60 percent, that means that more than half of the differences *among individuals* in their levels of that trait are due to differences in their genes. By definition, the other 40 percent is due to differences in their environments. Some traits, like height, are highly heritable: The heritability of height in adults is between 70 and 80 percent (Silventoinen et al., 2003). In contrast, other traits, like religious affiliation (which religion we choose), are due almost entirely to environment and therefore have a heritability of about zero. Our religious affiliation, not surprisingly, is influenced substantially by the beliefs with which we were raised. Interestingly, though, the depth of our religious belief is moderately heritable (Turkheimer, 1998), perhaps because it stems partly from personality traits, which are themselves heritable.

HERITABILITY: MISCONCEPTIONS AND CONCEPTIONS Heritability isn't as simple a concept as it appears, and it confuses even some psychologists. So before discussing how psychologists use heritability in different studies, we'll address three misunderstandings about what heritability is, and correct them with accurate knowledge:

Misconception 1: *Heritability applies to a single individual rather than to differences among individuals.*

Fact: Heritability applies only to groups of people. If someone asks you, "What's the heritability of your IQ?" you should promptly hand that person a copy of this text. Heritability tells us about the causes of differences among people, not within a person.

Misconception 2: *Heritability tells us whether a trait can be changed.*

Fact: Heritability technically says little or nothing about how malleable (alterable) a trait is. Many people believe that if a trait is highly heritable, then by definition we can't change it. Yet a trait can in principle have a heritability of 100 percent and still be extremely malleable. Imagine ten plants that differ markedly in height, with some of them only two or three inches tall and others five or six inches tall. Further imagine that they're only a few days old and that since their germination we've exposed them to *exactly equal* environmental conditions: the same amount of water and identical soil and lighting conditions. What's the heritability of height in this group of plants? It's 100 percent: The causes of differences in their heights *must be* completely genetic, because we've kept all environmental influences constant. Now imagine we suddenly decide to stop watering these plants and providing them with light. All of the plants will soon die, and their heights will become zero inches. So, even though the heritability of height in these plants was 100 percent, we can easily change their heights by changing their environments.

Behavioral geneticists refer to *reaction range* as the extent to which genes set limits on how much a trait can change in response to new environments (Gottlieb, 2003; Platt & Sanislow, 1988). Eye color has a limited reaction range, because it won't change much over our lifetimes, even in the presence of radical environmental changes. In contrast, at least some genetically influenced psychological traits, like intelligence, probably have a larger reaction range, because they can change—in either a positive or negative direction—in response to environmental changes, like early enrichment or early deprivation. However, the true reaction range of intelligence is unknown.

Misconception 3: *Heritability is a fixed number.*

Fact: Heritability can differ dramatically across different time periods and populations. Remember that heritability is the extent to which differences among people in a trait are due to genetic influences. So if we reduce the range of environmental influences on a trait within a population, the heritability of that trait will increase because more of the differences in that trait will be due to genetic factors. Conversely, if we increase the range of environmental influences on a trait within a population, heritability will go down because fewer of the differences in that trait will be due to genetic factors.

BEHAVIORAL GENETIC DESIGNS. Scientists estimate heritability using one of three behavioral genetic designs: *family studies*, *twin studies*, and *adoption studies*. In such studies, scientists track the presence or absence of a trait among different relatives. These studies help them determine how much both genes and environment contribute to that trait.

Even though differences in height among plants may be largely heritable, watering these plants—an environmental manipulation—can result in substantial increases in their height. The bottom line: High heritability doesn't imply unchangeability.

Family Studies. In **family studies**, researchers examine the extent to which a characteristic "runs" or goes together in intact families, namely, those in which all family members are raised in the same home. This information can be useful for estimating the risk of a disorder among the relatives of people afflicted with that disorder. Nevertheless, family studies have a crucial drawback: Relatives share a similar environment as well as similar genetic material. As a consequence, family studies don't allow us to disentangle the effects of nature from nurture. Investigators have therefore turned to more informative research designs to separate these influences and rule out alternative hypotheses about the effects of genes versus environments.

Twin Studies. To understand **twin studies,** most of which examine differences between identical and fraternal twins in traits, we first need to say a bit about the birds and the bees. Two different things can happen when a sperm fertilizes an egg. First, a single sperm may fertilize a single egg, producing a *zygote*, or fertilized egg. For reasons that scientists still don't fully understand, that zygote occasionally (in about one in 250 births) splits into two, yielding two identical genetic copies. Researchers refer to these identical twins as *monozygotic* (MZ), because they originate from one zygote. Identical twins are essentially genetic clones of each other because they share 100 percent of their genes. In other cases, two different sperm may fertilize two different eggs, resulting in two zygotes. These twins are *dizygotic* (DZ), or, more loosely, fraternal. In contrast to identical twins, fraternal twins share only 50 percent of their genes on average and are no more alike genetically than ordinary brothers or sisters.

Identical twin fetuses developing in utero. Behavior geneticists compare identical with fraternal twins to estimate genetic and environmental influences on psychological traits.

The logic of twin studies rests on the fact that identical twins are more similar genetically than are fraternal twins. Consequently, if identical twins are more alike on a psychological characteristic, such as intelligence or extraversion, than are fraternal twins, we can infer that this characteristic is genetically influenced, assuming the environmental influences on the characteristic we're studying are the same in identical and fraternal twins (Kendler et al., 1993).

Adoption Studies. As we've noted, studies of intact family members are limited because they can't disentangle genetic from environmental influences. To address this shortcoming, psychologists have turned to **adoption studies,** which examine the extent to which children adopted into new homes resemble their adoptive as opposed to their biological parents. Children adopted into other homes share genes, but not environment, with their biological relatives. As a consequence, if adopted children resemble their biological parents on a psychological characteristic, we can typically assume it's genetically influenced.

One potential confound in adoption studies is *selective placement*: Adoption agencies frequently place children in homes similar to those of their biological parents (DeFries & Plomin, 1978). This confound can lead investigators to mistakenly interpret the similarity between adoptive children and their biological parents as a genetic effect. In adoption studies, researchers try to control for selective placement by correcting statistically for the correlation between biological and adoptive parents in their psychological characteristics.

Psychologists have come to appreciate that genetic and environmental influences intersect in complex ways to shape our nervous systems, thoughts, feelings, and behaviors. For example, they've learned that people

family study
analysis of how characteristics run in intact families

twin study
analysis of how traits differ in identical versus fraternal twins

adoption study
analysis of how traits vary in individuals raised apart from their biological relatives

with certain genetic makeups tend to seek out certain environments (Plomin, DeFries, & McClearn, 1977) and react differently than people with other genetic makeups to certain environments (Kim-Cohen et al., 2006). They've also learned that many environmental influences, like life stressors and maternal affection, actually work in part by turning certain genes on or off (Weaver et al., 2004). Nature and nurture, although different sources of psychological influence, are turning out to be far more intertwined than we'd realized.

Assess Your Knowledge — FACT or FICTION?

Study and Review in MyPsychLab

1. Brain evolution is responsible for humans' advanced abilities.   True / False

2. The fact that the human brain is smaller than an elephant's shows that brain size is unrelated to intelligence.   True / False

3. Heritability values can't change over time within a population.   True / False

4. Identical twins have similar phenotypes (observable traits) but may have different genotypes (sets of genes).   True / False

5. Adoption studies are useful for distinguishing nature influences from nurture influences.   True / False

Answers: 1. T; 2. F; 3. F; 4. F; 5. T

YOUR COMPLETE REVIEW SYSTEM

Biological Psychology

Nerve Cells: Communication Portals

1 DISTINGUISH THE PARTS OF NEURONS AND WHAT THEY DO.

The neuron has a cell body, which contains a nucleus, where proteins that make up our cells are manufactured. Neurons have dendrites, long extensions that receive messages from other neurons and an axon, which extends from the cell body of each neuron and is responsible for sending messages.

1. The central region of the neuron, which manufactures new cell components is called the _____ _____.

2. The receiving ends of a neuron, extending from the cell body like tree branches, are known as _____.

3. _____ are long extensions from the neuron at the cell body that _____ messages from one neuron to another.

4. The space between two connecting neurons where neurotransmitters are released is called the _____.

5. The autoimmune disease multiple sclerosis is linked to the destruction of the glial cells wrapped around the axon, called the _____ _____.

2 DESCRIBE ELECTRICAL RESPONSES OF NEURONS AND WHAT MAKES THEM POSSIBLE.

Neurons exhibit excitatory and inhibitory responses to inputs from other neurons. When excitation is strong enough, the neuron generates an action potential, which travels all the way down the axon to the axon terminal. Charged particles crossing the neuronal membrane are responsible for these events.

6. The electrical charge difference across the membrane of the neuron when it's not being stimulated is called the _____ _____.

7. Label the image showing the process of action potential in a neuron. Include (a) axon, (b) arrow depicting the direction of the action potential, and (c) neurotransmitters.

3 EXPLAIN HOW NEURONS USE NEUROTRANSMITTERS TO COMMUNICATE WITH EACH OTHER.

Neurotransmitters are the chemical messengers neurons use to communicate with each other or to cause muscle contraction. The axon terminal releases neurotransmitters at the synapse. This process produces excitatory or inhibitory responses in the receiving neuron.

8. Neurotransmission can be halted by _____ of the neurotransmitter back into the axon terminal—a process by which the synaptic vesicle reabsorbs the neurotransmitter.

9. What "natural narcotic" produced by the brain helps athletes endure intense workouts or pain?

4 DESCRIBE HOW THE BRAIN CHANGES AS A RESULT OF DEVELOPMENT, LEARNING, AND INJURY.

The brain changes the most before birth and during early development. Throughout the life span the brain demonstrates some degree of plasticity, which plays a role in learning and memory. Later in life, healthy brain plasticity decreases and neurons can show signs of degeneration.

10. Scientists are working to improve ways to encourage neurogenesis, the adult brain's ability to create new _____.

The Brain–Behavior Network

5 IDENTIFY WHAT ROLES DIFFERENT PARTS OF THE CENTRAL NERVOUS SYSTEM PLAY IN BEHAVIOR.

The cerebral cortex consists of the frontal, parietal, temporal, and occipital lobes. Cortex involved with vision lies in the occipital lobe, cortex involved with hearing in the temporal lobe, and cortex involved with touch in the parietal lobe. Association areas throughout the cortex analyze and reanalyze sensory inputs to build up our perceptions. The motor cortex in the frontal lobe, the basal ganglia, and the spinal cord work together with the somatic nervous system to bring about movement and action. The somatic nervous system has a sensory as well as a motor component, which enables touch and feedback from the muscles to guide our actions.

11. The brain and spinal cord combine to form the superhighway known as the _____ _____ _____.

12. Outside of the CNS, the _____ _____ system works to help us control behavior and express emotion.

13. Label the various parts of the central nervous system.

Central Nervous System	
(a)	**Frontal Lobe:** performs executive functions that coordinate other brain areas, motor planning, language, and memory. **Parietal Lobe:** processes touch info, integrates vision and touch **Temporal Lobe:** processes auditory information, language, and autobiographical memory **Occipital Lobe:** processes visual information
(b)	control movement and motor planning
(c)	**Thalamus:** conveys sensory information to cortex **Hypothalamus:** oversees endocrine and autonomic nervous system **Amygdala:** regulates arousal and fear **Hippocampus:** processes memory for spatial locations
(d)	controls balance and coordinated movement
(e)	**Midbrain:** tracks visual stimuli and reflexes triggered by sound **Pons:** conveys information between the cortex and cerebellum **Medulla:** regulates breathing and heartbeats
(f)	conveys information between the brain and the body

14. The brain component responsible for analyzing sensory information and our ability to think, talk, and reason is called the _____ _____.

15. Fill in the function of each brain component identified in this figure.

Motor cortex
(a)

Primary sensory cortex
(b)

Prefrontal cortex
(i)

Visual association cortex
(c)

Broca's area
(h)

Primary visual cortex
(d)

Primary auditory cortex
(g)

Auditory association cortex
(f)

Wernicke's area
(e)

16. Parkinson's disease is the result of damage to the _____ _____, which play a critical role in voluntary movement.

17. The _____ _____ system connects to the forebrain and cerebral cortex and plays a key role in arousal.

6 CLARIFY HOW THE SOMATIC AND AUTONOMIC NERVOUS SYSTEMS WORK IN EMERGENCY AND EVERYDAY SITUATIONS.

The somatic nervous system carries messages from the CNS to the body's muscles. The autonomic nervous system consists of the parasympathetic and sympathetic divisions. Whereas the parasympathetic nervous system is active during rest and digestion, the sympathetic division propels the body into action during an emergency or crisis. Sympathetic arousal also occurs in response to everyday stressors.

18. Our ability to execute messages or commands of our central nervous system, through physical action, is dependent on the _____ _____ system.

19. Our ability to react physically to a perceived threat is dependent on the _____ division of the autonomic system.

20. Sympathetic activation triggers a variety of physical responses, including increased heart rate, _____, and _____.

The Endocrine System

7 DESCRIBE WHAT HORMONES ARE AND HOW THEY AFFECT BEHAVIOR.

Hormones are chemicals released into the bloodstream that trigger specific effects in the body. Activation of the sympathetic nervous system triggers the release of adrenaline and cortisol by the adrenal glands, which energize our bodies. Sex hormones control sexual responses.

21. The nervous system interfaces with the _____ _____, a network of glands that release hormones into the bloodsteam.

22. The gland once called the "master gland" which, under the control of the hypothalamus, directs all other body glands is known as the _____ _____.

23. Label the major endocrine glands of the body.

a
b
c

d

e

f

g

h

24. The pituitary hormone called _____ is responsible for a variety of reproductive functions including stretching the cervix and vagina during birth and aiding milk flow in nursing mothers.

25. Psychologists sometimes call the _____ _____ the emergency centers of the body.

26. When under threat or attack, how does the body prepare for fight or flight?

Answers are located at the end of the text.

27. Many anxiety disorders are associated with elevated levels of _____.

28. The testes make the male sex hormone, called _____, and the ovaries make the female sex hormone, called _____.

29. Males and females (do/don't) both manufacture some amount of sex hormone associated with the opposite sex.

30. Most researchers (accept/reject) the hypothesis that testosterone influences female sex drive.

Mapping the Mind: The Brain in Action

8 IDENTIFY THE DIFFERENT BRAIN-STIMULATING, -RECORDING, AND -IMAGING TECHNIQUES.

Electrical stimulation of the brain can elicit vivid imagery or movement. Methods such as electroencephalography (EEG) and magnetoencephalography (MEG) enable researchers to record brain activity. Imaging techniques provide a way to see the brain's structure or function. The first imaging techniques included computed tomography (CT) and magnetic resonance imaging (MRI). Imaging techniques that allow us to see how the brain's activity changes in response to psychological stimuli include positron emission tomography (PET) and functional MRI (fMRI).

31. Franz Joseph Gall made one of the earliest attempts to connect mind and brain by measuring head bumps, a technique known as _____.

32. Early efforts by Hans Berger to measure electrical activity in the brain resulted in the development of the _____.

33. Neuroscientists interested in measuring thought and emotion (would/wouldn't) employ a CT scan.

34. What do functional MRIs (fMRI), such as the one pictured here, measure?

9 EVALUATE RESULTS DEMONSTRATING THE BRAIN'S LOCALIZATION OF FUNCTION.

Stimulating, recording, and imaging techniques have shown that specific brain areas correspond to specific functions. Although these results provide valuable insight into how our brains delegate the many tasks we perform, many parts of the brain contribute to each specific task. Because individual brain areas participate in multiple functions, many cognitive functions cannot be neatly localized.

35. Neuroscientists have confirmed that there (are/aren't) parts of the brain that remain completely inactive and unutilized.

36. The phenomenon known as _____ explains how many cognitive functions rely on one cerebral hemisphere more than another.

37. Severing the corpus callosum to reduce the incidence of epileptic seizures is known as _____ surgery.

38. In this experiment, researchers flashed a chicken claw to a split-brain patient's left hemisphere and a snow scene to his right hemisphere. How can we explain his response?

39. The _____ hemisphere of the brain is related to coarse language skills and visuospatial skills whereas the _____ hemisphere is related to fine-tuned language skills and actions.

40. Artists and other creative thinkers (are/aren't) able to make use only of their right hemisphere.

Nature and Nurture: Did Your Genes—or Parents—Make You Do It?

10 DESCRIBE GENES AND HOW THEY INFLUENCE PSYCHOLOGICAL TRAITS.

Genes are composed of deoxyribonucleic acid (DNA), which are arranged on chromosomes. We inherit this genetic material from our parents. Each gene carries a code to manufacture a specific protein. These proteins influence our observable physical and psychological traits.

41. How many chromosomes do humans have? How many are sex-linked?

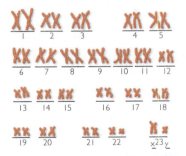

42. _____ are the thin threads within a nucleus that carry genes.

43. _____ are made up of deoxyribonucleic acid (DNA), the material that stores everything cells need to reproduce themselves.

44. Our _____ is the set of our observable traits, and our genetic makeup is our _____.

45. (Recessive/Dominant) genes work to mask other genes' effects.

46. The evolutionary principle that organisms that possess _____ survive and reproduce at a higher rate than other organisms is known as natural selection.

❚❚ EXPLAIN THE CONCEPT OF HERITABILITY AND THE MISCONCEPTIONS SURROUNDING IT.

Heritability refers to how differences in a trait across people are influenced by their genes as opposed to their environments. Highly heritable traits can sometimes change within individuals and the heritability of a trait can also change over time within a population.

47. Scientists use _____ _____ to examine the roles of nature and nurture in the origins of traits, such as intelligence.

48. Heritability applies only to (a single individual/groups of people).

49. Does high heritability imply a lack of malleability? Why or why not?

50. Analyses of how traits vary in individuals raised apart from their biological relatives are called _____ _____.

Apply Your Scientific Thinking Skills

Use your scientific thinking skills to answer the following questions, referencing specific scientific thinking principles and common errors in reasoning whenever possible.

1. Many websites and magazine articles exaggerate the notion of brain lateralization. Find two examples of products designed for either a "left-brained" or "right-brained" person. Are the claims made by these products supported by scientific evidence? Explain.

2. As we've learned in this text, scientists still aren't sure what causes women's sex drives to increase at certain times, although many view testosterone as a key influence. Locate alternative explanations for this hypothesis in the popular media and evaluate each using your scientific thinking skills.

3. The news media sometimes report functional brain imaging findings accurately, but often report them in oversimplified ways, such as implying that researchers identified a single brain region for Capacity X (like religion, morality, or political affiliation). Locate two media reports on functional brain imaging (ideally using fMRI or PET) and evaluate the quality of media coverage. Did the reporters interpret the findings correctly, or did they go beyond the findings? For example, did the reporters avoid implying that the investigators located a single brain "spot" or "region" underlying a complex psychological capacity?

Further Your Understanding

EXTEND YOUR KNOWLEDGE WITH THE MYPSYCHLAB VIDEO SERIES
Watch these videos in MyPsychLab. Follow the "Video Series" link.

👁 **The Basics: How the Brain Works** Find out about neurons: their parts, how they communicate, and their function in the brain.

👁 **The Basics: How the Brain Works** Find out about the nervous system: how it's divided and processes information, the significance of each brain structure, and how neuronal transmission works.

👁 **In the Real World: Neurotransmitters** Learn about the neurotransmitter dopamine and what happens when there is an imbalance of dopamine as a result of natural causes or drugs.

👁 **In the Real World: Taking Control of Our Genes** Dig deeper into the field of epigenetics and its role in disease prevention; explore an experiment on gene expression and addiction.

👁 **The Basics: Genetic Mechanisms and Behavioral Genetics** Learn about basic genetics and inheritance, trait correlation, and what family, adoption, and twin studies can tell us.

EXPERIENCE PSYCHOLOGICAL RESEARCH WITH MYPSYCHLAB SIMULATIONS
Access these simulations in MyPsychLab. Follow the "Simulations" link.

⊙ **Hemispheric Specialization** Judge whether a string of letters in your peripheral vision is a real word and test whether language functions are lateralized in the brain.

⊙ **Do You Fly or Fight?** Participate in a survey to discover if you flee or fight under stressful conditions.

APPLY YOUR CRITICAL THINKING SKILLS WITH MYPSYCHLAB WRITING ASSESSMENTS
Complete these writing assignments in MyPsychLab.

Your best friends invite you over for pizza and a friendly game of cards. Describe how the following parts of the brain are involved during your evening of eating pizza, socializing, and playing cards: Broca's area, hippocampus, hypothalamus, and occipital lobe.

How might you determine whether flute-playing ability is a highly heritable trait? If you want to improve your flute playing and someone tells you that musical ability is heritable, should you stop practicing?

Answer Key

NERVE CELLS: COMMUNICATION PORTALS

1. cell body
2. dendrites
3. Axons; send
4. synapse
5. myelin sheath
6. resting potential
7. a) axon is long extension in middle of diagram; b) arrow should go left to right; c) neurotransmitter release is represented by dots on right side of diagram
8. reuptake
9. endorphins
10. neurons

THE BRAIN-BEHAVIOR NETWORK

11. central nervous system
12. peripheral nervous
13. a) cortex; b) basal ganglia; c) limbic system; d) cerebellum; e) brain stem; f) spinal cord
14. cerebral cortex
15. a) generates signals responsible for voluntary movements; b) receives data about sensations in skin, muscles, and joints; c) analyzes visual data to form images; d) receives information from the optic nerve, transmitted through the visual thalamus; e) interprets spoken and written language; f) analyzes data about sound so that we can recognize words and melodies; g) detects discrete qualities of sound, such as pitch and volume; h) vital for the formation of speech; i) associated with various aspects of behavior, personality, planning, and reasoning
16. basal ganglia
17. reticular activating
18. somatic nervous
19. sympathetic
20. respiration; perspiration

THE ENDOCRINE SYSTEM

21. endocrine system
22. pituitary gland
23. a) hypothalamus; b) pineal gland; c) pituitary; d) thyroid; e) adrenal glands; f) pancreas; g) testes; h) ovaries
24. oxytocin
25. adrenal glands
26. The nerves of the sympathetic nervous system signal the adrenal glands to release adrenaline, which prepares us for counterattack (fight) or escape (flight).
27. cortisol
28. testosterone; estrogen
29. do
30. accept

MAPPING THE MIND: THE BRAIN IN ACTION

31. phrenology
32. electroencephalograph (EEG)
33. wouldn't
34. the change in blood oxygen level
35. aren't
36. lateralization
37. split-brain
38. The subject's right hemisphere recognizes the snow scene, leading her to point with her left hand (controlled by the right hemisphere) to the shovel, but her left hemisphere recognizes the claw, leading her to indicate verbally that the chicken is the matching object.
39. right; left
40. aren't

NATURE AND NURTURE: DID YOUR GENES—OR PARENTS—MAKE YOU DO IT?

41. 46; just 1 pair
42. Chromosomes
43. Genes
44. phenotype; genotype
45. Dominant
46. adaptations
47. behavioral genetics
48. groups of people
49. No, because environmental manipulation is still possible and could result in substantial changes. In fact, heritability can actually change over time.
50. adoption studies

References

Aamodt, S., & Wang, S. (2008). *Welcome to your brain: Why you lose your car keys but never forget how to drive and other puzzles of everyday life.* London, England: Bloomsbury.

Adolphs, R., Tranel, D., Damasio, H., & Damasio, A. (1994). Impaired recognition of emotion in facial expressions following bilateral damage to the human amygdala. *Nature, 372,* 669–672.

Aimone, J. B., Wiles, J., & Gage, F. H. (2006). Potential role for adult neurogenesis in the encoding of time in new memories. *Nature Neuroscience, 9,* 723–727.

Andreasen, N. C., O'Leary, D. S., Flaum, M., Nopoulos, P., Watkins, G. L., Boles Ponto, L. L., & Hichwa, R. D, (1997). Hypofrontality in schizophrenia: Distributed dysfunctional circuits in neuroleptic-naive patients. *Lancet, 349,* 1730–1734.

Angier, N. (2009, June 22). When an ear witness decides the case. *New York Times.* Retrieved from http://www.nytimes.com/2009/06/23/science/23angi.html

Azevedo, F. A., Carvalho, L. R. B., Grinberg, L. T., Farfel, J. M., Ferretti, R. E. L., Leite, R. E. P., . . . Herculano-Houzel, S. (2009). Equal numbers of neuronal and nonneuronal cells make the human brain an isometrically scaled-up primate brain. *Journal of Comparative Neurology, 513,* 532–541.

Bancroft, J. (2005). The endocrinology of sexual arousal. *Journal of Endocrinology, 186,* 411–427.

Beauregard, M., & Paquette, V. (2006). Neural correlates of a mystical experience in Carmelite nuns. *Neuroscience Letters, 405,* 186–190.

Bennett, C. M., Baird, A. A., Miller, M. B., & Wolford, G. L. (2009, June). *Neural correlates of interspecies perspective taking in the post-mortem Atlantic Salmon: An argument for multiple comparisons correction.* Poster presented at the 15th Annual Meeting of the Organization for Human Brain Mapping, San Francisco, CA.

Bennett, M. R. (1998). Monoaminergic synapses and schizophrenia: 45 years of neuroleptics. *Journal of Psychopharmacology, 12,* 289–304.

Berger, H. (1929). Ueber das Elektroenkephalogramm des Menschen. *Archiv für Psychiatrie und Nervenkrankheiten, 87,* 527–570.

Bernhardt, P. C., Dabbs, J. M., Fielden, J. A., & Lutter, C. D. (1998). Testosterone changes during vicarious experiences of winning and losing among fans at sporting events. *Physiology and Behavior, 65,* 59–62.

Beyerstein, B. L. (1999). Whence cometh the myth that we only use ten percent of our brains? In S. Della Sala (Ed.), *Mind myths: Exploring everyday mysteries of the mind and brain* (pp. 1–24). Chichester, England: Wiley.

Block, J. (2006). In whom should Americans trust? Jeff Block's personal idea fountain. Retrieved from http://jeffblock.wordpress.com/?s=in+whom+should+americans+trust&searchbutton=go%21

Blood, A. J., & Zatorre, R. J. (2001). Intensely pleasurable responses to music correlate with activity in brain regions implicated in reward and emotion. *Proceedings of the National Academy of Sciences, 98,* 11818–11823.

Boyer, P. (2003). Religious thought and behavior as by-products of brain function. *Trends in Cognitive Sciences, 7,* 119–124.

Boyke, J., Driemeyer, J., Gaser, C., Büchel, C., & May, A. (2008). Training-induced brain structure changes in the elderly. *Journal of Neuroscience, 28,* 7031–7035.

Bradbury, J. (2005). Molecular insights into human brain evolution. *PLoS Biology, 3,* 50.

Broca, P. P. (1861). Loss of speech, chronic softening and partial destruction of the anterior left lobe of the brain. *Bulletin de la Société Anthropologique, 2,* 235–238.

Bruce, V., & Young, A.W. (1986). Understanding face recognition. *British Journal of Psychology, 81,* 305–327.

Buckle, S., Dawson, K., & Singer, P. (1989). The syngamy debate: When precisely does a human life begin? *Law, Medicine, and Health Care, 17,* 174–181.

Buller, D. J. (2009, January). Evolution of the mind: 4 fallacies of psychology. *Scientific American, 300*(1).

Busigny, T., Joubert, S., Felician, O., Ceccaldi, M., & Rossion, B. (2010). Holistic perception of the individual face is specific and necessary: Evidence from an extensive case study of acquired prosopagnosia. *Neuropsychologia, 48*(14), 4057–4092. http://dx.doi.org/10.1016/j.neuropsychologia.2010.09.017

Buss, D. M. (1995). Evolutionary psychology: A new paradigm for psychological science. *Psychological Inquiry, 6,* 1–30.

Cacioppo, J. T., Berntson, G. G., Lorig, T. S., Norris, C. J., Rickett, E., & Nusbaum, H. (2003). Just because you're imaging the brain doesn't mean you can stop using your head: A primer and set of first principles. *Journal of Personality and Social Psychology, 85,* 650–661.

Cai, K., Haris, M., Singh, A., Kogan, F., Greenberg, J. H., Hariharan, H., . . . Reddy, R. (2012). Magnetic resonance imaging of glutamate. *Nature Medicine, 18*(2), 302–306.

Calvin, W. H. (2004). *A brief history of the mind: From apes to intellect and beyond.* New York, NY: Oxford University Press.

Cartwright, J. (2000). *Evolution and human behaviour.* London, England: Macmillan.

Chayer, C., & Freedman, M. (2001). Frontal lobe functions. *Current Neurology & Neuroscience Reports, 1,* 547–552.

Clark, M. (1997). *Reason to believe.* New York, NY: Avon Books.

Compton, M.T., & Broussard, B. (2009). *The first episode of psychosis: A guide for patients and their families.* New York, NY: Oxford University Press.

Consumer Reports. (2006, November 1). *Flip up or flip out.* Retrieved from http://www.accessmylibrary.com/coms2/summary_0286-29406170_ITM

Corballis, M. C. (1999). Are we in our right minds? In S. Della Sala (Ed.), *Mind myths* (pp. 26–42). Chichester, England: Wiley.

Cotter, D. R., Pariante, C. M., & Eerall, I. P. (2001). Glial cell abnormalities in major psychiatric disorders: The evidence and implications. *Brain Research Bulletin, 55,* 585–595.

Culham, J. C., & Valyear, K. F. (2006). Human parietal cortex in action. *Current Opinion in Neurobiology, 16*, 205–212.

Darwin, C. (1859). *On the origin of species.* London, England: John Murray.

Davis, M., & Shi, C. (2000). The amygdala. *Current Biology, 10*, R131.

Davis, S. R., Davison, S. L., Donath, S., & Bell, R. J. (2005). Circulating androgen levels and self-reported sexual function in women. *Journal of the American Medical Association, 294*, 91–96.

Devilbiss, D. M., & Berridge, C. W. (2006). Low-dose methylphenidate actions on tonic and phasic locus coeruleus discharge. *Journal of Pharmacology & Experimental Therapeutics, 319*, 1327–1335.

Duchaine, B., & Nakayama, K. (2006). Developmental prosopagnosia: A window to content-specific face processing. *Current Opinion in Neurobiology, 16*, 166–173.

Dunbar, R. (2003). Psychology: Evolution of the social brain. *Science, 302*, 1160–1161.

Esch, T., & Stefano, G. B. (2005). The neurobiology of love. *Neuro Endocrinology Letters, 26*, 175–192.

Evans, C. J. (2004). Secrets of the opium poppy revealed. *Neuropharmacology, 47*(Suppl. 1), 293–299.

Fagg, G. E., & Foster, A. C. (1983). Amino acid neurotransmitters and their pathways in the mammalian central nervous system. *Neuroscience, 9*, 701–719.

Feinstein, J. S., Adolphs, R., Damasio, A., & Tranel, D. (2011). The human amygdala and the induction and experience of fear. *Current Biology, 21*(1), 34–38.

Fields, R. D. (2009). *The other brain: From dementia to schizophrenia, how discoveries about the brain are revolutionizing medicine and science.* New York, NY: Simon & Schuster.

Finger, S. (2000). *Minds behind the brain: A history of the pioneers and their discoveries.* New York, NY: Oxford University Press.

Fredericks, C. M. (1996). Disorders of the cerebellum and its connections. *Pathophysiology of the Motor Systems, 445–466.*

Freire, R., & Cheng, H. W. (2004). Experience-dependent changes in the hippocampus of domestic chicks: A model for spatial memory. *European Journal of Neuroscience, 20*, 1065–1068.

Fukuda, H., & Takahashi, J. (2005). Embryonic stem cells as a cell source for treating Parkinson's disease. *Expert Opinion on Biological Therapy, 5*, 1273–1280.

Fuster, J. M. (2000). Executive frontal functions. *Experimental Brain Research, 133*, 66–70.

Gage, F. H. (2002). Neurogenesis in the adult brain. *Journal of Neuroscience, 22*, 612–613.

Garrido, L., Furl, N., Draganski, B., Weiskopf, N., Stevens, J., Tan, G. C., ... Duchaine, B. (2009). VBM reveals reduced gray matter volume in the temporal cortex of developmental prosopagnosics. *Brain, 132*, 3443–3455.

Gautier, B. (2011, May 4). Top ten bizarre mental case studies. *Listverse.* http://list-verse.com/2011/05/04/top-10-bizarre-mental-case-studies

Gazzaniga, M. S. (2000). Cerebral specialization and interhemispheric communication: Does the corpus callosum enable the human condition? *Brain, 123*, 1293–1326.

Gerard, S., & Aybala, S. (2007). GABAergic contributions to the pathophysiology of depression and the mechanism of antidepressant action. *CNS & Neurological Disorders—Drug Targets, 6*, 127–140.

Gibbs, M. E., & Bowser, D. N. (2009). Astrocytes and interneurons in memory processing in the chick hippocampus: Roles for G-coupled protein receptors, GABA(B) and mGluRi. *Neurochemical Research, 34.*

Gobel, S. M., & Rushworth, M. F. (2004). Cognitive neuroscience: Acting on numbers. *Current Biology, 14*, R517–R519.

Goff, D. C., & Coyle, J. T. (2001). The emerging role of glutamate in the pathophysiology and treatment of schizophrenia. *American Journal of Psychiatry, 158*, 1367–1377.

Gottesmann, C. (2002). GABA mechanisms and sleep. *Neuroscience, 111*, 231–239.

Gottlieb, G. (2003). On making behavioral genetics truly developmental. *Human Development, 46*, 337–355.

Gould, E., & Gross, C. G. (2002). Neurogenesis in adult mammals: Some progress and problems. *Journal of Neuroscience, 22*, 619–623.

Gould, S. J. (1997). Nonoverlapping magisteria. *Natural History, 106*, 16–22.

Graybiel, A. M., Aosaki, T., Flaherty, A. W., & Kimura, M. (1994). The basal ganglia and adaptive motor control. *Science, 265*, 1826–1831.

Gu, Q. (2002). Neuromodulatory transmitter systems in the cortex and their role in cortical plasticity. *Neuroscience, 111*, 815–835.

Hamilton, R. H., & Pascual-Leone, A. (1998). Cortical plasticity associated with Braille learning. *Trends in Cognitive Neuroscience, 2*, 168–174.

Harlow, J. M. (1848). Passage of an iron rod through the head. *Boston Medical and Surgical Journal, 39*, 389–393. (Republished in *Journal of Neuropsychiatry and Clinical Neuroscience, 1991, 11*, 281–283.)

Herbert, M. R. (2005). Large brains in autism: The challenge of pervasive abnormality. *Neuroscientist, 11*, 417–440.

Herrmann, N. (1996). *The whole brain business book.* New York, NY: McGraw-Hill.

Hesketh, P. J. (2008). Chemotherapy-induced nausea and vomiting. *New England Journal of Medicine, 358*(23), 2482–2494.

Hess, R. A. (2003). Estrogen in the adult male reproductive tract: A review. *Reproductive and Biological Endocrinology, 9*, 1–52.

Hill, E. L., & Frith, U. (2003). Understanding autism: Insights from mind and brain. In U. Frith & E. Hill (Eds.), *Autism: Mind and brain* (pp. 1–19). New York, NY: Oxford University Press.

Hines, T. (1987). Left brain/right brain mythology and implications for management and training. *The Academy of Management Review, 12*, 600–606.

Holahan, M. R., Rekart, J. L., Sandoval, J., & Routtenberg, A. (2006). Spatial learning induces presynaptic structural remodeling in the hippocampal mossy fiber system of two rat strains. *Hippocampus, 16*, 560–570.

Holden, J. E., Jeong, Y., & Forrest, J. M. (2005). The endogenous opioid system and clinical pain management. *AACN Clinical Issues, 16*, 291–301.

Holloway, R. L. (1983). Cerebral brain endocast pattern of *Australopithecus afarensis* hominid. *Nature, 303*, 420–422.

Hounsfield, G. N. (1973). Computerized transverse axial scanning (tomography). 1. Description of system. *British Journal of Radiology, 46*, 1016–1022.

Jacobson, L. H., Kelly, P. H., Bettler, B., Kaupmann, K., & Cryan, J. F. (2007). Specific roles of GABA B(1) receptor isoforms in cognition. *Behavioural Brain Research, 181*, 158–162.

Jerison, H. J. (1983). The evolution of the mammalian brain as an information processing system. In J. F. Eisenberg & D. G. Kleiman (Eds.), Advances in the study of mammalian behavior. *American Society of Mammalogists Special Publication, 7*, 632–661.

Jones, B. E. (2003). Arousal systems. *Frontiers in Bioscience, 8*, 438–451.

Joseph, R. (1988). Dual mental functioning in a split-brain patient. *Journal of Clinical Psychology, 44*, 770–779.

Kamrin, M. A. (1988). *Toxicology: A primer on toxicology principles and applications.* Boca Raton, FL: Lewis.

Karlen, S. J., & Krubitzer, L. (2006). The evolution of the neocortex in mammals: Intrinsic and extrinsic contributions to the cortical phenotype. *Novartis Found Symposium, 270*, 159–169.

Karlsson, R. M., Tanaka, K., Hellig, M., & Holmes, A. (2008). Loss of glial glutamate and aspartate transporter (Excitatory amino acid transporter 1) causes locomotor hyperactivity and exaggerated responses to psychotomimetics: Rescue by haloperidol and metabotropic glutamate 2/3 agonist. *Biological Psychiatry, 64*, 810–814.

Kendler, K. S., Neale, M. C., Kessler, R. C., Heath, A. C., & Eaves, L. J. (1993). A test of the equal-environment assumption in twin studies of psychiatric illness. *Behavior Genetics, 23*, 21–27.

Kenneally, C. (2006). The deepest cut—Radical neurosurgery and the brain's adaptability. *New Yorker, 82*(20), 36–42.

Kenrick, D. T., Li, N. P., & Butner, J. (2003). Dynamical evolutionary psychology: Individual decision rules and emergent social norms. *Psychological Review, 110*(1), 3–28. http://dx.doi.org/10.1037/0033-295X.110.1.3

Kim-Cohen, J., Caspi, A., Taylor, A., Williams, B., Newcombe, R., Craig, I., & Moffitt, T. (2006). MAOA, maltreatment, and gene-environment interaction predicting children's mental health: New evidence and a meta-analysis. *Molecular Psychiatry, 11*, 903–913.

Kitcher, P. (1985). *Vaulting ambition: Sociobiology and the quest for human nature.* Cambridge, MA: MIT Press.

Koob, A. (2009). *The root of thought: Unlocking glia—the brain cell that will help us sharpen our wits, heal injury, and treat brain disease.* New York, NY: FT Press.

Kosfeld, M., Heinrichs, M., Zaks, P., Fischbacher, U., & Fehr, E. (2005). Oxytocin increases trust in humans. *Nature, 435*, 673–676.

Kozorovitskiy, Y., & Gould, E. (2003). Adult neurogenesis: A mechanism for brain repair? *Journal of Clinical & Experimental Neuropsychology, 25*, 721–732.

Krubitzer, L., & Kaas, J. (2005). The evolution of the neocortex in mammals: How is phenotypic diversity generated? *Current Opinion in Neurobiology, 15*, 444–453.

Lambert, K. G. (2003). The life and career of Paul MacLean: A journey toward social and neurobiological harmony. *Physiology & Behavior, 79*, 373–381.

Lauterbur, P. (1973). Image formation by induced local interaction: Examples employing magnetic resonance. *Nature, 242*, 192.

LeDoux, J. E. (2000). Emotion circuits in the brain. *Annual Review of Neuroscience, 23*, 155–184.

Leek, F. F. (1969). The problem of brain removal during embalming by the ancient Egyptians. *Journal of Egyptian Archeology, SS*, 112–116.

Leggio, M. G., Mandolesi, L., Federico, F., Spirito, F., Ricci, B., Gelfo, F., & Petrosini, L. (2005). Environmental enrichment promotes improved spatial abilities and enhanced dendritic growth in the rat. *Behavioral Brain Research, 163*, 78–90.

Lehman, E. J., Hein, M. J., Baron, S. L., & Gersic, C. M. (2012). Neurodegenerative causes of death among retired National Football League players. *Neurology, 79*(19), 1970–1974.

Lezak, M. Howieson, D. B., Bigler, E. D., & Tranel, D. (2012). *Leader of the pack neuropsychological assessment.* New York, NY: Oxford University Press.

Lilienfeld, S. O. (1999a, March/April). ABC's *20/20* features segment on "goggle therapy" for depression and anxiety. *Skeptical Inquirer, 23*, 8–9.

Lilienfeld, S. O., & Byron, R. (2013) Your brain on trial. *Scientific American Mind, 23*, 44–53.

Limb, C. J. (2006). Structural and functional neural correlates of music perception. *Anatomical Record, Part A, Discoveries in Molecular, Cellular, and Evolutionary Biology, 288*, 435–446.

Lopez, D. J. (2002). Snaring the Fowler: Mark Twain debunks phrenology. *Skeptical Inquirer, 26* (1), 33–36.

MacKinnon, E. (2012). Eduardo Leite dubbed modern-day Phineas Gage after pole pierces his brain. *Life's Little Mysteries*. Retrieved from http://www.lifeslittlemysteries.com

Macmillan, M. (2000). Restoring Phineas Gage: A 150th retrospective. *Journal of the History of Neuroscience, 9*, 46–66.

Maguire, E. A., Gadian, D. G., Johnsrude, I. S., Good, C. D., Ashburner, J., Frackowiak, R. S., & Frith, C. D. (2000). Navigation-related structural change in the hippocampi of taxi drivers. *Proceedings of the National Academy of Sciences, 97*, 4398–4403.

Maier, I. C., & Schwab, M. E. (2006). Sprouting, regeneration and circuit formation in the injured spinal cord: Factors and activity. *Philosophical Transactions of the Royal Society London B Biological Sciences, 361*, 1611–1634.

Mann, E., & Mody, I. (2008). The multifaceted role of inhibition in epilepsy: Seizure-genesis through excessive GABAergic inhibition in autosomal dominant nocturnal frontal lobe epilepsy. *Current Opinion in Neurology, 21*, 155–160.

Mantella, R. C., Butters, M. A., Amico, J. A., Mazumdar, S., Rollman, B. L., Begley, A. E., ... Lenze, E. J. (2008). Salivary cortisol is associated with diagnosis and severity of late-life generalized anxiety disorder. *Psychoneuroendocrinology, 33*, 773–781.

Marino, L., McShea, D. W., & Uhen, M. D. (2004). Origin and evolution of large brains in toothed whales. *Anatomical Record Part A: Discoveries in Molecular, Cellular, & Evolutionary Biology, 281*, 1247–1255.

Marsh, A. A., Finger, E. C., Mitchell, D. G., Reid, M. E., Sims, C., Kosson, D. S., ... Blair, R. J. (2008). Reduced amygdala response to fearful expressions in children and adolescents with callous-unemotional traits and disruptive behavior disorders. *American Journal of Psychiatry, 165*, 712–720.

Mathews, V., Wang, Y., Kalnin, A. J., Mosier, K. M., Dunn, D. W., & Kronenberger, W. G. (2006). *Short-term effects of violent video game playing: An fMRI study.* Annual Meeting of the Radiological Society of North America, Chicago, IL.

Mattingley, J. B. (1999). Attention, consciousness, and the damaged brain: Insights from parietal neglect and extinction. *Psyche, 5*, 14.

McCabe, D. P., & Castel, A. D. (2008). Seeing is believing: The effect of brain images on judgments of scientific reasoning. *Cognition, 107*, 343–352.

McClearn, G. E., Johansson, B., Berg, S., Pedersen, N. L., Ahern, F., Petrill, S. A., & Plomin, R. (1997). Substantial genetic influence on cognitive abilities in twins 80 or more years old. *Science, 276*, 1560–1563.

McKinney, M., & Jacksonville, M. C. (2005). Brain cholinergic vulnerability: Relevance to behavior and disease. *Biochemical Pharmacology, 70*, 1115–1124.

Metea, M. R., & Newman, E. A. (2006). Glial cells dilate and constrict blood vessels: A mechanism of neurovascular coupling. *Journal of Neuroscience, 26*, 2862–2870.

Miller, G. (2010). Beyond DSM: Seeking a brain-based classification of mental illness. *Science, 327*(5972), 1437–1437.

Miller, R. H. (2006). The promise of stem cells for neural repair. *Brain Research, 1091*, 258–264.

Mobbs, D., Greicius, M. D., Abdel-Azim, E., Menon, V., & Reiss, A. L. (2003). Humor modulates the mesolimbic reward centers. *Neuron, 40*, 1041–1048.

Moscovitch, M., Rosenbaum, R. S., Gilboa, A., Addis, D. R., Westmacott, R., Grady, C., ... Nadel, L. (2005). Functional neuroanatomy of remote episodic, semantic and spatial memory: A unified account based on multiple trace theory. *Journal of Anatomy, 207*, 35–66.

Muller, F. J., Snyder, E. Y., & Loring, J. F. (2006). Gene therapy: Can neural stem cells deliver? *Nature Reviews Neuroscience, 7*, 75–84.

Nachev, P., & Husain, M. (2006). Disorders of visual attention and the posterior parietal cortex. *Cortex, 42*, 766–773.

Nakayama, K., Garrido, L., Russell, R., Chabris, C. F., Gerbasi, M., & Duchaine, B. C. (2006). Developmental prosopagnosia: Phenotypes and estimated prevalence. Paper presented at the Annual Meeting of the Society for Neuroscience, Atlanta, GA.

Nesse, R., & Ellsworth, P. (2009). Evolution, emotions, and emotional disorders. *American Psychologist, 64*, 129–139.

O'Donohue, W. T., Lilienfeld, S. O., & Fowler, K. A. (2007). Science is an essential safeguard against human error. In S. O. Lilienfeld & W. T. O'Donohue (Eds.), *The great ideas of clinical science: 17 principles that every mental health professional should understand* (pp. 3–27). New York, NY: Routledge.

Ogawa, S., Lee, T. M., Kay, A. R., & Tank, D. W. (1990). Brain magnetic resonance imaging with contrast dependent on blood oxygenation. *Proceedings of the National Academy of Sciences, 87*, 9868–9872.

Oosterlaan, J., Geurts, H. M., Knol, D. L., & Sergeant, J. A. (2005). Low basal salivary cortisol is associated with teacher-reported symptoms of conduct disorder. *Psychiatry Research, 134*(1), 1–10. http://dx.doi.org/10.1016/j.psychres.2004.12.005

Oppenheim, R. W. (1991). Cell death during development of the nervous system. *Annual Review of Neuroscience, 14*, 453–501.

Panksepp, J., & Panksepp, J. B. (2000). The seven sins of evolutionary psychology. *Evolution and Cognition, 6*, 108–131.

Penfield, W. (1958). *The excitable cortex in conscious man.* Liverpool, England: Liverpool University Press.

Pert, C. B., Pasternak, G., & Snyder, S. H. (1973). Opiate agonists and antagonists discriminated by receptor binding in brain. *Science, 182*, 1359–1361.

Peterson, C., & Seligman, M. E. P. (2003). *Character strengths and virtues: A handbook and classification.* New York, NY: Oxford University Press.

Platt, S. A., & Sanislow, C. A. (1988). Norm-of-reaction: Definition and misinterpretation of animal research. *Journal of Comparative Psychology, 102*, 254–261.

Plomin, R., & Crabbe, J. C. (2000). DNA. *Psychological Bulletin, 126*, 806–828.

Poldrack, R. A. (2011). The iPhone and the brain. *New York Times, 5*.

Pollard, K. S., Salama, S. R., King, B., Kern, A. D., Dreszer, T., Katzman, S., ... Hassler, D. (2006, October 13). Forces shaping the fastest evolving regions in the human genome. *PLoS Genetics, 2*(10), 168.

Racine, E., Bar-Ilan, O., & Illes, J. (2006). Brain imaging: A decade of coverage in the print media. *Science Communication, 28*, 122–142.

Ramon, M., Busigny, T., & Rossion, B. (2010). Impaired holistic processing of unfamiliar individual faces in acquired prosopagnosia. *Neuropsychologia, 48*, 933–944.

Raulin, M. L. (2003). *Abnormal psychology.* Boston, MA: Allyn & Bacon.

Rilling, J. K., King-Casas, B., & Sanfey, A. G. (2008). The neurobiology of social decision-making. *Current Opinion in Neurobiology, 18*, 159–165.

Roskies, A. L. (2007). Are neuroimages like photographs of the brain? *Philosophy of Science, 74*, 860–872.

Rotshtein, P., Vuilleumier, P., Winston, J., Driver, J., & Dolan, R. (2007). Distinct and convergent visual processing of high and low spatial frequency information in faces. *Cerebral Cortex, 17*(11), 2713–2724.

Roy-Byrne, P. P. (2005). The GABA-benzodiazepine receptor complex: Structure, function, and role in anxiety. *Journal of Clinical Psychiatry, 66*(Suppl. 2), 14–20.

Russell, R., Duchaine, B., & Nakayama, K. (2009). Super-recognizers: People with extraordinary face recognition ability. *Psychonomic Bulletin & Review, 16*, 252–257.

Saba, G., Schurhoff, F., & Leboyer, M. (2006). Therapeutic and neurophysiologic aspects of transcranial magnetic stimulation in schizophrenia. *Neurophysiologie Clinique, 36*, 185–194.

Sacks, O. (1985). *The man who mistook his wife for a hat: And other clinical tales.* New York, NY: Touchstone.

Sacks, O. (2010, June). A man of letters: Why was the morning paper suddenly in a foreign language? *New Yorker.*

Sanchez-Andres, J. V., Olds, J. L., & Alkon, D. L. (1993). Gated informational transfer within the mammalian hippocampus: A new hypothesis. *Behavioral Brain Research, 54*, 111–106.

Schacter, D. L. (1996). *Searching for memory: The brain, the mind, and the past.* New York, NY: Basic Books.

Schatzberg, A. F. (1998). Noradrenergic versus serotonergic antidepressants: Predictors of treatment response. *Journal of Clinical Psychiatry, 59*(Suppl. 14), 15–18.

Schmahmann, J. D. (2004). Disorders of the cerebellum: Ataxia, dysmetria of thought, and the cerebellar cognitive affective syndrome. *Journal of Neuropsychiatry & Clinical Neurosciences, 16*, 367–378.

Schroeter, M. L., Abdul-Khaliq, H., Krebs, M., Dieferibacher, A., & Blasig, I. E. (2009). Neuron-specific enolase is unaltered whereas S100B is elevated in serum of patients with schizophrenia—Original research and meta-analysis. *Psychiatry Research, 167*, 66–72.

Schultz, W. (2002). Getting formal with dopamine and reward. *Neuron, 36*(2), 241–263.

Seger, C. A., & Spiering, B. J. (2011). A critical review of habit learning and the basal ganglia. *Frontiers in Systems Neuroscience, 5*, 66. http://dx.doi.org/10.3389/fnsys.2011.00066

Shermer, M. (2008, October). Five ways brains scans mislead. *Scientific American.* http://www.scientificamerican.com/article.cfm?id=five-ways-brain-scans-mislead-us

Shomstein, S., & Yantis, S. (2006). Parietal cortex mediates voluntary control of spatial and nonspatial auditory attention. *Journal of Neuroscience, 26*, 435–439.

Silventoinen, K., Sammalisto, S., Perola, M., Boomsma, D. I., Cornes, B. K., Davis, C., ... Kaprio, J. (2003). Heritability of adult body height: A comparative study of twin cohorts in eight countries. *Twin Research, 6*, 399–408.

Solomon, R. (2002). *That takes ovaries! Bold females and their brazen acts.* New York, NY: Three Rivers Press.

Sperry, R. W. (1974). Lateral specialization in the surgically separated hemispheres. In F. Schmitt & F. Worden (Eds.), *Neurosciences third study program* (pp. 5–19). Cambridge, MA: MIT Press.

Suter, M. R., Wen, Y. R., Decosterd, I., & Ji, R. R. (2007). Do glial cells control pain? *Neuron Glia Biology, 3*, 255–268.

Swain, R. A., Kerr, A. L., & Thompson, R. F. (2011). The cerebellum: A neural system for the study of reinforcement learning. *Frontiers in Behavioral Neuroscience, 5*, 8. http://dx.doi.org/10.3389/fnbeh.2011.00008

Talbott, S. (2002). *The cortisol connection diet: The breakthrough program to control stress and lose weight.* Alameda, CA: Hunter House.

Tang, Y., Nyengaard, J. R., De Groot, D. M., & Gundersen, H. J. (2001). Total regional and global number of synapses in the human brain neocortex. *Synapse, 41*, 258–273.

Turkheimer, E. (1998). Heritability and biological explanation. *Psychological Review, 105*, 782–791.

Uttal, W. R. (2001). *The new phrenology: The limits of localizing cognitive processes in the brain.* Cambridge, MA: Bradford Books/MIT Press.

Volkow, N. D., Wang, G. J., Fowler, J. S., & Ding, Y. (2005). Imaging the effects of methylphenidate on brain dopamine: New model on its therapeutic actions for attention-deficit/hyperactivity disorder. *Biological Psychiatry, 57*, 1410–1415.

Vrba, J., & Robinson, S. E. (2001). Signal processing in magnetoencephalography. *Methods, 25*, 249–271.

Vul, E., Harris, C., Winkielman, P., & Pashler, H. (2009). Puzzlingly high correlations in fMRI studies of emotion, personality, and social cognition. *Perspectives on Psychological Science, 4*, 274–290.

Waldman, I. D. (2007). Gene-environment interactions reexamined: Does mother's marital stability interact with the dopamine receptor D2 gene in the etiology of childhood attention-deficit/hyperactivity disorder? *Development and Psychopathology, 19*(4), 1117–1128.

Wang, D. D., & Kriegstein, A. R. (2009). Defining the role of GABA in cortical development. *The Journal of Physiology, 187*, 1873–1879.

Wang, R., Li, J., Fang, H., M. Tian, & J. Liu. (2012). Individual differences in holistic processing predict face recognition ability. *Psychological Science, 23*, 169–177.

Weaver, I. C., Cervoni, N., Champagne, F. A., D'Alessio, A. C., Sharma, S., Seckl, J. R., . . . Meaney, M. J. (2004). Epigenetic programming by maternal behavior. *Nature Neuroscience, 8*, 847–854.

Weisberg, D. S., Keil, F. C., Goodstein, J., Rawson, E., & Gray, J. R. (2008). The seductive allure of neuroscience explanations. *Journal of Cognitive Neuroscience, 20*, 470–477.

Weisberg, L. A., Garcia, C., & Strub, R. L. (1996). Diseases of the peripheral nerves and motor neurons. In L. Weisberg, C. Garc'a, R. Strub, & E. Bouldin (Eds.), *Essentials of clinical neurology* (pp. 458–494). St. Louis: Mosby.

Wilgus, J., & Wilgus, B. (2009). Face to face with Phineas Gage. *Journal of the History of the Neurosciences, 18*, 340–345.

Winkelman, J. W., Buxton, O. M., Jensen, J. E., Benson, K. L., O'Connor, S. P., Wang, W., & Renshaw, P. F. (2008). Reduced brain GABA in primary insomnia: Preliminary data from 4T proton magnetic resonance spectroscopy (1HMRS). *Sleep, 31*, 1499–1506.

Woolf, N. J. (1991). Cholinergic systems in mammalian brain and spinal cord. *Progress in Neurobiology, 37*, 475–524.

Woolf, N. J. (2006). Microtubules in the cerebral cortex: Role in memory and consciousness. In J. A. Tuszynski (Ed.), *The emerging physics of consciousness* (pp. 49–94). Berlin, Germany: Springer-Verlag.

Young, L. J., & Wang, Z. X., (2004) The neurobiology of pair bonding. *Nature Neuroscience, 7*, 1048–1054.

Zaidel, D. W. (1994). A view of the world from a split brain perspective. In E. M. R. Critchley (Ed.), *The neurological boundaries of reality* (pp. 161–174). London, England: Farrand Press.

Zak, P. J. (2012). *The moral molecule: The source of love and prosperity.* New York, NY: Dutton.

Credits

Credits listed in order of appearance.

Photo Credits

Photo Credits listed in order of appearance.

Sensation and Perception

From Chapter 4 of *Psychology: From Inquiry to Understanding*, Third Edition. Scott O. Lilienfeld, Steven Jay Lynn, Laura L. Namy, Nancy J. Woolf. Copyright © 2014 by Pearson Education, Inc. All rights reserved.

Sensation and Perception

HOW WE SENSE AND CONCEPTUALIZE THE WORLD

140

Think About It

Do some people "taste" shapes or "hear" colors?

Can our eyes detect only a single particle of light?

Can certain blind people still "see" some of their surroundings?

Can we perceive invisible stimuli?

Can we "read" someone else's thoughts?

FIGURE 1 Separating Sensation from Perception. Hold this page about 10 inches from your face. Close your right eye and keep focusing on the white circle. Can you see the white *X*? Now slowly move the page toward your face and then away from it; at some point the white *X* will disappear and then reappear. Surprisingly, your brain supplies an illusory background pattern that fills in the white space occupied by the *X*.

illusion
perception in which the way we perceive a stimulus doesn't match its physical reality

sensation
detection of physical energy by sense organs, which then send information to the brain

perception
the brain's interpretation of raw sensory inputs

Watch in **MyPsychLab** the **Video:** The Basics: In Full Appreciation of the Cookie

---

Sensation and Perception

((•)) **Listen** in **MyPsychLab** to chapter audio

Before you read any further, try the exercise in **FIGURE 1**. Were you surprised that the white "X" disappeared from view? Were you even more surprised that you filled the missing space occupied by the "X" with a mental image exactly matching the fancy background pattern?

Sensation and perception are the underlying processes operating in this visual illusion; it's an **illusion** because the way you perceived the stimulus doesn't match its physical reality. Your brain—not your eyes—perceived a complete pattern even though some of it was missing. **Sensation** refers to the detection of physical energy by our sense organs, including our eyes, ears, skin, nose, and tongue, which then relay information to the brain. **Perception** is the brain's *interpretation* of these raw sensory inputs. Simplifying things just a bit, sensation first allows us to pick up the signals in our environments, and perception then allows us to assemble these signals into something meaningful.

We often assume that our sensory systems are infallible and that our perceptions are perfect representations of the world around us. We term these beliefs *naive realism*. We'll discover in this chapter that naive realism is wrong, because the world isn't precisely as we see it. Somewhere in our brains we reconstructed that fancy pattern in the figure and put it smack in the middle of the empty space, a perceptual process called *filling-in*, which occurs entirely without our awareness (Weil & Rees, 2011). Most of the time, filling-in is adaptive, as it helps us make sense of our often confusing and chaotic perceptual worlds. But sometimes it can fool us, as in the case of visual illusions.

Perception researchers have studied filling-in by showing participants incomplete objects on computer screens and determining which *pixels,* or picture elements, participants rely on to make perceptual judgments about the object (Gold et al., 2000). The pixels that participants use to perceive images are often located next to regions where there's no sensory information, demonstrating that we use available sensory information to make sense of what's missing and thereby identify incomplete objects. In other words, we often blend the real with the imagined, going beyond the information given to us. By doing so, we simplify the world, and often make better sense of it in the process.

Two Sides of the Coin: Sensation and Perception

1. Identify the basic principles that apply to all senses.
2. Discuss the role of attention and the nature of the binding problem.

How do signals that make contact with our sense organs—like our eyes, ears, and tongue—become translated into information that our brains can interpret and act on? And how does the raw sensory information delivered to our brains become integrated with what we already know about the world, allowing us to recognize objects, avoid accidents, and find our way out the door each morning?

Here's how. Our brain picks and chooses among the types of sensory information it uses, often relying on expectations and prior experiences to fill in the gaps and simplify processing. The end result often differs from the sum of its parts—and sometimes it's a completely wrong number! Errors in perception, like the illusion in Figure 1 and others we'll examine in this chapter, are often informative, not to mention fun. They show us which parts of our sensory experiences are accurate and which parts our brains fill-in for us.

We'll first discover what our sensory systems can accomplish and how they manage to transform physical signals in the outside world into neural activity in the "inside world"—our brains. Then we'll explore how and when our brains flesh out the details, moving beyond the raw sensory information available to us.

Sensation: Our Senses as Detectives

Our senses enable us to see majestic scenery, hear glorious music, feel a loving touch, maintain balance as we walk across a stage, and taste wonderful food. Despite their differences, all of our senses rely on a mere handful of basic principles.

TRANSDUCTION: GOING FROM THE OUTSIDE WORLD TO WITHIN. The first step in sensation is converting external energies or substances into a "language" the nervous system understands. **Transduction** is the process by which the nervous system converts an external stimulus, like light or sound, into electrical signals within neurons. A specific type of **sense receptor,** or specialized cell, transduces a specific stimulus. As we'll learn, specialized cells at the back of the eye transduce light, cells in a spiral-shaped organ in the ear transduce sound, odd-looking endings attached to axons embedded in deep layers of the skin transduce pressure, receptor cells lining the inside of

(© ScienceCartoonsPlus.com)

the nose transduce airborne odorants, and taste buds transduce chemicals containing flavor.

For all of our senses, activation is greatest when we first detect a stimulus. After that, our response declines in strength, a process called **sensory adaptation**. What happens when we sit on a chair? After a few seconds, we no longer notice it, unless it's an extremely hard seat, or worse, has a thumbtack on it. The adaptation takes place at the level of the sense receptor. This receptor reacts strongly at first and then tamps down its level of responding to conserve energy and attentional resources. If we didn't engage in sensory adaptation, we'd be attending to just about everything around us, all of the time.

PSYCHOPHYSICS: MEASURING THE BARELY DETECTABLE. Back in the 19th century, when psychology was gradually distinguishing itself as a science apart from philosophy, many researchers focused on sensation and perception. In 1860, German scientist Gustaf Fechner published a landmark work on perception. Out of his efforts grew **psychophysics,** the study of how we perceive sensory stimuli based on their physical characteristics.

Absolute Threshold. Imagine that a researcher fits us with a pair of headphones and places us in a quiet room. She asks repeatedly if we've heard one of many very faint tones. Detection isn't an all-or-none state of affairs because human error increases as stimuli become weaker in magnitude. Psychophysicists study phenomena like the **absolute threshold** of a stimulus—the lowest level of a stimulus we can detect on 50 percent of the trials when no other stimuli of that type are present. Absolute thresholds demonstrate how remarkably sensitive our sensory systems are. On a clear night, our visual systems can detect a single candle from 30 miles away. We can detect a smell from as few as 50 airborne odorant molecules; the salamander's exquisitely sensitive sniffer can pull off this feat with only one (Menini, Picco, & Firestein, 1995).

Just Noticeable Difference. Just how much of a difference in a stimulus makes a difference? The **just noticeable difference (JND)** is the smallest change in the intensity of a stimulus that we can detect. The JND is relevant to our ability to distinguish a stronger from a weaker stimulus, like a soft noise from a slightly louder noise. Imagine we're playing a song on an iPod but the volume is turned so low that we can't hear it. If we nudge the volume dial up to the point at which we can *just* begin to make out the song, that's a JND. **Weber's law** states that there's a constant proportional relationship between the JND and the original stimulus

transduction
the process of converting an external energy or substance into electrical activity within neurons

sense receptor
specialized cell responsible for converting external stimuli into neural activity for a specific sensory system

sensory adaptation
activation is greatest when a stimulus is first detected

psychophysics
the study of how we perceive sensory stimuli based on their physical characteristics

absolute threshold
lowest level of a stimulus needed for the nervous system to detect a change 50 percent of the time

just noticeable difference (JND)
the smallest change in the intensity of a stimulus that we can detect

Weber's Law
there is a constant proportional relationship between the JND and original stimulus intensity

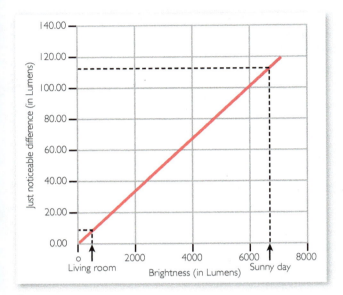

FIGURE 2 Just Noticeable Differences (JNDs) Adhere to Weber's Law. In this example, changes in light are shown measured in lumens, which are units equaling the amount of light generated by one candle standing one foot away. Weber's law states that the brighter the light, the more change in brightness is required for us to be able to notice a difference.

TABLE 1 Distinguishing Signals from Noise. In signal detection theory there are true positives, false negatives, false positives, and true negatives. Subject biases affect the probability of "yes" and "no" responses to the question "Was there a stimulus?"

	RESPOND "YES"	RESPOND "NO"
Stimulus present	True Positive	False Negative
Stimulus absent	False Positive	True Negative

intensity (see **FIGURE 2**). In plain language, the stronger the stimulus, the bigger the change needed for a change in stimulus intensity to be noticeable. Imagine how much light we'd need to add to a brightly lit kitchen to notice an increase in illumination compared with the amount of light we'd need to add to a dark bedroom to notice a change in illumination. We'd need a lot of light in the first case and only a smidgeon in the second.

Signal Detection Theory. David Green and John Swets (1966) developed **signal detection theory** to describe how we detect stimuli under uncertain conditions, as when we're trying to figure out what a friend is saying on a cell phone when there's a lot of static in the connection—that is, when there's high background noise. We'll need to increase the signal by shouting over the static or else our friend won't understand us. If we have a good connection, however, our friend can easily understand us without our shouting. This example illustrates the *signal-to-noise ratio*: It becomes harder to detect a signal as background noise increases.

Green and Swets were also interested in *response biases,* or tendencies to make one type of guess over another when we're in doubt about whether a weak signal is present or absent under noisy conditions. They developed a clever way to take into account some people's tendency to say "yes" when they're uncertain and other people's tendency to say "no" when they're uncertain. Instead of always delivering a sound, they sometimes presented a sound, sometimes not. This procedure allowed them to detect and account for participants' response biases. As we can see in **TABLE 1**, participants can report that they heard a sound when it was present (a *true positive*, or hit), deny hearing a sound when it was present (a *false negative*, or miss), report hearing a sound that wasn't there (a *false positive*, or false alarm), or deny hearing a sound that wasn't there (a *true negative*, or correct rejection). The frequency of false negatives and false positives helps us measure how biased participants are to respond "yes" or "no" in general.

Sensory Systems Stick to One Sense—Or Do They? Back in 1826, Johannes Müller proposed the doctrine of *specific nerve energies,* which states that even though there are many distinct stimulus energies—like light, sound, or touch—the sensation we experience is determined by the nature of the sense receptor, not the stimulus. To get a sense of this principle in action, the next time you rub your eyes shortly after waking up, try to notice phosphenes— vivid sensations of light caused by pressure on your eye's receptor cells. Many phosphenes look like sparks, and some even look like multicolored shapes in a kaleidoscope. Some people have speculated that phosphenes may explain certain reports of ghosts and UFOs (Neher, 1990).

Why do phosphenes occur? In the cerebral cortex, different areas are devoted to different senses. It doesn't matter to our brain whether light or touch activated the sense receptor: Our brains react the same way in either case. That is, once our visual sense receptors send their signals to the cortex, the brain interprets their input as visual, regardless of how our receptors were stimulated in the first place.

Most areas of the cortex are connected to cortical areas devoted to the same sense: Vision areas tend to be connected to other vision areas, hearing areas to other hearing areas, and so on. Yet scientists have found many examples of cross modal processing that produce different perceptual experiences than either modality provides by itself. One striking example is the *McGurk effect* (McGurk & MacDonald, 1976; Nahorna et al., 2012). This effect demonstrates that we integrate visual and auditory information when processing spoken language, and our brains automatically calculate the most probable sound given the information from the two sources. In the McGurk effect, hearing the audio track of one syllable (such as "ba") spoken repeatedly while seeing a video track of a different syllable being spoken (such as "ga") produces the perceptual experience of a different third sound

signal detection theory
theory regarding how stimuli are detected under different conditions

(such as "da"). This third sound is the brain's best "guess" at integrating the two conflicting sources of information.

Another fascinating example is an illusion that shows how our senses of touch and sight interact to create a false perceptual experience (Erhsson, Spence, & Passingham, 2004; Knox et al., 2006). This illusion involves placing a rubber hand on top of a table with the precise positioning that a participant's hand would have if she were resting it on the table. The participant's hand is placed under the table, out of her view. A researcher simultaneously strokes the participant's hidden hand and rubber hand gently with a paintbrush. When the strokes match each other, the participant experiences an eerie illusion: The rubber hand seems to be her own hand.

As we've seen, these cross-modal effects may reflect "cross-talk" among different brain regions. But there's an alternative explanation: In some cases, a single brain region may serve double duty, helping to process multiple senses. For example, neurons in the auditory cortex tuned to sound also respond weakly to touch (Fu et al., 2003). Visual stimuli enhance touch perception in the somatosensory cortex (Taylor-Clarke, Kennett, & Haggard, 2002). The reading of Braille by people blind from birth activates their visual cortex (Gizewski et al., 2003). And monkeys viewing videos with sound display increased activity in their primary auditory cortex compared with exposure to sound alone (Kayser et al., 2007).

Sir Francis Galton (1880) was the first to describe **synesthesia**, a rare condition in which people experience cross-modal sensations, like hearing sounds when they see colors—sometimes called "colored hearing"—or even tasting or smelling colors (Cytowic & Eagleman, 2009; Marks, in press). Synesthesia may be an extreme version of the cross-modal responses that most of us experience from time to time (Rader & Tellegen, 1987). No one knows for sure how widespread synesthesia is. An early estimate put it at no higher than about 1 in 2,000 people (Baron-Cohen et al., 1993); however, a more recent survey of 500 British university students estimated the prevalence to be about 4 percent, implying that it might not be as rare as once thought (Simner et al., 2006).

In the past, some scientists questioned the authenticity of synesthesia, yet research demonstrates that the condition is genuine (Ramachandran & Hubbard, 2001). **FIGURE 3** illustrates a clever test that detects grapheme-color synesthesia. Specific parts of the visual cortex become active during most synesthesia experiences, verifying that these experiences are associated with brain activity (Paulesu et al., 1995; Rouw et al., 2011).

The Role of Attention

In a world in which our brains are immersed in a sea of sensory input, flexible attention is critical to our survival and well-being. To zero in on a video game we play in the park, for example, we must ignore that speck of dust on our shirt, the shifting breeze, and the riot of colors and sounds in the neighborhood. Yet at any moment we must be prepared to use sensory information that signals a potential threat, such as an approaching thunderstorm. Fortunately, we're superbly well equipped to meet the challenges of our rich and ever-changing sensory environments.

SELECTIVE ATTENTION: HOW WE FOCUS ON SPECIFIC INPUTS. If we're constantly receiving inputs from all our sensory channels, like a TV set with all channels switched on at once, how do we keep from becoming hopelessly bewildered? **Selective attention** allows us to select one channel and turn off the others, or at least turn down their volume.

Donald Broadbent's (1957) *filter theory of attention* views attention as a bottleneck through which information passes. This mental filter enables us to pay attention to important stimuli and ignore others. Broadbent tested his theory using a task called *dichotic listening*—in which participants hear two different messages, one delivered to the left ear and one to the right ear. When Broadbent asked participants to ignore messages delivered to one of the ears, they seemed to know little or nothing about these messages. Anne Treisman (1960) replicated these findings, elaborating on them by asking participants to repeat the messages they heard. Although participants could only repeat the messages to which they'd attended, they'd sometimes mix in some of the information they were

---

synesthesia
a condition in which people experience cross-modal sensations

selective attention
process of selecting one sensory channel and ignoring or minimizing others

◀ **RULING OUT RIVAL HYPOTHESES**
Have important alternative explanations for the findings been excluded?

FIGURE 3 Are You Synesthetic? Although most of us see the top image as a bunch of jumbled numbers, some grapheme-color synesthetes, who "see" certain numbers as colors, perceive it as looking like the image on the bottom. Synesthesia makes it much easier to find the 2s embedded in a field of 5s.

Simulate in **MyPsychLab** the **Experiment:** Selective Attention

◀ **REPLICABILITY**
Can the results be duplicated in other studies?

FIGURE 4 The Cocktail Party Effect. The cocktail party effect helps explain how we can become aware of stimuli outside of our immediate attention when it's relevant to us—like our names.

FIGURE 5 An ESP Trick? Try It and Find Out. Try this "ESP trick," adapted from a demonstration by Clifford Pickover. This remarkable trick will demonstrate that we—the authors of this book—can read your mind! Select one of the six cards and be sure to recall it. To help you remember it, repeat its name out loud several times. Once you're sure you have the card in mind, check your answer shown on the next page.

supposed to ignore, especially if it made sense to add it. If the attended ear heard, "I saw the girl … song was wishing," and the unattended ear heard, "me that bird … jumping in the street," a participant might hear "I saw the girl jumping in the street," because the combination forms a meaningful sentence. The information we've supposedly filtered out of our attention is still being processed at some level—even when we're not aware of it (Beaman, Bridges, & Scott, 2007).

An attention-related phenomenon called the *cocktail party effect* refers to our ability to pick out an important message, like our name, in a conversation that doesn't involve us. We don't typically notice what other people are saying in a noisy restaurant or at a party unless it's relevant to us—and then suddenly, we perk up. This finding tells us that the filter inside our brain, which selects what will and won't receive our attention, is more complex than just an "on" or "off" switch. Even when seemingly "off," it's ready to spring into action if it perceives something significant (see **FIGURE 4**).

INATTENTIONAL BLINDNESS. Before reading on, try the ESP trick in **FIGURE 5**. We're going to try to read your mind. Then come back and read the next paragraph.

We're surprisingly poor at detecting stimuli in plain sight when our attention is focused elsewhere (Henderson & Hollingworth, 1999; Levin & Simons, 1997; McConkie & Currie, 1996). In an astonishing demonstration of this phenomenon, called **inattentional blindness**, Daniel Simons and Christopher Chabris (1999, 2010) asked subjects to watch a video of people tossing a basketball back and forth quickly, and required them to keep track of the number of passes. Then, smack in the middle of the video, a woman dressed in a gorilla suit strolled across the scene for a full 9 seconds. Remarkably, about half the viewers failed to notice the hairy misfit even though she paused to face the camera and thumped her chest. This and other findings demonstrate that we often need to pay close attention to pick out even dramatic changes in our environments (Koivisto & Revonsuo, 2007; Rensink, O'Regan, & Clark, 1997).

A closely related phenomenon, called *change blindness*, is a failure to detect obvious changes in one's environment (if you've tried the ESP trick we mentioned, you'll know what we mean). Change blindness is a particular concern for airplane pilots, who may fail to notice another plane taxiing across the runway as they're preparing to land (Podczerwinski, Wickens, & Alexander, 2002). You may be relieved to hear that industrial/organizational psychologists are working actively with aviation agencies to reduce the incidence of this problem.

The Binding Problem: Putting the Pieces Together

The *binding problem* is one of the great mysteries of psychology. When we perceive an apple, different regions of our brains process different aspects of it. Yet somehow—we don't really know how—our brains manage to combine or "bind" these diverse pieces of information into a unified whole. An apple looks red and round, feels smooth, tastes sweet and tart, and smells, well, like an apple. Any one of its characteristics in isolation isn't an apple or even a part of an apple. One hypothesis is that rapid, coordinated activity across

inattentional blindness
failure to detect stimuli that are in plain sight when our attention is focused elsewhere

146

multiple cortical areas assists in binding (Engel & Singer, 2001). Binding may explain many aspects of perception and attention. When we see the world, we rely on shape, motion, color, and depth cues, each of which requires different amounts of time to detect individually (Bartels & Zeki, 2006). Yet our minds seamlessly combine these visual cues into a unified perception of a scene. To better understand how perception and attention work together, we'll next discuss the different senses we rely on to make our way in the world, starting with the visual system.

from inquiry to understanding

HOW DOES MAGIC WORK?

When you think of the astonishing tricks of stage magicians, does psychological science come to mind? Probably not. Yet in the past decade, psychologists and neuroscientists have partnered with famous magicians, including the Amazing Randi and Teller (of Penn & Teller fame) (Macknik et al., 2008), to establish a "science of magic." This science promises to unravel the psychological mechanisms of the reality-bending illusions that magicians create (Kuhn et al., 2008; Stone, 2012). Magic tricks that confound and astound us can yield their secrets (only a few spoilers here) to researchers, and contribute to our understanding of perception.

Many of us have heard the old saying, "The hand is quicker than the eye" with regard to the ability of stage magicians to create mind-boggling stunts involving sleight of hand. Yet this adage actually reflects a popular misconception, as most magic tricks are carried out at a normal speed (Kuhn et al., 2008). Researchers have discovered that a more accurate phrase to capture how magicians fool us is "The hand is quicker than the brain."

Consider the following example. A stage magician can get people to believe that a coin has disappeared after it is seemingly transferred from his right to left hand, because the audience can't tell that he secretly concealed (palmed) the coin in the right hand. The magician takes advantage of a little-known fact: viewers don't consciously register information for a small fraction of second after it arrives in the brain, making it appear that the coin is still in the left hand, when it actually has been removed and hidden in the right hand (Stone, 2012). Because the onlooker's visual neurons keep firing for one-hundredth of a second after the coin is transferred (Libet et al., 1983), it ensures that the coin will appear to be in the left hand just long enough to fool observers. So when the magician opens his left hand, to the amazement of the stunned audience, the coin appears to have vanished!

Researchers have studied the vanishing ball illusion to understand how mental predictions and expectancies, rather than reality, affect perception. Here's how this fascinating illusion works. The magician throws two balls into the air, one at a time, and catches each in his hand. On both throws, his head and eyes look up to track the flight of the ball. The third time, the magician pretends to throw the ball, but secretly palms it in his hand as he moves his head up to follow the imaginary ball. In one study of this illusion (Kuhn & Land, 2006), two-thirds of the observers who viewed this trick perceived the ball to leave the magician's hand and disappear in mid-flight. In a second condition, rather than move his head to follow the flight of the imaginary ball, the magician looked at the hand that concealed the ball. When this occurred, less than a third of the participants said the ball vanished. The success of the trick depended on the head direction of the magician, a social cue that created the expectation that the ball was in flight, which never actually happened.

Stage magicians also trick people by other means, such as by misdirecting attention and awareness. This technique fools us because we're consciously aware of and attend to only a tiny part of the information that enters our eyes (Kuhn et al., 2008; Rensink et al., 1997). By riveting the audience's attention to a grand theatrical movement, such as pulling the proverbial rabbit out of a hat, the performer distracts onlookers from noticing a less obvious movement related to a secret prop that's essential to the next trick. So the next time you witness the likes of "The Fabulous Fabrini" performing captivating feats of magic on stage or screen, don't be surprised if scientists are studying him to sleuth how attention, awareness, and perception can play tricks on our minds.

Stage magicians capitalize on tricks of perception. In the case of the vanishing coin trick, there's a delay between the time something is "seen" and when the information about the event arrives in the brain; in the case of the vanishing ball illusion, cues—the magician's head moving upwards—shape the perception of the ball moving in the air and disappearing when it's actually in his palm.

Study and Review in MyPsychLab

Assess Your Knowledge   FACT or FICTION?

1. Perception is an exact translation of our sensory experiences into neural activity.
   True / False

2. In signal detection theory, false positives and false negatives help us measure how much someone is paying attention. **True / False**

3. Cross-modal activation produces different perceptual experiences than either modality provides by itself. **True / False**

4. The rubber hand illusion shows how our senses of smell and touch interact to create a false perceptual experience. **True / False**

5. Selective attention allows us to pay attention to important stimuli and ignore others. **True / False**

Answers: 1. F, 2. F, 3. T, 4. F, 5. T

Seeing: The Visual System

3 Explain how the eye starts the visual process.

4 Identify the different kinds of visual perception.

5 Describe different visual problems.

The first thing we see after awakening is typically unbiased by any previous image. If we're on vacation and sleeping somewhere new, we may not recognize our surroundings for a moment or two. Building up an image involves many external elements, such as light, biological systems in the eye and brain that process images for us, and our past experiences.

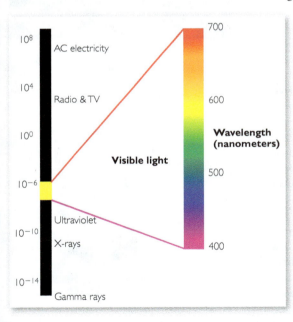

FIGURE 6 The Visible Spectrum Is a Subset of the Electromagnetic Spectrum. Visible light is electromagnetic energy between ultraviolet and infrared. Humans are sensitive to wavelengths ranging from slightly less than 400 nanometers (violet) to slightly more than 700 nanometers (red).

Light: The Energy of Life

One of the central players in our perception of the world is light, a form of electromagnetic energy—energy composed of fluctuating electric and magnetic waves. Visible light has a *wavelength* in the hundreds of nanometers (a nanometer is one billionth of a meter). As we can see in **FIGURE 6**, we respond only to a narrow range of wavelengths of light; this range is the human visible spectrum. Each animal species detects a specific visible range, which can extend slightly above or below the human visible spectrum. Butterflies are sensitive to all of the wavelengths we detect in addition to ultraviolet light, which has a shorter wavelength than violet light. We might assume that the human visible spectrum is fixed, but increasing the amount of vitamin A in our diets can increase our ability to see infrared light, which has a longer wavelength than red light (Rubin & Walls, 1969).

When light reaches an object, part of that light gets reflected by the object and part gets absorbed. Our perception of an object's *brightness* is influenced directly by the intensity of the reflected light that reaches our eyes. Completely white objects reflect all of the light shone on them and absorb none of it, whereas black objects do the opposite. So white and black aren't really "colors:" white is the presence of all colors, black the absence of them. The brightness of an object depends not only on the amount of reflected light, but also on the overall lighting surrounding the object.

Psychologists call the color of light **hue**. We're maximally attuned to three primary colors of light: red, green, and blue. The mixing of varying amounts of these three colors—called *additive color mixing*—can produce any color (see **FIGURE 7**). Mixing equal amounts of red, green, and blue light produces white light. This process differs from the mixing of colored pigments in paint or ink, called *subtractive color mixing*. As we can see in most printer color ink cartridges, the primary colors of pigment are yellow, cyan, and magenta. Mixing them produces a dark color because each pigment absorbs certain wavelengths. Combining them absorbs most or all wavelengths, leaving little or no color (see Figure 7).

hue
color of light

148

The Eye: How We Represent the Visual Realm

Without our eyes we couldn't sense or perceive much of anything about light, aside from the heat it generates. Keep an "eye" on **FIGURE 8** as we tour the structures of the eye.

HOW LIGHT ENTERS THE EYE. Different parts of our eye allow in varying amounts of light, permitting us to see either in bright sunshine or in a dark theater. Structures toward the front of the eyeball influence how much light enters our eye, and they focus the incoming light rays to form an image at the back of the eye.

The Sclera, Iris, and Pupil. Although poets have told us that the eyes are the windows to the soul, when we look people squarely in the eye all we can see is their sclera, iris, and pupil. The sclera is simply the white of the eye. The iris is the colored part of the eye, and is usually blue, brown, green, or hazel. Like the shutter of a camera, the iris controls how much light enters our eyes.

FIGURE 7 Additive and Subtractive Color Mixing. Additive color mixing of light differs from subtractive color mixing of paint.

Fovea
The part of the retina where light rays are most sharply focused

Optic nerve
Transmits impulses from the retina to the rest of the brain

Retina
Innermost layer of the eye, where incoming light is converted into nerve impulses

Eye muscle
One of six surrounding muscles that rotate the eye in all directions

Lens
Transparent disk that focuses light rays for near or distant vision

Cornea
Curved, transparent dome that bends incoming light

Iris
Colored area containing muscles that control the pupil

Pupil
Opening in the center of the iris that lets in light

Sclera
The white of the eye

FIGURE 8 The Key Parts of the Eye.

The **pupil** is a circular hole through which light enters the eye. The closing of the pupil is a reflex response to light or objects coming toward us. If we walk out of a building into bright sunshine, our eyes respond with the pupillary reflex to decrease the amount of light allowed into them. This reflex occurs simultaneously in both eyes (unless there's neurological damage), so shining a flashlight into one eye triggers it in both.

pupil
circular hole through which light enters the eye

Research demonstrates that men tend to find the faces of women with larger pupils (in this case, the face on the left) more attractive than those with smaller pupils, even when they're unaware of the reason for their preference. (*Source:* Hess, 1965; Tombs & Silverman, 2004).

The dilation (expansion) of the pupil also has psychological significance. Our pupils dilate when we're trying to process complex information, like difficult math problems (Beatty, 1982; Karatekin, 2004). They also dilate when we view someone we find physically attractive, and reflect sexual interest of homosexual as well as heterosexual individuals (Rieger & Savin-Williams, 2012; Tombs & Silverman, 2004). These findings may help to explain why people find faces with large pupils more attractive than faces with small pupils, even when they're oblivious to this physical difference (Hess, 1965; Tomlinson, Hicks, & Pelligrini, 1978). Researchers found that when they're in the fertile phase of their menstrual cycles, women are especially prone to prefer men with large pupils (Caryl et al., 2009). For centuries European women applied a juice from a poisonous plant called belladonna (Italian for "beautiful woman"), sometimes also called deadly nightshade, to their eyes to dilate their pupils, and thereby make themselves more attractive to men. Today, magazine photographers often enlarge the pupils of models, reasoning it will increase their appeal.

The Cornea, Lens, and Eye Muscles. The **cornea** is a curved, transparent layer covering the iris and pupil. Its shape bends incoming light to focus the incoming visual image at the back of the eye. The **lens** also bends light, but unlike the cornea, the lens changes its curvature, allowing us to fine-tune the visual image. The lens consists of some of the most unusual cells in the body: They're completely transparent, allowing light to pass through them.

In a process called **accommodation**, the lenses change shape to focus light on the back of the eyes; in this way, they adapt to different perceived distances of objects. So, nature has generously supplied us with a pair of "internal" corrective lenses, although they're often far from perfect. Accommodation can either make the lens "flat" (that is, long and skinny) enabling us to see distant objects, or "fat" (that is, short and wide) enabling us to focus on nearby objects. For nearby objects, a fat lens works better because it more effectively bends the scattered light and focuses it on a single point at the back of the eye.

(a) Nearsighted eye

(b) Farsighted eye

FIGURE 9 Nearsighted and Farsighted Eyes. Nearsightedness or farsightedness results when light is focused in front of or behind the retina, respectively.

 Explore in **MyPsychLab** the **Concept:** Normal Vision, Nearsightedness, and Farsightedness

The Shape of the Eye. How much our eyes need to bend the path of light to focus properly depends on the curve of our corneas and overall shape of our eyes. Nearsightedness, or *myopia*, results when images are focused in front of the rear of the eye due to our cornea being too steep or our eyes too long (see **FIGURE 9a**). Nearsightedness, as the name implies, is an ability to see close objects well coupled with an inability to see far objects well. Farsightedness, or *hyperopia,* results when our cornea is too flat or our eyes too short (see **FIGURE 9b**). Farsightedness, as the name implies, is an ability to see far objects well coupled with an inability to see near objects well. Our vision tends to worsen as we become older. That's because our lens can accommodate and overcome the effects of most mildly misshapen eyeballs until it loses its flexibility due to aging. This explains why only a few first-graders need eyeglasses, whereas most senior citizens do.

THE RETINA: CHANGING LIGHT INTO NEURAL ACTIVITY. The **retina**, which according to many scholars is technically part of the brain, is a thin membrane at the back of the eye. The **fovea** is the central part of the retina and is responsible for **acuity**, or sharpness of vision. We need a sharp image to read, drive, sew, or do just about anything requiring fine detail. We can think of the retina as a "movie screen" onto which light from the world is projected. It contains 100 million sense receptor cells for vision, along with cells that process visual information and send it to the brain.

Rods and Cones. Light passes through the retina to sense receptor cells located in its outermost layer. The retina contains two types of receptor cells. The far more plentiful **rods**, which are long and narrow, enable us to see basic shapes and forms. We rely on rods to see in low levels of light. When we enter a dimly lit room, like a movie theater, from a bright environment, **dark adaptation** occurs. Dark adaptation takes about 30 minutes, or about the time it takes rods to regain their maximum sensitivity to light (Lamb & Pugh, 2004). Some have even

cornea
part of the eye containing transparent cells that focus light on the retina

lens
part of the eye that changes curvature to keep images in focus

accommodation
changing the shape of the lens to focus on objects near or far

retina
membrane at the back of the eye responsible for converting light into neural activity

fovea
central portion of the retina

acuity
sharpness of vision

rods
receptor cells in the retina allowing us to see in low levels of light

dark adaptation
time in dark before rods regain maximum light sensitivity

speculated that pirates of old, who spent many long, dark nights at sea, might have worn eye patches to facilitate dark adaptation. There are no rods in the fovea, which explains why we should tilt our heads slightly to the side to see a dim star at night. Paradoxically, we can see the star better by *not* looking at it directly. By relying on our peripheral vision, we allow more light to fall on our rods.

The less numerous **cones**, which are shaped like—you guessed it—small cones, give us our color vision. We put our cones to work when reading because they're sensitive to detail; however, cones also require more light than do rods. That's why most of us have trouble reading in a dark room.

Different types of receptor cells contain *photopigments,* chemicals that change following exposure to light. The photopigment in rods is *rhodopsin.* Vitamin A, found in abundance in carrots, is needed to make rhodopsin. This fact led to the urban legend that eating carrots is good for our vision. Unfortunately, the only time vitamin A improves vision is when vision is impaired due to vitamin A deficiency.

The Optic Nerve. The *ganglion cells,* cells in the retinal circuit that contain axons, bundle all their axons together and depart the eye to reach the brain. The **optic nerve**, which contains the axons of ganglion cells, travels from the retina to the rest of the brain. After the optic nerves leave both eyes, they come to a fork in the road called the optic chiasm. Half of the axons cross in the optic chiasm and the other half stay on the same side. Within a short distance, the optic nerves enter the brain, turning into the optic tracts. The optic tracts send most of their axons to the visual part of the thalamus and then to the primary visual cortex—called V1—the primary route for visual perception (see **FIGURE 10**). The remaining axons go to structures in the midbrain, particularly the *superior colliculus.* These axons play a key role in reflexes, like turning our heads to follow something interesting.

The place where optic nerve connects to the retina is a **blind spot**, a part of the visual field that we can't see. It's a region of the retina containing no rods or sense receptors (refer back to Figure 8). We have a blind spot because the axons of ganglion cells push everything else aside. The exercise we performed at the outset of this chapter made use of the blind spot to generate an illusion (refer back to Figure 1). Our blind spot is there all of the time, creating perhaps the most remarkable of all visual illusions—one we experience every moment of our seeing lives. Our brain fills in the gaps created by the blind spot, and because each of our eyes supplies us with a slightly different picture of the world, we don't ordinarily notice it.

HOW WE PERCEIVE SHAPE AND CONTOUR. In the 1960s, David Hubel and Torsten Wiesel sought to unlock the secrets of how we perceive shape and form; their work eventually garnered them a Nobel Prize. They used cats as subjects because their visual systems are much like ours. Hubel and Wiesel recorded electrical activity in the visual cortexes of cats while presenting them with visual stimuli on a screen (see **FIGURE 11**). At first, they were unaware of

FIGURE 10 Perception and the Visual Cortex Visual information from the retina travels to the visual thalamus. Next, the visual thalamus sends inputs to the primary visual cortex (V1), then along two visual pathways to the secondary visual cortex (V2). One pathway leads to the parietal lobe, which processes visual form, position, and motion; and one to the temporal lobe, which processes visual form and color.

Factoid

Our eyes do not emit tiny particles of light, which allow us to perceive our surroundings. Many children and about 50 percent of college students (including those who've taken introductory psychology classes) harbor this belief, often called "emission theory" (Winer et al., 2002). Nevertheless, there's no scientific evidence for this theory, and considerable evidence against it.

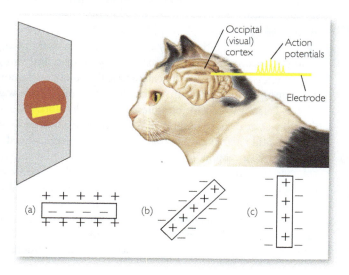

FIGURE 11 Cells Respond to Slits of Light of a Particular Orientation. *Top:* Hubel and Wiesel studied activity in the visual cortex of cats viewing slits of light on a screen. *Bottom:* Visual responses were specific to slits of dark on light (minuses on pluses—a) or light on dark (pluses on minuses—b) that were of particular orientations, such as horizontal, oblique, or vertical—(c). Cells in the visual cortex also detected edges.

cones
receptor cells in the retina allowing us to see in color

optic nerve
nerve that travels from the retina to the brain

blind spot
part of the visual field we can't see because of an absence of rods and cones

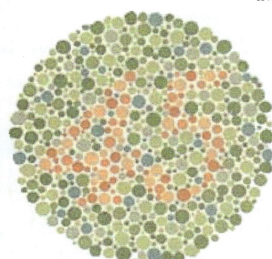

We're not alone when it comes to detecting edges and corners. In this example, a computer program detects edges (*blue*) and corners (*red*).

which stimuli would work best, so they tried many types, including bright and dark spots. At one point, they put up a different kind of stimulus on the screen, a long slit of light. As the story goes, one of their slides jammed in the slide projector slightly off-center, producing a slit of light (Horgan, 1999). Cells in the brain area V1 suddenly went haywire, firing action potentials at an amazingly high rate when the slit moved across the screen. Motivated by this surprising result, Hubel and Wiesel devoted years to figuring out which types of slits elicited such responses.

Here's what they found (Hubel & Wiesel, 1962; 1963). Many cells in V1 respond to slits of light of a specific orientation, for example, vertical, horizontal, or oblique lines or edges (refer again to Figure 11). Some cells in the visual cortex, *simple cells*, display "yes–no" responses to slits of a specific orientation, but these slits need to be in a specific location. Other cells, *complex cells,* are also orientation-specific, but their responses are less restricted to one location. This feature makes complex cells much more advanced than simple cells.

Feature Detection. Our ability to use certain minimal patterns to identify objects is called *feature detection*. Although simple and complex cells are **feature detector cells** in that they detect lines and edges, there are more complex feature detector cells at higher, that is, later levels of visual processing. They detect lines of specific lengths, complex shapes, and even moving objects. We use our ability to detect edges and corners to perceive many human-made objects, like furniture, laptops, and even the corners of the page you're reading at this moment.

As we saw in Figure 10, visual information travels from V1 to higher visual areas, called V2, along two major routes, one of which travels to the upper parts of the parietal lobe, and the other of which travels to the lower part of the temporal lobe. Numerous researchers have proposed a model of visual processing in which successively higher cortical regions process more and more complex shapes (Riesenhuber & Poggio, 1999). The many visual processing areas of the cortex enable us to progress from perceiving basic shapes to the enormously complex objects we see in our everyday worlds.

HOW WE PERCEIVE COLOR. Color delights our senses and stirs our imagination, but how does the brain perceive it? Scientists have discovered that we use the lower visual pathway leading to the temporal lobe to process color (refer back to Figure 10), but it hardly starts there. Different theories of color perception explain different aspects of our ability to detect color, enabling us to see the world, watch TV, and enjoy movies, all in vibrant color.

FIGURE 12 The Ishihara Test for Red–Green Color Blindness. If you can't see the two-digit number, you probably have red–green color blindness. This condition is common, especially among males.

Trichromatic Theory. **Trichromatic theory** proposes that we base our color vision on three primary colors—blue, green, and red. Trichromatic theory dovetails with our having three kinds of cones, each maximally sensitive to different wavelengths of light. Given that the three types of cones were discovered in the 1960s (Brown & Wald, 1964), it's perhaps surprising that Thomas Young and Hermann von Helmholtz described trichromatic theory over a century earlier. Young (1802) suggested that our vision is sensitive to three primary colors of light, and von Helmholtz (1850) replicated and extended his proposal by examining the colors that color-blind individuals could see. The Young-Helmholtz trichromatic theory of color vision was born.

REPLICABILITY ▶

Can the results be duplicated in other studies?

Persons with **color blindness** can't see all colors. Color blindness is most often due to the absence or reduced number of one or more types of cones stemming from genetic abnormalities. Still another cause is damage to a brain area related to color vision. Contrary to a popular misconception, *monochromats*—who have only one type of cone and thereby lose all color vision—are extremely rare, making up only about 0.0007 percent of the population. Most color-blind individuals can perceive a good deal of their world in color because they're *dichromats,* meaning they have two cones and are missing only one. Red–green dichromats see considerable color but can't distinguish reds as well as can people with normal color vision. We can find a test for red–green color blindness in **FIGURE 12**; many males have this condition but don't know it because it doesn't interfere much with their everyday functioning.

feature detector cell
cell that detects lines and edges

trichromatic theory
idea that color vision is based on our sensitivity to three primary colors

color blindness
inability to see some or all colors

Humans, apes, and some monkeys are *trichromats*, meaning we and our close primate relatives possess three kinds of cones. Most other mammals, including dogs and cats, see the world with only two cones, much like people with red–green color blindness (the most frequent form of color blindness). Trichromatic vision evolved about 35 million years ago, perhaps because it allowed animals to easily pick ripe fruit out of a green background. Recent fossil evidence suggests an alternative hypothesis, namely, that trichromatic vision may have enabled primates to find young, reddish, tender leaves that were nutritionally superior (Simon-Moffat, 2002). All scientists agree that seeing more colors gave our ancestors a leg up in foraging for food.

Opponent Process Theory. Trichromatic theory accounts nicely for how our three cone types work together to detect the full range of colors. But further research revealed a phenomenon that trichromatic theory can't explain—afterimages. Afterimages occur when we've stared at one color for a long time and then look away. We'll often see a different colored replica of the same image, as in **FIGURE 13**. Trichromatic theory doesn't easily explain why looking at one color consistently results in seeing another color in the afterimage, such as afterimages for red always appearing green. It turns out that afterimages arise from the visual cortex's processing of information from our rods and cones.

Some people occasionally report faint negative afterimages surrounding objects or other individuals. This phenomenon may have given rise to the paranormal idea that we're all encircled by mystical "auras" consisting of psychical energy (Neher, 1990). Nevertheless, because no one's been able to photograph auras under carefully controlled conditions, there's no support for this extraordinary claim (Nickel, 2000).

A competing model, which provides an explanation for afterimages, **opponent process theory**, holds that we perceive colors in terms of three pairs of opponent cells: red or green, blue or yellow, or black or white. Afterimages, which appear in complementary colors, illustrate opponent processing. Ganglion cells of the retina and cells in the visual area of the thalamus that respond to red spots are inhibited by green spots. Other cells show the opposite responses, and still others distinguish yellow from blue spots. Our nervous system uses both trichromatic and opponent processing principles during color vision, but different neurons rely on one principle more than the other. There's a useful lesson here that applies to many controversies in science: Two ideas that seem contradictory are sometimes both partly correct—they're merely describing differing aspects of the same phenomenon.

When We Can't See or Perceive Visually

We've learned how we see, and how we don't always see exactly what's there. Yet some 39 million people worldwide can't see at all (World Health Organization, 2012).

BLINDNESS. Blindness is the inability to see, or more specifically, the presence of vision less than or equal to 20/200 on the familiar Snellen eye chart, on which 20/20 is perfect vision. For people with 20/200 vision, objects at 20 feet appear as they would at 200 feet in a normally sighted person. The majority of cases of blindness—from cataracts, a clouding of the lens of the eye, and glaucoma, a disease that causes pressure on the eye and damages the optic nerve—are treatable, and are most likely to occur as people age.

The blind cope with their loss of vision in various ways—often relying more on other senses, including touch. This issue has been controversial over the years, with studies both replicating and contradicting a heightened sense of touch in the blind. Recent studies suggest that tactile (touch) sensitivity is indeed heightened in blind adults, giving them the same sensitivity as someone 23 years younger (Goldreich & Kanics, 2003). It's further known that the visual cortex of blind persons undergoes profound changes in function, rendering it sensitive to touch inputs (Sadato, 2005).

◀ **RULING OUT RIVAL HYPOTHESES**
Have important alternative explanations for the findings been excluded?

Factoid

There's preliminary evidence that a small proportion of women are *tetrachromats*, meaning their eyes contain four types of cones: the three cone types most of us possess plus an additional cone for a color between red and green (Jameson, Highnote, & Wasserman, 2001).

◀ **EXTRAORDINARY CLAIMS**
Is the evidence as strong as the claim?

◀ **RULING OUT RIVAL HYPOTHESES**
Have important alternative explanations for the findings been excluded?

FIGURE 13 Opponent Processes in Action. Find a patch of blank white wall or place a blank sheet of white paper nearby before you begin. Then relax your eyes and fix your gaze on the white dot in the image above for at least 30 seconds without looking around or away. Afterward, stare at the white wall or paper for a few seconds. What do you see?

opponent process theory
theory that we perceive colors in terms of three pairs of opponent colors: either red or green, blue or yellow, or black or white

◀ **REPLICABILITY**
Can the results be duplicated in other studies?

Ben Underwood has developed an amazing ability to use human echolocation to overcome many of the limitations of his blindness. Humans don't usually rely much on echolocation, although many whales do.

OCCAM'S RAZOR ▶

Does a simpler explanation fit the data just as well?

RULING OUT RIVAL HYPOTHESES ▶

Have important alternative explanations for the findings been excluded?

See, we read your mind! Now look at the cards again; you'll notice that one is missing. We've removed the card you picked! **How did we do it?** (See answer upside down.)

Answer: It's not an ESP trick after all. All five cards are different from those in the initial batch, but you probably didn't notice the change. The trick illustrates change blindness, a failure to notice obvious alterations in our environments.

This means they can devote more cortex—somatosensory cortex and visual cortex—to a touch task, such as reading Braille.

BLINDSIGHT: HOW ARE SOME BLIND PEOPLE ABLE TO NAVIGATE THEIR WORLDS? Recently, researchers (de Gelder et al., 2008) reported that a blind person, known by the initials TN, was able to walk around an obstacle course, with no assistance at all, side-stepping office equipment, boxes, and a variety of smaller objects. With normal eyes, TN is cortically blind—following several strokes, his brain fails to register sensory input. TN's rare ability may be the most impressive demonstration to date of a remarkable phenomenon called blindsight—the ability of blind people with damage to their cortex (Hamm et al., 2003) to make correct guesses about the appearance of things around them (Hamm et al., 2003; Weiskrantz, 1986). In TN's case, researchers used high-tech brain imaging to show that he was able to recognize facial expressions in angry, fearful, or joyous faces.

Because blindsight operates outside the bounds of conscious activity, some nonscientists have suggested that it may be a paranormal phenomenon. Yet there's a parsimonious natural explanation: People with blindsight have suffered damage to V1, the primary visual cortex, so that route of information flow to visual association areas is blocked. Coarser visual information still reaches the visual association cortex through an alternative pathway and bypasses V1. This visual information probably accounts for blindsight (Moore et al., 1995; Stoerig & Cowey, 1997; Weiskrantz, 1986).

Because TN was not deprived of auditory cues, the question arises of whether he might have been able to pull of his navigation feat with another equally amazing ability—echolocation. Certain animals, such as bats, dolphins, and many whales, emit sounds and listen to their echoes to determine their distance from a wall or barrier, a phenomenon called *echolocation*.

Remarkably, there's evidence that humans are capable of a crude form of echolocation. Echolocation might account for the fact that blind persons can sometimes detect objects a few feet away from them (Schörnich et al., 2012; Teng et al., 2011) and for TN's stumble free-walk. Ben Underwood, who was blinded at age 3 by retinal cancer, learned to make clicking noises that bounced off surfaces and clued him in to his surroundings. He rides his skateboard and plays basketball and video games. Recently, scientists have discovered that when blind people expert in echolocation use their ability to navigate in their environments, the same parts of the brain associated with visual images in sighted people become highly active (Thaler et al., 2011).

Although the echolocation explanation can't be ruled out completely, the researchers who studied TN argue that echolocation is unlikely in that it is not a particularly effective way to detect the small objects TN successfully avoided. What's clear is that blindsight and echolocation are remarkable examples of how even subtle signals from neural pathways can impact our rich sensory experience of the world.

VISUAL AGNOSIA. *Visual agnosia* is a deficit in perceiving objects. A person with this condition can tell us the shape and color of an object, but can't recognize or name it. At a dinner party, such a person might say, "please pass that eight-inch silver thing with a round end" rather than, "please pass the serving spoon." Oliver Sacks's 1985 book, *The Man Who Mistook His Wife for a Hat,* includes a case study of a man with visual agnosia who did exactly as the title suggests; he misperceived his wife as a fashion accessory.

Assess Your Knowledge   FACT or FICTION?

Study and Review in MyPsychLab

1. The visible spectrum of light differs across species and can differ across individuals.
   True / False

2. The lens of the eye changes shape depending on the perceived distance of objects.
   True / False

3. Red-green color blindness results when rods are missing but cones are intact.
   True / False

4. Only nonhuman animals, like bats, engage in echolocation.   **True / False**

5. People with visual agnosia have problems naming objects.   **True / False**

Answers: 1. T; 2. T; 3. F; 4. F; 5. T

Hearing: The Auditory System

6 Explain how the ear starts the auditory process.

7 Identify the different kinds of auditory perception.

If a tree falls in the forest and no one is around to hear it, does it make a sound? Ponder that age-old question while we explore our sense of hearing: **audition**. Next to vision, hearing is probably the sensory modality we rely on most to acquire information about our world.

Sound: Mechanical Vibration

Sound is vibration, a kind of mechanical energy traveling through a medium, usually air. The disturbance created by vibration of molecules of air produces sound waves. Sound waves can travel through any gas, liquid, or solid, but we hear them best when they travel through air. In a perfectly empty space (a vacuum), there can't be sound because there aren't any airborne molecules to vibrate. That should help us answer our opening question: Because there are air molecules in the forest, a falling tree most definitely makes a loud thud even if nobody can hear it.

PITCH. Sounds have *pitch,* which corresponds to the frequency of the wave. Higher frequency corresponds to higher pitch, lower frequency to lower pitch. Scientists measure pitch in cycles per second, or hertz (Hz) (see **FIGURE 14**). The human ear can pick up frequencies ranging from about 20 to 20,000 Hz (see **FIGURE 15**). When it comes to sensitivity to pitch, age matters. Younger people are more sensitive to higher pitch tones than older adults. A ring tone for cell phones has ingeniously exploited this simple fact of nature, allowing teenagers to hear their cell phones ring while many of their parents or teachers can't (Vitello, 2006).

A high school student responds to the "teenagers only" ringtone.

Watch in MyPsychLab the Video: Ear Ringing

(a) Long-wavelength (low-frequency) sound

(b) Short-wavelength (high-frequency) sound

FIGURE 14 Sound Wave Frequency and Amplitude. Sound wave frequency (cycles per second) is the inverse of wavelength (cycle width). Sound wave amplitude is the height of the cycle. The frequency for middle C (a) is lower than that for middle A (b).

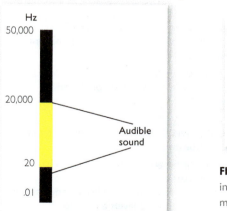

FIGURE 15 The Audible Spectrum (in Hz).
The human ear is sensitive to mechanical vibration from about 20 Hz to 20,000 Hz.

audition
our sense of hearing

155

LOUDNESS. The amplitude—or height—of the sound wave corresponds to *loudness*, measured in decibels (dB) (refer again to Figure 14). Loud noise results in increased wave amplitude because there's more mechanical disturbance, that is, more vibrating airborne molecules. **TABLE 2** lists various common sounds and their typical loudness.

TIMBRE. **Timbre** refers to the quality or complexity of the sound. Different musical instruments sound different because they differ in timbre, and the same holds for human voices.

The Structure and Function of the Ear

Just as sense receptors for vision transduce light into neural activity, sense receptors for hearing transduce sound into neural activity. The ear has three parts: outer, middle, and inner, each of which performs a different job (see **FIGURE 16**). The *outer ear*, consisting of the *pinna* (the part of the ear we see, namely, its skin and cartilage flap) and ear canal, has the simplest function; it funnels sound waves onto the *eardrum*.

On the other side of the eardrum lies the *middle ear*, containing the *ossicles*—the three tiniest bones in the body—named the hammer, anvil, and stirrup, after their shapes. These ossicles vibrate at the frequency of the sound wave, transmitting it from the eardrum to the inner ear.

Once sound waves enter the *inner ear*, the **cochlea** converts vibration into neural activity. The outer part of the spiral-shaped cochlea is bony, but its inner cavity is filled with a thick fluid. Vibrations from sound waves disturb this fluid and travel to the base of the cochlea, where pressure is released and transduction occurs.

Also located in the inner ear, the **organ of Corti** and **basilar membrane** are critical to hearing because *hair cells* are embedded within them (see Figure 16). Hair cells are where transduction of auditory information takes place: They convert acoustic information into action potentials. Here's how. Hair cells contain cilia (hairlike structures) that protrude into the fluid of the cochlea. When sound waves travel through the cochlea, the resulting pressure deflects these cilia, exciting the hair cells (Roberts, Howard, & Hudspeth, 1988). That information feeds into the *auditory nerve,* which travels to the brain, through the thalamus, which is a sensory relay station.

TABLE 2 Common Sounds. This decibel (dB) table compares some common sounds and shows how they rank in potential harm to hearing.

SOUND	NOISE LEVEL (DB)	EFFECT
Jet Engines (near)	140	We begin to feel pain at about 125 dB
Rock Concerts (varies)	110–140	
Thunderclap (near)	120	Regular exposure to sound over 100 dB for more than one minute risks permanent hearing loss
Power Saw (chainsaw)	110	
Garbage Truck/ Cement Mixer	100	No more than 15 minutes of unprotected exposure is recommended for sounds between 90 and 100 dB
Motorcycle (25 ft)	88	Very annoying 85
Lawn Mower	85–90	dB is the level at which hearing damage (after 8 hours) begins
Average City Traffic	80	Annoying; interferes with conversation;
Vacuum Cleaner	70	constant exposure may cause damage
Normal Conversation	50–65	Intrusive; interferes with telephone conversation Comfortable hearing levels are under 60 dB
Whisper	30	Very quiet
Rustling Leaves	20	Just audible

(*Source:* NIDCD)

timbre
complexity or quality of sound that makes musical instruments, human voices, or other sources sound unique

cochlea
bony, spiral-shaped sense organ used for hearing

organ of Corti
tissue containing the hair cells necessary for hearing

basilar membrane
membrane supporting the organ of Corti and hair cells in the cochlea

FIGURE 16 The Human Ear and Its Parts. A cutaway section through the human ear and a close-up diagram of the hair cells.

Eardrum
Membrane that vibrates in response to sound waves

Semicircular canal
One of three fluid-filled structures that play a role in balance

Cochlea
Converts vibration into neural activity

Ear canal
Conducts sound waves to the eardrum

Pinna
Flexible outer flap of the ear, which channels sound waves into the ear canal

Outer hair cells   **Auditory nerve fibers**   **Inner hair cells**

Outer Ear   Middle Ear   Inner Ear

Once the auditory nerve enters the brain, it makes contacts with the brain stem, which sends auditory information higher—all the way up the auditory cortex. At each stage, perception becomes increasingly complex. In this respect, auditory perception is like visual perception.

The primary auditory cortex processes different tones in different places (see **FIGURE 17**). That's because each place receives information from a specific place in the basilar membrane. Hair cells located at the base of the basilar membrane are most excited by high-pitched tones, whereas hair cells at the top of the basilar membrane are most excited by low-pitched tones. Scientists call this model of pitch perception **place theory**, because a specific place along the basilar membrane—and in the auditory cortex, too—matches a tone with a specific pitch (Békésy, 1949). Place theory accounts only for our perception of high-pitched tones, namely those from 5,000 to 20,000 Hz.

There are two routes to perceiving low-pitched tones. We'll discuss the simpler way first. In **frequency theory**, the rate at which neurons fire action potentials faithfully reproduces the pitch. This method works well up to 100 Hz, because many neurons have maximal firing rates near that limit. *Volley theory* is a variation of frequency theory that works for tones between 100 and 5,000 Hz. According to volley theory, sets of neurons fire at their highest rate, say 100 Hz, slightly out of sync with each other to reach overall rates up to 5,000 Hz.

When it comes to listening to music, we're sensitive not only to different tones, but to the arrangement of tones into melodies (Weinberger, 2006). We react differently to pleasant and unpleasant melodies. In one study, music that literally provoked feelings of "chills" or "shivers" boosted activity in the same brain regions corresponding to euphoric responses to sex, food, and drugs (Blood & Zatorre, 2001). So there may be a good reason why "sex," "drugs," and "rock and roll" often go together.

A   B   C   D   E   F   G   A   B   C   D   E   F
440 Hz

Basilar membrane

Response to low frequency

Response to high frequency

20 Hz   440 Hz   20,000 Hz

FIGURE 17 The Tone-Based Organization of the Basilar Membrane. Hair cells at the base of the basilar membrane respond to high-pitched tones, whereas hair cells at the top of the basilar membrane respond to low-pitched tones.

place theory
specific place along the basilar membrane matches a tone with a specific pitch

frequency theory
rate at which neurons fire the action potential reproduces the pitch

When We Can't Hear

About one in 1,000 people are deaf: They suffer from a profound loss of hearing. Many others have hearing deficits, called being "hard of hearing." There are several causes of deafness, some largely genetic, others deriving from disease, injury, or exposure to loud noise (Pascolini & Smith, 2009). *Conductive deafness* is due to a malfunctioning of the ear, especially a failure of the eardrum or the ossicles of the inner ear. In contrast, *nerve deafness* is due to damage to the auditory nerve.

If your grandmother warns you to "Turn down the sound on your iPod, or you'll go deaf by the time you're my age," there's more than a ring of truth in her warning. Loud sounds, especially those that last a long time or are repeated, can damage our hair cells and lead to *noise-induced hearing loss*. This type of hearing loss is often accompanied by tinnitus, a ringing, roaring, hissing, or buzzing sound in the ears that can be deeply disturbing (Nondahl et al., 2007). Hearing loss can also occur after exposure to one extremely loud sound, such as an explosion. But most of us lose some hearing ability as we age—especially for high-frequency sounds—as a by-product of the loss of sensory cells and degeneration of the auditory nerve, even if we've never attended a rock concert without earplugs (Ohlemiller & Frisina, 2008).

Study and **Review** in **MyPsychLab**

Assess Your Knowledge   FACT or FICTION?

1. The amplitude of the sound wave corresponds to loudness. **True / False**

2. Sound waves are converted to neural impulses by creating vibrations of fluid inside the cochlea. **True / False**

3. Place theory states that each hair cell in the inner ear has a particular pitch or frequency to which it's most responsive. **True / False**

4. Volley theory is a variation of frequency theory. **True / False**

5. As we age, we tend to lose hearing for low-pitched sounds more than high-pitched sounds. **True / False**

Answers: 1. T; 2. T; 3. T; 4. T; 5. F

Smell and Taste: The Sensual Senses

8 Identify how we sense and perceive odors and tastes.

Without smell and taste many of our everyday experiences would be bland. Cuisines of the world feature characteristic spices that enliven their dishes. Similarly, smell and taste stimulate our senses and elevate our spirits. The term "comfort food" refers to familiar dishes that we crave because of the warm memories they evoke.

Smell is also called **olfaction**, and taste **gustation**. These senses work hand in hand, enhancing our liking of some foods and our disliking of others. Smell and taste are the chemical senses because we derive these sensory experiences from chemicals in substances.

Animals use their sense of smell for many purposes—tracking prey, establishing territories, and recognizing the opposite sex, to name but a few. We humans aren't the most smell-oriented of creatures. The average dog is at least 100,000 times more sensitive to smell than we are, which explains why police use trained dogs rather than nosy people to sniff for bombs and banned substances.

The most critical function of our chemical senses is to sample our food before swallowing it. The smell and taste of sour milk are powerful stimuli that few of us can ignore even if we want to. An unfamiliar bitter taste may signal dangerous bacteria or poison in our food. We develop food preferences for "safe" foods and base them on a combination of smell and taste. One study of young French women found that only those who already liked red meat—its smell and its taste—responded favorably to pictures of it (Audebert, Deiss, & Rousset, 2006). We like what smells and tastes good to us.

olfaction
our sense of smell

gustation
our sense of taste

Culture also shapes what we perceive as delicious or disgusting. The prospect of eating sacred cow meat (as in a hamburger) would be as off-putting to Hindus as eating fried tarantulas, a delicacy in Cambodia, or Casu Marzu, a Sardinian cheese filled with insect larvae, would be to most Americans. Even within a society there are pronounced differences in food choices, as American meat lovers and vegans enjoy vastly different diets. We can acquire food preferences by means of learning, including modeling of eating behaviors.

What Are Odors and Flavors?

Odors are airborne chemicals that interact with receptors in the lining of our nasal passages. Our noses are veritable smell connoisseurs, capable of detecting between 2,000 and 4,000 different odors. Not everything, though, has an odor. Clean water, for example, has no odor or taste. Not all animals smell airborne molecules. The star-nosed mole, named for its peculiarly shaped snout, can detect odors underwater (Catania, 2006). The animal blows out air bubbles and "sniffs" them back in to find food underwater and underground.

In contrast, we can detect only a few tastes. We're sensitive to five basic tastes—sweet, salty, sour, bitter, and umami, the last of which is a recently uncovered "meaty" or "savory" taste. There's preliminary evidence for a sixth taste, one for fatty foods (Gilbertson et al., 1997).

Sense Receptors for Smell and Taste

We humans have over 1,000 olfactory (smell) genes, 347 of which code for olfactory receptors (Buck & Axel, 1991). Each olfactory neuron contains a single type of olfactory receptor, which "recognizes" an odorant on the basis of its shape. This lock-and-key concept is similar to how neurotransmitters bind to receptor sites. When olfactory receptors come into contact with odor molecules, action potentials in olfactory neurons are triggered.

We detect taste with **taste buds** on our tongues. Bumps on the tongue called *papillae* contain numerous taste buds (**FIGURE 18**). There are separate taste buds for sweet, salty, sour, bitter, and umami (Chandrashekar et al., 2006).

It's a myth, however, that a "tongue taste map" describes the tongue's sensitivity to different flavors, even though some books still contain this map (see **FIGURE 19**). In reality, there's only a weak tendency for individual taste receptors to concentrate at certain locations on the tongue, and any location on the tongue is at least slightly sensitive to all tastes. Try this exercise: Place a bit of salt on the tip of your tongue. Can you taste it? Now try placing a small amount of sugar on the back of your tongue. Chances are good you'll taste both the salt and the sugar, even though you placed them outside the mythical "tongue taste map." That's because receptors that detect sweet tastes are often located on the tip of the tongue and receptors that detect salt are often on the sides, but there's a good mix of receptors everywhere on the tongue.

Umami taste receptors were controversial until physiological studies replicated earlier results and showed that these receptors were present on taste buds (Chandrashekar et al., 2006). That was nearly a century after Kikunae Ikeda isolated the molecules responsible for the savory flavor found in many Japanese foods, such as broth or dried seaweed (Yamaguchi & Ninomiya, 2000). These molecules producing a savory or meaty flavor all had one thing in common: They contained a lot of the neurotransmitter glutamate. Monosodium glutamate (MSG), a derivative of glutamate, is a well-known flavor enhancer (the commercial flavor enhancer *Accent* consists almost entirely of MSG). Today, most scientists consider umami the fifth taste.

A similar controversy swirls around taste receptors for fat. It's clear that fat does something to our tongues. Richard Mattes (2005) and his associates found that merely putting fat on people's tongues alters their blood levels of fat. This means that as soon as fat enters our mouths it starts to affect our bodies' metabolism of fat. At first, researchers thought the responses were triggered by an olfactory receptor for fat. This hypothesis was ruled out when they showed that smelling fat didn't alter blood levels of fat; the fat had to make contact with the tongue.

FIGURE 18 How We Detect Taste. The tongue contains many taste buds, which transmit information to the brain as shown in this close-up.

FIGURE 19 The "Tongue Taste Map" Myth. Although diagrams of the tongue, like this one, appear in many popular sources, they're more fiction than fact.

◄ **REPLICABILITY**
Can the results be duplicated in other studies?

> **taste bud**
> sense receptor in the tongue that responds to sweet, salty, sour, bitter, umami, and perhaps fat

◄ **RULING OUT RIVAL HYPOTHESES**
Have important alternative explanations for the findings been excluded?

taste buds

 The two photographs above show the tongues of two people, one a super-taster and one a non-supertaster. **Which tongue belongs to a supertaster and why?** (See answer upside down on bottom of page.)

With only five or six taste receptors, why do we taste so many flavors? The secret lies in the fact that our taste perception is biased strongly by our sense of smell, which explains why we find food much less tasty when our noses are stuffed from a cold. Far more than we realize, we find certain foods "delicious" because of their smell. If you're not persuaded, try this exercise. Buy some multiflavored jelly beans, open the bag, and close your eyes so you can't see which color you're picking. Then pinch your nose with one hand and pop a jelly bean into your mouth. At first you won't be able to identify the flavor. Then gradually release your fingers from your nose and you'll be able to perceive the jelly bean's taste.

Our tongues differ in their number of taste receptors. Linda Bartoshuk (2004) calls those of us with a marked overabundance of taste buds—about 25 percent of people— "supertasters." If you find broccoli, coffee, and dark chocolate (we hope not) to be unbearably bitter, and sugary foods to be unbearably sweet, the odds are high you're a supertaster. At age 10, supertasters are most likely to be in the lowest 10 percent of height, probably a result of their sensitivity to bitter tastes and their fussy eating habits (Golding et al., 2009). Supertasters, who are overrepresented among women and people of African or Asian descent, are also especially sensitive to oral pain, and tend to avoid bitter tastes as a result. They also tend to avoid bitter tastes in alcohol and smoking tobacco, which may make them healthier than the rest of us (Bartoshuk, 2004).

Olfactory and Gustatory Perception

Our perceptions of smell and taste are often remarkably sensitive, and more informative than we consciously realize, although we're often not especially good at identifying odors by name. Babies can identify their mothers' odor and siblings can recognize each other on the basis of odor. Research suggests that women can even tell whether people just watched a happy or a sad movie from samples of their armpit odor (Wysocki & Preti, 2004). Should we perhaps call sad movies sweat-jerkers rather than tear-jerkers?

How do odors and tastes excite our receptors for smell and taste? After odors interact with sense receptors in the nasal passages, the resulting information enters the brain, reaching the olfactory cortex and parts of the limbic system (see **FIGURE 20**). Similarly, after taste information interacts with taste buds, it enters the brain, reaching a taste-related area called gustatory cortex, somatosensory cortex (because food also has texture), and parts of the limbic system. A region of the frontal cortex.

We analyze the intensity of smell and determine whether it's pleasing. Parts of the limbic system, such as the amygdala, help us to distinguish pleasant from disgusting smells (Anderson et al., 2003). Taste can also be pleasant or disgusting. Both tasting disgusting food and viewing facial expressions of disgust.

Emotional disorders, like anxiety and depression, can distort taste perception (Heath et al., 2006). Certain neurotransmitters, such as serotonin and norepinephrine—the same chemical messengers whose activity is enhanced by antidepressants—make us more sensitive to tastes. Tom Heath and his colleagues (2006) found that antidepressant drugs rendered participants more sensitive to various combinations of sweet, sour, and bitter tastes. Their research may shed light on appetite loss, which is a frequent symptom of depression.

Smell plays a particularly strong role in sexual behavior. Mice with a genetic defect in smell don't even bother to mate (Mandiyan, Coats, & Shah, 2005). Is smell central to human sexuality, too? Many perfume and cologne manufacturers sure seem to think so. Curiously, though, it may not be fragrant odors, but **pheromones**—odorless chemicals that serve as social signals to members of one's species—that alter our sexual behavior. There's evidence that rodents respond to pheromones during mating and social behavior (Biasi, Silvotti, & Tirindelli, 2001). So do most other mammals, including whales and horses (Fields, 2007). Most mammals use the *vomeronasal organ,* located in the bone between the

Perfume manufacturers have long advertised fragrances as increasing attraction and romance. But at least in nonhuman animals, the chemicals that produce the most potent effects on sexual behaviors are actually odorless pheromones.

Watch in **MyPsychLab** the **Video:**
Thinking Like a Psychologist: Can Smells Alter Mood and Behavior?

pheromone
odorless chemical that serves as a social signal to members of one's species

Answer: The tongue on the left, because supertasters have more taste buds on their tongues than do other people.

nose and the mouth, to detect pheromones. The vomeronasal organ doesn't develop in humans (Witt & Wozniak, 2006), causing some to suggest that humans are insensitive to pheromones. An alternative hypothesis is that humans detect pheromones via a different route. This idea is supported by the discovery of human pheromones (Pearson, 2006). A nerve that's only recently received attention, called "nerve zero," may step in to enable pheromones to trigger responses in the "hot-button sex regions of the brain" (Fields, 2007).

Still, we should be cautious about shelling out sizable chunks of our salaries on pheromone-based products that promise to stir up romance. Scientific evidence suggests they probably won't work. Pheromones are large molecules, so although it's easy to transfer a pheromone from one person to another during a passionate kiss, sending them across a restaurant table is definitely a stretch. Moreover, there's far more to human romance than physical chemistry; psychological chemistry matters, too.

Smells other than pheromones may contribute to human sexual behavior. Remarkably, human sperm cells may contain smell receptors that help them to find their way to female eggs (Spehr et al., 2003). Sometimes truth *is* stranger than fiction.

When We Can't Smell or Taste

About 2 million Americans suffer from disorders of taste, smell, or both. Gradual loss of taste and smell can be a part of normal aging, as the number of taste buds, routinely replaced when we're younger, declines. But these losses can also result from diseases, such as diabetes and high blood pressure.

There are many disorders of olfaction (Hirsch, 2003). Although not as serious as blindness or deafness, they can pose several dangers, such as an inability to detect gas leaks and smell spoiled food before we eat it. Damage to the olfactory nerve, along with brain damage caused by such disorders as Parkinson's and Alzheimer's disease can damage our sense of smell and ability to identify odors (Doty, Deems, & Stellar, 1988; Murphy, 1999; Wilson et al., 2007).

Losing our sense of taste can also produce negative health consequences. Cancer patients who lose their sense of taste have a worse prognosis than other patients, because they eat less and die sooner (Schiffman & Graham, 2000). This effect isn't due merely to a lack of nutrition. Adding flavor enhancers to the diet appreciably improves patients' health status. So taste may add an essential "zest" to life; a psychological flavoring that can help to ward off disease by boosting appetite.

◀ **RULING OUT RIVAL HYPOTHESES**
Have important alternative explanations for the findings been excluded?

Somatosensory cortex
Thalamus
Olfactory cortex
Olfactory bulb
Orbitofrontal cortex
Pons
Medulla oblongata

Smell
Taste

FIGURE 20 Smell and Taste. Our senses of smell and taste enter the brain by different routes but converge in the orbitofrontal cortex.

Advocates of aromatherapy claim that essential oils derived from plants have special healing powers. Many claim that such oils can cure depression, anxiety disorders, insomnia, and other ailments. Although the pleasant smells of such plants can no doubt lift our moods a bit, there's little evidence that they possess magical curative power (McCutcheon, 1996).

Assess Your Knowledge — FACT or FICTION?

1. The most critical function of our chemical senses is to sample our food before we swallow it.   **True / False**

2. Humans can detect only a small number of odors but thousands of tastes.   **True / False**

3. There's good evidence for a "tongue taste map," with specific taste receptors located on specific parts of the tongue.   **True / False**

4. The limbic system plays a key role in smell and taste perception.   **True / False**

5. The vomeronasal organ helps to detect pheromones in many mammals but doesn't develop in humans.   **True / False**

Answers: 1. T; 2. F; 3. F; 4. T; 5. T

 Study and **Review** in **MyPsychLab**

Philippe Petit, famous high-wire artist, demonstrates his extraordinary sense of balance walking between two buildings.

Our Body Senses: Touch, Body Position, and Balance

9   Describe the three different body senses.

10   Explain how pain perception differs from touch perception.

11   Describe the field of psychology called human factors.

Using only the chalk on his hands and climbing shoes, Alain Roberts, nicknamed "The French Spiderman," has scaled the world's tallest skyscrapers. To do so, he must rely on his senses of touch, body position, and balance. One miscalculation, one slip of his foot or his hand, and he would plummet from the heights of buildings more than 80 stories tall.

Fortunately for Roberts, he, like the rest of us, has three body senses that work in tandem. The system we use for touch and pain is the **somatosensory** (*somato-*, for "body") system. We also have a body position sense, called *proprioception*, or kinesthetic sense, and a sense of equilibrium or balance, called the *vestibular sense*.

The Somatosensory System: Touch and Pain

The stimuli that activate the somatosensory system come in a variety of types. In this respect, this sense differs from vision and audition, each of which is devoted mainly to a single stimulus type.

PRESSURE, TEMPERATURE, AND INJURY. Our somatosensory system responds to stimuli applied to the skin, such as light touch or deep pressure, hot or cold temperature, or chemical or mechanical (touch-related) injury that produces pain. Somatosensory stimuli can be very specific, such as the embossed patterns of a letter written in Braille, or generalized to a large area of the body. Damage to internal organs sometimes causes "referred pain"—pain in a different location—such as an ache felt throughout the left arm and shoulder during a heart attack.

SPECIALIZED AND FREE NERVE ENDINGS IN THE SKIN. We sense light touch, deep pressure, and temperature with *specialized nerve endings* located on the ends of sensory nerves in the skin (see **FIGURE 21**). We also sense touch, temperature, and especially pain with *free nerve endings*, which are far more plentiful than specialized nerve endings. Nerve endings of all types are distributed unevenly across our body surface. Most of them are in our fingertips (which explains why it really stings when we cut our finger, say, in a paper cut), followed by our lips, face, hands, and feet. We have the fewest in the middle of our backs, perhaps explaining why even a strenuous deep back massage rarely makes us scream in agony.

HOW WE PERCEIVE TOUCH AND PAIN. Information about body touch, temperature, and painful stimuli travels in our somatic nerves before entering the spinal cord. Touch information travels more quickly than information about pain stimuli. Many of us have discovered this fact when stubbing our toes on a piece of furniture: We first feel our toes hitting the furniture, but don't experience the stinging pain (ouch!) until a second or two later. That's because touch and pain have different functions. Touch informs us of our immediate surroundings, and keys us into urgent matters, such as when something feels hot to avoid a serious burn, whereas pain alerts us to take care of injuries, which can often wait a little while.

Often touch and pain information activate local spinal reflexes.

After activating spinal reflexes, touch and pain information travels upward through parts of the brain stem and thalamus to reach the somatosensory cortex (Bushnell et al., 1999). Additional cortical areas are active during the localization of touch information, such as association areas of the parietal lobe.

somatosensory
our sense of touch, temperature, and pain

As we've all discovered, pain comes in many varieties: sharp, stabbing, throbbing, burning, and aching. Many of the types of pain perception relate to the pain-causing stimulus—thermal (heat-related), chemical, or mechanical pain can also be acute, that is, short-lived, or chronic, that is, enduring, perhaps even lasting years. Each kind of pain-producing stimulus has a *threshold,* or point at which we perceive it as painful. People differ in their pain thresholds. Surprisingly, one study showed that people with naturally red hair require more anesthetic than do people with other hair colors (Liem et al., 2004). Of course, this correlational finding doesn't mean that red hair causes lower pain thresholds. Instead, some of the differences in people's thresholds are probably due to genetic factors that happen to be associated with hair color.

We can't localize pain as precisely as touch. Moreover, pain has a large emotional component. That's because pain information goes partly to the somatosensory cortex and partly to limbic centers in the brain stem and forebrain. The experience of pain is frequently associated with anxiety, uncertainty, and helplessness.

Scientists believe we can control pain in part by controlling our thoughts and emotions in reaction to painful stimuli (Moore, 2008). This belief has been bolstered by stories of people withstanding excruciating pain during combat or natural childbirth. According to the **gate control model** of Ronald Melzack and Patrick Wall (1965, 1970), pain under these circumstances is blocked from consciousness because neural mechanisms in the spinal cord function as a "gate," controlling the flow of sensory input to the central nervous system. The gate-control model can account for how pain varies from situation to situation depending on our psychological state. Most of us have experienced becoming so absorbed in an event, such as an interesting conversation or television program, that we forgot about the pain we were feeling from a headache or a trip to the dentist's office. The gate control model proposes that the stimulation we experience competes with and blocks the pain from consciousness. Because pain demands attention, distraction is an effective way of short-circuiting painful sensations (Eccleston & Crombez, 1999; McCaul & Malott, 1984). For example, scientists discovered that they could relieve the pain of burn patients undergoing physical therapy, wound care, and painful skin grafts by immersing them in a virtual environment populated by snowmen and igloos (Hoffman & Patterson, 2005). On the flip side, when people dwell on catastrophic thoughts about pain (such as "I won't be able to bear it") it can open the floodgates of distress.

What's the evidence for the involvement of the spinal cord in the gate control model? Patrick Wall (2000) showed that the brain controls activity in the spinal cord, enabling us to turn up, damp down, or in some cases ignore pain. The placebo effect exerts a strong response on subjective reports of pain. Falk Eippert and his colleagues (Eippert et al., 2009) used brain imaging to demonstrate that pain-related activity in the spinal cord is sharply reduced when participants receive an application of a placebo cream they're told would alleviate pain. Placebos may also stimulate the body's production of its natural painkillers: endorphins (Glasser & Frishman, 2008). Scientists are investigating ways of boosting endorphins while deactivating glial cells.

For many years the scientific consensus has been that we can ignore pain, or at least withstand it, with a stoic mind-set (Szasz, 1989). There's evidence that people of certain cultural backgrounds, such as American Indians, Cambodians, Chinese, and Germans, are more reserved and less likely to communicate openly about pain, whereas South and Central Americans consider it more acceptable to moan and cry

◀ **CORRELATION VS. CAUSATION**
Can we be sure that A causes B?

Meissner's corpuscle
(specialized for light touch)

Ruffini ending
(specialized for skin stretching)

Free nerve ending
(pain receptor)

Pacinian corpuscle
(specialized for deep pressure)

FIGURE 21 The Sense of Touch. The skin contains many specialized and free nerve endings that detect mechanical pressure, temperature, and pain.

gate control model
idea that pain is blocked or gated from consciousness by neural mechanisms in spinal cord

Watch in **MyPsychLab** the **Video:** In the Real World: Managing Pain

Why do you think the designers of this virtual world chose imagery of snowmen and igloos for burn patients? What imagery would you choose, and why?

RULING OUT RIVAL HYPOTHESES ▶
Have important alternative explanations for the findings been excluded?

Although firewalking seminars are extremely popular, there is nothing magical or mysterious about firewalking—but don't try it at home.

The mirror box consists of a two-chamber box with a mirror in the center. When the participant looks at her right hand in the box, it creates the illusion that the mirror image of her right hand is her left hand. This box can sometimes alleviate the discomfort of phantom limb pain by positioning the intact limb as the phantom limb appears to be positioned, and then moving it to a more comfortable position.

phantom pain
pain or discomfort felt in an amputated limb

proprioception
our sense of body position

out when in pain (Ondeck, 2003). Although these descriptions of average behavior may help physicians deal with diverse populations, the premise that pain perception varies with ethnicity isn't universally accepted. An alternative hypothesis is that health care professionals treat certain ethnic groups differently. Blacks and Hispanics are less likely than Caucasians to receive analgesic (anti-pain) medication during emergency room visits (Bonham, 2001), which could account for some of the differences in reports of pain.

Are there any unusual activities for which a stoic mind-set may come in handy? Some popular psychology gurus certainly think so. Firewalkers, popular in India, Japan, North Africa, and the Polynesian islands, have walked 20- to 40-foot-long beds of burning embers. Although the practice has been around since as early as 1200 B.C., there's recently been a glut of "Firewalking Seminars" in California, New York, and other states. These motivational classes promise ordinary people everything from heightened self-confidence to spiritual enlightenment—all by walking down an 8- to 12-foot-long path of burning embers. Contrary to what we might learn at these seminars, success in firewalking has nothing to do with pain sensitivity and everything to do with physics. The type of coal or wood used in firewalking has a low rate of heat exchange, such that it burns red hot in the center while remaining less hot on the outside (Kurtus, 2000). So any of us can firewalk successfully just so long as we walk (or even better, run) over the burning embers quickly enough. Still, accidents can occur if the fire isn't prepared properly or if the firewalker walks too slowly.

PHANTOM LIMB ILLUSION. Persons with amputated limbs often experience the eerie phenomenon of **phantom pain**, pain or discomfort in the missing limb. About 50 to 80 percent of amputees experience phantom limb sensations (Pühse et al., 2010; Sherman, Sherman, & Parker 1984). The missing limb often feels as if it's in an uncomfortably distorted position.

Vilayanur Ramachandran and colleagues developed a creative treatment for phantom limb pain called the *mirror box* (Ramachandran & Rogers-Ramachandran, 1996). Phantom limb patients position their other limb so that it's reflected in exactly the position that the amputated limb would assume. Then the patient performs the "mirror equivalent" of the exercise the amputated limb needs to relieve a cramp or otherwise get comfortable. For the mirror box to relieve pain or discomfort in the amputated limb, the illusion must be realistic. Seventeen out of 18 patients were successfully treated for phantom limb pain with the mirror box following amputation of one or more lower limbs resulting from injuries suffered as a result of the 2010 earthquake in Haiti (Miller et al., 2012).

*psycho*mythology

PSYCHIC HEALING OF CHRONIC PAIN

Many people believe in the power of mind over pain, but some individuals claim to possess supernatural abilities or "gifts" that enable them to reduce others' pain. Is this fact or fiction? In the summer of 2003, the Australian television show *A Current Affair* approached psychologists at the University of Bond to conduct a double-blind, randomized, controlled test of psychic healing powers.

Using a newspaper advertisement, the researchers located volunteers suffering from pain caused by cancer, chronic back conditions, and fibromyalgia (a chronic condition of muscle, joint, and bone pain and fatigue) (Lyvers, Barling, & Harding-Clark, 2006). The researchers assigned half of the chronic pain participants to a group that received psychic healing and the other half to a control condition that didn't. Neither the participants nor those interacting with them knew who was assigned to which group. In the healing condition, the psychic healer viewed and touched photographs of the chronic pain participants in another room. The healer was given all the time deemed necessary.

The researchers used the McGill Pain Questionnaire (Melzack, 1975) to test chronic pain participants' level of discomfort before and after the trial. Then, researchers compared their before and after scores. On average the scores showed no change before and after treatment, with half the participants reporting more pain and half reporting less pain regardless of whether psychic healing occurred.

These results agreed with earlier results obtained by British researchers on spiritual healing (Abbot et al., 2001). In a study of 120 chronic pain sufferers, they similarly used the McGill Pain Questionnaire. These researchers compared pain reports before and after face-to-face versus distant spiritual healing compared with no spiritual healing. The results suggested that despite the popularity of spiritual healing in England, this method lacks scientific support. A different research team, however, reported an improvement in neck pain following spiritual healing (Gerard, Smith, & Simpson, 2003). But because their study lacked a placebo treatment or blinding of the therapist, these authors couldn't rule out a placebo effect.

Lyvers and colleagues (2006) addressed the placebo effect with a double-blind design, and rated their chronic pain participants on a five-point scale that assessed the degree to which they believed in psychic phenomena. They found no correlation between psychic healing and decreased pain; however, they found that decreases in reported pain correlated with increased belief in psychic phenomena. So beliefs in the paranormal may create reality, at least psychological reality.

WHEN WE CAN'T FEEL PAIN. Just as some people are blind or deaf, others experience disorders that impair their ability to sense pain. Although pain isn't fun, research on pain insensitivity shows that pain serves an essential function. Pain insensitivity present from birth is an extremely rare condition that is sometimes inherited (Victor & Ropper, 2001). For the most part, children with this condition are completely unable to detect painful stimuli. Lacking any awareness of pain, they may chew off parts of their bodies, like their fingertips or the ends of their tongues, or suffer bone fractures without realizing it. Needless to say, this condition can be exceedingly dangerous. Other individuals show an indifference to painful stimuli: They can identify the type of pain, but experience no significant discomfort from it.

Proprioception and Vestibular Sense: Body Position and Balance

Right at this moment you're probably sitting somewhere. You may not be thinking about body control or keeping your head and shoulders up, because your brain is kindly taking care of all that for you. If you decided to stand up and grab a snack, you'd need to maintain posture and balance, as well as navigate bodily motion. **Proprioception**, also called our *kinesthetic sense*, helps us keep track of where we are and move efficiently. The **vestibular sense**, also called our *sense of equilibrium*, enables us to sense and maintain our balance as we move about. Our senses of body position and balance work together.

PROPRIOCEPTORS: TELLING THE INSIDE STORY. We use *proprioceptors* to sense muscle stretch and force. From these two sources of information we can tell what our bodies are doing, even with our eyes closed. There are two kinds of proprioceptors: stretch receptors embedded in our muscles, and force detectors embedded in our muscle tendons. Proprioceptive information enters the spinal cord and travels upward through the brain stem and thalamus to reach the somatosensory and motor cortexes (Naito, 2004). There, our brains combine information from our muscles and tendons, along with a sense of our intentions, to obtain a perception of our body's location (Proske, 2006).

THE VESTIBULAR SENSE: A BALANCING ACT. In addition to the cochlea, the inner ear contains three **semicircular canals** (see **FIGURE 22**). These canals, which are filled with fluid, sense equilibrium and help us maintain our balance. Vestibular information reaches parts of the brain stem that control eye muscles and triggers reflexes that coordinate eye and head movements (Highstein, Fay, & Popper, 2004). Vestibular information also travels to the cerebellum, which controls bodily responses that enable us to catch our balance when we're falling.

◀ **RULING OUT RIVAL HYPOTHESES**
Have important alternative explanations for the findings been excluded?

Ashlyn Blocker has congenital insensitivity to pain with anhidrosis (CIPA). *Congenital* means "present at birth," and *anhidrosis* means "inability to sweat." CIPA is a rare disorder that renders people unable to detect pain or temperature; those affected also can't regulate body temperature well because of an inability to sweat. Her parents and teachers need to monitor her constantly because she's prone to eating scalding hot food without the slightest hesitation. She may badly injure herself on the playground and continue to play.

FIGURE 22 How We Sense Motion. The semicircular canals of the inner ear detect movement and gravity.

vestibular sense
our sense of equilibrium or balance

semicircular canals
three fluid-filled canals in the inner ear responsible for our sense of balance

165

The vestibular sense isn't heavily represented in our cerebral cortex, so our awareness of this sense is limited. We typically become aware of this sense only when we lose our sense of balance or experience dramatic mismatches between our vestibular and visual inputs, which occur when our vestibular system and our eyes tell us different things. We commonly experience dizziness and nausea following these mismatches, such as when we're moving quickly in a car while not looking outside at the road whizzing past us.

Ergonomics: Human Engineering

How do our bodies interact with new technologies? A field of psychology called *human factors* optimizes technology to better suit our sensory and perceptual capabilities. We can use what we know about human psychology and sensory systems—ranging from our body position sense to vision—to build more *ergonomic,* or worker-friendly, gadgets and tools of the trade.

As Donald Norman (1998) pointed out, many everyday objects are designed without the perceptual experiences of users in mind. As a result, they can be extremely difficult to figure out how to operate. Have you ever tried to repeatedly push open a door that needed to be pulled open, or spent several minutes trying to figure out how to turn on a shower in an apartment or hotel room? Poor design kept the United States in limbo for five weeks following the 2000 presidential election between George W. Bush and Al Gore, when a bewildering election ballot in some Florida counties left state officials unable to figure out which candidate voters picked.

Fortunately, human factors psychologists have applied their extensive knowledge of sensation and perception to improve the design of many everyday devices. To take just one example, many people hold jobs that require them to sit at a computer terminal most of the day. This means that a new design for a computer screen, keyboard, or mouse that enables them to better reach for their computers or see their screens can increase their efficiency. Human factors psychologists design not only computer components, but devices that assist surgeons in performing delicate operations, workstations to improve comfort and decrease injuries on the job, and control panels on aircraft carriers, to make them safer and easier to use. The psychology of human factors reminds us that much of what we know about sensation and perception has useful applications to many domains of everyday life.

? Psychologist Donald Norman, posing in his office behind a teapot. Can you figure out what makes this teapot design a poor one? (See answer upside down on bottom of page.)

✓ **Study** and **Review** in **MyPsychLab**

Assess Your Knowledge   FACT or FICTION?

1. Pain information travels more quickly to the spinal cord than does touch information. **True / False**

2. Pain thresholds vary depending on the person and type of pain (stabbing, burning, or aching, for example). **True / False**

3. Firewalking requires both insensitivity to pain and extremely high levels of motivation. **True / False**

4. Proprioception enables us to coordinate our movements without having to look at our bodies. **True / False**

5. The inner ear plays a key role in our ability to keep our balance. **True / False**

Answers: 1. F; 2. T; 3. F; 4. T; 5. T

Answer: The handle is directly underneath the spout, which would cause hot tea to pour directly onto your hand.

Perception: When Our Senses Meet Our Brains

12 Track how our minds build up perceptions.

13 Describe how we perceive people, objects, and sounds in our environment.

14 Distinguish subliminal perception from subliminal persuasion.

15 Analyze the scientific evidence for and against the existence of ESP.

Now that we've learned how we process sensory information, we'll embark on an exciting voyage into how our minds organize the bits of sensory data into more meaningful concepts. What's so remarkable about our brain's ability to bring together so much data is that it doesn't rely only on what's in our sensory field. Our brain pieces together (a) what's in the sensory field, along with (b) what was just there a moment ago, and (c) what we remember from our past. When we perceive the world, we sacrifice small details in favor of crisp and often more meaningful representations. In most cases, the trade-off is well worth it, because it helps us make sense of our surroundings.

Parallel Processing: The Way Our Brain Multitasks

We can attend to many sense modalities simultaneously, a phenomenon called **parallel processing** (Rumelhart & McClelland, 1987). Two important concepts that go along with parallel processing are **bottom-up processing** and **top-down processing**. In bottom-up processing, we construct a whole stimulus from its parts. An example is perceiving an object on the basis of its edges. Bottom-up processing starts with the raw stimuli we perceive and ends with our synthesizing them into a meaningful concept. This kind of processing begins with activity in the primary visual cortex. In contrast, top-down processing starts with our beliefs and expectations, which we then impose on the raw stimuli we perceive. Top-down processing starts with processing in the association cortex, followed by processing in the primary visual cortex.

Some perceptions rely more heavily on bottom-up processing (Koch, 1993), others on top-down processing (McClelland & Plaut, 1993). In most cases, though, these two kinds of processing work hand in hand (Patel & Sathian, 2000). We can illustrate this point by how we process ambiguous figures (see **FIGURE 23**). Depending on our expectations, we typically perceive these figures differently. The top-down influence that we're thinking of a jazz musician biases our bottom-up processing of the shapes in Figure 23 and increases the chances we'll perceive a saxophone player. In contrast, if our top-down expectation were of a woman's face, our sensory-based bottom-up processing would change accordingly. Can you see both figures?

Perceptual Hypotheses: Guessing What's Out There

Because our brains rely so much on our knowledge and experiences, we can usually get away with economizing in our sensory processing and making educated guesses about what sensory information is telling us. Moreover, a pretty decent guess with fewer neurons is more efficient than a more certain answer with a huge number of neurons. As cognitive misers.

PERCEPTUAL SETS. We form a **perceptual set** when our expectations influence our perceptions—an example of top-down processing. We may perceive a misshapen letter as an "H" or as an "A" depending on the surrounding letters and the words that would result from our interpretation (see **FIGURE 24**). We also tend to perceive the world in accord with our preconceptions. An ambiguous cartoon drawn by W. E. Hill raises the question: Is it a young woman or an old witch? Participants placed in the perceptual set of a young woman by viewing a version of the cartoon exaggerating those features (see **FIGURE 25**)

FIGURE 23 What Do You See? Due to the influence of top-down processing, reading the caption "saxophone player" beneath this ambiguous figure tends to produce a different perception than reading the caption "woman."

FIGURE 24 Context Influences Perception. Depending on the perceptual set provided by the context of the surrounding letters, the middle letter can appear as an "H" or as an "A." Most of us read this phrase as "THE BAT" because of the context.

Old woman   Young woman

FIGURE 25 An Example of Perceptual Set. Depending on our perspective, the drawing on top can appear to be a young woman or an old one. Which did you perceive first? Look at the biased pictures (turn the page upside down) to alter your perceptual set. (*Source:* Hill, 1915)

parallel processing
the ability to attend to many sense modalities simultaneously

bottom-up processing
processing in which a whole is constructed from parts

top-down processing
conceptually driven processing influenced by beliefs and expectancies

perceptual set
set formed when expectations influence perceptions

FIGURE 26 Shape Constancy. We perceive a door as a door whether it appears as a rectangle or a trapezoid.

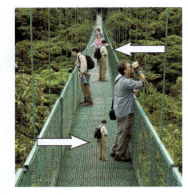

The man standing toward the back of the bridge looks to be of normal size, but the exact duplicate image appears in the foreground and looks like a toy because of size constancy.

FIGURE 27 The Checker-Shadow Illusion. We perceive a checkerboard pattern of black and white alternating squares, and because of color constancy, we ignore the dramatic change due to the shadow cast by the green cylinder. Believe it or not, the A and B squares are identical. (*Source:* © 1995 Edward H. Adelson)

perceptual constancy
the process by which we perceive stimuli consistently across varied conditions

reported seeing a young woman. In contrast, participants placed in the perceptual set of an old woman by viewing a version of the cartoon exaggerating those features reported seeing an old woman (Boring, 1930).

PERCEPTUAL CONSTANCY. The process by which we perceive stimuli consistently across varied conditions is **perceptual constancy**. Without perceptual constancy, we'd be hopelessly confused, because we'd be seeing our worlds as continually changing. Yet our brain allows us to correct from these minor changes. There are several kinds of perceptual constancy: shape, size, and color constancy. Consider a door we view from differing perspectives (see **FIGURE 26**). Because of *shape constancy,* we still see a door as a door whether it's completely shut, barely open, or more fully open, even though these shapes look almost nothing like each other.

Or take *size constancy,* our ability to perceive objects as the same size no matter how far away they are from us. When a friend walks away from us, her image becomes smaller. But we almost never realize this is happening, nor do we conclude that our friend is mysteriously shrinking. Outside of our conscious awareness, our brains mentally enlarge figures far away from us so that they appear more like similar objects in the same scene.

Color constancy is our ability to perceive color consistently across different levels of lighting. Consider a group of fire fighters dressed in bright yellow jackets. Their jackets look bright yellow even in very low levels of light. That's because we evaluate the color of an object in the context of background light and surrounding colors. Take a moment to examine **FIGURE 27**. The checkerboard appears to contain all black and white squares, but they're actually varying shades of gray. Remarkably, the A and B squares (one from the black set and one from the white set) are exactly the same shade of gray. Dale Purves and colleagues (2002) applied the same principle to cubes composed of smaller squares that appear to be of different colors, even though some of the smaller squares are actually gray (see **FIGURE 28**). We base our perception of color in these smaller squares on the surrounding context.

GESTALT PRINCIPLES. As we have learned, much of our visual perception involves analyzing an image in the context of its surroundings and our expectations. Our brains often provide missing information about outlines, a phenomenon called *subjective contours.* Gaetano Kanizsa sparked interest in this phenomenon in 1955. His figures illustrate how a mere hint of three or four corners can give rise to the perception of an imaginary shape (see **FIGURE 29**).

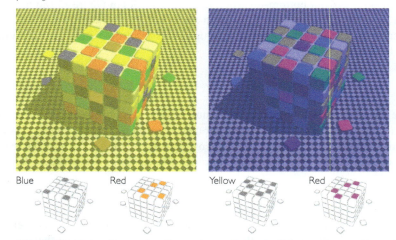

FIGURE 28 Color Perception Depends on Context. Gray can appear like a color depending on surrounding colors. The blue-colored squares on the top of the cube at the left are actually gray (*see map below the cube*). Similarly, the yellow-colored squares on the top of the cube at the right are actually gray (*see map below the cube*). (*Source:* © Dale Purves and R. Beau Lotto, 2002)

Gestalt principles are rules governing how we perceive objects as wholes within their overall context (*Gestalt* is a German word roughly meaning "whole"). Gestalt principles of perception help to explain why we see much of our world as consisting of unified figures or forms rather than confusing jumbles of lines and curves. These principles provide a road map for how we make sense of our perceptual worlds.

Here are the main Gestalt principles, formulated by psychologists Max Wertheimer, Wolfgang Kohler, and Kurt Koffka in the early 20th century (see **FIGURE 30**):

1. **Proximity:** Objects physically close to each other tend to be perceived as unified wholes (Figure 30a).

2. **Similarity:** All things being equal, we see similar objects as comprising a whole, much more so than dissimilar objects. If patterns of red circles and yellow circles are randomly mixed, we perceive nothing special. But if the red and yellow circles are lined up horizontally, we perceive separate rows of circles (Figure 30b).

3. **Continuity:** We still perceive objects as wholes, even if other objects block part of them. The Gestalt principle of continuity leads us to perceive the cross shown in Figure 30c as one long vertical line crossing over one long horizontal line rather than four smaller line segments joining together.

4. **Closure:** When partial visual information is present, our brains fill in what's missing. When the missing information is a contour, this principle is essentially the same as subjective contours. This Gestalt principle is the main illusion in the Kanizsa figures (Figure 30d).

5. **Symmetry:** We perceive objects that are symmetrically arranged as wholes more often than those that aren't. Figure 30e demonstrates that two symmetrical figures tend to be grouped together as a single unit.

6. **Figure–ground:** Perceptually, we make an instantaneous decision to focus attention on what we believe to be the central figure, and largely ignore what we believe to be the background. We can view some figures, such as Rubin's vase illusion, in two ways (Figure 30f). The vase can be the figure, in which case we ignore the background. If we look again, we can see an image in the background: two faces looking at each other.

Rubin's vase illusion is an example of a *bistable* image, one we can perceive in two ways. Another example is the Necker Cube in **FIGURE 31**. When we look at bistable images, we can typically perceive them only one way at a time, and there are limits to how quickly we can shift from one view to the other. A concept related to the bistable image is *emergence*—a perceptual gestalt that almost jumps out from the page and hits us all at once. Try to find the Dalmatian dog in the image on the next page. If you have trouble, keep staring at the black-and-white image until the dog emerges. It's worth the wait.

HOW WE PERCEIVE FACES. Our ability to recognize familiar faces, including our own, lies at the core of our social selves. After all, don't we refer to a friend as "a familiar face"? Even nonhuman primates can recognize faces (Pinsk et al., 2005).

Simulate in **MyPsychLab** the **Experiment:** Gestalt Laws of Perception

FIGURE 29 Kanizsa Square. This Kanizsa square illustrates subjective contours. The square you perceive in the middle of this figure is imaginary.

(a) Proximity

(b) Similarity

(c) Continuity

$+ = | + - \text{ not } -|-$

(d) Closure

(e) Symmetry

$\blacktriangleright\blacktriangleleft \ \blacktriangleright\blacktriangleleft = (\blacktriangleright\blacktriangleleft)(\blacktriangleright\blacktriangleleft)$
$\text{not } (\blacktriangleright)(\blacktriangleleft\blacktriangleright)(\blacktriangleleft)$

(f) Figure–ground

FIGURE 30 Gestalt Principles of Perception. As Gestalt psychologists discovered, we use a variety of principles to help us organize the world.

FIGURE 31 The Necker Cube. The Necker cube is an example of a bistable image.

Watch in **MyPsychLab** the **Video:** Special Topics: Recognizing Faces

Embedded in this photograph is an image of a Dalmatian dog. Can you find it?

FALSIFIABILITY ▶

Can the claim be disproved?

OCCAM'S RAZOR ▶

Does a simpler explanation fit the data just as well?

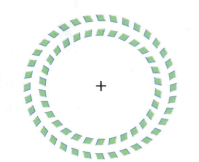

FIGURE 32 Moving Spiral Illusion. Focus on the plus sign in the middle of the figure and move the page closer to your face and then farther away. The two rings should appear to move in opposite directions, and those directions should reverse when you reverse the direction in which you move the page.

---

depth perception
ability to judge distance and three-dimensional relations

monocular depth cues
stimuli that enable us to judge depth using only one eye

binocular depth cues
stimuli that enable us to judge depth using both eyes

We don't need an exact picture of a face to recognize it. Caricature artists have long capitalized on this fact and amused us with their drawings of famous faces, usually with some feature exaggerated way out of proportion. Yet we can recognize wacky faces because our brains get by with only partial information, filling in the rest for us. Do individual neurons respond specifically to certain faces? Scientists have known for some time that the lower part of the temporal lobe responds to faces (refer back to Figure 10). Researchers have identified neurons in the human hippocampus that fire selectively in response to celebrity faces, such as those of Jennifer Aniston and Halle Berry (Quiroga et al., 2005). In the 1960s, Jerry Lettvin half-jokingly proposed that each neuron might store a single memory, like the recollection of our grandmother sitting in our living room when we were children. He coined the term "grandmother cell" to describe this argument, assuming it could be easily falsified (Horgan, 2005).

Certain neurons, such as those responding to Jennifer Aniston, are suggestive of grandmother cells, but we shouldn't be too quick to accept this possibility. Even though individual cells may respond to Aniston, many other neurons in other brain regions probably chime in, too. Researchers can only make recordings from a small number of neurons at once, so we don't know what the rest of the brain is doing. At present, the most parsimonious hypothesis is that sprawling networks of neurons, rather than single cells, are responsible for face recognition.

HOW WE PERCEIVE MOTION. The brain judges how things in our world are constantly changing by comparing visual frames, like those in a movie. Perceiving the motion of a car coming toward us as we cross the street relies on this kind of motion detection, and we couldn't cross the street, let alone drive a car, without it. We can also be fooled into seeing motion when it's not there. Moving closer to and farther from certain clever designs produces the illusion of motion, as we can see in **FIGURE 32**. The *phi phenomenon*, discovered by Max Wertheimer, is the illusory perception of movement produced by the successive flashing of images, like the flashing lights that seem to circle around a movie marquee. These lights are actually jumping from one spot on the marquee to another, but they appear continuous. The phi phenomenon shows that our perceptions of what's moving and what's not are based on only partial information, with our brains taking their best guesses about what's missing. Luckily, many of these guesses are accurate, or at least accurate enough for us to get along in everyday life.

Motion blindness is a serious disorder in which patients can't seamlessly string still images processed by their brains into the perception of ongoing motion. As we noted earlier, motion perception is much like creating a movie in our heads. Actual movies contain 24 frames of still photos per second, creating the illusory perception of motion. In patients with motion blindness, many of these "frames" are missing. This disability interferes with many simple tasks, like crossing the street. Imagine a car appearing to be 100 feet away and then suddenly jumping to only one foot away a second or two later. Needless to say, the experience would be terrifying. Life indoors isn't much better. Simply pouring a cup of coffee can be enormously challenging, because the person doesn't see the cup fill up. First, it's empty and then is overflowing with coffee onto the floor only a moment later.

HOW WE PERCEIVE DEPTH. Depth perception is the ability to see spatial relations in three dimensions; it enables us to reach for a glass and grasp it rather than knock it over and spill its contents. We need to have some idea of how close or far we are from objects to navigate around our environments. We use two kinds of cues to gauge depth: **monocular depth cues**, which rely on one eye alone, and **binocular depth cues**, which require both eyes.

Monocular Cues. We can perceive three dimensions using only one eye. We do so by relying on *pictorial cues* to give us a sense of what's located where in stationary scenes. The following pictorial cues help us to perceive depth.

- **Relative size:** All things being equal, more distant objects look smaller than closer objects.

- **Texture gradient:** The texture of objects becomes less apparent as objects move farther away.

- **Interposition:** One object that's closer blocks our view of an object behind it. From this fact, we know which object is closer and which is farther away.

- **Linear perspective:** The outlines of rooms or buildings converge as distance increases, a fact exploited by artists. We can trace most lines in a scene to a point where they meet—the *vanishing point*. In reality, lines in parallel never meet, but they appear to do so at great distances. Some *impossible figures*—figures that break physical laws—possess more than one vanishing point. Artist M. C. Escher was fond of violating this rule in his prints.

- **Height in plane:** In a scene, distant objects tend to appear higher, and nearer objects lower.

- **Light and shadow:** Objects cast shadows that give us a sense of their three-dimensional form.

One additional monocular cue that's not pictorial is *motion parallax:* the ability to judge the distance of moving objects from their speed. Nearby objects seem to move faster than those far away traveling at the same speed. Motion parallax also works when we're moving. Stationary objects nearer to us pass us more quickly than objects farther away, a fact we'll discover when looking out of the windows of a moving car. Our brains quickly compute these differences in speed and calculate approximate distances from us.

Binocular Cues. Our visual system is set up so that we view each of our two visual fields with both eyes. We'll recall that half of the axons in the optic nerve cross to the other side and half stay on the same side before entering the brain. Visual information from both sides is sent to neighboring cells in the visual cortex, where our brains can make comparisons. These comparisons form the basis of binocular depth perception; we use several binocular cues to perceive depth in our worlds.

- **Binocular disparity:** Like the two lenses from a pair of binoculars, our left and right eyes transmit quite different information for near objects but see distant objects similarly. To demonstrate this cue, close one of your eyes and hold a pen up about a foot away from your face, lining the top of it up with a distant point on the wall (like a doorknob or corner of a picture frame). Then, hold the pen steady while alternating which of your eyes is open. You'll find that although the pen is lined up with one eye, it's no longer lined up when you switch to the other eye. Each eye sees the world a bit differently, and our brains ingeniously make use of this information to judge depth.

Gisela Leibold is unable to detect motion. She's understandably concerned about important information she might miss riding down an escalator in Munich.

This painting depicts a scene that provides monocular cues to depth.

1. Relative size: The house is drawn approximately as high as the fence post, but we know the house is much bigger, so it must be considerably farther away.

2. Texture gradient: The grasses in front of the fence are drawn as individual blades but those in the field behind are shown with almost no detail.

3. Interposition: The tree at the corner of the house is blocking part of the house, so we know that the tree is closer to us than the house is.

This lithograph by M. C. Escher titled *Belvedere* (1958) features two vanishing points, resulting in an impossible structure. Can you locate the vanishing points off the page?

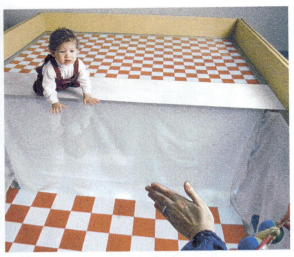

The visual cliff tests infants' ability to judge depth.

👁 **Watch** in **MyPsychLab** the **Video:** Classic Footage of Eleanor Gibson, Richard Walk, and the Visual Cliff

Sound source

Path of sound to far (right) ear

Path of sound to near (left) ear

Extra distance sound must travel to reach right ear

Sound shadow

FIGURE 33 How We Locate Sounds. When someone standing to our left speaks to us, the sound reaches our left ear slightly earlier than it reaches our right. Also, the intensity detected by the left ear is greater than the intensity detected by the right ear, because the right ear lies in a sound shadow produced by the head and shoulders.

FALSIFIABILITY ▶

Can the claim be disproved?

👁 **Watch** in **MyPsychLab** the **Video:** What's In It For Me?: Perceptual Magic in Art

• **Binocular convergence:** When we look at nearby objects, we focus on them reflexively by using our eye muscles to turn our eyes inward, a phenomenon called *convergence*. Our brains are aware of how much our eyes are converging, and use this information to estimate distance.

Depth Perception Appears in Infancy. We can judge depth as soon as we learn to crawl. Eleanor Gibson established this phenomenon in a classic setup called the *visual cliff* (Gibson, 1991; Gibson & Walk, 1960). The typical visual cliff consists of a table and a floor several feet below, both covered by a checkered cloth. A clear glass surface extends from the table out over the floor, creating the appearance of a sudden drop. Infants between 6 and 14 months of age hesitate to crawl over the glass elevated several feet above the floor, even when their mothers beckon. The visual cliff demonstrates that depth cues present soon after birth are probably partly innate, although they surely develop with experience.

HOW WE PERCEIVE WHERE SOUNDS ARE LOCATED. Cues play an important role as well in localizing (locating) sounds. We use various brain centers to localize sounds with respect to our bodies. When the auditory nerve enters the brain stem, some of its axons connect with cells on the same side of the brain, but the rest cross over to the other side of the brain. This clever arrangement enables information from both ears to reach the same structures in the brain stem. Because the two sources of information take different routes, they arrive at the brain stem slightly out of sync with each other. Our brains compare this difference between our ears—a so-called *binaural cue*—to localize sound sources (**FIGURE 33**). There's also a loudness difference between our ears, because the ear closest to the sound source is in the direct path of the sound wave, whereas the ear farthest away is in a sound shadow, created by our head. We rely mostly on binaural cues to detect the source of sounds. But we also use monaural cues, heard by one ear only. The cues help us distinguish sounds that are clear from those that are muffled due to obstruction by the ear, head, and shoulders, allowing us to figure out where sounds are coming from.

When Perception Deceives Us

Sometimes the best way to understand how something works is to see how it doesn't work—or works in unusual circumstances. We've already examined some illusions that illustrate principles of sensation and perception. Now we'll examine further how illusions and other unusual phenomena shed light on everyday perception.

• The *moon illusion*, which has fascinated people for centuries, is the illusion that the moon appears larger when it's near the horizon than high in the sky. Scientists have put forth several explanations for this illusion, but none is universally accepted. A common misconception is that the moon appears larger near the horizon due to a magnification effect caused by Earth's atmosphere. But we can easily refute this hypothesis.

Although Earth's atmosphere does alter the moon's color at the horizon, it doesn't enlarge it. Let's contrast this common misconception with a few better-supported explanations. The first is that the moon illusion is due to errors in perceived distance. The moon is some 240,000 miles away, a huge distance we've little experience judging. When the moon is high in the sky, there's nothing else around for comparison. In contrast, when the moon is near the horizon, we may perceive it as farther away because we can see it next to things we know to be far away, like buildings, mountains, and trees. Because we know these things are large, we perceive the moon as larger still. Another explanation is that we're mistaken about the three-dimensional space in which we live, along with the moon. For example, many people have the misperception that the sky is shaped like a flattened dome, leading us to see the moon as farther away on the horizon than at the top of the sky (Rock & Kaufman, 1962; Ross & Plug, 2002).

- The startling *Ames room illusion*, developed by Adelbert Ames, Jr. (1946), is shown in **FIGURE 34**. This distorted room is actually trapezoidal; the walls are slanted and the ceiling and floor are at an incline. Insert two people of the same size and the Ames room creates the bizarre impression of a giant person on the side of the room where the ceiling is lower (but doesn't appear to be) and of a tiny person on the side of the room where the ceiling is higher. This illusion is due to the relative size principle. The height of the ceiling is the key to the illusion, and the other distortions in the room are only necessary to make the room appear normal to the observer. Hollywood special effects wizards have capitalized on this principle in movies such as the *Lord of the Rings* and *Charlie and the Chocolate Factory* to make some characters appear gargantuan and others dwarf-like.

- In the *Müller-Lyer illusion*, a line of identical length appears longer when it ends in a set of arrowheads pointing inward than in a set of arrowheads pointing outward (see **FIGURE 35a**). That's because we perceive lines as part of a larger context. Three researchers (Segall, Campbell, & Herskovitz, 1966) found that people from different cultures displayed differing reactions to the Müller-Lyer illusion. The Zulu, who live in round huts and plow their fields in circles rather than rows, are less susceptible to the Müller-Lyer illusion, probably because they have less experience with linear environments (McCauley & Henrich, 2006).

- In the *Ponzo illusion*, also called the railroad tracks illusion, converging lines enclose two objects of identical size, leading us to perceive the object closer to the converging lines as larger (see **FIGURE 35b**). Our brain "assumes" that the object closer to the converging lines is farther away—usually it would be correct in this guess—and compensates for this knowledge by making the object look bigger.

- The *horizontal–vertical illusion* causes us to perceive the vertical part of an upside-down "T" as longer than the horizontal part, because the horizontal part is divided in half by the vertical part (see **FIGURE 35c**).

- The *Ebbinghaus–Titchener* illusion leads us to perceive a circle as larger when surrounded by smaller circles and smaller when surrounded by larger circles (see **FIGURE 35d**). Although this illusion fools our eyes, it doesn't fool our hands! Studies in which participants have to reach for the center circle indicate that their grasp remains on target (Milner & Goodale, 1995), although some scientists have recently challenged this finding (Franz et al., 2003).

The moon illusion causes us to perceive the moon as larger near the horizon than high in the sky.

(a) Which horizontal line is longer?

(b) Which line above is longer, and which circle is bigger?

(c) Which line is longer?

(d) Which center circle is bigger?

FIGURE 35 How Well Can You Judge Relative Size? The Müller-Lyer (a), Ponzo (b), horizontal–vertical (c), and Ebbinghaus–Titchener (d) illusions.

Actual position of person A

Actual and apparent position of person B

Apparent position of person A

Apparent shape of room   Viewing peephole

FIGURE 34 The Ames Room. Viewed through a small peephole, the Ames room makes small people look impossibly large and large people look impossibly small. Who is the younger and smaller child in this picture?

Subliminal and Extrasensory Perception

We've seen numerous examples of our ability to be cognitive misers. One way we scrimp and save our attentional resources is to process many of the sensory inputs to which we're exposed unconsciously. In fact, many of our actions occur with little or no forethought or deliberation (Hassin, Uleman, & Bargh, 2005). Consider that our lives would grind to a standstill if we had to think carefully before uttering every word, typing every sentence, or making the minor corrections in steering needed to drive a car safely. Under ordinary circumstances, we don't direct our attention consciously to these activities, yet we constantly adjust to the flow of sensory experience. Might some sensory inputs be so subtle that they aren't registered consciously, yet still affect our everyday lives? Put another way, if we can detect stimuli without our knowing it, does that affect our behavior?

SUBLIMINAL PERCEPTION AND PERSUASION. You're home on a Sunday afternoon, curled up on your couch watching a movie on TV. Suddenly, within a span of a few minutes you see three or four extremely quick flashes of light on the screen. Only a few minutes later, you're seized with an uncontrollable desire to eat a cheeseburger. Did the advertiser fiendishly insert several photographs of a cheeseburger in the midst of the film, so rapidly you couldn't detect them?

The American public has long been fascinated with the possibility of **subliminal perception**—the processing of sensory information that occurs below the limen, that is, the level of conscious awareness (Cheesman & Merikle, 1986; Rogers & Smith, 1993). To study subliminal perception, researchers typically present a word or photograph very quickly, say at 50 milliseconds (one twentieth of a second). They frequently follow this stimulus immediately with another stimulus (like a pattern of dots or lines) that blocks out mental processing of the subliminal stimulus. When participants can't correctly identify the content of the stimulus at better than chance levels, researchers deem it subliminal. The claim for subliminal perception may seem extraordinary, but the evidence for it is compelling (Seitz & Watanabe, 2003).

When investigators subliminally trigger emotions by exposing participants to words related to anger, these participants are more likely to rate other people as hostile (Bargh & Pietromonaco, 1982). In one study, researchers subliminally presented participants with words such as church, saint, and preacher, and then provided them with an opportunity to cheat on a different task. None of the participants who subliminally received religious words cheated, compared with 20 percent of those who subliminally received neutral, nonreligious words (Randolph-Seng & Nielson, 2007). For unclear reasons, the effects of subliminal information often vanish when participants become aware of or even suspect attempts to influence them subliminally (Glaser & Kihlstrom, 2005).

Even though we're subject to subliminal perception, that doesn't mean we numbly succumb to *subliminal persuasion,* that is, subthreshold influences over our votes in elections, product choices, and life decisions. Subliminally presented words related to thirst, such as "drink," may slightly influence how much people drink, but specific words related to brand names, such as "cola," don't influence beverage choice (Dijksterhuis, Aarts, & Smith, 2005). This may be because we can't engage in much,

? In 2000, the Republican National Committee ran this ad criticizing Al Gore's health care plan in which the word "RATS" appears for a fraction of a second. Would this subliminal message persuade viewers that Gore's plan is bad? (See answer upside down at bottom of page.)

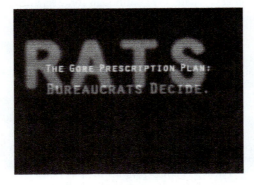

subliminal perception
perception below the limen or threshold of conscious awareness

Answer: No, because even if viewers were subject to subliminal perception they wouldn't have engaged in in-depth processing of the meaning of the word "RATS."

if any, in-depth processing of the *meaning* of subliminal stimuli (Rosen, Glasgow, & Moore, 2003). As a result, these stimuli probably can't produce large-scale or enduring changes in our attitudes, let alone our decisions.

Still, subliminal self-help audiotapes and videotapes are a multimillion-dollar-a-year industry in the United States alone. They purportedly contain repeated subliminal messages (such as "Feel better about yourself") designed to influence our behavior or emotions. Scores of studies show that subliminal self-help tapes are ineffective (Eich & Hyman, 1991; Moore, 1992). Nevertheless, those who listen to them believe they have improved, even when there is no evidence to support improvement (Greenwald et al., 1991). Phil Merikle (1988) uncovered another reason why subliminal self-help tapes don't work: His auditory analyses revealed that many of these tapes contain no message at all!

Some people even claim that *reversed* subliminal messages influence behavior. In 1990, the rock band Judas Priest was put on trial for the suicide of a teenager and the attempted suicide of another. While listening to a Judas Priest song, the boys supposedly heard the words "Do it" played backward. The prosecution claimed that this reversed message led the boys to shoot themselves. In the end, the members of Judas Priest were acquitted (Moore, 1996). As the expert witnesses noted, forward subliminal messages can't produce major changes in behavior, so it's even less likely that backward messages can do so. In some cases, extraordinary claims remain just that—extraordinary claims with no scientific support.

◄ **EXTRAORDINARY CLAIMS**
Is the evidence as strong as the claim?

SUBLIMINAL PERSUASION CDS

evaluating **CLAIMS**

The Internet is chock-full of advertisements for subliminal self-help CDs that promise to change your life, despite the fact that scientific research shows these products to be ineffective. The manufacturers of these CDs claim to be able to send messages to your unconscious mind that influence your actions. Let's evaluate some of these claims, which are modeled after actual advertisements for subliminal persuasion CDs.

"Over one million people have discovered the power of our CDs."

Does the sheer number of people who purchase a product provide evidence of its effectiveness? Is there necessarily a correlation between how many people use a product and its effectiveness?

"Your CDs are the best I've ever tried—they changed my life!"—*Andrew from Atlanta, GA*

Why are claims based only on testimonials and anecdotal evidence not trustworthy?

"Our CDs will *improve all aspects of your life.* You will conquer your fears, increase your IQ, lose weight, and attract a mate."

Extraordinary claims about subliminal persuasion require extraordinary evidence, and the ad provides no such evidence. To date, scientists have failed to document the ability of subliminal persuasion to produce profound personal changes.

EXTRASENSORY PERCEPTION (ESP): FACT OR FICTION? Proponents of **extrasensory perception (ESP)** argue that we can perceive events outside of the known channels of sensation, like seeing, hearing, and touch. Before we examine the evidence for this extraordinary claim, we first address the question…

EXTRAORDINARY CLAIMS ▶
Is the evidence as strong as the claim?

WHAT'S ESP, ANYWAY? *Parapsychologists*—investigators who study ESP and related psychic phenomena—have subdivided ESP into three major types (Hines, 2003; Hyman, 1989):

1. **Precognition:** acquiring knowledge of future events before they occur through paranormal means, that is, mechanisms that lie outside of traditional science. (You knew we were going to say that, didn't you?);

2. **Telepathy:** reading other people's minds; and

3. **Clairvoyance:** detecting the presence of objects or people that are hidden from view.

The Zener cards, named after a collaborator of Joseph B. Rhine, have been used widely in ESP research.

IS THERE SCIENTIFIC EVIDENCE FOR ESP? In the 1930s, Joseph B. Rhine, who coined the term *extrasensory perception,* launched the full-scale study of ESP. Rhine used a set of stimuli called *Zener cards,* which consist of five standard symbols: squiggly lines, star, circle, plus sign, and square. He presented these cards to participants in random order and asked them to guess which card would appear (precognition), which card another participant had in mind (telepathy), and which card was hidden from view (clairvoyance). Rhine (1934) initially reported positive results, as his participants averaged about seven correct Zener card identifications per deck of 25, where five would be chance performance.

REPLICABILITY ▶
Can the results be duplicated in other studies?

But there was a problem, one that has dogged ESP research for well over a century: Try as they might, other investigators couldn't replicate Rhine's findings. Moreover, scientists later pointed out serious flaws in Rhine's methods. Some of the Zener cards were so worn down or poorly manufactured that participants could see the imprint of the symbols through the backs of the cards (Alcock, 1990; Gilovich, 1991). In other cases, scientists found that Rhine and his colleagues hadn't properly randomized the order of the cards, rendering his analyses essentially meaningless. Eventually, enthusiasm for Zener card research dried up.

The problem with replication has come up more recently with research using the *Ganzfeld technique* in which the experimenter covers participants' eyes with goggles that look like the halves of ping-pong balls to create a uniform visual field when a red floodlight is directed toward the eyes. Another person (the "sender") attempts to mentally transmit a target picture while the participant reports mental images that come to mind. The participant then rates each of four pictures for how well it matches the mental imagery experienced. Only one of the pictures is the target the sender tried to transmit.

A participant in a Ganzfeld experiment attempting to receive images from a sender. The uniform sensory field he's experiencing is designed to minimize visual and auditory "noise" from the environment, supposedly permitting him to detect otherwise weak ESP signals.

Studies have found that the size of Ganzfeld effects was small and corresponded to chance differences in performance (Bem & Honorton, 1994; Milton & Wiseman, 1999). Other ESP paradigms have proven equally disappointing. For example, research conducted over three decades ago suggested that people could mentally transmit images to dreaming individuals (Ullman, Krippner, & Vaughn, 1973). Yet later investigators couldn't replicate these results, either.

The latest concern about replication stems from studies of precognition in which Cornell University researcher Daryl Bem

extrasensory perception (ESP)
perception of events outside the known channels of sensation

(2011) recently claimed that nine out of 10 experiments he conducted indicated that people's ability to acquire knowledge of future events affects their present behavior. Each of Bem's studies reversed the typical order of presentation of stimuli and responses by exposing participants to stimuli *after,* rather than before they respond to an experimental task. For example, in many psychology studies, researchers have found that when participants rehearse words (i.e., the stimuli) their recall is improved (i.e., the responses) relative to non-studied words. However, what if participants rehearse words *after* a recall test, and their memory for the rehearsed words improves on the earlier test, relative to the non-rehearsed words? This astonishing finding would throw a monkey wrench into the idea that causes precede effects and imply that people can somehow "see into the future" to affect their prior responses. Yet this is exactly what Bem found. Future events (i.e., rehearsing words after the test) seemed to predict past behaviors (i.e., test performance).

Even before Bem's study saw the light of publication in a prestigious psychology journal, it set ablaze a firestorm of criticism based on methodological and statistical concerns (Francis, in press; Wagenmakers et al., 2011). Still, scientists' mantra regarding whether a finding is reliable is *replication, replication, replication.* So Stuart Ritchie, Richard Wiseman, and Christopher French—scientists at three different universities—jumped at the opportunity to replicate Bem's memory rehearsal study, the one that claimed to provide the strongest evidence of all for reverse causality. The result? All three researchers failed to replicate Bem's findings: there was no recall difference across studied and non-studied words.

Other recent attempts to replicate Bem's controversial work have yielded similarly disconfirming results, but other attempts will surely follow (Galak, LeBoeuf, Nelson, & Simmons, 2012). If some studies repeat Bem's findings but others don't, it will be important to figure out why this is the case. But for now, the common-sense view of causes preceding effects seems not to be under serious threat. The many non-replications of ESP findings underscore the absence of a feature that's a hallmark of mature sciences: an "experimental recipe" that yields replicable results across independent laboratories (Hyman, 1989).

In the absence of scientific supporting evidence, many ESP proponents have come up with ad hoc hypotheses. Already the failures to replicate Bem (2011) have been attributed to the skepticism of the experimenters, an attitude claimed to inhibit ESP and dubbed the *experimenter effect.* Psi missing refers to significantly worse than chance performance on ESP tasks (Gilovich, 1991). Some ESP proponents have even argued that psi missing demonstrates the existence of ESP, because below chance performance indicates that individuals with ESP are deliberately selecting incorrect answers! Such ad hoc hypotheses render claims about ESP extremely difficult to falsify.

WHY PEOPLE BELIEVE IN ESP. The extraordinary claim of ESP isn't matched by equally extraordinary evidence. Yet surveys indicate that 41 percent of American adults believe in ESP (Haraldsson & Houtkooper, 1991; Moore, 2005). Moreover, two-thirds of Americans say they've had a psychic experience, like a dream foretelling the death of a loved one or a premonition about a car accident that came true (Greeley, 1987). In light of more than 150 years of failed replications, it's reasonable to ask why our beliefs in ESP are so strong given that the research evidence for it is so weak.

Illusory correlation offers one likely answer. We attend to and recall events that are striking coincidences and ignore or forget events that aren't. Imagine we're in a new city and thinking of an old friend we haven't seen in years. A few hours later, we run into that friend on the street. "What a coincidence!" we tell ourselves. This remarkable event is evidence of ESP, right? Perhaps. But we're forgetting about the thousands of times we've been in new cities and thought about old friends whom we never encountered (Presley, 1997).

Factoid

Beginning in 1972, the U.S. government invested $20 million in the Stargate program to study the ability of "remote viewers" to acquire militarily useful information in distant places, like the locations of nuclear facilities in enemy countries through clairvoyance. The government discontinued the program in 1995, apparently because the remote viewers provided no useful information and sometimes were wildly wrong (Hyman, 1996).

◄ **REPLICABILITY**
Can the results be duplicated in other studies?

◄ **FALSIFIABILITY**
Can the claim be disproved?

◄ **EXTRAORDINARY CLAIMS**
Is the evidence as strong as the claim?

◄ **REPLICABILITY**
Can the results be duplicated in other studies?

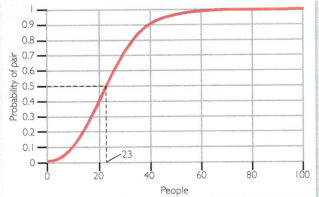

Further contributing to belief in ESP is our tendency to underestimate the frequency of coincidences. Most of us don't realize just how probable certain seemingly "improbable" events are. Take a crack at this question: *How large must a group of people be before the probability of two people sharing the same birthday exceeds 50 percent?*

Many participants respond with answers like 365, 100, or even 1,000. To most people's surprise, the correct answer is 23. That is, in a group of 23 people it's more likely than not that at least two people have the same birthday (see **FIGURE 36**). Once we get up to a group of 60 people, the odds exceed 99 percent. Because we tend to underestimate the likelihood of coincidences, we may be inclined to attribute them incorrectly to psychic phenomena.

FIGURE 36 The "Birthday Paradox."

As we reach a group size of 23 people, the probability that at least two people share the same birthday exceeds 0.5, or 50 percent. Research demonstrates that most people markedly underestimate the likelihood of this and other coincidences, sometimes leading them to attribute these coincidences to paranormal events.

PSYCHIC PREDICTIONS. For many years, science journalist Gene Emery tracked failed psychic predictions. In 2005, he found that psychics predicted that an airplane would crash into the Egyptian pyramids, astronauts would discover a Nazi flag planted on the moon, Earth's magnetic field would reverse, and a participant on a television reality show would cannibalize one of the contestants, none of which have occurred. Conversely, no psychic predicted any of the significant events that *did* occur in 2005, like Hurricane Katrina, which inflicted terrible loss of life and property damage on New Orleans and neighboring areas (Emery, 2005).

Many psychic forecasters make use of *multiple end points,* meaning they keep their predictions so open-ended that they're consistent with almost any conceivable set of outcomes (Gilovich, 1991). A psychic may predict, "A celebrity will get caught in a scandal this year." But aside from being vague, this prediction is extremely open-ended. What counts as a "celebrity?" Sure, we'd all agree that Lady Gaga and Brad Pitt are celebrities, but does our congressional representative count? What about a local television newscaster? Similarly, what counts as a "scandal?"

What about psychics, like John Edward or James von Pragh, who claim to tell us things about ourselves or our dead relatives that they couldn't possibly have known? Most of these psychics probably rely on a set of skills known as *cold reading,* the art of persuading people we've just met that we know all about them (Hines, 2003; Hyman, 1977). If you want to impress your friends with a cold reading, **TABLE 3** contains some tips to keep in mind.

Cold reading works for one major reason: we humans seek meaning in our worlds and often find it even when it's not there. So in many respects we're reading into the cold reading at least as much as the cold reader is reading into us.

Crystal ball readers claim to be able to tell us a great deal about ourselves and our futures. Yet many of them probably rely on cold-reading techniques that most of us could duplicate with relatively little training.

TABLE 3 Cold-Reading Techniques.

TECHNIQUE	EXAMPLE
Let the person know at the outset that you won't be perfect.	"I pick up a lot of different signals. Some will be accurate, but others may not be."
Start off with a *stock spiel*, a list of general statements that apply to just about everyone.	"You've recently been struggling with some tough decisions."
Fish for details by peppering your reading with vague probes.	"I'm sensing that someone with the letter M or maybe N has been important in your life lately."
Use the technique of *sleight of tongue*, meaning that you toss out so many guesses in rapid-fire fashion that at least a few of them are bound to be right.	"Has your father been ill?"; "How about your mother?"; "Hmmm … I sense that someone in your family is ill or worried about getting ill."
Use a prop.	A crystal ball, set of tarot cards, or horoscope convey the impression that you're basing your reading on mystical information.
Make use of *population stereotypes*, responses or characteristics reported by many or even most people.	"I believe you have a piece of clothing, like an old dress or blouse, that you haven't worn in years but have kept for sentimental value."
Look for physical cues to the individual's personality or life history.	A traditional manner of dress often suggests a conventional and proper person, a great deal of shiny jewelry often suggests a flamboyant person, and so on.
Remember that "flattery will get you everywhere."	Tell people what they want to hear, like "I see a great romance on the horizon."

(*Source*: Hines, 2003; Hyman, 1977; Rowland, 2001)

Factoid

To persuade people you have ESP, try the following demonstration in a large group of friends. Tell them, "I want you to think of an odd two-digit number that's less than 50, the only catch being that the two digits must be different—because that would make it too easy for me." Give them a few moments, and say, "I get the sense that some of you were thinking of 37." Then pause and say, "I was initially thinking of 35, but changed my mind. Was I close?" Research shows that slightly more than half of people will pick either 37 or 35, which are population stereotypes (see Table 3) that can convince many people you possess telepathic powers (French, 1992; Hines, 2003).

Assess Your Knowledge   FACT or FICTION?

1. In top-down processing, we construct a whole stimulus from its parts.   **True / False**

2. We perceive depth only when we have two slightly different views from our eyes.   **True / False**

3. The earth's atmosphere enlarges the appearance of the moon, creating the moon illusion.   **True / False**

4. Reversed subliminal messages can lead to violent actions.   **True / False**

5. Belief in ESP can be partly explained by our tendency to underestimate the probability of coincidences.   **True / False**

Answers: 1. F; 2. F; 3. F; 4. F; 5. T

✓ **Study** and **Review** in **MyPsychLab**

Your Complete Review System

 Study and **Review** in **MyPsychLab**

Two Sides of the Coin: Sensation and Perception

1 IDENTIFY THE BASIC PRINCIPLES THAT APPLY TO ALL SENSES.

Transduction is the process of converting an external energy, such as light or sound vibration, into electrical activity within neurons. The doctrine of specific nerve energies refers to how each of the sensory modalities is handled by specific regions of the brain. Even though most connections in the brain are faithful to one sense modality, brain regions often respond to information from a different sense.

1. The process of converting external stimulus energy into neural activity is called _____.

2. A _____ _____ is a specialized cell that transduces a specific stimulus.

3. The _____ _____ is the lowest level of a stimulus needed for the nervous system to detect a change 50 percent of the time.

4. _____ _____ states that there is a constant proportional relationship between the JND and the original stimulus intensity.

5. A striking example of cross-modal processing is the _____ effect.

6. Sir Francis Galton (1880) was the first to describe _____, a condition in which people experience cross-modal sensations, like hearing sounds when they see colors—sometimes called "colored hearing"—or even tasting colors.

2 DISCUSS THE ROLE OF ATTENTION AND THE NATURE OF THE BINDING PROBLEM.

To adapt to the challenges of an ever-changing environment, flexible attention is critical to survival and well-being. Yet attention must also be selective so that we are not overwhelmed by sensory inputs. One of the great mysteries of psychology is how we are able to bind different pieces of sensory information and cues together into a unified whole.

7. Donald Broadbent's (1957) _____ theory of attention views attention as a bottleneck through which information passes.

8. What does the cocktail party effect tell us about our ability to monitor stimuli outside of our immediate attention?

9. When we're unable to detect stimuli that are in plain sight when our attention is focused elsewhere, it is called _____ _____.

10. _____ refers to the mysterious way our mind combines different visual cues into a unified perception of a scene.

Seeing: The Visual System

3 EXPLAIN HOW THE EYE STARTS THE VISUAL PROCESS.

The lens in the eye accommodates to focus on images both near and far by changing from "fat" to "flat." The lens optimally focuses light on the retina, which lies at the rear of the eye. The retina contains rods and cones filled with pigments. Additional cells in the retina transmit information about light to ganglion cells, and the axons of these cells combine to form the optic nerve.

11. The _____ spectrum refers to the range of wavelengths of light that humans can see.

12. The intensity of reflected light that reaches our eyes is called _____.

13. Consisting of cells that are completely transparent, the _____ changes its curvature to keep images in focus.

14. We can think of the _____ as a "movie screen" onto which light from the world is projected.

15. _____ are receptor cells that allow us to see in low light, and _____ are receptor cells that allow us to see in color.

16. Identify each eye component and its function.

(a) _____
(b) _____
(c) _____
(d) _____
(e) _____
(f) _____
(g) _____
(h) _____

4 IDENTIFY THE DIFFERENT KINDS OF VISUAL PERCEPTION.

Our visual system is sensitive to shape and color. We use different parts of the visual cortex to process these different aspects of visual perception. V1 cells are sensitive to lines of a particular orientation. Color perception involves a mixture of trichromatic and opponent processing.

17. The idea that color vision is based on our sensitivity to three different colors is called the _____ theory.

18. _____ _____ is our ability to use minimal patterns to identify objects.

19. The ability to see afterimages after staring at the figure on the next page is explained by the _____ _____ theory.

5 DESCRIBE DIFFERENT VISUAL PROBLEMS.

Blindness is a worldwide problem, especially in underdeveloped countries. There are several types of color blindness, the most common being red–green. The phenomenon of blindsight demonstrates that some blind people can make decent guesses about the location of objects in their environments.

20. A person with _____ _____ can tell us the shape and color of an object, but can't recognize or name it.

Hearing: The Auditory System

6 EXPLAIN HOW THE EAR STARTS THE AUDITORY PROCESS.

Sound waves created by vibration of air molecules are funneled into the outer ear. These vibrations perturb the eardrum, causing the three small bones in the middle ear to vibrate. This process creates pressure in the cochlea, which contains the basilar membrane and organ of Corti, in which hair cells are embedded. The hair cells then bend, thereby exciting them. The message is relayed through the auditory nerve.

21. Identify the items in the figure showing sound waves.

22. _____ refers to the frequency of the sound wave, and is measured in hertz (Hz).

23. The height of the sound wave corresponds to _____ and is measured in decibels (dB).

24. We refer to _____ to describe the complexity or quality of a sound.

25. The _____ lies in the inner ear and converts vibration into neural activity.

26. The organ of Corti and basilar membrane are especially critical to hearing because _____ _____ are embedded within them.

27. Identify the components and their functions in the hearing process.

7 IDENTIFY THE DIFFERENT KINDS OF AUDITORY PERCEPTION.

Place theory is pitch perception based on where along the basilar membrane hair cells are maximally excited. Frequency theory is based on hair cells reproducing the frequency of the pitch in their firing rates. In volley theory, groups of neurons stagger their responses to follow a pitch.

28. The perception of high-pitched tones by the basilar membrane can be explained by the _____ theory.

29. Two theories related to perceiving low-pitched tones are the _____ theory and _____ theory.

30. _____ _____ is due to a malfunctioning of the ear, especially a failure of the eardrum or the ossicles of the inner ear.

Smell and Taste: The Sensual Senses

8 IDENTIFY HOW WE SENSE AND PERCEIVE ODORS AND TASTES.

The tongue contains taste receptors for sweet, sour, bitter, salty, umami, and perhaps fat. Our ability to taste foods relies largely on smell. Olfactory receptors in our noses are sensitive to hundreds of different airborne molecules. We react to extremely sour tastes, which may be due to food spoilage, with disgust. We also appear sensitive to pheromones, odorless molecules that can affect sexual responses.

31. Airborne chemicals that interact with receptors in the lining of our nasal passages are called _____.

32. We detect taste with _____ _____ that are on our tongue.

33. We're sensitive to _____ basic tastes, the last of which, _____, was recently discovered.

34. There is a (weak/strong) tendency for individual taste receptors to concentrate at certain locations on the tongue.

35. Our taste perception (is/isn't) dependent largely on our sense of smell.

36. Both tasting disgusting food and viewing facial expressions of disgust activate the _____ _____.

37. What chemicals do some perfume advertisers inaccurately claim are contained in their products which, when worn, allegedly trigger a physical response from others?

Answers are located at the end of the text.

38. A region of the _____ _____ is a site of convergence for smell and taste.

39. Label the brain components involved in the processes of smell and taste.

Smell
Taste

(a)
(b)
(c)
(d)
(e)
(f)
(g)

40. Researchers have showed that cancer patients who lose their sense of taste have a (better/worse) prognosis.

Our Body Senses: Touch, Body Position, and Balance

9 DESCRIBE THE THREE DIFFERENT BODY SENSES.

The three body senses are called "somatosensory" for body sensation, "proprioception" for muscle position sense, and "vestibular sense" for the sense of balance and equilibrium. The somatosensory system responds to light touch, deep pressure, hot and cold temperature, and tissue damage. Our muscles contain sense receptors that detect stretch and others that detect force. We calculate where our bodies are located from this information. We're typically unaware of our sense of equilibrium.

41. The body's system for touch and pain is the _____ system.

42. Our sense of body position is called _____.

43. The _____ _____, also called the sense of equilibrium, enables us to sense and maintain our balance.

10 EXPLAIN HOW PAIN PERCEPTION DIFFERS FROM TOUCH PERCEPTION.

There's a large emotional component to pain perception that's not present with touch. This is because pain information activates parts of the limbic system in addition to the somatosensory cortex.

44. We sense touch, temperature, and especially pain, with _____ _____ _____.

45. Our fingertips have the (least/most) nerve endings.

46. Information about body touch, temperature, and painful stimuli travels in the _____ nerves before entering the spinal cord.

47. Touch information travels more (slowly/quickly) than pain stimuli information.

48. Explain the process by which humans detect physical pressure, temperature, and pain.

Meissner's corpuscle (specialized for light touch)

Ruffini ending (specialized for skin stretching)

Free nerve ending (pain receptor)

Pacinian corpuscle (specialized for deep pressure)

49. Describe the "mirror box" treatment and identify its role in helping people who have lost limbs.

11 DESCRIBE THE FIELD OF PSYCHOLOGY CALLED HUMAN FACTORS.

The field of human factors starts with what psychologists have learned about sensation and perception, and then designs user-friendly devices, like computer keyboards and airplane cockpits, with this knowledge in mind.

50. Psychologists can use what we know about human psychology and sensory systems—ranging from our body position sense to vision—to build more _____, or worker-friendly, gadgets and tools of the trade.

Perception: When Our Senses Meet Our Brains

12 TRACK HOW OUR MINDS BUILD UP PERCEPTIONS.

Information travels from primary sensory to secondary sensory cortex and then on to association cortex. Along the way, perception becomes increasingly complex. We also process many different inputs simultaneously, a phenomenon called parallel processing. In addition to sensory inputs, our perceptual sets and expectations influence our perceptions. Perceptual constancy allows us to perceive stimuli across varied conditions.

51. In (top-down/bottom-up) processing, we construct a whole stimulus from its parts.

52. Name the processing model taking place when you look at this image with a caption of "woman" versus a caption of "saxophone player."

53. The process by which we perceive stimuli consistently across varied conditions is _____ _____.

54. The Gestalt principle illustrated by the image of the incomplete circle and rectangle is _____.

13 DESCRIBE HOW WE PERCEIVE PEOPLE, OBJECTS, AND SOUNDS IN OUR ENVIRONMENT.

Many neurons assembled in vast neural networks are probably responsible for face recognition. We perceive motion based on comparing visual frames like those in a movie, and we perceive depth by using both monocular and binocular cues. Cues also play an important role in locating sounds. Sometimes perception deceives us and we experience illusions.

55. The _____ _____ is the illusion of movement created by successive flashing images.

56. To perceive three dimensions using only one eye, it is necessary to use _____ cues.

57. In the Müller-Lyer illusion a line of identical length appears (longer/shorter) when it ends in a set of arrowheads pointing inward than in a set of arrowheads pointing outward.

14 DISTINGUISH SUBLIMINAL PERCEPTION FROM SUBLIMINAL PERSUASION.

Subliminal perception refers to the processing of sensory information that occurs below the limen or threshold of conscious awareness. Subliminal persuasion refers to subthreshold influences over our attitudes, choices, or behaviors.

58. If a stimulus cannot be identified at better than chance levels, it is considered to be _____.

59. Subthreshold influence over our votes in an election is a good example of subliminal _____.

15 ANALYZE THE SCIENTIFIC EVIDENCE FOR AND AGAINST THE EXISTENCE OF ESP.

Most people accept the existence of ESP without the need for scientific evidence, in part because they greatly underestimate how likely it is that a coincidence occurs by chance.

60. Research suggests that the extraordinary claim of ESP (is/isn't) matched by equally extraordinary evidence.

Apply Your Scientific Thinking Skills

Use your scientific thinking skills to answer the following questions, referencing specific scientific thinking principles and common errors in reasoning whenever possible.

1. We can find scores of subliminal self-help tapes and MP3s advertised online despite the fact that studies show they are ineffective. Locate two examples of these products and examine their claims scientifically. Apart from the illusory placebo effect, what are other reasons that people who purchase these products might think they work?

2. Go online and locate psychic predictions for the *upcoming* year from at least two different sites. What common techniques do they employ (such as multiple end points)? Now try to find predictions for the *past* year. How many of them were accurate? And how might those who made the predictions try to explain why they didn't come true?

3. Research the claims that proponents of aromatherapy make about the health benefits of essential oils. What does scientific research tell us about these claims?

Further Your Understanding

EXTEND YOUR KNOWLEDGE WITH THE MYPSYCHLAB VIDEO SERIES

Watch these videos in MyPsychLab. Follow the "Video Series" link.

The Basics: In Full Appreciation of the Cookie Watch how the simple act of eating a chocolate chip cookie involves all of our senses, and several parts of the brain are involved in forming our perception of that experience.

In the Real World: Pain Management See how injury is communicated to the brain, how pain signals can be intensified or blocked, and what the safest, most effective methods are for pain management.

What's In It For Me? Perceptual Magic in Art and Movies Investigate the ways in which artists play on and exploit sensation and perception to create works of art and illusion.

EXPERIENCE PSYCHOLOGICAL RESEARCH WITH MYPSYCHLAB SIMULATIONS

Access these simulations in MyPsychLab. Follow the "Simulations" link.

Ambiguous Figures View ambiguous figures and find out if what you "see" can be influenced by what you've viewed previously.

APPLY YOUR CRITICAL THINKING SKILLS WITH MYPSYCHLAB WRITING ASSESSMENTS

Complete these writing assignments in MyPsychLab.

The Gestalt psychologists maintained that when people perceive sensory elements, their tendency is to see things in terms of the entire form or pattern rather than as individual parts. Identify and describe these basic principles of perceptual organization from the Gestalt perspective: figure-ground, similarity, proximity, and closure.

Answer Key

TWO SIDES OF THE COIN: SENSATION AND PERCEPTION

1. transduction
2. sense receptor
3. absolute threshold
4. Weber's law
5. McGurk
6. synesthesia
7. filter
8. The *cocktail party effect* refers to our ability to pick out an important message, like our name, in a conversation that *doesn't* involve us. This finding tells us that the filter inside our brain, which selects what will and won't receive our attention, is more complex than just an "on" or "off" switch.
9. inattentional blindness
10. Binding

SEEING: THE VISUAL SYSTEM

11. visible
12. brightness
13. lens
14. retina
15. Rods; cones
16. a) fovea: part of the retina where light rays are most sharply focused; b) optic nerve: transmits impulses from the retina to the rest of the brain; c) retina: innermost layer of the eye, where incoming light is converted into nerve impulses; d) eye muscle: one of six surrounding muscles that rotates the eye in all directions; e) lens: transparent disk that focuses light rays for near or distant vision; f) cornea: curved, transparent dome that bends incoming light; g) iris: colored area containing muscles that control the pupil; h) pupil: opening in the center of the iris that lets in light
17. trichromatic
18. Feature detection
19. opponent process
20. visual agnosia

HEARING: THE AUDITORY SYSTEM

21. a) Amplitude; b) Wavelength
22. Pitch
23. loudness
24. timbre
25. cochlea
26. hair cells
27. a) eardrum: membrane that vibrates in response to sound waves; b) semicircular canal: one of three fluid-filled structures that plays a role in balance; c) cochlea: converts vibration into neural activity; d) pinna: flexible outer flap of the ear that channels sound waves into the ear canal; e) ear canal: conducts sound waves to the eardrum
28. place
29. frequency; volley
30. Conductive deafness

SMELL AND TASTE: THE SENSUAL SENSES

31. odors
32. taste buds
33. five; umami
34. weak
35. is
36. gustatory cortex
37. Pheromones
38. orbitofrontal cortex
39. a) somatosensory cortex; b) thalamus; c) olfactory cortex; d) olfactory bulb; e) orbitofrontal cortex; f) pons; g) medulla oblongata
40. worse

OUR BODY SENSES: TOUCH, BODY POSITION, AND BALANCE

41. somatosensory
42. proprioception
43. vestibular sense
44. free nerve endings
45. most
46. somatic
47. quickly
48. The skin contains many different types of receptors and free nerve endings specialized for detecting mechanical pressure, stretching, and pain.
49. The mirror box consists of a two-chamber box with a mirror in the center. When the participant looks at her right hand in the box, it creates the illusion that the mirror image of her right hand is her left hand. This box can sometimes alleviate the discomfort of phantom limb pain by positioning the intact limb as the phantom limb appears to be positioned and then moving it to a more comfortable position.
50. ergonomic

PERCEPTION: WHEN OUR SENSES MEET OUR BRAIN

51. bottom-up
52. Top-down processing: the top-down influence that we're thinking of a jazz musician biases our bottom-up processing of the shapes in this figure and increases the chances we'll perceive a saxophone player.
53. perceptual constancy
54. closure
55. phi phenomenon
56. pictorial
57. longer
58. subliminal
59. persuasion
60. isn't

References

Abbot, N. C., Harkness, E. F., Stevinson, C., Marshall, F. P., Conn, D. A., & Ernst, E. (2001). Spiritual healing as a therapy for chronic pain: A randomized, clinical trial. Pain, 91, 79–89.

Alcock, J. E. (1990). *Science and supernature: A critical appraisal of parapsychology.* Buffalo, NY: Prometheus.

Ames, A., Jr. (1946) Binocular vision as affected by relations between uniocular stimulus patterns in commonplace environments. *American Journal of Psychology, 59,* 333–357.

Anderson, C. A., Berkowitz, L., Donnerstein, E., Huesmann, L. R., Johnson, J. D., Linz, D.,… Wartella, E. (2003). The influence of media violence on youth. *Psychological Science in the Public Interest, 4,* 81–110.

Audebert, O., Deiss, V., & Rousset, S. (2006). Hedonism as a predictor of attitudes of young French women towards meat. *Appetite, 46,* 239–247.

Bargh, J. A., & Pietromonaco, P. (1982). Automatic information processing and social perception: The influence of trait information presented outside of conscious awareness on impression formation. *Journal of Personality and Social Psychology, 43,* 437–449.

Baron-Cohen, S., Harrison, J., Goldstein, L. H., & Wyke, M. (1993). Coloured speech-perception: Is synaesthesia what happens when modularity breaks down? *Perception, 22,* 419–426.

Bartels, A., & Zeki, S. (2006). The temporal order of binding visual attributes. *Vision Research, 46,* 2280–2286.

Bartoshuk, L. M. (2004). Psychophysics: A journey from the laboratory to the clinic. *Appetite, 43,* 15–18.

Beaman, C. P., Bridges, A. M., & Scott, S. K. (2007). From dichotic listening to the irrelevant sound effect: A behavioural and neuroimaging analysis of the processing of unattended speech. *Cortex, 43,* 124–134.

Beatty, J. (1982). Task-evoked pupillary responses, processing load, and the structure of processing resources. *Psychological Bulletin, 91,* 276–292.

Békésy, G. (1949). On the resonance curve and the decay period at different points along the cochlear partition. *Journal of the Acoustical Society of America, 21,* 245–254.

Bem, D. J., & Honorton, C. (1994). Does psi exist? Replicable evidence for an anomalous process of information transfer. *Psychological Bulletin, 115,* 4–18.

Biasi, E., Silvotti, L., & Tirindelli, R. (2001). Pheromone detection in rodents. *Neuroreport, 12,* A81–A84.

Blood, A. J., & Zatorre, R. J. (2001). Intensely pleasurable responses to music correlate with activity in brain regions implicated in reward and emotion. *Proceedings of the National Academy of Sciences, 98,* 11818–11823.

Bonham, V. L. (2001). Race, ethnicity, and pain treatment: Striving to understand the causes and solutions to the disparities in pain treatment. *Journal of Law & Medical Ethics, 29,* 52–68.

Boring, E. G. (1930). A new ambiguous figure. *American Journal of Psychology, 42,* 444.

Broadbent, D. E. (1957). A mechanical model for human attention and immediate memory. *Psychological Review, 54,* 205–215.

Brown, P. K., & Wald, G. (1964). Visual pigments in single rods and cones of the human retina. *Science, 144,* 45–52.

Buck, L., & Axel, R. (1991). A novel multigene family may encode odorant receptors: A molecular basis for odor recognition. *Cell, 65,* 175–183.

Bushnell, M. C., Duncan, G. H., Hofbauer, R. K., Ha, B., Chen, J. I., & Carrier, B. (1999). Pain perception: Is there a role for primary somatosensory cortex? *Proceedings of the National Academy of Sciences, 96,* 7705–7709.

Caryl, P. G., Bean, J. E., Smallwood, E. B., Barron, J. C., Tully, L., & Allerhand, M. (2009). Women's preference for male pupil-size: Effects of conception risk, sociosexuality and relationship status. *Personality and Individual Differences, 46,* 50–508.

Catania, K. C. (2006). Olfaction: Underwater "sniffing" by semi-aquatic mammals. *Nature, 444,* 1024–1025.

Chandrashekar, J., Hoon, M. A., Ryba, N. J., & Zuker, C. S. (2006). The receptors and cells for mammalian taste. *Nature, 444,* 288–294.

Cheesman, J., & Merikle, P. M. (1986). Distinguishing conscious from unconscious perceptual processes. *Canadian Journal of Psychology, 40,* 343–367.

Cytowic, R. E., & Eagleman, D. M. (2009). *Wednesday is indigo blue.* Cambridge and London, England: MIT Press.

de Gelder, B., Tamietto, M., van Boxtel, G., Goebel, R., Sahraie, A., van den Stock, J., . . . Pegna, A. (2008). Intact navigation skills after bilateral loss of striate cortex. *Current Biology, 18*(24). http://dx.doi.org/10.1016/j.cub.2008.11.002

Dijksterhuis, A., Aarts, H., & Smith, P. K. (2005). The power of the subliminal: On subliminal persuasion and other potential applications. In R. R. Hassin, J. S. Uleman, & J. A. Bargh (Eds.), *The new unconscious* (pp. 77–106). New York, NY: Oxford University Press.

Doty, R. L., Deems, D., & Stellar, S. (1988). Olfactory dysfunction in Parkinson's disease: A general deficit unrelated to neurologic signs, disease stage, or disease duration. *Neurology, 38*, 1237–1244.

Eccleston, C., & Crombez, G. (1999). Pain demands attention: A cognitive-affective model of the interruptive function of pain. *Psychological Bulletin, 125*, 356–366.

Ehrsson, H. H., Spence, C., & Passingham, R. E. (2004). That's my hand! Activity in premotor cortex reflects feeling of ownership of a limb. *Science, 305*, 875–877.

Eich, E., & Hyman, R. (1991). Subliminal self help. In D. Druckman & R. A. Bjork (Eds.), *In the mind's eye: Enhancing human performance* (pp. 107–119). Washington, DC: National Academies Press.

Eippert, F., Finsterbusch, J., Binger, U., & Buchel, C. (2009). Direct evidence for spinal cord involvement in placebo analgesia. *Science, 326*, 404.

Emery, G. (2005). Psychic predictions 2005. *Skeptical Inquirer, 29*(2), 7–8.

Engel, A. K., & Singer, W. (2001). Temporal binding and the neural correlates of sensory awareness. *Trends in Cognitive Science, 5*, 6–25.

Fields, R. D. (2007, February/March). Sex and the secret nerve. *Scientific American Mind*, 21–27.

Francis, G. (in press). Too good to be true: Publication bias in two prominent studies from experimental psychology. *Psychonomic Bulletin & Review.*

Franz, V. H., Bulthoff, H. H., & Fahle, M. (2003). Grasp effects of the Ebbinghaus illusion: Obstacle avoidance isn't the explanation. *Experimental Brain Research, 149*, 470–477.

French, C. C. (1992). Population stereotypes and belief in the paranormal: Is there a relationship? *Australian Psychologist, 27*, 57–58.

Fu, K. M., Johnston, T. A., Shah, A. S., Arnold, L., Smiley, J., Hackett, T. A.,... Schroeder, C. E. (2003). Auditory cortical neurons respond to somatosensory stimulation. *Journal of Neuroscience, 23*, 7510–7515.

Galton, F. (1880). Statistics of mental imagery. *Mind, 5*, 301–318.

Gerard, S., Smith, B. H., & Simpson, J. A. (2003). A randomized controlled trial of spiritual healing in restricted neck movement. *Journal of Alternative and Complementary Medicine, 9*, 467–477.

Gibson, E. J. (1991). *An odyssey in learning and perception.* Cambridge, MA: MIT Press.

Gibson, E. J., & Walk, R. D. (1960). The "visual cliff." *Scientific American, 202*, 64–71.

Gilbertson, T. A., Fontenot D. T., Liu, L., Zhang, H., & Monroe, W. T. (1997). Fatty acid modulation of K+ channels in taste receptor cells: Gustatory cues for dietary fat. *American Journal of Physiology, 272*(4 Pt. 1), C1203–C1210.

Gizewski, E. R., Gasser, T., de Greiff, A., Boehm, A., & Forsting, M. (2003). Cross-modal plasticity for sensory and motor activation patterns in blind subjects. *Neuroimage, 19*, 968–975.

Glaser, J., & Kihlstrom, J. F. (2005). Compensatory automaticity: Unconscious volition is not an oxymoron. In R. Hassin, J. S. Uleman, & J. A. Bargh (Eds.), *The new unconscious* (pp. 171–195). Oxford, England: Oxford University Press.

Gold, J. M., Murray, R. F., Bennett, P. J., & Sekuler, A. B. (2000). Deriving behavioural receptive fields for visually completed contours. *Current Biology, 10*, 663–666.

Goldreich, D., & Kanics, I. M. (2003). Tactile acuity is enhanced in blindness. *Journal of Neuroscience, 23*, 3439–3445.

Greeley, A. M. (1987). Mysticism goes mainstream. *American Health, 6*, 47–49.

Green, D. M., & Swets, J. A. (1966). *Signal detection theory and psychophysics.* New York, NY: Wiley.

Greenwald, A. G., Spangenberg, E. R., Pratkanis, A. R., & Eskenazi, J. (1991). Double-blind tests of subliminal self-help audio tapes. *Psychological Science, 2*, 119–122.

Hamm, A. O., Weike, A. I., Schupp, H. T., Treig, T., Dressel, A., & Kessler, C. (2003). Affective blindsight: Intact fear conditioning to a visual cue in a cortically blind patient, *Brain, 126*, 267–275.

Haraldsson, E., & Houtkooper, J. (1991). Psychic experience in the multinational human-values study: Who reports them. *Personality and Individual Differences, 13*, 1085–1096.

Hassin, R. R., Uleman, J. S., & Bargh, J. A. (2005). *The new unconscious.* New York, NY: Oxford University Press.

Heath, T. P., Melichar, J. K., Nutt, D. J., & Donaldson, L. F. (2006). Human taste thresholds are modulated by serotonin and noradrenaline. *Journal of Neuroscience, 26*, 12664–12671.

Helmholtz, H. (1850). Ueber die Fortpflanzungsgeschwindigkeit der Nervenreizung. *Annalen der Physik, 155*, 329–330.

Henderson, J. M., & Hollingworth, A. (1999). The role of fixation position in detecting scene changes across saccades. *Psychological Science, 10*, 438–443.

Hess, E. H. (1965). Attitude and pupil size. *Scientific American, 212*(4), 46–54.

Highstein, S. M., Fay, R. R., & Popper A. N. (2004). *The vestibular system.* Berlin, Germany: Springer-Verlag.

Hirsch, A. R., (2003). Handbook of olfaction and gustation. *Journal of the American Medical Association, 290*, 3257–3258.

Hoffman, H., & Patterson, D. (2005). Virtual reality pain distraction. *APS Bulletin, 15*(2).

Horgan, J. (1999). *The undiscovered mind: How the human brain defies replication, medication, and explanation.* New York, NY: Free Press.

Horgan, J. (2005, June). Can a single brain cell think? *Discover.* Retrieved from http://cbcl.mit.edu/news/files/kreiman-hogan-5-05.htm

Hubel, D. H, & Wiesel, T. N. (1962). Receptive fields, binocular interaction and functional architecture in the cat's visual cortex. *Journal of Physiology, 160*, 106–154.

Hyman, R. (1977). Cold reading: How to convince strangers that you know all about them. *The Zetetic, 1*(2), 18–37.

Hyman, R. (1996). The evidence for psychic functioning: Claims vs. reality. *Skeptical Inquirer, 20*, 24–26.

Jameson, K. A., Highnote, S., & Wasserman, L. (2001). Richer color experience in observers with multiple photopigment opsin genes. *Psychonomic Bulletin and Review, 8*, 244–261.

Karatekin, C. (2004). Development of attentional allocation in the dual task paradigm. *International Journal of Psychophysiology, 52*, 7–21.

Kayser, C., Petkov, C. I., Augath, M., & Logothetis, N. K. (2007). Functional imaging reveals visual modulation of specific fields in auditory cortex. *Journal of Neuroscience, 27*, 1824–1835.

Knox, J. J., Coppieters, M. W., & Hodges, P. W. (2006). Do you know where your arm is if you think your head has moved? *Experimental Brain Research, 173*, 94–101.

Koch, C. (1993). Computational approaches to cognition: The bottom-up view. *Current Opinion in Neurobiology, 3*, 203–208.

Koivisto, M., & Revonsuo, A. (2007). How meaning shapes seeing. *Psychological Science, 18*, 845–849.

Kuhn, G., Amlani, A. A., & Rensink, R. A. (2008). Towards a science of magic. *Trends in Cognitive Sciences, 12*, 349–354.

Kuhn, G., & Land, M. F. (2006). There's more to magic than meets the eye. *Current Biology, 16*(22), R950.

Kurtus, R. (2000). I walked on fire (and lived to tell about it). Retrieved from http://www.school-for-champions.com/excellence/firewalk.htm

Lamb, T. D., & Pugh, E. N., Jr. (2004). Dark adaptation and the retinoid cycle of vision. *Progress in Retinal and Eye Research, 23*, 307–380.

Levin, D. T., & Simons, D. J. (1997). Failure to detect changes to attended objects in motion pictures. *Psychonomic Bulletin and Review, 4*, 501–506.

Libet, B., Gleason, C. A., Wright, E. W., & Pearl, D. K. (1983) Time of conscious intention to act in relation to onset of cerebral activity (readiness-potential). The unconscious initiation of a freely voluntary act. *Brain, 106*, 623–642.

Lie, D. C., Song, H., Colamarino, S. A., Ming, G. L., & Gage, F. H. (2004). Neurogenesis in the adult brain: New strategies for central nervous system diseases. *Annual Review of Pharmacology & Toxicology, 44*, 399–421.

Lyvers, M., Barling, N., & Harding-Clark, J. (2006). Effect of belief in "psychic healing" on self-reported pain in chronic pain sufferers. *Journal of Psychosomatic Research, 60*, 59–61.

Macknik, S. L., King, M., Randi, J., Robbins, A., Teller, J., Thompson, J., & Martinez-Conde, S. (2008). Attention and awareness in stage magic: Turning tricks into research. *Nature Reviews Neuroscience, 9*, 871–879.

Mandiyan, V. S., Coats. J. K., & Shah, N. M. (2005). Deficits in sexual and aggressive behaviors in Cnga2 mutant mice. *Nature Neuroscience, 8*, 1660–1662.

Marks, L. E. (in press). Synesthesia: A teeming multiplicity. In E. A. Cardeña, S. J. Lynn, & S. C. Krippner (Eds.), *Varieties of anomalous experience: The state of the science* (2nd ed.). Washington, DC: American Psychological Association.

Mattes, R. D., Hollis, J., Hayes, D., & Stunkard, A. J. (2005). Appetite measurement and manipulation misgivings. *Journal of the American Dietetic Association, 105*, 87–97.

McCaul, K. D., & Malott, J. M. (1984). Distraction and coping with pain. *Psychological Bulletin, 95*, 516–533.

McCauley, R. N., & Henrich, J. (2006). Susceptibility to the Müller-Lyer Illusion, theory neutral observation, and the diachronic cognitive penetrability of the visual input system. *Philosophical Psychology, 19*, 79–101.

McClelland, J. L., & Plaut, D. C. (1993). Computational approaches to cognition: Top-down approaches. *Current Opinion in Neurobiology, 3*, 209–216.

McConkie, G. W., & Currie, C. B. (1996). Visual stability across saccades while viewing complex pictures. *Journal of Experimental Psychology: Human Perception & Performance, 22*, 563–581.

McCutcheon, L. (1996, May/June). What's that I smell? The claims of aromatherapy. *Skeptical Inquirer*, 35–37.

McGurk, H., & MacDonald, J. (1976). Hearing lips and seeing voices. *Nature, 264*, 746–748.

Melzack, R. (1975). The McGill Pain Questionnaire: Major properties and scoring methods. *Pain, 1*, 277–299.

Melzack, R. R., & Wall, P. (1965). Pain mechanisms: A new theory. *Science, 50*, 971–979.

Menini, A., Picco, C., & Firestein, S. (1995). Quantal-like current fluctuations induced by odorants in olfactory receptor cells. *Nature, 373*, 435–437.

Merikle, P. M. (1988). Subliminal auditory tapes: An evaluation. *Psychology and Marketing, 46*, 355–372.

Miller, C., Seckel, E., & Ramachandran, V. S. (2012). Using mirror box therapy to treat phantom pain in Haitian earthquake victims. *Journal of Vision, 12.* Retrieved from http://w.journalofvision.org/content/12/9/1323.short

Milner, A. D., & Goodale, M. A. (1995). The visual brain in action (Vol. 27). *Oxford Psychology Series.* Oxford, England: Oxford University Press.

Milton, J., & Wiseman, R. (1999). Does psi exist? Lack of replication of an anomalous process of information transfer. *Psychological Bulletin, 125*, 387–391.

Moore, D. W. (2005, June 16). Three in four Americans believe in the paranormal. *Gallup Poll News Service.* Retrieved from http://www.gallup.com/poll/16915/three-four-americans-believe-paranormal.aspx

Moore, R. J. (Ed.). (2008). *Biobehavioral approaches to pain.* Netherlands: Springer.

Moore, T. E. (1992). Subliminal perception: Facts and fallacies. *Skeptical Inquirer, 16*, 273–281.

Moore, T. E. (1996). Scientific consensus and expert testimony: Lessons from the Judas Priest trial. *Skeptical Inquirer, 20*, 32–38.

Murphy, C. (1999). Loss of olfactory function in dementing disease. *Physiology & Behavior, 66*, 177–182.

Nahorna, O., Berthommier, F., & Schwartz, J. L. (2012). Binding and unbinding the auditory and visual streams in the McGurk effect. *Acoustical Society of America, 132*(2), 1061–1077.

Naito, E. (2004). Sensing limb movements in the motor cortex: How humans sense limb movement. *Neuroscientist, 10*, 73–82.

Neher, A. (1990). *The psychology of transcendence.* New York, NY: Dover.

Nickel, J. (2000, May/June). Aura photography: A candid shot. *Skeptical Inquirer, 24*, 15–17.

Nondahl, D. M., Cruickshanks, K. J., Dalton, D. S., Klein, B., Klein, R., Schubert, C. R.,... Wiley, T. L. (2007). The impact of tinnitus on quality of life in older adults. *Journal of the American Academy of Audiology, 18*, 257–266.

Norman, D. (1998). *The design of everyday things.* London, England: MIT Press.

Ohlemiller, K. K., & Frisina, R. D. (2008). Age-related hearing loss and its cellular and molecular bases. In J. Schacht, A. N. Popper, & R. R. Fay (Eds.), *Springer handbook of auditory research: Auditory trauma, protection, and repair* (pp.145–162). Netherlands: Springer.

Ondeck, D. M. (2003). Impact of culture on pain. *Home Health Care Management Practice, 15*, 255–257.

Pascolini, D., & Smith, A. (2009). Hearing impairment in 2008: A compilation of available epidemiological studies. *International Journal of Audiology, 48*(7), 473–485.

Patel, G. A., & Sathian, K. (2000). Visual search: Bottom-up or top-down? *Frontiers in Bioscience, 5*, D169–D193.

Paulesu, E., Harrison, J., Baroncohen, S., Watson, J. D. G., Goldstein, L., Heather, J., ... Frith C. D. (1995). The physiology of colored hearing—A PET activation study of color-word synesthesia. *Brain, 118*, 661–676.

Pearson, H. (2006). Mouse data hint at human pheromones. *Nature, 442*, 495.

Pinsk, M. A., DeSimone, K., Moore, T., Gross, C. G., & Kastner, S. (2005). Representations of faces and body parts in macaque temporal cortex: A functional MRI study. *Proceedings of the National Academy of Sciences, 102*, 6996–7001.

Podczerwinski, E. S., Wickens, C. D., & Alexander, A. L. (2002) *Technical Report ARL-01-8/NASA-01-04.* Moffett Field, CA: NASA Ames Research Center.

Presley, S. (1997). *Why people believe in ESP for the wrong reasons.* Retrieved from http://www.rit.org/essays/esp.php

Proske, U. (2006). Kinesthesia: The role of muscle receptors. *Muscle Nerve, 34*, 545–558.

Pühse, G., Wachsmuth, J. U., Kemper, S., Husstedt, I. W., Kliesch, S., & Evers, S. (2010). Phantom testis syndrome: Prevalence, phenomenology, and putative mechanisms. *International Journal of Andrology, 33*(1), e-216–e.220.

Purves, D., Lotto, R. B., & Nundy, S. (2002). Why we see what we do. *American Scientist, 90*, 236.

Quiroga, R. Q., Reddy, L., Kreiman, G., Koch, C., & Fried, I. (2005). Invariant visual representation by single neurons in the human brain. *Nature, 435*, 1102–1107.

Rader, C. M., & Tellegen, A. (1987). An investigation of synesthesia. *Journal of Personality and Social Psychology, 52*, 981–987.

Ramachandran, V. S., & Hubbard, E. M. (2001). Synaesthesia: A window into perception, thought and language. *Journal of Consciousness Studies, 8*, 33–34.

Ramachandran, V. S., & Rogers-Ramachandran, D. C. (1996). Synaesthesia in phantom limbs induced with mirrors. *Proceedings of the Royal Society of London, 263*, 377–386.

Randoph-Seng, B., & Nielsen, M. E. (2007). Honesty: On effect of primed religious representations. *The International Journal for the Psychology of Religion, 17*, 303–315.

Rensink, R. A., O'Regan, J. K., & Clark, J. (1997). To see or not to see: The need for attention to perceive changes in scenes. *Psychological Science, 8*, 368–373.

Rieger, G., & Savin-Williams, R. C. (2012) The eyes have it: Sex and sexual orientation differences in pupil dilation patterns. *PLoS One, 7*(8), e40256. http://dx.doi.org/10.1371/journal.pone.0040256

Riesenhuber, M., & Poggio, T. (1999). Hierarchical models of object recognition in cortex. *Nature Neuroscience, 2*, 1019–1025.

Roberts, W. M., Howard, J., & Hudspeth, A. J. (1988). Hair cells: Transduction, tuning, and transmission in the inner ear. *Annual Review of Cell Biology, 4*, 63–92.

Rock, I., & Kaufman, L. (1962). The moon illusion, part 2. *Science, 136*, 1023–1031.

Rogers, M., & Smith, K. H. (1993). Public perceptions of subliminal advertising. *Journal of Advertising Research, 33*, 10–18.

Rosen, G. M., Glasgow, R. E., & Moore, T. E. (2003). Self-help therapy: The science and business of giving psychology away. In S. O. Lilienfeld, S. J. Lynn, & J. M. Lohr (Eds.), *Science and pseudoscience in clinical psychology* (pp. 399–424). New York, NY: Guilford Press.

Ross, H., & Plug, C. (2002). *The mystery of the moon illusion.* Oxford, England: Oxford University Press.

Rouw, R., Scholte, H. S., & Colizoli, O. (2011). Brain areas involved in synaesthesia: A review. *Journal of Neuropsychology, 5*, 214-242

Rowland, I. (2001). *The full facts on cold reading* (2nd ed.). London, England.

Rubin, M. L., & Walls, G. L. (1969). *Fundamentals of visual science* (p. 546). Springfield, IL: Charles C. Thomas.

Rumelhart, D. E., & McClelland, J. L. (1987). *Parallel distributed processing* (Vol. 1). Cambridge, MA: MIT Press.

Sadato, N. (2005). How the blind "see" Braille: Lessons from functional magnetic resonance imaging. *Neuroscientist, 11*, 577–582.

Schiffman, S. S., & Graham, B. G. (2000). Taste and smell perception affect appetite and immunity in the elderly. *European Journal of Clinical Nutrition, 54* (Suppl. 3), S54–S63.

Schörnich, S., Nagy, A., &Wiegrebe, L. (2012). Discovering your inner bat: Echo-acoustic target ranging in humans. *Journal of the Association for Research in Otolaryngology.* http://dx.doi.org/10.1007/s10162-012-0338-z

Segall, M. H., Campbell, D. T., & Herskovits, M. J. (1966). *The influence of culture on visual perception.* Indianapolis, IN: Bobbs-Merrill.

Seitz, A. R., & Watanabe, T. (2003). Psychophysics: Is subliminal learning really passive? *Nature, 422*, 36.

Sherman, R. A., Sherman, C. J., & Parker, L. (1984). Chronic phantom and stump pain among American veterans: Results of a survey. *Pain, 18*, 83–95.

Simner, J., Mulvenna, C., Sagiv, N., Tsakanikos, E., Withery, S.A., Fraser, C., ... Ward, J. (2006). Synaesthesia: The prevalence of atypical cross-modal experiences. *Perception, 35*, 1024–1033.

Simon-Moffat, A. (2002). New fossils and a glimpse of evolution. *Science, 25*, 613–615.

Simons, D. J., & Chabris, C. F. (1999). Gorillas in our midst: Sustained inattentional blindness for dynamic events. *Perception, 28*, 1059–1074.

Spehr, M., Gisselmann, G., Poplawski, A., Riffel, J. A., Wetzel, C. H., Zimmer, R. K., & Hatt, H. (2003). Identification of a testicular odorant receptor mediating human sperm chemotaxis. *Science, 299*, 2054–2058.

Stoerig, P., & Cowey, A. (1997). Blindsight in man and monkey. *Brain, 120*, 535–559.

Stone, A. (2012). *Fooling Houdini: Magicians, mentalists, math geeks, and the hidden powers of the mind.* New York, NY: HarperCollins.

Szasz, T. S. (1989). *Pain and pleasure: A study of bodily feelings.* Syracuse, NY: Syracuse University Press.

Taylor-Clarke, M., Kennett, S., & Haggard, P. (2002). Vision modulates somatosensory cortical processing. *Current Biology, 12*, 233–236.

Teng, S., Puri, A., & Whitney, D. (2011). Crossmodal transfer of object information in human echolocation. *I-Perception, 2*(8), 894.

Thaler, L., Arnott, S., and Goodale, M. (2011). Neural correlates of natural human echolocation in early and late blind echolocation experts. *PLoS One, 6*(5).

Tombs, S., & Silverman, I. (2004). Pupillometry—A sexual selection approach. *Evolution and Human Behavior, 25*, 221–228.

Tomlinson, N., Hicks, R. A., & Pellegrini R. J. (1978). Attributions of female college students to variations in pupil size. *Bulletin of the Psychonomic Society, 12*, 477–478.

Ullman, M., Krippner, S., & Vaughan, A. (1973). *Dream telepathy.* New York, NY: Macmillan.

Weil, R. S., & Rees, G. (2011). A new taxonomy for perceptual filling-in. *Brain Research Reviews, 67*(1-2), 40–55.

Weinberger, N. M. (2006). Music and the brain. *Scientific American, 291*(5), 88–95.

Weiskrantz, L. (1986). *Blindsight: A case study and its implications.* Oxford, England: Oxford University Press.

Wilson, R. S., Scherr, P. A., Schneider, J. A., Tang, Y., & Bennett, D. A. (2007). Relation of cognitive activity to risk of developing Alzheimer disease. *Neurology, 69*, 1911–1920.

Winer, G. A., Cottrell, J. E., Gregg, V., Fournier, J. S., & Bica, L. A. (2002). Fundamentally misunderstanding visual perception. Adults' belief in visual emissions. *American Psychologist, 57*, 417–424.

Witt, M., & Wozniak, W. (2006). Structure and function of the vomeronasal organ. *Advances in Otorhinolaryngology, 63*, 70–83.

World Health Organization (WHO) (2012). Visual impairments and blindness, Fact Sheet Number 282. Retrieved from http://www.who.int/mediacentre/factsheets/fs282/en

Wysocki, C. J., & Preti, G. (2004). Facts, fallacies, fears, and frustrations with human pheromones. *Anatomical Record: Discoveries in Molecular, Cellular, & Evolutionary Biology, 281*, 1201–1211.

Yamaguchi, S., & Ninomiya, K. (2000). Umami and food palatability. *Journal of Nutrition, 130*(4S Suppl.), 921S–926S.

Young, T. (1802). On the theory of light and colours. *Philosophical Transactions of the Royal Society of London, 92*, 12–48.

Credits

Credits listed in order of appearance.

Figure 3: Published by kind permission of Journal of Consciousness Studies, Imprint Academic, Exeter, UK. **Text:** Triesman, Anne M. 1960. Contextual Cues in Selective Listening. Quarterly Journal of Experimental Psychology 12:242-249. **Figure:** Adapted from St. Luke's Cataract & Laser Institute. **Text:** Fields, R.D., (2007, February/March) Sex and the Secret Nerve, Scientific American Mind, 2127. **Table 2:** NICDC. **Table 3:** Hines, T. (2003).

Pseudoscience and the paranormal: A critical examination of the evidence (2nd ed.). Buffalo, NY: Prometheus; Hyman, R. (1977). Cold reading: How to convince strangers that you know all about them. The Zetetic, 1(2); Rowland, I. (2001). The full facts on cold reading (2nd ed.). London, England:Author. **Figure 25:** Hill, 1915, "My Wife and My Mother-in-Law." Puck, 11. "**Figure 27:** © 1995 Edward H. Adelson. Reprinted by permission. **Figure 28:** © Dale Purves and R. Beau Lotto, 2002. Why we see what we do. American Scientist. Printed with permission from Dale Purves.

Photo Credits

Photo Credits listed in order of appearance.

Pressmaster/Shutterstock; DWImages Europe/Alamy; **(top center):** Sidney Harris/Science Cartoons Plus; **(center right):** Lawrence Manning/Corbis; **(bottom right):** Volodymyr Baleha/Shutterstock; **(top left):** vadim yerofeyev/Fotolia; **(top left):** Kevin German/Zuma Press/Newscom; **(center right):** Ladanyiphoto/Fotolia; **(top left):** Gustoimages/Science Source; **(top left):** Eye Ubiquitous/SuperStock; **(bottom left):** Alamy Limited; **(bottom right):** Dimitrije Paunovic/Dishapaun/iStockphoto; **(top left):** AP Images; **(bottom right):** Hunter Hoffman; **(top left):** St Petersburg Times/Zuma/Newscom; **(center right):** Stephen Morton/AP Images; **(top center):** Steve Kagan Photography; **(center left):** Jan Csernoch/Alamy; **(center):** Chris Madden/Alamy; **(top right):** Joe McNally/Getty Images News/Getty Images; **(center right):** John W. Johnston Watercolour by John W Johnston, Northampton, UK. www.JWJarts.com; **(bottom center):** M.C. Escher; **(top right):** Gary/Fotolia; **(bottom left):** Mauro Fermariello/Photo Researchers, Inc.; **(bottom center):** Reuters/Corbis; **(bottom center):** Yuri_arcurs/Dreamstime; **(bottom center):** Pearson Education; **(bottom left):** Patrick Blake/Alamy; **(center right):** Alamy.

Consciousness

Consciousness

EXPANDING THE BOUNDARIES OF PSYCHOLOGICAL INQUIRY

Think About It

Can we trust people's reports that they've been abducted by aliens?

Does a person's consciousness leave the body during an out-of-body experience?

Do people who have a near-death experience truly catch a glimpse of the afterlife?

Does hypnosis produce a trance state?

Is alcohol a stimulant drug?

Sleep paralysis has been reported in many cultures, with the terrifying nighttime visitors ranging from an "old hag" to demonlike entities, as depicted in this painting, *The Nightmare*, by Henry Fuseli.

RULING OUT RIVAL HYPOTHESES ▶

Have important alternative explanations for the findings been excluded?

sleep paralysis
state of being unable to move just after falling asleep or right before waking up

consciousness
our subjective experience of the world, our bodies, and our mental perspectives

Consciousness

 Listen in **MyPsychLab** to chapter audio

Consider this summary of a fascinating story related by a participant in Susan Clancy's (2005) landmark research on people who come to believe they were kidnapped by aliens.

The participant reported that he awakened from what seemed to be the worst dream he ever experienced, with something that wasn't human on top of him, suffocating and immobilizing him. The experience was so memorable and disturbing that he shared it with his therapist. Troubling images of aliens like those he saw in the movie *Signs* with Mel Gibson started to come to mind, and he couldn't turn off the thought that he was abducted. His therapist referred him to a psychologist who treated people with similar beliefs. When he broke down tearfully in the psychologist's office, the therapist reassured him that this was a normal response to his emerging awareness of what happened and that people can recover memories of what really took place if they undergo hypnosis (Clancy, 2005, pp. 30–31).

This person isn't alone. Nearly one-fifth of college students in one survey endorsed the belief that extraterrestrials (ETs) can actually visit us in dreams, and 10 percent claimed to have "experienced or met an extraterrestrial" (Kunzendorf et al., 2007–2008). But did they *really* encounter ETs, as Clancy's participants claimed? Clancy and her Harvard University colleagues (Clancy et al., 2002; McNally & Clancy, 2005) say there's a slim chance at best. But they happened on a startling discovery that may explain the abduction reports.

Many of the people they interviewed shared a history of **sleep paralysis**—a strange experience of being unable to move just after falling asleep or immediately upon awakening. This puzzling phenomenon is surprisingly common. One-third to one-half of college students have had at least one episode of sleep paralysis, which typically is no cause for concern (Fukuda et al., 1998). Sleep paralysis is caused by a disruption in the sleep cycle and is often associated with anxiety or even terror, feelings of vibrations, humming noises, and the eerie sense of menacing figures close to or on top of the immobile person. There are cultural differences in how people interpret this strange experience. In Thailand, people attribute it to a ghost, but in Newfoundland, people attribute it to an "old hag"—an elderly witch sitting on the person's chest. According to Susan Blackmore (2004), the "latest sleep paralysis myth may be alien abduction".

Unfortunately, the therapist that Clancy's participant consulted didn't consider sleep paralysis as an alternative explanation for her symptoms. Nor did he tell his client that hypnosis isn't a trustworthy means of unearthing accurate memories. In fact, we'll soon learn that hypnosis can often help to create false memories. In many of the cases Clancy reported, it's not a big leap for people who suspect they were abducted to elaborate on their story during hypnosis and to imagine that aliens performed medical experiments on them. After all, that's what filmmakers and science fiction writers often lead people to believe happens when the aliens come calling.

Sleep paralysis is only one of many remarkable sleep-related experiences we'll encounter in this chapter, along with other fascinating examples of alterations in **consciousness**—our subjective experience of the world and ourselves. Consciousness encompasses our ever-changing awareness of thoughts, emotions, bodily sensations, events, and actions. By one definition, "Consciousness is what you lose when you fall into a deep sleep at night and what you gain when you wake up in the morning" (Sanders, 2012, p. 22). Yet we'll see that even when we sleep, some of us retain self-awareness and know we're dreaming on occasion.

Our sleeping and waking experiences shade subtly into one another. On average, we spend about 30 percent of our waking hours mind-wandering, fantasizing, and flitting from one task-irrelevant or dream-like thought to another (Kane et al., 2007; Klinger, 2000; Smallwood & Schooler, 2006). Some so-called *fantasy-prone personalities* (about 2–4 percent of the population) say they spend at least half of their waking lives caught up in vivid daydreams and fantasies (Lynn & Rhue, 1988; Wilson & Barber, 1981). A common view is that is fantasy is an unhealthy escape from reality. However, fantasies and daydreams are perfectly normal and can help us plan for the future, solve problems, and express our creativity (Klinger, 1988). Honed by hundreds of thousands of years of natural selection, most of us can easily focus our attention when needed to respond to virtually any situation or threat efficiently, seamlessly, and often unconsciously (Kirsch & Lynn, 1998; Wegner, 2004).

In this chapter, we'll encounter numerous examples of how the spotlight of our awareness and level of alertness changes continually and how consciousness is sensitively attuned to changes in our brain chemistry, expectations, and culture. We'll come to appreciate how scientists are taking advantage of high tech tools to measure neural events and explore the most basic biological processes that sculpt our stream of consciousness. Finally, we'll examine how the unity of consciousness can break down in unusual ways, such as during sleepwalking, when we're unconscious yet move about as if awake, and déjà vu, when we feel as though we're reliving an event we've never experienced (Voss, Baym, & Paller, 2008). As in many cases in psychology, abnormalities in functioning can often shed light on normal functioning (Cooper, 2003; Harkness, 2007).

The Biology of Sleep

1 Explain the role of the circadian rhythm and how our bodies react to a disruption in our biological clocks.

2 Identify the different stages of sleep and the neural activity and dreaming behaviors that occur in each.

3 Identify the features and causes of sleep disorders.

We spend as much as one-third or more of our lives in one specific state of consciousness. No, we don't mean zoning out during a boring lecture. We're referring to sleep. Although it's clear that sleep is of central importance to our health and daily functioning, psychologists still don't know for sure why we sleep. Some theories suggest that sleep plays a critical role in storing memories and remembering emotional information (Payne & Kensinger, 2010); others suggest that it's critical for the immune system. Other models emphasize the possible role of sleep in promoting insight and problem solving (Wagner, et al., 2004) as well as neural development and neural connectivity more generally (Bushey et al., 2011; Mignot, 2008). J. Allan Hobson (2009) suggested that brain activation during sleep is essential to waking consciousness and our ability to plan, reason, and function to the best of our ability. Alternatively, some evolutionary theorists have proposed that sleep contributes to our survival by conserving our energy, taking us out of circulation at times when we might be most vulnerable to unseen predators, and restoring our strength to fend them off (Siegel, 2005). There may be considerable truth to several or even all of these explanations.

The Circadian Rhythm: The Cycle of Everyday Life

Long before scientists began to probe the secrets of sleep in the laboratory, primitive hunters were keenly aware of daily cycles of sleep and wakefulness. **Circadian rhythm** is a fancy term ("circadian" is Latin for "about a day") for changes that occur on a roughly 24-hour basis in many of our biological processes, including hormone release, brain waves, body temperature, and drowsiness. Popularly known as the brain's **biological clock**, a meager 20,000 neurons located in the hypothalamus make us feel drowsy at different times of the day and night. Many of us have noticed that we feel like taking a nap at around three or four in the afternoon. Indeed, in many European and Latin American countries, a midafternoon nap (a "siesta" in Spanish) is part of the daily ritual. This sense of fatigue is triggered by our biological clocks. The urge to snooze comes over us at night as well because levels of the hormone *melatonin*, which triggers feelings of sleepiness, increase after dark.

The biological clock even ticks in marine algae and red blood cells too (Edgar et al., 2012). When humans' biological clocks are disrupted, such as when we work late shifts, or travel across time zones and experience jet lag, it disturbs sleep and increases the risk of injuries, fatal accidents, and health problems, including diabetes and heart disease

Explore in **MyPsychLab** the **Concept:** The Big Picture: States of Consciousness

circadian rhythm
cyclical changes that occur on a roughly 24-hour basis in many biological processes

biological clock
term for the area of the hypothalamus that's responsible for controlling our levels of alertness

The tragic crash of Colgan Air Flight 3409 outside of Buffalo, New York, has been blamed on sleep deprivation, as both the pilot and co-pilot had been sleep-deprived prior to the flight.

Watch in **MyPsychLab** the **Video:** In the Real World: Sleep, Memory, and Learning

RULING OUT RIVAL HYPOTHESES ▶
Have important alternative explanations for the findings been excluded?

(Åkerstedt et al., 2002; Kirkcaldy, Levine, & Shephard, 2000). Scientists are hot on the trail of drugs that target melatonin receptors in the brain to re-sync our brain's biological clock (Rajaratnam et al., 2009). That's because melatonin plays a key role in regulating circadian rhythms.

How much sleep do we need? The answer varies, but most of us need about 7 to 10 hours. Newborns are gluttons for sleep and need about 16 hours over the course of a day. At the other extreme are the lucky few—less than 1 percent of the population—who carry a mutation in a gene called DEC2 that allows them to get away with sleeping as little as six hours a night without "crashing" the next day (He et al., 2009). College students may need as many as nine hours of sleep a night, although most sleep no more than six hours (Maas, 1999), creating a powerful urge to nap the next day (Rock, 2004). One common misconception is that the elderly need less sleep than the rest of us, only six or seven hours a night. In reality, they probably need just as much sleep, but they sleep more fitfully (Ohayon, 2002).

Ordinarily, there don't seem to be many negative consequences of losing one night's sleep other than feeling edgy, irritable, and unable to concentrate well the next day. Yet after a few nights of sleep deprivation, we feel more "out of it" and begin to accumulate a balance of "sleep debt," which can require at least several nights of sleeping a few extra hours to pay off. People deprived of multiple nights of sleep, or who cut back drastically on sleep, often experience mild depression, difficulties in learning new information and paying attention, problems in thinking clearly and solving problems, and slowed reaction times (Cohen, et al., 2010; Gangswisch et al., 2010). After more than four days of severe sleep deprivation, we may even experience brief hallucinations, such as hearing voices or seeing things (Wolfe & Pruitt, 2003). Sleep deprivation is associated with a variety of adverse health outcomes: weight gain (we burn off a lot of calories just by sleeping); increased risk for high blood pressure, diabetes, and heart problems; and a less vigorous immune response to viral infections (Dement & Vaughan, 1999; Motivala & Irwin, 2007). This last effect probably explains why you're more likely to get a cold after going for several days with little sleep. Some researchers even believe that the massive increase in obesity and diabetes in the United States over the past few decades is due largely to Americans' chronic sleep deprivation (Buxton et al., 2012; Hasler et al., 2004), although this claim is scientifically controversial. Loss of sleep has also been tied to friendly fire incidents in the 1991 Persian Gulf War, in which soldiers mistook their comrades for the enemy, resulting in senseless casualties (Kennedy, 2009).

Recent data point to a racial dimension to sleep loss as well: minorities, African-Americans in particular, appear to sleep less—and less well—than Whites. The reasons for this difference aren't clear. It remains even after taking into account differences between African-Americans and Whites in social class and education, so other factors, like race differences in everyday life stressors, appear to be at play (Carnethon et al., 2012; Quenqua, 2012).

Stages of Sleep

For much of human history, people believed there was something like a switch in our brains that turned consciousness on when we were awake and off when we snoozed. But one night in 1951, a discovery in Nathaniel Kleitman's sleep laboratory at the University of Chicago changed how we think about sleep and dreaming. Eugene Aserinsky, Kleitman's graduate student, monitored his 8-year-old son's eye movements and brain waves while he slept. Aserinsky was astonished to observe that his son's eyes danced periodically back and forth under his closed lids. Whenever the eye movements occurred, the boy's brain pulsed with electrical activity, as measured by an electroencephalogram (EEG), much as it did when he was awake (Aserinsky, 1996).

The fledgling scientist had the good sense to know that he was onto something of immense importance. The slumbering brain was hardly an inert tangle of neurons; rather, it was abuzz with activity, at least at various intervals. Aserinsky further suspected that his son's eye movements reflected episodes of dreaming. Aserinsky and Kleitman (1953) confirmed this hunch when they awakened participants while they were displaying **rapid eye movement (REM)**. In almost all cases, they reported vivid dreams. In contrast, participants were much less likely to report vivid dreams when researchers awakened them from sleep when they were not displaying REM, although later research showed that vivid dreams occasionally happened then, too.

In landmark research using all night-recording devices, Kleitman and William Dement (Dement & Kleitman, 1957) went on to discover that during sleep we pass repeatedly through five stages every night. Each cycle lasts about 90 minutes, and each stage of sleep is clearly distinguishable from awake states, as shown in **FIGURE 1**.

STAGE 1 SLEEP. Has someone ever nudged you to wake up, and you weren't even sure whether you were awake or asleep? Perhaps you even replied, "No, I wasn't really sleeping," but your friend insisted, "Yes, you were. You were starting to snore." If so, you were probably in stage 1 sleep. In this light stage of sleep, which lasts for 5 to 10 minutes, our brain activity powers down by 50 percent or more, producing *theta* waves, which occur four to seven times per second. These waves are slower than the *beta* waves of 13 or more times per second produced during active alert states, and the alpha waves of eight to 12 times per second when we're quiet and relaxed. As we drift off to deeper sleep, we become more relaxed, and we may experience *hypnagogic imagery*—scrambled, bizarre, and dream-like images that flit in and out of consciousness. We may also experience sudden jerks (sometimes called *myoclonic jerks*) of our limbs as if being startled or falling. In this state of sleep, we're typically quite confused. Some scientists speculate that many reports of ghosts and other spirits stem from hypnagogic imagery that sleepers misinterpret as human figures (Hines, 2003).

STAGE 2 SLEEP. In stage 2 sleep, our brain waves slow down even more. Sudden intense bursts of electrical activity called sleep spindles of about 12–14 cycles a second, and occasional sharply rising and falling waves known as K-complexes, first appear in the EEG (Aldrich, 1999). K-complexes appear only when we're asleep. As our brain activity decelerates, our heart rate slows, our body temperature decreases, our muscles relax even more, and our eye movements cease. We spend as much as 65 percent of our sleep in stage 2.

STAGES 3 AND 4 SLEEP. After about 10 to 30 minutes, light sleep gives way to much deeper slow-wave sleep, in which we can observe *delta waves,* which are as slow as one to two cycles a second, in the EEG. In stage 3, delta waves appear 20 to 50 percent of the time, and in stage 4, they appear more than half the time. To feel fully rested in the morning, we need to experience these deeper stages of sleep throughout the night. In this context, a common myth is that drinking alcohol is a good way to catch up on sleep. Not quite. Having several drinks before bed usually puts us to bed sooner, but it usually makes us feel more tired the next day, because alcohol suppresses delta wave sleep. Children are famously good sleepers because they spend as much as 40 percent of their sleep time in "deep sleep" and are difficult to awaken. In contrast, adults spend only about one-quarter of their sleep "sleeping like a baby," in deep sleep.

STAGE 5: REM SLEEP. After 15 to 30 minutes, we return to stage 2 before our brains shift dramatically into high gear, with high frequency, low-amplitude waves resembling those of wakefulness. We've entered stage 5, known commonly as **REM sleep**. In contrast, stages 1–4 are known as **non-REM (NREM) sleep**.

Our hyped brain waves during REM sleep are accompanied by increased heart rate and blood pressure, as well as rapid and irregular breathing, a state that occupies about 20 to 25 percent of our night's sleep. After 10 to 20 minutes of REM sleep, the cycle starts up again, as we glide back to the early stages of sleep and then back into deeper sleep yet

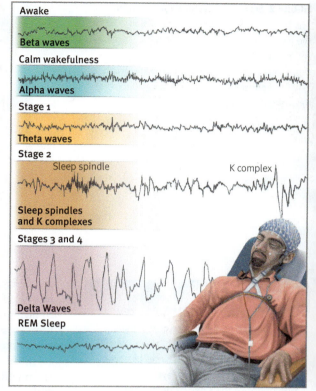

FIGURE 1 The Stages of Sleep. The EEG allows scientists to distinguish among the major stages of sleep, along with two levels of wakefulness. As we can see, brain activity during REM sleep is similar to that when we're awake and alert, because our brains during REM are typically engaged in vivid dreaming.

Watch in **MyPsychLab** the **Video:** The Basics: Rhythms of Consciousness

rapid eye movement (REM)
darting of the eyes underneath closed eyelids during sleep

REM sleep
stage of sleep during which the brain is most active and during which vivid dreaming most often occurs

non-REM (NREM) sleep
stages 1 through 4 of the sleep cycle, during which rapid eye movements do not occur and dreaming is less frequent and vivid

FIGURE 2 Stages of Sleep in a Typical Night.
The graph shows the typical progression through the night of stages 1–4 and REM sleep. Stages 1–4 are indicated on the *y* axis, and REM stages are represented by the green curves on the graph. The REM periods occur about every 90 minutes throughout the night (Dement, 1974).

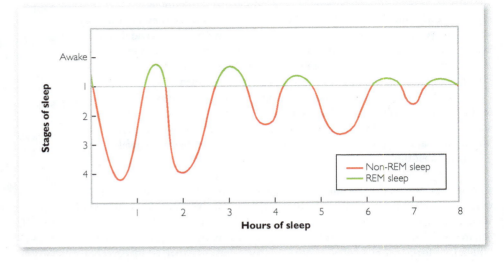

Factoid

Dolphins and some other aquatic animals (such as seals and sea lions) "sleep" with one of their brain's hemispheres asleep and the other awake. The eye on the side opposite the sleeping hemisphere typically remains shut, with the other eye remaining open. After a few hours, the other hemisphere and eye take over as sleep continues. This remarkable arrangement permits these animals to sleep while remaining on the lookout for predators and obstacles, as well as to rise periodically to the surface of the water to breathe (Ridgway, 2002).

? Research demonstrates that REM and non-REM dreams tend to differ in content. Would this dream image be more likely in a REM dream or a non-REM dream? (See answer upside-down below.)

Answer: It would be more likely in a REM dream.

again. Each night, we circle back to REM sleep five or six times (see **FIGURE 2**). Contrary to a belief held by Sigmund Freud and others, dreams occur for more than a few seconds. In fact, our later REM periods toward the early morning typically last for half an hour or more, compared with the 10 to 20 minutes we spend in REM after falling asleep. So if it seems like one of your dreams has lasted for 45 minutes, that's often because it has.

We don't dream *only* during REM sleep, although we dream *more* in REM (Domhoff, 1996, 1999). Many REM dreams are emotional, illogical, and prone to sudden shifts in plot (Foulkes, 1962; Hobson, Pace-Schott, & Stickgold, 2000). In contrast, non-REM dreams often are shorter (Antrobus, 1983; Foulkes & Rechtschaffen, 1964), more thought-like and repetitive, and deal with everyday topics of current concern to us, like homework, shopping lists, or taxes (Hobson, 2002; Rechtschaffen, Verdone, & Wheaton, 1963). Nevertheless, as the night wears on, dream reports from NREM sleep (starting with stage 2) resemble REM dream reports, leading some researchers to suggest that REM and NREM dreams aren't as distinct as once believed (Antrobus, 1983; Foulkes & Schmidt, 1983; McNamara et al., 2005).

REM sleep is biologically important and probably essential. Depriving rats of REM sleep typically leads to their death within a few weeks (National Institute on Alcohol Use and Alcoholism, 1998), although rats die even sooner from total sleep deprivation (Rechtschaffen, 1998). When we humans are deprived of REM for a few nights, we experience *REM rebound*: The amount and intensity of REM sleep increases, suggesting that REM serves a critical biological function (Ocampo-Garces et al., 2000). Many of us have observed REM rebound when we haven't slept much for a few nights in a row. When we finally get a good night's sleep, we often experience much more intense dreams, even nightmares, probably reflecting a powerful bounce-back of REM sleep. Yet scientists are still debating the biological functions of REM sleep.

Some researchers once believed that the darting movements of REM sleep served to scan the images of dreams (Dement, 1974; Siegel, 2005). William Dement once observed a person during REM engaging in a striking pattern of back-and-forth horizontal eye movements. When Dement awakened him, he reported dreaming of a Ping-Pong match. Nevertheless, the evidence for this "scanning hypothesis" of REM is mixed, and the fact that individuals who are blind from birth engage in REM calls it into question (Gross, Byrne, & Fisher, 1965). During REM the muscles of our middle ears become active, almost as though they're assisting us to hear sounds in the dream (Pessah & Roffwarg, 1972; Slegel et al., 1991).

During REM sleep, our supercharged brains are creating dreams, but our bodies are relaxed and, for all practical purposes, paralyzed. For this reason, scientists sometimes call REM sleep *paradoxical sleep* because the brain is active at the same time the body is inactive. If REM didn't paralyze us, we'd act out our dreams, something that people with a strange—and fortunately very rare—condition called REM behavior disorder (RBD) do on occasion. In one case of RBD, for 20 years a 77-year-old minister acted out violent dreams in his sleep and occasionally injured his wife (Mahowald & Schenck, 2000). Fortunately, only about one person in 200 has symptoms of RBD, which occurs most frequently in men over the age of 50. In this condition, the brain stem structures that ordinarily prevent us from moving during REM sleep don't function properly. Recently, it has come to light that RBD may be a very early marker of dementia and Parkinson's disease, with RBD emerging an average of 14 to 25 years before major symptoms of neurodegenerative diseases first appear (Boeve, 2010; Schenck, Boeve, & Mahowald, 2013).

Classic work by Michel Jouvet (1962) showed that lesioning a brain stem region called the locus coeruleus, which is responsible for keeping us paralyzed during REM, leads cats to act out their dreams. If Jouvet gave cats a ball of yarn to play with during the day, they'd often reenact this play behavior in their dreams.

Lucid Dreaming

We've been talking about sleeping and waking as distinct stages, but they may blend gradually into one another (Antrobus, Antrobus, & Fisher, 1965; Voss et al., 2009). A phenomenon that challenges the idea that we're either totally asleep or totally awake is described in the following example: "I briefly looked back. The person following me did not look like an ordinary human being; he was as tall as a giant.... Now it was fully clear to me that I was undergoing a dream.... Then it suddenly occurred to me that I did not have to escape but was capable of doing something else...So... I turned around, and allowed the pursuer to approach me. Then I asked him what it actually was that he wanted. His answer was: "How am I supposed to know?! After all, this is your dream and, moreover, you studied psychology and not me." (Tholey, 1987, p. 97 translated in Metzinger, 2009, p. 146).

If, like this slumberer, you've ever dreamed and known you were dreaming, you've experienced **lucid dreaming** (Blackmore, 1991; LaBerge, 1980, in press; Van Eeden, 1913). Most of us have experienced at least one lucid dream, and about one-fifth of Americans report dreaming lucidly on a monthly basis (Snyder & Gackenbach, 1988). Many lucid dreamers become aware they're dreaming when they see something so bizarre or improbable that they conclude (correctly) that they're having a dream.

Using brain imaging, researchers (Dresler et al., 2012) recently discovered that when participants experience a lucid dream, parts of their cerebral cortex associated with self-perceptions and with evaluating thoughts and feelings rev up with activity. Another study (Voss, Holzmann, Tuin, & Hobson, 2009), which measured electrical activity in the brain, suggested that lucid dreams are a hybrid or mixed state of consciousness with features of both waking and REM sleep. If these studies can be replicated, it would imply that it's possible to remain asleep yet self-aware, and that we don't merely report that dreams have a lucid quality after we awaken.

Lucid dreaming opens up the possibility of controlling our dreams (Kunzendorf et al., 2006–2007). The ability to become lucid during a nightmare usually improves the dream's outcome (Levitan & LeBerge, 1990; Spoormaker & Van den Bout, 2006). Nevertheless, there's no good evidence that changing our lucid dreams can help us to overcome depression, anxiety, or other adjustment problems, despite the claims of some popular psychology books, Internet sites, and even telephone applications that claim to increase dream lucidity (Mindell, 1990).

Disorders of Sleep

Nearly all of us have trouble falling asleep or staying asleep from time to time. When sleep problems recur, interfere with our ability to function at work or school, or affect our health, they can exact a dear price. The cost of sleep disorders in terms of lost work productivity alone amounts to as much as $63 billion per year in the United States (Kessler et al, 2011). We can also gauge the cost in terms of human lives, with an estimated 1,500 Americans who fall asleep at the wheel killed each year (Fenton, 2007). These grim statistics are understandable given that 30 to 50 percent of people report some sort of sleep problem (Althius et al., 1998; Blay, Andreoli, & Gastal, 2008).

👁 **Watch** in **MyPsychLab** the **Video:** Lucid Dreaming

◀ **REPLICABILITY**
Can the results be duplicated in other studies?

👁 **Watch** in **MyPsychLab** the **Video:** Special Topics: Sleep Disorders

lucid dreaming
experience of becoming aware that one is dreaming

To ensure that the effects of sleeping pills don't carry over to when we're awake, it's important to monitor how we react to them and ensure that we have plenty of time to sleep before needing to be active again.

Lucas Carlton suffers from narcolepsy and sleeps 20 hours a day. He's shown here at home in England in one of his narcoleptic states.

insomnia
difficulty falling and staying asleep

narcolepsy
disorder characterized by the rapid and often unexpected onset of sleep

INSOMNIA. The most common sleep disturbance is insomnia. **Insomnia** can take the following forms: (a) having trouble falling asleep (regularly taking more than 30 minutes to doze off), (b) waking too early in the morning, and (c) waking up during the night and having trouble returning to sleep. An estimated 9 to 15 percent of people report severe or longstanding problems with insomnia (Morin & Edinger, 2009).

People who suffer from depression, continual pain, or a variety of medical conditions report especially high rates of insomnia (Katz & McHorney, 2002; Smith & Haythornthwaite, 2004). Brief bouts of insomnia are often due to stress and relationship problems, medications and illness, working late or variable shifts, jet lag, drinking caffeine, or napping during the day. Insomnia can become recurrent if we become frustrated and anxious when we can't fall asleep right away (Spielman, Conroy, & Glovinsky, 2003). Many people don't realize that even most "good sleepers" take 15 to 20 minutes to fall asleep. If you have trouble drifting off to sleep and counting sheep doesn't help, James Maas (1999) recommends that you try the following: hide clocks to avoid becoming preoccupied with the inability to fall asleep quickly; sleep in a cool room; go to sleep and wake up at regular times; and avoid caffeine, naps during the day, reading in bed, and watching television or surfing the Web right before bedtime.

Although sleeping pills can be effective in treating insomnia, researchers have discovered that brief psychotherapy is more effective than Ambien, a popular sleeping pill (Jacobs et al., 2004). Recently, it's come to light that in rare instances, people who use Ambien engage in odd and even dangerous behaviors, including preparing food and eating raw food, walking, making phone calls, and even driving while asleep. Like Ambien, another popular sleeping medication, Lunesta, can cause amnesia for events that occur after taking it (Schenck, 2006). Longstanding use of many sleeping pills can create dependency and make it more difficult to sleep once people stop taking them. So, in an ironic twist, sleeping pills can actually cause insomnia (Bellon, 2006).

NARCOLEPSY. **Narcolepsy** is a dramatic disorder in which people experience bouts of sudden sleep lasting anywhere from a few seconds to several minutes and, less frequently, as long as an hour. The overwhelming urge to sleep can strike at any moment, as in the case of a patient with narcolepsy who fell asleep in all sorts of situations: during his favorite movies, in the shower, and while driving. He was a prison guard, but he couldn't stay awake on the job. He feared his boss would fire him and stifled many a yawn in his presence.

Surprise, elation, or other strong emotions—even those associated with laughing at a joke or engaging in sexual intercourse—can lead some people with narcolepsy to experience *cataplexy,* a complete loss of muscle tone. During cataplexy, people can fall because their muscles become limp as a rag doll. Cataplexy occurs in healthy people during REM sleep. But in narcolepsy, people experiencing cataplexy remain alert, even though they can't move. Ordinarily, sleepers don't enter REM sleep for more than an hour after they fall asleep. But when people who experience an episode of narcolepsy doze off, they plummet into REM sleep immediately, suggesting that it results from a sleep–wake cycle that's badly off-kilter. Vivid hypnagogic hallucinations often accompany the onset of narcoleptic episodes, raising the possibility that REM intrusions are one cause of brief waking hallucinations.

Genetic abnormalities boost the risk of narcolepsy, and some people develop narcolepsy after an accident that causes brain damage. The hormone *orexin* plays a key role in triggering sudden attacks of sleepiness (Mieda et al., 2004). Indeed, people with narcolepsy have abnormally few brain cells that produce orexin. When sleep-deprived rhesus monkeys were given orexin in a nasal spray their performance on cognitive tasks equaled that of well-rested monkeys (Deadwyler et al., 2007). Medications that either replace orexin or mimic its effects in the brain may one day cure narcolepsy.

SLEEP APNEA. In 2008, a 53-year-old Go Airlines pilot and his copilot fell asleep during the flight, failed to respond to air traffic controllers for nearly 20 minutes, and overshot the runway by about 30 miles before they woke up (CNN, August 3, 2009).

What happened? The pilot suffered from **sleep apnea**, a serious sleep disorder that afflicts between 2 and 20 percent of the general population, depending on how broadly or narrowly it's defined (Shamsuzzaman, Gersh, & Somers, 2003; Strohl & Redline, 1996). Apnea is caused by a blockage of the airway during sleep, as shown in **FIGURE 3**. This problem causes people with apnea to snore loudly, gasp, and sometimes stop breathing for more than 20 seconds. Struggling to breathe rouses the person many times—often several hundred times—during the night and interferes with sleep, causing fatigue the next day. Yet most people with sleep apnea have no awareness of these multiple awakenings. A lack of oxygen and the buildup of carbon dioxide can lead to many problems, including night sweats, weight gain, fatigue, hearing loss, an irregular heartbeat (Sanders & Givelber, 2006) and up the risk for dementia or other cognitive impairments (Yaffe et al., 2011). A 10-year study of 6,441 men and women underscored the dangerous effects of sleep apnea. The researchers found that the disorder raised the overall risk of death by 17 percent; in men 40–70 years old with severe apnea, the increase in risk shot up to 46 percent compared with healthy men of the same age (Punjabi et al., 2009).

Because apnea is associated with being overweight, doctors typically recommend weight loss as a first treatment option. When enlarged tonsils cause apnea in children, doctors can remove them surgically. But in adults, surgical procedures often don't work well. Many people benefit from wearing a facemask attached to a machine that blows air into their nasal passages, forcing the airway to remain open. Nevertheless, adjusting to this rather uncomfortable machine can be challenging (Wolfe & Pruitt, 2003).

NIGHT TERRORS. Night terrors are often more disturbing to onlookers than to sleepers. Parents who witness a child's night terrors can hardly believe that the child has no recollection of what occurred. Screaming, crying, perspiring, confused, and wide-eyed, the child may thrash about before falling back into a deep sleep. Such episodes usually last for only a few minutes, although they may seem like an eternity to a distraught parent.

Despite their dramatic nature, **night terrors** are typically harmless events that occur almost exclusively in children. Parents often learn not to overreact and even ignore the episodes if the child isn't in physical danger. Night terrors occasionally occur in adults, especially when they're under intense stress. Despite what most people believe, night terrors aren't associated with vivid dreaming; in fact, they occur exclusively in non-REM sleep.

SLEEPWALKING AND SEXSOMNIA. For many of us, the image of a "somnambulist," or sleepwalker, is a person with eyes closed, arms outstretched, and both hands at shoulder height, walking like a zombie. In actuality, a sleepwalking person often acts like any fully awake person,

FIGURE 3 Flow of Air and Quality of Sleep. When the flow of air is blocked, as in sleep apnea, the quality of sleep can be seriously disrupted.

Person using a device to combat sleep apnea at home

? What's wrong with this picture? Does it capture how a sleepwalking person would actually appear to an onlooker? (See answer upside down at bottom of page.)

Answer: Sleepwalkers typically walk just like regular people, not like zombies.

Factoid

Moms and dads typically worry about their sleep-deprived teenagers. But the parents of 15-year-old Louisa Ball, who lives in south England, were concerned for another reason—their daughter routinely slept for two weeks straight without interruptions, unless she received medication. Louisa suffers from a rare neurological condition called Kleine-Levin Syndrome, aptly nicknamed "Sleeping Beauty Disorder." Her parents need to wake her every 22 hours to feed her and take her to the bathroom, after which she falls immediately asleep.

sleep apnea
disorder caused by a blockage of the airway during sleep, resulting in daytime fatigue

night terrors
sudden waking episodes characterized by screaming, perspiring, and confusion followed by a return to a deep sleep

Factoid

We can fall asleep with our eyes open. In a 1960 study, an investigator taped the eyes of three volunteers—one of them severely sleep-deprived—wide open while flashing bright lights at them, blasting loud music into their ears, and administering periodic electric shocks to their legs. They fell sound asleep within 12 minutes (Boese, 2007).

☑ **Study** and **Review** in **MyPsychLab**

although a sleepwalker may be somewhat clumsier. Some 15 to 30 percent of children and 4 to 5 percent of adults sleepwalk occasionally (Mahowald & Bornemann, 2005). **Sleepwalking**—walking while fully asleep—often involves relatively little activity, but sleepwalkers have been known to drive cars and turn on computers while asleep (Underwood, 2007). In fact, a few people who committed murder have used sleepwalking as a legal defense. In one controversial case, a young man who drove almost 20 miles, removed a tire iron from a car, and used it to kill his mother-in-law. He also strangled his father-in-law to unconsciousness and stabbed them both with a knife. The man was declared innocent because he had slept through the whole event and wasn't responsible for his behavior (McCall, Smith, & Shapiro, 1997).

In a strange condition known as sleep sex or *sexsomnia*, people engage in sexual acts while asleep and don't remember what occurred after they awaken. In a number of controversial legal cases, people have been found not guilty of sexual assault by claiming they suffered from sexsomnia (Bothroyd, 2010).

Contrary to popular misconception, sleepwalkers aren't acting out their dreams, because sleepwalking almost always occurs during non-REM (especially stage 3 or 4) sleep. For most people, sleepwalking is harmless, and sleepwalkers rarely remember their actions after awakening. If someone is sleepwalking, it's perfectly safe to wake him or her up, despite what we may have seen in movies (Wolfe & Pruitt, 2003).

Assess Your Knowledge — FACT or FICTION?

1. The average adult needs about six hours of sleep a night. **True / False**

2. People move slowly through the first four stages of sleep but then spend the rest of the night in REM sleep. **True / False**

3. When we dream, our brains are much less active than when awake. **True / False**

4. Sleep apnea is more common in thin than in overweight people. **True / False**

5. Night terrors usually last only a few minutes and are typically harmless. **True / False**

Answers: 1. F; 2. F; 3. F; 4. F; 5. T

Dreams

4 Describe Freud's theory of dreams.

5 Explain three major modern theories of dreaming.

Dreaming is a virtually universal experience. Some people insist they never dream, but research shows this phenomenon is almost always due to a failure to recall their dreams rather than a failure to experience them. When brought into a sleep laboratory, just about everyone reports vivid dreaming when awakened during a REM period (Dement, 1974; Domhoff & Schneider, 2004), although a mysterious handful of people don't (Butler & Watson, 1985; Pagel, 2003). Even people who are blind dream. But whether their dreams contain visual imagery depends on when they became blind. People blinded before age 4 don't experience visual dream imagery, whereas those blinded after age 7 do so, suggesting that between ages 4 to 6 is the window within which the ability to generate visual imagery develops (Kerr, 1993; Kerr & Domhoff, 2004).

Whether we're researchers in Timbuktu or New York City, we'll find cross-culturally consistent patterns in dreaming. Virtually all of us experience dreams that contain more aggression than friendliness, more negative than positive emotions, and more misfortune than good fortune. At least a few differences in dreams are associated with cultural factors.

sleepwalking
walking while fully asleep

For example, the dreams of people in more technologically advanced societies feature fewer animals than those in small, traditional societies (Domhoff, 1996, 2001a).

Scientists still don't know for sure why we dream, but evidence from a variety of sources suggests that dreams are involved in (a) processing emotional memories (Maquet & Franck, 1997); (b) integrating new experiences with established memories to make sense of and create a virtual reality model of the world (Hobson, 2009; Stickgold, James, & Hobson, 2002); (c) learning new strategies and ways of doing things, like swinging a golf club (Walker et al., 2002); (d) simulating threatening events so we can better cope with them in everyday life (Revonsuo, 2000); and (e) reorganizing and consolidating memories (Crick & Mitchison, 1983; Diekelmann & Born, 2010). Still, the function of dreams remains a puzzle because research evidence concerning the role of learning and memory in dreams is mixed. We'll discuss four major theories of dreams, beginning with the granddaddy of them all: Sigmund Freud.

Freud's Dream Protection Theory

Humans have been trying to decipher the meaning of dreams for thousands of years. The Babylonians believed that dreams were sent by the gods, the Assyrians thought that dreams contained signs or omens, the Greeks built dream temples in which visitors awaited prophecies sent by the gods during dreams, and North American Indians believed that dreams revealed hidden wishes and desires (Van de Castle, 1994).

Sigmund Freud sided with the Native Americans. In his landmark book, *The Interpretation of Dreams* (1900), Freud described dreams as the guardians of sleep. During sleep, the ego, which acts as a sort of mental censor, is less able than when awake to keep sexual and aggressive instincts at bay by repressing them. If not for dreams, these instincts would bubble up, disturbing sleep. The *dream-work* disguises and contains the threatening sexual and aggressive impulses by transforming them into symbols that represent *wish fulfillment*—how we wish things could be.

According to Freud, dreams don't surrender their secrets easily—they require interpretation to reverse the dream-work and reveal their true meaning. He distinguished between the details of the dream itself, which he called the *manifest content,* and it's true, hidden meaning, which he called the *latent content*. For example, a dream about getting a flat tire (manifest content) might signify anxiety about the loss of status at our job (latent content).

Most scientists have rejected the dream protection and wish fulfillment theories of dreams (Domhoff, 2001a). Contrary to Freud's dream protection theory, some patients with brain injuries report that they don't dream, yet sleep soundly (Jus et al., 1973). If, as Freud claimed, "wish fulfillment is the meaning of each and every dream" (Freud, 1900, p. 106), we'd expect dream content to be mostly positive. Yet although most of us have occasional dreams of flying, winning the lottery, or being with the object of our wildest fantasies, these themes are less frequent than dreams of misfortune. Freud also believed that many or most dreams are sexual in nature. But sexual themes account for as little as 10 percent of the dreams we remember (see **TABLE 1**) (Domhoff, 2003). Of course, though a determined Freudian might argue that we're merely forgetting about many sexual dreams, this hypothesis has never been tested.

Another challenge to Freud's dream theory is that many dreams don't appear to be disguised, as he contended. As many as 90 percent of dream reports are straightforward descriptions of everyday activities and problems, like talking to friends (Domhoff, 2003; Dorus, Dorus, & Rechtschaffen, 1971). A final problem with wish fulfillment theory is that people who've experienced highly traumatic events often experience repetitive nightmares (Barratt, 1996). But nightmares clearly aren't wish fulfillments, and they aren't at all uncommon in either adults or children. So, if you have an occasional nightmare, rest assured: It's perfectly normal.

TABLE 1 Most Frequent Dream Themes.

1. Being chased or pursued
2. Being lost, late, or trapped
3. Falling
4. Flying
5. Losing valuable possessions
6. Sexual dreams
7. Experiencing great natural beauty
8. Being naked or dressed oddly
9. Injury or illness

(*Source:* Domhoff, 2003)

◄ **FALSIFIABILITY**
Can the claim be disproved?

Nightmares are most frequent in children, but are also common in adults.

FIGURE 4 Activation-Synthesis Theory. According to activation-synthesis theory, the pons transmits random signals to the thalamus, which relays information to the forebrain of the cerebral cortex. The forebrain in turn attempts to create a story from the incomplete information it receives.

RULING OUT RIVAL HYPOTHESES ▶

Have important alternative explanations for the findings been excluded?

FALSIFIABILITY ▶

Can the claim be disproved?

activation–synthesis theory
theory that dreams reflect inputs from brain activation originating in the pons, which the forebrain then attempts to weave into a story

Activation–Synthesis Theory

Starting in the 1960s and 1970s, Alan Hobson and Robert McCarley developed **activation–synthesis theory** (Hobson & McCarley, 1977; Hobson, Pace-Schott, & Stickgold, 2000), which proposes that dreams reflect brain activation in sleep, rather than repressed unconscious wishes, as Freud claimed. Far from having deep, universal meaning, Hobson and McCarley maintained that dreams reflect the activated brain's attempt to make sense of random and internally generated neural signals during REM sleep.

Throughout the day and night, the balance of neurotransmitters in the brain shifts continually. REM is turned on by surges of the neurotransmitter acetylcholine, as the neurotransmitters serotonin and norepinephrine are shut down. Acetylcholine activates nerve cells in the pons, located at the base of the brain, while dwindling levels of serotonin and norepinephrine decrease reflective thought, reasoning, attention, and memory. The activated pons sends incomplete signals to the thalamus is a relay station for sensory information, to the language and visual areas of the forebrain, as shown in **FIGURE 4**. That's the activation part of the theory. The forebrain does its best to cobble together the signals it receives into a meaningful story. That's the synthesis part of the theory. Nevertheless, the bits of information it receives are haphazard and chaotic, so the narrative is rarely coherent or logical. The amygdala is also ramped up, adding the emotional colors of fear, anxiety, anger, sadness, and elation to the mix. According to activation–synthesis theory, the net result of these complex brain changes is what we experience as a dream, which may bear slim to no relation to our everyday lives.

If dreams mirrored our life circumstances, as most other dream theories propose, we'd expect the dreams of people with disabilities to be very different from those of individuals with no disabilities. But when Hobson and his colleagues (Voss, Tuin, Schermelleh-Engel, & Hobson, 2009) examined the dreams of people who were either deaf-mute or paraplegic from the time of birth, they found that the form and content of their dreams were no different from the dreams of people without disabilities. Clearly, as activation–synthesis theory predicts, dreams often take on a life of their own, far removed from everyday reality.

Dreaming and the Forebrain

An alternative to the activation–synthesis theory emphasizes the role of the forebrain in dreaming. Mark Solms (1997; Solms & Turnbull, 2002) surveyed 332 cases of patients with brain damage from stroke, tumors, and injury. From this gold mine of data, he determined that damage to the parietal lobes and to the deep frontal white matter—which connects different parts of the cortex to the lower parts of the brain—can lead to a complete loss of dreaming. It's likely that the damaged brain areas are pathways that allow brain centers involved in dreaming to communicate. When they're disconnected, dreaming stops.

Thus, damage to the forebrain can eliminate dreams entirely, even when the brain stem is working properly. This finding seems to refute the claim of activation–synthesis theory that the brain stem plays an exclusive role in producing dreams and underscores the role of the forebrain in dreaming. According to Solms, dreams are driven largely by the motivational and emotional control centers of the forebrain as the logical "executive" parts of the brain snooze.

Answers are located at the end of the text.

DREAM INTERPRETATIONS   evaluating **CLAIMS**

We all dream, and many of us are curious about what, if anything, our dreams mean. According to many popular websites and books, our dreams are trying to tell us something through their symbols. Let's evaluate some of these claims, which are modeled after actual dream interpretation books and websites.

"Your dreams are *hidden messages* sent from your subconscious to help guide your life."

Is there extraordinary evidence to support this extraordinary claim? In fact, most dream reports are straightforward descriptions of everyday activities and problems rather than hidden or disguised messages.

"*Seeing a coconut in your dreams means* that you will receive an unexpected sum of money."

Scientific evidence doesn't support the claim that specific symbols in our dreams possess a deeper meaning or predict something in our lives. Many dreams have no special meaning at all, and some dreams reflect everyday preoccupations.

"Using the *ancient art of dream analysis*, we can uncover hidden meanings in your dreams."

Does the fact that dream interpretations have been around a long time mean they're valid?

Neurocognitive Perspectives on Dreaming

Scientists who've advanced a **neurocognitive theory** of dreaming argue that explaining dreams only in terms of neurotransmitters and random neural impulses doesn't tell the full story. Instead, they contend, dreams are a meaningful product of our cognitive capacities, which shape what we dream about. For example, children under the age of 7 or 8 recall dreaming on only 20 to 30 percent of occasions when awakened from REM sleep compared with 80 to 90 percent of adults (Foulkes, 1982, 1999). Until they reach the age of 9 or 10, children's dreams tend to be simple, lacking in movement, and apart from an occasional nightmare, less emotional and bizarre than adult dreams (Domhoff, 1996). A typical 5-year-old's dream may be of a pet or animal in a zoo. According to the neurocognitive perspective, complex dreams are cognitive achievements that parallel the gradual development of visual imagination and other advanced cognitive abilities. We begin to dream like adults when our brains develop the "wiring" to do so (Domhoff, 2001a).

According to the neurocognitive perspective, the fact that dreams are often rather ordinary and dramatize concerns that are important to us when we're not in slumberland implies that they reflect more than random neural impulses generated by the brain stem (Domhoff, 2011; Foulkes, 1985; Revonsuo, 2000). Content analyses of tens of thousands of adult dreams (Hall & Van de Castle, 1966) reveal that many are associated with everyday activities, emotional concerns, and preoccupations (Domhoff, 1996; Hall & Nordby, 1972;

neurocognitive theory
theory that dreams are a meaningful product of our cognitive capacities, which shape what we dream about

Smith & Hall, 1964), including playing sports, preparing for tests, feeling self-conscious about our appearance, and being single (Pano, Hilscher, & Cupchik, 2008–2009). Moreover, dream content is surprisingly stable over long time periods. In a journal containing 904 dreams that a woman kept for more than five decades, six themes (eating or thinking of food, the loss of an object, going to the toilet, being in a small or messy room, missing a bus or train, doing something with her mother) accounted for more than three-fourths of the contents of her dreams (Domhoff, 1993). Additionally, 50 to 80 percent of people report recurrent dreams, like missing a test, over many years (Cartwright & Romanek, 1978; Zadra, 1996).

As we've seen, there are sharp disagreements among scientists about the role of the brain stem and REM sleep, and the role that development plays in dreaming. Nevertheless, scientists generally agree that (1) acetylcholine turns on REM sleep and (2) the forebrain plays an important role in dreams.

Assess Your Knowledge   FACT or FICTION?

1. Dreams often reflect unfulfilled wishes, as Freud suggested.   True / False

2. Activation–synthesis theory proposes that dreams result from incomplete neural signals generated by the pons.   True / False

3. REM sleep is triggered by the neurotransmitter acetylcholine.   True / False

4. Damage to the forebrain can eliminate dreams.   True / False

5. Recurrent dreams are extremely rare.   True / False

Answers: 1. F; 2. T; 3. T; 4. T; 5. F

When astronauts train for missions in whirling centrifuge devices that force oxygen enriched blood out of their brains as they accelerate, some experience vivid hallucinations (Birbaumer et. al., 2005).

Other Alterations of Consciousness and Unusual Experiences

6 Determine how scientists explain unusual and seemingly "mystical" alterations in consciousness.

7 Distinguish myths from realities concerning hypnosis.

As the stages of sleep demonstrate, consciousness is far more complicated than just "conscious" versus "unconscious." Moreover, there are other variations on the theme of consciousness besides sleep and waking. Some of the more radical alterations in consciousness include hallucinations, as well as out-of-body, near-death, and déjà vu experiences.

Hallucinations: Experiencing What Isn't There

Hallucinations, ranging from seeing ghost-like apparitions or scenes of splendid beauty, to hearing voices in the head commanding people to engage in unspeakable acts of violence, to feeling bugs marching on the skin, can seem amazingly real. Hallucinations are realistic perceptual experiences in the absence of any external stimuli, and they can occur in any sensory modality. Brain scans reveal that when people report visual hallucinations, their visual cortex becomes active, just as it does when they see a real object (Allen et al., 2008; Bentall, in press). The same correspondence holds true for other senses, like hearing and touch, underscoring the link between our perceptual experiences and brain activity.

A frequent misconception is that hallucinations occur only in psychologically disturbed individuals (Aleman & Laroi, 2008). Yet surveys reveal that between 10 and 14 percent (Tien, 1991) to as many as 39 percent (Ohayon, 2000; Posey & Losch, 1983) of college students and people in the general population report having hallucinated during the day at least once—even when not taking drugs or experiencing psychological problems (Ohayon, 2000). Some non-Western cultures, including some in Africa, value hallucinations as gifts of wisdom from the gods and incorporate them into their religious rituals. People in these societies may even go out of their way to induce hallucinations by means of prayer, fasting, and hallucinogenic drugs (Al-Issa, 1995; Bourguignon, 1970).

Visual hallucinations can also be brought about by oxygen and sensory deprivation, epilepsy, fever, dementia, and migraine headaches (Manford & Andermann, 1998). Auditory hallucinations (those involving sound) can occur when patients mistakenly attribute their thoughts, or inner speech, to an external source (Bentall, 1990, in press; Frith, 1992). The auditory verbal hallucinations of psychotic and well-functioning non-psychotic individuals are similar in many respects. But they differ in that the voices that psychotic individuals hear are much more negative and perceived to be less controllable (Daalman et al., 2010).

People who float in lukewarm saltwater in dark and silent sensory deprivation tanks, hallucinate to compensate for the lack of sensory stimulation (Smith, 2009).

Out-of-Body and Near-Death Experiences

Carlos Alvarado (2000) described a 36-year-old police officer's account of an **out-of-body experience (OBE)**, an extraordinary sense of her consciousness leaving her body, when she pursued an armed suspect on her first night on patrol. "When I and three other officers stopped the vehicle and started getting (to) the suspect… I was afraid. I promptly went out of my body and up into the air maybe 20 feet above the scene. I remained there, extremely calm, while I watched the entire procedure—including myself—do exactly what I had been trained to do." Alvarado reported that "[s]uddenly, [she] found herself back in her body after the suspect had been subdued".

OBEs are surprisingly common: About 25 percent of college students and 10 percent of the general population report having experienced one or more of them (Alvarado, 2000). In many cases, individuals describe themselves as floating above their bodies, calmly observing themselves from above, implying that our sense of ourselves need not be subjectively locked into our bodies (Smith, 2009). People who are prone to OBEs frequently report other unusual experiences, including vivid fantasies, lucid dreams, hallucinations, perceptual distortions, and strange body sensations in everyday life (Blackmore, 1984, 1986). Some people also experience OBEs when they're medicated, using psychedelic drugs, experiencing migraine headaches or seizures, or either extremely relaxed or under extreme stress.

Yet are people really able to roam outside their bodies during an OBE? Laboratory studies have compared what's reported during an OBE against sights and sounds known to be present in a given location, like a hidden ledge 10 feet above a bed. Interestingly, even though many participants report they can see or hear what's occurring at a distant place, their reports are generally inaccurate or, at best, a "good guess" when they are accurate. When researchers have reported positive results, these results have virtually never been replicated (Alvarado, 2000). So there's no good evidence that people are truly floating above their bodies during an OBE, although it certainly seems that way to them (Cheyne & Girard, 2009). These findings appear to falsify the claim that people genuinely emerge from their bodies during OBEs.

What, then, are some possible explanations for these dramatic changes in consciousness? Our sense of self depends on a complex interplay of sensory information. Research suggests that when our senses of touch and vision are scrambled, the result is a disruption of our experience of our physical body with striking similarities to an OBE (Ehrsson, 2007; Lenggenhager et al., 2007). The "club drug," ketamine (widely known as "Special K"), which users often report produces bizarre out-of-body experiences and feelings of detachment from the physical world, disrupts patterns of brain activity

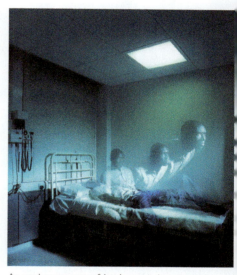

As real as an out-of-body experience seems to the person having it, research has found no evidence that consciousness exists outside the body.

◄ **REPLICABILITY**
Can the results be duplicated in other studies?

◄ **FALSIFIABILITY**
Can the claim be disproved?

out-of-body experience (OBE)
sense of our consciousness leaving our body

Although there are many variations of a "near-death experience," most people in our culture believe it involves moving through a tunnel and toward a white light.

that bring about a unified sense of the self and body by reducing transmission of the neurotransmitter glutamate (Wilkins, Girard, & Cheyne, 2011). OBEs remind us that one of the human brain's great achievements is its ability to integrate sensory information from different pathways into a unified experience. Yet when this ability is disrupted, it can trick us into thinking our physical selves are separate from our bodies (Cheyne & Girard, 2009; Terhune, 2009).

OBEs also sometimes occur in **near-death experiences (NDEs)** reported by people who've nearly died or thought they were going to die. In fact, about one quarter of patients with NDEs experience their consciousness outside their bodies (van Lommel et al., 2001). Ever since Raymond Moody (1975) cataloged them over 30 years ago, Americans have become familiar with the classical elements of the NDE that are widely circulated in books and movies—passing through a dark tunnel; experiencing a white light as a spiritual being, such as a deceased loved one or angel; the life review (seeing our lives pass before our eyes); and meeting spiritual beings or long-dead relatives, all before "coming back into the body" (see **TABLE 2**). Not all reports of NDEs follow this exact script, but most are close, as the case that follows illustrates. Dr. Elizabeth Kübler-Ross (1973) reported the tale of a man who was critically injured by a large truck and then observed the accident scene from above his body. He then saw his family, surrounded by an aura of light. Experiencing the family's wondrous, unconditional love, he decided to return to his body to share his experiences with others.

Roughly 6 to 33 percent of people who've been close to death report NDEs (Blanke & Dieguez, 2009; Greyson, in press; Ring, 1984; Sabom, 1982; van Lommel et al., 2001). NDEs differ across persons and cultures, suggesting they don't provide a genuine glimpse of the afterlife, but are constructed from prevalent beliefs about the hereafter in response to the threat of death (Ehrenwald, 1974; Noyes & Kletti, 1976). People from Christian and Buddhist cultures frequently report the sensation of moving through a tunnel, but native people in North America, the Pacific Islands, and Australia rarely do (Kellehear, 1993).

It's tempting to believe that NDEs prove that when we die we'll all be ushered into the afterlife by friends or loved ones. Nevertheless, the evidence is insufficient to support this extraordinary claim. Scientists have offered alternative explanations for NDEs based on changes in the chemistry of the brain associated with cardiac arrest, anesthesia, and other physical traumas (Blackmore, 1993). For example, a feeling of complete peace that can accompany an NDE may result from the massive release of *endorphins* in a dying brain, and buzzing, ringing, or other unusual sounds may be the rumblings of an oxygen-starved brain (Blackmore, 1993).

EXTRAORDINARY CLAIMS ▶
Is the evidence as strong as the claim?

RULING OUT RIVAL HYPOTHESES ▶
Have important alternative explanations for the findings been excluded?

(© www.CartoonStock.com)

TABLE 2 Common Elements in Adult Near-Death Experiences.

- Difficulty describing the experience in words
- Hearing ourselves pronounced dead
- Feelings of peace and quiet
- Hearing unusual noises
- Meeting "spiritual beings"
- Experiencing a bright light as a "being of light"
- Panoramic "life review," that is, seeing our entire life pass before our eyes
- Experiencing a realm in which all knowledge exists
- Experiencing cities of light
- Experiencing a realm of ghosts and spirits
- Sensing a border or limit
- Coming back "into the body"

(*Based on:* Greyson, 2000; Moody, 1975, 1977)

near-death experience (NDE)
experience reported by people who've nearly died or thought they were going to die

Moreover, many, if not all, of the experiences associated with NDEs occur in circumstances in which people don't face imminent death. For example, NDE-like experiences can be triggered by (a) electrical stimulation of the brain's temporal lobes (Persinger, 1994); (b) lack of oxygen to the brain in rapid acceleration during fighter pilot training (Whinnery, 1997); and (c) psychedelic (such as LSD and mescaline) and anesthetic (such as ketamine) drugs (Jansen, 1991). Until more definitive evidence is marshaled to demonstrate that NDEs reflect anything more than changes in physiology in the dying brain, there seems to be no reason to discard this more parsimonious explanation for NDEs (Lynn et al., 2010).

◄ **OCCAM'S RAZOR**
Does a simpler explanation fit the data just as well?

from inquiry to understanding

WHY DO WE EXPERIENCE DÉJÀ VU?

Have you ever been talking to a friend and noticed that the conversation and surroundings seemed strangely familiar? Or traveled somewhere new and felt like you've been there before? When your text's author first visited his undergraduate alma mater, Cornell University, he had the unmistakable feeling of having seen the campus even though he'd never been there before. If you've had one or more of these eerie 10–30 second flashes of familiarity, you've experienced **déjà vu**, which is French for "already seen." More than two-thirds of us have experienced at least one episode of déjà vu (Adachi et al., 2008). How can we explain the origins of déjà vu?

Although some have proposed that the déjà vu experience is a memory from a past life, this explanation is unfalsifiable and therefore outside the boundaries of science (Stevenson, 1960). Research conducted in the field of biopsychology offers more promising clues. An excess of the neurotransmitter dopamine in the temporal lobes may play a role in déjà vu (Taiminen & Jääskeläinen, 2001). In addition, people who experience small seizures in the right temporal lobe, which is largely responsible for feelings of familiarity, sometimes experience déjà vu right before a seizure (Bancaud et al., 1994). Other work on rodents raises the possiblity that closely interconnected brain areas that normally allow organisms to distinguish between two similar physical contexts may occasionally fail to communicate, perhaps explaining déjà vu experiences in humans (McHugh et al., 2007). Yet until recently, the hallmark of these fleeting illusions—the simultaneous sense of newness and familiarity—has not been well understood or studied under carefully controlled laboratory conditions.

A team of researchers recently used virtual reality technology to test the hypothesis that déjà vu arises when a present experience resembles an earlier one. Their research was guided by the idea that the sense of familiarity occurs when we don't consciously recall the previous experience. Perhaps we've driven by a park many times without ever noticing it, but our minds processed the information unconsciously (Strayer, Drews, & Johnston, 2003). So when we drive by the park some time later, it's "déjà vu all over again."

Anne Cleary and her colleagues (Cleary et al., 2012) outfitted participants with a head-mounted display that gave the impression they were immersed inside a 3-dimensional scene. Participants could turn their heads left or right, or look up or down to view the scene from different angles and perspectives. Cleary asked them to report whether they experienced déjà vu while viewing the scene, and defined déjà vu for participants as, "A feeling of having been somewhere or done something before, despite knowing that the current situation is new". According to the researchers' familiarity hypothesis, déjà vu arises when the arrangement of elements within a scene maps onto an arrangement previously seen, but the previous scene fails to come to mind. When participants viewed a novel scene whose key elements were arranged in a similar manner to a previously-viewed scene, such as a bedroom or a bowling alley, but failed to recall that scene, they reported higher familiarity ratings and more frequent déjà vu than for completely novel scenes. The more the new scenes resembled the previously viewed scenes, the more often they reported déjà vu.

◄ **FALSIFIABILITY**
Can the claim be disproved?

(© Chris Slane)

déjà vu
feeling of reliving an experience that's new

The researchers concluded that the matching of features of the scenes produces familiarity and déjà vu when participants can't recall the previous scene.

This conclusion may fit with findings that people who are frequently travelers often experience déjà vu (Brown, 2003, 2004a), because they have many opportunities to encounter similar scenes in different places. Still, Cleary and co-authors' fascinating research leaves open the question of why certain people, especially those who are young and politically liberal (Brown, 2004a), are prone to déjà vu. Some of the mysteries of déjà vu remain to be solved.

Mystical Experiences

A 30-year-old male who was listening to the rock band ABBA described a profound mystical experience in this way. He imagined gazing at a star-studded night sky; suddenly, his consciousness, not his physical body, started to travel up toward the stars. While he no longer paid attention to the music, even though it continued to play, he experienced his consciousness accelerating and expanding at a tremendous rate into the cosmos before finally returning to his body (Mystical Experience Registry, 2012).

Mystical experiences, like those reported by this lover of ABBA's music, can last for only a few moments yet often leave lasting, even lifelong, impressions. These experiences, although often difficult to put into words, often involve a sense of unity or oneness with the world, transcendence of time and space, and feelings of wonder and awe. These phenomena often have strong spiritual overtones and may have contributed to the formation of many world religions and have been reported through the ages in association with prayer, fasting, meditation, and social isolation (Wulff, in press). Yet they differ across religious faiths. Christians often describe mystical experiences in terms of an awe-inspiring merging with God's presence. In contrast, Buddhists, whose spiritual practices focus more on achieving personal enlightenment than worship of a deity, often describe mystical incidents in terms of bliss and selfless peace. Although shaped by learning and culture, each person's mystical experience is probably unique. As many as 35 percent of Americans say they've felt very close to a powerful, uplifting spiritual force at least once (Greeley, 1975).

Because intense mystical experiences are rare, unpredictable, and often fleeting, they're difficult to study in the laboratory (Wulff, in press). Nevertheless, scientists have recently begun to probe their mysteries. One approach is to induce mystical experiences and examine their consequences. Adopting this approach, researchers used fMRI to scan the brains of 15 Roman Catholic nuns after asking them to close their eyes and relive the most intense mystical occurrence they'd ever experienced (Beauregard & Paquette, 2006). They also instructed them to relive the most intense state of union with another human they'd felt as a nun. Compared with a condition in which the nuns sat quietly with eyes closed and the condition in which the nuns relived the interpersonal experience, the "mystical experiences" condition produced distinctive patterns of brain activation. In fact, at least 12 areas of the brain associated with emotion, perception, and cognition became active when the nuns relived mystical experiences. We can question whether the researchers actually captured mystical experiences. Reliving an experience in the laboratory may differ from more spontaneous mystical events produced by fasting, prayer, fevers, seizures in the temporal lobes, or meditation (Geschwind, 1983; Persinger, 1987).

In the second approach, neuroscientists (Griffiths et al., 2008; Griffiths et al., 2011) asked 36 participants without any personal or family history of mental illness to ingest psilocybin, a hallucinogenic drug that affects serotonin receptors and is the active ingredient in the sacred mushroom, used for centuries in religious ceremonies. At follow-up 14 months later, 58 percent of participants who ingested psilocybin reported a mystical experience they claimed was one of the most meaningful events of their lives. Additionally, about two thirds of the participants rated the experience as one of their top five most spiritually significant moments and reported increases in life satisfaction. The percentages of mystical and positive experiences were much lower among participants

mystical experience
feelings of unity or oneness with the world, often with strong spiritual overtones

who ingested a placebo. People who ingested psilocybin also reported increases in their ability to be open to experience (MacLean et al., 2012). In another study (Grob et al., 2011), patients with advanced cancer reported improvements in mood and anxiety following psilocybin that lasted for three months. Still, we should keep in mind that even with tightly controlled and emotionally supportive experimental procedures in place, some participants (31%, Griffiths et al, 2008) reported extreme fears and paranoia during the session, whereas in the placebo condition, none reported such fears. This research offers a glimpse of the promise of studying mystical experiences in the laboratory, while reminding us that caution is called for in using hallucinogenic drugs that can induce negative as well as positive feelings.

Hypnosis

Hypnosis is a set of techniques that provides people with suggestions for alterations in their perceptions and sensations, thoughts, feelings, memories, and behaviors (Kirsch & Lynn, 1998). To increase people's suggestibility, most hypnotists use an *induction method*, which typically includes suggestions for relaxation, calmness, and well-being, along with instructions to imagine or think about pleasant experiences (Kirsch, 1994). When suggestions are self-administered, the procedures are called self-hypnosis.

Once regarded as largely pseudoscientific, hypnosis has moved into the mainstream of science and clinical practice. Based on reliable and valid scales, scientists have established that approximately 15 to 20 percent of people pass very few (0–3 out of 12) suggestions (low suggestibles); another 15 to 20 percent pass 9–12 of the suggestions (high suggestibles); and the remaining 60 to 70 percent pass 5–8 suggestions (medium suggestibles).

Hypnosis enjoys a wide range of clinical applications. Studies show that hypnosis enhances the effectiveness of cognitive-behavioral psychotherapies (Kirsch, 1990; Kirsch, Montgomery, & Sapirstein, 1995). Hypnosis is also useful for treating pain, medical conditions, obesity, anxiety, and habit disorders (such as smoking addiction; Lynn, Rhue, & Kirsch, 2011) (see **FIGURE 5**). Nevertheless, the extent to which the benefits associated with hypnosis in these cases are attributable to something unique to hypnosis itself, as opposed to relaxation or enhanced expectancies for improvement, remains unclear. Because there's no evidence that hypnosis is an effective treatment by itself, we should be skeptical of professional "hypnotherapists" (many of whom we can find in our local Yellow Pages or the Internet who use nothing but hypnosis to treat serious psychological problems).

MYTHS AND FACTS ABOUT HYPNOSIS: WHAT HYPNOSIS ISN'T AND WHAT IT IS Despite the increasingly warm embrace of hypnosis by the professional community, public knowledge about hypnosis hasn't kept pace with scientific developments. We'll first examine six misconceptions about hypnosis and correct them with scientifically-based evidence. Then, we'll evaluate two prominent theories of how hypnosis works.

Myth and Fact 1: Hypnosis Produces a Trance State in Which "Amazing" Things Happen. Consider a sampling of movies that portray the hypnotic trance state as so overpowering that otherwise normal people will: (a) commit suicide (*The Garden Murders*); (b) disfigure themselves with scalding water (*The Hypnotic Eye*); (c) assist in blackmail (*On Her Majesty's Secret Service*); (d) perceive only a person's internal beauty (*Shallow Hal*); (e) experience total bliss (*Office Space*), (f) steal (*Curse of the Jade Scorpion*); and our favorite, (g) fall victim to brainwashing by alien preachers using messages in sermons (*Invasion of the Space Preachers*).

PARIS, DELARUE Éditeur 5, R des GRANDS AUGUSTINS

Hypnosis has fascinated scientists and clinical practitioners for more than two centuries, yet the basic methods for inducing hypnosis have changed little over the years.

Watch in **MyPsychLab** the **Video:** Thinking Like a Psychologist: The Uses and Limitations of Hypnosis

◄ **RULING OUT RIVAL HYPOTHESES** Have important alternative explanations for the findings been excluded?

Stop Smoking Forever with Hypnosis.

FIGURE 5 Anti-Smoking Ad. Many advertisements for the effectiveness of hypnosis in treating smoking are misleading and exaggerated. Still, hypnosis can sometimes be combined with well-established treatment approaches as a cost-effective means of helping some people quit smoking.

hypnosis
set of techniques that provides people with suggestions for alterations in their perceptions, thoughts, feelings, and behaviors

This classic picture of a person suspended between two chairs illustrates the "human plank phenomenon," often demonstrated at stage hypnosis shows as "proof" of the special powers of hypnosis. In actuality, people who stiffen their bodies can do this without hypnosis; however, we don't recommend you try it. If the chairs aren't placed properly, the person can be injured.

Other popular stereotypes of hypnosis derive from *stage hypnosis* shows, in which hypnotists seemingly program people to enact commands ranging from quacking like a duck to playing a wicked air guitar to the music of U2. But the wacky actions of people in movies and onstage have nothing to do with a trance state. In stage shows, the hypnotist carefully selects potential performers by observing how they respond to waking imaginative suggestions, which are highly correlated with how people respond to hypnotic suggestions (Braffman & Kirsch, 1999). Those whose outstretched hands drop or sag when asked to imagine holding a heavy dictionary are likely to be invited onstage because they're probably highly suggestible to begin with. Moreover, "hypnotized" volunteers often feel compelled to do outlandish things because they're under intense pressure to entertain the audience. Some stage hypnotists even whisper instructions to volunteers to get people to comply and make it a lively show ("When I snap my fingers, bark like a dog": Meeker & Barber, 1971). What's more, some of the tricks we see in stage hypnosis shows, like suspending volunteers between the tops of two chairs, are easily duplicated in highly motivated participants without hypnosis.

Actually, hypnosis doesn't have a great impact on suggestibility. A person who responds to six out of 12 suggestions without being hypnotized might respond to seven or eight after hypnosis (Kirsch & Lynn, 1995). In addition, people can resist and even oppose hypnotic suggestions at will (Lynn, Rhue, & Weekes, 1990). So, Hollywood thrillers aside, hypnosis can't turn a mild-mannered person into a mindless robot or cold-blooded murderer.

People who perform in stage hypnosis shows are carefully selected before the performance for high suggestibility.

RULING OUT RIVAL HYPOTHESES ▶
Have important alternative explanations for the findings been excluded?

Myth and Fact 2: Hypnotic Phenomena Are Unique. Scientists haven't yet identified any unique physiological states or markers of hypnosis (Dixon & Laurence, 1992; Hasegawa & Jamieson, 2002; Sarbin & Slagle, 1979; Wagstaff, 1998). Still, Kallio and colleagues (2011) recently claimed to have found evidence that the "hypnotic stare" is a unique marker of the trance state supposedly associated with hypnosis. The researchers tested a single highly hypnotizable participant whose eyes appeared to be wide and glassy during hypnosis, much like those of hypnotized participants portrayed in movies. What intrigued the researchers was that this participant did not show typical automatic eye movements in response to visual stimuli presented during hypnosis, and participants low in hypnotizability who tried to fake being hypnotized could not duplicate this feat. The problem in drawing conclusions from this study is that the result is based on only one participant, so it's questionable whether other highly suggestible people would respond similarly. The researchers might have done little more than identified a person who displays highly unusual responses to visual stimuli regardless of whether she was hypnotized. In fact, contrary to popular belief, people can experience many hypnotic phenomena, such as hallucinations and pain insensitivity, when they receive suggestions alone, even without hypnosis (Barber, 1969; Sarbin & Coe, 1979; Spanos, 1986, 1991).

Myth and Fact 3: Hypnosis Is a Sleeplike State. James Braid (1843), a Scottish physician, claimed that the hypnotized brain produces a condition akin to sleep. Braid labeled the phenomenon *neurohypnosis* (from the Greek word hypno, meaning "sleep"), and the shortened term "hypnosis" eventually stuck. Yet people who are hypnotized don't show brain waves similar to those of sleep. What's more, people are just as responsive to hypnotic suggestions administered while exercising on a stationary bicycle as they are following hypnotic suggestions for sleep and relaxation (Bányai & Hilgard, 1976; Wark, 2006).

Myth and Fact 4: Hypnotized People Are Unaware of Their Surroundings. Another popular idea is that hypnotized people are so entranced that they lose touch with their surroundings. Actually, most hypnotized people are fully aware of their immediate surroundings and can even recall the details of a telephone conversation they overheard during hypnosis (Lynn, Weekes, & Milano, 1989).

Myth and Fact 5: Hypnotized People Forget What Happened during Hypnosis. In the 1962 film *The Manchurian Candidate,* remade in 2004, a person is programmed by hypnosis to commit an assassination and has no memory of what occurred during hypnosis. In real life, *spontaneous amnesia* for what happens during hypnosis is rare and mostly limited to people who expect to be amnesic following hypnosis (Simon & Salzberg, 1985; Young & Cooper, 1972).

Myth 6: Hypnosis Enhances Memory. In 1976 in Chowchilla, California, three young men intent on committing the "perfect crime" kidnapped 26 children and their bus driver. The blundering criminals didn't expect their captives to escape after being hidden underground for six hours. After police apprehended the criminals, the bus driver was hypnotized and correctly provided numbers from the license plate of the kidnappers' car. The media used this now famous case to publicize the power of hypnosis to enhance recall. The problem is that the anecdote doesn't tell us whether hypnosis was responsible for what the driver remembered. Perhaps the driver recalled the event because people often can remember additional details when they try to recall an event a second time, regardless of whether they're hypnotized.

Moreover, the media tend not to report the scores of cases in which hypnosis fails to enhance memory, such as a Brinks armored car robbery that took place in Boston (Kihlstrom, 1987). In this case, the witness was hypnotized and confidently recalled the license plate of the car of the president of Harvard University, where the witness was employed. Apparently, he confused a car he'd seen multiple times with the car involved in the robbery.

Scientific studies generally reveal that hypnosis doesn't improve memory (Erdelyi, 1994; Mazzoni, Heap, & Scoboria, 2010). Hypnosis does increase the amount of information we recall, but much of it is inaccurate (Erdelyi, 1994; Steblay & Bothwell, 1994; Wagstaff, 2008). To make matters worse, hypnosis tends to increase eyewitnesses' confidence in inaccurate, as well as accurate, memories (Green & Lynn, 2005). Indeed, courts in most U.S. states have banned the testimony of hypnotized witnesses out of concerns that their inaccurate statements will sway a jury and lead to wrongful convictions.

THEORIES OF HYPNOSIS. Researchers have attempted to explain hypnosis in terms of unconscious drives and motivations, a willingness to overlook logical inconsistencies, enhanced receptivity to suggestion, and an inhibition of the brain's frontal lobes (Lynn & Rhue; 1991; Nash & Barnier, 2008; Sheehan & McConkey, 1986). Each of these theories has contributed valuable insights into hypnotic phenomena. Nevertheless, two other models, the sociocognitive theory and the dissociation theory, have received the lion's share of attention.

Sociocognitive Theory. Sociocognitive theorists (Barber, 1969; Coe & Sarbin, 1991; Lynn, Kirsch, & Hallquist, 2008; Spanos, 1986) reject the idea that hypnosis is a trance state or unique state of consciousness. Instead, they explain hypnosis in the same way they explain everyday social behaviors. According to **sociocognitive theory**, people's attitudes, beliefs, motivations, and expectations about hypnosis, as well as their ability to respond to waking imaginative suggestions, shape their responses to hypnosis.

Consistent with sociocognitive theory, peoples' expectations of whether they'll respond to hypnotic suggestions are correlated with how they respond (Kirsch & Council, 1992). Still, this correlation doesn't necessarily mean that people's expectations cause them to be susceptible to hypnosis. Studies in which participants' responses vary

Hypnotists frequently present participants with the suggestion that one of their arms is lifting involuntarily.

◀ **RULING OUT RIVAL HYPOTHESES**
Have important alternative explanations for the findings been excluded?

sociocognitive theory
approach to explaining hypnosis based on people's attitudes, beliefs, expectations, and responsiveness to waking suggestions

◀ **CORRELATION VS. CAUSATION**
Can we be sure that A causes B?

Researchers have used the Poggendorf illusion, shown above, to study the effects of hypnotic age regression. Adults tend to see the two segments of the black line as misaligned (in reality, they're perfectly aligned), whereas children don't. When adult participants are age-regressed to childhood, they still see the two segments of the black line as misaligned, suggesting that hypnotic age regression doesn't make adults' perceptions more childlike (Ascher, Barber, & Spanos, 1972; Nash, 1987).

psycho**mythology**

AGE REGRESSION AND PAST LIVES

One of the most popular myths of hypnosis is that it can help people retrieve memories of events as far back in time as birth. A televised documentary (Bikel, 1995) showed a group therapy session in which a woman was age-regressed through childhood, to the womb, and eventually to being trapped in her mother's fallopian tube. The woman provided a highly emotional demonstration of the discomfort that one would experience if one were indeed stuck in such an uncomfortable position. Although the woman may have believed in the reality of her experience, we can be quite certain that it wasn't memory based (after all, she didn't have a brain yet, because she wasn't even a fertilized egg at this point). Instead, age-regressed participants behave the way they think children should behave. Age-regressed adults don't show the expected patterns on many indices of development. For example, when regressed to childhood, they exhibit the brain waves (EEGs) typical of adults rather than of children. No matter how compelling, age-regressed experiences aren't exact mental replicas of childhood experiences (Nash, 1987).

Some therapists believe that they can trace their patients' current problems to previous lives and practice **past-life regression therapy** (Weiss, 1988). Typically, they hypnotize and age-regressed patients to "go back to" the source of their present-day problems. For example, some practitioners of past-life regression therapy claim that neck and shoulder pains may be signs of having been executed by hanging or by a guillotine in a previous life.

With rare exceptions (Stevenson, 1974), researchers believe that reports of a past life are the products of imagination and what hypnotized participants know about a given time period. When checked against known facts (such as whether the country was at war or peace, the face on the coin of the time), participants' descriptions of the historical circumstances of their supposed past lives are rarely accurate. When they are, we can often explain this accuracy by "educated guesses" and knowledge of history (Spanos et al., 1991). For example, one participant regressed to ancient times claimed to be Julius Caesar, emperor of Rome, in 50 B.C., even though the designations of B.C. and A.D. weren't adopted until centuries later and even though Julius Caesar died decades before the first Roman emperor came to power.

past-life regression therapy
therapeutic approach that hypnotizes and supposedly age-regresses patients to a previous life to identify the source of a present-day problem

dissociation theory
approach to explaining hypnosis based on a separation between personality functions that are normally well integrated

RULING OUT RIVAL HYPOTHESES ▶

Have important alternative explanations for the findings been excluded?

as a function of what they're told about hypnosis provide more convincing evidence of causality. Participants told that hypnotized people can resist suggestions find themselves able to resist, whereas those told that hypnotized people can't resist suggestions often fail to resist (Lynn et al., 1984; Spanos, Cobb, & Gorassini, 1985).

Studies show that a training program that increases people's positive feelings and expectancies about hypnosis and their willingness to imagine along with suggestions increases their ability to respond to hypnosis (Gorassini & Spanos, 1998). About half of participants who initially scored at the lowest range of suggestibility tested at the top range after training. These findings both challenge the idea that hypnotic suggestibility is a stable trait that can't be modified (Piccione, Hilgard, & Zimbardo, 1989) and offer support for sociocognitive theory.

Dissociation Theory. Ernest Hilgard's (1977, 1986, 1994) **dissociation theory** is an influential alternative to sociocognitive theories of hypnosis (Kihlstrom, 1992, 1998; Woody & Sadler, 2008). Hilgard (1977) defined *dissociation* as a division of consciousness, in which attention, effort, and planning are carried out without awareness. He hypothesized that hypnotic suggestions result in a separation between personality functions that are normally well integrated.

Hilgard (1977) happened on a discovery that played a key role in the development of his theory. During a demonstration of hypnotically suggested deafness, a student asked whether some part of the person could hear. Hilgard then told the participant that when he touched the participant's arm he'd be able to talk to the part that could hear if such a part existed. When Hilgard placed his hand on the participant's arm, the participant described what people in the room said. However, when Hilgard removed his hand, the participant was again "deaf." Hilgard invented the metaphor of the *hidden observer* to describe the dissociated, unhypnotized "part" of the mind that he could access on cue.

Later researchers suggested an alternative explanation for the hidden observer phenomenon (Kirsch & Lynn, 1998; Spanos, 1986, 1991). Nicholas Spanos (1991) believed that the hidden observer arises because the hypnotist suggests it directly or indirectly. That is, participants pick up on the fact that the instructions used to bring forth the hidden observer imply they should act as though a separate, nonhypnotized part of the person can communicate with the hypnotist. Spanos hypothesized that changing the instructions should change what the hidden observer reports. That's exactly what he found. Changing the instructions led hidden observers to experience more pain or less pain, or to perceive a number normally or in reverse (Spanos & Hewitt, 1980). In short, the hidden observer appears to be no different from any other suggested hypnotic response: It's shaped by what we expect and believe.

According to a revision of Hilgard's dissociation theory (Woody & Bowers, 1994), hypnosis bypasses the ordinary sense of control we exert over our behaviors. Thus, suggestions directly bring about responses with little or no sense of effort or conscious control (Jamieson & Sheehan, 2004; Sadler & Woody, 2010). This theory does a good job of describing what people experience during hypnosis and fits nicely with sociocognitive theories that emphasize the unconscious, automatic nature of most behaviors both within and apart from the context of hypnosis (Lynn & Green, 2011).

◀ **RULING OUT RIVAL HYPOTHESES**
Have important alternative explanations for the findings been excluded?

Assess Your Knowledge — FACT or FICTION?

1. College students rarely, if ever, report that they hallucinate.   **True / False**

2. OBEs are related to the ability to fantasize.   **True / False**

3. Many of the experiences associated with a NDE can be created in circumstances that have nothing to do with being "near death."   **True / False**

4. Déjà vu experiences often last for as long as an hour.   **True / False**

5. A hypnosis induction greatly increases suggestibility beyond waking suggestibility.
True / False

Answers: 1. F, 2. T, 3. T, 4. F, 5. F

✓ **Study** and **Review** in **MyPsychLab**

Drugs and Consciousness

8 Identify possible influences on substance use.

9 Distinguish different types of drugs and their effects on consciousness.

Virtually every culture has discovered that certain plants can alter consciousness, often dramatically. Knowledge of the mind-bending qualities of fermented fruits and grains, the juice of the poppy, boiled coffee beans and tea leaves, the burning tobacco or marijuana leaf, certain molds that grow on crops, and the granulated extract of the coca leaf has been handed down to us from ancient times. We now know that these **psychoactive drugs** contain chemicals similar to those found naturally in our brains and that their molecules alter consciousness by changing chemical processes in neurons. Some psychoactive drugs are used to treat physical and mental illness, but others are used almost exclusively for recreational purposes. The precise psychological and physical effects depend on the type of drug and dosage, as we've summarized in **TABLE 3**.

psychoactive drug
substance that contains chemicals similar to those found naturally in our brains that alter consciousness by changing chemical processes in neurons

TABLE 3 Major Drug Types and Their Effects.

DRUG TYPE	EXAMPLES	EFFECT ON BEHAVIOR
Depressants	Alcohol, barbiturates, Quaaludes, Valium	Decreased activity of the central nervous system (initial high followed by sleepiness, slower thinking, and impaired concentration)
Stimulants	Tobacco, cocaine, amphetamines, methamphetamine	Increased activity of the central nervous system (sense of alertness, well-being, energy)
Opiates	Heroin, morphine, codeine	Sense of euphoria, decreased pain
Psychedelics	Marijuana, LSD, Ecstasy	Dramatically altered perception, mood, and thoughts

But as we'll see, the effects of drugs depend on far more than their chemical properties. *Mental set*—beliefs and expectancies about the effects of drugs—the settings in which people take these drugs, and their cultural heritage and genetic endowment all play a part in accounting for the highs and lows of drug use.

Substance Use Disorders

Drugs are substances that change the way we think, feel, or act. It's easy to forget that alcohol and nicotine are drugs, because they're typically commonplace and legal. Still, the misuse of both legal and illegal drugs is a serious societal problem. According to a national survey (Johnston et al., 2009a), 66 percent of young people (ages 29–30) reported having tried marijuana, and 48 percent report having tried other illegal drugs, like cocaine, heroin, and hallucinogens.

DIAGNOSIS OF SUBSTANCE USE DISORDER. Generally speaking, people qualify for a diagnosis of *substance use disorder* when they experience recurrent significant impairment or distress associated with one or more drugs (APA, 2013). Substance use disorder is a new diagnostic category to appear in the forthcoming editon of the American Psychiatric Association's diagnostic manual. The new diagnosis combines the previous diagnostic categories of substance abuse, which encompasses recurrent problems with substances in the home, work, school, or with the law, and substance dependence, which includes symptoms of tolerance and withdrawal. The new diagnostic scheme considers the full range of alcohol-related problems and emphasizes the severity of these problems, rather than a sharp distinction between the former categories of substance abuse and dependence.

Tolerance, a key feature of substance use disorders, occurs when people need to consume an increased amount of a drug to achieve intoxication. Alternatively, people who develop tolerance may not obtain the same reaction or "kick" from a drug after using it for some time. Tolerance is often associated with increases in the amount of drugs people consume. When people use drugs for long periods of time and then either stop or cut down on their use, they're likely to experience **withdrawal** symptoms that vary with the drug they use. Alcohol withdrawal symptoms, for example, can range from insomnia and mild anxiety to more severe symptoms such as seizures, confusion, and bizarre visual hallucinations (Bayard et al., 2004). People exhibit **physical dependence** on a drug when they continue to take it to avoid withdrawal symptoms. In contrast, people can develop **psychological dependence** when their continued use of a drug is motivated by intense cravings. According to one survey (Knight et al., 2002), within a 12-month period, 6 percent of college students reported severe symptoms of alcohol use, including tolerance and withdrawal and 31 percent reported significant problems with alcohol that met criteria for substance abuse.

tolerance
reduction in the effect of a drug as a result of repeated use, requiring users to consume greater quantities to achieve the same effect

withdrawal
unpleasant effects of reducing or stopping consumption of a drug that users had consumed habitually

physical dependence
dependence on a drug that occurs when people continue to take it to avoid withdrawal symptoms

psychological dependence
dependence on a drug that occurs when continued use of the drug is motivated by intense cravings

 Watch in **MyPsychLab** the **Video:**
Speaking Out: Chris: Alcoholism

EXPLANATIONS FOR SUBSTANCE USE. People often begin using drugs when they become available, when their family or peers approve of them, and when they don't anticipate serious consequences from their use (Pihl, 1999). Illegal drug use typically starts in early adolescence, peaks in early adulthood, and declines sharply thereafter. Fortunately, later in life, pressures to be employed and establish a family often counteract earlier pressures and attitudes associated with drug use (Newcomb & Bentler, 1988). In the sections to come, we'll focus on the causes of alcohol use disorders because they're the forms of drug misuse that scientists best understand.

Sociocultural Influences. Cultures or groups in which drinking is strictly prohibited, such as Muslims or Mormons, exhibit low rates of alcoholism (substance use disorder, with tolerance and withdrawal symptoms; Chentsova-Dutton & Tsai, 2006). In Egypt, the annual rate of alcohol dependence is only 0.2 percent (World Health Organization, 2004), whereas in France and Italy, where they view drinking as a healthy part of daily life, the rates are considerably higher. In Poland, the annual rate is 11.2 percent. Some researchers attribute these differences to cultural differences in attitudes toward alcohol and its abuse. Nevertheless, these differences could also be due in part to genetic influences, and the cultural attitudes themselves may reflect these differences.

◀ **RULING OUT RIVAL HYPOTHESES**
Have important alternative explanations for the findings been excluded?

Is There an Addictive Personality? Important as they are, sociocultural factors don't easily explain individual differences *within* cultures. We can find alcoholics in societies with strong sanctions against drinking and teetotalers in societies in which drinking is widespread. To explain these facts, popular and scientific psychologists alike have long wondered whether certain people have an "addictive personality" that predisposes them to abuse alcohol and other drugs (Shaffer, 2000). On the one hand, research suggests that common wisdom to the contrary, there's no single addictive personality profile (Rozin & Stoess, 1993). On the other hand, researchers have found that certain personality traits predispose to alcohol and drug abuse. In particular, studies have tied substance abuse to impulsivity (Baker & Yardley, 2002; Kanzler & Rosenthal, 2003; Kollins, 2003), sociability (Wennberg, 2002), and a propensity to experience negative emotions, like anxiety and hostility (Jackson & Sher, 2003). But some of these traits may partly result from, rather than cause, substance misuse. Also, as we'll soon learn, genetic influences appear to account at least in part for both antisocial behavior and alcoholism risk (Slutske et al., 1998).

◀ **CORRELATION VS. CAUSATION**
Can we be sure that A causes B?

Learning and Expectancies. According to the tension reduction hypothesis (Cappell & Herman, 1972; Sayette, 1999; Sher, 1987), people consume alcohol and other drugs to relieve anxiety. Such self-medication reinforces drug use, increasing the probability of continued use. Alcohol affects brain centers involved in reward (Koob, 2000) as well as dopamine, which plays a crucial role in reward. Nevertheless, people probably drink to relieve anxiety only when they believe alcohol is a stress reducer (Greeley & Oei, 1999), so expectancies almost certainly play a role, too. But once individuals become dependent on alcohol, the discomfort of their withdrawal symptoms can motivate drug-seeking behavior and continued use.

Genetic Influences. Alcoholism tends to run in families (Sher, Grekin, & Williams, 2005). But this doesn't tell us whether this finding is due to genes, shared environment, or both. Twin and adoption studies have resolved the issue: They show that genetic factors play a key role in the vulnerability to alcoholism (McGue, 1999). Multiple genes are probably involved (NIAAA, 2000), but what's inherited? No one knows for sure, but researchers have uncovered a genetic link between people's response to alcohol and their risk of developing alcoholism. A strong negative reaction to alcohol use decreases the risk of alcoholism, whereas a weak response increases this risk. A mutation in the aldehyde 2 (ALDH2) gene causes a distinctly unpleasant response to alcohol: facial flushing, heart palpitations (feeling one's heart beating), and nausea (Higuchi et al., 1995). This gene is present in about 40 percent of people of Asian descent, who are at low risk for alcoholism and drink less alcohol than people in most other ethnic groups (Cook & Wall, 2005).

◀ **RULING OUT RIVAL HYPOTHESES**
Have important alternative explanations for the findings been excluded?

Like some people of Asian heritage, this person shows a pronounced flushing response after having a drink, as seen in this before and after panel. **Based on the research literature, is he likely to be at increased or decreased risk for alcohol problems in later life compared with most people?** (See answer upside-down at bottom of page).

Marc Schuckit (1994) argued that a genetically influenced weak response to alcohol contributes to a desire to drink heavily to achieve the pleasurable effects of intoxication. To determine whether reactions to alcohol predict alcohol abuse, Schuckit (1998) followed 435 20-year-olds for 10 years. Those with an initial weak response to alcohol displayed a fourfold increase in their risk for alcoholism at age 30. Recently, researchers confirmed Schuckit's claim and identified a gene on chromosome 15 that, perhaps in conjunction with unknown environmental factors, may be associated with a weak response to alcohol (Joslyn et al., 2008).

Depressants

Alcohol and sedative-hypnotics (barbiturates and benzodiazepines) are depressant drugs, so-called because they depress the effects of the central nervous system. By the way, **sedative** means "calming," and **hypnotic** means "sleep-inducing" (despite its name, it doesn't mean "hypnosis-inducing"). In contrast, stimulant drugs, like nicotine and cocaine, which we'll review in the next section, rev up our central nervous systems. We'll learn that the effects of alcohol are remarkably wide-ranging, varying from stimulation at low doses to sedation at higher doses.

ALCOHOL. Humanity has long had an intimate relationship with alcohol. Some scientists speculate that a long-forgotten person from the late Stone Age, perhaps 10,000 years ago, accidentally partook of a jar of honey that had been left out too long (Vallee, 1988). He or she became the first human to drink alcohol, and the human race has never been quite the same since. Today, alcohol is the most widely used and abused drug. By late adolescence, 78.2 percent of young adults have consumed alcohol (Swendsen et al., 2012). The majority (51.8 percent) of adult men in our society report they regularly use alcohol (at least 12 drinks in the past year; Centers for Disease Control, 2011), and 39 percent of 8th graders report that they tried alcohol at one time (Johnston et al., 2009b).

We must look to the effects of alcohol to understand its powerful appeal. Although many people believe that alcohol is a stimulant, physiologically it's primarily a depressant. Alcohol behaves as an emotional and physiological stimulant only at relatively low doses because it depresses areas of the brain that inhibit emotion and behavior (Pohorecky, 1977; Tucker, Vucinich, & Sobell, 1982). Small amounts of alcohol can promote feelings of relaxation, elevate mood, increase talkativeness and activity, lower inhibitions, and impair judgment. In most states, a BAC of 0.08 is the cutoff for legal intoxication while operating a vehicle; at this point the operation of an automobile is hazardous. At higher doses, when the blood alcohol content (BAC)—the concentration of alcohol in the blood—reaches 0.05 to 0.10, the sedating and depressant effects of alcohol generally become more apparent. Brain centers become depressed, slowing thinking and impairing concentration, walking, and muscular coordination (Erblich et al., 2003). At higher doses, users sometimes experience a mix of stimulating and sedating effects (King et al., 2002).

The short-term effects of intoxication are directly related to the BAC. Contrary to popular myth, switching among different types of alcohol—like beer, wine, and hard liquor—is no more likely to lead to drunkenness than sticking with one type of alcohol (see **TABLE 4**). The feeling of intoxication depends largely on the rate of absorption of alcohol by the bloodstream, mostly through the stomach and intestines. The more food in our stomach, the less quickly alcohol is absorbed. This fact explains why we feel more of an effect of alcohol on an empty stomach. Compared with men, women have more body fat (alcohol isn't fat-soluble) and less water in which to dilute alcohol. So a woman whose weight equals that of a man, and has consumed the same amount of alcohol, will have a higher BAC than he will (Kinney & Leaton, 1995). **FIGURE 6** shows the relationship between the amounts of beverage consumed and alcohol concentration in the blood. Because absorption varies as a function of variables like stomach contents and body weight, these effects vary across persons and occasions.

Although drug effects are influenced by the dose of the drug, the user's expectancies also play a substantial role. The *balanced placebo design* is a four-group

sedative
drug that exerts a calming effect

hypnotic
drug that exerts a sleep-inducing effect

Answer: Decreased.

TABLE 4 Six Other Alcohol Myths and Facts. Although we've addressed some popular misconceptions about alcohol in the text, there are scores of others. How many of these have you heard?

MISCONCEPTION	TRUTH
1. Every time we drink, we destroy about 10,000 brain cells.	Scientists haven't precisely determined the effect of a single drink on brain cell loss. Heavy drinking over time is associated with brain damage and memory problems.
2. It's okay to drive a few hours after drinking.	Coordination can be affected as much as 10–12 hours after drinking, so it's not safe to drink and drive. Binge-drinking (five or more drinks at a time if male; four, if female) is associated with 80 percent of traffic accidents (Marczinski, Harrison, & Fillmore, 2008).
3. To avoid a hangover, take two or three acetaminophen tablets, a common alternative to aspirin, or an energy drink with caffeine.	Taking acetaminophen tablets can increase the toxicity of alcohol to the liver. Energy drinks do not affect blood alcohol levels and increase the likelihood of binge drinking three-fold (Thombs et al., 2010).
4. Our judgment isn't impaired until we're extremely drunk.	Impaired judgment can occur well before obvious signs of intoxication appear.
5. A "blackout" is passing out from drinking.	A "blackout" is a loss of memory for a period of time while drunk, and has nothing to do with passing out.
6. Mixing diet drinks with alcohol reduces the risk of intoxication.	Mixing diet soda with alcohol increases breath alcohol concentrations by 18 percent, increasing the risk of intoxication (Marczinski & Stamates, 2012).

FIGURE 6 Influences on BAC. A person's blood alcohol content (BAC) depends on a variety of factors beyond the number of drinks consumed. The person's weight, gender, and stomach contents all play a role. This graph shows how body weight and gender influence BAC. For both men and women, heavier people have a lower BAC, but at both 120 pounds and 160 pounds, women have a higher BAC than men.

FIGURE 7 The Four Groups of the Balanced Placebo Design. The balanced-placebo design includes four groups in which participants (a) are told they're receiving a drug and in fact receive a drug, (b) are told they're receiving a drug but actually receive a placebo, (c) are told they're receiving a placebo but actually receive a drug, and (d) are told they're receiving a placebo and in fact receive a placebo.

design (see **FIGURE 7**) in which researchers tell participants they either are, or aren't, receiving an active drug and, in fact, either do or don't receive it (Kirsch, 2003). This clever design allows researchers to tease apart the relative influence of expectancies (placebo effects) and the physiological effects of alcohol and other drugs.

The results of balanced placebo studies show that at low alcohol dose levels, culturally learned expectancies influence mood and complex social behaviors. Remarkably, participants who ingest a placebo drink mixed to taste just like alcohol display many of the same subjective effects of drunkenness as participants who ingest an actual alcoholic drink. Expectancies are often more important than the physiological effects of alcohol in influencing social behaviors, such as aggression (Lang et al., 1975). Alcohol may provide some people with an excuse to engage in actions that are socially prohibited or discouraged, like flirting (Hull & Bond, 1986). In males, expectancies may override the pharmacological effects of alcohol in enhancing humor, anxiety reduction, and sexual responsivity. In contrast, nonsocial behaviors, such as reaction time and motor coordination, are more influenced by alcohol itself than by expectancies (Marlatt & Rosenow, 1980). Expectancies that drinking will produce positive outcomes predict who'll drink and how much they'll drink, and expectancies that drinking will produce negative outcomes predict who'll abstain (Goldman, Darkes, & Del Boca, 1999; Leigh & Stacy, 2004).

The *setting*, or social context in which people consume alcohol, also influences its effects. For example, participants tested in a barlike situation with drinking companions feel more friendly and elated when they drink, and consume nearly twice as much alcohol as participants who drink by themselves (Lindman, 1982; Sher et al., 2005).

THE SEDATIVE-HYPNOTICS. When people have problems falling asleep or are excessively anxious, they may consult a physician to obtain sedative-hypnotic drugs. Because these drugs produce depressant effects, they're dangerous at high dosages and can produce unconsciousness, coma, and even death.

Factoid

The Rolling Stones song "Mother's Little Helper" (released in 1966) is about Valium. The song's refrain refers to Valium as a little yellow pill to calm the mother.

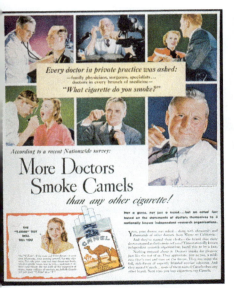

For years, cigarette companies published advertisements claiming that smoking is good for people's health, as in this 1946 ad boasting of Camel's popularity among physicians.

 Watch in **MyPsychLab** the **Video:**
Smoking Damage

 Watch in **MyPsychLab** the **Video:**
Cocaine

Factoid

Recent research suggests that trace (tiny) amounts of cocaine are present on 90 percent of dollar bills (and other paper money) in the United States. These amounts are highest in U.S. cities with the highest prevalence of drug problems; in Washington, DC, for example, 96 percent of paper money contained at least some cocaine (Raloff, 2009).

stimulant
drug that increases activity in the central nervous system, including heart rate, respiration, and blood pressure

At the turn of the twentieth century, many nonprescription products, such as the then-new soft drink Coca-Cola, contained tiny amounts of cocaine.

Researchers usually group sedative-hypnotics into three categories: *barbiturates* (for example, Seconal, Nembutal, and Tuinal); *nonbarbiturates* (for example, Sopor and Methaqualone, better known as Quaalude); and *benzodiazepines*. Benzodiazepines, including Valium, were extremely popular in the 1960s and 1970s and are still widely used today to relieve anxiety. Barbiturates produce a state of intoxication very similar to that of alcohol. Barbiturates have the greatest abuse potential, which is troubling because the consequences of overdose are often fatal.

Stimulants

Nicotine, cocaine, and amphetamines are **stimulants** because they rev up our central nervous system. In contrast to depressants, they increase heart rate, respiration, and blood pressure.

NICOTINE. Over the course of human history, people have consumed tobacco in various ways: smoking, chewing, dipping, licking, and even drinking (Gritz, 1980). As cigarette companies have long known but were reluctant to admit, the nicotine in tobacco is a potent and addictive drug. It reaches the brain about 10 seconds after it's inhaled. Nicotine activates receptors sensitive to the neurotransmitter acetylcholine, and smokers often report feelings of stimulation as well as relaxation and alertness.

Like many other drugs taken for nonmedical purposes, nicotine has *adjustive value*, meaning it can enhance positive emotional reactions and minimize negative emotional reactions, including the distress experienced when the nicotine level drops (Leventhal & Cleary, 1980). For many young people, positive images associated with smoking enhance its appeal.

COCAINE. Cocaine is the most powerful natural stimulant. Cocaine users commonly report euphoria, enhanced mental and physical capacity, stimulation, a decrease in hunger, indifference to pain, and a sense of well-being accompanied by diminished fatigue. Cocaine comes from a shrub that grows in abundance in South America. By the late 1800s, doctors prescribed cocaine for a wide range of illnesses. Around the turn of the century, many medicines, alcoholic tonics and even Coca-Cola contained cocaine. Cocaine came under strict government control in the United States in 1906.

According to surveys, 2.7 percent of 12th graders reported having used cocaine in the past year, and 40 percent of people by the age of 50 report having used cocaine at least once (Johnston et al, 2009a,b; Johnson et al., 2012). Cocaine is a powerful reinforcer. When

conditioned to self-inject cocaine, rhesus monkeys remain intoxicated for long periods of time. They may even "dose themselves to death" when unlimited quantities of cocaine are available (Johanson, Balster, & Bonese, 1976). Heavy intake of cocaine by humans also produces an intense drive to use it (Spotts & Shontz, 1976, 1983). Cocaine increases the activity of the neurotransmitters dopamine and perhaps serotonin, which contribute to its reinforcing effects.

Cocaine users can inject it intravenously. But they more commonly inhale or "snort" it through the nose, where the nasal mucous membranes absorb it. *Crack cocaine* is a highly concentrated dose of cocaine produced by dissolving cocaine in an alkaline (basic) solution and boiling it until a whitish lump, or "rock" remains that can be smoked. Crack's popularity is attributable to the intense euphoria it generates and its relative affordability. But the "high" is short-lived and followed by unpleasant feelings, which often leads to consuming cocaine whenever available to regain the high (Gottheil & Weinstein, 1983).

AMPHETAMINES. Amphetamines are among the most commonly abused of all drugs, with 37 percent of Americans trying them at least once by age 50 (Johnston et al., 2009a). Amphetamines illustrate how different patterns of use can produce different subjective effects. The first pattern involves occasional use of small doses of oral amphetamines to postpone fatigue, elevate mood while performing an unpleasant task, cram for a test, or experience well-being. In this case, intake of amphetamines doesn't become a routine part of the users' lifestyle. In the second pattern, users obtain amphetamines from a doctor, but ingest them on a regular basis for euphoria-producing effects rather than for their prescribed purpose. In these cases, a potent psychological dependence on the drug may occur, followed by depression if regular use is interrupted. The third pattern is associated with street users—"speed freaks"—who inject large doses of amphetamines intravenously to achieve the "rush" of pleasure immediately following the injection. These users are likely to be restless, talkative, and excited, and to inject amphetamines repeatedly to prolong euphoria. Inability to sleep and loss of appetite are also hallmarks of the so-called speed binge. Users may become increasingly suspicious and hostile and develop paranoid delusions (believing that others are out to get them).

In recent years, *methamphetamine,* a drug closely related chemically to amphetamines, has emerged as a widely abused drug. As many as 1 in 20 high school students report using methamphetamine (Johnston et al., 2009b). In its crystalline and highly addictive form, it's known as crystal meth or simply "meth." When users smoke it, they experience intense exhilaration, followed by euphoria that can last 12 to 16 hours. Crystal meth is more powerful than amphetamines, generally has a higher purity level, and carries a high risk of overdose and dependence. Meth can destroy tissues and blood vessels and cause acne; it can also lead to weight loss, tremors, and dental problems.

Narcotics

The opiate drugs heroin, morphine, and codeine are derived from the opium poppy, a plant found in abundance in Asia. Morphine is the major ingredient in opium. The action of heroin is virtually identical to that of morphine, but heroin is about three times as powerful and now accounts for 90 percent of opiate abuse. The opiates often are called **narcotics** because they relieve pain and induce sleep.

At first glance, heroin's psychological effects might appear mostly pleasurable: "Heroin is the king of drugs…. It leaves you floating on a calm sea where nothing seems to matter and everything is okay…. Suddenly the emptiness disappears…. The terrible growing inadequacy has vanished. And in its place is the power and comfort that's called confidence. No one can get to you when you keep nodding" (Rosenberg, 1973, pp. 25–26). This description conveys a sense of the euphoria that opiate users may experience. But these pleasurable effects are limited to the three or four hours that the usual dose lasts. If people addicted to heroin don't take another dose within four to six hours, they experience withdrawal symptoms, which include abdominal cramps, vomiting, craving for the drug, yawning, runny nose, sweating, and chills. With continued use, the drug's euphoric effects gradually diminish. The addict may continue using heroin as much to avoid withdrawal symptoms as to experience the intense high of the first few injections (Hutcheson et al., 2001; Julien, 2004).

About 1 to 2 percent of young adults have tried heroin (Johnston, O'Malley, & Bachman, 2003; Johnston et al., 2012). The sleep-inducing properties of heroin derive largely from its depressant effects on the central nervous system: drowsiness follows injection, breathing and pulse rate slow, and pupils constrict. At higher doses, coma and death may follow.

Even infrequent users risk becoming addicted to heroin. Contrary to popular conception, heroin addiction isn't inevitable (Sullum, 2003). For example, people who use opiates for medical purposes don't necessarily become addicted.

Smoking crack, a highly concentrated form of cocaine, is more dangerous than snorting regular cocaine.

This billboard contrasts the appearance of a woman before (on the left) and after (on the right) she became addicted to methamphetamine.

narcotic
drug that relieves pain and induces sleep

The ground-up leaves of the hemp plant are the source of marijuana.

CORRELATION VS. CAUSATION ▶
Can we be sure that A causes B?

hallucinogenic
causing dramatic alterations of perception, mood, and thought

Since the introduction of the powerful opiate pain reliever OxyContin in the mid-1990s, drug abusers have turned to it increasingly for "highs." Unfortunately, injecting or taking OxyContin in pill form in combination with alcohol and other depressant drugs can be lethal (Cone et al., 2004).

Psychedelics

Scientists describe such drugs as LSD, mescaline, PCP, and Ecstasy as **hallucinogenic** or *psychedelic* because they produce dramatic alterations in perception, mood, and thought. Because the effects of marijuana aren't as "mind-bending" as those of LSD, some researchers don't classify marijuana as a hallucinogen. In contrast, others describe it as a "mild hallucinogen." Interestingly, marijuana may also have sedative or hypnotic qualities.

MARIJUANA. Marijuana is the most frequently used illegal drug in the United States. By the age of 50, 74 percent of adults report having used it at least once (Johnston et al., 2009a). Known in popular culture as pot, grass, herb, Mary Jane, 420, and weed, marijuana comes from the leaves and flowering part of the hemp plant (*Cannabis sativa*). The subjective effects of marijuana are produced by its primary ingredient, THC (delta-9-tetrahydrocannabinol). People experience a "high" feeling within a few minutes, which peaks within a half hour. Hashish, manufactured from the buds and flowers of female plants, contains much greater concentrations of THC than marijuana and is more potent.

Whether marijuana is smoked or, less frequently, eaten or consumed in tea, users report short-term effects, including a sense of time slowing down, enhanced sensations of touch, increased appreciation for sounds, hunger ("the munchies"), feelings of well-being, and a tendency to giggle. Later, they may become quiet, introspective, and sleepy. At higher doses, users may experience disturbances in short-term memory, exaggerated emotions, and an altered sense of self. Some reactions are more unpleasant, including difficulty concentrating, slowed thought, depersonalization (a sense of being "out of touch" or disconnected from the self), and, more rarely, extreme anxiety, panic, and psychotic episodes (Earleywine, 2005). Driving while intoxicated with marijuana is hazardous, especially at high doses (Ramaekers et al, 2006).

The intoxicating effects of marijuana can last for two or three hours, but begin when THC courses through the bloodstream and travels to the brain, where it stimulates cannabinoid receptors. These specialized receptors are concentrated in areas of the brain that control pleasure, perception, memory, and coordinated body movements. The most prominent physiological changes are increases in heart rate, reddening of the eyes, and dryness of the mouth.

Scientists are striving to better understand the long-term physical and psychological effects of marijuana use. Although marijuana produces more damage to cells than tobacco smoke (Maertens et al., 2009), aside from an increased risk of lung and respiratory disease (Tetrault et al., 2007), scientists haven't found consistent evidence for serious physical health or fertility consequences of marijuana use. Still, chronic, heavy use of marijuana can impair attention and memory. Fortunately, normal cognitive functioning is typically restored after a month of abstinence (Pope, Gruber, & Yurgelun-Todd, 2001). Questions about cause-and-effect relationships come into play when interpreting research regarding the dangers of marijuana use. High school students who use marijuana earn lower grades and are more likely to get in trouble with the law than other students (Kleinman et al., 1988; Substance Abuse and Mental Health Services Administration, 2001, 2012). But high school students who use marijuana might do so because they have troubled home lives or psychological problems and do poorly in school *before* using marijuana (Shedler & Block, 1990). Indeed, there may be some truth to both scenarios.

Some researchers have argued that marijuana is a "gateway" drug that predisposes users to try more serious drugs, like heroin and cocaine (Kandel, Yamaguchi, & Chen, 1992). In a study of identical twin pairs in which one twin tried marijuana in adolescence but the other didn't, the twin who tried marijuana was later at heightened risk for abusing alcohol and other drugs (Lynskey et al., 2003). Nevertheless, evaluating whether marijuana is a gateway drug isn't easy. Merely because one event precedes another doesn't mean it causes it. For example, eating baby foods in infancy doesn't cause us to eat "grown-up" foods in adulthood. Teens may tend to use marijuana before other drugs because it's less threatening, more readily available, or both. The scientific debate continues.

LSD AND OTHER HALLUCINOGENS. On Friday, April 16, 1943, an odd thing happened to Swiss chemist Albert Hofmann. In 1938, Hofmann synthesized a chemical compound, d-lysergic acid diethylamide-25 (LSD), from chemicals found in a fungus that grows on rye. Five years later, when Hofmann again decided to work on the compound, he absorbed some of it unknowingly through his skin. When he went home, he felt restless, dizzy, and "perceived an uninterrupted stream of fantastic pictures, extraordinary shapes with intense, kaleidoscopic play of colors. After some two hours this condition faded away" (Hofmann, 1980, p. 5). Hoffman was the first of millions of people to experience the mind-altering effects of LSD.

By the age of 40, about 20 percent of Americans have tried the hallucinogen d-lysergic acid diethylamide-25, better known as LSD (Johnston, O'Malley, & Bachman, 2002). The psychedelic effects of LSD may stem from its interference with the action of the neurotransmitter serotonin at the synapse. The effects of LSD are also associated with areas of the brain rich in receptors for the neurotransmitter dopamine. Even tiny amounts of LSD can produce dramatic shifts in our perceptions and consciousness. Pills about the size of two aspirins can provide more than 6,000 "highs." Some users report astonishingly clear thoughts and fascinating changes in sensations and perceptions, including synesthesia (the blending of senses—for example, the "smelling of noises". Some users also report mystical experiences (Pahnke et al., 1970).

But LSD and other hallucinogens can also produce panic, paranoid delusions, confusion, depression, and bodily discomfort. Occasionally, psychotic reactions persist long after a psychedelic experience, most often in people with a history of psychological problems (Abraham & Aldridge, 1993). People who are suspicious and insecure before ingesting LSD are most anxious during an LSD session (Linton & Langs, 1964). *Flashbacks*—recurrences of a psychedelic experience—occur occasionally (Baggot et al., 2011). Curiously, there's no known pharmacological basis for their occurrence. One explanation is that they're triggered by something in the environment or an emotional state associated with a past psychedelic experience.

Unlike LSD, Ecstasy, also known as MDMA (methylenedioxymethamphetamine), has both stimulant and hallucinogenic properties. It produces cascades of the neurotransmitter serotonin in the brain, which increases self-confidence and well-being, and produces powerful feelings of empathy for others. But its use has a serious downside: Its side effects can include high blood pressure, depression, nausea, blurred vision, liver problems, sleep disturbance, and possibly memory loss and damage to neurons that rely on serotonin (Kish, 2002; Soar, Parrott, & Fox, 2004).

Drugs, like other means of altering consciousness, remind us that the "brain" and the "mind" are merely different ways of looking at the same phenomenon. They also illustrate the fluid way we experience the world and ourselves. Although a precise grasp of consciousness eludes us, appreciating the nuances of consciousness and their neurological correlates bring us closer to understanding the biological and psychological underpinnings of our waking and sleeping lives.

Factoid

LSD's subjective effects proved so fascinating to the Central Intelligence Agency (CIA) that in 1953 it launched a research program called MKULTRA to explore LSD's potential as a mind-control drug. This secret program involved administering LSD to unsuspecting individuals, including army scientists. After one of the scientists experienced a psychotic reaction and jumped to his death from a hotel window, the CIA turned to testing the effects of LSD on drug-dependent persons and prostitutes. The full scope of this operation came to light only after the program was discontinued in 1972. The researchers didn't find LSD to be a promising mind-control agent because its subjective effects were so unpredictable.

All-night dance parties termed "raves," in which Ecstasy and other psychedelic drugs are widely available, became popular in the mid-1990s in the United States.

✔ **Study** and **Review** in **MyPsychLab**

Assess Your Knowledge   **FACT** or **FICTION**?

1. The effects of many drugs depend on the expectations of the user. **True / False**

2. Alcohol is a central nervous system depressant. **True / False**

3. Tobacco is the most potent natural stimulant drug. **True / False**

4. A causal link between marijuana and poor school performance has been well established. **True / False**

5. Drug flashbacks are common among people who use LSD. **True / False**

Answers: 1. T; 2. T; 3. F; 4. F; 5. F

Your Complete Review System

 Study and **Review** in **MyPsychLab**

The Biology of Sleep

1 EXPLAIN THE ROLE OF THE CIRCADIAN RHYTHM AND HOW OUR BODIES REACT TO A DISRUPTION IN OUR BIOLOGICAL CLOCKS.

Sleep and wakefulness vary in response to a circadian rhythm that regulates many bodily processes over a 24-hour period. The "biological clock" is located in the hypothalamus.

1. As a college student you may like to sleep late in the morning because your _____ _____ is set that way.

2. The result of a disruption of our body's circadian rhythms that occurs when you fly across the country is called _____ _____.

2 IDENTIFY THE DIFFERENT STAGES OF SLEEP AND THE NEURAL ACTIVITY AND DREAMING BEHAVIORS THAT OCCUR IN EACH.

In the 1950s, researchers identified five stages of sleep that include periods of dreaming in which participants' eyes move rapidly back and forth (rapid eye movement, or REM, sleep). Although vivid, bizarre, and emotional dreams are most likely to occur in REM sleep, dreams occur in non-REM sleep as well. In stage 1 sleep, we feel drowsy and quickly transition to stage 2 sleep in which our brain waves slow down, heart rate slows, body temperature decreases, and muscles relax. In stages 3 and 4 sleep ("deep sleep"), large amplitude delta waves (1 or 2 cycles/second) become more frequent. In stage 5, REM sleep, the brain is activated much as it is during waking life.

3. Label the types of brain waves displayed at each sleep stage.

4. REM and non-REM dreams differ in that _____ dreams tend to be emotional and illogical and _____ dreams are shorter, more repetitive, and deal with everyday topics of current concern.

5. When humans are deprived of REM for a few nights, we experience _____ _____, during which the amount and intensity of REM sleep increases.

 Listen in **MyPsychLab** to chapter audio

3 IDENTIFY THE FEATURES AND CAUSES OF SLEEP DISORDERS.

Insomnia (problems falling asleep, waking in the night, or waking early) is the most common sleep disorder and is costly to society in terms of fatigue, missed work, and accidents. Episodes of narcolepsy, which can last as long as an hour, are marked by the rapid onset of sleep. Sleep apnea is also related to daytime fatigue and is caused by a blockage of the airways during sleep. Night terrors and sleepwalking, both associated with deep sleep, are typically harmless and are not recalled by the person on awakening.

6. Researchers have discovered that brief psychotherapy is (more/less) effective than Ambien, a popular sleeping pill, in the treatment of insomnia.

7. People who have _____ fall asleep suddenly and at inopportune times, like while driving a car.

8. What factors can contribute to cataplexy in people or animals with narcolepsy?

9. During a(n) _____ _____, a child can experience a dramatic episode of crying or thrashing during non-REM sleep, and won't remember it in the morning.

10. Sleepwalking is most frequent in (childhood/adulthood).

Dreams

4 DESCRIBE FREUD'S THEORY OF DREAMS.

Freud theorized that dreams represent disguised wishes. However, many dreams involve unpleasant or undesirable experiences, and many involve uninteresting reviews of routine daily events. Thus, Freud's dream theory hasn't received much empirical support.

11. In the era before rigorous laboratory research, *The Interpretation of Dreams*, by _____ _____ played an influential role in how people thought about dreams.

12. Freud distinguished between the details of the dream itself, which he called the _____ _____, and the true, hidden meaning, which he called the _____ _____.

13. Nightmares, which are common in both children and adults, challenge which theory about dreams?

5 EXPLAIN THREE MAJOR MODERN THEORIES OF DREAMING.

According to activation–synthesis theory, the forebrain attempts to interpret meaningless signals from the brain stem (specifically, the pons). Another theory of dreaming suggests that reduction of activity in the prefrontal cortex results in vivid and emotional, but logically disjointed, dreams. Neurocognitive theories hold that our dreams depend in large part on our cognitive and visuospatial abilities.

14. Evidence suggests that dreams (are/are not) involved in processing emotional memories and integrating new experiences with established memories to make sense of the world.

15. Hobson and McCarley's activation synthesis theory links dreams to _____ _____.

16. REM sleep is activated by surges of the neurotransmitter _____, which activates nerve cells in the pons.

17. Label the brain components (a, b, c, d) that the activation–synthesis theory suggests are involved in dreaming.

(a)
(b)
(c)
(d)

18. People who have an injury to the _____, as researched by Solms, do not dream.

19. Scientists who take a(n) _____ view of dreaming contend that we must consider our cognitive capacities, which shape the content of our dreams.

20. Children's dreams tend to be (less/more) emotional and bizarre than adult dreams.

Other Alterations of Consciousness and Unusual Experiences

6 DETERMINE HOW SCIENTISTS EXPLAIN UNUSUAL AND SEEMINGLY "MYSTICAL" ALTERATIONS IN CONSCIOUSNESS

Hallucinations and mystical experiences are associated with fasting, sensory deprivation, hallucinogenic drugs, prayer, and like near-death experiences, vary considerably in content across cultures. During out of body experiences, people's consciousness doesn't actually exit their bodies, and some NDEs are experienced by people who aren't near death. Déjà vu experiences don't represent a memory from a past life, but may be triggered by

small seizures in the temporal lobe or when a present experience resembles an earlier one that is forgotten.

21. _____ are realistic perceptual experiences in the absence of any external stimuli.

22. Why do people who float in lukewarm saltwater in dark and silent sensory deprivation tanks (such as the one pictured here) hallucinate?

23. Although there are many variations depending on one's religion and culture, many people in our culture associate a(n) _____ experience with approaching a white light.

24. One of the most common alterations in consciousness, _____ _____ is the sensation that you're reliving something even though you know the situation is new, or that you've been somewhere, even though you've never been there before.

7 DISTINGUISH MYTHS FROM REALITIES CONCERNING HYPNOSIS.

Contrary to popular belief, hypnosis isn't a sleeplike state, participants generally don't report having been in a "trance," people are aware of their surroundings and don't forget what happened during hypnosis, the type of induction has little impact, and hypnosis doesn't improve memory. In fact, hypnosis can lead to more false memories that are held with confidence, regardless of their accuracy. According to the sociocognitive model of hypnosis, the often dramatic effects associated with hypnosis may be attributable largely to preexisting expectations and beliefs about hypnosis. The dissociation model is another influential explanation for hypnosis. This model emphasizes divisions of consciousness during hypnosis or the automatic triggering of responses by hypnotic suggestion.

25. To increase people's suggestibility, most hypnotists use an _____ _____, which typically includes suggestions for relaxation and calmness.

26. Hypnosis in clinical practice (has/has not) demonstrated positive effects in treating pain and habit disorders, such as smoking.

27. Would the person shown in this drawing have to be in an altered state of consciousness to achieve this position? Why or why not?

Answers are located at the end of the text.

28. One of the most popular myths about hypnosis is that it can make people remember a past life using a therapy called _____ _____ _____ _____.

29. For _____ theorists, people's expectations about hypnosis, including the cues they receive from hypnotists, shape their responses.

30. Hilgard's _____ theory explains hypnosis based on a separation of the part of the personality responsible for planning from the part of the personality that controls awareness.

Drugs and Consciousness

8 IDENTIFY POSSIBLE INFLUENCES ON SUBSTANCE USE.

Substance use disorder is associated with recurrent problems related to the drug and may be associated with symptoms of tolerance and withdrawal. Cultures that prohibit drinking, such as Muslim cultures, generally exhibit low rates of alcoholism. Many people take drugs and alcohol in part to reduce tension and anxiety.

31. People qualify for a diagnosis of _____ _____ _____ when they experience recurrent problems related to the drug.

32. People can develop _____ _____ when their continued use of a drug is motivated by intense cravings.

33. Cultures in which drinking is strictly prohibited exhibit (low/high) rates of alcoholism.

34. According to the _____ _____ _____ people consume alcohol and other drugs to relieve anxiety.

9 DISTINGUISH DIFFERENT TYPES OF DRUGS AND THEIR EFFECTS ON CONSCIOUSNESS.

The effects of drugs are associated with the dose of the drug, as well as with users' expectancies, personality, and culture. Nicotine, a powerful stimulant, is responsible for the effects of tobacco on consciousness. Smokers often report feeling stimulated as well as tranquil, relaxed, and alert. Cocaine is the most powerful natural stimulant, with effects similar to those of amphetamines. Cocaine is highly addictive. Alcohol is a central nervous system depressant, like the sedative-hypnotic drugs such as Valium. Sedative-hypnotic drugs reduce anxiety at low doses and induce sleep at moderate doses. Expectancies influence how people react

to alcohol. Heroin and other opiates are highly addictive. Heroin withdrawal symptoms range from mild to severe. The effects of marijuana, sometimes classified as a mild hallucinogen, include mood changes, alterations in perception, and disturbances in short-term memory. LSD is a potent hallucinogen. Although flashbacks are rare, LSD can elicit a wide range of positive and negative reactions.

35. To show the balanced placebo design, insert the proper drug conditions in each of the four boxes.

36. Some people abuse _____ to postpone fatigue or elevate their mood while performing an unpleasant task.

37. In recent years, as many as one in 20 high school students report using methamphetamine, which in its crystalline form is known as _____ _____.

38. Opiate drugs—heroin, morphine, and codeine—are often called _____ because they relieve pain and induce sleep.

39. Hoffman created the mind-altering hallucinogenic drug _____ by accident while creating a compound from chemicals in a fungus.

40. Complete the table by adding the effects and examples for each drug type listed.

DRUG TYPE	EXAMPLES	EFFECT ON BEHAVIOR
Depressants	_____	_____
Stimulants	_____	_____
Opiates	_____	_____
Psychedelics	_____	_____

Apply Your Scientific Thinking Skills

Use your scientific thinking skills to answer the following questions, referencing specific scientific thinking principles and common errors in reasoning whenever possible.

1. As we've learned in this chapter, insomnia is the most common sleep disorder. Locate three treatment options for insomnia, being sure to include both behavioral and biomedical or drug treatments. Use your scientific thinking skills to determine which of these treatments would be the most effective and why.

2. Hypnosis has a wide range of clinical applications, including pain management and smoking cessation. Using the Internet or self-help books, choose two examples of hypnosis being used in a clinical setting and evaluate whether each example accurately portrays the benefits and limitations of hypnosis. Be sure to refer to this chapter's list of common misconceptions about hypnosis.

3. There is debate surrounding whether marijuana is physically and psychologically harmful to users. Research this debate further and find several media articles on both sides of the issue. What arguments does each side make to support its viewpoint? What rival hypotheses, if any, might each side have neglected to consider?

Further Your Understanding

EXTEND YOUR KNOWLEDGE WITH THE MYPSYCHLAB VIDEO SERIES

Watch these videos in MyPsychLab. Follow the "Video Series" link.

The Big Picture: States of Consciousness Learn why consciousness is so difficult to define and how various states differ.

The Basics: Rhythms of Consciousness Understand why sleep is one of our most basic biological needs and learn what goes on during the various sleep stages.

Special Topics: Sleep Disorders Find out what causes sleep disorders and how they can be treated.

Thinking Like a Psychologist: The Uses and Limitations of Hypnosis Explore what hypnosis is, what it is not, and how and why it works for some people and not others.

In the Real World: Sleep, Memory, and Learning Explore the sleeping and social habits of college students and how sleep deprivation can affect our waking hours.

What's In It For Me?: Altered States of Consciousness Look at the pathways and changes in brain activity that contribute to the feeling of an altered state.

EXPERIENCE PSYCHOLOGICAL RESEARCH WITH MYPSYCHLAB SIMULATIONS

Access these simulations in MyPsychLab. Follow the "Simulations" link.

Are Dreams Meaningful? Participate in a survey to discover trends in your dreaming and what these trends might mean.

What Altered States Have You Experienced? Participate in a survey to discover what altered states you and your classmates have experienced and the trends and motivations behind them.

What Drugs Have You Used? Participate in a survey on what hallucinogenic drugs you have used and discover trends in motivation and type of use.

APPLY YOUR CRITICAL THINKING SKILLS WITH MYPSYCHLAB WRITING ASSESSMENTS

Complete these writing assignments in MyPsychLab.

Your roommate has been coming back to the dorm at all hours of the night, disrupting your sleep. Describe a typical night's sleep cycle and then describe how your sleep deprivation impacts your ability to learn and your health.

Answer Key

THE BIOLOGY OF SLEEP

1. biological clock
2. jet lag
3. a) Beta waves; b) Alpha waves; c) Theta waves; d) Sleep spindles and K complexes; e) Delta waves
4. REM, non-REM
5. REM rebound
6. more
7. narcolepsy
8. Surprise, elation, or other strong emotions can lead people or animals with narcolepsy to experience cataplexy, a complete loss of muscle tone.
9. night terror
10. childhood

DREAMS

11. Sigmund Freud
12. manifest content, latent content
13. Freud's wish fulfillment theory
14. are
15. brain activity
16. acetylcholine
17. a) cerebral cortex; b) thalamus; c) pons; d) spinal cord
18. forebrain
19. neurocognitive
20. less

OTHER ALTERATIONS OF CONSCIOUSNESS AND UNUSUAL EXPERIENCES

21. Hallucinations
22. To compensate for the lack of sensory stimulation
23. near-death
24. déjà vu
25. induction method
26. has
27. No, people who stiffen their bodies can do this without hypnosis.
28. past life regression therapy
29. sociocognitive
30. dissociation

DRUGS AND CONSCIOUSNESS

31. substance use disorder
32. psychological dependence
33. low
34. tension reduction hypothesis

35.

Drug effect + Placebo effect	Placebo effect
Drug effect	Baseline

36. amphetamines
37. crystal meth
38. narcotics
39. LSD

40.

DRUG TYPE	EXAMPLES	EFFECT ON BEHAVIOR
Depressants	Alcohol, barbiturates, Quaaludes, Valium	Decreased activity of the central nervous system (initial high followed by sleepiness, slower thinking, and impaired concentration)
Stimulants	Tobacco, cocaine, amphetamines, methamphetamine	Increased activity of the central nervous system (sense of alertness, well-being, energy)
Opiates	Heroin, morphine, codeine	Sense of euphoria, decreased pain
Psychedelics	Marijuana, LSD, Ecstasy	Dramatically altered perception, mood, and thoughts

References

Abraham, H. D., & Aldridge, A. M. (1993). Adverse consequences of lysergic acid diethylamide. *Addiction, 88,* 1327–1334.

Adachi, N., Akanu, N., Adachi, T., Takekawa, Y., Adachi, Y., Ito, M., & Ikeda, H. (2008). Déjà vu experiences are rarely associated with pathological dissociation. *Journal of Nervous and Mental Disease, 196,* 417–419.

Akerstedt T, Fredlund, P., Gillberg, M., & Jansson, B. (2002). A prospective study of fatal occupational accidents—relationship to sleeping difficulties and occupational factors. *Journal of Sleep Research, 11,* 69–71.

Aldrich, M. S. (1999). *Sleep medicine.* New York, NY: Oxford University Press.

Aleman, A., & Laroi, F. (2008). *Hallucinations: The science of idiosyncratic perception.* Washington, DC: American Psychological Association.

Al-Issa, I. (1995). The illusion of reality or the reality of illusion: Hallucinations and culture. *British Journal of Psychiatry, 166,* 368–373.

Allen, P., Laroi, F., McGuire, P. K., & Aleman, A. (2008). The hallucinating brain: A review of structural and functional neuroimaging studies of hallucinations. *Neuroscience & Biobehavioral Reviews, 32,* 175–191.

Althius, M. D., Fredman, L., Langenberg, P. W., & Magaziner, J. (1998). The relationship between insomnia and mortality among community-dwelling older women. *Journal of the American Geriatric Society, 46,* 1270–1273.

Alvarado, C. S. (2000). Out-of-body experiences. In E. Cardeña, S. J. Lynn, & S. Krippner (Eds.), *The variety of anomalous experiences* (pp. 183–218). Washington, DC: American Psychological Association.

American Psychiatric Association. (2013). *Diagnostic and statistical manual of mental disorders* (5th ed.). Washington, DC: Author.

Antrobus, J. S. (1983). REM and NREM sleep reports: Comparison of word frequencies by cognitive classes. *Psychophysiology, 20,* 562–568.

Antrobus, J. S., Antrobus, J. S., & Fisher, C. (1965). Discrimination of dreaming and nondreaming sleep. *Archives of General Psychiatry, 12,* 395–401.

Ascher, L. M., Barber, T. X., & Spanos, N. P. (1972). Two attempts to replicate the Parrish-Lundy-Leibowitz experiment on hypnotic age regression. *American Journal of Clinical Hypnosis, 14,* 178–185.

Aserinsky, E. (1996). Memories of famous neuropsychologists: The discovery of REM sleep. *Journal of the History of the Neurosciences, 5,* 213–227.

Aserinsky, E., & Kleitman, N. (1953). Regularly occurring periods of ocular motility and concomitant phenomena during sleep. *Science, 118,* 361–375.

Baggott, M. J., Coyle, J. R., Erowid, E., Erowid, F., & Robertson, L. C. (2011). Abnormal visual experiences in individuals with histories of hallucinogen use: A web-based questionnaire. *Drug and Alcohol Dependence, 114*(1), 61–67.

Baker, J. R., & Yardley, J. K. (2002). Moderating effect of gender on the relationship between sensation-seeking impulsivity and substance use in adolescents. *Journal of Child and Adolescent Substance Abuse, 12,* 27–43.

Bancaud, J., Brunet-Bourgin, F., Chauvel, P., & Halgren, E. (1994). Anatomical origin of déjà vu and vivid "memories" in human temporal lobe epilepsy. *Brain, 117,* 71–90.

Bányai, E. I., & Hilgard, E. R. (1976). A comparison of active-alert hypnotic induction with traditional relaxation induction. *Journal of Abnormal Psychology, 85,* 218–224.

Barber, T. X. (1969). *Hypnosis: A scientific approach.* New York, NY: Van Nostrand Reinhold.

Barratt, D. (1996). *Trauma and dreams.* Cambridge, MA: Harvard University Press.

Bayard, M., Mcintyre, J., Hill, K. R., & Woodside, J. (2004). Alcohol withdrawal syndrome. *American Family Physician, 69,* 1442–1450.

Beauregard, M., & Paquette, V. (2006). Neural correlates of a mystical experience in Carmelite nuns. *Neuroscience Letters, 405,* 186–190.

Bellon, A. (2006). Searching for new options for treating insomnia: Are melatonin and ramelteon beneficial? *Journal of Psychiatric Practice, 12,* 229–243.

Bentall, R. (in press). In E. Cardeña, S. Lynn, & S. Krippner (Eds.), *Varieties of anamalous experience: Examining the scientific evidence* (2nd ed.). Washington, DC: American Psychological Association.

Bentall, R. P. (1990). The illusion of reality: A review and integration of psychological research on hallucinations. *Psychological Bulletin, 107,* 82–95.

Bikel, O. (Producer). (1995, April 11). *Frontline* [Television broadcast: "Divided Memories"]. New York, NY: Public Broadcasting Service.

Blackmore, S. (1984). Accounting for out-of-body experiences. *Bulletin of the British Psychological Society, 37,* A53.

Blackmore, S. (1991). Lucid dreaming: Awake in your sleep? *Skeptical Inquirer, 15,* 362–370.

Blackmore, S. (1993). *Dying to live: Near-death experiences.* Buffalo, NY: Prometheus.

Blackmore, S. (2004). *Consciousness: An introduction.* New York, NY: Oxford University Press.

Blanke, O., & Dieguez, S. (2009). Leaving body and life behind: Out-of-body and near death experience. In S. Laureys (Ed.), *The neurology of consciousness* (pp. 303–325). Amsterdam: Elsevier.

Blay, S. L., Andreoli, S. B., & Gastal, F. L. (2008). Prevalence of self-reported sleep disturbance among older adults and the association of sleep with service demand and medical conditions. *International Psychogeriatrics, 20,* 582–595.

Boeve, B.F. (2010). REM sleep behavior disorder: Updated review of the core features, the REM sleep behavior disorder-neurodegenerative disease association, evolving concepts, controversies, and future directions. *Annals of the New York Academy of Sciences, 1184,* 15–54.

Bothroyd, S. (2010). Man not guilty in "sexsomnia" rape trial. *ABC News.* Retrieved from http://www.abc.net.au/news/2010-02-12/man-not-guilty-in-sexsomnia-rape-trial/329486

Bourguignon, E. (1970). Hallucinations and trance: An anthropologist's perspective. In W. Keup (Ed.), *Origins and mechanisms of hallucination* (pp. 183–190). New York, NY: Plenum Press.

Braffman, W., & Kirsch, I. (1999). Imaginative suggestibility and hypnotizability: An empirical analysis. *Journal of Personality and Social Psychology, 77,* 578–587.

Brown, A. S. (2003). A review of the déjà vu experience. *Psychological Bulletin, 129,* 394–413.

Brown, A. S. (2004b). The déjà vu illusion. *Current Directions in Psychological Science, 13,* 256–259.

Bushey, D., Tononi, G., & Cirelli, C. (2011). Sleep and synaptic homeostasis: Structural evidence in Drosophila. *Science, 332*(6037), 1576–1581.

Butler, S., & Watson, R. (1985). Individual differences in memory for dreams: The role of cognitive skills. *Perceptual and Motor Skills, 53,* 841–864.

Buxton, O. M., Cain, S.W, O'Connor, S.P., Porter, J. H., Duffy, J. F., Wang, W.,... Shea, S.A. (2012). Adverse metabolic consequences in humans of prolonged sleep restriction combined with circadian disruption. *Science Translational Medicine, 4,* 129–143.

Cappell, H., & Herman, C. (1972). Alcohol and tension reduction: A review. *Quarterly Journal of Studies in Alcohol, 33,* 33–64.

Carnethon, M., Knutson, K. L., Kim, K., de Chavez, P. J., Goldberger, J., Ng, J.,... Zee, P. (2012). Racial/ethnic differences in sleep duration and quality in a population sample. Annual Meeting of the Associated Professional Sleep Societies (APSS), Boston, June 13.

Cartwright, R., & Romanek, I. (1978). Repetitive dreams of normal subjects. *Sleep Research, 7,* 7–15.

Centers for Disease Control and Prevention (2011). Summary Health Statistics for U.S. Adults: National Health Inverview Survey, 2011. Vital and Health Statistics, Series 10, Number 256. Hyattsville, MD: U.S. Depeartment of Health and Human Services.

Cheyne, J. A., & Girard, T. A. (2009). The body unbound: Vestibular-motor hallucinations and out of body experiences. *Cortex, 45,* 201–215.

Clancy, S. A., McNally, R. J., Schachter, D. L., Lenzenweger, M. F., & Pitman, R. K. (2002). Memory distortion in people reporting abduction by aliens. *Journal of Abnormal Psychology, 111,* 455–461.

Cleary, A. M., Brown, A. S., Sawyer, B. D., Nomi, J. S., Ajoku, A. C., & Ryals, A. J. (2012). Familiarity from the configuration of objects in 3-dimensional space and its relation to déjà vu: A virtual reality investigation. *Consciousness and Cognition, 21*(2), 969–975.

CNN (August 3, 2009). *Apnea, early starts blamed in Hawaii pilots' nap.* Retrieved from http://www.cnn.com/2009/US/08/03/sleepy.pilots.apnea

Coe, W. C., & Sarbin, T. R. (1991). Role theory: Hypnosis from a dramaturgical and narrational perspective. In S. J. Lynn & J. W. Rhue (Eds.), *Theories of hypnosis: Current models and perspectives* (pp. 303–323). New York, NY: Guilford Press.

Cohen, D. A., Wang, W., Wyatt, J. K., Kronauer, R. E., Dijk, D. J., Czeisler C. A., & Klerman, E. B. (2010). Uncovering residual effects of chronic sleep loss on human performance. *Science Translational Medicine, 2,* 14ra3.

Cone, E. J., Fant, R. V., Rohay, J. M., Caplan, Y, Ballina, M., Reder, R. F., & Haddox, J. D. (2004). Oxycodone involvement in drug abuse deaths. II. Evidence for toxic multiple drug–drug interactions. *Journal of Analytical Toxicology, 28,* 217–225.

Cook, T. A. R., & Wall, T. L. (2005). Ethnicity and the subjective effects of alcohol. In M. Earleywine (Ed.), *Mind-altering drugs: The science of subjective experience* (pp. 154–182). Washington, DC: American Psychological Association.

Cooper, R. P. (2003). Mechanisms for the generation and regulation of sequential behavior. *Philosophical Psychology, 16,* 389–416.

Crick, F., & Mitchison, G. (1983). The function of dream sleep. *Nature, 304,* 111–114.

Daalman, K., Boks, M. P., Diederen, K. M., de Weijer, A. D., Blom, J. D., Kahn, R. S., & Sommer, I. E. (2010). Same or different? Auditory verbal hallucinations in healthy and psychotic individuals. *Schizophrenia Research, 117*(2), 188–189.

Deadwyler, S. A., Porrino, L., Siegel, J. M., & Mampson, R. (2007). Systemic and nasal delivery of orexin-A (Hypocretin-I) reduces the effects of sleep deprivation on cognitive performance in nonhuman primates. *Journal of Neuroscience, 27,* 14239–14247.

Dement, W. C. (1974). *Some must watch while some must sleep.* San Francisco, CA: W. H. Freeman.

Dement, W. C., & Kleitman, N. (1957). The relation of eye movements during sleep to dream activity: An objective method for the study of dreaming. *Journal of Experimental Psychology, 53,* 339–346.

Dement, W. C., & Vaughan, C. (1999). *The promise of sleep: A pioneer in sleep medicine explores the vital connection between health, happiness, and a good night's sleep.* New York, NY: Dell Trade Paperbacks.

Diekelmann, S., & Born, J. (2010). The memory function of sleep. *Nature Reviews Neuroscience, 11,* 114–126.

Dixon, M., & Laurence, J. (1992). Two hundred years of hypnosis research: Questions resolved? Questions unanswered! In E. Fromm and M. Nash (Eds.), *Contemporary hypnosis research* (pp. 34–66). New York, NY: Guilford Press.

Domhoff, G. W. (1993). The repetition of dreams and dream elements: A possible clue to a function of dreams. In A. Moffitt, M. Kramer, & R. Hoffman (Eds.), *The functions of dreams* (pp. 293–320). Albany, NY: SUNY Press.

Domhoff, G. W. (1996). *Finding meaning in dreams: A quantitative approach.* New York, NY: Plenum.

Domhoff, G. W. (2001a). A new neurocognitive theory of dreams. *Dreaming, 11,* 13–33.

Domhoff, G. W. (2003). Dreaming—An introduction to the science of sleep. *Science, 299,* 1987–1988.

Domhoff, G.W. (2011). Dreams are embodied simulations that dramatize conceptions and concerns: The continuity hypothesis in empirical, theoretical, and historical context. *International Journal of Dream Research, 4*(2), 50–62.

Domhoff, G. W., & Schneider, A. (2004). Much ado about very little: The small effect size when home and laboratory dreams are compared. *Dreaming, 19,* 139–151.

Dorus, E., Dorus, W., & Rechtschaffen, A. (1971). The incidence of novelty in dreams. *Archives of General Psychiatry, 25,* 364–368.

Dresler, M., Wehrle, R., Spoormaker, V. I., Koch, S. P., Holsboer, F., Steiger, A.,... Samann, P. G. (2012). Neural correlates of dream lucidity obtained from contrasting lucid versus non-lucid REM sleep: A combined EEG/fMRI case study. *Sleep, 35*(7), 1017–1020.

Earleywine, M. (2005). *Mind-altering drugs: The science of subjective experience.* Oxford, England: Oxford University Press.

Edgar, R. S., Green, E. W., Zhao, Y., van Ooijen, G., Olmedo, M., Qin, X.,... Reddy, A. B. (2012). Peroxiredoxins are conserved markers of circadian rhythms. *Nature, 485,* 459–464)

Ehrenwald, J. (1974). Out-of-the-body experiences and the denial of death. *Journal of Nervous and Mental Disease, 159,* 227–233.

Ehrsson, H. H. (2007). The experimental induction of out-of-body experiences. *Science, 317,* 1048.

Erblich, J., Earleywine, M., Erblich, B., & Bovjerg, D. H. (2003). Biphasic stimulant and sedative effects of ethanol: Are children of alcoholics really different? *Addictive Behaviors, 28,* 1129–1139.

Erdelyi, M. (1994). Hypnotic hypermnesia: The empty set of hypermnesia. *International Journal of Clinical and Experimental Hypnosis, 42,* 379–390.

Fenton, R. (2007, November 2). Drowsy driving is big killer in U.S. Reuters. Retrieved from http://www.reuters.com/article/2007/11/02/us-usa-highways-sleep-idUSN3130250920071102

Foulkes, D. (1962). Dream reports from different stages of sleep. *Journal of Abnormal and Social Psychology, 65,* 14–25.

Foulkes, D. (1982). *Children's dreams.* New York, NY: Wiley.

Foulkes, D. (1985). *Dreaming: A cognitive-psychological analysis.* New York, NY: Erlbaum.

Foulkes, D., & Rechtschaffen, A. (1964). Presleep determinants of dream content: Effects of two films. *Perceptual and Motor Skills, 19,* 983–1005.

Foulkes, D., & Schmidt, M. (1983) Temporal sequence and unit composition in dream reports from different stages of sleep. *Sleep, 6,* 265–280.

Frith, C. D. (1992). *The cognitive neuropsychology of schizophrenia.* Hillsdale, NJ: Erlbaum.

Fukuda, K., Ogilvie, R., Chilcott, L., Venditteli, A., & Takeuchi, T. (1998). High prevalence of sleep paralysis in Canadian and Japanese college students. *Dreaming, 8,* 59–66.

Gangswisch, J. E., Babiss, L. A., Malaspina, D., Turner, J. B., Zammit, G. K., & Posner, K. (2010). Earlier parental set bedtimes as a protective factor against depression and suicidal ideation, *Sleep, 33,* 97–106.

Geschwind, N. (1983). Interictal behavior changes in epilepsy. *Epilepsia, 24*(Suppl. 1), S23–S30.

Goldman, M. S., Darkes, J., & Del Boca, F. K. (1999). Expectancy mediation of biopsychosocial risk for alcohol use and alcoholism. In I. Kirsch (Ed.), *How expectancies shape experience* (pp. 232–262). Washington, DC: American Psychological Association.

Gorassini, D. R., & Spanos, N. P. (1998). The Carleton Skill Training Program. In I. Kirsch, A. Capafons, E. Cardeña, & S. Amigo (Eds.), *Clinical hypnosis and self-regulation: Cognitive-behavioral perspectives* (pp. 141–177). Washington, DC: American Psychological Association.

Gottheil, E., & Weinstein, S. O. (1983). Cocaine: An emerging problem. In S. Akhtar (Ed.), *New psychiatric syndromes; DSM III and beyond.* New York, NY: Jason Aronson.

Greeley, A. M. (1975). *The sociology of the paranormal: A reconnaissance* (Sage Research Papers in the Social Sciences, Vol. 3, Series No. 90-023). Beverly Hills, CA: Sage.

Greeley, J., & Oei, T. (1999). Alcohol and tension reduction: 1987–1997. In K. E Leonard & H. T. Blane (Eds.), *Psychological theories of drinking and alcoholism* (2nd ed., pp.14–53). New York, NY: Guilford Press.

Green, J. P., & Lynn, S. J. (2005). Hypnosis vs. relaxation: Accuracy and confidence in dating international news events. *Applied Cognitive Psychology, 19,* 679–691.

Greyson, B. (in press). Near-death experiences. In E. Cardeña, S. J. Lynn, & S. Krippnes (Eds.), *Varieties of Anomolous Experiences.*Washington, DC: American Psychological Association.

Griffiths, R. R., Johnson, M. W., Richards, W. A., Richards, B. D., McCann, U., & Jesse, R. (2011). *Psychopharmacology, 218,* 649–665.

Griffiths, R. R., Richards, W. A., Johnson, M. W., McCann, U. D., & Jesse, R. (2008). Mystical-type experiences occasioned by psilocybin mediate the attribution of personal meaning and spiritual significance 14 months later. *Journal of Psychopharmacology, 22,* 621–632.

Gritz, E. R. (1980). Smoking behavior and tobacco abuse. In N. K. Mello (Ed.), *Advances in substance abuse, Vol. 1* (pp. 91–158). Greenwich, CT: JAI Press.

Grob C. S., Danforth A. L., Chopra G. S., Hagerty, M., McKay, C. R., Halberstadt, A. L., & Greer, G. R. (2011) Pilot study of psilocybin treatment for anxiety in patients with advanced-stage cancer. *Archives of General Psychiatry, 68,* 71–78.

Gross, J., Byrne, J., & Fisher, C. (1965). Eye movements during emergent Stage 1 EEG in subjects with lifelong blindness. *Journal of Nervous and Mental Disease, 141,* 365–370.

Hall, C. S., & Nordby, V. J. (1972). *The individual and his dreams.* Winnipeg, Manitoba, Canada: New American Library.

Hall, C. S., & Van de Castle, R. (1966). *Content analysis of dreams.* New York, NY: Appleton-Century-Crofts.

Harkness, A. R. (2007). Personality traits are essential for a complete clinical science. In S. O. Lilienfeld and W. O'Donohue (Eds.), *The great ideas of clinical science: 17 concepts that every mental health professional should understand* (pp. 263–290). New York, NY: Routledge.

Hasegawa, H., & Jamieson, G. A. (2002). Conceptual issues in hypnosis research: Explanations, definitions and the state/non-state debate. *Contemporary Hypnosis, 19,* 103–117.

Hasler, G., Buysse, D. J., Klaghofer, R., Gamma, A., Ajdacic, V., Eich, D.,... Angst, J. (2004). The association between short sleep duration and obesity in young adults: A 13-year prospective study. *Sleep, 27,* 661–666.

He, Y., Jones, C. R., Fujiki, N., Xu, Y., Guo, B., Holder, J. L.,... Fu, Y. (2009). The transcriptional repressor DEC2 regulates sleep length in mammals. *Science, 325,* 866–870.

Higuchi, S., Matsushita, S., Murayama, M., Takagai, S., & Hayashida, M. (1995). Alcohol and aldehyde dehydrogenase polymorphisms and the risk for alcoholism. *American Journal of Psychiatry, 152,* 1219–1221.

Hilgard, E. R. (1977). *Divided consciousness: Multiple controls in human thought and action.* New York, NY: Wiley.

Hobson, J. A. (2002). *Dreaming: An introduction to the science of sleep.* New York, NY: Oxford University Press.

Hobson, J. A. (2009). REM sleep and dreaming: Towards a theory of protoconsciousness. *Nature Reviews Neuroscience, 10,* 803–813.

Hobson, J. A., & McCarley, R. M. (1977). The brain as a dream state generator: An activation-synthesis hypothesis. *American Journal of Psychiatry, 134,* 1335–1348.

Hobson, J. A., Pace-Schott, E., & Stickgold, R. (2000). Dreaming and the brain: Towards a cognitive neuroscience of conscious states. *Behavioral and Brain Sciences, 23,* 793–842.

Hofmann, A. (1980). *LCD: My problem child.* New York, NY: McGraw-Hill.

Hull, J. G., & Bond, C. F. (1986). Social and behavioral consequences of alcohol consumption and expectancy: A meta-analysis. *Psychological Bulletin, 99,* 347–360.

Hutcheson, D. M., Everitt, B. J., Robbins, T. W., & Dickinson, A. (2001). The role of withdrawal in heroin addiction: Enhances reward or promotes avoidance? *Nature Neuroscience, 4,* 943–947.

Jackson, K. M., & Sher, K. J. (2003). Alcohol use disorders and psychological distress: A prospective state-trait analysis. *Journal of Abnormal Psychology, 112,* 599–613.

Jacobs, G. D., Pace-Schott, E. F., Stickgold, R., & Otto, M. W. (2004). Cognitive behavior therapy and pharmacotherapy for insomnia: A randomized controlled trial and direct comparison. *Archives of Internal Medicine, 164,* 1888–1896.

Jansen, K. L. R. (1991). Transcendental explanations and the near-death experience. *Lancet, 337,* 207–243.

Johanson, C. E., Balster, R. L., & Bonese, K. (1976). Self-administration of psychomotor stimulant drugs: The effects of unlimited access. *Pharmacology, Biochemistry, and Behavior, 4,* 45–51.

Johnston, L. D., O'Malley, P. M., & Bachman, J. G. (2002). *Monitoring the future national results on adolescent drug use: Overview of key findings, 2001.* Bethesda, MD: National Institute on Drug Abuse (DHHS/PHS).

Johnston, L. D., O'Malley, P. M., & Bachman, J. G. (2003). *Monitoring the future national results on adolescent drug use: Overview of key findings, 2002.* Bethesda, MD: National Institute on Drug Abuse (DHHS/PHS).

Johnston, L. D., O'Malley, P. M., Bachman, J. G., & Schulenberg, J. E. (2009). *Monitoring the future national survey results on drug use, 1975–2007. Volume I: Secondary school students* (NIH Publication No. 08-6418A). Bethesda, MD: National Institute on Drug Abuse.

Joslyn, G., Brusch, G., Robertson, M., Smith, T. L., Kalmijn, J., Schuckit, M., & White, R. L. (2008). Chromosome 15q25.1 genetic markers associated with level of response to alcohol in humans. *Proceedings of the National Academy of Sciences.* http://dx.doi.org/10.1073/pnas.0810970105

Julien, R. M. (2004). *A primer of drug action* (10th ed.). San Francisco, CA: W. H. Freeman.

Jus, A., Jus, K., Gautier, J., Villenueve, A., Pires, P., Lachance, R., & Villenueve, R. (1973). Dream reports after reserpine in chronic lobotomized schizophrenic patients. *Vie Médicale au Canada Français, 2,* 843–848.

Kandel, D., Yamaguchi, K., & Chen, K. (1992). Stages of progression in drug involvement from adolescence to adulthood: Further evidence for the gateway theory. *Journal of Studies of Alcohol, 53,* 447–457.

Kane, M. J., Brown, L. H., McVay, J. C., Silvia, P. J., Myin-Germeys, I., & Kwapil, T. R. (2007). For whom the mind wanders, and when: An experience-sampling study of working memory and executive control in daily life. *Psychological Science, 18*(7), 614–621.

Kanzler, H. R., & Rosenthal, R. N. (2003). Dual diagnosis: Alcoholism and co-morbid psychiatric disorders. *American Journal of Addiction, 12*(Suppl. 1), 21–40.

Katz, D. A., & McHorney, C. A. (2002). The relationship between insomnia and health-related quality of life in patients with chronic illness. *Journal of Family Practice, 51,* 229–235.

Kellehear, A. (1993). Culture, biology, and the near-death experience: A reappraisal. *Journal of Nervous and Mental Disease, 181,* 148–156.

Kennedy, K. (2009). Sleep starved: Too little sleep could be more dangerous than you may think. *Army Times.* Retrieved from http://www.armytimes.com/offduty/health/offduty_sleep_051906

Kerr, N. H. (1993) Mental imagery, dreams, and perception. In C. Cavallero & D. Foulkes (Eds.), *Dreaming as cognition* (pp. 18–37). Hertfordshire, England: Harvester Wheatsheaf.

Kerr, N. H., & Domhoff, G. W. (2004). Do the blind literally "see" in their dreams? A critique of a recent claim that they do. *Dreaming, 14,* 230–233.

Kessler, R. C., Berglund, P. A., Coulouvrat, C., Hajak, G., Roth, T., Shahly, V.,... Walsh, J. K. (2011). Insomnia and the performance of US workers: Results from the America Insomnia Survey, *Sleep, 34*(9), 1161–1171.

Kihlstrom, J. F. (1992). Hypnosis: A sesquicentennial essay. *International Journal of Clinical and Experimental Hypnosis, 40,* 301–314.

King, A. C., Houle, T., de Wit, H., Holdstock, L., & Schuster, A. (2002). Biphasic alcohol response differs in heavy versus light drinkers. *Alcoholism: Clinical and Experimental Research, 26,* 827–835.

Kinney, J., & Leaton, G. (1995). *Loosening the grip: A handbook of alcohol information* (5th ed.). St. Louis, MO: Mosby.

Kirkcaldy, B. D., Levine, R., & Shephard, R. J. (2000). The impact of working hours on physical and psychological health of German managers. *European Review of Applied Psychology, 50,* 443–449.

Kirsch, I. (1994). Clinical hypnosis as a nondeceptive placebo: Empirically derived techniques. *American Journal of Clinical Hypnosis, 37,* 95–106.

Kirsch, I. (2003). Hidden administration as ethical alternatives to the balanced placebo design. *Prevention & Treatment, 6,* Article 5. Retrieved from http://psycnet.apa.org/journals/pre/6/1/5c

Kirsch, I., & Council, J. R. (1992). Situational and personality correlates of suggestibility. In E. Fromm & M. Nash (Eds.), *Contemporary hypnosis research* (pp. 267–292). New York, NY: Guilford Press.

Kirsch, I., & Lynn, S. J. (1995). The altered state of hypnosis: Changes in the theoretical landscape. *American Psychologist, 50,* 846–858.

Kirsch, I., Montgomery, G., & Sapirstein, G. (1995). Hypnosis as an adjunct to cognitive behavioral psychotherapy: A meta-analysis. *Journal of Consulting and Clinical Psychology, 63,* 214–220.

Kish, S. J. (2002). How strong is the evidence that brain serotonin neurons are damaged in human users of ecstasy? *Pharmacology, Biochemistry, and Behavior, 71,* 845–855.

Kleinman, A. (1988). *Rethinking psychiatry: From cultural category to personal experience.* New York, NY: Free Press.

Klinger, E. (2000). Daydreams. In A. E. Kazdin (Ed.), *Encyclopedia of psychology.* New York, NY: Oxford University Press/American Psychological Association.

Klinger, E., & Cox, W. M. (1987–1988). Dimensions of thought flow in everyday life. *Imagination, Cognition and Personality, 7,* 105–128.

Knight, J. R., Wechsler, H., Kuo, M., Seibring, M., Weitzman, E. R., & Schuckit, M. (2002). Alcohol abuse and dependence among U.S. college students. *Journal of Studies on Alcohol, 63,* 263–270.

Kollins, S. H. (2003). Delay discounting is associated with substance use in college students. *Addictive Behaviors, 28,* 1167–1173.

Kallio, S., Hyönä, J., Revonsuo, A., Sikka, P., & Nummenmaa, L. (2011) Altered eye movements reveal a hypnotic state. *PLoS One, 6*(10), e26374.

Koob, G. F. (2000) Animal models of craving for ethanol. *Addiction, 95,* S73–S81.

Krakow, B., Hillifield, M., Johnston, L., Koss, M., Schrader, R., Warner, T.D.,... Prince, H. (2001). Imagery rehearsal therapy for chronic nightmares in sexual assault survivors with posttraumatic stress disorder: A randomized controlled trial. *Journal of the American Medical Association, 286*(5), 537–545.

Kunzendorf, R. G., Treantafel, N., Taing, B., Flete, A., Savoie, S., & Williams, R. (2006–2007). The sense of self in lucid dreams: "Self as subject" vs. "self as agent" vs. "self as object." *Imagination, Cognition, and Personality, 26,* 303–323.

Kunzendorf, R. G., Watson, G., Monroe, L., Tassone, S., Papoutsakis, E., McArdle, E., & Gauthier, A. (2007–2008). The archaic belief in dream visitations as it relates to "seeing ghosts," meeting the lord," as well as "encountering extraterrestrials." *Imagination, Cognition, and Personality, 27,* 71–85.

LaBerge, S. (1980). *Lucid dreaming: An exploratory study of consciousness during sleep*. Unpublished doctoral dissertation, Stanford University, Stanford, CA.

Lang, A. R., Goeckner, D. J., Adesso, V. J., & Marlatt, G. A. (1975). Effects of alcohol on aggression in male social drinkers. *Journal of Abnormal Psychology, 84*, 509–518.

Leigh, B. C., & Stacy, A. (2004). Alcohol expectancies and drinking in different age groups. *Addiction, 99*, 215–227.

Lenggenhager, B., Tadi, T., Metzinger, T., & Blanke, O. (2007). Video ergo sum: Manipulating bodily self-consciousness. *Science, 317*, 1096–1099.

Leventhal, H., & Cleary, P. D. (1980) The smoking problem: A review of the research and theory in behavioral risk modification. *Psychological Bulletin, 88*, 370–405.

Levitan, L., & LaBerge, S. (1990). Beyond nightmares: Lucid resourcefulness vs. helpless depression. *NightLight, 2*, 1–6.

Lindman, R. (1982). Social and solitary drinking: Effects on consumption and mood in male social drinkers. *Physiology and Behavior, 28*, 1093–1095.

Linton, H. B., & Langs, R. J. (1964). Subjective reactions to lysergic acid diethylamide (LSD-25) measured by a questionnaire. *Archives of General Psychiatry, 10*, 469–485.

Lynn, S. J., Cleere, C., Accardi, M., & Krackow, E. (2010). Near-death experiences: Out of body and out of mind? *Psychology of Religion and Spirituality, 2*(2), 117–118.

Lynn, S. J., Kirsch, I., & Hallquist, M. (2008). Social cognitive theories of hypnosis. In M. R. Nash & A. M. Barnier (Eds.), *Oxford handbook of hypnosis* (pp. 111–140). New York, NY: Oxford Press.

Lynn, S. J., Nash, M. R., Rhue, J. W., Frauman, D. C., & Sweeney, C. A. (1984). Nonvolition, expectancies, and hypnotic rapport. *Journal of Abnormal Psychology, 93*, 295–303.

Lynn, S. J., & Rhue, J. W. (1988). Fantasy proneness: Hypnosis, developmental antecedents, and psychopathology. *American Psychologist, 43*, 35–44.

Lynn, S. J., & Rhue, J. W. (1991). An integrative model of hypnosis. In S. J. Lynn & J. W. Rhue (Eds.), *Theories of hypnosis: Current models and perspectives* (pp. 397–438). New York, NY: Guilford Press.

Lynn, S. J., Rhue, J. W., & Weekes, J. R. (1990). Hypnotic involuntariness: A social-cognitive analysis. *Psychological Review, 97*, 169–184.

Lynn, S. J., Weekes, J. R., & Milano, M. (1989). Reality versus suggestion: Pseudomemory in hypnotizable and simulating subjects. *Journal of Abnormal Psychology, 98*, 75–79.

Lynskey, M. T., Heath, A. C., Bucholz, K. K., Slutske, W. S., Madden, P. A. F., Nelson, E. C.,... Martin, N. G. (2003). Escalation of drug use in early-onset cannabis users vs. co-twin controls. *Journal of the American Medical Association, 289*, 427–433.

Maas, J. B. (1999). *Power sleep: The revolutionary program that prepares your mind for peak performance*. New York, NY: Collins.

MacLean, K. A., Johnson, M. W., & Griffiths, R. R. (2011). Mystical experiences occasioned by the hallucinogen psilocybin lead to increases in the personality domain of openness. *Journal of Psychopharmacology, 25*(11), 1453–1461.

Maertens, R. M., White, P. A., Rickert, W, Levasseur, G., Douglas, G. R., Bellier, P. V.,... Desjardins, S. (2009). The genotoxicity of mainstream and sidestream marijuana and tobacco smoke condensates. *Chemical Research in Toxicology, 22*, 1406–1414.

Mahowald, M., & Schenck, C. (2000). *Principles and practice of sleep medicine*. New York, NY: W. B. Saunders.

Mahowald, M. W., & Bornemann, M. A. C. (2005). NREM sleep-arousal parasomnias. In M. H. Kryger, T. Roth, & W. C. Dement (Eds.), *Principles and practice of sleep medicine* (4th ed., pp. 889–896). Philadelphia, PA: Elsevier Saunders.

Manford, M., & Andermann, F. (1998). Complex visual hallucinations: Clinical and neurobiological insights. *Brain, 121*, 1819–1840.

Maquet, P., & Franck, G. (1997). REM sleep and the amygdala. *Molecular Psychiatry, 2*, 195–196.

Marczinski, C. A., Harrison, E. L., & Fillmore, M. T. (2008). The effects of alcohol on simulated drinking and perceived driving impairment in binge drinkers. *Alcohol: Clinical and Experimental Research, 32*, 1329–1337.

Marczinski, C. A., & Stamates, A. L. (2012). Artificial sweeteners versus regular mixers increase breath alcohol concentrations in male and female social drinkers. *Alcoholism: Clinical and Experimental Research.*

Marlatt, G. A., & Rosenhow, D. J. (1980). Cognitive processes in alcohol use: Expectancy and balanced placebo design. In N. K. Mello (Ed.), *Advances in substance abuse: Behavioral and biological research* (pp. 159–199). Greenwich, CT: JAI Press.

Mazzoni, G., Heap, M., & Scoboria, A. (2010). Hypnosis and memory: Theory, laboratory research, and application. In S. J. Lynn, J. W. Rhue, & I. Kirsch (Eds.), *Handbook of clinical hypnosis*. Washington, DC: American Psychological Association.

McCall Smith, A., & Shapiro, C. M. (1997). Sleep disorders and the criminal law. In C. Shapiro & A. McCall Smith (Eds.), *Forensic aspects of sleep* (pp. 29–64). Chichester, England: Wiley.

McGue, M. (1999). The behavioral genetics of alcoholism. *Current Directions in Psychological Science, 8*, 109–115.

McHugh, L., Barnes-Holmes, Y., Barnes-Holmes, D., Whelan, R., & Stewart, I. (2007). Knowing me, knowing you: Deictic complexity in false-belief understanding. *The Psychological Record, 57*(4), 533–542. Retrieved from http://search.proquest.com/docview/621929403?accountid=14168

McNally, R. J., & Clancy, S. A. (2005). Sleep paralysis, sexual abuse, and space alien abduction. *Transcultural Psychiatry, 42*, 113–122.

McNamara, P., McLaren, D., Smith, D., Brown, A, & Stickgold, R. (2005) A "Jekyll and Hyde" within—Aggressive versus friendly interactions in REM and non-REM dreams. *Psychological Science, 16*, 130–136.

Meeker, W., & Barber, T. (1971). Toward an explanation of stage hypnosis. *Journal of Abnormal Psychology, 77*, 61–70.

Metzinger, T. (2009). *The ego tunnel: The science of the mind and the myth of the self*. New York, NY: Basic Books.

Mieda, M., Willie, J. T., Hara, J., Sinton, C. M., Sakurai, T., & Yanagisawa, M. (2004). Orexin peptides prevent cataplexy and improve wakefulness in an orexin neuron-ablated model of narcolepsy in mice. *Proceedings of the National Academy of Sciences, 10*, 4649–4654.

Mignot, E. (2008). Why we sleep: The temporal organization of recovery. *PLoS Biology, 6*(April), e106. http://dx.doi.org/10.1371/journal.pbio.0060106

Mindell, A. (1990). *Working on yourself alone: Inner dreambody work*. New York, NY: Arkana.

Moody, R. A. (1975). *Life after life*. Covington, GA: Mockingbird Books.

Morewedge, C. K., & Norton, M. I. (2009). When dreaming is believing: The (motivated) interpretation of dreams. *Journal of Personality and Social Psychology, 96*, 249–264.

Morin, C. M., & Edinger, J. D. (2009). Sleep/wake disorders. In P. H. Blaney & T. Millon (Eds.), *Oxford textbook of psychopathology* (pp. 506–526). New York, NY: Oxford University Press.

Motivala, S., & Irwin, M. R. (2007). Sleep and immunity: Cytokine pathways linking sleep and health outcomes. *Psychological Science, 16*, 21–25.

Mystical Experience Registry (2012). Mystical experience registry. Inner experiences explored. Retrieved from http://www.bodysoulandspirit.net/mystical_experiences/read/visitors/new_submissions.shtml

Nash, M. R. (1987). What, if anything, is regressed about hypnotic age regression? A review of the empirical literature. *Psychological Bulletin, 102*, 42–52.

Nash, M. R., & Barnier, A. (Eds.). (2008). *The Oxford handbook of hypnosis*. New York, NY: Oxford Press.

National Institute on Alcohol Abuse and Alcoholism. (2000, July). *Alcohol alert. From genes to geography: The cutting edge of alcohol research*, No. 48. Retrieved from http://pubs.niaaa.nih.gov/publications/aa48.htm

Newcomb, M. D., & Bentler, P. M. (1988). Impact of adolescent drug use and social support on problems of young adults: A longitudinal analysis. *Journal of Abnormal Psychology, 97*, 64–75.

Noyes, R., & Kletti, R. (1976). Depersonalization in the face of life-threatening danger: An interpretation. *Omega, 7*, 103–114.

Ocampo-Garces, A., Molina, E., Rodriguez, A., & Vivaldi, E. A. (2000). Homeostasis of REM sleep after total and selective sleep deprivation in the rat. *Journal of Neurophysiology, 84*, 2699–2702.

Ohayon, M. M. (2000). Prevalence of hallucinations and their pathological associations in the general population. *Psychiatry Research, 97*, 153–164.

Ohayon, M. M. (2002). Epidemiology of insomnia: What we know and what we still need to learn. *Sleep Medicine Reviews, 6*, 97–111.

Pagel, J. F. (2003). Non-dreamers. *Sleep Medicine, 4*, 235–241.

Pahnke, W. N., Kurland, A. A., Unger, S., Savage, C., & Grof, S. (1970). Experimental use of psychedelic (LSD) psychotherapy. *Journal of the American Medical Association, 212*, 1856.

Pano, E. G., Hilscher, M. C., & Cupchik, G. C. (2008–2009). Responding to self-consciousness: An examination of everyday and dream episodes. *Imagination, Cognition, and Personality, 28*, 173–198.

Persinger, M. A. (1987). *Neuropsychological bases of God beliefs*. New York, NY: Praeger.

Persinger, M. A. (1994). Near-death experiences: Determining the neuroanatomical pathways by experiential patterns and simulation in experimental settings. In L. Besette (Ed.), *Healing: Beyond suffering or death* (pp. 277–286). Chabanel, Quebec, Canada: MNH.

Pessah, M. A., & Roffwarg, H. P. (1972). Spontaneous middle ear muscle activity in man: A rapid eye movement sleep phenomenon. *Science, 178*, 773–776.

Piccione, C., Hilgard, E. R., & Zimbardo, P. G. (1989). On the degree of stability of measured hypnotizability over a 25-year period. *Journal of Personality and Social Psychology, 56*, 289–295.

Pihl, R. O. (1999). Substance abuse: Etiological considerations. In T. Millon, P. Blaney, & R. D. Davis (Eds.), *Oxford handbook of psychopathology* (pp. 249–276). New York, NY: Oxford University Press.

Pohorecky, L. (1977). Biphasic action of ethanol. *Biobehavioral Review, 1*, 231–240.

Pope, H. G., Gruber, A. J., & Yergelun-Todd, D. (2001). Residual neuropsychologic effects of cannabis. *Current Psychiatry Report, 3*, 507–512.

Posey, T. B., & Losch, M. E. (1983). Auditory hallucinations of hearing voices in 375 normal subjects. *Imagination, Cognition and Personality, 3*, 99–113.

Punjabi, N. M., Caffo, B. S., Goodwin, J. L., Gottlieb, D. J., Newman, A. B., O'Connor, G. T.,... Samet, J. M. (2009) Sleep-disordered breathing and mortality: A prospective cohort study. *PLoS Medicine, 6*(8), e1000132. http://dx.doi.org/10.1371/journal.pmed.1000132

Quenqua, D. (2012, February). They're, like, way ahead of the linguistic currrrve. *New York Times*, 28.

Rajaratnam, S. M., Polymeropoulos, M. H., Fisher, D. M., Roth, T., Scott, C., Birznieks, G., & Klerman, E. B. (2009). Melatonin agonist tasimelteon (VEC-162) for transient insomnia after sleep-time shift: Two randomised controlled multicentre trials. *Lancet, 373,* 482–491.

Raloff, J. (2009, September 12). Drugged money. *Science News, 176*(6), 9.

Ramaekers, J. G., Kauert, G., van Ruitenbeek, P., Theunissen, E. L., Schneider, E., & Moeller, M. R. (2006). High-potency marijuana impairs executive function and inhibitory motor control. *Neuropsychopharmacology, 31,* 2296–2303.

Rechtschaffen, A. (1998). Current perspectives on the function of sleep. *Perspectives in Biology and Medicine, 41,* 359–390.

Rechtschaffen, A., Verdone, P., & Wheaton, J. (1963). Reports of mental activity during sleep. *Canadian Psychiatry, 8,* 409–414.

Revonsuo, A. (2000). The reinterpretation of dreams: An evolutionary hypothesis of the function of dreaming. *Behavioral and Brain Sciences, 23,* 877–901.

Ridgway, S. H. (2002). Asymmetry and symmetry in brain waves from dolphin left and right hemispheres: Some observations after anesthesia, during quiescent hanging behavior, and during visual obstruction. *Brain, Behavior, and Evolution, 60,* 265–274.

Ring, K. (1984). *Healing toward omega: In search of the meaning of the near-death experience.* New York, NY: Morrow.

Rock, A. (2004). *The mind at night: The new science of how and why we dream.* New York, NY: Basic Books.

Rosenberg, P. (1973). The effects of mood altering drugs: Pleasures and pitfalls. In R. E. Hardy & J. G. Cull (Eds.), *Drug dependence and rehabilitation approaches.* Springfield, IL: Charles C. Thomas.

Rozin, P., & Stoess, C. (1993). Is there a general tendency to become addicted? *Addictive Behaviors, 18,* 81–87.

Sabom, M. (1982). *Recollections of death: A medical investigation.* New York, NY: Harper & Row.

Sanders, L. (2012, February). Emblems of awareness. *Science News.*

Sanders, M. H., & Givelber, R. J. (2006). Overview of obstructive sleep apnea in adults. In T. L. Lee Chiong (Ed.), *Sleep: A comprehensive handbook* (pp. 231–247). Hoboken, NJ: Wiley.

Sarbin, T. R., & Coe, W. C. (1979). Hypnosis and psychopathology: Replacing old myths with fresh metaphors. *Journal of Abnormal Psychology, 88,* 506–526.

Sarbin, T. R., & Slagle, R. W. (1979). Hypnosis and psychophysiological outcomes. In E. Fromm & R. E. Shor (Eds.), *Developments in research and new perspectives* (pp. 273–303). New York, NY: Aldine.

Sayette, M. A. (1999). Does drinking reduce stress? *Alcohol Research and Health, 23,* 250–255.

Schenck, C. H. (2006). Paradox lost: Midnight in the battleground of sleep and dreams. Retrieved from http://www.parasomnias-rbd.com

Schenck, C. H., Boeve, B. F., & Mahowald, M. W. (2013, January 21). Delayed emergence of a parkinsonian disorder or dementia in 81% of older males initially diagnosed with idiopathic REM sleep behavior disorder (RBD): 16 year update on a previously reported series. *Sleep Medicine.*

Schuckit, M. A. (1994). A clinical model of genetic influences in alcohol dependence. *Journal of Studies of Alcohol, 55,* 5–17.

Shaffer, H. J. (2000). Addictive personality. In A. E. Kazdin (Ed.), *Encyclopedia of psychology* (Vol. 1, pp. 35–36). Washington, DC: American Psychological Association and Oxford University Press.

Shamsuzzaman, A. S., Gersh, B. J., & Somers, V. K. (2003). Obstructive sleep apnea: Implications for cardiac and vascular disease. *Journal of the American Medical Association, 290,* 1906–1914.

Shedler, J., & Block, J. (1990). Adolescent drug use and psychological health: A longitudinal inquiry. *American Psychologist, 45,* 612–630.

Sher, K. J. (1987). Stress response dampening. In H. T. Blane & K. E. Leonard (Eds.), *Psychological theories of drinking and alcoholism* (pp. 227–271). New York, NY: Guilford Press.

Sher, K. J., Grekin, E. R., & Williams, N. A. (2005). The development of alcohol use disorders. In S. Nolen-Hoeksema, T. D. Cannon, & T. Widiger (Eds.), *Annual Review of Clinical Psychology, 1,* 493–524.

Sher, K. J., Wood, M. D., Richardson, A. E., & Jackson, K. M. (2005). Subjective effects of alcohol 1: Effects of the drink and drinking context. In M. Earleywine (Ed.), *Mind-altering drugs: The science of subjective experience* (pp. 86–134). Washington, DC: American Psychological Association.

Siegel, J. (2005). Clues to the function of mammalian sleep. *Nature, 437,* 1264–1271.

Simon, M. J., & Salzberg, H. C. (1985). The effect of manipulated expectancies on posthypnotic amnesia. *International Journal of Clinical and Experimental Hypnosis, 33,* 40–51.

Slegel, D. E., Benson, K. L., Zarcone, V. P., & Schubert, E. D. (1991). Middle-ear muscle activity and its association with motor activity in the extremities and head in sleep. *Lancet, 337,* 597–599.

Slutske, W. S., Heath, A. C., Dinwiddie, S. H., Madden, P. A., & Bucholz, K. K. (1998). Common genetic risk factors for conduct disorder and alcohol dependence. *Journal of Abnormal Psychology, 107,* 363–374.

Smallwood, J., & Schooler, J. W. (2006). The restless mind. *Psychological Bulletin, 132*(6), 946–958.

Smith, M., & Hall, C. S. (1964). An investigation of regression in a long dream series. *Journal of Gerontology, 19,* 66–71.

Smith, M. T., & Haythornthwaite, J. A. (2004). How do sleep disturbance and chronic pain inter-relate? Insights from the longitudinal and cognitive-behavioral clinical trials literature. *Sleep Medicine Review, 8,* 119–132.

Snyder, T. J., & Gackenbach, J. (1988). Individual differences associated with lucid dreaming. In J. Gackenbach & S. Laberge (Eds.), *Conscious mind, sleeping brain: Perspectives on lucid dreaming* (pp. 221–260). New York, NY: Plenum.

Soar, K., Parrott, A. C., & Fox, H. C. (2004). Persistent neuropsychological problems after 7 years of abstinence from recreational ecstasy (MDMA): A case study. *Psychological Reports, 95,* 192–196.

Solms, M., & Turnbull, O. (2002). *The brain and the inner world.* New York, NY: Other Press.

Spanos, N. P. (1986). Hypnotic behavior: A social-psychological interpretation of amnesia, analgesia, and "trance logic." *The Behavioral and Brain Sciences, 9,* 499–502.

Spanos, N. P., Cobb, P. C., & Gorassini, D. (1985). Failing to resist hypnotic test suggestions: A strategy for self-presenting as deeply hypnotized. *Psychiatry, 48,* 282–292.

Spanos, N. P., & Hewitt, E. C. (1980). The hidden observer in hypnotic analgesia: Discovery or experimental creation? *Journal of Personality and Social Psychology, 39,* 1201–1214.

Spanos, N. P., Menary, E., Gabora, M. J., DuBreuil, S. C., & Dewhirst, B. (1991). Secondary identity enactments during hypnotic past-life regression: A sociocognitive perspective. *Journal of Personality and Social Psychology, 61,* 308–320.

Spielman, A., Conroy, D., & Glovinsky, P. B. (2003). Evaluation of insomnia. In M. L. Perlis & K. L. Lichstein (Eds.), *Treating sleep disorders: Principles and practice of behavioral sleep medicine* (pp. 190–213). Hoboken, NJ: Wiley.

Spoormacher, V., & Van den Bout, J. (2006). Lucid dreaming treatment for nightmares: A pilot study. *Psychotherapy and Psychosomatics, 75,* 389–394.

Spotts, J. F., & Shontz, F. C. (1983). Drug-induced ego states. 1. *The International Journal of the Addictions, 18,* 119–151.

Steblay, N. M., & Bothwell, R. K. (1994). Evidence for hypnotically refreshed testimony: The view from the laboratory. *Law and Human Behavior, 18,* 635–651.

Stevenson, I. (1960). The evidence for survival from claimed memories of former incarnations. Part I: Review of the data. *Journal of the American Society for Psychical Research, 54,* 51–71.

Stevenson, I. (1974). *Twenty cases suggestive of reincarnation* (2nd rev. ed.), Charlottesville, VA: University Press of Virginia.

Stickgold, R., James, L., & Hobson, J. A. (2002). Visual discrimination learning requires sleep after training. *Nature Neuroscience, 3,* 1235–1236.

Strayer, D. L., Drews, F. A., & Johnston, W. A. (2003). Cell phone-induced failures of visual attention during simulated driving. *Journal of Experimental Psychology: Applied, 9,* 23–32.

Strohl, K. P., & Redline, S. (1996). Recognition of obstructive sleep apnea. *American Journal of Respiratory and Critical Care Medicine, 154,* 279–289.

Substance Abuse and Mental Health Services Administration (2001). *2001 National household survey on drug abuse.* Retrieved from http://www.oas.samhsa.gov/nhsda/2k1nhsda/vol1/toc.htm

Sullum, J. (2003). *Saying yes: In defense of drug use.* New York, NY: Tarcher/Putnam.

Swendsen, J., Burstein, M., Case, B., Conway, K. P., Dierker, L., He, J., & Merikangas, K. R. (2012). Use and abuse of alcohol and illicit drugs in US adolescents: Results of the National Comorbidity Survey-Adolescent Supplement. *Archives of General Psychiatry, 69*(4), 390–398.

Taiminen, T., & Jääskeläinen, S. K. (2001). Intense and recurrent déjà vu experiences related to amantadine and phenylpropanolamine in a healthy male. *Journal of Clinical Neuroscience, 8,* 460–462.

Terhune, D. B. (2009). The incidence and determinants of visual phenomenology during out-of-body experiences. *Cortex, 45,* 236–242.

Tetrault, J. M., Crothers, K., Moore, B. A., Mehra, R., Concato, J., & Fiellin, D. A. (2007). Effects of marijuana smoking on pulmonary function and respiratory complications: A systematic review. *Archives of Internal Medicine, 167,* 221–228.

Thombs, D. L., O'Mara, R. J., Tsukamoto, M., Rossheim, M., Weiler, R. M., Merves, M. L., & Goldberger B. A. (2010). Event-level analyses of energy drink consumption and alcohol intoxication in bar patrons. *Addictive Behaviors, 35,* 325–330.

Tucker, J. A., Vucinich, R., & Sobell, M. (1982). Alcohol's effects on human emotions. *International Journal of the Addictions, 17,* 155–180.

Underwood, A. (2007, June 12). It's called "sexsomnia." *Newsweek,* 53.

Vallee, B. L. (1988, June). Alcohol in the Western world: A history. *Scientific American, 278,* 80–85.

Van de Castle, R. (1994). *Our dreaming mind.* New York, NY: Ballantine Books.

Van Eeden, F. (1913). A study of dreams. *Proceedings of the Society for Psychical Research, 26,* 431–461.

Van Lommel, P., van Wees, R., Meyers, V., & Elfferich, I. (2001). Near-death experiences in survivors of cardiac arrest: A prospective study in the Netherlands. *Lancet, 358,* 2039–2045.

Voss, J. L., and Paller, K. A. (2008). Brain substrates of implicit and explicit memory: The importance of concurrently acquired neural signals of both memory types. *Neuropsychologia, 46,* 3021–3029.

Voss, U., Holzmann, R., Tuin, I., & Hobson, J. A. (2009). Lucid dreaming: A state of consciousness with features of both waking and non-lucid dreaming. *Sleep, 32*(9), 1191–2000.

Wagner, U., Gais, S., Haider, H., Verleger, R., & Born, J. (2004). Sleep inspires insight. *Nature, 427,* 352–355.

Wagstaff, G. (1998). The semantics and physiology of hypnosis as an altered state: Towards a definition of hypnosis. *Contemporary Hypnosis, 15,* 149–165.

Wagstaff, G. (2008). Hypnosis and the law. *Criminal Justice and Behavior, 35,* 1277–1294.

Walker, M. P., Brakefield, A., Morgan, J., Hobson, J. A., & Stickgold, R. (2002). Practice, with sleep, makes perfect. *Neuron, 35,* 205–211.

Wark, D. M. (2006). Alert hypnosis: A review and case report. *American Jounral of Clinical Hypnosis, 48,* 291–300.

Wegner, D. M. (2004). Précis of the illusion of conscious will. *Behavioral and Brain Sciences, 27,* 649–692.

Weiss, B. L. (1988). *Many lives, many masters.* New York, NY: Simon & Schuster.

Wennberg, P. (2002). The development of alcohol habits in a Swedish male birth cohort. In S. P. Shohov (Ed.), *Advances in psychology research, Vol. 15* (pp. 121–155). Hauppauge, NY: Nova Science.

Whinnery, J. E. (1997). Psychophysiologic correlates of unconsciousness and near-death experiences. *Journal of Near-Death Studies, 15,* 231–258.

Wilkins, L. K., Girard, T., & Cheyne, J. A. (2011). Ketamine as a primary predictor of out-of-body experiences associated with multiple substance use. *Consciousness and Cognition, 20*(3), 943–950.

Wilson, S. C., & Barber, T. X. (1981). Vivid fantasy and hallucinatory abilities in the life histories of excellent hypnotic subjects ("somnambules"): Preliminary report with female subjects. In E. Klinger (Ed.), *Imagery: Concepts, results, and applications* (pp. 133–149). New York, NY: Plenum Press.

Wolfe, V. A., & Pruitt, S. D. (2003). Insomnia and sleep disorders. In L. M. Cohen, D. E. McChargue, & F. L. Collins (Eds.), *The health psychology handbook* (pp. 425–440). Thousand Oaks, CA: Sage.

Woody, E. Z., & Bowers, K. S. (1994). A frontal assault on dissociated control. In S. J. Lynn & J. W. Rhue (Eds.), *Dissociation: Clinical and theoretical perspectives* (pp. 52–79). New York, NY: Guilford Press.

Woody, E. Z., & Sadler, P (2008). Dissociation theories of hypnosis. In M. R. Nash & A. J. Barnier (Eds.), *The Oxford handbook of hypnosis* (pp. 81–110). New York, NY: Oxford University Press.

World Health Organization (WHO) (2004). *Global status report on alcohol 2004.* Geneva, Switzerland: WHO, Department of Mental Health and Substance Abuse.

Wulff, D.M. (in press). Mystical experiences. In E. Cardeña, S. Lynn, & S. Krippner (Eds.), *Varieties of anamalous experience: Examining the scientific evidence* (2nd ed.). Washington, DC: American Psychological Association.

Yaffe, K., Laffan, A. M., Harrison, S. L., Redline, S., Spira, A.P., Ensrud, K.E.,... Stone, K. L. (2011). Sleep-disordered breathing, hypoxia, and risk of mild cognitive impairment and dementia in older women. *Journal of the American Medical Association, 306*(6), 613–619.

Young, J., & Cooper, L. M. (1972). Hypnotic recall amnesia as a function of manipulated expectancy. *Proceedings of the 80th Annual Convention of the American Psychological Association, 7,* 857–858.

Zadra, A. (1996). Recurrent dreams: Their relation to life events. In D. Barrett (Ed.), *Trauma and dreams* (pp. 231–247). Cambridge, MA: Harvard University Press.

Credits

Photo Credits

Learning

Learning

HOW NURTURE CHANGES US

Think About It

How do phobias and fetishes develop?

How do trainers get animals to do cute tricks, like dancing or water skiing?

Does watching violence on tv really teach children to become violent?

Why do we sometimes avoid a delicious food for decades after only one negative experience?

Can we learn in our sleep?

Learning the information in this textbook is altering your brain in ways that psychologists are increasingly coming to understand.

learning
change in an organism's behavior or thought as a result of experience

Learning

Listen in **MyPsychLab** to chapter audio

Before reading further, try your hand at the following three items.

1. Ivan Pavlov, the discoverer of classical conditioning, was known to be a
   a. slow eater.
   b. fast walker.
   c. terrible cook.
   d. I have no idea.

2. John B. Watson, the founder of behaviorism, was tossed out of Johns Hopkins University for
   a. plagiarizing a journal article.
   b. stabbing one of his faculty colleagues.
   c. having an affair with his graduate student.
   d. I have no idea.

3. As a college student, B. F. Skinner, the founder of radical behaviorism, once spread a false rumor that which of the following individuals was coming to campus?
   a. silent movie comedian Charlie Chaplin
   b. psychoanalyst Sigmund Freud
   c. President Theodore Roosevelt
   d. I have no idea.

Now, read the following paragraph.

The three most famous figures in the psychology of learning were each colorful characters in their own way. The discoverer of classical conditioning, Ivan Pavlov, was a notoriously compulsive fellow. He ate lunch every day at precisely 12 noon, went to bed at exactly the same time every night, and departed St. Petersburg, Russia, for vacation the same day every year. Pavlov was such a rapid walker that his wife frequently had to run frantically to keep up with him. The life of the founder of behaviorism, John B. Watson, was rocked with scandal. Despite becoming one of the world's most famous psychologists, he was booted out of the Johns Hopkins University for having an affair with his graduate student, Rosalie Rayner. B. F. Skinner, the founder of radical behaviorism, was something of a prankster during his undergraduate years at Hamilton College in New York. He and a friend once spread a false rumor that comedian Charlie Chaplin was coming to campus. This rumor nearly provoked a riot when Chaplin didn't materialize as expected.

Now go back and try again to answer the three questions at the beginning of this chapter.

If you got more questions right the second time than the first—and odds are high that you did—then you've experienced something we all take for granted: learning. (The answers, by the way, are b, c, and a.) By **learning,** we mean a change in an organism's behavior or thought as a result of experience. When we learn our brains change along with our behaviors. Remarkably, your brain is physically different now than it was just a few minutes ago, because it underwent chemical changes that allowed you to learn novel facts. Learning lies at the heart of just about every domain of psychology. Virtually all behaviors are a complex stew of genetic predispositions and learning. Without learning, we'd be unable to do much; we couldn't walk or talk, let alone read an introductory psychology textbook chapter about learning.

Psychologists have long debated how many distinct types of learning there are. We won't try to settle this controversy here. Instead, we'll review several types of learning that psychologists have studied in depth, starting with the most basic.

Before we do, place your brain on pause, put down your pen or highlighter, close your eyes, and attend to several things that you almost never notice: the soft buzzing of the lights in the room, the feel of your clothing against your skin, the sensation of your tongue on your teeth or lips. Unless someone draws our attention to these stimuli, we don't even realize they're there, because we've learned to ignore them. **Habituation** is the process by which we respond less strongly over time to repeated stimuli. It helps explain why loud snorers can sleep peacefully through the night while keeping their irritated roommates wide awake. Chronic snorers have become so accustomed to the sound of their own snoring that they no longer notice it.

Habituation is the simplest and probably earliest form of learning to emerge in humans. Fetuses display habituation as early as 32 weeks. When researchers apply a gentle vibrator to the mother's stomach, the fetus first jerks around in response to the stimulus, but stops moving after repeated vibrations (Morokuma et al., 2004). What was first a jolt to the fetus's system later became a mere annoyance that it could safely ignore.

In research that earned him the Nobel Prize in 2000, neurophysiologist Eric Kandel uncovered the biological mechanism of habituation of *Aplysia,* a five-inch-long sea slug. Prick *Aplysia* on a certain part of its body, and it retracts its gill in a defensive maneuver. Touch *Aplysia* in the same spot repeatedly, and it begins to ignore the stimulus. This habituation, Kandel found, is accompanied by a progressive decrease in release of the neurotransmitter serotonin at *Aplysia*'s synapses (Siegelbaum, Camardo, & Kandel, 1982). This discovery helped psychologists unravel the neural bases of learning (see **FIGURE 1**).

Psychologists have studied habituation by measuring—of all things—sweat. Because perspiration on our fingertips is a good indicator of anxiety (Fowles, 1980), scientists measure it by using an electrical conductivity measure called the skin conductance response. Most research shows that our hands stop sweating sooner for weak stimuli than they do for strong stimuli, meaning that weak stimuli stop producing anxiety fairly quickly compared with strong stimuli. In the case of very strong stimuli, like painful electric shocks, we often see no habituation at all—people continue to sweat anxiously at the same high levels—even across many trials (Lykken et al., 1988).

This research suggests that habituation makes good sense from an evolutionary standpoint. We wouldn't want to attend to every tiny sensation that comes across our mental radar screens, because most pose no threat. Yet we wouldn't want to habituate to stimuli that could be dangerous. Fortunately, not all repeated stimuli lead to habituation, only those that we deem safe or worth ignoring do.

Some cases of repeated exposure to stimuli don't lead to habituation but to *sensitization*—that is, responding *more strongly* over time. Sensitization is most likely when a stimulus is dangerous, irritating, or both. Many organisms, from *Aplysia* to humans, show sensitization as well as habituation. Have you ever tried to study when the person next to you was whispering, and the whispering kept getting more annoying to the point that you couldn't concentrate? If so, you've experienced sensitization.

FIGURE 1 Habituation in a Simple Animal. *Aplysia californicus* is a sea slug about five inches long that retracts its gill when pricked, but then habituates (stops retracting its gill) if pricked repeatedly.

Habituating to background noise while studying can be difficult, especially if the noise is loud.

Classical Conditioning

1 Describe Pavlov's model of classical conditioning and discriminate conditioned stimuli and responses from unconditioned stimuli and responses.

2 Explain the major principles and terminology associated with classical conditioning.

3 Explain how complex behaviors can result from classical conditioning and how they emerge in our daily lives.

The story of habituation could hardly be more straightforward. We experience a stimulus, respond to it, and then stop responding after repeated exposure. We've learned something significant, but we haven't learned to forge connections between two stimuli. Yet a great deal of learning depends on associating one thing with another. If we never learned to connect one stimulus, like the appearance of an apple, with another stimulus, like its taste, our everyday life would be a world of disconnected sensory experiences.

habituation
process of responding less strongly over time to repeated stimuli

The rock band Barenaked Ladies accurately described classical conditioning in their song, "Brian Wilson." They sing about Pavlov and how a bell sound comes to trigger salivation. Not bad for a group of nonpsychologists!

Watch in **MyPsychLab** the **Video:**
Classical Footage of Pavlov

Factoid

Classical conditioning can occur even among people who are in a vegetative state. In one study, researchers repeatedly delivered a musical note, followed by a puff of air to the eyes—a UCS that produces a UCR of blinking—to 22 patients in vegetative or minimally conscious states (Bekinschtein et al., 2009). Eventually, the musical note became a CS, producing eye blinking even in these largely or entirely unconscious individuals.

classical (Pavlovian) conditioning
form of learning in which animals come to respond to a previously neutral stimulus that had been paired with another stimulus that elicits an automatic response

unconditioned stimulus (UCS)
stimulus that elicits an automatic response

unconditioned response (UCR)
automatic response to a nonneutral stimulus that does not need to be learned

conditioned response (CR)
response previously associated with a non-neutral stimulus that is elicited by a neutral stimulus through conditioning

conditioned stimulus (CS)
initially neutral stimulus that comes to elicit a response due to association with an unconditioned stimulus

In the nineteenth century, a school of thinkers called the *British Associationists* believed that we acquire virtually all of our knowledge by *conditioning*, that is, by forming associations among stimuli. Once we form these links, like the connection between our mother's voice with her face, we need only recall one element of the pair to retrieve the other. The British Associationists believed that simple connections provided the mental building blocks for all of our more complex ideas. Their armchair conjectures were to be confirmed by a pioneering Russian physiologist who demonstrated these processes of association in the laboratory.

Pavlov's Discovery of Classical Conditioning

That physiologist's name was Ivan Pavlov. Pavlov's primary research was on digestion in dogs—in fact, his discoveries concerning digestion, not classical conditioning, earned him the Nobel Prize in 1904. Pavlov placed dogs in a harness and inserted a collection tube into their salivary glands to study their digestive responses to meat powder. In doing so, he observed something unexpected: Dogs began salivating (more informally, they started to drool), not only to the meat powder itself, but to previously neutral stimuli that had become associated with it, such as research assistants who brought in the powder. Indeed, the dogs even salivated to the sound of these assistants' footsteps as they approached the laboratory. The dogs seemed to be anticipating the meat powder and responding to stimuli that signaled its arrival.

We call this process of association **classical conditioning** (or **Pavlovian conditioning**): a form of learning in which animals come to respond to a previously neutral stimulus that had been paired with another stimulus that elicits an automatic response. Yet Pavlov's initial observations were merely anecdotal, so like any good scientist he soon put his informal observations to a more rigorous test.

Here's how Pavlov first demonstrated classical conditioning systematically (see **FIGURE 2**):

1. He started with an initially neutral stimulus, one that didn't elicit any particular response. In this case, Pavlov used a metronome, a clicking pendulum that keeps time (in other studies, Pavlov used a tuning fork or whistle; contrary to popular belief, he didn't use a bell).

2. He then paired the neutral stimulus again and again with an **unconditioned stimulus (UCS),** a stimulus that elicits an automatic—that is, a reflexive—response. In the case of Pavlov's dogs, the unconditioned stimulus is the meat powder, and the automatic, reflexive response it elicits is the **unconditioned response (UCR).** For Pavlov's dogs, the unconditioned response was salivation. The key point is that the animal doesn't need to learn to respond to the unconditioned stimulus with the unconditioned response: Dogs naturally drool in response to food. The animal generates the unconditioned response without any training at all, because the response is a product of nature (genes), not nurture (experience).

3. As Pavlov repeatedly paired the neutral stimulus with the unconditioned stimulus, he observed something remarkable. If he now presented the metronome alone, it elicited a response, namely, salivation. This new response is the **conditioned response (CR):** a response previously associated with a nonneutral stimulus that comes to be elicited by a neutral stimulus. Lo and behold, learning has occurred. The metronome had become a **conditioned stimulus (CS)**—a previously neutral stimulus that comes to elicit a conditioned response as a result of its association with an unconditioned stimulus. The dog, which previously did nothing when it heard the metronome except perhaps turn its head toward it, now salivates when it hears the metronome. The conditioned response, in contrast to the unconditioned response, is a product of nurture (experience), not nature (genes).

In most cases, the CR is fairly similar to the UCR, but it's rarely identical to it. For example, Pavlov found that dogs salivated less in response to the metronome (the CS) than to the meat powder (the UCS).

Few findings in psychology are as replicable as classical conditioning. We can apply the classical conditioning paradigm to just about any animal with an intact nervous system, and demonstrate it repeatedly without fail. If only all psychological findings were so dependable!

Principles of Classical Conditioning

We'll next explore the major principles underlying classical conditioning. Pavlov noted, and many others have since confirmed, that classical conditioning occurs in three phases—acquisition, extinction, and spontaneous recovery. In addition, as we'll see, once classical conditioning to a stimulus occurs, it often extends to a host of related stimuli, making its everyday life influence surprisingly powerful.

◀ **REPLICABILITY**
Can the results be duplicated in other studies?

 Like many people, this girl found her first ride on a roller coaster terrifying. Now, all she needs to do is to see a photograph of a roller coaster for her heart to start pounding. **In this scenario, what three classical conditioning terms describe (a) her first roller coaster ride, (b) a photograph of a roller coaster, and (c) her heart pounding in response to this photograph?** (See answers upside down at bottom of page.)

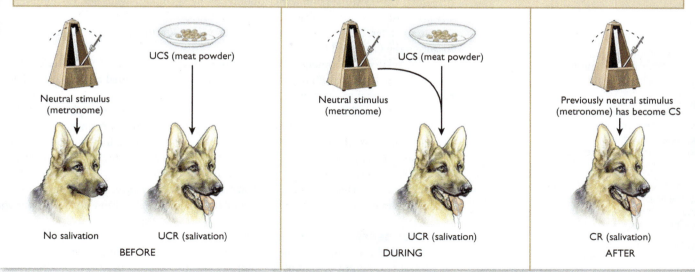

FIGURE 2 Pavlov's Classical Conditioning Model. UCS (meat powder) is paired with a neutral stimulus (metronome clicking) and produces UCR (salivation). Then the metronome is presented alone, and CR (salivation) occurs.

Classical Conditioning

Neutral stimulus (metronome)	UCS (meat powder)	Neutral stimulus (metronome)	UCS (meat powder)	Previously neutral stimulus (metronome) has become CS
No salivation	UCR (salivation)		UCR (salivation)	CR (salivation)
BEFORE		DURING		AFTER

FIGURE 3 Acquisition and Extinction. Acquisition is the repeated pairing of UCS and CS, increasing the CR's strength (a). In extinction, the CS is presented again and again without the UCS, resulting in the gradual disappearance of the CR (b).

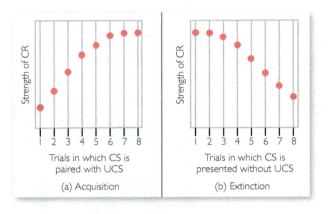

(a) Acquisition — Trials in which CS is paired with UCS — Strength of CR

(b) Extinction — Trials in which CS is presented without UCS — Strength of CR

Factoid

Backward conditioning—in which the UCS is presented *before* the CS—is extremely difficult to achieve. So, if we repeatedly present a dog with meat power, and then a metronome sound a second or two later, the metronome won't later trigger much, if any, salivation on its own. For conditioning to work efficiently, the CS must forecast the appearance of the UCS.

The renewal effect: A person hiking through the woods may experience fear when she approaches an area if she's previously spotted a dangerous animal there.

acquisition
learning phase during which a conditioned response is established

extinction
gradual reduction and eventual elimination of the conditioned response after the conditioned stimulus is presented repeatedly without the unconditioned stimulus

spontaneous recovery
sudden reemergence of an extinct conditioned response after a delay in exposure to the conditioned stimulus

renewal effect
sudden reemergence of a conditioned response following extinction when an animal is returned to the environment in which the conditioned response was acquired

stimulus generalization
process by which conditioned stimuli similar, but not identical, to the original conditioned stimulus elicit a conditioned response

ACQUISITION. In **acquisition,** we gradually learn—or acquire—the CR. If we look at **FIGURE 3a**, we'll see that as the CS and UCS are paired over and over again, the CR increases progressively in strength. The steepness of this curve varies somewhat depending on how close together in time we present the CS and UCS. In general, the closer in time the pairing of CS and UCS, the faster learning occurs, with about a half second delay typically being the optimal pairing for learning. Longer delays usually decrease the speed and strength of the organism's response.

EXTINCTION. In a process called **extinction,** the CR decreases in magnitude and eventually disappears when the CS is repeatedly presented alone, that is, without the UCS (see **FIGURE 3b**). After numerous presentations of the metronome without meat powder, Pavlov's dogs eventually stopped salivating. Most psychologists once believed that extinction was similar to forgetting: The CR fades away over repeated trials, just as many memories gradually decay. Yet the truth is more complicated and interesting than that. Extinction is an active, rather than passive, process. During extinction, a new response, which in the case of Pavlov's dogs was the *absence* of salivation, gradually "writes over" or inhibits the CR, namely, salivation. The extinguished CR doesn't vanish completely; it's merely overwritten by the new behavior. This contrasts with some forms of traditional forgetting, in which the memory itself disappears. Interestingly, Pavlov had proposed this hypothesis in his writings, although few people believed him at the time. How do we know he was right? Read on.

SPONTANEOUS RECOVERY. In a phenomenon called **spontaneous recovery,** a seemingly extinct CR reappears (often in somewhat weaker form) if we present the CS again, say, hours or even days later. It's as though the CR were lurking in the background, waiting to emerge following another presentation of the CS. In a classic study, Pavlov (1927) presented the CS (tone from a metronome) alone again and again and extinguished the CR (salivation) because there was no UCS (mouth-watering meat powder) following it. Two hours later, he presented the CS again and the CR returned. The animal hadn't really forgotten the CR, it had just suppressed it.

A related phenomenon is the **renewal effect,** which occurs when we extinguish a response in a setting different from the one in which the animal acquired it. When we restore the animal to the original setting, the extinguished response reappears (Bouton, 1994; Verliet et al., 2012). The renewal effect may help to explain why people with *phobias*—intense, irrational fears—who've overcome their phobias often experience a reappearance of their symptoms when they return to the environment in which they acquired their fears (Denniston, Chang, & Miller, 2003). Even though it may sometimes lead to a return of phobias, the renewal effect is often adaptive. If we've been bitten by a snake in one part of a forest, it makes sense to experience fear when we find ourselves there again, even years later. That same snake or his slithery descendants may still be lying in wait in the same spot.

STIMULUS GENERALIZATION. Pavlov found that following classical conditioning, his dogs salivated not merely to the original metronome sound, but to sounds similar to it. This phenomenon is **stimulus generalization:** the process by which CSs that are similar, but not identical, to the original CS elicit a CR. Stimulus generalization occurs along a *generalization gradient:* The more similar to the original CS the new CS is, the stronger the CR will be (see **FIGURE 4**). Pavlov found that his dogs showed their largest amount of salivation to the original sound, with progressively less salivation to sounds that were less and less similar to it in pitch. Stimulus generalization is typically adaptive, because it allows us to transfer what we've learned to new things. For example, once we've learned to drive our own car, we can borrow a friend's car without needing a full tutorial on how to drive it.

STIMULUS DISCRIMINATION. The flip side of the coin to stimulus generalization is **stimulus discrimination;** it occurs when we exhibit a less pronounced CR to CSs that differ from the original CS. Stimulus discrimination helps us understand why we can enjoy scary movies. Although we may hyperventilate a bit while watching television footage of a ferocious tornado tearing through a small town, we'd respond much more strongly if the tornado were headed straight for our home. Thankfully, we've learned to discriminate between a televised stimulus and the real-world version of it, and to modify our response as a result. Like stimulus generalization, stimulus discrimination is usually adaptive, because it allows us to distinguish among stimuli that share some similarities but that differ in important ways. Without it, we'd be scared to pet a new dog if we were bitten by a similar-looking dog last week.

Higher-Order Conditioning

Taking conditioning a step further, organisms learn to develop conditioned associations to previously neutral stimuli that come to be associated with the original CS. If after conditioning a dog to salivate to a tone, we pair a picture of a circle with that tone, a dog eventually salivates to the circle as well as to the tone. That's **higher-order conditioning:** the process by which organisms develop classically conditioned responses to previously neutral stimuli that later become associated with the original CS (Gewirtz & Davis, 2000). With higher-order conditioning, each progressive level results in weaker conditioning, just as a verbal message becomes less accurate as it's passed from one person to another. So second-order conditioning—in which a new CS is paired with the original CS—tends to be weaker than garden-variety classical conditioning, and third-order conditioning—in which a third CS is in turn paired with the second-order CS—is even weaker. Fourth-order conditioning and beyond is typically difficult or impossible to achieve.

Higher-order conditioning allows us to extend classical conditioning to a host of new stimuli. It helps explain why we feel thirsty after someone merely says "Coke" on a sweltering summer day. We've already come to associate the sight, sound, and smell of a Coca-Cola with quenching our thirst, and we eventually came to associate the word *Coke* with these CSs.

Applications of Classical Conditioning to Daily Life

Without classical conditioning, we couldn't develop physiological associations to stimuli that signal biologically important events, like things we want to eat—or that want to eat us. Many of the physiological responses we display in classical conditioning contribute to our survival. Salivation, for instance, helps us to digest food. Skin conductance

FIGURE 4 Generalization Gradient. The more similar to the original CS the new CS is, the stronger the CR will be. Pavlov used a tone pitched close to the original tone's pitch.

Higher-order conditioning helps explain the seemingly mysterious "power of suggestion." Merely hearing "Want a Coke?" on a hot summer day can make us feel thirsty.

Factoid

Many addictions are shaped in part by higher-order conditioning, with the context or setting in which people take the drugs serving as higher-order CSs (Sullum, 2003). One research team (Robins, Helzer, & Davis, 1975) examined 451 Vietnam veterans who returned to the United States with serious heroin addictions. Surprisingly, 86 percent of them lost their addiction shortly after returning to the United States. Because the context had changed from Vietnam to the United States, the veterans' classically conditioned responses to heroin extinguished.

stimulus discrimination
process by which organisms display a less pronounced conditioned response to conditioned stimuli that differ from the original conditioned stimulus

higher-order conditioning
developing a conditioned response to a conditioned stimulus by virtue of its association with another conditioned stimulus

Advertisers use higher-order classical conditioning to get customers to associate their products with an inherently enjoyable stimulus.

REPLICABILITY ▶
Can the results be duplicated in other studies?

RULING OUT RIVAL HYPOTHESES ▶
Have important alternative explanations for the findings been excluded?

Explore in MyPsychLab the Concept:
Classical Conditioning of Little Albert

FALSIFIABILITY ▶
Can the claim be disproved?

latent inhibition
difficulty in establishing classical conditioning to a conditioned stimulus we've repeatedly experienced alone, that is, without the unconditioned stimulus

responses probably were important to our primate ancestors (Stern, Ray, & Davis, 1980), who found that sticky fingers and toes came in handy for grasping tree limbs while fleeing from predators. Slightly moist fingertips help us adhere to things, as you'll discover if you moisten the tip of your index finger while turning to the next page of this text.

Classical conditioning isn't limited to salivating dogs in old Russian laboratories; it applies to daily life, too. We'll consider four everyday applications of classical conditioning here: advertising, the acquisition of fears and phobias, the acquisition of fetishes, and disgust reactions.

CLASSICAL CONDITIONING AND ADVERTISING. Few people grasp the principles of classical conditioning, especially higher-order conditioning, better than advertisers. By repeatedly pairing the sights and sounds of products with photographs of handsome hunks and scantily clad beauties, marketing whizzes aim to establish classically conditioned connections between their brands and positive emotions. They do so for a good reason: Research shows that it works. So does another favorite trick of advertisers: repeatedly pairing pictures of products with pictures our favorite celebrities (Till, Stanley, & Priluck, 2008).

One researcher (Gorn, 1982) paired slides of either blue or beige pens (the CSs) with music that participants had rated as either enjoyable or not enjoyable (the UCSs). Then he gave participants the opportunity to select a pen upon departing the lab. Whereas 79 percent of participants who heard music they liked picked the pen that had been paired with music, only 30 percent of those who heard music they disliked picked the pen that had been paired with music.

Not all researchers who've paired products, like familiar brands of cereal, with pleasurable stimuli have successfully replicated classical conditioning effects (Gresham & Shimp, 1985; Smith, 2001). But many of these negative findings are open to a rival explanation: latent inhibition. **Latent inhibition** refers to the fact that when we've experienced a CS alone many times, it's difficult to classically condition it to another stimulus (Palsson et al., 2005; Vaitl & Lipp, 1997). Because some investigators who failed to obtain classical conditioning effects for products relied on brands with which participants were already familiar, their negative findings may be attributable to latent inhibition. Indeed, when researchers have used novel brands, they've generally been able to show classical conditioning effects (Stuart, Shimp, & Engle, 1987).

THE ACQUISITION OF FEARS AND PHOBIAS: THE STRANGE TALE OF LITTLE ALBERT. Can classical conditioning help explain how we come to fear or avoid stimuli? John B. Watson, the founder of behaviorism, answered this question in 1920 when he and his graduate student, Rosalie Rayner, performed what's often regarded as one of the most ethically questionable studies in the history of psychology. Here's what they did.

Watson and Rayner (1920) set out in part to falsify the Freudian view of phobias, which proposes that phobias stem from deep-seated conflicts buried in the unconscious. To do so, they recruited a 9-month-old infant who'll be forever known in the psychological literature as Little Albert. Little Albert was fond of furry little creatures, like white rats. But Watson and Rayner were about to change that.

Watson and Rayner first allowed Little Albert to play with a rat. But only seconds afterward, Watson snuck up behind Little Albert and struck a gong with a steel hammer, creating an earsplitting noise, startling him out of his wits, and making him cry. After seven such pairings of the rat and UCS (the loud sound from the gong), Little Albert displayed a CR (crying) to the rat alone, demonstrating that the rat had now become a CS. That conditioned response was still present when Watson and Rayner exposed Little Albert to the rat five days later. Little Albert also displayed stimulus generalization, crying not only in response to rats, but also to a rabbit, a dog, a furry coat, and, to a lesser extent, a Santa Claus mask and John B. Watson's hair. Fortunately, Little Albert also demonstrated at least some stimulus discrimination, as he didn't display much fear toward cotton balls or the hair of Dr. Watson's research assistants.

Incidentally, no one knows for sure what became of poor Little Albert (see Factoid). His mother withdrew him from the study about a month after it began, never to be heard from again. Needless to say, because inducing a phobia-like condition in an infant raises a host of troubling ethical questions, Watson and Rayner's Little Albert study would never get past a modern-day college or university Institutional Review Board.

Stimulus generalization, like that experienced by Little Albert, allows our learning to be remarkably flexible—which is often, although not always, a good thing. It allows us to develop fears of many stimuli. Certain phobias, like those of snakes, spiders, heights, water, and blood, are considerably more widespread than others (American Psychiatric Association, 2000). And some are downright strange, as **TABLE 1** illustrates.

The good news is that if classical conditioning can contribute to our acquiring phobias, it can also contribute to our overcoming them. Mary Cover Jones, a student of Watson, treated a 3-year-old named Little Peter, who had a phobia of rabbits. Jones (1924) treated Peter's fear successfully by gradually introducing him to a white rabbit while giving him a piece of his favorite candy. As she moved the rabbit increasingly close to him, the sight of the rabbit eventually came to elicit a new CR: pleasure rather than fear. Modern-day psychotherapists, although rarely feeding their clients candy, use similar practices to eliminate phobias. They may pair feared stimuli with relaxation or other pleasurable stimuli (Wolpe, 1990).

FETISHES On the flip side of the coin from phobias, **fetishism**—sexual attraction to nonliving things—may also arise in part from classical conditioning (Akins, 2004; Hoffmann, 2011). Like phobias, fetishes come in a bewildering variety of forms: shoes, stockings, dolls, stuffed animals, automobile engines (yes, that's right), and just about anything else (Lowenstein, 2002).

Classic study in which a 9-month-old boy was conditioned to fear white furry objects. Here, Little Albert, with John B. Watson and Rosalie Rayner, is crying in response to a Santa Claus mask.

Factoid

One team of psychologists has recently claimed that Little Albert was actually "Douglas Merritte," who was born to a nurse in 1919 at Johns Hopkins University Hospital and died at age 6 due to a build-up of fluid in his brain (Beck, Levinson, & Irons, 2009). But a few other psychologists doubt that Little Albert has been discovered, so the debate continues (Powell, 2010; Reese, 2010).

TABLE 1 Phobias Galore. This sampling of phobias—a few relatively common, most quite rare—illustrates just how enormously varied people's fears can be. Many of these phobias may be acquired at least partly by classical conditioning.

PHOBIA	FEAR OF
Alliumphobia	garlic
Arachibutyrophobia	peanut butter sticking to the roof of one's mouth
Aulophobia	flutes
Brontophobia	thunderstorms
Bufonaophobia	toads
Catoptrophobia	mirrors
Coulrophobia	clowns
Epistaxiaophobia	nosebleeds
Lachanophobia	vegetables
Melissophobia	bees
Peladophobia	bald people
Pogonophobia	beards
Pteronophobia	being tickled by feathers
Rhytiphobia	getting wrinkles
Samhainophobia	Halloween
Taphephobia	being buried alive
Xyrophobia	razors

fetishism
sexual attraction to nonliving things

243

Michael Domjan and his colleagues used classical conditioning to instill a fetish in male quails.

In a series of studies, Michael Domjan and his colleagues classically conditioned fetishes in male Japanese quails. For example, they presented male quails with a cylindrical object made of terrycloth, followed by a female quail with which they happily mated. After 30 such pairings, about half of the male quails attempted to mate with the cylindrical object when it appeared alone (Köksal et al., 2004). Although the generalizability of these findings to humans is unclear, at least some people appear to develop fetishes by the repeated pairing of neutral objects with sexual activity (Rachman & Hodgson, 1968; Weinberg, Williams, & Calhan, 1995).

DISGUST REACTIONS. Imagine that a researcher asked you to eat a piece of fudge. No problem, right? Well, now imagine the fudge were shaped like dog feces. If you're like most subjects in the studies of Paul Rozin and his colleagues, you'd hesitate (D'Amato, 1998; Rozin, Millman, & Nemeroff, 1986).

Rozin (who's earned the nickname "Dr. Disgust") and his colleagues have found that we acquire disgust reactions with surprising ease. In most cases, these reactions are probably a product of classical conditioning. CSs—like a photograph of rotten eggs—that are associated with disgusting UCSs—like the smell and taste of rotten eggs in our mouths—may themselves come to elicit disgust. In many cases, disgust reactions are tied to stimuli that are biologically important to us, like animals or objects that are dirty or potentially poisonous (Connolly et al., 2008; Rozin & Fallon, 1987).

In another study, Rozin and his collaborators asked participants to drink from two glasses of water, both of which contained sugar (sucrose). In one case, the sucrose came from a bottle labeled "Sucrose"; in another, it came from a bottle labeled "Sodium Cyanide, Poison." The investigators told subjects that both bottles were completely safe. They even asked subjects to select which label went with which glass, proving the labels were meaningless. Even so, subjects were hesitant to drink from the glass that contained the sucrose labeled as poisonous (Rozin, Markwith, & Ross, 1990). Participants' responses in this study were irrational, but perhaps understandable: They were probably relying on the heuristic "better safe than sorry." Classical conditioning helps keep us safe, even if it goes too far on occasion (Engelhard, Olatunji, & de Jong, 2011).

James McConnell and his colleagues paired a light with an electric shock, which caused the planaria worm to contract reflexively.

psychomythology

ARE WE WHAT WE EAT?

Many of us have heard that "we are what we eat," but in the 1950s the psychologist James McConnell took this proverb quite literally. McConnell became convinced he'd discovered a means of chemically transferring learning from one animal to another. Indeed, for many years psychology textbooks informed undergraduates that scientists could chemically transfer learning across animals.

McConnell's animal of choice was the planaria, a flatworm that's typically no more than a few inches long. Using classical conditioning, McConnell and his colleagues exposed planaria to a light, which served as the CS, while pairing it with a one-second electric shock, which served as the UCS. When planaria receive an electric shock, they contract reflexively. After numerous pairings between light and shock, the light itself causes planaria to contract (Thompson & McConnell, 1955).

McConnell wanted to find out whether he could chemically transfer the memory of this classical conditioning experience to another planaria. His approach was brutally simple. Relying on the fact that many planaria are miniature cannibals, he chopped up the trained planaria and fed them to their fellow worms. Remarkably, McConnell (1962) reported that planaria who'd gobbled up classically conditioned planaria acquired classically conditioned reactions to the light more quickly than planaria who hadn't.

Understandably, McConnell's memory transfer studies generated enormous excitement. Imagine if McConnell were right! You could sign up for your introductory psychology class, swallow a pill containing all of the psychological knowledge you'd need to get an A, and ... voila, you're now an expert psychologist. Indeed, McConnell went directly to the general public with his findings, proclaiming in *Time, Newsweek,* and other popular magazines that scientists were on the verge of developing a "memory pill" (Rilling, 1996).

Yet it wasn't long before the wind went out of McConnell's scientific sails: Although researchers at over 50 labs tried to replicate his findings, many couldn't (Stern, 2010). What's more, researchers brought up a host of alternative explanations for his results. For one, McConnell hadn't ruled out the possibility that his findings were attributable to *pseudoconditioning*, which occurs when the CS by itself triggers the UCR. That is, he hadn't excluded the possibility that the light itself caused the planaria to contract (Collins & Pinch, 1993), perhaps leading him to the false conclusion that the cannibalistic planaria had acquired a classically conditioned reaction to the light. Eventually, after years of intense debate and mixed or negative results, the scientific community concluded that McConnell may have fooled himself into seeing something that was never there: He'd become a likely victim of confirmation bias. His planaria lab closed its doors in 1971, and was never heard from again.

Still, McConnell may yet have the last laugh. Even though his studies may have been flawed, some scientists have conjectured that memory may indeed be chemically transferrable in some cases (Smalheiser, Manev, & Costa, 2001). As is so often the case in science, the truth will win out.

◀ **REPLICABILITY**
Can the results be duplicated in other studies?

◀ **RULING OUT RIVAL HYPOTHESES**
Have important alternative explanations for the findings been excluded?

Assess Your Knowledge — FACT or FICTION?

✔ **Study** and **Review** in **MyPsychLab**

1. Habituation to meaningless stimuli is generally adaptive.   True / False
2. In classical conditioning, the conditioned stimulus (CS) initially yields a reflexive, automatic response.   True / False
3. Conditioning is generally most effective when the CS precedes the UCS by a short period of time.   True / False
4. Extinction is produced by the gradual "decay" of the CR over time.   True / False
5. Once a CS is established, it's almost impossible to extend to it to novel stimuli. True / False

Answers: 1. T; 2. F; 3. T; 4. F; 5. F

Operant Conditioning

4 Distinguish operant conditioning from classical conditioning.
5 Describe Thorndike's law of effect.
6 Describe reinforcement and its effects on behavior and distinguish negative reinforcement from punishment.
7 Identify the four schedules of reinforcement and the response pattern associated with each.
8 Describe some applications of operant conditioning.

What do the following four examples have in common?

- Using bird feed as a reward, a behavioral psychologist teaches a pigeon to distinguish paintings by Monet from paintings by Picasso. By the end of the training, the pigeon is a veritable art aficionado.
- Using fish as a treat, a trainer teaches a dolphin to jump out of the water, spin three times, splash in the water, and propel itself through a hoop.

Animal trainers use operant conditioning techniques to teach animals to perform tricks, like jumping through hoops.

- In his initial attempt at playing tennis, a frustrated 12-year-old hits his opponent's serve into the net the first 15 times. After two hours of practice, he returns his opponent's serve successfully more than half the time.
- A hospitalized patient with dissociative identity disorder (formerly known as multiple personality disorder), displays features of an "alter" personality whenever staff members pay attention to him. When they ignore him, his alter personality seemingly vanishes.

The answer: All are examples of operant conditioning. The first, incidentally, comes from an actual study (Watanabe, Sakamoto, & Wakita, 1995). **Operant conditioning** is learning controlled by the consequences of the organism's behavior (Staddon & Cerutti, 2003). In each of these examples, superficially different as they are, the organism's behavior is shaped by what comes after it, namely, reward. Psychologists also refer to operant conditioning as *instrumental conditioning,* because the organism's response serves an instrumental function. The organism "gets something" out of the response, like food, sex, attention, or avoiding something unpleasant.

Behaviorists refer to the behaviors produced by the animal to receive a reward as *operants,* because the animal "operates" on its environment to get what it wants. Dropping a dollar into a soda machine is an operant, as is asking out an appealing classmate. In the first case, our reward is a refreshing drink and in the second, a hot date—if we're lucky.

Distinguishing Operant Conditioning from Classical Conditioning

Operant conditioning differs from classical conditioning in three important ways, which we've highlighted in **TABLE 2**.

1. In classical conditioning, the organism's response is *elicited,* that is, "pulled out" of the organism by the UCS, and later the CS. Remember that in classical conditioning the UCR is a reflexive and automatic response that doesn't require training. In operant conditioning, the organism's response is *emitted,* that is, generated by the organism in a seemingly voluntary fashion.
2. In classical conditioning, the organism's reward is independent of what it does. Pavlov gave his dogs meat powder regardless of whether, or how much, they salivated. In operant conditioning, the animal's reward is contingent—that is, dependent—on what it does. If the animal doesn't emit a response, it comes out empty-handed (or in the case of a dog, empty-pawed).
3. In classical conditioning, the organism's responses depend primarily on the autonomic nervous system. In operant conditioning, the organism's responses depend primarily on the skeletal muscles. In contrast to classical conditioning, in which learning involves changes in heart rate, breathing, perspiration, and other bodily systems, in operant conditioning learning involves changes in voluntary motor behavior.

TABLE 2 Key Differences between Operant and Classical Conditioning.

	CLASSICAL CONDITIONING	OPERANT CONDITIONING
Target behavior is ...	Elicited automatically	Emitted voluntarily
Reward is ...	Provided unconditionally	Contingent on behavior
Behavior depends primarily on ...	Autonomic nervous system	Skeletal muscles

The Law of Effect

The famous **law of effect,** put forth by psychologist E. L. Thorndike, forms the basis of much of operant conditioning: *If a response, in the presence of a stimulus, is followed by a satisfying state of affairs, the bond between stimulus and response will be strengthened.* This statement isn't as

operant conditioning
learning controlled by the consequences of the organism's behavior

law of effect
principle asserting that if a stimulus followed by a behavior results in a reward, the stimulus is more likely to give rise to the behavior in the future

complicated as it appears. It means that if we're rewarded for a response to a stimulus, we're more like to repeat that response to the stimulus in the future. Psychologists sometimes refer to early forms of behaviorism as S-R psychology (S stands for *stimulus*, R for *response*). According to S-R theorists, most of our complex behaviors reflect the progressive accumulation of associations between stimuli and responses: the sight of a close friend and saying hello, or the smell of a delicious hamburger and reaching for it on our plate. S-R theorists maintain that almost everything we do voluntarily—driving a car, eating a sandwich, or planting a kiss on someone's lips—results from the gradual buildup of S-R bonds due to the law of effect. Thorndike (1898) discovered the law of effect in a classic study of cats and puzzle boxes. Here's what he did.

Thorndike placed a hungry cat in a box and put a tantalizing piece of fish just outside. To escape from the box, the cat needed to hit upon (literally) the right solution, which was pressing on a lever or pulling on a string inside the box (see **FIGURE 5**).

When Thorndike first placed the cat in the puzzle box, it typically flailed around aimlessly in a frantic effort to escape. Then, by sheer accident, the cat eventually found the correct solution, scurried out of the box, and gobbled up its delectable treat. Thorndike wanted to find out what would happen to the cat's behavior over time. Once it figured out the solution to the puzzle, would it then get it right every time?

Thorndike found that the cat's time to escape from the puzzle box decreased *gradually* over 60 trials. There was no point at which the cat abruptly realized what it needed to do to escape. According to Thorndike, his cats were learning by trial and error through the steady buildup of S-R associations. Indeed, Thorndike and many other S-R theorists went so far as to conclude that all learning, including all human learning, occurs only by trial and error. For them, S-R bonds are gradually "stamped into" the organism by reward.

These findings, Thorndike concluded, provide a crushing blow to the hypothesis that cats learn by **insight,** that is, by grasping the underlying nature of the problem. Had his cats possessed insight into the nature of the problem, the results presumably would have looked like what we see in **FIGURE 6**. This figure illustrates what psychologists term the *aha reaction:* "Aha—I got it!" Once the animal solves the problem, it gets it correct just about every time after that. Yet Thorndike never found an Aha! moment: The time to a correct solution decreased only gradually.

FIGURE 5 Thorndike's Puzzle Box. Thorndike's classic puzzle box research seemed to suggest that cats solve problems solely through trial and error.

FIGURE 6 "Aha Reaction." Insight learning: Once an individual solves the problem, he or she gets the answer right almost every time after that.

B. F. Skinner and Reinforcement

Thorndike's pioneering discoveries on the law of effect laid the groundwork for research on operant conditioning. B. F. Skinner then kicked it up a notch using electronic technology.

Skinner found Thorndike's experimental setup unwieldy because the researcher needed to stick around to place the unhappy cat back into the puzzle box following each trial. This limitation made it difficult to study the buildup of associations in ongoing operant behavior over hours, days, or weeks. So he

FIGURE 7 Rat in Skinner Box and Electronic Device for Recording the Rat's Behavior. B. F. Skinner devised a small chamber (the Skinner box) containing a bar that the rat presses to obtain food, a food dispenser, and often a light that signals when reward is forthcoming. An electronic device graphs the rat's responses in the researcher's absence.

developed what came to be known as a **Skinner box** (more formally, an operant chamber), which electronically records an animal's responses and prints out a graph (technically called a cumulative record) of the animal's activity. A Skinner box typically contains a bar that delivers food when pressed, a food dispenser, and often a light that signals when reward is forthcoming (see **FIGURE 7**). With this setup, Skinner studied the operant behavior of rats, pigeons, and other animals and mapped out their responses to reward. By allowing a device to record behavior without any direct human observation, Skinner ran the risk of missing some important behaviors that the box wasn't designed to record. Nonetheless, his discoveries forever altered the landscape of psychology.

insight
grasping the underlying nature of a problem

Skinner box
small animal chamber constructed by Skinner to allow sustained periods of conditioning to be administered and behaviors to be recorded unsupervised

"Oh, not bad. The light comes on, I press the bar, they write me a check. How about you?"

Forcing a student to see the principal is typically a form of punishment; nevertheless, it can instead serve as a negative reinforcement if it allows the student to escape from an unpleasant class.

reinforcement
outcome or consequence of a behavior that strengthens the probability of the behavior

positive reinforcement
presentation of a stimulus that strengthens the probability of the behavior

negative reinforcement
removal of a stimulus that strengthens the probability of the behavior

punishment
outcome or consequence of a behavior that weakens the probability of the behavior

Terminology of Operant Conditioning

To understand Skinner's research, we need to make our way through a bit of psychological jargon. Here we'll discuss three key concepts in Skinnerian psychology: reinforcement, punishment, and discriminative stimulus.

REINFORCEMENT. Up to this point, we've used the term *reward* to refer to any consequence that makes a behavior more likely to occur. Yet Skinner found this term imprecise, because it doesn't tell us how the organism's behavior changes in response to the reward. He preferred the term **reinforcement,** meaning any outcome that strengthens the probability of a response (Skinner, 1953, 1971).

Skinner distinguished **positive reinforcement,** when we administer a stimulus, from **negative reinforcement,** when we take away a stimulus. Positive reinforcement could be giving a child a Hershey's Kiss when he picks up his toys; negative reinforcement could be ending a child's time-out for bad behavior once she's stopped whining. In both cases, the most frequent outcome is an increase or strengthening of the response. Note, though, that Skinner would call these actions "reinforcements" *only* if they make the response more likely to occur in the future.

Hundreds of psychology students over the years have demonstrated the power of positive reinforcement using an unconventional participant: their professor. In the game Condition Your Professor (Vyse, 1997), a class of introductory psychology students agrees to provide positive reinforcement—such as smiling or nodding their heads—to their professor whenever he or she moves in a particular direction, such as to the far left side of the room. Your authors know of one famous introductory psychology teacher who spent almost all of his time lecturing from behind his podium. During one class, his students smiled profusely and nodded their heads whenever he ventured out from behind the podium. Sure enough, by the end of class the professor was spending most of his time away from the podium. You and your classmates might want to attempt a similar stunt with your introductory psychology professor: Just don't mention we suggested it.

PUNISHMENT. We shouldn't confuse negative reinforcement with **punishment,** which is any outcome that *weakens* the probability of a response. Like reinforcements, punishments can be either positive or negative. If a punishment involves administering a stimulus then it's positive; if it's taking away a stimulus then it's negative (see **TABLE 3**).

Positive punishment typically involves administering a stimulus that the organism wants to avoid, such as a physical shock or a spanking, or an unpleasant social outcome, like laughing at someone. Negative punishment involves the removal of a stimulus that the organism wishes to experience, such as a favorite toy or article of clothing.

We also shouldn't confuse punishment with the disciplinary practices often associated with it; discipline is punishment only if it decreases the probability of the

TABLE 3 Distinguishing Reinforcement from Punishment.

	PROCEDURE	EFFECT ON BEHAVIOR	TYPICAL EXAMPLE
Positive Reinforcement	Presenting a stimulus	Increases target behavior	Giving a gold star on homework, resulting in a student studying more
Negative Reinforcement	Removing a stimulus	Increases target behavior	Static on phone subsides when you stand in a specific spot in your room, causing you to stand there more often
Positive Punishment	Presenting a stimulus	Decreases target behavior	Scolding by a pet owner, reducing a dog's habit of chewing on shoes
Negative Punishment	Removing a stimulus	Decreases target behavior	Taking away a favorite toy, stopping a child from throwing future tantrums

behavior. Skinner, who insisted on precision in language, argued that certain actions that might superficially appear to be punishments are actually reinforcers. He defined reinforcers and punishments solely in terms of their consequences. Consider this scenario: A mother rushes into her 3-year-old son's bedroom and yells "Stop that!" each time she hears him kicking the wall. Is she punishing his demanding behavior? There's no way to tell without knowing the effect on his behavior. If he kicks the wall more often following the scolding, then the mother is actually reinforcing his behavior—strengthening the probability of a response. If his kicking decreases or stops altogether after he was scolded, then the mother's scolding is a punishment—weakening the probability of a response.

Try labeling each of the following examples as an instance of either negative reinforcement or punishment and explain why (you can find the answers upside down in the margin at the bottom of this page):

1. A boy keeps making noise in the back of a classroom despite a teacher's repeated warnings. The teacher finally sends him to the principal's office. When he returns 2 hours later, he's much quieter.

2. A woman with diabetes works hard to control her blood sugar through diet and exercise. As a result, her doctor allows her to discontinue administering her unpleasant daily insulin shots, which increases her attempts to eat healthily and exercise.

3. A parole board releases a previously aggressive criminal from prison early for being a "model citizen" within the institution over the past 5 years. Following his release, he continues to behave in a law-abiding manner.

4. A woman yells at her roommate for leaving dirty clothing scattered all around her apartment. Her roommate apologizes and never makes a mess again.

Does punishment work in the long run? Popular wisdom tells us that it usually does: "Spare the rod, spoil the child." Yet Skinner (1953) and most of his followers argued against the routine use of punishment to change behavior. They believed that reinforcement alone could shape most human behaviors for the better.

According to Skinner and others (Azrin & Holz, 1966), punishment has several disadvantages:

1. Punishment tells the organism only what *not* to do, not what *to* do. A child who's punished for throwing a tantrum won't learn how to deal with frustration more constructively.

2. Punishment often creates anxiety, which can interfere with future learning.

3. Punishment may encourage subversive behavior, prompting people to become sneakier about the situations in which they can and can't display forbidden behavior. A child who's punished for grabbing his brother's toys may learn to grab his brother's toys only when his parents aren't looking.

4. Punishment from parents may provide a model for children's aggressive behavior (Straus, Sugarman, & Giles-Sims, 1997). A child whose parents slap him when he misbehaves may "get the message" that slapping is acceptable.

Numerous researchers have reported that the use of physical punishment by parents is positively correlated with aggressive behavior in children (Fang & Corso, 2007; Gershoff, 2002), although scientists disagree about the size of this correlation (Paolucci & Violato, 2004). Across many studies, Murray Straus and his colleagues (for example, Straus & McCord, 1998) found that physical punishment is associated with more behavioral problems in children. In a study of 1,575 subjects drawn from the general population, Cathy Widom further found that physically abused children are at heightened risk for aggressiveness in adulthood (Widom, 1989a, 1989b). Many researchers interpreted this finding as implying that early physical abuse causes aggression.

 Listen in **MyPsychLab** to the **Podcast:** Punishment and Reinforcement

Skinner and his followers believed that reinforcement is generally much more effective than punishment in shaping children's behavior.

Answers: (1) punishment; because the boy's teacher reduced his rate of noise-making. (2) negative reinforcement; because her doctor increased the woman's rates of eating well and exercising. (3) negative reinforcement; because the parole board increased the prisoner's rate of law-abiding behavior. (4) punishment; because the woman decreased her roommate's rate of messy behavior.

Widom (1989a) concluded that her findings reveal the operation of a "cycle of violence," whereby parental aggression begets childhood aggression. When these children become parents, many become abusers themselves. Similarly, Elizabeth Gershoff (2002) reviewed 88 studies of corporal punishment based on a whopping 39,309 participants. Although she found that corporal punishment is sometimes associated with short-term improvements in children's behavior, she also found that a history of such punishment in childhood is associated with an increased probability of becoming an abuser in adulthood.

CORRELATION VS. CAUSATION ▶
Can we be sure that A causes B?

Yet let's remember that these studies are correlational and don't demonstrate causality. Other interpretations are possible (Jaffee, Strait, & Odgers, 2012). For example, because children share half of their genes with each parent, and because aggression is partly heritable (Krueger, Hicks, & McGue, 2001), the correlation between parents' physical aggression and their children's aggression may be due to the fact that parents who are physically aggressive pass on this genetic predisposition to their children (Boutwell et al., 2011; DiLalla & Gottesman, 1991; Lynch et al., 2006). It's also conceivable that the causal arrow is reversed: Aggressive children may be difficult to control and therefore evoke physical abuse from their parents. This hypothesis doesn't in any way excuse physical abuse or imply that it's acceptable, but it may help to explain why it occurs. In addition, it's possible that mild levels of punishment are effective, but that severe forms of punishment, including abuse, aren't (Baumrind, Larzelere, & Cowan, 1992; Lynch et al., 2006).

Making matters more complicated, the association between physical punishment and childhood behavior problems may vary by race and culture. In some studies, spanking and other forms of physical discipline have correlated positively with childhood behavior problems in Caucasian families, but correlated negatively in African American families (Lansford et al., 2004). Still, not all researchers have replicated these findings, so the issue requires further investigation (Gershoff et al., 2012). Moreover, spanking tends to be more predictive of higher levels of childhood aggression and anxiety in countries in which

REPLICABILITY ▶
Can the results be duplicated in other studies?

spanking is rare, like China or Thailand, than in countries in which it's common, like Kenya or India (Lansford et al., 2005). The reasons for this difference aren't clear, although children who are spanked in countries in which spanking is more culturally accepted may feel less stigmatized than children in countries in which it's culturally condemned.

Still, that's not to say that we should never use punishment, only that we should use it sparingly. Most research suggests that punishment works best when it's delivered consistently and follows the undesired behavior promptly (Brennan & Mednick, 1994). In particular, immediate punishment sometimes tends to be effective, whereas delayed punishment is often useless (Church, 1969; McCord, 2006; Moffitt, 1983). Punishment of an undesired behavior also works best when we simultaneously reinforce a desired behavior (Azrin & Holz, 1966).

In some countries, such as China and Thailand, spanking is uncommon.

DISCRIMINATIVE STIMULUS. Another critical term in operant conditioning lingo is the **discriminative stimulus,** any stimulus that signals the presence of reinforcement (be careful not to confuse this term with "stimulus discrimination"). When we snap our fingers at a dog in the hopes of having it come over to us, the dog may approach us for a much-appreciated petting. For the dog, our finger snapping is a discriminative stimulus: It's a signal that if it approaches us, it will receive reinforcement. According to behaviorists, we're responding to discriminative stimuli virtually all the time, even if we're not consciously aware of it. A friend's waving at us from across campus is another common discriminative stimulus: It often signals to us that our friend wants to chat with us, thereby reinforcing us for responding to her wave.

SAME SONG, SECOND VERSE. *Acquisition, extinction, spontaneous recovery, stimulus generalization,* and *stimulus discrimination* are all terms with which we've crossed paths in our discussion of classical conditioning. These terms apply just as much to operant conditioning, too. We can find their definitions in **TABLE 4.** Here, we'll examine how three of these concepts apply to operant conditioning.

discriminative stimulus
stimulus that signals the presence of reinforcement

Learning

TABLE 4 Definition Reminders of Key Concepts in Classical and Operant Conditioning.

TERM	DEFINITION
Acquisition	Learning phase during which a response is established
Extinction	Gradual reduction and eventual elimination of a response after a stimulus is presented repeatedly
Spontaneous Recovery	Sudden reemergence of an extinguished response after a delay
Stimulus Generalization	Displaying a response to stimuli similar to but not identical to the original stimulus
Stimulus Discrimination	Displaying a less pronounced response to stimuli that differ from the original stimulus

When parents stop giving this boy his favorite toy when he screams, he'll initially scream harder to get what he wants. Eventually he'll realize it won't work and give up the screaming behavior.

Extinction. In operant conditioning, extinction occurs when we stop delivering reinforcers following a previously reinforced behavior. Gradually, this behavior declines in frequency and disappears. If parents give a screaming child a toy to quiet her, they may be inadvertently reinforcing her behavior, because she's learning to scream to get something. If parents buy earplugs and stop placating the child by giving toys, the screaming behavior gradually extinguishes. In such cases we often see an *extinction burst*. That is, shortly after withdrawing the reinforcer the undesired behavior initially increases in intensity, probably because the child is trying harder to get reinforced. So there's some truth to the old saying that things sometimes need to get worse before they get better.

Stimulus Discrimination. As we mentioned earlier, one group of investigators used food reinforcement to train pigeons to distinguish paintings by Monet from those of Picasso (Watanabe et al., 1995). That's stimulus discrimination, because the pigeons learned to tell the difference between two different types of stimuli.

Stimulus Generalization. Interestingly, these investigators found that their pigeons also displayed stimulus generalization. Following operant conditioning, they distinguished paintings by impressionist artists whose styles were similar to Monet's, such as Renoir, from paintings by cubist artists similar to Picasso, such as Braque.

Schedules of Reinforcement

Skinner (1938) found that animals' behaviors differ depending on the **schedule of reinforcement,** that is, the pattern of delivering reinforcement. In the simplest pattern, **continuous reinforcement,** we reinforce a behavior every time it occurs. **Partial reinforcement,** sometimes called *intermittent reinforcement*, occurs when we reinforce responses only some of the time.

Try answering this question: If we want to train a dog to perform a trick, like catching a Frisbee, should we reinforce it for (a) each successful catch or (b) only some of its successful catches? If you're like most people, you'd answer (a), which seems to match our commonsense notions regarding the effects of reinforcement. At first blush, it seems logical to assume that the more consistent the reinforcement, the more consistent will be the resulting behavior.

Nevertheless, Skinner's principle of partial reinforcement shows that our commonplace intuitions about reinforcement are backward. According to the principle of partial reinforcement, behaviors we reinforce only occasionally are slower to extinguish than those we reinforce continuously, that is, every time. Does this idea seem counterintuitive? Think of it this way: If the dog has learned that he'll be rewarded for catching the Frisbee only occasionally, he's more likely to continue trying to catch it in the hopes of getting reinforcement.

So if we want an animal to maintain a trick for a long time, we should actually reinforce it for correct responses only every once in a while. Skinner (1969) noted that continuous reinforcement allows animals to learn new behaviors more quickly, but that

? If we want this dog to retain this dancing trick in the future, should we reinforce it each time if performs the trick, or only some of the time? (See answer upside down at bottom of page.)

schedule of reinforcement
pattern of reinforcing a behavior

continuous reinforcement
reinforcing a behavior every time it occurs, resulting in faster learning but faster extinction than only occasional reinforcement

partial reinforcement
only occasional reinforcement of a behavior, resulting in slower extinction than if the behavior had been reinforced continually

Answer: Only some of the time

partial reinforcement leads to a greater resistance to extinction. This principle may help to explain why some people remain trapped for years in terribly dysfunctional, even abusive, relationships (Dutton & Painter, 1993). Some relationship partners provide intermittent reinforcement to their significant others, treating them miserably most of the time but treating them well on rare occasions. This pattern of partial reinforcement may keep individuals "hooked" in relationships that aren't working—and aren't likely to work in the long run.

Although there are numerous schedules of reinforcement, we'll discuss the four major ones here. Remarkably, the effects of these reinforcement schedules are consistent across species as diverse as cockroaches, pigeons, rats, and humans. That's impressive replicability.

REPLICABILITY ▶
Can the results be duplicated in other studies?

The principal reinforcement schedules vary along two dimensions:

1. *The consistency of administering reinforcement.* Some reinforcement contingencies are *fixed,* whereas others are *variable.* That is, in some cases reinforcement occurs on a regular (fixed) basis, whereas in others it occurs on an irregular (variable) basis.

   Variable schedules tend to yield more consistent rates of responding than do fixed schedules. This finding makes intuitive sense. If we never know when our next treat is coming, it's in our best interests to keep emitting the response to ensure we've emitted it enough times to earn the reward.

2. *The basis of administering reinforcement.* Some reinforcement schedules operate on *ratio* schedules, whereas others operate on *interval* schedules. In ratio schedules, the animal is reinforced on the basis of the *number of responses* it's emitted. In interval schedules, it's reinforced on the basis of the *amount of time* elapsed since the last reinforcement.

   Ratio schedules tend to yield higher rates of responding than do interval schedules. This finding also makes intuitive sense. If a dog gets a treat every 5 times he rolls over, he's going to roll over more often than if he gets a treat every 5 minutes, regardless of whether he rolls over once or 20 times during that interval.

We can combine these two dimensions to arrive at four major schedules of reinforcement, each of which yields a distinctive pattern of responding (see **FIGURE 8**):

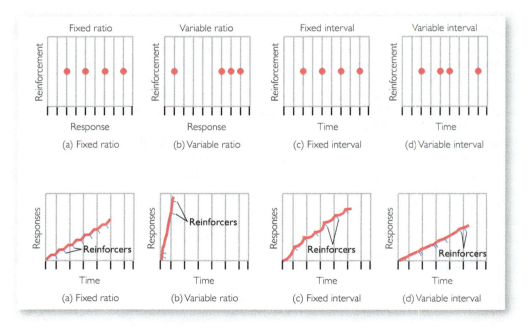

FIGURE 8 Four Major Reinforcement Schedules and Their Response Patterns. The four major reinforcement schedules are (a) fixed ratio, (b) variable ratio, (c) fixed interval, and (d) variable interval. Note the "scalloped" pattern in (c), the fixed interval response pattern. The subject decreases the reinforced behavior immediately after receiving a reinforcer, then increases the behavior in anticipation of reinforcement as the time for reinforcement approaches.

1. In a **fixed ratio (FR) schedule,** we provide reinforcement after a regular number of responses. For example, we could give a rat a pellet after it presses the lever in a Skinner box 15 times.

2. In a **variable ratio (VR) schedule,** we provide reinforcement after a specific number of responses on average, but the precise number of responses required during any given period varies randomly. A pigeon on a variable ratio schedule with an average ratio of 10 might receive a piece of bird feed after 6 pecks, then after 12 pecks, then after 1 peck, then after 21 pecks, with the average of these ratios being 10.

   Variable ratio (VR) schedules usually yield the highest rates of responding of all. It's for this reason that there's one place where we can be guaranteed to find a VR schedule: a casino. Roulette wheels, slot machines, and other casino devices deliver cash rewards on an irregular basis, and they do so based on the gambler's responses. Sometimes the gambler has to pull the arm of the slot machine (the "one-armed bandit") hundreds of times before receiving any money at all. At other times, the gambler pulls the arm only once and makes out like a bandit himself, perhaps walking away with thousands of dollars for a few seconds of work. The extreme unpredictability of the VR schedule is precisely what keeps gamblers hooked, because a huge reinforcement can come at any time.

   VR schedules keep pigeons hooked, too. Skinner (1953) found that pigeons placed on VR schedules sometimes continue to peck on a disk for food after more than 150,000 nonreinforced responses. In some cases, they literally ground down their beaks in the process. Like desperate gamblers in a Las Vegas casino hoping for a huge payoff, they don't give up despite repeated disappointments.

3. In a **fixed interval (FI) schedule,** we provide reinforcement for producing the response at least once after a specified amount of time has passed. For example, a worker in a clock factory might get paid every Friday for the work she's done, as long as she's generated at least one clock during that 1-week interval.

   Fixed interval schedules are especially distinctive in the behaviors they yield; they're associated with a "scalloped" pattern of responding (refer back to Figure 8). This pattern reflects the fact that the animal "waits" for a time after it receives reinforcement, and then increases its rate of responding just before the interval is up as it begins to anticipate reinforcement.

4. In a **variable interval (VI) schedule,** we provide reinforcement for producing the response after an average time interval, with the actual interval varying randomly. For example, we could give a dog a treat for performing a trick on a variable interval schedule with an average interval of 8 minutes. This dog may have to perform the trick sometime during a 7-minute interval the first time, then a 1-minute interval the second time, then a 20-minute interval, and then a 4-minute interval, with the average of these intervals being 8 minutes.

Applications of Operant Conditioning

Operant conditioning plays a role in a surprising number of everyday experiences and in some special circumstances, as well. As we've noted, operant conditioning is central to some parenting practices. It's also relevant to a wide array of other situations ranging from animal training to weight loss plans—and even to learning to master a video game. Here we'll explore a few well-studied examples of operant conditioning in action.

ANIMAL TRAINING. If you've ever seen animals perform at a circus, zoo, or aquarium, you might wonder how on earth they learned such elaborate routines. There's an old joke that just as magicians pull rabbits out of hats, behaviorists pull habits out of rats—and other animals, too. They

? Imagine that this football player received a salary bonus for every five touchdowns he scored. **What reinforcement schedule would he be on?** (See answer upside down on bottom of page.)

Factoid

The *gambler's fallacy* describes the error of believing that random events have "memories." After losing 10 roulette spins in a row, the gambler often concludes that he's now "due" to win. Yet his odds of winning on the 11th spin are no higher than they were on his first 10 spins.

fixed ratio (FR) schedule
pattern in which we provide reinforcement following a regular number of responses

variable ratio (VR) schedule
pattern in which we provide reinforcement after a specific number of responses on average, with the number varying randomly

fixed interval (FI) schedule
pattern in which we provide reinforcement for producing the response at least once following a specified time interval

variable interval (VI) schedule
pattern in which we provide reinforcement for producing the response at least once during an average time interval, with the interval varying randomly

Answer: Fixed ratio

Simulate in **MyPsychLab** the
Experiment: Shaping

Skinner's shaping principles are used today to train service animals.

CORRELATION VS. CAUSATION ▶
Can we be sure that A causes B?

typically do so by means of a procedure called **shaping.** Using shaping, we reinforce behaviors that aren't exactly the target behavior but that are progressively closer versions of it. Typically, we shape an organism's response by initially reinforcing most or all responses that are close to the desired behavior, and then gradually *fading* (that is, decreasing the frequency of) our reinforcement for the not-exactly-right behaviors over time.

Animal trainers often combine shaping with a technique called *chaining,* in which they link a number of interrelated behaviors to form a longer series. Each behavior in the chain becomes a cue for the next behavior in the chain, just as A becomes a cue for B, B for C, and so on when we're learning the alphabet.

By means of shaping and chaining, Skinner taught pigeons to play Ping-Pong, although they weren't exactly Olympic-caliber table tennis players. To do so, he first reinforced them for turning toward the paddles, then approaching the paddles, then placing the paddles in their beaks, then picking up the paddles with their beaks, and so on. Then, he chained later behaviors, like swinging the paddle and then hitting the ball, to the earlier behaviors. Skinner began his training by reinforcing initial approximations to the desired response. As we might imagine, shaping and chaining complex animal behaviors requires patience, as the process can take days or weeks. Still, the payoff can be substantial, because we can train animals to engage in numerous behaviors that lie well outside their normal repertoires. Indeed, all contemporary animal trainers rely on Skinnerian principles.

OVERCOMING PROCRASTINATION: I'LL GET TO THAT LATER. Be honest: Did you put off reading this chapter until the last moment? If so, don't feel ashamed, because procrastination is one of the most frequent study problems that college students report. Although widespread, procrastination may not be harmless. The stress it causes may be bad for our physical and psychological health. Moreover, procrastinators tend to perform more poorly in their classes than do early birds (Tice & Baumeister, 1997). Although these findings are correlational and don't establish that procrastination causes bad grades, they certainly suggest that putting things off isn't ideal.

How can we overcome procrastination? Don't put off reading the rest of this paragraph, because we have a possible remedy for dilly-dallying. Although there are several potential solutions for procrastination, among the best is probably the one discovered by David Premack (1965). In his research on monkeys, Premack found that we can positively reinforce a less frequently performed behavior with a more frequently performed behavior (Danaher, 1974). Although not a foolproof rule (Knapp, 1976), this principle typically works surprisingly well. Research suggests this approach may help people to stop putting off things they've long avoided, like going to the dentist (Ramer, 1980).

If you find yourself putting off a reading or writing task, think of behaviors you'd typically perform if given the chance—perhaps hanging out with a few close friends, watching a favorite TV program, or treating yourself to an ice cream cone. Then, reinforce yourself with these higher frequency behaviors *only* after you've completed your homework.

from inquiry to understanding

WHY ARE WE SUPERSTITIOUS?

How many of the following behaviors do you perform?
- Never opening an umbrella indoors
- Not walking under a ladder
- Crossing the street whenever you see a black cat
- Carrying a lucky charm or necklace
- Going out of your way not to step on cracks in the sidewalk
- Knocking on wood
- Crossing your fingers
- Avoiding the number 13 (like not stopping on the thirteenth floor of a building)

shaping
conditioning a target behavior by progressively reinforcing behaviors that come closer and closer to the target

If you've engaged in several of these actions, you're at least somewhat superstitious. You're also in good company (Lindeman & Svedholm, 2012). Twelve percent of Americans are afraid of walking under a ladder, while 14 percent are afraid of crossing paths with a black cat (Vyse, 1997). So many people are afraid of the number 13 (a fear called *triskaidekaphobia*) that the floor designations in many tall buildings skip directly from 12 to 14 (Hock, 2002). In Paris, triskaidekaphobics who are going out to dinner with 12 other people can hire a *quatorzieme*, a person paid to serve as a fourteenth guest. As many as 90 percent of college students engage in one or more superstitious rituals before taking an exam, such as using a "lucky" pen or wearing a "lucky" piece of jewelry (Vyse, 1997).

How do superstitions arise? In a classic operant conditioning study, B.F. Skinner (1948) placed eight food-deprived pigeons in a Skinner box while delivering reinforcement (bird feed) every 15 seconds *independent of their behavior*. That is, the birds received reinforcement regardless of what they did. After a few days, Skinner observed something surprising. He found that 6 of the 8 pigeons had acquired remarkably strange and varied behaviors, like making two or three turns between reinforcements or swinging their heads from right to left.

You may have observed similarly odd behaviors in pigeons that people are feeding in city parks; some may prance around or walk rapidly in circles in anticipation of reinforcement. According to Skinner, his pigeons had developed *superstitious behavior:* Actions linked to reinforcement by sheer coincidence (Morse & Skinner, 1957). There's no actual association between superstitious behavior and reinforcement, although the animal acts as though there is. The behavior that the pigeon just happened to be performing immediately prior to being reinforced was strengthened—remember that reinforcement increases the probability of a response—so the pigeon kept on doing it (this kind of accidental operant conditioning is sometimes called *superstitious conditioning*).

Not all studies replicated these findings in pigeons (Staddon & Simmelhag, 1971), although at least some animal—and human—superstitions probably develop in the fashion Skinner described (Bloom et al., 2007; Garcia-Montes et al., 2008). So if we happened to be wearing a certain pair of socks prior to a big test and got an A, we may develop the false belief that these socks somehow contributed to our good performance. We might then wear that same pair of socks before our next exam. Over time, we may become dependent on superstitions. In a series of studies, researchers showed that relying on "lucky" objects, like a favorite charm, actually improves performance on such skills as golfing and memory tasks, probably because doing so boosts our self-confidence (Damisch, Stoberock, & Mussweiler, 2010). Athletes are notoriously superstitious (Ofori, Biddle, & Lavalee, 2012). Interestingly, the prevalence of superstitions in sports depends on the extent to which the outcomes are due to chance (Vyse, 1997). That's exactly what Skinner would have predicted, because partial reinforcement schedules are more likely to produce enduring behaviors than are continuous reinforcement schedules. In baseball, hitting is much less under players' control than is fielding: Even the best hitters succeed only about 3 out of 10 times, whereas the best fielders succeed 9.8 or even 9.9 out of 10 times. So hitting is controlled by a partial reinforcement schedule, whereas fielding is controlled by something close to a continuous reinforcement schedule. As we might expect, baseball players have far more hitting-related superstitions— like drawing a favorite symbol in the sand in the batter's box—than fielding-related superstitions (Gmelch, 1974; Vyse, 1997).

Of course, human superstitions aren't due entirely to operant conditioning. Many superstitions are spread partly by word-of-mouth (Herrnstein, 1966). If our mother tells us over and over again that black cats bring bad luck, we may become wary of them. Still, for many superstitions, operant conditioning probably plays an important role.

So many people are afraid of the number 13 that many buildings don't have a thirteenth floor.

◄ REPLICABILITY
Can the results be duplicated in other studies?

THERAPEUTIC APPLICATIONS OF OPERANT CONDITIONING. We can apply operant conditioning to clinical settings as well. One of the most successful applications of operant conditioning has been the *token economy*. Token economies are systems, often set up in psychiatric hospitals, for reinforcing appropriate behaviors and extinguishing inappropriate ones (Carr, Frazier, & Roland, 2005; Kazdin, 1982). Typically, psychologists who construct token economies begin by identifying target behaviors, that is, actions they hope to make more frequent. Staff members reinforce patients who exhibit these behaviors using tokens, chips, points, or other **secondary reinforcers.** Secondary reinforcers are neutral objects that become associated with **primary reinforcers**—things, like a favorite food or drink, that naturally increase the target behavior.

One of the authors of your textbook worked in a psychiatric hospital unit consisting of children with serious behavior problems, including yelling and cursing. In this unit, one target behavior was being polite to staff members. So whenever a child was especially polite to a staff member, he was rewarded with points, which he could trade in for something he wanted, like ice cream or attending a movie with staff members. Whenever a child was rude to a staff member, he was punished with a loss of points.

Research suggests that token economies are often effective in improving behavior in hospitals, group homes, and juvenile detention units (Ayllon & Milan, 2002; Paul & Lentz, 1977). Nevertheless, token economies are controversial, because the behaviors learned in institutions don't always transfer to the outside world (Carr et al., 2005; Wakefield, 2006). That's especially likely if the patients return to settings, like deviant peer groups, in which they're reinforced for socially inappropriate behaviors.

Operant conditioning has also been helpful in the treatment of individuals with autism, especially in improving their language deficits. *Applied behavior analysis* (ABA) for autism makes extensive use of shaping techniques; mental health professionals offer food and other primary reinforcers to individuals with autism as they reach progressively closer approximations to certain words and, eventually, complete sentences.

Ivar Lovaas and his colleagues have pioneered the best-known ABA program for autism (Lovaas, 1987; McEachin, Smith, & Lovaas, 1993). The results of Lovaas's work have been promising. Children with autism who undergo ABA training emerge with better language and intellectual skills than do control groups of children with autism who don't undergo such training (Green, 1996; Matson et al., 1996; Romanczyk et al., 2003).

Nevertheless, because Lovaas didn't randomly assign children with autism to experimental and control groups, his findings are vulnerable to a rival explanation: Perhaps the children in the experimental group had higher levels of functioning to begin with. Indeed, there's evidence this was the case (Schopler, Short, & Mesibov, 1989). The current consensus is that ABA isn't a miracle cure for the language deficits of autism, but that it can be extremely helpful in many cases (Herbert, Sharp, & Gaudiano, 2002).

Putting Classical and Operant Conditioning Together

Up to this point, we've discussed classical and operant conditioning as though they were two entirely independent processes. Yet the truth is more complicated. The similarities between classical and operant conditioning, including the fact that we find acquisition, extinction, stimulus generalization, and so on, in both, have led some theorists to argue that these two forms of learning aren't as different as traditionally believed (Brown & Jenkins, 1968; Staddon, 2003).

Although there are certainly important similarities between classical and operant conditioning, brain imaging studies demonstrate that these two forms of learning are associated with activations in different brain regions. Classically conditioned fear reactions are based largely in the amygdala (LeDoux, 1996; Likhtik et al., 2008; Veit et al., 2002), whereas operantly conditioned responses are based largely in brain areas rich in dopamine, which are linked to reward (Robbins & Everitt, 1998; Simmons & Neill, 2009).

These two types of conditioning often interact. We've already discovered that certain phobias arise in part by classical conditioning: A previously neutral stimulus (the CS)—say, a dog—is paired with an unpleasant stimulus (the UCS)—a dog bite—resulting in the CR of fear. So far, so good.

The token economy is one of the most successful applications of operant conditioning. Some teachers use a variation of the token economy, the point chart, to reinforce pupils' positive behaviors.

RULING OUT RIVAL HYPOTHESES ▶
Have important alternative explanations for the findings been excluded?

secondary reinforcer
neutral object that becomes associated with a primary reinforcer

primary reinforcer
item or outcome that naturally increases the target behavior

But this tidy scheme doesn't answer an important question: Why doesn't the CR of fear eventually extinguish? Given what we've learned about classical conditioning, we might expect the CR of fear to fade away over time with repeated exposure to the CS of dogs. Yet this often doesn't happen (Rachman, 1977). Many people with phobias remain deathly afraid of their feared stimulus for years, even decades. Indeed, only about 20 percent of untreated adults with phobias ever get over their fears (American Psychiatric Association, 2000). Why?

Enter *two-process theory* to the rescue as an explanation (Mowrer, 1947; Schactman & Reilly, 2011). According to this theory, we need both classical and operant conditioning to explain the persistence of anxiety disorders. Here's how: People acquire phobias by means of classical conditioning. Then, once they have a phobia, they start to avoid their feared stimulus whenever they encounter it. If they have a dog phobia, they may cross the street whenever they see someone walking toward them with a large German shepherd. When they do, they experience a reduction in anxiety, which *negatively reinforces* their fear. Recall that negative reinforcement involves the removal of a stimulus, in this case anxiety, that makes the behavior associated with it more likely. So, by avoiding dogs whenever they see them, people with a dog phobia are negatively reinforcing their fear. Ironically, they're operantly conditioning themselves to make their fears more likely to persist. They're exchanging short-term gain for long-term pain.

✔ **Study** and **Review** in **MyPsychLab**

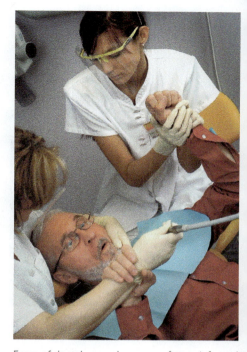

Fears of dental procedures are often reinforced by avoidance behavior over many years, such as a refusal to go to the dentist until it's absolutely necessary.

Assess Your Knowledge   FACT or FICTION?

1. In classical conditioning, responses are emitted; in operant conditioning, they're elicited.   **True / False**

2. Negative reinforcement and punishment are superficially different, but they produce the same short-term effects on behavior.   **True / False**

3. The correlation between spanking and children's behavioral problems appears to be positive in Caucasians but negative in African Americans.   **True / False**

4. The principle of partial reinforcement states that behaviors reinforced only some of the time extinguish more rapidly than behaviors reinforced continuously.   **True / False**

5. We can reinforce less frequent behaviors with more frequent behaviors.   **True / False**

Answers: 1. F, 2. T, 3. F, 4. F, 5. T

Where did I come from? Why am I here?

Cognitive Models Of Learning

9 Outline the evidence that supports latent learning and observational learning.

10 Identify evidence of insight learning.

Thus far, we've largely omitted one word when discussing how we learn: *thinking*. That's not accidental, because early behaviorists didn't believe that thought played much of a causal role in learning. Skinner (1953) was an advocate of what he called *radical behaviorism*, so-called because he believed that observable behavior, thinking, and emotion are all governed by the same laws of learning, namely, classical and operant conditioning. For radical behaviorists, thinking and emotion *are* behaviors, they're just not observable.

Skinner believed that humans and other intelligent animals think (deBell & Harless, 1992; Wyatt, 2001). But he didn't believe that thinking is any different in principle from any other behavior. For Skinner, this view is far more parsimonious than invoking different laws of learning for thinking than for other behaviors. Skinner (1990) even went so far to liken proponents of cognitive psychology, who believe that thinking

Skinner and other radical behaviorists acknowledged that people and other intelligent animals think, but they viewed thinking as no different from other behaviors, except that it just happens to be unobservable.

◄ **OCCAM'S RAZOR**
Does a simpler explanation fit the data just as well?

257

plays a central role in causing behavior, to pseudoscientists. Cognitive psychology, he argued, invokes unobservable and ultimately meaningless concepts—like "mind"—to explain behavior.

S-O-R Psychology: Throwing Thinking Back into the Mix

Few psychologists today share Skinner's harsh assessment of cognitive psychology. In fact, most psychologists now agree that the story of learning in humans is incomplete without at least some role for thinking (Bolles, 1979; Kirsch et al., 2004; Pinker, 1997).

Over the past 30 or 40 years, psychology has moved increasingly away from a simple S-R (stimulus-response) psychology to a more complex S-O-R psychology, with *O* being the organism that interprets the stimulus before producing a response (Mischel, 1973; Woodworth, 1929). For S-O-R psychologists, the link between S and R isn't mindless or automatic. Instead, the organism's response to a stimulus depends on what this stimulus *means* to it. The S-O-R principle helps to explain a phenomenon we've likely all encountered.

You've probably had the experience of giving two friends the same mild criticism (like, "It bothers me a little when you show up late") and found that they reacted quite differently: One was apologetic, the other defensive. To explain these differing reactions, Skinner would probably have invoked your friends' differing *learning histories,* in essence how each friend had been trained to react to criticism. In contrast, S-O-R theorists, who believe that cognition is central to explaining learning, would contend that the differences in your friends' reactions stem from how they *interpreted* your criticism. Your first friend may have viewed your criticism as constructive feedback, your second friend as a personal attack.

S-O-R theorists don't deny that classical and operant conditioning occur, but they believe that these forms of learning usually depend on thinking. Take a person who's been classically conditioned by tones and shock to sweat in response to the tones. Her skin conductance response will extinguish suddenly if she's told that no more shocks are on the way (Grings, 1973). This phenomenon of *cognitive conditioning,* whereby our interpretation of the situation affects conditioning, suggests that conditioning is more than an automatic, mindless process (Brewer, 1974; Kirsch et al., 2004).

S-O-R theorists also emphasize the role of expectations in learning. They point out that classical conditioning occurs only if the CS regularly predicts the occurrence of the UCS (Rescorla, 1990; Rescorla & Wagner, 1972). If we repeatedly present the CS and UCS close together in time, that alone won't do the trick when it comes to producing classical conditioning. Organisms show classically conditioned reactions only when the CS reliably forecasts the UCS, suggesting that they're building up expectations about what comes next. So according to S-O-R theorists, whenever Pavlov's dogs heard the ticking of the metronome, they thought—and the word "thought" is crucial here—"Ah, I think some meat powder is on the way."

To explain psychology's gradual transition from behaviorism to cognitivism, we need to tell the story of a pioneering psychologist and his rats.

Latent Learning

One of the first serious challenges to the radical behaviorist account of learning was mounted by Edward Chace Tolman (1886–1959), whose contribution to the psychology of learning can't be overestimated. Tolman suspected that reinforcement wasn't the be-all and end-all of learning. To understand why, answer this question: "Who was one of the first psychologists to challenge the radical behaviorist account of learning?" If you've been paying attention, you answered "Tolman." Yet immediately before we asked that question, you knew the answer, even though you had no opportunity to demonstrate it. According to Tolman (1932), you engaged in **latent learning**: learning that isn't directly observable (Blodgett, 1929). We learn many things without showing them. Putting it a bit differently, there's a crucial difference between *competence*—what we know—and *performance*—showing what we know (Bradbard et al., 1986).

Although few of us enjoy criticism, some of us react to it well, whereas others of us don't. According to S-O-R psychologists, this difference hinges on our interpretation of what the criticism means.

latent learning
learning that's not directly observable

Why is this distinction important? Because it implies that *reinforcement isn't necessary for learning.* Here's how Tolman and C. H. Honzik (1930) demonstrated this point systematically.

They randomly assigned three groups of rats to go through a maze over a 3-week period (see **FIGURE 9**). One group always received reinforcement in the form of cheese when it got to the end of the maze. A second group never received reinforcement when it got to the end of the

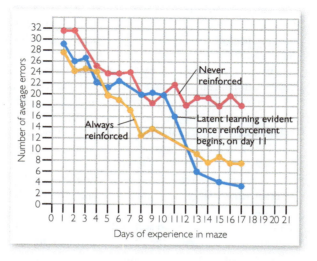

FIGURE 9 Tolman and Honzik's Maze Trials. Graph from Tolman and Honzik's classic study of latent learning in rats. Pay particular attention to the blue line. The rats in this group weren't reinforced until day 11; note the sudden drop in the number of their errors on receiving reinforcement. The rats were learning all along, even though they weren't showing it. (*Source:* Based on Tolman & Honzik, 1930)

maze. The first group made far fewer errors; that's no great surprise. The third group of rats received no reinforcement for the first 10 days, and then started receiving reinforcement on the 11th day.

As we can see in Figure 9, the rats in the third group showed a large and abrupt drop in their number of errors after receiving their very first reinforcer. In fact, within only a few days their number of errors didn't differ significantly from the number of errors among the rats who were always reinforced.

Tolman argued that the rats in the third group had been learning all along. They just hadn't bothered to show it because they had nothing to gain. Once there was a payoff for learning, namely, a tasty morsel of cheese, they promptly became miniature maze masters.

According to Tolman (1948), the rats had developed **cognitive maps**—spatial representations—of the maze. If you're like most college students, you were hopelessly confused the first day you arrived on your campus. Over time, however, you probably developed a mental sense of the layout of the campus, so that you now hardly ever become lost. That internal spatial blueprint, according to Tolman, is a cognitive map.

In a clever demonstration of cognitive maps, three investigators (McNamara, Long, & Wilke, 1956) had one set of rats run repeatedly through a maze to receive reinforcement. They put another set of rats in little moving "trolley cars," in which the rats could observe the layout of the maze but not obtain the experience of running through it. When the researchers gave the second group of rats the chance to run through the maze, they did just as well as the rats in the first group. As rodent tourists in trolley cars, they'd acquired cognitive maps of the maze.

The latent learning research of Tolman and others challenged strict behavioral models of learning, because their work suggested that learning could occur without reinforcement. To many psychologists, this research falsified the claim that reinforcement is necessary for all forms of learning. It also suggested that thinking, in the form of cognitive maps, plays a central role in at least some forms of learning.

Cats have cognitive maps, too. (© Hilary B. Price. King Features Syndicate)

◄ **FALSIFIABILITY**
Can the claim be disproved?

Observational Learning

According to some psychologists, one important variant of latent learning is **observational learning:** learning by watching others (Bandura, 1965). In many cases, we learn by watching *models:* parents, teachers, and others who are influential to us. Many psychologists regard observational learning as a form of latent learning because it allows us to learn without reinforcement. We can merely watch someone else being reinforced for doing something and take our cues from them.

cognitive map
mental representation of how a physical space is organized

observational learning
learning by watching others

Observational learning spares us the expense of having to learn everything firsthand (Bandura, 1977). Most of us aren't experts in skydiving, but from our observations of people who've gone skydiving we learn that it's generally a wise idea to have a parachute on before jumping out of a plane. Note that we didn't need to learn this useful tidbit of advice by trial and error, or else we wouldn't be here to talk about it. Observational learning can spare us from serious, even life-threatening, mistakes. But it can also contribute to our learning of maladaptive habits.

OBSERVATIONAL LEARNING OF AGGRESSION. In classic research in the 1960s, Albert Bandura and his colleagues demonstrated that children can learn to act aggressively by watching aggressive role models (Bandura, Ross, & Ross, 1963).

These researchers asked preschool boys and girls to watch an adult (the model) interact with a large Bobo doll, a wobbly doll that bounces back to its original upright position after being hit (Bandura, Ross, & Ross, 1961). The experimenters randomly assigned some children to watch the adult model playing quietly and ignoring the Bobo doll, and others to watch the adult model punching the Bobo doll in the nose, hitting it with a mallet, sitting on it, and kicking it around the room. As though that weren't enough, the aggressive model shouted out insults and vivid descriptions of his actions while inflicting violence: "Sock him in the nose," "Kick him," "Pow."

Bandura and his coworkers then brought the children into a room with an array of appealing toys, including a miniature fire engine, a jet fighter, and a large doll set. Just as children began playing with these toys, the experimenter interrupted them, informing them that they needed to move to a different room. This interruption was intentional, as the investigators wanted to frustrate the children to make them more likely to behave aggressively. Then the experimenter brought them into a second room, which contained a Bobo doll identical to the one they'd seen.

On a variety of dependent measures, Bandura and his colleagues found that previous exposure to the aggressive model triggered significantly more aggression against the Bobo doll than did exposure to the nonaggressive model. The children who'd watched the aggressive model yelled at the doll much as the model had done, and they even imitated many of his verbal insults. In a later study, Bandura and his colleagues (Bandura, Ross, & Ross, 1963) replicated these results when they displayed the aggressive models to children on film rather than in person.

MEDIA VIOLENCE AND REAL-WORLD AGGRESSION. The Bandura studies and scores of later studies of observational learning led psychologists to examine a theoretically and socially important question: Does exposure to media violence, such as in films, movies, or video games, contribute to real-world violence? The research literature addressing this question is as vast as it is confusing, and could easily occupy an entire book by itself. So we'll only briefly touch on some of the research highlights here.

Hundreds of investigators using correlational designs have reported that children who watch many violent television programs are more aggressive than other children (Wilson & Herrnstein, 1985). But do these findings demonstrate that media violence causes real-world violence? If you answered "No," give yourself a favored reinforcer. They could indicate merely that highly aggressive children are more likely than other children to tune in to aggressive television programs (Freedman, 1984). Alternatively, these findings could be due to a third variable, such as children's initial levels of aggressiveness. That is, highly aggressive children may be more likely than other children to both watch violent television programs *and* to act aggressively.

Investigators have tried to get around this problem by using longitudinal designs, which track individuals' behavior over time. Longitudinal studies show that children who choose to watch many violent television shows commit more aggressive acts years later than do children who choose to watch fewer violent television shows, even when researchers have equated children in their initial levels of aggression (Huesmann et al., 2003; see **FIGURE 10**). These studies offer somewhat more

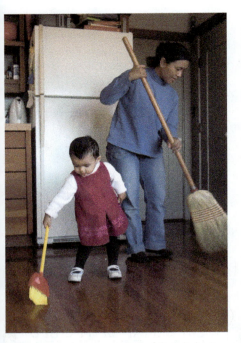

Children acquire a great deal of their behavior by observational learning of adults, especially their parents.

Watch in **MyPsychLab** the **Video:**
Bandura's Bobo Doll Experiment

REPLICABILITY ▶
Can the results be duplicated in other studies?

CORRELATION VS. CAUSATION ▶
Can we be sure that A causes B?

compelling evidence for a causal link between media violence and aggression than do traditional correlational studies. But even they don't demonstrate a causal association, because they're not true experiments. Participants in these studies aren't randomly assigned to conditions, but instead select which television shows to watch. As a consequence, unmeasured personality variables, like impulsivity, or social variables, like weak parental supervision, might account for these findings. Moreover, just because variable *A* precedes variable *B* doesn't mean that variable *A causes* variable *B*. For example, if we found that most common colds start with a scratchy throat and a runny nose, we shouldn't conclude that scratchy throats and runny noses cause colds, only that they're early signs of a cold.

Still other investigators have examined whether the link between media models and later aggression holds up under the tightly controlled conditions of the laboratory. In most of these studies, researchers have exposed subjects to either violent or nonviolent media presentations and seen whether subjects in the former groups behaved more aggressively, such as by yelling at the experimenter or delivering electric shocks to another subject when provoked. In general, these studies strongly suggest a causal association between media violence and laboratory aggression (Wood, Wong, & Chachere, 1991). The same conclusion may hold for the relation between violent video games and aggression (Anderson, Gentile, & Buckley, 2007; Bushman & Anderson, 2001), although the causal link here is controversial and less well established (Ferguson, 2009). In particular, some researchers argue that the link between violent video games and real-world violence is attributable to alternative explanations, such as the tendency of aggressive children to both watch these games and to engage in physical aggression (Ferguson, in press).

Finally, some investigators have conducted *field studies* of the link between media violence and aggression (Anderson & Bushman, 2002). In field studies, researchers examine the relation between naturally occurring events and aggression in the real world. For example, one investigator (Williams, 1986) conducted a field study of a small, isolated mountain town in Canada that had no television before 1973. She called it "Notel," short for "*no tele*vision." Compared with school-age children in two other Canadian towns that already had television, children in Notel showed a marked increase in physical and verbal aggression 2 years later. Nevertheless, these findings are difficult to interpret in light of a potential confound: At around the same time that Notel received television, the Canadian government constructed a large highway that connected Notel to nearby towns. This highway might have introduced the children in Notel to negative outside influences, including crime from other cities.

So what can we make of all of the research on media violence and aggressive behaviors? We're confronted with four lines of evidence—correlational studies, longitudinal studies, laboratory studies, and field studies—each with its own strengths and weaknesses. Correlational, longitudinal, and field studies tend to be strong in *external validity*, that is, generalizability to the real world, but weak in *internal validity*, that is, the extent to which they permit cause-and-effect inferences. Laboratory studies, in contrast, tend to be weak in external validity but strong in internal validity. Yet despite their shortcomings, all four types of studies point in the same direction: at least some causal relation between media violence and aggression (Anderson et al., 2003; Carnegay, Anderson, & Bartholow, 2007). Scientific conclusions are usually the most convincing when we base them on findings from different research designs, each with a slightly different set of imperfections (Shadish, Cook, & Campbell, 2002). As a result, most psychological scientists today agree that media violence contributes to aggression in at least some circumstances (Anderson & Bushman, 2002a; Bushman & Anderson, 2001).

Nevertheless, it's equally clear that media violence is only one small piece of a multifaceted puzzle. We can't explain aggression by means of media violence alone because the substantial majority of individuals exposed to high levels of such violence don't become aggressive (Freedman, 2002; Wilson & Herrnstein, 1985).

◄ **RULING OUT RIVAL HYPOTHESES**
Have important alternative explanations for the findings been excluded?

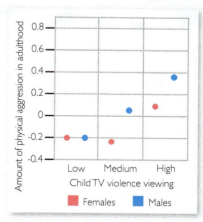

FIGURE 10 Longitudinal Study of Individuals Who Watched Violent TV as Children. In both females and males, there's a positive correlation between viewing violent television in childhood and violent behavior in adulthood. But this correlation doesn't demonstrate causality. Why? (*Source:* Based on Huesmann et al., 2003)

◄ **RULING OUT RIVAL HYPOTHESES**
Have important alternative explanations for the findings been excluded?

 Simulate in **MyPsychLab** the **Experiment:** Media Violence

Mirror Neurons and Observational Learning

Mirror neurons become active when we watch someone similar to us performing a behavior.

You find yourself alone in a new city standing in line behind someone using an ATM. Like so many other cash machines, this one is slightly—and annoyingly—different from all the other ones you've seen. You watch as the person in front of you inserts her card, pushes a few buttons, and grabs her money from the slot at the bottom of the machine. Now it's your turn, and you know exactly what to do. You learned by watching. But how? Although the question of how our brains engage in observational learning is still shrouded in mystery, neuroscientists have recently begun to pinpoint a potential physiological basis for it.

When a monkey watches another monkey perform an action, such as reaching for an object, a group of neurons in its prefrontal cortex, near its motor cortex, becomes active (Rizzolatti et al., 1996). These cells are called **mirror neurons** because they're the same cells that would have become active had the monkey performed the same movement. It's as though these neurons are "imagining" what it would be like to perform the behavior.

Mirror neurons appear to be remarkably selective. They don't become active when a monkey sees another monkey that remains stationary or sees a piece of food that another monkey grabbed. Instead, they become active only when a monkey sees another monkey engaging in an action, like grabbing. Moreover, these neurons seem tuned to extremely specific behaviors. Investigators have found one mirror neuron in monkeys that fires only when the monkey itself or a person it's observing grabs a peanut, and a different mirror neuron that fires only when the monkey itself or a person it's observing eats a peanut (Winerman, 2005). Using brain imaging techniques, researchers have identified what appears to be a similar mirror neuron system in humans (Gallese & Goldman, 1998; Molenberghs, Cunnington, & Mattingley, 2012), but they've yet to identify individual mirror neurons, as they have in monkeys. No one knows for sure what mirror neurons do or why they're in our brains. But some neuroscientists have conjectured that such neurons play a central role in empathy (Azar, 2005; Iacoboni, 2009; Ramachandran, 2000), including feeling others' emotional states and emulating their movements (Fabbri-Destro & Rizzolatti, 2008). When we see an athlete suffer an injury during a sporting event, like a baseball player grimacing in agony after a bruising slide into home plate, we wince in pain along with him. In some sense, we may be "feeling his pain," because the mirror neurons that correspond to the neurons in his motor areas are becoming activated. Some psychologists have gone further to speculate that mirror neuron abnormalities play a key role in infantile autism, which is often associated with difficulties in adopting the perspectives of others (Dingfelder, 2005; Kana, Wadsworth, & Travers, 2011). But whether these neurons play a role in causing autism is unknown, as the findings are only correlational (Dinstein et al., 2008). It's possible that that lower activity of the mirror neuron system in autism is a consequence, rather than a cause, of the empathy deficits often observed in this condition.

CORRELATION VS. CAUSATION ▶
Can we be sure that A causes B?

Even so, the discovery of mirror neurons may ultimately provide valuable insights into how we learn from others. This discovery also helps us appreciate that even when we're alone, we're often not really alone. Even when we're sitting by ourselves watching television, our brain and the brain of that baseball player sliding into home plate may be in sync, our mirror neurons and his lighting up in unison.

Insight Learning

Latent learning and observational learning were by no means the only holes poked in behaviorist theory. Another serious challenge came from a German psychologist during World War I: Wolfgang Köhler.

Around the same time that psychologists were conducting the first latent learning studies, Köhler (1925), a founder of Gestalt psychology, was posing assorted problems to four chimpanzees in the Canary Islands off the coast of Africa. His favorite of the four was a genius of an ape named Sultan, who was especially adept at solving puzzles. In one case Köhler placed a tempting bunch of bananas outside of the cage, well out of Sultan's reach, along with two bamboo sticks inside the cage.

mirror neuron
cell in the prefrontal cortex that becomes activated when an animal performs an action or observes it being performed

Neither stick was long enough to reach the bananas. After what appeared to be some heavy-duty pondering, Sultan suddenly hit upon the solution: Stick one bamboo stick inside the other, creating one extra-long bamboo stick.

What was notable, argued Köhler, was that his chimpanzees seemed to experience the "aha reaction" we discussed earlier. Their solutions to his problems didn't appear to reflect trial and error, as it did with Thorndike's cats, but rather *insight*, the sudden understanding of the solution to a problem. That is, their solutions resembled what we saw back in Figure 6. The chimps seemed to suddenly "get" the solution to the problem, and from then on they got it right just about every time.

Still, Köhler's findings and conclusions weren't without shortcomings. His observations were anecdotal and unsystematic. Because Köhler videotaped only some of his chimpanzees' problem solving, it's difficult to rule out the possibility that at least some of his chimps had engaged in trial and error before figuring out each problem (Gould & Gould, 1994). Moreover, because the chimps were often in the same cage, they might have engaged in observational learning. Still, Köhler's work suggests that at least some smart animals can learn through insight rather than trial and error. There's good evidence that humans can, too (Dawes, 1994).

◀ **RULING OUT RIVAL HYPOTHESES**
Have important alternative explanations for the findings been excluded?

Köhler's apes also figured out how to get to a banana suspended well above their heads: Stack a bunch of boxes atop each other, and climb to the top box.

✔ **Study** and **Review** in **MyPsychLab**

Assess Your Knowledge — FACT or FICTION?

1. According to Skinner, animals don't think or experience emotions.   **True / False**

2. Proponents of latent learning argue that reinforcement isn't necessary for learning.   **True / False**

3. Research on observational learning demonstrates that children can learn aggression by watching aggressive role models.   **True / False**

4. There's no good research evidence for insight learning.   **True / False**

Answers: 1. F; 2. T; 3. T; 4. F

Biological Influences on Learning

11   Explain how biological predispositions can facilitate learning of some associations.

For many decades, most behaviorists regarded learning as distinct from biology. The animal's learning history and genetic makeup were like two ships passing in the night. Yet we now understand that our biology influences the speed and nature of our learning in complex and fascinating ways. Here are three powerful examples.

Conditioned Taste Aversions

One night in the 1970s, psychologist Martin Seligman went out to dinner with his wife. He ordered a filet mignon steak flavored with sauce béarnaise, his favorite topping. About 6 hours later, while at the opera, Seligman felt nauseated and became violently ill. He and his stomach recovered, but his love of sauce béarnaise didn't. From then on, Seligman couldn't even think of, let alone taste, sauce béarnaise without feeling like throwing up (Seligman & Hager, 1972).

The *sauce béarnaise syndrome,* also known as *conditioned taste aversion,* refers to the fact that classical conditioning can lead us to develop avoidance reactions to the taste of food. Before reading on, ask yourself a question: Does Seligman's story contradict the other examples of classical conditioning we've discussed, like that of Pavlov and his dogs?

In fact, it does in at least three ways (Garcia & Hankins, 1977):

1. In contrast to most classically conditioned reactions, which require repeated pairings between CS and UCS, conditioned taste aversions typically require *only one trial* to develop.

Psychological science has helped many cancer patients undergoing chemotherapy to minimize conditioned taste aversions to their favorite foods.

Explore in **MyPsychLab** the **Concept:** Conditioned Taste Aversions

US (radiation box)   UR (nausea)

Neutral stimulus (flavored water)

No response

The CS is paired with the US

CS (flavored water) US (radiation box)

CS (flavored water)   CR (nausea)

FIGURE 11 Conditioned Taste Aversion. The work of John Garcia and his colleagues demonstrated that animals tend to develop conditioned taste aversions only to certain stimuli, namely, those that trigger nausea in the real world.

2. The delay between CS and UCS in conditioned taste aversions can be as long as 6 or even 8 hours (Rachlin & Logue, 1991).

3. Conditioned taste aversions tend to be remarkably specific and display little evidence of stimulus generalization. One of the earliest childhood memories of one of your text's authors is that of eating a delicious piece of lasagna and then becoming violently ill several hours later. For more than 20 years, he avoided lasagna at all costs while thoroughly enjoying spaghetti, manicotti, veal parmigiana, and virtually every other Italian dish despite its similarity to lasagna. He finally forced himself to get over his lasagna phobia, but not without a momentous struggle.

These differences make good sense from an evolutionary standpoint (O'Donnell, Webb, & Shine, 2010). We wouldn't want to have to experience horrific food poisoning again and again to learn a conditioned association between taste and illness. Doing so would not only be incredibly unpleasant, but we'd sometimes be dead after the first trial. The long lag time between eating and illness violates typical classical conditioning because close timing between the CS and UCS is usually necessary for learning. But in this case, the delayed association between CS and UCS is adaptive, because it teaches us to avoid dangerous foods we might have ingested hours earlier.

Conditioned taste aversions are a particular problem among cancer patients undergoing chemotherapy, which frequently induces nausea and vomiting. As a result, they often develop an aversion to any food that preceded chemotherapy, even though they realize it bears no logical connection to the treatment. Fortunately, health psychologists have developed a clever way around this problem. Capitalizing on the specificity of conditioned taste aversions, they ask cancer patients to eat an unfamiliar *scapegoat food*— a novel food of which they aren't fond—prior to chemotherapy. In general, the taste aversion becomes conditioned to the scapegoat food rather than to patients' preferred foods (Andresen, Birch, & Johnson, 1990).

John Garcia and one of his colleagues helped to demonstrate biological influences on conditioned taste aversions. They found that rats exposed to X-rays, which make them nauseated, developed conditioned aversions to a specific taste but not to a specific visual or auditory stimulus presented after the X-rays (Garcia & Koelling, 1966). In other words, the rats more readily associated nausea with taste than with other sensory stimuli after a single exposure (see **FIGURE 11**). Conditioned taste aversions aren't much fun, but they're often adaptive. In the real world, poisoned drinks and foods, not sights and sounds, make animals feel sick. As a consequence, animals more easily develop conditioned aversions to stimuli that tend to trigger nausea in the real world.

This finding contradicts the assumption of *equipotentiality*—the claim that we can classically condition all CSs equally well to all UCSs—a belief held by many traditional behaviorists (Plotkin, 2004). Garcia and others had found that certain CSs, such as those associated with taste, are easily conditioned to certain UCSs, such as those associated with nausea (Rachman, 1977; Thorndike, 1911). Recall that following his night out with his wife, Martin Seligman felt nauseated at the thought of sauce béarnaise, but not at the thought of the opera or—thankfully, for his marriage—his wife.

Preparedness and Phobias

A second challenge to the equipotentiality assumption comes from research on phobias. If we look at the distribution of phobias in the general population, we'll find something curious: People aren't always afraid of things with which they've had the most frequent unpleasant experiences. Phobias of the dark, heights, snakes, spiders, deep water, and blood are commonplace, even though many people who fear these stimuli have never had a frightening encounter with them. In contrast, phobias of razors, knives, the edges of furniture, ovens, and electrical outlets are extremely rare, although many of us have been cut, bruised, burned, or otherwise hurt by them.

Seligman (1971) proposed that we can explain the distribution of phobias in the population by means of **preparedness:** We're evolutionarily predisposed to fear certain stimuli more than others. According to Seligman, that's because certain stimuli, like steep cliffs and poisonous animals, posed

This coyote, eating from a sheep carcass that's been tainted with a mild poison, will become sick several hours later. The coyote will avoid sheep from then on. Ranchers have made use of this technique to keep coyotes from attacking their livestock.

a threat to our early human ancestors (Hofmann, 2008; Ohman & Mineka, 2001). In contrast, household items and appliances didn't, because they weren't around back then. In the words of Susan Mineka (1993), prepared fears are "evolutionary memories": emotional legacies of natural selection.

Mineka and Michael Cook (1993) showed lab-reared rhesus monkeys, who had no previous exposure to snakes, a videotape of fellow monkeys reacting in horror to snakes. Within less than half an hour, the monkeys acquired a fear of snakes by observational learning (surprisingly, rhesus monkeys who've never been exposed to snakes show no fear of them). The researchers then edited the videotape to make it appear that the same monkeys were reacting in horror, but this time in response to flowers, a toy rabbit, a toy snake, or a toy crocodile. They then showed these doctored videotapes to different groups of monkeys who had no experience with flowers, rabbits, snakes, or crocodiles. The monkeys who observed these altered videotapes acquired fears of the toy snake and toy crocodile, but not the flowers or toy rabbit. From the standpoint of preparedness, this finding is understandable. Snakes and crocodiles were dangerous to our primate ancestors, but flowers and rabbits weren't (Ohman & Mineka, 2003).

Preparedness may render us likely to develop *illusory correlations* between fear-provoking stimuli and negative consequences (Fiedler, Freytag, & Meiser, 2009; Tomarken, Mineka, & Cook, 1989). An illusory correlation is a statistical mirage; it's the perception of a nonexistent association between two variables. One team of investigators administered intermittent electrical shocks to subjects—some of whom feared snakes and some of whom didn't—while they watched slides of snakes and damaged electrical outlets. The pairings of the slide stimuli with the shocks were random, so that the actual correlation between them was zero. Yet subjects with high levels of snake fear perceived a marked correlation between the occurrence of the snake slides, but not the electrical outlets, with the electric shocks. Subjects with low levels of snake fear didn't fall prey to this illusory correlation (Tomarken, Sutton, & Mineka, 1995). Snake-fearful people were on the lookout for any threatening stimuli that might signal snakes, so they overestimated how often snake slides co-occurred with electric shock. Interestingly, they showed no such overestimation for electrical outlets, even though they're more closely linked in our minds than are snakes to electric shock. This finding suggests that preparedness may be at work, because snakes, but not electrical outlets, posed threats to our primate ancestors (Grupe & Nitschke, 2011).

Still, the laboratory evidence for preparedness isn't completely consistent. When researchers have paired either prepared stimuli—like snakes or spiders—or unprepared stimuli—like flowers or mushrooms—with electric shocks, they haven't invariably replicated the finding that subjects more rapidly acquire fears to prepared than unprepared stimuli (Davey, 1995; McNally, 1987). Moreover, some authors have proposed that preparedness findings may be due to an alternative explanation that isn't evolutionary in nature: latent inhibition. As we'll recall from earlier in the chapter, latent inhibition refers to the fact that CSs that have appeared alone (that is, without a UCS) many times are especially difficult to classically condition to a stimulus. Because we routinely encounter electric sockets, stoves, knives, and the like, without experiencing any negative consequences, these stimuli may be resistant to classical conditioning. In contrast, because few of us have regular encounters with snakes, cliffs, deep water, and so on, these stimuli may be more easily classically conditioned to aversive outcomes (Bond & Siddle, 1996).

Mineka and Cook (1993) showed that monkeys can acquire fears of snakes by means of observational learning. Nevertheless, these monkeys didn't acquire fears of nondangerous stimuli, like flowers, suggesting a role for evolutionary predispositions in the development of fears.

◄ **REPLICABILITY**
Can the results be duplicated in other studies?

◄ **RULING OUT RIVAL HYPOTHESES**
Have important alternative explanations for the findings been excluded?

preparedness
evolutionary predisposition to learn some pairings of feared stimuli over others owing to their survival value

Aside from preparedness, genetic influences probably play a role in the acquisition of certain phobias. Individuals with a dog phobia don't differ from those without a dog phobia in their number of negative experiences with dogs, such as bites (DiNardo et al., 1988). Moreover, only about half of people with a dog phobia have ever had a scary encounter with a dog; the same holds for people with many other phobias. These results make it unlikely that classical conditioning alone can explain all cases of phobia. Instead, some people may be predisposed genetically to develop phobias *given* a history of certain classical conditioning experiences (Czajkowoski et al., 2011; Kendler et al., 1992).

Instinctive Drift

Animal trainers Marian and Keller Breland taught pigeons, chickens, raccoons, pigs, and a host of other creatures to perform a variety of tricks—much like those we might see on David Letterman's Stupid Pet Tricks segment—for circuses and television advertisers. As students of B. F. Skinner at Harvard, they relied on traditional methods of operant conditioning to shape their animals' behavior.

In the process of their animal training adventures, the Brelands discovered that their little charges didn't always behave as anticipated. In one case they tried to train raccoons to drop tokens into a piggy bank. Although they successfully trained the raccoons to pick up the coins using food reinforcement, they soon ran headfirst into a surprising problem. Despite repeated reinforcement for dropping the coins into the piggy bank, the raccoons began rubbing the coins together, dropping them, and rubbing them together again instead.

The raccoons had reverted to an innate behavior, namely, rinsing. They were treating the tokens like pieces of food, like the small hard shells they extract from the beds of ponds and streams (Timberlake, 2006). Breland and Breland (1961) referred to this phenomenon as **instinctive drift:** the tendency for animals to return to innate behaviors following repeated reinforcement. Researchers have observed instinctive drift in other animals, including rats (LeFrancois, 2011; Powell & Curley, 1984). Psychologists don't fully understand the reasons for such drift. Nevertheless, instinctive drift suggests that we can't fully understand learning without taking into account innate biological influences, because these influences place limits on what kinds of behaviors we can train through reinforcement.

Instinctive drift is the tendency to return to an evolutionarily selected behavior.

Study and **Review** in **MyPsychLab**

Assess Your Knowledge — FACT or FICTION?

1. Many conditioned taste aversions are acquired in only a single trial.   True / False

2. Most research suggests that the assumption of equipotentiality is false.   True / False

3. The phenomenon of preparedness helps explain why virtually all major phobias are equally common in the general population.   True / False

4. With progressively more reinforcement, animals typically drift further and further away from their instinctive patterns of behavior.   True / False

Answers: 1. T; 2. T; 3. F; 4. F

Learning Fads: Do They Work?

12   Evaluate popular techniques marketed to enhance learning.

If you've made it all the way to this point in the chapter (congratulations!), you know that learning new information is hard work. Perhaps because learning new things requires so much time and effort on our part, many mental health professionals have marketed a motley assortment of techniques that supposedly help us to learn more quickly, or more easily, than we currently do. Do these newfangled methods work? We'll find out by examining four popular techniques.

instinctive drift
tendency for animals to return to innate behaviors following repeated reinforcement

Sleep-Assisted Learning

Imagine that you could master all of the information in this text while getting a few nights of sound sleep. You could pay someone to audio-record the entire book, play the recording over the span of several weeknights, and you'd be all done. You could say goodbye to those late nights in the library or dorm room reading about psychology.

As in many areas of psychology, hope springs eternal. Many proponents of *sleep-assisted learning*—learning new material while asleep—have made some extraordinary claims regarding this technique's potential. For example, on Amazon.com, we can download various audio clips that can purportedly help us to learn languages, stop procrastinating, lose weight, or boost our self-confidence, all while we're comfortably catching up on our *zzzzs*.

These assertions are certainly quite remarkable. Does the scientific evidence for sleep-assisted learning stack up to its proponents' impressive claims?

◀ **EXTRAORDINARY CLAIMS**
Is the evidence as strong as the claim?

As is so often the case in life, things that sound too good to be true often are. Admittedly, the early findings on sleep-assisted learning were encouraging. One group of investigators exposed sailors to Morse code (a shorthand form of communication that radio operators sometimes use) while asleep. These sailors mastered Morse code 3 weeks faster than did other sailors (Simon & Emmons, 1955). Other studies from the former Soviet Union seemingly provided support for the claim that people could learn new material, such as tape-recorded words or sentences, while asleep (Aarons, 1976).

Nevertheless, these early positive reports neglected to rule out a crucial alternative explanation: The recordings may have awakened the subjects. The problem is that almost all of the studies showing positive effects didn't monitor subjects' electroencephalograms (EEGs) to ensure they were asleep while listening to the tapes (Druckman & Bjork, 1994; Druckman & Swets, 1988; Lilienfeld et al., 2010). Better-controlled studies that monitored subjects' EEGs to make sure they were asleep offered little evidence for sleep-assisted learning. So to the extent that sleep-learning recordings "work," it's probably because subjects hear snatches of them while drifting in and out of sleep. As for that quick fix for reducing stress, we'd recommend skipping the audio recordings and just getting a good night's rest.

◀ **RULING OUT RIVAL HYPOTHESES**
Have important alternative explanations for the findings been excluded?

Answers are located at the end of the text.

SLEEP-ASSISTED LEARNING   evaluating CLAIMS

When you think of learning, what's the first thing that pops into your head—textbooks, classrooms, or late-night study sessions? For proponents of sleep-assisted learning, it might be a cozy bed. Numerous websites and books claim that you can master a foreign language, become a better public speaker, and even improve your marriage while you're sound asleep. Let's evaluate some of these claims, which are modeled after actual ads for sleep-assisted learning products.

"Join the *thousands of people* who have increased their learning."
Does the fact that thousands of people believe in a claim make it true? What logical fallacy does this ad commit?

"Sleep learning is a more efficient way to learn because *the information flows directly to our subconscious mind.* (While your conscious mind relaxes!)"
What's the problem with this extraordinary claim?

"Risk-free, 100% money-back *guarantee.*"
We should be skeptical of guarantees, as virtually no psychological technique is foolproof.

"Designed using *proven research* conducted all over the world …"
What questions should you ask about how this research was conducted? Can we assume that "proven" means the research has been replicated?

"Use your brain's full potential. The average mind uses only *5% of its* capacity."
Is there scientific support for the claim that we use only a small portion of our brain?

At the same time, there may be a tiny core of truth in claims regarding sleep-assisted learning. Recent evidence demonstrates that while asleep, participants can acquire classically conditioned responses to smells. When investigators repeatedly paired tones with specific odors—which elicited sniffing—while participants slept, participants later sniffed to the tones alone when awake (Arzu et al., 2012). Still, this is a far cry from the claims made by proponents of sleep-assisted learning: The fact that we can learn classically conditioned associations while asleep doesn't mean that we can learn new facts—let alone new languages—while asleep.

Accelerated Learning

Still other companies promise consumers ultrafast techniques for learning. These methods, known as Superlearning or Suggestive Accelerative Learning and Teaching Techniques (SALTT), supposedly allow people to pick up new information at anywhere from 25 to several hundred times their normal learning speeds (Wenger, 1983). SALTT relies on a mixture of several techniques, such as generating expectations for enhanced learning (telling students they'll learn more quickly), getting students to visualize information they're learning, playing classical music during learning, and breathing in a regular rhythm while learning (Lozanov, 1978). When combined, these techniques supposedly allow learners to gain access to intuitive aspects of their minds that otherwise remain inaccessible.

EXTRAORDINARY CLAIMS ▶
Is the evidence as strong as the claim?

RULING OUT RIVAL HYPOTHESES ▶
Have important alternative explanations for the findings been excluded?

Again, however, the evidence for the effectiveness of SALTT and similar methods doesn't come close to matching the extraordinary claims (Della Sala, 2006). Almost all studies show that SALTT doesn't produce enhanced learning (Dipamo & Job, 1990; Druckman & Swets, 1988). Even when researchers have reported positive results for SALTT, these findings have been open to rival explanations. That's because many of the studies conducted on SALTT compared this method with a control condition in which students did little or nothing. As a result, the few positive results reported for SALTT could be attributable to placebo effects, especially because one of the major components of SALTT is raising learners' expectations (Druckman & Swets, 1988).

Discovery Learning

As we've discovered throughout this text, learning how to *rule out rival explanations* for findings is a key ingredient of scientific thinking. But science educators haven't always agreed on how to teach this crucial skill.

RULING OUT RIVAL HYPOTHESES ▶
Have important alternative explanations for the findings been excluded?

One increasingly popular way of imparting this knowledge is *discovery learning*: giving students experimental materials and asking them to figure out the scientific principles on their own (Klahr & Nigram, 2004). For example, a psychology professor who's teaching operant conditioning might set her students up with a friendly rat, a maze, and a plentiful supply of cheese and ask them to figure out which variables affect the rat's learning. For instance, does the rat learn the maze most quickly when we reinforce it continuously or only occasionally?

Nevertheless, as David Klahr and others have shown, the old-fashioned method of *direct instruction,* in which we simply tell students how to solve problems, is usually more effective and efficient than discovery learning (Alfieri et al., 2011). In one study, investigators examined third- and fourth-graders' ability to isolate the variables that influence how quickly a ball rolls down a ramp, such as the ramp's steepness or length. Only 23 percent of students assigned to a discovery learning condition later solved a slightly different problem on their own, whereas 77 percent of students assigned to a direct instruction condition did (Klahr & Nigram, 2004).

That's not to say that discovery learning has no role in education, as in the long-term it may encourage students to learn how to pose scientific questions on their own (Alferink, 2007; Kuhn & Dean, 2005). But because many students may never figure out how to solve certain scientific problems independently, it's ill-advised as a stand-alone approach (Kirschner, Sweller, & Clark, 2006; Mayer, 2004).

Learning Styles

Few claims about learning are as widespread as the belief that all individuals have their own distinctive **learning styles**—their preferred means of acquiring information. According to proponents of this view, some students are "analytical" learners who excel at breaking down problems into different components, whereas others are "holistic" learners who excel at

The view that students with certain learning styles benefit from specific types of instructional materials is popular in educational psychology. Yet scientific research provides little evidence for this belief.

viewing problems as a whole. Still others are "verbal" learners who prefer to talk through problems, whereas others are "spatial" learners who prefer to visualize problems in their heads (Cassidy, 2004; Desmedt & Valcke, 2004). Some educational psychologists have claimed to boost learning dramatically by matching different methods of instruction to students' learning styles. According to them, children who are verbal learners should learn much faster and better with written material, children who are spatial learners should learn much faster and better with visual material, and so on.

Appealing as these assertions are, they haven't stood the test of careful research (Lilienfeld et al., 2009; Pashler et al., 2009; Rohrer & Paschler, 2012). For one thing, it's difficult to assess learning style reliably (Snider, 1992; Stahl, 1999). *Reliability* refers to consistency in measurement. In this case, different measures designed to assess people's learning styles often yield very different answers about their preferred mode of learning. In part, that's probably because few of us are purely analytical or holistic learners, verbal or spatial learners, and so on; most of us are a blend of multiple styles. Moreover, studies have generally revealed that tailoring different methods to people's learning styles doesn't result in enhanced learning (Kavale & Forness, 1987; Kratzig & Arbuthnott, 2006; Tarver & Dawson, 1978). Instead, most research shows that certain teaching approaches, like setting high standards for students and providing them with the motivation and skills to reach these standards, work best regardless of students' learning styles (Geake, 2008; Zhang, 2006). Like a number of other fads in popular psychology, the idea of learning styles seems to be more fiction than fact (Alferink, 2007; Pashler et al., 2009; Stahl, 1999).

Assess Your Knowledge   FACT or FICTION?

1. Sleep-assisted learning techniques only work if subjects stay completely asleep during learning.   **True / False**

2. The few positive results for accelerated learning in the SALTT program may be due to placebo effects.   **True / False**

3. Discovery learning tends to be more efficient than direct instruction for solving most scientific problems.   **True / False**

4. There's little evidence that matching teaching methods to people's learning styles enhances learning.   **True / False**

Answers: 1. F; 2. T; 3. F; 4. T

 Study and **Review** in **MyPsychLab**

learning style
an individual's preferred or optimal method of acquiring new information

✓ **Study** and **Review** in **MyPsychLab**

((ɛ **Listen** in **MyPsychLab** to chapter audio

Classical Conditioning

1 DESCRIBE PAVLOV'S MODEL OF CLASSICAL CONDITIONING AND DISCRIMINATE CONDITIONED STIMULI AND RESPONSES FROM UNCONDITIONED STIMULI AND RESPONSES.

In classical conditioning, animals come to respond to a previously neutral stimulus that had been paired with another stimulus (the CS) that elicits a reflexive, automatic response. After repeated pairings with the UCS, which elicits an automatic, reflexive response (the UCR) from the organism, the CS comes to elicit a conditioned response (CR).

1. A change of an organism's behavior or thought as a result of experience is called _____.

2. The process of _____ occurs when we respond less strongly over time to repeated stimuli.

3. Identify the steps of the classical conditioning model used in Pavlov's dog research.

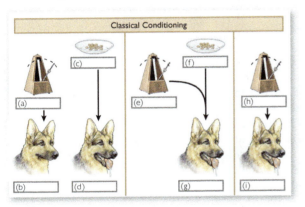

Classical Conditioning

4. If the dog continues to salivate at the sound of the metronome when the meat powder is absent, psychologists call this process _____ _____.

2 EXPLAIN THE MAJOR PRINCIPLES AND TERMINOLOGY ASSOCIATED WITH CLASSICAL CONDITIONING.

Acquisition is the process by which we gradually learn the CR. Extinction is the process whereby following repeated presentation of the CS alone, the CR decreases in magnitude and eventually disappears. Extinction appears to involve an "overwriting" of the CR by new information rather than a forgetting of this information.

5. The learning phase during which a conditioned response is established is called _____.

6. After numerous presentations of the metronome without meat powder, Pavlov's dogs eventually stopped salivating; this is the process of _____.

7. A sudden reemergence of an extinguished conditioned response after a delay in exposure to the conditioned stimulus is called _____ _____.

8. Being able to enjoy a scary movie while still being scared of real world stimuli is an example of stimulus (generalization/discrimination).

3 EXPLAIN HOW COMPLEX BEHAVIORS CAN RESULT FROM CLASSICAL CONDITIONING AND HOW THEY EMERGE IN OUR DAILY LIVES.

Higher-order conditioning occurs when organisms develop classically conditioned responses to CSs associated with the original CS. Such conditioning allows us to expand our learning to a host of different, but related, stimuli in everyday life.

9. _____ _____ refers to the fact that when we've experienced a CS by itself many times, it can be difficult to later condition to another stimulus.

10. Describe the methods used by Watson and Rayner to condition fear in Little Albert and explain why their work couldn't be replicated today for ethical reasons.

Operant Conditioning

4 DISTINGUISH OPERANT CONDITIONING FROM CLASSICAL CONDITIONING.

Operant conditioning is learning controlled by its consequences. Operant conditioning involves many of the same processes, including acquisition and extinction, as does classical conditioning. Nevertheless, in operant conditioning, responses are emitted rather than elicited, the reinforcement is contingent on behavior, and responses mostly involve skeletal (voluntary) muscles rather than the autonomic nervous system.

11. Complete the table to show the differences between classical and operant conditioning.

	CLASSICAL CONDITIONING	OPERANT CONDITIONING
Target behavior is …	_____	_____
Reward is …	_____	_____
Behavior depends primarily on …	_____	_____

12. In (classical/operant) conditioning, the reward is contingent on behavior.

5 DESCRIBE THORNDIKE'S LAW OF EFFECT.

Thorndike's law of effect tells us that if a response, in the presence of a stimulus, is followed by a reward, it's likely to be repeated, resulting in the gradual "stamping in" of S-R (stimulus-response) connections.

13. Thorndike's findings provided a crushing blow to the hypothesis that cats invariably learn by _____, that is, by grasping the nature of the problem.

6 DESCRIBE REINFORCEMENT AND ITS EFFECTS ON BEHAVIOR AND DISTINGUISH NEGATIVE REINFORCEMENT FROM PUNISHMENT.

Reinforcement can be either positive (presentation of an outcome) or negative (withdrawal of an outcome). Negative reinforcement increases the rate of a behavior, whereas punishment decreases it. One disadvantage of punishment is that it tells the organism only what *not* to do, not what *to* do.

14. A physics professor announces to his class that students who are earning 90 percent or higher in the class don't have to take the midterm. This is an example of (positive/negative) reinforcement.

15. Reinforcement _____ the probability of a response, whereas punishment _____ the probability of a response.

16. According to Skinner, one disadvantage of punishment is that it often creates _____, which interferes with future learning.

7 IDENTIFY THE FOUR SCHEDULES OF REINFORCEMENT AND THE RESPONSE PATTERN ASSOCIATED WITH EACH.

There are four major schedules of reinforcement: fixed ratio, fixed interval, variable ratio, and variable interval. These four schedules differ along two dimensions: consistency of administering reinforcement (fixed or variable) and the basis of administering reinforcement (ratio or interval).

17. Identify the typical response patterns for the four reinforcement schedule types.

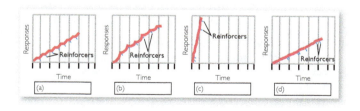

18. Casino gambling is a prime example of a _____ _____ schedule.

8 DESCRIBE SOME APPLICATIONS OF OPERANT CONDITIONING.

Operant conditioning has a number of applications to everyday life, including shaping—which is a fundamental technique of animal training—and overcoming procrastination. Psychologists have also harnessed operant conditioning principles to develop token economies and other therapeutically useful applications. Operant

conditioning principles probably also help to explain certain irrational behaviors in everyday life, including superstitions.

19. Animal trainers often combine the technique of _____, when they reinforce behaviors that aren't exactly the target behavior but that are progressively closer versions of it, with _____, in which they link a number of interrelated behaviors to form a longer series.

20. One of the most successful applications of operant conditioning has been the _____ _____, which is a system, often set up in psychiatric hospitals, for reinforcing appropriate behaviors and extinguishing inappropriate ones.

Cognitive Models of Learning

9 OUTLINE THE EVIDENCE THAT SUPPORTS LATENT LEARNING AND OBSERVATIONAL LEARNING.

S-O-R psychologists believe that the organism's interpretation of stimuli plays a central role in learning. Tolman's work on latent learning, which showed that animals can learn without reinforcement, challenged the radical behaviorists' view of learning. Research suggests that individuals can acquire aggressive behavior by observational learning. Correlational studies, longitudinal studies, laboratory studies, and field studies suggest that media violence contributes to aggression, although questions regarding the strength of this relationship remain.

21. Skinner was an advocate of _____ behaviorism, in which observable behavior, thinking, and emotion are all governed by the same laws of learning.

22. Early behaviorists (believed/didn't believe) that thought played an important causal role in learning.

23. In the past few decades, psychology has increasingly moved away from a simple S-R (stimulus-response) psychology to a more complex _____ psychology, where the link between S and R isn't automatic.

24. When talking to employees about their performance, why might managers want to adapt their style depending on the person to whom they're talking?

25. According to Tolman, the rats in his study had developed spatial representations of the maze termed _____ _____.

Answers are located at the end of the text.

26. What type of learning is taking place in this photo, and what is the basis of the learning process shown?

27. In classic research in the 1960s, _____ _____ and his colleagues demonstrated that children can learn to act aggressively by watching aggressive role models.

28. Longitudinal studies that correlate the amount of violent TV watched in childhood with the amount of aggressive acts committed in adulthood (have/have not) demonstrated causality.

29. Cells in the prefrontal cortex that become activated by specific motions when an animal performs or observes an action are called _____ _____.

10 IDENTIFY EVIDENCE OF INSIGHT LEARNING.

Kohler's work suggested that apes can learn through insight, and later work with humans suggests the same conclusion. This research calls into question Thorndike's conclusion that all learning occurs through trial and error.

30. Kohler's work with chimpanzees suggested that at least some smart animals can learn through _____ rather than trial and error.

Biological Influences on Learning

11 EXPLAIN HOW BIOLOGICAL PREDISPOSITIONS CAN FACILITATE LEARNING OF SOME ASSOCIATIONS.

Psychologists have increasingly recognized that our genetic endowment influences learning. Conditioned taste aversions refer to the phenomenon whereby classical conditioning can lead us to develop avoidance reactions to the taste of food. John Garcia and his colleagues showed that conditioned taste aversions violate the principle of equipotentiality, because they demonstrate that certain CSs are more easily conditioned than others to certain UCSs. Research on preparedness suggests that we are evolutionarily predisposed to learn to fear some stimuli more easily than others.

31. Conditioned taste aversions typically require (one trial/many trials) to develop.

32. Explain how health psychologists can help cancer patients undergoing chemotherapy to minimize conditioned taste aversions to their favorite foods.

33. Through his research with rats, Garcia helped to demonstrate the _____ influences on conditioned taste aversions.

34. The rats in Garcia's study more readily associated nausea with _____ than with any other sensory stimuli.

35. Conditioned taste aversions aren't much fun, but they're often _____ in the real world. An example would be an animal that develops a conditioned taste aversion to a poisoned food or drink.

36. Garcia and others challenged the assumption of _____, the belief of many behaviorists that we can pair all CSs equally well with all UCSs.

37. According to Seligman, we're evolutionarily predisposed to fear certain stimuli more than others by means of _____.

38. In Mineka's and Cook's study, the monkeys (acquired/didn't acquire) fears of nondangerous stimuli, such as flowers.

39. Mineka's and Cook's study was clearly a case of learning because the monkeys were (afraid/unafraid) of snakes prior to the experiment.

40. Describe the phenomenon whereby animals return to evolutionarily selected behaviors, and explain how that phenomenon has affected researchers' understanding of learning.

Learning Fads: Do They Work?

12 EVALUATE POPULAR TECHNIQUES MARKETED TO ENHANCE LEARNING.

Proponents of sleep-assisted learning claim that individuals can learn new material while asleep. Nevertheless, early reports of successful learning during sleep appear attributable to a failure to carefully monitor subjects' EEGs to ensure that they were asleep. Studies of accelerated learning techniques also show few or no positive effects, and positive results appear attributable to placebo effects and other artifacts. Although popular in science education, discovery learning approaches are often less effective and efficient than direct instruction. Some educational psychologists claim to be able to boost learning by matching individuals' learning styles with different teaching methods, but studies that have matched learning styles with teaching methods have typically yielded negative results.

41. The problem with early findings on sleep-assisted learning is that almost all of the studies showing positive effects didn't monitor subjects' _____ to ensure they were asleep while listening to the tapes.

42. Explain the extraordinary claims about how sleep-assisted learning works and identify shortcomings in researchers' attempts to validate those claims.

43. Methods of accelerated learning, such as _____ _____ _____ _____ _____ supposedly allow people to pick up new information anywhere from 25 to several hundred times their normal learning speed.

44. SALTT relies on such techniques as getting students to _____ information they're learning, and playing _____ music while they're learning.

45. Any scattered positive results for SALTT could be due in part to _____ effects because one of the components of the program is raising learners' expectations.

46. When you give students experimental materials and ask them to figure out a scientific principle on their own, this is known as _____ _____.

47. Klahr and his colleagues have shown that the old-fashioned method of _____ _____, in which we simply tell students how to solve problems, is often most efficient and effective.

48. Individuals' preferred or optimal method of acquiring new information are referred to as _____ _____.

49. Proponents of this view believe that some students are _____ learners who excel at breaking down problems into different components, while others are _____ learners who excel at viewing problems as a whole.

50. Provide a valid argument against teaching to students' learning styles.

Apply Your Scientific Thinking Skills

Use your scientific thinking skills to answer the following questions, referencing specific scientific thinking principles and common errors in reasoning whenever possible.

1. Skinner and his followers believed that reinforcement is more effective than punishment in shaping children's behavior. Yet there still exists a wide variety of opinion over the best way to raise and discipline children. Read several sources of parenting advice offered in the popular media, locating some examples that favor reinforcement and others that favor punishment. What arguments does each side use to support its preferred parenting style? What claims do they make about shaping children's behaviors, and are they supported by scientific evidence?

2. Researchers have used different types of studies to examine the connection between exposure to media violence and aggressive behavior. Read a few newspaper, magazine, or Internet articles on this topic (their focus can be on violent television, movies, songs, or video games), choosing at least one that argues for a connection between media violence and aggression and at least one that argues against such a connection. What arguments does each side make? How accurately did they interpret the research? Are there explanations or variables that these articles neglected to consider?

3. This chapter discussed four popular learning fads: sleep-assisted learning, accelerated learning, discovery learning, and learning styles. Identify and evaluate some other popular learning techniques (Hint: Perform a Google search for "learning techniques" or "learning methods"). Do these techniques make extraordinary claims regarding their benefits? What research support, if any, do they offer for their claims?

Further Your Understanding

EXTEND YOUR KNOWLEDGE WITH THE MYPSYCHLAB VIDEO SERIES
Watch these videos in MyPsychLab. Follow the "Video Series" link.

The Big Picture: What Does It Mean to Learn? See how other students define "learning," and find out about different types of learning that can occur through associations, consequences, and observation.

Special Topics: Learning to Overcome Phobias Look at how phobias can arise and be reinforced through conditioning and explore how they can be effectively treated.

In the Real World: Learning Aggression Explore some of the ways children learn aggressive behaviors and examine the power of the media in influencing them.

What's In It For Me? How to Make Healthier Choices See how principles of learning can help individuals break bad habits and create new, healthier ones.

EXPERIENCE PSYCHOLOGICAL RESEARCH WITH MYPSYCHLAB SIMULATIONS
Access these simulations in MyPsychLab. Follow the "Simulations" link.

What Learning Techniques Do You Use? Participate in a survey to understand better how you learn, teach, and incentivize learning.

APPLY YOUR CRITICAL THINKING SKILLS WITH MYPSYCHLAB WRITING ASSESSMENTS
Complete these writing assignments in MyPsychLab.

Imagine you are asked by a roommate to help him devise a weight loss program to increase his chances of making the football team. Create a one month behavior modification program based on the principles of operant conditioning which will get him started towards his goal. Be sure to describe how you will measure your roommate's progress and what schedules of reinforcement will be included in your program.

Answer Key

CLASSICAL CONDITIONING

1. learning
2. habituation
3. a) neutral stimulus (metronome); b) no salivation;
   c) UCS (meat powder); d) UCR (salivation);
   e) neutral stimulus; f) UCS; g) UCR (salivation);
   h) previously neutral stimulus is now CS; i) CR (salivation)
4. classical conditioning
5. acquisition
6. extinction
7. spontaneous recovery
8. discrimination
9. Latent inhibition
10. Little Albert initially liked small furry animals. Watson and Rayner first allowed Little Albert to play with a white rat. But only seconds afterward, Watson sneaked up behind Little Albert and struck a gong with a steel hammer, creating an earsplitting noise and startling him out of his wits. After seven such pairings of CS (rat) and UCS (loud sound from gong), Little Albert displayed a CR (fear) to the rat alone. Because inducing a prolonged fear response in an infant raises a host of serious ethical questions, the study would never get past a modern IRB.

OPERANT CONDITIONING

11.

	CLASSICAL CONDITIONING	OPERANT CONDITIONING
Target behavior is …	Elicited automatically	Emitted voluntarily
Reward is …	Provided unconditionally	Contingent on behavior
Behavior depends primarily upon …	Autonomic nervous system	Skeletal muscles

12. operant
13. insight
14. negative
15. strengthens; weakens
16. anxiety
17. a) fixed ratio; b) fixed interval; c) variable ratio; d) variable interval
18. variable ratio
19. shaping; chaining
20. token economy

COGNITIVE MODELS OF LEARNING

21. radical
22. didn't believe
23. S-O-R
24. S-O-R theorists believe that cognition is central to explaining learning and contend that people respond differently because they interpret the criticism in different ways. So managers need to take into account individual reactions when offering performance evaluations.
25. cognitive maps
26. Observational learning takes place by watching others. Children acquire a great deal of their behavior by observing and imitating the behaviors of adults, especially their parents.
27. Albert Bandura
28. have not
29. mirror neurons
30. insight

BIOLOGICAL INFLUENCES ON LEARNING

31. one trial
32. By using a scapegoat food, they can minimize conditioned taste aversions to their favorite foods.
33. biological
34. taste
35. adaptive
36. equipotentiality
37. preparedness
38. didn't acquire
39. unafraid
40. Instinctive drift is the tendency for animals to return to innate behaviors following repeated reinforcement to perform a different behavior. Psychologists don't fully understand the reasons for such drift, but it does suggest that we can't fully understand learning without taking into account innate biological influences, as these influences often place limits on what kind of behaviors we can train.

LEARNING FADS: DO THEY WORK?

41. electroencephalograms (EEGs)
42. Proponents of sleep-assisted learning claim we can learn languages or learn how to stop smoking, lose weight, or reduce stress while asleep. The problem with almost all of the studies showing positive effects of sleep-assisted learning is they didn't monitor participants' EEGs to ensure they were actually asleep while listening to the tapes.
43. Suggestive Accelerative Learning and Teaching Techniques
44. visualize; classical
45. placebo
46. discovery learning
47. direct instruction
48. learning style
49. analytical; holistic
50. Scientific research provides little evidence that tailoring teaching to individual learning styles enhances learning. In addition, it's difficult to assess students' learning styles reliably.

References

Aarons, L. (1976). Sleep-assisted instruction. *Psychological Bulletin, 83,* 1–40.

Akins, C. K. (2004). The role of Pavlovian conditioning in sexual behavior: A comparative analysis of human and nonhuman animals. *International Journal of Comparative Psychology, 17,* 241–262.

Alferink, L. A. (2007). Educational practices, superstitious behavior, and mythed opportunities. *Scientific Review of Mental Health Practice, 5*(2), 21–30.

American Psychiatric Association. (2000). *Diagnostic and statistical manual of mental disorders: DSM-IV-TR* (4th ed.). Washington, DC: Author.

Anderson, A. K., Christoff, K., Stappen, I., Panitz, D., Ghahremani, D. G., Glover, G.,... Sobel, N. (2003). Dissociated neural representations of intensity and valence in human olfaction. *Nature Neuroscience, 6,* 196–202.

Anderson, C. A., & Bushman, B. J. (2002a). The effects of media violence on society. *Science, 295,* 2377–2378.

Anderson, C. A., Gentile, D. A., & Buckley, K. E. (2007). *Violent video game effects on children and adolescents: Theory, research, and public policy.* Oxford, England: Oxford University Press.

Andresen, G. V., Birch, L. L., & Johnson, P. A. (1990). The scapegoat effect on food aversions after chemotherapy. *Cancer, 66,* 1649–1653.

Arkowitz, H., & Lilienfeld, S. O. (2009, January). Why science tells us not to rely on eyewitness accounts. *Scientific American Mind.* http://www.scientificamerican.com/article.cfm?id=do-the-eyes-have-it

Ayllon, T., & Milan, M. (2002). Token economy: Guidelines for operation. In M. Hersen & W. Sledge, *Encyclopedia of psychotherapy* (pp. 829–833). New York, NY: Academic Press.

Azar, B. (2005, October). How mimicry begat culture. *American Psychological Association Monitor, 36*(9). Retrieved from http://www.apa.org/monitor/oct05/mimicry.aspx

Azrin, N. H., & Holz, W. C. (1966). Punishment. In W. K. Honig (Ed.), *Operant behavior: Areas of research and application* (pp. 380–447). New York, NY: Appleton-Century-Crofts.

Bandura, A. (1965). Vicarious processes: A case of no-trial learning. In L. Berkowitz (Ed.), *Advances in experimental social psychology* (Vol. 2, pp. 3–55). New York, NY: Academic Press.

Bandura, A. (1977). Self-efficacy: Toward a unifying theory of behavioral change. *Psychological Review, 84,* 191–215.

Bandura, A., Ross, D., & Ross, S. A. (1961). Transmission of aggression through imitation of aggressive models. *Journal of Abnormal and Social Psychology, 63,* 575–582.

Bandura, A., Ross, D., & Ross, S. A. (1963). Imitation of film mediated aggressive models. *Journal of Abnormal and Social Psychology, 66,* 3–11.

Beck, H. P., Levinson, S., & Irons, G. (2009). A journey to John B. Watson's infant laboratory. *American Psychologist, 64,* 605–614.

Bekinschtein, T. A., Shalom, D. E., Forcato, C., Herrera, M., Coleman, M. R., Manes, F. F., & Sigman, M. (2009). Classical conditioning in the vegetative and minimally conscious state. *Nature Neuroscience, 12,* 1343–1349.

Blodgett, H. C. (1929). The effect of the introduction of reward upon the maze performance of rats. *University of California Publications in Psychology, 4,* 113–134.

Bloom, C., Venard, J., Harden, M., & Seetharaman, S. (2007). Non-contingent positive and negative reinforcement schedules of superstitious behaviors. *Behavioural Processes, 75,* 8–13.

Bolles, R. C. (1979). *Learning theory.* New York, NY: Holt, Rinehart and Winston.

Bond, N. W., & Siddle, D. A. T. (1996). The preparedness account of social phobia: Some data and alternative explanations. In R. M. Rapee (Ed.), *Current controversies in the anxiety disorders* (pp. 291–316). London, England: Guilford Press.

Bouton, M. E. (1994). Context, ambiguity, and classical conditioning. *Current Directions in Psychological Science, 3*, 1–5.

Bradbard, M. R., Martin, C. L., Endsley, R. C., & Halverson, C. F. (1986). Influence of sex stereotypes on children's exploration and memory: A competence versus performance distinction. *Developmental Psychology, 22*, 481–486.

Breland, K., & Breland, M. (1961). The misbehavior of organisms. *American Psychologist, 16*(11), 681–684.

Brennan, P. A., & Mednick, S. A. (1994). Learning theory approach to the deterrence of criminal recidivism. *Journal of Abnormal Psychology, 103*, 430–440.

Brewer, W. F. (1974). There is no convincing evidence for operant or classical conditioning in adult humans. In W. B. Weimer & D. S. Palemo (Eds.), *Cognition and the symbolic processes* (pp. 1–42). Hillsdale, NJ: Erlbaum.

Brown, P. L., & Jenkins, H. M. (1968). Auto-shaping of pigeons key-peck. *Journal of the Experimental Analysis of Behavior, 11*, 1–18.

Bushman, B. J., & Anderson, C. A. (2001). Media violence and the American public: Scientific facts versus media misinformation. *American Psychologist, 56*, 477–489.

Carnagey, N. L., Anderson, C. A., & Bartholow, B. D. (2007). Media violence and social neuroscience: New questions and new opportunities. *Current Directions in Psychological Science, 16*, 178–182.

Carr, J. E., Fraizer, T. J., & Roland, J. P. (2005). Token economy. In A. M. Gross & R. S. Drabman (Eds.) *Encyclopedia of behavior modification and cognitive behavior therapy—Volume 2: Child clinical applications* (pp. 1075–1079). Thousand Oaks, CA: Sage.

Cassidy, K. L. (2004). The adult learner rediscovered: Psychiatry residents' push for cognitive–behavioral therapy training and a learner-driven model of educational change. *Academic Psychiatry, 28*, 215–220.

Church, R. M. (1969). Response suppression. In B. Campbell & R. Church (Eds.), *Punishment and aversive behavior* (pp. 111–156). New York, NY: Appleton-Century-Crofts.

Collins, H., & Pinch, T. (1993) *The Golem: What you should know about science.* Cambridge, England: Cambridge University Press.

Connolly, K. M., Lohr, J. M., & Olatunji, B. O. (2008). Information processing in contamination fear: A covariation bias examination of fear and disgust. *Journal of Anxiety Disorders, 23*, 60–68.

D'Amato, E. (1998, January/February). Mystery of disgust. *Psychology Today.* Retrieved from http://www.psychologytoday.com/articles/200909/mystery-disgust

Danaher, B. C. (1974). Theoretical foundations and clinical applications of the Premack principle: Review and critique. *Behavior Therapy, 5*, 307–324.

Davey, G. C. L. (1995). Rumination and the enhancement of fear: Some laboratory findings. *Behavioural and Cognitive Psychotherapy, 23*, 203–215.

Dawes, R. M. (1994). *House of cards: Psychology and psychotherapy built on myth.* New York, NY: Free Press.

DeBell, C. S., & Harless, D. K. (1992) B. F. Skinner: Myth and misperception. *Teaching of Psychology, 19*(2), 68–73.

Denniston, J. C., Chang, R., & Miller, R. R. (2003). Massive extinction prevents the renewal effect. *Learning and Motivation, 34*, 68–86.

Desmedt, E., & Valcke, M. (2004). Mapping the learning styles "jungle": An overview of the literature based on citation analysis. *Educational Psychology, 24*, 445–464.

DiLalla, L. F., & Gottesman, I. I. (1991). Biological and genetic contributors to violence—Widom's untold tale. *Psychological Bulletin, 109*, 125–129.

DiNardo, P. A., Guzy, L. T., & Bak, R. M. (1988). Anxiety response patterns and etiological factors in dog-fearful and non-fearful subjects. *Behaviour Research and Therapy, 26*, 245–251.

Dingfelder, S. F. (2005, October). Autism's smoking gun? *American Psychological Association Monitor, 36*(9). Retrieved from http://www.apa.org/monitor/oct05/autism.html

Dinstein, I., Thomas, C., & Behrmann, M. (2008) A mirror up to nature. *Current Biology, 18*, R13–R18.

Druckman, D., & Bjork, R. A. (Eds.). (1994). *Learning, remembering, believing: Enhancing human performance.* Washington, DC: National Academies Press.

Druckman, D., & Swets, J. A. (Eds.). (1988). *Enhancing human performance: Issues, theories, and techniques.* Washington, DC: National Academies Press.

Fabbri-Destro, M., & Rizzolatti, G. (2008). Mirror neurons and mirror systems in monkeys and humans. *Physiology, 23*, 171–179.

Fang, X., & Corso, P. S. (2007). Child maltreatment, youth violence, and intimate partner violence: Developmental relationships. *American Journal of Preventive Medicine, 33*, 281–290.

Ferguson, C. J. (2009) Violent video games: Dogma, fear, and pseudoscience. *Skeptical Inquirer, 33*(5), 38–54.

Fiedler, K., Freytag, P., & Meiser, T. (2009). Pseudocontingencies: An integrative account of an intriguing cognitive illusion. *Psychological Review, 116*, 187–206.

Fowles, D. C. (1980). The three arousal model: Implications of Gray's two-factor learning theory for heart rate, electrodermal activity, and psychopathy. *Psychophysiology, 17*, 87–104.

Freedman, J. L. (1984). Effect of television violence on aggressiveness. *Psychological Bulletin, 96*, 227–246.

Freedman, J. L. (2002). *Media violence and its effects on aggression: Assessing the scientific evidence.* Toronto, Ontario, Canada: University of Toronto Press.

Gallese, V., & Goldman, A. (1998) Mirror neurons and the simulation theory of mind-reading. *Trends in Cognitive Sciences, 2*, 493–501.

Garcia, J., & Hankins, W. G. (1977). On the origin of food aversion paradigms. In L. M. Barker, M. R. Best, & M. Domjan (Eds.), *Learning mechanisms in food selection* (pp. 3–22). Houston, TX: Baylor University Press.

Garcia, J., & Koelling, R. A. (1966). The relation of cue to consequence in avoidance learning. *Psychonomic Science, 4*, 123–124.

García-Montes, J. M., Álvarez, M. P., Sass, L. A., & Cangas, A. J. (2008). The role of superstition in psychopathology. *Philosophy, Psychiatry, & Psychology, 15*, 227–237.

Geake, J. (2008). Neuromythologies in education. *Educational Research, 80*, 123–133.

Gershoff, E. T. (2002). Corporal punishment by parents and associated child behaviors and experiences: A meta-analytic and theoretical review. *Psychological Bulletin, 128*, 539–579.

Gewirtz, J. C., & Davis, M. (2000). Using Pavlovian "higher-order" conditioning paradigms to investigate the neural substrates of emotional learning and memory. *Learning and Memory, 7*, 257–266.

Gorn, G. J. (1982). The effects of music in advertising on choice behavior: A classical conditioning approach. *Journal of Marketing, 46*, 94–101.

Gould, J. L., & Gould, C. G. (1994) *The animal mind.* New York, NY: Scientific American Library/Scientific American Books.

Green, G. (1996). Early behavioral intervention for autism: What does research tell us? In C. Maurice, G. Green, & S. Luce (Eds.), *Behavioral intervention for young children with autism: A manual for parents and professionals* (pp. 29–44). Austin, TX: PRO-E.

Gresham, L. G., & Shimp, T. A. (1985). Attitude toward the advertisement and brand attitudes: A classical conditioning perspective. *Journal of Advertising, 14*, 10–17, 49.

Grings, W. W. (1973). Cognitive factors in electrodermal conditioning. *Psychological Bulletin, 79*, 200–210.

Herbert, J. D., Sharp, I. R., & Gaudiano, B. A. (2002). Separating fact from fiction in the etiology and treatment of autism: A scientific review of the evidence. *Scientific Review of Mental Health Practice, 1*, 25–45.

Herrnstein, R. J. (1966). Superstition: A corollary of the principles of operant conditioning. In W. K. Honig (Ed.), *Operant behavior: Areas of research and application* (pp. 33–51). New York, NY: Appleton-Century-Crofts.

Hock, R. R. (2002). *Forty studies that changed psychology: Explorations into the history of psychological research* (4th ed.). Upper Saddle River, NJ: Prentice Hall.

Hofmann, S. G. (2008). Cognitive processes in fear acquisition and extinction in animals and humans: Implications for exposure therapy of anxiety disorders. *Clinical Psychology Review, 28*, 199–210.

Huesmann, L. R., Moise-Titus, J., Podolski, C., & Eron, L. D. (2003). Longitudinal relations between children's exposure to TV violence and their aggressive and violent behavior in young adulthood: 1977–1992. *Developmental Psychology, 39*, 201–221.

Iacoboni, M., (2009). Imitation, empathy, and mirror neurons. *Annual Review of Psychology, 60*, 653–670.

Jones, M. C. (1924). The elimination of children's fears. *Journal of Experimental Psychology, 7*, 382–390.

Kähler, W. (1925) An aspect of Gestalt psychology. *Pediatric Seminars, 32*, 691–723.

Käksal, F., Domjan, M., Kurt, A., Sertel, O., Orüng, S., Bowers, R., & Kumru, G. (2004). An animal model of fetishism. *Behaviour Research and Therapy, 42*, 1421–1434.

Kavale, K. A., & Forness, S. R. (1987). Substance over style—Assessing the efficacy of modality testing and teaching. *Exceptional Children, 54*, 228–239.

Kazdin, A. E. (1982). The token economy: A decade later. *Journal of Applied Behavior Analysis, 15*, 431–445.

Kendler, K. S., Neale, M. C., Kessler, R. C., Heath, A. C., & Eaves, L. J. (1992) The genetic epidemiology of phobias in women: The interrelationship of agoraphobia, social phobia, situational phobia, and simple phobia. *Archives of General Psychiatry, 49*, 273–281.

Kirsch, I., Lynn, S. J., Vigorito, M., & Miller, R. R. (2004). The role of cognition in classical and operant conditioning. *Journal of Clinical Psychology, 60*, 369–392.

Kirschner, P. A., Sweller, J., & Clark, R. E. (2006). Why minimal guidance during instruction does not work: An analysis of the failure of constructivist, discovery, problem-based, experiential, and inquiry-based teaching. *Educational Psychologist, 41*, 75–86.

Klahr, D., & Nigam, M. (2004). The equivalence of learning paths in early science instruction: Effects of direct instruction and discovery learning. *Psychological Science, 15*, 661–667.

Knapp, T. J. (1976). Premack principle in human experimental and applied settings. *Behaviour Research and Therapy, 14*, 133–147.

Kratzig, G. P., & Arbuthnott, K. D. (2006). Perceptual learning style and learning proficiency: A test of the hypothesis. *Journal of Educational Psychology, 98*, 238–246.

Krueger, R. F., Hicks, B. M., & McGue, M. (2001). Altruism and antisocial behavior: Independent tendencies, unique personality correlates, distinct etiologies. *Psychological Science, 12*, 397–402.

Kuhn, D., & Dean, D. (2005). Is developing scientific thinking all about learning to control variables? *Psychological Science, 16*, 866–870.

Lansford, J. E., Chang, L., Dodge, K. A., Malone, P. S., Oburu, P., Palmérus, K., . . . Quinn, N. (2005). Physical discipline and children's adjustment: Cultural normativeness as a moderator. *Child Development, 76*, 1234–1246.

Lansford, J. E., Deater-Deckard, K., Dodge, K. A., Bates, J. E., & Pettit, G. S. (2004). Ethnic differences in the link between physical discipline and later adolescent externalizing behaviors. *Journal of Child Psychology and Psychiatry, 45,* 801–812.

LeDoux, J. (1996). *The emotional brain: The mysterious underpinnings of emotional life.* New York, NY: Simon & Schuster.

Likhtik, D. Popa, J., & Apergis-Schoute, G.A. (2008). Amygdala intercalated neurons are required for expression of fear extinction. *Nature, 45,* 642–645.

Lovaas, O. I. (1987) Behavioral treatment and normal educational and intellectual functioning in young autistic children. *Journal of Consulting and Clinical Psychology, 55,* 3–9.

Lowenstein, L. F.(2002). Fetishes and their associated behavior. *Sexuality and Disability, 20,* 135–147.

Lozanov, G. (1978) *Suggestology and outlines of suggestopedy* (M. Hall-Pozharlieva & K. Pashmakova, Trans.). Oxford, England: Gordon & Breach.

Lykken, D. T., Iacono, W. G., Harioan, K., McGue, M., & Bouchard, T. J. (1988). Habituation of the skin-conductance response to strong stimuli—A twin study, *Psychophysiology, 25,* 4–15.

Lynch, S. K., Turkheimer, E., D'Onofrio, B., Mendle, J., Emery, R. E., Slutske, W. S., & Martin, N. G. (2006). A genetically informed study of the association between harsh punishment and offspring behavior problems. *Family Psychology, 20,* 190–198.

Matson, J. L., Benavidez, D. A., Compton, L. S., Paclawskyj, T., & Baglio, C. (1996) Behavioral treatment of autistic persons: A review of research from 1980 to the present. *Research in Developmental Disabilities, 17,* 433–465.

Mayer, R. (2004). Should there be a three-strikes rule against pure discovery learning? The case for guided methods of instruction. *American Psychologist, 59,* 14–19.

McConnell, J. V. (1962). Memory transfer through cannibalism in planarians. *Journal of Neuropsychiatry, 3*(Suppl. 1), 542–548.

McCord, J. (2006). Punishments and alternate routes to crime prevention. In A. K. Hess & I. B. Weiner (Eds.), *The handbook of forensic psychology* (3rd ed., pp. 701–721). Hoboken, NJ: Wiley.

McEachin, J. J., Smith, T., & Lovaas, O. I. (1993) Long-term outcome for children with autism who received early intensive behavioral treatment. *American Journal on Mental Retardation, 97,* 359–372.

McNally, R. J. (1987). Preparedness and phobias—A review. *Psychological Bulletin, 101,* 283–303.

McNamara, H. J., Long, J. B., & Wike, E. L. (1956). Learning without response under two conditions of external cues. *Journal of Comparative and Physiological Psychology, 49,* 477–480.

Mineka, S., & Cook, M. (1993). Mechanisms involved in the observational conditioning of fear. *Journal of Experimental Psychology: General, 122,* 23–38.

Mischel, W. (1973). Toward a cognitive social learning reconceptualization of personality. *Psychological Review, 80,* 252–283. http://dx.doi.org/10.1037/h0035002

Moffitt, T. E. (1983). The learning theory model of punishment: Implications for delinquency deterrence. *Criminal Justice and Behavior, 10,* 131–158.

Morokuma, S., Fukushima, K., Kawai, N., Tomonaga, M., Satoh, S., & Nakano, H. (2004). Fetal habituation correlates with functional brain development. *Behavioural Brain Research, 153,* 459–463.

Morse, W. H., & Skinner, B. F. (1957). A second type of superstition in the pigeon. *American Journal of Psychology, 70,* 308–311.

Mowrer, O. H. (1947). On the dual nature of learning—A re-interpretation of "conditioning" and "problem-solving." *Harvard Educational Review, 17,* 102–148.

Ohman, A., & Mineka, S. (2001). Fears, phobias, and preparedness: Toward an evolved module of fear and fear learning. *Psychological Review, 108,* 483–522.

Ohman, A., & Mineka, S. (2003). The malicious serpent: Snakes as a prototypical stimulus for an evolved module of fear. *Current Directions in Psychological Science, 12,* 5–9.

Palsson, E., Klamer, D., Wass C., Archer, T., Engel, J. A., & Svensen, L. (2005). The effects of phencyclidine on latent inhibition in taste aversion conditioning: Differential effects of preexposure and conditioning. *Behavioural Brain Research, 157,* 139–146.

Paolucci, E. O., & Violato, C. (2004). A meta-analysis of the published research on the affective, cognitive and behavioral effects of corporal punishment. *Journal of Psychology, 138,* 197–221.

Pashler, H., McDaniel, M., Rohrer, D., & Bjork, R. (2009). Learning styles: Concepts and evidence. *Psychological Science in the Public Interest, 9,* 105–119.

Paul, G., & Lentz, R. J. (1977). *Psychosocial treatment of chronic mental patients: Milieu versus social-learning programs.* Cambridge, MA: Harvard University Press.

Pavlov, I. P. (1927). *Conditioned reflexes.* Oxford, England: Oxford University Press.

Pinker, S. (1997). *How the mind works.* New York, NY: Norton.

Plotkin, H. (2004). *Evolutionary thought in psychology: A brief history.* Oxford, England: Blackwell.

Powell, R. A. (2010). Little Albert still missing. *American Psychologist, 65,* 299–300.

Powell, R. W., & Curley, M. (1984). Analysis of instinctive drift. 2. The development and control of species-specific responses in appetitive conditioning. *Psychological Record, 34,* 363–379.

Premack, D. (1965). Reinforcement theory. In D. Levine (Ed.), *Nebraska Symposium on Motivation* (pp. 123–180). Lincoln, NE: University of Nebraska Press.

Rachlin, H., & Logue, A. W. (1991). Learning. In M. Hersen, A. E. Kazdin, & A. S. Bellack (Eds.), *The clinical psychology handbook* (2nd ed., pp. 170–184). Elmsford, NY: Pergamon Press.

Rachman, S. (1977). The conditioning theory of fear-acquisition: A critical examination. *Behaviour Research and Therapy, 15,* 375–387.

Rachman, S., & Hodgson, R. J. (1968). Experimentally induced "sexual fetishism": Replication and development. *Psychological Record, 18,* 25–27.

Ramachandran, V. S. (2000). Mirror neurons and imitation learning as the driving force behind "the great leap forward" in human evolution. Edge. Retrieved from http://www.edge.org/3rd_culture/ramachandran/ramachandran_p1.html

Ramer, D. G. (1980) The Premack Principle, self-monitoring, and the maintenance of preventive dental health behaviour. *Dissertation Abstracts International, 40*(11-B), 5415–5416.

Rescorla, R. A. (1990). The role of information about the response-outcome relation in instrumental discrimination learning. *Journal of Experimental Psychology: Animal Behavior Processes, 16,* 262–270.

Rescorla, R. A., & Wagner, A. R. (1972). A theory of Pavlovian conditioning: Variations in effectiveness of reinforcement and non-reinforcement. In A. H. Black & W. F. Prokasy (Eds.), *Classical conditioning II: Current research and theory,* (pp. 64–98). New York, NY: Appleton-Century-Crofts.

Rilling, M. (1996). The mystery of the vanished citations: James McConnell's forgotten 1960s quest for planarian learning, a biochemical engram, and celebrity. *American Psychologist, 51,* 1039.

Rizzolatti, G., Fadiga, L., Gallese, V., & Fogassi, L. (1996) Premotor cortex and the recognition of motor actions. *Cognitive Brain Research, 3,* 131–141.

Robins, L. N., Helzer, J. E., & Davis, D. H. (1975). Narcotic use in Southeast Asia and afterward: An interview study of 898 Vietnam returnees. *Archives of General Psychiatry, 32,* 955–961.

Romanczyk, R. G., Arnstein, L., Soorya, L. V., & Gillis, J. (2003). The myriad of controversial treatments for autism: A critical evaluation of efficacy. In S. O. Lilienfeld, S. J. Lynn, & J. M. Lohr (Eds.), *Science and pseudoscience in clinical psychology* (pp. 363–395). New York, NY: Guilford Press.

Rozin, P., & Fallon, A. (1987). A perspective on disgust. *Psychological Review, 94,* 23–41.

Rozin, P., Markwith, M., & Ross, B. (1990). The sympathetic magical law of similarity, nominal realism and neglect of negatives in response to negative labels. *Psychological Science, 1,* 383–384.

Schopler, E., Short, A., & Mesibov, G. (1989) Relation of behavioral treatment to "normal functioning": Comment on Lovaas. *Journal of Consulting and Clinical Psychology, 57,* 162–164.

Seligman, M. E. P. (1971). Phobias and preparedness. *Behavior Therapy, 2,* 307–320.

Seligman, M. E. P., & Hager, J. L. (1972). Sauce-bearnaise syndrome. *Psychology Today, 6*(3), 59.

Shadish, W. R., Cook, T. D., & Campbell, D. T. (2002). *Experimental and quasi-experimental designs for generalized causal inference.* Boston, MA: Houghton Mifflin.

Siegelbaum, S. A., Camardo, J. S., & Kandel, E. R. (1982, September 30). Serotonin and cyclic AMP close single K+ channels in Aplysia sensory neurons. *Nature, 299,* 413–417.

Simmons, D. A., & Neill. D. B. (2009) Functional interaction between the basolateral amygdala and the ventral striatum underlies incentive motivation for food reward. *Neuroscience, 159,* 1264–1273.

Simon, C. W., & Emmons, W. H. (1955). Learning during sleep? *Psychological Bulletin, 52,* 328–342.

Skinner, B. F. (1938). *The behavior of organisms: An experimental analysis.* New York, NY: Appleton-Century-Crofts.

Skinner, B. F. (1948). Superstition in the pigeon. *Journal of Experimental Psychology, 38,* 168–172.

Skinner, B. F. (1953). *Science and human behavior.* New York, NY: Macmillan.

Skinner, B. F. (1969). *Contingencies of reinforcement.* East Norwalk, CT: Appleton-Century-Crofts.

Skinner, B. F. (1990). Can psychology be a science of mind? *American Psychologist, 4,* 1206–1210.

Smalheiser, N. R., Manev, H., & Costa, E. (2001) RNAi and memory: Was McConnell on the right track after all? *Trends in Neuroscience, 24,* 216–218.

Snider, V. E. (1992). Learning styles and learning to read: A critique. *RASE: Remedial & Special Education, 13,* 6–18.

Staddon, J. E. R., & Cerutti, D. T. (2003) Operant behavior. *Annual Review of Psychology, 54,* 115–144.

Staddon, J. E. R., & Simmelhag, V. L. (1971). Superstition experiment—A reexamination of its implications for principles of adaptive behavior. *Psychological Review, 78,* 3.

Stahl, S. (1999). Different strokes for different folks? A critique of learning styles. *American Educator, 23,* 27–31.

Stern, J. M., Ray, W. J., & Davis, C. M. (1980). *Psychophysiological recording.* New York, NY: Oxford University Press.

Straus, M. A., & McCord, J. (1998). Do physically punished children become violent adults? In S. Nolen-Hoeksema (Ed.), *Clashing views on abnormal psychology: A taking sides custom reader* (pp. 130–155). Guilford, CT: Dushkin/McGraw-Hill.

Straus, M. A., Sugarman, D. B., & Giles-Sims, J. (1997). Spanking by parents and subsequent antisocial behavior of children. *Archives of Pediatrics and Adolescent Medicine, 151,* 761–767.

Stuart, E. W., Shimp, T. A., & Engle, R. W. (1987). Classical conditioning of consumer attitudes: Four experiments in an advertising context. *Journal of Consumer Research, 14,* 334–349.

Sullum, J. (2003). *Saying yes: In defense of drug use.* New York, NY: Tarcher/Putnam.

Tarver, S. G., & Dawson, M. M. (1978). Modality preference and teaching of reading: Review. *Journal of Learning Disabilities, 11*(1), 5–17.

Thompson, R., & McConnell, J. (1955). Classical conditioning in the planarian, *Dugesia dorotocephala. Journal of Comparative and Physiological Psychology, 48,* 65–68.

Thorndike, E. L. (1898). *Animal intelligence: An experimental study of the associative processes in animals.* New York, NY: Macmillan.

Thorndike, E. L. (1911). *Animal intelligence: Experimental studies.* New York, NY: Macmillan.

Tice, D. M., & Baumeister, R. F. (1997). Longitudinal study of procrastination, performance, stress, and health: The costs and benefits of dawdling. *Psychological Science, 8,* 454–458.

Till, B. D., Stanley, S. M., & Priluck, R. (2008). Classical conditioning and celebrity endorsers: An examination of belongingness and resistance to extinction. *Psychology & Marketing, 25,* 179–196.

Timberlake, W. (2006). Evolution-based learning mechanisms can contribute to both adaptive and problematic behavior. In S. O. Lilienfeld & W. T. O'Donohue (Eds.), *The great ideas of clinical science: 17 principles that every mental health professional should understand* (pp. 187–218). New York, NY: Routledge.

Tolman, E. C. (1932). *Purposive behavior in animals and men.* Oxford, England: Appleton-Century-Crofts.

Tolman, E. C. (1948). Cognitive maps in rats and men. *Psychological Review, 55,* 189–208.

Tolman, E. C., & Honzik, C. H. (1930). Introduction and removal of reward, and maze performance in rats. *University of California Publications in Psychology, 4,* 257–275.

Tomarken, A. J., Mineka, S., & Cook, M. (1989) Fear-relevant selective associations and covariation bias. *Journal of Abnormal Psychology, 98,* 381–394.

Tomarken, A. J., Sutton, S. K., & Mineka, S. (1995) Fear-relevant illusory correlations: What types of associations promote judgmental bias? *Journal of Abnormal Psychology, 104,* 312–326.

Veit, R., Flor, H., Erb, M., Hermann, C., Lotze, M., Grodd, W., & Birbaumer, N. (2002). Brain circuits involved in emotional learning in antisocial behavior and social phobia in humans. *Neuroscience Letters, 328*(3), 233–236.

Wakefield, J. C. (2006). Is behaviorism becoming a pseudo-science? Power versus scientific rationality in the eclipse of token economies by biological psychiatry in the treatment of schizophrenia. *Behavior and Social Issues, 15,* 202–221.

Watanabe, S., Sakamoto, J., & Wakita, M. (1995). Pigeons' discrimination of paintings by Monet and Picasso. *Journal of the Experimental Analysis of Behavior, 63,* 65–174.

Watson, J. B., & Rayner, R. (1920). Conditioned emotional reactions. *Journal of Experimental Psychology, 3,* 1–14.

Weinberg, M. S., Williams, C. J., & Calhan, C. (1995). If the shoe fits... Exploring male-homosexual foot fetishism. *Journal of Sex Research, 31,* 17–27.

Wenger, W. (1983). Toward a taxonomy of methods for improving teaching and learning. *Journal of the Society for Accelerative Learning and Teaching, 8,* 75–90.

Widom, C. S. (1989a). The cycle of violence. *Science, 244,* 160–166.

Widom, C. S. (1989b) Child abuse, neglect, and adult behavior: Research design and findings on criminality, violence, and child abuse. *American Journal of Orthopsychiatry, 59,* 355–367.

Williams, T. M. (Ed.). (1986). *The impact of television: A naturalistic study in three communities.* Orlando, FL: Academic Press.

Wilson, J. Q., & Herrnstein, R. J. (1985). *Crime and human nature: The definitive study of the causes of crime.* New York, NY: Simon & Schuster.

Winerman, L. (2005, October). The mind's mirror. *American Psychological Association Monitor, 36*(9). Retrieved from http://www.apa.org/monitor/oct05/mirror.html

Wolpe, J. (1990). *The practice of behavior therapy* (4th ed.). Elmsford, NY: Pergamon Press.

Wood, W., Wong, F. Y., & Chachere, J. G. (1991). Effects of media violence on viewers' aggression in unconstrained social interaction. *Psychological Bulletin, 109,* 371–383.

Woodworth, R. S. (1929). *Psychology* (Rev. ed.). Oxford, England: Holt.

Wyatt, W. J. (2001) Some myths about behaviorism that are undone by B. F. Skinner's "The Design of Cultures." *Behavior and Social Issues, 11,* 28–30.

Zhang, L. (2006). Does student-teacher thinking style match/mismatch matter in students' achievement? *Educational Psychology, 26,* 395–409.

Credits

Credits listed in order of appearance.

Figure 9: Tolman, E. C., & Honzik, C. H. (1930). Introduction and removal of reward, and maze performance in rats. University of California Publications in Psychology. **Figure 10:** Huesmann, L. R., Moise-Titus, J., Podolski, C., & Eron, L. D. (2003). Longitudinal relations between children's exposure to TV violence and their aggressive and violent behavior in young adulthood: 1977–1992. Developmental Psychology.

Photo Credits

Memory

From Chapter 7 of *Psychology: From Inquiry to Understanding,* Third Edition. Scott O. Lilienfeld, Steven Jay Lynn, Laura L. Namy, Nancy J. Woolf. Copyright © 2014 by Pearson Education, Inc. All rights reserved.

Memory

CONSTRUCTING AND RECONSTRUCTING OUR PASTS

Think About It

Do we really remember everything that's ever happened to us?

Do memory aids like "ROY G. BIV" (for the colors of the rainbow) really help us to remember?

What are infants' earliest memories?

Do witnesses to a crime always remember what they observed accurately?

Can people recover repressed memories of traumatic experiences?

Memory

 Listen in **MyPsychLab** to chapter audio

Consider the following memorable tales of memory, both true.

True Story 1. A woman in her forties, known only by the initials A. J., has such an astounding memory that she's left even seasoned psychological researchers shaking their heads in bewilderment. Although emotionally quite normal, A. J. is markedly abnormal in one way: She remembers just about everything she's ever experienced. When given a date, like March 17, 1989, she can report precisely what she was doing on that day—taking a test, eating dinner with a good friend, or traveling to a new city. The claims here are extraordinary, but they've now been confirmed by research. Scientists have confirmed that she's almost always right. Moreover, she remembers on what day of the week that date fell. In 2003, a team of investigators asked A. J. to remember all of the dates of Easter over the past 24 years. She got all but two correct and reported accurately what she'd done each day (Parker, Cahill, & McCaugh, 2006).

A. J., like about a dozen other people identified thus far, "suffers" from an exceedingly rare condition called hyperthymestic syndrome: memory of life events that's too good. Or does she really suffer? It's not entirely clear, because she regards her remarkable memory as both a curse and a blessing (Price & Davis, 2008). A. J. says that she sometimes remembers painful events that she'd prefer to forget, but also that she'd never want to give up her special memory "gift." As to the causes of hyperthymestic syndrome, scientists are baffled (Foer, 2007). Nevertheless, recent research suggests subtle differences in brain structure between people with and without this condition, especially involving brain regions involved in autobiographical memory (LePort et al., 2012).

True Story 2. In 1997, Nadean Cool, a 44-year-old nurse's aide in Wisconsin, won a $2.4 million malpractice settlement against her psychotherapist. Nadean entered treatment with relatively mild emotional problems, such as depressed mood and binge eating. Yet after five years of treatment, Nadean supposedly "recovered" childhood memories of having been a member of a murderous satanic cult, of being raped, and of witnessing the murder of her 8-year-old childhood friend. Her therapist also persuaded her that she harbored more than 130 personalities, including demons, angels, children, and a duck. (Her therapist apparently even listed her treatment as group therapy on the grounds that he needed to treat numerous different personalities.)

All of these memories surfaced after Nadean participated in repeated sessions involving *guided imagery*—in which therapists ask clients to imagine past events—and *hypnotic age regression*—in which therapists use hypnosis to "return" clients to the psychological state of childhood. The therapist also subjected Nadean to an exorcism and 15-hour marathon therapy sessions. As therapy progressed, she became overwhelmed by images of terrifying memories she was convinced were genuine. Eventually, however, Nadean came to doubt the reality of these memories, and she terminated treatment.

In a very real sense, we *are* our memories. Our memories define not only our past, but also our sense of identity. For A. J., life is like "a movie in her mind that never stops," as she puts it. Her recollections of her life and interactions with friends are remarkably vivid and emotionally intense. A. J.'s memory has shaped her personality in profound ways.

Moreover, when our memories change, as did Nadean Cool's, so do our identities. Following psychotherapy, Nadean came to believe she was a victim of brutal and repeated child abuse. She even came to believe she suffered from a severe condition, namely, *dissociative identity disorder*, or DID (known formerly as multiple personality disorder), which is supposedly characterized by the existence of "alter" personalities, or *alters*.

How Memory Operates: The Memory Assembly Line

1 Identify the ways that memories do and don't accurately reflect experiences.

2 Explain the function, span, and duration of each of the three memory systems.

3 Differentiate the subtypes of long-term memory.

We can define **memory** as the retention of information over time. We have memories for many different kinds of information, ranging from our sixteenth birthday party, to how to ride a bike, to the shape of a pyramid. Our memories work pretty well most of

memory
retention of information over time

the time. Odds are high that tomorrow you'll find your way into school or work just fine and that, with a little luck, you'll even remember some of what you read in this chapter. Yet in other cases, our memories fail us, often when we least expect it. How many times have you misplaced your keys or cell phone or forgotten the names of people you've met over and over again? We call this seeming contradiction the *paradox of memory:* Our memories are surprisingly good in some situations and surprisingly poor in others.

The Paradox of Memory

To a large extent, this chapter is the story of this paradox. As we'll see, the answer to the paradox of memory hinges on a crucial fact: *The same memory mechanisms that serve us well in most circumstances can sometimes cause us problems in others.*

Salvador Dali's classic painting *The Persistence of Memory* is a powerful reminder that our memories are much more like melting wax than hardened metal. They often change over time, far more than we realize.

WHEN OUR MEMORIES SERVE US WELL. Research shows that our memories are often astonishingly accurate. Most of us can recognize our schoolmates decades later and recite the lyrics to dozens, even hundreds, of songs. Consider a study in which college students viewed 2,560 photographs of objects or scenes for a few seconds each. Three days later, the researchers showed these students each original photograph paired with a new one. Remarkably, the students correctly picked out the original photographs 93 percent of the time (Standing, Conezio, & Haber, 1970). In another case, a researcher contacted participants 17 years(!) after they'd viewed over 100 line drawings for one to three seconds in a laboratory study. They identified these drawings at better-than-chance rates compared with participants who'd never seen the drawings (Mitchell, 2006).

The memories of a small subset of individuals with a condition known as *infantile autism* are even more astonishing. Contrary to popular misconception (Stone & Rosenbaum, 1988), most individuals with autism lack specialized memory abilities, but there are impressive exceptions. Take the case of Kim Peek, who was the inspiration for the 1998 Academy Award–winning film *Rain Man* (Peek died in 2009). Peek's IQ was 87, noticeably below the average of approximately 100. Yet Peek memorized about 12,000 books word for word, the ZIP Codes of every town in the United States, and the number of every highway connecting every city in the United States (Foer, 2007; Treffert & Christensen, 2005). Kim Peek was also a *calendar calculator:* If you gave him any past or future date, like October 17, 2094, he'd give you the correct day of the week in a matter of seconds. Not surprisingly, Kim earned the nickname of "Kim-puter" among researchers who studied his astonishing memory feats.

Kim Peek, the "real Rain Man" (who passed away in 2009), exhibited phenomenal memory despite low overall intelligence.

Yet as we learned with A. J., it's not only people with autism who possess remarkable memory capacities. Consider the case of Rajan Mahadevan (better known simply as Rajan), now a lecturer in the psychology department of the University of Tennessee. Rajan's memory feats are so spectacular that they were spoofed on an episode of the cartoon show *The Simpsons*. Rajan had somehow managed to memorize the number *pi*— the ratio of a circle's diameter to its radius—to a remarkable 38,811 digits (see **FIGURE 1**). When he recited them, it took him three hours at a rate of more than three digits per second (by the way, if you're curious, the world record for remembering pi is now up to over 80,000 digits; Foer, 2007). Yet Rajan also provides a wonderful illustration of the paradox of memory. Despite finding pi to be a piece of cake, he kept forgetting the location of the men's restroom at the University of Minnesota psychology department although it was just down the hall from where he'd been tested repeatedly (Biederman et al., 1992).

How did Rajan pull off his amazing feat? We'll find out later in the chapter.

Pi=3.					
1415926535	8979323846	2643383279	5028841971	6939937510	(50)
5820974944	5923078164	0628620899	8628034825	3421170679	(100)
8214808651	3282306647	0938446095	5058223172	5359408128	(150)
4811174502	8410270193	8521105559	6446229489	5493038196	(200)
4428810975	6659334461	2847564823	3786783165	2712019091	(250)
4564856692	3460348610	4543266482	1339360726	0249141273	(300)
7245870066	0631558817	4881520920	9628292540	9171536436	(350)
7892590360	0113305305	4882046652	1384146951	9415116094	(400)
3305727036	5759591953	0921861173	8193261179	3105118548	(450)
0744623799	6274956735	1885752724	8912279381	8301194912	(500)
9833673362	4406566430	8602139494	6395224737	1907021798	(550)
6094370277	0539217176	2931767523	8467481846	7669405132	(600)
0005681271	4526356082	7785771342	7577896091	7363717872	(650)
1468440901	2249534301	5654958537	1050792279	6892589235	(700)
4201995611	2129021960	8640344181	5981362977	4771309960	(750)
5187072113	4999999837	2978049951	0597317328	1609631859	(800)
5024459455	3469083026	4252230825	3344685035	2619311881	(850)
7101000313	7838752886	5875332083	8142061717	7669147303	(900)
5982534904	2875546873	1159562863	8823537875	9375195778	(950)
1857780533					

FIGURE 1 Rajan's Demonstration Sheet of Digits of Pi. Rajan's feats demonstrate the uppermost end of the capacity of human memory.

Memory

WHEN OUR MEMORIES FAIL US. In some exceedingly rare cases, as with A. J., memory is virtually perfect. Many others of us have extremely good memories in one or two narrow domains, like art history, baseball batting averages, or Civil War trivia. Yet as the case of Nadean Cool illustrates, memory can be surprisingly malleable and prone to error.

Most and perhaps all of us are vulnerable to false memories under the right conditions. Here's a simple demonstration that requires only a pen or pencil and a sheet of paper (for maximum effect, you may want to try this demonstration along with a group of friends). Read the list of words below, taking about a second per word. Read the left column first, then the middle column, then the right. Ready? Okay, begin.

Bed	Cot	Sheets
Pillow	Dream	Rest
Tired	Snore	Yawn
Darkness	Blanket	Couch

Now, put down your textbook, and take a minute or so to jot down as many of these words as you can recall.

Did you remember *couch*? If so, give yourself a point. How about *snore*? If so, good—give yourself another point.

Okay, how about *sleep*? If you're like about a third of typical people, you "remembered" seeing the word *sleep*. But now take a close look at the list. The word *sleep* isn't there. If you or your friends remembered seeing this word on the list, you experienced a **memory illusion**: a false but subjectively compelling memory (Brainerd, Reyna, & Zember, 2011; Deese, 1959; Roediger & McDermott, 1995, 1999). Like visual illusions, most memory illusions are by-products of our brain's generally adaptive tendency to go beyond the information available to it. By doing so, our brain helps us make sense of the world, but it sometimes leads us astray (Gilovich, 1991; Kida, 2006). In this case, you may have remembered seeing the word *sleep* because it was linked closely in meaning to the other words on the list—namely, bed, dream, and rest. As a consequence, you may have been fooled into remembering that the word *sleep* was there. By relying on the *representativeness heuristic*—like goes with like—we simplify things to make them easier to remember. In this case, though, our use of this handy heuristic comes with a modest price: a memory illusion.

The Reconstructive Nature of Memory

This demonstration drives home a crucial point: Our memories frequently fool us and fail us. Indeed, a central theme of this chapter is that our memories are far more reconstructive than reproductive. When we try to recall an event, we *actively reconstruct* our memories using the cues and information available to us. We don't *passively reproduce* our memories, as we would if we were downloading information from a web page. Remembering is largely a matter of patching together our often fuzzy recollection with our best hunches about what really happened. When we recall our past experiences, we rarely, if ever, reproduce precise replicas of them (Neisser & Hyman, 1999; Mori, 2008). We should therefore be skeptical of claims that certain vivid memories or even dreams are exact "photocopies" of past events (van der Kolk et al., 1984).

In fact, it's easy to show that our memories are often reconstructive. After reading this sentence, close your eyes for a few moments and picture your most recent walk along a beach, lake, or pond. Then, after opening your eyes, ask yourself what you "saw."

Did you see yourself as if from a distance, seeing yourself as an outside observer would? Many people report this visual perspective. As Sigmund Freud noted well over a century ago, such memories provide an existence proof that at least some of our memories are reconstructive (Schacter, 1996). You couldn't possibly have *seen* yourself from a distance, because you don't see yourself when you look at

memory illusion
false but subjectively compelling memory

284

your surroundings: You must have constructed that memory rather than recalled it in its original form (Nigro & Neisser, 1983). Interestingly, Asians are more likely than European Americans to see themselves at a distance in such memories (Cohen & Gunz, 2002; Martin & Jones, 2012). This result fits with findings that members of many Asian cultures are more likely than members of Western cultures to adopt others' perspectives. So our memories are probably shaped by not only our hunches and expectations, but also by our cultural backgrounds.

The science of memory offers yet another striking example of how research contradicts popular opinion (Alvarez & Brown, 2001). A survey of the general public revealed that 64 percent of Americans believe that "human memory works like a video camera, accurately recording the events we see and hear" (Simons & Chabris, 2011, p. 3). In that survey, 38 percent of respondents said that once a memory is formed, it never changes. Even most psychotherapists believe that everything we learn is permanently stored in the mind (Loftus & Loftus, 1980; Yapko, 1994). Yet as we'll soon discover, research paints a very different picture of human memory. How can our memories be so good in some cases and so bad in others? How can we explain both the astonishing memories of people like A. J. and Rajan and the faulty memories of people like Nadean Cool? To grasp the paradox of memory, we need to figure out how some of our experiences make it into our memories, whereas so many others never do. To do so, let's embark on a guided tour of the factory assembly line inside our heads.

When you picture yourself taking a recent walk on the beach, do you see yourself as an outside observer would? If so, such a recollection provides compelling evidence that memory can be reconstructive.

The Three Systems of Memory

Up to this point, we've been talking about memory as though it were a single thing. It isn't. Most psychologists distinguish among three major *systems* of memory: sensory memory, short-term memory, and long-term memory, as depicted in **FIGURE 2** (Atkinson & Shiffrin, 1968; Waugh & Norman, 1965). These systems serve different purposes and vary along at least two important dimensions: *span*—how much information each system can hold—and *duration*—over how long a period of time that system can hold information.

In reality, the distinctions among these three memory systems aren't always clear-cut. Moreover, many modern researchers suspect that there are more than three memory systems (Baddeley, 1993; Healy & McNamara, 1996). For the sake of simplicity, we'll begin by discussing the three-systems model, although we'll point out some ambiguities along the way.

We can think of these three systems much like different factory workers along an assembly line. The first system, *sensory memory*, is tied closely to the raw materials of our experiences, our perceptions of the world; it holds these perceptions for just a few seconds or less before passing *some* of them on to the second system. This second system, *short-term memory*, works actively with the information handed to it, transforming it into more meaningful material before passing *some* of it on to the third system. Short-term memory holds on to information longer than sensory memory does, but not much longer. The third and final system, *long-term memory*, permits us to retain important information for minutes, days, weeks, months, or even years. In some cases, the information in long-term memory lasts for a lifetime. The odds are high, for example, that you'll remember your first kiss and your high school graduation for many decades, perhaps until the last day of your life. As you can tell from our use of the word *some* in the previous sentences, we lose a great deal of information at each relay station in the memory assembly line.

SENSORY MEMORY. If you're anywhere near a television set, turn it on for 10 seconds or so. What did you see?

Regardless of what program you were watching, you almost certainly experienced a steady and uninterrupted stream of visual information. In reality, that continuous stream of images was an illusion, because television programs and movies consist of a series of

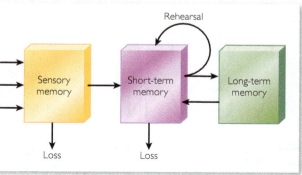

FIGURE 2 The Three-Memory Model. This model subdivides memory into sensory, short-term, and long-term memory. Information flows from left to right, but also from right to left in the case of information retrieved from long-term memory and moved into short-term memory (Atkinson & Shiffrin, 1968).

 Explore in **MyPsychLab** the **Concept:** Key Processes in Stages of Memory

Iconic memory: After a lightning strike, we retain a visual image of it for about one second. (*Source:* © Ralph Wetmore.)

FIGURE 3 Display of 12 Letters as Used in Sperling's 1960 Study. Sperling's partial report method demonstrated that all displayed letters were held in sensory memory, but decayed rapidly before all of them could be transferred to short-term memory (Sperling, 1960).

sensory memory
brief storage of perceptual information before it is passed to short-term memory

iconic memory
visual sensory memory

echoic memory
auditory sensory memory

disconnected frames, each separated by an extremely brief interlude of darkness you can't perceive. Yet your brain sees these frames as blending together into a seamless whole, in part because it continues to detect each frame for an extremely brief period of time after it disappears.

That is, our brains retain each frame in our sensory memory, the first factory worker in the assembly line of memory. Sensory memory briefly maintains our perceptions in a "buffer" area before passing them on to the next memory system, which is short-term memory. Sensory memory is a helpful system, because it buys our brains a bit of extra time to process incoming sensations. It also allows us to "fill in the blanks" in our perceptions and see the world as an unbroken stream of events.

Psychologists believe that each sense, including vision, hearing, touch, taste, and smell, has its own form of sensory memory. In the case of television or movie clips, we experience an iconic memory, the type of sensory memory that applies to vision (Persuh, Genzer, & Melara, 2012). Iconic memories last for only about a second, and then they're gone forever.

Psychologist George Sperling (1960) conducted a pioneering study that demonstrated the existence of iconic memory. He quickly flashed participants a display of 12 letters, with four letters arranged in three rows, as shown in **FIGURE 3**. The display lasted only about one-twentieth of a second, and participants had to recall as many letters within the display as they could. Sperling found that most participants could recall only four or five letters. Surprisingly, different participants remembered different letters. This finding suggested to Sperling that all 12 letters had an equal chance of being recalled but that no one person could recall them all. This finding was puzzling. After all, if participants had remembered the whole visual display, why could they recall only a handful of letters and no more?

To find out, Sperling had a "flash" of insight, pun intended. Immediately after he flashed the 12 letters, he presented a tone (high, medium, or low) to signal participants which of the three rows (top, middle, or bottom) to report. Then he randomly instructed participants to report only one of the three rows. When he used this technique, he found that virtually all participants now got almost all letters in that row correct. This finding confirmed Sperling's hunch: Participants had access to all 12 letters in their memories. Sperling concluded that our iconic memories fade so quickly that we can't access all the information before it disappears. So Sperling's participants were able to take in all of the information, but retained it in memory only long enough to read off a few letters.

Iconic memory may help to explain the remarkable, and exceedingly rare, phenomenon of *eidetic imagery*, popularly called "photographic memory." People with eidetic memory, most of them children, can supposedly hold a visual image in their minds with such clarity that they can describe it perfectly or almost perfectly (see **FIGURE 4**). Some psychologists believe that eidetic memory reflects an unusually long persistence of the iconic image in some fortunate people. Nevertheless, it's not clear that any memories are truly photographic, because even these memories often contain minor errors, such as information that wasn't in the original visual stimulus (Minsky, 1986; Rothen, Meier, & Ward, 2012).

Sensory memory applies to hearing, too. Now read that last sentence aloud: "Sensory memory applies to hearing, too." If you pause for a few moments after saying it, you'll be able to replay the words precisely as you heard them for a few seconds, much like a soft echo reverberating from a mountaintop. That's why psychologists call this form of sensory memory echoic memory (Neisser, 1967). In contrast to iconic memories, echoic memories can last as long as 5 to 10 seconds (Cowan, Lichty, & Grove, 1990), conveniently permitting you to take notes on your psychology professor's most recent sentence even after he or she has finished saying it. Interestingly, there's also some evidence of eidetic memories for hearing, in which a few fortunate individuals report that their echoic memories persist for unusually long periods of time. Now, wouldn't that make taking lecture notes a breeze?

SHORT-TERM MEMORY. Once information makes it past our sensory buffers, it passes into our **short-term memory**, a second system for retaining information in our memories for brief periods of time. Short-term memory is the second factory worker in our memory assembly line. Short-term memory is closely related to what psychologists call *working memory*, which refers to our ability to hold on to information we're currently thinking about, attending to, or processing actively (Baddeley, 1993; Baddeley & Hitch, 1974; Unsworth & Engle, 2007). If sensory memory is what feeds raw materials into the assembly line, short-term memory is the workspace where construction happens. After construction takes place, we either move the product into the warehouse for long-term storage or, in some cases, scrap it altogether.

If short-term memory is a short stop on the assembly line, just how brief is it? In the late 1950s, a husband-and-wife team decided to find out.

The Duration of Short-Term Memory. Lloyd and Margaret Peterson (1959) presented participants with lists of three letters each, such as MKP or ASN, and then asked them to recall these three-letter strings. In some cases, they made participants wait only three seconds before recalling the letters; in other cases, they made them wait up to 18 seconds. Each time, they told participants to count backward by threes while they were waiting.

Many psychologists were surprised by the Petersons' results, and you may be, too. They found that after about 10 or 15 seconds, most participants *did no better than chance*. So the duration of short-term memory is quite brief; it's probably no longer than about 20 seconds. Some researchers believe it's even shorter than that, perhaps even less than five seconds, because some participants in the Peterson and Peterson study may have been able to silently rehearse the letters even when counting backward (Sebrects, Marsh, & Seamon, 1989). Incidentally, many people misuse the term *short-term memory* in everyday language. For example, they may say that their "short-term memory isn't working" because they forgot what they had for dinner yesterday. As we've seen, the duration of short-term memory is far briefer than that.

Memory Loss from Short-Term Memory: Decay versus Interference. Why did the Petersons' participants lose their short-term memories so quickly, just as we quickly lose our memories of phone numbers we've just heard? The most obvious explanation is that short-term memories **decay**, that is, fade away over time. The longer we wait, the less is left. Yet there's a competing explanation for the loss of information from short-term memory: **interference**. According to this view, our memories get in the way of each other. That is, our memories are very much like radio signals. They don't change over time, but they're harder to detect if they're jammed by other signals.

As it turns out, there's evidence for both decay and interference. Recent physiological evidence for decay comes from research suggesting that the birth of new neurons in the hippocampus leads to the decay of memories in that brain region (Kitamura et al., 2009). As we create new memories, our old ones gradually fade away. Nevertheless, there's even stronger evidence for the role of interference in memory loss. For example, two investigators (Waugh & Norman, 1965) presented participants with many different lists of 16 digits, such as 6 2 7 1 8 5 3 4 2 6 9 7 4 5 8 3. Right after participants saw each list, the researchers gave them one "target" digit to focus on and then asked participants which digit came after this target digit. In all cases, this target digit appeared twice in the list, and participants had to remember the digit that came after its *first* presentation in the list. In the digit list above, the target item might be "8," so we'd search for the first 8 in the list—and the correct response would be 5.

FIGURE 4 Alice with Cheshire Cat. Memory psychologists have used variations of this drawing from Lewis Carroll's *Alice's Adventures in Wonderland* to test for eidetic imagery. To find out if you have eidetic memory, look at the drawing for no longer than 30 seconds and then cover it with a sheet of paper. Do that now before reading on. Now, can you remember how many stripes were on the cat's tail? Few adults can remember such details (Gray & Gummerman, 1975), although eidetic memory is much more prevalent among elementary school children (Haber, 1979).

👁 **Watch** in **MyPsychLab** the **Video:** Randall Engle: What Is Working Memory?

◀ **RULING OUT RIVAL HYPOTHESES**
Have important alternative explanations for the findings been excluded?

short-term memory
memory system that retains information for limited durations

decay
fading of information from memory over time

interference
loss of information from memory because of competition from additional incoming information

RULING OUT RIVAL HYPOTHESES ▶

Have important alternative explanations for the findings been excluded?

? This player is actively engaged in a racquetball match. If she was an experienced tennis player before attempting racquetball, the odds are high that her tennis swings would initially get in the way of her learning how to swing a racquetball racquet properly. That is, it will take her a while to "unlearn" her tennis swings. **What kind of interference is she experiencing?** (See answer upside down.)

---

retroactive interference
interference with retention of old information due to acquisition of new information

proactive interference
interference with acquisition of new information due to previous learning of information

Magic Number
the span of short-term memory, according to George Miller: seven plus or minus two pieces of information

---

 Simulate in **MyPsychLab** the **Experiment:** Digit Span

Answer: Proactive interference (the old interfering with the new).

As an ingenious means of ruling out alternative hypotheses, the experimenters manipulated two variables to figure out which of them influenced forgetting. Specifically, they manipulated (1) where in the list the target digit appeared (early or late) and (2) how rapidly they presented digits to participants—either quickly (one digit every second) or slowly (one digit every four seconds). They told participants to listen carefully to each digit, but not to rehearse it mentally. Now, if decay were the principal culprit in forgetting, participants' performance should become worse when researchers read the list slowly because more time had passed between digits. In contrast, if interference were the principal culprit, participants' performance should become worse when the target digit appeared later rather than earlier in the list, regardless of speed, because memory for later digits is hampered by memory for earlier digits.

The results showed that interference is the major factor in forgetting. Participants' forgetting is due almost entirely to where in the list the target digit appears, rather than to the speed of presentation (Keppel & Underwood, 1962). Still, most researchers believe that both decay and interference play some role in short-term memory loss (Altmann & Schunn, 2002).

We're not quite done with our examination of interference yet, because it turns out that there are two different kinds of interference (Ebert & Anderson, 2009; Underwood, 1957). One kind, **retroactive interference**, occurs when learning something new hampers earlier learning: The new interferes with the old (think of the prefix *retro-*, because retroactive interference works in a reverse direction). If you've learned one language, say Spanish, and then later learned a somewhat similar language, perhaps Italian, you probably found that you started making mistakes in Spanish you'd never made before. Specifically, you may have found yourself using Italian words, like *buono*, for Spanish words, like *bueno* (both *buono* and *bueno* mean "good").

In contrast, **proactive interference** occurs when earlier learning gets in the way of new learning: The old interferes with the new. For example, knowing how to play tennis might interfere with our attempt to learn to play racquetball, which requires a much smaller racquet. Not surprisingly, both retroactive and proactive interference are more likely to occur when the old and new stimuli that we've learned are similar. Learning a new language doesn't much affect our ability to master a new spaghetti recipe.

The Capacity of Short-Term Memory: The Magic Number. We've already seen that short-term memory doesn't last very long. Twenty seconds, or even less, and—poof—the memory is gone, unless we've made an extra-special effort to retain it. But how large is the *span* of short-term memory?

Try reading each of the following rows of numbers, one row at a time, at a rate of one number per second. Once you're done with each row, close your eyes and try writing down what you remember. Ready? Okay, begin.

$$9 - 5 - 2$$
$$2 - 9 - 7 - 3$$
$$5 - 7 - 4 - 9 - 2$$
$$6 - 2 - 7 - 3 - 8 - 4$$
$$2 - 4 - 1 - 8 - 6 - 4 - 7$$
$$3 - 9 - 5 - 7 - 4 - 1 - 8 - 9$$
$$8 - 4 - 6 - 3 - 1 - 7 - 4 - 2 - 5$$
$$5 - 2 - 9 - 3 - 4 - 6 - 1 - 8 - 5 - 7$$

You've just taken a test of "digit span." How'd you make out? Odds are that you breezed through three digits, started to find four digits a bit tricky, and maxed out at somewhere between five and nine digits. It's unlikely you got the ten-digit list completely right; if you did, you've earned the right to call yourself a memory superstar.

That's because the digit span of most adults is between five and nine digits, with an average of seven digits. Indeed, this finding is so consistent among people that psychologist George Miller (1956) referred to seven plus or minus two pieces of information as the **Magic Number**.

According to Miller, the Magic Number is the universal limit of short-term memory, and it applies to just about all information we encounter: numbers, letters, people, vegetables, and cities. Because it's hard to retain much more than seven plus or minus two pieces of information in our short-term memory, it's almost surely not a coincidence that telephone numbers in North America are exactly seven digits long, not counting the area code (some European phone numbers are slightly longer, but few exceed nine, the upper limit for the Magic Number). Some psychologists have since argued that Miller's Magic Number may overestimate the capacity of short-term memory, and that the true Magic Number may be as low as four (Cowan, 2001; Mathy & Feldman, 2011). Regardless of who's right, it's clear that the capacity of short-term memory is extremely limited.

Chunking. If our short-term memory capacity is no more than nine digits, and perhaps much less, how do we manage to remember larger amounts of information than this for brief periods of time? Read the following sentence; then wait a few seconds and recite it back to yourself: **Harry Potter's white owl Hedwig flew off into the dark and stormy night.** Were you able to remember most or even all of it? The odds are high that you were. Yet this sentence contained 13 words, which exceeds the Magic Number. How did you accomplish this feat?

We can expand our ability to remember things in the short term by using a technique called **chunking**: organizing material into meaningful groupings. For example, look at the following string of 15 letters for a few seconds, and then try to recall them:

K A C F J N A B I S B C F U I

How'd you do? Odds are you didn't do too well, probably right around the Magic Number, that is, only a subset of the letters listed. Okay, now try this 15-letter string.

C I A U S A F B I N B C J F K

Did you do any better this time? It's the same 15 letters, but you probably noticed something different about this group than the first group: They consisted of meaningful abbreviations. So you probably "chunked" these 15 letters into five meaningful groups of three letters each: CIA, USA, FBI, NBC, JFK. In this way, you reduced the number of items you needed to remember from 15 to only 5. In fact, you might have gotten this number down to less than five by combining CIA and FBI (both the initials of U.S. government intelligence agencies) into one chunk.

Chunking explains how Rajan performed his remarkable pi memorization feats. He memorized enormous numbers of area codes, dates of famous historical events, and other meaningful numbers embedded within the list of pi digits to effectively reduce more than 30,000 digits to a much smaller number.

Experts rely on chunking to help them recall complicated information. For example, chess masters recall *realistic* chess positions far better than do novices, yet do no better than novices at recalling random chess positions, suggesting that experts organize meaningful chess positions into broader patterns (Chase & Simon, 1973; Gobet & Simon, 1998).

Rehearsal. Whereas chunking increases the span of short-term memory, a strategy called rehearsal extends the duration of information in short-term memory. **Rehearsal** is repeating the information mentally, or even aloud. In that way, we keep the information "alive" in our short-term memories, just as a juggler keeps a bunch of bowling pins "alive" by continuing to catch them and toss them back into the air. Of course, if he pauses for a second to scratch his nose, the bowling pins come crashing to the ground. Similarly, if we stop rehearsing and shift our attention elsewhere, we'll quickly lose material from our short-term memory.

There are two major types of rehearsal. The first, **maintenance rehearsal**, simply involves repeating the stimuli in their original form; we don't attempt to change the original stimuli in any way. We engage in maintenance rehearsal whenever we hear a phone number and keep on repeating it—either aloud or in our minds—until we're ready to dial the number. In this way, we keep the information "alive" in our short-term memory. Of course, if someone interrupts us while we're rehearsing, we'll forget the number.

Master chess players recall realistic chess positions, like the one above, better than do beginners. But they do no better than beginners at recalling unrealistic chess positions. So the experts' edge stems not from raw memory power, but from chunking.

chunking
organizing information into meaningful groupings, allowing us to extend the span of short-term memory

rehearsal
repeating information to extend the duration of retention in short-term memory

maintenance rehearsal
repeating stimuli in their original form to retain them in short-term memory

FIGURE 5 Word Pairs. Using elaborative rehearsal helps us recall the word pair *dog–shoe* (Paivio, 1969).

The second type of rehearsal, **elaborative rehearsal**, usually takes more effort. In this type of rehearsal, we "elaborate" on the stimuli we need to remember by linking them in some meaningful way, perhaps by visualizing them or trying to understand their interrelationship (Craik & Lockhart, 1972).

To grasp the difference between maintenance and elaborative rehearsal, let's imagine that a researcher gave us a *paired-associate task*. In this task, the investigator first presents us with various pairs of words, such as *dog–shoe*, *tree–pipe*, *key–monkey*, and *kite–president*. Then, she presents us with the first word in each pair—*dog*, *tree*, and so on—and asks us to remember the second word in the pair. If we used maintenance rehearsal, we'd simply repeat the words in each pair over and over again as soon as we heard it—*dog–shoe*, *dog–shoe*, *dog–shoe*, and so on. In contrast, if we used elaborative rehearsal, we'd try to link the words in each pair in a meaningful way. One effective way of accomplishing this goal is to come up with a meaningful, perhaps even absurd, visual image that combines both stimuli (Ghetti et al., 2008; Paivio, 1969) (see **FIGURE 5**). Research shows that we're especially likely to remember the two stimuli if we picture them interacting in some fashion (Blumenfeld et al., 2010; Wollen, Weber, & Lowry, 1972). That's probably because doing so allows us to chunk them into a single integrated stimulus. So to remember the word pair *dog–rocket*, for example, we could picture a dog piloting a rocket ship or a rocket ship barking like a dog.

Elaborative rehearsal usually works better than maintenance rehearsal (Harris & Qualls, 2000). This finding demolishes a widely held misconception about memory: that rote memorization is typically the best means of retaining information. There's a take-home lesson here when it comes to our study habits. To remember complex information, it's almost always better to connect that information with things we already know than to merely keep repeating it. *deeper processing → Better memory*

Depth of Processing. This finding is consistent with a **levels-of-processing** model of memory. According to this model, the more deeply we process information, the better we tend to remember it. This model identifies three levels of processing of verbal information (Craik & Lockhart, 1972): visual, phonological (sound-related), and semantic (meaning-related). Visual processing is the most shallow; phonological, somewhat less shallow; and semantic, the deepest. To understand the differences among these three levels, try to remember the following sentence:

ALL PEOPLE CREATE THEIR OWN MEANING OF LIFE.

If you relied on *visual* processing, you'd hone in on how the sentence looks. For example, you might try to focus on the fact that the sentence consists entirely of capital letters. If you relied on *phonological* processing, you'd focus on how the words in the sentence sound. Most likely, you'd repeat the sentence again and again until it began to sound boringly familiar. Finally, if you relied on *semantic* processing, you'd emphasize the sentence's meaning. You might elaborate on how you've tried to create your own meaning of life and how doing so has been helpful to you. Research shows that deeper levels of processing, especially semantic processing, tend to produce more enduring long-term memories (Craik & Tulving, 1975).

Still, some psychologists have criticized the levels-of-processing model as largely unfalsifiable (Baddeley, 1993). According to them, it's virtually impossible to determine how deeply we've processed a memory in the first place, so we could never independently test the claim that more deeply processed memories are better remembered. Moreover, critics claim that proponents of the levels-of-processing model are merely equating "depth" with how well participants later remember. There may well be some truth to this criticism. Still, it's safe to say that the more meaning we can supply to a stimulus, the more likely we are to recall it in the long term.

LONG-TERM MEMORY. Now that the second factory assembly line worker—short-term memory—has finished her construction job, what does she pass on to the third and final worker? And how does what the third worker receives differ from what the second worker

Simulate in MyPsychLab the **Experiment:** Depth of Processing

FALSIFIABILITY ▶
Can the claim be disproved?

elaborative rehearsal
linking stimuli to each other in a meaningful way to improve retention of information in short-term memory

levels of processing
depth of transforming information, which influences how easily we remember it

started out with? **Long-term memory**, the third worker, is our relatively enduring store of information. It includes the facts, experiences, and skills we've acquired over our lifetimes.

Differences between Long-Term and Short-Term Memory. Long-term memory differs from short-term memory in several important ways. First, in contrast to short-term memory, which can typically hold at most seven to nine stimuli in hand at a single time, the capacity of long-term memory is huge. Just how huge? No one knows for sure. Some scientists estimate that a typical person's memory holds about as much information as 500 huge online encyclopedias, each about 1,500 pages long (Cordón, 2005). So if someone praises you on your "encyclopedic memory," accept the compliment. They're probably right.

Second, although information in short-term memory vanishes after only about 20 seconds at most, information in long-term memory often endures for years, even decades—and sometimes permanently. Consider the work of psychologist Harry Bahrick, who has studied individuals' memory for languages they learned in school over many decades. In **FIGURE 6**, we can see that people's memory declines markedly about two to three years after taking a Spanish course. Yet after about two years, the decline becomes quite gradual. Indeed, it begins to level out after a while, with almost no additional loss for up to 50 years after they took the course (Bahrick & Phelps, 1987). Bahrick referred to this kind of long-term memory, which remains "frozen" over time, as **permastore**, as an analogy to the permafrost found in the Arctic or Antarctic that never melts. ↳ long-term memory is frozen over time.

Third, the types of mistakes we commit in long-term memory differ from those we make in short-term memory. Long-term memory errors tend to be *semantic*, that is, based on the meaning of the information we've received. So we might misremember a "poodle" as a "terrier." In contrast, short-term memory errors tend to be *acoustic*, that is, based on the sound of the information we've received (Conrad, 1964; Wickelgren, 1965). So we might misremember hearing "noodle" rather than "poodle."

Primacy and Recency Effects. When we try to remember a large number of items, such as a grocery list or a schedule of events, we often forget some of them. To some extent, psychologists can predict which items we're more likely to forget and which we're more likely to remember.

To demonstrate this point, read the list of 20 words below, either to yourself or aloud. Read the left column first, then the middle column, then the right one. Then, turn away from your book and take a few minutes to try to recall as many of these words as you can in any order you'd like. Ready? Begin.

Ball	Sky	Store
Shoe	Desk	Pencil
Tree	Car	Grass
Dog	Rope	Man
Paper	Dress	Cloud
Bird	Xylophone	Hat
House	Knife	Vase

If you're like most people, you probably did a bit better with the early words, like *ball*, *shoe*, and *tree*, than with the words in the middle of the list. That's the **primacy effect**: the tendency to remember stimuli, like words, early in a list. Also, you may have done a bit better with the later words, like *cloud*, *hat*, and *vase*. That's the **recency effect**: the tendency to remember stimuli later in a list. As an aside, there's a decent chance you remembered the word *xylophone*, which seems to be something of an oddball in the list. That's because

FIGURE 6 Long-Term Memory Retention. The classic work of Harry Bahrick (1984) shows that retention of a foreign language remains remarkably constant for spans of almost 50 years after an initial drop. (*Source:* Adapted from Bahrick, 1984, Figure 3)

long-term memory
relatively enduring (from minutes to years) retention of information stored regarding our facts, experiences, and skills

permastore
type of long-term memory that appears to be permanent

primacy effect
tendency to remember words at the beginning of a list especially well

recency effect
tendency to remember words at the end of a list especially well

FIGURE 7 The Serial Position Curve. Most psychologists believe that the primacy and recency effects in this curve are the telltale signs of two different memory systems: long-term and short-term memory, respectively.

serial position curve
graph depicting both primacy and recency effects on people's ability to recall items on a list

semantic memory
our knowledge of facts about the world

episodic memory
recollection of events in our lives

explicit memory
memories we recall intentionally and of which we have conscious awareness

implicit memory
memories we don't deliberately remember or reflect on consciously

we tend to remember stimuli that are distinctive in some way (Neath & Surprenant, 2003; Radvansky, Gibson, & McNerny, 2011).

If we averaged your results along with those of a few hundred other participants, we'd end up with the graph depicted in **FIGURE 7**, called the **serial position curve**. As we can see, this curve clearly displays the primacy and recency effects.

Most researchers agree that primacy and recency effects reflect the operation of different memory systems. Because the last few words in the list were probably lingering in your short-term memory, you were probably especially likely to recall them. So, the recency effect seems to reflect the workings of short-term memory.

What explains the primacy effect? This one is trickier, but there's good evidence that you were more likely to recall the earlier words in the list because you had more opportunity to rehearse them silently—and perhaps even to chunk them. As a consequence, these words were more likely to be transferred from short-term memory into long-term memory. So the primacy effect seems to reflect the operation of long-term memory.

Types of Long-Term Memory. As we mentioned earlier, some psychologists argue that there are actually more than three memory systems. In particular, they claim that long-term memory isn't just one system, but many.

To find out why, try your hand at the following four questions.

1. In what year did the United States become independent from Great Britain?
2. What Republican candidate for president did Barack Obama defeat in the 2012 U.S. election?
3. How old were you when you first tried to ride a bicycle?
4. Where did you celebrate your last birthday?

According to Endel Tulving (1972) and many other memory researchers (Renoult et al., 2012), our answers to the first two questions rely on different memory systems than our answers to the last two. Our answers to the first two questions (1776 and John McCain) depend on **semantic memory**, our knowledge of facts about the world. In contrast, our answers to the last two questions, which are unique to us, depend on **episodic memory**, our recollection of events in our lives. A. J., whom we discussed at the beginning of the chapter, experiences remarkably accurate episodic memories. There's good evidence that these two types of memory are housed in different brain regions. Semantic memory tends to activate the left frontal cortex more than the right frontal cortex, and vice versa for episodic memory (Cabeza & Nyberg, 1997).

Still, semantic and episodic memory both require conscious effort and awareness. Whether we're trying to recall the definition of "chunking" from earlier in this chapter or our first kiss, we *know* we're trying to remember. Moreover, when we recall this information, we have a conscious experience of accessing it. That is, both semantic and episodic memory are examples of **explicit memory**, the process of recalling information intentionally. (Some researchers refer to the information recalled by explicit memory as *declarative memory*.)

Explicit memory differs from **implicit memory**, the process of recalling information we don't remember deliberately. Implicit memories don't require conscious effort on our part (Gopie, Craik, & Hasher, 2011). For example, each of us can go through the steps of unlocking our front doors without consciously recalling the sequence of actions required to do so. In fact, we probably can't tell without reenacting it in our heads or actually standing in front of our doors which way the key turns in the lock and how we hold the key in our hands while unlocking the door.

Studies of people with brain damage provide remarkable *existence proofs* for the distinction between implicit and explicit memory. Antonio Damasio (2000) has studied a patient named David, whose left and right temporal lobes were largely obliterated by a virus. David has virtually no explicit memory for anyone he's met; when Damasio shows him photographs of people with whom he's recently interacted, he can't recognize any of them. Yet when Damasio asks David which of these people he'd ask for help if he needed it, he points to those who've been kind to him, utterly clueless of who they are. David has no explicit memory for who's helped him, but his implicit memory remains intact.

Procedural memory is memory for how to do things, even things we do automatically without thinking about how to do them.

To make matters still more complicated, there are several subtypes of implicit memory. We'll discuss two here: procedural memory and priming. However, according to most psychologists, implicit memory also includes habituation, classical conditioning, and other forms of learning.

One subtype of implicit memory, **procedural memory**, refers to memory for motor skills and habits. Whenever we ride a bicycle or open a soda can, we're relying on procedural memory. In contrast to semantic memory, which is "know what" memory, procedural memory is "know how" memory. Our procedural and semantic memories for the same skills are sometimes surprisingly different. For those of you who are avid typists, find a computer or smart phone keyboard and type the word *the*. That's a breeze, right? Now turn away from the keyboard for a moment, and try to remember where the *t, h,* and *e* are located, but without moving your fingers. If you're like most people, you'll draw a blank. You may even find that the only way to remember their location is to use your fingers to type the imaginary letters in midair. Although your procedural memory for locating letters on a keyboard is effortless, your semantic memory for locating them is a different story.

A second subtype of implicit memory, **priming**, refers to our ability to identify a stimulus more easily or more quickly when we've previously encountered similar stimuli. Imagine that a researcher flashes the word *QUEEN*, interspersed with a few hundred other words, very quickly on a computer screen. An hour later, she asks you to perform a task that requires you to fill in the missing letters of a word. In this case, the stem completion task is K _____. Research shows that having seen the word *QUEEN*, you're more likely to complete the stem with *KING* (as opposed to *KILL* or *KNOW*, for example) than are participants who haven't seen *QUEEN* (Neely, 1976). This is true, incidentally, even for participants who insist they can't even remember having seen the word *QUEEN* (Bargh, 1994). This memory is implicit because it doesn't require any deliberate effort on our part. (Yeh, He, & Cavanagh, 2012).

If you're having a hard time keeping all of these subtypes of long-term memory straight, **FIGURE 8** summarizes the major subtypes of explicit and implicit memory.

Is the drawing at the bottom a duck or a rabbit? This illusion, originally concocted by psychologist Joseph Jastrow around the turn of the century, affords a good illustration of priming you can try on your friends. Show some of your friends only Photograph A (covering up Photograph B; then show other friends only Photograph B (covering up Photograph A). Ask them what they see in the drawing below. Your friends primed with Photograph A will be more likely to "see" the related image of a duck, and your friends primed with Photograph B will be more likely to "see" the related image of a rabbit.

FIGURE 8 The Many Subtypes of Memory. A summary of the subtypes of explicit and implicit memory.

procedural memory
memory for how to do things, including motor skills and habits

priming
our ability to identify a stimulus more easily or more quickly after we've encountered similar stimuli

---

Assess Your Knowledge   **FACT** or **FICTION**?

1. Most of us can accurately recognize thousands of faces we've seen only a few days earlier.   **True / False**

2. Memory is more reconstructive than reproductive.   **True / False**

3. The major reason for forgetting information from short-term memory appears to be the decay of memories.   **True / False**

4. Chunking can permit us to greatly increase the number of digits or letters we hold in our short-term memories.   **True / False**

5. Information in long-term memory often lasts for years or decades.   **True / False**

Answers: 1. T; 2. T; 3. F; 4. T; 5. T

The Three Processes of Memory

4 Identify methods for connecting new information to existing knowledge.

5 Identify the role that schemas play in the storage of memories.

6 Distinguish ways of measuring memory.

7 Describe how the relation between encoding and retrieval conditions influences remembering.

How do we get information into our long-term memories? Memory psychologists agree that there are three major *processes* of memory: *encoding, storage,* and *retrieval.* By the way, we shouldn't confuse these three processes with the three *systems* of memory we just discussed (sensory, short-term, and long-term). Whereas the three systems refer to the *what* of memory, the three processes we're about to discuss refer to the *how* of memory. They explain how information gets transferred into long-term memory and gets back out again when we need it (see **FIGURE 9**).

To understand these three processes of memory, picture yourself working as a librarian at your college or university library. When a new book arrives, you first give it a number to identify it; that's encoding. Then you file it away on the bookshelf; that's storage. Then, when you want to find the book a few weeks, months, or even years later, you go to the shelves and fetch it; that's retrieval. Of course, like all metaphors, this one is an oversimplification, because the memories we retrieve are rarely identical to those we

FIGURE 9 Three Processes of Memory.
The process of remembering is similar in some ways to the process of filing and fetching a library book.

Process 1 Encoding: Using a computer, a librarian enters the cataloguing information for a book into the library's database. In the process, the librarian finds out where the book needs to be shelved. The computer prints out a label (what we might think of as an encoding label) that the librarian affixes to the book's spine so that everyone will know where the book should be stored.

Process 2 Storage: The librarian puts the books in the proper section of the library, according to how they've been catalogued.

Process 3 Retrieval: When the librarian wants to access the book, he looks up the cataloguing information and then goes to the appropriate shelf with his computer printout showing the catalogue location of the book to retrieve it.

initially encoded. Some of the "books" in our mental library may become yellow with age; others become marked up or even damaged beyond recognition.

Encoding: The "Call Numbers" of the Mind

Encoding refers to the process of getting information into our memory banks. To remember something, we first need to make sure the information is in a format our memories can use. To a far greater extent than we realize, many of our memory failures are actually failures of encoding. To go back to our library analogy, imagine that the librarian assigns an identification number to some of the books that come in for processing but later decides to toss some of them in the trash instead. These books never make it to the shelves. Once we lose the chance to encode an event, we'll never remember it. No encoding, no memory.

THE ROLE OF ATTENTION. To encode something, we must first attend to it. Have you ever had the embarrassing experience of going to a party and being introduced to several people at the same time and then realizing that you'd immediately forgotten all of their names? Odds are high you were so nervous or distracted that you never encoded their names in the first place.

That principle helps to explain why the popular belief that our brains preserve a record of every event we've ever encountered (Alvarez & Brown, 2001) can't be right. Most events we've experienced are never encoded, and almost all events we do encode include only some of the details of the experience. Much of our everyday experience never gets into our brain in the first place. For instance, consider this example of an everyday object we've seen hundreds, even thousands, of times. Take a look at **FIGURE 10**, where you'll see an array of six pennies. Which of these pennies is the real one?

If you flunked this miniature test of "common cents," don't feel too bad. When two researchers conducted a similar version of this test about three decades ago, they found that fewer than half of 203 Americans identified the correct penny (Nickerson & Adams, 1979). We see pennies almost every day, yet how often do we actually pay attention to the details of them?

Encoding also helps to explain the familiar *next-in-line effect*. You've experienced this phenomenon if you've ever been in a class when the instructor called on several students in a row to answer a question or say their names. You probably found that your memory was especially poor for what the person immediately before you said (Bond, Pitre, & van Leeuwen, 1991; Innes, 2011). That's because you were so preoccupied with what you were going to say that you weren't paying much attention to what the person right before you was saying.

MNEMONICS: VALUABLE MEMORY AIDS. What do the following strange passages have in common?

1. Please Excuse My Dear Aunt Sally.
2. Thirty days hath September, April, June, and November. All the rest have 31, except for February, which has 28, and you probably think it's great. Or maybe it's when fine, on leap year, it has 29.
3. Every Good Boy Does Fine.

Each is a **mnemonic** (pronounced "nee-MAH-nik"): a learning aid, strategy, or device that enhances recall. Mnemonics help us encode memories in a way that makes them easier to recall. From time to time, virtually all of us use recall boosters, like making lists or writing appointments on a calendar, cell phone, or portable computer (Intons-Peterson & Fournier, 1986; McCabe, Osher, Roche, & Susser, 2011). Nevertheless, mnemonics differ from these "external" memory aids in that they rely on internal mental strategies, namely, strategies we use during encoding that help us later retrieve useful information. Item 1 specifies the proper order of mathematical operations (parentheses, exponents, multiplication, division, addition, subtraction) by having each

"In one ear and out the other," so the saying goes. If you have met someone and forgotten his or her name a minute later, you probably never encoded it in the first place.

? **FIGURE 10** Penny Array from Nickerson and Adams (1979). Which of these pennies is the real one? Try to guess before pulling one out of your pocket. (*Source:* Based on Nickerson & Adams, 1979)

Music students use the mnemonic "Every good boy does fine" to remember the names of the lines (E, G, B, D, F) in the treble clef.

encoding
process of getting information into our memory banks

mnemonic
a learning aid, strategy, or device that enhances recall

Answer: The correct answer is (b).

FIGURE 11 Pegword Method. The pegword method can be a useful mnemonic for helping us recall lists of objects in order. See the text for an explanation of this fanciful illustration.

word start with the same letter as the mathematical operation. Item 2 is a rhyme that's a handy way of remembering the number of days in each month. Item 3 stands for the notes on the lines of the treble clef in musical notation (E, G, B, D, F).

Mnemonic devices share two major features. First, we can apply them to just about anything and everything: the names of planets, the elements of the periodic table, the bones of the hand, the order of geological time periods, and the colors of the rainbow (the last being ROY G. BIV for red, orange, yellow, green, blue, indigo, and violet). Second, most mnemonics depend on our having a store of knowledge to begin with. We need to know something about mathematical operations for the mnemonic about Aunt Sally to make any sense. So in general, mnemonics are most helpful as mental shortcuts for recalling lists of information we've already learned. There are many other mnemonic approaches in addition to those we've discussed: We'll review three here.

Pegword Method. By elementary school age, most of us were well acquainted with the exploits of Jack and Jill, Little Bo Peep, and Little Jack Horner. Songs ranging from "Twinkle, Twinkle Little Star" to the hip-hop songs of the Black Eyed Peas are easy to remember because they contain rhymes.

Rhyming is a key component of the *pegword method*, often used to recall ordered lists of words. To master this mnemonic, first associate each number in a list with a word that rhymes with the number, such as "One is a bun." The word associated with the number is a "pegword." It's essential to memorize a list like the one that follows, but the fact that the numbers and words rhyme makes it easy to do so: (1) One is a bun, (2) Two is a shoe, (3) Three is a tree, and (4) Four is a door.

Suppose you need to learn four words associated with memory concepts for your psychology class (don't you wish there were only four new terms in this chapter?) and that you need to recall them in the following order: chunking, elaboration, hippocampus, and decay. After you've memorized the pegword associated with each number (such as "one is a bun"), create an image that associates the word you want to remember with the pegword (such as *bun*). For the first word, *chunking*, you could imagine a bun (the pegword) with a chunk missing or broken up into chunks. For two—*elaboration*—you might imagine a shoe with elaborate beading, sequins, and bows. For three—*hippocampus*—imagine a tree with a hippo camping under it. For number four, *decay*, you might picture a rotting, decaying door on an old house. When you need to remember the third item on your list, for example, you'd say to yourself that three is a tree, which would prompt recall of the hippo camping under it, and you'd know that the third word on the list is hippocampus (see **FIGURE 11**). Researchers have found that repeated use of the pegword method enhanced students' delayed recall for ordered lists of unfamiliar terms, suggesting that the method may be a useful study strategy for improving vocabulary (Carney & Levin, 2011).

Method of Loci. The *method of loci* (pronounced "low-sigh") relies on imagery of places, that is, *locations,* hence the name of the mnemonic (Bellezza, 1999; Foer, 2011). The method is straightforward: Think of a path with which you're familiar and can imagine vividly. Perhaps it's the route from your dorm to the cafeteria or a stroll through the rooms in your apartment. Think of the path you take and the things that you encounter in a set order. For example, to get to the cafeteria, first you get in the elevator, then you walk under a huge tree before you pass by a fountain, and so on. If you need to remember five words in a particular order, think of five things you'll encounter on your way to the cafeteria; if you need to recall ten words, imagine ten locations along your route. If you were trying to remember the list of memory terms with the method of loci, you might imagine chunks of rock or glass on the floor of the elevator.

Keyword Method. If you've taken a foreign language course, you may be familiar with the *keyword method.* This strategy depends on your ability to think of an English word (the keyword) that reminds you of the word you're trying to remember. Take the Spanish word *casa*, which means "house" in English. Think of an English word, like *case*, that sounds like or brings to mind *casa*. Now think of an image that combines *case* (or another word of your choice) and *house*. Perhaps you can picture a case of soda on the roof of your house. When you think of this image, it should help you retrieve the meaning of *casa*. People who learn foreign vocabulary benefit from the keyword strategy compared with more traditional methods, such as rote memorization (Beaton et al., 2005; Gruneberg & Sykes, 1991). Likewise, researchers have found that the keyword strategy was effective for third-graders, including students with learning disabilities, in mastering new vocabulary words (Uberti, Scruggs, & Mastropieri, 2003).

Music. Can putting material-to-be-learned to a familiar melody like "Pop Goes the Weasel" or "Yankee Doodle Dandy" assist in learning? That's what one pair of researchers set out to determine (Rainey & Larson, 2002). They included lists of names in the two songs, and participants either listened to one or the other tune or heard the words in the lists spoken. The researchers found no initial recall advantage for people who learned the names with musical accompaniment. However, those who heard the sung version required fewer trials to relearn the names a week later, suggesting that learning information put to a melody improves long-term retention.

Generally speaking, mnemonics can be helpful if we're motivated to practice them on a regular basis. Mnemonics require training, patience, and even a dash of creativity.

Ginkgo and other supposed memory-enhancing drugs are a multimillion-dollar industry in the United States. These pills are popular, but do they work?

psychomythology

SMART PILLS

The next time you're in your local drugstore, stop by the aisle containing herbal remedies. There you'll find a virtual museum of so-called smart pills designed to enhance memory: ginkgo; vitamin E; and even drugs with unpronounceable, but scientific-sounding, names like phosphatidylserine, citicoline, and piracetam. Can any of them help us remember where we mislaid our keys this morning, memorize the names of the ten people we met at last night's party, or recall how to spell *phosphatidylserine*?

Probably the best-known herbal remedy for memory is ginkgo (whose scientific name is *Ginkgo biloba*), an ancient Chinese medicine extracted from the leaves of the ginkgo tree. Although it might be tempting to assume that ginkgo is effective because it's been used for many centuries, this would be an example of the *argument from antiquity fallacy*, the error of concluding that something must be effective because it's been around for a long time. The manufacturers of ginkgo claim that it can markedly improve normal people's memory in as little as four weeks. Like many other memory boosters, ginkgo presumably works in part by increasing the level of the brain's acetylcholine, a neurotransmitter that plays a key role in memory.

Ginkgo is remarkably popular; Americans spend $249 million on it per year (DeKosky et al., 2008). Yet controlled studies comparing ginkgo with a placebo show that its effects on memory in normal individuals are minimal, even nonexistent (Gold, Cahill, & Wenk, 2002; Elsabagh et al., 2005). If ginkgo produces any effects on normal memory at all, they appear to be about equal to those of drinking a glass of lemonade or any sugary liquid (sugar is the brain's fuel). Ginkgo's effects on memory in people with Alzheimer's disease or other forms of dementia are slight (Gold et al., 2002) and perhaps even nonexistent (DeKosky et al., 2008; Vellas et al., 2012). There's no good evidence that it can reverse severe memory loss or stave off age-related cognitive decline (Snitz et al., 2009). Moreover, like many herbal remedies, ginkgo can be harmful in certain cases; it can interfere with the effects of blood-thinning medicines and thereby cause excessive bleeding. As for the other smart pills we mentioned with fancy names, the evidence for their effects on memory is too preliminary to draw strong conclusions (McDaniel, Maier, & Einstein, 2002).

Finally, what about pills designed to boost attention and keep us awake, perhaps just long enough to study for that dreaded final exam? Not surprisingly, some of these drugs are becoming popular on college campuses. Surveys show that up to 30 percent of college students have used Ritalin, Adderall, and similar stimulants, widely prescribed for attention-deficit/hyperactivity disorder, to help them concentrate while studying or taking exams (Greely et al., 2008; Garnier-Dykstra et al., 2012). One team of investigators compared students taking the SAT, some of whom believed they were ingesting Ritalin and some whom believed they were ingesting a dummy pill. The former students reported better mental functioning and attention—but their SAT scores weren't any higher. Yet *both* groups had actually received a dummy pill, suggesting that Ritalin's "impact" on test taking may be due to a placebo effect (Gowin, 2009). Still other evidence suggests that stimulants may be helpful in consolidating declarative memories, like memories of facts, but the evidence is too preliminary to draw firm conclusions (Smith & Farah, 2011).

Modafinil (its brand name is Provigil), commonly prescribed for narcolepsy, sleep apnea, and other sleep disorders, is also popular as an aid for maintaining wakefulness and alertness. Nevertheless, research suggests that although Modafinil may be about as effective as caffeine for enhancing attention in sleep-deprived people, at least some of its effects on fatigue may not exceed those of a placebo (Drabiak-Syed, 2011; Kumar, 2008). Because the Food and Drug Administration (FDA) no longer regulates diet supplements and herbal remedies, including those intended to enhance memory, it's anybody's guess whether they work, or even whether any might be harmful (Bent, 2008). As is so often the case in pop psychology, the best advice for those of us hoping to become memory whizzes overnight is *caveat emptor:* Let the buyer beware.

Storage: Filing Away Our Memories

Once we've filed away a library book on the shelf, it sits there, often for years at a time, collecting dust and cobwebs. We've stored it, perhaps to be retrieved one day by a student or professor who needs it for a writing project. **Storage** refers to the process of keeping information in memory.

Yet where in the library we choose to file this text depends on our *interpretation and expectations* regarding the book's content. Let's imagine a new book entitled *The Psychology of Dating* has just arrived in the library. Should we file this text in the psychology section, along with books on personality, emotion, and social psychology, or in the relationships section, along with books on dating, attraction, and marriage? The answer depends on what we think is most important or relevant about the book's content. Similarly, how we store our experiences in memory depends on our interpretations and expectations of these events.

THE VALUE OF SCHEMAS. Consider this scenario. You and your friends go to a brand new sit-down restaurant. Although this is your first visit, you've got a pretty good idea of what's in store. That's because you possess a schema for eating at a nice restaurant. A **schema** is an organized knowledge structure or mental model that we've stored in memory. Our schema for restaurants is characterized by a set order of events, sometimes called a *script* (Schank & Abelson, 1977). You're seated at a table, given menus from which you order food, wait while your food is prepared, eat the food, get the check, and pay for the food before leaving. And don't forget the tip! There's even a standard sequence in ordering, at least in U.S. culture. We order drinks first, followed by appetizers, soup or salad, entrees, and finally dessert and coffee.

Schemas serve a valuable function: They equip us with frames of reference for interpreting new situations. Without schemas, we'd find some information almost impossible to comprehend (Bransford & Johnson, 1972). For example, if you've ever switched suddenly to a new computer system or smart phone, you know how confusing doing so can be at first. You may not have an understanding of how the keyboard is arranged, of what buttons are in which places, or perhaps even in which order you're supposed to type different instructions.

Our interpretation of ambiguous events in everyday life, like an animated conversation on the street, depends in part on our schemas.

storage
process of keeping information in memory

schema
organized knowledge structure or mental model that we've stored in memory

SCHEMAS AND MEMORY MISTAKES. Valuable as they are, schemas can sometimes create problems, because they can lead us to remember things that never happened. Schemas simplify, which is good because they help us make sense of the world. But schemas sometimes *oversimplify*, which is bad because they can produce memory illusions. Schemas provide one key explanation for the paradox of memory: They enhance memory in some cases, but lead to memory errors in others.

For example, Mark Snyder and Seymour Uranowitz (1978) presented participants with a case study of the life of a woman, Betty K. After reading this case study, some participants learned that Betty was now living a heterosexual lifestyle; others learned that she was living a homosexual lifestyle. Snyder and Uranowitz then gave participants a recognition test for the details in the passage. They found that participants distorted their memories of the original information, such as her relationship with her father and past dating habits, to be in line with their schema—their beliefs about her current lifestyle. For example, participants who believed Betty to be homosexual mistakenly recalled her as never having dated men in high school. If we're not careful, our schemas can lead us to overgeneralize, painting all members of a category with the same broad brush.

Answers are located at the end of the text.

MEMORY BOOSTERS

evaluating **CLAIMS**

Many of us would love to improve our memories—to perform better in our courses or at work; remember birthdays, anniversaries, and other important dates; or just remember where we left our keys. Scores of products on the market purport to improve our memories and overall brain function. Let's evaluate some of these claims, which are modeled after actual ads for memory-enhancing supplements.

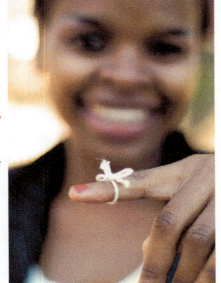

"Never misplace your keys again! Use our product and *cure your absentmindedness!*"
The claim that this product is a cure is extraordinary. What kind of evidence is needed to support this claim?

"*Scientifically proven* to improve your memory."
The claim talks of "proof," yet scientific knowledge is rarely, if ever, conclusive. What information would you need to evaluate whether the studies were conducted properly?

"Our formula is a *synergistic blend of antioxidants, gotu kola, brainy aromatics, amino acids, and specific neurotransmitter nutrients* to help maintain *healthy cellular energy production by promoting healthy mitochondrial function, scavenging free radicals, and promoting blood circulation* to the brain."
We should beware of meaningless "psychobabble" that uses scientific-sounding words that are lacking in substance.

"*75% of Americans are turning to complementary and alternative medicine* to improve their memory—by taking our all-natural memory enhancers you can be one of them."
Does the claim that a large number of Americans use complementary and alternative medicines mean this product is effective? Why or why not?

TABLE I Demonstration of Retrieval Cues.
Find a friend and read each category, followed by the word that goes along with it. Then, ask your friend to recall only the words, in any order. For each word your friend forgot, ask whether he or she remembers something from that word's category. As you'll see, this demonstration helps to make a simple point: Many memory failures are actually failures of retrieval.

TABLE I Demonstration of Retrieval Cues.

CATEGORY	WORD
A metal	Silver
A precious stone	Pearl
A relative	Niece
A bird	Canary
Type of reading material	Journal
A military title	Major
A color	Violet
A four-legged animal	Mouse
A piece of furniture	Dresser
A part of the body	Finger
A fruit	Cherry
A weapon	Cannon
A type of dwelling	Mansion
An alcoholic beverage	Brandy
A crime	Kidnapping
An occupation	Plumber
A sport	Lacrosse
An article of clothing	Sweater
A musical instrument	Saxophone
An insect	Wasp

retrieval
reactivation or reconstruction of experiences from our memory stores

retrieval cue
hint that makes it easier for us to recall information

recall
generating previously remembered information

recognition
selecting previously remembered information from an array of options

relearning
reacquiring knowledge that we'd previously learned but largely forgotten over time

Retrieval: Heading for the "Stacks"

To remember something, we need to fetch it from our long-term memory banks. This is **retrieval**, the third and final process of memory. Yet, as we mentioned earlier, this is where our metaphor of a library begins to break down, because what we retrieve from our memory often doesn't match what we put into it. Our memories are reconstructive, often transforming our recollections to fit our beliefs and expectations.

Many types of forgetting result from failures of retrieval: Our memories are still present, but we can't access them. It's pretty easy to demonstrate this point. If a friend is nearby, try the following demonstration, courtesy of psychologist Endel Tulving (even if you don't have a friend handy, you can still follow along). Read each category in **TABLE I** to your friend, followed by the word that goes along with it. Tell your friend that after you're done reading all of the categories and their corresponding words, you'll ask him or her to recall just the words—in any order—not the categories.

After you read the list to your friend, ask him or her to take a few minutes to write down as many words as he or she can remember. Almost certainly, your friend missed some of them. For those missing words, prompt your friend with the category. So if your friend missed *Finger*, ask, "Do you remember the word that went with 'A part of the body'?" You'll probably find that these prompts help your friend to remember some of the forgotten words. In psychological lingo, the category names serve as **retrieval cues**: hints that make it easier for us to recall information. So your friend's long-term memory contained these missing words, but he or she needed the retrieval cues to remember them.

MEASURING MEMORY. Psychologists assess people's memory in three major ways: recall, recognition, and relearning. Think of them as the three Rs (another mnemonic device, by the way).

Recall and Recognition. What kind of exam do you find the toughest: essay or multiple choice? For sure, we've all taken multiple-choice tests that are "killers." Still, all else being equal, essay tests are usually harder than multiple-choice tests. That's because **recall**, that is, generating previously remembered information on our own, tends to be more difficult than **recognition**, selecting previously remembered information from an array of options (Bahrick, Bahrick, & Wittlinger, 1975). To demonstrate what we mean, try recalling the sixth president of the United States. Unless you're an American history buff, you may be stumped. If so, try this question instead.

The sixth president of the United States was:

(a) George Washington   (c) Bill Clinton

(b) John Quincy Adams   (d) Sarah Palin

With a bit of thought, you probably figured out that (b) was the correct answer. You could safely eliminate (a) because you know George Washington was the first president, (c) because you know Bill Clinton was a much more recent president, and (d) because you know Sarah Palin hasn't been president. Moreover, you may well have recognized John Quincy Adams as an early U.S. president, even if you didn't know he was number six.

Why is recall usually harder than recognition? In part, it's because recalling an item requires two steps—generating an answer and then determining whether it seems correct—whereas recognizing an item takes only one step: determining which item from a list seems most correct (Haist, Shimamura, & Squire, 1992).

Relearning. A third way of measuring memory is **relearning**: how much more quickly we learn information when we study something we've already studied relative to when we studied it the first time. For this reason, psychologists often call this approach the method of *savings*: Now that we've studied something, we don't need to take as much time to refresh our memories of it (that is, we've "saved" time by studying it).

The concept of relearning originated with the pioneering work of German researcher Hermann Ebbinghaus (1885) well over a century ago. Ebbinghaus used hundreds of "nonsense syllables," like ZAK and BOL, to test his own recollection across differing time intervals. As we can see in **FIGURE 12**, he found that most of our forgetting occurs almost immediately after learning new material, with less and less forgetting after that. However, he also found that when he attempted to relearn the nonsense syllables he'd forgotten after a delay, he learned them much more quickly the second time around.

Imagine you learned to play the guitar in high school but haven't played it for several years. When you sit down to strum an old song, you're rusty at first. Although you need to go back to your notes to remind yourself the first couple of times you sit down to play, you'll probably find that it doesn't take you nearly as long to get the hang of the song the second time around. That's relearning. Relearning shows that a memory for this skill was still lurking in your brain—somewhere.

Relearning is a more sensitive measure of memory than either recall or recognition. That's because relearning allows us to assess memory using a relative amount (how much faster was material learned the second time?) rather than the simple "right" or "wrong" we obtain from recall or recognition (MacLeod, 2008; Nelson, 1985). It also allows us to measure memory for procedures, like driving a car or playing a piano piece, as well as for facts and figures.

When memorizing his nonsense syllables, Ebbinghaus happened on a crucial principle that applies to most forms of learning: the law of **distributed versus massed practice** (Donovan & Radosevich, 1999; Willingham, 2002). Simply put, this law tells us that we tend to remember things better in the long run when we spread our learning over long intervals than when we pack it into short intervals. This principle is probably one of the best-replicated effects in all of psychology (Cepeda et al., 2006). Even infants show it (Cornell, 1980).

Herein lies another word to the wise. Cramming for an exam helps us remember the information for *that exam*, but it typically produces poor long-term retention. If you want to master the information in your psychology course—or any course, for that matter—you should spread out your review of the material over long intervals. So when one of your teachers nags you to "start studying at least a week before the exam rather than waiting until the last minute," you have Ebbinghaus to thank—or blame.

TIP-OF-THE-TONGUE PHENOMENON. We've all experienced retrieval failure in the form of the frustrating **tip-of-the-tongue (TOT) phenomenon**, in which we're sure we know the answer to a question, but can't come up with it (Brown, 1991; Ecke, 2009; Schwartz, 1999). It's surprisingly easy to generate this phenomenon (Baddeley, 1993). Read the names of the ten U.S. states in **TABLE 2**, and try to name their capital cities. Now focus on the states for which you're *unsure* of whether you know the right answer, and keep trying. If you're still stuck, look at the list that follows, which gives you the first letter of the capital of each state: Georgia (A), Wisconsin (M), California (S), Louisiana (B), Florida (T), Colorado (D), New Jersey (T), Arizona (P), Nebraska (L), and Kentucky (F).

Did the first letters help? Research shows when we experience the TOT phenomenon, they often will. The fact that we sometimes experience TOT tells us that there's a difference between something we've forgotten because it didn't get *stored* in memory and something that's in there somewhere that we can't quite *retrieve*.

Two investigators showed that when people believe that something is on the tip of their tongues, they're frequently right (Brown & McNeill, 1966). They presented participants with the definitions of relatively rare words (such as "to give up the throne") and asked them to come up with the word (in this case, *abdicate*). About 10 percent of the time, participants reported a TOT experience; they were pretty sure they "knew" the word, but couldn't generate it. In these cases, the researchers asked participants to guess the first letter of the word or the number of syllables in it. Interestingly, the participants did much better than chance. So participants *did* know something about the word; they just couldn't spit it out whole.

FIGURE 12 Ebbinghaus's Curve of Forgetting. This graph from Ebbinghaus's classic memory research shows the percent "savings," or how much faster information he relearned the second time following various delays (plotted in hours).

 Watch in **MyPsychLab** the **Video:** IT Video: Cramming

◄ **REPLICABILITY**
Can the results be duplicated in other studies?

TABLE 2 TOT Phenomenon. First try to come up with the capital of each state. Then, return to the text for some hints. (Answers are located upside-down at the bottom of the page.)

STATE	CAPITAL
Georgia	
Wisconsin	
California	
Louisiana	
Florida	
Colorado	
New Jersey	
Arizona	
Nebraska	
Kentucky	

distributed versus massed practice studying information in small increments over time (distributed) versus in large increments over a brief amount of time (massed)

tip-of-the-tongue (TOT) phenomenon experience of knowing that we know something but being unable to access it

Answers: Atlanta, Madison, Sacramento, Baton Rouge, Tallahassee, Denver, Trenton, Phoenix, Lincoln, Frankfort.

Memory

FIGURE 13 Research Shows That the Word Learning of Scuba Divers Depends on Context. If the divers learned words underwater, they recalled them best when underwater again (Godden & Baddely, 1975).

REPLICABILITY ▶
Can the results be duplicated in other studies?

encoding specificity
phenomenon of remembering something better when the conditions under which we retrieve information are similar to the conditions under which we encoded it

context-dependent learning
superior retrieval of memories when the external context of the original memories matches the retrieval context

state-dependent learning
superior retrieval of memories when the organism is in the same physiological or psychological state as it was during encoding

REPLICABILITY ▶
Can the results be duplicated in other studies?

ENCODING SPECIFICITY: FINDING THINGS WHERE WE LEFT THEM. Why is it easier to retrieve some things from memory than others? One answer to this mystery lies in the principle of **encoding specificity** introduced by Endel Tulving (1982; Tulving & Thompson, 1973). We're more likely to remember something when the conditions present at the time we encoded it are also present at retrieval. We can see this principle at work in several psychological phenomena, two of which we'll examine here: context-dependent learning and state-dependent learning.

Context-Dependent Learning. **Context-dependent learning** refers to superior retrieval when the external context of the original memories matches the retrieval context (Vlach & Sandhofer, 2011). Duncan Godden and Alan Baddeley (1975) provided an example of this effect in an ingenious study of scuba divers. They presented divers with 40 unrelated words while the divers were either standing on the beach or submerged in about 15 feet of water. Godden and Baddeley then tested the divers in either the same or a different context from which they originally presented the words. The divers' memory was best when the original context matched the retrieval context, regardless of whether they were on land or underwater, as shown in **FIGURE 13**.

There's even evidence for context-dependent learning when undergraduates take exams. Students tend to do slightly better on their exams when tested in the same classroom in which they learned the material (Smith, 1979). You may want to gently remind your introductory psychology instructor of this fact when he or she schedules the room for your next test. Still, this effect isn't all that powerful, and not all researchers have replicated it (Saufley, Otaka, & Bavaresco, 1985). That's probably because you've acquired the information not only in the classroom but also in other settings, such as the room in which you're now reading this text.

State-Dependent Learning. Despite its name, state-dependent learning doesn't mean that if you learned something while on vacation in the state of Montana, you need to go back to Montana to recall it. Instead, state-dependent learning is similar to context-dependent learning, except that it refers to the internal "state" of the organism rather than the external context. That is, **state-dependent learning** refers to superior retrieval of memories when the organism is in the same physiological or psychological state as it was during encoding (McNamara, Trimmer, & Houston, 2012).

There's anecdotal evidence for this phenomenon among alcoholics, who often report that they need to get drunk to locate items—including their favorite bottles of liquor—that they'd hidden while drinking (Goodwin, 1995). Of course, we've learned that anecdotes are limited as sources of scientific evidence. However, in this case, controlled studies bear out the anecdotes: People who've learned a task while under the influence of alcohol tend to remember it better when under the influence than when sober (Goodwin et al., 1969). Still, researchers haven't always replicated these findings (Lisman, 1974), suggesting that state-dependent effects probably depend in complex ways on the participants tested and stimuli administered.

State-dependent learning sometimes extends to mood, in which case it's termed *mood-dependent learning* (Bower, 1981). Studies show that both younger and older adults find it easier to recall and recognize unpleasant memories than pleasant ones when they're sad and easier to recall and recognize pleasant memories than unpleasant ones when they're happy (Knight, Maines, & Robinson, 2002; Nelson & Craighead, 1977; Robinson & Rollings, 2011).

Mood-dependent learning can create nasty difficulties for researchers who want to draw conclusions about people's life histories. Specifically, it can result in a *retrospective bias:* Our current psychological state can distort memories of our past (Dawes, 1988; Ross, 1989; Taylor, Russ-Eft, & Taylor, 2009). For example, most individuals with clinical depression report having been treated more harshly by their parents in childhood than do individuals without clinical depression. One explanation for this finding is that harsh parental treatment predisposes to later depression. But there's another explanation: Perhaps people's bad moods distort their memories of their childhoods.

To evaluate this possibility, researchers asked three groups of participants—(1) people who had clinical depression, (2) people who had a history of depression but weren't currently depressed, and (3) people who'd never been depressed—about how their parents treated them as children. Currently depressed participants recalled their parents as having been more rejecting and domineering toward them as children than did participants in the other two groups (Lewinsohn & Rosenbaum, 1987). So participants' moods seem to have influenced their evaluations of how their parents had treated them. In this case, we don't know whether the participants with clinical depression were less *accurate* than the participants in the other groups, only that their memories were different.

◀ **RULING OUT RIVAL HYPOTHESES**
Have important alternative explanations for the findings been excluded?

Assess Your Knowledge   FACT or FICTION?

1. We encode virtually all of our life experiences, even though we can't retrieve more than a tiny proportion of them.   **True / False**

2. We need to practice mnemonics to use them successfully.   **True / False**

3. Schemas only distort memories, but don't enhance them.   **True / False**

4. In general, recall is more difficult than recognition.   **True / False**

5. Cramming for exams, although stressful, is actually a good strategy for enhancing long-term recall of material.   **True / False**

Answers: 1. F 2. T 3. F 4. T 5. F

 Study and **Review** in **MyPsychLab**

The Biology of Memory

8   Describe the role of long-term potentiation in memory.

9   Distinguish different types of amnesia and the relevance of amnesia to the brain's organization of memory.

10   Identify the key impairments of Alzheimer's disease.

Although few of us think about it, the biology of memory plays a pivotal role in our daily lives, whether it's remembering where we left our keys or the name of that friendly person we met at last night's party. What's more, understanding how our brains store memory may help us find ways of treating devastating diseases that impair our ability to recall everyday events.

Explore in **MyPsychLab** the **Concept:**
Virtual Brain: Learning and Memory

The Neural Basis of Memory Storage

Locating where a library book is stored is generally pretty easy. We look it up in our library's online system, write down its number, go to the shelf, and—unless someone's recently plucked it away—find it. If we're lucky, it's right there on the shelf where it's supposed to be. Yet as we'll soon see, memory storage in the brain isn't quite this cut and dry.

THE ELUSIVE ENGRAM. Beginning in the 1920s, psychologist Karl Lashley went in search of the *engram:* the physical trace of each memory in the brain. He taught rats how to run mazes and lesioned different parts of their brains to see if they forgot how

Glutamate

AMPA   NMDA

FIGURE 14 Neural Basis of Long-Term Potentiation. LTP enhances the release of glutamate and activates postsynaptic receptors for NMDA and AMPA

REPLICABILITY ▶
Can the results be duplicated in other studies?

RULING OUT RIVAL HYPOTHESES ▶
Have important alternative explanations for the findings been excluded?

Factoid

One source of evidence for the role of the hippocampus in memory comes from research on Clark's nutcracker, a remarkable North American bird. To help it prepare for long winters, Clark's nutcracker buries up to 33,000 seeds in about 5,000 places spread over about 150 square miles—and manages to locate most of them months later—even though they're often buried under several feet of snow! Clark's nutcracker has an unusually large hippocampus, which may help to explain its exceptional spatial memory (Basil et al., 1996).

long-term potentiation (LTP)
gradual strengthening of the connections among neurons from repetitive stimulation

to find their way. By doing so, Lashley hoped to discover where memory is stored in the brain. Yet after years of painstaking work, he came up empty-handed.

Still, Lashley learned two important things. First, the more brain he removed, the worse the rat performed on the maze: There's no great surprise there. Second, no matter where he removed brain tissue, the rats retained at least some memory of the maze (Lashley, 1929). Even removing up to half of the rat's cortex didn't erase the memory. These findings led Lashley to conclude that we can't simply point to a spot in the brain and say, "There's the memory of my first kiss," because that memory isn't located in a single place, like a library book sitting on a shelf. Instead, as scientists have since learned, memories of different features of experiences, like their sound, sight, and smell, are almost certainly stored in different brain.

Over a half century ago, Donald Hebb (1949) suggested that the engram is instead located in *assemblies* (organized groups) of neurons in the brain. According to Hebb, one neuron (A) becomes connected to another neuron (B) when it repeatedly activates that neuron. Neurons, fed by a rich blend of neurotransmitters, form circuits, integrate sensory information in meaningful ways, and transform our experience of the world into lasting, perhaps even lifelong, memories.

LONG-TERM POTENTIATION—A PHYSIOLOGICAL BASIS FOR MEMORY. Long-term **potentiation (LTP)** refers to a gradual strengthening of the connections among neurons by repetitive stimulation over time (Abrari et al., 2009; Bliss, Collingridge, & Morris, 2004). Terje Lomo first observed LTP in the hippocampus of rabbits in 1966, a finding replicated by many later researchers in other animals and humans. The gist of what neuroscientists have learned since the discovery of LTP is that neurons that "fire together wire together" (Malenka & Nicoll, 1999). To a large extent, Hebb was right.

Today, many researchers believe that our ability to store memories depends on strengthening the connections among neurons arranged in sprawling networks that extend to the far and deep recesses of our brains (Shors & Matzel, 1999). The question of whether LTP is directly responsible for the storage of memories or whether it affects learning indirectly by increasing arousal and attention, remains unresolved (Shors & Matzel, 1999). Still, most scientists agree that LTP plays a key role in learning and that the hippocampus plays a key role in forming lasting memories.

LTP and Glutamate LTP tends to occur at synapses where the sending neuron releases the neurotransmitter glutamate into the synaptic cleft—the space between the sending and receiving neuron. As shown in **FIGURE 14**, glutamate interacts with receptors for NMDA and another substance (AMPA). LTP enhances the release of glutamate into the synaptic cleft, resulting in enhanced learning (Lisman & Raghavachari, 2007; Navakkode & Korte, 2012). A research team was even able to create a "super smart mouse" by manipulating its genes to create extra receptors for NMDA. Compared with everyday mice, the super-smart mouse is an especially quick and effective learner (Lee & Silva, 2009; Tsien, 2000).

Where Is Memory Stored?

Clearly, the hippocampus is critical to memory. Some researchers have even identified neurons in the hippocampus that fire in response only to certain celebrities, such as actress Halle Berry (Quiroga et al., 2005).

But is the hippocampus, or any single brain structure, the site of the elusive engram? We can say with some certainty that the answer is no. fMRI studies reveal that learned information isn't stored permanently in the hippocampus itself. Rather, the prefrontal cortex seems to be one of the major "banks" from which we withdraw our memories (Zeinah et al., 2003). But as Lashley discovered, damage to isolated areas of the prefrontal cortex—or other cortical regions, for that matter—doesn't wipe out long-established memories. Much as the smell of a rose diffuses throughout a room, our memories distribute themselves throughout many areas of the cortex.

AMNESIA—BIOLOGICAL BASES OF EXPLICIT AND IMPLICIT MEMORY. Earlier we learned about explicit and implicit memory. Research demonstrates that two forms of memory are governed largely by different brain systems (Squire, 1987; Voss & Paller, 2008). The best evidence comes from individuals with severe amnesia. The two most common types of amnesia are **retrograde amnesia**, in which we lose some memories of our past, and **anterograde amnesia**, in which we lose the capacity to form new memories.

Amnesia Fictions and Facts. Contrary to popular belief, generalized amnesia—in which people have lost all details of their previous life (American Psychiatric Association, 2000), is quite rare (Baxendale, 2004). Even retrograde amnesia isn't especially common; anterograde amnesia is much more frequent among people with brain damage (Lilienfeld et al., 2010). Also, although many Hollywood films depict memory recovery from amnesia as abrupt, recovery from amnesia tends to occur gradually, if at all (APA, 2000).

Case Studies of Amnesia: H. M. and Clive Wearing. By far the best-known person with amnesia in the psychological literature was a man from Connecticut known only by the initials H. M. He suffered from severe epileptic seizures that his doctors couldn't control with medication. In March 1953, in a last-ditch attempt to eliminate these seizures, surgeons removed large chunks of H. M.'s temporal lobes, including both his left and right hippocampi, where they had reason to believe the seizures originated. (The surgeons of the time didn't anticipate the disastrous impact of this radical operation, which would probably never be performed today.) At the time, H. M. was 26 years old. Following the operation, H. M. developed virtually complete anterograde amnesia: He could recall almost no new information. Although he also experienced some retrograde amnesia for the 11 years prior to the surgery (Corkin, 1984), his memories from the first 15 years of his life remained pretty much intact.

In the decades following his surgery, H. M.'s life was, for all intents and purposes, frozen in time. H. M. himself put it eloquently: "Every day is alone by itself, whatever enjoyment I have had, whatever sorrow I have had." Among other things, he was oblivious to the fact that he had undergone surgery. Two years after the operation, in 1955, he reported the current date as March 1953. H. M. read the same magazines and completed the same jigsaw puzzles over and over again without any awareness of having seen them before. He didn't recall having met physicians whom he met just a few minutes earlier or remember what he ate for lunch 30 minutes ago (Milner, 1972; Scoville & Milner, 1957). Even when informed repeatedly of the death of his uncle, he showed the same dramatic grief to the news each time (Shimamura, 1992). H. M.'s identity was revealed as Henry Molaison only after his death in December 2008 at the age of 82. For 55 years, he acquired virtually no new explicit memories.

H. M.'s tragic case, like that of Damasio's patient David, illustrates a striking dissociation between explicit and implicit memory. Researchers asked H. M. to trace simple geometrical shapes from a mirror (see **Figure 15**), a task that just about all people find infuriatingly difficult when they first try it. Although H. M. had no recollection of ever having performed this task before, his performance improved steadily over time (Milner, 1964, 1965). So although H. M. had no explicit memory for this task, he displayed clear-cut implicit—specifically, procedural—memory for it.

When researchers examined H. M.'s brain using imaging techniques, they found that not only his hippocampus but also his surrounding cortex and neighboring amygdala were damaged (Corkin et al., 1997). This finding and others led researchers to hypothesize that large circuits connecting different parts of the limbic system, including the hippocampus, and amygdala, are critical to memory (see **FIGURE 16** on page 270).

Similar evidence for a distinction between explicit and implicit memory comes from the case of Clive Wearing, a former music producer in Great Britain whose hippocampi (along with several other brain structures) were destroyed by a herpes virus in 1985

FIGURE 15 A Mirror Tracing Task Similar to That Administered to H. M. How well can you draw while looking in a mirror? On this task, used to assess implicit memory, participants must trace a star while looking only at a mirror.

👁 **Watch** in **MyPsychLab** the **Video:** Special Topics: When Memory Fails

retrograde amnesia
loss of memories from our past

anterograde amnesia
inability to encode new memories from our experiences

Thalamus
Corpus callosum

Amygdala
(Emotional
component
of memories)

Hippocampus
(Factual
component
of memories)

FIGURE 16 Emotional Memories and the Brain. Research suggests that the amygdala helps us recall the fear associated with scary experiences and the hippocampus helps us recall the experiences themselves.

Watch in **MyPsychLab** the **Video:** In the Real World: The Memories We Don't Want

(Wearing, 2005). Like H. M., Clive has virtually complete anterograde amnesia. When his wife leaves the room for a few minutes and returns, he showers her with immense affection, as though he hasn't seen her in years. Yet Clive shows implicit memory in the form of priming effects. When his wife says "St. Mary's," he quickly responds "Padding-ton," entirely oblivious of why he says that. The name of the hospital to which Clive Wearing was taken after his viral infection was—you guessed it—St. Mary's Paddington (Wearing, 2005). The bottom line: Damage to the hippocampus impairs explicit memory, but leaves implicit memory intact.

EMOTIONAL MEMORY. We usually think of memory as our good friend, as a lifelong companion that helps us to store useful information, allowing us to cope with our environment. Yet our memories can also bring us distress, as in the case of a 53-year-old woman who reported olfactory (smell) memories tracking back to a brutal gang rape decades earlier (Vermetten & Bremner, 2003). Olfactory hallucinations of leather, alcohol, and the aftershave Old Spice—all of which were present at the rape scene—triggered intense fear responses that led her to retreat to a closet and engage in self-destructive behavior.

The Role of the Amygdala The amygdala is where the emotional components of these and other memories, especially those governing fear, are stored. The amygdala interacts with the hippocampus during the formation of memory, but each structure contributes different information (refer again to Figure 16). Researchers uncovered the specific roles of the amygdala and hippocampus in a study of two patients identified by their initials, S. M. and W. S. The first suffered damage to the amygdala; the second, to the hippocampus (LeBar & Phelps, 2005). The patient with amygdala damage (S. M.) remembered facts about the fear-producing experience, but not the fear. In contrast, the patient with hippocampal damage (W. S.) remembered the fear, but not the facts about the fear-producing experience. So the amygdala and hippocampus play distinctive roles in memory, with the amygdala helping us recall the emotions associated with fear-provoking events and the hippocampus helping us recall the events themselves (Fitzgerald et al., 2011; Marschner et al., 2008).

Erasing Painful Memories What if it were possible to erase or take the sting out of traumatic or painful memories, like witnessing someone's death or experiencing the devastating breakup of a relationship?

As we've learned, emotional memories can persist, even if they often become distorted over time. The hormones adrenaline and norepinephrine are released in the face of stress and stimulate protein (beta-adrenergic) receptors on nerve cells, which solidify emotional memories.

Lawrence Cahill and James McGaugh (1995) demonstrated the staying power of emotional memories in an elegant study. They created two stories regarding 12 slides they showed to participants. They told half of the participants an emotionally neutral story about a boy's visit to a hospital where his father works. They told the other half a far more disturbing story about the same slides; in the middle of the story, they informed participants that the boy was injured and operated on at a hospital to reattach his severed legs. Participants returned for a memory test 24 hours later, and Cahill and McGaugh asked them what they remembered. Participants who heard the emotionally arousing story displayed the best recall for the part of the story about the boy's trauma. In contrast, participants who heard the neutral story recalled the same amount of detail for all parts of the story.

Cahill and his colleagues (Cahill et al., 1994) conducted a similar experiment with an interesting twist. This time, they gave some participants a drug called *propranolol*, which blocks the effects of adrenaline on beta-adrenergic receptors (doctors also use it to treat high blood pressure). When participants' adrenaline was inhibited by propranolol, they didn't display especially good recall for the emotionally arousing part of the story. In fact, their recall was no different from that of individuals who listened to the emotionally neutral story.

Psychiatrist Roger Pitman reasoned that propranolol might blunt the memories of real-life traumas, such as automobile accidents. Pitman and his colleagues (Pitman et al., 2002) administered propranolol to people for 10 days after they experienced a traumatic event, such as a car accident and, a month later, examined their physical reactions to individually prepared tapes that replayed key aspects of the event. Forty-three percent of participants who received a placebo showed a physical response to the tape that re-created their traumatic experience. Yet none of the people who received the drug did.

Pitman's pill only dampened the effects of traumatic memories; it didn't erase them. These findings have been replicated by other investigators using different designs (Brun et al., 2011; Kindt, Soeter, & Vervliet, 2009). Still, this research hasn't laid to rest difficult questions about whether such procedures are ethical, much less desirable. After all, if we could choose to forget every negative experience, would we learn and grow from our mistakes? The mere fact that we *can* do something doesn't mean we *should*, so the debate continues.

◀ **REPLICABILITY**
Can the results be duplicated in other studies?

The Biology of Memory Deterioration

As we humans pass the ripe old age of 65, we usually begin to experience memory problems and some degeneration in the brain. Yet despite what many people believe (Lilienfeld et al., 2010), senility isn't an unavoidable part of aging, and some manage to make it past 100 with only modest amounts of everyday forgetfulness. But scientists disagree as to how much memory loss is "normal" during the advanced years. Some argue that we needn't accept any memory impairment as normal. Nevertheless, a longitudinal study of participants aged 59 to 84 years at baseline showed small but consistent reductions in the overall area of the cortex at two-year and four-year intervals (Resnick et al., 2003). We might assume that subtle cognitive decline would accompany these tissue losses, but alternative hypotheses are possible. For example, cognition may be fully preserved until a critical amount of tissue loss occurs.

◀ **RULING OUT RIVAL HYPOTHESES**
Have important alternative explanations for the findings been excluded?

Many people equate senility with one cause: Alzheimer's disease. Yet Alzheimer's disease is only the most frequent cause of senility, accounting for about 50 to 60 percent of cases of *dementia*, that is, severe memory loss (another common cause of senility is the accumulation of multiple small strokes in the brain). Alzheimer's disease occurs at alarming rates as people age—one American develops Alzheimer's disease every 72 seconds (Alzheimer's Disease Facts and Fictions, 2007). The risk for Alzheimer's disease is 13 percent for those over 65 years of age, but a whopping 42 percent for those over 85 years of age. With the "graying" (aging) of the U.S. population, Alzheimer's disease is expected to become even more of a concern in coming decades, with approximately 13 million Americans projected to develop the disease by 2050 if a cure can't be found (Alzheimer's Association, 2012).

The cognitive impairments of Alzheimer's disease are both memory- and language-related, which corresponds to the patterns of cortical loss in this illness (see **FIGURE 17**). The memory loss begins with recent events, with memories of the distant past being the last to go. Patients with Alzheimer's forget their grandchildren's names well before forgetting their children's names. They also experience disorientation and are frequently at a loss as to where they are, what year it is, or who the current president is.

The Alzheimer's brain contains many senile plaques and neurofibrillary tangles. These abnormalities contribute to the loss of synapses and death of cells in the hippocampus and cerebral cortex. They may also contribute to memory loss and intellectual decline. Loss of synapses is correlated with intellectual status, with greater loss as the disease progresses (Scheff et al., 2007). But this result doesn't necessarily mean that the reduction in synapses causes the memory decline. Along with loss of synapses comes degeneration and death of acetylcholine neurons in the forebrain. Accordingly, the

FIGURE 17 Changes in the Brain of Patients with Alzheimer's Disease. Changes include enlargement of the ventricles and severe loss of the cortex in areas involved in language and memory. (*Source:* Courtesy of Alzheimer's Disease Research, a program of the American Health Assistance Foundation)

◀ **CORRELATION VS. CAUSATION**
Can we be sure that A causes B?

In 2001, the year of the *Time* magazine photoessay on the "Nun Study," Sister Ester was 106, the oldest nun in the order. The results of this study suggest that physical and mental activity may protect against memory loss.

CORRELATION VS. CAUSATION ▶
Can we be sure that A causes B?

most common treatments for Alzheimer's disease today are drugs, like Donepezil (whose genetic name is *Aricept*), that boost the amount of acetylcholine in the brain by inhibiting its breakdown. There are also experimental procedures, such as gene therapies that enhance the production of neurotrophic (growth) factors, which enable acetylcholine neurons to survive and thrive. Still other promising medications block the actions of the neuorotransmitter glutamate (Francis, 2008), tends to be toxic to neurons in high doses. Yet no treatment to date halts or reverses the course of Alzheimer's disease. At best, these treatments only slow its progression slightly (Birks, 2012).

For this reason, researchers have evaluated people's lifestyles to see if anything can be done to reduce the risk of Alzheimer's disease. A massive study assessing over 4,000 people over 65 years of age showed that being physically active reduces the risk of cognitive impairment and Alzheimer's disease (Laurin et al., 2001). This large study dovetails with earlier findings from a small but telling study of 678 nuns who were hard-working, were active, and had strong social networks. What's most remarkable about these nuns is their advanced age—ranging from 87 to over 100 years—along with their low incidence of cognitive impairment, including Alzheimer's disease (Snowdon, 2003). Numerous other studies suggest that people who are highly educated and intellectually active are at decreased risk of Alzheimer's disease (Ngandu et al., 2007; Sattler et al., 2012). Admittedly, these correlational findings are ambiguous in their causal direction: Perhaps people who are more mentally and physically fit have more brain capacity to begin with. Yet these findings certainly raise the possibility that the old maxim "use it or lose it" may contain more than a grain of truth (Cracchiolo et al., 2007; Wilson et al., 2007).

✔ **Study** and **Review** in **MyPsychLab**

Assess Your Knowledge — FACT or FICTION?

1. Long-term potentiation appears to play a key role in learning.   True / False
2. The hippocampus is the site of the engram.   True / False
3. Memory recovery from amnesia is usually quite sudden.   True / False
4. Explicit and implicit memory are controlled by the same brain structures.   True / False
5. Alzheimer's disease is only one cause of dementia.   True / False

Answers: 1. T; 2. F; 3. F; 4. F; 5. T

The Development of Memory: Acquiring a Personal History

11   Identify how children's memory abilities change with age.

How early can children remember, and what do they remember? The answer depends on what kind of memory we're discussing. In one sense, we can remember information even before we're born. That's because fetuses display *habituation*—a decrease in attention to familiar stimuli. Fetuses as young as 32 weeks exhibit a decline in their reactions to vibratory stimulators over time. Habituation is a form of implicit memory—to interpret a stimulus as familiar, we need to recall we've experienced it before. It's a far cry from explicitly recalling the words to a song or remembering what we wore to our last birthday party, but it's still a form of remembering.

Memory over Time

Memory changes as we age, but there's considerable continuity over the course of development. On average, infants have worse memories than do children, who have worse memories than adults, and young adults have better memories than older adults. But the same basic processes operate across the life span. For example, infants display a serial position curve just as adults do (Cornell & Bergstrom, 1983; Gulya et al., 2001). Nevertheless, the span of memory and the ability to use strategies increase dramatically across the infant, toddler, preschool, and elementary school years.

Over time, children's memories become increasingly sophisticated. Several factors explain why. First, children's memory spans increase with age (Pascual-Leone, 1989). In fact, their Magic Number doesn't become seven plus or minus two until age 12 or so. If we ask a 3-year-old to remember a string of letters or numbers, she'll remember only about three on average. A 5-year-old will remember about four. By age 9, children are getting close to the adult's Magic Number, remembering six items on average.

Is this increase in span a result of better use of strategies, like rehearsal? That's certainly part of the story (Flavell, Beach, & Chinsky, 1966; McGilly & Siegler, 1989), but there's a large physical maturational component, too. So in an odd turn of events, shoe size is actually more highly correlated with memory span in children than with either age or intelligence. Nevertheless, we can assure you that this correlation isn't a causal one! Because different children grow at different rates, this correlation reflects a biological maturity component to memory span, for which variables like shoe size and height are the best predictors.

Second, our conceptual understanding increases with age. This fact is important because our ability to chunk related items and store memories in meaningful ways depends on our knowledge of the world. For example, without knowing that "CIA" stands for Central Intelligence Agency, children can't chunk the letters *C*, *I*, and *A* into one unit.

Third, over time, children develop enhanced **meta-memory** skills: knowledge about their memory abilities and limitations. These skills help children to identify when they need to use strategies to improve their memories, as well as which strategies work best (Schneider, 2008; Schneider & Bjorklund, 1998; Weinert, 1989; Zabrucky & Ratner, 1986). If we show a 4-year-old ten pictures and ask her how many she thinks she can remember, she'll probably tell you with supreme confidence that she can remember all ten. She can't. Children at this age don't appreciate their own memory limitations and overestimate their capacities as a result. Older children, who actually remember *more* than younger children do, estimate they'll remember *less*. As a result, they're more accurate in their ability to gauge their recall (Flavell, Friedrichs, & Hoyt, 1970).

Infants' Implicit Memory: Talking with Their Feet

Carolyn Rovee-Collier developed an innovative technique to study infants' implicit memory. Her research capitalizes on the fact that we can operantly condition infants to perform specific behaviors. Rovee-Collier placed infants in a crib with a mobile positioned over their heads. She first watched their behaviors for a few minutes to assess their activity levels in a "baseline" condition. Then, she took a ribbon tied to the mobile and attached it to the infant's ankle. The next time the infant kicked her foot, she was in for a pleasant surprise: The mobile shook and jiggled in response. Infants find the motion of the mobile inherently reinforcing. Because the movement is dependent on infants' behavior, they quickly become conditioned to kick their legs to get the mobile moving.

Once she conditioned infants to kick their legs in response to the mobile, Rovee-Collier sent them home. Then, after a delay—of a day, a week, or even a month—she brought them back to the lab and placed them in the crib again. This time, the mobile wasn't attached to the infant's leg, so there was no reinforcement. The question was: Would infants show an increased kicking rate in response to seeing the mobile? If so, it would imply that they remembered the conditioning experience.

◀ **CORRELATION VS. CAUSATION**
Can we be sure that A causes B?

Carolyn Rovee-Collier and other researchers have used mobiles to study infants' implicit memory. Although infants can't tell you they remember the mobiles, their memories "vote with their feet."

meta-memory
knowledge about our own memory abilities and limitations

Rovee-Collier (1993) found that children as young as two months retained a memory of this experience, although they forgot it after just a few days. Nevertheless, their span of recall increased quickly. Three-month-olds could remember the conditioning for over a week, and six-month-olds for over two weeks. Infants' memories of the experience were surprisingly specific. If researchers modified even a few elements of the mobile or changed the pattern of the crib liner ever so slightly, infants didn't seem to recognize the mobile: Their kicking rate returned to baseline.

? Some people claim to remember their own birth. **What well-established psychological phenomenon renders this claim extremely implausible?** (See answer upside down on bottom of page.)

infantile amnesia
inability of adults to remember personal experiences that took place before an early age

EXTRAORDINARY CLAIMS ▶
Is the evidence as strong as the claim?

from inquiry to understanding

WHY CAN'T WE REMEMBER THE FIRST FEW YEARS OF OUR LIVES?

Take a brief break from reading this chapter, and try to recall your earliest memory. What was it, and how old were you? Most students say their earliest memory falls somewhere between 3 and 5 years of age. **Infantile amnesia** is the inability of adults to retrieve accurate memories before an early age (Malinoski, Lynn, & Sivec, 1998; Wetzler & Sweeney, 1986).

Few, if any, of us correctly recall events before 2 or 3 years of age, the lowest cutoff for infantile amnesia (West & Bauer, 1999; Winograd & Killinger, 1983), although there are differences among people in the boundary of this amnesia (Peterson, Warren, & Short, 2011). Memories before that age just aren't trustworthy. So if you have a distinct memory of something that happened at age 1 or before, it's almost certainly either a false memory or a true memory of something that happened several years later.

Recent research suggests that culture may shape the age and content of our first memories. European Americans report earlier first memories than do people from Taiwan. Moreover, European Americans' earliest memories more often focus on themselves, whereas Taiwanese's earliest memories more often focus on others (Wang, 2006). These findings dovetail with research showing that European-American cultures tend to be individually oriented, whereas many Asian cultures tend to be other-oriented (Lehman, Chiu, & Schaller, 2004).

Unfortunately, proponents of some fringe psychological treatments have largely ignored the scientific evidence concerning infantile amnesia. Many advocates of hypnotic age regression, which Nadean Cool's therapist used, claim to be able to retrieve memories from well before age 2, sometimes even before birth (Nash, 1987). At least one therapist even tried to recover his female client's memory of being trapped as an egg in her mother's fallopian tube prior to fertilization (*Frontline*, 1995). Similarly, proponents of the school of Scientology, popular among many Hollywood celebrities, believe that long-buried memories of negative statements overheard by fetuses, embryos, and even zygotes can be reactivated in adulthood, especially under stress. These memories, Scientologists claim, can trigger low self-esteem and other psychological problems (Carroll, 2003; Gardner, 1958). For example, if a fetus overhears her mother say "I hate you" during a bitter argument with her husband, the grown adult may later misinterpret this statement as referring to her rather than to her father. Fortunately, for both fetuses and adults, there's no evidence for this extraordinary claim. Fetuses can't accurately make out most sentences they hear from outside the womb (Smith et al., 2003), let alone remember them decades later.

No one knows for sure why the first few years of our lives are lost to us forever, but psychological science offers several promising leads (Bauer, 2006). The hippocampus, which as we learned plays a key role in long-term memory, especially episodic memory, is only partially developed in infancy (Mishkin, Malamut, & Bachevalier, 1984; Schacter & Moscovitch, 1984;

Zola, 1997). So before age 2 or so, we may not possess the brain architecture needed to retain memories of events (Josselyn & Frankland, 2012).

Also, as infants, we possess little or no concept of self (Fivush, 1988; Howe & Courage, 1993). Before about 18 months of age, infants can't recognize themselves in mirrors (Lewis, Brooks-Gunn, & Jaskir, 1985). Without a well-developed schema of self, infants may not be able to encode or store memories of their experiences in a meaningful fashion. So these experiences will never be remembered.

Research suggests that other than humans, gorillas, orangutans, dolphins, and perhaps elephants are among the handful of species that exhibit mirror self-recognition—often regarded as one important indicator of the presence of a self-concept (Plotnik, de Waal, & Reiss, 2006). Here a baby reacts to his mirror image.

 Study and **Review** in **MyPsychLab**

Assess Your Knowledge — FACT or FICTION?

1. Most young children underestimate their memory abilities.   **True / False**
2. Children as young as two months have implicit memories of their experiences. **True / False**
3. Most adults can accurately recall events that took place before they were 3 years old.   **True / False**
4. One explanation for infantile amnesia is that the hippocampus is only partially developed in infancy.   **True / False**

Answers: 1. F; 2. T; 3. F; 4. T

False Memories: When Good Memory Goes Bad

12 Identify factors that influence people's susceptibility to false memories and memory errors.

13 Describe some of the real-world implications of false memories and memory errors.

We generally trust our memories to provide us with an accurate recounting of our past. In many cases, our memories do the job well enough. Over the past few decades, however, researchers have shown that our memories can be more fallible than any of us could have imagined. Moreover, we're often far more confident of our recollections of events than we should be.

False Memories

At first blush, our everyday experience strongly suggests that we can safely rely on our memories, because many of our recollections seem to be as crisp as scenes from a movie. Do you remember where you were and what you were doing when you heard about the terrorist attacks on September 11, 2001? Most Americans say yes, and many say that, even today, they can "relive" those frightening moments with astonishing clarity. Many older Americans report equally vivid memories of the assassination of President John F. Kennedy on November 22, 1963. Powerful memories of the attempted assassination of President Ronald Reagan (Pillemer, 1984), the explosion of the space shuttle *Challenger* (McCloskey, Wible, & Cohen, 1988), and the deaths of Princess Diana (Krackow, Lynn, & Payne, 2005–2006) and singer Michael Jackson are other examples.

FLASHBULB MEMORIES. It's no wonder that Roger Brown and James Kulik (1977) referred to these recollections as **flashbulb memories**, emotional memories that seem so vivid that people appear to recount them in remarkable, even photographic, detail.

flashbulb memory
emotional memory that is extraordinarily vivid and detailed

A photo of then-president George W. Bush being told about the September 11 terrorist attacks by his chief of staff, Andrew Card. Two months later, while answering a question, Bush said that he vividly recalled watching the first plane hit the World Trade Center tower on television. Yet Bush's recollection must have been a false memory, because video footage of the first plane hitting the tower wasn't released until a number of days after the attacks (Chabris & Simons, 2010; Greenberg, 2004).

REPLICABILITY ▶

Can the results be duplicated in other studies?

OCCAM'S RAZOR ▶

Does a simpler explanation fit the data just as well?

They further argued that flashbulb memories don't decay over time like ordinary memories. So flashbulb memories suggest that our memories sometimes operate like video cameras or DVDs after all, right?

Maybe not. Ulric Neisser and Nicole Harsch (1992) decided to find out whether extremely vivid memories were accurate by studying college students' recollection of the explosion of the space shuttle *Challenger* in 1986. For many people, this was a particularly tragic and memorable event because, for the first time, a non-astronaut—a schoolteacher named Christa McAuliffe—was on board. Neisser and Harsch discovered that two and a half to three years after the *Challenger* explosion, 75 percent of college students' reports of the event didn't match their recollections from only a few days following this event. Moreover, about a third of the students' stories changed dramatically over time. Consider this recollection from one of their participants almost immediately after the *Challenger* explosion.

Initial Recollection (January 1986): "I was in my religion class and some people walked in and started talking about the explosion. I didn't know any details except that it had exploded and the schoolteacher's students had all been watching, which I thought was so sad. Then after class I went to my room and watched the TV program talking about it and I got all the details from that."

Here's the recollection from the *same* student more than two and a half years later:

Later Recollection (September 1988): "When I first heard about the explosion I was sitting in my freshman dorm room with my roommate and we were watching TV. It came on a news flash and we were both totally shocked. I was really upset and went upstairs to talk to a friend of mine, and then I called my parents."

When Neisser and Harsch presented students with their written recollections from several years earlier, some insisted that they must have been written by someone else! The authors coined the term *phantom flashbulb memory* to capture the idea that many seeming flashbulb memories are false. This phenomenon has been replicated with a group of students asked to recall their memory of the 1995 verdict of the O. J. Simpson murder trial (Schmolk, Buffalo, & Squire, 2000). After 32 months, 40 percent of the memory reports contained "major distortions" relative to their initial recollection only three days after the verdict. Still, flashbulb memories typically contain substantial kernels of accuracy. For example, people who learned about the terrorist attacks of September 11, 2001, were usually correct in their recall about where they were when they heard about the attacks, but often wrong about what they were doing at the time or who told them (Rimmele, Davachi, & Phelps, 2012).

This research indicates that so-called flashbulb memories change over time, just like all other memories. Moreover, the rate of forgetting flashbulb memories is similar to that of ordinary memories (Hirst et al., 2009; Talarico & Rubin, 2007). Flashbulb memories remind us that much as our memories may seem to work like video cameras, they don't. We don't need to invoke an entirely new set of explanations to explain vivid recollections. The most parsimonious hypothesis is that flashbulb memories aren't a separate class of memories; they're much like other memories, just more intense.

SOURCE MONITORING: WHO SAID THAT? Think back to a conversation you had yesterday with a friend. How do you know it really happened? About 25 percent of undergraduates report experiencing a distinct memory of an event but feeling unsure of whether it actually occurred or was part of a dream (Rassin, Merckelbach, & Spaan, 2001). This is an example of a **source monitoring confusion**, a lack of clarity about the origin of a memory.

According to a *source monitoring* view of memory (Johnson, Hashtroudi, & Lindsay, 1993; Johnson & Raye, 1981), we try to identify the origins of our memories by seeking cues about how we encoded them. Source monitoring refers to our efforts to identify the origins (sources) of a memory. We rely on source monitoring to recall which information source provided the information—did you hear it on the news or from a friend? Have you ever started to tell someone a joke or story only to realize that he or she

ce monitoring confusion
    ïty about the origin of a memory

was the one who told it to you in the first place? Whenever we try to figure out whether a memory really reflects something that happened or whether we merely imagined it, we're engaging in source monitoring. For example, we typically rely on cues regarding how vivid and detailed our memories are. All things being equal, memories of our recent past that are more vivid and detailed are more likely to reflect actual events (Lynn et al., 2003a), although as we've learned, even these memories are sometimes inaccurate. If our memory of a conversation with a friend on campus is vague and fuzzy, we may begin to wonder whether it really happened or was merely a product of our overactive imagination.

In many cases, source monitoring works well by helping us avoid confusing our memories with our fantasies. This ability comes in handy when we're trying to recall whether we actually punched our obnoxious boss in the nose or just fantasized about doing so. Yet because cues regarding the vividness and detail of memories are far from perfect, source monitoring isn't perfect either. We can sometimes be fooled, and, as we've learned, false memories can result.

Source monitoring failure can account for why some people mistakenly recall that they engaged in an action even though they didn't perform the action, but instead observed someone else doing it (Lindner et al., 2010). Consider another example of source monitoring failure. Foster and Garry (2012) asked participants to build LEGO vehicles (such as a police car or train) and to complete some but not all steps in constructing the vehicles. While participants kept their eyes closed, the experimenter completed the steps the participants hadn't completed. When tested the following day, participants confidently remembered having completed steps they hadn't actually completed. Participants mentally filled in the actions related to the missing steps and later confused what they believed had occurred with their real actions.

A source monitoring perspective helps us understand why some people are especially receptive to false memories. Remember the memory illusion test with all of the sleepy words earlier in the chapter? (No, it's not a false memory.) Some studies suggest that people who are fantasy-prone are more likely to experience memory illusions on this task (Geraerts et al., 2005; Winograd, Peluso, & Glover, 1998). So are the elderly (Jacoby & Rhodes, 2006) and even people who believe they've been abducted by space aliens (Clancy et al., 2002) or report improbable memories of a previous life (Meyersburg et al., 2009). All of these groups of people, as well as young children (Peters et al., 2007; Thierry & Spence, 2002), are probably more likely to confuse their imaginations with reality.

Many other memory errors reflect confusion in source monitoring. Take the phenomenon of **cryptomnesia** (literally meaning "hidden memory"), whereby we mistakenly forget that one of "our" ideas originated with someone else. Some cases of plagiarism probably reflect cryptomnesia (Brown & Murphy, 1989). When the late George Harrison, a former member of the Beatles, wrote his hit song "My Sweet Lord," he apparently forgot that the melody of the song was virtually identical to that of the Chiffons' song "He's So Fine," which had appeared about ten years earlier. After the copyright owners of the Chiffons' song sued Harrison, he used cryptomnesia as a legal defense, arguing that he mistakenly believed he'd invented the melody himself. The judge awarded money to the copyright owners of the original song, although he ruled that Harrison probably didn't commit the plagiarism intentionally.

Implanting False Memories in the Lab

Three decades ago, psychologist Elizabeth Loftus (Loftus, 1979; Loftus, Miller, & Burns, 1978; Wells & Loftus, 1984) opened researchers' eyes to the dramatic effects of misleading suggestions on both everyday memories and eyewitness reports. She found that **suggestive memory techniques**—procedures that strongly encourage people to recall memories—often create recollections that were never present to begin with (Lynn et al., 2003a).

In 2006, Kaavya Viswanathan, a Harvard sophomore and author of the book *How Opal Mehta Got Kissed, Got Wild, and Got a Life,* was accused of plagiarism when reporters revealed that numerous passages in her book were suspiciously similar to those in several other books. Viswanathan's defense was cryptomnesia. She claimed to have read these books and forgotten their source (she also claimed to possess a photographic memory, making it difficult for her to forget the original passages).

cryptomnesia
failure to recognize that our ideas originated with someone else

suggestive memory technique
procedure that encourages patients to recall memories that may or may not have taken place

?

Watch in **MyPsychLab** the **Video:**
Elizabeth Loftus: Memory

Her pioneering work demonstrated that our memories are far more malleable than most psychologists had assumed.

MISINFORMATION EFFECT. In a classic study, Loftus and John Palmer (1974) showed participants brief clips of traffic accidents and asked them to estimate the speed of the vehicles involved. They varied the wording of the question "About how fast were the cars going when they _____ each other?" by inserting different words in the blank, like *contacted*, *hit*, *bumped*, *collided*, and *smashed*. When the inserted word suggested a greater degree of contact between the cars, participants reported higher speeds. For example, when they heard the word *smashed*, they rated the speed as nine miles per hour faster than when they heard the word *contacted* (40.8 when *smashed* was used versus 31.8 when *contacted* was used). In a second study, Loftus and Palmer replicated these findings by using the words *hit* and *smashed* and a week later asked participants if they recalled seeing any broken glass at the scene. Sure enough, compared with those who heard the *hit* word, participants who heard the *smashed* word more often reported seeing glass.

REPLICABILITY ▶
Can the results be duplicated
in other studies?

In a later study, Loftus and her colleagues asked participants to watch a slide sequence of an accident in which a car passed through an intersection and struck a pedestrian. They asked participants questions about the event. Some of the questions contained misleading suggestions. For example, in the actual slide sequence, the sign at the intersection was a yield sign. Yet Loftus and her colleagues phrased one of the questions "While the car was stopped at the stop sign, did a red Datsun pass by?" Afterward, participants who received the misleading questions were more likely to say that the sign was a stop sign than a yield sign. In contrast, most participants who didn't receive the phony information recalled the yield sign accurately. This phenomenon is the **misinformation effect**: Providing people with misleading information after an event can lead to fictitious memories (Loftus, Miller, & Burns, 1978). Older adults are particularly vulnerable to misinformation effects, partly due to difficulties with source monitoring (Roediger & Geraci, 2007)

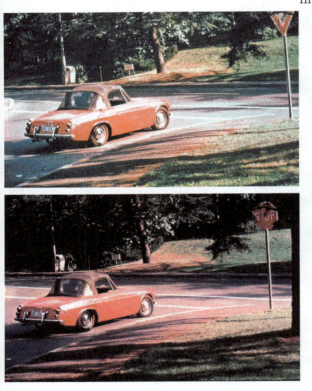

In the 1978 study by Loftus and her colleagues, participants saw a car stopped at a yield sign (*top*). Yet when prompted with the information that the car had been stopped at a stop sign (*bottom*), they later "remembered" seeing the stop sign.

LOST IN THE MALL AND OTHER IMPLANTED MEMORIES. Loftus's famous "lost in the mall study" demonstrates that we can implant elaborate memories of a made-up event that never happened. Loftus and her colleagues (Loftus, Coan, & Pickrell, 1996; Loftus & Pickrell, 1995) asked the relatives of 24 participants to describe events that participants had experienced in childhood. They then presented participants with a booklet that contained the details of three events the relatives reported, along with a fourth event that the relatives verified never occurred: being lost in a shopping mall as a child. Participants wrote about each event they could recall. In follow-up interviews, a quarter of the participants claimed to distinctly remember being lost in the mall as a child. Some even provided surprisingly detailed accounts of the event.

Many investigators followed in the path of Loftus's groundbreaking work. Using suggestive questions and statements, researchers have successfully implanted memories of a wide variety of events in about 20 to 25 percent of college students, ranging from accidentally spilling a bowl of punch on the parents of the bride at a wedding reception, to surviving a serious animal attack, to being bullied in childhood (Bernstein et al., 2005; DeBreuil, Garry, & Loftus, 1998; Hyman, Husband, & Billings, 1995; Mazzoni et al., 1999; Porter, Yuille, & Lehman, 1999).

Do participants' reports in false memory studies reflect actual changes in their memories? Or could the reports merely reflect demand characteristics, attempts to please experimenters or give experimenters the answers participants believe they're seeking? Probably not, because even when researchers have told participants they implanted the memories, many continue to insist that the memories are genuine (Ceci et al., 1994). Moreover, the fact that many investigators, using different experimental

misinformation effect
creation of fictitious memories by providing misleading information about an event after it ~lace

designs, have replicated the finding that memories are malleable provides strong support for the claim that memory is reconstructive.

EVENT PLAUSIBILITY. As we might imagine, there are limits to how far we can go in implanting false memories. How likely is it you could be convinced that you won the lottery or an international trivia contest last year? Not likely, we suspect. That's because it is easier to implant a memory of something that's plausible than something that isn't (Pezdek, Finger, & Hodge, 1997). In addition, it is easier to implant a fictitious memory of an event from the distant past for which we have hazy or no recall than of an event from the recent past we are likely to remember.

MEMORIES OF IMPOSSIBLE OR IMPLAUSIBLE EVENTS. Most of the studies we've reviewed are open to at least one major criticism. Perhaps participants actually experienced the suggested event, such as being lost in a mall, but forgot about it until the suggestion reminded them of it. Studies of impossible or highly implausible memories rule out this alternative hypothesis. Indeed, researchers have devised clever *existence proofs* demonstrating that it's possible to create elaborate memories of events that never happened. Here are some "memorable" examples.

One team of researchers (Wade et al., 2002) showed participants a fake photograph of a hot-air balloon into which they'd pasted photographs of the participant and a relative. Family members had confirmed that the participant had never experienced a hot-air balloon ride. The investigators showed participants the fake photograph and asked them to describe "everything you can remember without leaving anything out, no matter how trivial it may seem." After two further interviews, 50 percent of participants recalled at least some of the fictitious hot-air balloon ride, and some embellished their reports with sensory details, like seeing a road from high up in the air. In another study (Braun, Ellis, & Loftus, 2002), investigators showed participants ads for Disneyland that featured Bugs Bunny and asked them about seeing Bugs at Disneyland as a child. Sixteen percent of participants said they remembered meeting and shaking hands with Bugs Bunny; some even remembered hearing him say, "What's up, doc?" What's so strange about that? Bugs Bunny is a Warner Brothers, not a Disney, cartoon character, so the memories must have been false.

In another study, researchers (Mazzoni et al., 2001) provided Italian undergraduate students with false newspaper articles implying that cases of demonic possession were more common in their culture than previously thought, thereby increasing the plausibility of such an event. After receiving this fictional information, 18 percent of the students came to believe that they probably had witnessed a demonic possession.

Generalizing from the Lab to the Real World

Suggestions can affect not only memory, but also our preferences and behaviors. Consider what is known as the "asparagus study" (Laney et al., 2008). The researchers provided participants with the suggestion that they loved to eat asparagus as children. Participants who received this suggestion became more confident that they liked asparagus the first time they had tried it compared with participants who received no such suggestion. After participants acquired these new (false) beliefs, they reported an increased liking for asparagus, a greater desire to eat asparagus in a restaurant, and a willingness to pay more for asparagus in the grocery store. In another study, investigators suggested to some participants that they'd become ill in childhood after eating egg salad (Geraerts et al., 2008). Later on, these participants ate significantly fewer egg salad sandwiches than participants who didn't receive this suggestion—even up to four months later.

◀ **REPLICABILITY**
Can the results be duplicated in other studies?

◀ **RULING OUT RIVAL HYPOTHESES**
Have important alternative explanations for the findings been excluded?

Research using fake photographs shows that we can "rewrite" parts of people's life histories. In one case, participants became convinced that they'd experienced a hot-air balloon ride as a child even when they hadn't.

 Simulate in **MyPsychLab** the **Experiment:** Creating False Memories

Ronald Cotton (*right*) was identified, convicted, and imprisoned for raping a college student in 1984. In 1995, a DNA test showed conclusively that Bobby Poole (*left*) was the actual rapist, and Cotton was released after spending 11 years in prison for a crime he didn't commit.

? Even though the teller may have a good look at the face of this bank robber, her eyewitness memory of his face is likely to be impaired by what factor? (See answer upside down at bottom of page.)

Watch in **MyPsychLab** the **Video:**
Thinking Like a Psychologist: Police Line-Up

Still, we should be cautious about generalizing experimental findings to the real world, because these laboratory studies may be low in *external validity*. Ethical limitations render it difficult, if not impossible, to determine whether we can implant memories of sexual and physical abuse inside or outside the laboratory. Yet research on false memories raises the possibility that memory errors bear important implications for real-world situations, like eyewitness identifications. Do they?

EYEWITNESS TESTIMONY. As of today, 306 prisoners have been acquitted of a crime and released because their DNA didn't match genetic material left by perpetrators. Consider Gene Bibbons, "Number 125," sentenced to life imprisonment for the sexual assault of a 16-year-old girl. The victim described the perpetrator as a man with long curly hair, wearing jeans, even though Bibbons had cropped hair at the time and was wearing shorts. Still, she identified Bibbons as the assailant. Years later, investigators located a biological specimen, and genetic testing confirmed that Bibbons's DNA didn't match the DNA at the crime scene. After maintaining his innocence for 16 years, Bibbons walked out of prison a free man.

If there's a thread that ties Bibbons to the more than 300 other unjustly imprisoned individuals, it's that an eyewitness misidentified him as guilty. More than 75 percent of prisoners acquitted by DNA testing are identified mistakenly by eyewitnesses (Duckworth et al., 2011; Schec, Neufeld, & Dwyer, 2000) and in about a third of cases by two or more eyewitnesses (Arkowitz & Lilienfeld, 2009). The fact that eyewitness misidentification is the most common cause of wrongful convictions (The Innocence Project, n.d.; Duke, Lee, & Pager, 2009) isn't so surprising when we consider that when witnesses seem sure they've identified a culprit, juries tend to believe them (Smith et al., 2001; Wells & Bradford, 1998). Even attorneys and judges are unduly influenced by confident yet inaccurate eyewitness testimony (Van Wallendael et al., 2007). Contrary to popular (mis)conception, the correlation between witnesses' confidence and the accuracy of their testimony is often modest (Bothwell, Deffenbacher, & Brigham, 1987; Kassin, Ellsworth, & Smith, 1989; Sporer et al., 1995).

Eyewitnesses sometimes provide invaluable evidence, especially when they have ample time to observe the perpetrator under good lighting conditions, when the criminal isn't disguised, and when little time elapses between witnessing the crime and identifying the guilty party (Memon, Hope, & Bull, 2003). But eyewitness testimony is far from accurate when these optimal conditions aren't met. Moreover, eyewitness testimony is less likely to be accurate when people observe individuals of races different from their own (Kassin et al., 2001; Pezdek, O'Brien, & Wasson, 2011; Meissner & Brigham, 2001); when they talk to other witnesses (Pezdek et al., 2011; Wells, Memon, & Penrod, 2006); when they catch only a brief glimpse of the criminal (Wells, Memon, & Penrod, 2006); or when they view a crime under stressful circumstances, such as when they feel threatened (Deffenbacher et al., 2004; Valentine & Mesout, 2009). Sometimes eyewitnesses also mistake someone they've seen shortly before the crime for the actual criminal (Deffenbacher, Bornstein, & Penrod, 2006). Eyewitness accuracy is also often impaired by *weapon focus:* When a crime involves a weapon, people understandably tend to focus on the weapon rather than the perpetrator's appearance (Pickel, 2007; Steblay, 1992). Psychologists can play a critical role in educating jurors about the science of eyewitness recall so that they can better weigh the evidence (Arkowitz & Lilienfeld, 2009).

Psychologists also can inform juries about the best way to conduct eyewitness lineups, a common fixture of television crime shows. Most research suggests that identification of suspects is more accurate with *sequential lineups*, in which witnesses view one person at a time (Carlson, 2011; Lindsay & Wells, 1985) than with *simultaneous lineups*, in which witnesses make the selection from a group of both suspects and decoys (Steblay et al., 2001). The major problem is that when the real criminal isn't in the lineup, witnesses are likely to mistakenly identify the person who most closely resembles the guilty perpetrator. Nevertheless, because this finding hasn't been universally replicated, some researchers have argued that it may be premature to substitute sequential with simultaneous lineups in real-world settings (McQuiston-Surrett, Malpass, & Tredoux, 2006). In addition, lineups tend to be more accurate when police tell witnesses that the true criminal might or might not be present in the lineup, as this procedure reduces demand characteristics on witnesses to "help" investigators by fingering a guilty person (Wells et al., 2006). A final crucial consideration is that the person who conducts the lineup should be blind to who the suspect is, because this knowledge could unintentionally bias eyewitnesses.

◄ **REPLICABILITY**
Can the results be duplicated in other studies?

Suggestibility and Child Testimony

Probably because they sometimes confuse fantasy with reality, children are especially vulnerable to suggestions to recall events that didn't occur (Ceci & Bruck, 1993). In one study, researchers (Otgaar et al., 2009) implanted memories in children of having been abducted by a UFO by providing them with newspaper articles suggesting that such experiences are relatively common. Younger children, 7–8 years old, were more likely to report "memories" of being abducted than were children 11–12 years old. Stephen Ceci and his colleagues (Ceci et al., 1994) asked preschool children to imagine real and fictitious events. Once a week, for a total of seven to ten interviews, they instructed children to "think real hard" about whether the events had occurred. For example, they asked the children to try to remember made-up events, like going to the hospital with a mousetrap on their fingers. Fifty-eight percent of children generated stories regarding at least one of these fictitious events. Interestingly, about a quarter of the children continued to insist that their memories were real even when their parents and the experimenter assured them that the events never happened. The fact that children cling to their false memories even when an authority figure tells them the memories are wrong suggests that such memories can be convincing. These findings are important for another reason: Many social workers and police officers who suspect that a child was abused question the child about this abuse repeatedly. Repeated questioning comes with a risk: Children may give investigators the answers they're seeking, even if the answers are wrong. Children and young adolescents also are more likely than adults to make a positive identification from a lineup, particularly when the real culprit is absent from the lineup (Keast, Brewer, & Wells, 2007).

This research carries a key practical suggestion: Psychologists and other health care workers need to use less suggestive procedures when questioning children. Indeed, most research demonstrates that many children can provide reasonably accurate memories when they're simply asked about an event once in a nonleading fashion (for example, "Can you tell me what happened?") (Ornstein et al., 1997).

Children's memories are also affected by schemas, especially their expectations about how others will act. To demonstrate this point, two researchers (Leichtman & Ceci, 1995) provided 3- to 6-year-old children with information that led them to hold a negative stereotype about a man, "Sam Stone," before he visited the classroom several weeks later. The researchers told the children various stories about Sam, a clumsy character who did things like accidentally break Barbie dolls and rip sweaters. When Sam actually visited, he wasn't clumsy at all, but the next day, the teacher showed the children a soiled teddy bear and a torn book. Afterward, the investigators interviewed some of the children on different occasions about what Sam did during the visit. They asked the children suggestive questions, such as "Did Sam Stone rip the book, or did he use scissors?" Then, during the final interview, they asked children to describe Sam's visit. In response to open-ended questions, 46 percent of 3- and 4-year-olds and 30 percent of 5- and 6-year-olds reported that Sam had ripped the book, soiled the teddy bear, or both. With further prompts, 72 percent of the younger preschoolers and 44 percent of the older preschoolers responded to the suggestion. Children in a control condition, who weren't interviewed or given negative stereotypes, rarely made these errors.

Factoid

Many therapists who treat patients with suspected sexual abuse histories prescribe "survivor books"—self-help books that often contain checklists of supposed telltale symptoms of past sexual abuse, such as fears of sex, low self-esteem, insecurity about one's appearance, or excessive dependency (Lynn et al., 2003b). Yet research shows that most of these symptoms are so vague and general that they can apply to virtually everyone (Emery & Lilienfeld, 2004).

THE FALSE MEMORY CONTROVERSY. One of the most divisive controversies in all of psychology centers on the possibility that memories of child abuse and other traumatic experiences can be shaped by suggestive techniques in psychotherapy. In fact, debates concerning false memories have become so bitter that some writers have referred to them as the "memory wars" (Crews, 1990).

On one side of the battle are memory recovery therapists, who claim that patients *repress* memories of traumatic events, such as childhood sexual abuse, and then *recover* them years, even decades, later (Brown, Scheflin, & Hammond, 1997). Most followers of Sigmund Freud believe that repression is a form of forgetting in which people push painful memories into their unconscious. According to recovered memory therapists, these repressed memories are the root cause of current life problems that must be addressed to make progress in psychotherapy (McHugh, 2008; McNally, 2003). Some, like Nadean Cool's therapist, claim that their clients have repressed memories of murderous satanic cults, even though investigations by the FBI have consistently failed to unearth any evidence of the cults (Lanning, 1989). By the mid-1990s, approximately 25 percent of psychotherapists in the United States and the United Kingdom reported in surveys (Polusny & Follette, 1996; Poole et al., 1995) that they used two or more potentially suggestive procedures, including dream interpretation, repeated questioning, guided imagery, and hypnosis, to help patients who had no recollection of sexual abuse to recover memories of it. More recent data from Canada point to similar numbers (Legault & Laurence, 2007), suggesting that these techniques are still widely used in many quarters.

Lined up on the opposing side of the false memory debate is a growing chorus of researchers who claim that there's slim evidence that people repress traumatic memories, including childhood sexual abuse. These researchers point to a mounting body of evidence that painful memories, such as memories of the Holocaust (Golier et al., 2002), are well remembered and, if anything, remembered too well (Loftus, 1993; McNally, 2003; Pope et al., 2007. According to them, there's serious reason to doubt that many memories can be repressed and then recovered years or decades later. These researchers have also voiced serious concerns about whether suggestive procedures can lead patients to conclude erroneously that family members abused them in childhood. Indeed, hundreds of individuals have been separated from their families, and in some cases even imprisoned, solely on the basis of recovered memory claims of child sexual abuse. According to this perspective, at least some memory recovery techniques can cause harm (Lilienfeld, 2007).

From a scientific and ethical standpoint, this state of affairs is deeply troubling, often tragic. Given what we now know about how fallible human memory is, recovered memories of child abuse shouldn't be trusted completely unless they're accompanied by clear-cut corroborating evidence. In the past decade, the false memory controversy has subsided somewhat, largely because a consensus has emerged that suggestive procedures can create false memories of childhood events in many, although perhaps not all, psychotherapy clients.

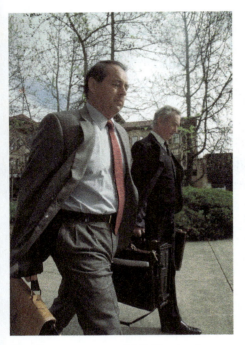

Gary Ramona, a successful California wine executive, was accused by his daughter, Holly, of sexually abusing her as a child. Siding with her daughter, his wife divorced him. Ramona eventually won a half-million-dollar lawsuit against Holly's psychiatrist. The jury agreed with Ramona that the psychiatrist's suggestive techniques had triggered false memories of sexual abuse in Holly.

Learning Tips: Getting the Science of Memory to Work for Us

As we've learned throughout this chapter, our memories are remarkable. They can allow us to recall staggering amounts of information, even over years and decades. Yet as we've also discovered, our memories are far from perfect. Many of our memories interfere with each other or fade with the passage of time; our schemas can bias our memories of events; and misleading information, such as leading questions, can lead us to "remember" occurrences that never happened (Schacter, 2001).

But none of this should lead us to despair. Indeed, as the story of Joshua Foer teaches us, even ordinary people can acquire extraordinary memories in at least some domains (Foer, 2011). Foer was a reporter with a perfectly normal memory who decided to see how much he could enhance his recall using mnemonic devices, including the method of loci. After a solid year of training, Foer won the U.S. Memory Championship, memorizing (among other things) the exact order of a full deck of 52 cards in 1 minute and 40 seconds.

Although few of us have the time or determination of Foer to become memory whizzes, there's good news: The science of memory we've encountered in this chapter can help us learn material—and study—more effectively and efficiently. So drawing on what we've learned, we leave you with a set of evidence-based tips to bear in mind as you study the material in this course—and other courses. These tips will be helpful for acquiring and consolidating your memories not only in college, but also in everyday life.

1. **Distributed versus massed study.** Spread out your study time—review your notes and textbook in increments rather than cramming.

2. **Testing effect.** Putting down what you've read, test yourself frequently on the material.

3. **Elaborative rehearsal.** Connect new knowledge with existing knowledge rather than simply memorizing facts or names.

4. **Levels of processing.** Work to process ideas deeply and meaningfully—avoid taking notes word for word from instructors' lectures or slides. Try capturing the information in your own words and using other concepts from the course.

5. **Mnemonic devices.** The more reminders or cues you can connect from your knowledge base to new material, the more likely you are to recall new material.

Journalist Joshua Foer had no background in mnemonics, but spent a year of his life mastering the method of loci and similar memory techniques. After doing so, he captured the 2006 U.S. Memory Championship by, among other things, memorizing the exact order of a deck of cards in 1 minute and 40 seconds (Foer, 2011).

Assess Your Knowledge   FACT or FICTION?

 Study and **Review** in **MyPsychLab**

1. Flashbulb memories almost never change over time.   True / False

2. People sometimes find it difficult to tell the difference between a true and a false memory.   True / False

3. It's almost impossible to create false memories of complex events, like witnessing a demonic possession.   True / False

4. One powerful way of creating false memories is to show people fake photographs of events that didn't happen.   True / False

5. Repeatedly asking children if they were abused leads to more accurate answers than asking only once.   True / False

Answers: 1. F, 2. T, 3. F, 4. T, 5. F

Your Complete Review System

How Memory Operates: The Memory Assembly Line

1 IDENTIFY THE WAYS THAT MEMORIES DO AND DON'T ACCURATELY REFLECT EXPERIENCES.

Memories can be surprisingly accurate over very long periods of time, but tend to be reconstructive rather than reproductive.

1. A(n) _____ _____ is a false but subjectively compelling memory.

2. Our memories are far more (reproductive/reconstructive) rather than (reproductive/reconstructive).

2 EXPLAIN THE FUNCTION, SPAN, AND DURATION OF EACH OF THE THREE MEMORY SYSTEMS.

Sensory memory, short-term memory, and long-term memory are stages of information processing that vary in how much information they hold and for how long they retain it. Short-term memory has a limited span of seven plus or minus two items that can be extended by grouping things into larger, meaningful units called chunks.

3. The three major systems of memory are measured by _____, or how much information each system can hold, and _____, or how long a period of time the system can hold information.

4. Map out the three-memory model process proposed by Atkinson and Shiffrin depicting memory flow.

5. _____ memory is the brief storage of perceptual information before it's passed to _____ memory.

6. _____ _____ is a type of sensory memory that applies to vision.

7. To extend the span of short-term memory, we organize information into meaningful groupings using a process called _____.

8. The tendency to remember words at the beginning of a list better than those in the middle of the list is known as the _____ _____.

3 DIFFERENTIATE THE SUBTYPES OF LONG-TERM MEMORY.

Explicit memory subtypes include semantic and episodic memory. Implicit memory types include procedural and priming memory.

9. _____ memory is the process of recalling information intentionally, and _____ memory is the process of recalling information we don't remember deliberately.

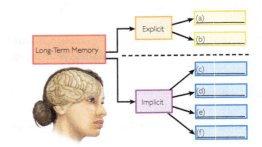

10. Complete the diagram to show the many subtypes of explicit and implicit memory.

The Three Processes of Memory

4 IDENTIFY METHODS FOR CONNECTING NEW INFORMATION TO EXISTING KNOWLEDGE.

Mnemonics are memory aids that link new information to more familiar knowledge. There are many kinds of mnemonics; they take effort to use but can assist recall.

11. The three major processes of memory are _____, _____, and _____.

12. _____ is the process of organizing information in a format that our memories can use.

13. If we use the phrase "Every good boy does fine" to remember the names of the lines (E, G, B, D, F) in the treble clef, we're using a(n) _____.

5 IDENTIFY THE ROLE THAT SCHEMAS PLAY IN THE STORAGE OF MEMORIES.

Schemas equip us with frames of reference for interpreting new situations. Nevertheless, they can sometimes lead to memory errors.

14. Organized knowledge structures that we've stored in memory are called _____.

6 DISTINGUISH WAYS OF MEASURING MEMORY.

Recall requires generating previously encountered information on our own, whereas recognition simply requires selecting the correct information from an array of choices. How quickly we relearn material previously learned and forgotten provides another measure of memory.

15. _____ is the reactivation or reconstruction of experiences from our memory stores.

16. _____ is reacquiring knowledge that we'd previously learned but largely forgotten over time.

17. The law of _____ _____ _____ _____ explains why cramming for a test is not the best way to remember things well in the long run.

18. _____ _____ is an experience of knowing that we know something but being unable to access it in our memory.

7 DESCRIBE HOW THE RELATION BETWEEN ENCODING AND RETRIEVAL CONDITIONS INFLUENCES REMEMBERING.

Individuals tend to remember better if they're tested under the same physical and emotional conditions as when they encoded the information.

19. _____ _____ is the phenomenon of remembering something better when the conditions under which we retrieve information are similar to the conditions under which we encoded it.

20. In _____ _____, our retrieval of memories is superior when the external context of the original memories matches the retrieval context, as shown in the figure below.

The Biology of Memory

8 DESCRIBE THE ROLE OF LONG-TERM POTENTIATION IN MEMORY.

Most scientists believe that long-term potentiation—a gradual strengthening of the connections among neurons from repetitive stimulation—plays a key role in the formation of memories and memory storage.

21. Lashley's studies with rats demonstrated that memory (is/isn't) located in one part of the brain.

22. Today most scientists agree that LTP plays a key role in _____.

23. The _____ plays a key role in forming lasting memories.

9 DISTINGUISH DIFFERENT TYPES OF AMNESIA AND THE RELEVANCE OF AMNESIA TO THE BRAIN'S ORGANIZATION OF MEMORY.

Evidence from studies of amnesia patients demonstrates that there are distinct memory systems, because people with amnesia for declarative memory often still form new procedural memories.

Retrograde amnesia causes forgetting of past experiences, whereas anterograde amnesia prevents us from forming memories of new experiences.

24. A person with _____ amnesia has lost some memories of his or her past.

25. The inability to encode new memories from our experiences is called _____ amnesia.

26. On this task, participants must trace a star while looking only at a mirror. What type of memory is this task designed to assess?

27. Damage to the hippocampus impairs _____ memory but leaves _____ memory intact.

28. Label and describe each component of the limbic system and its role in memory.

1) _____

2) _____

3) _____

4) _____

_____

_____

10 IDENTIFY THE KEY IMPAIRMENTS OF ALZHEIMER'S DISEASE

The memory loss of patients with Alzheimer's disease begins with that of recent events, with memories of events of the distant past typically being the last to go. Alzheimer's disease is marked by loss of synapses and acetylcholine neurons.

29. Senility (is/isn't) an unavoidable part of aging.

30. Alzheimer's disease accounts for only 50 to 60 percent of cases of _____, or severe memory loss.

The Development of Memory: Acquiring a Personal History

11 **IDENTIFY HOW CHILDREN'S MEMORY ABILITIES CHANGE WITH AGE.**

Infants display implicit memory for events; both infants' and children's memories are influenced by some of the same factors as adults' memory. Children's memory improves in part because of maturational changes in the brain that extend the span of memory. Over time, children become better able to use mnemonic and rehearsal strategies and become more aware of their memory limitations.

31. Over time, children develop their enhanced _____ skills that provide knowledge about their memory ability and limitations.

32. Rovee-Collier's experiments utilized operant conditioning to study infants' _____ _____.

33. How did Carolyn Rovee-Collier and others use infants' kicking behavior to study memory in infants?

34. Rovee-Collier found that infants' memories of the experience were surprisingly (general/specific).

35. _____ _____ is the inability to remember personal experiences that took place before the age of three or so.

36. European Americans report (earlier/later) first memories than do people from Taiwan.

37. There (is/isn't) evidence that we can remember things that took place at or prior to birth

38. The _____, which is critical for the establishment of long-term memory, is only partially developed in infancy.

39. Infants have little sense of _____, which makes it difficult for them to encode or store experiences in ways that are meaningful.

40. Which important ability relevant to the presence of a self-concept do humans and chimpanzees exhibit?

False Memories: When Good Memory Goes Bad

12 **IDENTIFY FACTORS THAT INFLUENCE PEOPLE'S SUSCEPTIBILITY TO FALSE MEMORIES AND MEMORY ERRORS.**

Flashbulb memories for highly significant events seem more crisp and vivid than do other memories but may be just as vulnerable to errors as other kinds of memory. One source of memory errors is ~~~monitoring difficulty; we can't always remember where or ~~~we learned something or whether it was a figment of our ~~~mes resulting in cryptomnesia. Our memories

for events are easily influenced by suggestions from others that the events happened differently than our observations suggested.

41. _____ _____ are memories that are extremely vivid and detailed and often highly emotional.

42. Whenever we try to figure out whether a memory reflects something that really happened, we're engaging in _____ _____.

43. The failure to recognize that our ideas come from another source is called _____.

44. Explain Elizabeth Loftus's misinformation effect and its influence on our memory.

45. Explain how we could have vivid memories of events we never experienced.

46. Research has shown that it's (impossible/possible) to implant memories of a made-up event that never happened.

13 **DESCRIBE SOME OF THE REAL-WORLD IMPLICATIONS OF FALSE MEMORIES AND MEMORY ERRORS.**

The fact that we're receptive to suggestions about whether and how events took place bears important implications for eyewitness testimony. Many scientists have argued that apparent "recovered memories" of early trauma may actually be due to the tendency of suggestive therapeutic procedures to induce false recollections.

47. The correlation between eyewitnesses' confidence in their testimony and the accuracy of this testimony is (modest /strong).

48. Research suggests that some _____ may be unintentionally implanting memories of traumatic events by means of suggestive procedures.

49. In an example proving that ordinary people can acquire extraordinary memory, Joshua Foer enhanced his recall using _____ _____, including the method of loci to win the U.S. Memory Championship.

50. Identify the five concepts below from memory research that can help you in studying for this course and others.

MEMORY CONCEPT	POINTER
1. _____	Spread out your study time—review your notes and textbook in increments rather than cramming.
2. _____	Connect new knowledge with existing knowledge rather than simply memorizing facts or names.
3. _____	Work to process ideas deeply and meaningfully—avoid taking notes word for word from instructors' lectures or slides. Try to capture the information in your own words.
4. _____	The more reminders or cues you can connect from your knowledge base to new material, the more likely you are to recall new material when tested.
5. _____	Test yourself frequently on the material you've read.

Apply Your Scientific Thinking Skills

Use your scientific thinking skills to answer the following questions, referencing specific scientific thinking principles and common errors in reasoning whenever possible.

1. As we've learned, our memories are often not as accurate as we assume. Think back to an early memory of an event (such as a childhood vacation) that you shared with friends or family. Write down as many details of the memory as you can. Now ask those friends or family members to write down their memories of the same event. In what ways do the memories differ? How can you explain the differences given what you now know about memory?

2. Search the Internet or popular magazines and find several examples of products designed to improve your memory, such as so-called "memory pills" or "smart pills." What kinds of claims do the promoters of these products make? Are their claims scientifically plausible given what you've learned about how memory works?

3. Locate at least three magazine articles or Internet sites that discuss repressed and recovered memory. What arguments do they make to support the existence and accuracy of these memories? Are these arguments supported by scientific knowledge? Are there rival hypotheses to consider? Explain your answers.

Further Your Understanding

EXTEND YOUR KNOWLEDGE WITH THE MYPSYCHLAB VIDEO SERIES

Watch these videos in MyPsychLab. Follow the "Video Series" link.

The Big Picture: The Woman Who Cannot Forget Hear the story of Jill Price, a woman with a phenomenal ability to remember things.

The Basics: Do You Remember When...? Learn how the brain is able to receive and retrieve information when it is needed.

Special Topics: When Memory Fails Learn about the famous case of "H. M.," the man whose memory only allowed him to live in 20-second increments.

Thinking Like a Psychologist: Police Lineup Learn how stress can affect the accuracy of eyewitness testimony.

What's In It for Me?: Making It Stick Perform well on tests by learning about study habits and whether "blocking" or "interleaving" is a better method for remembering information long term.

EXPERIENCE PSYCHOLOGICAL RESEARCH WITH MYPSYCHLAB SIMULATIONS

Access these simulations in MyPsychLab. Follow the "Simulations" link.

Digit Span Use chunking to increase your working memory capacity and recall series of digits and letters.

Serial Position Effect Test the limits of your working memory with lists.

What Do You Remember? Participate in a survey to discover how and what you remember and the strategies you use to aid long- and short-term memory.

APPLY YOUR CRITICAL THINKING SKILLS WITH MYPSYCHLAB WRITING ASSESSMENTS

Complete these writing assignments in MyPsychLab.

You are reading your text and studying for an upcoming exam in psychology. Identify and describe each step in the process required for remembering information from your text in order to do well on the exam. Discuss a strategy for improving memory and provide an example of how it could help you on the exam.

Answer Key

HOW MEMORY OPERATES: THE MEMORY ASSEMBLY LINE

1. memory illusion
2. reconstructive; reproductive
3. span; duration
4. a) sensory memory; b) short-term memory; c) long-term memory
5. Sensory; short-term
6. Iconic memory
7. chunking
8. primacy effect
9. Explicit; implicit
10. a) semantic; b) episodic; c) procedural; d) priming; e) conditioning; f) habituation

THE THREE PROCESSES OF MEMORY

11. encoding; storage; retrieval
12. Encoding
13. mnemonic
14. schemas
15. Retrieval
16. Relearning
17. distributed versus massed practice
18. Tip-of-the-tongue phenomenon
19. Encoding specificity
20. context-dependent learning

THE BIOLOGY OF MEMORY

21. isn't
22. learning
23. hippocampus
24. retrograde
25. anterograde
26. implicit memory
27. explicit; implicit
28. 1) thalamus; 2) corpus callosum; 3) amygdala/ helps us recall the emotions associated with fear-provoking events; 4) hippocampus/ helps us recall the events themselves
29. isn't
30. dementia

THE DEVELOPMENT OF MEMORY: ACQUIRING A PERSONAL HISTORY

31. metamemory
32. implicit memory
33. Rovee-Collier and others used mobiles to study infants' implicit memory. She conditioned infants to kick in a circular setting to see a mobile move. Although infants can't tell you they remember the mobile when they see it again, their kicking behavior gives us insight into whether they recall the mobile and for how long.
34. specific
35. Infantile amnesia
36. earlier
37. isn't
38. hippocampus
39. self
40. mirror self-recognition

FALSE MEMORIES: WHEN GOOD MEMORY GOES BAD

41. Flashbulb memories
42. source monitoring
43. cryptomnesia
44. The misinformation effect is the creation of fictitious memories by providing misleading information about an event after it takes place.
45. By using powerful suggestions and fake photographs, researchers have demonstrated that it's possible to create elaborate memories of events that never happened.
46. possible
47. modest
48. therapists
49. mnemonic devices
50. 1) Distributed versus massed study; 2) elaborative rehearsal; 3) levels of processing; 4) mnemonic devices; 5) testing effect

References

Abrari, K., Rashidy-Pour, A., Semnanian, S., & Fathollahi, Y. (2009). Post-training administration of corticosterone enhances consolidation of contextual fear memory and hippocampal long-term potentiation in rats. *Neurobiology of Learning and Memory, 91,* 260–265.

Altmann, E. M., & Schunn, C. D. (2002). Integrating decay and interference: A new look at an old interaction. In the *Proceedings of the 24th Annual Conference of the Cognitive Science Society.* Mahwah, NJ: Erlbaum.

Alvarez, C. A., & Brown, S. W. (2001). *What people believe about memory despite the research evidence.* Paper presented at the Annual Convention of the American Psychological Association, San Francisco, CA.

Alzheimer's Association. (2012). *Alzheimer's disease information: Facts and fiction.* Retrieved from http://www.psychtreatment.com/alzheimer.htm

American Psychiatric Association. (2000). *Diagnostic and statistical manual of mental disorders: DSM-IV-TR* (4th ed.). Washington, DC: Author.

Arkowitz, H., & Lilienfeld, S. O. (2009, January). Why science tells us not to rely on eyewitness accounts. *Scientific American Mind.* http://www.scientificamerican.com/article.cfm?id=do-the-eyes-have-it

Atkinson, R. C., & Shiffrin, R. M. (1968). Human memory: A proposed system and its control processes. In K. W. Spence and J. T. Spence (Eds.), *The psychology of learning and motivation: Advances in research and theory* (Vol. 2, pp. 89–195). New York, NY: Academic Press.

Baddeley, A. D. (1993). *Your memory: A user's guide* (2nd ed.). London, England: Lifecycle Publications.

Baddeley, A. D., & Hitch, G. J. (1974). Working memory. In G. A. Bower (Ed.), *Recent advances in learning and motivation* (Vol. 8, pp. 47–90). New York, NY: Academic Press.

Bahrick, H. P. (1984). Semantic memory content in permastore: Fifty years of memory for Spanish learning in school. *Journal of Experimental Psychology: General, 113,* 1–29.

Bahrick, H. P., Bahrick, P. O., & Wittlinger, R. P. (1975). Fifty years of memory for names and faces: A cross-sectional approach. *Journal of Experimental Psychology: General, 104,* 54–75.

Bahrick, H. P., & Phelps, E. (1987). Retention of Spanish vocabulary over 8 years. *Journal of Experimental Psychology: Learning, Memory, & Cognition, 13,* 344–349.

Bargh, J. A. (1994). The four horsemen of automaticity: Awareness, efficiency, intention, and control in social cognition. In R. S. Wyer, Jr., & T. K. Srull (Eds.), *Handbook of social cognition* (2nd ed., pp. 1–40). Hillsdale, NJ: Erlbaum.

Basil, J. A., Kamil, A. C., Balda, R., & Fite, K. V. (1996). Differences in hippocampal volume among food storing corvids. *Brain Behavior and Evolution, 47,* 156–154.

Bauer, P. J. (2006). Constructing a past in infancy: A neuro-developmental account. *Trends in Cognitive Sciences, 10,* 175–181.

Baxendale, S. (2004). Memories aren't made of this: Amnesia at the movies. *British Medical Journal, 18,* 1480–1483.

^ A., Gruneberg, M. M., Hyde, C., Shufflebottom, A., & Sykes, R. N. (2005). ...on of receptive and productive foreign vocabulary learning using the ...od: The role of image quality. *Memory, 13*(5), 458–471.

Bellezza, F. S. (1999). Mnemonic devices. In A. E. Kazdin (Ed.), *Encyclopedia of psychology.* Washington, DC: American Psychological Association.

Bent, S. (2008). Herbal medicine in the United States: Review of efficacy, safety, and regulation: Grand rounds at University of California, San Francisco Medical Center. *Journal of General Internal Medicine, 23,* 854–859.

Bernstein, D. M., Laney, C., Morris, E. K., & Loftus, E. F. (2005). False memories about food can lead to food avoidance. *Social Cognition, 23,* 11–34.

Biederman, I., Cooper, E. E., Fox, P. W., & Mahadevan, R. S. (1992). Unexceptional spatial memory in an exceptional memorist. *Journal of Experimental Psychology: Learning, Memory, and Cognition, 18,* 654–657.

Birks, J. (2012). Cholinesterase inhibitors for Alzheimer's disease. *Cochrane Library.* Retrieved from http://onlinelibrary.wiley.com/doi/10.1002/14651858.CD005593/pdf/standard

Bliss, T., Collingridge, G., & Morris, R. (2004). Long-term potentiation: Enhancing neuroscience for 30 years. Oxford, England: Oxford University Press.

Blumenfeld R. S., Parks C. M., Yonelinas, A.P., & Ranganath, C. (2010). Putting the pieces together: The role of dorsolateral prefrontal cortex in relational memory encoding. *Journal of Cognitive Neuroscience, 23,* 257–65.

Bond, C. F., Jr., Pitre, U., & Van Leeuwen, M. D. (1991). Encoding operations and the next-in-line effect. *Personality and Social Psychology Bulletin, 17,* 435–441.

Bothwell, R. K., Deffenbacher, K. A., & Brigham, J. C. (1987). Correlation of eyewitness accuracy and confidence: Optimality hypothesis revisited. *Journal of Applied Psychology, 72,* 691–695.

Bower, G. H. (1981). Mood and memory. *American Psychologist, 36,* 129–148.

Brainerd, C. J., Reyna, V. F., & Zember, E. (2011). Theoretical and forensic implications of developmental studies of the DRM illusion. *Memory & Cognition, 39*(3), 365–380. http://dx.doi.org/10.3758/s13421-010-0043-2

Bransford, J. D., & Johnson, M. K. (1972). Contextual prerequisites for understanding: Some investigations of comprehension and recall. *Journal of Verbal Learning and Verbal Behavior, 11,* 717–726.

Braun, K. A., Ellis, R., & Loftus, E. F. (2002). Make my memory. *Psychology and Marketing, 19,* 1–23.

Brown, A. S. (1991). A review of the tip of the tongue phenomenon. *Psychological Bulletin, 109,* 204–223.

Brown, A. S., & Murphy, D. R. (1989). Cryptomnesia: Delineating inadvertent plagiarism. *Journal of Experimental Psychology: Learning, Memory, and Cognition, 15,* 432–442.

Brown, D., Scheflin, A. W., & Hammond, C. (1997). *Trauma, memory, treatment, and the law.* New York, NY: Norton.

Brown, R., & Kulik, J. (1977). Flashbulb memories. *Cognition, 5,* 73–99.

Brown, R. W., & McNeill, D. (1966). The "tip-of-the-tongue" phenomenon. *Journal of Verbal Learning and Verbal Behavior, 5,* 325–337.

Brunet, A., Poundja, J., Tremblay, J., Bui, É., Thomas, É., Orr, S. P.,... Pitman, R. K. (2011). Trauma reactivation under the influence of propranolol decreases posttraumatic stress symptoms and disorder: 3 open-label trials. *Journal of Clinical Psychopharmacology, 31,* 547–550.

Cabeza, R., & Nyberg, L. (1997). Imaging cognition: An empirical review of PET studies with normal subjects. *Journal of Cognitive Neuroscience, 9*, 1–26.

Cahill, L., & McGaugh, J. L. (1995). A novel demonstration of enhanced memory associated with emotional arousal. *Consciousness and Cognition, 4*, 410–421.

Cahill, L., Prins, B., Weber, M., & McGaugh, J. L. (1994). Beta-adrenergic activation and memory for emotional events. *Nature, 371*, 702–704.

Carlson, C. A. (2011). Influence of a perpetrator's distinctive facial feature on eyewitness identification from simultaneous versus sequential lineups. *Applied Psychology in Criminal Justice, 7*(2), 77-92. Retrieved from http://search.proquest.com/docview/927683183?accountid=14168

Carney, R. N., & Levin, J. R. (2011). Delayed mnemonic benefits for a combined peg-word–keyword strategy, time after time, rhyme after rhyme. *Applied Cognitive Psychology, 25*(2), 204–211. http://dx.doi.org/10.1002/acp.1663

Carroll, R. T. (2003). *The skeptic's dictionary: A collection of strange beliefs, amusing deceptions, and dangerous delusions.* New York, NY: Wiley.

Ceci, S. J., & Bruck, M. (1993). Suggestibility of the child witness: A historical review and synthesis. *Psychological Bulletin, 113*, 403–439.

Ceci, S. J., Crotteau-Huffman, M., Smith, E., & Loftus, E. W. (1994). Repeatedly thinking about non-events. *Consciousness & Cognition, 3*, 388–407.

Cepeda, N. J., Pashler, H., Vul, E., Wixted, J. T., & Rohrer, D. (2006). Distributed practice in verbal recall tasks: A review and quantitative synthesis. *Psychological Bulletin, 132*, 354–380.

Chabris, C., & Simons, D. (2010). *The invisible gorilla and other ways our intuitions deceive us.* New York, NY: Crown.

Chase, W. G., & Ericsson, K. A. (1981). Skilled memory. In J. R. Anderson (Ed.), *Cognitive skills and their acquisition* (pp. 141–189). Hillsdale, NJ: Erlbaum.

Chase, W. G., & Simon, H. A. (1973). The mind's eye in chess. In W. G. Chase (Ed.), *Visual information processing* (pp. 215–281). New York, NY: Academic Press.

Clancy, S. A., McNally, R. J., Schachter, D. L., Lenzenweger, M. F., & Pitman, R. K. (2002). Memory distortion in people reporting abduction by aliens. *Journal of Abnormal Psychology, 111*, 455–461.

Clark, A., Nash, R. A., Fincham, G., & Mazzoni, G. (2012). Creating non-believed memories for recent autobiographical events. *PLoS One, 7*(3), e32998. Epub Mar 9.

Cohen, D., & Gunz, A. (2002). As seen by the other...: Perspectives on the self in the memories and emotional perceptions of Easterners and Westerners. *Psychological Science, 13*, 55–59.

Conrad, R. (1964). Acoustic confusion and immediate memory. *British Journal of Psychology, 55*, 75–84.

Cordón, L. A. (2005). *Popular psychology: An encyclopedia.* Westport, CT: Greenwood.

Corkin, S. (1984). Lasting consequences of bilateral medial temporal lobectomy: Clinical course and experimental findings. In S. M. Kosslyn & R. A. Anderson (Eds.), *Frontiers in cognitive neuroscience* (pp. 516–526). London, England: MIT Press.

Corkin, S., Amaral, D. G., Gonzalez, R. G., Johnson, K. A., & Hyman, B. T. (1997). H.M.'s medial temporal lobe lesion: Findings from magnetic resonance imaging. *Journal of Neuroscience, 17*, 3964–3979.

Cornell, E. H. (1980). Distributed study facilitates infants' delayed recognition memory. *Memory and Cognition, 8*, 539–542.

Cornell, E. H., & Bergstrom, L. I. (1983). Serial-position effects in infants' recognition memory. *Memory and Cognition, 11*, 494–499.

Cowan, N. (2001). The magical number 4 in short-term memory: A reconsideration of mental storage capacity. *Behavioral and Brain Sciences, 24*, 87–185.

Cowan, N., Lichty, W., & Grove, T. R. (1990). Properties of memory for unattended spoken syllables. *Journal of Experimental Psychology: Learning, Memory, & Cognition, 16*, 258–269.

Cracchiolo, J. J., Mori, T., Nazian, S., Tan, J., Potter, H. G., & Adrendash, G. W. (2007). Enhanced cognitive activity—over and above social or physical activity—is required to protect Alzheimer's mice against cognitive impairment, reduce Aβ deposition, and increase synaptic immunostaining. *Neurobiology of Learning & Memory, 88*, 277–294.

Craik, F. I. M., & Lockhart, R. (1972). Levels of processing: A framework for memory research. *Journal of Verbal Learning & Verbal Behavior, 11*, 671–684.

Crews, F. (1990). *The memory wars: Freud's legacy in dispute.* New York, NY: New York Times Review of Books.

Damasio, A. (2000). *The feeling of what happens: Body, emotion and the making of consciousness.* Cambridge, MA: MIT Press.

Dawes, R. M. (1988). *Rational choice in an uncertain world.* Orlando, FL: Harcourt-Brace Jovanovich.

DeBreuil, S. C., Garry, M., & Loftus, E. F. (1998). Tales from the crib: Age regression and the creation of unlikely memories. In S. J. Lynn & K. M. McConkey (Eds.) *Truth in memory* (pp. 137–160). New York, NY: Guilford Press.

Deese, J. (1959). On the prediction of occurrence of particular verbal intrusions in immediate recall. *Journal of Experimental Psychology, 58*, 17–22.

Deffenbacher, K. A., Bornstein, B. H., & Penrod, S. D. (2006). Mugshot exposure effects: Retroactive interference, mugshot commitment, source confusion, and unconscious transference. *Law and Human Behavior, 30*, 287–307.

Deffenbacher, K. A., Bornstein, B. H., Penrod, S. D., & McGorty, E. K. (2004). A meta-analytic review of the effects of high stress on eyewitness memory.

Law and Human Behavior, 28, 687–706.

DeKosky, S. T., Williamson, J. D., Fitzpatrick, A. L., Kronmal, R. A., Ives, D. G., Saxton, J. A.,... Furberg, C. D. (2008). Ginkgo biloba for prevention of dementia: A randomized controlled trial. *Journal of the American Medical Association, 300*, 2253–2262.

Donovan, J. J., & Radosevich, D. R. (1999). A meta-analytic review of the distribution of practice effect: Now you see it, now you don't. *Journal of Applied Psychology, 84*, 795–805.

Drabiak-Syed, K. (2011). Reining in the pharmacological enhancement train: We should remain vigilant about regulatory standards for prescribing controlled substances. *The Journal of Law, Medicine & Ethics, 39*(2), 272–279.

Duckworth, T. S., Kreiner, D. S., Stark-Wroblewski, K., & Marsh, P. A. (2011). Effects of experiencing the eyewitness identification procedure on juror decisions. *Journal of Police and Criminal Psychology, 26*(1), 11–19. http://dx.doi.org/10.1007/s11896-010-9071-x

Duke, S. B., Lee, A., & Pager, C. (2009). A picture's worth a thousand words: Conversational versus eyewitness testimony in criminal convictions. *Yale Faculty Scholarship Series*, Paper 829. Retrieved from http://digitalcommons.law.yale.edu/fss_papers/829

Ebbinghaus, H. (1885). *Memory: A contribution to experimental psychology.* New York, NY: Teachers College, Columbia University.

Ebert, P. L., & Anderson, N. D. (2009). Proactive and retroactive interference in young adults, healthy older adults, and older adults with amnestic mild cognitive impairment. *Journal of the International Neuropsychological Society, 15*(1), 83.

Ecke, P. (2009). The tip-of-the-tongue phenomenon as a window on (bilingual) lexical retrieval. In A. Pavlenko (Ed.), *The bilingual mental lexicon: Interdisciplinary approaches* (pp. 185–208). Bristol, England: Multilingual Matters.

Elsabagh, S., Hartley, D. E., Ali, O., Williamson, E. M., & File, S. E. (2005). Differential cognitive effects of *Ginkgo biloba* after acute and chronic treatment in healthy young volunteers. *Psychopharmacology, 179*(2), 437–446. http://dx.doi.org/10.1007/s00213-005-2206-6

Emery, C., & Lilienfeld, S. O. (2004). The validity of child sexual abuse survivor checklists in the popular psychology literature: A Barnum effect? *Professional Psychology: Science and Practice, 35*, 268–274.

Fitzgerald, D. A., Arnold, J. F., Becker, E. S., Speckens, A. E., Rinck, M., Rijpkema, M.,... Tendolkar, I. (2011). How mood challenges emotional memory formation: An fMRI investigation. *Neuroimage, 56*(3), 1783–1790.

Fivush, R. (1988). The functions of event memory: Some comments on Nelson and Barsalou. In U. Neisser & E. Winograd (Eds.), *Remembering reconsidered: Ecological and traditional approaches to the study of memory* (pp. 277–282). New York, NY: Cambridge University Press.

Flavell, J., Friedrichs, A., & Hoyt, J. (1970). Developmental changes in memorization processes. *Cognitive Psychology, 1*, 324–340.

Flavell, J. H., Beach, D. H., & Chinsky, J. M. (1966). Spontaneous verbal rehearsal in a memory test as a function of age. *Child Development, 37*, 283–299.

Foer, J. (2007). Memory. *National Geographic.* Retrieved from http://ngm.nationalgeographic.com/2007/11/memory/foer-text

Foer, J. (2011). *Moonwalking with Einstein: The art and science of remembering everything.* New York, NY: Penguin Press.

Foster, J. L., & Garry, M. (2012). Building false memories without suggestions. *The American Journal of Psychology, 125*(2), 225–232. http://dx.doi.org/10.5406/amerjpsyc.125.2.0225

Francis P. T. (2008). Glutamatergic approaches to the treatment of cognitive and behavioural symptoms of Alzheimer's disease. *Neurodegenerative Diseases, 5*, 241–243.

Frontline (1995). *Divided memories* [Video]. Retrieved from http://www.youtube.com/watch?v=VWoxGEr0nmw

Gardner, M. (1958). *Fads and fallacies in the name of science.* New York, NY: Dover.

Garnier-Dykstra, L., Caldeira, K. M., Vincent, K. B., O'Grady, K. E., & Arria, A. (2012). Nonmedical use of prescription stimulants during college: Four-year trends in exposure opportunity, use, motives, and sources. *Journal of American College Health, 60*(3), 226–234. http://dx.doi.org/10.1080/07448481.2011.589876

Geraerts, E., Bernstein, D. M., Merckelbach, H., Londers, C., Raymaekers, L., & Loftus, E. F. (2008). Lasting beliefs and their behavioral consequences. *Psychological Science, 19*, 749–753.

Geraerts, E., Smeets, E., Jelicic, M., van Heerden, J., & Merckelbach, H. (2005). Fantasy proneness, but not self-reported trauma is related to DRM performance of women reporting recovered memories of childhood sexual abuse. *Consciousness and Cognition, 14*, 602–612.

Ghetti, S., Lyons, K. E., Lazzarin, F., & Cornoldi, C. (2008). The development of metamemory monitoring during retrieval: The case of memory strength and memory absence. *Journal of Experimental Child Psychology, 99*, 157–181.

Gilovich, T. (1991). *How we know what isn't so: The fallibility of human reason in everyday life.* New York, NY: Free Press.

Gobet, F., & Simon, H. A. (1998). Expert chess memory: Revisiting the chunking hypothesis. *Memory, 6*, 225–255.

Godden, D. R., & Baddeley, A. D. (1975). Context dependency in two natural environments: On land and underwater. *British Journal of Psychology, 91*, 99–1

Gold, P. E., Cahill, L., & Wenk, G. L. (2002). Gingko biloba: A cognitive enhan

Psychological Science in the Public Interest, 3, 2–11.

Golier, J. A., Yehuda, R., Lupien, S. J., Harvey, P. D., Grossman, R., & Elkin, A. (2002). Memory performance in Holocaust survivors with posttraumatic stress disorder. *American Journal of Psychiatry, 159,* 1682–1688.

Goodwin, D. W. (1995). Alcohol amnesia. *Addiction, 90,* 315–317.

Goodwin, D. W., Powell, B., Brenner, D., Hoine, H., & Sterne, J. (1969). Alcohol and recall: State dependent effects in man. *Science, 163,* 1358–1360.

Gowin, J. (2009, September 29). How "smart drugs" enhance us. *Psychology Today.* Retrieved from http://www.psychologytoday.com/blog/you-illuminated/200909/how-smart-drugs-enhance-us

Gray, C. R., & Gummerman, K. (1975). The enigmatic eidetic image: A critical examination of methods, data, and theories. *Psychological Bulletin, 82,* 383–407.

Greely H., Sahakian, B., Harris, J., Kessler, R. C., Gazzaniga, M., Campbell, P., & Farah, M. J. (2008). Towards responsible use of cognitive-enhancing drugs by the healthy. *Nature, 456,* 702–705.

Greenberg, D. L. (2004). President Bush's False 'Flashbulb' Memory of 9/11/01. *Applied Cognitive Psychology, 18,* 363–370.

Gruneberg, M. M., and Sykes, R. N. (1991). Individual differences and attitudes to the keyword method of foreign language learning. *Language Learning Journal, 4,* 60–62.

Gulya, M., Galluccio, L., Wilk, A., & Rovee-Collier, C. (2001). Infants' long-term memory for a serial list: Recognition and reactivation. *Developmental Psychobiology, 38,* 174–185.

Haber, R. N. (1979). Twenty years of haunting eidetic imagery: Where's the ghost? *Behavioral and Brain Sciences, 2,* 583–629.

Haist, F., Shimamura, A. P., & Squire, L. R. (1992). On the relationship between recall and recognition memory. *Journal of Experimental Psychology: Learning, Memory, and Cognition, 18,* 691–702.

Harris, J. L., & Qualls, C. D. (2000). The association of elaborative or maintenance rehearsal with age, reading comprehension, and verbal working memory performance. *Aphasiology, 14,* 515–526.

Healy, A. F., & McNamara, D. S. (1996). Verbal learning and memory: Does the modal model still work? *Annual Review of Psychology, 47,* 143–172.

Hebb, D. O. (1949). *The organization of behavior.* New York, NY: Wiley.

Hirst, W., Phelps, E. A., Buckner, R. L., Budson, A. E., Cuc, A., Gabrieli, J. D. E.,... Vaidya, C. J. (2009). Long-term memory for the terrorist attack of September 11: Flashbulb memories, event memories, and the factors that influence their retention. *Journal of Experimental Psychology: General, 138*(2), 161–176. http://dx.doi.org/10.1037/a0015527

Howe, M., & Courage, M. (1993). On resolving the enigma of infantile amnesia. *Psychological Bulletin, 113,* 305–326.

Hyman, I. E., Husband, T. H., & Billings, F. J. (1995). False memories of childhood experiences. *Applied Cognitive Psychology, 9,* 181–197.

Innocence Project (n.d.) Retrieved from http://www.innocenceproject.org

Intons-Peterson, M. J., & Fournier, J. (1986). External and internal memory aids: When and how often do we use them? *Journal of Experimental Psychology: General, 115,* 267–280.

Jacoby, L. L., & Rhodes, M. G. (2006). False remembering the aged. *Current Directions in Psychological Science, 15,* 49–53.

Johnson, M. K., Hashtroudi, S., & Lindsay, D. S. (1993). Source monitoring. *Psychological Bulletin, 114,* 3–28.

Johnson, M. K., & Raye, C. L. (1981). Reality monitoring. *Psychological Review, 88,* 67–85.

Josselyn, S. A., & Frankland, P. W. (2012). Infantile amnesia: A neurogenic hypothesis. *Learning & Memory, 19,* 423–433.

Kassin, S. M., Ellsworth, P. C., & Smith, V. L. (1989). The "general acceptance" of psychological research on eyewitness testimony: A survey of the experts. *American Psychologist, 44,* 1089–1098.

Kassin, S. M., Tubb, V. A., Hosch, H. M., & Memon, A. (2001). On the "general acceptance" of eyewitness testimony research. *American Psychologist, 56,* 405–416.

Keast, A., Brewer, N., &Wells, G. L. (2007). Children's metacognitive judgments in an eyewitness identification *task. Journal of Experimental Child Psychology, 97,* 286–314.

Keppel, G., & Underwood, B. J. (1962). Proactive inhibition in short-term retention of single items. *Journal of Verbal Learning and Verbal Behavior, 1,* 153–161.

Kida, T. (2006). *Don't believe everything you think: The 6 basic mistakes we make in thinking.* Amherst, NY: Prometheus.

Kindt, M., Soeter, M., & Vervliet, B. (2009). Beyond extinction: Erasing human fear responses and preventing the return of fear. *Nature Neuroscience, 12,* 256–258.

Kitamura T., Saitoh, Y., Takashima, N., Murayama, A., Niibori, Y., Ageta, H.,. .. Inokuchi, K. (2009). Adult neurogenesis modulates the hippocampus-dependent period of associative fear memory. *Cell, 139,* 814–827.

Knight, B. G., Maines, M. L., & Robinson, G. S. (2002). The effects of sad mood on memory in older adults: A test of the mood congruence effect. *Psychology and Aging, 17*(4), 653–661. http://dx.doi.org/10.1037/0882-7974.17.4.653

Lynn, S. J., & Payne, D. (2005–2006). Death of Princess Diana: memory enhancement procedures on flashbulb memories. *...tion, and Personality, 25,* 197–220.

Kumar, R. (2008) Approved and investigational uses of modafinil: An evidence-based review. *Drugs, 68,* 1803–1839.

Laney, C., Morris, E. K., Bernstein, D. M., Wakefield, B. M., & Loftus, E. F. (2008). Asparagus, a love story: Healthier eating could be just a false memory away. *Experimental Psychology, 55*(5), 291–300. http://dx.doi.org/10.1027/1618-3169.55.5.291

Lanning, K. V. (1989). *Child sex rings: A behavioral analysis.* Washington, DC: National Center for Missing and Exploited Children.

Lashley, K. S. (1929). *Brain mechanisms and intelligence.* Chicago, IL: University of Chicago Press.

Laurin, D., Verreault, R., Lindsay, J., MacPherson, K., & Rockwood, K. (2001). Physical activity and risk of cognitive impairment and dementia in elderly persons. *Archives of Neurology, 58,* 498–504.

LeBar K. S., & Phelps E. A. (2005). Arousal mediated memory consolidation: Role of the medial temporal lobe in humans. *Psychological Science, 9,* 490–493.

Lee, Y. S. (2009). The role of genes in the obesity epidemic. *Annals of the Academy of Medicine Singapore, 38,* 45–47.

Legault, E., & Laurence, J. R. (2007). Recovered memories of childhood sexual abuse: Social worker, psychologist, and psychiatrist reports of beliefs, practices and cases. *Australian Journal of Clinical and Experimental Hypnosis, 35,* 111–133.

Lehman, D. R., Chiu, C. Y., & Schaller, M. (2004). Psychology and culture. *Annual Review of Psychology, 55,* 689–714.

Leichtman, M., & Ceci, S. (1995). The effects of stereotypes and suggestions on preschoolers' reports. *Developmental Psychology, 31,* 568–578.

LePort, A. K., Mattfeld, A. T., Dickinson-Anson, H., Fallon, J. H., Stark, C. E., Kruggel, F. R.,... McGaugh, J. L. (2012). Behavioral and neuroanatomical investigation of Highly Superior Autobiographical Memory (HSAM). *Neurobiology of Learning and Memory, 98,* 78–92.

Lewinsohn, P. M., & Rosenbaum, M. (1987). Recall of parental behavior by acute depressives, remitted depressives, and nondepressives. *Journal of Personality and Social Psychology, 52,* 611–620.

Lewis, M., Brooks-Gunn, J., & Jaskir, J. J. (1985). Individual differences in visual self-recognition as a function of mother–infant attachment relationship. *Developmental Psychobiology, 21,* 1181–1187.

Lilienfeld, S. O. (1997). The relation of anxiety sensitivity to higher and lower order personality dimensions: Implications for the etiology of panic attacks. *Journal of Abnormal Psychology, 106,* 539–544.

Lilienfeld, S. O., Lynn, S. J., Ruscio, J., & Beyerstein, B. L. (2010). *50 great myths of popular psychology: Shattering widespread misconceptions about human behavior.* Malden, MA: Wiley-Blackwell.

Lindner, I., Echterhoff, G., Davidson, P. S. R., & Brand, M. (2010). Observation inflation: Your actions become mine. *Psychological Science, 21,* 1291–1299.

Lindsay, R. C. L., & Wells, G. L. (1985). Improving eyewitness identifications from lineups: Simultaneous versus sequential lineup presentation. *Journal of Applied Psychology, 70,* 556–564.

Lisman, J., & Raghavachari, S. (2007). A unified model of the presynaptic and postsynaptic changes during LTP at CA1 synapses. *Science STKE, 10,* 11.

Lisman, S. A. (1974). Alcohol "black-out": State dependent learning? *Archives of General Psychiatry, 30,* 46–53.

Loftus, E. F. (1979). *Eyewitness testimony.* Cambridge, MA: Harvard University Press.

Loftus, E. F. (1993). The reality of repressed memories. *American Psychologist, 48,* 518–537.

Loftus, E. F., Coan, J. A., & Pickrell, J. E. (1996). Manufacturing false memories using bits of reality. In L. M. Reder (Ed.), *Implicit memory and metacognition* (pp. 195–220). Mahwah, NJ: Erlbaum.

Loftus, E. F., & Loftus, G. R. (1980). On the permanence of stored information in the human brain. *American Psychologist, 35,* 409–420.

Loftus, E. F., Miller, D. G., & Burns, H. J. (1978). Semantic integration of verbal information into a visual memory. *Human Learning and Memory, 4,* 19–31.

Loftus E. F., & Palmer, J. C. (1974). Reconstruction of automobile destruction: An example of the interaction between language and memory. *Journal of Learning and Verbal Behavior, 13,* 585–589.

Loftus, E. F., & Pickrell, J. E. (1995). The formation of false memories. *Psychiatric Annals, 25,* 720–725.

Lynn, S. J., Lock, T., Loftus, E. F., Krackow, E., & Lilienfeld, S. O. (2003a). The remembrance of things past: Problematic memory recovery techniques in psychotherapy. In S. O. Lilienfeld, S. J. Lynn, & J. Lohr (Eds.), *Science and pseudoscience in clinical psychology* (pp. 205–239). New York, NY: Guilford Press.

Lynn, S. J., Pintar, J., Sandberg, D., Fite, R. F., Ecklund, K., & Stafford, J. (2003b). Towards a social narrative model of revictimization. In L. Koenig, A. O'Leary, L. Doll, & W. Pequenat (Eds.), *From child sexual assault to adult sexual risk: Trauma, revictimization, and intervention* (pp. 281–313). Washington, DC: American Psychological Association.

MacLeod, C. M. (2008). Implicit memory tests: Techniques for reducing conscious intrusion. In J. Dunlosky R. A. Bjork (Eds.), *Handbook of metamemory and memory* (pp. 245–263). New York, NY: Psychology Press.

Malenka, R. C., & Nicoll, R. A. (1999). Long-term potentiation—A decade of progress? *Science, 285,* 1870–1874.

Malinoski, P., Lynn, S. J., & Sivec, H. (1998). The assessment, validity, and determinants of early memory reports: A critical review. In S. J. Lynn & K. McConkey (Eds.), Truth in memory (pp. 109–136). New York, NY: Guilford Press.

Marschner, A., Kalisch, R., Vervliet, B., Vansteenwegen, D., & Büchel, C. (2008) Dissociable roles for the hippocampus and the amygdala in human cued versus context fear conditioning. Journal of Neuroscience, 28, 9030–9036.

Martin, M., & Jones, G. V. (2012). Individualism and the field viewpoint: Cultural influences on memory perspective. Consciousness and Cognition: An International Journal, 21(3), 1498–1503. Retrieved from http://search.proquest.com/docview/1020052255?accountid=14168

Mathy, F., & Feldman, J. (2011). What's magic about magic numbers? Chunking and data compression in short-term memory. Cognition, 122, 346–362.

Mazzoni, G., Scoboria, A., & Harvey, L. (2010). Non-believed memories. Psychological Science, 21(9), 1334–1340.

Mazzoni, G. A., Loftus, E. F., Seitz, A., & Lynn, S. J. (1999). Changing beliefs and memories through dream interpretation. Applied Cognitive Psychology, 13, 125–144.

Mazzoni, G. A. L., Loftus, E. F., & Kirsch, I. (2001). Changing beliefs about implausible autobiographical events: A little plausibility goes a long way. Journal of Experimental Psychology: Applied, 7, 31–39.

McCabe, J. A., Osha, K. L., Roche, J. A., & Susser, J. A. (2011, May). Undergraduates' knowledge and use of mnemonics: A survey study. Poster presented at the 18th Annual APS-STP Teaching Institute, at the 23rd Annual Association for Psychological Science Convention, Washington, DC.

McCloskey, M., Wible, C. G., & Cohen, N. J. (1988). Is there a special flashbulb-memory mechanism? Journal of Experimental Psychology: General, 117, 171–181.

McDaniel, M. A., Maier, S. F., & Einstein, G. O. (2002). "Brain-specific" nutrients: A memory cure? Psychological Science in the Public Interest, 3, 12–38.

McHugh P. R. (2008). Try to remember: Psychiatry's clash over meaning, memory, and mind. New York, NY: Dana Press.

McNally, R. J. (2003). Remembering trauma. Cambridge, MA: Belknap Press.

McNamara, J. M., Trimmer, P. C., & Houston, A. I. (2012). The ecological rationality of state-dependent valuation. Psychological Review, 119, 114–119.

McQuiston-Surrett, D., Malpass, R. S., & Tredoux, C. G. (2006). Sequential vs. simultaneous lineups: A review of methods, data, and theory. Psychology, Public Policy, and Law, 12, 137–169.

Meissner, C. A., & Brigham, J. C. (2001). Thirty years of investigating the own-race bias in memory for faces: A meta-analytic review. Psychology, Public Policy, and Law, 7, 3–35.

Memon, A., Hope, L., & Bull, R. (2003). Exposure duration: Effects on eyewitness accuracy and confidence. British Journal of Psychology, 94, 339–354.

Meyersburg, C. A., Bogdan, R., Gallo, D. A., & McNally, R. J. (2009). False memory propensity in people reporting recovered memories of past lives. Journal of Abnormal Psychology, 118, 399–404.

Miller, G. A. (1956). The magical number seven, plus or minus two: Some limits on our capacity for processing information. Psychological Review, 63, 81–97.

Milner, B. (1964) Some effects of frontal lobectomy in man. In J. M. Warren & K. Akert (Eds.), The frontal granular cortex and behavior (pp. 313–334). New York, NY: McGraw-Hill.

Milner, B. (1972). Disorders of learning and memory after temporal lobe lesions in man. Clinical Neurosurgery, 19, 421–446.

Minsky, M. (1986). The society of mind. New York, NY: Simon & Schuster.

Mishkin, M., Malamut, B., & Bachevalier, J. (1984). Memories and habits: Two neural systems. In G. Lynch, J. McGaugh, & N. Weinberger (Eds.), Neurobiology of Learning and Memory (pp. 65–77). New York, NY: Guilford Press.

Mitchell, D. B. (2006). Nonconscious priming after 17 years—Invulnerable implicit memory? Psychological Science, 17, 925–929.

Mori, N. (2008). Styles of remembering and types of experience: An experimental investigation of reconstructive memory. Integrative Psychological & Behavioral Science, 42(3), 291–314.

Nash, M. R. (1987). What, if anything, is regressed about hypnotic age regression? A review of the empirical literature. Psychological Bulletin, 102, 42–52.

Navakkode, S., & Korte, M. (2012). Cooperation between cholinergic and glutamatergic receptors are essential to induce BDNF-dependent long-lasting memory storage. Hippocampus, 22(2), 335–346. http://dx.doi.org/10.1002/hipo.20902

Neath, I., & Saint-Aubin, J. (2011). Further evidence that similar principles govern recall from episodic and semantic memory: The Canadian prime ministerial serial position function. Canadian Journal of Experimental Psychology, 65, 77–83.

Neath, I., & Surprenant, A. M. (2003). Human memory (2nd ed.). Pacific Grove, CA: Wadsworth.

Neely, J. (1976) Semantic priming and retrieval from lexical memory: Evidence for facilitory and inhibitory processes. Memory and Cognition, 4, 648–654.

Neisser, U. (1967). Cognitive psychology. New York, NY: Appleton-Century-Crofts.

Neisser, U., & Harsch, N. (1992). Phantom flashbulbs: False recollections of hearing the news about Challenger. In E. Winograd & U. Neisser (Eds.), Affect and accuracy in recall: Studies of flashbulb memories (pp. 9–31). Cambridge, England: Cambridge University.

Neisser, U., & Hyman, I. (Eds.). (1999). Memory observed: Remembering in natural contexts. New York, NY: Worth.

Nelson, R. E., & Craighead, W. E. (1977), Selective recall of positive and negative feedback, self-control behaviors, and depression. Journal of Abnormal Psychology, 86, 379–388.

Nelson, T. O. (1985). Ebbinghaus's contribution to the measurement of retention: Savings during relearning. Journal of Experimental Psychology: Human Learning and Memory, 11, 472–479.

Ngandu, T., von Strauss, E., Helkala, E. L., Winbland, B., Nissinen, A., Tuomilehto, J.,... Kivipelto, M. (2007). Education and dementia: What lies behind the association? Neurology, 69, 1442–1450.

Nickerson, R. S., & Adams, J. J. (1979). Long-term memory for a common object. Cognitive Psychology, 11, 287–307.

Nigro, G., & Neisser, N. (1983). Point of view in personal memories. Cognitive Psychology, 15, 467–482.

Ornstein, P. A., Baker-Ward, L., Gordon, B. N., & Merritt, K. A. (1997). Children's memory for medical experiences: Implications for testimony. Applied Cognitive Psychology, 11, S87–S104.

Otgaar, H., Candel, I., Merckelbach, H., & Wade, K. (2009). Abducted by a UFO: Prevalence information affects young children's false memories for an implausible event. Applied Cognitive Psychology, 23(1), 115–125. http://dx.doi.org/10.1002/acp.1445

Otgarr, H., Scoboria, A., & Smeets, T. (2012). Experimentally evoking nonbelieved memories for childhood events. Journal of Experimental Psychology: Learning, Memory, and Cognition. Retrieved from http://www.ncbi.nlm.nih.gov/pubmed/22905934

Paivio, A. (1969). Mental imagery in associative learning and memory. Psychological Review, 76, 341–363.

Parker, E. S., Cahill, L., & McGaugh, J. L. (2006). A case of unusual autobiographical remembering. Neurocase, 12, 35–49.

Pascual-Leone, J. (1989). An organismic process model of Witkin's field dependence-independence. In T. Globerson and T. Zelniker (Eds.), Cognitive style and cognitive development (pp. 36–70). Norwood, NJ: Ablex.

Persuh, M., Genzer, B., & Melara, R. D. (2012). Iconic memory requires attention. Frontiers in Human Neuroscience, 6, 1–8.

Peters, M. J. V., Horselenberg, R., Jelicic, M., & Merckelbach, H. (2007). The false fame illusion in people with memories about a previous life. Consciousness and Cognition: An International Journal, 16(1), 162–169. http://dx.doi.org/10.1016/j.concog.2006.02.002

Peterson, C., Warren, K. L., & Short, M. M. (2011). Infantile amnesia across the years: A 2-year follow-up of children's earliest memories. Child Development, 82(4), 1092–1105. http://dx.doi.org/10.1111/j.1467-8624.2011.01597.x

Peterson, L. R., & Peterson, M. J. (1959). Short-term retention of individual verbal items. Journal of Experimental Psychology, 58, 193–198.

Pezdek, K., Finger, K., & Hodge, D. (1997). Planting false childhood memories: The role of event plausibility. Psychological Science, 8, 437–441.

Pezdek, K., O'Brien, M., & Wasson, C. (2011). Cross-race (but not same-race) face identification is impaired by presenting faces in a group rather than individually. Law and Human Behavior (0147-7307) http://dx.doi.org/10.1037/h0093933

Pickel, K. L. (2007). Remembering and identifying menacing perpetrators: Exposure to violence and the weapon focus effect. In R. C. L. Lindsay, D. F. Ross, J. D. Read, & M. P. Toglia (Eds.), The handbook of eyewitness psychology, volume II: Memory for people (pp. 339–360). Mahwah, NJ: Erlbaum.

Pillemer, D. B. (1984). Flashbulb memories of the assassination attempt on President Reagan. Cognition, 16, 63–80.

Pitman, R. K., Sanders, K. M., Zusman, R. M., Healy, A. R., Cheema, F., Lasko, N. B.,... Orr, S. P. (2002). Pilot study of secondary prevention of posttraumatic stress disorder with propranolol. Biological Psychiatry, 51, 189–192.

Plotnik, J. M., de Waal, F. B. M., & Reiss, D. (2006). Self-recognition in an Asian elephant. Proceedings of the National Academy of Sciences, 103, 17053–17057.

Polusny, M. A., & Follette, V. M. (1996). Remembering childhood sexual abuse: A national survey of psychologists' clinical practices, beliefs, and personal experiences. Professional Psychology: Research and Practice, 27, 41–52.

Poole, D. A., Lindsay, D. S., Memon, A., & Bull, R. (1995). Psychotherapists' opinions, practices, and experiences with recovery of memories of incestuous abuse. Journal of Consulting and Clinical Psychology, 68, 426–437.

Pope, H. G., Jr., Poliakoff, M. B., Parker, M. P., Boynes, M., & Hudson, J. I. (2007). Is dissociative amnesia a culture-bound syndrome? Findings from a survey of historical literature. Psychological Medicine, 37, 225–233.

Porter, S., Yuille, J. C., & Lehman, D. R. (1999). The nature of real, implanted, and fabricated memories for emotional childhood events. Law and Human Behavior, 23, 517–537.

Price, J., & Davis, B. (2008). The woman who can't forget: The extraordinary story of living with the most remarkable memory known to science. New York, NY: Free Press.

Quiroga, R. Q., Reddy, L., Kreiman, G., Koch, C., & Fried, I. (2005). Invariant visual representation by single neurons in the human brain. Nature, 435, 1102–1107.

Radvansky, G. A., Gibson, B. S., & McNerney, M. W. (2011). Synesthesia and memory: Color congruency, von restorff, and false memory effects. Journal (

Experimental Psychology: Learning, Memory, and Cognition, 37(1), 219–229. http://dx.doi.org/10.1037/a0021329

Rainey, D. W., & Larsen, J. D. (2002). The effect of familiar melodies on initial learning and long-term memory for unconnected text. *Music Perception, 20*, 173–186.

Rassin, E., Merckelbach, H., & Spaan, V. (2001). When dreams become a royal road to confusion: Realistic dreams, dissociation, and fantasy proneness. *Journal of Nervous and Mental Disease, 189*, 478–481.

Renoult, L., Davidson, P. S., Palombo, D. J., Moscovitch, M., & Levine, B. (2012). Personal semantics: At the crossroads of semantic and episodic memory. *Trends in Cognitive Sciences, 16*, 550–558.

Resnick, S. M., Pham, D. L., Kraut, M. A., Zonderman, A. B., & Davatzikos, C. (2003). Longitudinal magnetic resonance imaging studies of older adults: A shrinking brain. *Journal of Neuroscience, 23*, 3295–3301.

Rimmele, U., Davachi, L., & Phelps, E. A. (2012). Memory for time and place contributes to enhanced confidence in memories for emotional events. *Emotion, 12*(4), 834–846. http://dx.doi.org/10.1037/a0028003

Robinson, S. J., & Rollings, L. J. L. (2011). The effect of mood-context on visual recognition and recall memory. *Journal of General Psychology, 138*(1), 66–79. http://dx.doi.org/10.1080/00221309.2010.534405

Roediger, H. L., & Crowder, R. G. (1976). A serial position effect in recall of United States presidents. *Bulletin of the Psychonomic Society, 8*, 275–278.

Roediger, H. L., & Geraci, L. (2007). Aging and the misinformation effect: A neuropsychological analysis. *Journal of Experimental Psychology: Learning, Memory, and Cognition, 33*(2), 321–334. http://dx.doi.org/10.1037/0278-7393.33.2.321

Roediger, H. L., & McDermott, K. B. (1995). Creating false memories: Remembering words not presented in lists. *Journal of Experimental Psychology: Learning, Memory, and Cognition, 21*, 803–814.

Ross, M. (1989). Relation of implicit theories to the construction of personal histories. *Psychological Review, 96*, 341–357.

Rothen, N., Meier, B., & Ward, J. (2012). Enhanced memory ability: Insights from synaesthesia. *Neuroscience & Biobehavioral Reviews*, awaiting volume and page numbers.

Rovee-Collier, C. (1993). The capacity for long-term memory in infancy. *Current Directions in Psychological Science, 2*, 130–135.

Sattler, C., Toro, P., Schönknecht, P., & Schröder, J. (2012). Cognitive activity, education and socioeconomic status as preventive factors for mild cognitive impairment and Alzheimer's disease. *Psychiatry Research, 196*(1), 90–95. http://dx.doi.org/10.1016/j.psychres.2011.11.012

Saufley, W. H., Otaka, S. R., & Bavaresco, J. L. (1985). Context effects: Classroom tests and context independence. *Memory & Cognition, 13*, 522–528.

Schacter, D. L. (1996). *Searching for memory: The brain, the mind, and the past.* New York, NY: Basic Books.

Schacter, D. L. (2001). *The seven sins of memory.* Boston, MA: Houghton-Mifflin.

Schacter, D. L., & Moscovitch, M. (1984). Infants, amnesics, and dissociable memory systems. In M. Moscovitch (Ed.), *Infant memory* (pp. 173–216). New York, NY: Plenum.

Schank, R. C., & Abelson, R. (1977). *Scripts, plans, goals, and understanding.* Hillsdale, NJ: Erlbaum.

Scheck, B., Neufeld, P., & Dwyer, J. (2000). *Actual innocence.* New York, NY: Random House.

Scheff, S. W., Price, D. A., Schmitt, F. A., DeKosky, S. T., & Mufson, E. J. (2007). Synaptic alterations in CA1 in mild Alzheimer disease and mild cognitive impairment. *Neurology, 68*, 1501–1508.

Schmolk, H., Buffalo, E. A., & Squire, L. R. (2000). Memory distortions develop over time. Recollections of the O. J. Simpson trial verdict after 15 and 32 months. *Psychological Science, 11*, 39–45.

Schneider, W. (2008). The development of metacognitive knowledge in children and adolescents: Major trends and implications for education. *Mind, Brain, and Education, 2*, 114–121.

Schneider, W., & Bjorklund, D. F. (1998). Memory. In W. Damon, R. S. Siegler, & D. Kuhn (Eds.), *Handbook of child psychology, Vol. 2* (pp. 467–521). New York, NY: Wiley.

Schwartz, B. L. (1999). Sparkling at the end of the tongue: The etiology of the tip-of-the-tongue phenomenology. *Psychonomic Bulletin & Review, 6*, 379–393.

Scoville, W. B., & Milner, B. (1957). Loss of recent memory after bilateral hippocampal lesions. *Journal of Neurology, Neurosurgery, and Psychiatry, 20*, 11–21.

Sebrechts, M. M., Marsh, R. L., & Seamon, J. G. (1989). Secondary memory and very rapid forgetting. *Memory & Cognition, 17*, 693–700.

Shimamura, A. P. (1992). Organic amnesia. In L. Squire (Ed.), *Encyclopedia of learning and memory* (pp. 30–35). New York, NY: Macmillan.

Shors, T. J., & Matzel, L. D. (1999). Long-term potentiation: What's learning got to do with it? *Behavioral and Brain Sciences, 20*, 597–655.

Simons, D. J., & Chabris, C. F. (2011). What people believe about how memory works: A representative survey of the U.S. population. *PLoS One, 6*(8), e22757. http://dx.doi.org/10.1371/journal.pone.0022757

M. E., & Farah, M. J. (2011). Are prescription stimulants "smart pills"? The ...ology and cognitive neuroscience of prescription stimulant use by ... individuals. *Psychological Bulletin, 137*, 717–741.

Smith, S. L., Gerhardt, K. J., Griffiths, S. K., Huang, X., & Abrams, R. M. (2003). Intelligibility of sentences recorded from the uterus of a pregnant ewe and from the fetal inner ear. *Audiology & Neuro-otology, 8*, 347–353.

Smith, S. M. (1979). Remembering in and out of context. *Journal of Experimental Psychology: Human Learning and Memory, 5*, 460–471.

Smith, S. M., Lindsay, R. C. L., Pryke, S., & Dysart, J. E. (2001). Postdictors of eyewitness errors: Can false identifications be diagnosed in the cross race situation? *Psychology, Public Policy, and Law, 7*, 153–169.

Snitz, B. E., O'Meara, E. S., Carlson, M. C., Arnold, A. M., Ives, D. G., Rapp, S. R., . . . DeKosky, S. T. (2009). *Ginkgo biloba* for preventing cognitive decline in older adults: A randomized trial. *Journal of the American Medical Association, 302*(24), 2663–2670. http://dx.doi.org/10.1001/jama.2009.1913

Snowdon, D. A. (2003). Healthy aging and dementia: Findings from the nun study. *Annals of Internal Medicine, 139*, 450–454.

Snyder, M., & Uranowitz, S. W. (1978). Reconstructing the past: Some cognitive consequences of person perception. *Journal of Personality and Social Psychology, 36*, 941–950.

Sperling, G. (1960). The information available in brief visual presentations. *Psychological Monographs: General and Applied, 74* (11, Whole No. 498), 1–29.

Sporer, S. L., Penrod, S., Read, D., & Cutler, B. (1995). Choosing, confidence, and accuracy: A meta-analysis of the confidence-accuracy relation in eyewitness identification studies. *Psychological Bulletin, 118*, 315–327.

Squire, L. R. (1987). *Memory and brain.* New York, NY: Oxford University Press.

Standing, L., Conezio, J., & Haber, R. N. (1970). Perception and memory for pictures: Single-trial learning of 2500 visual stimuli. *Psychonomic Science, 19*, 73–74.

Steblay, N. M. (1992). A meta-analytic review of the weapon focus effect. *Law and Human Behavior, 16*, 413–424.

Steblay, N. M., Dysart, J., Fulero, S., & Lindsay, R. C. L. (2001). Eyewitness accuracy rates in sequential and simultaneous lineup presentations: A meta-analytic comparison. *Law and Human Behavior, 25*, 459–474.

Stone, W. L., & Rosenbaum, J. L. (1988). A comparison of teacher and parent views of autism. *Journal of Autism and Developmental Disorders, 18*, 403–414.

Talarico, J. M., & Rubin, D. C. (2007). Flashbulb memories are special after all; in phenomenology, not accuracy. *Applied Cognitive Psychology, 21*(5), 557–578. http://dx.doi.org/10.1002/acp.1293

Taylor, P., Russ-Eft, D., & Taylor, H. (2009). Gilding the outcome by tarnishing the past: Inflationary biases in retrospective pretests. *American Journal of Evaluation, 30*, 31–43.

Thierry, K. L., & Spence, M. J. (2002). Source-monitoring training facilitates preschoolers' eyewitness memory performance. *Developmental Psychology, 38*(3), 428–437. http://dx.doi.org/10.1037/0012-1649.38.3.428

Thompson, R., Emmorey, K., & Gollan, T. (2005). Tip-of-the-fingers experiences by ASL signers: Insights into the organization of a sign-based lexicon. *Psychological Science, 16*, 856–860.

Treffert, D. A., & Christensen, D. D. (2005, December). Inside the mind of a savant. *Scientific American, 293*, 108–113.

Tsien, J. Z. (2000). Linking Hebb's coincidence-detection to memory formation. *Current Opinions in Neurobiology, 10*, 266–273.

Tulving, E. (1972). Episodic and semantic memory. In E. Tulving & W. Donaldson (Eds.), *Organization of memory* (pp. 378–402). New York, NY: Academic Press.

Tulving, E. (1982). Synergistic ecphory in recall and recognition. *Canadian Journal of Psychology, 36*, 130–147.

Tulving, E., & Thomson, D. M. (1973). Encoding specificity and retrieval processes in episodic memory. *Psychological Review, 80*, 352–373.

Uberti, H. Z., Scruggs, T. E., & Mastropieri, M. A. (2003). Keywords make the difference! Mnemonic instruction in inclusive classrooms. *TEACHING Exceptional Children, 35*(3), 56–61.

Underwood, B. J. (1957) Interference and forgetting. *Psychological Review, 64*, 49–60.

Unsworth, N., & Engle, R. W. (2007). On the division of short-term and working memory: An examination of simple and complex spans and their relation to higher-order abilities. *Psychological Bulletin, 133*, 1038–1066.

Valentine, T., & Mesout, J. (2009). Eyewitness identification under stress in the London dungeon. *Applied Cognitive Psychology, 23*(2), 151–161. http://dx.doi.org/10.1002/acp.1463

van der Kolk, B., Britz, R., Burr, W., Sherry, S., & Hartmann, E. (1984). Nightmares and trauma: A comparison of nightmares after combat with lifelong nightmares in veterans. *American Journal of Psychiatry, 141*, 187–190.

Van Wallendael, L. R., Cutler, B. L., Devenport, J., & Penrod, S. D. (2007). Mistaken identification = erroneous conviction? Assessing and improving legal safeguards. In M. P. Toglia, D. F. Ross, J. D. Read, & R. C. L. Lindsay (Eds.), *Handbook of eyewitness psychology, Vol II: Memory for people* (pp. 557–572). Mahwah, NJ: Erlbaum.

Vellas, B., Coley, N., Ousset, P. J., Berrut, G., Dartigues, J. F., Dubois, B., . . . Andrieu, S. (2012). Long-term use of standardised ginkgo biloba extract for the prevention of Alzheimer's disease (GuidAge): A randomised placebo-controlled trial. *The Lancet Neurology, 11*, 851–859.

Vermetten, E., & Bremner, J. D. (2003). Olfaction as a traumatic reminder in posttraumatic stress disorder: Case reports and review. *Journal of Clinical Psychiatry, 64,* 202–207.

Vlach, H. A., & Sandhofer, C. M. (2011). Developmental differences in children's context-dependent word learning. *Journal of Experimental Child Psychology, 108,* 394–401.

Voss, J. L., and Paller, K. A. (2008). Brain substrates of implicit and explicit memory: The importance of concurrently acquired neural signals of both memory types. *Neuropsychologia, 46,* 3021–3029.

Wade, K. A., Garry, M., Read, J. D., & Lindsay, D. S. (2002). A picture is worth a thousand lies: Using false photographs to create false childhood memories. *Psychonomic Bulletin & Review, 9,* 597–603.

Wang, Q. (2006). Culture and the development of self-knowledge. *Current Directions in Psychological Science, 15,* 182–187.

Waugh, N. C., & Norman, D. A. (1965). Primary memory. *Psychological Review, 72,* 89–104.

Wearing, D. (2005). *Forever today.* New York, NY: Doubleday.

Weinert, F. (1989). The impact of schooling on cognitive development: One hypothetical assumption, some empirical results, and many theoretical implications. *EARLI News, 8,* 3–7.

Wells, G. L., & Bradford, A. L. (1998). "Good, you identified the suspect": Feedback to eyewitnesses distorts their reports of the witnessing experience. *Journal of Applied Psychology, 83,* 360–376.

Wells, G. L., & Loftus, E. F. (Eds.). (1984). *Eyewitness testimony: Psychological perspectives.* New York, NY: Cambridge University Press.

Wells, G. L., Memon, A., & Penrod, S. D. (2006). Eyewitness evidence: Improving its probative value. *Psychological Science in the Public Interest, 7,* 45–75.

West, T. A., & Bauer, P. J. (1999). Assumptions of infantile amnesia: Are there differences between early and later memories? *Memory, 7,* 257–278.

Wetzler, S. E., & Sweeney, J. A. (1986). Childhood amnesia: An empirical demonstration. In D. C. Rubin (Ed.), *Autobiographical memory* (pp. 191–201). New York, NY: Cambridge University Press.

Wickelgren, W. A. (1965). Acoustic similarity and retroactive interference in short-term memory. *Journal of Verbal Learning and Verbal Behavior, 4,* 53–61.

Willingham, D. T. (2002). *Allocating student study time: "Massed" versus "distributed" practice.* Retrieved from http://www.aft.org/newspubs/periodicals/ae/summer2002/willingham.cfm

Winograd, E., & Killinger, W. A., Jr. (1983). Relating age at encoding in early childhood to adult recall: Development of flashbulb memories. *Journal of Experimental Psychology: General, 112,* 413–422.

Winograd, E., Peluso, J. P., & Glover, T. A. (1998). Individual differences in susceptibility to memory illusions. *Applied Cognitive Psychology, 12,* S5–S27.

Wollen, K. A., Weber, A., & Lowry, D. H. (1972). Bizarreness versus interaction of mental images as determinants of learning. *Cognitive Psychology, 3,* 518–523.

Yapko, M. D. (1994). *Suggestions of abuse: True and false memories of childhood sexual trauma.* New York, NY: Simon & Schuster.

Yeh, S.-L., He, S., & Cavanagh, P. (2012). Semantic priming from crowded words. *Psychological Science, 23,* 608–616.

Zabrucky, K., & Ratner, H. H. (1986). Children's comprehension monitoring and recall of inconsistent stories. *Child Development, 57,* 1401–1418.

Zeinah, M. M., Engel, S. A., Thompson, P. M., & Bookheimer, S. Y. (2003). Dynamics of the hippocampus during encoding and retrieval of face-name pairs. *Science, 299,* 577–580.

Zola, S. (1997). The neurobiology of recovered memory, *Journal of Neuropsychiatry and Clinical Neurosciences, 9,* 449–459.

Credits

Credits listed in order of appearance.

Text: Simons & Chabris, 2011. **Figure 2:** Atkinson & Shiffrin, 1968. **Figure 3:** Sperling, 1960. **Figure 6:** Bahrick, H. p. (1984). Semantic memory content in permastore: Fifty years of memory for Spanish learning in school. Journal of Experimental Psychology: General. **Figure 17:** The medical illustration is provided courtesy of Alzheimer's Disease Research, a program of BrightFocus Foundation (c) 2013 http://www.brightfocus.org/alzheimers. **Text:** Loftus and John Palmer (1974).

Photo Credits

Photo Credits listed in order of appearance.

Christopher Robbins/Getty Images; Imagebroker/Alamy; **(top right):** Topham/The Image Works; **(center right):** Neno Images/PhotoEdit; **(top right):** Alamy Limited; **(top left):** Stefan Arendt/Glow Images; **(center):** Pearson Education; **(top left):** Stockbyte/Getty Images; **(bottom center):** Zuma Press/Alamy; **(top center):** Alamy Limited; **(top right):** Marcin Perkowski/Shutterstock; **(top right):** Juniors Bildarchiv/Alamy; **(top right):** SuperStock/Glow Images; **(top right):** Bob Daemmrich/PhotoEdit; **(top left):** Pearson Education; **(center right):** T. Bannor/Custom Medical Stock Photo Custom Medical Stock Photo/Newscom; **(bottom center):** Alistair Cotton/Shutterstock; **(top left):** Steve Liss/Time Life Pictures/Getty Images; **(bottom right):** Gareth Brown/Corbis/Glow Images; **top left:** Liba Taylor/Alamy; p**(top right):** Superstock; **(top left):** Reuters/Win McNamee/Landov; **(center right):** Bloomberg/Getty Images; **(center left):** Dr. Elizabeth Loftus; **(center right):** Jeff Greenberg/PhotoEdit; **(top left):** Burlington Police Department/AP Images; **(center left):** Colchester Police/AP Images; **(top left):** Al Francis/AP Images; **(top right):** Dan Eckstein/Zuma/Newscom; **(center left):** Gareth Brown/Corbis/Glow Images; **(bottom left):** Superstock; **(top right):** Dr. Elizabeth Loftus; **(center right):** Jeff Greenberg/PhotoEdit.

329

Thinking, Reasoning, and Language

From Chapter 8 of *Psychology: From Inquiry to Understanding,* Third Edition. Scott O. Lilienfeld, Steven Jay Lynn, Laura L. Namy, Nancy J. Woolf. Copyright © 2014 by Pearson Education, Inc. All rights reserved.

Thinking, Reasoning, and Language

GETTING INSIDE OUR TALKING HEADS

Think About It

Which are more accurate: first impressions or in-depth analyses?

What's the best way to make important decisions?

Do nonhuman animals have language?

Are children who learn two languages at a disadvantage?

Does speed-reading work?

One of the most valuable lessons psychology can teach us is to appreciate mental capacities we normally take for granted. Take thinking and language. We rely on them almost every second of our waking hours but rarely notice the complexity that goes into them. Picture this scenario:

> Two friends decide to go fishing. Jason is responsible for bringing the fishing gear, and Tre is responsible for bringing snacks and drinks. After a long drive, they reach their favorite fishing hole. As they are unpacking the car, Jason says, "Oh no! I forgot to bring the sinkers. Now we won't have anything to weigh down the fishing line; it's just going to float at the top of the water." Tre thinks for a second and then snaps his fingers. "I've got some keys to my uncle's old apartment rattling around in my backpack." "Nice one!" says Jason.

What just happened? Tre generated a novel solution to a problem by thinking of something that was about the right size and weight to hold down the fishing line and that had a hole through which the fishing line could be threaded. Problem solving in action! Notice also that although Tre never actually spelled out his solution ("I know. We can use some old keys as weights instead!"), Jason (and you) figured out what he meant when he announced that he had some old keys in his bag. The simple act of following the implications of that conversation required both reasoning and language skills.

These are the kinds of abilities we'll explore in this chapter. First, we'll examine our thinking and reasoning processes in everyday life and discover how we make decisions and solve problems. Then we'll examine how we communicate and comprehend meaning using words, and the enormous challenges we face—and overcome—when doing so.

Thinking and Reasoning

1. Identify methods for achieving cognitive economy.
2. Describe what factors affect our reasoning about the world.

Generally speaking, we can define **thinking** as any mental activity or processing of information. It includes learning, remembering, perceiving, communicating, believing, and deciding. All are fundamental aspects of what psychologists call cognition.

Behaviorists attempted to explain mental activity in terms of stimulus and response, reinforcement and punishment. Yet psychologists have long known that our minds often go beyond the available information, making leaps of insight and drawing inferences. Our minds fill in the gaps to create information that isn't present in its environmental inputs. Behaviorism's "black box psychology" can't easily account for this phenomenon.

Cognitive Economy—Imposing Order on Our World

Given the complexity of the cognitive tasks we must perform every day, our brains have adapted by finding ways to streamline the process. That's where cognitive economy enters the picture. We're *cognitive misers*. We economize mentally in a variety of ways that reduce our mental effort, but enable us to get things right most of the time. Yet, cognitive economy can occasionally get us in trouble, especially when it leads us not merely to simplify, but *over* simplify.

Our minds use a variety of heuristics, or mental shortcuts, to increase our thinking efficiency (Ariely, 2008; Herbert, 2010; Kahneman, 2011). From an evolutionary perspective, heuristics may have enhanced our survival. Even though these shortcuts can backfire if we're not careful, we've developed them for a reason: They're often useful in everyday life (Gigerenzer, 2007; Gilovich, Griffin, & Kahneman, 2002).

We process an enormous amount of information every minute of every day. From the moment we wake up, we must take into account what time it is, notice if there are any obstacles on the floor (like a roommate's shoes) between us and the shower, plan

thinking
any mental activity or processing of information, including learning, remembering, perceiving, communicating, believing, and deciding

what time we need to get to class or work, and collect everything we need to take with us. Of course, that's all before we've even stepped out the door. If we were to attend to and draw conclusions about every aspect of our experience all the time, we'd be so overwhelmed that we'd be paralyzed psychologically.

We draw inferences that provide mental shortcuts many times a day, and most of the time, they steer us right. If a roommate's keys are lying on the dining table, we might infer that our roommate is home. We might conclude that the stressed-looking woman walking briskly by might not be the best person to stop and ask to contribute to our charity. Without actually tasting it (or better yet, conducting a microscopic bacterial analysis), we typically can decide that the three-week-old milk in our refrigerator has gone bad based on its smell. Each of these conclusions is unwarranted under rigorous standards of evidence-based reasoning. Yet most of these guesses are probably accurate enough to be safe bets.

Cognitive economy allows us to simplify what we attend to and keep the information we need for decision making to a manageable minimum. Gerd Gigerenzer and his colleagues (Gigerenzer & Goldstein, 1996; Gigerenzer, Hertwig, & Pachur, 2011) referred to this type of cognitive economy as "fast and frugal" thinking. He argued that it serves us well most of the time. In fact, in many cases, the heuristics we use are more valid than an exhaustive (and exhausting!) analysis of all potential factors (Gladwell, 2005).

One study revealed that untrained observers can make surprisingly accurate judgments about people on the basis of limited information. Samuel Gosling and his colleagues asked a group of untrained observers to make personality judgments about students by viewing their dorm rooms or bedrooms for only a few minutes. The researchers gave observers no instructions about what features of the room to focus on and covered all photos in the rooms so that observers couldn't determine the sex, race, or age of the rooms' occupants. Yet observers accurately gauged several aspects of the occupants' personalities, such as their emotional stability, openness to new experiences, and conscientiousness (Gosling, 2008). Presumably, observers were relying on mental shortcuts to draw conclusions about occupants' personalities because they had no first-hand experience with them.

Nalini Ambady and Robert Rosenthal (1993) provided another remarkable example of how cognitive economy serves us well. They showed participants 30-second silent clips of instructors teaching and asked them to evaluate the instructors' nonverbal behaviors. Participants' ratings on the basis of only 30 seconds of exposure were correlated significantly with the teachers' end-of-course evaluations by their students; in fact, their ratings were still predictive of course evaluations even when the clips were only six seconds long. Ambady and Rosenthal referred to our ability to extract useful information from small bits of behavior as "thin slicing." John Gottman and his colleagues also showed that after observing just 15 minutes of a couple's videotaped interaction, they could predict with more than 90 percent accuracy which couples would divorce within the next 15 years. It turns out that the emotion of contempt—perhaps surprisingly, not anger—is one of the best predictors (Carrère & Gottman, 1999).

But cognitive economy is a mixed blessing, because it can also lead us to faulty conclusions (Lehrer, 2009; Myers, 2002). Although our snap judgments are usually accurate (or at least accurate enough to get by), we can occasionally be wildly wrong (Gigerenzer, 2007; Krueger & Funder, 2005; Shepperd & Koch, 2005).

Heuristics and Biases: Double-Edged Swords

Psychologists have identified many more heuristics and **cognitive biases**, predispositions and default expectations that we use to interpret our experiences, that operate in our everyday lives. We'll examine a few of them here.

Research by Samuel Gosling and his collaborators suggests that observers can often infer people's personality traits at better-than-chance levels merely by inspecting their rooms. What might you guess about the level of conscientiousness of this room's occupant?

cognitive bias
systematic error in thinking

Factoid

Are there more words in the English language with the letter *k* as the first letter in the word or the third letter in the word? If you're like most people, you guessed that there are more words beginning with the letter *k* than with *k* in the third position. In fact, there are more than twice as many words with *k* in the third position as there are words beginning with the letter *k*. Most of us get this question wrong because we rely on the availability heuristic: Because of how our brains categorize words, we find it easier to think of words with *k* in the first position (like *kite* and *kill*) than words with *k* in the third position (like *bike* and *cake*).

FIGURE 1 A Floral Demonstration of Base Rates. This bouquet includes purple irises and yellow and purple tulips. If we were to choose a purple flower at random, would it be more likely to be an iris or a tulip? Even though all of the irises are purple and most of the tulips are yellow, the purple flower we chose is more likely to be a tulip because there are twice as many purple tulips as there are purple irises. That means that the base rate of purple tulips in this bouquet is higher than the base rate of purple irises.

representative heuristic
heuristic that involves judging the probability of an event by its superficial similarity to a ~~~e~~~

335

~~~istic or behavior is~~~

REPRESENTATIVENESS HEURISTIC. The **representativeness heuristic** involves judging the probability of an event based on how prevalent that event has been in past experience (Kahneman, Slovic, & Tversky, 1982; Tversky & Kahneman, 1974). If we meet someone who is shy, awkward, and a tournament chess player, we might guess that he is more likely to be a computer science major than a communications major. If so, we relied on a representativeness heuristic, because this person matched our stereotype of a computer science major.

Stereotyping is a form of cognitive economy, and it's often a result of our overgeneralizing from experiences with individuals in a minority group (such as African-Americans or Muslim Americans) to all individuals in that group. So the representativeness heuristic can sometimes lead us to incorrect conclusions. Imagine we met another student who is Asian-American, is bilingual in English and Chinese, and is vice president of the college's Chinese Students Association. We might judge that she's more likely to be an Asian-American Studies major than a psychology major. However, in this case, the representativeness heuristic may have misled us. Although this student's characteristics may be consistent with those of many Asian-American Studies majors, we also must consider the fact that even within the broad group of Asian-American students, there are many more psychology majors than there are Asian-American Studies majors. So the odds would actually predict that she's more likely to be a psychology major.

The challenge to our reasoning in this example is that we are poor at taking into account *base rate* information. **Base rate** is a fancy term for how common a behavior or characteristic is in general (Finn & Kamphuis, 1995; Meehl & Rosen, 1955). When we say that alcoholism has a base rate of about 5 percent in the U.S. population (American Psychiatric Association, 2000), we mean that about 1 in 20 Americans experiences alcoholism on average. When evaluating the probability that a person belongs to a category (for example, Asian-American Studies major), we need to consider not only how similar that person is to other members of the category, but also how prevalent that category is overall, the base rate (see **FIGURE 1**).

AVAILABILITY HEURISTIC. We also rely heavily on the **availability heuristic** in our everyday lives. Based on this heuristic, we estimate the likelihood of an occurrence based on how easily it comes to our minds—on how "available" it is in our memories (Kahneman et al., 1982). Like representativeness, availability often works well. If we ask you whether there's a higher density of trees (a) on your college campus or (b) in the downtown area of the nearest major city, you're likely to answer (a). Odds are you'd be right (unless, of course, your college campus is *in* a downtown area). When you answered the question, it's unlikely you actually calculated the precise proportion of trees you've observed in each place. Instead, you probably called to mind mental images of your campus and of a downtown area and observed that the examples of the campus that came to mind more often had trees in them than the examples of downtown areas that came to mind.

But now consider this example, which you may want to try on your friends (Jaffe, 2004). Ask half of your friends to guess the number of murders per year in Michigan and the other half to guess the number of murders per year in Detroit, Michigan. If you average the answers for each group, based on the availability heuristic, you will probably find that your friends give higher estimates for the number of murders in Detroit, Michigan, than for the entire state of Michigan! In one study, people who were asked about the state of Michigan estimated about 100 murders per year, but those asked about Detroit estimated 200 murders per year (Kahneman, 2011).

This paradoxical result is almost certainly due to our reliance on the availability heuristic. When we imagine the state of Michigan, we conjure up images of sprawling farms and peaceful suburbs. Yet when we imagine the city of Detroit, we conjure up images of dangerous inner-city areas and run-down buildings. So thinking of Detroit makes the idea of murder more readily available to us.

from inquiry to understanding

WHY DO WE WORRY ABOUT THE WRONG THINGS?

Try answering the following four questions:

In the United States, which causes more deaths?

(1) All types of accidents combined or strokes?

(2) All motor vehicle (car, truck, bus, and motorcycle) accidents combined or digestive cancer?

(3) Diabetes or homicide?

(4) Sharks or cattle?

The answers are (1) strokes (by about twofold), (2) digestive cancer (by about threefold), (3) diabetes (by about fourfold), and (4) cattle (by about twenty-fold). If you got one or more questions wrong, you're in good company, because most people do. In fact, a large body of data demonstrates that we're poor at estimating risks. We worry a lot about things that aren't all that dangerous and don't worry enough about things that are dangerous (Daley, 2012; Ropeik, 2010). Why?

Scientific research shows that the availability heuristic is a major culprit (Hertwig, Pachur, & Kurzenhauser, 2005; Tversky & Kahneman, 1974). Because the news media provide far more coverage of dramatic accidents and homicides than they do strokes, digestive cancer, or diabetes, we overestimate the probability of accidents and homicides and underestimate the probability of many common diseases. For example, because the media feature so many emotional stories of famous women who've developed breast cancer, the availability heuristic makes us think of breast cancer as a more frequent and deadly illness than heart disease, when the truth is just the opposite (Slovic, Finucane, Peters, & MacGregor, 2012). Heart disease is probably less newsworthy precisely because it's more commonplace than cancer. These errors in judgment can be costly: If women believe heart disease isn't a health threat, they may not change their lifestyles to minimize their risk.

These errors can also shape our decision making. If you learned that four jumbo jets at full capacity crashed every day in the United States, you'd probably never get on a commercial airplane again. Yet the equivalent of that number—about 1,200 people—die each day in America from smoking-related causes (Centers for Disease Control and Prevention, 2005), and still, millions of Americans take up smoking every year. What are the odds that we'll die in a commercial plane crash? Infinitesimally small. We'd need to fly in commercial airliners for about 10,000 years straight—that is, around the clock without any breaks—before the odds of our dying in a plane crash exceed 50 percent. But because big plane crashes make big news, we overestimate their frequency, leading many people to avoid flying altogether.

Overall, we underestimate the frequency of the most common causes of death and overestimate the occurrence of the least common causes of death (Lichtenstein, Slovic, Fischhoff, et al., 1978). As John Ruscio (2000) points out, this tendency sometimes leads to a negative correlation between the actual risk of events and their perceived risk. The less likely something is, the more likely the media is to cover it and, as a result, the more common we believe it to be. So in an ironic twist, not only do we often worry about the wrong things, we often worry about the safest things.

Our mental images of Michigan (top) and Detroit, Michigan (bottom), conjure up markedly different estimates of violent crime. In this case, the availability heuristic can lead us to faulty conclusions.

Simulate in MyPsychLab the Experiment: Heuristics

HINDSIGHT BIAS. Hindsight bias, sometimes also known as the "I knew it all along" effect, refers to our tendency to overestimate how accurately we could have predicted something happening once we know the outcome (Fischoff, 1975; Kunda, 1999). As the old saying goes, "Hindsight is 20/20." This is also where the term "Monday Morning Quarterbacking" comes from—when commentators and spectators of a football game played Sunday evening point out after the fact that a different strategy would have worked better. Even if they are correct, it's much easier to say "It would have worked better if…" once you already know that the action taken hasn't worked.

availability heuristic
heuristic that involves estimating the likelihood of an occurrence based on the ease with which it comes to our minds

hindsight bias
our tendency to overestimate how well we could have predicted something after it has already occurred

We're also prone to a powerful cognitive bias called *confirmation bias*, which is our tendency to seek out evidence that supports our hypotheses or beliefs and to deny, dismiss, or distort evidence that doesn't. The scientific method helps us compensate for this bias in research but, as we'll discover later in this chapter, it can also have consequences for our real-world decision making.

Top-Down Processing

Our brains have evolved to streamline processing in other ways besides heuristics and biases. One key example is that we fill in the gaps of missing information using our experience and background knowledge. Psychologists call this phenomenon *top-down processing*. We can contrast top-down processing with bottom-up processing, in which our brain processes only the information it receives, and constructs meaning from it slowly and surely by building up understanding through experience. Perception differs from sensation because our perceptual experiences rely not only on raw sensory input, but also on stored knowledge that our brains access to interpret those experiences. Chunking is a memory aid that relies on our ability to organize information into larger units, expanding the span and detail of our memories. Each of these examples highlights our brain's tendency to simplify our cognitive functioning by using preexisting knowledge to spare us from reinventing the wheel.

One common source of top-down processing that helps us to think and reason is our use of concepts and schemas. **Concepts** are our knowledge and ideas about objects, actions, and characteristics that share core properties. We have concepts of the properties that all motorcycles share of what feature unifies all purple things. Sschemas are concepts we've stored in memory about how certain actions, objects, and ideas relate to each other. They help us to mentally organize *events* that share core features, say, going to a restaurant, cleaning the house, or visiting the zoo. As we acquire knowledge, we create schemas that enable us to draw on our knowledge when we encounter something new.

A concept allows us to have all of our general knowledge about dogs, for example, at our disposal when dealing with a new dog, Rover. We don't need to discover from scratch that Rover barks, pants when he's hot, and has a stomach. All of these things come "for free" once we recognize Rover as a dog. Similarly, when we go to a new doctor's office, no one has to tell us to check in with the receptionist and sit in the waiting room until someone calls us to enter an examining room, because our schema for doctors' visits tells us that this is the standard script. Of course, our concepts and schemas don't apply to all real-world situations. Rover may be unable to bark because of a throat disorder. Yet most of the time, our concepts and schemas safely allow us to exert less cognitive effort over basic knowledge, freeing us to engage in more complex reasoning and emotional processing.

? Nostradamus was a sixteenth-century prophet whose four-line poems supposedly foretold the future. Here's a famous one:

Beasts ferocious with hunger will cross the rivers, The greater part of the battlefield will be against the Hister. Into a cage of iron will the great one be drawn, When the child of Germany observes nothing.

After reading it, can you guess what historical event it supposedly predicted? (The answer is upside down at the bottom of this page.) Odds are high you won't. Yet after discovering the answer, you're likely to find that the poem fits the event quite well. This is an example of hindsight bias. (Yafeh & Heath, 2003).

concept
our knowledge and ideas about a set of objects, actions, and characteristics that share core properties

An example of top-down processing comes from mondegreens—commonly misheard song lyrics. For example, one of your textbook'stext's authors thought that Soulja Boy was singing "Shook my leg in the mirror" in his song "Turn My Swag On" (much to her teenage son's chagrin). The real lyric was "Took a look in the mirror."

Answer: Adolph Hitler's rise to power.

Assess Your Knowledge   FACT or FICTION?

 Study and **Review** in **MyPsychLab**

1. Fast and frugal processing almost always leads to false conclusions.   **True / False**

2. Concepts are a form of cognitive economy because they don't rely on any specific knowledge or experience.   **True / False**

3. Assuming that someone must play basketball because he or she is extremely tall is an example of the availability heuristic.   **True / False**

4. Humans are typically biased to consider base rates when calculating the likelihood that something is true.   **True / False**

5. Top-down processing involves drawing inferences from previous experience and applying them to current situations.   **True / False**

Answers: 1. F, 2. F, 3. T, 4. F, 5. T

Thinking at Its Hardest: Decision Making and Problem Solving

3   Discover what influences our decision making.

4   Describe some common problem-solving strategies and challenges.

5   Describe various models of the human mind.

Probably the most difficult and effortful thinking we do is that involved in making decisions and solving problems. Psychologists call these aspects of thinking "higher-order" cognition because they require us to take all of the more basic aspects of cognition, such as perception, knowledge, memory, language, and reasoning, and integrate them to generate a plan of action.

Decision Making: Choices, Choices, and More Choices

Decision making is the process of selecting among a set of alternatives. Should I order fries or a salad with my sandwich? Should I major in philosophy or physics? Which outfit looks better?

Each decision we make seems deceptively simple: It's an either/or choice. But many factors enter in to most decisions. Let's take the seemingly straightforward question of whether to order a salad or fries. Such a choice often depends on a variety of factors, such as whether we're watching our weight, whether we like the type of fries and salad dressings available at the restaurant, and maybe even what everyone else at our table is ordering. For many of these small decisions, we often weigh the considerations quickly and implicitly, that is, below conscious awareness. This often involves System 1 thinking, which is rapid and intuitive (Kahneman, 2011). But for some other decisions, such as where to go to college or whether to get married, the decisions have much larger consequences and require more careful deliberation. In these cases, decision making often becomes more explicit and deliberate. We mull over the options; sometimes identify and list the pros and cons of each option; and may solicit the advice and opinions of friends, family, and trusted advisers such as professors, clergy, and coaches. Here, we're relying on System 2 thinking, which is slow and analytical.

Is explicitly analyzing the situation before making a decision a good idea? It depends (Lehrer, 2009). Timothy Wilson and his colleagues gave female college students a choice among five art posters to take home. The investigators asked half of the students to just "go with their gut" and pick the poster they liked and the other half to carefully list each of the pros and cons of each poster. When the researchers recontacted the participants a few weeks later, those who went with their gut reported that they were much happier with their choice (Wilson et al., 1993). When it comes to emotional preferences, like which art we like or which people we find attractive, thinking too much may get us in trouble. Ironically, this may be especially

decision making
the process of selecting among a set of possible alternatives

true for complex emotionally laden decisions, like which car to buy, because our brains can easily become overwhelmed by excessive information (Dijksterhuis et al., 2006). In such cases, listing all of the pros and cons can sometimes confuse us, producing a "paralysis by analysis."

Yet when it comes to evaluating scientific claims in the laboratory and in real life, such careful analysis may be the better bet (Lilienfeld et al., 2010; Myers, 2002). In fact, business communities are increasingly encouraging managers to be more strategic in their decision making about personnel, resources, and organizational structure. The new field of "decision management" attempts to bring scientific evidence into the business world to help organizations prosper through sound decision making and avoid bias (Yates & Potworowski, 2012).

Marketing researchers, advertising executives, and political pollsters have long known that an additional factor influences our decision making: **framing**, that is, how we formulate the question about what we need to decide (Tversky & Kahneman, 1986). Imagine you've been diagnosed with lung cancer and your doctor gives you a choice. She tells you, "We can treat your cancer with surgery, which has a 90 percent post-procedure survival rate and a 34 percent five-year survival rate, *or* we can treat it with radiation, which has a 100 percent post-procedure survival rate and a 22 percent five-year survival rate." Which option would you choose? Most people in this situation pick surgery. But imagine that your doctor reworded the question to emphasize a different aspect of the decision: "We can treat your cancer with surgery, which has a 10 percent post-procedure fatality rate and a 66 percent five-year fatality rate, *or* we can treat it with radiation, which has a 0 percent post-procedure fatality rate and a 78 percent five-year fatality rate." When the question is framed that way, more people choose radiation. Suddenly the fact that we might not live through surgery becomes much more noticeable. Even though both questions contain the same information, one emphasizes survival; the other, death. That's framing.

? The ad on the left emphasizes a percent reduction in sugar; the ad on the right highlights the total amount. Both emphasize the low amount of sugar in the product but present the information differently. **What concept do the differences between these two ads demonstrate?** (See answer upside down at bottom of page.)

Researchers in a newly minted field called *neuroeconomics* have become interested in how the brain works while making financial decisions (Glimcher et al., 2008; Hasler, 2012). By using fMRI to identify brain areas that become active in specific decision-making situations—such as when interacting with a person who's stingy or selfish—researchers hope to better predict and understand how emotion, reasoning, and arousal influence our decisions (Kato et al., 2009). For example, one team of investigators imaged the brains of participants asked to make risky monetary decisions. When participants received advice from a financial expert, brain regions involved in decision making—such as certain areas of their frontal lobes—became less active than when they received no financial advice (Engelmann et al., 2009). This new field has the potential to help us understand why decision making goes wrong in some individuals. For example, clinical psychologists have recently begun exploring ways to use neuroeconomics approaches to diagnose and characterize psychological disorders (Sharp, Monterosso, & Read Montague, 2012).

framing
the way a question is formulated that can influence the decisions people make

problem solving
generating a cognitive strategy to accomplish a goal

👁 **Watch** in **MyPsychLab** the **Video:** The Basics: The Mind Is What the Brain Does

Problem Solving: Accomplishing Our Goals

Many times a day, we're faced with problems to solve. Some are as simple as figuring out where we left our favorite pair of shoes, but others involve attempting to recover a corrupted computer file or figuring out how to get to a restaurant in an unfamiliar part of town. **Problem solving** is generating a cognitive strategy to accomplish a goal.

Answer: Framing. Seeing f different decision-making proc. of information are in the foreground.

APPROACHES TO SOLVING PROBLEMS. We've encountered a variety of heuristics, like availability and representativeness, that we use to draw conclusions and solve problems in a fast and frugal way. Although these heuristics are often effective, we can draw on a variety of more deliberate solutions, too. In particular, we can solve many problems following step-by-step learned procedures known as **algorithms**. Algorithms come in handy for problems that depend on the same basic steps for arriving at a solution every time the solution is required, such as replacing the starter on a car, performing a tonsillectomy, or making a peanut-butter-and-jelly sandwich. Algorithms ensure that we address all steps when we solve a problem, but they're pretty inflexible. Imagine you had an algorithm for cooking a mushroom omelet that includes melting some butter but you ran out of butter. You'd be stuck. As a result, you could either give up—or, instead, "use your head" to engage in a more flexible solution.

Another more flexible approach is to break down a problem into subproblems that are easier to solve. If we're trying to construct a doghouse, we might break down the problem into identifying the size and dimensions of the doghouse, purchasing the materials, constructing the floor, and so on. By breaking down the problem into bite-sized chunks, we can often solve it more quickly and easily. Another effective approach involves reasoning from related examples, such as realizing that because oil is often substituted for butter in baking recipes, it might work for an omelet, too (Gentner et al., 2009). Many breakthroughs in scientific problems in the laboratory and real world have come from drawing *analogies* between two distinct topics. These analogies solve problems with similar structures. For example, after observing how burrs stuck to his dog's fur by using a series of tiny hooks that attached to individual strands of fur, George de Mestral invented Velcro in 1948.

OBSTACLES TO PROBLEM SOLVING. Although we use a variety of effective strategies to solve problems, we also face a variety of hurdles—cognitive tendencies that can interfere with the use of effective problem-solving strategies. We'll consider three obstacles to solving problems correctly: salience of surface similarities, mental sets, and functional fixedness.

Salience of Surface Similarities. Salience refers to how attention-grabbing something is. We tend to focus our attention on the surface-level (superficial) properties of a problem, such as the topic of an algebra word problem, and try to solve problems the same way we solved problems that exhibited similar surface characteristics. When one algebra word problem calls for subtraction and another calls for division, the fact that both deal with trains isn't going to help us. Ignoring the surface features of a problem and focusing on the underlying reasoning needed to solve it can be challenging.

Imagine learning about two problems. In one problem, a general wants to capture a fortress but realizes that taking all his forces down a single path makes them vulnerable to attack, so he divides the forces up into many smaller units who each attack along a different path. By surrounding the fortress along many paths, the fortress is taken without significant loss of troops. In the second problem, a doctor is attempting to treat a stomach tumor by use of a laser but realizes that sending the full-intensity beam required to destroy the tumor will damage the healthy tissue in its path. Can you think of a solution that destroys the tumor but protects the healthy tissue? Hint: the second problem involves the same reasoning process as the first. Did you realize that the same solution—sending lots of low-intensity beams in from lots of directions—would work for the tumor problem? In one study, only 20 percent of students who saw the fortress problem figured out the tumor problem (Gick & Holyoak, 1983). But when researchers told students that the fortress problem could help them solve the tumor problem, their success shot up to 92 percent. The students hadn't noticed that the fortress solution was relevant.

Mental Sets. Once we find a workable solution that's dependable, we often get stuck in that solution mode; we have trouble generating alternatives or "thinking outside the box." Psychologists term this phenomenon a **mental set**. When attempting to pick a topic for a term paper, we may have trouble thinking of topics the professor hasn't already covered in class. Ironically, a friend who hasn't taken the class may be able to come up with more creative ideas because our thinking has become "boxed in" by our experiences.

Watch in **MyPsychLab** the **Video:** IT Video: Water Lilly

Simulate in **MyPsychLab** the **Experiment:** Obstacles to Problem Solving

 Explore in **MyPsychLab** the **Concept:** Intuition and Discovery in Problem Solving

algorithm
step-by-step learned procedure used to solve a problem

mental set
phenomenon of becoming stuck in a sp problem-solving strategy, inhibiting ou to generate alternatives

A	B	C	Target
I	127	21	3	100
2	94	20	I	72
3	95	25	5	50

FIGURE 2 Mental Set Problems. Solve these problems by figuring out how to add and remove precise amounts of water using the jars provided. The first two problems use the same formula: Add the amount in the first jug (A), subtract the amount from the second jug (B), and then subtract the amount from the third jug (C) twice (A – B – C – C = Target amount). The third problem requires a different solution. Can you figure it out? If you're stuck, you may be experiencing a "mental set."

RULING OUT RIVAL HYPOTHESES ▶
Have important alternative explanations for the findings been excluded?

FIGURE 3 Functional Fixedness. A classic demonstration of functional fixedness requires participants to figure out how to mount a candle on a wall given only a candle, a book of matches, and a box of tacks (Duncker, 1945). For the solution, see the upside-down figure

In a classic study of mental sets, participants solved a series of problems that required measuring out a precise amount of water by adding and subtracting water given only three odd measuring jars (such as filling a jug with precisely 100 quarts using only a 21-quart jar, a 127-quart jar, and a 3-quart jar; see **FIGURE 2**). Half the participants solved eight problems that used the same formula (A – B – C – C = Target amount) before working on a problem that used a different formula, and the other half solved only the ninth problem without working on the first eight. Only 36 percent of participants who solved the first eight problems the same way generated the correct solution on the ninth one. In contrast, participants who solved the ninth problem first generated a correct solution 95 percent of the time (Luchins, 1946). Solving the first eight problems actually made solving the ninth more difficult, because the eight problems created a mental set from which subjects had a hard time breaking free.

More recent research has explored some of the ways to break out of mental sets. One study showed that giving people actual jars to manipulate made participants less likely to get stuck in a mental set. This approach worked especially well for participants with strong visual-spatial skills (Vallée-Tourangeau, Euden, & Hearn, 2011). Studies using fMRI suggest that being able to break free of a mental set depends on activation of the frontal and parietal lobes, probably because these regions help us to inhibit previous responses and allow us to generate new strategies (Witt & Stevens, 2012).

Functional Fixedness. **Functional fixedness** occurs when we experience difficulty conceptualizing that an object typically used for one purpose can be used for another (German & Defeyter, 2000). That is, we become "fixated" on one conventional use for an object. Have you ever needed a hammer, tape, or scissors but didn't have any of these items around? Were you able to come up with an alternative solution? Functional fixedness can prevent us from realizing that we could use a shoe as a hammer or a mailing label as tape. Remember our buddy Tre who realized that a key could weigh down a fishing line? His clever idea is a clear example of overcoming functional fixedness.

One famous technique for measuring functional fixedness asked participants to figure out a way to mount a candle on a wall given only a candle, a book of matches, and a box of tacks, as shown in **FIGURE 3** (Duncker, 1945). Can you figure out how to do it? Most of us find this problem difficult because it forces us to use conventional objects in unconventional ways. Nevertheless, one study challenged the idea of functional fixedness as an explanation for this finding. The researchers showed that individuals from a rural area of Ecuador who live in a traditional nontechnological society and consequently have few expectations about the functional roles of these objects still had difficulty solving the problem (German & Barrett, 2005). So functional fixedness may occur even when we've had little or no experience with the objects in question.

Models of the Mind

Given everything we've learned about our fast and frugal processing, our heuristics and biases, and our abilities and limitations as problem solvers, what's the best model—or unifying explanation—for how the mind works? In the 1980s, many psychologists adopted a computer analogy to explain the mind's tendency to process information, fill in gaps, and draw inferences. Perhaps thinking is akin to running data through a computer program. From this perspective, the brain's algorithms are like preprogrammed abilities; the brain runs data through its "software program" and spits out an answer.

Although some modern psychologists still rely on the computer model, most believe that a computer analogy doesn't do a good job of explaining how we think (Searle, 1990). In fact, some of the tasks that humans find simplest are among the most difficult for computers. Although we can perceive and recognize speech without difficulty, anyone who's attempted to use voice commands on an automated phone menu knows that computers are notoriously poor at this task. One reason humans beat out computers on such tasks is that we can take context into account and draw subtle inferences that computers can't.

cific
ability

an object typically
e used for another

For example, we might hear someone say something that sounds a lot like "I frog," but that occurs in the context of him apologizing for not bringing you something he promised. So we could guess correctly that he meant to say "I forgot." In contrast, a computer won't be able to use top-down knowledge to resolve this ambiguity.

Another important way that human thinking differs from computers is that computers don't have a chance to explore and interact with the world. From infancy, we act on the world and observe the consequences of our actions. We learn that sitting on a surface that isn't designed to hold our weight can cause us to fall or that telling someone "You're a jerk" usually produces a different emotional reaction than telling her "I'm upset about what you said."

Recent models of the mind have attempted to reflect the physically interactive nature of our knowledge and experience by developing *embodied* accounts of thinking. According to embodiment models, our knowledge is organized and accessed in a manner that enables us to simulate our actual experiences (Lakoff, 2012). For example, people who hear the sentence "The man saw the eagle in the sky" and then see a picture of an eagle are quicker to label the eagle if its wings are spread (consistent with how it would look in the scenario described in the sentence) than if its wings are folded close to its body (Fischer & Zwaan, 2008). Neuroimaging studies of brain activation are consistent with an embodied approach to thinking (Barsalou, 2008). These studies show that the brain's sensory areas (for example, visual, auditory, and motor cortex) become activated when people think about objects, actions, and events.

Human cognitive processing is remarkably flexible and creative, taking advantage of past experience, context, imagination, and mental shortcuts to provide us with rapid and efficient solutions to problems. Our fast and frugal thinking serves us remarkably well much of the time. Nevertheless, one of our major goals in this text is to raise awareness about how our cognitive systems can lead us astray—and just as important, how we can guard against it. Such awareness can help us recognize situations in which we're vulnerable to faulty reasoning and to think twice about our intuitions. When we hear on the news that one presidential candidate is leading in the polls or that bilingual schooling is bad for children, we should pause to think about the information on which the media based these conclusions. When deciding whether that incredible deal on laptops ("Laptops for only $200, and they're five times faster than your home computer!") or the financing on the car you're thinking of buying is too good to be true, you should consider whether the information is sufficient to warrant the remarkable claims. When deciding whether a diet plan we're considering is effective, we should think about what scientific research says instead of relying on a handful of anecdotes from friends. Cognitive economy has a lot going for it, but being aware of its pitfalls will make us more informed consumers of information in our everyday lives.

◀ **EXTRAORDINARY CLAIMS**
Is the evidence as strong as the claim?

✓ **Study** and **Review** in **MyPsychLab**

Assess Your Knowledge — FACT or FICTION?

1. Decision making is always an implicit process subtly influenced by how we frame the problem.   **True / False**

2. Performing careful analysis of pros and cons is typically most useful when making decisions about emotional preferences.   **True / False**

3. Neuroeconomics has the potential to use brain imaging to identify personality differences and psychiatric disorders.   **True / False**

4. Comparing problems that require similar reasoning processes but different surface characteristics can help us overcome deceptive surface similarities.   **True / False**

5. Functional fixedness is a product of Western technology-dependent society.   **True / False**

Answers: 1. F; 2. F; 3. T; 4. T; 5. F

TABLE 1 How's That Again? Ambiguous News Headlines. Language can be ambiguous and even unintentionally humorous when taken out of context. The examples in (A) are ambiguous because they use words that possess multiple meanings. The examples in (B) possess ambiguous grammar, resulting in two possible interpretations.

(A) Ambiguous Word Meaning
Drunk Gets Nine Months in Violin Case
Iraqi Head Seeks Arms
Man Struck by Lightning Faces Battery Charge
Old School Pillars Are Replaced by Alumni
Two Convicts Evade Noose, Jury Hung

(B) Grammatically Ambiguous
Eye Drops Off Shelf
British Left Waffles on Falkland Islands
Killer Sentenced to Die for Second Time in 10 Years
Ban on Soliciting Dead in Trotwood
Include Your Children When Baking Cookies
Juvenile Court to Try Shooting Defendant

"Sorry, but I'm going to have to issue you a summons for reckless grammar and driving without an apostrophe."

© The New Yorker Collection 1987 Michael Maslin from cartoonbank.com. All Rights Reserved.)

Language
largely arbitrary system of communication that combines symbols (such as words and gestural signs) in rule-based ways to create meaning

Phoneme
category of sounds our vocal apparatus produces

Morpheme
smallest meaningful unit of speech

Syntax
grammatical rules that govern how words are [combined] to meaningful strings

...mation
...hat aren't part
...t are critical to

Answer to F:

How Does Language Work?

6 Describe the four levels of analysis that make up language.

7 Trace the development of language acquisition in children.

8 Identify the pros and cons of bilingualism.

9 Distinguish human language from nonhuman animal communication.

We tend to think that words possess fixed meanings, like the ones we find in the dictionary. But how we interpret a word depends on its context. Many funny (and sometimes not so funny) misunderstandings can arise when contextual information is missing. **TABLE 1** presents examples of actual newspaper headlines in which interpreting the words literally result in unintentionally humorous interpretations.

Language is a system of communication that combines symbols, such as words or gestural signs, in rule-based ways to create meaning. One hallmark of language is that it tends to be arbitrary: Its sounds, words, and sentences bear no clear relation to their meaning. For example, there's nothing about the word *dog* that resembles a friendly, furry animal that barks, and the word *tarantula* is much longer than the word *pig*, even though tarantulas are (thankfully) a lot smaller than pigs. Language serves several crucial functions. The most obvious is the transmission of information. When we tell our roommate "The party starts at nine" or we place an order at a coffee shop for a "skim latte," we're communicating information that enables us or someone else to accomplish a goal, like getting to the party on time or making sure our latte is nonfat.

Language serves key social and emotional functions, too. It enables us to express our thoughts about social interactions, such as conveying "I thought you were mad at me" or "That guy was hilarious." We spend much of our conversational time establishing or maintaining our relationships with others (Dunbar, 1996).

The Features of Language

We take language for granted because it's a highly practiced and automatic cognitive process. By *automatic*, we mean that using and interpreting language usually requires little attention, enabling us to perform other tasks, such as walking, cooking, or exercising, without speech getting in the way (Posner & Snyder, 1975). We don't realize how complex language is until we try to learn or use a new one. In fact, our ability to use language requires the coordination of an enormous number of cognitive, social, and physical skills. Even the mere ability to produce the sounds of our language requires the delicate interplay among breath control, vocal cords, throat and mouth position, and tongue movement.

We can think about language at four levels of analysis, all of which we need to coordinate to communicate effectively. These levels are (1) **phonemes**, the sounds of our language; (2) **morphemes**, the smallest units of meaningful speech; (3) **syntax**, the grammatical rules that govern how we compose words into meaningful strings; and (4) **extralinguistic information**, elements of communication that aren't part of the content of language but are crucial to interpreting its meaning, such as facial expressions and tone of voice. We can think of each level as similar to the different levels of specificity involved in preparing a meal—ranging from the individual ingredients to the menu items to the meal itself and, last but not least, to the overall dining experience.

PHONEMES: THE INGREDIENTS. Phonemes are categories of sounds produced by our vocal apparatus. These categories are influenced by elements of our vocal tract, including our lips, teeth, tongue placement, vibration of the vocal cords, opening and closing of our throat, and other physical manipulations of our throat and mouth.

Experts disagree on the total number of phonemes across all of the world's languages—probably around 100 in total—but they agree that each language includes only a subset of them. English contains between 40 and 45 phonemes, depending on how we count them. Some languages have as few as about 15; others, more than 60. Although there's some overlap across languages, some languages contain sounds that don't occur in other languages. This fact certainly adds to the challenge of learning a second language. The most famous example of this principle (at least among English speakers) is the Japanese *R/L* distinction. Japanese has a single sound category that encompasses both "r" and "l" sounds, a fact that's difficult for English speakers to understand because the sounds seem so different. However, there are similar examples that turn the tables on English speakers. English speakers easily distinguish "d" sounds from "t" sounds. But the Hindi language (spoken in many parts of India) has a third sound category that's partway between a *d* and a *t*, produced as if pronouncing the letter *d* but with the tongue pressed against the back of the teeth. This third category sounds just as distinct to Hindi speakers as *r* and *l* do to English speakers, and yet English speakers can't make out this difference (Werker & Tees, 2002). They hear it as either a *d* or a *t*.

MORPHEMES: THE MENU ITEMS. Morphemes are the smallest units of meaning in a language. They're created by stringing phonemes together. Most of our morphemes are words such as *dog* and *happy*. Morphemes convey information about **semantics**—meaning derived from words and sentences. Nevertheless, we also have strings of sounds that aren't words by themselves, but modify the meaning of words when they're tacked onto them. These are morphemes, too, although they don't stand alone as words. For example, the morpheme *re-* as in *recall* and *rewrite* means "to do again," and the morpheme *-ish* as in *warmish* and *pinkish* means "to a moderate degree."

SYNTAX: PUTTING THE MEAL TOGETHER. Syntax is the set of rules of a language by which we construct sentences. For instance, the string of words *I ate pizza for dinner* forms a complete sentence that follows the syntactic rules of English. In contrast, *Pizza ate I for dinner* doesn't follow English syntax, although it follows the syntactic rules of some other languages. Syntax isn't just word order, though; it also includes *morphological markers* and sentence structure. Morphological markers are morphemes (which means they change the meaning of a word but they do so based on a grammatical rule). For example, in English, we add *s* for plural, *ed* for past tense, and *ing* for ongoing action.

Although syntactic rules describe how language is organized, real-world language rarely follows them perfectly. If you were to write down word for word what your psychology professor says at the beginning of your next class, you'd find that he or she violates at least one or two syntactic rules. So syntax describes an idealized form of language, much like the formal language we read in written documents.

EXTRALINGUISTIC INFORMATION: THE OVERALL DINING EXPERIENCE. We often think of language as self-explanatory: We say what we mean and mean what we say (most of the time, anyway). Yet we take a great deal of additional information for granted when we interpret the language we hear. Extralinguistic information isn't part of language, but it plays an essential role in allowing us to interpret it. Some examples include previous statements made by others in the conversation and the speaker's nonverbal cues—such as his or her facial expression, posture, gestures, and tone of voice. Misunderstandings can easily arise if people aren't attentive to this information or if some of it is blocked, such as during a phone conversation or in a text message.

Suppose we hear someone say, "It's just awful in here!" This sentence doesn't provide enough information to figure out what the speaker means. To understand her, we need to look at her facial expressions and gestures and consider where she is, what she's doing, and what people were talking about just prior to her making the statement. If she's waving her hand in front of her face and wiping her forehead while standing in a hot kitchen, we'd probably infer that she's referring to the temperature of the room. If she's

How we interpret a sentence depends a great deal on the context. How would your interpretation of the sentence "It's just awful in here!" differ in these two contexts?

semantics
meaning derived from words and se

holding her nose and looking disgusted while standing in a seafood shop, we'd probably infer that she's referring to a dreadful smell. And if she has a frustrated look on her face and someone just commented on the huge number of people at the event she's attending, we might infer she's referring to how crowded the room is.

LANGUAGE DIALECTS: REGIONAL AND CULTURAL DIFFERENCES IN DINING HABITS. Although each language has its own set of phonemes, morphemes, and syntactic rules, there's variability in these elements within, as well as across, languages. **Dialects** are variations of the same language used by groups of people from specific geographic areas, social groups, or ethnic backgrounds. Dialects aren't distinct languages, because speakers of two different dialects can, for the most part, understand each other (Labov, 1970; Tang & van Heuven, 2009). Different dialects may employ slight variations of the standard pronunciations, vocabulary, and syntax of the language. For instance, many people from Boston (and from England) are known for dropping their *r*'s ("I pahked my cah") and many Texans are known for their "twang." Similarly, you may refer to the same drink as "soda," "pop," "tonic," or "Coke" depending on where you live. It's important to understand that speakers of dialects that differ from the "standardized" version of the native language aren't making pronunciation or grammatical errors.

Many people assume that speakers of nondominant dialects are trying but failing to speak the majority (standard) version of the dialect (Smitherman-Donaldson & van Dijk, 1988). This assumption can lead to unwarranted and misguided prejudice (Baugh, 2000). Speakers of these dialects are using consistent syntactic rules in their speech, even though these rules differ from those used by the "mainstream" dialect (Ellis, 2006; Rickford & Rickford, 2000). For example, speakers of African-American Vernacular English might say "plug it *up*" instead of "plug it *in*." Speakers of Appalachian dialect, spoken by many people living in the Appalachian Mountains, might say, "He had *went* to the store" instead of "He had *gone* to the store." As long as they're using these constructions systematically, they're using an equally valid rule-based form of communication.

Frank and Ernest

© 1997 Thaves. Reprinted with permission. Newspaper dist. by NEA, Inc.

(© 1997 Thaves. Reprinted with permission.)

How and Why Did Language Come About?

Scientists have long debated the question of how language evolved and what possible advantages such a complicated communication system offers. One clear advantage is that language allows us to communicate extremely complex thoughts. Some evolutionary theorists argue that language evolved into a complex system as our early apelike ancestors began to engage in increasingly complex social organizations and activities like coordinated group hunting. One thing on which evolutionary theorists agree is that language must provide the human species a strong survival advantage to offset its disadvantages. Indeed, there are plenty of disadvantages. For example, language requires a lengthy learning period and hefty brainpower. In addition, possessing a vocal tract that allows us to make a wide array of sounds actually increases our chances of choking (Lieberman, 2007).

One challenge to explaining how language evolved is the fact that language is generally arbitrary. Most phonemes, words, and syntactic rules are unrelated to things to which they refer. That seems like an unintuitive "design feature." Many scholars argue that language is arbitrary for a good reason. Using arbitrary words allows us more flexibility to express complex ideas that don't have sounds naturally associated with them. Still, there are intriguing examples of nonarbitrary language in which words *do* resemble their meaning. The most obvious is *onomatopoeia*, or words that resemble the sounds to which they refer, like *buzz*, *meow*, *beep*, and *zoom*. Another example is that across the world's languages, the word for mother nearly always starts with an *m* or *n*, whereas the word for father nearly always starts with a *b*, *p*, or *d*. This fact is probably more than a coincidence, particularly because these phonemes tend to be those that children acquire earliest; in the case of mother, "m" is a sound that babies make while nursing. Research on *sound symbolism*—the fact that certain

roup of people
nity or ethnic
tences

speech sounds seem to be associated with particular meanings—challenges the idea of language as completely arbitrary (Aveyard, 2012; Imai et al., 2008; Nygaard, Cook, & Namy, 2009; see **FIGURE 4**). For example, in Japanese, the word *hayai* means "fast." English speakers told that *hayai* means "fast" learn this information more easily than those taught that it means "sweet" (Nygaard et al., 2009). This finding suggests that *hayai* sounds like its *real* meaning. The fact that at least some sound symbolism is consistent across languages raises the intriguing possibility that connections between auditory and other sensory systems in the brain influenced how languages evolved.

FIGURE 4 A Classic Example of Sound Symbolism. Which object looks like a "maluma" and which looks like a "takete"? If you're like most people (children *and* adults the world over), you'll say that the "maluma" is on the left and the "takete" is on the right.

How Do Children Learn Language?

Language is among the few documented cases in which children are more efficient learners than adults are. The language-learning process starts long before children begin talking. In fact, it begins even before they're born. By the fifth month of pregnancy, the auditory systems of unborn infants are developed enough that they can begin to make out their mother's voice, learn to recognize some characteristics of their mother's native language, and even recognize specific songs or stories they've heard repeatedly (DeCasper & Spence, 1988).

We know this to be true because researchers have developed a clever way to test newborn infants' ability to distinguish sounds, namely, a method that capitalizes on operant conditioning. The technique is the *high-amplitude sucking procedure* that takes advantage of one of the few behaviors over which infants have good control at birth—sucking. Two-day-old infants suck more on a pacifier when they hear their mother's native language than when they hear a foreign language, even when total strangers speak both languages. Even at this early age, they display a clear preference for their mother's native language. This is true of infants of English-speaking and Spanish-speaking mothers alike: Infants whose mothers speak English suck harder when they hear English rather than Spanish, and those whose mothers speak Spanish suck harder when they hear Spanish rather than English (Moon, Cooper, & Fifer, 1993). The fact that researchers tested babies with English- and Spanish-speaking mothers is an elegant experimental design feature. It allowed researchers to rule out the possibility that all babies prefer English over another language, regardless of which language their mothers speak.

PERCEIVING AND PRODUCING THE SOUNDS OF LANGUAGE. During the first year or so after birth, infants learn much more about the sounds of their native language. They begin to figure out the phonemes of their language and how to use their vocal apparatus to make specific sounds. Although children's babbling seems like nonsense—and it usually is—it plays an important role in language development by enabling babies to figure out how to move their vocal tracts to generate certain sounds. **Babbling** refers to any intentional vocalization (sounds other than crying, burping, sighing, and laughing, which are less intentional) that lacks meaning. Babbling evolves over the first year of life and follows a progression of stages demonstrating infants' increasing control of their vocal tract (Kent & Miolo, 1995). By the end of their first year, infants' babbling takes on a conversational tone that sounds meaningful even though it isn't (Goldstein & Schwade, 2008).

Factoid

Related words often have similar-sounding initial consonant clusters, a phenomenon called phonesthemes (Hutchins, 1999; Bergen, 2004). For example, in English the "sn" sound is associated with a large number of nose-related activities, including sneeze, sniff, snore, snooze, snicker, snort, snoop (what a "nosy" person does, after all), and even snot! What other sound sequences occur in a cluster of related words?

Fetuses can learn about the melody and rhythm of their native language and learn to recognize their mother's voice before birth. They even can learn to recognize a specific story read to them before birth (DeCasper & Spence, 1988).

◄ **RULING OUT RIVAL HYPOTHESES**
Have important alternative explanations for the findings been excluded?

babbling
intentional vocalization that lacks specific meaning

 Watch in **MyPsychLab** the **Video:** Language Development

As infants are fine-tuning their vocal tracts, they're fine-tuning their ears, too. As we've learned, different languages have different phonemes; so to be successful users of their native language, infants must learn which sets of sounds are relevant for their language. All babies initially share the same basic phoneme categories regardless of their parents' native language. However, babies adjust their phonemes rapidly over the course of the first year to match their native language. By ten months, infants' phoneme categories are very much like those of the adult speakers of their native language (Werker & Tees, 1984).

? Very young children with limited vocabularies can't talk very well and are often shy about talking in front of strangers. **Can you think of ways researchers could measure what words children understand without depending on their ability to tell them?** (See answer upside down at bottom of page.)

LEARNING WORDS. How and when do children begin to communicate using words? One key principle characterizes early word learning: *Comprehension precedes production.* Children learn to recognize and interpret words well before—sometimes months before—they can produce them. That's because they have only a limited ability to coordinate sounds to produce recognizable words. They may be perfectly aware that *elephant* refers to a large gray animal with a long trunk, but they may be unable to produce this big word.

Children start to *produce* their first words around their first birthdays, although there's considerable variability in this milestone. They acquire their first words slowly. Between one and one-and-a-half years of age, they gradually accumulate a vocabulary of between 20 and 100 words. As children become more experienced in learning new words, the rate at which they acquire words increases and the difference between the number of words they know and those they can say continues to narrow (Golinkoff et al., 2000; Smith, 2000). By the time they turn two, most children can produce several hundred words. By kindergarten, their vocabularies have ballooned to several thousand words.

Yet children typically make some mistakes in interpreting what words mean and how to use them, often over- and underextending. This means that they apply words in a broader sense (overextension, like referring to all adult men as "Daddy") than adults do or in a narrower sense (underextension, like thinking that the word *cat* applies only to their pet cat). Of course, most of the time, children manage to get word meanings exactly right, which is a remarkable achievement.

? A child who uses the word grandpa to apply to any gray-haired man is committing what kind of mistake? (See answer upside down at bottom of page.)

SYNTACTIC DEVELOPMENT: PUTTING IT ALL TOGETHER. The first major milestone in children's syntactic development is combining words into phrases. Children start off speaking in the **one-word stage**, during which they use individual words to convey entire thoughts. A child may use the word *doggie* to mean "There's a doggie!" "Where's the doggie?" or even "The doggie licked me!" Interpreting what children mean in the one-word stage can be challenging. By the time children turn two, most of them start to combine words into simple two-word phrases. Although these phrases are still far from complete sentences, they go a long way toward improving comprehensibility. For example, the child can now say "more juice" to request a refill or "uh-oh juice" to notify mom that his juice just spilled. Children at this stage have already grasped something about syntactic rules. For example, they tend to use words in the correct order, even if they're leaving some of them out.

Answer (bottom photo): Overextension.

Answer (top photo): Researchers often ask infants to show what they know ("Which one is the ball?") or measure whether children look longer at the correct object when hearing a familiar word.

As is the case with word learning, children comprehend some basic syntactic rules before they can display them. Among other things, they understand how word order relates to meaning before they can generate complete sentences. Two researchers showed 17-month-olds two videos side by side, one showing Cookie Monster tickling Big Bird and another showing Big Bird tickling Cookie Monster. The experimenter asked the children, "Show me where Big Bird is tickling Cookie Monster." The children pointed toward the correct video, demonstrating they could determine from word order who was the "tickler" and who was the "ticklee" (Hirsh-Pasek & Golinkoff, 1996). (See **FIGURE 5** for a different example using a pig and a dog.)

Several months after they've begun using two-word phrases, children use more complex sentences involving three- and four-word combinations. Around the same time, they begin to produce morphological markers such as *-s* for plural and *-ed* for past tense in English. They acquire most syntactic rules by preschool age, but continue to acquire more complex rules in their early school years (Owens, 2011).

FIGURE 5 Children Display Comprehension of Word Order Prior to Sentence Production. Children can display their grasp of syntax by pointing to a video that matches a sentence they have heard. Here, a 17-month-old child is displaying her comprehension of the sentence *The pig is tickling the dog* by pointing to the video that corresponds to the sentence.

Critical Periods for Language Learning

As we noted earlier, younger children are better at learning language than are older children and adults. Much of the evidence for this conclusion derives from studies of second language acquisition. This research has focused on whether there's a *critical period* for developing language. Critical periods are windows of time in development during which an organism must learn an ability if it's going to learn it at all. We can look at the age of exposure to language to discover whether such exposure must occur during a specific time window for language to be learned.

For obvious ethical reasons, we'd never intentionally deprive a child of language exposure until a particular age for the sake of science. Nevertheless, several tragic cases have served as "natural experiments" in this regard. They provide important information about whether critical periods for learning language exist. For example, a girl named Genie was seriously neglected and abused, chained to a potty seat in a back bedroom for much of the first 13 years of her life, and deprived almost entirely of social interaction or language input (Curtiss, 1977). Once rescued from this abusive situation and exposed to language, Genie displayed a rudimentary ability to communicate. But she, and others like her, failed to use language fluently. Nevertheless, there are alternative explanations for impairment in these cases, such as the severe emotional and physical neglect these children experienced. Case studies like Genie's tend to be limited in their ability to exclude rival hypotheses.

Susan Goldin-Meadow discovered an alternative way to study language deprivation, one that ruled out many of the rival explanations that plague cases like Genie's. She began studying children who were deaf but whose parents were hearing and didn't know any sign language. Unlike Genie, these children are loved, cared for, fed, and given the opportunity to develop normally in all respects except language. Goldin-Meadow found that many children who are deaf of hearing parents invent their own signs, even when not instructed in sign language. This phenomenon, called **homesign**, shows impressive ingenuity (and motivation to communicate) on the part of children, because they've invented these signs without guidance from adults (Goldin-Meadow et al., 2009). *Still, without being exposed systematically to a language model*, such as American Sign Language, homesigners never develop full-blown language. Still, this research doesn't directly address whether there's a specific age at which language exposure must occur for children to become fluent.

A young girl named Genie, who was deprived of language until adolescence, failed to learn to use language fluently. This is consistent with the idea of a critical period for language learning, although her abusive upbringing makes it difficult to draw firm conclusions.

◀ **RULING OUT RIVAL HYPOTHESES**
Have important alternative explanations for the findings been excluded?

homesign
system of signs invented by children who are deaf and born of hearing parents and therefore receive no language input

More recently, researchers have examined evidence of critical periods by studying children born deaf to hearing parents who have received *cochlear implants* at various ages. Cochlear implants allow these children's brains to receive auditory input. The implants tend to produce more positive effects on language among younger than older children (Svirsky, Chin, & Jester, 2007). It's not clear whether these age effects are due to the brain's ability to process and interpret the auditory stimulation in general or the ability to learn language specifically.

In another classic study, researchers found a different way to examine the critical period for language by studying how *second* language proficiency varies based on the age of exposure to that language. The goal was to measure the English grammar skills of adults who'd immigrated to the United States from China and Korea at various ages. The test required participants to detect grammatical errors such as "The man climbed the ladder up carefully" and "The little boy is speak to a policeman." The investigators found that overall language proficiency was near native levels for adults who'd first been exposed to English between one and seven years of age. But skills dropped off for adults who weren't exposed to English until after age seven (Johnson & Newport, 1989; see **FIGURE 6**). Notice, however, in Figure 8 that after the age of 7, the drop-off is gradual rather than abrupt. Syntax and pronunciation are more vulnerable to effects of the age of exposure than is vocabulary (Johnson & Newport, 1989; Piske, MacKay, & Flege, 2001).

It is clear that age of acquisition influences language learning. But there's no evidence in humans for strict critical periods, at least when it comes to language. Instead, language learning is typically marked by what psychologists call a *sensitive period*, an interval during which people are more receptive to learning and can acquire new knowledge more easily. We don't fully understand why older children and adults are less capable of learning new languages than younger children are. The most promising account is Elissa Newport's (1990) "less is more" hypothesis (Newport, Bavelier, & Neville, 2001). According to this hypothesis, children have more limited information-processing abilities, fewer analytic skills, and less specific knowledge about how language works than do adults. As a result, they learn language more naturalistically and gradually from the "ground up." In contrast, adults try to impose more organization and structure on their learning, ironically making learning a language more challenging.

RULING OUT RIVAL HYPOTHESES ▶
Have important alternative explanations for the findings been excluded?

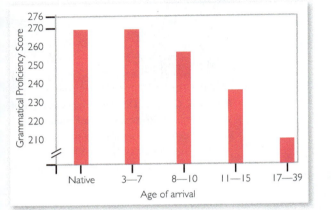

FIGURE 6 Proficiency in Second Language Depends on the Age of Exposure. Adults first exposed to English before age seven displayed proficiency comparable to that of native English speakers, whereas those who learned English after age 7 were significantly less proficient. (Based on Johnson & Newport, 1989)

Special Cases of Language Learning

Children learning language sometimes confront special challenges. These challenges may prevent, slow down, or complicate acquiring a language. We'll review two of them: sign language learning and bilingual language acquisition.

SIGN LANGUAGE. Sign language is a type of language developed by members of deaf communities that allows them to use visual rather than auditory communication. It involves using the hands, face, body, and "sign space"—the space immediately in front of the signer—to communicate. Just as there are many spoken languages, there are many sign languages used in different countries and deaf communities.

Many people hold a variety of misconceptions about sign languages (see **TABLE 2**). People often think of sign language as an elaborate form of gesturing, a charades-like attempt to act out silently what people would otherwise speak. This couldn't be further from the truth. Sign language is called "language" for a reason. It's a linguistic system of communication with its own phonemes, words, syntax, and extralinguistic information (Newport & Meier, 1985; Poizner, Klima, & Bellugi, 1987; Stokoe, Casterline, & Croneberg, 1976). Linguists who've analyzed the structure and organization of various sign languages (American Sign Language, French Sign Language, even Nicaraguan Sign Language) have confirmed that sign languages exhibit the same features as spoken languages, including a complex set of syntactic rules that determine when a string of signs is a grammatical sentence.

s of a deaf
ier than

TABLE 2 Common Misconceptions about Deafness and Sign Language.

MYTH	REALITY
1. Deaf people don't need sign language because they can lip-read.	Even the most skilled lip-readers can pick up only about 30 to 35 percent of what's being said because most of the work is done behind the scenes by the throat, tongue, and teeth. Our lips look virtually identical when saying *nice* and *dice*—even words like *queen* and *white* look the same to lip-readers.
2. Learning to sign slows down deaf children's ability to learn to speak.	Historically, deaf education programs tried to prevent deaf children from learning to sign because they feared children would never learn to talk. It's now clear that learning a sign language actually speeds up the process of learning to talk.
3. American Sign Language is English translated word for word into signs.	American Sign Language (ASL) bears no resemblance to English; the syntax in particular differs completely from English syntax. Some deaf communities use what's called Signed English instead of ASL; Signed English translates English sentences word for word into signs from ASL.

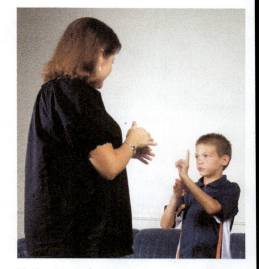

Unlike this deaf child whose parent is a fluent signer, most deaf babies are born to hearing parents who don't begin learning sign language until after their babies are born (or sometimes even later).

Further evidence that sign language works like any other language comes from two sources. First, the same brain areas involved in processing spoken languages become active in sign languages (Hickok, Bellugi, & Klima, 2011; Poizner et al., 1987). In fact, native signers' brains involve both traditional "language areas" and other brain areas that play roles in visual and spatial processing (Newman et al., 2002). Second, babies who learn sign languages pass through the same developmental stages at about the same ages as babies who learn spoken languages (Newport & Meier, 1985; Orlanksy & Bonvillian, 1984; Petitto & Marentette, 1991).

BILINGUALISM. Many of us have tried to learn a second language, and some of us are **bilingual**, adept at speaking and comprehending two languages. Given that so many of us have attempted to master a second language, why can so few of us call ourselves bilingual? Part of the answer lies in how we encounter a second language. We usually master a language more easily by living in a community where this language is spoken than by learning it in a classroom (Baker & MacIntyre, 2000; Genesee, 1985). Not surprisingly, our motivation to learn a new language also plays a key role (Ushioda & Dornyei, 2012). But as we observed in Figure 6, the best predictor of whether we'll become fluent is the age of acquisition: All things being equal, the earlier, the better (Johnson & Newport, 1989).

In most bilingual persons, one language is dominant. It's typically the first language learned, the one they heard most often as a child, and the one they use most often. There are cases in which a child is introduced to two languages from the outset, as when the parents speak two languages or the child has a full-time caretaker who speaks a different language from that of her parents. How do bilingual persons fluent in two languages keep them straight? How are these languages organized in their brain?

Children learning two languages follow the same stages in the same order for each language as do *monolingual* children—those learning a single language. There's some evidence that bilingual children experience a delay in syntax development in each of their languages relative to their monolingual counterparts (Gathercole, 2002a, b), although vocabulary development is relatively unimpaired (Pearson & Fernández, 1994; Pearson, Fernández, & Oller, 1993). Moreover, the delays that occur early in development are balanced out by a variety of long-term benefits (Bialystok, Craik, & Luk, 2012). Not only can bilingual individuals converse with two language communities rather than one, but the process of figuring out how two languages work gives them heightened **metalinguistic** insight—awareness of how language is structured and used. As a result, they tend to perform better on language tasks in general (Bialystok, 1988; Galambos & Hakuta, 1988; Ricciardelli, 1992). In fact, recent research suggests that bilingualism may even offer protection from cognitive decline in patients with Alzheimer's disease and other forms of dementia (Schweizer, Ware, Fischer, et al., 2012).

A growing number of children hear one language spoken at home and another at school. Some are instructed in two different languages at school. Although bilingualism may slow the learning of some aspects of both languages, it promotes metalinguistic insight in the long run.

 Watch in **MyPsychLab** the **Video:** Bilingual Education

bilingual
proficient and fluent at speaking and comprehending two distinct languages

metalinguistic
awareness of how language is struct[...] and used

Studies of brain activation during language processing demonstrate that bilingual persons who learned a second language early in development process the two languages using similar brain areas (Buchweitz, Shinkareva, Mason, et al., 2012; Fabbro, 1999). In contrast, those who learned a second language later in development use different brain areas (Kim et al. 1997), suggesting that the brain may separate their first and second languages into different regions. An alternative hypothesis is that the distinct brain areas observed for later-age exposure to second language are due to the fact that people who acquire languages later are less proficient and require more brain involvement to master their second language as a result (Abutalebi, Cappa, & Perani, 2005).

Theoretical Accounts of Language Acquisition

Given children's impressive ability to learn to use such a complex system at an early age, what explains children's language learning? Some explanations fall more heavily on the nature side of the nature–nurture debate; others, on the nurture side. Yet even the strongest nature account acknowledges that children aren't born knowing their specific language; they learn what they hear. Similarly, the strongest nurture account acknowledges that children's brains are set up in a way that's receptive to learning and organizing language input. Here, we'll review four major theoretical accounts of language acquisition.

THE "PURE" NATURE AND NURTURE ACCOUNTS. The simplest explanation of children's language learning is that they learn through imitation. In this respect, this account is the most parsimonious hypothesis. Babies hear language used in systematic ways and learn to use language as adults use it. This is certainly true in one sense, because babies learn the language they hear. But a purely imitation-based explanation is unlikely tell the whole story for one reason: Language is **generative**. *Generativity* means that language isn't just a set of predefined sentences that we can pull out and apply in appropriate contexts. Instead, it's a system that allows us to create an infinite number of sentences, producing new statements, thoughts, and ideas never previously uttered (indeed, it's unlikely anyone has ever written the exact sentence you just read). The strongest nature view is the **nativist** account, which says that children come into the world with some basic knowledge of how language works. Nativists propose that children are born with expectations that there will be syntactic rules that influence how sentences are constructed (Chomsky, 1972), although the precise rules for their native language need to be determined through exposure. Noam Chomsky, who essentially invented the field of contemporary linguistics, hypothesized that humans possess a specific language "organ" in the brain that houses these rules. He called it the **language acquisition device** and argued that it comes preprogrammed to enable children to use language.

A key weakness of the nativist view is that many of its claims are difficult to falsify. Critics point out that children learn syntax gradually and that even adults use grammatically incorrect sentences. The nativist would reply that different aspects of grammar take more or less time to "set" and that ungrammatical sentences don't imply lack of knowledge of grammar. These are certainly reasonable explanations, but the theory's weakness is that it's hard to think of an outcome that nativists couldn't explain. A theory that can explain every conceivable outcome essentially explains nothing Two less extreme accounts of language acquisition have stronger evidence on their side.

THE SOCIAL PRAGMATICS ACCOUNT. The **social pragmatics** account suggests that specific aspects of the social environment structure language learning. According to this model, children use the context of a conversation to infer its topic from the actions, expressions, gestures, and other behaviors of speakers (Bloom, 2000). Still, this account has its weaknesses. Explaining child language on the basis of social understanding requires us to assume that infants understand a great deal about how other people are thinking. In addition, we can explain most social pragmatic abilities without requiring as much insight on the part of the child (Samuelson & Smith, 1998). For example, social

---

generative
allowing an infinite number of unique sentences to be created by combining words in novel ways

nativist
account of language acquisition that suggests children are born with some basic knowledge of how language works

language acquisition device
...ical organ in the brain in which ...nowledge of syntax resides

...that proposes
... and sentences
...al interactions

pragmatic theorists might say that children learn to interpret meaning from pointing because children recognize that the speaker's communicative goal is to direct the child's attention to a particular object, like a toy. But children might use a simpler process altogether. Perhaps they notice that every time their caretaker points to a specific object, he or she utters the same word. In this way, children may infer that pointing is correlated with word meaning. This deduction doesn't require children to take into account the social context or communicative intentions of others.

◀ **OCCAM'S RAZOR**
Does a simpler explanation fit the data just as well?

THE GENERAL COGNITIVE PROCESSING ACCOUNT. A final explanation for how children learn language is the *general cognitive processing* account. It proposes that children's ability to learn language results from general skills that children apply across a variety of activities. Children's ability to perceive, learn, and recognize patterns may be all they need to learn language. If so, there'd be no need to propose a language acquisition device as Chomsky did.

Still, there are challenges to this account, too. One is that children are better at learning languages than adults are, whereas adults are better at learning things in general. Another is that specific areas of the brain, especially the left temporal lobe (see **FIGURE 7**), are more active in language processing than in other types of learning, memory, and pattern recognition activities (Gazzaniga, Ivry, & Mangun, 2002). This finding implies that at least some distinct cognitive processes occur during language as opposed to other cognitive activities.

FIGURE 7 Language Processing Areas of the Brain. Two areas of the brain that play key roles in language processing are Broca's area, involved in speech production, and Wernicke's area, involved in speech comprehension.

---

psycho**mythology**

DO TWINS HAVE THEIR OWN LANGUAGE?

The idea of being a twin has a certain appeal and allure. It's only natural to expect a special bond between two people who've been together from the moment of conception. One commonly held belief is that this special bond enables twins to invent their own secret language, one only they can understand—a phenomenon known as *cryptophasia*.

As fascinating as this notion is, the truth is less exotic, but no less interesting. Cases of apparent cryptophasia among twins turn out to be a result of phonological impairment and other types of language delay (Bishop & Bishop, 1998; Dodd & McEvoy, 1994) that are more prevalent among twins than among singletons (children born one at a time). Twin pairs who've supposedly developed a secret language are simply attempting to use their native language, but with poor articulation and significant pronunciation errors. These difficulties are serious enough to render their speech largely incomprehensible to the rest of us. This problem sometimes results in longer-term language impairment well into elementary school. Because twin pairs tend to make similar kinds of phonological errors, their speech is more understandable to each other than it is to their parents or nonrelated children (Dodd & McEvoy, 1994; Thorpe, et al., 2001).

? Popular psychology tells us that twins sometimes develop their own language.
What does research indicate is really going on here? (See answer upside down at bottom of page.)

Watch in **MyPsychLab** the **Video:** Bird and Language

Nonhuman Animal Communication

The communication systems of different animal species differ in type and complexity. Some species use scent marking as their primary form of communication. Others rely on visual displays, such as baring their teeth or flapping their wings. Still others, like we humans, use vocal communication. Most species have a fixed number of ways of expressing a fixed number of messages but no means of communicating completely new ideas.

aren't developing their own language; instead, ᴚɥɐ very similar-sounding speech production

FIGURE 8 Communication among Honeybees. Honeybees use the waggle dance to communicate to other bees the location of a food source: in which direction it lies, how far away it is, and how plentiful it is.

Watch in **MyPsychLab** the **Video:** Classic Footage of Chimpanzees and Sign Language

FIGURE 9 A Bonobo Uses Lexigrams to Communicate with Caretakers. This ape has been trained to associate colored shapes with meanings such as "juice," "fruit," and "tickle."

HOW ANIMALS COMMUNICATE. In most nonhuman animals, the two circumstances in which communication most often takes place are—you guessed it—sex and violence. Male songbirds, such as canaries and finches, produce a specific song to attract mates and another song to convey the message "This is my territory; back off" (Kendeigh, 1941). Chimpanzees use a combination of vocalizations and visual displays, such as making facial expressions and slapping the ground, to convey aggression (de Waal, 1989). When it comes to mating rituals, male chimpanzees squat with their knees spread to display their penises as an invitation to mate (admittedly, chimpanzees aren't known for their subtlety).

A fascinating example of nonhuman communication that provides information exchange beyond aggression and mating is the waggle dance of honeybees. Bees use this dance to communicate with their fellow bees about the location of a food source (see **FIGURE 8**). (Riley et al., 2005; von Frisch, 1967). The bee's waggle dance is one of the few nonhuman examples of communication about something beyond the here and now.

Vervet monkeys provide another interesting example; they use different alarm calls to signal different predators (Seyfarth & Cheney, 1997). They produce one type of call when they see a leopard, a second when they see a snake, and a third when they see a hawk or another flying predator. These alarm calls are the closest thing to words scientists have observed outside human language, because specific sounds correspond to specific meanings.

TEACHING HUMAN LANGUAGE TO NONHUMAN ANIMALS. Concerted efforts to teach animals human language have been largely unsuccessful. The earliest attempts to teach chimpanzees, one of our nearest living genetic relatives, fell flat. The researchers assumed incorrectly that chimpanzees possess a vocal apparatus similar to ours: Chimpanzees' vocal apparatus doesn't permit anywhere near the range and coordination of sounds we can achieve (Lieberman, Crelin, & Klatt, 1972). Later researchers tried to teach chimpanzees to use either sign language or a lexigram board, which allows them to point to printed visual symbols that stand for specific words (see **FIGURE 9**).

These attempts were more promising, but there were crucial limits. They required many trials with reinforcement to learn the associations between signs or lexigrams and their meanings. Even then, chimpanzees learned only a limited vocabulary. They also never mastered syntactic rules.

Two animal species appear to do a bit better. One is the bonobo, once thought to be a type of chimpanzee but now recognized as a distinct species that's genetically even more closely related to humans. The few studies conducted on bonobos suggest a different learning pathway, which more closely resembles human learning (Savage-Rumbaugh, 1986). Bonobos (1) learn better as young animals than as adults, (2) tend to learn through observation rather than direct reinforcement, and (3) use symbols to comment on or engage in social interactions rather than simply for food treats. Yet bonobos, like their chimpanzee cousins, seem to get stuck when learning syntax.

One species that may be able to use spoken language much as we do is the African gray parrot. An Einstein of a parrot named Alex, who died in 2007 at the age of 31, was renowned for his ability to speak and to solve cognitive tasks. Parrots are, of course, famous (and sometimes infamous) for their ability to mimic sounds. But at least some African gray parrots, including Alex, appear to go beyond mere mimicry. They use language in a more humanlike manner, generating new and meaningful combinations of words and even mastering syntactic rules (Pepperberg, 2006). Yet their learning process is more like that of chimpanzees than bonobos and humans. It's a result of many repetitions rather than observation and interaction with the world.

We humans are unique in our ability to use language in such sophisticated ways. Of course, complexity in and of itself doesn't make us better, although it may make us "smarter" in some crucial ways. Squirrels and cockroaches do a pretty decent job of keeping themselves going with whatever communication systems they have to work with. For their purposes, they're every bit as effective in their communication as we are.

1. Nonstandard dialects of English follow syntactic rules that differ from but are just as valid as the rules in standard American English. **True / False**

2. Children's two-word utterances typically violate syntactic rules. **True / False**

3. Children who are deaf learn to sign at an older age than hearing children who are learning to talk. **True / False**

4. Bilingual individuals usually have one dominant language, which they learned earlier in development. **True / False**

5. Few nonhuman animal communication systems involve exchanges of information beyond the here and now. **True / False**

Answers: 1. T; 2. F; 3. F; 4. T; 5. T

Study and **Review** in **MyPsychLab**

Alex (an African gray parrot) was famous for his impressive language skills.

Communication and the Mind: Connecting Thinking, Language, and Reading

10 Identify how our language may influence our thinking.

11 Identify the skills required to learn to read.

12 Analyze the relationship between reading speed and reading comprehension.

Given how complex language is, we might wonder how it corresponds to the equally complex ways that our thinking works. In this section, we'll explore how our thoughts are translated into spoken words and how our spoken words are translated into print.

Do We Think in Words? The Relation Between Language and Thought

We've all had times when we realized we were conversing with ourselves; we may have even started talking aloud to ourselves. Clearly, we sometimes think in words. What about the rest of the time? One early and since rejected hypothesis, proposed by John B. Watson, the founder of behaviorism, is that thinking is a form of internal speech. For Watson, there's no thinking without language, and all of our thoughts—our memories, decisions, ruminations, and fantasies—are merely verbal descriptions in our minds. Watson believed that thinking is simply subvocal talking, moving the vocal tract as if talking, but below hearing level.

The proposal that all thought is represented verbally implies that children don't think at all until they've mastered language and that the language we speak shapes how we perceive and interact with the world. What does the evidence say?

LINGUISTIC DETERMINISM: WE SPEAK; THEREFORE, WE THINK. The view that we represent all thinking linguistically is called **linguistic determinism**. One of the best-known examples of how language can influence thought is the belief that Inuits (formerly called Eskimos) possess about a thousand words for snow. Linguistic determinists argue that having so many words for snow enables Inuits to perceive incredibly subtle distinctions among types of snow. It's a good story. But there are several reasons to believe this conclusion may not be warranted.

1. Although Inuits make several fine distinctions among types of snow, research shows that a thousand is a substantial exaggeration of these types.

2. English speakers actually use many terms to describe different types of snow, such as *slush*, *powder*, and even *crud*. In fact, we have just about as many terms as do the Inuits.

It's common lore that the Inuit have a thousand words to refer to different types of snow, and as a result, they make finer distinctions among types of snow than do people who speak English. In fact, this claim is a myth: Inuit languages have about the same number of words for snow as does English.

linguistic determinism
view that all thought is represented and that, as a result, our language thinking

3. Even assuming that the Inuits have more terms for snow than we do, we can't infer that the greater number of terms *caused* the Inuit to make finer distinctions. It's just as likely that Inuits and other people who work in snowy conditions, like skiers and hikers, find it helpful to draw fine distinctions among types of snow. If so, language may reflect people's thinking about snow rather than the other way around. The correlation between the number of words and number of distinctions doesn't mean that the words produced distinctions that wouldn't otherwise have been there.

It's challenging to think of ways to test linguistic determinism. One strong test would be to compare the thought processes of people who can use language with those of people who can't to see if their thinking is similar (see **FIGURE 10**). Of course, nearly everyone learns language, and those few who don't are typically severely cognitively impaired or have suffered such serious abuse and neglect that they're deeply disturbed emotionally. So we need to turn to other evidence to see whether normal thinking can exist without language.

This evidence gives us reason to doubt linguistic determinism. First, children can perform many complex cognitive tasks long before they can talk about them. A second compelling argument against linguistic determinism comes from neuroimaging studies of problem solving, thinking, remembering, and reading (see **FIGURE 11**). These studies show that although language areas often become activated when people engage in certain cognitive tasks such as reading, those areas of the brain aren't especially active during other tasks such as spatial tasks and visual imagery (Gazzaniga, Ivry, & Mangun, 2002). These studies suggest that thought can occur without language.

LINGUISTIC RELATIVITY: LANGUAGE GIVES THOUGHT A GENTLE NUDGE. Clearly, linguistic determinism—at least in its original form—doesn't have much going for it. Nevertheless, there's some promise for a less radical perspective, called **linguistic relativity**. Proponents of this view maintain that characteristics of language shape our thought processes. This idea is also called the *Sapir-Whorf hypothesis*, named after the two scholars who proposed it (Sapir, 1929; Whorf, 1956). There's evidence both for and against linguistic relativity.

Several studies suggest that language can affect thinking (Majid, 2010; McDonough, Choi, & Mandler, 2003). Two researchers examined the memories of Russians who moved to the United States and achieved fluency in English. These participants recalled events that happened in Russia more accurately when speaking Russian and recalled events that happened in the United States more accurately when speaking English even though they were in the United States when they recalled both sets of events (Marian & Neisser, 2000).

Yet in other cases, language doesn't appear to influence thought. One example is color categorization (Lenneberg, 1967). Different languages contain different numbers of basic color terms. In English, we generally use a set of 11 basic color terms: red, blue, green, yellow, white, black, purple, orange, pink, brown, and gray. Nevertheless, some languages contain fewer basic color terms. A language community may use a single word to refer to all things that are either blue or green. When it becomes important to distinguish blue from green things, speakers may say "blue/green like the sky" versus "blue/green like the leaves." In a small number of non-Westernized cultures such as the Dani of New Guinea, there are no true color terms at all, only "dark" and "bright." Yet even those who have no specific color terms still perceive colors as dividing into roughly the same color categories as English speakers do (Rosch, 1973).

So does this mean that speakers of all languages end up thinking in precisely the same ways? No, because the evidence suggests that language shapes some, but not all, aspects of perception, memory, and thought. Nevertheless, when researchers identify language-related differences in thought, it's not easy to disentangle the influences of language from culture. Different language communities also have different priorities, emphases, and values that shape how they think about the world. Because nearly all

"I did not know that I am. I lived in a world that was a no-world. . . . I did not know that I knew aught [anything] or that I lived or acted or desired. I had neither will nor intellect" (Keller, 1910, pp. 113–114).

FIGURE 10 Could Helen Keller Think Before She Learned To Communicate? Helen Keller, who lost her hearing and sight at 19 months due to illness, eventually learned to communicate through signs performed against the palm of her hand. After learning to communicate through sign and writing, she described her experience of the world before learning language.

FIGURE 11 Brain Activation during Language Tasks. This PET scan shows the areas in the left temporal lobe that become especially active when people are trying to figure out the meanings of words.

Factoid

Stroke patients who have damage to the left hemisphere of their brain often exhibit pronounced language deficits, but damage to the right temporal and frontal lobes can also disrupt the ability to interpret or use nonliteral speech such as ⌐d sarcasm.

cross-linguistic comparisons are correlational rather than experimental, language and culture are nearly always confounded. We therefore must be careful when drawing causal conclusions about the impact of language on thinking.

Reading: Recognizing the Written Word

Reading, like spoken language, eventually becomes an automatic process, one that doesn't consume our attentional resources, except when we're reading something particularly challenging or engaging. Odds are high you could munch on potato chips while reading this chapter without it affecting your comprehension. In fact, reading becomes so automatic by the time we reach college age that we can't turn it off even when we want to. Usually, this is a good thing because it means we can read street signs while driving even when the person sitting next to us is gabbing away. But the automatic nature of reading can be less than ideal when we glimpse someone's open diary or intimately personal Facebook message on a nearby computer. In these cases, we almost can't help but violate others' privacy, because we can't put the brakes on our brain to stop us from processing what we see.

A compelling demonstration of the automaticity of language—for better or for worse—is the Stroop color-naming task, named after the researcher who invented it, J. Ridley Stroop (1935). This task requires participants to identify the color of ink used to print words. That sounds simple enough. The catch is that the printed words are color names that contradict the ink color (see **FIGURE 12**). Most people experience enormous difficulty ignoring the printed words, even though the task doesn't require them to read. The Stroop task shows that reading is automatic and hard to inhibit (MacLeod, 1991). Interestingly, children who are still getting the hang of reading don't experience interference in the Stroop task, so they find it easier than adults (Schadler & Thissen, 1981). Because their reading is effortful, they can turn off their attention to the words and pay attention only to ink color. As children become more practiced readers, they begin to do worse on the Stroop.

Beginning readers must master two skills to become experts. The first is learning to recognize familiar words when they see them printed on a page. Without this skill, reading can't become automatic. We need to recognize common words without having to sound out each word as if it were the first time we've seen it. The average reader uses **whole word recognition** to read the vast majority of printed words (LaBerge & Samuels, 1974). Still, this obviously can't be the whole story because we need to develop strategies for reading new words, especially when we're just learning to read. For these words, we use a second strategy, called **phonetic decomposition** or *phonics* (National Research Council, 1998). This strategy involves sounding out words by figuring out the correspondences between printed letters and sounds. For words like *livid*, this task is simple because each printed consonant (*l*, *v*, and *d*) corresponds to a single phoneme in English and the vowel (*i*) has the same sound in both instances. Nevertheless, not all sounds in the English language are linked to a unique letter (or even combination of letters) corresponding to them. For example, sounding out the word *pleasure* based on letter-to-phoneme correspondences won't get us far; we'll end up with something way off base, like "plee-ah-sir-eh." In these cases, we need to memorize how the word's spelling translates to the spoken word.

There's been heated debate about whether whole word recognition or phonics is the best strategy for teaching reading. For a long time, educators in the United States believed that teaching children to recognize whole words was the best approach.

◀ **CORRELATION VS. CAUSATION**
Can we be sure that A causes B?

The Dani language has only words for "dark" and "bright," not individual colors, but Dani people can distinguish colors just as we do.

Control Condition	Stroop Interference Condition
Rabbit	Red
House	Blue
Blanket	Green
Dance	Yellow
Flower	Purple
Key	Orange
Seven	Black
Dance	Yellow
House	Blue
Key	Orange
Seven	Purple
Flower	Black
Rabbit	Red
Blanket	Green

FIGURE 12 The Stroop Effect. The Stroop task demonstrates that reading is automatic. Go down each column and say aloud the color of ink in which each word is printed. Try the control list first—you'll find that it's relatively straightforward task. Then try the Stroop interference list. You'll probably find the task considerably more difficult.

whole word recognition
reading strategy that involves identifying common words based on their appearance without having to sound them out

phonetic decomposition
reading strategy that involves sounding out words by drawing correspondences between printed letters and sounds

Although these educators were right that mature readers rely mostly on whole word recognition, they mistook the correlation between reading proficiency and the whole word recognition strategy as causal. They concluded incorrectly that whole word recognition *leads to* better reading. In fact, experiments show that training children to be aware of sound–letter correspondences enhances reading (Bradley & Bryant, 1983; Gibb & Randall, 1988; Lundberg, Frost, & Petersen, 1988) and is a more effective way to get and keep children reading (Rayner et al., 2002).

Does Speed-Reading Work?

We can find ads for training programs in speed-reading, also known as photoreading, megaspeed-reading, and alphanetics, in magazines, web ads, and on bulletin boards on campus. Some universities even offer their own sponsored courses to boost students' reading rates. Does it work?

Speed-reading "works" in the sense that it speeds up our reading rate. So what's the catch? Beyond a certain point, our comprehension suffers enormously (Graf, 1973). Reading is subject to a speed–accuracy trade-off: The faster we read, the more we miss. The average college student reads about 200–300 words per minute (Carver, 1990). Controlled studies indicate that reading faster than 400 words per minute results in comprehension rates below 50 percent (Cunningham, Stanovich, & Wilson, 1990).

So why are speed-reading programs so popular? Because they're based on a genuine finding, namely, that reading speed is correlated with comprehension. Nevertheless, this correlation doesn't necessarily imply that if we start reading faster, we'll comprehend more. Proficient readers tend to be both faster at reading and better at comprehending compared with poorer readers, but reading speed doesn't cause comprehension.

Speed-reading programs promise to increase our reading rates many times over, to 1,000 or even 2,000 words per minute. There have even been extraordinary claims of people who can read between 15,000 and 30,000 words per minute. Yet the truth turns out to be far less than extraordinary. Speed readers are no better than average readers at finding specific words (Homa, 1983) and understand less than 50 percent of what they read.

? We can often spot posters and fliers like this one on college campuses, in coffee shops, and in our spam. Such speed-reading programs claim to increase our reading rate from 2 to 100 times over the average reading rate (which is 200–300 words per minute). **Why should we not trust these claims?** (See answer upside down below.)

Is there any hope of improving our reading speed while not diminishing our comprehension? Fortunately, there *are* tutoring approaches that can increase reading speed, but only within the expected reading range of 200–400 words per minute. Even more important, students who increase their reading speed within this range typically also improve their comprehension, especially on timed reading tasks such as exams. Why? Because they can cover more material in the same amount of time.

Answer: Although our reading rate increases, our comprehension suffers.

Answers are located at the end of the text.

SPEED-READING COURSES
evaluating CLAIMS

How much time do you spend reading textbooks, lecture notes, and other course materials? Probably a lot. Wouldn't it be great to cut that time in half—or even more—and spend more time hanging out with your friends? Let's evaluate some of these claims, which are modeled after actual advertisements for speed-reading courses.

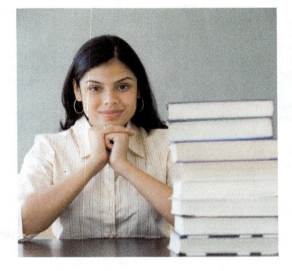

"Improve your reading speed, comprehension, retention, and recall with our course."

The ad claims to improve reading speed and comprehension, but research shows that speed-reading has negative consequences on comprehension.

"Learn how to double or triple your reading speed in under 15 minutes."

What kind of evidence would you need to support this extraordinary claim?

"This course was developed by a team of professionals who researched speed-reading at colleges and universities around the world."

What would you need to know about these "professionals" and how they conducted their research?

"Our course will teach you how to skim excessively detailed documents."

This claim acknowledges that most of the success of "speed-reading" actually comes from skimming—that is, not reading some material at all.

Assess Your Knowledge
FACT or FICTION?

✔ **Study** and **Review** in **MyPsychLab**

1. We can't determine whether the fine distinctions Inuits make among different kinds of snow are a cause or a consequence of the many terms for snow in their language.   **True / False**

2. People who speak languages that lack terms for distinguishing colors can't tell these colors apart.   **True / False**

3. The Stroop color-naming task demonstrates that reading is automatic.   **True / False**

4. Phonetic decomposition is a straightforward linking of printed letters to phonemes.   **True / False**

5. Whole word recognition is the most efficient reading strategy for fluent readers and the best way to teach children to read.   **True / False**

Answers: 1. T; 2. F; 3. T; 4. F; 5. F

Your Complete Review System

Thinking and Reasoning

I IDENTIFY METHODS FOR ACHIEVING COGNITIVE ECONOMY.

Cognitive economy is a necessary aspect of our cognitive functioning. We would be unable to function effectively without some way of streamlining our information processing. Heuristics and top-down processing are examples of cognitive economy that we use routinely. There are downsides to cognitive economy, including errors in reasoning.

1. We define _____ as any mental activity or processing of information.

2. _____ _____ allows us to simplify what we need to attend to and keep the information we need to make decisions to a manageable minimum.

3. Ambady and Rosenthal referred to our ability to extract useful information from small bits of behavior as _____ _____.

2 DESCRIBE WHAT FACTORS AFFECT OUR REASONING ABOUT THE WORLD.

Heuristics and cognitive biases are often useful, but can lead us to make costly mistakes in reasoning if we apply them uncritically. The representativeness heuristic is a quick way of estimating the likelihood of a particular event based on past experience, but it can lead to overgeneralizations. This is often due to a failure to take base rates into account. The availability heuristic involves generating estimates about the probability of an event based on how easily we can think of examples of that event. Confirmation bias can often lead us to overlook contradictory evidence and seek only evidence consistent with our expectations.

4. Jules is going to buy a new vehicle. Selena knows that Jules is passionate about recycling and composting. Which kind of car would Selena probably assume Jules is buying, a big gas-guzzling truck that gets only 13 miles to the gallon or a small hybrid vehicle that gets 50 miles to the gallon?

5. Racial profiling, such as selectively searching Arab Americans at airport security checkpoints, is based on the idea that Arab Americans are more likely to be terrorists than are Americans of other ethnicities. This type of profiling is an example of the _____ heuristic.

6. In this example, someone who failed to take base rates into account would predict that a purple flower picked at random is more likely to be a(n) _____ (iris/tulip).

7. The fact that people estimate higher numbers of murders for the city of Detroit than for the entire state of Michigan demonstrates which heuristic or bias?

8. "Monday Morning Quarterbacking" is an example of _____ _____.

9. _____ processing involves filling in gaps of information from our experiences and background knowledge.

10. A mental representation of a set of objects, actions, or events that share core features is a(n) _____.

Thinking at Its Hardest: Decision Making and Problem Solving

3 DISCOVER WHAT INFLUENCES OUR DECISION MAKING.

Many of our daily decisions are made quickly and implicitly (without conscious awareness) relying on heuristics, which is a type of System 1 thinking. For bigger decisions, we may attempt to analyze the pros and cons on a more explicit level and consult experts, trusted friends, and advisers, which is slower and more deliberate—a case of System 2 thinking. Although it makes sense to make bigger decisions more carefully, overanalyzing can sometimes overwhelm us. Framing, which refers to how decisions are presented to us, has a substantial impact on these decisions even when the underlying information relevant to these decisions is identical.

11. System 1 thinking appears to lead to better decision making about _____ (emotional preferences/business decisions) than System 2 thinking.

12. As these two cereal advertisements demonstrate, _____ can affect decision making.

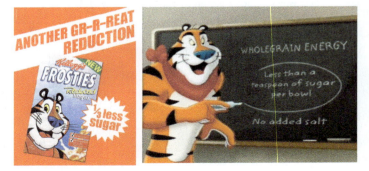

13. The new field of _____ explores brain activity during financial decision making.

4 DESCRIBE SOME COMMON PROBLEM-SOLVING STRATEGIES AND CHALLENGES.

Many daily problems are solved using heuristics, but others involve more deliberate strategies. Algorithms are step-by-step procedures for solving routine problems, but they aren't very flexible. Other solutions involve breaking down problems into subproblems and reasoning based on analogies to other problems in seemingly unrelated areas. Three hurdles to effective problem solving are being distracted by the salience of surface similarities, being stuck in a mental set, and falling prey to functional fixedness.

14. When we generate a cognitive strategy to accomplish a specific goal, we are engaging in _____ _____.

15. Which problem-solving approach is more creative and flexible: algorithms or analogies?

16. Steve is feeling overwhelmed by how much work he must do to prepare for his upcoming physics test. His tutor encourages him to take the studying process in stages: organize his notes, prepare flashcards, review the flashcards, etc. This is an example of solving a problem by breaking it into _____.

17. Participants in the jar study who had trouble solving their final problem were experiencing a(n) _____ _____.

18. _____ _____ occurs when we experience difficulty conceptualizing that an object typically used for one purpose can be used for another.

5 DESCRIBE VARIOUS MODELS OF THE HUMAN MIND.

Scientists once believed that the mind worked much like a computer, running programs to compute answers to problems and execute mental commands. Nevertheless, it's is now clear that the computer is a poor analogy for the human mind. We draw inferences, instantly take context into account, and draw on top-down knowledge in a way that computers don't. Our ability to interact physically with the world also exerts a big impact on our thinking abilities. Embodied accounts of thinking seem to better

explain our thinking and reasoning abilities and are supported by neuroimaging studies demonstrating that our brain's perceptual and motor areas are activated during thought.

19. Why does the computer turn out to be a poor model of the mind?

20. According to _____ _____ of cognition, our knowledge is organized and accessed in a manner that enables us to simulate our actual experiences.

How Does Language Work?

6 DESCRIBE THE FOUR LEVELS OF ANALYSIS THAT MAKE UP LANGUAGE.

To fully understand the complexity of language, we must analyze phonemes, morphemes, syntax, and extralinguistic information. These four levels work together to create meaning and transmit information. Morphemes are the smallest units of language that convey meaning, known as semantics. Extralinguistic information such as tone of voice, facial expression, gestures, contextual cues, and cultural conventions enter into how we interpret language. Dialects are regional, social, and ethnic group variations in the ways a language is spoken, all of which are equally valid versions of the language.

21. List the four levels of analysis we use to analyze language.

1. _____
2. _____
3. _____
4. _____

22. English contains between 40 and 45 categories of sounds, or _____.

23. We can use _____ information about this woman's facial expressions and gestures to determine what she means when she says, "It's just awful in here."

24. A language variation used by a group of people who share geographic proximity or ethnic background is a(n) _____.

7 TRACE THE DEVELOPMENT OF LANGUAGE ACQUISITION IN CHILDREN.

Infants' babbling becomes more sophisticated over the course of their first year as control over their vocal tracts increases. They also fine-tune their perception of phonemes over the course of the first year of listening to their native language. Children's word and syntax comprehension precedes their production of language. They acquire their first words around their fir[st] birthday and typically begin combining words into rudi[mentary] phrases by their second birthday. Understanding of ex[tralin]guistic aspects of communication develops graduall[y] preschool and elementary school years. Sign languages possess the same linguistic features and complexity as spoken language does. Children learning sign language from native signing parents acquire their language at the same age and rate as children learning spoken language. Children learn languages more easily than adolescents and adults do.

25. By what month of pregnancy are fetuses' auditory systems developed enough for them to detect sounds? How much do they learn about their mother's language and voices in utero?

26. Infants and toddlers produce words (before/at the same time as/after) they begin to comprehend them.

27. The (same/different) brain areas involved in processing spoken languages become active in using sign languages.

8 IDENTIFY THE PROS AND CONS OF BILINGUALISM.

Bilingual individuals typically have one dominant language. Learning two languages slows some aspects of the acquisition process, but ultimately results in stronger metalinguistic skills. Bilingualism also seems to offer some protection against cognitive decline in old age.

28. Bilingual individuals tend to perform (better/worse) on metalinguistic tasks than do individuals who speak only one language.

29. Bilinguals are (more/less) likely to show evidence of dementia in old age.

9 DISTINGUISH HUMAN LANGUAGE FROM NONHUMAN ANIMAL COMMUNICATION.

Most nonhuman animal communication systems involve aggression and mating displays but little else, and they lack the generativity of human language systems. Attempts to teach language to nonhuman animals have been only modestly successful. Chimpanzees and African gray parrots can learn the basics of linguistic communication, but they don't learn the way humans do. Bonobos seem to learn more like humans do, but don't exceed the proficiency level of about a two-and-a-half-year-old human.

30. What makes honeybees' communication distinct from many other nonhuman animals' communication systems?

Communication and the Mind: Connecting Thinking, Language, and Reading

...OW OUR LANGUAGE MAY INFLUENCE OUR THINKING.

...ge completely determines our thinking
... little or no scientific support.
... the idea that language can
...hinking (linguistic relativity).

31. The view that all thought is represented linguistically, as evidenced by the different Inuit words for snow, is called _____ _____.

32. Recent neuroimaging studies suggest that thought (can/can't) occur without language.

33. How does the fact that the Dani of New Guinea can perceive different color categories present a challenge to the Sapir-Whorf hypothesis?

34. When researchers identify language-related differences in thought, it (is/isn't) easy to disentangle the influences of language from culture.

11 IDENTIFY THE SKILLS REQUIRED TO LEARN TO READ.

Reading is a skill that, for most of us, becomes so automatic that we can't stop doing it, even when we want to. We generally use two strategies when learning to read: whole word recognition and phonetic decomposition. Whole word recognition is more efficient when reading familiar words, but phonetic decomposition is critical for less familiar words. There is no perfect correspondence between printed letters and spoken sounds, which makes sounding out printed words challenging.

35. The Stroop task shows that reading is _____.

36. The average reader uses _____ _____ _____ to read the vast majority of printed words.

37. With a reading strategy called _____ _____, we sound out new words by drawing correspondences between printed letters and sounds.

Control Condition	Stroop Interference Condition
Rabbit	Red
House	Blue
Blanket	Green
Dance	Yellow
Flower	Purple
Key	Orange
Seven	Black
Dance	Yellow
House	Blue
Key	Orange
Seven	Purple
Flower	Black
Rabbit	Red
Blanket	Green

38. There's been heated debate about whether awareness of sound–letter correspondences, known as _____, is the best strategy for teaching children to read.

12 ANALYZE THE RELATIONSHIP BETWEEN READING SPEED AND READING COMPREHENSION.

Speed-reading courses are ineffective. Although we can learn to increase our speed as readers, reading faster than 400 words per minute seriously impairs text comprehension.

39. Reading speeds (are/aren't) correlated with comprehension.

40. Controlled studies indicate that reading faster than _____ words per minute results in comprehension rates below 50 percent.

Apply Your Scientific Thinking Skills

Use your scientific thinking skills to answer the following questions, referencing specific scientific thinking principles and common errors in reasoning whenever possible.

1. Communication depends on more than just our words. It also includes our facial expressions, posture, gestures, and tone of voice. Create a list of several different ways we communicate in our personal, academic, and professional lives (for example, face-to-face conversations, text messages, email, Facebook). Which aspects of communication are preserved and omitted in each of these communication forms? What types of communication errors might arise as a result? How can we use scientific thinking and our knowledge of language and communication to prevent these errors from occurring?

2. Examine the role that framing plays in our decision making. Select a current topic of debate, like health care, foreign policy, or gun control laws, and research how each opposing side frames its arguments. How can you use your knowledge of decision making and your scientific thinking skills to make an informed decision about this issue?

3. Try to think of a recent time when you were trying to solve a problem—say, a problem in your personal life or a homework problem assigned to you in one of your classes—and got stuck despite repeated attempts. To which of the obstacles to effective problem solving discussed in this chapter might you have fallen prey? What helped you, or might have helped you, resolve this problem?

Further Your Understanding

EXTEND YOUR KNOWLEDGE WITH THE MYPSYCHLAB VIDEO SERIES

Watch these videos in MyPsychLab. Follow the "Video Series" link.

The Big Picture: I Am, Therefore I Think Discover how we take in and understand the information around us using concepts, algorithms, and heuristic strategies to process information.

The Basics: The Mind Is What the Brain Does Learn how concepts are formed and how we build on, use, and share them with others and why individuals don't always share the same prototypes and mental images of the same concepts.

Special Topics: Mental Imagery: In the Mind's Eye Learn where mental imagery is processed in the brain and why the mental images we see in our mind can feel as real as the tangible objects we see in front of us.

Thinking Like a Psychologist: Speaking One's Mind Find out about the many stages of language acquisition and the incredible ability of babies to learn hundreds of complex sounds and word labels.

In the Real World: Changing Your Mind Learn more about our problem-solving abilities, the professions that require quick decision-making skills versus deliberation, and our ability to acquire and improve decision-making skills over time.

What's In It for Me?: Making Choices Explore how our brains, emotions, and cultures affect our decision making and what happens when we are faced with too many options.

EXPERIENCE PSYCHOLOGICAL RESEARCH WITH MYPSYCHLAB SIMULATIONS

Access these simulations in MyPsychLab. Follow the "Simulations" link.

Depth of Processing Discover whether depth of processing affects recall and memory.

Stroop Illustrate the Stroop effect by responding to questions about words and colors.

APPLY YOUR CRITICAL THINKING SKILLS WITH MYPSYCHLAB WRITING ASSESSMENTS

Complete this writing assignment in MyPsychLab.

Maria's method of studying worked effectively throughout high school until she took her first foreign language course. In this course, her grades were much lower than usual. How might mental set have played a role in Maria's academic problem?

Answer Key

THINKING AND REASONING

1. thinking
2. Cognitive economy
3. thin slicing
4. the hybrid
5. representativeness
6. iris
7. availability heuristic
8. hindsight bias
9. Top-down
10. concept

THINKING AT ITS HARDEST: DECISION MAKING AND PROBLEM SOLVING

11. emotional preferences
12. framing
13. neuroeconomics
14. problem solving
15. analogies
16. subproblems
17. mental set
18. Functional fixedness
19. Computers can't draw inferences and utilize top-down knowledge as humans can.
20. embodied accounts

HOW DOES LANGUAGE WORK?

21. 1) phonemes; 2) morphemes; 3) syntax; 4) extralinguistic information
22. phonemes
23. extralinguistic
24. dialect
25. Babies begin to hear inside the womb by the fifth month of pregnancy. They can learn to recognize their mother's voice and some characteristics of their mother's native language; they even can recognize specific songs or stories they've heard over and over again.
26. after
27. same
28. better
29. less
30. Honeybees, unlike most other nonhuman animals, can communicate beyond the here and now about distant food sources.

COMMUNICATION AND THE MIND: CONNECTING THINKING, LANGUAGE, AND READING

31. linguistic determinism
32. can
33. If language influences thought, someone from the Dani, whose language contains only two color terms, should have a harder time distinguishing blue from green than those of us whose language contains separate terms for these two colors. But Rosch (1973) demonstrated that the Dani perceive colors as dividing up into roughly the same color categories as those of English speakers.
34. isn't
35. automatic
36. whole word recognition
37. phonetic decomposition
38. phonics
39. are
40. 400

References

Abutalebi, J., Cappa, S. F., & Perani, D. (2005). What can functional neuroimaging tell us about the bilingual brain? In Kroll, J. F., & de Groot, A. M. B. (Eds.), *Handbook of bilingualism: Psycholinguistic approaches* (pp. 497–515). New York, NY: Oxford University Press.

Ambady, N., & Rosenthal, R. (1993). Half a minute: Predicting teacher evaluations from thin slices of nonverbal behavior and physical attractiveness. *Journal of Personality and Social Psychology, 64,* 431–441.

Ariely, D. (2008). *Predictably irrational: The hidden forces that shape our decisions.* New York, NY: HarperCollins.

Aveyard, M. E. (2012). Some constants sound curvy: Effects of sound symbolism on object recognition. *Memory & Cognition, 40,* 83–92.

Baker, S. C., & MacIntyre, P. D. (2000). The role of gender and immersion in communication and second language orientations. *Language Learning, 50,* 311–341.

Barsalou, L. W. (2008). Cognitive and neural contributions to understanding the conceptual system. *Current Directions in Psychological Science, 17,* 91–95.

Baugh, J. (2000). *Beyond Ebonics: Linguistic pride and racial prejudice.* New York, NY: Oxford University Press.

Bergen, B. K. (2004). The psychological reality of phonaesthemes. *Language, 80,* 290–311.

Bialystok, E. (1988). Levels of bilingualism and levels of linguistic awareness. *Developmental Psychology, 24,* 560–567.

Bialystok, E., Craik, F. I. M., & Luk, G. (2012). Bilingualism: Consequences for mind and brain. *Trends in Cognitive Sciences, 16,* 240–250.

Bishop, D. V. M., & Bishop, S. J. (1998). "Twin language": A risk factor for language impairment? *Journal of Speech, Language & Hearing Research, 41,* 150–160.

Bloom, P. (2000). *How children learn the meanings of words.* Boston, MA: MIT Press.

Bradley, L., & Bryant, P. E. (1983). Categorizing sounds and learning to read: A causal connection. *Nature, 301,* 419–421.

Buchweitz, A., Shinkareva, S. V., Mason, R. A., Mitchell, T. M., & Just, M. A. (2012). Identifying bilingual semantic neural representations across languages. *Brain and Language, 120,* 282–289.

Carrère, S., & Gottman, J. (1999). Predicting divorce among newlyweds from the first three minutes of a marital conflict discussion. *Family Process, 30,* 293–301.

Carver, R. P. (1990). *Reading rate: A review of research and theory.* San Diego, CA: Academic Press.

Centers for Disease Control and Prevention (2005). *Cigarette smoking among adults: United States, 2003. MMWR Highlights, 54*(20), United States Department of Health and Human Services. Atlanta, GA: Author.

̵ ̵ ̵, N. (1972). *Language and mind.* New York, NY: Harcourt Brace ̵ ̵ch.

Stanovich, K. E., & Wilson, M. R. (1990). Cognitive varia- ̵students differing in reading ability. In T. H. Carr & B. ̵ ̵d its development: Component skills approaches ̵cademic Press.

tic study of a modern-day "wild child." ̵ss.

8). Prenatal maternal speech influences new- ̵unds. In S. Chess, A. Thomas, & M. Hertzig

(Eds.), *Annual progress in child psychiatry and child development, 1987* (pp. 5–25). Philadelphia, PA: Brunner/Mazel.

de Waal, F. B. M. (1989). The myth of a simple relation between space and aggression in captive primates. *Zoo Biology, 8,* 141–148.

Dijksterhuis, A., Bos, M. W., Nordgren, L. F., & van Baaren, R. B., (2006). On making the right choice: The deliberation-without-attention effect. *Science, 311,* 1005–1007.

Dodd, B., & McEvoy, S. (1994). Twin language or phonological disorder? *Journal of Child Language, 21,* 273–289.

Dunbar, R. (1996). *Grooming, gossip, and the evolution of language.* London, England: Faber & Faber.

Duncker, K. (1945). *On problem-solving.* Psychological Monographs (No. 270).

Ellis, M. (2006). Appalachian English and Ozark English. In R. Abramson & J. Haskell (Eds.), *The Encyclopedia of Appalachia* (pp. 1008–1011). Knoxville, TN: University of Tennessee Press.

Engelmann, J. B., Capra, M. S., Noussair, C., & Berns, G. S. (2009). Expert financial advice neurobiologically "offloads" financial decision-making under risk. *PLoS One, 4*(3), e4957.

Fabbro, F. (1999). *The neurolinguistics of bilingualism. An introduction.* Hove, England: Psychology Press.

Finn, S. E., & Kamphuis, J. H. (1995). What a clinician needs to know about base rates. In J. N. Butcher (Ed.), *Clinical personality assessment: Practical approaches* (pp. 224–235). New York, NY: Oxford University Press.

Fischer, M. H., & Zwaan, R. A. (2008). Embodied language: A review of the role of the motor system in language comprehension. *Quarterly Journal of Experimental Psychology, 61,* 825–850.

Galambos, S. J., & Hakuta, K. (1988). Subject-specific and task-specific characteristics of metalinguistic awareness in bilingual children. *Applied Psycholinguistics, 9,* 141–162.

Gathercole, V. C. M. (2002a). Command of the mass/count distinction in bilingual and monolingual children: An English morphosyntactic distinction. In D. K. Oller & R. E. Eilers (Eds.), *Language and literacy in bilingual children* (pp. 175–206). Clevedon, England: Multilingual Matters.

Gazzaniga, M. S., Ivry, R., & Mangun, G. R. (2002). *Fundamentals of cognitive neuroscience* (2nd ed.). New York, NY: Norton.

Genesee, F. (1985). Second language learning through immersion: A review of U.S. programs. *Review of Educational Research, 55,* 541–561.

Gentner, D., Loewenstein, J., Thompson, L., & Forbus, K. D. (2009). Reviving inert knowledge: Analogical abstraction supports relational retrieval of past events. *Cognitive Science, 33,* 1343–1382.

German, T. P., & Barrett, H. C. (2005). Functional fixedness in a technologically sparse culture. *Psychological Science, 16,* 1–5.

German, T. P., & Defeyter, M. A. (2000). Immunity to functional fixedness in young children. *Psychonomic Bulletin & Review, 7,* 707–712.

Gibb, C., & Randall, P. E. (1988). Metalinguistic abilities and learning to read. *Educational Research, 30,* 135–141.

Gigerenzer, G. (2007). *Gut feelings: The intelligence of the unconscious.* New York, NY: Viking Press.

Gigerenzer, G., & Goldstein, D. G. (1996). Reasoning the fast and frugal way: Models of bounded rationality. *Psychological Review, 103,* 650–669.

Gigerenzer, G., Hertwig, R., & Pachur, T. (Eds.). (2011). *Heuristics: The foundations of adaptive behavior*. New York, NY: Oxford University Press.

Gilovich, T., Griffin, D., & Kahneman, D. (Eds.). (2002). *Heuristics and biases: The psychology of intuitive judgment*. New York, NY: Cambridge University Press.

Gladwell, M. (2005). *Blink: The power of thinking without thinking*. Boston, MA: Little, Brown.

Glimcher, P. W., Camerer, C. F., Fehr, E., & Poldrack, R. A. (2008). *Neuroeconomics: Decision-making and the brain*. San Diego, CA: Academic Press.

Goldin-Meadow, S., Ozyurek, A., Sancar, B., & Mylander, C. (2009). Making language around the globe: A crosslinguistic study of homesign in the United States, China, and Turkey. In J. Guo, E. Lieven, N. Budwig, S. Ervin-Tripp, K. Nakamura, & S. Ozcaliskan (Eds.) *Crosslinguistic approaches to the psychology of language: Research in the tradition of Dan Isaac Slobin* (pp. 27–39). New York, NY: Psychology Press.

Goldstein, M. H., & Schwade, J. A. (2008). Social feedback to infants' babbling facilitates rapid phonological learning. *Psychological Science, 19*, 515–523.

Golinkoff, R. M., Hirsh-Pasek, K., Bloom, L., Smith, L. B., Woodward, A. L., Akhtar, N.,... Hollich, G. (2000). *Becoming a word learner: A debate on lexical acquisition*. New York, NY: Oxford University Press.

Gosling, S. D. (2008). Personality in non-human animals. *Social and Personality Psychology Compass, 2*, 985–1002.

Graf, R. G. (1973). Speed reading: Remember the tortoise. *Psychology Today, 7*, 112–113.

Hasler, G. (2012). Can the neuroeconomics revolution revolutionize psychiatry? *Neuroscience and Biobehavioral Reviews, 36*, 64–78.

Herbert, W. (2010). *On second thought: Outsmarting your mind's hard-wired habits*. New York, NY: Crown.

Hertwig, R., Pacur, T., & Kurzenhauser, S. (2005). Judgments of risk frequencies: Tests of possible cognitive mechanisms. *Journal of Experimental Psychology: Learning, Memory, and Cognition, 31*, 621–642.

Hickok, G., Bellugi, U., & Klima, E. S. (2011). The basis of the neural organization for language: Evidence from sign language aphasia. *Reviews in the Neurosciences, 8*, 205–222.

Hirsh-Pasek, K., & Golinkoff, R. (1996). *The origins of grammar*. Cambridge, MA: MIT Press.

Homa, D. (1983). An assessment of two extraordinary speed-readers. *Bulletin of the Psychonomic Society, 21*, 123–126.

Hutchins, S. S. (1999). *The psychosocial reality, variability, and the compositionality of English phonesthemes*. Unpublished doctoral dissertation, Emory University, Atlanta, GA.

Imai, M., Kita, S., Nagumo, M., & Okada, H. (2008). Sound symbolism facilitates early verb learning. *Cognition, 109*, 54–65.

Jaffe, E. (2004). What was I thinking? Kahneman explains how intuition leads us astray. *Association for Psychological Science Observer, 17*, 5.

Johnson, J. S., & Newport, E. L. (1989). Critical period effects in second language learning: The influence of maturational state on the acquisition of English as a second language. *Cognitive Psychology, 21*, 60–99.

Kahneman, D. (2011). *Thinking, fast and slow*. New York, NY: Farrar, Straus & Giroux.

Kahneman, D., Slovic, P., & Tversky, A. (Eds.). (1982). *Judgment under uncertainty: Heuristics and biases*. New York, NY: Cambridge University Press.

Kato, J., Ide, H., Kabashima, I., Kadota, H., Takano, K., & Kansaku, K. (2009). Neural correlates of attitude change following positive and negative advertisements. *Frontiers in Behavioral Neuroscience, 3*, ArtID 6.

Kendeigh, S. C. (1941). Territorial and mating behavior of the house wren. *Illinois Biographical Monographs, 18*(3) (Serial No. 120).

Kent, R. D., & Miolo, G. (1995). Phonetic abilities in the first year of life. In P. Flether & B. MacWhinney (Eds.), *The handbook of child language* (pp. 303–334). San Diego, CA: Academic Press.

Kim, J. H. S., Relkin, N. R., Lee, K. M., & Hirsch, J. (1997). Distinct cortical areas associated with native and second languages. *Nature, 388*, 171–174.

LaBerge, D., & Samuels, S. J. (1974). Towards a theory of automatic information processing in reading. *Cognitive Psychology, 6*, 293–323.

Labov, W. (1970). The logic of non-standard English. In F. Williams (Ed.), *Language and Poverty*, 153–189. Chicago, IL: Markham.

Lakoff, G. (2012). Explaining embodied cognition results. *Topics in Cognitive Science*. http://dx.doi.org/10.1111/j.1756-8765.2012.01222.x

Lehrer, J. (2009). *How we decide*. Boston, MA: Houghton-Mifflin.

Lenneberg, E. (1967). *Biological foundations of language*. New York, NY: Wiley.

Lichtenstein, S., Slovic, P., Fischhoff, B., Layman, M., & Combs, B. (1978). Judged frequency of lethal events. *Journal of Experimental Psychology: Human Learning and Memory, 4*, 551–578.

Lieberman, P. (2007). The evolution of human speech: Its anatomical and neural bases. *Current Anthropology, 48*, 39–66.

Lieberman, P., Crelin, E. S., & Klatt, D. H. (1972). Phonetic ability and related anatomy of the newborn and adult human, Neanderthal man, and the chimpanzee. *American Anthropologist, 74*, 287–307.

Luchins, A. S. (1946). Classroom experiments on mental set. *American Journal of Psychology, 59*, 295–298.

Lundberg, I., Frost, J., & Petersen, O. (1988). Effects of an extensive program for stimulating phonological awareness in preschool children. *Reading Research Quarterly, 23*, 263–284.

MacLeod, C. M., (1991). Half a century of research on the Stroop effect: An integrative review. *Psychological Bulletin, 109*, 163–203.

Majid, A. (2010). How words categorize the body: The mapping of perceptual parts to natural language. In B. C. Malt, & P. Wolff (Eds.), *Words and the world: How words capture human experience*. New York, NY: Oxford University Press.

Marian, V., & Neisser, U. (2000). Language-dependent recall of autobiographical memories. *Journal of Experimental Psychology: General, 129*, 361–368.

McDonough, L., Choi, S., & Mandler, J. M. (2003). Understanding spatial relations: Flexible infants, lexical adults. *Cognitive Psychology, 46*, 229–259.

Meehl, P. E., & Rosen, A. (1955). Antecedent probability and the efficiency of psychometric signs, patterns, or cutting scores. *Psychological Bulletin, 52*, 194–216.

Moon, C., Cooper, R. P., & Fifer, W. P. (1993). Two-day-olds prefer their native language. *Infant Behavior & Development, 16*, 495–500.

Myers, D. G. (2002). *Intuition: Its powers and perils*. New Haven, CT: Yale University Press.

National Research Council. (1998). Preventing reading difficulties in young children. In C. E. Snow, M. S. Burns, & P. Griffin (Eds.), Washington, DC: National Academies Press.

Newman, A. J., Bavelier, D., Corina, D., Jezzard, P., & Neville, H. J. (2002). A critical period for right hemisphere recruitment in American Sign Language processing. *Nature Neuroscience, 5*, 76–80.

Newport, E. L. (1990). Maturational constraints on language learning. *Cognitive Science, 14*, 11–28.

Newport, E. L., Bavelier, D., & Neville, H. J. (2001). Critical thinking about critical periods: Perspectives on a critical period for language acquisition. In E. Dupoux (Ed.), *Language, brain and cognitive development: Essays in honor of Jacques Mehler*. Cambridge, MA: MIT Press.

Newport, E. L., & Meier, R. (1985). The acquisition of American Sign Language. In D. Slobin (Ed.), *The cross-linguistic study of language acquisition, Vol. 1* (pp. 881–938). Hillsdale, NJ: Erlbaum.

Nygaard, L. C., Cook, A. E., & Namy, L. L. (2009). Sound to meaning correspondences facilitate word learning. *Cognition, 112*, 181–186.

Orlanksy, M. D., & Bonvillian, J. (1984). The role of iconicity in early sign language acquisition. *Journal of Speech and Hearing Disorders, 49*, 287–292.

Owens, R. E. (2011). *Language development: An introduction* (8th ed.). Upper Saddle River, NJ: Pearson.

Pearson, B. Z., & Fernández, S. C. (1994). Patterns of interaction in the lexical growth in two languages of bilingual infants and toddlers. *Language Learning, 44*, 617–653.

Pearson, B. Z., Fernández, S. C., & Oller, D. K. (1993). Lexical development in bilingual infants and toddlers: Comparison to monolingual norms. *Language Learning, 43*, 93–120.

Pepperberg, I. M. (2006). Cognitive and communicative abilities of grey parrots. *Applied Animal Behaviour Science, 100*, 77–86.

Petitto, L. A., & Marentette, P. F. (1991). Babbling in the manual mode: Evidence for the ontogeny of language. *Science, 251*, 1493–1496.

Piske, T., MacKay, I. R. A., & Flege, J. E. (2001). Factors affecting degree of foreign accent in an L2: A review. *Journal of Phonetics, 29*, 191–215.

Poizner, H., Klima, E. S., & Bellugi, U. (1987). *What the hands reveal about the brain*. Cambridge, MA: MIT Press.

Posner, M. I., & Snyder, C. R. R. (1975). Facilitation and inhibition in the processing of signals. In P. M. A. Rabbitt & S. Dornic (Eds.), *Attention and performance* (pp. 669–682). New York, NY: Academic Press.

Rayner, K., Foorman, B. R., Perfetti, C. A., Pesetsky, D., & Seidenberg, M. S. (2002). How should reading be taught? *Scientific American, 286*, 84.

Ricciardelli, L. A. (1992). Bilingualism and cognitive development in relation to threshold theory. *Journal of Psycholinguistic Research, 21*, 301–316.

Rickford, J. R., & Rickford, R. J. (2000). *Spoken soul: The story of Black English*. New York, NY: Wiley.

Riley, J. R., Greggers, U., Smith, A. D., Reynolds, D. R., & Menzel, R. (2005) The flight paths of honeybees recruited by the waggle dance. *Nature, 435*, 205–207.

Ropeik, D. (2010). *How risky is it, really?: Why our fears don't always match the facts*. New York, NY: McGraw-Hill.

Rosch, E. (1973). Natural categories. *Cognitive Psychology, 4*, 328–350.

Ruscio, J. (2000). Risky business: Vividness, availability, and the media paradox. *Skeptical Inquirer, 24*, 22–26.

Samuelson, L. K., & Smith, L. B. (1998). Memory and attention make smart word learning: An alternative account of Akhtar, Carpenter, and Tomasello. *Chil Development, 69*, 94–104.

Sapir, E. (1929). The status of linguistics as a science. *Language, 5*, 209.

Savage-Rumbaugh, E. S. (1986). *Ape language: From conditioned response to* New York, NY: Columbia University Press.

Schadler, M., & Thissen, D. M. (1981). The development of automatic wr recognition and reading skill. *Memory & Cognition, 9*, 132–141.

Schweizer, T., Ware, J., Fischer, C. E., Craik, F. I. M., & Bialystok, E. (2012). Bilingualism as a contributor to cognitive reserve: Evidence from brain atrophy in Alzheimer's disease. *Cortex, 48*, 991–996.

Searle, J. (1990). Is the brain's mind a computer program? *Scientific American, 262* (1), 26–31.

Seyfarth, R. M., & Cheney, D. L. (1997). Behavioral mechanisms underlying vocal communication in nonhuman primates. *Animal Learning & Behavior, 25*, 249–267.

Sharp, C., Monterosso, J., & Read Montague, P. (2012). Neuroeconomics: A bridge for translational research. *Biological Psychiatry, 72*, 87–92.

Shepperd, J. A., & Koch, E. J. (2005). Pitfalls in teaching judgment heuristics. *Teaching of Psychology, 32*, 43–46.

Slovic, P., Finucane, M., Peters, E., & MacGregor, D. G. (2012). Risk as feeling: Some thoughts about affect, reason, risk and rationality. L. Asveld & S. Roeser (Eds.) *The Ethics of Technological Risk*, 163–182.

Smith, L. B. (2000). Learning how to learn words: An associative crane. In *Becoming a Word Learner*. New York, NY: Oxford University Press.

Smitherman-Donaldson, G., & van Dijk, T. (1988). *Discourse and discrimination*. Detroit: Wayne State University Press.

Stokoe, W. C., Casterline, D. C., & Croneberg, C. G. (1976). *A dictionary of American Sign Language on linguistic principles*. Silver Spring, MD: Linstok.

Stroop, J. R. (1935). Studies of interference in serial verbal reactions. *Journal of Experimental Psychology, 18*, 643–662.

Svirsky, M. A., Chin, S. B., & Jester, A. (2007). The effects of age at implantation on speech intelligibility in pediatric cochlear implant users: Clinical outcomes and sensitive periods. *Audiological Medicine, 5*, 293–306.

Tang, C., & van Heuven, V. J. (2009). Mutual intelligibility of Chinese dialects experimentally tested. *Lingua, 119*, 709–732.

Thorpe, K., Greenwood, R., Eivers, A., & Rutter, M. (2001). Prevalence and developmental course of "secret language." *International Journal of Language & Communication Disorders, 36*, 43–62.

Tversky, A., & Kahneman, D. (1974). Judgment under uncertainty: Heuristics and biases. *Science, 185*, 1124–1131.

Tversky, A., & Kahneman, D. (1986). Rational choice and the framing of decisions. *Journal of Business, 59*, S251–S278.

Ushioda, E., & Dornyei, Z. (2012). Motivation. In S. Gass and A. Mackey (Eds.), *The Routledge handbook of second language acquisition* (pp. 396–409). Abingdon, England: Routledge.

Vallée-Tourangeau, F., Euden, G., & Hearn, V. (2011). Eistellung defused: Interactivity and mental set. *Quarterly Journal of Experimental Psychology, 64*, 1889–1895.

von Frisch, K. (1967). *The dance language and orientation of bees*. London, England: Oxford University Press.

Werker, J. F., & Tees, R. C. (2002). Cross-language speech perception: Evidence for perceptual reorganization during the first year of life. *Infant Behavior & Development, 25*, 121–133.

Whorf, B. L. (1956). *Language, thought, and reality: Selected writings of Benjamin Lee Whorf*. J. B. Carroll (Ed.). Cambridge, MA: MIT Press.

Wilson, T., Lisle, D., Schooler, J., Hodges, S. D., Klaaren, K. J., & LaFleur, S. J. (1993). Introspecting about reasons can reduce post-choice satisfaction. *Personality and Social Psychology Bulletin, 69*, 331–339.

Witt, S. T., & Stevens, M. C. (2012). Overcoming residual interference in mental set switching: Neural correlates and developmental trajectory. *NeuroImage, 62*, 2055–2064.

Yafeh, M., & Heath, C. (2003, September/October). Nostradamus' clever clairvoyance: The power of ambiguous specificity. *Skeptical Inquirer, 27*, 36–40.

Yates, J. F., & Potworowski, G. A. (2012). Evidence-based decision management. In D. Rousseau (Ed.), *The Oxford handbook of evidence-based management* (pp. 198–222). Oxford, England: Oxford University Press.

Credits

Credits listed in order of appearance.

Photo Credits

Photo Credits listed in order of appearance.

Intelligence and IQ Testing

From Chapter 9 of *Psychology: From Inquiry to Understanding*, Third Edition. Scott O. Lilienfeld, Steven Jay Lynn, Laura L. Namy, Nancy J. Woolf. Copyright © 2014 by Pearson Education, Inc. All rights reserved.

Intelligence and IQ Testing

CONTROVERSY AND CONSENSUS

Think About It

Is human intelligence related to brain size?

Are IQ scores stable over time?

Do IQ tests predict anything useful?

Are IQ tests biased against certain minority groups?

Are all intelligent people creative?

Watch in **MyPsychLab** the **Video:** The Basics: Theories of Intelligence

Intelligence and IQ Testing

Listen in **MyPsychLab** to chapter audio

If you were to see Chris Langan on the street, you'd almost surely pass right by him. Now in his early sixties, Langan's face is unfamiliar to the overwhelming majority of the general public. Yet according to some psychologists, Langan may be the smartest person in the United States (Gladwell, 2008). Like many geniuses, Langan was a *child prodigy:* someone who displays astounding intellectual achievements at an early age (Morelock & Feldman, 1993). According to reports, he began speaking at 6 months of age and taught himself to read by age 3. When tested on a standard intelligence test, his approximate IQ—intelligence quotient—was an astonishing 195; the psychologist who examined him had to estimate it because the scores on standard IQ tests don't go up that high. Langan received a perfect score of 1600 on his SAT, a widely used college admissions test, and he dropped out of two colleges in part because he felt that he knew more than his professors—he may have been right. In 2008, Langan won $250,000 on NBC's game show "1 vs. 100." In his spare time, he wrote a book introducing his "Cognitive-Theoretical Model of the Universe," a comprehensive theory linking the mind to reality, which contains sentences like "No matter what else happens in this evolving universe, it must be temporally embedded in this dualistic self-inclusion operation" (no, we don't understand it, either).

What, you might ask, does Chris Langan do for a living? Is he a laboratory scientist, a university professor, or a famous computer programmer? If you guessed any of these three, you'd be wrong. For about 20 years, Chris Langan worked as a bar bouncer while holding other jobs, including construction worker and firefighter. Today, he works on a farm in Missouri with his wife. Even though Langan long yearned to earn a doctoral degree and to become a great scientist, he never got close. Why? He seemed to have a knack for offending others, including his college professors, without intending to. Moreover, he appeared unwilling to tolerate the minor bureaucratic frustrations of academic life. To this day, Langan's grand theory remains obscure, as he's never submitted it to a peer-reviewed journal.

How do people like Chris Langan achieve stratospheric levels of IQ? And how can we explain why Langan, in contrast to many others with extremely high IQs, failed to achieve great academic success? In this chapter, we won't find definitive answers, but we'll uncover a few tantalizing cues.

What Is Intelligence? Definitional Confusion

1 Identify different models and types of intelligence.

2 Describe the connection between intelligence and brain size and efficiency.

One of the problems that renders psychology so challenging—and at times exasperating—is the lack of clear-cut definitions for many of its concepts. No area of psychology illustrates this ongoing challenge better than does the field of intelligence. Even today, psychologists can't agree on the precise definition of intelligence (Sternberg, 2003b; Sternberg & Detterman, 1986).

Psychologist Edwin Boring (1923) discovered an easy way around the nagging question of what intelligence is. According to Boring, intelligence is whatever intelligence tests measure. Yes, it's that simple. Some modern psychologists have embraced this definition, which lets us off the hook from having to figure out what intelligence is. Yet because this definition sidesteps the central question of what makes some people smarter than others—or whether some people are actually smarter than others across the board—it doesn't really get us all that far. The definition of intelligence must go beyond Boring's definition. With that point in mind, let's examine the most influential attempts to define and understand intelligence.

Intelligence as Sensory Capacity: Out of Sight, Out of Mind

Sir Francis Galton (1822–1911) was a prominent scientist, inventor, and cousin of the great biologist Charles Darwin, co-developer of the theory of evolution by natural selection. Following in the footsteps of his cousin, Galton—himself a creative genius in many respects—was interested in the potential adaptive advantages of high intellect. Perhaps as a consequence of his own exceptional intelligence, he was fascinated by the question of what makes some people especially smart.

Galton proposed a radical hypothesis: Intelligence is the by-product of sensory capacity. He reasoned that most knowledge first comes through the senses, especially vision and hearing. Therefore, he assumed, people with superior sensory capacities, like better eyesight, should acquire more knowledge than will other people.

For a six-year period beginning in 1884, Galton set up a laboratory at a museum in London, England. There, he administered a battery of 17 sensory tests to more than 9,000 visitors (Gillham, 2001). He measured just about everything under the sun relating to sensory ability: the highest and lowest pitch of sounds that individuals could detect; their reaction times to various stimuli; and their ability to discriminate the weights of similar objects. James McKeen Cattell, who worked under Galton, imported Galton's tests to America, administering them to thousands of college students to find out what they were measuring. Like his teacher, Cattell assumed that intelligence was a matter of raw sensory ability.

Yet later research showed that one exceptional sense, like heightened hearing, doesn't bear much of a relation to other exceptional senses, like heightened vision (Acton & Schroeder, 2001). Nor are measures of sensory ability highly correlated with overall intelligence (Li, Jordanova, & Lindenberger, 1998). These findings falsify Galton's claim that intelligence equals sensory ability. Whatever intelligence is, it's more than just good eyesight, hearing, and smell. A moment's reflection reveals that this must be the case: According to Galton, Helen Keller, the blind and deaf woman who became a brilliant author and social critic would almost by definition have had mental retardation. Galton's definition can't be right.

◀ **FALSIFIABILITY**
Can the claim be disproved?

Still, as we'll learn later, Galton may have been onto something. Recent research suggests that some forms of sensory ability relate modestly to intelligence, although these two concepts clearly aren't identical.

Intelligence as Abstract Thinking

Early in the last century, the French government wanted to find a way to identify children in need of special educational assistance. In 1904, the Minister of Public Instruction in Paris tapped two individuals, Alfred Binet (pronounced "Bee-NAY") and Théodore Simon (pronounced "See-MOAN"), to develop an objective psychological test that would separate "slower" learners from other children without having to rely on the subjective judgments of teachers.

Binet and Simon experimented with many different items (an item is a question on a measure, including an intelligence or personality test) designed to distinguish students whom teachers perceived as plodding learners from other students. In 1905, they developed what most psychologists regard as the first **intelligence test**, a diagnostic tool designed to measure overall thinking ability.

Their items were remarkably diverse in content. They involved naming objects, generating the meanings of words, drawing pictures from memory, completing incomplete sentences ("The man wrote a letter using his _____."), determining the similarities between two objects ("In what way are a dog and a rose alike?"), and constructing a sentence from three words (*woman*, *house*, and *walked*). Despite the superficial differences among these items, they had one thing in common that Binet and Simon (1905) recognized: *higher mental processes*. These processes included reasoning, understanding, and judgment (Siegler, 1992). In this respect, their items differed sharply from those of Galton, which had relied solely on sensation. Virtually all items on modern intelligence tests have followed Binet and Simon's lead.

Indeed, most experts agree that whatever intelligence is, it has something to do with **abstract thinking**: the capacity to understand hypothetical concepts, rather than concepts in the here and now (Gottfredson, 1997; Sternberg, 2003b). In 1921, a panel of

Galton's laboratory on display at the International Health Exhibition in London in 1884. The exhibit later moved to the South Kensington Museum where, between 1886 and 1890, thousands of visitors took a battery of 17 sensory tests.

intelligence test
diagnostic tool designed to measure overall thinking ability

abstract thinking
capacity to understand hypothetical concepts

371

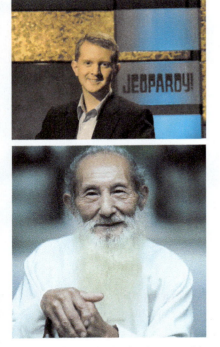

Ken Jennings *(top)*, who broke the record for winnings on the game show *Jeopardy!*, would be regarded as especially intelligent by most individuals in Western culture. In contrast, a village elder *(bottom)* who can impart wisdom would be regarded as especially intelligent by many individuals in Chinese culture.

REPLICABILITY ▶
Can the results be duplicated
in other studies?

g (general intelligence)
hypothetical factor that accounts for overall differences in intellect among people

14 American experts generated a list of definitions of intelligence. They didn't succeed in hammering out a single definition, but they mostly agreed that intelligence consists of the abilities to:

- Reason abstractly.
- Learn to adapt to novel environmental circumstances.
- Acquire knowledge.
- Benefit from experience.

Interestingly, research on how laypeople view intelligence yields similar conclusions, at least in the United States. Most Americans view intelligence as consisting of the capacity to reason well and reason quickly ("to think on one's feet"), as well as to amass large amounts of knowledge in brief periods of time (Sternberg et al., 1981). In contrast, in some non-Western countries, laypersons view intelligence as reflecting people's wisdom and judgment more than their intellectual brilliance (Baral & Das, 2003). For example, in China, people tend to view intelligent individuals as those who perform actions for the greater good of the society and are humble (Yang & Sternberg, 1997). Geniuses who "toot their own horns" might be showered with fame and fortune in the United States, but they might be viewed as hopeless braggarts in the eyes of many Chinese. This difference is consistent with findings that Chinese culture tends to be more focused on group harmony than is American culture (Triandis, 2001).

Intelligence as General versus Specific Abilities

There was one other crucial way that Binet and Simon's items differed from Galton's. When researchers looked at the correlations among these items, they were in for a surprise. Even though Binet and Simon's items differed enormously in content, the correlations among them were all positive: People who got one item correct were more likely than chance to get the others correct. Admittedly, most of these correlations were fairly low, say .2 or .3, but they were almost never zero or negative. Interestingly, this finding has held up with items on modern IQ tests (Alliger, 1988; Carroll, 1993). Given that some of Binet and Simon's items assessed vocabulary, others assessed spatial ability, and still others assessed verbal reasoning, this finding was puzzling.

The phenomenon of positive correlations among intelligence test items caught the attention of psychologist Charles Spearman (1927). To account for these correlations, Spearman hypothesized the existence of a single shared factor across all these aspects—*g* **(general intelligence)**—that explained the overall differences in intellect among people. All intelligence test items are positively correlated, he believed, because they reflect the influence of overall intelligence.

Spearman wasn't sure what produces individual differences in *g*, although he speculated that it has something to do with "mental energy" (Sternberg, 2003b). For Spearman, *g* corresponds to the strength of our mental engines. Just as some cars possess more powerful engines than others, he thought, some people have more "powerful"—more effective and efficient—brains than others. They have more *g*.

The meaning of *g* remains exceedingly controversial (Gould, 1981; Herrnstein & Murray, 1994; Jensen, 1998). All because of this little letter, some intelligence researchers are barely on speaking terms. Why? Because *g* implies that some people are just plain smarter than others. Many people find this view distasteful, because it smacks of elitism. Others, like the late Stephen Jay Gould, have argued that *g* is merely a statistical artifact. In his influential book *The Mismeasure of Man*, Gould (1981) maintained that the idea that all people can be ranked along a single dimension of general intelligence is mistaken. Yet Gould's critics have responded that *g* is unlikely to be a statistical illusion, because scientists have consistently found that intelligence test items are positively correlated with each other regardless of their content (Gottfredson, 2009). Spearman (1927) didn't believe that *g* tells the whole story about intelligence. For every intelligence test item, He also proposed the existence of a factor called *s* (**specific abilities**), that is unique to each item. According to Spearman, how well we perform on a given mental task depends not only on our general smarts (*g*), but also on our particular skills in narrow domains (*s*). For example, our ability to solve the spatial problem in **FIGURE 1** is due not only to our general problem-solving ability, but also to our specific talents with spatial tests, tasks examining the location of objects in physical space. Even if we're really smart—high in overall *g*—we might flunk this item because we have a specific deficiency when it comes to spatial problems. That deficiency may mean either that we're not inherently adept at spatial tasks or that we haven't had much experience with them.

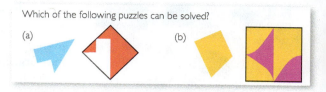

Which of the following puzzles can be solved?

FIGURE 1 Spatial Task. Try it! For each of the two puzzles shown, try to complete the figure using the shape on the left.

Fluid and Crystallized Intelligence

Later researchers found that Spearman's *g* wasn't as uniform as he'd believed (Carroll, 1993; Vernon, 1971). In the 1930s, Louis Thurstone (1938) discovered that some intelligence test items relate more highly to each other than do other items: These items form clumps corresponding to different intellectual capacities. Later, Raymond Cattell (no relation to James McKeen Cattell) and John Horn distinguished fluid from crystallized intelligence, arguing that what we call "intelligence" is actually a mixture of two capacities.

Fluid intelligence refers to the capacity to learn new ways of solving problems. We depend on our fluid intelligence the first time we try to solve a puzzle we've never seen or the first time we try to operate an apparatus, like a new type of cell phone, we've never used. In contrast, **crystallized intelligence** refers to the accumulated knowledge of the world we acquire over time (Cattell, 1971; Ghisletta et al., 2012; Horn, 1994). We rely on our crystallized intelligence to answer questions such as What's the capital of Italy? or How many justices sit on the U.S. Supreme Court? According to Cattell and Horn, knowledge from newly learned tasks "flows" into our long-term memories, "crystallizing" into lasting knowledge (see **FIGURE 2**). Most modern researchers don't believe that the existence of fluid and crystallized intelligence undermines the existence of *g*. Instead, they view them as "facets" or more specific aspects of *g* (Messick, 1992).

Fluid IQ

Crystallized IQ

FIGURE 2 Knowledge "Flowing" into a Flask. According to Cattell and Horn's model, there are two kinds of intelligence, fluid and crystallized. Fluid intelligence "flows" into crystallized intelligence over time.

There's some evidence for the fluid–crystallized distinction. Fluid abilities are more likely to decline with age than are crystallized abilities (Nisbett et al., 2012). In fact, some researchers have found that crystallized abilities often increase with age, including old age (Salthouse, 1996; Schaie, 1996). In addition, fluid abilities are more highly related to *g* than are crystallized abilities (Blair, 2006; Gustafsson, 1988). This finding suggests that of the two abilities, fluid intelligence may better capture the power of the "mental engine" to which Spearman referred.

I.Q. TEST FOR BIRDS

? According to Cattell and Horn, would this bird IQ test primarily be a measure of (a) fluid or (b) crystallized intelligence? Why? (See answer upside down on bottom of page.)

Crystallized intelligence, but not fluid intelligence, is moderately and positively associated (a correlation of about .3) with the personality trait *openness to experience* (Ackerman & Heggestad, 1997; DeYoung, Peterson, & Higgins, 2005; Gignac, Stough, & Loukomitis, 2004). People with high levels of openness to experience are imaginative; intellectually curious; and excited about exploring new ideas, places, and things (Goldberg, 1993; Nusbaum & Silvia, 2011). We don't fully understand the causal direction here. Higher crystallized intelligence could give rise to greater openness to experience, as people who know more things to begin with may find learning new things to be easier and therefore more enjoyable. Alternatively, greater openness to experience could give rise to greater crystallized intelligence, as people who are intellectually curious may expose themselves to more knowledge and learn more things (Ziegler et al., 2012).

s (**specific abilities**)
particular ability level in a narrow domain

fluid intelligence
capacity to learn new ways of solving problems

crystallized intelligence
accumulated knowledge of the world acquired over time

◄ **CORRELATION VS. CAUSATIC**
Can we be sure that A causes B?

because it assesses accumulated
orld.

Multiple Intelligences: Different Ways of Being Smart

Up to this point, we've been talking about "intelligence" as though it were only one overarching intellectual ability. But in recent decades, several prominent psychologists have argued for the existence of **multiple intelligences**: entirely different domains of intellectual skill. According to them, the concept of *g* is wrong, or at least incomplete. For them, we need multiple intelligences to explain the story of people like Chris Langan, who are extremely successful in some intellectual domains yet unsuccessful in others. Moreover, these psychologists maintain that we can't simply say that Sally is smarter than Bill, because there are many ways of being smart (Guilford, 1967). Even Spearman's concept of *s* is a partial acknowledgement of the existence of multiple intelligences, because it recognizes that people with equal levels of *g* can have different intellectual strengths and weaknesses. But in contrast to Spearman, most proponents of multiple intelligences insist that *g* is only one component of intelligence.

FRAMES OF MIND. Howard Gardner's (1983, 1999) theory of multiple intelligences has been enormously influential in educational practice and theory over the past two decades. According to Gardner, there are numerous "frames of mind," or different ways of thinking about the world. Each frame of mind is a different and fully independent intelligence in its own right.

Gardner (1983) outlined a number of criteria for determining whether a mental ability is a separate intelligence. Among other things, researchers must demonstrate that different intelligences can be isolated from one another in studies of people with brain damage; people with damage to a specific brain region must show deficits in one intelligence but not others. In addition, different intelligences should be especially pronounced in people with exceptional talents. For example, Gardner believed that the existence of *autistic savants*, provides evidence for multiple intelligences. These individuals show remarkable abilities in one or two narrow domains, such as knowing the precise batting averages of all active baseball players, but not in most other domains. Gardner also suggested that different intelligences should make sense from an evolutionary standpoint: They should help organisms survive or make it easier for them to meet future mates.

Gardner (1999) proposed eight different intelligences ranging from linguistic and spatial to musical and interpersonal, as described in **TABLE 1**. He also tentatively proposed the existence of a ninth intelligence, called *existential* intelligence: the ability to grasp deep philosophical ideas like the meaning of life.

Gardner's model has inspired thousands of teachers to tailor their lesson plans around children's individual profiles of multiple intelligences (Armstrong, 2009). For example, in a class of students with high levels of bodily-kinesthetic intelligence but low levels of logico-mathematical intelligence, a teacher might encourage students to learn arithmetic problems like 3 + 4 = 7 by dividing them into groups of three and four, having them stand in front of the class, and all join hands to form a bigger group of seven.

(a)

(b)

(c)

According to Gardner, individuals vary in the types of intelligence at which they excel. (a) Martin Luther King, Jr., was a great orator with high linguistic (and probably interpersonal) intelligence; (b) Taylor Swift is a musician ~renowned musical intelligence; and ~nal tennis player Serena Williams ~lv-kinesthetic intelligence.

Answer: Crystallized knowledge of the
evels
ual skill

TABLE 1 Howard Gardner's Multiple Intelligences.

INTELLIGENCE TYPE	CHARACTERISTICS OF HIGH SCORERS
Linguistic	Speak and write well
Logico-mathematical	Use logic and mathematical skills to solve problems such as scientific questions
Spatial	Think and reason about objects in three-dimensional space
Musical	Perform, understand, and enjoy music
Bodily-kinesthetic	Manipulate the body in sports, dance, or other physical endeavors
Interpersonal	Understand and interact effectively with others
Intrapersonal	Understand and possess insight into self
Naturalistic	Recognize, identify, and understand animals, plants, and other living things

Yet this approach may not be a good idea, and even Gardner himself has said he isn't entirely comfortable with it (Willingham, 2004). After all, if a child has a weakness in a specific skill domain like vocabulary or mathematics, it may make more sense to try to teach "to" that domain rather than "away" from it. Otherwise, we may allow the child's already poor skills to decay, much like a weak muscle we choose not to exercise. In addition, research hasn't supported the claim that matching teaching styles to students' learning styles enhances learning outcomes (Reiner & Willingham, 2010; Stahl, 1999).

The scientific reaction to Gardner's model has been mixed. All researchers agree with Gardner that we vary in our intellectual strengths and weaknesses. Gardner also deserves credit for highlighting the point that all intelligent people aren't smart in the same way. But much of Gardner's model is vague and difficult to test. In particular, it's not clear why certain mental abilities, but not others, qualify as multiple intelligences. According to Gardner's criteria, there should probably also be "humor" and "memory" intelligences (Willingham, 2004). Or given Gardner's emphasis on evolutionary adaptiveness, why not "romantic" intelligence, the ability to attract sexual partners? It's also not clear that all of Gardner's "intelligences" are genuinely related to intelligence. Some, such as bodily-kinesthetic intelligence, seem much closer to talents that depend heavily on nonmental abilities like athletic skills (Scarr, 1985; Sternberg, 1988b).

Moreover, because Gardner hasn't developed formal tests to measure his intelligences, his model is difficult to falsify (Klein, 1998). In particular, there's no good evidence that his multiple intelligences are truly independent, as he claims (Lubinski & Benbow, 1995). If measures of these intelligences were all positively correlated, that could suggest that they're all manifestations of *g*, just as Spearman argued. Even research on autistic savants doesn't clearly support Gardner's model, because autistic savants tend to score higher on measures of general intelligence than do other individuals with autism (Miller, 1999). This finding suggests that their highly specialized abilities are due at least partly to *g*.

◀ **FALSIFIABILITY**
Can the claim be disproved?

THE TRIARCHIC MODEL. Like Gardner, Robert Sternberg has argued that there's more to intelligence than *g*. Sternberg's (1983, 1988b) **triarchic model** posits the existence of three largely distinct intelligences (see **FIGURE 3**). Moreover, in conjunction with the College Board, he's been developing measures of the second and third intelligence, which he believes are largely unrepresented in standard IQ tests (Gillies, 2011; Hunt 2010). These three intelligences are:

1. **Analytical intelligence:** the ability to reason logically. In essence, analytical intelligence is "book smarts." It's the kind of intelligence we need to do well on traditional IQ tests and college admissions exams, the kind of intelligence possessed by Chris Langan. According to Sternberg, this form of intelligence is closely related to *g*. But for him, it's only one component of intelligence and not necessarily the most crucial. Indeed, Sternberg has long complained about a "*g*-ocentric" view of intelligence, one in which school-related smarts is the only kind of intelligence that psychologists value (Sternberg & Wagner, 1993).

2. **Practical intelligence:** also called "tacit intelligence," the ability to solve real-world problems, especially those involving other people. In contrast to analytical intelligence, this form of intelligence is akin to "street smarts." It's the kind of smarts we need to "size up" people we've just met or figure out how to get ahead on the job. Practical intelligence also relates to what some researchers call *social intelligence,* or the capacity to understand others (Guilford, 1967). Sternberg and his colleagues have developed measures of practical intelligence to assess how well employees and bosses perform in business settings, how well soldiers perform in military settings, and so on.

3. **Creative intelligence:** also called "creativity," our ability to come up with novel and effective answers to questions. It's the kind of intelligence we need to find new and effective solutions to problems, like composing an emotionally moving poem or exquisite piece of music. Sternberg argues that practical and creative intelligences predict outcomes, like job performance, that analytical intelligence doesn't (Sternberg & Wagner, 1993; Sternberg et al., 1995).

FIGURE 3 Sternberg's Triarchic Model of Intelligence. Sternberg's model proposes three kinds of intelligence: analytical, practical, and creative.

 Watch in **MyPsychLab** the **Video:** Practical Intelligence

triarchic model
model of intelligence proposed by Robert Sternberg positing three distinct types of intelligence: analytical, practical, and creative

Our intuitions tell us that these three types of intellect don't always go hand in hand. We can all think of people who are extremely book smart but who possess all of the social skills of a block of concrete. Similarly, we can think of people who have high levels of street smarts but who do poorly on school-related tests.

Yet, like virtually all anecdotes, such examples have their limitations. Indeed, some scientists have questioned the bases of Sternberg's claims. In particular, Sternberg hasn't demonstrated convincingly that practical intelligence is independent of g (Gottfredson, 2003; Jensen, 1993). Like crystallized intelligence, it may merely be one specialized subtype of g. Furthermore, Sternberg's work-related measures of practical intelligence may actually be measures of job knowledge. Not surprisingly, people who know the most about a job tend to perform it the best (Schmidt & Hunter, 1993). Moreover, the causal direction of this correlation isn't clear. Although more practical knowledge may lead to better job performance, better job performance may lead to more practical knowledge (Brody, 1992). Moreover, even creative intelligence is probably not independent of g. As we'll learn later in the chapter, measures of these two constructs tend to be at least moderately correlated (Preckel, Holling, & Wiese, 2006).

Thus, the concept of multiple intelligences remains controversial. Unquestionably, we all possess different intellectual strengths and weaknesses, but it's not clear that they're as independent of each other as Gardner and Sternberg assert. So there may still be a general intelligence dimension after all.

Revisiting Chris Langan, we can see how Spearman, on the one hand, and Gardner and Sternberg, on the other, would conceptualize his genius. Spearman would have viewed Langan as possessing extremely high g, as well as high specific abilities (s) in language, theoretical understanding, and other mental capacities. Gardner and Sternberg, while acknowledging that Langan has remarkable analytical abilities—book smarts—and perhaps even creative abilities, might emphasize that he appears to have difficulty understanding others and therefore may be below average in interpersonal (Gardner) or practical (Sternberg) intelligence.

Biological Bases of Intelligence

One popular notion about intelligence is that it's related positively to brain size. We speak of smart people as "brainy" or having "lots of marbles upstairs." But to what extent is intelligence related to the brain's size and efficiency?

INTELLIGENCE AND BRAIN STRUCTURE AND FUNCTION. For years, almost all psychology textbooks informed students that although brain size correlates with intelligence *across* species, it's uncorrelated with intelligence *within* species, including humans. Yet several studies demonstrate that brain volume, as measured by structural MRI scans, correlates positively—between .3 and .4—with measured intelligence (McDaniel, 2005; Willerman et al., 1991). So when we refer to the supersmart kid in class as a "brain,"—the one who gets 100s on all of his exams without studying—we may not be entirely off base. Still, the correlation between brain volume and IQ is complicated and may hold more for verbal than for spatial abilities (Witelson, Beresh, & Kiger, 2006).

Moreover, we don't know whether these findings reflect a direct causal association. Perhaps bigger brains contribute to higher intelligence. Or perhaps some third variable, like better nutrition before or shortly after birth, leads to both. In addition, a correlation of less than .4 tells us that the association between brain size and intelligence is far less than perfect. For example, Albert Einstein's brain actually weighed about 1230 grams, slightly less than the average brain. Interestingly, though, the lower part of Einstein's parietal cortex, an area that becomes active during spatial reasoning tasks, was 15 percent wider than normal (Witelson, Kigar, & Harvey, 1999). This finding may explain Einstein's remarkable capacity for visual imagery (Falk, 2009). In addition, Einstein's brain also had an unusually high density of neurons and glial cells, suggesting that his brain packed more mass than the average brain (Anderson & Harvey, 1996).

CORRELATION VS. CAUSATION ▶
Can we be sure that A causes B?

CORRELATION VS. CAUSATION ▶
Can we be sure that A causes B?

Recent studies on brain development suggest that there may be more to the story. A study using structural MRI revealed that highly intelligent (IQs in the top 10 percent) 7-year-olds have a *thinner* cerebral cortex than do other children. The cortexes of these children then thicken rapidly, peaking at about age 12 (Shaw et al., 2006). We don't yet know what these findings mean, and independent investigators haven't replicated them. But they may indicate that, like fine wines, intelligent brains take longer to mature than others.

Functional brain imaging and laboratory studies of information processing offer intriguing clues regarding what intelligence is and where in the brain it resides. Over the span of about a month, Richard Haier and his colleagues (Haier et al., 1992) taught a group of eight undergraduates to play the computer video game Tetris. All participants improved over time, and those with the highest scores on a measure of intelligence improved the most. Surprisingly, participants with higher levels of intelligence exhibited *less* brain activity in many areas than participants with lower levels of intelligence (Haier et al., 2009). Haier's explanation? The brains of the more intelligent students were especially efficient. Much like well-conditioned athletes who barely break a sweat while running a five-mile race, they could afford to slack off a bit while learning the task (Haier, 2009). Admittedly, not all researchers have replicated Haier's results (Fidelman, 1993), but these findings raise the possibility that intelligence in part reflects efficiency of mental processing (Langer et al., 2011).

◀ **REPLICABILITY**
Can the results be duplicated in other studies?

? Here are functional brain images of two people who've been playing the computer game Tetris. As is standard in brain images, red depicts high levels of brain activation; blue, low levels of brain activation. **According to research by Richard Haier and colleagues, which brain is likely to come from someone with a high IQ? Why?** (See answer upside down on bottom of page.)

◀ **REPLICABILITY**
Can the results be duplicated in other studies?

THE LOCATION OF INTELLIGENCE. Where in the brain is intelligence located? This may seem like a silly question, as it's unlikely that a neurosurgeon can point to a specific region of the brain and say "Right there. . . that's what makes us smart." Yet intelligence is more localized to certain areas of the cortex than others. One group of investigators administered a number of reasoning tasks that are highly "g-loaded"—substantially related to general intelligence (see **FIGURE 4**). These tasks all activated the prefrontal cortex (Duncan et al., 2000), a brain region that plays key roles in planning, impulse control, and short-term memory. More recent evidence demonstrates that intelligence is associated with the density of neural connections between the prefrontal cortex (especially on the left side of the brain) and other brain regions, suggesting that the prefrontal cortex may be a "command and control center" that pulls together information from other parts of the brain to help us think (Cole, Yarkoni, Repovs, Anticevic, & Braver, 2012).

(a)   (b)

(c)   (d)

(e)

? **FIGURE 4** Sample Task (a Highly *g*-Loaded Item). This sample item is similar to items that researchers have identified as highly "g-loaded," meaning that it's a good predictor of general intelligence. In this item, one of the five choices differs from the others. **Can you figure out which one it is?** (The answer is printed upside down at the bottom of the page.)

FIGURE 5 Reaction-Time Apparatus. Psychologists have used a reaction-time box to study the relation between intelligence and response to simple stimuli. Typically, the red lights turn on, and then as soon as one turns off, the participant tries as quickly as possible to press the blue button next to the unlit

Nevertheless, the prefrontal cortex doesn't tell the whole story when it comes to intelligence. For example, regions of the parietal lobe, which is intimately involved in spatial abilities, also appear to be associated with intelligence (Haier, 2009; Jung & Haier, 2007).

INTELLIGENCE AND REACTION TIME. When speaking loosely, we sometimes refer to people who don't seem as intelligent as other people as "slow." Psychologists have transported this folk belief to the laboratory by studying the relation of intelligence to *reaction time*, or the speed of responding to a stimulus (Jensen, 2006). Imagine being seated in front of the reaction time box shown in **FIGURE 5** (Hick, 1952), which features a semicircle of eight buttons, with lights alongside them. On each trial, anywhere from one to eight of the lights turn on, and then one of them suddenly turns off. Your job is to hit the button next to the light that turned off—and to do so as quickly as possible. The results of numerous studies indicate that measured intelligence correlates negatively (about −.3 to −.4) with reaction time on this task (Deary, Der, & Ford, 2001; Detterman, 1987): People with higher intelligence react more quickly than other people do when the light turns off (Brody, 1992). So Galton may not have been completely wrong in believing that speed of sensory processing contributes to intelligence, although these two concepts clearly aren't identical.

INTELLIGENCE AND MEMORY. Intelligence also bears an intimate connection to memory capacity. Many researchers have examined the relation of tasks that assess "working memory" to intelligence. This type of memory is closely related to short-term memory, and it reflects especially our ability to juggle multiple bits of information in our minds at the same time. A typical working memory task might require particpants to perform a test of digit span while trying to figure out the meaning of a proverb (such as "What does the saying 'A bird in the hand is worth two in the bush' mean?"). Scores on working memory tasks are moderately correlated (about .5) with scores on intelligence tests (Ackerman, Beier, & Boyle, 2005; Engle, 2002; Kane, Hambrick, & Conway, 2005). Indeed, an increasing number of researchers argue that differences among people in their working memory may help to explain why some people process information more quickly than others, and hence score better on standard measures of IQ (Conway, Getz, Macnamara, & Engel de Abreu, 2011; Redick, Unsworth, Kelly, & Engle, 2012).

In light of the findings we have just reviewed, several commercial companies now market computerized products, like *BrainTwister* and *BrainFitness Pro*, to boost working memory (say, by teaching them to recognize when a number in a sequence matches a previous number in that sequence). These companies claim that by doing so they can increase IQ. Yet controlled studies suggest that although these products may increase working memory, they don't increase IQ (Redick et al., 2012; Shipstead, Redick, & Engle, 2012). So although working memory and IQ are correlated, these findings remind us that one can't assume that improving working memory will *cause* increases in general intelligence.

CORRELATION VS. CAUSATION ▶
Can we be sure that A causes B?

PULLING IT ALL TOGETHER. If there's one central theme to these diverse findings, it's that intelligence is related to efficiency or speed of information processing (Schmiedek et al., 2007; Vernon, 1987). So here, common sense may be partly correct: People who are rapid thinkers tend to be especially intelligent. Still, the associations are far less than a perfect correlation of 1.0, which tells us that whatever intelligence, it's more than quickness of thinking. These results also suggest that the capacity to retrieve short-term information—and to keep this information active while we process it online—is related to intelligence, although the causal direction of this association isn't clear.

 Study and **Review** in **MyPsychLab**

Assess Your Knowledge   FACT or FICTION?

1. Most research suggests that intelligence is almost entirely a function of sensory ability. **True / False**

2. All or almost all items on modern intelligence tests tend to be positively correlated with each other. **True / False**

3. According to Sternberg, practical intelligence is essentially the same thing as book smarts. **True / False**

4. Within humans, brain size tends to be moderately positively correlated with measured intelligence. **True / False**

5. Intelligence is unrelated to reaction time. **True / False**

Answers: 1. F; 2. T; 3. F; 4. T; 5. F

Intelligence Testing: The Good, the Bad, and the Ugly

3   Determine how psychologists calculate IQ.

4   Explain the history of misuse of intelligence tests in the United States.

5   Describe tests of intelligence used today and evaluate the reliability and validity of IQ scores.

6   Distinguish the unique characteristics of mental retardation and genius.

Psychologists have long struggled with the thorny question of how to measure people's intelligence. The simplest way to do so, of course, would be to ask them "How smart are you?" Tempting as this approach might be, it's unlikely to work. Self-estimates of IQ correlate only .2 to .3 with objective measures of intelligence (Hansford & Hattie, 1982; Paulhus, Lysy, & Yik, 1998). Making matters more complicated, evidence suggests that people with poor cognitive skills are especially likely to overestimate their intellectual abilities (Dunning, Heath, & Suls, 2004; Kruger & Dunning, 1999). This curse may explain why some people perform poorly in school and on the job, even though they're convinced they're performing well. It may also help to explain the embarrassing behavior of some singers on television shows like *American Idol*, who seem utterly oblivious of the fact that they have no more musical talent than the average person off the street. *Metacognitive skills* play a key role in this phenomenon (Koriat & Bjork, 2005). Metacognition refers to knowledge of our own knowledge. People with poor metacognitive skills in a given domain may overestimate their performance, because they don't know what they don't know (Dunning et al., 2004; Sinkavich, 1995).

These findings confirm the intuitions of Binet, Simon, and other psychologists that we need systematic tests to measure intelligence, because self-assessments of intelligence won't do. When Binet and Simon created the first intelligence test more than a century ago, however, they had no inkling that they'd alter the landscape of psychology. Yet their invention has changed how we select people for schools, jobs, and the military; it's changed schooling and social policies; and it's changed how we think about ourselves. The history of intelligence testing begins where Binet and Simon left off.

How We Calculate IQ

Shortly after Binet and Simon introduced their test to France, Lewis Terman of Stanford University developed a modified and translated version called the **Stanford-Binet IQ test**, first published in 1916 and still used today in its revised fifth edition. Originally developed for children but since extended to adults, the Stanford-Binet consists of a wide variety of tasks like those Binet and Simon used, such as measures that involve testing vocabulary and memory for pictures, naming familiar objects, repeating sentences, and following commands (Janda, 1998). Terman's great achievement was to establish a set of *norms*, baseline scores in the general population from which we can compare each individual's score. Using norms, we can ask whether a given person's score on intelligence test items are above or below those of similar-aged people and by how much. All modern intelligence tests contain norms for different age groups, such as adults between 30 and 54 and between 55 and 69.

Shortly before World War I, German psychologist Wilhelm Stern (1912) invented the formula for the **intelligence quotient**, which will forever be known by two letters: *IQ*. Stern's formula for computing IQ was simple: Divide *mental age* by *chronological age* and multiply the resulting number by 100. **Mental age**, a concept introduced by Binet, is the age corresponding to the average person's performance on an intelligence test. A girl who takes an IQ test and does as well as the average 6-year-old has a mental age of 6, regardless of her actual age. Her chronological age is simply her actual age in years. So if a 10-year-old child does as well on an IQ test

Stanford-Binet IQ test
intelligence test based on the measure developed by Binet and Simon, adapted by Lewis Terman of Stanford University

intelligence quotient (IQ)
systematic means of quantifying differences among people in their intelligence

mental age
age corresponding to the average individual's performance on an intelligence test

Watch in **MyPsychLab** the **Video:** Special Topics: Intelligence Testing, Then and Now

Watch in **MyPsychLab** the **Video:** Classic Footage of Language Assessment Portions of Stanford-Binet Intelligence Scale

as the average 8-year-old, his or her IQ according to Stern's formula would be 80 (a mental age of 8 divided by a chronological age of 10, multiplied by 100). Conversely, if an 8-year-old child does as well on an IQ test as the average 10-year-old, his or her IQ according to Stern's formula would be 125 (a mental age of 10 divided by a chronological age of 8 multiplied by 100).

Although Stern's formula does a respectable job of estimating intelligence for children and young adolescents, it soon became evident that the formula contains a critical flaw. Mental age scores increase progressively in childhood, but start to level out at around age 16 (Eysenck, 1994). Once we hit 16 or so, our performance on IQ test items doesn't increase by much. Because our mental age levels off but our chronological age increases with time, Stern's formula would result in everyone's IQ getting lower as they get older.

That's why almost all modern intelligence researchers rely on a statistic called **deviation IQ** when computing IQ for adults (Wechsler, 1939). Basically, using a statistical measure of variability, the deviation IQ expresses each person's IQ relative to the norms for his or her age group. An IQ of 100, which is average, means that a person's IQ is exactly typical of people of his or her age group. An IQ of 80 is a standard amount below average for any age group, and an IQ of 120 is a standard amount above. In this way, the deviation IQ gets rid of the problem posed by Stern's formula, because it doesn't result in IQs decreasing after age 16.

The Eugenics Movement: Misuses and Abuses of IQ Testing

Soon after French psychologists Binet and Simon had developed their test, researchers in other countries began translating it into various languages. Among the first was American psychologist Henry Goddard, who translated it into English in 1908. In only a matter of years, IQ testing became a booming business in the United States. It was no longer merely a vehicle for targeting schoolchildren in need of special help, however, but a means of identifying adults deemed intellectually inferior.

The IQ testing movement quickly spiraled out of control. Examiners frequently administered these tests in English to new American immigrants who barely knew the language. It's hardly surprising, then, that about 40 percent of these immigrants were classified as having mental retardation. Moreover, Goddard and others adapted childhood tests for use in testing adults, without fully understanding how the IQ scores applied to adults (Kevles, 1985). As a consequence, legions of adults given his tests, including prison inmates and delinquents, scored in the range of mental retardation.

Eventually, concern with the low IQs of many immigrants and some Americans led to a social movement called **eugenics** (meaning "good genes"), a term coined by none other than Sir Francis Galton (Gillham, 2001). Eugenics was the effort to improve a population's "genetic stock" by encouraging people with "good genes" to reproduce, by discouraging people with "bad genes" from reproducing, or both. Galton had been a proponent of only the first type of eugenics, but many later psychologists advocated both.

Although eugenics was by no means unique to America (Kuntz & Bachrach, 2006), it became immensely popular there in the early twentieth century, especially from 1910 to 1930. Dozens of universities, including several Ivy League schools, offered courses in eugenics (Selden, 1999). Most high school and college biology texts presented eugenics as a scientific enterprise.

Acceptance of eugenics brought about some disturbing practices. Beginning in the 1920s, the U.S. Congress passed laws designed to restrict immigration from other countries supposedly marked by low intelligence, especially those in eastern and southern Europe (Gould, 1981). Even worse, 33 U.S. states passed laws requiring the sterilization of low-IQ individuals with the aim of halting the supposed deterioration of

Factoid

The popularity of the eugenics movement of the early twentieth century led the name *Eugene* to become one of the most frequently used boys' names in the United States.

deviation IQ

expression of a person's IQ relative to his or her same-aged peers

twentieth century
genetic stock
... to
genes

the population's intelligence (see **FIGURE 6**). When all was said and done, about 66,000 North Americans, many of them African Americans and other poor minorities, underwent forced sterilizations (Reynolds, 2003). Disturbingly, the U.S. Supreme Court upheld these sterilization practices in 1927 in the case *Buck v. Bell*. Ruling to uphold the sterilization of 18-year-old Carrie Buck, who'd come from two generations of purportedly "feeble-minded" ancestors, Justice Oliver Wendell Holmes wrote that "three generations of imbeciles are enough." Fortunately, the practice of sterilization slowed in the 1940s and had subsided almost completely by the early 1960s, although involuntary sterilization laws remained on the books in America for years. Virginia became the last state to repeal them in 1974.

 We can still feel the impact of the eugenics movement today. Many people are understandably suspicious of claims regarding IQ and its genetic bases, as these claims remind them of the efforts by eugenics advocates to "purge" low-IQ individuals from the gene pool. Still, we must be careful not to confuse a claim's validity with the people who advocate it (otherwise known as the error of "guilt by association"). It's true that many eugenics supporters were strong proponents of IQ testing and research on the genetic bases of IQ. But this fact doesn't, by itself, imply that we should dismiss the science of IQ testing or research on genetic bases of IQ. Although it's entirely appropriate to be dismayed by the tragic history of the eugenics movement in America, the two issues are logically separable.

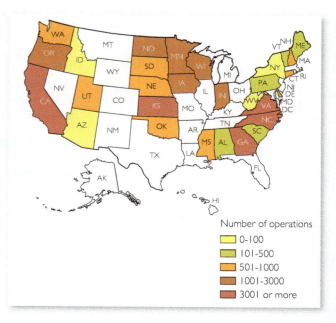

FIGURE 6 A Sterilization Map of the United States. Between 1905 and 1979, many U.S. states had mandatory sterilization laws, a legacy of the eugenics movement.

Number of operations
- 0-100
- 101-500
- 501-1000
- 1001-3000
- 3001 or more

IQ Testing Today

Today, the IQ test stands as one of psychology's best-known, yet most controversial, accomplishments. In 1989, the American Academy for the Advancement of Science listed the IQ test as one of the 20 greatest scientific achievements of the twentieth century (Henshaw, 2006). Whether we agree with this assessment, there's no question that IQ testing has been remarkably influential. Although psychologists have developed dozens of IQ tests, a mere handful have come to dominate the modern testing scene. We'll discuss these tests next, along with standardized tests like the SAT and measures of infant intelligence.

COMMONLY USED ADULT IQ TESTS. The IQ test administered most widely to assess intelligence in adults is the **Wechsler Adult Intelligence Scale (WAIS)** (Watkins et al., 1995). Ironically, David Wechsler, a psychologist who developed this test, was a Romanian immigrant to the United States who was among those classified as feebleminded by early flawed IQ tests. Perhaps not surprisingly, Wechsler's negative experience led him to construct an IQ test based on more than verbal abilities. The most recent version of his test, the WAIS-IV (Wechsler, 2008), consists of 15 "subtests," or specific tasks, designed to assess such varied mental abilities as vocabulary, arithmetic, spatial ability, reasoning about proverbs, and general knowledge about the world. We can find sample items from several of these subtests in **FIGURE 7**. The WAIS-IV yields five major scores: (1) overall IQ, (2) verbal comprehension, (3) perceptual reasoning, (4) working memory, and (5) processing speed. Verbal comprehension relates primarily to crystallized intelligence, while perceptual reasoning, working memory, and processing speed relate primarily to fluid intelligence.

COMMONLY USED CHILDHOOD IQ TESTS. Two widely used IQ tests for children are the Wechsler Intelligence Scale for Children (WISC) and the Wechsler Primary and Preschool Scale of Intelligence (WPPSI; pronounced "WHIP-see"), the former in its fourth edition

Lee Anderson, 87, shown August 8, 2006, at her home in Fayetteville, North Carolina, was involuntarily sterilized in 1950 by the Eugenics Board of North Carolina after the birth of her last child.

Wechsler Adult Intelligence Scale (WAIS)
most widely used intelligence test for today, consisting of 15 subtests to a' different types of mental abilities

Intelligence and IQ Testing

and the latter in its third edition. Both measures are versions of the WAIS adapted for older children and adolescents (the WISC-IV) or younger children aged 2 1/2 to 7 years old (the WPPSI-III) (Kaplan & Sacuzzo, 2008).

CULTURE-FAIR IQ TESTS. One longstanding criticism of IQ tests has been their heavy reliance on language. Test takers who aren't fluent in the native language may do poorly on IQ tests largely because they don't comprehend the test instructions or the questions

Wechsler Adult Intelligence Scale (WAIS) Sample Items*		
Test	Description	Example
Information	Taps general range of information	On which continent is France?
Comprehension	Tests understanding of social conventions and ability to evaluate past experience	Why do people need birth certificates?
Arithmetic	Tests arithmetic reasoning through verbal problems	How many hours will it take to drive 150 miles at 50 miles per hour?
Similarities	Asks in what way certain objects or concepts are similar; measures abstract thinking	How are a calculator and a typewriter alike?
Digit span	Tests attention and rote memory by orally presenting series of digits to be repeated forward or backward	Repeat the following numbers backward: 2 4 3 5 1 8 6
Vocabulary	Tests ability to define increasingly difficult words	What does *repudiate* mean?
Digit symbol	Tests speed of learning through timed coding tasks in which numbers must be associated with marks of various shapes	Shown: 1 2 3 4 Fill in: 4 2 1 3
Picture completion	Tests visual alertness and visual memory through presentation of an incompletely drawn figure; the missing part must be discovered and named	Tell me what is missing:
Block design	Tests ability to perceive and analyze patterns presenting designs that must be copied with blocks	Assemble blocks to match this design:
Visual Puzzles	Tests ability to organize parts of a figure into a larger spatial array	Which three of these pieces go together to make this puzzle?
Figure Weights	Tests ability to reason logically about numbers	Which one of these goes here to balance the scale?

381

themselves. Moreover, cultural factors can affect people's familiarity with test materials—and in turn their performance on intellectual tasks (Neisser et al., 1996). In one study, a researcher asked schoolchildren in England and Zambia (a country in southern Africa) to reproduce a series of visual patterns using both paper and pencil—a medium with which British children tend to be familar—and wire—a medium with which Zambian children tend to be familiar. The British children did better than the Zambian children when using paper and pencil, but the Zambian children did better than the British children when using wire (Serpell, 1979).

As a consequence of these problems, psychologists have developed a variety of **culture-fair IQ tests**, which consist of abstract-reasoning items that don't depend on language (Cattell, 1949). Presumably, these tests are less influenced by cultural differences than standard IQ tests are.

Perhaps the best-known culture-fair test is Raven's Progressive Matrices, used widely in Great Britain as a measure of intelligence, especially fluid intelligence (Raven, Raven, & Court, 1998). As **FIGURE 8** shows, this test requires examinees to pick out the final geometrical pattern in a sequence (the matrices are "progressive" because they start off easy and become increasingly difficult). Raven's Progressive Matrices is an excellent measure of *g* (Neisser et al., 1996; Nisbett et al., 2012).

FIGURE 8 Item Similar to That on Raven's Progressive Matrices. An item similar to those in the *Raven's Progressive Matrices—Advanced Progressive Matrices*. The answer is positioned upside down at the bottom of the page.

psychomythology

DO COLLEGE ADMISSIONS TESTS PREDICT GRADES?

Psychologists designed the SAT, ACT, Graduate Record Exam (GRE), and other admissions tests to forecast performance in undergraduate and graduate courses. Yet the correlations between these tests and college grades are often below .5 and in a few cases close to zero (Morrison & Morrison, 1995). Moreover, although SATs and GREs tend to predict first-year grades at reasonable levels, they generally do a worse job of predicting performance in later years of college (Kuncel & Hezlett, 2007).

These low correlations have prompted many critics to conclude that the SAT and GRE aren't helpful for making predictions about grades (Oldfield, 1998; Sternberg & Williams, 1997). More than one-fourth of major liberal arts colleges in the United States no longer require the SAT, and these numbers are growing (Lewin, 2006). Ralph Nader, a consumer advocate and former presidential candidate, argued that the SAT is so invalid that it should be banned (Kaplan, 1982; Nairn, 1980). In 2001, the chancellor of the University of California State system, Richard Atkinson—himself a prominent psychologist—argued that the SAT is only weakly predictive of students' actual achievement (Atkinson, 2001).

Are Nader and Atkinson right? Yes and no. They're right that the SAT and GRE are highly imperfect predictors and that they don't correlate highly with future grades. But they're wrong that this fact renders the tests largely useless. To understand why, let's look at the graph in **FIGURE 9a**. We call this graph a *scatterplot*, because it's a plot of the correlation between two variables, in this case between SAT scores and grade point average (GPA) in college. As we can see, the SAT scores (combined across all three subtests) range from 700 to 2,300, and GPA ranges from 1.5 to almost 4.0. The correlation in this scatterplot is .65, which is fairly high. High positive correlations display a pronounced upward tilt.

But let's now look at **FIGURE 9b**, which is a close-up of the dots that are 1,500 or higher on the *x* (horizontal) axis. As we can see, the range of SAT scores is now between only 1,500 and 2,300 combined. This range is typical of what we find at many highly competitive colleges. That's because few people with SAT scores much below 1,500 combined get into these colleges. What does the correlation look like now? As we can see, it's much lower than that in Figure 9a; in fact, the correlation is close to zero (it's even slightly negative). The upward tilt of this correlation has clearly disappeared.

culture-fair IQ test
abstract reasoning measure that doesn't depend on language and is often belie to be less influenced by cultural fact other IQ tests are

FIGURE 9 Scatterplot of Correlation between SAT Scores and College GPA. In the graph depicted in (a), SAT scores are clearly correlated with GPA. We can see an upward slant to the data points as we move from lower to higher scores. In the graph depicted in (b), the same data are depicted but only for the narrow range of higher SAT scores (1,500–2,300). As we can see, there is no clear correlation between SAT scores and GPA in this range.

These two scatterplots illustrate a crucial phenomenon overlooked by many critics of the SAT and GRE (for example, Sternberg & Williams, 1997): restriction of range. *Restriction of range* refers to the fact that correlations tend to go down when we limit the range of scores on one or both variables (Alexander et al., 1987). To understand restriction of range, think of the relation of height to basketball playing ability. In a group of ordinary people playing a pickup basketball game on a Saturday afternoon, height will correlate highly with who scores more points. But in a game of professional basketball players, height barely matters, because almost everyone who makes it to a professional basketball team is tall.

Restriction of range helps to explain why the SAT and GRE aren't highly predictive of scores in college and graduate school: Colleges and graduate schools rarely admit low scorers (Camara, 2009). Indeed, when two researchers examined the validity of the GRE in a graduate department that admitted applicants regardless of their GRE score, the GRE correlated highly (between .55 and .70) with measures of graduate GPA (Huitema & Stein, 1993). So when we remove restriction of range, the GRE becomes highly predictive of later grades. Restriction of range also probably accounts for why SATs and GREs are less predictive of later grades than of first-year grades. When students get to pick the classes in which they do well, they tend to obtain higher grades, thereby limiting the range of GPAs (Sackett, Borneman, & Connelly, 2008).

To return to the question posed at the outset—Do standardized tests predict grades?—the answer is, "When we measure the full range of scores, yes, although by no means perfectly."

Among professional basketball players, height isn't an especially good predictor of who scores the most points, because the range of heights is dramatically restricted.

College Admissions Tests: What Do They Measure?

The odds are high you've taken at least one, and perhaps many, college admissions tests in your life. In fact, to get into college you may have endured the misery of the SAT, once called the Scholastic Assessment Test, and before that, the Scholastic Aptitude Test (oddly enough, the initials "SAT" no longer stand for anything) or the ACT (which formerly stood for the American College Test, which also no longer stands for anything). The SAT now consists of three sections—Mathematics, Critical Reading, and Writing—with scores on each ranging from 200 to 800.

COLLEGE ADMISSIONS TESTS AND IQ. College admissions tests are designed either to test overall competence in a specific domain or to predict academic success. For many years, the Educational Testing Service apparently collected data on the correlation between the SAT and IQ, but didn't release them until about a decade ago (Seligman, 2004). When Murphy Frey and Douglas Detterman (2004) analyzed these data, they found that the SAT correlates highly (between about .7 and .8) with two standard measures of intelligence, including the Raven's Progressive Matrices. So the SAT is clearly linked to measured intelligence.

COACHING ON COLLEGE ADMISSIONS TESTS. You've probably heard of companies such as Princeton Review and Kaplan that prepare students for the SAT and other college admissions tests. Many of these companies guarantee whopping increases of 100 points or more when taking the tests a second time (Powers & Rock, 1999).

Nevertheless, the actual benefits of these courses aren't entirely clear (DerSimonian & Laird, 1983). There's definitely a positive *correlation* between whether people take coaching courses and their SAT scores, but this association may be due to a third variable: Students who take coaching courses tend to be more educated and better prepared for these tests to begin with (Camara, 2009). Still, the evidence suggests that commercial coaching improves SAT scores slightly, probably by 10 to 15 points on average per section (Kulik, Bangert-Drowns, & Kulik, 1984; Powers, 1993).

In addition, the companies are probably neglecting to consider an alternative explanation for their advertised increases in test scores: practice effects (Shadish, Cook, & Campbell, 2002). By *practice effects*, we mean that people frequently improve on tests as a result of practice alone. So the companies may be concluding mistakenly that people who take their courses are improving *because* of these courses rather than merely *after* them. When researchers have controlled for practice effects by including a control group of people who take the SAT a second time but haven't taken an SAT preparation course, the improvements resulting from these courses has been much smaller than the companies claimed (Camara, 2009; Powers & Rock, 1999).

Reliability of IQ Scores: Is IQ Forever?

We often think of people's IQ scores in much the same way we think of their Social Security numbers: as sticking with them for life. Joe's a 116, Maria's a 130, and Bill's a 97. Yet IQ scores aren't fixed. They almost never remain the same over time; in fact, they occasionally shift for the same person by as much as 10 points or more over a matter of months.

STABILITY OF IQ IN ADULTHOOD. IQ scores usually remain reasonably stable in adulthood. *Reliability* refers to consistency of measurement. And one important type of reliability is *test-retest reliability,* which refers to the extent to which scores on a measure remain stable over time. For adult IQ tests like the WAIS-IV, test-retest reliabilities tend to be about .95 over an interval of several weeks (Wechsler, 1997). As you may recall, .95 is an extremely high correlation, nearly but not quite perfect. Even across long stretches of time, IQ scores tend to be reasonably stable (Gow et al., 2011). In one study of 101 Scottish schoolchildren followed up over time, IQ scores obtained at age 11 correlated .73 with their IQ scores at age 77 (Deary et al., 2000).

STABILITY OF IQ IN INFANCY AND CHILDHOOD. There's a key exception to the rule regarding the high test-retest reliability of IQ tests. Prior to age 2 or 3 in children, IQ tests aren't stable over time. In fact, IQ measured in the first six months of life correlates just about zero with adult IQ (Brody, 1992). Nor do IQ scores obtained in the first few years of life do a good job of forecasting outcomes, unless they're extremely low, such as under 50; such scores tend to be predictive of later mental retardation. IQ tests designed for very young children assess the sensory abilities that Galton emphasized, which bear little association with intelligence. In contrast, IQ tests designed for older children and beyond assess the abstract reasoning emphasized by Binet and Simon. This reasoning, as we've discovered, lies at the heart of what we call intelligence.

Some measures of infant intelligence are slightly more promising when it comes to predicting later IQ. One is speed of habituation. Habituation refers to the tendency to stop responding to repeated presentations of the same stimulus. Infants who habituate to a visual stimulus (like a red circle) more quickly—as measured by how long they stare at it—turn out to have higher IQs in later childhood and adolescence than do other children, with most correlations in the .3 to .5 range (McCall & Carriger, 1993; Slater, 1997).

It's not entirely clear why this is so. Perhaps this correlation reflects a direct causal association between intelligence and habituation: Infants who are smart "take in" information from novel stimuli quickly, so they're ready to move on to new things. Alternatively, this correlation may reflect the influence of a third variable, like interest in new stimuli (Colombo, 1993). Maybe infants who are more interested in new things habituate more quickly *and* learn more things, resulting in higher intelligence later on.

◀ **CORRELATION VS. CAUSATION**
Can we be sure that A causes B?

◀ **RULING OUT RIVAL HYPOTHESES**
Have important alternative explanations for the findings been excluded?

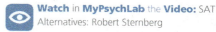
Watch in **MyPsychLab** the **Video:** SAT Alternatives: Robert Sternberg

Seated comfortably on mom's lap, a baby takes an experimental measure of infant intelligence that assesses response to novelty. The baby had previously viewed a number of identical pairs of photos of two people playing with toys and is now viewing two different photos of people playing with different toys. The extent to which infants look at the novel photo modestly predicts their adult intelligence.

◀ **CORRELATION VS. CAUS**
Can we be sure that A causes

A related approach presents babies with pairs of pictures, like photos of faces. For many trials, the two faces are the same. Then suddenly, a novel face appears along with the familiar face. Infants who attend more to the new face later tend to have higher IQs in childhood and adolescence than other infants (DiLalla et al., 1990; Rose et al., 2012; Smith, Fagan, & Ulvund, 2002). Still, this measure has its problems. In particular, its test-retest reliability is fairly low (Benasich & Bejar, 1992).

It remains to be seen whether researchers will develop even better measures of infant intelligence. Ultimately, these measures may yield clues regarding how intelligence develops and perhaps even what intelligence is.

Validity of IQ Scores: Predicting Life Outcomes

Whatever we think of IQ tests, there's little question that they're valid for at least some purposes. *Validity* refers to the extent to which a test measures what it purports to measure. One important indicator of a test's validity is its ability to relate to outcomes measured at about the same time the test is administered, or what psychologists call "concurrent" validity (think of the word *current*). Modern IQ tests possess strong concurrent validity; for example, they correlate moderately to highly with other IQ tests given during the same session (Wechsler, 1988).

Another important indicator of a test's validity is its capacity to forecast future outcomes, or what psychologists call "predictive" validity. IQ scores do a good job of predicting academic success; they correlate about .5 with grades in high school and college (Neisser et al., 1996). Still, because this correlation is considerably lower than 1.0, it tells us there's more to school success than IQ. Motivation, intellectual curiosity, effort, and *mental energy*—the ability to focus on difficult problems for long periods of time (Lykken, 2005)—also play crucial roles. IQ scores also forecast other important life behaviors; for example, people with high IQs tend to be more politically active regardless of their views (Deary, Batty, & Gale, 2008).

How typical are people like Chris Langan, who have extremely high IQs but unremarkable occupational success? Less than we might think. IQ scores predict performance across a wide variety of occupations, with the average correlation again being about .5 (Chen & Furnham, 2012; Ones, Viswesvaran, & Dilchert, 2005; Sackett et al., 2008). By comparison, the correlation between ratings of how well people do in job interviews and job performance is only about .15, which is ironic given that many employers place heavier weight on interviews than on IQ when selecting job applicants (Dawes, Faust, & Meehl, 1989; Hunter & Hunter, 1984). The correlation between IQ and job performance is higher in more mentally demanding occupations such as physician and lawyer than in less mentally demanding occupations like clerk and newspaper delivery person (Salgado et al., 2003). Using estimates from biographers and historians, one researcher found that presidents' estimated IQ predicted the quality of leadership among U.S. presidents, with correlations in the .3 to .4 range (Simonton, 2006).

Perhaps the link between IQ and achievement is more complex than we've implied. Some people, like journalist Malcolm Gladwell, author of the best-selling book *Outliers* (2009), claim that the correlation between high IQ and life accomplishments holds up to only a moderate IQ level, after which the correlation becomes essentially nonexistent. This phenomenon, which psychologists call a *threshold effect*, implies that above a certain level of IQ, intelligence is no longer predictive of important real-world accomplishments. Yet the evidence doesn't support that assertion: The correlation between IQ and life achievements remains essentially identical even at extremely high levels of IQ (Kuncel, Ones, & Sackett, 2010; Lubinksi, 2009; Sackett et al., 2008).

IQ also predicts a variety of important real-world behaviors outside the classroom and workplace. For example, low IQ is associated with health-related

Watch in **MyPsychLab** the **Video:** Are Intelligence Tests Valid: Robert Guthrie

a. DO NOT CHEW OR CRUSH, SWALLOW WHOLE.

b. FOR EXTERNAL USE ONLY

c. YOU SHOULD **AVOID** PROLONGED OR EXCESSIVE EXPOSURE TO DIRECT AND/OR ARTIFICIAL **SUNLIGHT** WHILE TAKING THIS MEDICATION.

Low levels of health literacy, which are associated with IQ, can lead to dangerous ...derstandings of medication instructions. ...nts in a study interpreted these ... a) you need to chew ... should use ... c) you

385

outcomes, including sickness and car accidents (Gottfredson, 2004; Johnson et al., 2011; Lubinski & Humphreys, 1992). At least some of the negative correlation between IQ and illness may be attributable to *health literacy*, the ability to understand health-related information such as instructions from doctors and on drug labels. People with low health literacy may have difficulty maintaining good health behaviors, such as getting enough exercise, eating the right foods, or taking the right dosage of their medications. IQ is also associated with criminal tendencies: The IQs of delinquent adolescents are about seven points lower than those of other adolescents (Wilson & Herrnstein, 1985).

But there's a potential confound here. IQ is positively associated with social class, as poorer people tend to have lower IQs (Strenze, 2007). So poverty, rather than IQ, may explain at least some of the associations we've discussed. Researchers have tried to address this rival hypothesis by determining whether the correlations hold up even when accounting for social class. In most cases, including the association between IQ and both health outcomes and crime, they do (Herrnstein & Murray, 1994; Johnson et al., 2011; Neisser et al., 1996). Still, to some extent, the causal arrow probably runs in both directions. Poverty may contribute to low IQs, but low IQs may also contribute to poverty, because people with low IQs may lack some of the cognitive abilities that allow them to obtain and keep well-paying jobs.

◀ **RULING OUT RIVAL HYPOTHESES**
Have important alternative explanations for the findings been excluded?

◀ **CORRELATION VS. CAUSATION**
Can we be sure that A causes B?

A Tale of Two Tails: From Mental Retardation to Genius

Within a population, IQ scores are distributed in a **bell curve**, across the range of possible IQ scores. In this distribution, discovered by the German mathematician Karl Friedrich Gauss (1777–1855), the bulk of the scores fall toward the middle, with progressively fewer scores toward the "tails" or extremes, forming the shape of a bell.

FIGURE 10 shows that the bell curve fits the distribution of IQ scores in the population fairly well, with one minor exception. Most of the scores fall in the broad middle of the distribution; about 95 percent of us have IQs between 70 and 130. The curve contains a small bump on the left, indicating that there are more very low IQ scores than we'd expect from a perfect bell curve. These extreme scores are probably the result of *assortative mating* (Mackintosh, 1998): the tendency of individuals with similar genes to have children. In this case, individuals with mental retardation are especially likely to parent a child with other individuals with mental retardation, probably because they frequent the same locations (such as special schools), then develop a relationship and have children.

Let's now look at what we know about the two tails of the IQ score distribution: mental retardation and genius.

FIGURE 10 Distribution of IQ Scores in the General Population. The bell curve roughly approximates the distribution of IQ scores in the general population.

MENTAL RETARDATION. Psychologists define **mental retardation**, sometimes now termed "intellectual disability," using three criteria, all of which must be present: (1) onset prior to adulthood; (2) IQ below approximately 70; and (3) inadequate adaptive functioning, as assessed by difficulties with dressing and feeding oneself, communicating with others, and managing other basic life skills (Greenspan & Switzky, 2003). The adaptive functioning criterion largely explains why about two-thirds of children with mental retardation lose this diagnosis in adulthood (Grossman, 1983); as individuals acquire life-functioning skills, they no longer qualify for this diagnosis. The definition of mental retardation has taken on new importance over the past decade with the 2002 Supreme Court decision of *Atkins vs. Virginia*, which ruled that criminals with mental retardation can't be executed.

Some experts also emphasize *gullibility* (the susceptibility to being duped by others) as a criterion for mental retardation, in part for social policy reasons. A diagnosis of mental retardation qualifies individuals for additional government services. For this reason, the

bell curve
distribution of scores in which the bulk of the scores fall toward the middle, with progressively fewer scores toward the "t[a]" or extremes

mental retardation
condition characterized by an onset adulthood, an IQ below about 7[0] inability to engage in adequate [c]

Most individuals with Down syndrome have mild or moderate mental retardation. Nevertheless, many have been successfully mainstreamed into traditional classrooms.

Factoid

The terms *moron*, *imbecile*, and *idiot*, today used in everyday language as insults, once referred to differing levels of mental retardation: mild (moron), moderate to severe (imbecile), and profound (idiot) (Scheerenberger, 1983).

inability to protect oneself from being taken advantage of by others should be weighted heavily in determining whether a person has mental retardation (Greenspan, Loughlin, & Black, 2001).

About 1 percent of persons in the United States, most of them males, fulfill the criteria for mental retardation (American Psychiatric Association, 2013). The current system of psychiatric diagnosis classifies mental retardation into four categories: mild (once called "educable"), moderate (once called "trainable"), severe, and profound. Contrary to popular conception, most individuals with mental retardation—at least 85 percent—fall into the "mild" category. In most cases, children with mild retardation can be integrated or *mainstreamed* into regular classrooms. Still, the term *mild mental retardation* is misleading, because individuals in this category still have significant deficits in adaptive functioning.

Contrary to what we might expect, the more severe the mental retardation, the *less* likely it is to run in families (Reed & Reed, 1965). Mild forms of mental retardation are typically due to a mix of genetic and environmental influences that parents pass on to their children. In contrast, severe forms of mental retardation are more often the result of rare genetic mutations or accidents during birth, neither of which tend to be transmitted within families.

There are at least 200 different causes of mental retardation. Two of the most common genetic conditions associated with mental retardation are fragile X syndrome, which is produced by a mutation on the X chromosome (females have two copies of this chromosome; males, only one), and Down syndrome, which is the result of an extra copy of chromosome 21. Most children with Down syndrome have either mild or moderate retardation. Nevertheless, a subset of individuals with Down syndrome known as *mosaics* (so called because only some of their cells contain an extra chromosome 21) have relatively normal IQs. People with Down syndrome typically exhibit a distinctive pattern of physical features, including a flat nose, upwardly slanted eyes, a protruding tongue, and a short neck. The prevalence of Down syndrome rises sharply with the birth mother's age; at age 30, it's less than one in 1,000, but by age 49, it's about one in 12 (Hook & Lindsjo, 1978).

Fortunately, societal attitudes toward individuals with mental retardation have improved dramatically over the past century. The Americans with Disabilities Act (ADA), passed in 1990, outlawed job and educational discrimination on the basis of mental and physical disabilities, and the Individuals with Disabilities Education Act (IDEA), passed in 1996, provided federal aid to states and local educational districts for accommodations for youth with mental and physical disabilities. Both ADA and IDEA have helped bring those with mental retardation out of institutions and into our workplaces and schools. As we increase our regular contact with these individuals, such laws may further erode the lingering stigma that some Americans feel toward these members of society.

IQ Score

Custodial workers
Truck drivers
Carpenters
Plumbers
Agricultural occupations
Auto mechanics
Law enforcement
Sales occupations
Teachers, K–5
Social workers, clergy
High school teachers
Finance, insurance, real estate
Technology
Natural sciences
Social sciences
Electrical engineers
College professors
Medical Doctors

■ 10th percentile IQ score   ■ 50th percentile IQ score   ■ 90th percentile IQ score

FIGURE 11 IQ Scores among Select
A study of IQ scores reveals
of professions, medicine,
engineering attract
However,
ofession
. (Source:

GENIUS AND EXCEPTIONAL INTELLIGENCE. Let's now turn to the opposite tail of the bell curve. If you're fortunate enough to score in the top 2 percent of the IQ range, you'll qualify for membership in an organization called Mensa. A large proportion of individuals with IQs at or near this range populate certain occupations, such as doctors, lawyers, engineers, and college professors (Herrnstein & Murray, 1994; Sorjonen et al., 2012) (see **FIGURE 11**). Yet we know relatively little about the psychological characteristics of individuals with high IQs or their academic, occupational, and social performance over time. Several research studies offer tantalizing clues.

Intelligence and IQ Testing

In the 1920s, Lewis Terman and his colleagues (Terman & Oden, 1959) initiated one of the classic studies of intellectually gifted individuals. From some 250,000 junior high school students in California, Terman selected about 1,500 who had IQs of about 135 or higher. He tracked these individuals, known affectionately as Terman's "Termites," for several decades (some are still alive today). Although Terman's study was flawed, in part because he didn't recruit a control group of individuals with average or low IQs, it refuted two common misconceptions regarding people with high IQs.

First, contradicting the common belief that almost all child prodigies "burn out" in adulthood, Terman's particpants became a highly distinguished group: 97 earned doctoral degrees, 57 earned medical degrees, and 92 earned law degrees. These numbers are all much higher than what we'd expect from the general population (Leslie, 2000). A later study of an even more select group—young adolescents who scored in the top .001 percent (that's 1 in 10,000) on tests of verbal or mathematical ability—generated similar results. By their early twenties, these individuals were attending graduate school at a rate more than 50 times higher than that in the general population and many had already published scientific or literary articles (Lubinski, 2009; Lubinski et al., 2006). Second, Terman's results disputed the popular notion that there's an intimate link between genius and madness. Although the absence of a control group makes it difficult to know for certain, his findings pointed to slightly lower rates of mental illness and suicide among his adult Termites compared with the general population. Later researchers have found broadly similar results (Simonton & Song, 2009), although a few have reported that exceedingly intelligent children, such as those with IQs over 180, may be at heightened risk for selected mental health problems, especially loneliness and depression (Janos & Robinson, 1985; Winner, 1999). These negative outcomes may stem from the greater ridicule and isolation that these children experience. Still, there's scant evidence that high intelligence is associated with high levels of severe mental illness.

What's the recipe for creating a genius like Chris Langan? We don't know, although as we'll soon discover, genetic factors probably play a significant role. Still, as the brilliant inventor Thomas Edison said famously, "Genius is 1 percent inspiration, 99 percent perspiration." Here common wisdom is correct: Practice makes perfect—or at least pretty darned good. The best predictor of exceptional career success in violin, piano, ballet, chess, and sports is the sheer amount of time we spend in practice. The most talented musicians practice twice as much as the less talented ones (Ericsson, Krampe, & Tesch-Römer, 1993; Gladwell, 2009). Of course, the causal arrow here isn't clear. Greater amounts of practice could be causing greater success, or greater levels of initial talent could be causing greater amounts of practice. We won't spend ten hours a day perfecting our guitar playing unless we're decent at it to begin with. In addition, research shows that across many domains, such as science, art, and music, individuals rarely attain remarkable intellectual accomplishments until they've dedicated themselves intensely for at least ten years—or to be a bit more precise, 10,000 hours—in that domain (Gladwell, 2009; Simonton, 1997). So the familiar Hollywood stereotype of the teenager or young adult who achieves astonishing intellectual brilliance with virtually no effort is exceedingly unrealistic.

? Are Hollywood movies like the 1997 movie *Good Will Hunting* accurate in their portrayal of childhood or adolescent geniuses exerting minimal effort to make astonishing intellectual discoveries? Why or why not? (See answer upside down on bottom of page.)

◄ **CORRELATION VS. CAUSATION**
Can we be sure that A causes B?

Assess Your Knowledge   FACT or FICTION?

1. Today, IQ is measured as mental age divided by chronological age, multiplied by 100.
   True / False

2. Standard IQ tests administered in infancy tend not to be highly predictive of later IQ scores.   **True / False**

3. Although IQ scores predict school achievement, they're almost useless for predicting occupational success.   **True / False**

4. The most prevalent form of mental retardation is mild retardation.   **True / False**

5. Research suggests a close link between extremely high intelligence and severe mental illness.   **True / False**

Answers: 1. F, 2. T, 3. F, 4. T, 5. F

research shows that such discoveries
—a decade or more of hard,
in a specific area.

Genetic and Environmental Influences on IQ

7   Explain how genetic influences can be determined from family, twin, and adoption studies.

8   Identify potential environmental influences on IQ.

Up to this point, we've talked at length about what intelligence is and how we measure it. But we've said little about its causes or about the relative roles of nature and nurture in its development. Over the past few decades, psychologists have obtained a better handle on the genetic and environmental contributors to IQ. As we'll discover, however, significant flash points of controversy remain.

Exploring Genetic Influences on IQ

Scientists can study genetic influences on psychological characteristics in three major ways: family studies, twin studies, and adoption studies. They've done so for intelligence, with surprisingly consistent results.

FAMILY STUDIES. *Family studies* allow us to determine the extent to which a trait "runs" or goes together in intact families, those in which all family members live in the same home. Sir Francis Galton, who coined the phrase *nature and nurture* (Galton, 1876), conducted one of the first family studies of intelligence. He gathered data on the extent to which persons renowned for their intellectual accomplishments had biological relatives who were also renowned for their intellectual accomplishments. He found that the proportion of relatives who'd achieved intellectual greatness declined steadily with increasing biological distance. Intellectually brilliant individuals had many first-degree relatives (parents, siblings, and children) who were also brilliant, but fewer second-degree relatives (such as cousins) and still fewer third-degree relatives (such as second cousins) who were brilliant. Later studies have confirmed that IQ runs in families: The correlation of IQ for brothers and sisters raised in the same family is about .45, whereas for cousins it's about .15 (Bouchard & McGue, 1981; Plomin & Petrill, 1997). Galton (1869) concluded that these findings demonstrated a genetic basis to intellectual greatness, but he overlooked a crucial limitation that applies to all family studies: *Studies of intact families don't allow us to distinguish the effects of genes from those of the environment.* As a consequence, when a trait runs in families, we don't know whether it's for genetic reasons, environmental reasons, or a mix of both.

TWIN STUDIES. Because family studies don't permit investigators to disentangle the effects of nature from those of nurture, they've turned to more informative research designs. These include *twin studies*, which compare correlations in a trait in two types of twins: identical (monozygotic) and fraternal (dizygotic).

The logic of the twin design is straightforward. Because identical twins share twice as many of their genes on average as fraternal twins, we can compare the correlations in IQ in these two twin types. Given a handful of assumptions we won't bother with here, higher identical than fraternal twin correlations strongly suggest genetic influence. In almost all cases, studies of twins reared together have offered evidence of considerably higher identical than fraternal twin correlations for IQ (Bouchard & McGue, 1981; Loehlin, Willerman, & Horn, 1988; Toga & Thompson, 2005). In typical studies of IQ, identical twin correlations have been in the .7 to .8 range, whereas fraternal twin correlations have been in the .3 to .4 range. Nevertheless, in all studies of twins raised together, identical twin correlations have been considerably lower than 1.0.

These findings tell us two things. First, the higher identical than fraternal twin correlations imply that IQ is influenced by genetic factors. The best estimate for the heritability of IQ falls somewhere between 40 and 70 percent (Brody, 1992; Devlin, Daniels, & Roeder, 1997). Interestingly, the heritability of IQ seems to increase from childhood to adulthood (McClearn et al., 1997), perhaps because people become less influenced by their environments, especially their parents, as they move away from home. Although the twin findings don't tell us which genes are relevant to intelligence, the past decade has witnessed progress

Explore in **MyPsychLab** the **Concept:**
Factors Affecting Intelligence

Twin studies of intelligence typically compare the mental performance of identical (*top*) versus fraternal (*bottom*) twins.

Explore in **MyPsychLab** the **Concept:**
Correlations Between IQ Scores of Persons of Varying Relationships

Answer: No, because almost always requi- concentrated wor/

in identifying specific genes for intelligence. These genes appear to cut across multiple domains of mental ability, including attention, working memory, and perhaps even risk for Alzheimer's disease (Plomin & Kovas, 2005; Posthuma & de Gues, 2006). Moreover, it's clear that intelligence isn't due to only one or even a small number of genes; instead, it appears to be tied to many genes, each exerting tiny effects on brain functioning (Davies et al., 2011). Nevertheless, although there have been numerous published findings linking specific genes to intelligence, these results haven't been consistently replicated (Chabris, 2013); as a consequence, the actual genes that predispose to intelligence are unknown.

There's one notable exception to the moderate to high heritability of IQ. Increasing evidence suggests that the heritability of IQ may be very low in individuals, especially children, at or below the poverty line (Deary, Spinath, & Bates, 2006; Nisbett et al., 2012; Rowe, Jacobson, & Van den Oord, 1999; Turkheimer et al., 2003). These findings raise the possibility that at high levels of environmental deprivation, the effects of environment on intelligence may largely swamp out the effects of genes. They also remind us that heritability isn't a fixed number, because it can be influenced by the range of environments in our sample. In this case, because people in poor neighborhoods often have restricted access to environmental resources like books and computers, there's less opportunity for them to realize their genetic potential for intelligence (Nisbett et al., 2012).

Second, twin findings provide convincing evidence for environmental influences on IQ, because the identical twin correlations for IQ are far less than perfect. Given that identical twins share 100 percent of their genes, they would correlate 1.0 if genetic influences alone were operative (assuming the IQ tests are reliable). The fact that they correlate less than 1.0 tells us that environmental influences also play a role, although the studies don't tell us what these influences are.

Thus far, we've discussed only studies of twins raised together. These studies are vulnerable to a rival hypothesis: Perhaps identical twins are more similar than fraternal twins because they spend more time together. To exclude this possibility, investigators have conducted studies of identical and fraternal twins reared apart since birth or shortly after birth. During the 1980s and 1990s, Thomas Bouchard and his colleagues at the University of Minnesota conducted the landmark study of twins reared apart. Remarkably, the results of this study revealed that a sample of over 40 identical twin pairs reared apart were just as similar on three measures of IQ (including the WAIS and Raven's Progressive Matrices) as were identical twins reared together (Bouchard et al., 1990). Other investigators have replicated these findings (Pederson et al., 1992); although because twins reared apart are extremely rare, the sample sizes of these studies are relatively low.

ADOPTION STUDIES. As we've seen, studies of intact family members are limited because they can't disentangle genetic from environmental influences. To address this shortcoming, psychologists have turned to *adoption studies*, which examine the extent to which children adopted into new homes resemble their adoptive versus biological parents. Adoption studies allow us to separate environmental from genetic effects on IQ, because adoptees are raised by parents with whom they share an environment but not genes. One potential confound in adoption studies is *selective placement*: Adoption agencies frequently place children in homes similar to those of the biological parents (DeFries & Plomin, 1978; Tully, Iacono, & McGue, 2008). This confound can lead investigators to mistakenly interpret the similarity between adoptive children and adoptive parents as an environmental effect. In adoption studies of IQ, researchers often try to control for selective placement by correcting statistically for the correlation in IQ between biological and adoptive parents.

Adoption studies have established a clear contribution of the environment in IQ. For example, adopted children who come from extremely deprived environments show an increase in IQ when adopted into homes that provide more enriched environments (Capron & Duyme, 1989). In one study of French children raised in a very poor environment, children who were adopted showed an average 16-point IQ edge over children who weren't (Schiff et al., 1982).

◀ REPLICABILITY
Can the results be duplicated in other studies?

◀ RULING OUT RIVAL HYPOTHESES
Have important alternative explanations for the findings been excluded?

◀ REPLICABILITY
Can the results be duplicated in other studies?

Many children adopted from environm severe deprivation, such as this orph Romania, show increases in IQ aft in a healthier and more attentiv environment.

But do adopted children's IQs resemble their biological parents' IQs? The results of adoption studies indicate that the IQs of adopted children tend to be similar to the IQs of their biological parents, offering evidence of genetic influence. As young children, adoptees tend to resemble the adoptive parents in IQ, but this resemblance dissipates once these children become older and approach adolescence (Loehlin, Horn, & Willerman, 1989; Phillips & Fulker, 1989; Plomin et al., 1997).

Exploring Environmental Influences on IQ

So twin and adoption studies paint a consistent picture: Both genes and environment affect IQ scores. But these studies leave a mysterious question unanswered: What exactly are these environmental factors? Psychologists don't know for sure, although they've made significant inroads toward identifying promising candidates. As we'll see, environmental influences can include not only the *social* environment, such as school and parents, but also the *biological* environment, such as the availability of nutrients and exposure to toxic substances (lead, for instance). We'll also discover that the evidence for some of these environmental influences is more convincing than for others.

DOES HOW WE THINK ABOUT INTELLIGENCE AFFECT IQ? Recent research suggests that how we conceptualize intelligence may actually influence our intelligence. Carol Dweck (2002, 2006) showed that people who believe that intelligence is a fixed entity that doesn't change tend to take fewer academic risks, such as enrolling in challenging classes. According to Dweck, they think, "If I do really poorly in a class, it probably means I'm stupid, and I can't do anything about that." After failing on a problem, they tend to become discouraged and give up, probably because they assume they can't boost their intelligence. In contrast, people who believe that intelligence is a flexible process that can increase over time tend to take more academic risks; they think, "If I do really poorly in a class, I can still do better next time." They tend to persist after failing on a problem, probably because they believe that effort can pay off. As a consequence, they may perform better in the long run on challenging intellectual tasks (Salekin, Lester, & Sellers, 2012). Nevertheless, because not all researchers have found that beliefs about intelligence are associated with performance on mental tests, these claims require further investigation (Glenn, 2010).

REPLICABILITY ▶
Can the results be duplicated in other studies?

BIRTH ORDER: ARE OLDER SIBLINGS WISER? In the 1970s, Robert Zajonc (whose name, oddly enough, rhymes with *science*), created a stir by arguing that later-born children tend to be less intelligent than earlier-born children (Zajonc, 1976). According to Zajonc, IQ declines steadily with increasing numbers of children in a family. He even authored an article in the popular magazine *Psychology Today* entitled "Dumber by the Dozen" (Zajonc, 1975).

In one respect, Zajonc was right: Later-born children tend to have slightly lower IQs (on the order of a few points) than do earlier-born children (Kristensen & Bjerkedal, 2007). But it's not clear that he interpreted this correlation correctly. Here's the problem. Parents with lower IQs are slightly more likely to have many children than are parents with higher IQs. As a consequence, when we look across families, birth order is associated with IQ, but only because low-IQ families have a larger number of later-born children than do high-IQ families. In contrast, when we look *within* families, the relationship between birth order and IQ becomes smaller and may even vanish (Michalski & Shackelford, 2001; Rodgers et al., 2000). So a more accurate way to state the correlation is that children who come from larger families have slightly lower IQs than do children who come from smaller families.

DOES SCHOOLING MAKE US SMARTER? Autopsy studies show that educated people have more synapses, that is, neural connections, than do less-educated people (Orlovskaya et al., 1999). In addition, the number of years of schooling correlates between .5 and .6 with IQ scores (Neisser et al., 1996). Although some authors have interpreted this correlation as meaning that schooling leads to higher IQ and perhaps even more synapses—it's equally possible that the causal arrow is reversed. Indeed, there's evidence

...SATION ▶
A causes B?

391

that individuals with high IQ scores enjoy taking classes more than do individuals with low IQ scores (Rehberg & Rosenthal, 1978). As a consequence, they may be more likely to stay in school and go on to college and beyond. This wouldn't be terribly surprising given that individuals with high IQ scores tend to do better in their classes.

Still, several lines of evidence suggest that schooling exerts a causal influence on IQ (Ceci, 1991; Ceci & Williams, 1997; Nisbett, 2009; Nisbett et al., 2012):

1. Researchers have examined pairs of children who are almost exactly the same age, but in which one child attended an extra year of school because he or she was born just a few days earlier (say, August 31 as opposed to September 2). This can occur because public schools often have hard-and-fast cutoff dates for how old children must be to begin school. In such cases, children who've attended an extra year of school tend to have higher IQs, despite being nearly identical in chronological age.

2. Children's IQs tend to drop significantly during summer vacations.

3. Students who drop out of school end up with lower IQs than do students who stay in school, even when they start out with the same IQ.

Children's IQs tend to drop significantly during summer vacations, suggesting an environmental influence on IQ.

BOOSTING IQ BY EARLY INTERVENTION. In a controversial article in the late 1960s, psychologist Arthur Jensen contended that IQ is highly heritable and therefore difficult to modify by means of environmental intervention (Jensen, 1969). In making this argument, Jensen fell prey to a logical error, namely, that heritability implies that a trait can't be changed. Yet he raised an important question: Can we boost IQ with early educational interventions?

Some of the best evidence comes from studies of *Head Start*, a preschool program launched in the 1960s to give disadvantaged children a "jump start" by offering them an enriched educational experience. The hope was that this program would allow them to catch up intellectually to other children. Dozens of studies of Head Start programs have yielded consistent results, and they've been largely disappointing. Although these programs produce short-term increases in IQ (Ludwig & Phillips, 2008), these increases don't typically persist after the programs end (Caruso, Taylor, & Detterman, 1982; Royce, Darlington, & Murray, 1983). Similar results emerge from studies of other early-intervention programs (Brody, 1992; Herrnstein & Murray, 1994).

At the same time, these programs appear to produce lasting and at times large increases in *school achievement*, which is hardly a meaningless accomplishment. Several studies indicate that Head Start and similar early-intervention programs result in lower rates of dropping out of high school and of being held back a grade compared with control conditions (Campbell & Ramey, 1995; Darlington, 1986; Neisser et al., 1996). They may also yield higher levels of early literacy and understanding of others' emotions (Bierman et al., 2008). In addition, there's preliminary evidence that they boost certain executive functions, which, include the ability to inhibit and modify one's impulses (Bierman et al., 2010).

The federal Head Start program was launched in the 1960s to give disadvantaged preschoolers a jump-start on their education. Studies show that Head Start programs typically produce short-term increases in IQ but that these increases fade with time.

A SELF-FULFILLING PROPHECY: EXPECTANCY EFFECTS ON IQ. In the 1960s, Robert Rosenthal and Lenore Jacobson wanted to examine the effects of teacher expectancies on IQ. The *experimenter expectancy effect* refers to the tendency of researchers to unintentionally influence the outcome of studies. In this case, Rosenthal and Jacobson (1966) looked at the expectancies of teachers rather than researchers. They administered an IQ test to students in the first through sixth grades, disguising it with a fake name ("The Harvard Test of Inflected Acquisition"). Then they gave teachers the results, which indicated that 20 percent of their students would display remarkable gains in intelligence during the subsequent eight months: These students were "bloomers" who'd soon reach their full intellectual potential. But Rosenthal and Jacobson misled the teachers. They had *randomly* assigned these 20 percent of students to be classified as bloomers, and these students' initial scores didn't differ from those of other students. Yet when Rosenthal and Jacobson retested all students a year later with the same IQ test, the 20 percent labeled as bloomers scored about four IQ points higher than the other students. Expectations had become reality.

Intelligence and IQ Testing

REPLICABILITY ▶
Can the results be duplicated in other studies?

This effect has since been replicated in a number of studies, although the size of the effect is usually only modest (Rosenthal, 1994; Smith, 1980). We don't know how this effect occurs, although there's evidence that teachers more often smile at, make eye contact with, and nod their heads toward students they incorrectly believe are smart compared with other students (Chaiken, Sigler, & Derlega, 1974). As a consequence, they may positively reinforce these students' learning. Still, the effects of expectancy on IQ have their limits. These effects are substantial only when teachers don't know their students well; when teachers have worked with students for at least a few weeks, the effects often disappear (Raudenbush, 1984). Once teachers form definite impressions of how smart their students are, it's hard to persuade them that their impressions are off base.

Lead exposure can arise from many sources in everyday life and may contribute to decreased IQ. Nevertheless, the causal association between lead intake and IQ remains controversial.

POVERTY AND IQ: SOCIOECONOMIC AND NUTRITIONAL DEPRIVATION. It's difficult to put a firm number on the effects of poverty, but there's reason to believe that social and economic deprivation can adversely affect IQ. Arthur Jensen (1977) studied a group of families in an extremely poor area of rural Georgia. For African-American (but not Caucasian) children, he found evidence for cumulative declines, that is, differences that increase over time. Older siblings consistently had lower IQs than did younger siblings, with a steady decrease of about 1.5 IQ points per year. Jensen's explanation was that siblings in this impoverished region experienced progressively more intellectual deprivation as they aged, leading them to fall further behind other children (Willerman, 1979). Moreover, because the environments of African-American children were even more impoverished than those of white children, the former children may have been especially likely to suffer this ill effect.

Along with poverty often comes inadequate diet. Studies from poor areas in Central America suggest that malnutrition in childhood, especially if prolonged, can lower IQ (Eysenck & Schoenthaler, 1997). In one investigation, researchers gave nutritional (protein) supplements to preschool children from an impoverished region of Guatemala. These children's school-related test scores were significantly higher than those of similar children who didn't receive supplements (Pollitt et al., 1993). The intake of high-fat and high-sugar foods in childhood is also linked to slightly lower IQ scores several years later, although these data are only correlational (Northstone et al., 2010) and could be due to unmeasured factors, like the extent to which parents play an active role in their children's upbringing. Poor children are also especially likely to be exposed to lead as a result of drinking lead-contaminated water, breathing lead-contaminated dust, or eating lead paint chips. Such exposure is also associated with intellectual deficits (Bellinger & Needleman, 2003; Canfield et al., 2003; Ris et al., 2004). Nevertheless, it's again unclear how much of this association is due to the direct effects of lead itself as opposed to poverty or other factors like malnutrition.

RULING OUT RIVAL HYPOTHESES ▶
Have important alternative explanations for the findings been excluded?

RULING OUT RIVAL HYPOTHESES ▶
Have important alternative explanations for the findings been excluded?

Scientific controversy has swirled around another potential nutritional influence: breast-feeding. On one side of the debate are researchers who claim that infants who are breast-fed end up with higher IQs—perhaps on the order of a few points—than are children who are bottle-fed (Mortensen et al., 2002; Quinn et al., 2001). Indeed, mothers' milk contains about 100 ingredients absent from milk formula, including several that speed up the myelinization of neurons. On the other side are researchers who contend that this IQ difference is due to one or more confounds: For example, mothers who breast-feed their babies tend to be somewhat higher in social class and IQ than are mothers who bottle-feed their babies (Der, Batty, & Deary, 2006; Jacobson, Chiodo, & Jacobson, 1999). These confounds could account for the seeming effect of breast-feeding on IQ. The debate rages on (Caspi et al., 2007).

GETTING SMARTER ALL THE TIME: THE MYSTERIOUS FLYNN EFFECT. In the 1980s, political scientist James Flynn noticed something decidedly odd (Dickens & Flynn, 2001; Flynn, 1981, 1987). Over time, the average IQ of the population was rising at a rate of about three points per decade, a phenomenon now known as the **Flynn effect** (Herrnstein & Murray, 1994; Nisbett et al., 2012). The magnitude of the Flynn effect is mind-boggling. It suggests that, on average, our IQs are a full 10 to 15 points higher than those of our grandparents (see **FIGURE 12**). It also appears to be occurring across much of the world, including the United States, Europe, and South American (Colom, Flores-Mendoza, & Abad, 2007). With a few exceptions (Mingroni, 2007; Rushton, 1999), most researchers agree that this effect is a result of unidentified environmental influences on IQ, because it's unlikely that genetic changes could account for such rapid rises in IQ over brief time periods.

What could these environmental influences be? Psychologists have proposed at least four explanations:

1. **Increased test sophistication.** According to this explanation, the rise in IQ scores results not from people becoming smarter, but from people becoming more experienced at taking tests (Flynn, 1998). There may be some truth to the test sophistication hypothesis, but there's a "fly in the ointment." The Flynn effect is most pronounced on "culture-fair" tests, such as Raven's Progressive Matrices, to which people have had the least exposure (Brouwers, Van de Vijver, & Van Hemert, 2009; Neisser, 1998).

2. **Increased complexity of the modern world.** With television, email, the Internet, Twitter, iPhones, and the like, we're forced to process far more information far more quickly than our parents and grandparents ever did. Modern schooling is also placing more emphasis on abstract reasoning, especially reasoning that involves geometrical objects, which play a starring role in many IQ tests (Blair et al., 2005). So the modern information explosion may be putting pressure on us to become more intelligent—or at least more adept at processing information rapidly (Greenfield, 1998; Schooler, 1998).

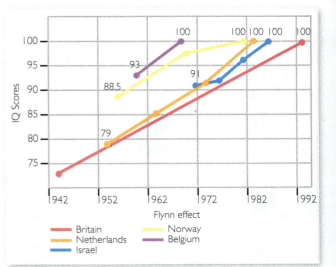

FIGURE 12 Flynn Effect. Research on the Flynn effect demonstrates that IQ scores have been increasing in many countries across several decades. The causes of this effect remain unclear. (*Source:* Flynn, 1999)

> **Flynn effect**
> finding that average IQ scores have been rising at a rate of approximately three points per decade

Answers are located at the end of the text.

IQ BOOSTERS
evaluating CLAIMS

A wide variety of books and websites claim to increase your IQ in a matter of days—some by as much as 200 points! Let's evaluate some of these claims, which are modeled after actual ads for products designed to increase your IQ.

"While the 'experts' argue about whether you can increase IQ or not, we promise real results!"

A warning sign of pseudoscience is the absence of connectivity to other research. This claim implies that the test developers can simply ignore what others have tried before—possible, but unlikely.

"Become a genius in 5 simple steps."

Does this claim seem plausible given the probable reaction range of intelligence? What kind of evidence would you need to support it?

"Credibly synthesize process-centric quantum wave outsourcing."

Beware of psychobabble; this claim sounds sophisticated but has little or no scientific meaning.

"Take our IQ test and expose you true creativity."

This claim implies that intelligence and ity are similar if not identical. What scientific research say?

One American differs from his Civil War ancestor.

Typical Civil War soldier	Typical modern American
(5 feet, 6 inches, 145 pounds)	(5 feet, 11 inches, 235 pounds)

As can be seen in the sizes of these men and their uniforms, most people are considerably larger today than they were in the era of the U.S. Civil War (1861–1865). That difference reflects dramatic differences in nutrition over the past 150 years. Some psychologists propose that enhanced nutrition may account for the Flynn effect.

3. **Better nutrition.** Most evidence suggests that the Flynn effect is affecting primarily the lower, but not the upper, tail of the bell curve. One potential explanation for this finding is diet. People are better fed than ever before, and the rates of severe malnutrition in many (although not all) parts of the world are declining (Lynn, 1998; Sigman & Whaley, 1998). As we've already learned, there's good evidence that nutrition can affect IQ.

4. **Changes at home and school.** Over the past several decades in the United States, families have become smaller, allowing parents to devote more time to their children. Parents also have more access to intellectual resources than ever. In addition, children and adolescents spend more years in school than in previous generations (Bronfenbrenner et al., 1996).

We don't fully understand the causes of the Flynn effect, and there may be some truth to several of these explanations. But the mystery doesn't end here. Recent data suggest that the Flynn effect may be subsiding or even reversing, at least in Europe (Sundet, Barlaug, & Torjussen, 2004; Teasdale & Owen, 2008). Some investigators have suggested that children's decreasing amounts of play with other children, perhaps resulting from greater computer and video game use, may be the culprit (Schneider, 2006), but no one knows for sure. The causes of the apparent end to the Flynn effect are as puzzling as the causes of its beginning.

 Study and **Review** in **MyPsychLab**

Assess Your Knowledge — FACT or FICTION?

1. Identical twins reared apart appear to be about as similar on IQ tests as identical twins reared together.   **True / False**

2. Children adopted at birth bear almost no resemblance in IQ to their biological parents.   **True / False**

3. There's good evidence that being removed from school can lower IQ scores.   **True / False**

4. Head Start programs produce lasting increases in IQ scores.   **True / False**

5. People's average performance on IQ tests has remained virtually unchanged over the past several decades.   **True / False**

Answers: 1. T; 2. F; 3. T; 4. F; 5. F

Group Differences in IQ: The Science and the Politics

9 Identify similarities and differences in mental ability between men and women.

10 Evaluate the evidence concerning racial differences in IQ.

Thus far, we've focused almost entirely on the thorny question of *individual differences* in IQ: Why does measured intelligence differ among people within a population? If you think that what we've discussed so far is controversial, fasten your seat belts. The topic of *group differences* in IQ is perhaps the most bitterly disputed in all of psychology. Here we'll look at what the research says about two group differences in IQ: (1) differences between men and women and (2) differences among races.

As we'll discover, the issues are as emotionally charged as they are scientifically complex. They've also become deeply entangled in politics (Hunt, 1999), with people on different sides of these debates accusing each other of biases and bad intentions.

Some have even gone so far as to argue that scientists should stay away altogether from studying group differences in IQ (Rose, 2009). When evaluating these issues, it's crucial that we try to be as objective as possible. That is, we must try to avoid *emotional reasoning*, or the affect heuristic, the tendency to judge the validity of an idea by our emotional reactions to it. Just because some of the ideas we'll encounter regarding intelligence may make us feel uneasy or even angry doesn't mean we should dismiss them out of hand. Difficult as it can be, we must try to evaluate these issues objectively with an open mind to scientific evidence.

Watch in **MyPsychLab** the **Video:** Gende Differences: Robert Sternberg

Sex Differences in IQ and Mental Abilities

In January 2005, then–Harvard University President Lawrence Summers created a furor. Speaking at an informal meeting of university faculty from around the country, Summers wondered aloud why so few women were in hard sciences like physics, chemistry, and biology (see **FIGURE 13**). He tentatively proposed a few reasons, one involving discrimination against women and a second involving women's preference for raising families instead of competing in grueling, cutthroat occupations. But it was Summers' third reason that really got people going. Summers conjectured that perhaps women enter the world with a genetic disadvantage in science and mathematics. Many people were appalled. One prominent woman biologist from the Massachusetts Institute of Technology stormed out of Summers' talk in protest. Within days, hundreds of Harvard faculty members were "calling for his head" (he resigned shortly thereafter). A firestorm of controversy regarding sex differences in mental abilities followed on the heels of Summers' provocative statements. In this section, we'll take a scientifically balanced look at the evidence.

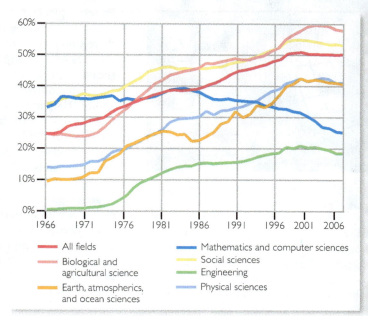

FIGURE 13 Bachelor's Degrees Earned by Women in Selected Fields, 1966–2008. Across a 40-year period, women have been underrepresented in most of the hard sciences comprising only a minority of those graduating with a degree in these areas of study. (Based on data from http://nces.ed.gov/programs/digest/d11/tables_1.asp)

SEX DIFFERENCES IN IQ. Do men and women differ in overall IQ? Probably not. A handful of researchers have reported that men have slightly higher IQs than women do—perhaps between up to three points (Irwing, 2012; Jackson & Rushton, 2006; Lynn & Irwing, 2004)—but these claims are controversial, to put it mildly. Indeed, most researchers have found few or no average sex differences in IQ (Flynn & Rossi-Case, 2011; Jensen, 1998).

Still, average differences don't tell the whole story. Numerous studies reveal that men are more *variable* in their overall IQ scores than women are (Hedges & Nowell, 1995; Johnson, Carothers, & Deary, 2009). So although men don't appear to have higher average IQs than women do, there are more men at both the low and the high ends of the IQ bell curve (see **FIGURE 14**). We don't know the reason for this difference; researchers have, not surprisingly, proposed both genetic and environmental explanations.

SEX DIFFERENCES IN SPECIFIC MENTAL ABILITIES. Even though there's little, if any, difference in overall IQ between men and women, the picture becomes more interesting—and more complicated—when we get to specific mental abilities. Men and women are quite similar when it comes to most intellectual abilities (Hyde, 2005; Maccoby & Jacklin, 1974), but a closer look reveals consistent sex differences in a few domains (Block, 1976; Halpern, 1992; Halpern et al., 2007; Pinker, 2005).

Women tend to do better than men on some verbal tasks, like spelling, writing, and pronouncing words (Feingold, 1988; Halpern et al., 2007; Kimura, 1999). This sex difference may have a hormonal component; even within women, some research suggests that verbal ability ebbs and flows along with the level of estrogen, a sex hormone that's more plentiful in women than in men. In one study, women were

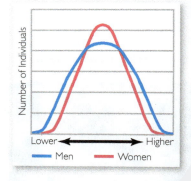

FIGURE 14 Distributions of Men and W in IQ Tests. The IQ distribution of me wider than the distribution of wom consequence, there are more me with both low and high IQ sco women with scores in the m

best at quickly repeating tongue twisters (like "A box of mixed biscuits in a biscuit mixer") when their estrogen levels were at their peak (Hampson & Kimura, 1988). Nevertheless, not all investigators have found that current levels of sex hormones are associated with mental abilities within males and females (Halari et al., 2005; Lurine, 2008). On average, females also do better than males in arithmetic calculation, like adding and subtracting numbers, although this difference appears to be present only in childhood (Hyde, Fennema, & Lamon, 1990). Finally, females tend to be better than males in detecting and recognizing feelings in others, especially when they reach adulthood (Hall, 1978; McClure, 2000). For example, they're usually better than men at distinguishing among faces that display different emotions, such as fear and anger. Incidentally, despite popular stereotypes, there's no good evidence that women talk more than men do. A study that tracked six samples of men and women in the United States and Mexico found that both sexes speak about 16,000 words per day (Mehl et al., 2007).

In contrast, men tend to do better than women on most tasks requiring spatial ability (Halpern et al., 2007). The largest difference emerges on *mental rotation* tasks, like the one shown in **FIGURE 15**, which require participants to determine which of a series of rotated blocks matches a target group of rotated blocks (Estes & Felker, 2012; Lippa, Collaer, & Peters, 2010; Voyer, Voyer, & Bryden, 1995). This sex difference appears as early as 3 months of age, raising the possibility that it's partly innate (Quinn & Liben, 2008). Interestingly, one of the largest reported psychological sex differences is in geography, an area of study that relies heavily on spatial ability. Among the 5 million children who've participated in the National Geographic Bee, 77 percent have been boys (Zernike, 2000). Males also tend to do better than females on mathematics tasks that involve complicated reasoning, like deriving proofs in geometry (Benbow & Stanley, 1980). This difference doesn't emerge until adolescence (Hyde et al., 1990), perhaps reflecting hormonal changes that occur around puberty. At the extreme tails of the bell curve, this difference is magnified. For example, in a recent study of students who received scores of 700 or above on the SAT math section, males outnumbered females by about 4 to 1 (Wai et al., 2010). But there are more males than females in the low tail of the test, too.

POTENTIAL CAUSES OF SEX DIFFERENCES So what's the bottom line? On the one hand, some sex differences in mental abilities, such as women's higher scores on certain verbal tasks and men's higher scores on spatial and complex math-solving tasks, may be rooted partly in genes. Indeed, despite many changes in men's and women's roles over the past several decades, sex differences in spatial ability haven't decreased much over time (Voyer et al., 1995). Moreover, some studies indicate that excess levels of prenatal testosterone, a hormone of which males have more than females, is associated with better spatial ability (Hampson, Rovert, & Altmann, 1998; Jones, Braithwaite, & Healy, 2003), although not all researchers have replicated this finding.

On the other hand, there's ample reason to suspect that some, perhaps even most, of the sex differences in science and math ability are environmental (Levine et al., 2006). For one thing, male and female infants show few or no differences in spatial or counting ability (Spelke, 2005). Even when sex differences in these abilities emerge later in life, they may be due more to sex differences in problem-solving strategies than in inherent abilities. For example, when researchers have encouraged both men and women to solve math problems using spatial imagery (which men usually prefer) rather than verbal reasoning (which women usually prefer), the sex difference in math performance becomes noticeably smaller (Geary, 1996). Moreover, data indicate that the percentage of women entering the hard sciences has been increasing steadily over the past three decades (Ceci, Williams, & Barnett, 2009). This finding suggests that at least some of the underrepresentation of women in the hard sciences is the result of societal factors such as discrimination and societal expectations rather than women's weaker science skills.

REPLICABILITY ▶

Can the results be duplicated in other studies?

? **FIGURE 15** Mental Rotation Task.
Men tend to do better than women on tests of mental rotation, many of which require participants to determine whether a "standard" shape (shown on the left) matches a "comparison" shape (shown on the right). You might want to try your hand—or your mind, to be exact—at this item: If the shape on the left is rotated in space, will it match the shape on the right? Turn the book upside down (or if you're really adventurous, mentally rotate the book!) to the find the answer.

REPLICABILITY ▶

Can the results be duplicated in other studies?

397

Racial Differences in IQ

Perhaps the most controversial, and at times troubling, findings in the study of intelligence are that average IQ scores differ among some races. The differences vary in size but have been replicated multiple times (Loehlin, Lindzey, & Spuhler, 1977; Gottfredson, 2009; Wicherts, Dolan, & van der Maas, 2010). On average, African Americans and Hispanic Americans score lower than Caucasians do on standard IQ tests (Hunt & Carlson, 2007; Lynn, 2006; Neisser et al., 1996), and Asian Americans score higher than Caucasians do (Lynn, 1996; Sue, 1993). Among Caucasians in the United States, the IQs of Jews are slightly higher than those of non-Jews (Lynn, 2003). The average IQ difference between Caucasians and African Americans, which some researchers have estimated to be as high as 15 points, has received the most attention. What do these differences tell us about the abilities and potential of individuals from different races and why these differences exist?

FOR WHOM THE BELL CURVE TOLLS. Over the years, some sectors of society have attempted to use these findings in a misguided attempt to argue that some races are innately superior to others. There are several problems with this claim. First, claims of inherent racial "superiority" lie outside the boundaries of science and can't be answered by data. Scientists can determine only the origins of racial differences, namely, whether they're genetic, environmental, or both. Second, the IQ differences among races may be narrowing over recent decades (Hauser, 1998). For example, evidence suggests that the gap between whites and African Americans has narrowed by about 5 points since the early 1970s (Dickens & Flynn, 2006; Nisbett, 2012). Third, the variability *within* any given race tends to be considerably larger than the variability *between* races (Nisbett, 1995, 2009). This finding means that the distributions of IQ scores for different races overlap substantially (see **FIGURE 16**). As a result, many African Americans and Hispanic Americans have higher IQs than do many Caucasians and Asian Americans. The bottom line is clear: We can't use race as a basis for inferring any given person's IQ.

In 1994, Richard Herrnstein and Charles Murray touched off a bitter dispute among scientists and politicians alike. In their explosive and still widely discussed book *The Bell Curve*, they argued that IQ plays a more important role in society than most people are willing to admit. People at the upper tail of the IQ bell curve, they maintained, tend to "rise to the top" of the social ladder, because they possess high levels of cognitive skills. As a consequence, they make more money, assume more positions of leadership, and enter more powerful occupations than do people at the lower tail.

Had Herrnstein and Murray (1994) stopped there, their book would probably have attracted scant public attention. But they went further, conjecturing that at least some of the IQ gap between races might be genetic in origin. Herrnstein and Murray were hardly the first to make this suggestion (Jensen, 1973; Rushton & Bogaert, 1987). Nevertheless, their claims received unprecedented press coverage, reawakening a bitter debate launched in the 1960s when Arthur Jensen proposed a genetic basis for racial differences in IQ. Jensen's work aroused widespread suspicions of racism and was even interpreted by some white supremacists as supporting claims that Caucasians are genetically superior to blacks. J. Philippe Rushton (1995) also became a controversial figure in the 1980s and 1990s when he offered an evolutionary explanation for racial differences in IQ. Although some researchers have advanced strong arguments for a genetic basis for these differences, we'll soon discover that the preponderance of evidence suggests that racial differences in IQ are largely or entirely environmental in origin. These differences in turn may reflect the different resources and opportunities available to individuals of different races.

RECONCILING RACIAL DIFFERENCES. To see why racial differences in IQ don't necessarily imply genetic differences in intelligence or learning potential, let's look at the two groups of plants in the upper panel of **FIGURE 17** (Lewontin, 1970).

◀ **REPLICABILITY**

Can the results be duplicated in other studies?

FIGURE 16 Diagram of African-American and Caucasian Distributions for IQ.

African-American and Caucasian IQ distributions differ by an average of 15 IQ points—but they show substantial overlap, as indicated by the shaded area.

Group 1   Group 2

FIGURE 17 Drawings of Two Groups of Plants. These two groups of plants are well matched in height to start, but one outstrips the other over time due to different environmental conditions. This demonstrates how group differences in IQ could be "real" but completely environmentally determined. (*Source:* Based on Lewontin, 1970)

As we can see, in this "thought experiment," the plants within each group differ in height. These differences in height reflect (at least in part) genetic influences on plants' tendencies to grow and flourish. Note, however, that at this point in the growth cycle, the plants in the two groups are, on average, roughly equal in height. Now let's imagine that we provide one of these groups of plants (in this case, the one on the left) with plenty of water and light, but provide the other group with minimal water and light. We twiddle our thumbs and wait a few weeks and then voila: We find that the plants on the left are, on average, much taller compared with the plants on the right. Although the two groups each had equal potential to grow and flourish, environmental influences resulted in one group growing taller than the other.

So what's the take-home message? The difference in height between these groups is *entirely environmental*—it's due to watering and light—so we can't explain the difference between the two groups in genetic terms. In other words, the between-group differences aren't at all heritable. If we think of children as little "human plants" (after all, the word *kindergarten* means "child garden" in German), we can easily imagine that different races begin life with few or no average genetic differences in IQ. But over time, the cumulative effects of such factors as social deprivation and prejudice may produce notable differences in IQ among racial groups, one that's entirely environmental in origin.

It's also important to note that although one group of plants in our example grew taller than the other group, one or two individual plants in the shorter group actually grew taller than some plants from the taller group. This point highlights the overlapping distributions of heights in the two groups, demonstrating that even within a relatively "deprived" group, some plants exceed the growth of some members of the more "privileged" group. This point reminds us why we can't use group differences in IQ to infer the intelligence of any given person. Although this example demonstrates that racial differences in IQ *could* be entirely environmental in nature, it doesn't demonstrate that they *are*. We need to turn to the scientific evidence for answers to that question.

WHAT ARE THE CAUSES OF RACIAL DIFFERENCES IN IQ? Some researchers have pointed out that IQ is heritable, and have concluded that racial differences must therefore be due at least partly to genetic influences. Yet this is a faulty conclusion based on a misunderstanding of how the heritability of a trait among individuals *within* a group relates to the heritability of this trait *between* groups.

Within-group heritability is the extent to which a trait, like IQ, is heritable within groups, such as Asian Americans and women. **Between-group heritability** is the extent to which the difference in this trait between groups, such as between Asian Americans and Caucasians and between men and women, is heritable. It's critical to keep in mind that *within-group heritability doesn't necessarily imply between-group heritability*. That is, just because IQ is heritable within groups doesn't imply that the difference between these groups has anything to do with their genes. Some researchers have confused within-group and between-group heritability, assuming mistakenly that because IQ is heritable within a group such as a race or gender, racial differences in IQ must themselves be heritable (Lilienfeld & Waldman, 2000; Nisbett, 1995, 2009). To return to our plant analogy, we must remember that within each group, some plants grew taller than others. These differences were caused by differences in the hardiness of the genetic strain of the individual plants within each group. Nevertheless, the differences between the two groups of plants were due entirely to environmental factors, even though within-group differences were due entirely to genes.

'thin

etween

So what's the evidence that racial differences in IQ result from environmental and *not* genetic factors? Most of this research comes from analyses of differences between African Americans and Caucasians, and it largely points away from a genetic explanation of racial IQ gaps.

One study conducted in Germany shortly after World War II compared the IQ scores of children of African-American soldiers and Caucasian-German mothers with the children of Caucasian-American soldiers and Caucasian-German mothers. In both groups, mothers raised the children, so the societal environment was approximately the same. The IQs of these two groups of children didn't differ (Eyferth, 1961). Thus, the different race-related genes appeared to have no bearing on children's IQ when environment was roughly equated. Other studies have examined whether African Americans with Caucasian-European ancestry obtain a "boost" in IQ relative to those with few European ancestors, which would be expected if racial differences were genetic. This research shows that African Americans with more ancestors of Caucasian descent don't differ significantly in IQ from those with few or no such ancestors (Nisbett, 2009; Scarr et al., 1977; Witty & Jenkins, 1934). One research team even found a slight tendency in the opposite direction: African Americans with more Caucasian-European ancestry had *lower* IQs (Loehlin, Vandenberg, & Osborne, 1973). In any case, these findings provide no evidence for a genetic explanation of the IQ gap between African Americans and Caucasians.

A classic study examined the effect of cross-racial adoption on IQ. This investigation showed that the IQs of African-American children adopted by middle-class Caucasian parents were higher at age 7 than those of either the average African-American or Caucasian child (Scarr & Weinberg, 1976). This finding suggests that what appears to be a race-related effect may be more related to socioeconomic status, because a much higher percentage of African and Hispanic Americans than Caucasians and Asian Americans live in poverty. A follow-up of these children revealed that their IQs declined over a ten-year period (Weinberg, Scarr, & Waldman, 1992), which may mean that the effects of socioeconomic status are short-lived. Or it may mean that the negative effects (such as discrimination) of being a member of an ethnic minority group in a predominantly Caucasian community gradually counteract the effects of a changed environment.

TEST BIAS. One popular explanation for race differences in IQ is that the tests are biased against certain groups and in favor of others. Test bias has a specific meaning for psychologists, which differs from the popular use of the term. In scientific terms, a test isn't biased merely because some groups perform better on it than others. Psychologists don't regard a tape measure as biased because men obtain higher average scores than women when we use it to measure height; the tape measure is picking up on actual differences in height between men and women.

When psychologists refer to **test bias**, they mean that a test predicts outcomes—such as grades or occupational success—better in one group than in another (Anastasi & Urbina, 1996; Reynolds, 1999; Kaplan & Saccuzzo, 2008). Putting it a bit differently, a biased test means different things in one group than in another. Suppose that the correlation between IQ scores and college grade point average (GPA) in Caucasians is .7, as shown in **FIGURE 18a**, but only .25 for Asian Americans, as shown in **FIGURE 18b**. This finding implies that IQ is a better predictor of GPA in Caucasians than in Asian Americans. In this case, the IQ test is biased *against* Asian Americans, even though the average IQ scores for that group are higher than those of Caucasians. Thus, average differences between groups *do not* necessarily indicate test bias.

So are IQ tests racially biased? The answer isn't entirely resolved, but the answer seems to be "generally no" (Brody, 1992; Lilienfeld et al., 2010; Neisser et al., 1996). In almost all studies, researchers have found that the correlations between IQ tests and both academic and occupational achievement are about equal across races (Brown, Reynolds, & Whitaker, 1999; Gottfredson, 2009; Hunter, Schmidt, & Hunter, 1979). There may be a few exceptions on specific IQ test items (Aguinis, Culpepper, & Pierce, 2010), but they aren't sufficiently large or frequent to account for overall differences across races in IQ.

(a)

(b)

FIGURE 18 Two Scatterplots Representing Test Bias. These two scatterplots display a made-up example of test bias. In (*a*), IQ scores correlate highly with GPA for Caucasians (.7 correlation), whereas in (*b*), correlations between IQ scores and GPA are much lower for Asian Americans (.25). Even though Asian Americans display higher IQs on average in this example, the te is biased against them because it's a weake predictor of GPA in that group.

test bias
tendency of a test to predic⁺
better in one group than ∂

Intelligence and IQ Testing

The finding of little or no race bias in IQ tests leads to the conclusion that IQ differences among races go hand in hand with differences in average *achievement* among races. Unfortunately, in U.S. society, some races tend to do better in school and have higher-ranking and higher-paying jobs than other races do. According to some psychologists, the most likely explanation for this state of affairs is that *society* itself is biased, leading to differences in IQ test performance and to differences in grades and career achievement among races. For example, African Americans and Hispanic Americans may receive lower scores on IQ tests because of prejudice, inferior schooling, and other environmental disadvantages. These disadvantages, in turn, leave many African and Hispanic Americans less prepared to compete in higher education and the job market. Nevertheless, the finding that IQ tests are also equally correlated with reaction time measures across races suggests that this explanation may not tell the whole story, because these measures are unlikely to be affected by social disadvantage (Jensen, 1980).

STEREOTYPE THREAT. One other environmental factor that may affect how individuals perform and achieve is **stereotype threat**. Stereotype threat refers to the fear that we may confirm a negative group stereotype, such as a view of our group as being less intelligent or less athletic than other groups. Stereotype threat creates a self-fulfilling prophecy in which those who are anxious about confirming a negative stereotype actually increase their likelihood of doing so. According to psychologist Claude Steele, stereotype threat can impair individuals' performance on IQ tests and standardized tests like the SAT. Here's his reasoning: If we're members of a group that has a reputation for doing poorly on IQ tests, the mere thought that we're taking an IQ test will arouse stereotype threat. We think, "I'm supposed to do really badly on this test." This belief, Steele (1997) contends, can itself influence behavior, leading some people who would otherwise do well to display reduced performance.

Steele has shown that stereotype threat can indeed depress African Americans' IQ scores, at least in the laboratory. When researchers gave African Americans items from an IQ test but told them the items were measuring something other than IQ, like "the ability to solve puzzles," they performed better than when the researchers told them the items were measuring IQ (Nguyen & Ryan, 2008; Steele & Aronson, 1995; Walton & Spencer, 2009). Stereotype threat manipulations may cause African-American participants to become stressed, preoccupied, or overly self-conscious, thereby impeding their performance (Logel et al., 2009; Schmader, Johns, & Forbes, 2008). Also, giving African Americans and Caucasians an in-class writing assignment designed to boost their personal identity—by asking them to identify their most important personal value, such as their friends, their family, or their need to express themselves through art—reduced the racial gap in academic performance by 40 percent (Cohen et al., 2006). The meaning of these intriguing findings isn't clear. One possibility is that thinking about what's important to us, or focusing on ourselves as individuals rather than as members of a group, renders us less vulnerable to stereotype threat. Still, most of these findings come from the tightly controlled world of the psychological laboratory and therefore may be of limited external validity. So the extent to which stereotype threat findings generalize to the real world remains an active area of investigation and debate (Danaher & Crandall, 2008; Stricker & Ward, 2004).

Some researchers (McCarty, 2001) and writers in the popular media (Chandler, 1999) have gone so far as to suggest that racial differences between African Americans and Caucasians on IQ tests are due completely to stereotype threat and self-fulfilling prophecies (Brown & Day, 2006). Nevertheless, most studies suggest that the effects of stereotype threat aren't large enough to account fully for this gap (Sackett, Hardison, & Cullen, 2004).

Our discussion leads us to the conclusion that broader societal differences in resources, opportunities, attitudes, and experiences are probably responsible for much, if not all, of the racial differences in IQ. The encouraging news, however, is that nothing in the research literature implies that racial differences in IQ are unchangeable. If environmental disadvantages can contribute to IQ differences, eradicating the disadvantages may reduce or eliminate those differences.

Research shows that in virtually every country ever studied, girls are better readers than boys (Halpern, 2004). Does this finding show that tests of reading are biased against boys? Why or why not? (See answer upside down at left.)

Watch in **MyPsychLab** the **Video**: In the Real World: Intelligence Tests and Stereotypes

Research suggests that stereotype threat can lead African-American students to perform worse on tests on which they believe members of their race tend to do poorly.

Outcomes other

401

dr

Answer: No, bec
two groups dor.

Assess Your Knowledge   FACT or FICTION?

1. There are few or no sex differences on spatial tasks such as mental rotation.
   True / False

2. The IQ difference between African Americans and Caucasians is smaller than the IQ difference within each group.   **True / False**

3. Within-group heritability necessarily implies between-group heritability.   **True / False**

4. Average differences between groups on a test don't necessarily indicate that the test is biased.   **True / False**

5. Stereotype threat may account for part of the IQ difference between African Americans and Caucasians.   **True / False**

Answers: 1. F; 2. T; 3. F; 4. T; 5. T

The Rest of the Story: Other Dimensions of Intellect

11 Describe how creativity and emotional intelligence relate to intelligence.

12 Explain why intelligence doesn't protect us from errors in thinking.

IQ, IQ, and still more IQ. Pretty much everything we've discussed in this chapter presumes that IQ is a good measure of intelligence. Although there's compelling evidence that IQ tests are valid indicators of what psychologists call intelligence, it's clear that there's far more than high IQ to living our lives intelligently. Many people without sky-high IQs are wise and thoughtful citizens of society, and many people with sky-high IQs behave in foolish, even disastrous ways. If you have any doubt about the latter, just look at the string of high-profile political sex scandals over the past decade in which well-educated and highly intelligent people got caught red-handed doing remarkably dumb things. We'll conclude the chapter with a survey of other psychological variables that can make us act intelligently—and not so intelligently.

Bernard Madoff, shown here after his arrest in 2009, swindled thousands of extremely intelligent and well-educated investors out of huge amounts of money—in some cases many millions of dollars each. Research shows that high levels of intelligence offer no guarantee against gullibility and uncritical thinking.

Creativity

By age 54, German composer Ludwig van Beethoven was almost completely deaf. Yet when he reached that age in 1824, he somehow managed to compose his monumental "Ninth Symphony," even though while conducting the orchestra performing its world premiere, he couldn't hear a note of it.

"Beethoven's Ninth," as musicologists call it, was astonishing in its originality and brilliance: It was unlike any piece of music ever written. As is often the case in response to works of music, art, and literature that break the mold, some critics condemned Beethoven's Ninth as being too abrasive, too reckless, and too "different" (Goulding, 1992). Yet today, many experts consider Beethoven's "Ninth Symphony" to be the greatest piece of music ever written.

Beethoven's music personifies creativity. But like former Supreme Court Justice Potter Stewart, who defined obscenity by saying, "I know it when I see it" (*Jacobellis v. Ohio*, 1964), psychologists have found creativity easier to identify than define. Nevertheless, most psychologists agree that creative accomplishments consist of two features: They are *novel* and *successful*. When we hear an exceptionally creative piece of music, like Beethoven's Ninth, or see an exceptionally creative painting, we nod our heads and say "Wow, that's amazing. He or she got it exactly right."

Psychologists often measure creativity using tests of **divergent thinking** (Guilford, 1967; Razoumnikova, 2000): the capacity to generate many different solutions to problems. For this reason, psychologists sometimes call it "outside-the-box" thinking. For example, in the "Uses for Objects" test, participants must generate as many uses for

divergent thinking
capacity to generate many di
to a problem

an ordinary object, like a paper clip or a brick, as they can (Hudson, 1967). It's likely, though, that tests of divergent thinking don't capture everything about creativity. To be creative, we also need to be good at **convergent thinking**: the capacity to find the single best answer to a problem (Bink & Marsh, 2000). As two-time Nobel Prize–winner Linus Pauling said, to be creative, we first need to come up with lots of ideas and then toss out all the bad ones.

We shouldn't confuse intelligence with creativity: Measures of these two capacities are only weakly or moderately associated, with correlations often in the .2 or .3 range (Furnham et al., 2006; Willerman, 1979). Many intelligent people aren't especially creative, and vice versa.

Highly creative people are an interesting lot. They tend to be bold and willing to take intellectual risks (Sternberg & Lubart, 1992). They also tend to be emotionally troubled while possessed of high self-esteem. Not surprisingly, they're not always the easiest folks to get along with (Barron, 1969; Cattell, 1971).

There's evidence of a link between creativity and *bipolar disorder*. People with bipolar disorder (once called manic depression) experience episodes of greatly elevated exuberance, energy, self-esteem, and risk taking (Furnham et al., 2008). They frequently report that thoughts race through their heads more quickly than they can speak them, and they can go for days without much sleep. During these dramatic bursts of heightened mood and activity (called manic episodes), individuals with bipolar disorder who have artistic talents may become especially productive. Nevertheless, there's not much evidence that their work increases in quality, only quantity (Weisberg, 1994).

Biographical evidence suggests that many great painters such as Vincent van Gogh, Paul Gauguin, and Jackson Pollack; great writers such as Emily Dickinson, Mark Twain, and Ernest Hemingway; and great composers such as Gustav Mahler, Peter Ilyich Tchaikovsky, and Robert Schumann probably suffered from bipolar disorder (Jamison, 1993; McDermott, 2001). More recently, actresses Carrie Fisher and Catherine Zeta-Jones, and singer Sinead O'Connor have spoken publicly about their struggles with the condition. Consistent with these anecdotal reports, studies show that highly creative individuals in artistic and literary professions have higher-than-expected levels of bipolar disorder and closely related conditions (Andreasen, 1987; Jamison, 1989; see **FIGURE 19**).

Because they're willing to take intellectual risks, creative people typically fall flat on their faces more often than do uncreative people. Even Beethoven composed one or two notable clunkers. Probably the best predictor of the *quality* of a person's creative accomplishments is the *quantity* of that person's output (Simonton, 1999). Extremely creative artists, musicians, and scientists produce far more stuff than other people. Some of it isn't especially good, but much of it is. And every once in a while, some of it is truly great.

Interests and Intellect

Research shows that people with different intellectual strengths tend to exhibit different personality traits and interest patterns (Ackerman & Beier, 2003). When we get to the level of specific mental abilities, we find that people with different intellectual strengths typically display different intellectual interests. People with high levels of scientific and mathematical ability tend to be especially interested in investigating the workings of nature and often describe themselves as enjoying the practical deeds of everyday life, like balancing checkbooks or fixing things around the house. People with high levels of verbal ability tend to be interested in art and music. And people who are poor at math and spatial ability tend to be especially interested in going into professions that involve helping others (Ackerman & Heggestad, 1997; Ackerman, Kanfer, & Goff, 2005). What we're good at—and not good at—tells us quite a bit about what we like to do.

Frank Lloyd Wright's architectural masterpiece Fallingwater is a prime example of a remarkable creative achievement. It still stands proudly in rural Pennsylvania.

FIGURE 19 A Graph of Robert Schumann's Productivity. The German composer Robert Schumann almost certainly had bipolar disorder. As we can see, his productivity increased dramatically during "hypomanic" (mild manic) episodes and decreased ~matically during depressive episodes ~t people with bipolar disorder ~*Source:* Based on data from

Emotional Intelligence: Is EQ as Important as IQ?

Emotional intelligence—the ability to understand our emotions and those of others and to apply this information to our everyday lives (Goleman, 1995; Mayer, Salovey, & Caruso, 2008; Salovey & Mayer, 1990)—is one of the most active topics in popular psychology today. According to some researchers, emotional intelligence consists of several subcomponents, such as the capacity to understand and recognize one's emotions, to appreciate others' emotions, to control one's emotions, and to adapt one's emotions to diverse situations (Bar-On, 2004). Most proponents of emotional intelligence maintain that "EQ" (one's emotional quotient) is just as, if not more, important as IQ for functioning effectively in the world.

Some items on emotional intelligence tests ask participants to report how good they are at handling their emotions under stress. Others ask participants to identify which emotion a face is expressing. Still others ask participants to predict what emotion a person will experience in a given situation, like meeting future in-laws for the first time or being asked an embarrassing question during a job interview (see **FIGURE 20**). Many American companies now provide their employees and bosses with formal training for boosting their emotional intelligence (Locke, 2005). Among other things, EQ training seminars teach workers to "listen" to their emotions when making decisions, find better means of coping with stressful job situations, and express empathy to coworkers.

When Anne's friend Maggie was feeling depressed over a recent break-up with her boyfriend, Anne took several hours off from studying for a big test to drive to Maggie's apartment and comfort her. Two weeks later, Anne was upset over an argument with her sister, and phoned Maggie to talk about it. Maggie told Anne she was busy packing for an upcoming trip and asked if they could put off talking until the following week. Anne felt _____. (Select the best choice.)

(a) sad   (b) nervous   (c) embarrassed   (d) resentful   (e) envious

FIGURE 20 Item Similar to That on a Test of Emotional Intelligence. How would you do on a test of emotional intelligence? Try your hand at this item, modeled after items on actual emotional intelligence measures. The correct answer is upside down at the bottom of the page.

Few would dispute that these are helpful skills on the job. In addition, people with low emotional intelligence are prone to some psychological problems, like depression, substance abuse (Hertel, Schutz, & Lammers, 2009), and perhaps psychopathic personality, a condition characterized by dishonesty, lack of guilt, and self-centeredness (Ermer et al., 2012).

Still, the emotional intelligence concept has its critics. In particular, it's not clear that this concept offers much beyond personality (Matthews, Zeidner, & Roberts, 2002). Most measures of emotional intelligence assess personality traits, such as extraversion, agreeableness, and openness to experience, at least as much they do intelligence (Conte, 2005). Moreover, although advocates of emotional intelligence claim that this concept predicts job performance beyond general intelligence (Mayer, Roberts, & Barsade, 2008; O'Boyle et al., 2010), at least some research suggests otherwise (Van Rooy & Viswesvaran, 2004). Nor is there much evidence that different measures of emotional intelligence are highly correlated (Conte, 2005). The most parsimonious hypothesis is that emotional intelligence isn't anything new; instead, it's a mixture of personality traits that psychologists have studied for decades.

◄ OCCAM'S RAZOR
Does a simpler explanation fit the data just as well?

emotional intelligence
ability to understand our own emotions and those of others and to apply this information to our daily lives

wisdom
application of intelligence toward a common good

Wisdom

Being intelligent isn't the same as being wise. Indeed, measures of intelligence are only moderately correlated with measures of wisdom (Helson & Srivastava, 2002). Robert Sternberg (2002) defined **wisdom** as the application of intelligence toward a common good. Wise people have learned to achieve a delicate balance among three often-competing interests: (1) concerns about oneself (self-interest), (2) concerns about others,

Answer to Figure 20: d

and (3) concerns about the broader society. Wise persons channel their intelligence into avenues that benefit others. To accomplish this end, they come to appreciate alternative points of view, even as they may disagree with them. To a substantial extent, wisdom is marked by an awareness of our biases and cognitive fallibilities (Meacham, 1990). In these respects, we can think of wise people as good scientific thinkers in everyday life (Lilienfeld, Ammirati, & Landfield, 2009). Wisdom sometimes, but by no means always, comes with age (Erikson, 1968).

Many modern scholars would agree that Tenzin Gyatso, the current Dalai Lama, exemplifies wisdom. Despite arguing forcefully for Tibet's independence from China, he has consistently advocated for nonviolence and a willingness to engage in constructive dialogue with his opponents.

from inquiry to understanding

WHY SMART PEOPLE BELIEVE STRANGE THINGS

We might assume that people with high IQs would be immune to weird ideas; if so, we'd be wrong. Data reveal that people with high IQs are at least as prone as other people to beliefs in conspiracy theories, such as the belief that President Kennedy's assassination was the result of a coordinated plot within the U.S. government (Goertzel, 1994) or that the administration of president George W. Bush orchestrated the September 11 attacks (Molé, 2006). Moreover, the history of science is replete with examples of brilliant individuals holding strange beliefs. Two-time Nobel Prize–winning chemist Linus Pauling, whom we encountered when discussing creativity, insisted that high levels of vitamin C could cure cancer, despite overwhelming evidence to the contrary.

As psychologist Keith Stanovich (2009) has shown, although IQ tests do a good job of assessing how efficiently we process information, they don't assess the ability to think scientifically. For example, measures of confirmation bias, like the Wason selection task, are barely correlated with IQ (Stanovich & West, 2008). So high levels of intelligence afford no guarantee against beliefs for which there's scant evidence (Hyman, 2002). Recent research also indicates that people with high IQs are just as prone to bias blind spot as are people with low IQs (West, Meserve, & Stanovich, 2012); bias blind spot (the "not me fallacy") is the tendency to believe that we're immune to biases, like confirmation bias and hindsight bias that afflict everyone else.

In many cases, smart people embrace odd beliefs because they're adept at finding plausible-sounding reasons to bolster their opinions (Shermer, 2002). IQ is correlated positively with the ability to defend our positions effectively, but correlated negatively with the ability to consider alternative positions (Perkins, 1981). High IQ may also be related to the strength of the **ideological immune system**: our defenses against evidence that contradicts our views (Shermer, 2002; Snelson, 1993). We've all felt our ideological immune systems kicking into high gear when a friend challenges our political beliefs (say, about capital punishment) with evidence we'd prefer not to hear. First, we feel defensive, and then we frantically search our mental knowledge banks to find arguments that could refute our friend's irksome evidence. Our knack for defending our positions against competing viewpoints can sometimes lead to confirmation bias, blinding us to information we should take seriously.

Robert Sternberg (2002) suggested that because people with high IQs tend to know many things, they're especially vulnerable to the sense that they know much more than

One of the photographs from the famous Cottingley fairies hoax that took in writer Arthur Conan Doyle. Even extremely intelligent people can be fooled by fake claims.

ideological immune system
our psychological defenses against evidence that contradicts our views

they do. Take the brilliant writer Sir Arthur Conan Doyle, who invented the character Sherlock Holmes. Conan Doyle, was a devoted believer in the paranormal who was taken in by an embarrassingly obvious prank (Hines, 2003). In the 1917 "Cottingley fairies" hoax, two young British girls insisted that they'd photographed themselves along with dancing fairies. Brushing aside the criticisms of doubters, Conan Doyle wrote a book about the Cottingley fairies and defended the girls against accusations of trickery. He'd forgotten the basic principle that extraordinary claims require extraordinary evidence. The girls eventually confessed to doctoring the photographs after someone discovered they'd cut the fairies out of a book (Randi, 1982). Conan Doyle, who had a remarkably sharp mind, may have assumed that he couldn't be duped.

The message here is that none of us is immune from errors in thinking. When intelligent people neglect the safeguards afforded by the scientific method, they'll often be fooled.

◀ **EXTRAORDINARY CLAIMS**
Is the evidence as strong as the claim?

Assess Your Knowledge   FACT or FICTION?

✔ **Study** and **Review** in **MyPsychLab**

1. Intelligence and creativity are highly correlated.   **True / False**

2. The work of highly creative people is almost always high in quality.   **True / False**

3. Emotional intelligence and personality aren't entirely independent.   **True / False**

4. People with high IQs are almost always better at considering alternative points of view than are people with low IQs.   **True / False**

Answers: 1. F; 2. F; 3. T; 4. F

Your Complete Review System

 Study and **Review** in **MyPsychLab**

 Listen in **MyPsychLab** to chapter audio

What Is Intelligence? Definitional Confusion

1 IDENTIFY DIFFERENT MODELS AND TYPES OF INTELLIGENCE.

Sir Francis Galton proposed that intelligence stems from sensory capacity. Binet and Simon, who developed the first intelligence test, argued that intelligence consists of higher mental processes such as reasoning, understanding, and judgment. Spearman observed that tests of mental ability tend to be positively correlated. To explain this pattern, he invoked the existence of *g*, or general intelligence, but also posited the existence of *s*, or specific factors unique to particular mental tasks. Some psychologists have argued for the existence of multiple intelligences. According to them, there are different ways of being smart. Nevertheless, it's not clear whether these proposed intelligences are independent of each other or of a more general intelligence factor.

1. According to Galton's conception of intelligence, someone who has excellent eyesight and hearing would also have (high/low) intelligence.

2. Binet and Simon developed what is considered to be the first _____ _____, which served as a model for many intelligence researchers who followed in their footsteps.

3. In trying to define intelligence, early twentieth-century researchers agreed that it was related to _____ _____.

4. The theory of _____ _____, developed by Charles Spearman, which accounted for the differences in intellect among people, could be explained by a single common factor.

5. According to Spearman, someone's intelligence is dependent not only on his or her general intelligence, or *g*, but also on his or her _____ or _____ _____.

6. When driving a vehicle you've never driven, you're relying on your capacity for _____ _____, but when you answer a question on a history test, you're relying on your capacity for _____ _____.

7. According to Gardner's model of multiple intelligences, there are many different types of intelligence, which he refers to as _____ _____ _____.

8. Identify the three kinds of intelligence in Sternberg's Triarchic Model of Intelligence.

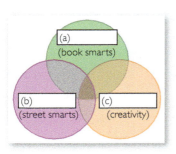
(a) (book smarts)
(b) (street smarts)
(c) (creativity)

2 DESCRIBE THE CONNECTION BETWEEN INTELLIGENCE AND BRAIN SIZE AND EFFICIENCY.

Brain size and intelligence are moderately positively correlated in humans. Some evidence suggests that people with high levels of intelligence possess especially efficient brains. Intelligence also seems related to faster reaction times, as well as working memory capacity, and probably stems in part from the activity of the prefrontal cortex.

9. Haier's study of college students who played the video game Tetris indicated that the brains of the more intelligent students were especially _____ at mental processing.

10. Which of these images displays a different pattern than the others? What underlying abilities might be required to enable someone to answer this *g*-loaded question correctly?

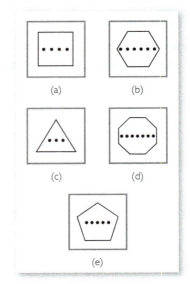
(a)   (b)
(c)   (d)
(e)

Intelligence Testing: The Good, the Bad, and the Ugly

3 DETERMINE HOW PSYCHOLOGISTS CALCULATE IQ.

Stern defined the intelligence quotient (IQ) as mental age divided by chronological age, with the result multiplied by 100. This simple formula becomes problematic in adolescence and adulthood, because mental age tends to level out at around age 16. As a consequence, most modern intelligence tests define IQ in terms of deviation IQ.

11. Using Wilhelm Stern's IQ formula, complete the equation and calculate IQ for the example provided. Then explain the flaw in this formula when applying it to two adults with a mental age of 18, the first an 18-year-old and the second a 35-year-old.

$$\underset{\substack{\text{(mental}\\\text{age)}}}{8} \div \underset{\substack{\text{(chronological}\\\text{age)}}}{10} = \underset{\text{(total)}}{\underline{\quad\quad}} \times \underline{\quad\quad} = \underset{\text{(IQ)}}{\underline{\quad\quad}}$$

12. When computing IQ, modern researchers rely on a statistic called _____ _____.

4 EXPLAIN THE HISTORY OF MISUSE OF INTELLIGENCE TESTS IN THE UNITED STATES.

Eugenics was the effort to improve a population's "genetic stock" by encouraging people with "good genes" to reproduce, by discouraging people with "bad genes" from reproducing, or both. IQ tests became an important tool of the eugenics movement, because many proponents of eugenics wanted to minimize the reproduction and immigration of individuals with low IQs. In part because of eugenics, many people today view IQ tests with skepticism.

13. _____ _____ is one of the extremely disturbing practices that came about as a result of the eugenics movement.

5 DESCRIBE TESTS OF INTELLIGENCE USED TODAY AND EVALUATE THE RELIABILITY AND VALIDITY OF IQ SCORES.

Psychologists have developed IQ tests for both adults, such as the WAIS-IV, and children, such as the WISC-IV. IQ scores are reasonably stable in adulthood, although they aren't especially stable in infancy or early childhood. IQ tests predict a variety of important real-world outcomes, including job performance and physical health.

14. Psychologists have developed many different adult IQ tests, but the most commonly used is the _____ _____ _____ _____.

15. Apply your knowledge of the WAIS by viewing each visual example and identifying its corresponding test and description.

Test	Description	Example
(a) _____		
(b) _____		
(c) _____		

16. The _____ of IQ tests indicates whether these tests accurately measure what they purport to measure.

6 DISTINGUISH THE UNIQUE CHARACTERISTICS OF MENTAL RETARDATION AND GENIUS.

There are four categories of mental retardation: mild, moderate, severe, and profound. At least 85 percent of individuals with mental retardation fall into the mild category. Terman's study of gifted schoolchildren helped to debunk widespread ideas that child prodigies "burn out" in adulthood and that genius often leads to insanity.

17. Three criteria define mental retardation: (1) onset prior to adulthood, (2) IQ below approximately _____, and (3) inadequate adaptive functioning.

18. About 1 percent of persons in the United States, most of them (females/males), fulfill the criteria for mental retardation.

19. _____ is an organization whose members score in the top _____ percent of the IQ range.

20. The results of Lewis Terman's classic studies of intellectually gifted individuals disputed the popular notion that there's an intimate link between genius and _____.

Genetic and Environmental Influences on IQ

7 EXPLAIN HOW GENETIC INFLUENCES CAN BE DETERMINED FROM FAMILY, TWIN, AND ADOPTION STUDIES.

Twin and adoption studies suggest that at least some of the tendency for IQ to run in families is genetically influenced, although these studies also offer convincing evidence of environmental effects on IQ. The heritability of IQ appears be relatively low, however, among extremely poor individuals, perhaps reflecting the adverse effects of environmental deprivation on the expression of genetic potential.

21. Galton conducted one of the first _____ _____ of intelligence to determine whether intellectual brilliance runs in families.

22. Twin studies tell us that IQ is influenced by both _____ and _____ factors.

23. _____ studies are a way for researchers to separate environmental effects from genetic effects on IQ and other psychological traits.

24. If a child from a deprived environment is adopted into an enriched family environment, we would expect this child's IQ to (increase/decrease/stay the same).

8 IDENTIFY POTENTIAL ENVIRONMENTAL INFLUENCES ON IQ.

Schooling is related to high IQ scores. Research suggests that both poverty and nutrition are causally related to IQ, although disentangling the effects of nutrition from other factors, such as social class, is challenging.

25. Environmental influences on intelligence can be divided into two types: the _____ environment, such as school and parents, and the _____ environment, such as nutrition and exposure to toxins.

26. What effect, according to Ceci, does summer vacation have on a child's IQ, and what does this finding suggest about the factors contributing to performance on IQ tests?

27. According to studies like Rosenthal and Jacobson's, if a teacher thinks a student has obtained a high IQ score, that teacher will give (more/less) attention to that student. This finding is related to the _____ _____ effect.

28. Studies from poor areas in Central America suggest that _____ in childhood can lower IQ.

29. If your IQ is higher than your grandparents' IQ scores, this difference may be attributable to the _____ _____.

30. Identify four possible environmental influences on IQ as seen in the Flynn effect.

1. _____
2. _____
3. _____
4. _____

Group Differences in IQ: The Science and the Politics

9 IDENTIFY SIMILARITIES AND DIFFERENCES IN MENTAL ABILITY BETWEEN MEN AND WOMEN.

Most research suggests little, if any, overall average sex difference in IQ between men and women. Nevertheless, studies indicate that men are more variable in their IQ scores than women are. Women tend to do better than men on some verbal tasks, whereas men tend to do better than women on some spatial tasks.

31. Comments about women in science and mathematics made by a former president of Harvard University sparked a firestorm about _____ differences in IQ.

32. Men and women (are/aren't) similar when it comes to most intellectual abilities.

33. Men tend to do better than women on some tasks requiring _____ ability, and women tend to do better than men on some tasks requiring _____ ability.

34. There's little evidence for sex differences in IQ overall, but research has revealed consistent differences between the sexes in some specific skills. Indicate below which sex (M/F) scores higher on each of the skills listed.

_____ Spelling

_____ Arithmetic calculation (in childhood)

_____ Complex mathematical tasks (in adolescence)

_____ Safe driving

_____ Geography

_____ Sociability

_____ Reading facial expression for emotion

_____ Spatial ability

35. From 1966–2001, the number of women entering the hard sciences (increased/decreased) steadily.

10 EVALUATE THE EVIDENCE CONCERNING RACIAL DIFFERENCES IN IQ.

On average, compared with Caucasians, African Americans score about 15 points lower on standard IQ tests. Asian Americans, compared with Caucasians, score about five points higher. Nevertheless, there's substantial overlap in the IQ distributions

across races. Test bias does not appear to be a viable interpretation of the IQ test gap between African Americans and Caucasians because IQ scores predict the same criteria in African Americans and Caucasians. Nevertheless, several studies offer good reasons to believe that much of the IQ between African Americans and Caucasians is environmental.

36. The authors of *The Bell Curve* revived a bitter public debate when they speculated that the IQ gap between races might be _____ in origin.

37. How can environmental influences explain how two sets of plants that started out at the same height can end up so different? What does this thought experiment tell us about potential environmental effects on IQ?

38. To demonstrate that there's no genetic explanation for the IQ gap between African Americans and Caucasian Americans, one needs to understand the difference between _____ heritability and _____ heritability.

39. When a test predicts outcomes better in one group than in another, this is known as _____ _____.

40. If you're a member of a group that has a reputation for doing poorly on standardized tests, you may do poorly when you take one merely because of _____ _____.

The Rest of the Story: Other Dimensions of Intellect

11 DESCRIBE HOW CREATIVITY AND EMOTIONAL INTELLIGENCE RELATE TO INTELLIGENCE.

Creative accomplishments consist of two features: They are novel and successful. Psychologists often measure creativity using tests of divergent thinking, which assess the capacity to generate many different solutions to a problem. Nevertheless, creativity also requires convergent thinking, the capacity to find the single best answer to a problem. Emotional intelligence refers to the ability to understand our own emotions and those of others and to apply this information to our daily lives. Although emotional intelligence is relevant to job performance, it's not clear how much it contributes beyond either intelligence or personality traits such as extraversion.

41. Intelligence, as measured by IQ, (is/isn't) the only dimension of intellect.

42. If you're good at thinking "outside the box," you'd probably score highly on a test that measures _____ thinking.

43. The ability to find the best single answer to a problem is called _____ _____.

44. Correlations between measures of intelligence and creativity tend to be (low/high).

45. Creative people tend to be (willing/not willing) to take intellectual risks.

46. What traits do highly creative people possess that other noncreative people lack?

47. There (is/isn't) evidence that different measures of emotional intelligence are highly correlated.

12 **EXPLAIN WHY INTELLIGENCE DOESN'T PROTECT US FROM ERRORS IN THINKING.**

Wisdom is the application of intelligence toward a common good. Wisdom isn't identical to intelligence, and it sometimes, but not

always, comes with age. Even highly intelligent people can believe strange things because standard IQ tests aren't especially good measures of scientific thinking capacity. Some people have even suggested that high intelligence may allow people to find false, but plausible-sounding, arguments to bolster their unsupported views.

48. IQ is (positively/negatively) correlated with the ability to consider alternative positions.

49. Nobel Prize–winning chemist Linus Pauling's belief that vitamin C cures cancer, despite overwhelming evidence to the contrary, suggests that he had a strong _____ immune system.

50. Why was the writer Arthur Conan Doyle fooled by the famous Cottingley fairies hoax?

Apply Your Scientific Thinking Skills

Use your scientific thinking skills to answer the following questions, referencing specific scientific thinking principles and common errors in reasoning whenever possible.

1. There's a widely held myth that highly stimulating early environments are critical for infant intellectual development. In reality, most normal environments provide adequate stimulation for infant development. Although research suggests a negative effect of severely deprived environments on intelligence, adding *more* stimulation to already healthy environments may not help much. Look for websites marketing "infant stimulation" products. In what way are these sites' claims consistent—or inconsistent—with scientific evidence?

2. Research three examples of companies or products that claim to improve your score on standardized tests. What methods

do they recommend for improving your score? Are there other explanations for the improvements in scores they advertise? Do they make any guarantees or exaggerated claims about how much your score will improve?

3. As the chapter notes, even highly intelligent people sometimes behave in foolish ways. Locate an example of a famous person—say, a political figure, a scientist, or an artist—who's clearly intelligent but who engaged in spectacularly unintelligent actions. What potential scientific explanations might you offer for the causes of his or her behavior?

Further Your Understanding

EXTEND YOUR KNOWLEDGE WITH THE MYPSYCHLAB VIDEO SERIES

Watch these videos in MyPsychLab. Follow the "Video Series" link.

The Big Picture: What is Intelligence? Explore your definition of intelligence and see that although it is a concept we value and measure, defining it and determining how it is acquired can be challenging.

The Basics: Theories of Intelligence Dig deeper into well-known intelligence theories developed by Spearman, Sternberg, and Gardner.

Intelligence Testing, Then and Now Look back into the history of intelligence testing at how the Stanford-Binet, WAIS, and IQ tests were developed and learn how intelligence tests today have evolved to help us better interpret an individual's specific strengths and weaknesses to improve overall ability at school and work.

Thinking Like a Psychologist: Intelligence Tests and Success Find out how IQ scores and overall success are correlated and how others' reactions to our IQ scores can shape our destiny.

In the Real World: Intelligence Tests and Stereotypes See how stereotype threat can negatively affect an individual's self esteem, performance, and sense of identity.

EXPERIENCE PSYCHOLOGICAL RESEARCH WITH MYPSYCHLAB SIMULATIONS

Access these simulations in MyPsychLab. Follow the "Simulations" link.

What Is Intelligence? Participate in a survey to learn about your definition of and stereotypes about intelligence.

APPLY YOUR CRITICAL THINKING SKILLS WITH MYPSYCHLAB WRITING ASSESSMENTS

Complete these writing assignments in MyPsychLab.

Provide real-world examples for the following types of intelligences as theorized by Gardner: verbal/linguistic, body-kinesthetic (movement), and logical/mathematical. Explain why each example represents one of the types of intelligence. Present some of the arguments critics have offered against Gardner's research.

Answer Key

WHAT IS INTELLIGENCE? DEFINITIONAL CONFUSION

1. high
2. intelligence test
3. abstract thinking
4. general intelligence
5. s; specific abilities
6. fluid intelligence; crystallized intelligence
7. frames of mind
8. a) analytical; b) practical; c) creative
9. efficient
10. d. General abilities such as reasoning, short-term memory, and pattern recognition could explain people's ability to answer this question correctly.

INTELLIGENCE TESTING: THE GOOD, THE BAD, AND THE UGLY

11. In the example provided, .8 × 100 = 80. If we apply this formula to an 18-year-old with a mental age of 18, we'd have the following: 18 (mental age)/18 (chronological age) = 1 × 100 = 100 (IQ). If we apply it to a 35-year-old who also has a mental age of 18, we'd have 18 (mental age)/35 (chronological age) = .51 × 100 = 51 (IQ). Because our mental age levels off but our chronological age increases with time, Stern's formula would result in everyone's IQ dropping lower and lower as he or she got older.
12. deviation IQ
13. Mandatory sterilization
14. Wechsler Adult Intelligence Scale (WAIS)
15. a) Digit symbol: tests speed of learning through timed coding tasks in which numbers must be associated with marks of various shapes; b) Picture completion: tests visual alertness and visual memory through presentation of an incompletely drawn figure; the missing part must be discovered and named; c) Block design: tests ability to perceive and analyze patterns by presenting designs that must be copied with blocks.
16. validity
17. 70
18. males
19. Mensa; 2
20. madness

GENETIC AND ENVIRONMENTAL INFLUENCES ON IQ

21. family studies
22. genetic; environmental
23. Adoption
24. increase
25. social; biological
26. Children's IQ tends to drop significantly during summer vacations, suggesting an environmental influence on IQ.
27. more; experimenter expectancy
28. malnutrition
29. Flynn effect
30. 1) increased test sophistication; 2) increased complexity of the modern world; 3) better nutrition; 4) changes at home and school

GROUP DIFFERENCES IN IQ: THE SCIENCE AND THE POLITICS

31. sex
32. are
33. spatial; verbal
34. F: spelling; F: arithmetic calculation; M: complex mathematical tasks; M: safe driving; M: geography; F: sociability; F: reading facial expression for emotion; M: spatial ability
35. increased
36. genetic
37. The two groups of plants started at the same height but were exposed to different environmental conditions. This demonstrates how group differences in IQ can be "real" but completely environmentally influenced.
38. within-group; between-group
39. test bias
40. stereotype threat

THE REST OF THE STORY: OTHER DIMENSIONS OF INTELLECT

41. isn't
42. divergent
43. convergent thinking
44. low
45. willing
46. Creative people tend to be bold and willing to take intellectual risks. They also tend to be emotionally troubled while possessing high self-esteem.
47. isn't
48. negatively
49. ideological
50. Because people with high IQs are especially vulnerable to the sense that they know much more than they do.

References

Ackerman, P. L., & Beier, M. E. (2003). Intelligence, personality, and interests in the career choice process. *Journal of Career Assessment, 11,* 205–218.

Ackerman, P. L., Beier, M. E., & Boyle, M. O. (2005). Working memory and intelligence: The same or different constructs? *Psychological Bulletin, 131,* 30–60.

Ackerman, P. L., & Heggestad, E. D. (1997). Intelligence, personality, and interests: Evidence for overlapping traits. *Psychological Bulletin, 121,* 219–245.

Acton, G. S., & Schroeder, D. H. (2001). Sensory discrimination as related to general intelligence. *Intelligence, 29*(3), 263–271. http://dx.doi.org/10.1016/S0160-2896(01)00066-6

Aguinis, H., Culpepper, S. A., & Pierce, C. A. (2010). Revival of test bias research in preemployment testing. *Journal of Applied Psychology, 95*(4), 648–680. http://dx.doi.org/10.1037/a0018714

Alexander, R. A., Carson, K. P., Alliger, G. M., & Carr, L. (1987). Correcting doubly truncated correlations: An improved approximation for correcting the bivariate normal correlation when truncation has occurred on both variables. *Educational and Psychological Measurement, 47,* 309–315.

Alliger, G. M. (1988). Do zero correlations really exist among measures of different intellectual abilities? *Educational & Psychological Measurement, 48,* 275–280.

American Psychiatric Association. (2013). *Diagnostic and statistical manual of mental disorders* (5th ed.). Washington, DC: Author.

Anastasi, A., & Urbina, S. (1996). *Psychological testing.* New York, NY: Prentice Hall.

Anderson B., & Harvey T. (1996). Alterations in cortical thickness and neuronal density in the frontal cortex of Albert Einstein. *Neuroscience Letters, 210,* 161–164.

Andreasen, N. C. (1987). Creativity and mental illness: Prevalence rates in writers and their first-degree relatives. *American Journal of Psychiatry, 144,* 1288–1292.

Armstrong, T. (2009). *Multiple intelligences in the classroom.* Alexandria, VA: Association for Supervision and Curriculum Development.

Atkinson, R. C. (2001, February 18). *Standardized tests and access to American universities.* The 2001 Robert H. Atwell Distinguished Lecture delivered at the 83rd Annual Meeting of the American Council on Education, Washington, DC. Retrieved from http://www.ucop.edu/news/sat/speech.html

Baral, B. D., & Das, J. P. (2003). Intelligence: What is indigenous to India and what is shared? In R. J. Sternberg (Ed.), *International handbook of intelligence* (pp. 270–301). Cambridge, England: Cambridge University Press.

Bar-On, R. (2004). The Bar-On Emotional Quotient Inventory (EQ-i): Rationale, description, and psychometric properties. In G. Geher (Ed.), *Measuring emotional intelligence: Common ground and controversy* (pp. 115–145). Hauppauge, NY: Nova Science.

Barron, F. (1969). *Creative person and creative process.* New York, NY: Holt, Rinehart and Winston.

Bellinger, D. C., & Needleman, H. L. (2003). Intellectual impairment and blood lead levels. *New England Journal of Medicine, 349,* 500–502.

Benasich, A. A., & Bejar, I. I. (1992). The Fagan Test of Infant Intelligence: A critical review. *Journal of Applied Developmental Psychology, 13,* 153–171.

Benbow, C. P., & Stanley, J. C. (1980). Sex differences in mathematical ability: Fact or artifact? *Science, 210,* 1262–1264.

Bierman, K. L., Coie, J. D., Dodge, K. A., Greenberg, M. T., Lochman, J. E., McMahon, R. J., & Pinderhughes, E. (2010). The effects of a multiyear universal social–emotional learning program: The role of student and school characteristics. *Journal of Consulting and Clinical Psychology, 78*(2), 156–168. http://dx.doi.org/10.1037/a0018607

Bierman, K. L., Domitrovich, C. E., Nix, R., Gest, S. D., Welsh, J. A., Greenberg, M. T.,... Jones, D. (2008). Promoting academic and social-emotional school readiness: The Head Start REDI program. *Child Development, 79,* 1802–1807.

Binet, A., & Simon, T. A. (1905). Méthode nouvelle pour le diagnostic du niveau intellectuel des anormaux. *L'Année Psychologique, 11,* 191–244.

Bink, M. L., & Marsh, R. L. (2000). Cognitive regularities in creative activity. *Review of General Psychology, 4,* 59–78.

Blair, C. (2006). How similar are fluid cognition and general intelligence? A developmental neuroscience perspective on fluid cognition as an aspect of human cognitive ability. *Behavioral and Brain Sciences, 29,* 109–160.

Blair, C., Gamson, D., Thorne, S., & Baker, D. (2005). Rising mean IQ: Cognitive demand of mathematics education for young children, population exposure to formal schooling, and the neurobiology of the prefrontal cortex. *Intelligence, 33*(1), 93–106. http://dx.doi.org/10.1016/j.intell.2004.07.008

Block, J. (1976). Issues, problems and pitfalls in assessing sex differences: A critical review of "The Psychology of Sex Differences." *Merrill Palmer Quarterly, 22,* 283–340.

Boring, E. G. (1923). Intelligence as the tests test it. *New Republic, 35,* 35–37.

Bouchard, T. J., Lykken, D. T., McGue, M., Segal, N. L., & Tellegen, A. (1990, October 12). Sources of human psychological differences: The Minnesota study of twins reared apart. *Science, 250,* 223–228.

Bouchard, T. J., & McGue, M. (1981). Familial studies of intelligence: A review. *Science, 212,* 1055–1059.

Brody, N. (1992). *Intelligence* (2nd ed.). San Diego, CA: Academic Press.

Bronfenbrenner, U., McClelland, P., Wethington, E., Moen, P., & Ceci, S. J. (1996). *The state of Americans: This generation and the next.* New York, NY: Free Press.

Brouwers, S. A., Van de Vijver, F. J. R., & Van Hemert, D. A. (2009). Variation in Raven's Progressive Matrices scores across time and place. *Learning and Individual Differences, 19,* 330–338.

Brown, R. P., & Day, E. A. (2006). The difference isn't black and white: Stereotype threat and the race difference on Raven's Progressive Matrices. *Journal of Applied Psychology, 91,* 979–985.

Brown, R. T., Reynolds, C. R., & Whitaker, J. S. (1999). Bias in mental testing since "Bias in Mental Testing." *School Psychology Quarterly, 14,* 208–238.

Camara, W. J. (2009). College admission testing: Myths and realities in an age of admissions hype. In R. Phelps (Ed.), *Correcting fallacies about educational and psychological testing* (pp. 147–180). Washington, DC: American Psychological Association.

Campbell, F. A., & Ramey, C. T. (1995). Cognitive and school outcomes for high-risk African-American students at middle adolescence: Positive effects of early intervention. *American Educational Research Journal, 32,* 743–772.

Canfield, R. L., Henderson, C. R., Jr., Cory-Slechta, D. A., Cox, C., Jusko, T. A., & Lanphear, B. P. (2003). Intellectual impairment in children with blood lead concentrations below 10 microg per deciliter. *New England Journal of Medicine, 348,* 1517–1526.

Capron, C., & Duyme, M. (1989). Assessment of effects of socioeconomic status on IQ in a full cross-fostering study. *Nature, 340,* 552–553.

Carroll, J. B. (1993). *Human cognitive abilities: A survey of factor analytic studies.* Cambridge, England: Cambridge University Press.

Caruso, D. R., Taylor, J., & Detterman, D. K. (1982). Intelligence research and intelligent policy. In D. K. Detterman & R. J. Sternberg (Eds.), *How and how much can intelligence be increased?* (pp. 45–65). Norwood, NJ: Ablex.

Caspi, A., Williams, B., Kim-Cohen J., Craig, I. W., Milne, B. J., Poulton, R.,... Moffitt, T. E. (2007). Moderation of breastfeeding effects on the IQ by genetic variation in fatty acid metabolism. *Proceedings of the National Academy of Sciences, 10,* 1073.

Cattell, R. B. (1949). *Culture Free Intelligence Test, Scale 1, Handbook.* Champaign, IL: Institute of Personality and Ability.

Cattell, R. B. (1971). *Abilities: Their structure, growth, and action.* Boston, MA: Houghton-Mifflin.

Ceci, S. J. (1991). How much does schooling influence general intelligence and its cognitive components? A reassessment of the evidence. *Developmental Psychology, 27,* 703–722.

Ceci, S. J., & Williams, W. M. (1997). Schooling, intelligence, and income. *American Psychologist, 52,* 1051–1058.

Ceci, S. J., Williams, W. M., & Barnett, S. M. (2009). Women's underrepresentation in science: Sociocultural and biological considerations. *Psychological Bulletin, 135*(2), 218–261. http://dx.doi.org/10.1037/a0014412

Chabris, C. F., Hebert, B. M., Benjamin, D. J., Beauchamp, J., Cesarini, D., van der Loos, M.,... Laibson, D. (2013). Most reported genetic associations with general intelligence are probably false positives. *Psychological Science.*

Chaiken, A. L., Sigler, F., & Derlega, V. J. (1974). Nonverbal mediators of supervisor expectancy effects. *Journal of Personality and Social Psychology, 30,* 144–149.

Chandler, M. (Writer & Director). (1999, October 4). "Secrets of the SAT." In M. Sullivan (Executive Producer), *Frontline.* Boston, MA: WGBH.

Cheng, H., & Furnham, A. (2012). Childhood cognitive ability, education, and personality traits predict attainment in adult occupational prestige over 17 years. *Journal of Vocational Behavior, 81,* 218–226.

Cohen, G. L., Garcia, J., Apfel, N., & Master, A. (2006). Reducing the racial achievement gap: A social-psychological intervention. *Science, 313,* 1307–1310.

Cole, M. W., Yarkoni, T., Repovs, G., Anticevic, A., & Braver, T. S. (2012). Global connectivity of prefrontal cortex predicts cognitive control and intelligence. *Journal of Neuroscience, 32*(26), 8988–8999. http://dx.doi.org/10.1523/JNEUROSCI.0536-12.2012

Colom, R., Flores-Mendoza, C., & Abad, F. J. (2007). Generational changes on the draw-A-man test: A comparison of Brazilian urban and rural children tested in 1930, 2002 and 2004. *Journal of Biosocial Science, 39*(1), 79–89. http://dx.doi.org/10.1017/S0021932005001173

Colombo, J. (1993). *Infant cognition: Predicting later intellectual functioning.* Newbury Park, CA: Sage.

Conte, J. M. (2005). A review and critique of emotional intelligence measures. *Journal of Organizational Behavior, 26*(4), 433–440. http://dx.doi.org/10.1002/job.319

Conway A. R., Getz, S. J., Macnamara, B., & Engel de Abreu, P. M. J. (2011). Working memory and intelligence. In R. J. Sternberg and S. B. Kaufman (Eds.), *The Cambridge handbook of intelligence* (pp. 394–418). Cambridge: Cambridge University Press.

Danaher, K., & Crandall, C. S. (2008). Stereotype threat in applied settings re-examined. *Journal of Applied Social Psychology, 38,* 1639–1655.

Darlington, R. B. (1986). Long-term effects of preschool programs. In U. Neisser (Ed.), *The school achievement of minority children.* Hillsdale, NJ: Erlbaum.

Davies, G., Tenesa, A., Payton, A., Yang, J., Harris, S. E., Liewald, D.,... Dreary, I. J. (2011). Genome-wide association studies establish that human intelligence is highly heritable and polygenic. *Molecular Psychiatry, 16*(10), 996–1005. http://dx.doi.org/10.1038/mp.2011.85

Davis, T. C., Wolf, M. S., Bass, P. F., Middlebrooks, M., Kennen, E., Baker, D. W.,... Parker, R. M. (2006). Low literacy impairs comprehension of prescription drug warning labels. *Journal of General Internal Medicine, 21,* 847–851.

Dawes, R. M., Faust, D., & Meehl, P. E. (1989). Clinical versus actuarial judgment. *Science, 243*(4899), 1668–1674. http://dx.doi.org/10.1126/science.2648573

Deary, I. J., Batty, G. D., & Gale, C. R. (2008a). Bright children become enlightened adults. *Psychological Science, 19*(1), 1–6. http://dx.doi.org/10.1111/j.1467-9280.2008.02036.x

Deary, I. J., Der, G., & Ford, G. (2001). Reaction time and intelligence differences: A population based cohort study. *Intelligence, 29,* 1–11.

Deary, I. J., Spinath, F. M., & Bates, T. C. (2006). Genetics of intelligence. *European Journal of Human Genetics, 14*(6), 690–700.

Deary, I. J., Whalley, L. J., Lemmon, H., Crawford, J. R., & Starr, J. M. (2000). The stability of individual differences in mental ability from childhood to old age: Follow-up of the 1932 Scottish Mental Survey. *Intelligence, 28,* 49–55.

DeFries, J. C., & Plomin, R. (1978). Behavioral genetics. *Annual Review of Psychology, 29,* 473–515.

Der, G., Batty, G. D., & Deary, I. J. (2006). Effect of breast feeding on intelligence in children: Prospective study, sibling pairs analysis, and meta-analysis. *British Medical Journal, 333,* 945–950.

DerSimonian, R., & Laird, N. M. (1983). Evaluating the effect of coaching on SAT scores: A meta-analysis. *Harvard Educational Review, 53,* 1–15.

Detterman, D. K. (1987). What does reaction time tell us about intelligence? In P. Vernon (Ed.), *Speed of information-processing and intelligence.* Norwood, NJ: Ablex.

Devlin, B., Daniels, M., & Roeder, K. (1997). The heritability of IQ. *Nature, 388,* 468–471.

DeYoung, C. G., Peterson, J. B., & Higgins, D. M. (2005). Sources of openness/intellect: Cognitive and neuropsychological correlates of the fifth factor of personality. *Journal of Personality, 73,* 825–858.

Dickens, W. T., & Flynn, J. R. (2001). Heritability estimates versus large environmental effects: The IQ paradox resolved. *Psychological Review, 108,* 346–369.

Dickens, W. T., & Flynn, J. R. (2006). Black Americans reduce the racial IQ gap: Evidence from standardization samples. *Psychological Science, 17*(10), 913-920. http://dx.doi.org/10.1111/j.1467-9280.2006.01802.x

Diener, E., & Seligman, M. E. P. (2004). Beyond money: Toward an economy of well-being. *Psychological Science in the Public Interest, 5,* 1–31.

DiLalla, L. F., Thompson, L. A., Plomin, R., Phillips, K., Fagan, J. F., Haith, M. M., . . . Fulker, D. W. (1990). Infant predictors of preschool and adult IQ: A study of infant twins and their parents. *Developmental Psychology, 26,* 759–769.

Duncan, J., Seitz, R. J., Kolodny, J., Bor, D., Herzog, H., Ahmed, A.,... Emslie, H. (2000). A neural basis for general intelligence. *Science, 289*(5478), 457–460.

Dunning, D., Heath, C., & Suls, J. (2004). Flawed self-assessment: Implications for health, education, and the workplace. *Psychological Science in the Public Interest, 5,* 69–106.

Dweck, C. S. (2002). Beliefs that make smart people dumb. In R. Sternberg (Ed.), *Why smart people can be so stupid* (pp. 24–41). New Haven. CT: Yale University Press.

Engle, R. W. (2002). Working memory capacity as executive attention. *Current Directions in Psychological Science, 11,* 19–23.

Ericsson, K. A., Krampe, R. Th., & Tesch-Römer, C. (1993). The role of deliberate practice in the acquisition of expert performance. *Psychological Review, 100,* 363–406.

Erikson, E. H. (1968). *Identity: Youth and crisis.* London, England: Faber & Faber.

Ermer, E., Kahn, R. E., Salovey, P., & Kiehl, K. A. (2012). Emotional intelligence in incarcerated men with psychopathic traits. *Journal of Personality and Social Psychology, 103,* 194–204.

Estes, Z., & Felker, S. (2012). Confidence mediates the sex difference in mental rotation performance. *Archives of Sexual Behavior, 41*(3), 557–570. http://dx.doi.org/10.1007/s10508-011-9875-5

Eyferth, K. (1961). Leistungen verschidener Gruppen von Besatzungskindern in Hamburg-Wechsler Intelligenztest fur Kinder (HAWIK) [Performance of different groups of occupation children on the Hamburg-Wechsler Intelligence Test for Children]. *Archhiv fur die gesamte Psychologie, 113,* 222–241.

Eysenck, H. J. (1994). *Test your IQ.* Toronto, Ontario, Canada: Penguin Books.

Eysenck, H. J., & Schoenthaler, S. J. (1997). Raising IQ level by vitamin and mineral supplementation. In R. Sternberg & E. Grigorenko (Eds.),

Intelligence, heredity, and environment (pp. 363–392). Cambridge, England: Cambridge University Press.

Falk, D. (2009). *New information about Albert Einstein's brain.* Frontiers in Evolutionary Neuroscience. Retrieved from http://frontiersin.org/evolution-aryneuroscience/paper/10.3389/neuro.18/003.2009/html

Feingold, A. (1988). Cognitive gender differences are disappearing. *American Psychologist, 43,* 95–103.

Fidelman, U. (1993). Intelligence and the brain's consumption of energy: What is intelligence? *Personality and Individual Differences, 14,* 283–286.

Flynn, J. R. (1981). The mean IQ of Americans: Massive gains 1932 to 1978. *Psychological Bulletin, 95,* 29–51.

Flynn, J. R. (1998). IQ gains over time: Toward finding the causes. In U. Neisser (Ed.), *The rising curve* (pp. 25–66). Washington, DC: American Psychological Association.

Flynn, J. R., & Rossi-Casé, L. (2011). Modern women match men on Raven's progressive matrices. *Personality and Individual Differences, 50*(6), 799–803. http://dx.doi.org/10.1016/j.paid.2010.12.035

Frey, M. C., & Detterman, D. K. (2004). Scholastic assessment or g? The relationship between the SAT and general cognitive ability. *Psychological Science, 15,* 373–398.

Furnham, A., Batey, M., Anand, K., & Manfield, J. (2008). Personality, hypomania, intelligence and creativity. *Personality and Individual Differences, 44,* 1060–1069.

Furnham, A., Zhang, J., & Chamorro-Premuzic, T. (2006) The relationship between psychometric and self-estimated intelligence, creativity, personality and academic achievement. *Imagination, Cognition and Personality, 25,* 119–145.

Galton, F. (1869). *Hereditary genius: An inquiry into its laws and consequences.* London, England: Macmillan.

Galton, F. (1876). The history of twin, as a criterion of the relative powers of nature and nurture. *Journal of the Anthropological Institute of Great Britain and Ireland, 5,* 391–406.

Gardner, H. (1983). *Frames of mind: The theory of multiple intelligences.* New York, NY: Basic Books.

Gardner, H. (1999). *Intelligence reframed: Multiple intelligences for the 21st century.* New York, NY: Basic Books.

Geary, D. C. (1996). Sexual selection and sex differences in mathematical abilities. *Behavioral and Brain Sciences, 19,* 229–284.

Gignac, G. E., Stough, C., & Loukomitis, S. (2004). Openness, intelligence, and self-report intelligence. *Intelligence, 32,* 133–143.

Gillham, N. W. (2001). *A life of Sir Francis Galton: From African exploration to the birth of eugenics.* New York, NY: Oxford University Press.

Gillies, R. M. (2011). Alternative views on intelligence. *International Journal of Disability, Development and Education, 58*(2), 189–193. http://dx.doi.org/10.1080/1034912X.2011.570507

Gladwell, M. (2008). *Outliers: The story of success.* Boston, MA: Little, Brown.

Glenn, D. (2010, May 9). Carol Dweck's attitude: It's not about how smart you are. *Chronicle of Higher Education.* Retrieved from http://chronicle.com/article/Carol-Dwecks-Attitude/65405

Goertzel, T. (1994). Belief in conspiracy theories. *Political Psychology, 15*(4), 731–742. http://dx.doi.org/10.2307/3791630

Goldberg, L. R. (1993). The structure of phenotypic personality traits. *American Psychologist, 48,* 26–34.

Goleman, D. (1995). *Emotional intelligence.* New York, NY: Bantam.

Gottfredson, L. S. (1997). Why g matters: The complexity of everyday life. *Intelligence, 24,* 79–132.

Gottfredson, L. S. (2003). On Sternberg's "Reply to Gottfredson." *Intelligence, 31,* 415–424.

Gottfredson, L. S. (2004). Intelligence: Is it the epidemiologists' elusive "fundamental cause" of social class inequalities in health? *Journal of Personality and Social Psychology, 86,* 174–199.

Gottfredson, L. S. (2009). Logical fallacies used to dismiss the evidence on intelligence testing. In R. Phelps (Ed.), *Correcting fallacies about educational and psychological testing* (pp. 11–65). Washington, DC: American Psychological Association.

Gould, S. J. (1981). *The mismeasure of man.* New York, NY: Norton.

Goulding, P. (1992). *Classical music: The 50 greatest composers and their 1000 greatest works.* New York, NY: Ballantine.

Gow, A. J., Johnson, W., Pattie, A., Brett, C. E., Roberts, B., Starr, J. M., & Deary, I. J. (2011). Stability and change in intelligence from age 11 to ages 70, 79, and 87: The lothian birth cohorts of 1921 and 1936. *Psychology and Aging, 26*(1), 232–240. http://dx.doi.org/10.1037/a0021072

Greenfield, P. (1998). The cultural evolution of IQ. In U. Neisser (Ed.), *The rising curve: Long-term gains in IQ and related measures* (pp. 81–122). Washington, DC: American Psychological Association.

Greenspan, S., Loughlin, G., & Black, R. S. (2001). Credulity and gullibility in people with developmental disabilities: A framework for future research. In L. M. Glidden (Ed.), *International Review of Research in Mental Retardation, Vol. 24* (pp. 101–135). New York, NY: Academic Press.

Greenspan, S., & Switzky, H. N. (Eds.). (2003). *What is mental retardation? Ideas for the new century.* Washington, DC: American Association on Mental Retardation.

Grossman, H. J. (Ed.). (1983). *Classification in mental retardation* (Rev. ed.). Washington, DC: American Association on Mental Deficiency.

Guilford, J. P. (1967). *The nature of human intelligence.* New York, NY: McGraw-Hill.

Gustafsson, J. E. (1988). Hierarchical models of individual differences in cognitive abilities. In R. J. Sternberg (Ed.), *Advances in the psychology of human intelligence, Vol. 4* (pp. 35–71). Hillsdale, NJ: Erlbaum.

Haier, R. J. (2009). Neuro-intelligence, neuro-metrics and the next phase of brain imaging studies. *Intelligence, 37*(2), 121–123. http://dx.doi.org/10.1016/j.intell.2008.12.006

Haier, R. J. (2009, November/December). What does a smart brain look like? *Scientific American Mind,* 26–33.

Haier, R. J., Siegel, B. V., MacLachlan, A., Soderling, E., Lottenberg, S., & Buchsbaum, M. S. (1992). Regional glucose metabolic changes after learning a complex visuospatial/motor task: A positron emission tomographic study. *Brain Research, 570,* 134–143.

Halari, R., Hines, M., Kumari, V., Mehrotra, R., Wheeler, M., Ng, V., & Sharma, T. (2005) Sex differences and individual differences in cognitive performance and their relationship to endogenous gonadal hormones and gonadotropins. *Behavioral Neuroscience, 119,* 104–117.

Hall, J. A. (1978). Gender effects in decoding nonverbal cues. *Psychological Bulletin, 85,* 845–857.

Halpern, D. F. (1992). *Sex differences in cognitive abilities* (2nd ed.). Hillsdale, NJ: Erlbaum.

Halpern, D. F. (2004). A cognitive-process taxonomy for sex differences in cognitive abilities. *Current Directions in Psychological Science, 13,* 135–139.

Halpern, D. F., Benbow, C. P., Geary, D. C., Gur, R. C., Hyde, J. S., & Gernsbacher, M. A. (2007). The science of sex differences in science and mathematics. *Psychological Science in the Public Interest, 8,* 1–51,

Hampson, E., & Kimura, D. (1988) Reciprocal effects of hormonal fluctuations on human motor and perceptual-spatial skills. *Behavioral Neuroscience, 102,* 456–459.

Hampson, E., Rovet, J. F., & Altmann, D. (1998). Spatial reasoning in children with congenital adrenal hyperplasia due to 21-hydroxylase deficiency. *Developmental Neuropsychology, 14,* 299–320.

Hansford, B., & Hattie, J. (1982). The relationship between self and achievement performance measures. *Review of Educational Research, 52,* 123–142.

Hauser, R. M. (1998). Trends in black-white test score differences: I. Uses and misuses of NAEP/SAT data. In U. Neisser (Ed.), *The rising curve: Long-term gains in IQ and related measures* (pp. 219–249). Washington, DC: American Psychological Association.

Hedges, L. V., & Nowell, A. (1995). Sex differences in mental test scores, variability, and numbers of high-scoring individuals. *Science, 269,* 41–45.

Helson, R., & Srivastava, S. (2002). Creativity and wisdom: Similarities, differences, and how they develop. *Personality and Social Psychology Bulletin, 28,* 1430–1440.

Henshaw, J. M. (2006). *Does measurement measure up? How numbers reveal and conceal the truth.* Baltimore, MD: Johns Hopkins University Press.

Herrnstein, R. J., & Murray, C. (1994). *The bell curve: Intelligence and class structure in American life.* New York, NY: Free Press.

Hertel, J., Schutz, A., & Lammers, C. H. (2009). Emotional intelligence and mental disorder. *Journal of Clinical Psychology, 65,* 942–954.

Hick, W. E. (1952). On the rate of gain of information. *Quarterly Journal of Experimental Psychology, 4,* 11–26.

Hines, T. (2003). *Pseudoscience and the paranormal: A critical examination of the evidence* (2nd ed.). Buffalo, NY: Prometheus.

Hook, E. B., & Lindsjo, A. (1978). Down syndrome in live births by single year maternal age interval in a Swedish study: Comparison with results from a New York State study. *American Journal of Human Genetics, 30,* 19–27.

Hudson, L. (1967). *Contrary imaginations: A psychological study of the English schoolboy.* Harmondsworth, England: Penguin.

Huitema, B. E., & Stein, C. R. (1993). Validity of the GRE without restriction of range. *Psychological Reports, 72,* 123–127.

Hunt, E. (1999). Intelligence and human resources: Past, present, and future. In P. L. Ackerman, P. C. Kyllonen, & R. D. Roberts (Eds.), *Learning and individual differences: Process, trait, and content determinants* (pp. 3–30). Washington, DC: American Psychological Association.

Hunt, E., & Carlson, J. (2007). Considerations relating to the study of group differences in intelligence. *Perspectives on Psychological Science, 2,* 194–213.

Hunt, E. B. (2010). *Human intelligence.* Cambridge, England: Cambridge University Press.

Hunter, J. E., & Hunter, R. F. (1984). Validity and utility of alternative predictors of job performance. *Psychological Bulletin, 96,* 72–98.

Hunter, J. E., Schmidt, F. L., & Hunter, R. (1979). Differential validity of employment tests by race: A comprehensive review and analysis. *Psychological Bulletin, 85,* 721–735.

Hyde, J. S. (2005). The gender similarities hypothesis. *American Psychologist, 60,* 581–592.

Hyde, J. S., Fennema, E., & Lamon, S. J. (1990). Gender differences in mathematics performance: A meta-analysis. *Psychological Bulletin, 107,* 139–155.

Hyman, R. (2002). When and why are smart people stupid? In R. Sternberg (Ed.), *Why smart people can be so stupid* (pp. 1–23). New Haven, CT: Yale University Press.

Irwing, P. (2012). Sex differences in *g*: An analysis of the US standardization sample of the WAIS-III. *Personality and Individual Differences, 53*(2), 126–131. http://dx.doi.org/10.1016/j.paid.2011.05.001

Jackson, D. N., & Rushton, J. P. (2006). Males have greater *g*: Sex differences in general mental ability from 100,000 17- to 18-year-olds on the Scholastic Assessment Test. *Intelligence, 34*, 479–486.

Jacobson, S. W., Chiodo, L. M., & Jacobson, J. L. (1999). Breastfeeding effects on intelligence quotient in 4- and 11-year-old children. *Pediatrics, 103*, e71.

Jamison, K. R. (1989). Mood disorders and patterns of creativity in British writers and artists. *Psychiatry, 52*, 125–134.

Jamison, K. R. (1993). *Touched with fire: Manic-depressive illness and the artistic temperament.* New York, NY: Free Press.

Janda, L. H. (1998). *Psychological testing, theory, and applications.* Boston, MA: Allyn & Bacon.

Janos, P. M., & Robinson, N. M. (1985). Psychosocial development in intellectually gifted children. In F. D. Horowitz & M. O'Brien (Eds.), *The gifted and talented: Developmental perspectives* (pp. 149–195). Washington, DC: American Psychological Association.

Jensen, A. R. (1969). How much can we boost I.Q. and scholastic achievement? *Harvard Educational Review, 33*, 1–123.

Jensen, A. R. (1973). *Educability and group differences.* London, England: Methuen.

Jensen, A. R. (1977). Cumulative deficit of blacks in the rural south. *Developmental Psychology, 13*, 184–191.

Jensen, A. R. (1980). *Bias in mental testing.* New York, NY: Free Press.

Jensen, A. R. (1993). Test validity: g versus "tacit knowledge." *Current Directions in Psychological Science, 2*, 9–10.

Jensen, A. R. (1998). *The g factor: The science of mental ability.* Westport, CT: Praeger.

Jensen, A. R. (2006). *Clocking the mind: Mental chronometry and individual differences.* Oxford, England: Elsevier.

Johnson, W., Carothers, A., & Deary, I. J. (2009). A role for the X chromosome in sex differences in variability in general intelligence? *Perspectives on Psychological Science, 4*, 598–611.

Johnson, W., Corley, J., Starr, J. M., & Deary, I. J. (2011). Psychological and physical health at age 70 in the Lothian Birth Cohort 1936: Links with early life IQ, SES, and current cognitive function and neighborhood environment. *Health Psychology, 30*(1), 1–11.

Jones, C. M., Braithwaite, V. A., & Healy, S. D. (2003). The evolution of sex differences in spatial ability. *Behavioral Neuroscience, 117*, 403–411.

Jung, R. E., & Haier, R. J. (2007). The parieto-frontal integration theory (P-FIT) of intelligence: Converging neuroimaging evidence. *Behavioral and Brain Sciences, 30*(2), 135–154. http://dx.doi.org/10.1017/S0140525X07001185

Kane, M. J., Hambrick, D. Z., & Conway, A. R. A. (2005). Working memory capacity and fluid intelligence are strongly related constructs: Comment on Ackerman, Beier, and Boyle (2004). *Psychological Bulletin, 131*, 66–71.

Kaplan, R. M. (1982). Nader's raid on the testing industry: Is it in the best interests of the consumer? *American Psychologist, 37*, 15–23.

Kaplan, R. M., & Saccuzzo, D. P. (2008). *Psychological testing: Principles, applications, and issues* (7th ed.). Belmont, CA: Wadsworth/Thomson.

Kevles, D. J. (1985). *In the name of eugenics: Genetics and the uses of human heredity.* New York, NY: Knopf.

Kimura, D. (1999). *Sex and cognition.* Cambridge, MA: MIT Press.

Klein, D. F. (1998). Listening to meta-analysis but hearing bias. *Prevention & Treatment, 1*, art. 0006c. Retrieved from http://psycnet.apa.org/index.cfm?fa=buy.optionToBuy&id=1999-11094-005

Koriat, A., & Bjork, R. A. (2005). Illusions of competence in monitoring one's knowledge during study. *Journal of Experimental Psychology: Learning, Memory, and Cognition, 31*, 187–194.

Kristensen, P., & Bjerkedal, T. (2007). Explaining the relation between birth order and intelligence. *Science, 316*, 1717.

Kruger, J., & Dunning, D. (1999). Unskilled and unaware of it: How difficulties in recognizing one's own incompetence lead to inflated self-assessments. *Journal of Personality and Social Psychology, 77*, 1121–1134.

Kulik, J. A., Bangert-Drowns, R. L., & Kulik, C.-L. C. (1984). Effectiveness of coaching for aptitude tests. *Psychological Bulletin, 95*, 179–188.

Kuncel, N. R., & Hezlett, S. A. (2007). Standardized tests predict graduate students' success. *Science, 315*, 1080–1081.

Kuncel, N. R., Ones, D. S., & Sackett, P. R. (2010). Individual differences as predictors of work, educational, and broad life outcomes. *Personality and Individual Differences, 49*(4), 331–336. http://dx.doi.org/10.1016/j.paid.2010.03.042

Kuntz, D., & Bachrach, S. (2006). *Deadly medicine: Creating the master race.* Washington, DC: United States Holocaust Memorial Museum.

Langer, N., Pedroni, A., Gianotti, L. R., Hänggi, J., Knoch, D., & Jäncke, L. (2012). Functional brain network efficiency predicts intelligence. *Human brain mapping, 33*(6), 1393–1406. http://dx.doi.org/10.1002/hbm.21297

Leslie, M. (2000). The vexing legacy of Lewis Terman. Retrieved from http://www.stanfordalumni.org/news/magazine/2000/julaug/articles/terman.html

Levine, S. C., Vasilyeva, M., Lourenco, S. F., Newcombe, N. S., & Huttenlocher, J. (2005). Socioeconomic status modifies the sex difference in spatial skill. *Psychological Science, 16*, 841–845.

Lewin, T. (2006, August 31). Students' path to small colleges can bypass SAT. *New York Times.* Retrieved from http://www.nytimes.com/2006/08/31/education/31sat.html?_r=1&n=Top/Reference/Times%20Topics/People/L/Lewin,%20Tamar&oref=slogin

Lewontin, R. C. (1970). Further remarks on race and the genetics of intelligence. *Bulletin of the Atomic Scientists, 26*, 23–25.

Li, S. C., Jordanova, M., & Lindenberger, U. (1998). From good senses to good sense: A link between tactile information processing and intelligence. *Intelligence, 26*, 99–122.

Lilienfeld, S. O., Ammirati, R., & Landfield, K. (2009). Giving debiasing away: Can psychological research on correcting cognitive errors improve human welfare? *Perspectives on Psychological Science, 4*, 390–398.

Lilienfeld, S. O., & Waldman, I. D. (2000, November 13). Race and IQ: What the science says. *Emory Report, 3.*

Lippa, R. A., Collaer, M. L., & Peters, M. (2010). Sex differences in mental rotation and line angle judgments are positively associated with gender equality and economic development across 53 nations. *Archives of Sexual Behavior, 39*, 990–997.

Locke, E. A. (2005). Why emotional intelligence is an invalid concept. *Journal of Organizational Behavior, 26*, 425–431.

Loehlin, J. C., Horn, J. M., & Willerman, L. (1989) Modeling IQ change—Evidence from the Texas adoption project. *Child Development, 60*, 993–1004.

Loehlin, J. C., Lindzey, G., & Spuhler, J. N. (1977). *Race differences in intelligence.* San Francisco, CA: W. H. Freeman.

Loehlin, J. C., Vandenberg, S. G., & Osborne, R. T. (1973). Blood group genes and Negro-white ability differences. *Behavior Genetics, 3*, 263–270.

Loehlin, J. C., Willerman, L., & Horn, J. M. (1988). Human behavior genetics. *Annual Review of Psychology, 39*, 101–133.

Logel, C., Iserman, E. C., Davies, P. G., Quinn, D. M., & Spencer, S. J. (2009). The perils of double consciousness: The role of thought suppression in stereotype threat. *Journal of Experimental Social Psychology, 45*, 299–312.

Lubinski, D. (2009). Exceptional cognitive ability: The phenotype. *Behavior Genetics, 39*(4), 350–358.

Lubinski, D., & Benbow, C. P. (1995). An opportunity for empiricism: Review of Howard Gardner's *Multiple Intelligences: The Theory in Practice. Contemporary Psychology, 40*, 935–938.

Lubinski, D., Benbow, C. P., Webb, R. M., & Bleske-Rechek, A. (2006). Tracking exceptional human capital over two decades. *Psychological Science, 17*, 194–199.

Lubinski, D., & Humphreys, L. G. (1992). Some bodily and medical correlates of mathematical giftedness and commensurate levels of socioeconomic status. *Intelligence, 16*, 99–115.

Ludwig, J., & Phillips, D. A. (2008). Long-term effects of Head Start on low-income children. *Annals of the New York Academy of Sciences, 1136*, 257–268.

Lykken, D. T. (2005). Mental energy. *Intelligence, 33*, 331–335.

Lynn, R. (1996). *Dysgenics: Genetic deterioration in modern populations.* Westport, CT: Praeger.

Lynn, R. (1998). In support of the nutrition theory. In U. Neisser (Ed.), *The rising curve: Long-term gains in IQ and related measures* (pp. 207–218). Washington, DC: American Psychological Association.

Lynn, R. (2003). The intelligence of American Jews. *Personality and Individual Differences, 36*, 201–206.

Lynn, R. (2006). *Race differences in intelligence: An evolutionary analysis.* Augusta, GA: Washington Summit Books.

Lynn, R., & Irwing, P. (2004). Sex differences on the Progressive Matrices: A meta-analysis. *Intelligence, 32*, 481–498.

Maccoby, E. E., & Jacklin, C. N. (1974). *Psychology of sex differences.* Stanford, CA: Stanford University Press.

Mackintosh, M. J. (1998). *IQ and human intelligence.* Oxford, England: Oxford University Press.

Matthews, G., Zeidner, M., & Roberts, R. (2002). *Emotional intelligence: Science and myth.* London, England: MIT Press.

Mayer, J., Roberts, R., & Barsade, S. G. (2008). Human abilities: Emotional intelligence. *Annual Review of Psychology, 59*, 507–536.

Mayer, J. D., Salovey, P., & Caruso, D. R. (2008). Emotional intelligence: New ability or eclectic traits? *American Psychologist, 63*, 503–517.

McCall, R. B., & Carriger, M. S. (1993). A meta-analysis of infant habituation and recognition memory performance as predictors of later IQ. *Child Development, 64*, 57–79.

McCarty, R. (2001, April). Negative stereotypes: A personal view. *Monitor on Psychology, 32*(4), 31.

McClearn, G. E., Johansson, B., Berg, S., Pedersen, N. L., Ahern, F., Petrill, S. A., & Plomin, R. (1997). Substantial genetic influence on cognitive abilities in twins 80 or more years old. *Science, 276*, 1560–1563.

McClure, E. B. (2000). A meta-analytic review of sex differences in facial expression processing and their development in infants, children, and adolescents. *Psychological Bulletin, 126*, 424–453.

McDaniel, M. A. (2005) Big-brained people are smarter: A meta-analysis of the relationship between in vivo brain volume and intelligence. *Intelligence, 33*, 337–346.

McDermott J. F. (2001). Emily Dickinson revisited: A study of periodicity in her work. *American Journal of Psychiatry, 158,* 686–690.

Meacham, J. (1990). The loss of wisdom. In R. J. Sternberg (Ed.), *Wisdom: Its nature, origins, and development* (pp. 181–211). New York, NY: Cambridge University Press.

Mehl, M. R., Vazire, S., Ram'rez-Esparza, N., Slatcher, R. B., & Pennebaker, J. W. (2007). Are women really more talkative than men? *Science, 317,* 82.

Messick, S. (1992). Multiple intelligence or multilevel intelligence? Selective emphasis on distinctive properties of hierarchy: On Gardner's *Frames of Mind* and Sternberg's *Beyond IQ* in the context of theory and research on the structure of human abilities. *Psychological Inquiry, 3,* 365–384.

Michalski, R. L., & Shackelford, T. K. (2001). Methodology, birth order, intelligence, and personality. *American Psychologist, 56,* 520–521.

Miller, L. K. (1999). The savant syndrome: Intellectual impairment and exceptional skill, *Psychological Bulletin, 125,* 31–46.

Mingroni, M. A. (2007). Resolving the IQ paradox: Heterosis as a cause of the Flynn effect and other trends. *Psychological Review, 114,* 806–829.

Molé, P. (2006). 9/11 conspiracy theories. *Skeptic, 12,* 30–42.

Morelock, M., & Feldman, D. H. (1993). Prodigies and savants: What they have to tell us about giftedness and human cognition. In K. Heller, F. Monks, & H. Passow (Eds.), *International handbook for research on giftedness and talent* (pp. 161–181). Oxford, England: Pergamon Press.

Morrison, T., & Morrison, M. (1995). A meta-analytic assessment of the predictive validity of the quantitative and verbal components of the Graduate Record Examination with grade point average representing the criterion of graduate success. *Educational & Psychological Measurement, 55,* 309–316.

Mortensen, E. L., Michaelson, K. F., Sanders, S. A., & Reinisch, J. M. (2002). The association between duration of breastfeeding and adult intelligence. *Journal of the American Medical Association, 287,* 2365–2371.

Nairn, A. (1980). *The reign of ETS: The corporation that makes up minds.* Washington, DC: Ralph Nader.

Neisser, U. (1998). *The rising curve: Long-term gains in IQ and related measures.* Washington, DC: American Psychological Association.

Neisser, U., Boodoo, G., Bouchard, T. J., Jr., Boykin, A. W., Brody, N., Ceci, S. J.,... Urbina, S. (1996). Intelligence: Knowns and unknowns. *American Psychologist, 51,* 77–101.

Nguyen, H. D., & Ryan, A. M. (2008). Does stereotype threat affect test performance of minorities and women? A meta-analysis of experimental evidence. *Journal of Applied Psychology, 93*(6), 1314–1334. http://dx.doi.org/10.1037/a0012702

Nisbett, R. E. (1995). Race, IQ and scientism. In S. Fraser (Ed.), *The bell curve wars* (pp. 36–57). New York, NY: HarperCollins.

Nisbett, R. E. (2009). *Intelligence and how to get it: Why schools and cultures count.* New York, NY: Norton.

Nisbett, R. E., Aronson, J., Blair, C., Dickens, W., Flynn, J., Halpern, D. F., & Turkheimer, E. (2012). Intelligence: New findings and theoretical developments. *American Psychologist, 67*(2), 130–159. http://dx.doi.org/10.1037/a0026699

Northstone, K., & Emmett, P. M. (2010). Dietary patterns of men in ALSPAC: Associations with socio-demographic and lifestyle characteristics, nutrient intake and comparison with women's dietary patterns. *European Journal of Clinical Nutrition, 64*(9), 978–986.

Nusbaum, E. C., & Silvia, P. J. (2011). Are intelligence and creativity really so different? Fluid intelligence, executive processes, and strategy use in divergent thinking. *Intelligence, 39*(1), 36–45.

O'Boyle, E. H., Humphrey, R. H., Pollack, J. M., Hawver, T. H., & Story, P. A. (2011). The relation between emotional intelligence and job performance: A meta-analysis. *Journal of Organizational Behavior, 32*(5), 788.

Oldfield, K. (1998). The GRE as fringe science. *Skeptic, 6*(1), 68–72.

Ones, D. S., Viswesvaran, C., & Dilchert, S. (2005). Personality at work: Raising awareness and correcting misconceptions. *Human Performance, 18,* 389–404.

Orlovskaya, D. D., Uranova, N. A., Zimina, I. S., Kolomeets, N. S., Vikhreva, O. V., Rachmanova, V. I.,... Greenough, W. T. (1999). Effect of professional status on the number of synapses per neuron in the prefrontal cortex of normal human and schizophrenic brain. *Society for Neuroscience Abstracts, 329,* 430.

Paulhus, D. L., Lysy, D. C., & Yik, M. S. M. (1998). Self-report measures of intelligence: Are they useful as proxy IQ tests? *Journal of Personality, 66*(4), 525–554. http://dx.doi.org/10.1111/1467-6494.00023

Pederson, N. L., Plomin, R., Nesselroade, J. R., & McClearn, G. E. (1992). A quantitative genetic analysis of cognitive abilities during the second half of the life span. *Psychological Science, 3,* 346–352.

Perkins, D. N. (1981). *The mind's best work.* Cambridge, MA: Harvard University Press.

Phillips, K., & Fulker, D. W. (1989). Quantitative genetic analysis of longitudinal trends in adoption designs with application to IQ in the Colorado Adoption Project. *Behavior Genetics, 19,* 621–658.

Pinker, S. (2005, February 14). The science of difference: Sex ed. *The New Republic, 232,*

Plomin, R., & Kovas, Y. (2005). Generalist genes and learning disabilities. *Psychological Bulletin, 131,* 592–617.

Plomin, R., & Petrill, S. A. (1997). Genetics and intelligence: What's new? *Intelligence, 24*(1), 53–77. http://dx.doi.org/10.1016/S0160-2896(97)90013-1

Pollitt, E., Gorman, K. S., Engle, P. L., Martorell, R., & Rivera, J. (1993). Early supplementary feeding and cognition: Effects over two decades. *Monographs of the Society for Research in Child Development, 58*(7, Serial No. 235).

Posthuma, D., & de Geus, E. J. C. (2006). Progress in the molecular-genetic study of intelligence. *Current Directions in Psychological Science, 15,* 151–155.

Powers, D. E. (1993). Coaching for the SAT: A summary of the summaries and an update. *Educational Measurement: Issues and Practice, 12,* 24–39.

Powers, D. E., & Rock, D. A. (1999). Effects of coaching on SAT I: Reasoning test scores. *Journal of Educational Measurement, 36*(2), 93–118. http://dx.doi.org/10.1111/j.1745-3984.1999.tb00549.x

Preckel, F., Holling, H., & Wiese, M. (2006). Relationship of intelligence and creativity in gifted and non-gifted students: An investigation of threshold theory. *Personality and Individual Differences, 40*(1), 159–170. http://dx.doi.org/10.1016/j.paid.2005.06.022

Quinn, P. C., & Liben, L. S. (2008). A sex difference in mental rotation in young infants. *Psychological Science, 19*(11), 1067–1070. http://dx.doi.org/10.1111/j.1467-9280.2008.02201.x

Quinn, P. J., O'Callaghan, M. J., Williams, G. M., Najman, J. M., Andersen, M. J., & Bor, W. (2001). The effect of breastfeeding on child development at 5 years: A cohort study. *Journal of Paediatrics and Child Health, 37,* 465–469.

Randi, J. (1982). *Flim-flam!* Amherst, NY: Prometheus.

Raudenbush, S. W. (1984). Magnitude of teacher expectancy effects on pupil IQ as a function of the credibility of expectancy induction: A synthesis of findings from 18 experiments. *Journal of Educational Psychology, 76,* 85–97.

Raven, J., Raven, J. C., & Court, J. H. (1998). *Manual for Raven's Advanced Progressive Matrices.* Oxford, England: Oxford Psychologists Press.

Razoumnikova, O. (2000). Functional organization of different brain areas during convergent and divergent thinking: An EEG investigation. *Cognitive Brain Research, 10,* 11–18.

Redick, T. S., Unsworth, N., Kelly, A. J., & Engle, R. W. (2012). Faster, smarter? Working memory capacity and perceptual speed in relation to fluid intelligence. *Journal of Cognitive Psychology, 24*(7), 844–854. http://dx.doi.org/10.1080/20445911.2012.704359

Reed, E. W., & Reed, S. C. (1965). *Mental retardation: A family study.* Philadelphia, PA: W. B. Saunders.

Rehberg, R. A., & Rosenthal, E. R. (1978). *Class and merit in the American high school.* New York, NY: Longman.

Reiner, C., & Willingham, D. (2010). The myth of learning styles. *Change: The Magazine of Higher Learning, 42*(5), 32–35.

Reynolds, C. R. (1999). Cultural bias in testing of intelligence and personality. In C. Belar (Ed.), Sociocultural and individual differences, Vol. 10 of M. Hersen & A. Bellack (Eds.), *Comprehensive clinical psychology* (pp. 53–92). Oxford, England: Elsevier Science.

Reynolds, D. (2003, April 25). Panel recommends counseling for sterilization survivors. *Inclusion Daily Express.* Retrieved from http://www.inclusiondaily.com/news/institutions/nc/eugenics.htm#042503

Ris, M. D., Dietrich, K. N., Succop, P. A., Berger, O. G., & Bornschein, R. L. (2004). Early exposure to lead and neuropsychological outcome in adolescence. *Journal of the International Neuropsychological Society, 10,* 261–270.

Rodgers, J., Cleveland, H., van der Oord, E., & Rowe, D. (2000). Resolving the debate over birth order, family size, and intelligence. *American Psychologist, 55,* 599–612.

Rose, S. (2009). Darwin 200: Should scientists study race and IQ? NO: Science and society do not benefit. *Nature, 457,* 786–788.

Rose, S. A., Feldman, J. F., Jankowski, J. J., & Van Rossem, R. (2012). Information processing from infancy to 11 years: Continuities and prediction of IQ. *Intelligence.* http://dx.doi.org/10.1016/j.intell.2012.05.007

Rosenthal, R. (1994) Interpersonal expectancy effects: A 30-year perspective. *Current Directions in Psychological Science, 3,* 176–179.

Rosenthal, R., & Jacobson, L. (1966). Teachers' expectancies: Determinants of pupils' IQ gains. *Psychological Reports, 1,* 115–118.

Rowe, D. C., Jacobson, K. C., & Van den Oord, E. J. (1999). Genetic and environmental influences on vocabulary IQ: Parental education level as moderator. *Child Development, 70*(5), 1151–1162.

Royce, J., Darlington, R., & Murray, H. (1983). Pooled analyses: Findings across studies. In Consortium for Longitudinal Studies (Ed.), *As the twig is bent: Lasting effects of preschool programs* (pp. 411–459). Hillsdale, NJ: Erlbaum.

Rushton, J. P. (1995). *Race, evolution, and behavior: An evolutionary perspective.* New Brunswick, NJ: Transaction.

Rushton, J. P. (1999). Secular gains in IQ note related to the g factor and inbreeding depression—Unlike black-white differences: A reply to Flynn. *Personality and Individual Differences, 26,* 381–389.

Rushton, J. P., & Bogaert, A. F. (1987). Race differences in sexual behavior: Testing an evolutionary hypothesis. *Journal of Research in Personality, 21,* 529–551.

Sackett, P. R., Borneman, M. J., & Connelly, B. S. (2008). High stakes testing in higher education and employment: Appraising the evidence for validity and fairness. *American Psychologist, 63*(4), 215–227. http://dx.doi.org/10.1037/0003-066X.63.4.215

Sackett, P. R., Hardison, C. M., & Cullen, M. J. (2004). On interpreting stereotype threat as accounting for black-white differences on cognitive tests. *American Psychologist, 59,* 7–13.

Salekin, R. T., Lester, W. S., & Sellers, M. (2012). Mental sets in conduct problem youth with psychopathic features: Entity versus incremental theories of intelligence. *Law and Human Behavior, 36*(4), 283–292. http://dx.doi.org/10.1037/h0093971

Salgado, J. F., Anderson, N., Mocsoso, S., Bertua, C., deFruyt, F., & Rolland, J. P. (2003). A meta-analytic study of general mental ability validity for different occupations in the European community. *Journal of Applied Psychology, 88,* 1068–1081.

Salovey, P., & Mayer, J. D. (1990). Emotional intelligence. *Imagination, Cognition, and Personality, 9,* 185–211.

Salthouse, T. A. (1996). The processing-speed theory of adult age differences in cognition. *Psychological Review, 103,* 403–428.

Scarr, S. (1985). An author's frame of mind (Review of *Frames of mind: The theory of multiple intelligences*). *New Ideas in Psychology, 3,* 95–100.

Scarr, S., Pakstis, A. J., Katz, S. H., & Barker, W. B. (1977). Absence of a relationship between degree of white ancestry and intellectual skills within a black population. *Human Genetics, 39,* 69–86.

Scarr, S., & Weinberg, R. A. (1976). IQ test performance of black children adopted by white families. *American Psychologist, 31,* 726–739.

Schaie, K. W. (1996). *Intellectual development in adulthood: The Seattle longitudinal study.* New York, NY: Cambridge University Press.

Scheerenberger, R. C. (1983). *A history of mental retardation.* Baltimore, MD: P. H. Brooks.

Schiff, M., Duyme, M., Dumaret, A., & Tomkiewicz, S. (1982). How much can we boost scholastic achievement and IQ scores? A direct answer from a French adoption study. *Cognition, 12,* 165–196.

Schmader, T., Johns, M., & Forbes, C. (2008). An integrated process model of stereotype threat on performance. *Psychological Review, 115,* 336–356.

Schmidt, F. L., & Hunter, J. E. (1993). Tacit knowledge, practical intelligence, general mental ability and job knowledge. *Current Directions in Psychological Science, 2,* 8–9.

Schmiedek F., Oberauer K., Wilhelm O., Süss H. M., & Wittmann W. W. (2007). Individual differences in components of reaction time distributions and their relations to working memory and intelligence. *Journal of Experimental Psychology: General, 136,* 414–429.

Schneider, D. (2006). Smart as we can get? *American Scientist, 94,* 311–312.

Schooler, C. (1998). Environmental complexity and the Flynn effect. In U. Neisser (Ed.), *The rising curve: Long-term gains in IQ and related measures* (pp. 67–79). Washington, DC: American Psychological Association.

Selden, S. (1999). *Inheriting shame: The story of eugenics and racism in America.* New York, NY: Teachers College Press.

Serpell, R. (1979). How specific are perceptual skills? *British Journal of Psychology, 70,* 365–380.

Shadish, W. R., Cook, T. D., & Campbell, D. T. (2002). *Experimental and quasi-experimental designs for generalized causal inference.* Boston, MA: Houghton Mifflin.

Shaw, P., Greenstein, D., Lerch, J., Clasen, L., Lenroot, R., Gogtay, N.,... Giedd, J. (2006). Intellectual ability and cortical development in children and adolescents. *Nature, 440,* 676–679.

Shermer, M. (2002). *Why people believe weird things: Pseudoscience, superstition, and other confusions of our time* (2nd ed.). New York, NY: W. H. Freeman.

Siegler, R. S. (1992). The other Alfred Binet. *Developmental Psychology, 28,* 179–190.

Sigman, M., & Whaley, S. E. (1998). The role of nutrition in the development of intelligence. In U. Neisser (Ed.), *The rising curve: Long-term gains in IQ and related measures* (pp. 155–182). Washington, DC: American Psychological Association.

Simonton, D. K. (1997). Creative productivity: A predictive and explanatory model of career trajectories and landmarks. *Psychological Review, 104,* 66–89.

Simonton, D. K. (1999). *Origins of genius.* New York, NY: Cambridge Press.

Simonton, D. K. (2006). Presidential IQ, openness, intellectual brilliance and leadership: Estimates and correlations for 42 U.S. chief executives. *Political Psychology, 27,* 511–526.

Simonton, D. K., & Song, A. V. (2009). Eminence, IQ, physical and mental health, and achievement domain: Cox's 282 geniuses revisited. *Psychological Science, 20,* 429–434.

Sinkavich, F. J. (1995). Performance and metamemory: Do students know what they don't know? *Instructional Psychology, 22,* 77–87.

Slater, A. (1997). Can measures of infant habituation predict later intellectual ability? *Archives of Diseases of the Child, 77,* 474–476.

Smith, L., Fagan, J. F., & Ulvund, S. E. (2002). The relation of recognition memory in infancy and parental socioeconomic status to later intellectual competence. *Intelligence, 30,* 247–259.

Smith, M. L. (1980). Teacher expectations. *Evaluation in Education, 4,* 53–55.

Snelson, J. S. (1993). The ideological immune system: Resistance to new ideas in science. *Skeptic, 1*(4), 44–55.

Sorjonen, K., Hemmingsson, T., Lundin, A., Falkstedt, D., & Melin, B. (2012). Intelligence, socioeconomic background, emotional capacity, and level of education as predictors of attained socioeconomic position in a cohort of Swedish men. *Intelligence, 40*(3), 269–277. http://dx.doi.org/10.1016/j.intell.2012.02.009

Spearman, C. (1927). *The abilities of man.* New York, NY: Macmillan.

Spelke, E. S. (2005). Sex differences in intrinsic aptitude for mathematics and

science: A critical review. *American Psychologist, 60,* 950–958.

Stahl, S. (1999). Different strokes for different folks? A critique of learning styles. *American Educator, 23,* 27–31.

Stanovich, K. E. (2009). *Decision making and rationality in the modern world.* New York, NY: Oxford University Press.

Stanovich, K. E., & West, R. F. (2008). On the failure of intelligence to predict myside bias and one-sided bias. *Thinking & Reasoning, 14,* 129–167.

Steele, C. M. (1997). A threat in the air: How stereotypes shape intellectual identity and performance. *American Psychologist, 52,* 613–629.

Steele, C. M., & Aronson, J. (1995). Stereotype threat and the intellectual test-performance of African-Americans. *Journal of Personality and Social Psychology, 69,* 797–811.

Stern, W. (1912). *The psychological methods of intelligence testing* (G. Whipple, Trans.). Baltimore, MD: Warwick and York.

Sternberg, R. J. (1983). Components of human intelligence. *Cognition, 15,* 1–48.

Sternberg, R. J. (1988b). *The triarchic mind: A new theory of human intelligence.* New York, NY: Penguin Press.

Sternberg, R. J. (2002). Smart people are not stupid, but they sure can be foolish: The imbalance theory of foolishness. In R. J. Sternberg (Ed.), *Why smart people can be so stupid.* New Haven, CT: Yale University Press.

Sternberg, R. J. (2003b). Intelligence. In I. B. Weiner & D. K. Freedheim (Eds.), *Comprehensive handbook of psychology, Vol. 1* (pp. 135–156). New York, NY: Wiley.

Sternberg, R. J., Conway, B. E., Ketron, J. L., & Bernstein, M. (1981). People's conceptions of intelligence. *Journal of Personality and Social Psychology, 41,* 37–55.

Sternberg, R. J., & Lubart, T. I. (1992). Buy low and sell high: An investment approach to creativity. *Current Directions in Psychological Science, 1,* 1–5.

Sternberg, R. J., & Wagner, R. K. (1993). *Thinking styles inventory.* Unpublished instrument.

Sternberg, R. J., Wagner, R. K., Williams, W. M., & Horvath, J. A. (1995). Testing common sense. *American Psychologist, 50,* 912–927.

Sternberg, R. J., & Williams, W. M. (1997). Does the Graduate Record Examination predict meaningful success in the graduate training of psychologists? A case study. *American Psychologist, 52,* 630–641.

Strenze, T. (2007). Intelligence and socioeconomic success: A meta-analytic review of longitudinal research. *Intelligence, 35*(5), 401–426. http://dx.doi.org/10.1016/j.intell.2006.09.004

Stricker, L. J., & Ward, W. C. (2004) Stereotype threat, inquiring about test takers' ethnicity and gender, and standardized test performance. *Journal of Applied Social Psychology, 34,* 665–693.

Sue, S. (1993, November). *Measurement, testing, and ethnic bias: Can solutions be found?* Keynote Address at the Ninth Buros-Nebraska Symposium on Measurement and Testing, Lincoln, NE.

Sundet, J. M., Barlaug, D. G., & Torjussen, T. M. (2004). The end of the Flynn effect? A study of secular trends in mean intelligence test scores of Norwegian conscripts during half a century. *Intelligence, 32,* 349–362.

Teasdale, T. W., & Owen, D. R. (2008). Secular declines in cognitive test scores: A reversal of the Flynn effect. *Intelligence, 36*(2), 121–126. http://dx.doi.org/10.1016/j.intell.2007.01.007

Terman, L. M., & Oden, M. H. (1959). *Genetic studies of genius: Vol. 5. The gifted group at mid-life.* Stanford, CA: Stanford University Press.

Thurstone, L. L. (1938). *Primary mental abilities.* Chicago, IL: University of Chicago Press.

Toga, A. W., & Thompson, P. M. (2005). Genetics of brain structure and intelligence. *Annual Review of Neuroscience, 28,* 1–23.

Triandis, H. C. (2001). Individiaulism-collectivism and personality. *Journal of Personality, 69,* 907–924.

Tully, E. C., Iacono, W. G., & McGue, M. (2008). An adoption study of parental depression as an environmental liability for adolescent depression and childhood disruptive disorders. *American Journal of Psychiatry, 165,* 1148–1154.

Turkheimer, E., Haley, A., D'Onofrio, B., Waldron, M., & Gottesman, I. (2003). Socioeconomic status modifies heritability of IQ in young children. *Psychological Science, 14,* 623–628.

Van Rooy, D. L., & Viswesvaran, C. (2004). Emotional intelligence: A meta-analytic investigation of predictive validity and nomological net. *Journal of Vocational Behavior, 65,* 71–95.

Vernon, P. A. (1987). *Speed of information processing and intelligence.* Norwood, NJ: Ablex.

Vernon, P. E. (1971). *The structure of human abilities.* London, England: Methuen.

Voyer, D., Voyer, S., & Bryden, M. P. (1995). Magnitude of sex differences in spatial abilities: A meta-analysis and consideration of critical variables. *Psychological Bulletin, 117,* 250–270.

Wai, J., Cacchio, M., Putallaz, M., & Makel, M. C. (2010). Sex differences in the right tail of cognitive abilities: A 30-year examination. *Intelligence, 38*(4), 412–423.

Walton, G. M., & Spencer, S. J. (2009). Latent ability: Grades and test scores systematically underestimate the intellectual ability of negatively stereotyped students. *Psychological Science, 20*(9), 1132–1139. http://dx.doi.org/10.1111/j.1467-9280.2009.02417.x

Watkins, C. E., Campbell, V. L., Nieberding, R., & Hallmark, R. (1995). Contemporary practice of psychological assessment by clinical psychologists. *Professional Psychology: Science and Practice, 26,* 54–60.

Wechsler, D. (1939). *The measurement of adult intelligence.* Baltimore, MD: Williams & Wilkins.

Wechsler, D. (1988). *Wechsler Intelligence Scale for Children—Revised (WISC R).* New York, NY: The Psychological Corporation.

Wechsler, D. (1997). *The Wechsler Adult Intelligence Scale—Third edition (WAIS-III).* San Antonio, TX: Harcourt Assessment.

Wechsler, D. (2008). *Wechsler Adult Intelligence Scale, Fourth edition (WAIS-IV).* Boston, MA: Pearson.

Weinberg, R. A., Scarr, S., & Waldman, I. D. (1992). The Minnesota Transracial Adoption Study: A follow-up of IQ test performance at adolescence. *Intelligence, 16,* 117–135.

Weisberg, R. W. (1994). Genius and madness? A quasi-experimental test of the hypothesis that manic-depression increases creativity. *Psychological Science, 5,* 361–367.

West, R. F., Meserve, R. J., & Stanovich, K. E. (2012). Cognitive sophistication does not attenuate the bias blind spot. *Journal of Personality and Social Psychology, 103,* 506–519.

Wicherts, J. M., Dolan, C. V., & van der Maas, H. L. J. (2010). A systematic literature review of the average IQ of sub-Saharan Africans. *Intelligence, 38,* 1–20.

Willerman, L. (1979). *The psychology of individual and group differences.* San Francisco, CA: Freedman.

Willerman, R., Schultz, J. N., Rutledge, J. N., & Bigler, D. D. (1991). In vivo brain size and intelligence. *Intelligence, 15,* 223–228.

Willingham, D. T. (2004). Reframing the mind: Howard Gardner became a hero among educators simply by redefining talents as "intelligences." *Education Next, 4,* 18–24.

Wilson, J. Q., & Herrnstein, R. J. (1985). *Crime and human nature: The definitive study of the causes of crime.* New York, NY: Simon & Schuster.

Winner, E. (1999). Uncommon talents: Gifted children, prodigies, and savants. *Scientific American Presents: Exploring Intelligence, 9,* 32–37.

Witelson, S. F., Beresh, H., & Kiger, D. L. (2006). Intelligence and brain size in 100 postmortem brains, sex, lateralization and age factors. *Brain, 129,* 386–398.

Witelson, S. F., Kigar, D. L., & Harvey, T. (1999). The exceptional brain of Albert Einstein. *Lancet, 353,* 2149–2153.

Witty, P. A., & Jenkins, M. D. (1934). The educational achievements of a group of gifted Negro children. *Journal of Educational Psychology, 25,* 585–597.

Yang, S., & Sternberg, R. J. (1997). Taiwanese Chinese people's conceptions of intelligence. *Intelligence, 25,* 21–36.

Zajonc, R. B. (1975). Birth order and intelligence: Dumber by the dozen. *Psychology Today, 8*(8), 37–43.

Zajonc, R. B. (1976). Family configuration and intelligence: Variations in scholastic aptitude scores parallel trends in family size and the spacing of children. *Science, 192,* 227–236.

Zernike, K. (2000, May 31). Girls a distant 2nd in geography gap among U.S. pupils. *New York Times.* Retrieved from http://www.nytimes.com/2000/05/31/nyregion/girls-a-distant-2nd-in-geography-gap-among-us-pupils.html?pagewanted=1

Ziegler, M., Danay, E., Heene, M., Asendorpf, J., & Bühner, M. (2012). Openness, fluid intelligence, and crystallized intelligence: Toward an integrative model. *Journal of Research in Personality, 46*(2), 173–183. http://dx.doi.org/10.1016/j.jrp.2012.01.002

Credits

Photo Credits

Human Development

From Chapter 10 of *Psychology: From Inquiry to Understanding*, Third Edition. Scott O. Lilienfeld, Steven Jay Lynn, Laura L. Namy, Nancy J. Woolf. Copyright © 2014 by Pearson Education, Inc. All rights reserved.

Human Development

HOW AND WHY WE CHANGE

Think About It

Do emotionally traumatic experiences in infancy typically scar children for life?

Do American parenting and schooling techniques give children a developmental advantage relative to approaches used in other countries?

Can adolescents make mature decisions?

How does becoming a parent affect people's quality of life?

Is the aging process all downhill?

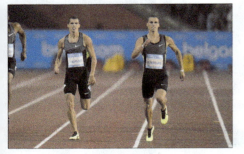

Olympic athletes Jonathan and Kevin Borlee share identical genes and nearly identical environments so it makes good sense that their running records are highly similar. Yet other identical twins are less similar. Investigating the combined influences of genes and environmental influences helps us to explain how such differences develop.

Human Development

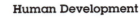

Jonathan and Kévin Borlée, Lucija and Ana Zaninović, Mo and Hassan Farah: three pairs of identical twins, six people with world-class athletic potential. Does that mean that these identical twins—who share 100 percent of their genes—have identical skills? If our skill development is a combination of nature (genes) and nurture (environment), then identical twins should attain identical achievements, right? Let's find out.

Jonathan and Kévin Borlée are Belgian sprinters trained by their father. Both specialize in the 400-meter race. Both attended Florida State University. Both have medaled in the European and World Championships. Both developed a stress fracture of the same bone in one of their feet within six weeks of each other. Both competed in the 400-meter finals in the 2012 London Olympics, where they came in fifth and sixth, finishing .02 seconds apart. Exactly what we'd predict, right? Identical genes, nearly identical environments, and nearly identical careers. Now let's look at another set of twins.

Mo and Hassan Farah were born in Somalia around the start of a bloody civil war. The brothers were inseparable, sleeping in the same bed and often eating from the same plate. Both boys could run like the wind, and when they raced, Hassan beat Mo just as often as Mo beat Hassan. As the civil war continued, their father sought safety in Great Britain but obtained permission to bring only one of the boys with him. Mo left for England at age 8 with his father, while Hassan remained in Africa. Twenty-one years later, how did their lives turn out? Hassan is a successful telecommunications engineer and a family man living a modest life in Somalia, but has had no athletic career. In contrast, Mo became a runner and competed in the 2012 Olympics for Great Britain. He won gold medals in the 5000- and 10,000-meter races. Why such different outcomes despite their identical DNA? The Farahs' story is a clear case of environmental differences influencing development. While Hassan was living in poverty with no resources to nourish his athletic potential, Mo was growing up in an environment that cultivated his talent. He had coaches, training facilities, sponsors, and opportunities to compete throughout his teens and twenties. Obviously, genes alone weren't enough to make an Olympic athlete, but the genes and environment combined did the trick.

Now let's look at one more twin pair. Lucija and Ana Zaninović are from Croatia, and both became fascinated with taekwondo at age 13 after seeing it debut as a competitive sport at the 2000 Sydney Olympics. They began training with the same coach, and both began winning. Ana holds a World Championship title; Lucija, a European Championship title. Neither qualified for the 2008 Beijing Olympics, but both competed in the 2012 London Olympics. Yet there was no risk that they would have to compete against each other. Why not? Because they compete in different weight classes! Lucija, who competed in the lighter weight class, won the bronze medal, whereas Ana was eliminated in the quarterfinals. How can individuals with identical genes and virtually identical environments develop not only different skills levels, but also different *weights*? The mathematical equation for predicting development must be far more complex than genes + environment = outcome.

Why did the sisters differ? We don't know for sure, but it's not uncommon for one twin to be born heavier than the other. This happens when one twin consumes more resources in the womb. So perhaps an early imbalance in weight and strength influenced their later weights and skill levels. Alternatively, perhaps the twins were treated differently because of their different sizes. Or perhaps the smaller of the two sisters was given more support, attention, or encouragement, enabling her to medal while her sister faltered.

The tales of these three twin pairs, like those of other case studies, raise far more questions than answers—in this case, about how genes and environments combine to lead to developmental outcomes, some similar, some different. Case studies are almost always better suited to raising questions than answering them. Fortunately, as we'll soon learn, psychologists have developed ingenious methods for shedding light on the causes of development over time.

Special Considerations in Human Development

1. Identify ways to think scientifically about developmental findings.
2. Clarify how nature and nurture can contribute to development.

Developmental psychology is the study of how behavior changes over the lifespan. Before we explore issues of how we develop, we need to come to grips with several challenges that often arise when investigating psychological development. Understanding these challenges, along with the scientific thinking principles we've encountered throughout this text, will provide us with the equipment we need to evaluate the causes of physical, cognitive, emotional, and social changes from childhood to old age.

Watch in **MyPsychLab** the **Video:** The Big Picture: Different Perspectives on the World

Post Hoc Fallacy

We've learned throughout the text that correlation between two variables measured at the same time doesn't mean that one causes the other. But when it comes to development, where things happen progressively over time, this logical fallacy can become particularly tempting. It's easy to assume that things that occur early in development cause things that come later. For example, if we learned that children who are shy are more likely to become engineers as adults, we could easily imagine plausible arguments for how shyness might lead to interests in engineering. But now imagine we learned that nearly 100 percent of serial killers drank milk as children. It would be silly to conclude that milk drinking creates mass murderers. We wouldn't have grounds for inferring causation from this linkage, because many factors could have influenced both behaviors. This logical error—the mistake of assuming that because A comes before B, A must cause B—is called the **post hoc fallacy** (*post hoc* is Latin for "after this").

◀ **CORRELATION VS. CAUSATION**
Can we be sure that A causes B?

Bidirectional Influences

Human development is almost always a two-way street: developmental influences are bidirectional. Children's experiences influence their development, but their development also influences what they experience. Psychological traffic from parents to children runs in both directions: Parents influence their children's behavior, which in turn influences parents' reactions, and so on (Bell, 1968; Collins et al., 2000; O'Connor et al., 1998). Children also change their environments by acting in ways that create changes in the behaviors of their siblings, friends, and teachers (Plomin, DeFries, & Loehlin, 1977; Steele, Rasbash, & Jenkins, 2012). Furthermore, as children grow older, they play an increasingly active role in selecting their own environments.

It's crucial to keep bidirectional influences in mind, because pop psychology is chock full of *unidirectional* explanations: those that attempt to explain development in terms of a one-headed arrow. Parents fight with each other → their children react negatively. Children witness violence at school → they become more aggressive. There's probably a kernel of truth in each of those explanations. Yet they typically tell only part of the story. That's why so many arrows in psychology contain two heads (↔), not one. In the study of human development, two "heads" are almost always better—or least more accurate—than one, at least as far as arrows are concerned.

? Can you think of both an environmental and genetic explanation for why adolescents in gangs become trouble makers?

(See answer upside down at bottom of page.)

Keeping an Eye on Cohort Effects

Imagine we conduct a study designed to examine how people's knowledge of computers changes with age. Our hypothesis is simple: People's knowledge of computers should increase steadily from adolescence until early adulthood, after which it should level off at about age 30. After about age 30, we predict, knowledge of computers should remain about the same or increase slightly. To test our hypothesis, we sample 100,000 people in the U.S. population, with a broad age range from 18 to 80. We carefully screen out people with dementia or other forms of brain damage to ensure that we're not accidentally including people with cognitive impairment. However, contrary to our hypothesis, we find that people's knowledge of computers declines dramatically with age, especially between the ages of 60 and 80. What did we do wrong?

developmental psychology
study of how behavior changes over the lifespan

post hoc fallacy
false assumption that because one event occurred before another event, it must have caused that event

Answer: Environmental explanation—kids who hang out with troublemakers can be persuaded to engage in troubled behaviors themselves. Genetic explanation—kids who are genetically predisposed to engage in destructive acts are driven to seek out other like-minded kids.

RULING OUT RIVAL HYPOTHESES ▶

Have important alternative explanations for the findings been excluded?

Older adults may be less comfortable or skilled with technology because it wasn't around when they were growing up, limiting our ability to compare performance of older adults with younger adults in a cross-sectional study.

RULING OUT RIVAL HYPOTHESES ▶

Have important alternative explanations for the findings been excluded?

Longitudinal designs track the lives of the same groups of people over time. The classic "Up Series" directed by Michael Apted used the same technique by tracing the lives of 14 British people, including Jackie, Lynn, and Sue, shown here, from age 7 all the way through age 56.

cross-sectional design
research design that examines people of different ages at a single point in time

cohort effect
effect observed in a sample of participants that results from individuals in the sample growing up at the same time

It turns out that we forgot to consider an alternative explanation for our findings. We started out by asking a perfectly sensible question. But in science, we also must make sure that the design we select is the right one to answer the question. In this case, it wasn't. We used a **cross-sectional design**, a design in which researchers examine people who are of different ages at a single point in time (Achenbach, 1982; Raulin & Lilienfeld, 2008). In a cross-sectional design, we obtain a "snapshot" of each person at a single age; we assess some people when they're 24, some when they're 47, others when they're 63, and so on.

The major problem with cross-sectional designs is that they don't control for **cohort effects**: effects due to the fact that sets of people who lived during one time period, called *cohorts*, can differ in some systematic way from sets of people who lived during a different time period. In the study we've described, cohort effects are a serious shortcoming, because before the late 1980s, few Americans used computers. So those over 60 years old may not be as computer savvy as younger folks for reasons that have nothing to do with aging, but everything to do with the era in which they grew up.

A longitudinal design is the only sure way around this problem. In a **longitudinal design**, psychologists track the development of the same group of participants over time (Shadish, Cook, & Campbell, 2002). Rather than obtaining a snapshot of each person at only one point in time, we obtain the equivalent of a series of home movies taken at different ages. This design allows us to examine true *developmental* effects: changes over time within individuals as a consequence of growing older (Adolph & Robinson, 2011). Without longitudinal designs, we can be tricked into concluding that event A comes before result B even when it doesn't. For example, much of the pop psychology literature warns us that divorce results in children engaging in disruptive behaviors such as throwing tantrums, breaking rules, defying authority figures, and committing crimes (Wallerstein, 1989). Yet a longitudinal study that tracked a sample of boys over several decades revealed otherwise: Boys whose parents divorced exhibited these behaviors *years before* the divorce occurred (Block & Block, 2006; Block, Block, & Gjerde, 1986). This raises some interesting unanswered questions about why parents with male children who engage in problem behaviors are more likely than other parents to get divorced. The key point is that the longitudinal nature of the design enabled us to rule out the plausible—but in this case incorrect—explanation that the boys' behaviors are a reaction to the divorce.

Although longitudinal designs are ideal for studying change over time, they can be costly and time-consuming. For example, our study of computer literacy would take about six decades to complete. Such studies also can result in *attrition*—participants dropping out of the study before it is completed. Attrition can be a particular problem when the participants who drop out differ in important ways from those who stay in. When longitudinal designs aren't feasible, we should interpret the results of cross-sectional studies with caution, bearing in mind that cohort effects may account for any observed changes at different ages. Nevertheless, there are some research questions for which cross-sectional designs are more useful than longitudinal designs. For example, when comparing the performance of 2-year-olds with 2½-year-olds on a memory test, the potential for cohort effects seems low. In fact, in such a study, a longitudinal design could be problematic because administering the same memory task to the same children twice so close together would probably result in better performance on the second test simply because the task was familiar. We should also bear in mind that most longitudinal studies don't use experimental designs , because we typically can't randomly assign individuals to conditions. As a result, we can't use most of these studies to infer cause-and-effect relationships.

The Influence of Early Experience

There's no doubt that early life experiences sometimes shape later development in powerful ways. Indeed, early input from the outside world exerts a significant impact on brain development. Yet these influences on brain and behavior don't stop after the first few years, but operate throughout the lifespan. Therefore, we shouldn't make the mistake of overestimating the impact of experiences during infancy on long-term development. Although such experiences are influential, they can often be reversed (Bruer, 1999; Clarke & Clarke, 1976; Kagan, 1998; Paris, 2000).

Indeed, most children are more resilient than we often believe. For example, contrary to popular psychology sources, separating an infant from its mother during the first few hours after birth has no negative consequences for children's emotional adjustment (Klaus & Kennell, 1976). There's no question that early experience plays an important role in children's physical, cognitive, and social development. But there's no reason to believe that later experiences play any less of a role in development than do early experiences. In fact, later positive experiences can often counteract the negative effects of early deprivation (Kagan, 1975; McGoron, Gleason, Smyke et al., 2012). Neuroscience research shows that the brain changes in important ways in response to experience throughout childhood and well into early adulthood (Greenough, 1997), supporting the notion that later experiences in life can be as influential as those in early childhood. Most children are also remarkably capable of withstanding stress and trauma, emerging from potentially traumatic experiences, including kidnappings and even sexual abuse, in surprisingly good shape (Bonanno, 2004; Cicchetti & Garmezy, 1993; Garmezy, Masten, & Tellegen, 1984; Rind, Tromovitch, & Bauserman, 1998; Salter et al., 2003). It's not uncommon for these children to show some short-term negative effects, including changes in behavior or sleep routines, and certainly some children experience long-term negative outcomes. But fortunately, most children bounce back from these events with little permanent damage to their well-being.

Clarifying the Nature–Nurture Debate

Both *nature*—our genetic endowment—and *nurture*—the environments we encounter—play powerful roles in shaping development. Yet as we'll soon see, disentangling their effects is far from simple, because nature and nurture intersect in a variety of fascinating ways, which we've summarized in **TABLE 1**.

In the mid-1990s, Betty Hart and Todd Risley (1995) published a now-classic longitudinal study that showed that parents who speak a lot to their children produce children with larger vocabularies than parents who don't. The study has been replicated using different populations and measures (Greenwood et al., 2011). Hart and Risley's finding provides evidence for a powerful environmental influence on children's vocabulary, right? Well, not so fast. In intact families, parents and children share not only environment, but genes, too. To use a term you may already know, genes and environment are *confounded*. So there's an alternative explanation for Hart and Risley's findings: Perhaps they reflect the fact that parents who speak a lot to their children have higher vocabularies themselves. Vocabulary size is partly influenced by genetic factors (Stromswold, 2001), so these parents may merely be passing on their genetic predisposition for better vocabularies to their children. Many studies of human development are subject to the same confound.

◀ **REPLICABILITY**
Can the results be duplicated in other studies?

◀ **RULING OUT RIVAL HYPOTHESES**
Have important alternative explanations for the findings been excluded?

GENE–ENVIRONMENT INTERACTION. Nature and nurture sometimes *interact* over the course of development, meaning that the effect of one depends on the contribution of the other. For example, some, but not all, studies shows that people who possess a gene that results in low production of an enzyme called *monoamine oxidase* (MAO) are at somewhat

TABLE 1 Intersections of Nature and Nurture. Nature and nurture are hard to disentangle—it's easy to mistake an environmental effect for a genetic effect, and vice versa. Here are some of the ways that genes and environment can intersect, making it difficult to separate out the influence of each.

NATURE–NURTURE INTERSECTIONS	DEFINITIONS
Gene–Environment Interactions	The impact of genes on behavior depends on the environment in which the behavior develops.
Nature via Nurture	Genetic predispositions can drive us to select and create particular environments that influence our behavior, leading to the mistaken appearance of a pure effect of nature.
Gene Expression	Some genes "turn on" only in response to specific environmental events.

longitudinal design
research design that examines development in the same group of people on multiple occasions over time

425

heightened risk for developing into violent criminals (Moore, Scarpa, & Raine, 2002). In 2002, Avshalom Caspi and his colleagues conducted a longitudinal study of children who possessed this gene, some of whom committed violent crimes and some of whom didn't. The researchers discovered that whether this genetic risk factor is associated with violent behavior depends on whether children were exposed to a specific environmental factor. Specifically, children with *both* the low MAO gene *and* a history of maltreatment (such as physical abuse) were at heightened risk for antisocial behaviors like stealing, assault, and rape. Children with the low MAO gene alone weren't at heightened risk, even when they were maltreated (Caspi et al., 2002; Kim-Cohen et al., 2006). This finding illustrates **gene–environment interaction**: in many cases, the effects of genes depend on the environment, and vice versa.

NATURE VIA NURTURE. Nature and nurture are rarely independent. In particular, children with certain genetic predispositions often seek out and create their own environments, a phenomenon termed **nature via nurture** (Lykken, 1995; Ridley, 2003). In this way, nurture affords children the opportunity to express their genetic tendencies (Scarr & McCartney, 1983). For example, as they grow older, highly fearful children tend to seek out environments that protect them from their anxieties (Rose & Ditto, 1983). Because highly fearful children select safer environments, it may appear that growing up in safe environments helps to create fearfulness, when in fact the environment is a consequence of children's genetic predispositions.

GENE EXPRESSION. Strange as it may sound, environmental experiences actually turn genes on and off throughout our lives. This phenomenon of **gene expression** is one of the most significant discoveries to hit psychology over the past several decades (Champagne & Mashoodh, 2009; Plomin & Crabbe, 2000). Every one of the 100 trillion or so (give or take a few trillion) cells in our bodies contains every one of our genes. Yet only some of these genes are active at any given time, and it sometimes takes environmental experiences to flip their switches to "on." For example, children with genes that predispose them to anxiety may never become anxious unless a highly stressful event (for example, the death of a parent early in development) triggers these genes to become active. Gene expression reminds us that nurture affects nature. In turn, nature affects how we react to nurture, and so on (Akbarian & Nestler, 2013).

✔ **Study** and **Review** in **MyPsychLab**

Assess Your Knowledge   FACT or FICTION?

1. Just because one event precedes a second event doesn't necessarily mean that the first event causes the second.   **True / False**

2. Research shows that most children are passive recipients of their parents' influence. **True / False**

3. Most children exposed to severe stressors end up with healthy patterns of psychological adjustment.   **True / False**

4. Gene expression is predetermined at birth and doesn't change in response to environmental experiences.   **True / False**

Answers: 1. T ; 2. F ; 3. T ; 4. F

gene–environment interaction
situation in which the effects of genes depend on the environment in which they are expressed

nature via nurture
tendency of individuals with certain genetic predispositions to seek out and create environments that permit the expression of those predispositions

gene expression
activation or deactivation of genes by environmental experiences throughout development

The Developing Body: Physical and Motor Development

3 Track the trajectory of prenatal development and identify barriers to normal development.

4 Describe how infants learn to coordinate motion and achieve major motor milestones.

5 Describe physical maturation during childhood and adolescence.

6 Explain which aspects of physical ability decline during aging.

The human body begins to take shape long before birth, as does the ability to perform coordinated movements. Learning, memory, and even preferences—for certain sounds or body positions, for example—are also well under way in unborn infants. Nevertheless, the form and structure of the body, including the brain, undergo radical changes throughout the lifespan, shaping the range of behaviors exhibited across development.

Conception and Prenatal Development: From Zygote to Baby

During the **prenatal** (prior to birth) period of development, the human body acquires its basic form and structure.

The most dramatic changes in prenatal development occur in the earliest stages of pregnancy. Following conception, when a sperm cell fertilizes an egg to produce a **zygote**, prenatal physical development unfolds in three stages. In the *germinal stage*, the zygote begins to divide and double, forming a **blastocyst**—a ball of identical cells that haven't yet begun to take on any specific function in a body part. The blastocyst keeps growing as cells continue to divide for the first week and a half or so after fertilization (see **FIGURE 1**). Around the middle of the second week, the cells begin to differentiate, taking on different roles as the organs of the body begin to develop.

Once cells start to assume different functions, the blastocyst becomes an **embryo**. The *embryonic stage* continues from the second to the eighth week of development, during which limbs, facial features, and major organs (including the heart, lungs, and brain) begin to take shape. During this stage, many things can go wrong in fetal development. Spontaneous miscarriages often occur when the embryo doesn't form properly (Roberts & Lowe, 1975), frequently without the mother even knowing she was pregnant.

By the ninth week, the major organs are established, and the heart begins to beat. This final milestone is called the *fetal stage* because it's the point at which the embryo becomes a **fetus**. The fetus's "job" for the rest of the pregnancy is physical maturation. This phase is more about fleshing out what's already there than establishing new structures. The last third of pregnancy in particular is devoted almost entirely to "bulking up."

BRAIN DEVELOPMENT: 18 DAYS AND BEYOND. The human brain begins to develop a mere 18 days after fertilization. Unlike most organs, which are completely formed by birth and continue to grow only in size, our brains continue to develop well into adolescence and probably even early adulthood (Caviness et al., 1996).

Between the eighteenth day of pregnancy and the end of the sixth month, neurons begin developing at an astronomical rate, a process called *proliferation*. Some estimates place the rate of neural development as high as an astonishing 250,000 brain cells per minute at peak times. The fetus ends up manufacturing far more neurons than it will need as an infant. In addition to producing all of these cells, the brain must organize them to perform coordinated functions. Starting in the fourth month and continuing throughout pregnancy, migration of cells begins to occur. Neurons start to sort themselves out, moving to their final positions in specific structures of the brain, such as the hippocampus and cerebellum.

This series of photos depicts the transition from blastocyst (a mass of identical cells) (*top*) to embryo (preliminary development of skeleton, organs, and limbs) (*middle*) to fetus (recognizably human form) (*bottom*) during the first three months of pregnancy.

Watch in **MyPsychLab** the **Video:** Fetal Development

prenatal
prior to birth

zygote
fertilized egg

blastocyst
ball of identical cells early in pregnancy that haven't yet begun to take on any specific function in a body part

embryo
second to eighth week of prenatal development, during which limbs, facial features, and major organs of the body take form

fetus
period of prenatal development from ninth week until birth after all major organs are established and physical maturation is the primary change

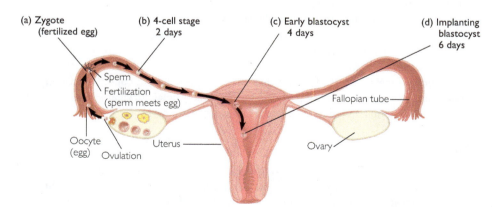

(a) Zygote (fertilized egg) (b) 4-cell stage 2 days (c) Early blastocyst 4 days (d) Implanting blastocyst 6 days

Sperm
Fertilization (sperm meets egg)
Fallopian tube
Oocyte (egg)
Ovulation
Uterus
Ovary

FIGURE 1 The Journey of a Fertilized Egg from Ovary to Uterus. After an egg is fertilized by a sperm cell, it begins traveling through the fallopian tube to the uterus. As it travels, cells begin to divide and duplicate, becoming a blastocyst. The blastocyst implants itself in the uterus by the sixth day. (Adapted from Marieb and Hoehn, 2007)

| 25 days | 35 days | 40 days | 50 days | 100 days |

| 5 months | 6 months | 7 months |

| 8 months | 9 months |

The fetal brain begins as a long tube that develops into a variety of different structures, with the brain stem (which controls basic functions like breathing and digestion) developing first, followed by cortical structures later in pregnancy. (Based on Restak, 1984)

CORRELATION VS. CAUSATION ▶
Can we be sure that A causes B?

Watch in MyPsychLab the Video: Fetal Alcohol Syndrome: Sidney

Different teratogens adversely affect different systems and may vary in their effects at different stages of pregnancy. For example, high levels of alcohol exposure can result in a collection of symptoms known as *fetal alcohol syndrome*. (Abel & Sokol, 1986)

OBSTACLES TO NORMAL FETAL DEVELOPMENT. Although most babies are born healthy and fully intact, fetal development can be disrupted in three ways: (1) exposure to hazardous environmental influences, (2) biological influences resulting from genetic disorders or errors in cell duplication during cell division, and (3) premature birth.

Hazardous Environmental Influences Most women don't even realize they're pregnant until after the fetus's body and brain development are well under way. As a result, women often engage unknowingly in activities that are potentially harmful to the fetus. **Teratogens** are environmental factors that can affect prenatal development negatively. They run the gamut from drugs and alcohol to chicken pox and X-rays. Even anxiety and depression in the mother are potential teratogens because they alter the fetus's chemical and physiological environment (Bellamy, 1998; Katz, 2012).

Alcohol exposure can result in **fetal alcohol syndrome**, which includes a host of symptoms, such as learning disabilities, physical growth retardation, facial malformations, and behavioral disorders (Abel, 1998). Cigarette smoking during pregnancy is one of the most prevalent teratogens. Mothers who smoke cigarettes or marijuana or who use other recreational drugs during pregnancy are particularly likely to deliver low birth weight babies, defined as less than 5½ pounds for a full-term baby (compared with an average birth weight of about 7½ pounds) (Pringle et al., 2005; Windham et al., 2000). Low birth weight is linked to a high risk of death, infection, developmental delays, and even psychological disorders such as depression and anxiety (Boyle et al., 2011; Copper et al., 1993; Schothorst & van Engeland, 1996). Nevertheless, it is unknown how many of these associations are due directly to low birth weight, as low birth weight may itself be a reflection of other difficulties during pregnancy.

Depending on the teratogen and when the embryo or fetus is exposed to it, some teratogens can influence how specific parts of the brain develop. Other teratogens exert a more general impact on brain development. Because the brain has such a long period of maturation relative to most other organs, it's particularly vulnerable to teratogens.

Genetic Disorders. Genetic disorders or random errors in cell division are another set of adverse influences on prenatal development. Often, a single cell, including the egg or sperm cell prior to fertilization, or even a family of cells is copied with some error or break in the genetic material. Like a page with a smudge that keeps being photocopied with that smudge preserved, these cells replicate with the error retained, resulting in impaired development of organs or organ systems. Any number of irregularities can result, some as minor as a birthmark and others as major as mental retardation, including Down syndrome, a disorder marked by specific facial and body malformations.

Premature Birth. A full-term baby is born after 40 weeks of pregnancy—actually closer to 9½ months than 9 months, as is commonly believed. Premature infants ("preemies") are those born at fewer than 36 weeks' gestation. The *viability* point, the point in pregnancy at which infants can typically survive on their own, is around 25 weeks. In rare cases, fetuses as young as 22 weeks have survived, but only with serious physical and cognitive impairments. Preemies have underdeveloped lungs and brains and are often unable to engage in basic physiological functions such as breathing and maintaining a healthy body temperature. They often experience serious delays in cognitive and physical development. With each week of pregnancy, the odds of fetal survival increase and the odds of developmental disorders decrease (Hoekstra et al., 2004).

Infant Motor Development: How Babies Get Going

Starting at birth, infants begin to learn how to make use of their bodies through movement and how to coordinate interactions with their environment. Some aspects of motor coordination are evident even at birth, but others develop gradually throughout infancy and early childhood.

SURVIVAL INSTINCTS: INFANT REFLEXES. Infants are born with a large set of automatic motor behaviors—or *reflexes*—that are triggered by specific types of stimulation. Reflexes fulfill important survival needs (Swaiman & Ashwal, 1999). One example is the *sucking reflex*, an automatic response to oral stimulation. If we put something in a baby's mouth (including a finger—try it sometime … with the parents' permission, of course!), she'll clamp down and begin sucking. A related reflex is the *rooting reflex*, which serves the same survival need: eating. If we softly stroke a hungry infant's cheek, she'll automatically turn her head toward our hand and begin casting about with her mouth, eagerly seeking a nipple to suck. These reflexes help keep infants alive; if they needed to learn through trial and error that sucking on an object yields nourishment, they might starve trying to get the hang of it.

LEARNING TO GET UP AND GO: COORDINATING MOVEMENT. But reflexes can get babies only so far; they must learn other motor behaviors through trial and error. **Motor behaviors** are bodily motions that occur as result of self-initiated force that moves the bones and muscles. The major motor milestones during development include sitting up, crawling, standing unsupported, and walking. The age at which different children reach these milestones varies enormously, although almost all children acquire them in the same order (see **FIGURE 2**).

We take for granted how easy it is to reach for a cup of coffee sitting on a table, yet the calculations our body makes—the physical adjustments that control our body's positioning and the direction and speed of our movements—to accomplish that act are incredibly complex. They're also customized to fit each situation, or we'd end up knocking our coffee to the floor most of the time (Adolph, 1997). As novices, babies haven't yet learned to perform the lightning-quick calculations needed for good hand-eye coordination and motor planning. Crawling and walking are even more complicated than reaching, because they involve supporting the infant's weight, coordinating all four limbs, and somehow keeping track of where the baby is heading.

FIGURE 2 The Progression of Motor Development. Different children typically achieve major motor milestones in the same order, although each milestone requires an entirely new set of motor coordination skills. For example, cruising, walking, and running look similar but require very different muscle groups and shifts in weight to accomplish movement.

FACTORS INFLUENCING MOTOR DEVELOPMENT. There's a wide range in the rate and manner in which children achieve motor milestones. Some crawl and walk much earlier than others do, and a few skip the crawling stage entirely. These findings suggest that these skills don't necessarily build on each other in a causal fashion, as the post hoc fallacy might lead us to believe. What remains to be explained, then, is why all children acquire motor milestones in the same order.

Physical maturation of both the body and the brain plays a key role in allowing children to become increasingly steady and flexible in their movements. Some motor developments may be a consequence of innately programmed patterns of motion that become activated in response to stimuli. Many motor achievements, such as crawling and walking, also depend on the physical maturation of the body, allowing children to acquire the necessary strength and coordination. Differences among children in the rate at which motor development unfolds are also tied to their body weight. Heavier babies tend to achieve milestones more gradually than lighter babies do because they need to build up their muscles more before they can support their weight (Thelen & Ulrich, 1991).

teratogen
an environmental factor that can exert a negative impact on prenatal development

fetal alcohol syndrome
condition resulting from high levels of prenatal alcohol exposure, causing learning disabilities, physical growth retardation, facial malformations, and behavioral disorders

motor behavior
bodily motion that occurs as result of self-initiated force that moves the bones and muscles

Cultural and parenting practices also play crucial roles in motor development (Thelen, 1995). Considerable variability exists in the timing of developmental milestones across cultures. In Peru and China, infants are tightly swaddled in blankets that provide warmth and a sense of security but prevent free movement of the limbs (Li et al., 2000). Swaddled babies tend to cry less and sleep more soundly, but prolonged swaddling over the first year of life slows down their motor development. In contrast, many African and West Indian mothers engage in a variety of stretching, massage, and strength-building exercises with their infants. This practice, which looks harmful to American eyes, speeds up infants' motor development (Hopkins & Westra, 1988). Even things as basic as cloth or disposable diapers, which are prevalent only in industrialized societies, slow down walking (Cole, Lingeman, & Adolph, 2012).

The practices of swaddling and stretching infants can seem extreme to many Americans, but these are our cultural perspectives. Although cultural variability in these practices influences the rate of motor development, none of these early physical experiences result in long-term advantages or impairments.

Growth and Physical Development Throughout Childhood

Our bodies continue to change dramatically through early childhood and adolescence. Careful inspection of an infant reveals that he has no apparent neck, a head almost half the size of his torso, and arms that don't even reach the top of his head. Over the course of childhood, different parts of the body grow at different rates and the ultimate proportions of the body are quite different than at birth. For example, the absolute size of the head continues to increase with development, but it grows at a slower pace than the torso or legs. As a result, an adolescent or young adult has a smaller head-size-to-body-size ratio than an infant (see **FIGURE 3**).

FIGURE 3 Changes in Body Proportions During Development. This figure displays the proportional size of the head, torso, and limbs across the lifespan when scaled to the same overall height. The size of the head relative to the body decreases dramatically over the course of development, whereas the relative length of the legs increases dramatically.

Throughout this text, we've sprinkled numerous examples of popular psychology wisdom that are false. Well, here's some common knowledge that's *true:* Growth spurts are real. Michael Hermanussen and his colleagues found "mini growth spurts" occurring every 30 to 55 days in children ages 3 to 16, followed by lulls during which growth was much slower (Hermanussen, 1998; Hermanussen et al., 1988). One study that measured three infants daily found that infants' growth occurs more suddenly. They showed no growth at all for days at a time, followed by overnight increases of as much as an inch (Lampl, Veldhuis, & Johnson, 1992)! Nevertheless, other studies have failed to replicate this finding, leading some researchers to propose that growth is actually more gradual, with shifts in the *rate* of growth at various points in development (Heinrichs et al., 1995; Hermanussen & Geiger-Benoit, 1995). The evidence suggests that there are spurts, but that the periods between them aren't marked by a total absence of growth. Interestingly, infants sleep longer and take more frequent naps during growth periods (Lampl & Johnson, 2011), although the direction of causality between sleep and growth isn't clear. In all likelihood, both sleep and growth are the result of a third variable, such as metabolism or gene expression.

REPLICABILITY ▶
Can the results be duplicated in other studies?

CORRELATION VS. CAUSATION ▶
Can we be sure that A causes B?

During the 2012 Olympic Games in London, female Chinese swimmer Ye Shiwen surprised the world by swimming as fast as many male Olympiads. Men's greater strength, on average, makes it challenging for women to compete at the men's level in athletics.

Physical Maturation in Adolescence: The Power of Puberty

Our bodies don't reach full maturity until **adolescence**—the transitional period between childhood and adulthood commonly associated with the teenage years. Adolescence is a time of profound physical changes, many of them hormonal. The pituitary gland stimulates physical growth, and the reproductive system releases sex hormones—estrogens and androgens —into the bloodstream, triggering growth and other physical changes. Many people think of androgens, such as testosterone, as male hormones and estrogens as female hormones. In fact, both types of hormones are present in both sexes in varying proportions. In boys, testosterone promotes increases in muscle tissue, growth of facial and body hair, and broadening of the shoulders. In girls, estrogens promote breast growth, uterus and vaginal maturation,

Acne
Beard
Voice change
Underarm hair, chest hair, muscle development
Pubic hair
Enlargement of penis, scrotum, testes
Ejaculation

Acne
Underarm hair
Breast development
Rounded body contours
Pubic hair
Enlargement of uterus, clitoris, labia
Menstruation

FIGURE 4 Physical and Sexual Maturation During the Preteen and Teenage Years. Hormones result in rapid growth to full adult height. They also trigger changes in the reproductive system and in secondary sex characteristics such as increased breast size and broader hips in girls and broader shoulders in boys.

hip broadening, and the onset of menstruation. Androgens in girls also induce physical growth and the growth of pubic hair (see **FIGURE 4**). Boys' muscle strength begins to exceed girls' in adolescence, and boys undergo a variety of changes in lung function and blood circulation. These changes result in greater average physical strength and endurance in boys than in girls, explaining the divergence between boys' and girls' athletic ability that emerges in adolescence (Beunen & Malina, 1996; Malina & Bouchard, 1991).

A crucial component of hormonal changes in adolescence is **puberty**, or *sexual maturation*—the attainment of physical potential for reproduction. Maturation includes changes in **primary sex characteristics**, which include the reproductive organs and genitals. Maturation also includes changes in **secondary sex characteristics**, which are sex-differentiating characteristics that don't relate directly to reproduction, such as breast enlargement in girls, deepening voices in boys, and pubic hair in both genders. In girls, **menarche**—the onset of menstruation—tends not to begin until they've achieved full physical maturity. Menarche is the body's insurance plan against allowing girls to become pregnant before their bodies can carry an infant to term and give birth safely (Tanner, 1990). There's variability in when menstruation begins because girls reach full physical maturity at different ages.

Spermarche, the first ejaculation, is the comparable milestone in boys; it occurs, on average, at around 13 years of age. Because boys need not be fully physically mature to bear children, spermarche isn't as closely tied to physical maturity as is menarche. In fact, boys often take much longer to mature fully than girls do, which is why we often see sixth- and seventh-grade girls towering above their male counterparts. The first signs of sexual maturation in boys are enlargement of the testicles and penis and growth of pubic hair (Graber, Petersen, & Brooks-Gunn, 1996). Later, boys begin to see signs of facial and body hair, and their voices deepen.

The timing of puberty in boys and girls is genetically influenced; identical twins tend to begin menstruating within a month of each other, whereas fraternal twins average about a year's difference in onset (Tanner, 1990). Still, a variety of environmental factors, some relating to physical health, affect when adolescents reach puberty. Adolescents from higher socioeconomic status households generally have access to better nutrition and health care and reach puberty earlier as a result (Eveleth & Tanner, 1976).

Factoid

The age of menarche in girls has decreased over the past 100 years, moving from around 15 to around 13 years of age on average. This change is probably due primarily to better nutrition and health care (Tanner, 1998) although other factors, such as increased exposure to hormones fed to livestock, may also contribute (Soto et al., 2008). Researchers have also found signs of puberty in American boys up to two years earlier than previously reported—age 9 on average for blacks, age 10 for whites and Hispanics (Herman-Giddens et al., 2012).

These seventh-grade students vary in physical height, but the girl (on the right) is the tallest of the bunch. Girls tend to mature earlier and more rapidly than boys do. The girl is probably close to reaching her adult height, whereas the boys still have a great deal of growing to do.

adolescence
the transition between childhood and adulthood commonly associated with the teenage years

puberty
the achievement of sexual maturation resulting in the potential to reproduce

primary sex characteristic
a physical feature such as the reproductive organs and genitals that distinguish the sexes

secondary sex characteristic
a sex-differentiating characteristic that doesn't relate directly to reproduction, such as breast enlargement in women and deepening voices in men

menarche
start of menstruation

spermarche
boys' first ejaculation

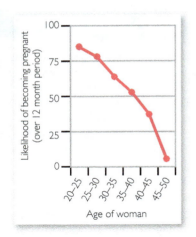

FIGURE 5 Fertility Peaks in the Twenties and Declines Thereafter. Women reach peak fertility between the ages of 20 and 25. The likelihood of a woman becoming pregnant drops dramatically between 30 and 50. This figure shows how the success of women becoming pregnant during one year's time declines with age.

Girls from wealthier countries tend to begin menstruating earlier than those from poorer countries. Girls in Japan and the United States usually start menstruating between 12½ and 13½ years of age, whereas girls in the poorest regions of Africa don't usually start menstruating until between the ages of 14 and 17 (Eveleth & Tanner, 1990).

Physical Development in Adulthood

After reaching full physical and sexual maturation during puberty, most of us reach our physical peaks in our early twenties (Larsson, Grimby, & Karlsson, 1979; Lindle et al., 1997). Strength, coordination, speed of cognitive processing, and physical flexibility also attain their highest levels in early adulthood.

PHYSICAL CHANGES IN MIDDLE ADULTHOOD. Americans spend millions of dollars each year on products and gimmicks marketed to make them look younger as they attempt to stave off the inevitable ravages of aging. Unfortunately, some of the effects of age on physical appearance and functioning are inescapable facts of life. As we age, we experience a decline in muscle tone and an increase in body fat. Basic sensory processes such as vision and hearing tend to decline too. Even our sense of smell becomes less sensitive when we reach our sixties or seventies.

Fertility in women declines sharply during their thirties and forties (see **FIGURE 5**), which has become a challenge for many women in contemporary society who opt to delay childbearing until they achieve career success. As a result, fertility treatments have been on the rise. The bad news is that the risks of serious birth defects in babies increase substantially among women who become pregnant in their thirties and forties.

One of the major milestones of physical aging in women is **menopause**—the termination of menstruation, signaling the end of a woman's reproductive potential. Menopause is triggered by a reduction in estrogen, which can result in "hot flashes"

Answers are located at the end of the text.

ANTI-AGING TREATMENTS

evaluating CLAIMS

Many people are in search of a "fountain of youth"—a quick, easy, and affordable way to reduce or even reverse the signs of aging. A variety of products such as creams and serums purport to do exactly this, yet which of them—if any—are effective? Let's evaluate some of these claims, which are modeled after actual ads for anti-aging products.

"We are affiliated with *various medical schools* and our product is *used by thousands of physicians* nationwide."

This claim indicates that the program is affiliated with medical schools and used by physicians, creating a sense of legitimacy, but it neglects to mention which medical schools. Moreover, this claim commits the argument from authority fallacy.

"We hold *exclusive worldwide rights* to a highly refined supplement and are making it *available to the public for a limited time* only so act now!"

Beware of ads that claim to have a scarcity of resources or promise you exclusive access to a product.

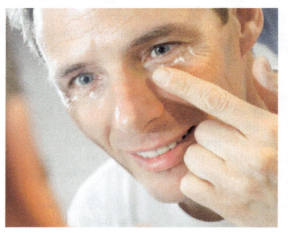

"See how natural looking and youthful our product will make you. We offer *no overnight miracles or quick-fixes*, but subtle results over time."

By explaining that the results may take time, this ad avoids exaggerated claims. It also doesn't promise any specific quantifiable results, only that your appearance will be more "natural looking" and "youthful."

"In a *randomized, double-blind human study* our product showed a significant effect on the signs of aging."

Randomization and double-blind condition assignment are crucial components of experimental research. What additional information would you need to know about this experiment to evaluate whether the product's claims are legitimate?

marked by becoming incredibly hot, sweaty, and dry-mouthed. Many women report mood swings, sleep disruption, and temporary loss of sexual drive or pleasure. Interestingly, the prevalence of these effects varies across cultures. Although about 50 percent of North American women report hot flashes, less than 15 percent of Japanese women do (Lock, 1998). Moreover, the meaning of menopause for women also differs across cultures. Whereas more than half of Australian women fear menopause as a sign of aging, more than 80 percent of Laotian women say menopause symptoms have no personal significance for them (Sayakhot, Vincent, & Teede, 2012). A common misconception is that menopause is a period of heightened depression. Research suggests that women in menopause are no more prone to depression than are women at other phases of life (Busch, Zonderman, & Costa, 1994; Dennerstein, Lehert, & Guthrie, 2002).

Men experience nothing comparable to menopause; they can continue to reproduce well into old age. Still, there's a gradual decline in sperm production and testosterone levels with age, and maintaining an erection and achieving ejaculation can become a challenge—as the popularity of Viagra and Cialis television ads targeted toward aging males attests Like older women, older men are at heightened risk for having children with developmental disorders, including autism (Callaway, 2012). Despite changes in the reproductive equipment of aging adults, most senior citizens continue to experience healthy sex drives.

CHANGES IN AGILITY AND PHYSICAL COORDINATION WITH AGE. There are individual and task-specific differences in the effects of aging on motor coordination. Complex tasks show greater effects of age than do simpler ones (Luchies et al., 2002; Welford, 1977); simple motor tasks, such as tapping a finger to a beat, display relatively small declines (Ruff & Parker, 1993). Elderly adults also find it more difficult to learn new motor skills like learning to drive a new car (Guan & Wade, 2000).

Some individuals display greater age-related decreases than others. Strength training and increased physical activity may minimize some of these declines and increase lifespan (Fiatarone et al., 1990; Frontera et al., 1988; Hurley, Hanson, & Sheaff, 2011). Many of the changes we typically associate with aging are actually due not to aging itself, but to diseases that are correlated with age, like heart disease and arthritis. Although chronological age and physical health are negatively correlated, the great variability in how people age refutes the popular notion that old age invariably produces physical decline.

Research suggests that physical activity and strength training are valuable in minimizing age-related declines.

◀ **CORRELATION VS. CAUSATION**
Can we be sure that A causes B?

✓ **Study** and **Review** in **MyPsychLab**

Assess Your Knowledge — FACT or FICTION?

1. A fetus's brain produces only as many neurons as it will need as an infant.   True / False

2. Fetuses exposed to teratogens, such as cigarette smoke from their mothers, tend to be low-birth-weight infants at birth.   True / False

3. Children tend to achieve motor milestones in the same order even though the age of acquisition varies within and across cultures.   True / False

4. Androgens cause changes in boys at puberty, whereas estrogens cause changes in girls.   True / False

5. Elderly people's hearing, sight, and other senses decline, but their ability to learn new motor skills are still intact.   True / False

Answers: 1. F ; 2. T ; 3. T ; 4. F ; 5. F

menopause
the termination of menstruation, marking the end of a woman's reproductive potential

The Developing Mind: Cognitive Development

7 Understand major theories of how children's thinking develops.

8 Explain how children acquire knowledge in important cognitive domains.

9 Describe how attitudes toward knowledge change during adolescence.

Cognitive development—how we acquire the ability to learn, think, communicate, and remember over time—sheds light on the mystery of how we come to understand our worlds. Yet only relatively recently have psychologists constructed systematic theories of cognitive development across the lifespan.

Theories of Cognitive Development

Psychologists have generated a variety of theoretical perspectives to explain how our thinking develops. Cognitive developmental theories differ in three core ways:

1. Some propose *stagelike* changes in understanding (sudden spurts in knowledge followed by periods of stability); others, more *continuous* (gradual, incremental) changes in understanding.

2. Some adopt a *domain-general* account of development; others, a *domain-specific* account. Domain-general accounts propose that changes in children's cognitive skills affect most or all areas of cognitive function in tandem. In contrast, domain-specific accounts propose that children's cognitive skills develop independently and at different rates across different domains, such as reasoning, language, and counting.

3. They differ in their views of the main source of learning. Some models emphasize physical experience (moving around in the world); others, social interaction (how parents and peers engage with them); and still others, biological maturation (innate programming of certain mental capacities).

PIAGET'S THEORY: HOW CHILDREN CONSTRUCT THEIR WORLDS The Swiss psychologist Jean Piaget (1896–1980) was the first person to present a comprehensive account of cognitive development. He attempted to identify the stages that children pass through on their way to adult-like thinking. Piaget's theory led to the formation of cognitive development as a distinct discipline, and for decades, most research in this field focused on substantiating—or more recently, refuting—his claims.

Perhaps Piaget's greatest contribution was his insight that children aren't miniature adults. He showed that children's understanding of the world differs fundamentally from adults', but is perfectly rational given their limited experience with the world. For example, children often believe that their teachers live at school, a reasonable assumption given that's the only place they've seen their teachers. Piaget also demonstrated that children aren't passive observers of their worlds, but rather active learners who seek information and observe the consequences of their actions.

Piaget was a *stage theorist*. He proposed that children's development is marked by radical reorganization of thinking at specific transition points—stages—followed by periods during which their understanding of the world stabilizes. He also believed that the end point of cognitive development is the achievement of the ability to reason logically about hypothetical problems. As we'll see, each stage is characterized by a certain level of abstract reasoning capacity, with the ability to think beyond the here and now increasing at each stage. Piaget's stages are domain-general, slicing across all areas of cognitive capacity. Thus, a child capable of a certain level of abstract reasoning in mathematics can also achieve this level in a spatial problem-solving task.

Piaget proposed that cognitive change is a result of children's need to achieve *equilibration*: maintaining a balance between their experience of the world and their understanding of it. Children, he argued, are motivated to match their thinking about reality with their observations. When the child experiences something new, she checks whether that experience fits with her understanding of how the world works. If the information

Jean Piaget was the first scientist to develop a comprehensive theory of cognitive development. His ideas rested on the assumption that children's thinking was not just an immature form of adult thinking, but was fundamentally different from that of adults.

---

cognitive development
study of how children acquire the ability to learn, think, reason, communicate, and remember

is inconsistent, as when a child experiences the world as flat but learns in school that the earth is round, something must give way. Piaget suggested that children use two processes—assimilation and accommodation—to keep their thinking about the world in tune with their experiences.

Assimilation and Accommodation. The process of absorbing new experience into our current understanding is **assimilation**. If a child who believes the earth is flat (see **FIGURE 6a**) learns that the earth is round, she might assimilate this knowledge by picturing a flat disk, like a coin (see **FIGURE 6b**). This adjustment allows her to absorb this fact without changing her belief that the earth is flat. Children use assimilation to acquire new knowledge within a stage. During assimilation, the child's cognitive skills and worldviews remain unchanged, so she reinterprets new experiences to fit with what she already knows.

The assimilation process can continue for only so long. Eventually, the child can no longer reconcile what she believes with what she experiences. A child confronted with a globe will have a difficult time assimilating this information into her conception of the earth as flat. When a child can no longer assimilate experiences into her existing knowledge structures, something has to budge. She's forced to engage in accommodation.

Accommodation is the process of altering beliefs about the world to make them more compatible with experience. Stage changes are the result of accommodation, because accommodation forces children to enter a new way of looking at the world, in this case, by changing their conception from flat to round (see **FIGURE 6c**). This process of assimilating and accommodating in tandem ensures a state of harmony between the world and mind of the child—equilibration.

Piaget's Stages of Development. Piaget identified four stages, each marked by a specific way of understanding reality and a specific set of cognitive limitations (see **TABLE 2**).

1. **Sensorimotor stage:** From birth to about 2 years, the **sensorimotor stage** is marked by a focus on the here and now. Children's main sources of knowledge, thinking, and experience are their physical interactions with the world. They acquire all information through perceiving information from the world and observing the physical consequences of their actions. The major milestone of this stage, which forces children to accommodate and enter a new stage, is *mental representation*—the ability to think about things that are absent from immediate surroundings, such as remembering previously encountered objects. Children in this stage lack **object permanence**, the understanding that objects continue to exist even when out of view.

FIGURE 6 An Example of Assimilation and Accommodation in Action. A child's initial belief that the earth is flat (a) is adjusted through assimilation (b) when she learns the earth is round. Once her assimilated belief no longer fits with her experience, her belief undergoes accommodation (c).

(a)

(b) Assimilation

(c) Accommodation

? This child appears to have forgotten that the toy continues to exist after it's been hidden from view. **What Piagetian concept does this photograph illustrate?** (See answer upside down at bottom of page.)

assimilation
Piagetian process of absorbing new experience into current knowledge structures

accommodation
Piagetian process of altering a belief to make it more compatible with experience

sensorimotor stage
stage in Piaget's theory characterized by a focus on the here and now without the ability to represent experiences mentally

object permanence
the understanding that objects continue to exist even when out of view

TABLE 2 Descriptions of the Four Stages of Cognitive Development in Piaget's Theory.

STAGE	TYPICAL AGES	DESCRIPTION
Sensorimotor	Birth to 2 years	No thought beyond immediate physical experiences
Preoperational	2 to 7 years	Able to think beyond the here and now, but egocentric and unable to perform mental transformations
Concrete Operations	7 to 11 years	Able to perform mental transformations but only on concrete physical objects
Formal Operations	11 years to adulthood	Able to perform hypothetical and abstract reasoning

Answer: Object permanence

FIGURE 7 Piaget's Three Mountain Task.
Piaget's three mountain task requires children to look at a display from one perspective (View 1) and infer what someone would see if viewing the mountains from a different perspective, such as View 2. Piaget argued that egocentric reasoning in the preoperational stage prevents children from succeeding at this task.

Watch in **MyPsychLab** the **Video:** Piaget: Sensorimotor Stage

FIGURE 8 Piaget's Conservation Tasks.
Piaget's conservation tasks ask the child to examine two equal amounts and then watch as the researcher manipulates one of the two amounts in some way. The researcher then asks the child to compare the two quantities. The conservation of liquid task is on the top; the conservation of number task, on the bottom. To succeed at the conservation task, children need to say that the amounts remain the same even though they appear unequal.

Explore in **MyPsychLab** the **Concept:** Piaget's Stages of Cognitive Development

preoperational stage
stage in Piaget's theory characterized by the ability to construct mental representations of experience but not yet perform operations on them

egocentrism
inability to see the world from others' perspectives

conservation
Piagetian task requiring children to understand that despite a transformation in the physical presentation of an amount, the amount remains the same

concrete operations stage
stage in Piaget's theory characterized by the ability to perform mental operations on physical events only

formal operations stage
stage in Piaget's theory characterized by the ability to perform hypothetical reasoning beyond the here and now

A ball that disappears behind the television is, for all intents and purposes, gone: "Out of sight, out of mind." *Deferred imitation*, the ability to perform an action observed earlier, is also absent from the sensorimotor stage. Both object permanence and deferred imitation require children to think beyond what is immediately present.

2. **Preoperational stage:** Piaget proposed that from 2 until about 7 years, children pass through the **preoperational stage**, marked by an ability to construct mental representations of experience. Children in this stage can use such symbols as language, drawings, and objects as representations of ideas. When a child holds a banana and pretends it's a phone, he's displaying symbolic behavior. He has a mental representation that differs from his physical experience. Similarly, playing house in which one child pretends to be the mommy, one the daddy, and one the baby demonstrates an ability to assume imaginary roles that differ from actual roles.

Although the preoperational stage is characterized by clear advances in thinking, Piaget believed that children in this stage were hampered by **egocentrism**—an inability to see the world from others' point of view (see **FIGURE 7**). The preoperational stage is called "preoperational" because of another limitation, the inability to perform mental operations. Although preoperational children have mental representations, they can't perform mental

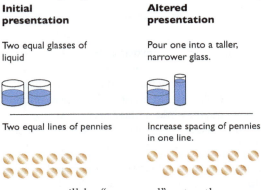

Initial presentation | Altered presentation

Two equal glasses of liquid | Pour one into a taller, narrower glass.

Two equal lines of pennies | Increase spacing of pennies in one line.

transformations ("operations") on them. For example, they can generate a mental image of a vase on a table if the vase isn't there. But they can't imagine what would happen to the vase if someone knocked it off the table. Piaget developed a set of **conservation** tasks like those shown in **FIGURE 8** to test children's ability to perform mental operations. These tasks ask children to determine whether a certain amount will be "conserved"—stay the same—following a physical transformation. Preoperational children routinely fail conservation tasks that older children find to be a breeze.

3. **Concrete operational stage:** Between 7 and 11 years old, according to Piaget, children enter the **concrete operations stage**, characterized by the ability to perform mental operations, but only for actual physical events. Children in this stage can now pass conservation tasks. They can also perform organizational tasks that require mental operations on physical objects, like sorting coins by size or setting up a battle scene with toy soldiers. But they're still poor at performing mental operations in abstract or hypothetical situations. They need physical experience as an anchor to which they can tether their mental operations.

4. **Formal operations stage:** Piaget's fourth and final stage, which he believed didn't emerge until adolescence, is the **formal operations stage**. It's then that children can perform what Piaget regarded as the most sophisticated type of thinking: hypothetical reasoning beyond the here and now, as in the pendulum task shown in **FIGURE 9**. This task requires children to experiment systematically with hypotheses and explain outcomes. Children at this stage can understand logical concepts, such as if–then statements ("If I'm late for school, then I'll get sent to the principal's office") and either–or statements ("Mom says I can either go to the game tonight or go to the sleepover tomorrow night."). They can also begin to think about abstract questions like the meaning of life.

Pros and Cons of Piaget's Theory. Piaget's theory was a significant landmark in psychology, as it helped us understand how children's thinking evolves into more adultlike thinking. Nevertheless, his theory turned out to be inaccurate in several ways. Subsequent research has revealed that much of development is more continuous than stagelike (Flavell, 1992; Klahr & MacWhinney, 1998; Siegler, 1995). Developmental change is also less domain-general than what Piaget proposed.

FIGURE 9 Pendulum Task. Piaget's pendulum task requires children to answer the question: "What makes a pendulum swing faster or slower?" Children have the opportunity to construct a pendulum using longer and shorter strings with heavier and lighter weights. Children in the formal operations stage can systematically manipulate various combinations of weights and lengths to observe how they influenced the speed of the swing.

Another criticism of Piaget's theory is that some phenomena he observed appeared to be at least partly a product of task demands. He often relied on children's ability to reflect and report on their reasoning processes. As a result, he probably underestimated children's abilities. Investigators using tasks that are less dependent on language have often failed to replicate Piaget's findings. In fact, many researchers have found that children can achieve important milestones such as object permanence and hypothesis testing at considerably earlier ages than reported by Piaget (Baillargeon, 1987; Gopnik, 2012).

◀ REPLICABILITY
Can the results be duplicated in other studies?

Piaget's methodologies may also have been culturally biased in that they elicited more sophisticated responses from children in Westernized societies with formal education than from children in non-Westernized societies. Indeed, non-Westernized children often reveal sophisticated insights when interviewed in a more culturally sensitive manner (Cole, 1990; Gellatly, 1987; Luria, 1976; Rogoff & Chavajay, 1995). Meanwhile, even in Western societies, a significant proportion of adolescents and even adults fail some formal operational tasks (Byrnes, 1988; Kuhn et al., 1995), suggesting that Piaget may have been overly optimistic about the typical course of cognitive development. Perhaps he based his conclusions on a particularly educated sample that skewed his estimates of the typical developmental trajectory. Piaget's observations themselves may also have been biased because many were based on tests of his own three children.

Despite these shortcomings, Piaget justifiably remains an important figure in the field of cognitive development (Lourenco & Machado, 1996). As a result of his legacy, psychologists today have reconceptualized cognitive development by:

1. Viewing children as different in kind rather than degree from adults.

2. Characterizing learning as an active rather than passive process.

3. Exploring general cognitive processes that may cut across multiple domains of knowledge, thereby accounting for cognitive development in terms of fewer—and more parsimonious—underlying processes.

◀ OCCAM'S RAZOR
Does a simpler explanation fit the data just as well?

VYGOTSKY'S THEORY: SOCIAL AND CULTURAL INFLUENCES ON LEARNING. At around the same time Piaget was developing his theory, Russian researcher Lev Vygotsky (1896–1934) was developing a different but equally comprehensive theory of cognitive development.

Vygotsky was particularly interested in how social and cultural factors influence learning. He noted that parents and other caretakers tend to structure the learning environment for children in ways that guide them to behave as if they've learned something before they have. This process is now known as **scaffolding**, a term borrowed from building construction (Wood, Bruner, & Ross, 1976). Just as builders provide external scaffolds for support while a building is under construction, parents provide a structure to aid their children. Over time, parents gradually remove structure as children become better able to complete tasks on their own, much like taking off training wheels from a bicycle.

scaffolding
Vygotskian learning mechanism in which parents provide initial assistance in children's learning but gradually remove structure as children become more competent

Lev Vygotsky (pictured here with his daughter) developed a theory of cognitive development that emphasized social and cultural information as the key sources of learning. Although Vygotsky's scholarly career was shortened by an early death (he died of tuberculosis at age 37), his theory is still extremely influential.

Watch in **MyPsychLab** the **Video:** Zone of Proximal Development: Cognitive

The term *scaffolding* is used to refer to the way parents structure the learning environment for their children. Here, the father is instructing his child on how to fit the shape onto a peg, but allowing the child to insert the shape herself.

zone of proximal development
phase of learning during which children can benefit from instruction

One of Vygotsky's most influential notions was developmental readiness for learning. He identified the **zone of proximal development** as the phase when children are receptive to learning a new skill but aren't yet successful at it. He suggested that for any given skill, children move from a phase when they can't learn it, even with assistance, to the zone of proximal development, during which they're ready to make use of scaffolding. In Vygotsky's view, children gradually learn to perform a task independently, but require guidance when getting started. Vygotsky also believed that different children can acquire skills and master tasks at different rates. For him, there were no domain-general stages.

Vygotsky's work has had a substantial impact on European, British, and American researchers and remains influential today, especially in educational settings, where guided learning and peer collaboration are popular (Gredler, 2012; Jaramillo, 1996; Rogoff, 1995; Tomasello, 2008). Whereas Piaget emphasized physical interaction with the world as the primary source of learning, Vygotsky emphasized social interaction.

CONTEMPORARY THEORIES OF COGNITIVE DEVELOPMENT. Theoretical accounts today are more diverse than when the field of cognitive development got off the ground, and few are strictly Piagetian or Vygotskian. Still, we can trace the roots of each theory to one of these two theorists.

General Cognitive Accounts. Several modern theories resemble Piaget's theories in that they emphasize general cognitive abilities and acquired rather than innate knowledge (Bloom, 2000; Elman, 2005). Contemporary theorists share Piaget's commitment to general cognitive processes and experience-based learning. Nevertheless, they differ from Piaget in that they regard learning as gradual rather than stagelike.

Sociocultural Accounts. These theories emphasize the social context and the ways in which interactions with caretakers and other children guide children's understanding of the world (Rogoff, 1998; Tomasello, 2000). Some sociocultural theorists emphasize experience-based learning; others, innate knowledge. But along with Vygotsky, they share a focus on the child's interaction with the social world as the primary source of development.

Modular Accounts. Like Vygotsky's theory, this class of theories emphasizes the idea of domain-specific learning, that is, separate spheres of knowledge in different domains (Carey, 1985; Waxman & Booth, 2001). For example, the knowledge base for understanding language may be independent of the ability to reason about space, with no overlapping cognitive skills between them.

Cognitive Landmarks of Early Development

We've already learned about some of the major cognitive developmental accomplishments within the realms of perception , memory , and language. But children must attain a variety of other cognitive skills to make sense of their worlds. Here, we'll review a few of the important milestones.

PHYSICAL REASONING: FIGURING OUT WHICH WAY IS UP. To understand their physical worlds, children must learn to reason about them. Children need to learn that objects are solid, they fall when dropped, and one object can disappear behind another and reappear on the other side. Adults take all of these concepts for granted, but they aren't obvious to novice experiencers of the world.

Piaget proposed that children don't master object permanence until between 8 and 12 months of age, because children younger than 8 months don't search for an object hidden under a cloth. Nevertheless, Renee Baillargeon (1987) showed that by five months and possibly younger, infants display an understanding of object permanence if given a task that doesn't require a physically coordinated search for the object.

psychomythology

THE MOZART EFFECT, BABY EINSTEIN, AND CREATING "SUPERBABIES"

For years, parents have yearned for a quick and easy educational method to boost their infants' intelligence. After all, in today's cutthroat world, what parents wouldn't want to place their child at a competitive advantage? To get a jump start, of course, parents must begin early, ideally soon after birth. This seemingly far-fetched hope that parents can turn their babies into miniature geniuses turned into apparent reality in 1993 with the publication of an article in the prestigious journal *Nature*. That paper reported that college students who listened to about ten minutes of a Mozart piano sonata showed a significant improvement on a spatial reasoning task compared with a group of students who listened to a relaxation tape (Rauscher, Shaw, & Ky, 1993). The *Mozart Effect*—the supposed enhancement in intelligence after listening to classical music (Campbell, 1997)—was born.

The 1993 finding didn't say anything about long-term enhancement of spatial ability, let alone intelligence in general. It applied only to a task administered almost immediately after listening to Mozart's music. And the findings were based entirely on college students. But this didn't stop the popular press and toy companies from taking the Mozart Effect ball and running with it. Companies soon marketed classical music recordings targeted toward babies, featuring claims that listening to the music of Mozart and other composers boosts infant intelligence. The state of Georgia even began issuing free Mozart recordings to all newborns to help enhance infant intelligence.

Unfortunately, for all those excited parents, attempts to replicate the Mozart Effect largely failed (Pietschnig, Voracek, & Formann, 2010). Many couldn't find the effect at all, and those who did discovered that it was trivial in magnitude (two IQ points or less) and of short duration (an hour or less; Chabris, 1999; Steele, Bass, & Crook, 1999). Later researchers helped to explain the Mozart Effect. The results of one study suggested that the effect may be due to the greater emotional arousal produced by listening to Mozart relative to other composers or silence (Thompson, Schellenberg, & Husain, 2001). In fact, listening to Mozart seems to be no better for improving spatial ability than listening to a similarly arousing passage from a scary story. These findings suggest that a more parsimonious explanation for the Mozart Effect is short-term arousal. Anything that boosts alertness is likely to increase performance on mentally demanding tasks, but it's unlikely to produce long-term effects on spatial ability or, for that matter, overall intelligence (Gray & Della Sala, 2007; Lilienfeld et al., 2009). Our advice: It's a wonderful idea to expose infants and children to great music. But don't expect it to turn babies into little geniuses.

The Mozart Effect is only one example of a research finding being overhyped to capitalize on parents' desires to boost their baby's intellect. In the 1980s, thousands of parents bombarded their newborn infants with foreign languages and advanced math in an effort to create "superbabies" (Clarke-Stewart, 1988). Alleged intelligence-improving products such as "Baby Einstein" toys and videos are a $100-million-a-year industry (Minow, 2005; Quart, 2006). Yet there's no evidence that these products work, either. In fact, research suggests that babies learn less from videos than from playing actively for the same time period (Anderson & Pempek, 2005; Zimmerman, Christakis, & Meltzoff, 2007).

Claims for the Mozart Effect have contributed to a huge industry of products for babies and young children, yet the scientific evidence for this effect is surprisingly weak.

◄ **REPLICABILITY**
Can the results be duplicated in other studies?

◄ **OCCAM'S RAZOR**
Does a simpler explanation fit the data just as well?

 Watch in **MyPsychLab** the **Video:**
Thinking Like a Psychologist: Smart Babies by Design

Baillargeon based her conclusions on studies of how long infants look at displays that are either consistent or inconsistent with object permanence. She hypothesized that young children failed Piaget's object permanence task not because they lacked object permanence, but because they lacked the ability to plan and perform a physical

◄ **RULING OUT RIVAL HYPOTHESES**
Have important alternative explanations for the findings been excluded?

search for the hidden toy. When Baillargeon eliminated these task demands by relying on a looking-based measure, an earlier mastery of object permanence emerged. Infants possess a basic understanding of some other aspects of how physical objects behave. For example, they know that unsupported objects should fall (Spelke, 1994). This knowledge becomes more refined with experience (see **FIGURE 10**) (Baillargeon & Hanko-Summers, 1990; Needham & Baillargeon, 1993). In particular, as we age, we become less reliant on intuitions and more reliant on evidence of how things actually work.

FIGURE 10 Children Learn Gradually That Unsupported Objects Will Fall. As early as 4½ months, infants expect objects that are completely unsupported, as in (a), to fall and objects that are completely supported, as in (e), not to fall. An understanding of how much support must be present to prevent an object from falling develops over time. Early on, infants expect that any contact with a support surface will prevent the object from falling, as in (b), (c), and (d). With experience, infants learn to expect that only those in (d) and (e), in which the majority of the weight is on the support surface, won't fall.

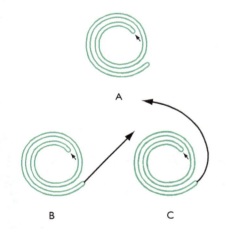

FIGURE 11 Intuitive Physics. Michael McCloskey (1983) posed the following problem to undergraduates: Imagine a ball enters a tube, as shown in drawing A. Which drawing illustrates how it will exit the tube, B or C? (See answer upside down at the bottom of the page.) If you got this wrong, don't feel bad, because many college students do, committing the same error that many school-age children do. This finding suggests that even as adults, we often don't fully outgrow mistaken notions of how the world works (Bloom & Weisberg, 2007) (*Source:* Reprinted by permission from the American Psychological Association)

Answer: B. Most people find C more intuitive, as this answer suggests that objects will continue in the same path of motion in which they began.

from inquiry to understanding

WHY IS SCIENCE DIFFICULT?

Many of us find science hard. Indeed, college students often find clever ways of avoiding courses in the so-called "hard sciences," such as physics and chemistry for this very reason. One reason science is challenging, to be sure, is that the "language" of science is mathematics, which many of us find difficult to master. Another reason is that science isn't intuitive: It doesn't come naturally to the human species. As a result, it needs to be learned and requires continual practice (Cromer, 1993; McCauley, 2012). Some psychologists, including Paul Bloom and Deena Weisberg (2007), have conjectured that the roots of our difficulties in grasping science stem partly from certain childhood notions that we never fully outgrow. Admittedly, in some ways, young children do act a bit like junior scientists: They are continually trying to figure out what causes what and sometimes draw correct conclusions in the process (Gopnik, 2012). Yet in other ways, children think unscientifically.

Take the work of Michael McCloskey (1983), who showed that many adults hold "commonsensical" but inaccurate ideas about physics, such as notions about the movement of objects. For example, children and most college students tend to get the problem shown in **FIGURE 11** wrong, because they expect objects to keep moving in the same trajectory in which they started moving. It's almost as though they attribute intention to the objects: They assume that the object "wants" to continue moving in the same direction in which it began. Similarly, most children incorrectly expect an object that is pushed off a flat surface, like a table, to keep moving horizontally in the air for some distance before it drops. This false belief is reinforced by cartoons, which frequently portray animals that fall off a cliff as traveling horizontally for several feet before realizing they are falling—and only then plummeting to the ground vertically.

In addition, young children assume that most animals, objects, and events have a purpose for existing (Kelemen, 1999; Kelemen, Rottman, & Seston, 2012). When asked why lions exist, 4-year-olds invoke a reason (such as "so that we can see them in the zoo"); the same holds true when they are asked why clouds exist (such as "to make it rain"; Bloom & Weisberg, 2007). Although adults partially outgrow this kind of reasoning, they may never do so entirely. In turn, this reasoning may render us prone to erroneous beliefs and resistant to certain scientific beliefs. For example, our tendency to detect intentions in purposeless events may render us likely to believe in ghosts, spirits, and other imaginary entities; it may also render us less willing to accept Darwin's theory of natural selection, which implies that organisms evolve without any long-term goal in mind.

If Bloom and Weisberg (2007) are right, science may be difficult because it conflicts with our deep-seated assumptions of how the world works and challenges our reliance on our impressions, intuitions, and observations. These natural tendencies may be rooted in early ways of thinking that still lurk within all of us (McCauley, 2012).

CONCEPTS AND CATEGORIES: CLASSIFYING THE WORLD. One of the most fundamental cognitive accomplishments is learning to categorize objects by kind. Children learn to recognize dogs even though dogs come in all shapes, sizes, and colors. They also learn to distinguish dogs from cats, horses, and goats. Categorization is crucial because it frees us from having to explore every object to find out what it is and does. Imagine if every time a baby were given a new bottle, she had to discover through trial and error what it was. Children, not to mention adults, wouldn't get very far without categories.

Even infants possess basic abilities to categorize. When shown a series of pictures of birds, infants eventually get bored with them and look away, but they exhibit fresh interest when shown a picture of a dinosaur. This finding implies that they've categorized birds as all of the same kind and therefore no longer new, but the dinosaur as belonging to a different category (Arterberry & Bornstein, 2012; Quinn & Eimas, 1996). Over the course of development, conceptual knowledge becomes richer, more detailed, and more flexible (Nelson, 1977). Children learn how objects are thematically related to each other, such as a dog and a bone being related because dogs eat bones. They also learn more about aspects of categories that explain how members of categories connect, such as that fruits taste sweet and grow on trees. This increased conceptual knowledge about categories assists them in reasoning about the world.

SELF-CONCEPT AND THE CONCEPT OF "OTHER": WHO WE ARE AND WHO WE AREN'T. Developing a sense of self as distinct from others is critical for children's development. Their ability to understand themselves as possessing unique identities mostly develops during the toddler and preschool years (Harter, 2012). But even by three months of age, infants possess some ability to distinguish themselves from others. Babies at this age who view videos of themselves side by side with another baby prefer to look at the image of the other baby (Bahrick, Moss, & Fadil, 1996; Rochat, 2001), suggesting that they recognize the other baby as being different from them. Even if all they can see is their legs and another infant's legs, they still prefer to watch the video of the other baby's legs. This finding demonstrates that babies' preference for another baby's face isn't merely a result of having seen their own face in the mirror or in photographs. As early as their first birthdays, children can recognize their images in a mirror (Amsterdam, 1972; Priel & deSchonen, 1986). By 2 years, they can recognize pictures of themselves and refer to themselves by name (Lewis & Brooks-Gunn, 1979). These accomplishments appear to be tied to development in a specific brain region, namely, the junction of the left temporal and parietal lobes (Lewis & Carmody, 2008). A further milestone is children's ability to understand that others' perspectives can differ from theirs—a capacity called **theory of mind** (Premack & Woodruff, 1978). Theory of mind refers to children's ability to reason about what other people believe. The big challenge for children on this front is to realize that "other people may not know what I know." In some sense, children know this fact by the time they're 1 or 2 years old, because they ask their parents questions like "Where's Daddy?" and "What's this?" revealing that they expect parents to know things they don't. Yet it's particularly challenging for children to realize that sometimes *they* know things that others don't.

A classic test of theory of mind is the *false-belief task* (Birch & Bloom, 2007; Wimmer & Perner, 1983), which evaluates children's ability to understand that someone else believes something they know to be wrong. In this task, children hear a story (often accompanied by illustrations like those in **FIGURE 12**) about a child who stores a special treat in one place, but a third party (such as the child's mother), unbeknownst to the child, moves the treat to another place. Researchers then ask the child where the child in the story will look for the treat when he returns. Children who pass

Children acquire concepts of events as well as objects. For example, young children rapidly learn what's likely to occur during routine events such as birthday parties, visits to the doctor's office, and trips to fast-food restaurants. Children depend so heavily on their expectations of events that they sometimes incorrectly recall a typical feature of an event that didn't occur. (Fivush & Hudson, 1990; Nelson & Hudson, 1988)

◀ **RULING OUT RIVAL HYPOTHESES**
Have important alternative explanations for the findings been excluded?

Infants who view a video image of their own legs side by side with a videotape of another infant's legs will look longer at the video of the other baby. This finding suggests that infants recognize the correspondence between the video images and their own bodies (Bahrick & Watson, 1985) and find their own actions less interesting to watch.

theory of mind
ability to reason about what other people know or believe

(a)   (b)   (c)   (d)

FIGURE 12 The False-Belief Task. In the false-belief task, the child participant knows something about which someone else is unaware. In this scenario, the child learns that Joey in the story believes the candy bar is in the cabinet. But because she's heard the whole story, the child knows the candy bar is really in the refrigerator. When asked where Joey thinks the candy is, will the child respond with her own knowledge of the true location, or will she realize that Joey is unaware of this change?

this task understand that although they know where the treat is actually hidden, the child in the story holds an incorrect belief about the treat's location. Those who fail the task believe that if they know where the treat is, the child in the story must know too.

Children typically don't succeed at this task until around age four or five. Yet how early children succeed on false-belief tasks varies depending on seemingly minor variations in the task, such as whether it's a story-book or real-world situation (Wellman, Cross, & Watson, 2001). Also, if researchers tell children the reason for the change was to "trick" someone, they're more successful at an earlier age. Thus, the age at which children pass the false-belief task is due partially to aspects of the task in addition to their understanding of others' knowledge (Dalke, 2011). Still, it's clear that the ability to understand others' perspectives increases with age.

NUMBERS AND MATHEMATICS: WHAT COUNTS. Counting and math are relatively recent achievements in human history. Humans developed the first counting system only a few thousand years ago. Unlike many cognitive skills that children acquire, counting and mathematics don't inevitably develop. In fact, in a few nonindustrialized cultures such as the Pirahã, a tribe in Brazil, conventional counting and mathematics appear not to exist (Gordon, 2004; Everett & Madora, 2012).

Learning to count is much more complex than it seems. Of course, many children learn to "count to ten" at a very early age, reciting "1-2-3-4-5-6-7-8-9-10" in rapid succession and waiting for applause to follow. But children must also learn a variety of more complex aspects of numbers, such as that (1) numbers are about amount, (2) number words refer to specific quantities (and not just "a bunch" or "a few"), and (3) numbers are ordered from smallest to largest in quantity (Gelman & Gallistel, 1978). Children must also master the idea that two elephants is the same number as two grains of rice—that the *size* of entities isn't relevant to quantity. Kelly Mix and her colleagues showed that this insight is extremely difficult for children (Mix, 1999; Mix, Huttenlocher, & Levine, 1996). Children find it easier to match two sets of the same quantity when the objects to be counted closely resemble each other than when they look different

RULING OUT RIVAL HYPOTHESES ▶
Have important alternative explanations for the findings been excluded?

Factoid

Not all cultures count to 10 on their fingers; many have much more elaborate systems of tracking amounts on their fingers, hands, arms, heads, and other body parts. Some systems have specific body locations assigned for numbers from 1 to as high as 74!

(see **FIGURE 13**). When similarity among the objects is high, children master this task at 3 years of age, but when the objects look different, children don't succeed until 3½ years. And when they have to match the quantity of a visual set with sets of sounds, they don't succeed until after age 4.

Counting and other mathematical skills in preschool- and school-aged children develop at different rates across cultures. Cross-cultural differences in how parents and teachers introduce counting to children seem to account, at least in part, for these differences. Differences in how linguistic counting systems are structured also play a role. For example, the English word *twelve* doesn't convey any information about what quantity it represents, whereas in Chinese, it's literally translated as "one ten, two," which appears to help children understand what quantity it represents (Gladwell, 2009; Miller et al., 1995).

Cognitive Changes in Adolescence

As Piaget noted, it's not until adolescence that we achieve our most abstract levels of reasoning ability. There are many reasons that cognitive development continues well into the teenage years. Part of the story here is about brain development, and part of it is about the kinds of problems, opportunities, and experiences we encounter for the very first time during adolescence.

Although most brain maturation occurs prenatally and in the first few years of life, the frontal lobes don't mature fully until late adolescence or early adulthood (Casey et al., 2000; Johnson, 1998). The frontal lobes are largely responsible for planning, decision making, and impulse control. The fact that the frontal lobes are still maturing during adolescence may explain some of the impulsive behaviors, like skateboarding down a steep incline, for which teens are notorious (Weinberger, Elvevag, & Giedd, 2005). Even on the simplest tasks, such as suppressing the impulse to look at a flashing light, teens have a more difficult time and require more brain processing than do adults (Luna & Sweeney, 2004). In addition, during adolescence, limbic structures of the brain involved in social rewards become more active, probably rendering teens susceptible to peer group influences, which can lead to further risk-taking (Steinberg, 2007).

Adolescents routinely encounter new adult-like opportunities to engage in potentially harmful activities, even though their brains aren't ready to make well-reasoned decisions. For example, they're often faced with decisions such as whether to have sex, engage in vandalism, or drive drunk. Adolescents must negotiate these choices without a "full deck" of decision-making cards. Nevertheless, there's debate over whether we can blame teen behavioral problems entirely on the "teen brain." Some researchers argue that these impulsive behaviors don't routinely appear in adolescents in non-Westernized cultures, suggesting that the causes of this phenomenon may be as much cultural as biological (Epstein, 2007; Schlegel & Barry, 1991).

A common assumption about teenagers is that they engage in risk-taking because they possess a sense of invincibility—they don't believe bad things can ever happen to them. But research calls this notion into question (Vartanian, 2000). Most adolescents don't actually underestimate the risks of such behaviors as driving fast or having early sex; they're often aware they're taking chances, but believe they're willing to accept the consequences (Reyna & Farley, 2006).

ATTITUDES TOWARD KNOWLEDGE IN ADOLESCENTS AND YOUNG ADULTS. Another critical cognitive change that takes place during the late high school and college years is in adolescents' and young adults' perspectives

FIGURE 13 Children Find It Easier to Match Quantities When the Objects Resemble Each Other. In Mix's studies, children match the display on the left with one of the displays on the right. Children find this much easier in the top figure (a), in which the disks resemble the dots, than in the bottom figure (b), in which the stimuli are different. (Based on Mix, 1999)

◄ **RULING OUT RIVAL HYPOTHESES**
Have important alternative explanations for the findings been excluded?

Lee Boyd Malvo participated in the Washington, D.C., sniper killings in October 2002. He was 17 years old at the time of the crimes. Some researchers argue that adolescents who commit crimes should be considered "less guilty by reason of adolescence" because their frontal lobes aren't fully mature, preventing them from making mature decisions regarding the consequences of their actions (Steinberg & Scott, 2003). Others disagree, noting that the overwhelming majority of adolescents don't commit violent crimes. What do you think?

toward knowledge. Students starting college are often frustrated to find few black-and-white answers to questions, including questions in their psychology courses. One of the hardest things for them to appreciate is that the answer to questions like "Which theory is better?" is often "It depends." William Perry (1970) cataloged the transitions that students undergo during the college years as they discover that their professors have few absolute answers to offer. He noted that over the course of their college years, students pass through a variety of "positions," or perspectives, on knowledge.

Students who expect clear right or wrong answers to all questions may initially resist changing their views and instead try to reconcile their expectations with what they're learning in the classroom (recall Piaget's assimilation process). They may understand that the "it depends" perspective is the one their professors want them to embrace. So they'll often say the "right things" on exams to get good grades, but believe deep down that there's a right and a wrong answer to most questions. With time and experience, students relax their expectations for absolute answers and construe knowledge as relative. Ultimately, students typically come to realize that they can't abandon the idea of "truth" or "reality" completely, but recognize that they can appreciate and respect differing points of view. Although the past three decades have witnessed minor modifications to Perry's stages, his overall model has withstood the test of time (Cano, 2005; Cano & Cardelle-Elawar, 2004).

REPLICABILITY ▶
Can the results be duplicated in other studies?

Cognitive Function in Adulthood

There are minuses and pluses to growing older. On the downside, many aging adults complain that they just can't remember things they used to. They're right: Many aspects of cognitive function *do* decline as people get older (Ghisletta et al., 2012). Our ability to recall information, especially the names of people, objects, and places, begins to decrease after age 30. Still, there's considerable variability in how much memory declines, with most people experiencing only modest decreases with age (Shimamura et al., 1995). People's overall speed of processing also declines, which is why teenagers can regularly beat older adults at video games and other speed-sensitive tasks (Cerella, 1985; Salthouse, 2004). These age-related declines are probably a result of brain changes that occur with age, because overall brain matter decreases over the course of adulthood. Age-related declines in brain volume are particularly pronounced in certain areas (Scahill et al., 2003), including the cortex and the hippocampus, which plays a key role in memory.

On the upside, some aspects of cognitive function are largely spared from age-related decline, and others actually improve with age:

When we consider that older adults have decades of accumulated knowledge and crystallized intelligence outstripping that of younger adults, we can see why many of the world's cultures honor and revere the elderly.

- Although free recall (being asked to generate items from memory) declines with age, cued recall and recognition remain intact (Schonfield & Robertson, 1966).

- Aging adults show relatively little decline when asked to remember material that's pertinent to their everyday lives, as opposed to the random lists of words often used in memory research (Graf, 1990; Perlmutter, 1983).

- Older adults perform better on most vocabulary and knowledge tests than do younger adults (Cattell, 1963). Crystallized intelligence , our accumulated knowledge and experience, tends to stay the same or increase with age (Baltes, Saudinger, & Lindenberger, 1999; Beier & Ackerman, 2001; Horn & Hofer, 1992). Here's a case in which common sense is true: Older *is* wiser!

Assess Your Knowledge   FACT or FICTION?

✓ Study and Review in MyPsychLab

1. Piaget argued that development was domain-general and continuous.   True / False

2. Vygotsky's theory proposes that individual children vary in the age at which they achieve developmental readiness for particular cognitive abilities.   True / False

3. The ability to count precise quantities is absent in some cultures.   True / False

4. Adolescents may not always make mature decisions about engaging in risky behaviors because their frontal lobes aren't fully mature.   True / False

5. Compared with younger adults, older adults perform worse on tests that require memory for random lists of words, but perform better on tests of knowledge and vocabulary.   True / False

Answers: 1. F; 2. T; 3. T; 4. T; 5. T

The Developing Personality: Social and Moral Development

10 Describe how and when children establish emotional bonds with their caregivers.

11 Explain the environmental and genetic influences on social behavior and social style in children.

12 Determine how morality and identity develop during adolescence and emerging adulthood.

13 Identify developmental changes during major life transitions in adults.

14 Summarize different ways of conceptualizing old age.

We humans are inherently social beings. Our work lives, school lives, romantic lives, and family lives all involve interaction with others. Because social relationships are so central to our everyday functioning, it's not surprising that our interpersonal relations change as we develop.

Social Development in Infancy and Childhood

Soon after birth, infants begin to take a keen interest in others. Infants prefer looking at faces over just about all other visual information. As early as four days after birth, infants show a marked preference for Mommy's face over that of other people (Pascalis et al., 1995). Infants' interest in others is a good thing because people—particularly familiar people like their parents—are valuable sources of information and provide the love and support infants need to flourish.

Infants become increasingly socially engaged and interactive with others over the first six or seven months. But then something changes dramatically. The same infant who was giggling on the floor with a perfect stranger at six months may scream in terror if approached by that same stranger only a few months later. This phenomenon, known as **stranger anxiety**, manifests itself in a fear of strangers beginning at about eight or nine months of age (Greenberg, Hillman, & Grice, 1973; Konner, 1990). It generally increases up until about 12 to 15 months of age and then declines steadily (see **FIGURE 14**). Stranger anxiety makes good evolutionary sense, because it occurs around the age most infants begin to crawl around on their own (Boyer & Bergstrom, 2011). As a result, it's the age at which infants can—and usually do—find a way to get themselves into trouble. So this anxiety may be an adaptive mechanism for keeping infants away from dangers, including unknown adults. Interestingly, the onset of stranger anxiety appears to be virtually identical across all cultures (Kagan, 1976).

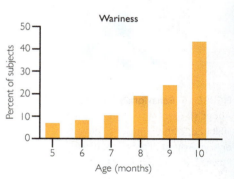

FIGURE 14 Stranger Anxiety. As we can see in this graph, infants' wariness when confronted with a stranger first begins at around 8 or 9 months and continues to increase. Typically, stranger anxiety reactions don't begin to decline until about 12 or 15 months. (*Based on:* Waters, Matas, & Sroufe, 1975)

stranger anxiety
a fear of strangers developing at 8 or 9 months of age

445

The majority of children fall into one of three temperament categories: (a) easy, (b) difficult, and (c) slow to warm up.

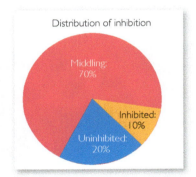

FIGURE 15 Behaviorally Inhibited Children. About 10 percent of children are behaviorally inhibited, with the majority either uninhibited or somewhere in between. (Based on Kagan, Reznick, & Snidman, 1988)

RULING OUT RIVAL HYPOTHESES ▶
Have important alternative explanations for the findings been excluded?

temperament
basic emotional style that appears early in development and is largely genetic in origin

attachment
the strong emotional connection we share with those to whom we feel closest

TEMPERAMENT AND SOCIAL DEVELOPMENT: BABIES' EMOTIONAL STYLES. As anyone who's spent time with infants can attest, babies vary widely in their social interaction styles. Some are friendly, others are shy and wary, and still others ignore most people altogether. These individual differences in children's social and emotional styles reflect differences in **temperament** (Mervielde et al., 2005). Temperament can be distinguished from other later appearing personality characteristics because it emerges early and appears to be largely genetically influenced.

In their studies of American children, Alexander Thomas and Stella Chess (1977) identified three major temperamental styles. *Easy* infants (about 40 percent of babies) are adaptable and relaxed, *difficult* infants (about 10 percent of babies) are fussy and easily frustrated, and *slow-to-warm-up* infants (about 15 percent of babies) are disturbed by new stimuli at first but gradually adjust to them. The remaining 35 percent of children don't fit neatly into any of these three categories.

Based initially on research with cats, Jerome Kagan identified another temperamental style he termed *behavioral inhibition* (Kagan et al., 2007). Like "scaredy cats," who crawl under the nearest bed at the sight of a new person or moving object, behaviorally inhibited human infants become frightened at the sight of novel or unexpected stimuli like unfamiliar faces, loud tones, or little moving robots (Kagan, Reznick, & Snidman, 1988). Their hearts pound, their bodies tense up, and their amygdalae become active (Schwartz et al., 2003). This last finding makes sense, because the amygdala plays a key role in processing fear. According to Kagan and his colleagues, we can find this temperamental style in about 10 percent of children (see **FIGURE 15**). Infants with high levels of behavioral inhibition are at heightened risk for shyness and anxiety disorders in childhood, adolescence, and adulthood (Biederman et al., 2001; Rotge et al., 2011; Turner, Beidel, & Wolff, 1996). Still, behavioral inhibition isn't all bad. Infants with extremely *low* levels of behavioral inhibition may be at increased risk for impulsive behaviors in later childhood (Burgess et al., 2003), so a certain amount of behavioral inhibition may be healthy. Like other temperaments, behavioral inhibition is genetically influenced but can still be shaped by environmental factors. For example, behaviorally inhibited children placed in daycare settings often adapt to this social environment by becoming less inhibited (Martin & Fox, 2006).

Certain cultural differences in temperament are evident even in newborns (Freedman & DeBoer, 1979). Daniel Freedman (1978; Freedman & Freedman, 1969) compared how Chinese-American and European-American four-day-old infants reacted when researchers placed a cloth over their faces. Chinese-American infants were considerably calmer than were European-American infants, many of whom struggled mightily to remove the offending cloths. These findings seem to suggest the presence of genetic differences across ethnicities. Nevertheless, there are several rival explanations. For example, different cultural practices in pregnant women (such as exercise and diet) could change the infant's prenatal environment. Alternatively, mothers of different cultures may differ in their patterns of hormone release during pregnancy, in turn altering their intrauterine (within the womb) environment.

ATTACHMENT: ESTABLISHING BONDS. Virtually all infants forge close emotional bonds with significant adults, usually their parents. This emotional connection we share with those to whom we feel closest is called **attachment**. There may be a good evolutionary reason for the attachment bond. As psychiatrist John Bowlby (1973) noted, it ensures that infants and children don't stray too far from the caretakers who feed and protect them. To understand the origins of attachment, we need to begin with the story of an Austrian zoologist and his birds.

Imprinting. In the 1930s, Konrad Lorenz—who went on to win a Nobel Prize for the work we're about to describe—was observing the behaviors of geese. By sheer accident, he discovered that goslings (young geese) seemed to follow around the first large moving object they saw after hatching, which, in 99 percent or more of cases, turns out to be none other than Mother Goose. Although Lorenz (1937) referred to this phenomenon as "stamping in" in German; it's come to be known in English as *imprinting*. Once a gosling has imprinted on something or someone, it becomes largely fixated on it and is unlikely to follow or bond with anything else. What happens when the mother goose isn't around? Goslings will imprint on whatever large moving object they see first, including large white bouncing balls, boxes on wheels, and even Lorenz himself.

We humans don't imprint onto our mothers the way geese do: We don't bond automatically to the first moving thing we see. Still, human infants and most mammalian infants exhibit a "softer" form of imprinting in which they forge strong bonds with those who tend to them shortly after birth.

Lorenz discovered that imprinting occurs only during a *critical period* (Almli & Finger, 1987): a specific window of time during which an event must occur. Lorenz reported that this critical period was about 36 hours. If the goslings didn't see their mothers until after that window closed, they never imprinted on her or on anything else for that matter. It turns out that critical periods rarely end as abruptly as Lorenz reported (Bruer, 1999). That's especially true of intelligent mammals like cats, dogs, and humans, whose behaviors are more flexible than those of geese. That's why psychologists typically use the term *sensitive period* to refer to developmental windows in creatures with a greater range of behaviors.

Do humans have sensitive periods for the development of healthy interpersonal relationships? Although the question is controversial, early and prolonged separation from attachment figures may produce detrimental effects on psychological adjustment, including social bonding.

Some of the best evidence for this possibility comes from a longitudinal study of infants adopted from Romanian orphanages. In the 1970s and 1980s, all forms of birth control were banned in Romania, resulting in catastrophic numbers of unplanned pregnancies and babies whose parents couldn't support them. Romanian orphanages were overwhelmed by vast numbers of infants for whom they had to provide care. As a result, these orphanages offered little social interaction or emotional care, and infants were often left in their cribs all day and night. These infants had no opportunity to develop bonds with adult caretakers until much later, when thousands of them were adopted by families in the United States and England. Sir Michael Rutter and his colleagues found that although infants from these orphanages adopted before six months of age fared well later, those who were older than six months of age when they were adopted often exhibited what appeared to be negative psychological effects of their early environment, including inattention, hyperactivity, and difficulties becoming attached to their adult caregivers (O'Connor & Rutter, 2000; Rutter et al., 2012). Nevertheless, there may be another explanation for these findings: The children who were adopted later may have had more emotional difficulties to begin with. As a consequence, they may have been more difficult to place in adoptive families. Nevertheless, the finding that early institutionalization is associated with later emotional problems has been replicated in numerous studies using different methodologies (Ames, 1997; Kreppner et al., 2001).

Contact Comfort: The Healing Touch. Given that human infants don't imprint onto attachment figures, on what basis do they bond to their parents? For decades, psychologists assumed that the primary basis for the attachment bond is the nourishment supplied by mothers. Children bond to those who provide them with milk and food, and in most cases this happens to be Mommy. This view fit with a behaviorist account, which proposes that reinforcement is the primary influence on our preferences.

Harry Harlow overturned this assumption in the 1950s with his research on infant rhesus monkeys, which are close genetic relatives of humans (Blum, 2002).

As Nobel Prize–winning biologist Konrad Lorenz goes for a swim, he's followed by three geese who imprinted on him almost immediately after they hatched.

"IT'S AN INTERESTING PSYCHOLOGICAL PHENOMENON. THEY THINK HE'S THEIR MOTHER. SO DOES HE."

◀ **RULING OUT RIVAL HYPOTHESES**
Have important alternative explanations for the findings been excluded?

◀ **REPLICABILITY**
Can the results be duplicated in other studies?

Harlow (1958) separated baby monkeys from their mothers only a few hours after birth. He then placed them in a cage with two "surrogate" mothers, both inanimate. One—the "wire mother"—consisted of an angular face and a cold, mangled mesh of uncomfortable metal wires. This wire mother did have one thing going for her, though: nourishment. She sported a little bottle of milk from which the baby monkey could drink. In sharp contrast, the second mother, the "terry cloth mother," had a round face and was made of foam rubber overlaid with a comfortable layer of terry cloth and heated with a lightbulb. Harlow found that although baby monkeys routinely went to wire mothers for milk, they spent much more of their time with terry cloth mothers. In addition, when Harlow exposed monkeys to a scary stimulus, like a toy robot playing a drum, they were much more likely to run to the terry cloth mother and cling to her for reassurance. Harlow termed this phenomenon **contact comfort**: the positive emotions afforded by touch. Contact comfort may help us understand why we human primates find simple touch, like holding the hand of a romantic partner, so reassuring. Indeed, Tiffany Field (2003) and her colleagues showed that gentle massage helps premature babies gain weight, sleep better, and bond more closely with their parents than does attention alone.

Attachment Styles: The Strange Situation. Although virtually all infants attach to their parents, different children exhibit this attachment in different ways. Some are cuddly and affectionate, some are clingy, and some seem almost angry with their parents. To investigate whether there are distinct styles of attachment between infants and caregivers, Mary Ainsworth and her colleagues (1978) developed the *Strange Situation*. The Strange Situation is a laboratory procedure designed to evaluate attachment style by observing 1-year-olds' reactions to being separated from and then reunited with their primary caregivers, usually their mothers. The Strange Situation starts out by placing the infant and mother in an unfamiliar room loaded with all kinds of interesting toys the infant is free to explore. The researchers observe (1) how comfortable the infant is exploring on his or her own, (2) the infant's emotional reaction when a stranger enters the room, (3) the infant's response to the mother leaving the infant alone with the stranger and (4) the infant's behavior when the mother returns (see **FIGURE 16**). Based on the infant's behavior in these stages of the Strange Situation, researchers classify infants' attachment relationships into one of four categories.

? When frightened by a novel object, Harlow's infant monkeys almost always preferred the terry cloth mother over the wire mother. **What does this finding tell us about the basis for attachment?** (See answer upside down at bottom of page.)

FIGURE 16 Physical Setup of the Strange Situation. In the Strange Situation, both the mother and a stranger are present before the mother leaves the child with the stranger. The child's response to the mother's departure and reaction when she returns are used to determine the child's attachment style.

contact comfort
positive emotions afforded by touch

1. **Secure attachment** (about 60 percent of U.S. infants). The infant explores the room but checks to make sure mom is watching, returns to mom when the stranger enters, reacts to mom's departure by becoming upset, but greets her return with joy. In essence, the infant uses mom as a *secure base:* a rock-solid source of support to which to turn in times of trouble (Bowlby, 1990).

2. **Insecure-avoidant attachment** (about 15–20 percent of U.S. infants). The infant explores the room independently without checking in with mom, is indifferent to the entry of the stranger, shows no distress at mom's departure, and displays little reaction upon her return.

3. **Insecure-anxious attachment** (about 15–20 percent of U.S. infants). The infant does not explore the toys without mom's assistance, shows distress when the stranger enters, reacts to mom's departure with panic, and shows a mixed emotional reaction upon her return, simultaneously reaching for her yet squirming to get away after she picks him or her up (for this reason, some psychologists refer to this style as "anxious-ambivalent").

4. **Disorganized attachment** (about 5–10 percent of U.S infants). This rarest of attachment styles wasn't included in the original classification, but was added

later by Mary Main and her colleagues (Main & Cassidy, 1988). Children with this pattern react to the toys, the stranger, and mom's departure and return with an inconsistent and confused set of responses. They may appear dazed when reunited with their mom.

Note that we wrote "U.S. infants" in parentheses following each classification. That's because there are cultural differences in attachment style. For example, more infants in Japan than in the United States fall into the insecure-anxious category, whereas more infants in the United States than in Japan fall into the insecure-avoidant category (Rothbaum et al., 2000). These differences may stem in part from the fact that Japanese babies experience fewer separations from their mothers in everyday life than do American babies. As a consequence, Japanese babies may find the Strange Situation even "stranger"— and more stressful—than do American babies (van Ijzendoorn & Sagi, 1999).

The attachment styles derived from the Strange Situation predict children's later behavior. Infants with a secure attachment style tend to grow up to be more well-adjusted, helpful, and empathic than do infants with other attachment styles (LaFreniere & Sroufe, 1985; Sroufe, 1983). In contrast, infants with an anxious attachment style are more likely to be disliked and mistreated by their peers later in childhood than are infants with other attachment styles.

Infants can form multiple attachments, bonding with both mothers and fathers and with siblings, grandparents, and other caregivers. Their attachment style exhibited with one caregiver doesn't necessarily predict their attachment style with other caregivers (van Ijzendorn & De Wolff, 1997). Developing an attachment to one adult figure in the infant's life doesn't necessarily undermine the ability to form other attachments. Infants placed in daycare may establish secure attachment relationships with their caretakers, although secure attachments are more likely with parents. Moreover, the quality of attachment to daycare workers depends on the quality and type of daycare (Ahnert et al., 2006). In two-parent households, infants typically display a strong early preference for the primary caregiver (usually the mother) that disappears by around 18 months.

Today, most attachment researchers rely on the Strange Situation to measure infants' attachment styles. Although this makes it easier to compare results across studies and individuals, relying on a single measure over and over again has its limitations (Shadish, Cook, & Campbell, 2002). The Strange Situation is, after all, simply one indicator of attachment, and attachment bonds involve many more scenarios than just reactions to novel experiences. To address this concern, some researchers have begun to develop alternative measures of attachment, such as interviews in adulthood designed to assess bonding to one's parents (Hesse, 1999).

The Strange Situation also isn't especially *reliable*. Reliability refers to the consistency of a measuring instrument. If the Strange Situation were a highly reliable measure of attachment, babies who are securely attached at 12 months, for example, should also be securely attached at 14 months. Yet many infants switch their attachment classifications over brief time periods (Lamb et al., 1984; Paris, 2000). In general, attachment styles remain consistent only when the family environment stays the same. For example, if parents undergo a change in job status, their children's attachment style often changes as well (Bruer, 1999; Thompson, 1998). Moreover, almost 40 percent of children display a different attachment style with their mother than with their father (van Ijzendorn & De Wolff, 1997), suggesting that many children can't be pigeonholed into a single attachment classification. Most attachment theorists assume that infants' attachment styles are attributable largely to their parents' responsiveness to them. For example, infants whose parents respond to their signals of distress by comforting them are more likely to develop a secure attachment style than are other infants (Ainsworth et al., 1978). For most attachment theorists, the cause → effect arrow runs from parent to child. In contrast, some psychologists have argued that the causal arrow is reversed and that children's temperament influences

Simulate in **MyPsychLab** the **Experiment:** Attachment Classifications in the Strange Situation

◄ **CORRELATION VS. CAUSATION**
Can we be sure that A causes B?

449

their attachment styles. That is, infants with certain temperaments may elicit certain attachment behaviors from their parents (Paris, 2000; Rutter, 1995). For example, irritable infants may provoke frustration in their parents, which in turn makes these infants still more irritable, and so on. This bidirectional influence may result in an insecure attachment style. So temperament may be a third variable that influences both certain parenting practices and certain attachment styles.

INFLUENCE OF PARENTING ON DEVELOPMENT. Over the past century, self-proclaimed parenting experts have bombarded nervous mothers and fathers with contradictory advice about how to raise their children (Hulbert, 2003; Rankin, 2005). In the 1950s and 1960s, pediatrician Dr. Benjamin Spock became a major proponent of a *child-centered*, or "soft," approach to parenting, in which parents should be highly responsive to their children's needs (Hulbert, 2003). Other experts have instead called for a *parent-centered*, or "hard," approach to parenting, in which parents don't indulge or reinforce children's calls for attention. Making matters more confusing, some parenting advice seems to be at odds with psychological research. Some parenting experts advocate spanking children as a disciplinary technique (Dobson, 1992), even though there's not much evidence that physical punishment is effective for promoting long-term behavioral change. Renewed interest in this topic was provoked by the publication of two books emphasizing cultural differences in parenting approaches. Amy Chua (2011) advocates the "Tiger Mother" approach espoused by many Chinese and Chinese Americans, which says that children's primary goal should be to strive to excel. In this approach, fun doesn't enter into the equation and achievement is the overriding aim. Pamela Druckerman (2012), an American mother living in Paris, France, argued that French children are better behaved than U.S. children because of French parents' quiet authority. They say "no" and mean it, and they expect their children to find ways to entertain themselves; moreover, although they are loving and nurturing, they are less child-focused. What does research say about which parenting styles are most effective for promoting healthy development?

Parenting Styles and Later Adjustment. Diana Baumrind's (1971, 1991) work may offer partial answers to this perennial question. Based on her observations of Caucasian middle-class families, Baumrind identified the following three major parenting styles:

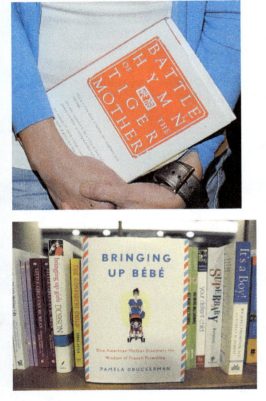

There are strong cultural differences in parenting approaches that reflect different attitudes towards childhood. For example, some cultures emphasize child achievement (as reflected in the book *Battle Hymn of the Tiger Mother*) and others emphasize self sufficiency (as reflected in the book *Bringing Up Bébé*).

- **Permissive.** Permissive parents tend to be lenient with their children, allowing them considerable freedom inside and outside the household. They use discipline sparingly, if at all, and often shower their children with affection.

- **Authoritarian.** Authoritarian parents tend to be strict with their children, giving their children little opportunity for free play or exploration and punishing them when they don't respond appropriately to their demands. They show little affection toward their children.

- **Authoritative.** Authoritative parents combine the best features of both permissive and authoritarian worlds. They're supportive of their children but set clear and firm limits.

Some authors refer to these three styles as "too soft," "too hard," and "just right," respectively. Since Baumrind developed her initial threefold classification, some authors (Maccoby & Martin, 1983) identified a fourth style of parenting:

- **Uninvolved.** Neglectful parents tend to ignore their children, paying little attention to either their positive or negative behaviors.

Baumrind (1991) and other investigators (Weiss & Schwarz, 1996) found that children with *authoritative* parents exhibit the best social and emotional adjustment and the lowest levels of behavior problems, at least among Caucasian middle-class American families. Children with uninvolved parents tend to fare the worst, and children with either permissive or authoritarian parents fall in between.

Superficially, these findings seem to suggest that parents should raise their children authoritatively. Yet Baumrind's findings are only correlational and don't permit us to draw cause-and-effect inferences. In fact, the correlations that Baumrind reported could be at least partly genetic in origin. For example, permissive parents may tend to be impulsive and pass on genes to their children that predispose them to impulsivity. Research shows that the fussiness of children in infancy forecasts whether parents will engage in physical punishment such as spanking, raising the possibility that child temperament may partly influence parenting style (Berlin et al., 2009).

There's another limitation to Baumrind's conclusions: They may not hold up well outside middle-class Caucasian-American families. The relationships between parenting style and children's adjustment aren't as strong in *collectivist* cultures like China as in *individualistic* cultures like the United States. Collectivist cultures place a high premium on group harmony, whereas individualist cultures place a high premium on achievement and independence (Triandis & Suh, 2002). Some data suggest that authoritarian parenting is associated with better outcomes in collectivist than in individualist societies (Sorkhabi, 2005; Steinberg, 2001), perhaps because in the former societies, there are more rigid expectations for adherence to societal values. Other research suggests that even within individualist cultures, there's variability in what seems most effective. For example, a hybrid parenting approach, one that includes harsh (often physical) punishments alongside a warm emotional bond, is tied to better outcomes for African-American families than are other parenting styles (Deater-Deckard & Dodge, 1997).

So what's the bottom line? The bulk of the research suggests that specific parenting styles may not matter as much as experts had once thought. By and large, so long as parents provide their children with what Heinz Hartmann (1939) termed the **average expectable environment**—an environment that provides children with basic needs for affection and appropriate discipline—most of their children will probably turn out just fine. As Donald Winnicott (1958) argued, parenting need only be *good enough*, not necessarily excellent (Paris, 2000). So contrary to what they may hear from parenting gurus, parents needn't lose sleep about everything they do or every word they utter.

Yet if parenting falls well below the range of the average expectable environment—if it's especially poor—children's social development can suffer. There's good reason to believe that many children raised by extremely abusive (so-called toxic) parents often experience ill effects later in life (Downey & Coyne, 1990; Lykken, 2000; Oshri, Rogosch, & Cicchetti, 2012). In addition, parenting quality matters when children enter the world with a strong genetic predisposition toward psychological disturbance or aggressiveness. For example, when children are genetically prone to high levels of impulsivity and violent behavior, parents probably need to exert especially firm and consistent discipline (Collins et al., 2000; Lykken, 1995). As we noted earlier, the effects of genes sometimes interact with those of the environment (Caspi et al., 2002; Kagan, 1994; Suomi, 1997).

Peers Versus Parents. In 1995, a controversy erupted when Judith Rich Harris published a paper in one of psychology's premier journals, *Psychological Review*, claiming that peers play an even more important role than parents in children's social development (Harris, 1995). She argued that most environmental transmission is "horizontal"—from children to other children—rather than "vertical"—from parents to children (Harris, 1998). Harris's model implies that parents may play much less of a role in children's development than previously believed. Nevertheless, twins who share many of the same peers are only slightly more similar in personality than are twins who share only a few of the same peers (Loehlin, 1997), raising questions about Harris's claims. Furthermore, the causal direction of this association isn't clear: Do similar peers lead twins to develop similar personalities, or do twins with similar personalities seek out similar peers? Regardless of whether peers play a stronger or weaker role in child development than parents do, peers clearly make up an important part of the developing child's environment.

◄ **CORRELATION VS. CAUSATION**
Can we be sure that A causes B?

Watch in **MyPsychLab** the **Video:** In the Real World: Parenting Styles and Socialization

In collectivist cultures, where obedience to authority is highly valued, authoritarian parenting may be associated with better outcomes than authoritative parenting.

◄ **CORRELATION VS. CAUSATION**
Can we be sure that A causes B?

average expectable environment
environment that provides children with basic needs for affection and discipline

"For the last time - don't throw him in the air so roughly!"

CORRELATION VS. CAUSATION ▶
Can we be sure that A causes B?

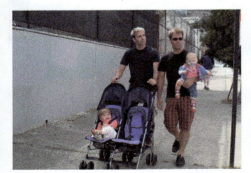

Although the popular stereotype of a family includes a husband, a wife, and several children, a surprisingly small number of families fit this mold. Single-parent families, same-sex parents, blended families following a second marriage, and childless couples are far more common than most people think.

The Role of the Father. Fathers differ from mothers in several ways in their interactions with their children. First, fathers and infants tend to share less mutual attention and show less affection than do mothers and their babies (Colonnesi et al., 2012). Second, they spend less time with their babies than mothers do, even in households in which both mothers and fathers are at home (Golombok, 2000). Third, when fathers interact with their children, they spend more of their time than do mothers in physical play (Parke, 1996). Fourth, both boys and girls tend to choose their fathers over their mothers as playmates (Clarke-Stewart, 1980). Despite these differences between mothers and fathers, fathers exert an important influence on children's psychological well-being and adjustment. Children benefit from warm, close relationships with their fathers regardless of how much time they spend with him (Lamb & Tamis-LeMonda, 2003).

"Nontraditional" Families: Science and Politics. Most child development research has been conducted on children in "traditional" families—those living in a household with two parents of opposite sex. But many children grow up in single-parent households or have same-sex parents. Politicians and the media have had much to say about the demise of the traditional American family and the need to protect traditional family values. What does research have to say about the effects of "nontraditional" parenting configurations?

The impact of single-parenthood on children is unclear. On the one hand, there's evidence that compared with children from two-parent families, children from single-parent families have more behavior problems, such as aggression and impulsivity (Golombok, 2000), and are at significantly higher risk for crime (Lykken, 1993, 2000). On the other hand, these data are only correlational, so we can't draw causal inferences from them. Single-parent households tend to differ from two-parent households in a variety of ways that may contribute to this correlation. For example, single mothers tend to be poorer, less educated, and marked by higher levels of life stress (Aber & Rappaport, 1994) than are married mothers. Single mothers also move more often, making it difficult for their children to form stable social bonds with peers (Harris, 1998).

Support for the idea that other variables explain child adjustment in single-parent households other than the absence of a second parent comes from research on widowed mothers. Even though these are also single-parent households, children in these families generally exhibit no higher rates of emotional or behavioral problems than do children from two-parent households (Felner et al., 1981; McLeod, 1991). This finding suggests that the apparent effects of single-mother parenting could be attributable to characteristics of the *father* or perhaps other unknown variables.

Of course, many single mothers do a fine job of raising their children, so being raised by a single mom doesn't necessarily doom children to later behavior problems. In addition, children raised by single fathers don't appear to differ in their behaviors from children raised by single mothers (Golombok, 2000; Hetherington & Stanley-Hagan, 2002). Although compared with other parents some single parents have children with more behavioral problems, the causes of this difference are unknown.

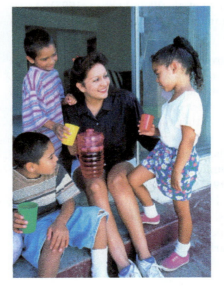

The evidence regarding the impact of same-sex parents on children's development is clearer. Children raised by same-sex couples don't differ from those raised by opposite-sex couples in social adjustment outcomes, academic performance, or sexual orientation (Gottman, 1990; Potter, 2012; Wainright et al., 2004). The bottom line is that having two parents who divide their roles into a primary caregiver and a secondary attachment figure who plays the rough-and-tumble role seen in fathers of traditional families is important for most children. But the gender composition of these caregivers may not matter.

Effects of Divorce on Children. Much of the popular psychology literature informs us that divorce often exacts a serious emotional toll on children. This belief was reinforced by the results of a widely publicized 25-year study of 60 families by Judith Wallerstein (1989), who reported that the negative effects of divorce were enduring: Many years later, the children of divorced parents had difficulties establishing career goals and stable romantic relationships. Yet Wallerstein didn't include a control group of families in which one or both parents had been separated from their children for other reasons, such as death or incarceration, so we can't tell whether the outcomes she observed were a consequence of divorce specifically.

Better-designed studies indicate that the substantial majority of children survive their parents' divorce without long-term emotional damage (Cherlin et al., 1991; Hetherington, Cox, & Cox, 1985). In addition, the effects of divorce seem to depend on the severity of conflict between parents before the divorce. When parents experience only mild conflict before the divorce, the seeming effects of divorce are actually *more* severe than when parents experience intense conflict before the divorce (Amato & Booth, 1997; Rutter, 1972). In the latter case, divorce typically produces no ill effects on children, probably because they find the divorce to be a welcome relief from their parents' incessant arguing.

Still, divorce can produce negative effects on *some* children. One group of investigators compared the children of identical twins, only one of whom had been divorced. The design provides an elegant control for genetic effects, because these twins are genetically identical. The researchers found that children of identical twins who'd divorced had higher levels of depression and substance abuse, as well as poorer school performance, than did the children of identical twins who hadn't divorced (D'Onofrio et al., 2006). These findings suggest that divorce can exert negative effects on some children, although the findings don't rule out the possibility that parental conflict prior to and during the divorce, rather than divorce itself, accounts for the differences (Hetherington & Stanley-Hagan, 2002).

SELF-CONTROL: LEARNING TO INHIBIT IMPULSES. A crucial ingredient of social development, and one that parents begin wishing for long before it emerges, is **self-control**: the ability to inhibit our impulses (Eigsti et al., 2006). We may be tempted to snag that unclaimed coffee at the Starbucks counter or tell our unbearably arrogant coworker what we really think of him, but we usually—and thankfully—restrain our desires to do so. Other times, we must put our desires on the back burner until we fulfill our obligations, such as putting off going to see a movie we're excited about until we've finished an important assignment.

Children are notoriously bad at delaying gratification, but some are better at it than others. As Walter Mischel and his colleagues discovered, children's early capacity to delay gratification is a good predictor of later social adjustment. To study delay of gratification, the experimenters leave a child alone in a room with a small reward (one cookie, for instance) and a little bell. Next, they tell the child that if she can wait 15 minutes, she can get an even bigger reward (for example, two cookies). If she can't wait that long, she can ring the bell to summon the experimenter. The children have several options: wait patiently, ring the bell and sacrifice the big reward, or throw caution to the wind and stuff the cookie in their mouths.

Children's ability to wait for the bigger reward at the age of 4 forecasts superior ability to cope with frustration in adolescence, probably because handling difficult situations hinges on an ability to inhibit negative reactions to distress. It even predicts teenagers' SAT scores (Mischel, Shoda, & Peake, 1988; Mischel, Shoda, & Rodriguez, 1989) and the likelihood of being overweight as adults (Schlam, Wilson, Shoda et al., 2012): Both studying a lot and resisting the temptation to overeat often require us to delay gratification. Of course, these findings don't prove that self-control causes these later outcomes. But they do suggest that the capacity to delay gratification in childhood is an early indicator of the capacity to restrain impulses, which is controlled in part by the frontal lobes (Eigsti et al., 2006; Mischel & Ayduk, 2004).

◀ **RULING OUT RIVAL HYPOTHESES**
Have important alternative explanations for the findings been excluded?

◀ **RULING OUT RIVAL HYPOTHESES**
Have important alternative explanations for the findings been excluded?

Children in Mischel's delay-of-gratification task must inhibit their desire to eat a cookie if they want to receive a bigger reward—eating both cookies—later.

◀ **CORRELATION VS. CAUSATION**
Can we be sure that A causes B?

self-control
ability to inhibit an impulse to act

Vanessa Sheridan is an influential transgendered woman who has worked with corporations and churches to help build acceptance and understanding of transgender issues.

Researchers have observed that when monkeys are given a choice of toys to play with, female monkeys *(left)* tend to prefer dolls, whereas male monkeys *(right)* tend to prefer trucks.

THE DEVELOPMENT OF GENDER IDENTITY. Whether we consider ourselves male or female is a fundamental aspect of our identity and our understanding of ourselves as social beings. Nevertheless, male/female distinctions aren't always as straightforward as we might assume. Most psychologists distinguish sex from gender, with *sex* referring to individuals' biological status as male or female and *gender* referring to the psychological characteristics—behaviors, thoughts, and emotions—that tend to be (but are not necessarily) associated with being male or female. **Gender role** refers to the behaviors that typically tend to be associated with being male or female, such as mowing the lawn (male) and nursing (female). But we're not done yet. **Gender identity** refers to people's sense of being male or female, which may or may not correspond to their biological sex. Some people, both children and adults, experience gender identities that conflict with their biological sex, and they either deny their biological sex or report feeling "trapped" in a body of the opposite sex. They may be biologically male yet feel like a woman, or vice versa. Many people who experience this kind of gender identity conflict opt to become *transgendered*, adopting the dress, mannerisms, gender roles, and sometimes the secondary sex characteristics of the opposite sex. Gender identity and gender role don't always go together. An adolescent may see herself as female, yet engage in "stereotypically" masculine behaviors like playing football and playing the role of class clown.

Biological Influences on Gender. A popular misconception is that gender differences don't emerge until socializing influences such as parenting practices have had the opportunity to act on children. Yet some gender differences are evident in early infancy, rendering this explanation unlikely.

As early as 1 year of age or less, boys and girls prefer to play with different types of toys, even if they've been exposed only to gender-neutral toys or have had equal access to toys associated with both genders (Alexander, & Saenz, 2012). Boys generally like balls, guns, and fire trucks; girls like dolls, stuffed animals, and cookware (Caldera, Huston, & O'Brien, 1989; Smith & Daglish, 1977). Infants as young as 3 months prefer to look at gender-consistent toys (Alexander et al., 2009). Remarkably, investigators have observed these preferences in nonhuman primates, including vervet monkeys. When placed in cages with toys, boy monkeys tend to choose trucks and balls, whereas girl monkeys tend to choose dolls and pots (Alexander & Hines, 2002). This finding suggests that toy preferences may reflect differences in biological predispositions such as aggressiveness and nurturance shared by many primates. Indeed, in humans, monkeys, and even mice, adult females exposed to excess levels of testosterone during birth tend to engage in more rough-and-tumble play than do other females (Berenbaum & Hines, 1992; Edwards, 1970; Young, Goy, & Phoenix, 1964).

As early as age three, boys prefer to hang out with other boys, and girls with other girls (LaFreniere, Strayer, & Gauthier, 1984; Whiting & Edwards, 1988). This phenomenon of *sex segregation* suggests that children understand the differences between genders and are aware that they fit better with one gender than the other. Sex segregation also emerges in rhesus monkeys between 6 and 12 months of age (Rupp, 2003), raising the possibility that this phenomenon has biological roots.

Social Influences on Gender. As we've discovered throughout this chapter, nature rarely if ever operates in a vacuum. Nature is almost always shaped or amplified by nurture, such as the reinforcing influences of parents, teachers, and peers. Research shows that parents tend to encourage children to engage in gender-stereotyped behaviors, such as achievement and independence among boys and dependence and nurturance among girls. Fathers are more likely than mothers to enforce these stereotypes (Lytton & Romney, 1991).

In a striking research demonstration of how social environment and social expectations can influence how gender stereotypes are reinforced, adults watched a video of a baby reacting to several emotionally arousing stimuli, like a jack-in-the-box popping open suddenly (Condry & Condry, 1976). The researchers told half the adults that the infant was a boy ("David") and the other half that the infant was a girl ("Dana"). The investigators randomly assigned the adults to these two conditions, making the study a true experiment. They found that observers' beliefs about the infant's reactions differed depending on their belief about the baby's gender. Adults who thought the infant was named David rated "his" startled reaction to the jack-in-the-box as reflecting anger, whereas adults who

gender role
a set of behaviors that tend to be associated with being male or female

gender identity
individuals' sense of being male or female

thought the infant was named Dana rated "her" startled reaction to the jack-in-the-box as reflecting fear. We can easily imagine how even such a small difference in interpretation of a reaction could eventually result in parents interacting differently with boys versus girls.

Teachers also tend to respond to boys and girls in accord with gender stereotypes. Teachers give boys more attention when they exhibit aggression and girls more attention when they exhibit dependent or "needy" behaviors (Serbin & O'Leary, 1975). Even when boys and girls are equally assertive and equally verbal, teachers tend to lavish assertive boys and verbal girls with greater amounts of attention (Fagot et al., 1985). In modern-day America, gender-role socialization tends to be stricter for boys than for girls. Parents tolerate and may even encourage cross-sex "tomboy" behavior in girls, like playing with both trucks and dolls, more than in boys, who tend to be stereotyped as "sissies" if they play with dolls (Langlois & Downs, 1980; Wood et al., 2002).

Research suggests that parents tend to be more accepting of "tomboyish" behaviors among girls than "sissyish" behavior among boys.

Social and Emotional Development in Adolescence

Common wisdom regards adolescence as one of the most traumatic times in development, and it's certainly a time of dramatic changes in body, brain, and social activities. Yet the teenage years can also be a wonderful time of discovery, of opportunity to participate in adultlike activities, and of deep friendships. We might characterize adolescence in the words of Charles Dickens: "It was the best of times, it was the worst of times." There's plenty of conflict with parents (Laursen, Coy, & Collins, 1998), risk-taking (Arnett, 1995), and anxiety (Larson & Richards, 1994) relative to younger children and adults. Yet most evidence suggests that the idea of adolescence as an inevitable roller-coaster ride is a myth (Arnett, 1999; Epstein, 2007): Only about 20 percent of adolescents experience marked turmoil (Offer & Schonert-Reichl, 1992). The remainder ride out the teenage years surprisingly smoothly. Recent research points to one reason for the popularity of the myth of adolescent turmoil: Teens may be less skilled than adults are at controlling their emotional reactions, so the adjustment problems they experience are more obvious (Silvers et al., 2012).

BUILDING AN IDENTITY. We've all asked ourselves "Who am I?" at some point. Indeed, one of the central challenges of adolescence is to get a firm handle on our **identity**, our sense of who we are, as well as our life goals and priorities. Erik Erikson (1902–1994) developed the most comprehensive theory of how identity develops.

Watch in **MyPsychLab** the **Video:** What's In It For Me?: Identity

According to Erikson, adolescence is a time of exploring who we are. Trying on different identities by acting and dressing in particular ways is part of this process.

Erikson's Model of Identity: The Identity Crisis. As an adolescent, Erikson wrestled with more than his share of identity issues. Although of Danish descent and unmistakably Scandinavian in appearance (he was tall, with blue eyes and blond hair), Erikson was raised Jewish. Largely as a consequence, he felt like an outsider at his synagogue, where he was teased for being Scandinavian, and his school, where he was teased for being Jewish (Hunt, 1993; Kushner, 1993). It's probably not merely coincidental that Erikson (1963, 1970) coined the term *identity crisis* to describe the confusion that most adolescents experience regarding their sense of self.

Erikson's theoretical work went well beyond the topic of adolescence. In contrast to Sigmund Freud, who believed that personality development stopped largely in late childhood, Erikson believed that personality growth continues throughout the lifespan. Erikson formulated an eight-stage model of human development from "womb to tomb," as psychologists like to say. In each of his "Eight Stages," we confront a different **psychosocial crisis**: a dilemma concerning our relations to other people, be they parents, teachers, friends, or society at large. For example, Erikson believed that infants face a dilemma about whether the world is a safe place in which they can depend on caregivers to treat them well. Later, children face a dilemma about whether to feel confident in their abilities. As we negotiate each stage, we acquire a more fleshed-out sense of who we are.

As we can see in **FIGURE 17** the fifth stage, "Identity versus Role Confusion," this is the period when adolescents grapple with perhaps the most fundamental question of all: who they are. In most cases, they emerge from this crisis relatively unscathed. But if they don't, they may be at risk for later psychological conditions marked by confusion regarding identity (such as borderline personality disorder). For Erikson, the successful resolution of each stage

identity
our sense of who we are, as well as our life goals and priorities

psychosocial crisis
dilemma concerning an individual's relations to other people

holds crucial implications for later in development. If we don't solve the challenges posed by earlier stages, we'll experience difficulty solving the challenges posed by later stages.

Although Erikson's theorizing has been influential, the research basis for many of his claims is slim. There's not much evidence that there are exactly eight stages or that we pass through them in the same order. There's some evidence that individuals who don't successfully navigate the early stages of development, like identity versus role confusion, experience more difficulty with later stages than do other individuals (Vaillant & Milofsky, 1980). Although consistent with Erikson's model, these findings are only correlational. As a consequence, they don't demonstrate that problems with early stages *produce* problems in later stages, as the post hoc fallacy reminds us.

CORRELATION VS. CAUSATION ▶
Can we be sure that A causes B?

1. **Infancy**
Trust versus mistrust
Developing general security, optimism, and trust in others

2. **Toddlerhood**
Autonomy versus shame and doubt
Developing a sense of independence and confident self-reliance, taking setbacks in stride

3. **Early childhood**
Initiative versus guilt
Developing initiative in exploring and manipulating the environment

4. **Middle childhood**
Industry versus inferiority
Enjoyment and mastery of the developmental tasks of childhood, in and out of school

5. **Adolescence**
Identity versus role confusion
Achievement of a stable and satisfying sense of role and direction

6. **Young adulthood**
Intimacy versus isolation
Development of the ability to maintain intimate personal relationships

7. **Adulthood**
Generativity versus stagnation
Satisfaction of personal and familial needs supplemented by development of interest in the welfare of others and the world in general

8. **Aging**
Ego integrity versus despair
Recognizing and adjusting to aging and the prospect of death with a sense of satisfaction about the future

FIGURE 17 Erikson's Eight Stages of Human Development. (Adapted from Good and Brophy, 1995)

emerging adulthood
period of life between the ages of 18 and 25 when many aspects of emotional development, identity, and personality become solidified

Emerging Adulthood. Until recently, developmental researchers regarded individuals under 18 as adolescents and those over 18 as adults. But of course there isn't a magical transition that happens at the stroke of midnight of the eighteenth birthday. Scientists have increasingly recognized that many changes in identity and emotional development take place in early adulthood that are distinct from later adult experiences. Researchers define the period of life between 18 and 25 as **emerging adulthood**, when many aspects of emotional development, identity, and personality become solidified (Arnett, 2004).

Many emerging adults struggle to figure out their identities and life goals, "trying on different hats" in an effort to see which one fits best. Psychologists call this process *role experimentation*. We may juggle "nerdy," "hipster," and "jock" friends at various times, scope out different potential majors, and even explore alternative religious and philosophical beliefs. Our identities undergo a variety of important changes over the course of emerging adulthood as we acquire the opportunity to fine-tune the fit between who we are and who we want to be.

MORAL DEVELOPMENT: KNOWING RIGHT FROM WRONG. Children begin to develop ideas of right and wrong as toddlers and preschoolers. But *moral dilemmas*—situations in which there are no clear right or wrong answers—arise more frequently in the teen and young adult years. Should I lie to my parents about where I've been so they don't worry about me? Should I avoid my nice but nerdy friend so that my popular friends will like me better? The approach we adopt to these and other moral problems changes over the course of development.

Children's Moral Development. There's good reason to believe that we can trace the roots of our moral understanding to *fear*. In infancy and childhood, we associate right with reward and wrong with punishment, so we learn not to do bad things to avoid punishment. Indeed, one of the best predictors of the strength of children's sense of morality is their level of fear years earlier (Frick & Marsee, 2006; Kochanska et al., 2002).

Piaget believed that children's moral development, like other aspects of their development, is constrained by their level of cognitive development (Loevinger, 1987).

For example, he argued that children in the concrete operational stage tend to evaluate people in terms of how much harm they've done, whereas later, their *intentions* to produce harm are more relevant than the actual outcome (Piaget, 1932). For example, if we ask a child who's more to blame—(a) a child who accidentally knocks over a stack of 20 kitchen plates or (b) a child who purposefully knocks over 10 kitchen plates because he was hopping mad at his parents—a 6- or 7-year-old is more likely to say (a), because it produced more damage. In contrast, a 12- or 13-year-old is more likely to say (b), because it was intentional. With age, children become better able to understand that there's more to personal responsibility than the sheer amount of damage one has wrought. Whether a person meant to inflict damage also counts.

Kohlberg and Morality: Finding the Moral High Ground.

Lawrence Kohlberg extended Piaget's thinking to identify how morality unfolds across the lifespan. He studied how morality changes with development by exploring how participants wrestle with moral dilemmas. Because Kohlberg's moral dilemmas don't have clear right or wrong answers, he didn't score the answers based on what participants would do in these situations; he scored only the *reasoning processes* they used to decide what was right or wrong.

We'll explain this point using one famous moral problem developed by Kohlberg. Consider Heinz's dilemma and think about how you'd handle it.

Heinz and the Drug

In Europe, a woman was near death from a special kind of cancer. There was one drug that the doctors thought might save her. It was a form of radium that a druggist in the same town had recently discovered. The drug was expensive to make, but the druggist was charging 10 times what the drug cost him to make. He paid $400 for the radium and charged $4,000 for a small dose of the drug. The sick woman's husband, Heinz, went to everyone he knew to borrow the money and tried every legal means, but he could only get together about $2,000, which is half of what it cost. He told the druggist that his wife was dying, and asked him to sell it cheaper or let him pay later. But the druggist said, "No, I discovered the drug and I'm going to make money from it." So, having tried every legal means, Heinz gets desperate and considers breaking into the man's store to steal the drug.

Question: Should Heinz steal the drug? Why or why not? (Kohlberg, 1981, p. 12)

After studying the responses of many children, adolescents, and adults to this and other dilemmas, Kohlberg (1976, 1981) concluded that morality develops in three major stages. We can see these stages, along with sample answers to the Heinz dilemma at each stage, in **TABLE 3**. The first level, *preconventional morality*, is marked by a focus on punishment and reward. What's right is what we're rewarded for; what's wrong is what we're punished for. The second level, *conventional morality*, is marked by a focus on societal values. What's right is what society approves of; what's wrong is what society disapproves of. The third level, *postconventional morality*, is marked by a focus on internal moral principles that may differ from conventional societal values. What's right is what protects fundamental human rights and values; what's wrong is what contradicts these rights and values. Reasonable people, Kohlberg reminded us, may disagree on what is right at each stage of morality, so what's important is their rationale for deciding what's right. Kohlberg believed that all people pass through these stages in a fixed order, although he acknowledged that different people pass through them at different rates. In fact, Kohlberg's research indicated that most adults never get past conventional morality to achieve postconventional morality.

Criticisms of Kohlberg's Work.

Kohlberg's work has been enormously influential; his research has shed light on the development of morality and informed educational efforts to enhance people's moral reasoning (Kohlberg & Turiel, 1971; Loevinger, 1987). Still, Kohlberg's findings have been met with more than their share of criticism; we'll examine several criticisms here.

Another moral dilemma, in this case adapted slightly from one of Kohlberg's: Imagine you've just learned that one of your next-door neighbors, whom you've known for many years as an extremely kind and caring person, is wanted for an attempted murder she committed as a young woman three decades ago (this scenario describes Sara Jane Olson, ex-member of a violent revolutionary organization, shown here with her daughter). Would you turn her in to the police? Why or why not?

 Watch in **MyPsychLab** the **Video:** Moral Development: Postconventional

TABLE 3 Kohlberg's Scheme of Moral Development and Sample Explanations. Kohlberg scored the reasoning processes underlying the answer to the Heinz dilemma, not the answers themselves.

LEVEL	HEINZ SHOULD STEAL THE DRUG BECAUSE …	HEINZ SHOULD *NOT* STEAL THE DRUG BECAUSE …
Preconventional Morality	He can get away with it.	He might get caught.
Conventional Morality	Others will look down on him if he lets his wife die.	It's against the law.
Postconventional Morality	The protection of human life is a higher moral principle that can overrule laws against stealing.	Doing so violates a basic social contract needed to preserve civilization: Thou shalt not steal.

457

Carol Gilligan suggested that women's more caring orientation may affect their responses to moral dilemmas. Yet women appear to score just as highly as men on Kohlberg's moral development scheme.

FALSIFIABILITY ▶

Can the claim be disproved?

RULING OUT RIVAL HYPOTHESES ▶

Have important alternative explanations for the findings been excluded?

- **Cultural Bias.** By and large, studies have shown that Kohlberg's stages generalize across cultures (Snarey, 1982). But some critics have accused Kohlberg of cultural bias, because people from different cultures tend to achieve different scores on his moral development scheme. For example, people from individualistic societies often score somewhat higher than do those in collectivist societies (Schweder, Mahapatra, & Miller, 1990). Still, group differences don't always imply bias, so the meaning of this finding is unclear.

- **Sex Bias.** Kohlberg's student Carol Gilligan (1982) broke from her mentor to argue that his system was biased against women. For Gilligan, Kohlberg's scheme unfairly favors males, who are more likely than women to adopt a "justice" orientation based on abstract principles of fairness, whereas women are more likely than men to adopt a "caring" orientation based on concrete principles of nurturance. Yet despite gender differences in strategies toward moral problems, there's little evidence that men score higher than women on Kohlberg's scheme (Moon, 1986; Sunar, 2002).

- **Low Correlation with Moral Behavior.** Scores on Kohlberg's scheme are only modestly related to real-world moral behavior (Krebs & Denton, 2005). For example, the correlation between Kohlberg's levels and moral behavior, such as honest and altruistic actions, tends to be only about .3 (Blasi, 1980). Kohlberg argued that his moral development system *shouldn't* correlate highly with real-world actions, because it measures people's thinking about moral problems, not their moral behaviors. People may perform the same behaviors for very different reasons: A person may steal a coat from a store because he wants to add it to his fashion collection or because he wants to keep his freezing children warm in the winter. Still, this kind of reasoning raises problems for the falsifiability of Kohlberg's system. If the scores in this system correlate with behavior, they provide evidence for it; if they don't correlate with behavior, they don't necessarily provide evidence against it.

- **Confound with Verbal Intelligence.** Responding effectively to Kohlberg's moral dilemmas requires some basic smarts. But that fact should make us a bit uneasy, because Kohlberg's scheme may be measuring people's ability to understand and talk about problems in general rather than moral problems in particular (Blasi, 1980). There's only one way to rule out this possibility: Measure verbal intelligence and moral development in the same study and see whether it washes out the findings. Some studies have found that intelligence may explain Kohlberg's findings (Sanders, Lubinski, & Benbow, 1995), but other studies haven't (Gibbs, 2006). The issue remains unresolved.

- **Causal Direction.** Kohlberg's model assumes that our moral reasoning precedes our emotional reactions to moral issues. Yet in some cases, our emotional reactions to morally laden stimuli, like photographs of assaults on innocent people, occur almost instantaneously (Luo et al., 2006). Moreover, we can know something is wrong without being able to explain why; for example, many people "know" intuitively that incest is immoral but can't offer a reason (Haidt, 2007). These findings suggest that moral reasoning may sometimes come after, rather than before, our emotional reactions.

Life Transitions in Adulthood

As we "emerge" into full-blown adulthood, many aspects of our lives begin to stabilize, but others begin to change even more dramatically. These changes tend to be associated with major transitions in lifestyle or societal status, such as shifting from student to wage earner, entering a serious relationship, or becoming a parent. Many of these transitions are wonderful experiences, but they can be stressful. We often think of adults as following a predictable life trajectory: attending college in the late teens and early twenties, getting that first job after graduation, falling in love with someone of the opposite sex, getting married, having children, watching them grow up, and growing old gracefully while rocking on the front porch. In reality, we vastly overestimate how many of us adhere to this tidy stereotype of the road of life (Coontz, 1992). Many college students are in their late twenties, thirties, and forties, attend school while maintaining a job, and have families who are financially dependent on them. Many family units consist of single parents, same-sex parents, unmarried parents, second families following a divorce, and childless couples. Census reports (U.S. Census Bureau, 2010) indicate that only about 20 percent of adults live in conventional nuclear families (mom, dad, and children).

CAREERS. One of the biggest sources of anxiety for young adults graduating from college—particularly those who haven't served in the workforce—is what they're going to do for a living. Many recent graduates cast around a bit for a career path that matches their qualifications and interests. For some, this strategy can be beneficial, because they end up discovering an unexpected career that is a good fit for their skills and passions. Although it was once the norm for people to work for one company or in one career for their entire life, this is no longer the case. A longitudinal study conducted by the Bureau of Labor Statistics (2006) revealed that the average American worker changed jobs 10.5 times between the ages of 18 and 40. Although changes were more frequent in the teens and early twenties, people between 36 and 40 changed jobs at least once on average.

Finding a satisfying job—one that's stimulating, draws on the employee's skills, and involves a supportive work environment—can be a challenge. But job satisfaction (or lack thereof) can have a big impact on our emotional well-being (Faragher, et al., 2005). Overall levels of job satisfaction change over the course of adulthood. Emerging adults who are starting their first professional position often report high levels of job satisfaction, but rates of satisfaction decline during middle adulthood, perhaps in part because the novelty has worn off. Nevertheless, job satisfaction increases again prior to retirement age, creating what psychologists call a U-shaped curve, in which satisfaction is high early and late in the game but hits a dip in the middle (Clark et al., 1996).

LOVE AND COMMITMENT. One of the most momentous adult transitions is finding a life mate. Romantic relationships, although often exciting and fulfilling, typically call for a major shift in lifestyle. Even something as simple as dividing up closet space can be a stressful experience. Nevertheless, there appear to be benefits to sharing life with a significant other. Physical and emotional intimacy is associated with greater physical health and lower stress (Coombs, 1991). Those in serious long-term relationships—both homosexual and heterosexual—report higher overall levels of happiness than those who are single (Gove, Hughes, & Style, 1983; Wayment & Peplau, 1995). Nevertheless, this finding is only correlational and could reflect a tendency for happier people to enter into stable relationships.

Although the average age of marriage in the United States has increased, from 20 for women and 22 for men in 1960 to about 25 for women and 27 for men today, more than 50 percent of adults in the United States are married and about 5 percent are cohabitating but unmarried. About 1 percent of all cohabitating couples are same-sex partnerships, almost evenly divided between male and female relationships (U.S. Census Bureau, 2011). The vast majority of people become part of a long-term committed relationship at some point during adulthood.

PARENTHOOD. Becoming a parent is probably the biggest transition that adults can undergo. Having a child involves a fundamental and often stressful shift in lifestyle because, suddenly, adults are completely responsible for the well-being of someone other than themselves. Becoming a parent can be immensely rewarding, but it requires a huge change in schedule, a reduction in sleep, and challenges associated with balancing competing demands of work and family. New parents are often unprepared for these changes, imagining that they'll just stick to their routine and bring baby along with them wherever they go—which almost never works the way they envision it. Research indicates that new parents who have the easiest time adjusting to parenthood are those whose expectations about the amount of change required are most realistic (Belsky & Kelly, 1994).

Although we usually think of college students as being in their late teens or early twenties and financially dependent on their parents, many "nontraditional" students enroll in college while working full-time and supporting families.

◄ **CORRELATION VS. CAUSATION**
Can we be sure that A causes B?

Having a baby is a significant and wonderful life event, but becoming a new parent is also a significant source of stress.

Most parents make the adjustment, although each year—and sometimes each month—can bring new challenges as children develop. Although most adults adjust to parenthood, longitudinal studies reveal that couples' marital satisfaction drops for both parents during the year following the birth of a child and remains low throughout the first several years of their child's life (Cowan & Cowan, 1995; Dew & Wilcox, 2011). Couples who are matched on initial level of marital satisfaction but don't have a child display no such decline (Schulz, Cowan, & Cowan, 2006). The good news is that parents' overall level of satisfaction with *life* doesn't decline after the birth of a child, only their satisfaction with their partner. Fortunately, marital satisfaction typically rebounds once children reach school age.

MIDLIFE TRANSITIONS. Major adjustments also take place as adults reach middle age and begin to see the first signs of gray hair and wrinkles. As adults begin to feel their age, they confront new challenges, such as having their children leave home or caring for aging parents whose health is declining. The "sandwich generation" refers to adults (typically in their thirties and forties) who are caring for *both* growing children and aging parents, a particularly difficult situation given the competing demands.

One popular misconception about middle age is that most men, and some women, undergo a **midlife crisis**, marked by emotional distress about the aging process and an attempt to regain their youth. The stereotype is of a man in his forties or fifties impulsively buying a motorcycle or leaving his similarly aged wife for a 25-year-old woman. Although psychologists once viewed this period of transition as a normal part of adult development (Gould, 1978), researchers have failed to replicate findings of an increase in emotional distress during middle age (Eisler & Ragsdale, 1992; Rosenberg, Rosenberg, & Farrell, 1999). The midlife crisis is more myth than reality.

REPLICABILITY ▶

Can the results be duplicated in other studies?

The parallel female version of the midlife crisis in popular psychology is the **empty-nest syndrome**, a supposed period of depression in mothers following the "flight" of their children from the home as they reach adulthood. The idea of the empty-nest syndrome, like the midlife crisis, is overstated. Most research suggests that there are cohort effects on the incidence of empty-nest syndrome. Women whose children left the "nest" during or just after World War II seem to have been less affected by the change in role than those whose children moved out of the home in the 1960s and 1970s. This cohort effect appears to relate to the percentage of women who had joined the workforce or were primarily homemakers, because a majority of women were employed outside the home during and just after World War II to aid in war efforts, followed by a decline in outside employment during the 1960s and 1970s (Borland, 1982).

Women who define themselves less exclusively in their roles as parents, even those who aren't employed outside the home, are less vulnerable to empty-nest syndrome than those who have more traditional attitudes toward women's roles in society (Harkins, 1978). Some researchers have even speculated that empty-nest syndrome is specific to Caucasian women who don't work outside the home. Studies of African-American and Mexican-American women and of women of lower socioeconomic status who more commonly work outside the home (and often have greater extended family demands) indicate less distress associated with children "flying the nest" (Borland, 1982; Woehrer, 1982). Fortunately, and contrary to popular belief, most empty nesters experience an *increase* in life satisfaction following their newfound flexibility and freedom (Black & Hill, 1984). Nonetheless, the shift in role, not to mention the sudden increase in free time, takes some adjustment (Walsh, 1999).

For women who worked outside the home during the years they raised their children, the "empty-nest" transition tends to be easier than for stay-at-home mothers.

SOCIAL TRANSITIONS IN LATER YEARS. In the early twenty-first century, people are living longer than ever. The life expectancy of the average American man is 75.3; for the American woman, it's 80.4 (Centers for Disease Control and Prevention, 2009). Contrast those numbers with those only a century ago, when the average lifespan was 48 for men and 51 for women (National Center for Health Statistics, 2005). A greater percentage of the population is elderly than ever before, now that the baby boomers are coming of age. Moreover, the elderly now have more options for living out their later years. Many opt not to retire until well after 70. Some retire and take on part-time work or volunteer for charities. Many enter retirement

midlife crisis
supposed phase of adulthood characterized by emotional distress about the aging process and an attempt to regain youth

empty-nest syndrome
alleged period of depression in mothers following the departure of their grown children from the home

communities and assisted living facilities that allow them to maintain active social lives even when they can no longer drive, shop, or cook for themselves. Contrary to popular belief, depression is less common among the elderly than it is among younger people (Lilienfeld et al., 2010). Across the population, happiness tends to increase through the sixties and perhaps even seventies (Nass, Brave, & Takayama, 2006). Nevertheless, about 15 percent of the elderly experience significant problems with depression. Perhaps not surprisingly, those with declining health and sleep disturbances are especially vulnerable to depression (Cole & Dendukuri, 2003), although the causal arrow may run in the other direction, with depression increasing risk for health and sleep problems (Wolkowitz, Reus, & Mellon, 2011).

How can we predict how aging will affect us? Chronological age doesn't necessarily forecast the changes that accompany aging (Birren & Renner, 1977). Other ways of measuring age may do a better job of capturing the impact of these changes in later life. Let's consider four indices other than chronological age (Birren & Renner, 1977):

1. **Biological age:** the estimate of a person's age in terms of biological functioning. How efficiently are the person's organ systems, such as heart and lungs, functioning? When a 65-year-old brags that his doctor says that he has "the body of a 40-year-old," this is what his doctor is talking about.

2. **Psychological age:** a person's mental attitudes and agility and the capacity to deal with the stresses of an ever-changing environment. Some people display little change in memory, ability to learn, and personality from adolescence to old age, whereas others deteriorate substantially.

3. **Functional age:** a person's ability to function in given roles in society. Functional age may provide a better basis for judging readiness to retire, replacing the arbitrary criterion of chronological age (for example, that people should retire at 65 or 70).

4. **Social age:** whether people behave in accord with the social behaviors appropriate for their age. When people judge a woman as "dressing too young for her age" or roll their eyes at an 80-year-old man cruising around in a convertible sports car, they're invoking expectations about social age.

Growing old isn't entirely a "state of mind," as the saying goes, because a host of physical and social factors influence how comfortably we age. But there's no question that remaining physically and mentally active can promote a younger body and mind no matter how many candles appear on our birthday cake.

◄ **CORRELATION VS. CAUSATION**
Can we be sure that A causes B?

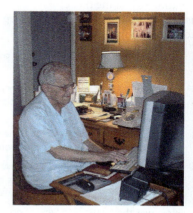

Until a few weeks before he died in 2013 at the age of 100, Mitchell Namy (the great-uncle of one of this text's authors) sent emails, surfed the Web, and traded stocks online. He played bridge weekly. Although his hearing and his knees declined in his nineties, his "functional age" was well below his chronological age.

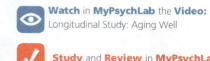

Watch in **MyPsychLab** the **Video:**
Longitudinal Study: Aging Well

Study and **Review** in **MyPsychLab**

Assess Your Knowledge   FACT or FICTION?

1. Studies of contact comfort suggest that nourishment isn't the principal basis for attachment in primates.   **True / False**

2. Studies suggest that within the broad range of the average expectable environment, parenting style may not be a crucial determinant of children's development.   **True / False**

3. Gender differences don't emerge until parenting practices have the opportunity to influence children's behavior.   **True / False**

4. In evaluating Kohlberg's moral dilemmas, the answers people give are more important than the reasoning processes they used to arrive at these answers.   **True / False**

5. Getting married and becoming a parent both exert an overall positive impact on adults' stress levels.   **True / False**

Answers: 1. T; 2. T; 3. F; 4. F; 5. F

Your Complete Review System

 Study and Review in MyPsychLab

Special Considerations In Human Development

1 IDENTIFY WAYS TO THINK SCIENTIFICALLY ABOUT DEVELOPMENTAL FINDINGS.

In evaluating how and why children change, we must resist the temptation to assume that events that happened prior necessarily cause events that happen later and keep in mind that cause and effect is often a two-way street.

1. The study of how behavior changes over time is called _____ _____.

2. The _____ _____ fallacy is the assumption that because one event happened before another event, the two events are causally related.

3. In a(n) _____ design, researchers obtain a "snapshot" of people of different ages at a single point in time.

4. _____ _____ can be observed when different samples of participants show different effects because they grew up during different time periods.

5. How was the classic "Up Series" documentary set up similar to longitudinal designs in psychology? Identify at least one positive and one negative aspect of utilizing longitudinal designs.

6. Research shows that most children (are/aren't) remarkably resilient and capable of withstanding stress.

2 CLARIFY HOW NATURE AND NURTURE CAN CONTRIBUTE TO DEVELOPMENT.

Genes and environment intersect in complex ways, so we can't always conclude that one or the other is driving behavior. For example, as children develop, how their genes are expressed often depends on their experiences.

7. Both _____ (our genetic endowment) and _____ (the environments we encounter) play powerful roles in shaping our development.

8. Many studies of human development are subject to a(n) _____, meaning it is difficult to identify the relative effects of genes and environment.

 Listen in MyPsychLab to chapter audio

9. Caspi and colleagues' longitudinal study of children with low levels of MAO illustrates the phenomenon of _____ _____, in which the effect of genes depends on environment, and vice versa.

10. Apply what you've learned about the nature–nurture debate by matching each nature–nurture intersection with the appropriate description.

____ Gene Expression	1. The impact of genes on behavior depends on the environment in which the behavior develops.
____ Gene-Environment Interactions	2. Genetic predispositions can drive us to select and create particular environments, leading to the mistaken appearance of a pure effect of nature.
____ Nature via Nurture	3. Some genes "turn on" only in response to specific environmental events.

The Developing Body: Physical and Motor Development

3 TRACK THE TRAJECTORY OF PRENATAL DEVELOPMENT AND IDENTIFY BARRIERS TO NORMAL DEVELOPMENT.

Many important aspects of fetal development occur early in pregnancy. The brain begins to develop 18 days after conception and continues to mature into adolescence. Teratogens such as drugs, alcohol, and even maternal stress can damage or slow fetal development. Although premature infants often experience developmental delays, low-birth-weight babies tend to have the least positive outcomes.

11. Early in pregnancy, a ball of identical cells that hasn't yet taken on a specific function is called the _____.

12. The embryo becomes a(n) _____ once the major organs are established and the heart has begun to beat.

13. Environmental factors that can have a negative effect on prenatal development are called _____.

14. The _____ point at which infants can typically survive on their own is 25 weeks, but a full-term baby is born at _____ weeks.

4 DESCRIBE HOW INFANTS LEARN TO COORDINATE MOTION AND ACHIEVE MAJOR MOTOR MILESTONES.

Children tend to achieve motor milestones such as crawling and walking in roughly the same order, although the ages when they accomplish these milestones vary. Infants are born with reflexes that help them get started, but experience plays a critical role in building children's muscles and motor coordination.

15. Children rely on _____ _____ as they learn how to coordinate their movements to reach or crawl.

16. Plot the progression of development in the figure by listing the age and major motor milestone depicted by each child.

(a)_____

(b)_____

(c)_____

(d)_____

(e)_____

(f)_____

17. Compared with those in the United States, how do child-rearing practices in other cultures (such as swaddling in Peru) affect children's short- and long-term motor development?

5 DESCRIBE PHYSICAL MATURATION DURING CHILDHOOD AND ADOLESCENCE.

During childhood, different parts of the body grow at different rates, with the head-to-body-size ratio becoming smaller than in infancy. Adolescence is marked by sexual maturation and significant physical changes.

18. Sexual maturation includes changes in _____ _____ _____, such as the reproductive organs and genitals, and _____ _____ _____, such as breast enlargement in girls and deepening voices in boys.

6 EXPLAIN WHICH ASPECTS OF PHYSICAL ABILITY DECLINE DURING AGING.

There are large individual differences in age-related changes in agility and physical coordination. One of the major milestones of physical aging in women is menopause.

19. Some aspects of physical decline may be related to decreasing _____ capacities.

20. Research suggests that women in menopause are (more/no more) prone to depression than women at other phases of life.

The Developing Mind: Cognitive Development

7 UNDERSTAND MAJOR THEORIES OF HOW CHILDREN'S THINKING DEVELOPS.

Piaget believed that development unfolds in four stages that influence all aspects of cognitive development. Vygotsky believed that different children develop skills in different domains at

different rates and that social structuring on the part of the parent facilitates children's learning and development. Researchers continue to debate whether learning happens in more general or domain-specific ways, whether learning is gradual or stagelike, and how much innate cognitive knowledge children possess.

21. According to Piaget, when children can no longer use _____ to absorb a new experience into their current knowledge structures, they will engage in _____ by altering an existing belief to make it more compatible with the new experience.

22. Using the descriptions provided, complete the table to show Piaget's four stages of cognitive development.

STAGE	TYPICAL AGES	DESCRIPTION
_____	_____	No thought beyond immediate physical experiences
_____	_____	Able to think beyond the here and now, but egocentric and unable to perform mental transformations
_____	_____	Able to perform mental transformations but only on concrete physical objects
_____	_____	Able to perform hypothetical and abstract reasoning

23. What ability does Piaget's three mountains task (below) measure? In what stage can children pass this task?

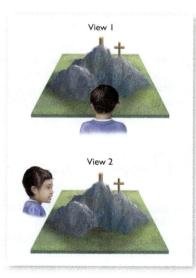

View 1

View 2

24. Modern research suggests that cognitive development is (less/more) continuous and (less/more) general than Piaget theorized.

25. Whereas Piaget emphasized children's exploration of the physical world, Vygotsky believed that _____ and _____ factors were children's primary source of learning.

26. Vygotsky identified the zone of _____ _____ as the phase when a child is receptive to learning a new skill and can make use of _____, the structure provided by parents to aid the child's learning.

8 EXPLAIN HOW CHILDREN ACQUIRE KNOWLEDGE IN IMPORTANT COGNITIVE DOMAINS.

Physical reasoning in infants involves basic, apparently innate knowledge and refinement of knowledge based on experience. Conceptual development requires children to acquire knowledge of how things look, how they are used, and in what contexts they appear. Self-recognition becomes increasingly sophisticated as children move from understanding they are physically distinct entities to understanding that others have minds distinct from their own. Numerical development requires a complex understanding of counting rules and the nature of precise quantities. This ability develops slowly and is easily disrupted. The ability to count doesn't appear in all cultures.

27. Work by Renee Baillargeon shows that infants (do/don't) have a basic understanding of the physics of an object's behavior.

28. A classic test of _____ _____ _____ is the false-belief task, which examines children's ability to reason about what other people know or believe.

9 DESCRIBE HOW ATTITUDES TOWARD KNOWLEDGE CHANGE DURING ADOLESCENCE.

Adolescents are confronted with more adultlike opportunities and decisions that their brain's relatively immature frontal lobes aren't always prepared to handle.

29. The "teen brain" can be distinguished from the adult brain because the _____ _____ are not yet fully developed.

30. William Perry noted that students pass through a variety of _____, or perspectives, on knowledge during their college years as they discover that their professors have few absolute answers to offer.

The Developing Personality: Social and Moral Development

10 DESCRIBE HOW AND WHEN CHILDREN ESTABLISH EMOTIONAL BONDS WITH THEIR CAREGIVERS.

Although infants may recognize and react positively to their caregivers, they don't develop a specific attachment bond until around 8 months of age. The type of attachment that infants form with their caregivers varies depending on parental style and the infant's temperament.

31. Usually starting at 8 or 9 months, babies can develop _____ _____, which may be an adaptive mechanism for keeping infants away from danger.

32. Lorenz showed that newborn goslings bonded to the first moving thing they saw, a phenomenon called _____.

33. Define Harlow's notion of contact comfort and describe the role each "mother" played in helping meet the monkey's needs.

34. Complete the table by describing the four attachment styles identified in Ainsworth's Strange Situation research.

ATTACHMENT STYLE	DESCRIPTION/CHILD'S REACTION
1. Secure attachment	_____
2. Insecure-avoidant attachment	_____
3. Insecure-anxious attachment	_____
4. Disorganized attachment	_____

11 EXPLAIN THE ENVIRONMENTAL AND GENETIC INFLUENCES ON SOCIAL BEHAVIOR AND SOCIAL STYLE IN CHILDREN.

Parenting style (permissive, authoritative, authoritarian, or uninvolved), family structure, and peers may all influence children's behaviors and emotional adjustment, although their precise causal role is controversial. Aspects of children, such as temperament and self-control, also affect their long-term social development.

35. Research suggests that specific parenting styles may not matter so much as whether the parent can provide the _____ _____ environment.

12 DETERMINE HOW MORALITY AND IDENTITY DEVELOP DURING ADOLESCENCE AND EMERGING ADULTHOOD.

Children's initial concepts of morality are based largely on fear of punishment, but over time become more sophisticated and based on intentions rather than consequences. Getting a handle on identity is one of the challenges of adolescence.

36. Erikson coined the term _____ _____ to describe the confusion that most adolescents experience regarding their sense of self.

37. According to Erikson's theory of human development, we travel through _____ stages and we face a different _____ crisis at each stage.

38. Kohlberg studied the development of _____ by scoring the _____ _____ people used as they wrestled with a moral dilemma.

13 IDENTIFY DEVELOPMENTAL CHANGES DURING MAJOR LIFE TRANSITIONS IN ADULTS.

Major life transitions, including career changes, finding a romantic partner, and having children, can be stressful for adults. Nevertheless, contrary to the claims of popular psychology, midlife crises are relatively rare.

39. One of the biggest transitions an adult can go through is becoming a _____.

14 SUMMARIZE DIFFERENT WAYS OF CONCEPTUALIZING OLD AGE.

Chronological age isn't a perfect predictor of physical, social, or cognitive ability in the elderly. Some aspects of cognitive and physical functions begin to decline as early as age 30. However, other cognitive abilities increase with age; how much we slow down depends on a host of factors, including our activity level.

40. A 65-year-old person who is in excellent health and top physical condition may have a(n) _____ _____ of 45.

Apply Your Scientific Thinking Skills

Use your scientific thinking skills to answer the following questions, referencing specific scientific thinking principles and common errors in reasoning whenever possible.

1. Parents now have an amazing amount of parenting advice at their disposal in books, on websites, and through parent Listservs and chat rooms. Research three sources of parenting information and create a list of the key topics they address (such as getting one's infant to sleep or eat better or disciplining one's child). What assumptions do they make about the role of nature versus nurture in parenting? How do these assumptions correspond to scientific research? What, if any, rival hypotheses about children's behaviors do these sources neglect to consider?

2. As we've learned, the frontal lobes don't fully mature until late adolescence or early adulthood, a biological reality that may affect teenage decision making. There is active debate regarding how many teenage behavioral problems stem from the "teen brain." Find three media articles related to this issue that discuss topics such as debates over changing the age at which teens can enlist in the military, drink alcohol legally, obtain a driving license, or stay out during an age-related "curfew." What arguments does each side use to support its case? What scientific or logical errors, if any, does each side make?

3. Based on the research we've discussed regarding the changes that come with age, what features would you include if someone asked you to design a senior center to help healthy aging adults maintain their physical, cognitive, and social well-being? What evidence would you cite to support each of your decisions?

Further Your Understanding

EXTEND YOUR KNOWLEDGE WITH THE MYPSYCHLAB VIDEO SERIES

Watch these videos in MyPsychLab. Follow the "Video Series" link.

The Big Picture: Different Perspectives on the World Watch these interviews and decide whether generational stereotypes are on target or way off base.

The Basics: How Thinking Develops Learn how cognitive development happens early in life. Hear psychologists discuss their work in infant cognition.

The Basics: Attachment See how the quality of the caregiver-child bond, also called attachment, can affect how a child relates to other people for the rest of his or her life.

Special Topics: Risky Behavior and Brain Development See how the adolescent brain is physically different from the adult brain and how these physical differences explain adolescent social behaviors.

Thinking Like a Psychologist: Babies by Design Hear a psychologist's concerns for how children are spending their time and what the best ways are for them to learn and grow.

In the Real World: Socialization Find out about goodness of fit, the four parenting styles, and the impact each has on the developing child.

What's In It for Me?: Identity Explore the importance of identity formation, particularly in emerging adulthood and learn how our modern culture has the unprecedented luxury of allowing ourselves the time to find out who we really are.

EXPERIENCE PSYCHOLOGICAL RESEARCH WITH MYPSYCHLAB SIMULATIONS

Access these simulations in MyPsychLab. Follow the "Simulations" link.

What Has Your Father Done for You? Participate in a survey to define the effects, perceptions, and importance of having a father during childhood and adolescence.

APPLY YOUR CRITICAL THINKING SKILLS WITH MYPSYCHLAB WRITING ASSESSMENTS

Complete these writing assignments in MyPsychLab.

Using specific examples, differentiate between the thinking patterns of a 3-year-old preschooler and a 9-year-old student according to Piaget's theory of cognitive development.

Answer Key

SPECIAL CONSIDERATIONS IN HUMAN DEVELOPMENT

1. developmental psychology
2. post hoc
3. cross-sectional
4. Cohort effects
5. Like a longitudinal design, the series traces the lives of the same group of British people over time, from age 7 all the way up through age 49. Longitudinal design allows us to examine true developmental effects: changes over time as a consequence of growing older. However, this type of design is time-consuming and is not experimental, so it can't be used to infer cause-and-effect relationships.
6. are
7. nature; nurture
8. confound
9. gene-environment interaction
10. 3 (Gene Expression); 1 (Gene-Environment Interaction); 2 (Nature via Nurture)

THE DEVELOPING BODY: PHYSICAL AND MOTOR DEVELOPMENT

11. blastocyst
12. fetus
13. teratogens
14. viability; 40
15. motor behaviors
16. a) sitting without support (6 months); b) crawling (9 months); c) standing (11 months); d) cruising (12 months); e) walking without assistance (13 months); f) running (18–24 months)
17. Although cultural variability in practices such as swaddling and stretching influences the rate of motor development, none of these early physical experiences results in long-term advantages or impairments.
18. primary sex characteristics; secondary sex characteristics
19. sensory
20. no more

THE DEVELOPING MIND: COGNITIVE DEVELOPMENT

21. assimilation; accommodation

22. From top to bottom: sensorimotor (birth to 2 years); preoperational (2 to 7 years); concrete operations (7 to 11 years); formal operations (11 years to adulthood)
23. The task measures egocentrism— the inability to see the world from others' perspectives. Children in the concrete operational stage can pass this task.
24. more; less
25. social; cultural
26. proximal development; scaffolding
27. do
28. theory of mind
29. frontal lobes
30. positions

THE DEVELOPING PERSONALITY: SOCIAL AND MORAL DEVELOPMENT

31. stranger anxiety
32. imprinting
33. Contact comfort refers to positive emotions afforded by touch. When frightened by a novel object, Harlow's infant monkeys almost always preferred the terry cloth mother over the wire mother even though the wire mother was the monkeys' source of food. Contact comfort prevails over nourishment.
34. 1) The infant becomes upset upon mom's departure but greets her return with joy. 2) The infant reacts with indifference to mom's departure and shows little reaction upon her return. 3) The infant reacts to mom's departure with panic and shows a mixed emotional reaction upon her return. 4) The infant reacts to mom's departure and return with an inconsistent and confused set of responses. The infant may appear dazed when reunited with her.
35. average expectable
36. identity crisis
37. eight; psychosocial
38. morality; reasoning processes
39. parent
40. biological age

References

Abel, E. L. (1998). *Fetal alcohol abuse syndrome.* New York, NY: Plenum Press.

Abel, E. L., & Sokol, R. J. (1986). Fetal alcohol syndrome is now leading cause of mental retardation. *Lancet, 2,* 1222.

Aber, M., & Rappaport, J. (1994). The violence of prediction: The uneasy relationship between social science and social policy. *Applied and Preventive Psychology, 3,* 43–54.

Achenbach, T. M. (1982). Research methods in developmental psychopathology. In P. C. Kendall & J. Butcher (Eds.), *Handbook of research methods in clinical psychology* (pp. 127–181). New York, NY: Wiley.

Adolph, K. E. (1997). Learning in the development of infant locomotion. *Monographs of the Society for Research in Child Development, 63,* Serial No. 251.

Adolph, K. E., & Robinson, S. R. (2011): Sampling development, *Journal of Cognition and Development, 12,* 411–423.

Ahnert, L., Pinquart, M., & Lamb, M. E. (2006). Security of children's relationships with nonparental care providers: A meta-analysis. *Child Development, 77*(3), 664–679.

Ainsworth, M. D. S., Blehar, M. C., Waters, E., & Wall, S. (1978). *Patterns of attachment: A psychological study of the Strange Situation.* Hillsdale, NJ: Erlbaum.

Akbarian, S., & Nestler, E. J. (2013) Epigenetic mechanisms in psychiatry. *Neuropsychopharmacology, 28,* 1–2.

Alexander, G. M., & Hines, M. (2002). Sex differences in response to children's toys in non-human primates (*cercopithecus aethiops sabaeus*). *Evolution and Human Behavior, 23,* 467–479.

Alexander, G. M., & Saenz, J. (2012). Early androgens, activity levels and toy choices of children in the second year of life. *Hormones and Behavior, 62,* 500–504.

Alexander, G. M., Wilcox, T., & Woods, R. (2009). Sex differences in infants' visual interest in toys. *Archives of Sexual Behavior, 38,* 427–433.

Almli, C. R., & Finger, S. (1987). Neural insult and critical period concepts. In M. H. Bornstein (Ed.), *Sensitive periods in development: Interdisciplinary perspectives* (pp. 123–143). Hillsdale, NJ: Erlbaum.

Amato, P. R., & Booth, A. (1997). *A generation at risk: Growing up in an era of family upheaval.* Cambridge, MA: Harvard University Press.

Ames, E. (1997). *The development of Romanian orphanage children adopted to Canada. Final report to National Welfare Grants Program: Human Resources Development, Canada.* Barnaby, British Columbia, Canada: Simon Fraser University.

Amsterdam, B. (1972). Mirror self-image reactions before the age of two. *Developmental Psychobiology, 5,* 297–305.

Anderson, D. R., & Pempek, T. A. (2005). Television and very young children. *American Behavioral Scientist, 48,* 505–522.

Arnett, J. J. (1995). The young and the reckless: Adolescent reckless behavior. *Current Directions in Psychological Science, 4,* 67–71.

Arnett, J. J. (1999). Adolescent storm and stress, reconsidered. *American Psychologist, 4,* 317–326.

Arnett, J. J. (2004). *Emerging adulthood: The winding road frm the late teens through the twenties.* Oxford, England: Oxford University Press.

Arterberry, M. E., & Bornstein, M. H. (2012). Categorization of real and replica objects by 14- and 18-month-old infants. *Infant Behavior and Development, 35,* 606–612.

Bahrick, L. E., Moss, L., & Fadil, C. (1996). The development of self recognition in infancy. *Ecological Psychology, 8,* 189–208.

Bahrick, L. E., & Watson, J. S. (1985). Detection of intermodal proprioceptive visual contingency as a potential basis of self-perception in infancy. *Developmental Psychology, 21,* 963–973.

Baillargeon, R. (1987). Object permanence in 3 ½ and 4 ½ month olds. *Developmental Psychology, 23,* 655–664.

Baillargeon, R., & Hanko-Summers, S. (1990). Is the top object adequately supported by the bottom object? Young infants' understanding of support relations. *Cognitive Development, 5,* 29–53.

Baltes, P. B., Staudinger, U. M., & Lindenberger, U. (1999). Lifespan psychology: Theory and application to intellectual functioning. *Annual Review of Psychology, 50,* 471–507.

Baumrind, D. (1971). Current patterns of parental authority. *Developmental Psychology Monographs, 4* (Pts. 1 & 2).

Baumrind, D. (1991). The influence of parenting style on adolescent competence and substance use. *Journal of Early Adolescence, 11,* 56–95.

Beier, M. E., & Ackerman, P. L. (2001). Current events knowledge in adults: An investigation of age, intelligence and non-ability determinants. *Psychology and Aging, 16,* 615–628.

Bell, R. (1968). A reinterpretation of the direction of effects in studies of socialization. *Psychological Review, 75,* 81–95.

Bellamy, C. (1998). *The state of the world's children 1998.* New York, NY: Oxford University Press.

Belsky, J., & Kelly, J. (1994). *The transition to parenthood.* New York, NY: Delacourte.

Berenbaum, S. A., & Hines, M. (1992). Early androgens are related to childhood sex-typed toy preference. *Psychological Science, 3,* 203–206.

Berlin, L. J., Ispa, J. M., Fine, M. A., Malone, P. S., Brooks-Gunn, J., Brady-Smith, C., . . . Bai, Y. (2009). Correlates and consequences of spanking and verbal punishment for low-income White, African American, and Mexican American toddlers. *Child Development, 80,* 1403–1420.

Beunen, G., & Malina, R. M. (1996). *The child and adolescent athlete.* Oxford, England: Blackwell.

Biederman, J., Hirshfeld-Becker, D. R., Rosenbaum, J. F., Herot, C., Friedman, D., Snidman, N., Faraone, S. V. (2001). Further evidence of association between behavioral inhibition and social anxiety in children. *American Journal of Psychiatry, 158,* 1673–1679.

Birch, S. A. J., & Bloom, P. (2007). The curse of knowledge in reasoning about false beliefs. *Psychological Science, 18,* 382–386.

Birren, J. E., & Renner, V. J. (1977). Research on the psychology of aging: Principles and experimentation. In J. E. Birren & K. W. Schaie (Eds.), *Handbook of the psychology of aging* (pp. 3–38). New York, NY: Van Nostrand Reinhold.

Black, S. M., & Hill, C. E. (1984). The psychological well-being of women in their middle years. *Psychology of Women Quarterly, 8,* 282–292.

Blasi, A. (1980). Bridging moral cognition and moral action: A critical review of the literature. *Psychological Bulletin, 88,* 593–637.

Block, J., & Block, J. H. (2006). Venturing a 30-year longitudinal study. *American Psychologist, 61,* 315–327.

Block, J. H., Block, J., & Gjerde, P. F. (1986). The personality of children prior to divorce: A prospective study. *Child Development, 57,* 827–840.

Bloom, P., & Weisberg, D. S. (2007, May 18). Childhood origins of adult resistance to science. *Science, 316,* 996–997.

Blum, D. (2002). *Love at Goon Park: Harry Harlow and the science of affection.* Cambridge, MA: Perseus.

Bonanno, G. A. (2004). Loss, trauma, and human resilience: Have we underestimated the human capacity to thrive after extremely aversive events? *American Psychologist, 59,* 20–28.

Borland, D. C. (1982). A cohort analysis approach to the empty nest syndrome among three ethnic groups of women: A theoretical position. *Journal of Marriage and the Family, 44,* 117–129.

Bowlby, J. (1973). *Attachment and loss. Vol. 2: Separation: Anxiety & anger.* London, England: Hogarth.

Bowlby, J. (1990). The study and reduction of group tensions in the family. In E. Trist, H. Murray, & B. Trist (Eds.), *The social engagement of social science: A Tavistock anthology, Vol. I: The socio-psychological perspective* (pp. 291–298). Philadelphia, PA: University of Pennsylvania Press.

Boyer, P., & Bergstrom, B. (2011). Threat-detection in child development: An evolutionary perspective. *Neuroscience and Biobehavioral Reviews, 35,* 1034–1041.

Boyle, M. H., Miskovic, V., Van Lieshout, R., Duncan, L., Schmidt, L. A., Hoult, L., . . . Saigal, S. (2011). Psychopathology in young adults born at extremely low birth weights. *Psychological Medicine, 41,* 1763–1774.

Bruer, J. T. (1999). *The myth of the first three years: A new understanding of brain development and lifelong learning.* New York, NY: Free Press.

Bureau of Labor Statistics. (2006). *Number of jobs held, labor market activity, and earnings growth among the youngest baby boomers: Results from a longitudinal survey.* Retrieved from http://www.bls.gov/news.release/nlsoy.nr0.htm

Burgess, K. B., Marshall, P., Rubin K. H., & Fox, N. A. (2003). Infant attachment and temperament as predictors of subsequent behavior problems and psychophysiological functioning. *Journal of Child Psychology and Psychiatry and Allied Disciplines, 44,* 1–13.

Busch, C. M., Zonderman, A. B., & Costa, P. T. (1994). Menopausal transition and psychological distress in a nationally representative sample: Is menopause associated with psychological distress? *Journal of Aging and Health, 6,* 209–228.

Byrnes, J. P. (1988). Formal operations: A systematic reformulation. *Developmental Review, 8,* 66–87.

Caldera, Y. M., Huston, A. C., & O'Brien, M. (1989). Social interactions and play patterns of parents and toddlers with feminine, masculine and neutral toys. *Child Development, 60,* 70–76.

Callaway, E. (2012). Fathers bequeath more mutations as they age. *Nature, 488,* 439.

Campbell, D. (1997). *The Mozart effect: Tapping the power of music to heal the body, strengthen the mind, and unlock the creative spirit.* New York, NY: Avon Books.

Cano, F. (2005). Epistemological beliefs and approaches to learning: Their change through secondary school and their influence on academic performance. *British Journal of Educational Psychology, 75,* 203–221.

Cano, F., & Cardelle-Elawar, M. (2004). An integrated analysis of secondary school students' conceptions and beliefs about learning. *European Journal of Psychology of Education, 19,* 167–187.

Carey, S. (1985). *Conceptual change in childhood.* Cambridge, MA: Bradford Books, MIT Press.

Casey, B., Giedd, J. N., & Thomas, K. M. (2000). Structural and functional brain development and its relation to cognitive development. *Biological Psychology, 54,* 241–257.

Caspi, A., McClay, J., Moffitt, T., Mill, J., Martin, J., Craig, I. W., . . . Poulton, R. (2002). Role of genotype in the cycle of violence in maltreated children. *Science, 297,* 851–854.

Cattell, R. B. (1963). Theory of fluid and crystallized intelligence: A critical experiment. *Journal of Educational Psychology, 54,* 1–22.

Caviness, V. S. Jr., Kennedy, D. N., Bates, J. F., & Makris, N. (1996). The developing human brain: A morphometric profile. In R. W. Thatcher, G. R. Lyon, J. Rumsey, & N. Krasnegor (Eds.), *Developmental neuroimaging: Mapping the development of brain and behavior* (pp. 3–14). San Diego, CA: Academic Press.

Centers for Disease Control and Prevention (2009). *NCHS Data Brief: Death in the United States, 2007.* Retrieved from http://www.cdc.gov/NCHS/data/databriefs/db26.htm

Cerella, J. (1985). Information processing rates in the elderly. *Psychological Bulletin, 98,* 67–83.

Chabris, C. F. (1999). Prelude or requiem for the "Mozart effect"? *Nature, 400,* 826–827.

Champagne, F. A., & Mashoodh, R. (2009). Genes in context: Gene-environment interplay and the origins of individual differences in behavior. *Current Directions in Psychological Science, 18,* 127–131.

Cherlin, A. J., Furstenberg, F. F., Chase-Lansdale, P. L., Kiernan, K. E., Robins, P.K., Morrison, D. R., & Teitler, J. O. (1991) Longitudinal studies of effects of divorce on children in Great Britain and the United States. *Science, 252,* 1386–1389.

Chua, A. (2011). *Battle hymn of the tiger mother.* New York, NY: Penguin Press.

Cicchetti, D., & Garmezy, N. (1993). Prospects and promises in the study of resilience. *Development and Psychopathology, 5,* 497–502.

Clark, A., Oswald, A., & Warr, P. (1996). Is job satisfaction U-shaped in age? *Journal of Occupational and Organizational Psychology, 69,* 57–81.

Clarke, A. M., & Clarke, A. D. B. (1976). *Early experience: Myth and evidence.* London, England: Open Books.

Clarke-Stewart, K. A. (1980). The father's contribution to children's cognitive and social development in early childhood. In F. A. Pedersen (Ed.), *The father-infant relationship: Observational studies in the family setting* (pp. 111–146). New York, NY: Praeger.

Clarke-Stewart, K. A. (1988). Parents' effects on children's development: A decade of progress? *Journal of Applied Developmental Psychology, 9,* 41–84.

Cole, M. (1990). Cultural psychology: A once and future discipline? In J. J. Berman (Ed.), *Nebraska Symposium on Motivation, 1989: Cross-cultural perspectives* (pp. 279–335). Lincoln, NE: University of Nebraska Press.

Cole, M. G., & Dendukuri, N. (2003). Risk factors for depression among elderly community subjects: A systematic review and meta-analysis. *American Journal of Psychiatry, 160,* 1147–1156.

Cole, W. G., Lingeman, J. M., & Adolph, K. E. (2012). Go naked: Diapers affect infant walking. *Developmental Science.*

Collins, A. W., Maccoby, E. E., Steinberg, L., Hetherington, M. E., & Bornstein, M. H. (2000). Contemporary research on parenting. *American Psychologist, 55,* 218–232.

Colonnesi, C., Zijlstra, B. J. H., van der Zande, A., & Bögels, S. M. (2012). Coordination of gaze, facial expressions and vocalizations of early infant communication with mother and father. *Infant Behavior and Development, 35,* 523–532.

Condry, J. C., & Condry, S. (1976). Sex differences: A study in the eye of the beholder. *Child Development, 47,* 812–819.

Coombs, R. H. (1991). Marital status and personal well-being: A literature review. *Family Relations: Journal of Applied Family and Child Studies, 40,* 17–102.

Coontz, S. (1992). *The way we never were: American families and the nostalgia trap.* New York, NY: Basic Books.

Copper, R. L., Goldenberg, R. L., Creasy, R. K., DuBard, M. B., Davis, R. O., Entman, S. S., . . . Cliver, S. P. (1993). A multicenter study of preterm, birth weight, and gestational age-specific neonatal mortality. *American Journal of Obstetrics and Gynecology, 168,* 78–84.

Cowan, C. P., & Cowan, P. A. (1995). Interventions to ease the transition to parenthood: Why they are needed and what they can do. *Family Relations, 44,* 412–423.

Cromer, A. (1993). *Uncommon sense: The heretical nature of science.* New York, NY: Oxford University Press.

Dalke, D. E. (2011). Explaining young children's difficulty on the false belief task: Representational deficits or context-sensitive knowledge? *British Journal of Developmental Psychology, 13,* 209–222.

Deater-Deckard, K., & Dodge, K. A. (1997). Externalizing behavior problems and discipline revisited: Nonlinear effects and variation by culture, context, and gender. *Psychological Inquiry, 8,* 161–175.

Dennerstein, L., Lehert, P., & Guthrie, J. (2002). The effects of the menopausal transition and biopsychosocial factors on well-being. *Archives of Women's Mental Health, 5,* 15–22.

Dew, J., & Wilcox, W. B. (2011). If Momma ain't happy: Explaining declines in marital satisfaction among new mothers. *Journal of Marriage and Family, 73,* 1–12.

Dobson, J. (1992). *The strong-willed child.* Carol Stream, IL: Tyndale.

D'Onofrio, B. M., Turkheimer, E. N, Emery, R., Slutske, W., Heath, A., Madden, P. A., & Martin, N. G. (2006). A genetically informed study of the processes underlying the association between parental marital instability and offspring adjustment. *Developmental Psychology, 42,* 486–499.

Downey, G., & Coyne, J. C. (1990). Children of depressed parents: An integrative review. *Psychological Bulletin, 108,* 50–76.

Druckerman, P. (2012) *Bringing up Bebe: One American mother discovers the wisdom of French parenting.* New York, NY: Penguin Press.

Edwards, D. A. (1970). Post-neonatal androgenization and adult aggressive behavior in female mice. *Physiology and Behavior, 5,* 465–467.

Eigsti, I. M., Zayas, V., Mischel, W., Shoda, Y., Ayduk, O., Dadlani, M. B., . . . Casey, B. J. (2006). Predicting cognitive control from preschool to late adolescence and young adulthood. *Psychological Science, 17,* 478–484.

Eisler, R. M., & Ragsdale, K. (1992). Masculine gender role and midlife transition in men. In V. B. Van Hasselt & M. Hersen (Eds.), *Handbook of social development: A lifespan perspective* (pp. 455–471). New York, NY: Plenum Press.

Elman, J. L. (2005). Connectionist models of cognitive development: Where next? *Trends in Cognitive Science, 9,* 111–117.

Epstein, R. (2007). Giving psychology away: A personal journey. *Perspectives on Psychological Science, 1,* 389–400.

Erikson, E. H. (1963). *Childhood and society* (2nd ed.). New York, NY: Norton.

Eveleth, P. B., & Tanner, J. M. (1976). *Worldwide variation in human growth*. Cambridge, England: Cambridge University Press.

Eveleth, P. B., & Tanner, J. M. (1990). *Worldwide variation in human growth* (2nd ed.). Cambridge, England: Cambridge University Press.

Everett, C., & Madora, K. (2012). Quantity recognition among speakers of an anumeric language. *Cognitive Science, 36*, 130–141.

Fagot, B., Hagan, R., Leinbach, M., & Kronsberg, S. (1985). Differential reactions to assertive and communicative acts of toddler girls and boys. *Child Development, 56*, 1499–1505.

Faragher, E. B., Cass, M., & Cooper C. L. (2005). The relationship between job satisfaction and health: A meta-analysis. *Occupational and Environmental Medicine, 62*, 105–112.

Felner, R. D., Ginter, M. A., Boike, M. F., & Cowen, E. L. (1981). Parental death or divorce in childhood: Problems, interventions, and outcomes in a school based mental health project. *Journal of Primary Prevention, 1*, 240–246.

Fiatarone, M. A., Marks, E. C., Ryan, N. D., Meredith, C. N., Lipsitz, L. A., & Evans, W. J. (1990). High-intensity strength training in nonagenarians. *Journal of the American Medical Association, 263*, 3029–3034.

Field, T. (2003). Stimulation of preterm infants. *Pediatrics in Review, 24*, 4–10.

Fivush, R., & Hudson, J. A. (Eds.). (1990). *Knowing and remembering in young children*. New York, NY: Cambridge University Press.

Flavell, J. H. (1992). Cognitive development: Past, present and future. *Developmental Psychology, 28*, 998–1005.

Freedman, D. G. (1978). Ethnic differences in babies. *Human Nature, 2*, 36–43.

Freedman, D. G., & DeBoer, M. (1979). Biological and cultural differences in early child development: A review. *Annual Review of Anthropology, 8*, 579–600.

Freedman, D. G., & Freedman, N. C. (1969). Behavioral differences between Chinese-American and European-American newborns. *Nature, 224*, 122.

Frick, P. J., & Marsee, M. A. (2006). Psychopathy and developmental pathways to antisocial behavior in youth. In C. J. Patrick (Ed.), *Handbook of psychopathy* (pp. 353–374). New York, NY: Guilford Press.

Frontera, W. R., Meredith, C. N., O'Reilly, K. P., Knuttgen, H. H., & Evans, W. J. (1988). Strength conditioning in older men: Skeletal muscle hypertrophy and improved function. *Journal of Applied Physiology, 64*, 1038–1044.

Garmezy, N., Masten, A. S., & Tellegen, A. (1984). The study of stress and competence in children: A building block for developmental psychopathology. *Child Development, 55*, 97–111.

Gellatly, A. R. (1987). Acquisition of a concept of logical necessity. *Human Development, 30*, 32–47.

Gelman, R., & Gallistel, C. (1978). *The child's understanding of number*. Cambridge, MA: Harvard University Press.

Ghisletta, P., Rabbitt, P., Lunn, M., & Lindenberger, U. (2012). Two thirds of the age-based changes in fluid and crystallized intelligence, perceptual speed, and memory in adulthood are shared. *Intelligence, 40*(3), 260–268. http://dx.doi.org/10.1016/j.intell.2012.02.008

Gibbs, J. C. (2006). Should Kohlberg's cognitive developmental approach to morality be replaced with a more pragmatic approach? Comment on Krebs and Denton (2005). *Psychological Review, 113*, 666–671.

Gilligan, C. (1982). *In a different voice: Psychological theory and women's development*. Cambridge, MA: Harvard University Press.

Golombok, S. (2000). *Parenting: What really counts?* London, England: Routledge.

Good, T. L., & Brophy, J. (1995). *Contemporary educational psychology*. Boston, MA: Longman.

Gopnik, A. (2012). Scientific thinking in young children: Theoretical advances, empirical research, and policy implications. *Science, 337*, 1623–1627.

Gordon, P. (2004). Numerical cognition without words: Evidence from Amazonia. *Science, 306*, 496–499.

Gottman, J. S. (1990). Children of gay and pesbian parents. In F. W. Bozett, & M. B. Sussman (Eds.), *Homosexuality and Family Relations* (pp. 177–196). London, England: The Hawthorne Press.

Gould, R. (1978). *Transformations: Growth and change in adult life*. New York, NY: Simon & Schuster.

Gove, W. R., Hughes, M., & Style, C. B. (1983). Does marriage have positive effects on the psychological well-being of the individual? *Journal of Health and Social Behavior, 24*, 122–131.

Graber, J. A., Petersen, A. C., & Brooks-Gunn, J. (1996). Pubertal processes: Methods, measures, and models. In J. A. Graber, J. Brooks-Gunn, & A. C. Petersen (Eds.), *Transitions through adolescence: Interpersonal domains and context* (pp. 23–53). Hillsdale, NJ: Erlbaum.

Graf, P. (1990). Life-span changes in implicit and explicit memory. *Bulletin of the Psychonomic Society, 28*, 353–358.

Gray, G., & Della Sala, S. (2007). The Mozart effect: It's time to face the music! In S. Della Sala (Ed.), *Tall tales about the mind and brain: Separating fact from fiction* (pp. 148–157). Oxford, England: Oxford University Press.

Gredler, M. E. (2012). Understanding Vygotsky for the classroom: Is it too late? *Educational Psychology Review, 24*, 113–131.

Greenberg, D. J., Hillman, D., & Grice, D. (1973). Infant and stranger variables related to stranger anxiety in the first year of life. *Development Psychology, 9*, 207–212.

Greenough, W. T. (1997). We can't just focus on the first three years. *American Psychological Association Monitor on Psychology, 28,* 19.

Greenwood, C. R., Thiemann-Bourque, K., Walker, D., Buzhardt, J., & Gilkerson, J. (2011). Assessing children's home language environments using automatic speech recognition technology. *Communication Disorders Quarterly*. http://dx.doi.org/10.1177/1525740110367826

Guan, J. H., & Wade, M. G. (2000). The effect of aging on adaptive eye–hand coordination. *Journals of Gerontology Series B—Psychological Sciences and Social Sciences, 55*, P151–P162.

Haidt, J. (2007) The new synthesis in moral psychology. *Science, 316*, 998–1002.

Harkins, E. B. (1978). Effects of empty nest transition on self-report of psychological and physical well-being. *Journal of Marriage and the Family, 40*, 549–556.

Harlow, H. F. (1958). The nature of love. *American Psychologist, 13*, 673–685.

Harris, E. C., & Barraclough, B. (1997). Suicide as an outcome for mental disorders—A meta-analysis. *British Journal of Psychiatry, 170*, 205–228.

Harris, J. R. (1995). Where is the child's environment? A group socialization theory of development. *Psychological Review, 102*, 458–489.

Harris, J. R. (2006). *No two alike: Human nature and human individuality*. New York, NY: Norton.

Hart, B., & Risley, T. R. (1995). *Meaningful differences in the everyday experience of young American children*. Baltimore, MD: Paul H. Brookes.

Harter, S. (2012). *Construction of the self* (2nd ed.). New York, NY: Guilford Press.

Hartmann, H. (1939). *Ego psychology and the problem of adaptation*. New York, NY: International Universities Press.

Heinrichs, C., Munson, P., Counts, D., Cutler, G., Jr., & Baron, J. (1995). Patterns of human growth. *Science, 268*, 442–447.

Herman-Giddens, M. E., Steffes, J., Harris, D., Slora, E., Hussey, M., Dowshen, S. A., . . . Reiter, E. O. (2012). Secondary sexual characteristics in boys: Data from pediatric research in office settings network. *Pediatrics*.

Hermanussen, M. (1998). The analysis of short-term growth. *Hormone Research, 49*, 53–64.

Hermanussen, M., & Geiger-Benoit, K. (1995). No evidence for saltation in human growth. *Annals of Human Biology, 22*, 341–345.

Hermanussen, M., Geiger-Benoit, K., Burmeister, J., & Sippell, W. G. (1988). Knemometry in childhood: Accuracy and standardization of a new technique of lower leg length measurement. *Annals of Human Biology, 15*, 1–16.

Hesse, E. (1999). The adult attachment interview: Historical and current perspectives. In J. Cassidy & P. Shaver (Eds.), *Handbook of attachment: Theory, research, and clinical applications* (pp. 395–433). New York, NY: Guilford Press.

Hetherington, E. M., Cox, M., & Cox, R. (1985). Long-term effects of divorce and remarriage on the adjustment of children. *Journal of the American Academy of Child Psychiatry, 24*, 518–530.

Hetherington, E. M., & Stanley-Hagan, M. (2002). Parenting in divorced and remarried families. In M. Bornstein (Ed.), *Handbook of parenting: Being and becoming a parent, Vol. 3*, 287–316. Mahwah, NJ: Erlbaum.

Hoekstra, R. E., Ferrara, T. B., Couser, R. J., Payne, N. R., & Connett, J. E. (2004). Survival and long-term neurodevelopmental outcome of extremely premature infants born at 23–26 weeks' gestation age at a tertiary center. *Pediatrics, 113*, e1–e6.

Hopkins, B., & Westra, T. (1988). Maternal handling and motor development: An intracultural study. *Genetic, Social, and General Psychology Monographs, 114*, 377–408.

Horn, J. L., & Hofer, S. M. (1992). Major abilities and development in the adult period. In R. J. Sternberg & C. A. Berg (Eds.), *Intellectual development* (pp. 44–99). New York, NY: Cambridge University Press.

Hulbert, A. (2003). *Raising America: Experts, parents, and a century of advice about children*. New York, NY: Knopf.

Hunt, M. (1993). *The story of psychology*. New York, NY: Doubleday.

Hurley, B. F., Hanson, E. D., & Sheaff, A. K. (2011). Strength training as a countermeasure to aging muscle and chronic disease. *Sports Medicine, 41*, 289–306.

Jaramillo, J. A., (1996). Vygotsky's sociocultural theory and contributions to the development of constructivist curricula. *Education, 117*, 133–140.

Johnson, M. H. (1998). The neural basis of cognitive development. In W. Damon (Ed.), *Handbook of child psychology: Vol. 2: Cognition, perception, and language* (pp. 1–49). Hoboken, NJ: Wiley.

Kagan, J. (1975). Resilience in cognitive development. *Ethos, 3*, 231–247.

Kagan, J. (1976). Emergent themes in human development. *American Scientist, 64*, 186–196.

Kagan, J. (1994). *Three seductive ideas*. Cambridge, MA: Harvard University Press.

Kagan, J. (1998). Biology and the child. In W. Damon & N. Eisenberg (Eds.), *Handbook of child psychology, Vol. 3: Social, emotional, and personality development* (5th ed., pp. 177–235). Hoboken, NJ: Wiley.

Kagan, J., Reznick, J. S., & Snidman, N. (1988). Biological bases of childhood shyness. *Science, 240*, 167–171.

Kagan, J., Snidman, N., Kahn, V., & Towsley, S. (2007). The preservation of two infant temperaments into adolescence. *SRCD Monographs, 72*(2).

Katz, V. L. (2012). Work and work-related stress in pregnancy. *Clinical Obstetrics & Gynocology, 55*, 765–773.

Kelemen, D. (1999). The scope of teleological thinking in preschool children. *Cognition, 70*, 241–272.

Kelemen, D., Rottman, J., & Seston, R. (2012). Professional physical scientists display tenacious teleological tendencies: Purpose-based reasoning as a cognitive default. *Journal of Experimental Psychology: General,* awaiting volume and page numbers.

Kim-Cohen, J., Caspi, A., Taylor, A., Williams, B., Newcombe, R., Craig, I., & Moffitt, T. (2006). MAOA, maltreatment, and gene-environment interaction predicting children's mental health: New evidence and a meta-analysis. *Molecular Psychiatry, 11,* 903–913.

Klahr, D., & MacWhinney, B. (1998). Information processing. In W. Damon (Ed.), *Handbook of child psychology: Vol. 2: Cognition, perception, and language* (pp. 631–678). Hoboken, NJ: Wiley.

Klaus, M. H., & Kennell, J. H. (1976). *Maternal–infant bonding.* St. Louis, MO: Mosby.

Kochanska, G., Gross, J. N., Lin, M.-H., & Nichols, K. E. (2002). Guilt in young children: Development, determinants, and relations with a broader system of standards. *Child Development, 73,* 461–482.

Kohlberg, L. (1976). Moral stages and moralization: The cognitive-developmental approach. In T. Lickona (Ed.), *Moral development and behavior: Theory, research and social issues* (pp. 31–53). New York, NY: Holt, Rinehart and Winston.

Kohlberg, L. (1981). *The philosophy of moral development: Moral stages and the idea of justice.* San Francisco, CA: Harper & Row.

Kohlberg, L., & Turiel, E. (1971). Moral development and moral education. In G. Lesser (Ed.), *Psychology and educational practice.* Chicago, IL: Scott Foresman.

Konner, M. (1990). *Why the reckless survive—And other secrets of human nature.* New York, NY: Viking Press.

Krebs, D. L., & Denton, K. (2005). Toward a more pragmatic approach to morality: A critical evaluation of Kohlberg's model. *Psychological Review, 112,* 629–649.

Kreppner, J. M., O'Connor, T. G., & Rutter, M. (2001). Can inattention/overactivity be an institutional deprivation syndrome? *Journal of Abnormal Child Psychology, 29,* 513–528.

Kuhn, D., Garcia-Mila, M., Zohar, A., & Andersen, C. (1995). Strategies of knowledge acquisition. *Monographs of the Society for Research in Child Development, 60,* Serial No. 4.

Kushner, H. I. (1993). Taking Erikson's identity seriously: Psychoanalyzing the psychohistorian. *Psychohistory Review, 22,* 7–34.

LaFreniere, P. J., & Sroufe, L. A. (1985). Profiles of peer competence in the preschool: Interrelations among measures, influence of social ecology, and relation to attachment history. *Developmental Psychology, 21,* 56–69.

LaFreniere, P. L., Strayer, F. F., & Gauthier, R. (1984). The emergence of same-sex affiliative preference among preschool peers: A developmental/etho-logical perspective. *Child Development, 55,* 1958–1965.

Lamb, M., & Tamis-LeMonda, C. (2003). The role of the father. In M. Lamb (Ed.), *The role of the father in child development* (4th ed., pp. 1–31). Hoboken, NJ: Wiley.

Lamb, M. E., Thompson, R. A., Gardner, W. P., Charnov, E. L., & Estes, D. (1984). Security of infantile attachment as assessed in the "strange situation": Its study and biological interpretation. *Behavioral and Brain Sciences, 7,* 127–171.

Lampl, M., & Johnson, M. L. (2011). Infant growth in length follows prolonged sleep and increased naps. *Sleep, 34,* 641–650.

Lampl, M., Veldhuis, J. D., & Johnson, M. L. (1992). Saltation and stasis—A model of human growth. *Science, 258,* 801–803.

Langlois, J. H., & Downs, A. C. (1980). Mothers, fathers, and peers as socialization agents of sex-typed play behaviors in young children. *Child Development, 51,* 1237–1247.

Larson, R., & Richards, M. (1994). *Divergent realities: The emotional lives of mothers, fathers, and adolescents.* New York, NY: Basic Books.

Larsson, L. G., Grimby, G., & Karlsson, J. (1979). Muscle strength and speed of movement in relation to age and muscle morphology. *Journal of Applied Physiology, 46,* 451–456.

Laursen, B., Coy, K. C., & Collins, W. (1998). Reconsidering changes in parent-child conflict across adolescence: A meta-analysis. *Child Development, 69,* 817–832.

Lewis, M., & Brooks-Gunn, J. (1979). *Social cognition and the acquisition of self.* New York, NY: Plenum.

Lewis, M., & Carmody, D. P. (2008). Self-representation and brain development. *Developmental Psychology, 44,* 1329–1334.

Li, Y., Liu, J., Liu, F., Guo, G., Anme, T., & Ushijima, H. (2000). Maternal child-rearing behaviors and correlates in rural minority areas of Yunnan, China. *Journal of Developmental & Behavioral Pediatrics, 21,* 114–122.

Lindle, R. S., Metter, E. J., Lynch, N. A., Fleg, J. L., Fozard, J. L., Tobin, J., . . . Hurley, B. F. (1997). Age and gender comparisons of muscle strength in 654 women and men aged 20–93 yr. *Journal of Applied Physiology, 83,* 1581–1587.

Lock, M. (1998). Menopause: Lessons from anthropology. *Psychosomatic Medicine, 60,* 410–419.

Loehlin, J. C. (1997). A test of J. R. Harris's theory of peer influences on personality. *Journal of Personality and Social Psychology, 72,* 1197–1201.

Loevinger, J. (1987). *Paradigms of personality.* New York, NY: W. H. Freeman.

Lorenz, K. (1937). The nature of instinct. In C. H. Schiller (Ed.), *Instinctive behavior: The development of a modern concept* (pp. 129–175). New York, NY: International Universities Press.

Lourenco, O., & Machado, A. (1996). In defense of Piaget's theory: A reply to 10 common criticisms. *Psychological Review, 103,* 143–164.

Luchies, C. W., Schiffman, J., Richards, L. G., Thompson, M. R., Bazuin, D., & DeYoung, A. J. (2002). Effects of age, step direction, and reaction condition on the ability to step quickly. *Journals of Gerontology: Series A: Biological Sciences and Medical Sciences, 57A,* M246–M249.

Luna, B., & Sweeney, J. A. (2004). The emergence of collaborative brain function: fMRI studies of the development of response inhibition. In R. E. Dahl & L. P. Spear (Eds.), *Adolescent brain development: Vulnerabilities and opportunities* (pp. 296–309). New York, NY: New York Academy of Sciences.

Luo, Q., Nakic, M., Wheatley, T., Richell, R., Martin, A., & Blair, R. J. R. (2006). The neural basis of implicit moral attitude—An IAT study using event-related fMRI. *NeuroImage, 30,* 1449–1457.

Luria, A. (1976). *Cognitive development: Its cultural and social foundations.* (M. Lopez-Morillas & L. Solotaroff, Trans.). Cambridge, MA: Harvard University Press.

Lykken, D. T. (1993). Predicting violence in the violent society. *Applied and Preventive Psychology, 2,* 13–20.

Lykken, D. T. (1995). *The antisocial personalities.* Mahwah, NJ: Erlbaum.

Lykken, D. T. (2000). The causes and costs of crime and a controversial cure. *Journal of Personality, 68,* 559–605.

Lytton, H., & Romney, D. M. (1991). Parents' differential socialization of boys and girls: A meta-analysis. *Psychological Bulletin, 109,* 267–296.

Maccoby, E. E., & Martin, J. A. (1983). Socialization in the context of the family: Parent–child interaction. In P. H. Mussen (Ed.) & E. M. Hetherington (Vol. Ed.), *Handbook of child psychology: Vol. 4. Socialization, personality, and social development* (4th ed., pp. 1–101). New York, NY: Wiley.

Main, M., & Cassidy, J. (1988). Categories of response to reunion with the parent at age 6: Predictable from infant attachment classifications and stable over a 1-month period. *Developmental Psychology, 24,* 415–426.

Malina, R. M., & Bouchard, C. (1991). *Growth, maturation, and physical activity.* Champaign, IL: Human Kinetics.

Marieb, E. N., & Hoehn, K. (2007). *Human anatomy and physiology* (7th ed.) San Francisco, CA: Pearson.

Martin, J. N., & Fox, N. A. (2006) Temperament. In McCartney, K., & Phillips, D. (Eds.), *Blackwell handbook of early childhood development* (pp. 126–146). Malden, MA: Blackwell.

McCauley, R. N. (2012). *Why religion is natural and science is not.* New York, NY: Oxford University Press.

McCloskey, M. (1983). Intuitive physics. *Scientific American, 248* (4), 122–130.

McGoron, L., Gleason, M. M., Smyke, A. T., Drury, S. S., Nelson, C. A., III, Gregas, M. C., . . . Zeanah, C. H. (2012). Recovering from early deprivation: Attachment mediates effects of caregiving on psychopathology. *Journal of the American Academy of Child & Adolescent Psychiatry, 51*(7), 683–693.

McLeod, J. D. (1991). Childhood parental loss and adult depression. *Journal of Health and Social Behavior, 32,* 205–220.

Mervielde, I., De Clercq, B., De Fruyt, F., & Van Leeuwen, K. (2005). Temperament, personality, and developmental psychopathology as childhood antecedents of personality disorders. *Journal of Personality Disorders, 19,* 171–201.

Miller, W. R., Brown, J. M., Simpson, T. L., Handmaker, N. S., Bien, T. H., Luckie, L. F., . . . Tonigan, J. S. (1995). What works? A methodological analysis of the alcohol treatment outcome literature. In R. K. Hester (Ed.), *Handbook of alcoholism treatment approaches: Effective alternatives* (2nd ed., pp. 12–44). Boston, MA: Allyn & Bacon.

Minow, N. (2005, December 14). Are "educational" baby videos a scam? Research lacking to support claims. *Chicago Tribune.* Retrieved from http:// blogfromthepond.blogspot.com/2005/12/are-educational-baby-videos-scam.html

Mischel, W., & Ayduk, O. (2004). Willpower in a cognitive-affective processing system: The dynamics of delay of gratification. In R. F. Baumeister & K. D. Vohs (Eds.), *Handbook of self-regulation: Research, theory, and applications* (pp. 99–129). New York, NY: Guilford Press.

Mischel, W., Shoda, Y., & Peake, P. K. (1988). The nature of adolescent competencies predicted by preschool delay of gratification. *Journal of Personality and Social Psychology, 54,* 687–696.

Mischel, W., Shoda, Y., & Rodriguez, M. L. (1989). Delay of gratification in children. *Science, 244,* 933–938.

Mix, K. S. (1999). Similarity and numerical equivalence appearances count. *Cognitive Development, 14,* 269–297.

Mix, K. S., Huttenlocher, J., & Levine, S. C. (1996). Do preschool children recognize auditory-visual numerical correspondences? *Child Development, 67,* 1592–1608.

Moon, Y. (1986). A review of cross-cultural studies on moral judgment development using the Defining Issues Test. *Behavior Science Research, 20,* 147–177.

Moore, T. M., Scarpa, A., & Raine, A. (2002). A meta-analysis of serotonin metabolite 5-HIAA and antisocial behavior. *Aggressive Behavior, 28,* 299–316.

Nass, C., Brave, S., & Takayama, L. (2006). Socializing consistency: From technical homogeneity to human epitome. In P. Zhang & D. Galletta (Eds.), *Human-computer interactions in management information systems: Foundations* (pp. 373–391). Armonk, NY: M.E. Sharpe.

National Center for Health Statistics. (2005). *Life expectancy at birth, 65 and 85 years of age, United States, selected years 1900–2004.* Retrieved from http://www.cdc

gov/nchs/data/hus/2011/022.pdf

Needham, A., & Baillargeon, R. (1993). Intuitions about support in 4.5-month-old infants. *Cognition, 47*, 121–148.

Nelson, K. (1977). The syntagmatic-paradigmatic shift revisited: A review of research and theory. *Psychological Bulletin, 84*, 93–116.

Nelson, K., & Hudson, J. (1988). Scripts and memory function relationships in development. In F. E. Weinert, & M. Perlmutter (Eds.) *Memory development: Universal changes and individual differences* (pp. 147–168). Hillsdale, NJ: Erlbaum.

O'Connor, T. G., Deater-Deckard, K., Fulker, D., Rutter, M., & Plomin, R. (1998). Genotype-environment correlations in late childhood and early adolescence: Antisocial behavioral problems and coercive parenting. *Developmental Psychology, 34*, 970–981.

O'Connor, T. G., & Rutter, M. (2000). Attachment disorder behavior following early severe deprivation: Extension and longitudinal follow-up. *Journal of the American Academy of Child and Adolescent Psychiatry, 39*, 703–712.

Offer, D., & Schoenert-Reichl, K. A. (1992). Debunking the myths of adolescence: Findings from recent research. *Journal of the American Academy of Child and Adolescent Psychiatry, 31*, 1003–1014.

Oshri, A., Rogosch, F. A., & Cicchetti, D. (2012). Child maltreatment and mediating influences of childhood personality types on the development of adolescent psychopathology. *Journal of Clinical Child & Adolescent Psychology, 42*. 187–201.

Paris, J. (2000). *Myths of childhood.* New York, NY: Brunner/Mazel.

Parke, R. (1996). *Fatherhood.* Cambridge, MA: Harvard University Press.

Pascalis, O., de Schonen, S., Morton, J., Deruelle, C., & Fabre-Grenet, M. (1995). Mother's face recognition by neonates: A replication and an extension. *Infant Behavior and Development, 18*, 79–85.

Perlmutter, M. (1983). Learning and memory through adulthood. In M. W. Riley, B. B. Hess, & K. Bond (Eds.), *Aging in society: Selected reviews of recent research.* Hillsdale, NJ: Erlbaum.

Perry, W. G., Jr. (1970). *Forms of intellectual and ethical development in the college years.* Oxford, England: Holt, Rinehart & Winston.

Piaget, J. (1932). *The moral judgment of the child.* London, England: Kegan Paul.

Pietschnig, J., Voracek, M., & Formann, A. K. (2010). Mozart effect-Schmozart effect: A meta-analysis. *Intelligence, 38*, 314–323.

Plomin, R., & Crabbe, J. C. (2000). DNA. *Psychological Bulletin, 126*, 806–828.

Plomin, R., DeFries, J. C., & Loehlin, J. C. (1977). Genotype-environment interaction and correlation in the analysis of human behavior. *Psychological Bulletin, 84*, 309–322.

Potter, D. (2012). Same-sex parent families and children's academic achievement. *Journal of Marriage and Family, 74*, 556–571.

Premack, D., & Woodruff, G. (1978). Does the chimpanzee have a theory of mind? *Behavioral and Brain Sciences, 1*, 515–526.

Priel, B., & de Schonen, S. (1986). Self-recognition: A study of a population without mirrors. *Journal of Experimental Child Psychology, 41*, 237–250.

Pringle, P. J., Geary, M. P. P., Rodeck, C. H., Kingdom, J. C. P., Kayamba-Kay's, S., & Hindmarsh, P. C. (2005). The influence of cigarette smoking on antenatal growth, birth size, and the insulin-like growth factor axis. *Journal of Clinical Endocrinology & Metabolism, 90*, 2556–2562.

Quart, E. (2006, July/August). Extreme parenting. *The Atlantic.* Retrieved from http://www.theatlantic.com/doc/prem/200607/parenting

Quinn, P. C., & Eimas, P. D. (1996). Perceptual cues that permit categorical differentiation of animal species by infants. *Journal of Experimental Child Psychology, 63*, 189–211.

Rankin, J. L. (2005). *Parenting experts: Their advice, the research, and getting it right.* Westport, CT: Praeger.

Raulin, M. L., & Lilienfeld, S. O. (2008). Research paradigms in the study of psychopathology. In P. H. Blaney & T. Milton (Eds.), *Oxford textbook of psychopathology.* (2nd ed., pp. 86–115). New York, NY: Oxford University Press.

Rauscher, F. H., Shaw, G. L., & Ky, K. N. (1993). Music and spatial task performance. *Nature, 365*, 611.

Restak, R. (1984). *The brain.* New York, NY: Bantam.

Reyna, V. F., & Farley, F. (2006). Risk and rationality in adolescent decision making: Implications for theory, practice, and policy. *Psychological Science in the Public Interest, 7*, 1–44.

Ridley, M. (2003). *Nature via nurture: Genes, experience, and what makes us human.* New York, NY: HarperCollins.

Rind, B., Tromovitch, P., & Bauserman, R. (1998). A meta-analytic examination of assumed properties of child sexual abuse using college samples. *Psychological Bulletin, 124*, 22–53.

Roberts, C. J., & Lowe, C. R. (1975). Where have all the conceptions gone? *Lancet, i*, 498–501.

Rochat, P. (2001). *The infant's world.* Cambridge, MA: Harvard University Press.

Rogoff, B. (1995). Observing sociocultural activities on three planes: Participatory appropriation, guided participation, and apprenticeship. In J. V. Wertsch, P. Pablo del R'o, & A. Alvarez (Eds.), *Sociocultural studies of mind* (pp. 139–163). Cambridge, England: Cambridge University Press.

Rogoff, B. (1998). Cognition as a collaborative process. In D. Kuhn & R. S. Seigler (Eds.), *Handbook of child psychology, Vol. 2: Cognition, perception, & language*

(5th ed., pp. 679–744). New York, NY: Wiley.

Rogoff, B., & Chavajay, P. (1995). What's become of research on the cultural basis of cognitive development? *American Psychologist, 50*, 859–877.

Rose, R. J., & Ditto, W. B. (1983). A developmental-genetic analysis of common fears from early adolescence to early adulthood. *Child Development, 54*, 361–368.

Rosenberg, S. D., Rosenberg, H. J., & Farrell, M. P. (1999). The midlife crisis revisited. *Journal of Personality and Social Psychology, 77*, 415–427.

Rotge, J-Y., Grabot, D., Aouizerate, B., Pelissolo, A., Lepine, J-P., & Tignol, J. (2011). Childhood history of behavioral inhibition and comorbidity status in 256 adults with social phobia. *Journal of Affective Disorders, 129*, 338–341.

Rothbaum, R., Weisz, J., Pott, M., Miyake, K., & Morelli, G. (2000). Attachment and culture: Security in Japan and the U.S. *American Psychologist, 55*, 1093–1104.

Ruff, R. M., & Parker, S. B. (1993). Gender- and age-specific changes in motor speed and eye-hand coordination in adults: Normative values for the Finger Tapping and Grooved Pegboard tests. *Perceptual and Motor Skills, 76*, 1219–1230.

Rupp, H. (2003). *Sex segregation in rhesus monkeys* (Macaca mulatta). Unpublished master's thesis, Emory University, Atlanta, GA.

Rutter, M. (1972). *Maternal deprivation reassessed.* Oxford, England: Penguin.

Rutter, M. (1995). Maternal deprivation. In M. H. Bornstein (Ed.), *Handbook of parenting, Vol. 4: Applied and practical parenting* (pp. 3–31). Hillsdale, NJ: Erlbaum.

Rutter, M., Kumsta, R., Schlotz, W., & Sonuga-Barke, E. (2012). Longitudinal studies using a "Natural Experiment" design: The case of adoptees from Romanian institutions. *Journal of the American Academy of Child & Adolescent Psychiatry, 51*, 762–770.

Salter, D., McMillan, D., Richards, M., Talbot, T., Hodges, J., Bentovim, A., . . . Skuse, D. (2003). Development of sexually abusive behaviour in sexually victimised males: A longitudinal study. *Lancet, 361*, 471–476.

Salthouse, T. A. (2004). Localizing age-related individual differences in a hierarchical structure. *Intelligence, 32*, 541–561.

Sanders, C. E., Lubinski, D., & Benbow, C. P. (1995). Does the Defining Issues Test measure psychological phenomena distinct from verbal ability? An examination of Lykken's query. *Journal of Personality and Social Psychology, 69*, 498–504.

Sayakhot, P., Vincent, A., & Teede, H. (2012). Cross-cultural study: Experience, understanding of menopause and related therapies in Australian and Laotian women. *Menopause.* http://dx.doi.org/10.1097/gme.0b013e31825fd14e

Scahill, R. I., Frost, C., Jenkins, R., Whitwell, J. L., Rosser, M. N., & Fox, N. C. (2003). A longitudinal study of brain volume changes in normal aging using serial registered magnetic resonance imaging. *Archives of Neurology, 60*, 989–994.

Scarr, S., & McCartney, K. (1983). How people make their own environments: A theory of genotype-environment effects. *Child Development, 54*, 424–435.

Schlam, T. R., Wilson, N. L., Shoda, Y., Mischel, W., & Ayduk, O. (2012). Preschoolers' delay of gratification predicts their body mass 30 years later. *The Journal of Pediatrics, 162*, 90–93.

Schlegel, A., & Barry, H., III. (1991). *Adolescence: An anthropological inquiry.* New York, NY: Free Press.

Schonfield, D., & Robertson, B. A. (1966). Memory storage and aging. *Canadian Journal of Psychology, 20*, 228–236.

Schothorst, P. F., & van Engeland, H. (1996). Long term behavioral sequelae of prematurity. *Journal of the American Academy of Child and Adolescent Psychiatry, 35*, 175–183.

Schulz, M. S., Cowan, C. P., & Cowan, P. A. (2006). Promoting healthy beginnings: A randomized controlled trial of preventive intervention to preserve marital quality during the transition to parenthood. *Journal of Consulting and Clinical Psychology, 74*, 20–31.

Schwartz, C. E., Wright, C. I., Shin, L. M., Kagan, J., & Rauch, S. L. (2003). Inhibited and uninhibited infants "grown up": Adult amygdalar response to novelty. *Science, 300*, 1952–1953.

Schweder, R., Mahapatra, M., & Miller, J. (1990). Culture and moral development. In J. Kagan & S. Lamb (Eds.), *The emergence of morality in young children* (pp. 1–83). Chicago, IL: University of Chicago Press.

Serbin, L. A., & O'Leary, K. D. (1975). How nursery schools teach girls to shut up. *Psychology Today, 9*(7), 56–58.

Shimamura, A. P., Berry, J. M., Mangels, J. A., Rusting, C. L., & Jurica, P. J. (1995). Memory and cognitive abilities in university professors: Evidence for successful aging. *Psychological Science, 6*, 271–277.

Siegler, R. S. (1995). Children's thinking: How does change occur? In F. E. Weinert & W. Schneider (Eds.), *Memory performance and competencies: Issues in growth and development* (pp. 405–430). Hillsdale, NJ: Erlbaum.

Silvers, J. A., McRae, K., Gabrieli, J. D. E., Gross, J. J., Remy, K. A., & Ochsner, K. N. (2012). Age-related differences in emotional reactivity, regulation, and rejection sensitivity in adolescence. *Emotion.* http://dx.doi.org/10.1037/a0028297

Smith, P. K., & Daglish, L. (1977). Sex differences in parent and infant behavior in the home. *Child Development, 48*, 1250–1254.

Snarey, J. (1982). *The social and moral development of kibbutz founders and Sabras: A cross-sectional and longitudinal cross-cultural study.* Thesis presented to the faculty of the Graduate School of Education, Harvard University, Cambridge, MA.

Sorkhabi, N. (2005). Applicability of Baumrind's parent typology to collective cultures: Analysis of cultural explanations of parent socialization effects. *International Journal of Behavioral Development, 29,* 552–563.

Soto Am, V. L., Vandenberg, L. N., Maffini, M. V., & Sonnenschein, C. (2008). "Does breast cancer start in the womb?" *Basic & Clinical Pharmacology & Toxicology, 102,* 125–133.

Spelke, E. S. (1994). Initial knowledge: Six suggestions. *Cognition, 50,* 431–445.

Sroufe, L. A. (1983). Infant-caregiver attachment and patterns of adaptations in preschool: The roots of maladaptations and competence. In M. Perlmutter (Ed.), *Minnesota Symposium on Child Psychology* (Vol. 16, pp. 41–81). Hillsdale, NJ: Erlbaum.

Steele, F., Rasbash, J., & Jenkins, J. (2012). A multilevel simultaneous equations model for within-cluster dynamic effects, with an application to reciprocal parent–child and sibling effects. *Psychological Methods.* http://dx.doi.org/10.1037/a0029316

Steele, K. M., Bass, K. E., & Crook, M. D. (1999). The mystery of the Mozart effect: Failure to replicate. *Psychological Science, 10,* 366–369.

Steinberg, L. (2001). We know some things: Adolescent-parent relationships in retrospect and prospect. *Journal of Research in Adolescence, 11,* 1–20.

Steinberg, L. (2007). Risk-taking in adolescence: New perspectives from brain and behavioral science. *Current Directions in Psychological Science, 16,* 55–59.

Steinberg, L., & Scott, E. S. (2003). Less guilty by reason of adolescence—Developmental immaturity, diminished responsibility, and the juvenile death penalty. *American Psychologist, 58,* 1009–1018.

Stromswold, K. (2001). The heritability of language: A review and metaanalysis of twin, adoption, and linkage studies. *Language, 77,* 647–723.

Sunar, D. (2002). The psychology of morality. In W. J. Lonner, D. L. Dinnel, S. Hayes, & D. N. Sattler (Eds.), *Online readings in psychology and culture* (Unit 2, Chap. 11), Center for Cross-Cultural Research, Western Washington University, Bellingham, WA.

Suomi, S. J. (1997). Early determinants of behaviour: Evidence from primate studies. *British Medical Bulletin, 53,* 170–184.

Swaiman, K. F., & Ashwal, S. (1999). *Pediatric neurology: Principles and practice* (3rd ed.). St. Louis, MO: Mosby.

Tanner, J. M. (1990). *Fetus into man: Physical growth from conception to maturity* (Rev. ed.). Cambridge, MA: Harvard University Press.

Tanner, J. M. (1998). Sequence, tempo, and individual variation in growth and development of boys and girls aged twelve to sixteen. In R. E. Muuss & H. D. Porton (Eds.), *Adolescent behavior and society: A book of readings* (5th ed., pp. 34–46). New York, NY: McGraw-Hill.

Thelen, E. (1995). Time-scale dynamics and the development of an embodied cognition. In R. F. Port & T. van Gelder (Eds.), *Mind as motion: Explorations in the dynamics of cognition* (pp. 69–100). Cambridge, MA: MIT Press.

Thelen, E., & Ulrich, B. D. (1991). Hidden skills: A dynamic systems analysis of treadmill stepping during the first year. *Monographs of the Society for Research in Child Development, 56,* Serial No. 223.

Thomas, A., & Chess, S. (1977). *Temperament and development.* New York, NY: Brunner/Mazel.

Thompson, R. A. (1998). Early sociopersonality development. In W. Damon (Series Ed.) & N. Eisenberg (Vol. Ed.), *Handbook of child psychology: Vol. 3. Social, emotional, and personality development* (5th ed., pp. 25–104). New York, NY: Wiley.

Thompson, W. F., Schellenberg, E. G., & Husain, G. (2001). Arousal, mood, and the Mozart effect. *Psychological Science, 12,* 248–251.

Tomasello, M. (2000). *The cultural origins of human cognition.* Cambridge, MA: Harvard University Press.

Tomasello, M. (2008). *Origins of human communication.* Cambridge, MA: MIT Press.

Triandis, H. C., & Suh, E. M. (2002). Cultural influences on personality. *Annual Review of Psychology, 53,* 133–160.

Turner, S. M., Beidel, D. C., & Wolff, P. L. (1996). Is behavioral inhibition related to the anxiety disorders? *Clinical Psychology Review, 16,* 57–172.

U.S. Census Bureau (2010). 2010 Census Data. Retrieved from http://www.census.gov/2010census/data

U.S. Census Bureau (2011). American Community Survey. Retrieved from http://www.census.gov/acs

Vaillant, E., & Milofsky, E. (1980). Natural history of male psychological health: IX. Empirical evidence for Erikson's model of the life cycle. *American Journal of Psychiatry, 137,* 1348–1359.

Van Ijzendoorn, M. H., & De Wolff, M. S. (1997). In search of the absent father: Meta-analyses on infant–father attachment. *Child Development, 68,* 604–609.

Van Ijzendoorn, M. H., & Sagi, A. (1999). Cross-cultural patterns of attachment: Universal and cultural dimensions. In J. Cassidy & P. R. Shaver (Eds.), *Handbook of attachment: Theory, research, and clinical applications* (pp. 713–734). New York, NY: Guilford Press.

Vartanian, L. R. (2000). Revisiting the imaginary audience and personal fable constructs of adolescent egocentrism: A conceptual review. *Adolescence, 35,* 639–661.

Wainright, J. L., Russell, S. T., & Patterson, C. J. (2004). Psychosocial adjustment, school outcomes, and romantic relationships of adolescents with same-sex parents. *Child Development, 75,* 1886–1898.

Wallerstein, J. S. (1989, January 22). Children after divorce: Wounds that don't heal. *New York Times Magazine, 19,* 42.

Walsh, F. (1999). Families in later life: Challenges and opportunities. In B. Carter & M. McGoldrick (Eds.), *The expanded family life cycle: Individual, family and social perspectives* (3rd ed., pp. 307–326). Boston, MA: Allyn & Bacon.

Waters, E., Matas, L., & Sroufe, L. A. (1975). Infants' reactions to an approaching stranger: Description, validation, and functional significance of wariness. *Child Development, 46,* 348–356.

Waxman, S. R., & Booth, A. E. (2001). On the insufficiency of domain-general accounts of word-learning: A reply to Bloom and Markson. *Cognition, 78,* 277–279.

Wayment, H. A., & Peplau, L. A. (1995). Social support and well-being among lesbian and heterosexual women: A structural modeling approach. *Personality and Social Psychology Bulletin, 21,* 1189–1199.

Weinberger, D. R., Elvevag, B., & Giedd, J. N., (2005). *The adolescent brain: A work in progress, The National Campaign to Prevent Teen Pregnancy.* Retrieved from http://www.teenpregnancy.org/resources/reading/pdf/BRAIN.pdf

Weiss, L. H., & Schwarz, J. C. (1996). The relationship between parenting types and older adolescents' personality, academic achievement, adjustment, and substance use. *Child Development, 67,* 2101–2114.

Welford, A. (1977). Mental workload as a function of demand, capacity, strategy and skill: Synthesis report. *Travail Humain, 40,* 283–304.

Wellman, H. M., Cross, D., & Watson, J. (2001). Meta-analysis of theory-of-mind development: The truth about false belief. *Child Development, 72,* 655–684.

Whiting, B. B., & Edwards, C. P. (1988). *Children of different worlds: The formation of social behavior.* Cambridge, MA: Harvard University Press.

Wimmer, H., & Perner, J. (1983). Beliefs about beliefs: Representation and constraining function of wrong beliefs in young children's understanding of deception. *Cognition, 13,* 103–128.

Windham, G. C., Hopkins, B., Fenster, L., & Swan, S. H. (2000). Prenatal active or passive tobacco smoke exposure and the risk of preterm delivery or low birth weight. *Epidemiology, 11,* 427–433.

Winnicott, D. (1958). *Collected papers—Through pediatrics to psychoanalysis.* New York, NY: Basic Books.

Woehrer, C. E. (1982). The influence of ethnic families on intergenerational relationships and later life transitions. In F. M. Berardo (Ed.), *The Annals of the American Academy of Political and Social Science* (pp. 65–78). Beverly Hills, CA: Sage.

Wolkowitz, O. M., Reus, V. I., & Mellon, S. H. (2011). Of sound mind and body: Depression, disease, and accelerated aging. *Dialogues in Clinical Neuroscience, 13,* 25–39.

Wood, D., Bruner, J. A., & Ross, G. (1976). Role of tutoring in problem-solving. *Journal of Child Psychology and Psychiatry and Allied Disciplines, 17,* 89–100.

Wood, E., Desmarais, S., & Gugula, S. (2002). The impact of parenting experience on gender stereotyped toy play of children. *Sex Roles, 47,* 39–49.

Young, W. C., Goy, R. W., & Phoenix C. H. (1964). Hormones and sexual behavior. *Science, 143,* 212–218.

Zimmerman, F. J., Christakis, D. A., & Meltzoff, A. N. (2007) Associations between media viewing and language development in children under age 2 years. *The Journal of Pediatrics, 151,* 364–368.

Credits

Credits listed in order of appearance.

Figure 1: Marieb, Elaine N.; Hoehn, Katja, Human Anatomy & Physiology, 7th Ed., © 2007, p.118 Reprinted and electronically reproduced by permission Pearson Education, Inc., Upper Saddle River, New Jersey. **Unnumbered Figure 1:** Adapted from Restak, R. (1984). *The brain.* New York: Bantam Books. **Figure 13:** Based on Mix, K. S. (1999). Similarity and numerical equivalence: appearances count. Cognitive Development, 14, 2, p. 269–297. **Figure 15:** Based on Kagan, J., Reznick, J. S., & Snidman, N. (1988). Biological bases of childhood shyness. Science, 240, 167–171. **Figure 17:** Good, Thomas L.; Brophy, Jere. Contemporary Educational Psychology, 5th Ed., (c)1995, p. 84. Reprinted and electronically reproduced by Pearson Education, Inc. Upper Saddle River, New Jersey. **Text:** Kohlberg, L. (1981). The philosophy of moral development: Moral stages and the idea of justice. San Francisco: Harper & Row.

Photo Credits

Photo Credits listed in order of appearance.

Image Source/Alamy; Bombaert Patrick/Alamy; **(bottom):** Panoramic/Zuma/Newscom; **(center right):** Sorge/Caro/Alamy; **(top left):** Ian Shaw Alamy; **(center left):** Bureau L.A. Collection/Corbis; **(top right):** RBM Online/epa/Corbis; **(center right):** Science Source; **(bottom right):** Claude Edelmann/Science Source/Photo Researchers; **(bottom):** Stuart Wong/KRT/Newscom; **(top left):** Keren Su/Encyclopedia/Corbis; **(top right):** Nick Obank/Barcroft Media/Landov; **(bottom left):** Ma Yan Xinhua News Agency/Newscom; **(center right):** Mary Kate Denny/PhotoEdit; **(bottom center):** BSIP/Photo Researchers; **(center right):** Robert Michael/Corbis; **(center left):** Bill Anderson/Photo Researchers; **(top right):** Doug Goodman/Photo Researchers; **(center right):** Doug Goodman/Photo Researchers; **(top left):** Marsists.org; **(center left):** James Shaffer/PhotoEdit; **(top right):** Stuart Gregory/Photodisc/Getty Images; **(center):** Lorraine E. Bahrick; **(bottom center):** Martin Smith-Rodden/Zuma/Newscom; **(bottom left):** Infocusphoto/Alamy; **(top left):** Elizabeth Crews/The Image Works; **(center left):** MGP/Photodisc/Getty Images; **(bottom left):** Michael Newman/PhotoEdit; **(top right):** Nina Leen/Time Life Pictures/Getty Images; **(center right):** Sidney Harris/Science Cartoons Plus; **(top left):** Photo Researchers; **(top left):** Eugene Gologursky/Getty Images; **(center left):** Timothy A. Clary/AFP/Getty Images/Newscom; **(center right):** Tanya Constantine/Getty Images; **(top left):** Richard Jolley/CartoonStock; **(bottom left):** Rachel Epstein/The Image Works; **(bottom center):** Tony Freeman/PhotoEdit, Inc.; **(center right):** Pearson Education; **(top right):** Zuma Wire Service/Alamy; **(center left):** Gerianne Alexander/KRT/Newscom; **(center right):** Gerianne Alexander/KRT/Newscom; **(top left):** Mira/Alamy; **(center right):** Ei Katsumata/Alamy; **(top right):** Eric Miller KRT/Newscom; **(top left):** Yellow Dog Productions/Getty Images; **(top right):** Alice Musbach/Alamy; **(bottom right):** Big Cheese Photos Photograph/FotoSearch; **(bottom left):** Peter Hvizdak/The Image Works; **(top):** Laura Namy; **(center left):** Bureau L.A. Collection/Corbis; **(center):** Keren Su/Encyclopedia/Corbis; **(top):** Photo Researchers, Inc.

Emotion and Motivation

From Chapter 11 of *Psychology: From Inquiry to Understanding,* Third Edition. Scott O. Lilienfeld, Steven Jay Lynn, Laura L. Namy, Nancy J. Woolf.

Emotion and Motivation

WHAT MOVES US

Are emotion and reason opposites of each other?

Is the polygraph test really a "lie detector"?

Are people who have good things happen to them happier than other people?

Does sexual desire disappear in old age?

Do opposites attract in romantic relationships?

Emotion and Motivation

Listen in **MyPsychLab** to chapter audio

Meet Elliott. He's a Caucasian male, 30 years of age. At first blush, Elliott looks and acts pretty much like everyone else. He's well dressed and socially appropriate, and his scores on tests of intelligence, memory, and language are boringly normal. Yet Elliott is different—very different—from the average person in two ways.

First, Elliott is missing a sizable chunk of tissue from his frontal lobe as a result of surgery to remove a brain tumor. In many respects, Elliott is a contemporary version of Vermont railroad worker Phineas Gage, who lost much of his frontal cortex in a catastrophic accident in 1848 (Damasio, 1994; Eslinger & Damasio, 1985).

Second, Elliott seems entirely devoid of emotion. Antonio Damasio (1994), who studied Elliott in depth, remarked that in his many hours of observing him, he never witnessed a hint of sadness, irritation, or any other fundamentally human emotions. When Damasio's colleague Daniel Tranel showed Elliott a series of upsetting photographs, including pictures of gruesome injuries, buildings crumbling during earthquakes, and houses in flames, Elliott displayed virtually no emotional response. Nor does Elliott express much joy when describing the wonderful moments of his life. As Damasio (1994) noted, to understand Elliott, we need to imagine a life devoid of pleasure in response to a beautiful painting or a favorite piece of music. Elliott knows that these experiences once moved him deeply, but he now feels essentially nothing when he encounters them.

What's more, Elliott's life is in utter shambles. Before the operation, Elliott was a successful businessman with a happy and balanced home life. But since then, he has made foolish decisions, investing all of his savings in a risky business venture and going bankrupt. He also married a woman who was a poor match for him, resulting in an abrupt divorce. His on-the-job performance is no better.

Elliott's case imparts a valuable lesson: emotion and reason aren't necessarily opposites. To the contrary, emotion is often the servant of reason (Levine, 1998). Without feelings, we have scant basis for rational decisions. Recent research suggests that college students who were made a bit angry by researchers (who asked the students to write about past infuriating experiences) are actually better than non-angry students at distinguishing strong from weak scientific arguments in research studies (Moons & Mackie, 2007). Elliott married the wrong woman in part because he'd lost access to his "gut feelings" concerning his attraction to members of the opposite sex. He based his choice of a romantic partner largely on reason alone, which is typically a recipe for disaster (Gigerenzer, 2007). Even though Mr. Spock of *Star Trek* fame is heralded as the epitome of pure reason, research suggests that a real-life version of Mr. Spock would actually be far more irrational than rational. His absence of emotional reactions would ultimately do him in as he attempted to generate solutions to everyday problems.

Popular wisdom teaches us that many emotions, especially negative ones, are bad for us. A slew of pop psychology books encourage us not to feel especially angry, guilty, ashamed, or sad. Such emotions, the books inform us, are unhealthy, even "toxic." Take the 2013 book *Your Killer Emotions*, which warns readers that strongly held emotions "can kill the accomplishment of your plans, the fulfillment of your dreams, and the attainment of the life you envision and so dearly want for yourself" (Linder, 2013, p. ix). Like many exaggerated claims in pop psychology, this one contains a kernel of truth. Pop psychologists are correct that excessive and unjustified anger, guilt, and the like can sometimes be self-destructive. "Everything in moderation," as our grandmother reminded us. But they're wrong to suggest we'd be better off without these feelings, because many emotions—even negative ones—are crucial to our survival.

Theories of Emotion: What Causes Our Feelings?

1 Describe the major theories of emotion.

2 Identify unconscious influences on emotion.

Elliott and Mr. Spock aside, virtually all of us experience **emotions**—mental states or feelings associated with our evaluation of our experiences. Although psychologists don't agree completely on what causes our emotions, we'll soon discover that they've made significant strides toward unraveling this and many other enduring mysteries.

emotion

mental state or feeling associated with our evaluation of our experiences

Discrete Emotions Theory: Emotions as Evolved Expressions

According to **discrete emotions theory**, humans experience only a small number of distinct emotions that combine in complex ways (Griffiths, 1997; Izard, 1994; Tomkins, 1962). Advocates of this theory propose that each basic emotion (1) has its own biological roots and (2) serves one or more distinctive evolutionary functions that are essentially the same in all of us (Ekman & Friesen, 1971). They further argue that because the brain's cortex, which plays a key role in thinking, evolved later than did the limbic system, which plays a key role in emotion, our emotional reactions to situations come before our thoughts about them (Zajonc, 1984, 2000).

SUPPORT FOR AN EVOLUTIONARY BASIS OF EMOTIONS. The fact that some emotional expressions emerge even without direct reinforcement suggests that they may be by-products of innate motor programs (Freedman, 1964; Panksepp, 2007). Newborn infants smile spontaneously during REM sleep, the sleep stage during which most vivid dreaming occurs. At about 6 weeks, babies start to smile whenever they see a favorite face, and at about 3 months, they may smile when they're learning to do something new, even when no one's around (Plutchik, 2003). Irenäus Eibl-Eibesfeldt (1973) showed that even 3-month-old babies who are blind from birth smile in response to playing and tickling and frown and cry when left alone.

Consider the emotion of *disgust*, which derives from the Latin term for "bad taste." Imagine we asked you to swallow a piece of food that you find repulsive, like a dried-up cockroach (apologies to those of you reading this chapter over lunch or dinner). The odds are high that you'd wrinkle your nose, contract your mouth, stick out your tongue, turn your head slightly to one side, and close your eyes at least partly (Phillips et al., 1997). Discrete emotions theorists would say that this coordinated set of reactions is evolutionarily adaptive. When you wrinkle your nose and contract your mouth, you're reducing the chances you'll ingest this substance; by sticking out your tongue, you're increasing the chances you'll expel it; by turning your head, you're doing your best to avoid it; and by closing your eyes, you're limiting the damage it can do to your visual system. Other emotions similarly prepare us for biologically important actions (Frijda, 1986). When we're angry, our teeth and fists often become clenched, readying us to bite and fight. And when we're afraid, our eyes open wide, allowing us to better spot potential dangers, like predators, lurking in our environment.

Charles Darwin (1872) was among the first to point out the similarities between the emotional expressions of humans and many nonhuman animals. He noted that the angry snarl of dogs, marked by the baring of their fangs, is reminiscent of the dismissive sneer of humans. Eugene Morton (1977, 1982) showed deep-seated similarities in communication across most animal species, especially mammals and birds, further suggesting that the emotions of humans and nonhuman animals share the same evolutionary heritage. For example, across the animal kingdom, high-pitched sounds are associated with friendly interactions; low-pitched sounds, with hostile interactions. Jaak Panksepp (2005) discovered that rats emit a high-pitched chirp, perhaps similar to human laughter, when tickled. The high-pitched panting of dogs during play also seems similar in many ways to human laughter, as does the chuckling of chimpanzees (Provine, 2012).

Of course, the mere fact that two things are superficially similar doesn't prove that they share evolutionary roots. In the case of emotions, however, we know that all mammals share an evolutionary ancestor. The fact that many mammals display similar emotional reactions during similar social behaviors, such as tickling and play, lends itself to a parsimonious hypothesis: perhaps these reactions share the same evolutionary origins.

CULTURE AND EMOTION. Another way of evaluating claims that discrete emotions are products of evolution is to examine the *universality* of emotional expressions. If we humans evolved to express emotions a certain way, we'd expect expressions to communicate the same meaning across cultures. We'd also expect people across the world to recognize emotions similarly.

People have recognized the facial reaction of disgust for centuries. This is a photograph from Charles Darwin's book on the expression of emotions, published in 1872.

Factoid

The facial characteristics associated with fear, including big eyes and an open mouth, are similar to the facial characteristics of babies. Some scholars speculate that these facial signals evolved to make others more likely to nurture and take care of us when we're afraid (Marsh, Adams, & Kleck, 2005).

David Matsumoto and Bob Willingham, themselves former national judo competitors, examined the facial expressions of judo competition winners and losers at the 2004 Athens Olympics. They found that competitors in 35 countries across six continents displayed extremely similar smiles and other facial reactions after winning a match or receiving a medal (Matsumoto & Willingham, 2006).

◄ **OCCAM'S RAZOR**
Does a simpler explanation fit the data just as well?

discrete emotions theory
theory that humans experience a small number of distinct emotions that are rooted in their biology

477

REPLICABILITY ▶
Can the results be duplicated
in other studies?

RULING OUT RIVAL HYPOTHESES ▶
Have important alternative explanations for
the findings been excluded?

(a)   (b)   (c)

(d)   (e)   (f)

? Six of the seven primary emotions
identified by Paul Ekman and his
colleagues. **Can you match each face to
the corresponding emotions of anger, disgust,
fear, happiness, sadness, and surprise?** (See
answer upside down at bottom of page.)

Some psychologists believe that pride is also a
discrete emotion. Pride tends to be associated
with a smile, along with the head pushed back,
the chest pushed forward, and one's hands
on the hips or in the air (Tracy & Robins,
2007)—as shown here.

primary emotions
small number (perhaps seven) of
emotions believed by some theorists to be
cross-culturally universal

▶ Simulate in **MyPsychLab** the
Experiment: Recognizing Facial
Expressions of Emotions

Recognition of Emotions Across Cultures. Indeed, one telling piece of evidence for discrete emotions theory derives from well-replicated research showing that college students and other participants in North American and European countries recognize and generate the same emotional expressions across cultures (Izard, 1971). Nevertheless, this research is vulnerable to a rival explanation: because these participants have all been exposed to Western culture, the similarities may be due to shared experiences rather than a shared evolutionary heritage.

To rule out this explanation, in the late 1960s, American psychologist Paul Ekman traveled to the wilds of southeastern New Guinea to study a group of people who'd been essentially isolated from Western culture and still used Stone Age tools. With the aid of a translator, Ekman read them a brief story (for example, "His mother has died, and he feels very sad"), along with a display of photographs of Americans depicting various emotions, like happiness, sadness, and anger. Then, Ekman asked them to select the photograph that matched the story. He later went further, asking U.S. college students to guess which emotions the New Guineans were displaying (Ekman & Friesen, 1971).

Ekman (1999) and his colleagues (Ekman & Friesen, 1986) concluded that a small number of **primary emotions**—perhaps seven—are cross-culturally universal. Specifically, they found that the facial expressions associated with these emotions are recognized across most, if not all, cultures. Discrete emotions theorists call these emotions "primary" because they're presumably the biologically based emotions from which other emotions arise:

- Happiness
- Sadness
- Surprise
- Anger
- Disgust
- Fear
- Contempt

As we can see in the photos, each emotion is linked with a characteristic set of muscular changes. Some research suggests that pride, which tends to be associated with a smile and an upward tilting of the head, may also be a cross-culturally universal emotion (Tracy & Robins, 2007). Other work raises the possibility that awe, the emotion we feel when we encounter something vast and mysterious, is also a primary emotion (Rudd, Vohs, & Aaker, 2013; Shiota, Keltner, & Mossman, 2007). Awe tends to be associated with a person staring upward while gaping. Nevertheless, the evidence that pride and awe are primary emotions is more preliminary than that for the "Big Seven" emotions we've listed.

In his cross-cultural work, Ekman and his colleagues found that certain primary emotions are easier to detect than others. Happiness tends to be the most easily recognized emotion (Ekman, 1994; Elfenbein & Ambady, 2002). In contrast, negative emotions are more difficult to recognize; many people confuse disgust with anger, anger with fear, and fear with surprise (Elfenbein & Ambady, 2002; Tomkins & McCarter, 1964). One challenge to discrete emotions theory, however, is that people across widely different cultures don't always agree on which facial expressions go with which emotions (Feldman Barrett & Bliss-Moreau, 2009; Jack, Garrod, Caldara, & Schyns, 2012; Russell, 1994). Nevertheless, as discrete emotion theory would predict, the levels of agreement are far higher than would be expected by chance alone, suggesting at least some cross-cultural universality in the recognition of emotion.

Primary emotions don't tell the whole story of our feelings. Just as talented painters create a magnificently complex palette of secondary paint colors, like various shades of

Answers: (a) happiness; (b) sadness; (c) fear; (d) surprise; (e) disgust; (f) anger.

green and purple, from a few primary paint colors, like blue and yellow, our brains "create" an enormous array of *secondary emotions* from a small number of primary emotions. The secondary emotion of "alarm" seems to be a mixture of fear and surprise, and the secondary emotion of "hatred" seems to be a mixture of anger and disgust (Plutchik, 2000).

Cultural Differences in Emotional Expression: Display Rules. The finding that certain emotions exist across most or all cultures doesn't mean that cultures are identical in their emotional expressions. In part, that's because cultures differ in **display rules**, societal guidelines for how and when to express emotions (Ekman & Friesen, 1975; Matsumoto et al., 2005). In Western culture, parents teach most boys not to cry, whereas they typically teach girls that crying is acceptable (Plutchik, 2003). Americans can be taken aback when a visitor from South America, the Middle East, or some European countries like Russia greets them by planting a kiss on their cheek.

In a study of display rules, Wallace Friesen (1972) videotaped Japanese and American college students without their knowledge as they watched films, either while alone or with an experimenter. He asked both individuals in each group of students to watch two film clips, one of a neutral travel scene (the control condition) and one of an incredibly gory film depicting a ritual genital mutilation (the experimental condition). When each student was alone, his or her facial reactions to the films was similar: Participants in both groups showed little emotional reaction to the neutral film but clear signs of fear, disgust, and distress to the gory film. Yet when an older experimenter entered the room, the role of culture became apparent. Although American students' reactions to the films didn't change, Japanese students typically smiled during the gory film, concealing their negative emotional reactions. In Japanese culture, deference to authority figures is the norm, so the students acted as though they were happy to see the films. In many cases, culture doesn't influence emotion itself; it influences its overt expression (Fok et al., 2008).

Still, display rules may not tell the full story of cultural differences in emotion. One research team asked North American participants to guess the nationality of either Japanese-American individuals or native Japanese individuals as they assumed either a neutral expression or an emotional expression in photographs. Participants were significantly more accurate in guessing individuals' nationality when they expressed emotion in photographs, suggesting that different cultures may be associated with different "nonverbal accents"—slight differences in facial expression depending on one's culture (Marsh, Elfenbein, & Ambady, 2003). The presence of nonverbal accents suggests that although discrete emotion theory may be largely right, culture can subtly shape how emotions are expressed (Elfenbein, 2013).

ACCOMPANIMENTS OF EMOTIONAL EXPRESSIONS. According to discrete emotions theorists, each primary emotion is associated with a distinctive constellation of facial expressions. In anger, our lips consistently narrow and our eyebrows move downward. In contempt, we frequently lift and tighten our lips on one side of our face, generating a smirk (Matsumoto & Ekman, 2004) or roll our eyes upward, in effect communicating "I'm above (superior to) you" (see **FIGURE I**).

Emotions and Physiology. We can differentiate at least some primary emotions by their patterns of physiological responding (Ax, 1953; Rainville et al., 2006). The mere act of making a face associated with a specific emotion alters our bodily reactions in characteristic ways (Ekman, Levenson, & Friesen, 1983). Our heart rates increase more when we make angry and fearful expressions than happy or surprised facial expressions (Cacioppo et al., 1997), probably because the first two emotions are more closely linked to the emergency reactions we experience when we're threatened. Our heart kicks into high gear when we're in danger, mobilizing us for action (Frijda, 1986). Yet even fear and anger differ physiologically. When we're afraid, our digestive systems tend to slow down. In contrast, when we're angry, our digestive systems tend to speed up, which explains why our "stomachs churn" when we're furious (Carlson & Hatfield, 1992).

In April 2007, American actor Richard Gere scandalized much of India by kissing Indian actress Shilpa Shetty's cheek on stage at an AIDS awareness rally. This action even resulted in a warrant being placed for Gere's arrest in India; it was later dropped. Gere was apparently unaware of display rules in India that strictly forbid kissing in public.

Pair I

Pair 2

FIGURE I Which Mask Conveys a Threat? In hunter–gatherer societies, people often construct masks to convey threat, especially anger. These two pairs of shapes are based on wooden masks worn in these societies. In both cases, the shape on the left communicates more threat. Even American college students can distinguish the threatening from nonthreatening mask at higher-than-chance levels. (*Source:* Aronoff, Barclay, & Stevenson, 1988)

display rules
cross-cultural guidelines for how and when to express emotions

Brain imaging data also provide at least some evidence for discrete emotions. For example, fear is relatively specific to the amygdala, disgust to the *insula*, a region within the limbic system, and anger to a region of the frontal cortex behind our eyes (Murphy, Nimmo-Smith, & Lawrence, 2003; Vytal & Hamann, 2010).

Yet in other cases, we can't distinguish different emotions by means of their physiology (Cacioppo, Tassinary, & Bernstson, 2000; Feldman Barrett et al., 2007; Lindquist et al., 2012). Surprisingly, happiness and sadness aren't all that different in their patterns of brain activation (Murphy et al., 2003). According to some researchers, these findings pose challenges to discrete emotion theory, because they suggest that different emotions aren't always associated with distinctive physiological signatures. Moreover, there's almost certainly no single "fear processor," "disgust processor," and so on, in the brain, because multiple brain regions participate in all emotions (Schienle et al., 2002).

Real Versus Fake Emotions. We can use certain components of facial expressions to help us distinguish real from fake emotions. In genuine happiness, we see an upward turning of the corners of the mouth, along with a drooping of the eyelids and a crinkling of the corners of the eyes (Ekman, Davidson, & Friesen, 1990). Emotion theorists distinguish this genuine expression, called the *Duchenne smile* after the neurologist who discovered it, from the fake or *Pan Am smile*, which is marked by a movement of the mouth but not the eyes. The term *Pan Am smile* derives from an old television commercial featuring the now defunct airline Pan Am, in which all of the flight attendants flashed obviously fake smiles. If you page through your family albums, you'll probably find an abundance of Pan Am smiles, especially in posed photographs.

As several research teams have shown, Duchenne smiles possess predictive validity for important life outcomes (Harker & Keltner, 2001). In one clever study, investigators found that among individuals whose spouse had died recently, those who displayed Duchenne smiles in conversations were more likely to recover emotionally from their loss than those who did not (Bonanno & Keltner, 1997).

Cognitive Theories of Emotion: Think First, Feel Later

As we've seen, for discrete emotions theorists, emotions are largely innate motor programs triggered by certain stimuli, and our emotional reactions to these stimuli come before our interpretation of them. Advocates of **cognitive theories of emotion** disagree. For them, emotions are products of our thinking rather than the other way around. The way we interpret a situation influences what we feel in response to it (Scherer, 1988). For example, the way we appraise situations influences whether we find them stressful (Lazarus & Folkman, 1984). If we see an upcoming job interview as a potential catastrophe, we'll be hopelessly stressed out; if we see it as a healthy challenge, we'll be appropriately geared up. Moreover, for cognitive theorists, there are no discrete emotions, because the boundaries across emotions are fuzzy. Moreover, some argue that because thinking essentially determines our emotions, there are as many different emotions as there are different kinds of thoughts (Feldman Barrett & Russell, 1999; Ortony & Turner, 1990).

JAMES–LANGE THEORY OF EMOTION. Perhaps the oldest cognitive theory of emotion owes its origins to the great American psychologist William James (1890). Because Danish researcher Carl Lange (1885) advanced a similar version of this theory around the same time, psychologists refer to it as the **James–Lange theory of emotion**. According to the James–Lange theory, emotions result from our interpretations of our bodily reactions to stimuli.

To take James's example, let's imagine that while hiking through the forest, we come upon a bear. What happens next? Common wisdom tells us that we become scared and then run away. Yet as James recognized, the link between our fear and running away is only a correlation; this link doesn't demonstrate that our fear *causes* us to run away. Indeed, James and Lange argued that the causal arrow is reversed: *we're afraid because we run away*. That is, we observe our physiological and behavioral reactions to a stimulus—in this

 Psychologist Paul Ekman, shown here, is demonstrating two smiles: a Duchenne (genuine) smile and a non-Duchenne smile. **Which is the Duchenne smile?** (See answer upside down at bottom of page.)

Watch in **MyPsychLab** the **Video:** The Big Picture: Motivation and Emotion

cognitive theories of emotion
theories proposing that emotions are products of thinking

James-Lange theory of emotion
theory proposing that emotions result from our interpretations of our bodily reactions to stimuli

CORRELATION VS. CAUSATION ▶
Can we be sure that A causes B?

Answer: Photo on top. One simple clue is more movement of the eyes in a Duchenne smile.

case our hearts pounding, our palms sweating, and our feet running—and then conclude that we must have been scared (see **FIGURE 2**).

In support of this theory, a researcher examined five groups of patients with injuries in different regions of their spinal cord (Hohmann, 1966). Patients with injuries high in their spinal cord had lost almost all of their bodily sensation, and those with lower injuries had lost only part of their bodily sensation. Just as James and Lange would have predicted, patients with higher spinal cord damage reported less emotion—fear and anger—than those with lower spinal cord damage. Presumably, patients with lower injuries could feel more of their bodies, which allowed them a greater range of emotional reactions. Some researchers have criticized these findings because of a possible experimenter expectancy effect: the researcher knew which spinal cord patients were which when he assessed their emotions, which could have biased the results (Prinz, 2004). Moreover, investigators haven't always replicated these findings: one research team found no differences in the happiness of patients with or without spinal cord injuries (Chwalisz, Diener, & Gallagher, 1988).

Few scientists today are strict believers in the James–Lange theory, but it continues to influence modern-day thinking. Antonio Damasio's (1994) **somatic marker theory** (*somatic* means "physical") proposes that we unconsciously and instantaneously use our "gut reactions"—especially our autonomic responses, like our heart rate and sweating—to gauge how we should act. According to Damasio, if we feel our hearts pounding during a first date, we use that information as a "marker" or signal to help us decide what to do next, like ask the person out for a second date. Elliott, whom we met in this chapter's opening, may have made irrational decisions because he'd lost much of his frontal cortex, an input station for information from the brain's sensory regions. In turn, he may have lost access to somatic markers of emotion (Damasio, 1994; Reimann & Bechara, 2010). Still, there's evidence that people can make decisions solely on the basis of external knowledge and without any bodily feedback (Maia & McClelland, 2004). One team of investigators examined patients who suffer from a rare condition called *pure autonomic failure* (PAF), which is marked by a deterioration of autonomic nervous system neurons beginning in middle age (Heims et al., 2004). These patients don't experience increases in autonomic activity, such as heart rate or sweating, following emotional stimuli. Yet they had no difficulty on a gambling task that required them to make decisions about monetary risks. These findings don't falsify somatic marker theory, as it's possible that somatic markers are helpful to us in making decisions. But they suggest that somatic markers aren't *necessary* for wise choices, even if they can give us a bit of extra guidance.

CANNON–BARD THEORY OF EMOTION. Walter Cannon (1929) and Philip Bard (1942) pointed out several flaws with James and Lange's reasoning. They noted that most physiological changes occur too slowly—often taking at least a few seconds—to trigger emotional reactions, which happen almost instantaneously. Cannon and Bard also argued that we aren't aware of many of our bodily reactions, like the liver or stomach contractions. So we can't use them to infer our emotions.

They proposed an alternative model for the correlation between emotions and bodily reactions. According to the **Cannon–Bard theory**, an emotion-provoking event leads simultaneously to an emotion and bodily reactions. To return to James's example, Cannon and Bard would say that when we see a bear while hiking in the forest, the sight of that bear triggers being afraid and running at the same time (again refer to Figure 2).

Although Cannon and Bard proposed that the *thalamus*, which is a relay station for the senses, triggers both an emotion and bodily reactions, later researchers showed that numerous regions of the limbic system, including the hypothalamus and the amygdala, also play key roles in emotion (Carlson & Hatfield, 1992; Lewis, Haviland-Jones, & Feldman Barrett, 2008; Plutchik & Kellerman, 1986). Still, Cannon and Bard's model of emotion encouraged investigators to explore the bases of emotion in the brain.

◀ **REPLICABILITY**
Can the results be duplicated in other studies?

FIGURE 2 What Triggers Emotions? The James–Lange and Cannon–Bard theories differ in their views of how emotions are generated.

◀ **FALSIFIABILITY**
Can the claim be disproved?

◀ **RULING OUT RIVAL HYPOTHESES**
Have important alternative explanations for the findings been excluded?

somatic marker theory
theory proposing that we use our "gut reactions" to help us determine how we should act

Cannon-Bard theory
theory proposing that an emotion-provoking event leads simultaneously to an emotion and to bodily reactions

481

According to Schachter and Singer's two-factor theory of emotion, we first experience arousal after an emotion-provoking event like a car accident; then we seek to interpret the cause of that arousal. The resulting label we attach to our arousal is the emotion.

In a study of "love at first fright," investigators tested Schachter and Singer's two-factor theory of emotion. They approached participants immediately before or after a roller-coaster ride and showed them a photograph of a member of the opposite sex. Participants who'd just gotten off the roller coaster rated the person as more attractive than did those who were just about to get on the roller coaster (Meston & Frohlich, 2003).

two-factor theory
theory proposing that emotions are produced by an undifferentiated state of arousal along with an attribution (explanation) of that arousal

TWO-FACTOR THEORY OF EMOTION. Stanley Schachter and Jerome Singer (1962) contended that the James–Lange and Cannon–Bard models were too simple. They agreed with James and Lange that our cognitive interpretations of our bodily reactions play a crucial role in emotions, but disagreed with James and Lange that these bodily reactions are sufficient for emotion. According to their **two-factor theory**, two psychological events are required to produce an emotion:

1. After encountering an emotion-provoking event, we experience an undifferentiated state of arousal, that is, alertness. By "undifferentiated," Schachter and Singer meant that this arousal is the same across all emotions.

2. We then seek to explain the source of this autonomic arousal. Once we attribute the arousal to an occurrence—either within us or in the external environment—we experience an emotion. Once we figure out what's making us aroused, we "label" that arousal with an emotion. This labeling process, Schachter and Singer proposed, typically occurs so rapidly that we're not aware of it. According to this view, emotions are the explanations we attach to our arousal.

To illustrate, imagine we're hiking in the forest yet again (you'd think we'd have learned by now that we might find a bear there). Then, sure enough, we come upon a bear. According to Schachter and Singer, we first become physiologically aroused; evolution assures that we do so to prepare us to fight—probably not an especially smart idea in this case—or flee. Then, we try to figure out the source of that arousal. One need not have a Ph.D. in psychology to infer that our arousal probably has something to do with the bear. So we label this arousal as fear, and that's the emotion we experience.

It's a good story, but do our emotions really work this way? In a classic study, Schachter and Singer (1962) decided to find out. As a "cover story," they informed participants that they were testing the effectiveness of a new vitamin supplement—"Suproxin"—on vision. In reality, they were testing the effects of *adrenaline*, a chemical that produces physiological arousal. Schachter and Singer randomly assigned some participants to receive an injection of Suproxin (again, actually adrenaline) and others an injection of a placebo. While the adrenaline was entering their system, Schachter and Singer randomly assigned participants to two additional conditions: (1) one in which a confederate (an undercover research assistant) acted in a happy fashion while completing questionnaires and (2) one in which a confederate acted in an angry fashion while completing questionnaires. The confederate was blind to whether participants had received adrenaline or placebo. Finally, Schachter and Singer asked participants to describe how strongly they had experienced various emotions.

The results dovetailed with two-factor theory. The emotions of participants who'd received the placebo weren't influenced by the behavior of the confederate, but those of the participants who had received adrenaline were. Participants exposed to the happy confederate reported feeling happier, and those exposed to the angry confederate reported feeling angrier—but in both cases *only* if they'd received adrenaline. Emotion, Schachter and Singer concluded, requires *both* physiological arousal *and* an attribution of that arousal to an emotion-inducing event.

The award for the most creative test of the two-factor theory probably goes to two researchers (Dutton & Aron, 1974) who asked an attractive female confederate to approach male undergraduates on the University of British Columbia campus. She asked them for help with a survey and gave them her phone number in case they had any questions. Half of the time, she approached them on a sturdy bridge that didn't move, and half of the time she approached them on a swaying bridge suspended 200 feet above a river. Although only 30 percent of males in the first condition called her, 60 percent of males in the second condition did. The wobbly bridge in the second condition presumably increased male students' arousal, leading them to feel more intense romantic emotions—just as Schachter and Singer would have predicted (Szczucka, 2012).

Support for two-factor theory has been mixed; not all researchers have replicated Schachter and Singer's (1962) results (Marshall & Zimbardo, 1979; Maslach, 1979). Moreover, research suggests that although arousal often intensifies emotions, emotions can occur in the absence of arousal (Reisenzein, 1983). Contrary to what Schachter and Singer claimed, arousal isn't necessary for all emotional experiences.

PUTTING IT ALL TOGETHER. So which of these theories should we believe? As is often the case in psychology, there's probably some truth to several explanations. Discrete emotions theory is probably correct that our emotional reactions are shaped in part by natural selection and that these reactions serve crucial adaptive functions. Nevertheless, as demonstrated by work on nonverbal accents, discrete emotion theory may underestimate cultural differences in the expression and perhaps experience of emotion. In addition, discrete emotions theory doesn't exclude the possibility that our thinking influences our emotions in significant ways, as cognitive theorists propose. Indeed, the James–Lange and somatic marker theories are probably correct in assuming that our inferences concerning our bodily reactions can influence our emotional states. Finally, two-factor theory may be right that physiological arousal plays a key role in the intensity of our emotional experiences, although it's unlikely that all emotions require such arousal.

Unconscious Influences on Emotion

In recent decades, researchers have become especially interested in *unconscious influences on emotion*: variables outside our awareness that can affect our feelings. One piece of evidence for unconscious influences on emotion comes from research on *automatic behaviors*.

AUTOMATIC GENERATION OF EMOTION. Rsome research suggests that a good deal of our behavior is produced automatically, that is, with no voluntary influence on our part (Bargh & Ferguson, 2000). Yet we often perceive such behavior as intentional (Bargh et al, 2012; Kirsch & Lynn, 1999; Wegner, 2002). Although not all psychologists agree, the same may hold for our emotional reactions; many may be generated automatically, much like the knee-jerk reflex that our doctor elicits when she taps on our knee with a hammer.

Two investigators visually presented some participants with a set of words describing positive stimuli (like *friends* and *music*) and other participants with words describing negative stimuli (like *cancer* and *cockroach*). These stimuli appeared so quickly that they were *subliminal*, that is, below the threshold for awareness. Even though participants couldn't identify what they saw at better-than-chance levels, those exposed to positive stimuli reported being in a better mood than those exposed to negative stimuli (Bargh & Chartrand, 1999). Other research shows that subliminal exposure to faces displaying a specific emotion, like fear, happiness, or disgust, produces changes in facial muscles corresponding to that emotion (Dimberg, Thunberg, & Elmehed, 2000). Nevertheless, these kinds of effects are often small in magnitude and difficult to replicate, so their size and existence remains controversial (Bartlett, 2013).

MERE EXPOSURE EFFECT.

> *Psychology: From Inquiry to Understanding*
> *Psychology: From Inquiry to Understanding*
> *Psychology: From Inquiry to Understanding*
> *Psychology: From Inquiry to Understanding*

After reading the four lines above, how do you feel about our textbook? Do you like it more or less than you did before? (We hope you answered "more.")

Popular wisdom would say no. It tells us that "familiarity breeds contempt": The more often we've seen or heard something, the more we come to dislike it. Yet research by Robert Zajonc and others on the **mere exposure effect** suggests that the opposite is more often the case; that is, familiarity breeds *comfort* (Zajonc, 1968). The mere exposure effect

◀ **REPLICABILITY**
Can the results be duplicated in other studies?

Stimuli can influence our emotional behavior even when we don't recognize them as the culprits. In one study, participants subtly reminded of money by watching a computer screensaver of floating currency (*above*) later put more physical distance between themselves and a stranger than did participants who watched a screensaver of floating fish (*below*), presumably because thinking of money makes people more self-centered (Vohs, Mead, & Goode, 2006).

◀ **REPLICABILITY**
Can the results be duplicated in other studies?

mere exposure effect
phenomenon in which repeated exposure to a stimulus makes us more likely to feel favorably toward it

Simulate in **MyPsychLab** the
Experiment: Mere Exposure

refers to the fact that repeated exposure to a stimulus makes us more likely to feel favorably toward it (Bornstein, 1989; Kunst-Wilson & Zajonc, 1980).

Of course, the finding that we like things we've seen many times before may not be terribly surprising. This correlation could be due merely to the fact that we repeatedly seek out things we like. If we love ice cream, we're likely to spend more time seeking ice cream than are people who hate ice cream, assuming such human beings actually exist. Better evidence for the mere exposure effect derives from experiments using meaningless material, for which individuals are unlikely to have any prior feelings. Experiments show that repeated exposure to various stimuli, such as nonsense syllables (like "zab" and "gar"), Chinese letters (to non-Chinese participants), and polygons of various shapes, results in greater liking toward these stimuli compared with little or no exposure (see **FIGURE 3**). These effects have been replicated by multiple investigators using quite different stimuli, including songs, attesting to their generality (Verrier, 2012). The mere exposure effect extends to faces, too. We tend to prefer an image of ourselves as we appear in the mirror to an image of ourselves as we appear in a photograph (Mita, Dermer, & Knight, 1977), probably because we see ourselves in the mirror just about every day. Our friends, in contrast, generally prefer the photographic image. Advertisers are well aware of the mere exposure effect and capitalize on it mercilessly (Baker, 1999; Fang, Singh, & AhluWalia, 2007; Morgenstern, Isensee & Hanewinkel, 2013). Repetitions of a commercial tend to increase our liking for the product, especially if we're positively inclined toward it to begin with.

REPLICABILITY ▶

Can the results be duplicated in other studies?

Polygon pairs

FIGURE 3 Which Polygon Do You Prefer? Pairs of polygons used in the mere exposure research of Robert Zajonc and his colleagues. Participants exposed repeatedly to only one polygon within the pair prefer that polygon, even if they don't recall having seen it. (*Source:* Epley, 2006)

There's evidence that the mere exposure effect can operate unconsciously, because it emerges even when experimenters present meaningless stimuli subliminally, below the threshold of awareness (Bornstein, 1989; Zajonc, 2001). Even when people aren't aware of having seen a stimulus, like a specific polygon, they report liking it better than stimuli, like slightly different polygons, they've never seen. Mere exposure effects may be even larger for subliminally than for *supraliminally* (consciously) presented stimuli (Bornstein, 1989). Still, there's controversy about just how enduring the mere exposure effect is. It seems to influence short-term, but not long-term, preferences (Lazarus, 1984).

No one knows why mere exposure effects occur. These effects may reflect *habituation*, a primitive form of learning. The more frequently we encounter a stimulus without anything bad happening, the more comfortable we feel in its presence. Alternatively, we may prefer things we find easier to process (Harmon-Jones & Allen, 2001; Mandler, Nakamura, & Van Zandt, 1987). The more often we experience something, the less effort it typically takes to comprehend it. In turn, the less effort something takes, the more we tend to like it—just as we generally prefer books that are easy to read over those that are hard to read (Herbert, 2011; Hertwig et al., 2008). We're *cognitive misers*: We prefer less mental work to more.

So now to the bottom line: All else being equal, you'll probably like this paragraph better after having read it a few times than after you read it the first time. That's a not-so-subtle hint to read it again!

FACIAL FEEDBACK HYPOTHESIS. If no one is near you, and you're not afraid of looking foolish, make a big smile and hold it for a while, maybe for 15 seconds. How do you feel (other than silly)? Next, make a big frown, and again hold it for a while. How do you feel now?

According to the **facial feedback hypothesis**, you're likely to feel emotions that correspond to your facial features—first happy and then sad or angry (Adelmann & Zajonc, 1989; Goldman & de Vignemont, 2009; Niedenthal, 2007). This hypothesis originated with none other than Charles Darwin (1872), although Robert Zajonc revived it in the 1980s. Zajonc went beyond Darwin by proposing that changes in the blood vessels of the face "feed back" temperature information to the brain, altering our emotions in predictable ways. Like James and Lange, Zajonc argued that our emotions typically arise

facial feedback hypothesis
theory that blood vessels in the face feed back temperature information in the brain, altering our experience of emotions

from our behavioral and physiological reactions. But unlike James and Lange, Zajonc viewed this process as purely biochemical and noncognitive, that is, as involving no thinking (Zajonc, Murphy, & Inglehart, 1989).

There's scientific support for the facial feedback hypothesis. In one study, researchers asked participants to rate how funny they found various cartoons (Strack, Martin, & Stepper, 1988). They randomly assigned some participants to watch cartoons while holding a pen with their teeth and others to watch cartoons while holding a pen with their lips. If you try this at home, you'll discover that when you hold a pen with your teeth, you tend to smile; when you hold a pen with your lips, you tend to frown. Sure enough, participants who held a pen with their teeth rated the cartoons as funnier than did other participants. In another study, experimenters asked participants to hold chopsticks in their mouths in one of three positions to which they were randomly assigned, one that produced a Duchenne (genuine) smile, one that produced a fake smile, and one that produced a neutral expression. Then, participants submerged their hands in ice water for a minute, a widely used laboratory technique for eliciting pain. Participants who engaged in smiles, especially Duchenne smiles, showed lower heart rates immediately following the task, suggesting that the smiles had tamped down their stress level (Kraft & Pressman, 2012). Still, it's not clear that these effects work by means of facial feedback to the brain, as Zajonc claimed. An alternative hypothesis for these effects is classical conditioning. Over the course of our lives, we've experienced countless conditioning "trials" in which we smile while feeling happy and frown while feeling unhappy. Eventually, smiles become conditioned stimuli for happiness; frowns, for unhappiness.

Most people prefer their mirror image to their image as taken by a photographer. In this case, this subject is more likely to prefer the photograph on the left, presumably because he is more accustomed to this view of himself.

◀ **RULING OUT RIVAL HYPOTHESES**
Have important alternative explanations for the findings been excluded?

from inquiry to understanding

WHY DO WE CRY?

Few behaviors are more obviously emotional than crying. Moreover, crying is familiar to all of us. On average, women cry about five times a month; men, once a month (Walter, 2006). Yet psychologists have yet to figure out what functions, if any, crying serves (Provine, 2012; Trimble, 2012). Still, they've begun to make a few promising inroads.

One widespread view is that we cry to make ourselves feel better; many of us say that when we're upset, we just need a "good cry." Indeed, 94 percent of popular articles tout crying as a good way of reducing negative emotions (Cornelius, 2001). Yet research by Jonathan Rottenberg and his colleagues suggests that crying actually tends to *increase* distress and arousal in most people (Rottenberg, Bylsma, & Vingerhoets, 2008). One explanation for this discrepancy is that when people look back on their crying episodes, they mistakenly recall them as having helped. Still, it's possible that crying has long-term benefits that researchers haven't uncovered.

Another hint comes from research on the timing of crying in early development. As all parents know, babies cry loudly from the moment of birth. Crying clearly has an impact on parents. For example, it triggers milk production in mothers who've recently given birth (Provine, 2000). Crying increases in frequency from birth until about 6 weeks of age, decreases a few months later, and then levels off until the age of 1, after which it drops again (Provine, 2012; Wolff, 1969). Perhaps not coincidentally, crying becomes less frequent when babies learn to talk, suggesting that crying initially serves the role of grabbing parents' attention. In this respect, crying functions as an "acoustical umbilical cord" (Ostwald, 1972). When babies can speak and communicate their distress more directly ("Mommy, I have a tummy ache"), they can snatch their parents' attention more effectively, so this "umbilical cord" is no longer needed. As we

Factoid

Injections of the chemical Botox, used to treat wrinkles by paralyzing the muscles surrounding them, results in diminished affective reactions to emotionally-arousing film clips compared with injections of substances that don't affect facial muscles (Davis et al., 2010). This finding, along with others (Finzi & Wasserman, 2006), is consistent with the facial feedback hypothesis, because Botox may dampen emotions by reducing facial movement.

age, crying may continue to play a similar attention-getting function with those who care about us, only less frequently. So even in adults, crying probably serves largely as a social signal, a cue to others that we're upset and in need of emotional comfort.

Interesting as it is, none of this addresses the related question of why we tear up when we cry. Interestingly, we humans appear to be unique in the animal kingdom in our tendency to shed tears when we're upset (Provine, 2012). One hypothesis holds that tearing helps us to get rid of stress hormones and other substances that produce unpleasant emotions (Frey, 1985). According to this view, tearing improves our moods by allowing us to release toxic substances that build up in our bloodstreams. Nevertheless, the amounts of stress hormones released in tears are extremely small, so it's unlikely to be a complete explanation. An alternative hypothesis is that by moistening the eyes, tears evolved to prevent damage to the blood vessels in infants' eyes when they cry loudly (Trimble, 2012).

The truth is that the mystery of crying remains unresolved. Crying may illustrate a key principle, namely, that most complex psychological phenomena have more than one explanation. Whatever the reasons, we can be sure that crying will continue to provide fascinating clues to the causes of human emotion.

RULING OUT RIVAL HYPOTHESES ▶
Have important alternative explanations for the findings been excluded?

Even presidents cry, as evidenced by the tears shed by Barack Obama during a December 14, 2012, news conference while discussing the child victims of the horrific school shooting in Newtown, Connecticut. Yet scientists still don't fully understand why humans cry; as is typically the case in psychology, there may be multiple explanations rather than one.

 Study and **Review** in **MyPsychLab**

Factoid

John Gray (1992), author of *Men Are from Mars, Women Are from Venus*, contended that men's and women's emotional communications are vastly different. For example, he argued that men are innately programmed to withdraw and not talk to others when upset, whereas women are innately programmed to do the opposite. Yet in fact, the overlap between men's and women's communication styles is substantial, and men and women are more similar than different in how they talk with others (Barnett & Rivers, 2004; Lilienfeld et al., 2009; Wilson, 2003).

nonverbal leakage
unconscious spillover of emotions into nonverbal behavior

Assess Your Knowledge   FACT or FICTION?

1. Psychological research demonstrates that emotion and reason are direct opposites of each other.   **True / False**

2. Some emotions, like happiness, appear to be recognized by a substantial majority of people in all cultures.   **True / False**

3. According to the James–Lange theory, emotions follow from our bodily reactions.   **True / False**

4. Two-factor theory proposes that arousal is necessary for emotion.   **True / False**

5. The mere exposure effect refers to the finding that repeated presentations of a stimulus lead to less liking of that stimulus.   **True / False**

Answers: 1. F; 2. T; 3. T; 4. T; 5. F

Nonverbal Expression of Emotion: The Eyes, Bodies, and Cultures Have It

3   Explain the importance of nonverbal expression of emotion.

4   Identify major lie detection methods and their pitfalls.

Much of our emotional expression is nonverbal. Not only do our facial expressions change frequently when we experience a strong emotion, so do our gestures and postures. As baseball Hall of Famer Yogi Berra (known for his funny words of wisdom) said, "You can observe a lot just by watching." What's more, our nonverbal behaviors are often more valid indicators of our emotions than our words are, largely because we're better at disguising our verbal language than our gestures and tone of voice (DePaulo, 1992; Jacob et al., 2012). **Nonverbal leakage**—an unconscious spillover of emotions into nonverbal behavior—is often a powerful cue that we're trying to hide an emotion. So when we ever so subtly roll our eyes while agreeing to our boss's unreasonable request to house-sit her dogs over the weekend ("Sure, I'd be happy to do it"), we can be confident that the "eyes have it."

The Importance of Nonverbal Cues

We often take for granted how important nonverbal behavior is to our everyday communication. Without nonverbal cues to our emotions, embarrassing miscommunications can arise. Many of us have experienced this effect when a person to whom we send an innocent or humorous text message or email ("Hey, don't worry—everybody fails a test now and then!") misinterprets it as hostile. Without being able to hear our vocal inflections or see our facial emotions, recipients may misinterpret what we meant to say. This problem is compounded by the fact that we overestimate how easily others can figure out the intended meanings of our e-mail messages (Kruger et al., 2005). More broadly, psychologists refer to this problem as the *curse of knowledge:* when we know something, in this case what we intend to say, we often make the mistake of assuming others know it, too (Birch & Bloom, 2003) (see **FIGURE 4**).

Body Language and Gestures

Our postures can convey a lot about our emotional states (see **FIGURE 5**). Slumped posture can convey sadness, and upright posture can convey happiness or excitement, although an upright posture involving a lot of body tension may also convey anger (Duclos et al, 1989). When interpreting the emotional states of others, we typically take both facial and body information into account. Research on embodied cognition even shows that our postures affect our readiness to engage in certain behaviors. When participants are insulted, they're more likely to display brain responses typical of anger (activation of the left frontal lobes) when sitting straight up than when reclining (Harmon-Jones & Peterson, 2009). That's probably because we're more prepared to strike others when we're upright than lying down. And when experimenters ask participants to adopt "high power" poses, which are marked by having one's body and arms spread open wide, participants are more likely to feel powerful and to gamble on money than participants who adopt "low power" poses (Carney, Cuddy, & Yap, 2010). So if you want to feel powerful, look powerful.

Gestures come in a seemingly endless variety of forms (Ekman, 2001). When talking, we often use *illustrators* (Ekman, 2001), gestures that highlight or accentuate speech, such as when we forcefully move our hands forward to make an important point. When stressed out, we may engage in *manipulators,* gestures in which one body part strokes, presses, bites, or otherwise touches another body part. For example, while cramming for an exam, we may twirl our hair or bite our fingernails.

We're all familiar with *emblems* (Ekman, 2001), gestures that convey conventional meanings recognized by members of a culture, such as the hand wave and nodding of the head. Some of these gestures are consistent across cultures, such as crossing one's fingers when hoping for good luck (Plutchik, 2003). Yet others differ across cultures, which should serve as a word of warning to unwary foreign travelers (Archer, 1997). The "thumbs up" is a sign of approval among Westerners, but an insult in much of the Muslim world. Some surprised American soldiers quickly discovered this awkward fact upon greeting Iraqi civilians following the U.S. invasion in 2003. The familiar American "hello" wave means "go away" in some European countries, and the American "OK sign" is a vulgar insult in Turkey (Axtell, 1997).

As useful as body language can be in communicating information about emotional states, we must be careful in drawing conclusions about its meaning for any given person (Ekman, 2001). Some pop psychologists specialize in "translating" body language into emotions, as if there were a universal dictionary of body language. Yet these psychologists overlook the fact that within a given culture, people differ greatly in the body language they use to express certain emotions. For instance, in June 2012, body language expert Tonya Reiman interpreted the fact that President Barack Obama put his hand on top of that of former president George W. Bush while shaking hands during a White House meeting as evidence that Obama was trying to assume a power role. But these kinds of interpretations overlook the fact that there's no simple one-to-one translation of bodily gestures into emotions, largely because these gestures often mean very different things for different people.

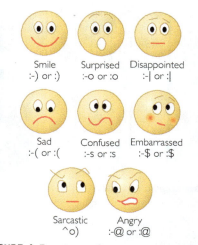

FIGURE 4 Emoticons. Because email messages are devoid of nonverbal cues, people have developed a variety of "emoticons" to convey various emotions that might not be obvious over email and instant messaging. (*Source:* Microsoft Corporation)

FIGURE 5 Emotional Expression through Posture. Even with the absence of facial features, it is easy to interpret the emotional states of these stick figures from their "body language" (Duclos et al., 1989).

(Sydney Harris, www.CartoonStock.com. Used by permission.)

Research points to cultural differences in personal space. For example, people from Middle Eastern countries often talk slightly closer to others than do people from European countries.

Factoid

Although survey data indicate that about 70 percent of people believe that "shifty eyes" are good indicators of lying (Bond, 2006), data indicate that shifty eyes are essentially unrelated to dishonesty. Indeed, pathological liars and psychopaths, who are notorious liars, tend to stare their victims straight in the eye (Ekman, 2001). Still, because shifty eyes might give away *bad* liars, they may be somewhat useful as emotional cues.

Personal Space

Have you ever walked into a virtually empty movie theater and taken a seat, only to find that someone sits right next to you? Or have you ever approached someone to whom you were attracted, only to find them taking a step away from you? These are among the phenomena addressed by **proxemics**—the study of personal space.

Anthropologist Edward Hall (1966) observed that personal distance is correlated positively with emotional distance. The farther we stand from a person, the less emotionally close we usually feel to him or her, and vice versa. But there are exceptions. When we're trying to intimidate people, we typically get closer to them. For example, lawyers tend to stand closer to witnesses they're challenging (Brodsky et al., 1999).

According to Hall, there are four levels of personal space. Nevertheless, like most distinctions in psychology, the separations between these levels aren't clear-cut:

1. **Public distance** (12 feet or more): typically used for public speaking, such as lecturing
2. **Social distance** (4–12 feet): typically used for conversations among strangers and casual acquaintances
3. **Personal distance** (1.5–4 feet): typically used for conversations among close friends or romantic partners
4. **Intimate distance** (0–1.5 feet): typically used for kissing, hugging, whispering "sweet nothings," and affectionate touching

When these implicit rules are violated, we usually feel uncomfortable, as when a stranger gets "in our face" to ask us for a favor. Hall (1976) argued that cultures differ in personal space. In many Latin and Middle Eastern countries, personal space is relatively close, whereas in many Scandinavian and Asian countries, personal space is more distant. Nevertheless, data suggest that although these cultural differences are genuine, they aren't as large as Hall believed (Jones, 1979). There are also sex differences in personal space, with women preferring closer space than men (Vrught & Kerkstra, 1984). Personal space also increases from childhood to early adulthood (Hayduk, 1983), perhaps because the young haven't yet developed clear interpersonal boundaries. Recent data suggest that even within cultures, personal space preferences are influenced by personality traits, such as fear-proneness. In a striking illustration of this principle, a woman with severe amygdala damage, who in turn was markedly fearless, displayed virtually no sense of personal space (Kennedy et al., 2009).

Lying and Lie Detection

We all lie. Diary studies suggest that college students tell an average of about two lies per day (DePaulo et al., 1996). Lying is so commonplace that the English language contains 112 different words for lying (Henig, 2006). Psychologists have long been interested in finding a dependable means of detecting lying. But how successful have they been?

HUMANS AS LIE DETECTORS. We spend a sizable amount of our everyday lives trying to figure out if others are "being straight" with us or putting us on. To do so, we frequently rely on people's nonverbal behaviors. Yet despite what most police officers believe, nonverbal cues tend to be less valid indicators of lying than verbal cues (Vrij, 2008; Vrij, Granhag, & Porter, 2010). The best way of finding out whether someone is lying is to listen to *what* they're saying rather than how they're saying it. For example, dishonest statements tend to contain fewer details and fewer qualifiers (such as "I'm not sure about this, but I think that …") than do truthful statements (DePaulo et al., 2003).

Although many of us are confident of our ability to detect lies, research suggests given a 50-50 chance of being right, most of us achieve only about 55 percent accuracy and few exceed 70 percent (Bond & DePaulo, 2006; Warren, Schertler, & Bull, 2009;

proxemics
study of personal space

Zuckerman, DePaulo, & Rosenthal, 1981). Moreover, occupational groups we might expect to be especially accurate detectors of lies, such as people who administer so-called lie detector (polygraph) tests, customs officials, and psychiatrists, usually do no better than the rest of us—meaning not much better than chance (DePaulo & Pfeifer, 1986; Ekman & O'Sullivan, 1991; Kraut & Poe, 1980). Researchers have found only a few groups, including secret service agents, clinical psychologists who study deception, and perhaps some judges and law enforcement officials, to be especially adept at lie detection (Ekman & O'Sullivan, 1991; Ekman, O'Sullivan, & Frank, 1999). These correlational findings may indicate that years of experience in spotting lies make people better at it: Practice makes perfect. Or perhaps the causal arrow is reversed: people who are interpersonally perceptive may pursue professions that allow them to exercise this talent (see **FIGURE 6**).

Another sobering finding is that there's typically little or no correlation between people's confidence in their ability to detect lies and their accuracy (Ekman, 2001). So when a juror proclaims with utmost confidence, "I could tell that the witness was lying; I'm positive about it," we should take it with a grain of salt.

THE POLYGRAPH TEST. The polygraph or "lie detector" test has long been one of the icons of popular psychology. It makes frequent cameo appearances in television courtroom dramas and daytime talk shows. Even popular psychologist Phillip McGraw (Dr. Phil) has promoted the polygraph test on his television show as a means of finding out which partner in a relationship is lying (Levenson, 2005). The largest organization of polygraph examiners in the United States claims that the test is 98 percent accurate (Koerner, 2002). Does research support this extraordinary claim?

The polygraph test, like most lie-detection techniques, rests on the assumption of the **Pinocchio response**: a perfect physiological or behavioral indicator of lying (Lykken, 1998; Ruscio, 2005; Vrij et al., 2010). Like Pinocchio's nose, people's bodily reactions supposedly give them away whenever they lie.

Modern polygraphs measure several physiological signals that often reflect anxiety, most typically blood pressure, respiration, and skin conductance, a measure of palm sweating. The assumption is that dishonest suspects experience anxiety—and heightened autonomic activity—when confronted with questions that expose their falsehoods. The most widely administered version of the polygraph test, the Controlled Question Test (CQT), measures suspects' physiological responses following three major types of yes–no questions (Lykken, 1998).

1. **Relevant questions,** or "Did you do it" questions, those bearing on the crime in question (Did you rob the bank on the afternoon of August 16?)

2. **Irrelevant questions,** those not bearing on the crime in question or on suspects' lies (Is your name Sam Jones?)

3. **Control questions,** those reflecting probable lies. They typically inquire about trivial misdeeds about which most people will lie, especially under intense pressure (Have you ever been tempted to steal anything from a store?). Suspects' physiological activity following these questions supposedly provides a "baseline" for gauging their responses during known lies.

If the suspect's autonomic activity following the relevant questions is higher than that following irrelevant and control questions, polygraph examiners label the CQT results "deceptive." Otherwise, they label them "truthful" (or inconclusive if the responses to irrelevant and control questions are about equal).

Evaluating the Polygraph Test: What's the Truth? Although the polygraph test does better than chance at detecting lies (Kircher, Horowitz, & Raskin, 1988), it yields a high rate (perhaps as up to 40 percent) of *false positives*, that is, innocent individuals whom the test labels incorrectly as guilty (Iacono & Patrick, 2006; National Research Council, 2003). This means that that *the polygraph test is biased against the innocent.* As a consequence, the results of polygraph tests aren't admissible in most U.S. courts (Saxe & Ben-Shakhar, 1999).

Pinocchio response
supposedly perfect physiological or behavioral indicator of lying

◄ **CORRELATION VS. CAUSATION**
Can we be sure that A causes B?

 Watch in **MyPsychLab** the **Video:** Special Topics: Detecting Lies

◄ **EXTRAORDINARY CLAIMS**
Is the evidence as strong as the claim?

FIGURE 6 Who Can Catch a Liar? Data from Paul Ekman and his colleagues on the accuracy levels of different occupational groups in detecting deception; the chance rate of accuracy in these studies is 50 percent. Several groups do only somewhat better than chance, with law enforcement officers (including police) actually doing slightly worse than chance. (Based on data from Ekman, O'Sullivan, & Frank, 1999)

The polygraph test assumes the existence of a Pinocchio response, a physiological reaction uniquely associated with lying. But does such a response exist?

Factoid

The principal developer of the polygraph test, William Marston (1893–1947), also created the comic-book character Wonder Woman, who proudly sported a "lasso of truth." When Wonder Woman wrapped the lasso around the waist of a potential criminal, she compelled him to tell the truth ("Yes, I did rob the bank … I admit it"). For Marston (1938), the polygraph test was the equivalent of Wonder Woman's lasso: it was an infallible detector of lies.

FALSIFIABILITY ▶

Can the claim be disproved?

The modern polygraph test relies on the assumption of a Pinocchio response, a perfect indicator of lying—much like that of Pinocchio's nose, which became longer whenever he fibbed. Yet psychological research calls the existence of the Pinocchio response into serious question. Some people exhibit physiological arousal when they don't lie, and some people don't exhibit physiological arousal when they do lie.

The problem is that the polygraph test confuses arousal with evidence of guilt. The polygraph test is misnamed: it's an "arousal detector," not a lie detector (Iacono, 2009; Saxe, 1991). Many people display arousal following relevant questions for reasons other than the anxiety associated with lying, such as the fear of being convicted of a crime they didn't commit. Polygraph enthusiasts' claims to the contrary, no Pinocchio response has yet been discovered by psychologists.

These problems plague other popular lie-detection methods. Some agencies use *voice stress analysis* to detect lies on the basis of findings that people's voices increase in pitch when they lie. Yet because most people's voices also go up in pitch when they're stressed out (Long & Krall, 1990), voice stress analyzers barely do better than chance at detecting lies (Agosta, Pezzoli, & Sartori, 2013; Gamer et al., 2006; Sackett & Decker, 1979).

The polygraph test may also yield a nontrivial number of *false negatives*, that is, guilty individuals whom the test incorrectly labels innocent. Many individuals can "beat" the test by using *countermeasures*—methods designed to alter their responses to control questions (Ben-Shakhar, 2011). To pass the polygraph test, as we've seen, we must exhibit a more pronounced physiological response to control questions than to relevant questions. With less than 30 minutes of preparation, half or more of participants can accomplish this goal by biting their tongues, curling their toes, or performing difficult mental arithmetic problems (such as counting backward from 1,000 by 17s) during control questions (Honts, Raskin, & Kircher, 1994; Iacono, 2001). Some psychologists also argue that people with psychopathic personality, who have low levels of guilt and fear, may be especially adept at beating the polygraph test because of their low levels of arousal in response to incriminating questions (Lykken, 1978), although research supporting this hypothesis is mixed (Patrick & Iacono, 1989; Waid & Orne, 1982).

If the polygraph is so flawed, why are polygraph examiners persuaded of its validity? The answer probably lies in the fact that the polygraph is often effective for eliciting confessions, especially when people fail the test (Lykken, 1998; Ruscio, 2005). As a result, polygraph examiners may come to believe the test works, because many people who fail the test later "admit" they were lying. Yet there's good evidence that many criminal confessions are false (Kassin & Gudjonsson, 2004). Moreover, polygraph examiners frequently conclude that suspects who failed the test and who didn't confess to crimes must actually be guilty. But without hard-and-fast criminal evidence against suspects, this assertion is unfalsifiable.

OTHER METHODS OF LIE DETECTION. The serious limitations of the polygraph test have led researchers to seek out alternatives to this technique.

Here we'll examine three other widely used lie detection methods.

Guilty Knowledge Test. To get around the polygraph test's shortcomings, David Lykken developed the **guilty knowledge test (GKT)**, which relies on the premise that criminals harbor concealed knowledge about the crime that innocent people don't (Ben-Shakhar, 2011; Lykken, 1959, 1960). In contrast to the polygraph, the GKT doesn't hinge on the assumption of a Pinocchio response, because it measures suspects' recognition of concealed knowledge, not lying.

To administer the GKT to a suspect, we'd concoct a series of multiple-choice questions in which only one choice contains the object at the crime scene, such as a red handkerchief, and we'd measure his or her physiological responses following each choice. If, across many items, the suspect consistently shows pronounced responses to only the objects at the crime scene, we can be reasonably certain that he or she was present at the crime—and probably committed it.

In contrast to the polygraph, the GKT has a low false-positive rate; that is, it misidentifies few innocent people as guilty. In this respect, it may be a useful investigative device for law enforcement officials. Nevertheless, the GKT has a fairly high false-negative rate, because many criminals may have not noticed or since forgotten key aspects of the crime scene (Ben-Shakhar & Elaad, 2003; Iacono & Patrick, 2006).

Tests Using Brain Scanning Techniques. Several researchers have attempted to improve on the traditional GKT by measuring suspects' EEGs (brain waves;) following each item (Bashore & Rapp, 1993; Farwell & Donchin, 1991), a technique sometimes called *brain fingerprinting.* Brain waves may be a more sensitive measure of the recognition of concealed knowledge than are skin conductance or other indices used in the traditional GKT (Farwell & Smith, 2001). Nevertheless, the scientific support for brain fingerprinting is preliminary. One problem is that most of the evidence for this technique comes from laboratory studies in which participants are forced to rehearse details of a simulated crime (like the color of a stolen purse or the type of jacket worn by a victim). In the real world, many criminals may forget these details, leading to lower accuracy rates (Meijer, Ben-Shakhar, Verschuere, & Donchin, 2012; Rosenfeld, 2005). Moreover, most of the evidence for brain fingerprinting hasn't been subjected to peer review, which is an essential safeguard against error in science.

Other investigators have turned to fMRI, a more direct brain imaging method than EEG, to assist them with detecting lies (Langleben, 2008). Studies show that when people lie, certain brain areas—such as the anterior cingulate cortex, a region that helps to monitor psychological conflict—often become activated. Nevertheless, there is presently no known brain "signature" of lying, because the pattern of brain activation differs across both different individuals and different types of lies (Langleben & Moriarty, 2012; Satel & Lilienfeld, 2013).

Other companies, like the California-based "No Lie MRI," claim to be able to use fMRI methods to distinguish truths from falsehoods (Stix, 2008). Yet these techniques aren't ready for widespread public consumption, because different studies often find activations in different brain regions during lying (Greely & Illes, 2007; Satel & Lilienfeld, 2013). Moreover, the brain activations associated with lying may be similar or identical to those associated with merely *thinking* about lying (Greene & Paxton, 2009). If so, fMRI methods may suffer from the same false-positive problem as the traditional polygraph.

psychomythology

IS "TRUTH SERUM" REALLY A TRUTH SERUM?

Scores of Hollywood movies portray truth serum as the chemical version of Wonder Woman's magical lasso (see preceding Factoid). In the 2004 comedy *Meet the Fockers*, a father injects his daughter's fiancé with truth serum to test whether he is worthy of marrying her. After a person receives truth serum, the embarrassing truth supposedly emerges, whether or not he wants it to.

Truth serum is a term for a broad class of drugs. Most of these medications are *barbiturates* such as Sodium Pentothal. These drugs typically relax people and, in high doses, make them fall asleep. During the 1930s and 1940s, truth serum was a popular tool in psychotherapy for unearthing supposedly unconscious material (Dysken et al., 1979; Mann, 1969; Winter, 2005). For several decades, the police and military occasionally administered truth serum to suspects in the hopes of dredging up concealed information. In 1963, the U.S. Supreme Court ruled that criminal confessions induced under truth serum were scientifically questionable and unconstitutional, effectively putting a halt to its use for most purposes. Still, fascination with truth serum never died. Following the terrorist attacks of September 11, 2001, some U.S. government organizations displayed a renewed interest in truth serum, largely for the purpose of interrogating suspected terrorists (Brown, 2006). In 2008, Indian police reportedly administered truth serum to the lone surviving gunman in the horrific Mumbai terrorist attacks (Borrell, 2008).

Yet scientific evidence demonstrates that truth serum is anything but infallible. Studies show that people can lie under the influence of truth serum, falsifying the claim that this chemical invariably produces truthful statements (Piper, 1993). Even more problematic is evidence suggesting that truth serum, like many suggestive memory-recovery techniques, doesn't enhance memory: it merely lowers the threshold for reporting all memories, both true and false (Lynn et al., 2003a; Piper, 1993). As a consequence, memories retrieved under the influence of truth serum aren't any more trustworthy—and may be less trustworthy—than other memories (Borrell, 2008). Indeed, because the physiological effects of barbiturates are similar to those of alcohol, the effects of truth serum are comparable to those of getting rip-roaring drunk. Our inhibitions are lowered, but what we say can't always be trusted.

◄ **FALSIFIABILITY**
Can the claim be disproved?

guilty knowledge test (GKT)
alternative to the polygraph test that relies on the premise that criminals harbor concealed knowledge about the crime that innocent people don't

Emotion and Motivation

More recently, some experts in national security have proposed that oxytocin, a hormone that often boosts trust, might be an effective truth serum (Tennison & Moreno, 2012), as it could lead spies and other suspects to become more willing to tell the truth to interrogators. Yet because oxytocin boosts trust only among members of our in-groups (such as friends within our culture), not our out-groups (such as enemies of a different culture; Van Ijzendoorn & Bakermans-Kranenburg, 2012), this possibility seems unlikely.

Integrity Tests. Rather than use complex equipment designed to measure people's physiological responses, an estimated 6,000 U.S. companies, including McDonald's, administer paper-and-pencil **integrity tests**, questionnaires that presumably assess workers' tendency to steal or cheat (Cullen & Sackett, 2004). Integrity test questions fall into several categories:

- **History of stealing** ("Have you ever stolen anything from your place of work?")
- **Attitudes toward stealing** ("Do you think that workers who steal property from a store should always be fired?")
- **Perceptions of others' honesty** ("Do you believe that most people steal from their companies every now and then?")

"Yes" responses to questions 1 and 3 and a "no" response to question 2 will put you well on your way to a "dishonest" score on integrity tests.

Integrity tests predict employee theft, absenteeism, and other workplace misbehavior at better-than-chance levels (Berry, Sackett, & Wiemann, 2007; Ones, Viswesvaran, & Schmidt, 1993; Sackett & Wanek, 1996). Yet because these tests yield numerous false positives, their validity for detecting dishonesty in the business world is often relatively weak (Lilienfeld, Alliger, & Mitchell, 1995; Office of Technology Assessment, 1990; Van Iddekinge et al., 2012). So integrity tests, like the polygraph, may be biased against the innocent.

✔ **Study** and **Review** in **MyPsychLab**

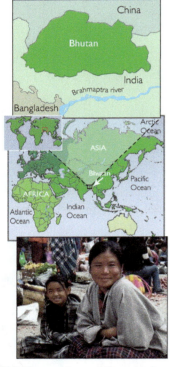

FIGURE 7 Bhutan, Home of Gross National Happiness. In the Himalayan country of Bhutan, the king has made increasing his country's Gross National Happiness a major domestic policy goal.

integrity test
questionnaire that presumably assesses workers' tendency to steal or cheat

Happiness and Self-Esteem: Science Confronts Pop Psychology

5 Identify common myths and realities about happiness and self-esteem.

6 Describe the emerging discipline of positive psychology.

The ruler of the tiny country of Bhutan, nestled in the Himalayan mountain range, recently had an unconventional idea (see **FIGURE 7**). Rather than focusing on increasing his nation's gross national product (GNP, a measure of economic success), the king decided to try to improve his nation's gross national happiness (GNH; Nettle, 2005). He hopes to boost Bhutan's GNH, as it's called, by preserving the beauty of its natural environment, promoting positive cultural values, and giving citizens more of a voice in government decisions. Until recently, almost all psychologists would have probably viewed the king as a naive idealist. Not anymore.

What Happiness Is Good For

For most of the twentieth century, psychologists largely dismissed happiness as a "fluffy" topic better suited to self-help books and motivational seminars than to rigorous research. Yet over the past few decades, a growing body of research has suggested that happiness—generally defined as people's sense of how satisfied they are with life—may produce enduring psychological and physical benefits.

Consider a study that has tracked a group of 180 nuns in Wisconsin for six decades. These nuns had kept daily diaries starting in the 1930s, when they were in their early twenties. Nuns whose sentences featured many positive words—such as those dealing with love, joy, and hope—outlived other nuns by an average of almost ten years (Danner, Snowdon, & Friesen, 2001). Of course, correlation doesn't imply causation, and the nuns who used more happy words may have differed in subtle ways from other nuns, such as in their exercise or health practices. Still, the findings are tantalizing.

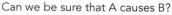

◄ CORRELATION VS. CAUSATION
Can we be sure that A causes B?

Like all primary emotions, happiness may serve evolutionarily adaptive functions. According to Barbara Fredrickson's (2001, 2003) **broaden and build theory**, happiness predisposes us to think more openly, allowing us to see the big picture we might have otherwise overlooked. As one test of this theory, doctors who received a small bag of candy made more accurate diagnoses of liver disease than did other doctors, apparently because being in a good mood allowed them to consider alternative diagnostic possibilities (Isen, Rosenzweig, & Young, 1991). So broader thinking may permit us to find novel solutions to problems. When we're happy, we see more of the world and seek out more opportunities, like romantic partners we wouldn't have considered (Keyes, Frederickson, & Park, 2012; Lyubomirsky, King, & Diener, 2005).

All else being equal, life is easier for those of us who are optimists. Optimists tend to be happier in everyday life compared with pessimists (Seligman & Pawelski, 2003), find it easier than pessimists to cope with life's rocky road (Watson & Clark, 1984), and may even live longer (see **FIGURE 8**). Optimism is even a plus in the bruising world of politics. One of the best predictors of who'll win a presidential election is which candidate's speeches contain the more hopeful language (Zullow et al., 1988).

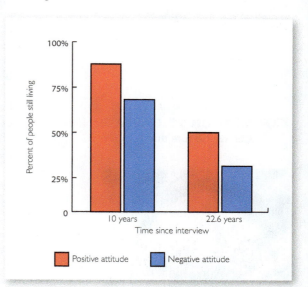

FIGURE 8 **Happily Living Longer** A study of over 600 people over age 50 found that those with positive attitudes about aging lived, on average, 7.5 years longer. Does this finding reflect a direct causal effect? Could we ever know? (*Based on:* Duenwald, 2002)

What Makes Us Happy: Myths and Realities

According to one recent estimate, Americans spend about $2 billion a year on self-help books designed to make them happy; moreover, Amazon.com lists about 400,000 books in the self-help category (Engelberg, 2012). Given this wealth of information, we might assume that we have all of the advice about happiness we need. Yet as psychologist Daniel Gilbert observed, "People have a lot of bad theories about happiness" (Martin, 2006). So to understand happiness, we first need to burst some pop psychology bubbles by countering them with surprising findings.

Finding #1: Life events don't determine happiness. Ed Diener and Martin Seligman screened more than 200 college students for their levels of happiness and compared the upper 10 percent with the middle and lowest 10 percent. The happiest students didn't experience any more positive life events than the other

broaden and build theory
theory proposing that happiness predisposes us to think more openly

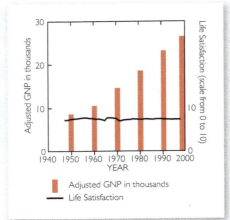

FIGURE 9 Does Wealth Bring Happiness? Over a 60-year span, the U.S. gross national product (a measure of economic prosperity) has increased dramatically. Yet Americans' average level of life satisfaction has stayed remarkably constant over the same time period. (*Based on:* Diener & Seligman, 2004)

CORRELATION VS. CAUSATION ▶
Can we be sure that A causes B?

? According to psychological research, what's wrong—or at least misleading—about this photo? (See answer upside down on bottom of page.)

positivity effect
tendency for people to remember more positive than negative information with age

Answer: Research suggests that money and material gifts don't buy us happiness, at least once we're financially comfortable.

groups did (Diener & Seligman, 2002). In another study, Daniel Kahneman and his colleagues tracked the moods and activities of over 900 women by asking them to record their experiences. The researchers found that life circumstances, such as the women's income and features of their job—like whether their jobs included good benefits—were essentially uncorrelated with women's current levels of happiness. In contrast, women's sleep quality and tendencies toward depression were good predictors of happiness (Kahneman et al., 2004).

Finding #2: Money usually doesn't make us happy. From what psychological research tells us, a lot of money can't buy long-term happiness (Kesebir & Diener, 2008; Wilson, 2002). Admittedly, when we're running short of it, money is a bit related to happiness (Helliwell & Putnam, 2004). Below about an annual salary of $75,000 per person, there's a modest association between how wealthy we are and how happy we are. But above this figure, additional money doesn't make us much happier (Kahneman & Deaton, 2010; see **FIGURE 9**). Still, most unhappy people are mistakenly convinced they'd be happier if they could only have more money. They may forget that higher salaries often require longer hours, which in turns means less free time—and in turn, often less happiness (Kahneman et al. 2006). One interesting exception to this is that more money *relative to other people* we know just might make us happier. Research shows that although our absolute amount of wealth isn't much related to our happiness, our position (ranking) of our wealth compared with those around us is (Boyce, Brown, & Moore, 2010).

Finding #3: The elderly are typically happier than younger people are. We're all familiar with the widespread stereotype of the sad old man or woman sitting all alone in a sparsely decorated room with no one to talk to. Yet happiness tends to increase with age, at least through the late sixties and perhaps seventies (Mroczek & Kolarz, 1998). Surveys suggest that the happiest group of people is men aged 65 and older (Martin, 2006). Only when people become quite old, typically in their eighties, does happiness decrease noticeably. Interestingly, happiness drops dramatically in the last year of life when people die of natural causes (Mroczek & Spiro, 2005). Although this correlation may reflect a causal effect of unhappiness on health, it may also reflect a causal effect of declining health on unhappiness.

The increase in happiness with old age appears to be due to the **positivity effect**: the tendency for individuals to remember more positive than negative information with age (Carstensen & Lockenhoff, 2003; Charles, Mather, & Carstensen, 2003). This effect appears to be due largely to elderly people's preferences for attending to, and thinking about, the bright side of life (Reed & Carstensen, 2012). The positivity effect is also accompanied by diminished activity of the amygdala (Mather et al., 2004), which plays a key role in the processing of negative emotions. So as we age, we may also be less affected by unpleasant information.

Finding #4: People on the West Coast are no happier than anyone else. Beautiful beaches, sunshine, warm weather, great celebrity watching ... who could ask for a better recipe for happiness? Maybe some Southern Californians. Even though non-Californians believe that Southern Californians are especially happy, Southern Californians are no happier than anyone else, including people in the chilly upper Midwest (Schkade & Kahneman, 1998). Non-Californians are probably falling prey to the *availability heuristic*. When we think of the West Coast, we think of surfers, glamorous actresses, and millionaires sipping martinis on the beach. We forget about the high cost of living, high crime rates, traffic congestion, and all of the other things that come with living in popular areas.

We've talked about four things that don't make us happy, but we haven't said much about what *does* make us happy. Fortunately, research offers some helpful clues (Martin, 2006; Myers, 1993b; Myers & Diener, 1996):

- **Marriage.** Married people tend to be happier than unmarried people (Mastekaasa, 1994), a well-replicated finding that holds across 42 countries studied by researchers (Diener et al., 2000). Moreover, among people who are married, happiness is a good predictor of marital satisfaction (Myers, 2000).

- **Friendships.** People with many friends tend to be happier than people with few friends (Diener & Seligman, 2002).

- **College.** People who graduate from college tend to be happier than people who don't (Martin, 2006).

- **Religion.** People who are deeply religious tend to be happier than people who aren't (Myers, 1993b). This finding might reflect the fact that religious individuals often feel connected to a larger community, as well as to a higher power.

- **Political affiliation.** Republicans tend to be happier than Democrats, both of whom tend to be happier than Independents (Haidt, 2012; Pew Research Center, 2006), although the reasons for these differences are unclear.

- **Exercise.** People who exercise regularly tend to be happier and less depressed than people who don't (Babyak et al., 2000; Stathopoulou et al., 2006), perhaps because exercise itself seems to be an antidepressant (Rozanski, 2012; Salmon, 2001).

- **Gratitude.** Merely asking participants on a daily basis to list reasons why they should be grateful about their lives, like having good friends, intimate romantic partners, and a fulfilling job, can enhance short-term happiness (Emmons & McCullough, 2003; Sheldon & Lyubomirsky, 2006), probably because doing so reminds them of what they have.

- **Giving.** Research in which experimenters give participants cash shows that spending money on others produces greater happiness than does spending it on ourselves (Dunn, Aknin, & Norton, 2008). This finding dovetails with research showing that we find performing empathic behaviors toward others pleasurable (de Waal, 2009).

- **Flow.** Mihaly Csikszentmihalyi (pronounced "cheeks sent me high") has found that individuals in the midst of *flow,* a mental state in which we're completely immersed in what we're doing, such as reading, writing, performing manual labor, or playing sports, tend to be especially happy (Csikszentmihalyi, 1990, 1997). During moments of flow, we're so intensely engaged in a rewarding activity that we screen out unpleasant distractions. We also feel a powerful sense of control over our actions.

Still, we should bear two cautions in mind when interpreting these findings. First, the associations between these variables and happiness are typically modest in magnitude, and there are many exceptions to the trends. For example, although there's a slight tendency for married people to be happier than unmarried people, there are plenty of unhappy married people and happy unmarried people (Lucas et al., 2003). Moreover, the apparent boost in happiness from marriage typically lasts only about two years (Luhmann et al., 2012).

Second, many of these findings derive from correlational research, so the direction of the causal arrow is often unclear. For example, although religious people tend to be happier than nonreligious people, happier people may find it easier than unhappy people to embrace a meaningful religious faith. Moreover, although frequent flow experiences probably contribute to long-term happiness, happy people may be especially prone to flow experiences.

◀ **REPLICABILITY**
Can the results be duplicated in other studies?

Contrary to popular conception, older adults are happier, on average, than younger people.

The state of "flow," in which we're totally absorbed in an activity and don't notice time passing, is associated with high levels of satisfaction and subjective well-being. We can experience flow in many work situations and enjoyable pastimes.

Factoid

The world champions of happiness are the Costa Ricans (Veenhoven, 2012), who recently dethroned the Danes (White, 2006). For unknown reasons, people in Costa Rica report the highest level of satisfaction in the world, with Vietnam coming in second.

◀ **CORRELATION VS. CAUSATION**
Can we be sure that A causes B?

If research tells us anything about how to find happiness, it's that consciously going out of our way to seek it out rarely works. As the concept of flow implies, happiness often emerges from the sheer act of enjoying what we do best, whether it's our work, hobbies, or romantic partners. Happiness lies in the pursuit of the prize, not the prize itself.

Forecasting Happiness

We're remarkably poor at **affective forecasting**: predicting our own and others' happiness (Gilbert et al., 1998; Wilson, 2002). Our affective forecasts aren't merely wrong; they're consistently incorrect in one direction. Specifically, *we overestimate the long-term impact of events on our moods* (Gilbert, 2006; Sevdalis & Harvey, 2007). That is, we display a **durability bias**: we believe that both our good and bad moods will last longer than they do (Frederick & Loewenstein, 1999; Gilbert et al., 1998; Wilson, 2002). Consider the following counterintuitive findings:

- Every month, tens of thousands of Americans wait on hour-long lines in the hopes of winning multimillion-dollar lotteries—and guaranteeing a life of never-ending bliss. Sure enough, lottery winners' happiness shoots up sky high immediately after hitting the big jackpot. Yet by two months, their happiness is back to normal—and not much higher than anyone else's (Brickman, Coates, & Janoff-Bulman, 1978; Diener & Biswas-Diener, 2008).

- Most people with paraplegia—people paralyzed from the waist down—have returned largely (although not entirely) to their baseline level of happiness only a few months after their accident (Brickman et al., 1978). People with other major physical disabilities similarly cope surprisingly well; for example, people who are blind are on average just as happy as people who can see (Feinman, 1978).

- Before taking an HIV test, people understandably predict that they'd be profoundly distressed were they to turn up HIV-positive. Yet only five weeks after discovering they're HIV-positive, people are considerably happier than they expected to be. Moreover, people who discovered they were HIV-negative are considerably less happy than they expected to be (Sieff, Dawes, & Loewenstein, 1999).

What's going on here? We underestimate how rapidly we adjust to our baseline levels of happiness or unhappiness. We forget that we're stuck on what Philip Brickman and Donald Campbell (1971) termed the **hedonic treadmill**: the tendency for our moods to adapt to external circumstances (*hedonic* means "associated with pleasure"). Just as our running speeds quickly adjust to match the speed of a treadmill—or else we'll fall flat on our faces—our levels of happiness adjust quickly to our ongoing life situations. When something good happens to us, we feel better in the short term. Yet we soon adapt to our positive life circumstances, bringing us back to emotional square one (Helson, 1948).

The hedonic treadmill hypothesis proposes that we begin life with a genetically influenced happiness "set point" from which we bounce up and down in response to short-term life events (Lykken, 2000; Lykken & Tellegen, 1996). With few exceptions, we return to that set point after a few days or weeks. We differ from each other in our happiness set points. Studies reveal that most of us are relatively happy most of the time, but others of us are chronically unhappy (Diener, Lucas, & Scollon, 2006) (see **FIGURE 10**). Our happiness set points are quite stable, but they can occasionally shift over time, especially following momentous life events (Diener, Kesebir, & Tov, 2012). This seems to be especially the case for negative experiences. Getting divorced, widowed, or laid off from work often seem to result in lasting increases in unhappiness that don't dissipate completely (Diener et al., 2006; Lucas et al., 2012).

There's a life lesson lurking in all of this. Here popular wisdom is correct: the grass *is* greener on the other side. It seems greener, that is, until we've been on the other side for a while and realize that the grass is still greener on yet another lawn.

Shortly after winning a big lottery, people are—not surprisingly—overjoyed. Yet research suggests that only a few months later, they are often not much happier than they were before winning the money.

Watch in **MyPsychLab** the **Video:** Thinking Like a Psychologist: Predicting Future Emotion and Desire

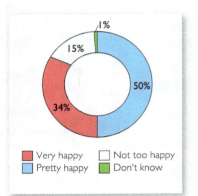

- Very happy
- Pretty happy
- Not too happy
- Don't know

1% 15% 50% 34%

FIGURE 10 How Happy Are Americans? Research shows that half of all Americans are pretty happy, with about a third describing themselves as "very happy." (*Based on:* Pew Research Center Report, 2006)

affective forecasting
ability to predict our own and others' happiness

durability bias
belief that both our good and bad moods will last longer than they do

hedonic treadmill
tendency for our moods to adapt to external circumstances

Self-Esteem: Important or Overhyped?

Many pop psychology sources tie virtually all psychological difficulties to one, and only one, core problem: low self-esteem (Branden, 1994; Reasoner, 2000). If you log on to Amazon.com, you'll find over 150,000 books, tapes, and other products devoted to boosting **self-esteem**, typically defined as people's evaluation of their worth. You can even find a self-esteem cereal bowl emblazoned with positive affirmations like "I'm talented!" and "I'm good-looking!" One American company has even established "Celebration Voice Mailboxes" to offer continual praise to its employees (Zaslow, 2007).

THE MYTHS AND REALITIES OF SELF-ESTEEM. All things being equal, high self-esteem isn't a bad thing: Self-esteem is positively correlated with happiness and negatively correlated with loneliness (Furnham & Cheng, 2000; Hudson, Elek, & Campbell-Grossman, 2000). Yet despite what the popular psychology industry tells us, there's no evidence that low self-esteem is the root of all unhappiness. This assertion is a prime example of a *single-variable explanation*, which reduces complex problems, like depression or aggression, to one cause. Although low self-esteem may play some causal role in these problems, it's unlikely to be the sole culprit. Indeed, the correlations between self-esteem and these difficulties are only modest in size.

What's more, the evidence linking self-esteem to life success is relatively feeble (Dawes, 1994; Marsh & Craven, 2006; Sommers & Satel, 2005). People with high self-esteem aren't any more likely than people with low self-esteem to have good social skills or to do well in school. They're also just about as likely to abuse alcohol and other drugs (Baumeister et al., 2003). When it comes to aggression, the story becomes more complex. Most of the popular psychology literature links aggression to low self-esteem. There may be some truth to this view (Donnellen et al., 2005). Yet most evidence suggests that a subset of people with high self-esteem is especially prone to aggression, especially when confronted with "ego threats": challenges to their self-worth.

In one study, Brad Bushman and Roy Baumeister asked participants to write essays concerning their attitudes toward abortion and told them that another participant would be evaluating their essay. In fact, Bushman and Baumeister had randomly assigned participants to receive either positive evaluations ("No suggestions, great essay!") or negative evaluations ("This is one of the worst essays I have read!"). Then, participants played a game in which they could retaliate against their essay evaluator with a loud blast of noise. Participants with high self-esteem who also had high levels of *narcissism*—extreme self-centeredness—responded to negative evaluations by bombarding their opponents with louder noises, but low self-esteem participants didn't (Bushman & Baumeister, 1998). In addition, in prisons, narcissistic prison inmates are especially likely to respond with verbal aggression when given orders by guards (Cale & Lilienfeld, 2006), and high-esteem students who are narcissistic are especially like to retaliate against teachers who give them low grades by punishing them with low course evaluations (Vaillancourt, 2012). These data suggest that high self-esteem can actually be more of a risk factor for hostility than low self-esteem, especially when high opinions of oneself are paired with narcissism.

THE REALITIES OF SELF-ESTEEM. Still, research suggests that self-esteem affords several apparent benefits along with somewhat greater happiness and social connectedness (Baumeister et al., 2003). High self-esteem is associated with greater initiative and persistence—that is, a willingness to attempt new challenges and to stick with them even when the going gets rough—and with resilience in the face of stress. Nevertheless, these findings are correlational and may not be causal. Self-esteem measures are also more predictive of specific life outcomes when they are more specific themselves. For example, although overall self-esteem doesn't correlate highly with general school achievement, people's self-esteem regarding their mathematics ability does tend to be highly correlated with their achievement in math courses (Swann, Chang-Schneider, & McClarty, 2007).

Happiness is largely a matter of comparison, as this photograph from the 2008 Beijing Summer Olympics demonstrates. Research shows that third-place finishers, such as American swimmer Ryan Lochte (*right*), tend to be happier—and in this case just about as happy as first-place finisher Michael Phelps (*middle*)—than second-place finishers, like Hungarian Laszlo Cseh (*left*). The second-place finishers are probably especially disappointed because they compare their outcome with what "might have been" (Medvec, Madey, & Gilovich, 1995).

Popular psychology typically encourages children to maintain or increase their self-esteem. What does research say about whether doing so is a good idea?

◀ **CORRELATION VS. CAUSATION**
Can we be sure that A causes B?

self-esteem
evaluation of our worth

On April 20, 1999, Eric Harris and Dylan Klebold murdered 12 students and a teacher at Columbine High School in Colorado. Although much of the popular press attributed the murders to low self-esteem, Harris and Klebold's diaries (released after their suicides) indicated that they perceived themselves as superior to their classmates.

Watch in **MyPsychLab** the **Video:** Positive Psychology

positive illusions
tendencies to perceive ourselves more favorably than others do

positive psychology
discipline that has sought to emphasize human strengths

defensive pessimism
strategy of anticipating failure and compensating for this expectation by mentally overpreparing for negative outcomes

Self-esteem is also related to **positive illusions**: tendencies to perceive ourselves more favorably than others do. Most high self-esteem individuals see themselves as more intelligent, attractive, and likable than do low self-esteem individuals. Yet they don't score any higher than low-self-esteem individuals on objective measures of these characteristics (Baumeister et al., 2003).

A slight positive bias may be adaptive, as it may lend us the self-assurance we need to take healthy risks, like asking people out for dates or applying for jobs. Positive illusions may also be good for romantic relationships, at least when they're not too extreme; research suggests that romantic partners who hold unrealistically positive views of each other are more likely to endure in their relationships than are other partners (Murray, Holmes, & Griffin, 1996). Yet when our positive biases become excessive, they may lead to psychological difficulties, including extreme self-centeredness, because these biases may prevent us from benefiting from constructive feedback (Kistner et al., 2006).

Positive Psychology: Psychology's Future or Psychology's Fad?

Much of contemporary psychology has done little to encourage adequately functioning people to achieve their full emotional potential (Keyes & Haidt, 2003). Some authors have argued that popular psychology has underestimated people's resilience in the face of stressful life events (Bonanno et al., 2002; Garmezy, Masten, & Tellegen, 1984). Since about the turn of the twenty-first century, the emerging discipline of **positive psychology** has sought to change that state of neglect by emphasizing human strengths such as resilience, coping, life satisfaction, love, and happiness (Myers & Diener, 1996; Seligman & Csikszentmihalyi, 2000). This field also focuses on helping people to find ways of enhancing positive emotions like happiness and fulfillment, as well as on building psychologically healthy communities (Sheldon & King, 2001). Christopher Peterson and Martin Seligman (2004) outlined numerous "character strengths and virtues" they view as essential to positive psychology. Several of them, such as curiosity, love, and gratitude, are positively associated with long-term life satisfaction (Park, Peterson, & Seligman, 2004). Across the country, positive psychologists have begun to teach students to incorporate these strengths and virtues into their daily lives (Max, 2007).

Yet some psychologists have condemned positive psychology as a "fad" (Lazarus, 2003) whose claims have outstripped the scientific evidence (Ehrenreich, 2009; Held, 2004; Max, 2007). Indeed, data suggest that although being happy is correlated with many indicators of life success, being *moderately* happy is actually tied to higher levels of income, education, and participation in politics (Oishi, Diener, & Lucas, 2007), raising the possibility that being too happy can make us complacent. Moreover, as Julie Norem (2001) observed, *defensive pessimism* serves a valuable function for many anxious people. **Defensive pessimism** is the strategy of anticipating failure and then compensating for this expectation by mentally overpreparing for negative outcomes. For example, defensive pessimists tend to respond "True" to items like "I often start out expecting the worst, even though I will probably do okay." This strategy helps certain people to improve their performance, probably because it encourages them to work harder (Norem & Cantor, 1986). Robbing defensive pessimists of their pessimism—say, by cheering them up—makes them perform worse (Norem & Chang, 2002).

Moreover, optimists' rose-colored glasses and tendency to gloss over their mistakes may sometimes prevent them from seeing reality clearly. For example, optimists tend to recall feedback about their social skills as better than it was (Norem, 2001), which could prevent them from learning from their interpersonal errors, like inadvertently offending others. In addition, optimists sometimes display greater physiological responses to stressors, such as bad health news, than do pessimists, perhaps because they don't spend enough time preparing for the worst (Segerstrom, 2005).

None of this takes away from the value of positive psychology for many people. But the problem of individual differences reminds us to be wary of "one size fits all" solutions to life's multifaceted problems. Positive thinking is a key ingredient in many people's recipe for happiness, but it may not be for everyone.

Assess Your Knowledge   FACT or FICTION?

1. Good moods often allow us to consider novel alternatives to problems.   True / **False**

2. Money is highly correlated with happiness, especially at high levels of income.
   True / False

3. Happiness tends to decline sharply after age 50.   True / **False**

4. A few months after hitting it big in a lottery, lottery winners aren't much happier than anyone else.   **True** / False

5. High self-esteem is essential for good mental health.   True / **False**

6. Pessimism is an adaptive strategy for some people.   **True** / False

Answers: 1. T; 2. F; 3. F; 4. T; 5. F; 6. T

Motivation: Our Wants and Needs

7   Explain basic principles and theories of motivation.

8   Describe the determinants of hunger, weight gain, and obesity.

9   Identify the symptoms of bulimia and anorexia.

10   Describe the human sexual response cycle and factors that influence sexual activity.

11   Identify common misconceptions about and potential influences on sexual orientation.

Up to this point, we've discussed how and why we experience emotions. Yet to explain *why* we do things in response to our emotions, we also need to understand the psychological forces that pull and push us in various, and sometimes opposing, directions. **Motivation** refers to the drives—especially wants and needs—that propel us in specific directions. When we're motivated to do something, like read an interesting book, talk to a friend, or avoid studying for an exam, we're driven to *move* toward or away from that act—both psychologically and physically.

The world of popular psychology is bursting at the seams with "motivational speakers" who line their pockets with cash from people hoping to receive inspiration in love or work. Although such speakers may get our adrenaline flowing and make us feel good in the short term, there's no evidence that they deliver long-term benefits (Wilson, 2003).

Motivation: A Beginner's Guide

One doesn't need to be a psychologist to realize that two of the most overpowering motivators in life are food and sex. We'll soon learn about the whys and the hows of these two great "facts of life." Before we do, we first need to learn about a few basic principles of motivation. Does our little teaser motivate you to read on? We hope so.

DRIVE REDUCTION THEORY. One of the most influential motivational concepts in psychology is **drive reduction theory**, formulated by Clark Hull (1943), Donald Hebb (1949), and others. According to this theory, certain *drives*, like hunger, thirst, and sexual frustration, motivate us to minimize negative feelings and seek pleasure (Dollard & Miller, 1950). Note that all of these drives are unpleasant, but that satisfaction of them reduces tension and results in pleasure. For example, the unpleasant feeling of hunger motivates food seeking and eating, which, in turn, produce satisfaction and pleasure.

From the standpoint of evolutionary theory, drives are geared to ensure our survival and reproduction. Yet some drives are more powerful than others. Thirst is more potent than hunger, and for good reason. Natural selection has probably ensured that our drive to quench our thirst is stronger than our drive to satisfy our hunger because most of us can survive only a few days without water but over a month

Motivational speakers like Anthony Robbins are adept at persuading their audiences that they can accomplish just about anything with enough drive and effort. Nevertheless, there's no solid research evidence that such speakers produce long-term changes in people's behavior.

motivation
psychological drives that propel us in a specific direction

drive reduction theory
theory proposing that certain drives, like hunger, thirst, and sexual frustration, motivate us to act in ways that minimize aversive states

FIGURE 11 Yerkes–Dodson Law. This law describes an inverted U-shaped relation between arousal on the one hand and performance or affect on the other. We tend to do our best—and are most content—when we experience intermediate levels of arousal.

Sports psychology research indicates that athletes who are too calm often don't perform at maximum capacity. So getting athletes "pumped up" —but not too pumped up—is a key goal for coaches and trainers.

FIGURE 12 Approach and Avoidance Over Time. As we get closer to a goal, the avoidance gradient becomes steeper than the approach gradient. Projects that seem desirable a few weeks in the future become more undesirable as the deadline approaches.

homeostasis
equilibrium

Yerkes–Dodson law
inverted U-shaped relation between arousal on the one hand and mood and performance on the other

without food. Most drive reduction theories propose that we're motivated to maintain a given level of psychological **homeostasis**, that is, equilibrium. To understand homeostasis, think of how a thermostat works to control the temperature in your house or apartment. It's set to a given temperature, say 68 degrees Fahrenheit, and when the room temperature deviates up or down from that set point, the thermostat "tells" your cooling or heating system to restore the equilibrium. Similarly, when we're hungry, we're motivated to satisfy that drive by eating, but ideally not too much. If we eat too much, our brain signals to us that we've overdone things and doesn't allow us to become hungry again for a while.

Drives and Arousal: Not Getting Ahead of the Curve. One factor that affects the strength of our drives is arousal. According to the **Yerkes–Dodson law** (Yerkes & Dodson, 1908), formulated about a century ago, there's an inverted U-shaped relation between arousal, on the one hand, and mood and performance, on the other (although its developers actually referred to the strength of stimuli rather than the strength of arousal; Winton, 1987). As we can see in **FIGURE 11**, for each of us, there's an optimal point of arousal, usually near the middle of the curve. If we're below that optimal point, we typically experience low motivation and don't perform well. If we're above that optimal point, we typically feel too anxious or stimulated and likewise don't perform well. Only when we're moderately aroused do we experience the ideal balance of motivation and control to accomplish our goals. Moreover, even within each of us, our arousal level often shifts depending on the time of day, substances we've ingested (like caffeine), and complexity of the tasks we're confronting (Revelle et al., 1980).

The Yerkes–Dodson law is popular among sports psychologists. Think of a swimmer who's underaroused before a major meet. She's unlikely to perform as well as she could, because she's not sufficiently motivated to do her best. So her sports psychologist may try to nudge her into the "psyched up" range of the Yerkes–Dodson curve, where she's feeling just aroused enough to want to do well but not so aroused she can't concentrate (Anderson, Revelle, & Lynch, 1989).

According to the Yerkes–Dodson law, when we're underaroused, we frequently experience "stimulus hunger," that is, a drive for stimulation. As Daniel Berlyne (1960) noted, underarousal can heighten our sense of curiosity, motivating us to explore stimuli that are complex or novel, like a challenging book or a piece of abstract art. In classic studies of *sensory deprivation* in the 1950s and 1960s, volunteers who entered isolation tanks for several hours often managed to create their own mental stimulation in this state of extreme underarousal (Jones, 1969; Zuckerman & Hopkins, 1966). Many experienced rich sensory images, and a few began to see or hear things that weren't there. Their brains yanked them out of the low end of the Yerkes–Dodson curve.

When Our Drives Clash: Approach and Avoidance. It's way past midnight. We're incredibly hungry, but too exhausted to get up off the couch to pop a dessert into the microwave. So we sit there frozen pathetically in place, spending several minutes deciding whether to remain on the couch or exert the monumental effort needed to walk the 10 feet to the kitchen. We're experiencing the often psychologically painful effects of conflicting drives.

Certain drives generate tendencies toward *approach,* that is, a predisposition toward certain stimuli, like food or objects of our sexual desire. In contrast, others generate tendencies toward *avoidance,* that is, a disposition away from certain stimuli, like rude people or frightening animals (Gray, 1982). As Kurt Lewin (1935) observed, approach and avoidance drives often conflict, as when we want to introduce ourselves to an attractive person across the room but are terrified of rejection. In other cases, two approach drives can conflict, as can two avoidance drives. As a general rule, the avoidance gradient is steeper than the approach gradient (Bogartz, 1965) (see **FIGURE 12**). This means that as we get closer to our goals, our tendencies to avoid increase more rapidly than our tendencies to approach. This phenomenon helps explain why we often agree to do things months in advance, only to regret them later. When we volunteer in June to organize our club's holiday party in December, the idea sounds like a lot of fun. But as the date of the party draws near, our sense of enjoyment is swamped by our sense of dread regarding all of the drudge work that lies ahead.

INCENTIVE THEORIES. As valuable as drive reduction theories have been to psychology, they don't explain why we often engage in behaviors even when our drives are satisfied. For example, drive reduction theories would predict that once Maya Angelou, Pablo Picasso, or Wolfgang Amadeus Mozart completed a masterpiece, their desire to generate another one would decrease, because they would have quenched their creative thirsts. Yet the opposite often happens; creative success seems to breed an even greater desire to create.

As a consequence, psychologists have come to recognize that drive reduction theories of motivation need to be supplemented by **incentive theories**, which propose that we're often motivated by positive goals, like the pleasure of creating a great painting or the glory of finishing first in a track meet. Many of these theories, in turn, distinguish *intrinsic motivation,* in which people are motivated by internal goals, from *extrinsic motivation,* in which people are motivated by external goals. If we're intrinsically motivated to do well in a psychology class, we're driven primarily by our desire to master the material; if we're extrinsically motivated to do well in this class, we're driven primarily by our desire to get a good grade.

Behaviorists define reinforcement as any outcome that makes the behavior that preceded it more likely. Yet there's evidence that certain rewards that we might expect to be reinforcers may *undermine* intrinsic motivation, making us less likely to perform behaviors we once enjoyed (Deci, 1971; Deci, Koestner, & Ryan, 1999). Mark Lepper and his colleagues (Lepper, Greene, & Nisbett, 1973) identified preschool children who were especially interested in drawing and randomly assigned them to three conditions: (1) one in which children agreed to draw pictures to receive an award (a fancy certificate with a gold seal and red ribbon); (2) one in which children drew pictures without knowing they'd receive an award, which they later all received; or (3) one in which no children received an award. Two weeks later, the experimenters again gave children the chance to draw pictures and observed them behind a one-way mirror. Interestingly, children in the first condition—who engaged in the activity to achieve a reward—showed significantly less interest in drawing than did children in the other two conditions. Many psychologists and some popular writers have interpreted these findings as implying that when we see ourselves performing a behavior to obtain an external goal, we conclude that we weren't all that interested in the behavior in the first place (Kohn, 1993). "I was only doing it to get the reward," we tell ourselves, "so I guess I wasn't really interested in it for its own sake." As a result, our intrinsic motivation for that behavior decreases.

Not all psychologists accept this interpretation (Carton, 1996; Eisenberger & Cameron, 1996). For one thing, some researchers haven't replicated the undermining effect (Cameron & Pierce, 1994). Still others have offered rival explanations for these findings. One is a *contrast effect:* once we receive reinforcement for performing a behavior, we anticipate that reinforcement again. If the reinforcement is suddenly withdrawn, we're less likely to perform the behavior. So we're not that different from a rat that's reinforced with a chunk of cheese for completing a maze. When the rat gets to the end of the maze and unexpectedly finds no cheese (the origin of the expression, "Rats!" perhaps?), he's less likely to run the maze quickly the next time (Crespi, 1942; Shoemaker & Fagen, 1984).

OUR NEEDS: PHYSICAL AND PSYCHOLOGICAL URGES. As anyone who's hungry or thirsty knows, some human needs take precedence over others. Starting with Henry Murray (1938), theorists have distinguished *primary needs*—biological necessities like hunger and thirst from *secondary needs*—psychological desires. Murray identified more than 20 secondary needs, including the *need for achievement.*

In everyday life, approach and avoidance drives often conflict, resulting in difficult decisions. For example, we may be tempted to eat a delicious desert (an approach drive) but also tempted to avoid it because it's bad for us (an avoidance drive); similarly, we may be tempted to eat an apple because it's good for us (an approach drive) but also tempted to avoid if we aren't fond of apples (an avoidance drive).

? Children who are motivated to draw for the fun of it rather than for an outside reward possess what kind of motivation?
(See answer upside down on bottom of page.)

◄ **REPLICABILITY**
Can the results be duplicated in other studies?

◄ **RULING OUT RIVAL HYPOTHESES**
Have important alternative explanations for the findings been excluded?

incentive theories
theories proposing that we're often motivated by positive goals

Answer: Intrinsic

Classic work conducted by David McClelland and his colleagues (McClelland et al., 1958; McClelland et al., 1953) demonstrated that individuals who display higher achievement-related imagery in response to ambiguous drawings (such as a boy looking at a violin) are more successful than other people in leadership positions, such as management and business.

According to Abraham Maslow's **hierarchy of needs** (1954, 1971), we must satisfy our primary needs, such as physiological needs and needs for safety and security, before we can progress to more complex secondary needs. These more complex needs include desires for belongingness and love; self-esteem; and finally self-actualization, the drive to realize our full psychological potential. As we progress up Maslow's hierarchy, we move away from needs produced by drives and toward needs produced by incentives. Maslow's hierarchy reminds us of an often-overlooked point: when people are starving or malnourished, they often aren't concerned about abstract principles of psychological growth such as achieving self-knowledge or obtaining democratic freedoms. First things must come first (see **FIGURE 13**).

Although Maslow's hierarchy is a helpful starting point, we shouldn't take it literally. For one thing, it isn't based on biological reality, as it omits important evolutionary needs like sexual and parenting drives (Kenrick et al., 2010). Also, although some needs are more crucial than others, there's evidence that people who haven't achieved lower levels of this hierarchy can sometimes attain higher levels (Rowan, 1998; Soper, Milford, & Rosenthal, 1995). The numerous cases of starving artists who continue to paint masterworks despite being hungry and poor appear to falsify Maslow's claim of an invariant hierarchy of needs (Zautra, 2003).

FALSIFIABILITY ▶
Can the claim be disproved?

Hunger, Eating, and Eating Disorders

If we're lucky, we don't experience the pangs of hunger very often or for very long and can refuel with a Big Mac, a veggie sandwich, or whatever satisfies our cravings. But for billions of less privileged people, hunger is a fact of everyday life. As unpleasant as feelings of hunger can be, our very survival depends on it. We experience hunger and thirst to motivate us to acquire food and drink, which provide us with nutrients and energy needed to be active and alert, and to maintain a properly functioning immune system (Mattes et al., 2005).

HUNGER AND EATING: REGULATORY PROCESSES. If food is available, we eat when we're hungry. And when we feel full (satiated), we stop eating. Simple, right? Not when we consider that inside our bodies, a complex series of events governing hunger and eating unfolds. One early idea, suggested by Walter Cannon and Alfred Washburn (1912), is that stomach contractions, which occur when our stomach is empty, cause hunger. To test this hypothesis, Washburn, Cannon's graduate student, swallowed a balloon that was inflated inside his stomach by means of a tube. (We don't recommend trying this at home.) The intrepid student's reports of hunger were associated with muscle contractions, measured by pressure on the balloon. Nevertheless, as we've learned, we can't infer causation from a correlational finding. Scientists have since observed that people still report hunger pangs when their stomachs are surgically removed and when surgeons cut the nerve to the stomach responsible for stomach contractions (Bray, 1985). These findings falsify the stomach contraction hypothesis.

CORRELATION VS. CAUSATION ▶
Can we be sure that A causes B?

FALSIFIABILITY ▶
Can the claim be disproved?

Children often point to their stomachs when they're hungry, but the brain is far more influential than the stomach as a command and control center for food cravings. Scientists began to get an inkling of this truth more than 50 years ago, when they learned that two areas of the hypothalamus play different roles in eating. Consider two rats in the same cage that couldn't look more different. Rat 1 is very large, some might say humongous. Rat 2 is scrawny to the point of requiring force-feeding to survive. Scientists supersized the first rat by electrically stimulating the lateral (side) parts of its hypothalamus (Delgado & Anand, 1952). The second rat became slimmer than a supermodel rodent

hierarchy of needs
model developed by Abraham Maslow proposing that we must satisfy physiological needs and needs for safety and security before progressing to more complex needs

when researchers destroyed its lateral hypothalamus by making a small lesion in it (Anand & Brobeck, 1951; Teitelbaum & Epstein, 1962). Based on these findings, scientists concluded that the lateral hypothalamus plays a key role in initiating eating.

Something remarkable happens when researchers stimulate the *ventromedial* or lower middle part of rats' hypothalamus: The furry creatures eat very little or stop eating entirely (Olds, 1959). When researchers lesion the same part of the brain, the rats become so hefty that they look like they're about to burst (Hetherington & Ranson, 1940; King, 2006). The ventromedial hypothalamus seems to let rats know when to stop eating.

Many psychology books have labeled the lateral hypothalamus a "feeding center" and the ventromedial hypothalamus a "satiety center," but this distinction is too simple. Other regions of the hypothalamus also respond to hunger and satiety signals (Coppari et al., 2005; Scott, McDade, & Luckman, 2007). In reality, a complex sequence of events mediated by different brain areas and body regions orchestrates eating (Grill & Kaplan, 2002). A distended or full stomach activates neurons in the hypothalamus, and in response, we resist our impulses to reach for that second cookie (Jordan, 1969; Smith, 1996; Stunkard, 1975). A hormone produced in the stomach called *ghrelin* communicates with the hypothalamus to increase hunger, whereas another hormone, called cholecystokinin (CCK), counteracts the effects of ghrelin and decreases hunger (Badman & Flier, 2005).

Glucose (blood sugar) provides our cells with high-octane energy to score a touchdown or flee from a hungry lion. Our bodies produce glucose from proteins, fats, and carbohydrates in the foods we eat. The hypothalamus is in tune with changing levels of glucose (Schwartz et al., 2000; Woods et al., 1998). According to **glucostatic theory** (Campfield et al., 1996; van Litalie, 1990), when our blood glucose levels drop, typically after we haven't eaten for some time, hunger creates a drive to eat to restore the proper level of glucose. In this way, we achieve homeostasis, the balance of energy we take in and expend. People gain weight when there's an imbalance, such that more energy is taken into the body than expended by way of exercise or the body's ability to "burn" excess calories through metabolic processes.

When our glucose levels drop substantially, we generally feel hungry (Levin, Dunn-Meynell, & Routh, 1999). But levels of blood glucose can be quite variable and don't always mirror the amount or types of food we eat. In fact, our self-reported hunger and desire for a meal are better predictors of our energy intake in our meals over a three-day period than are our glucose levels (Pittas et al., 2005). Far more than glucose is involved in regulating eating.

WEIGHT GAIN AND OBESITY: BIOLOGICAL AND PSYCHOLOGICAL INFLUENCES. When we go "people watching" in the mall, we can't help but notice that adults and children come in more shapes and sizes than varieties of Campbell's soup. If that mall or supermarket is in the United States, we'll also observe that about two-thirds of the passersby are overweight or obese. In our evolutionary history, stocking up on tasty and energy-loaded fatty foods was probably necessary for survival and may partly explain our preference for such foods. In today's food-rich society of all-you-can-eat buffets and oversized portions, however, people typically consume far more calories than they need to ensure their survival (Capaldi, 1996; Konner, 2003). Here we'll examine the physiology and psychology of eating and overeating.

Chemical Messengers and Eating. When we eat a candy bar, some of the glucose from the treat may get converted into fat, which stores energy for the long term. The more stored energy in fat cells, the more they produce a hormone called **leptin**. Leptin signals the hypothalamus and brain stem to reduce appetite and increase the amount of energy used (Grill et al., 2002; Williams, Scott, & Elmquist, 2009). Researchers discovered a clue to the causes of obesity when they found that mice that lacked the gene for leptin become obese at an early age (Hamann & Matthaei, 1996). Interestingly, people who are obese seem resistant to the effects of leptin.

Individuals who are obese also find food difficult to resist because they think about food a lot and find the tasty qualities of food especially rewarding. The mere sight, taste, smell, and thought of plentiful food in our environment can trigger the release of neurotransmitters,

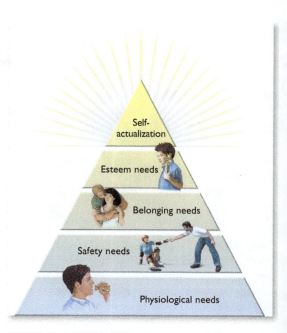

FIGURE 13 Maslow's Hierarchy of Needs. According to Abraham Maslow, our needs are arranged in a hierarchy or pyramid, with the most "basic" needs at the bottom. If our basic needs aren't satisfied, Maslow claimed, we can't progress up the hierarchy. Does research support this assertion?

Explore in **MyPsychLab** the **Concept:** Virtual Brain Hunger and Eating

glucostatic theory
theory that when our blood glucose levels drop, hunger creates a drive to eat to restore the proper level of glucose

leptin
hormone that signals the hypothalamus and brain stem to reduce appetite and increase the amount of energy used

People differ in their genetic tendency toward obesity, so differences in food consumption and weight may be apparent at an early age. A mutation in the melanocortin-4 receptor gene may play a role in some early cases of obesity.

Brian Wansink, shown here, has shown that people tend to eat more popcorn when it's served in a large rather than small bucket—an example of what psychologists call "unit bias." So beware of those "You can get an extra-large portion for only 75 cents more" pitches from movie vendors.

CORRELATION VS. CAUSATION ▶

Can we be sure that A causes B?

set point
value that establishes a range of body and muscle mass we tend to maintain

including serotonin, that activate the brain's pleasure circuits (Ciarella et al., 1991; Lowe & Levine, 2005). People who are obese also may overeat to provide comfort or distraction to counter negative emotions (Hoppa & Hallstrom, 1981; Stice et al., 2005).

The Set Point. Another reason the battle of the bulge isn't easy to win is that each of us may have a genetically programmed **set point**, a value—much like that on our car's fuel gauge—that establishes a range of body fat and muscle mass we tend to maintain (Mrosovsky & Powley, 1977). When we eat too little and drop below our set point, regulatory mechanisms kick in to increase our appetite or decrease our metabolism (Knecht, Elllger, & Levine, 2007). In this way, our bodies defend against weight loss (Nisbett, 1972).

No one knows for sure what "sets" the set point, but compared with thin people, individuals who are obese may be born with more fat cells, with lower metabolic rates at which their bodies burn calories, or with less sensitivity to leptin. Some people seem to gain weight no matter how little they eat, whereas others remain thin no matter how much they eat.

Still, some findings raise suspicions about the set point hypothesis. David Levitsky and his colleagues (Levitsky, 2005) determined how many calories study participants consumed during a 14-day baseline period and then overfed the participants so that they consumed 35 percent more calories than they did at baseline. During a third period in which participants could eat whatever they wanted, they didn't restrict their food intake enough to return to baseline levels, as predicted by set point theory. What's clear is that we're not fated to remain at a fixed weight; there's a range of weights we can "settle into." Most of us can control and modify our weight, within limits, by staying active and eating a healthy diet.

The Role of Genes in Obesity. Genes probably exert a substantial influence on our weight. In about 6 percent of cases of severe obesity, a mutation in a major *melanocortin-4 receptor gene* is responsible (Todorovic & Haskell-Lueuvano, 2005). People born with this mutation never seem to feel full, regardless of whether they've eaten a strawberry or half a strawberry pie. In effect, their brains don't let them know when to stop eating. Scientists have identified other genes, including the leptin gene, but a combination of many genes associated with appetite, amount of fat stored in the body, and metabolism probably work together to increase the likelihood of obesity (Choquet & Meyre, 2011).

Sensitivity to Cues and Expectations. But genes don't completely determine our weight. External cues such as time of day, the opportunity to observe others sample multiple portions of tempting desserts, and expectations also play prominent roles in food consumption. The supersizing of portions—called *portion distortion*—has probably contributed to the supersizing of Americans (Geier, Rozin, & Doros 2006; Wansink, 2009). In the United States, from 1977 to 1996, portion sizes of food served on dinner plates in restaurants ballooned by 25 percent (Young & Nestle, 2002). When people are served M&Ms with a large spoon, they eat substantially more of them than when they're served in a small spoon (Geier et al., 2006). Brian Wansick and his colleagues (Wansink, Painter, & North, 2005) fooled participants by having them unknowingly drink soup from "bottomless bowls"—bowls that remained full by means of a flowing tube. They consumed a whopping 73 percent more soup than participants who consumed soup from regular bowls. Because we think in terms of "units" of things as the optimal amount—a heuristic called *unit bias* (Geier et al., 2006)—controlling portions of food consumed is a good way to control our weight. A nifty trick to keep in mind is to eat food on a smaller plate: doing so will make portions appear bigger and limit the amount we eat.

Scores on a delay of gratification task administered to preschoolers at age 4 predicted body mass index (BMI) approximately 30 years later. For each additional minute that a child was able to delay gratification, BMI was reduced by.2 in adulthood. Still, the findings are correlational and do not permit causal conclusions about the link between delay of gratification and BMI (Schlam et al., 2013).

Stanley Schachter proposed the **internal–external theory**, which holds that relative to other people, people with obesity are motivated to eat more by external cues like portion size, as well as the taste, smell, and appearance of food, than by internal cues like a growling stomach or feelings of fullness (Canetti, Bachar, & Berry 2002; Schachter, 1968). According to this theory, individuals are at risk for obesity when they continue to eat even after being full and base their food choices on the appealing qualities of food, time of day, or social circumstances. In laboratory studies, people who are obese are more likely than other people to overeat after researchers manipulate clocks in the room to fool participants into thinking it's dinnertime (Schachter & Gross, 1968). Nevertheless, another possibility, which research favors, is that the oversensitivity to external cues is a consequence rather than a cause of eating patterns (Nisbett, 1972).

EATING DISORDERS: BULIMIA AND ANOREXIA. People with eating disorders are strongly motivated to stay thin or lose weight, while they often are preoccupied with food and experience guilt and other negative emotions during and after eating. The eating disorder of **bulimia nervosa** (better known simply as *bulimia*) is associated with a pattern of *bingeing*—eating large amounts of highly caloric foods in brief periods of time—followed by *purging*—vomiting or other means of drastic weight loss, like frantic exercise or extreme dieting. During a binge, some people gorge themselves with food equaling more than 10,000 calories in a two-hour period and average about 3,500 calories per binge. That amounts to about six Big Macs (Walsh, 1993; Walsh et al., 1992).

Bulimia literally means "ox hunger." Bingeing can be frightening because it's often accompanied by the feeling that it's impossible to stop eating. After a binge, most people with bulimia feel guilt and anxiety over the loss of control and the prospect of gaining weight. Frequently, their answer to this problem is to purge, which typically takes the form of self-induced vomiting, but sometimes involves abusing laxatives or diet pills or exercising excessively (Williamson et al., 2002).

Bingeing and purging set up a vicious cycle. Purging is reinforcing because it relieves anxious feelings after overeating and sidesteps weight gain. But it sets the stage for bouts of overeating. For example, vomiting allows people with bulimia to "undo" the binge and rationalize later bouts of overeating ("I can always get rid of the ice cream"). After bingeing, they may resolve to go on a strict diet. Yet severe dieting leads to hunger and increases preoccupation with food and the temptation to binge (Stice et al., 1999; Stice et al., 2005). When eating spirals out of control, concerns about dieting and the likelihood of another

◀ **RULING OUT RIVAL HYPOTHESES**
Have important alternative explanations for the findings been excluded?

internal–external theory
theory holding that obese people are motivated to eat more by external cues than internal cues

bulimia nervosa
eating disorder associated with a pattern of bingeing and purging in an effort to lose or maintain weight

Answers are located at the end of the text.

DIETS AND WEIGHT-LOSS PLANS

evaluating CLAIMS

We Americans are always looking for a new, quicker way to lose weight and achieve our ideal body size and shape. The creators of diets and weight-loss plans are only too happy to oblige. Some claim we can lose weight by avoiding carbohydrates; others, by drinking protein shakes; and still others, by consuming only one type of soup or grapefruit. How many of these diet tips have you heard? Let's evaluate some of these claims, which are modeled after actual ads for diets and weight-loss plans.

"We help you lose weight by changing your everyday habits. Learn how to eat *smaller portions*, choose more *nutritious foods*, and make *exercise* a part of your daily routine."

This ad doesn't make any promises about how much weight you'll lose and correctly notes that reducing calories (through smaller portions of nutritious foods) and exercise are necessary components of a sensible diet.

"I have a whole new lease on life—I lost *98 pounds in only four months*!"

The anecdotal claim that someone lost almost 100 pounds in four months is extraordinary—that would be an average of over six pounds lost each week. Note that the ad doesn't mention potential adverse health effects of such dramatic weight loss. In addition, no reason is given for the weight loss, so we can't assume that diet is the cause. What rival explanations can you think of for such a drastic weight loss?

"Our *revolutionary research* shows that you can lose weight without dieting or exercise. Click here to learn more."

Beware of claims based on "revolutionary" new studies. The principle of connectivity reminds us that science builds with previous research. Moreover, to be trusted, results should be replicated in independent studies.

CORRELATION VS. CAUSATION ▶
Can we be sure that A causes B?

Anorexia isn't limited to women, although it's comparatively rare among men. It's associated with body image distortion, which contributes to a fear of being fat despite being severely underweight.

binge escalate, thereby completing the self-destructive circle (Fairburn, Cooper, & Shafran, 2003). This binge-purge cycle can be physically hazardous, resulting in heart problems, tears to the esophagus, and wearing away of tooth enamel (Mehler, 2003).

Bulimia is the most common eating disorder, afflicting 1 to 3 percent of the population (Craighead, 2002; Keski-Rahkonen et al., 2008). About 95 percent of people with this diagnosis are women. An additional 8–16 percent of young women, including many in college, fall short of a diagnosis of bulimia (one binge a week for three months) but show signs of disordered eating, such as repeated bingeing. People with bulimia report high levels of body dissatisfaction and often see themselves as obese when they're of normal weight (Johnson & Wardle, 2005). Twin studies suggest that bulimia is influenced by genetic factors (Bulik, Sullivan, & Kendler, 1998; Root et al., 2010). Nevertheless, bulimia is probably also triggered in part by sociocultural expectations concerning the ideal body image. In modern society, the media equate beauty with a slender female figure. Movies, sitcoms, and magazines feature extremely underweight females, typically 15 percent below women's average weight (Johnson, Tobin, & Steinberg, 1989). So it's no wonder that women who frequently view television programs featuring extremely thin women experience higher levels of body image dissatisfaction than do other women (Himes & Thompson, 2007; Thompson et al., 2004; Tiggemann & Pickering, 1996). It's possible that women who are already concerned about their body image may tend to watch television programs featuring idealized images of women, so the causal arrow could run in the opposite direction. Still, there's compelling circumstantial evidence for at least some causal effect of the media on eating disorders. Following the introduction of American and British television onto the remote Pacific island of Fiji, the symptoms of eating disorders in teenage girls increased fivefold within only four years (Becker et al., 2002).

Anorexia nervosa, or anorexia, is less common than bulimia, with rates ranging from .5 percent to 1 percent of the population (Craighead, 2002). But like bulimia, anorexia usually begins in adolescence and is sometimes fueled by sociocultural pressures to be thin. Although anorexia is more common in girls than boys, as many as 25 percent of people diagnosed with anorexia are male adolescents (Woolridge & Lytle, 2012). Whereas individuals with bulimia tend to be in the normal weight range, those with anorexia become emaciated in their relentless pursuit of thinness (Golden & Sacker, 1984). Along with a "fear of fatness," individuals with anorexia—like those with bulimia—have a distorted perception of their body size. Even those with bones showing through their skin may describe themselves as fat.

Psychologists diagnose anorexia when individuals display a refusal to maintain body weight at or above a healthy weight expected for age and height, with a significantly low body weight due to restriction of food or energy intake. Individuals with anorexia often lose between 25 percent and 50 percent of their body weight.

With continued low weight, a loss of menstrual periods, hair loss, heart problems, life-threatening electrolyte imbalances, and fragile bones may result (Gottdiener et al., 1978; Katzman, 2005). An anorexic patient treated by your text's second author broke her femur (the long bone in the thigh) during an ordinary game of tennis. Some researchers put the mortality rate for anorexia at 5–10 percent, making it one of the most life-threatening of all psychological conditions (Birmingham et al., 2005; Sullivan, 1995).

Anorexia is present not only in Western countries but also in regions that have had little exposure to Western media, including some Middle Eastern nations and parts of India (Keel & Klump, 2003; Lynn et al., 2007). Although anorexia appears to be more culturally and historically universal compared with bulimia, societal *explanations* for its causes have differed across time and place. For example, historical descriptions suggest that some young Catholic nuns in medieval times who starved themselves probably had anorexia. Yet they explained their fasting behaviors as efforts to purify their souls for God (Keel & Klump, 2003; Smith, Spillane, & Annus, 2006).

Sexual Motivation

Sexual desire—called *libido*—is a wish or craving for sexual activity and sexual pleasure (Regan & Berscheid, 1999). Sexual desire is deeply rooted in our genes and biology, but as we'll see, it's also influenced by social and cultural factors.

anorexia nervosa
eating disorder associated with excessive weight loss and the irrational perception that one is overweight

SEXUAL DESIRE AND ITS CAUSES. The sex hormone testosterone can sometimes enhance sexual interest in the short term, but other biological influences are also at play when it comes to sexual desire. For example, low levels of sexual desire are associated with high levels of the neurotransmitter serotonin (Houle et al., 2006). Researchers have discovered that variations in a gene that produces DRD4, a protein related to dopamine transmission, are correlated with students' reports of sexual desire and arousal (Zion et al., 2006). The scientists estimated that approximately 20 percent of the population possesses the mutation for increased sexual desire, whereas another 70 percent possesses a variant of the gene that depresses sexual desire. These findings dovetail with research showing that dopamine plays a key role in reward.

Many people believe that men have a stronger desire for sex than do women. This stereotype may hold more than a kernel of truth (Baumeister, Catanese, & Vohs, 2001). Compared with women, men desire sex more frequently and experience more sexual arousal (Hiller, 2005; Klusmann 2002), have a greater number and variety of sexual fantasies (Laumann et al., 1994; Leitenberg & Henning, 1995), masturbate more frequently (Oliver & Hyde, 1993), want to have more sexual partners (Buss & Schmitt, 1993), and desire sex earlier in a relationship (Sprecher, Barbee, & Schwartz, 1995). Women tend to experience greater variability than men in their sex drive (Lippa, 2009), and women with high sex drives tend to be attracted to both men and women (Chivers & Bailey, 2005). In contrast, men with high sex drives tend to be attracted to one sex or the other, depending on their sexual orientation (Lippa, 2006). In contrast to men, women's appetite for sex—but not their need for romantic tenderness—appears to decline after they form a secure relationship (Murray & Milhausen, 2012). Of course, none of these findings about sex necessarily apply to any individual man or woman, and there's tremendous variability in sexual interest among men and women—indeed, at least as much variability as there is between men and women.

Socialization may help explain why men and women appear to differ in sexual desire. Women are socialized to be less assertive and aggressive in many spheres of life, including the expression of their sexual desires. So perhaps women and men actually experience comparable sexual drives, but women don't express or admit their desires as much (Fisher, 2009). Although the data tilt toward the conclusion that men have an inherently stronger sex drive than do women, the evidence isn't definitive.

THE PHYSIOLOGY OF THE HUMAN SEXUAL RESPONSE. In 1954, the husband and wife team of William Masters and Virginia Johnson launched their pioneering investigations of sexual desire and the human sexual response. Their observations included sexual behaviors under virtually every imaginable condition—and some virtually unimaginable. Masters and Johnson's laboratory wasn't exactly a prescription for romantic intimacy: in addition to a bed, it contained monitoring equipment to measure physiological changes, cameras, and a probe that contained a camera to record changes in the vagina during intercourse. Yet most people who volunteered for their studies accommodated to the laboratory with surprising ease.

Masters and Johnson (1966) reported that the basic sexual arousal cycle was the same for men and women. Based on their research and other observations (Kaplan, 1977), scientists define the *sexual response cycle* in terms of four phases: (1) excitement, (2) plateau, (3) orgasm, and (4) resolution (see **FIGURE 14**).

The **excitement phase** is initiated by whatever prompts sexual interest. People often experience little sexual desire when they're tired, distracted, stressed out, in pain, or ill. Lack of attraction to a partner, depression, anxiety, and resentment can also inhibit sexual desire. In the excitement phase, people experience sexual pleasure and start to notice physiological changes, such as penile erection in men and vaginal swelling and lubrication in women. During the **plateau phase**, sexual tension builds, and if it continues, ultimately leads to orgasm. In the **orgasm (climax) phase**, sexual pleasure and physical changes peak, there are involuntary rhythmic contractions in the muscles of the

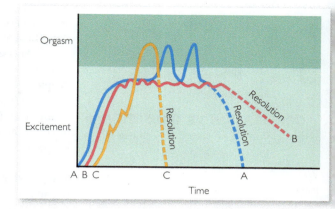

FIGURE 14 Variations in Female Sexual Response Cycle. This figure depicts the sexual arousal cycle for four different women, each represented by a different color. Three of the four women experienced at least one orgasm. The woman whose response is traced by the red line experienced excitement but no orgasm. (*Source:* Rathus, Nevid, & Fichner-Rathus, 2008)

◀ **RULING OUT RIVAL HYPOTHESES**
Have important alternative explanations for the findings been excluded?

excitement phase
phase in human sexual response in which people experience sexual pleasure and notice physiological changes associated with it

plateau phase
phase in human sexual response in which sexual tension builds

orgasm (climax) phase
phase in human sexual response marked by involuntary rhythmic contractions in the muscles of genitals in both men and women

genitals in men and women, and men ejaculate. After orgasm, people report relaxation and a sense of well-being in the **resolution phase**, as the body returns to its unstimulated state (Belliveau & Richter, 1970; Resnick & Ithman, 2009).

Masters and Johnson's groundbreaking efforts didn't capture a crucial fact: People's sexuality is deeply embedded in their relationships and feelings for each other. People experience more frequent and consistent orgasms when they love their partner and feel loved in return (Birnbaum, Glaubman, & Mikulincer, 2001) and feel satisfied in their relationship (Brody & Weiss, 2011; Young et al., 2000). But we can question the causal direction between relationship quality and the frequency and consistency of orgasms. Frequent orgasms may not merely reflect healthy relationships, but contribute to them.

FREQUENCY OF SEXUAL ACTIVITIES AND AGING. Early in their marriage, couples have sex on average about twice a week (Laumann et al., 1994). As people age, the frequency of their sexual activities decreases but their sexual satisfaction doesn't. Perhaps people expect their sexual activity to decrease as they age, so they're not disappointed by this change.

Contrary to the myth that sexual activities virtually cease for senior citizens, many people are sexually active well into their seventies and eighties, especially when they're healthy, are in happy marriages, and perceive that their partner desires a sexual relationship (Call, Sprecher, & Schwartz, 1995). In a survey of 1,491 individuals aged 40–80 years, 79.4 percent of men and 69.3 percent of women reported having engaged in sexual intercourse during the year prior to the study (Laumann et al., 2009). Women experience complex and sometimes striking changes in hormones during menopause, although there's another explanation for the difference between older men's and women's sexual activities. By the age of 80, women have less opportunity to find male partners; for every 100 women, there are only 39 men (Meston, 1997).

SEXUALITY AND CULTURE. People's expression of sexual desires is shaped by social norms and culture. Clellan Ford and Frank Beach's (1951) fascinating observations reveal how cultural norms influence people's ideas of what's sexually appropriate or inappropriate. When members of the Tsonga tribe in Africa first saw Europeans kissing, they laughed and remarked, "Look at them—they eat each other's saliva and dirt" (Ford & Beach, 1951). Admittedly, they have a point. Members of the Apinaly society in Brazil don't kiss, but women of the tribe may bite off their lovers' eyebrows and noisily spit them to one side. Women of the island Turk are even less kind, at least by Western standards: they customarily poke a finger into the man's ear when they're sexually excited.

David Buss (1989) found that residents of non-Western societies, including India, Iran, and China, place a much greater value on chastity in a potential partner than do individuals in Western European countries, including Sweden, Holland, and France. Americans are divided on whether they approve (59 percent) or disapprove (41 percent) of premarital sex (Widmer, Treas, & Newcomb, 1998). This latter percentage stands at odds with the prevalence of premarital sex in the United States, with men reporting rates of 85 percent and women rates of 80 percent (Laumann et al., 1994).

SEXUAL ORIENTATION: SCIENCE AND POLITICS. What motivates attraction to same versus opposite sex sexual partners? Same-sex romantic relationships develop in virtually all cultures and have done so since the dawn of recorded history. Biologists have documented homosexual behaviors in some 450 species (Bagemihl, 1999). People differ in their sexual orientation or interest in same (homosexual), opposite (heterosexual), or both (bisexual) sex sexual partners. We should keep in mind that sexual orientation isn't the same as sexual activity. For example, people may restrict their sexual partners to opposite sex individuals, yet be sexually attracted to same-sex individuals, or vice versa. People also differ in how they think and feel about their homosexuality. Many people who engage in occasional homosexual activities don't view themselves as gay, and many people participate in both homosexual and heterosexual activity (Bell & Weinberg, 1978).

Explore in **MyPsychLab** the **Concept:** The Sexual Response Cycle

CORRELATION VS. CAUSATION ▶
Can we be sure that A causes B?

Watch in **MyPsychLab** the **Video:** Special Topics: Cultural Norms and Sexual Behavior

RULING OUT RIVAL HYPOTHESES ▶
Have important alternative explanations for the findings been excluded?

Research indicates that gay people are as likely as heterosexual people to provide supportive environments for children.

Watch in **MyPsychLab** the **Video:** Thinking Like a Psychologist: Sexual Orientation

resolution phase

phase in human sexual response following orgasm, in which people report relaxation and a sense of well-being

Prevalence of Different Sexual Orientations. Research suggests that about 2.8 percent of males and 1.4 percent of females 18 or older identify themselves as gay, lesbian, or bisexual (Laumann et al., 1994; National Opinion Research Center, 2003). Nevertheless, even the best estimates may not represent the general population, because researchers often conduct surveys in prisons, college dorms, or military barracks or under the sponsorship of gay organizations, all of which may result in sampling bias.

Since Alfred Kinsey's famous "Kinsey Report" of the 1940s and 1950s, which presented his groundbreaking research on human sexuality, scientists have acquired a better understanding of homosexuality and challenged common misconceptions about gay men, lesbians, and bisexuals. Contrary to the stereotype that one person in a gay relationship adopts a masculine role whereas the other adopts a feminine role, less than a fourth of gay men and women fit neatly into those categories (Jay & Young, 1979; Lever, 1995). A good deal of media coverage also implies that gay individuals recruit others to become gay, are especially likely to sexually abuse children and adolescents, and are unfit to be parents. Yet scientific evidence supports none of these views (Bos, van Balen, & van den Boom, 2007; Freund, Watson & Rienzo, 1989; Patterson, 1992).

Can Sexual Orientation Be Changed? Is it possible to change the sexual orientation of gay men and women who wish to become heterosexual? Robert Spitzer (2003) evaluated 200 cases of people who underwent sexual reorientation therapy. He reported many instances in which people changed from a predominantly homosexual to heterosexual orientation for a five-year period or longer. In a striking published statement nearly a decade later, however, Spitzer (2012) acknowledged that a fatal flaw in the study was that he had no way to gauge the validity of participants' claims of changed sexual orientation. For example, the participants could have been lying to investigators or deceiving themselves about their sexual orientation. Going further, Spitzer apologized to the gay community for making unsubstantiated claims and to gay individuals who had wasted time and energy engaging in reparative therapy based on exaggerated reports of its effectiveness. The American Psychological Association (APA, 2009) affirmed that same-sex sexual and romantic attractions are normal variations of human sexuality and concluded that insufficient evidence supports the use of psychological interventions to change sexual orientation.

Prior to 1973, homosexuality was included in the American Psychiatric Association's formal list of mental disorders, the Diagnostic and Statistical Manual (Bayer & Spitzer, 1985), but scientific and social attitudes have changed markedly over the past three and a half decades, as the APA's recent statement indicates. Although gay men and women report relatively high rates of anxiety and depression (Biernbaum & Ruscio, 2004; Ferguson, Horwood, & Beautrais, 1999), in many or most cases, gay individuals' psychological problems may reflect their reaction to social oppression and intolerance of their lifestyles and genetic factors, rather than preexisting mental disturbance (Zietsch et al., 2012). Accordingly, gay individuals who participate in reorientation therapy and don't achieve the changes they seek may become even more dissatisfied. There's growing consensus that evidence-based treatments that value cultural diversity are well-positioned to help many currently distressed people accept and live with their homosexuality, rather than change their sexual orientation (Bartoli & Gillem, 2008; Glassgold et al., 2009).

GENETIC AND ENVIRONMENTAL INFLUENCES ON SEXUAL ORIENTATION. Bearing in mind the caveat that heritability doesn't imply that a characteristic can't be changed, most scientists are skeptical about the ability of gay individuals to change their sexual orientation because there are indications of inborn differences between homosexual and heterosexual individuals. Because many gay men and women report they've felt different from others for as long as they can remember, it's plausible that biological differences are sometimes present even before birth.

Sexual Orientation: Clues from Twin Studies. In a study conducted in Australia with 1,538 male twin pairs, Michael Bailey and his associates (Bailey, Dunne, & Martin, 2000) used a strict standard for defining sexual orientation and found a concordance rate

Canadian singers and songwriter twins Tegan and Sarah Quin, who are openly gay, don't want their music to be defined by their sexual orientation.

◄ **RULING OUT RIVAL HYPOTHESES**
Have important alternative explanations for the findings been excluded?

in twins (*concordance* refers to the proportion of co-twins who exhibit a characteristic, in this case, homosexuality, when the other twin also exhibits this characteristic) of 20 percent for homosexuality in identical twins and 0 percent in fraternal twins. In another study, they found concordance rates for lesbians of 48 percent in identical twins and 16 percent in fraternal twins (Bailey et al., 1993). The finding that a substantial percentage of identical twins aren't concordant tells us that environmental influences play a key role in homosexuality, although it doesn't tell us what these influences are.

Exotic Becomes Erotic. Nestled within Bailey's studies are clues related to the causes of sexual orientation. Gay men reported that they were often feminine boys and lesbians that they were often masculine girls, suggesting a potential genetic influence on childhood gender nonconformity.

Daryl Bem (1996, 2000) and others (Bailey & Zucker, 1995; Green, 1987; Zuger, 1988) proposed that childhood gender nonconformity plays a pivotal role in homosexuality. Boys who lack aggressiveness and avoid rough-and-tumble play may prefer the company of girls, and thus be gender-nonconforming. According to Bem's theory, called *exotic becomes erotic*, nonconforming children feel different and estranged from their peers and perceive their same-sex peers as unfamiliar and exotic (Bem, 2000). Children's sense of being different from their same-sex peers, and possibly being the subject of teasing or ridicule, arouses their autonomic nervous systems. Later in life, this arousal is transformed into attraction for same-sex peers. It's unlikely that Bem's theory accounts for all or even most gay individuals' sexual preferences, because only about half of gay men and lesbian women report having been feminine and masculine, respectively, in childhood (Bell et al., 1981). Still, one strength of Bem's theory is its acknowledgment of the interplay of genetic and environmental influences, including play activities and peers' reactions.

Sex Hormones, Prenatal Influences, and Sexual Orientation. When the fetus develops, sex hormones called androgens influence whether the brain sets the child on a path toward more masculine than feminine characteristics, or vice versa. According to one theory, girls exposed to excessive testosterone in the womb develop masculinized brains, and boys exposed to too little testosterone develop feminized brains (Ellis & Ames, 1987; Hines, 2010). These hormonal influences affect temperament and set the stage for childhood gender nonconformity and a homosexual orientation in later life (Bem, 1996).

Having older brothers increases the odds of male homosexuality by 33 percent for each older brother, amounting to an increase in the rate of homosexuality from about 3–5 percent (Blanchard & Bogaert, 1996). One explanation is that male fetuses produce substances that trigger the mother's immune system to develop anti-male antibodies that affect the sexual differentiation of the fetus's brain, with the effect intensifying with the birth of each succeeding male child. Researchers recently qualified the original finding by showing that older brothers increase the odds of homosexuality in right-handed but not left-handed males (Blanchard, 2008). Perhaps left-handed fetuses may not be sensitive to the anti-male antibodies, or the mothers of left-handed fetuses may not produce these antibodies.

Fingerprints, finger length, and handedness are all determined largely before birth, and gay and heterosexual individuals differ with respect to each of these characteristics (Hall & Kimura, 1994; Lalumière, Blanchard, & Zucker, 2000; Williams et al., 2000). So there's some justification for pointing the finger (pun intended) at prenatal influences, even though we can't yet specify which influences, such as exposure to sex hormones, are most important.

Sexual Orientation: Brain Differences. In 1981, Simon LeVay created a stir among scientists and laypersons alike by reporting that a small cluster of neurons in the hypothalamus, no larger than a millimeter, was less than half the size in gay compared with heterosexual men. The study is open to several criticisms: LeVay examined gay men's brains at autopsy, and the men died from AIDS-related complications. Still, it's unlikely that the differences LeVay uncovered are due entirely to AIDS, because a number of the heterosexual men also died of AIDS-related complications. The changes LeVay observed in the hypothalamus might also have been the result, rather than the cause, of homosexuality and differences in lifestyles between gay and heterosexual men. Yet another limitation was that LeVay's sample of gay men with AIDS wasn't representative of all gay men, so replicating his results will be especially important.

REPLICABILITY ▶
Can the results be duplicated in other studies?

Researchers have looked beyond the hypothalamus to find biological indicators of sexual orientation and discovered that the brain's corpus callosum is larger in homosexual than heterosexual men (Witelson et al., 2008). The scientists suggested that this finding implies that homosexuality is influenced by genetic factors, because the size of the corpus callosum is inherited. Nevertheless, we should again bear in mind that both brain size and brain activity could be a consequence, rather than a cause, of sexual orientation.

Scientists have yet to discover a dependable biological marker of sexual orientation. For example, many gay men have more older sisters than older brothers, and the size of the hypothalamus is comparable in most gay and non-gay individuals. In all likelihood, social and cultural influences that remain to be understood, in conjunction with genetic factors, play important roles in shaping people's sexual orientation.

◀ CORRELATION VS. CAUSATION
Can we be sure that A causes B?

✓ **Study** and **Review** in **MyPsychLab**

Assess Your Knowledge   FACT or FICTION?

1. According to the Yerkes–Dodson law, we generally do best when we're at our highest levels of arousal. **True / False**

2. Obese individuals seem resistant to the effects of leptin. **True / False**

3. Starvation can lead to at least some symptoms of anorexia nervosa. **True / False**

4. Few people are sexually active into their seventies and eighties. **True / False**

5. Scientists have yet to discover a dependable biological marker of sexual orientation. **True / False**

Answers: 1. F; 2. T; 3. T; 4. F; 5. T

Attraction, Love, and Hate: The Greatest Mysteries of Them All

12   Identify principles and factors that guide attraction and relationship formation.

13   Describe the major types of love and the elements of love and hate.

In 1975, psychologists Ellen Berscheid and Elaine Hatfield received a dubious distinction (Benson, 2006). They became the first individuals to receive the Golden Fleece Award, an "honor" (actually, a dishonor) bestowed on them by then–Wisconsin Senator William Proxmire. Proxmire had cooked up this award as a way of drawing public attention to projects that he regarded as colossal wastes of taxpayer money. Berscheid and Hatfield, it so happens, had won this award for their government-funded research on the psychological determinants of attraction and love (look for their names in the section you're about to read). Proxmire found the very idea of studying these topics scientifically to be absurd:

> "I'm strongly against this," he said, "not only because no one—not even the National Science Foundation—can argue that falling in love is a science; not only because I am sure that even if they spend 84 million or 84 billion they wouldn't get an answer that anyone would believe. I'm also against it because I don't *want* to know the answer!" (Hatfield & Walster, 1978, viii)

Of course, Proxmire was entitled not to know the answer. Yet more than three decades of research have since shown that Proxmire was woefully wrong in one crucial respect: Psychologists *can* study love scientifically. In this respect, we've come a long way from the 1970s. None of this takes away from the profound mysteries of falling in love, but it suggests that love may not be quite as unfathomable as we—or the thousands of poets who've written about it across the centuries—might believe.

Social Influences on Interpersonal Attraction

How can two people meet and become lovers in a world teeming with nearly 7 billion people? Of course, attraction is only the initial stage in a relationship, but we need to feel a twinkle of chemistry with someone before deciding whether we're compatible enough with

The origins of love are remarkably old, even ancient. In 2007, archaeologists unearthed these skeletons of a male and female couple in Italy (coincidentally, only 25 miles from Verona, the site of Shakespeare's legendary *Romeo and Juliet*), frozen in an embrace over 5,000 years ago.

him or her in our core values and attitudes before proceeding any further (Murstein, 1977). We might ascribe finding our true love to the fickle finger of destiny, but scientists suggest that friendship, dating, and mate choices aren't random. Three major principles guide attraction and relationship formation: proximity, similarity, and reciprocity (Berscheid & Reis, 1998; Luo & Klohnen, 2005; Sprecher, 1998).

PROXIMITY: WHEN NEAR BECOMES DEAR. A simple truth of human relationships is that our closest friends often live, study, work, or play closest to us. Many years after high school, the second author of your textbook married the woman who sat in front of him in numerous classes. Because their last names started with the letter *L*, the fact that the seats were arranged alphabetically ensured they'd have an opportunity to become acquainted. After their 30-year high school reunion brought them together again, they fell in love and married.

This example illustrates how physical nearness—or **proximity**—affords relationship formation. Like reunited schoolmates, people in classrooms with alphabetically assigned seats tend to have friends with last names that start with the same letter or a letter close in the alphabet (Segal, 1974). We're most likely to be attracted to and befriend people nearby whom we see on a regular basis (Nahemow & Lawton, 1975). Leon Festinger, Stanley Schachter, and Kurt Back (1950) asked individuals living in apartments for married students at the Massachusetts Institute of Technology to name three of their closest friends. Of these friends, 65 percent lived in the same building, and 41 percent lived next door.

The effects of mere exposure we encountered earlier in the chapter may explain why seeing someone on a frequent basis, whether in the supermarket or workout room, heightens attraction. In a study conducted in a college classroom, four women with similar appearances posed as students and attended 0, 5, 10, or 15 sessions (Moreland & Beach, 1992). At the end of the semester, the experimenters showed participants slides of the women and asked them to rate attendees' attractiveness. Although the posers didn't interact with any of the students, participants judged women who attended more classes as more attractive.

SIMILARITY: LIKE ATTRACTS LIKE. Would you rather be stranded on a desert island with someone very much like yourself or very different? Perhaps if you like Mozart and your island mate prefers rap, you'd have a lot to talk or at least debate about. Yet with little in common, you might find it difficult to establish a personal connection. This point brings us to our next principle: **similarity**, the extent to which we have things in common with others.

Scientists have found that there's more truth to the adage "Birds of a feather flock together" than the equally well-worn proverb "Opposites attract." Whether it's art, music, food preferences, educational level, physical attractiveness, or values, we're attracted to people who are similar to us (Byrne, 1971; Montoya, Horton, & Kirchner, 2008; Swann & Pelham, 2002). We're also more likely to befriend, date, and marry compatible people (Curran & Lippold, 1975; Knox, Zusman, & Nieves, 1997). There's even evidence that pet owners tend to select dogs who resemble them (Roy & Christenfeld, 2004), although not all researchers are persuaded by these findings (Levine, 2005).

Online dating services have caught on to the fact that similarity breeds content (Finkel et al., 2012; Hill, Rubin & Peplau, 1976). One service, eHarmony.com, matches prospective partners on the basis of personality similarity, although there's little evidence that they're successful at doing so (Epstein, 2007). In addition, the claims of most online dating sites are overstated, in part because similarity better predicts what people *say* they like in relationship partner than what they actually like (Finkel et al., 2012). Still, actual similarity generally pays off in the long run. Married couples who share similar traits are more likely to stay together than are dissimilar couples (Meyer & Pepper, 1977).

Similarity greases the wheels of social interaction for a few reasons. First, when people's interests and attitudes overlap, the foundation is paved for mutual understanding. Second, we assume we'll be readily accepted and liked by others who see eye to eye with us. Third, people who share our likes and dislikes provide validation for our views and help us feel good about ourselves. There may even be considerable truth to the saying "The enemy of my enemy is my friend" (Heider, 1958). Research demonstrates that a glue that binds

Watch in **MyPsychLab** the **Video:**
Interpersonal Attraction

Psychological research shows that physical proximity, such as being seated next to each other in a classroom, can set the stage for later attraction.

Most commercial online dating sites capitalize on the principle of similarity: birds of a feather flock together. Nevertheless, most of the claims of these sites are poorly supported scientifically, in part because similarity is a better predictor of what people say they want in a prospective relationship partner than what they end up wanting.

proximity
physical nearness, a predictor of attraction

similarity
extent to which we have things in common with others, a predictor of attraction

friendships, especially in the early stages, is sharing negative impressions about others (Bosson et al., 2006). Negative gossip may permit us to elevate ourselves at the expense of others, thereby enhancing our self-esteem.

RECIPROCITY: ALL GIVE AND NO TAKE DOES NOT A GOOD RELATIONSHIP MAKE. For a relationship to move to deeper levels, the third principle of attraction—**reciprocity**, or the rule of give and take—is often crucial. Across cultures, there's a norm of reciprocity (Gouldner, 1960) that begins to kick into motion as early as 11 years of age (Rotenberg & Mann, 1986). That is, we tend to feel obligated to give what we get and maintain equity in a relationship (Walster, Berscheid, & Walster, 1973). Liking begets liking, and revealing personal information begets disclosure. When we believe people like us, we're inclined to feel attracted to them (Brehm et al., 2002; Carlson & Rose, 2007). When we believe that our partner finds us attractive or likable, we generally act more likable in response to this ego-boosting information (Curtis & Miller, 1986). Talking about meaningful things is a vital element of most friendships. In particular, disclosure about intimate topics often brings about intimacy. When one person talks about superficial topics or discusses intimate topics in a superficial way, low levels of disclosure often result (Lynn, 1978). Although a complete lack of reciprocity can put a relationship into the deep freeze, absolute reciprocity isn't required to make a relationship hum, especially when one partner responds to our disclosures with sympathy and concern (Berg & Archer, 1980).

PHYSICAL ATTRACTION: LIKE IT OR NOT, WE JUDGE BOOKS BY THEIR COVERS. Some important scientific discoveries arise from *serendipity*, that is, sheer luck. So it was with a study that Elaine Hatfield and her colleagues conducted over 40 years ago (Hatfield et al., 1966). They administered a battery of personality, attitude, and interest measures to 725 incoming college men and women during freshman "Welcome Week." Hatfield and her coworkers paired these students randomly for a leisurely date and dance lasting two-and-a-half hours, giving them the chance to get acquainted. Which variables, the researchers wondered, would predict whether the partners were interested in a second date? Much to their surprise, the only variable that significantly predicted attraction was one the researchers had included only as an afterthought (Gangestad & Scheyd, 2005): people's level of physical attractiveness as rated by their partners (Hatfield et al., 1966).

Physically attractive people tend to be more popular than physically unattractive people (Dion, Berscheid, & Walster, 1972; Fehr, 2008). Yet what makes us find others attractive? Is it all merely a matter of "chemistry," an inexplicable process that lies beyond the grasp of science, as Senator Proxmire believed? Or is there a science to "love at first sight," or at least attraction at first sight?

SEX DIFFERENCES IN WHAT WE FIND ATTRACTIVE: NATURE, NURTURE, OR BOTH? Although physical attractiveness is important to both sexes when it comes to choosing our romantic partners, it's especially important to men (Buunk et al., 2002; Feingold, 1992). David Buss (1989) conducted a comprehensive survey of mate preferences among heterosexuals in 37 cultures across six continents, with countries as diverse as Canada, Spain, Finland, Greece, Bulgaria, Venezuela, Iran, Japan, and South Africa. Although he found that the importance people attach to physical attractiveness varies across cultures, men consistently place more weight on looks in women than women do in men. Men also prefer women who are somewhat younger than they are. Conversely, Buss found that women tend to place more emphasis than do men on having a partner with a high level of financial resources. In contrast to men, women prefer partners who are somewhat older than they are. Still, men and women value most of the same things. Both sexes put a premium on having a partner who's intelligent, dependable, and kind (Buss, 1994).

Evolutionary Models of Attraction. Putting aside these commonalities, how can we make sense of sex differences in mate preferences? Evolutionary theorists point out that because most men produce an enormous number of sperm—an average of about 300 million

 Simulate in **MyPsychLab** the **Experiment:** Perceptions of Attractiveness

reciprocity
rule of give and take, a predictor of attraction

per ejaculation—they typically pursue a mating strategy that maximizes the chances that at least one of these sperm will find a receptive egg at the end of its long journey (Symons, 1979). As a consequence, evolutionary psychologists contend, men are on the lookout for cues of potential health and fertility such as physical attractiveness and youth. Women, in contrast, typically produce only one egg per month, so they must be choosy. In a study of speed dating—a technique invented by Los Angeles Rabbi Yaacov Deyo in 1998 to help Jewish singles get acquainted—men and women interacted with potential dates for three minutes (Kurzban & Weeden, 2005). Men chose to have further contact with half of the women they met, whereas women were decidedly pickier, selecting one in three men to meet again. Women tend to pursue a mating strategy that maximizes the chances that the man with whom they mate will provide well for their offspring. Hence, women prefer men who are well off monetarily and a bit more experienced in the ways of life (Buunk et al., 2002).

Social Role Theory. Some researchers have offered alternatives to evolutionary models of attraction. According to Alice Eagly and Wendy Wood's (1999) *social role theory*, biological variables play a role in men's and women's preferences, but not in the way that evolutionary psychologists contend. Instead, biological factors constrain the roles that men and women adopt (Eagly, Wood, & Johannesen-Schmidt, 2004). Because men tend to be bigger and stronger compared with women, they've more often ended up playing the roles of hunter, food provider, and warrior. Moreover, because men don't bear children, they have considerable opportunities to pursue high-status positions. In contrast, because women bear children, they've more often ended up playing the role of child care provider and have been more limited in pursuing high-status positions.

Some of these differences in traditional roles may help to explain men's and women's different mate preferences. For example, because women have typically held fewer high-status positions than men have, they may have preferred men who are dependable financial providers (Eagly et al., 2004). Consistent with social role theory, men and women have become more similar in their mate preferences over the past half century (Buss et al., 2001), perhaps reflecting the increasing social opportunities for women across that time period. So although nature may channel men and women into somewhat different roles and therefore different mate preferences, nurture may shape these roles and preferences in significant ways.

IS BEAUTY IN THE EYE OF THE BEHOLDER? Popular wisdom tells us that "beauty is in the eye of the beholder." To some extent, that saying is true. Yet it's also an oversimplification. People tend to agree at considerably higher-than-chance levels about who is and isn't physically attractive (Burns & Farina, 1992). This is the case not only within a race, but also across races; Caucasian and African-American men tend to agree on which women are attractive, as do Caucasian and Asian-American men (Cunningham et al., 1995). Even across vastly different cultures, men and women tend to agree on whom they find physically attractive (Langlois et al., 2000).

Furthermore, men and women prefer certain body shapes in members of the opposite sex. Men tend to be especially attracted to women with a waist-to-hip ratio of about .7, that is, with a waist about 70 percent as large as their hips (Pazhoohi & Liddle, 2012; Singh, 1993), although this ratio is often less important than other variables, like body weight (Furnham, Petrides, & Constantinides, 2005; Tassinary & Hansen, 1998). In contrast, women generally prefer men with a higher waist-to-hip ratio (Singh, 1995). According to evolutionary psychologist Donald Symons (1979), these findings imply that "beauty lies in the adaptations of the beholder." Women's waist-to-hip ratio tends to decline as they become older, so this ratio is a cue—although a highly imperfect one—to fertility.

Still, there are differences in physical preferences within and across cultures (Swami & Furnham, 2008). For example, men from African-American and Caribbean cultures often find women with a large body size more physically attractive than do men of European cultures (Rosenblum & Lewis, 1999). Furthermore, preferences toward thinness have frequently shifted over historical time, as even a casual inspection of paintings of nude women over the past few centuries reveals.

Although standards of beauty differ somewhat within and across cultures, research suggests that both most African-American men and most Caucasian men agree on which Caucasian women (such as Jennifer Aniston, *left*) and African-American women (such as Beyoncé, *right*) are physically attractive.

WHEN BEING "JUST AVERAGE" IS JUST FINE. Which person are we more likely to find attractive: (a) someone who's exotic, unusual, or distinctive in some way or (b) someone who's just plain average? If you're like most people, you'd assume (a). Indeed, we sometimes insult people's appearance by calling women "plain Janes" and men "average Joes." Yet as Judith Langlois and Lori Roggman (1990) showed, being average has its pluses. By using a computer to digitize the faces of students and then combine them progressively, these researchers found that people generally prefer faces that are most average. In their study, people preferred average faces a whopping 96 percent of the time (see **FIGURE 15**; to try your hand at averaging faces, see a demonstration at www.faceresearch.org/tech/demos/average). Although some psychologists found these results difficult to believe, many investigators have replicated them for European, Japanese, and Chinese faces (Gangestad & Scheyd, 2005; Komori, Kawamura, & Ishihara, 2009; Rhodes, Halberstadt, & Brajkovich, 2001). Average faces are also more symmetrical than nonaverage faces, so our preferences for average faces might be due to their greater symmetry. Yet studies show that even when faces are symmetrical, people still prefer faces that are more average (Valentine, Darling, & Donnelly, 2004).

Evolutionary psychologists have speculated that "averageness" in a face tends to reflect an absence of genetic mutations, serious diseases, and other abnormalities. As a consequence, we could be drawn to people with such faces, as they're often better "genetic catches." Maybe. But studies show that people prefer not merely average faces, but average animals like birds and fish and even average objects like cars and watches (Halberstadt & Rhodes, 2003). So our preference for average faces may be due to an alternative mechanism, namely, a more general preference for anything that's average. Perhaps we find average stimuli to be more familiar and easier to process mentally, because they reflect stimuli we've seen before many times (Gangestad & Scheyd, 2005).

Love: Science Confronts the Mysterious

Elizabeth Barrett Browning wrote famously: "How do I love thee? Let me count the ways." According to some psychologists, we may not need to count all that high. We'll explain. Psychologists are no different from the rest of us. They've tried to understand the myriad varieties of love, with some concluding that there's only one type of love; others, that love comes in many shapes and sizes. According to Elaine Hatfield and Richard Rapson (1996), there are two major types of love: passionate and companionate. Robert Sternberg, as we'll soon see, puts the number at seven.

PASSIONATE LOVE: LOVE AS A HOLLYWOOD ROMANCE. Passionate love is marked by a powerful, even overwhelming, longing for one's partner. It's a strange mix of delirious happiness when we're around the object of our desire and utter misery when we're not. It's the stuff of which Hollywood movies are made. As Romeo and Juliet knew all too well, passionate love is fueled when obstacles, such as seemingly insurmountable physical distance or the strenuous objection of parents, are placed in the way of romance (Driscoll, Davis, & Lipetz, 1972). Such hurdles may heighten arousal, thereby intensifying passion, as Schachter and Singer's two-factor theory would predict (Kenrick, Neuberg, & Cialdini, 2005). In a study that followed participants for one month after a speed dating event, individuals who experienced anxiety about a potential partner's romantic involvement expressed greater preference for a serious relationship than for a one-night stand (Eastwick & Finkel, 2008). Uncertainty about how relationships will unfold, combined with hope that romantic feelings will be reciprocated, fuel attachment and desire (Tennov, 1979). The good news is that long-term passionate love is possible: In one survey, 40 percent of couples assessed after ten years or more of marriage reported that they were "very intensely in love" (O'Leary et al., 2012).

COMPANIONATE LOVE: LOVE AS FRIENDSHIP. Companionate love is marked by a sense of deep friendship and fondness for one's partner (Acevedo & Aron, 2009). Romantic relationships tend to progress over time from passionate to companionate love

◄ REPLICABILITY
Can the results be duplicated in other studies?

FIGURE 15 Which Face Is Most Attractive? The two columns depict faces that have been averaged with other faces (from *top* to *bottom*) 4, 8, 16, and 32 times. Most people find the faces on the bottom, which are most "average," to be the most attractive (Langlois & Roggman, 1990). Remarkably, Sir Francis Galton (1878) anticipated these findings well over a century ago. (*Source:* Langlois & Roggman, 1990)

passionate love
love marked by powerful, even overwhelming, longing for one's partner

companionate love
love marked by a sense of deep friendship and fondness for one's partner

(Wojciszke, 2002), although most healthy relationships retain at least a spark of passion. In older couples, companionate love may be the overriding emotion in the relationship.

There's growing evidence that companionate and passionate love are psychologically independent. Studies indicate that people can "fall in love" with partners in the sense of caring deeply about them, yet experience little or no sexual desire toward them (Diamond, 2004). In addition, these two forms of love may be associated with different brain systems (Diamond, 2003; Gonzaga et al., 2006). Animal research suggests that emotional attachment to others is influenced largely by such hormones as oxytocin, which plays a key role in pair bonding and interpersonal trust. In contrast, sexual desire is influenced by sex hormones such as testosterone and estrogen.

THE THREE SIDES OF LOVE. Robert Sternberg believes that the "two types of love" model is too simple. In his *triangular theory of love*, Sternberg (1986, 1988a) proposed three major elements of love: (1) intimacy ("I feel really close to this person"), (2) passion ("I'm crazy about this person"), and (3) commitment ("I really want to stay with this person"). These elements combine to form seven varieties of love (see **FIGURE 16**). Sternberg's model is more a description of love types than an explanation of why people fall in love, but it's a helpful road map toward understanding one of life's great mysteries.

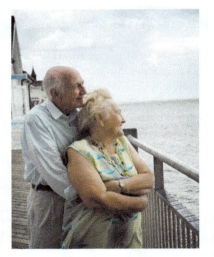

Companionate love is often the primary form of love among the elderly. It can be a powerful emotional bond between couples across the lifespan.

Watch in **MyPsychLab** the **Video:**
Triangluar Theory of Love: Robert Sternberg

FIGURE 16 What Is Love? According to Sternberg's triangular theory of love, intimacy, passion, and commitment combine to form seven varieties of love, with "consummate love" being the ultimate form of love marked by high levels of all three components.

Hate: A Neglected Topic

Until recently, psychologists didn't want to have much to do with the topic of hate. Most introductory psychology textbooks don't even list the word *hate* in their indices. Yet with the horrific events of September 11, 2001, and the burgeoning problem of terrorism around the globe, it's clear that psychologists can no longer turn a blind eye to the question of why some people despise others, at times to the point of wanting to destroy them (Bloom, 2004; Sternberg, 2004). Of course, hate can assume a variety of less violent but still pernicious forms in everyday life, including extreme forms of racism, sexism, anti-Semitism, homophobia, and occasionally even excessive political partisanship. Without question, hatred toward individuals who differ markedly from us, such as people from other cultures, is fueled by the Internet, which can create "virtual communities" of like-minded people who share similar hostile views (Post, 2010).

Using his triangular theory of love as a starting point, Robert Sternberg (2003a) developed a theory of hate, with hatred consisting of three elements:

1. Negation of intimacy ("I would never want to get close to these people")

2. Passion ("I absolutely and positively despise these people.")

3. Commitment ("I'm determined to stop or harm these people.")

As in his theory of love, different forms of hate arise from combinations of these three elements, with "burning hate"—the most severe—reflecting high scores on all three. For Sternberg, the key to fueling hate is propaganda. Groups and governments that "teach" hatred of other groups are experts at portraying these groups as evil and worthy of disdain (Keen, 1986; Lilienfeld, Ammirati, & Landfield, 2009; Sternberg, 2003a).

The good news is that if we can learn hate, we can probably unlearn it. Teaching individuals to overcome their confirmation bias toward perceiving only the negative attributes of individuals or groups they dislike may be an essential first step (Harrington, 2004; Lilienfeld et al., 2009). Recognizing that "there's good and bad in everyone," as the saying goes, may help us combat our deep-seated animosity toward our enemies—and more broadly, members of other races, cultures, and groups whose views differ from our own.

Assess Your Knowledge — FACT or FICTION?

Study and **Review** in **MyPsychLab**

1. When it comes to romantic chemistry, opposites attract. True / False

2. In general, people find average faces the most physically attractive. True / False

3. Companionate and passionate love appear to be psychologically and physiologically independent. True / False

4. Passion and commitment play a key role in love, but are irrelevant to hate. True / False

Answers: 1. F; 2. T; 3. T; 4. F

Your Complete Review System

Theories of Emotion: What Causes Our Feelings?

1 DESCRIBE THE MAJOR THEORIES OF EMOTION.

According to discrete emotions theory, people experience a small number (perhaps seven) of distinct biologically influenced emotions. According to cognitive theories, including the James–Lange theory, emotions result from our interpretation of stimuli or our bodily reactions to them. According to the Cannon–Bard theory, emotion-provoking events lead to both emotions and bodily reactions. Schachter and Singer's two-factor theory proposes that emotions are the explanations we attach to our general state of arousal following an emotion-provoking event.

1. According to _____ _____ theory, humans experience a small number of distinct emotions that combine in complex ways.

2. One of the first researchers to study how emotional expressions of humans and nonhumans are similar, _____ _____ observed that the angry snarl of dogs bears a resemblance to the dismissive sneer of humans.

3. What kind of smile, marked by the turning upward of the corners of the mouth and changes in the eyelids and corners of the eye, is Paul Ekman displaying in this photo?

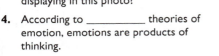

4. According to _____ theories of emotion, emotions are products of thinking.

5. According to the _____ theory of emotion, emotions result from our interpretations of our bodily reactions to stimuli.

6. According to Damasio's somatic marker theory, we (do/don't) use our "gut reactions" to help us determine how we should act.

7. According to the Cannon–Bard theory, an emotion-provoking event leads _____ to an emotion and to bodily reactions.

8. Describe how we experience emotions during an event like a car accident, according to Schachter and Singer's two-factor theory of emotion.

2 IDENTIFY UNCONSCIOUS INFLUENCES ON EMOTION.

Many emotional experiences are generated automatically and operate unconsciously, as illustrated by research on the mere exposure effect and the facial feedback hypothesis.

9. According to the mere exposure effect, repeated exposure to a stimulus makes us (more/less) likely to feel favorably toward it.

10. According to the facial feedback hypothesis, we're more likely to feel emotions that correspond to our _____ _____.

Nonverbal Expression of Emotion: The Eyes, Bodies, and Cultures Have It

3 EXPLAIN THE IMPORTANCE OF NONVERBAL EXPRESSION OF EMOTION.

Much of emotional expression is nonverbal; gestures highlight speech (illustrators), involve touching our bodies (manipulators), or convey specific meanings (emblems). Nonverbal expressions are often more valid indicators of emotions than are words.

11. The unconscious spillover of emotions into nonverbal behavior is known as _____ _____.

12. How do emoticons help to ensure that an email or text message is interpreted in the manner it was intended?

13. When talking, we often use _____, gestures that highlight or accentuate speech.

Smile
:-) or :)

Surprised
:-o or :o

14. When stressed or nervous, you may engage in _____, such as biting your fingernails or twirling your hair.

15. Gestures that convey specific meanings, such as a hand wave or the OK sign, are called _____.

4 IDENTIFY MAJOR LIE DETECTION METHODS AND THEIR PITFALLS.

The polygraph test measures physiological responses to questions designed to expose falsehoods. The Controlled Question Test (CQT) contains questions relevant and irrelevant to the crime and control questions that reflect presumed lies. Greater physiological reactivity in response to relevant questions supposedly suggests deception. Nevertheless, the CQT detects general arousal rather than guilt and results in numerous false positives. False negatives can result when individuals employ countermeasures (such as biting their tongue or curling their toes). The Guilty Knowledge Test (GKT) relies on the premise that criminals harbor concealed knowledge about the crime. The GKT has a low false-positive rate but a fairly high false-negative rate.

16. Typically, the correlation between people's confidence in their ability to detect lies and their accuracy in doing so is (low/high).

17. The most widely administered version of the polygraph test, the _____ _____ _____, measures people's physiological responses following three major types of yes–no questions.

18. Research shows that the primary problem with the polygraph test is its high rate of (false positives/false negatives).

19. How does the polygraph rely on the assumption of the Pinocchio response?

20. Some employers administer paper-and-pencil _____ tests in an attempt to assess workers' tendency to steal or cheat.

Happiness and Self-Esteem: Science Confronts Pop Psychology

5 IDENTIFY COMMON MYTHS AND REALITIES ABOUT HAPPINESS AND SELF-ESTEEM.

Myths: the prime determinant of happiness is what happens to us, money makes us happy, happiness declines in old age, and people on the West Coast are happiest. Realities: happiness is associated with being married, having a college education, and being religious; voting Republican; exercising; being thankful; and immersing ourselves in what we're doing ("flow"). We tend to overestimate the long-term impact of events on our happiness. Myth: low self-esteem is the root of all unhappiness. Reality: self-esteem is only modestly associated with mental health but is associated with greater initiative, persistence, and positive illusions—the tendency to perceive ourselves more favorably than others do.

21. Explain how the King of Bhutan plans to increase the Gross National Happiness of his country and why this initiative may be beneficial to all.

22. According to Frederickson's _____, _____ _____ theory, happiness predisposes us to think more openly.

23. According to psychological research, money (can/can't) buy long-term happiness.

24. The increase in happiness with old age appears to be due to the _____ effect.

25. The ability to predict our own and others' happiness is called _____ _____.

26. When we believe that both our good and bad moods will last longer than they do, we're suffering from a(n) _____ _____.

27. Why do second-place finishers tend to be less happy than third-place finishers?

28. Most individuals with high self-esteem have _____ _____ in that they see themselves as more intelligent, attractive, and likeable than other individuals.

6 DESCRIBE THE EMERGING DISCIPLINE OF POSITIVE PSYCHOLOGY.

Positive psychology emphasizes strengths, love, and happiness. Nevertheless, some critics have argued that positive psychology's "look on the bright side of life" approach may have its downsides, in part because excessive happiness may sometimes be maladaptive.

29. Peterson and Seligman identified numerous _____ _____ and _____ as essential to positive psychology.

30. _____ _____ is a strategy of anticipating failures and compensating for this expectation by mentally overpreparing for negative outcomes.

Motivation: Our Wants and Needs

7 EXPLAIN BASIC PRINCIPLES AND THEORIES OF MOTIVATION.

Motivation refers to the drives—especially our wants and needs—that propel us in specific directions. Drive reduction theory states that drives (such as hunger and thirst) pull us to act in certain ways. The Yerkes–Dodson law posits an inverted U-shaped relation between arousal and mood/performance. Approach and avoidance often drive conflict. According to incentive theories, positive goals are motivators. These motivators include primary (biological) and secondary (psychological desires/achievement, self-actualization) needs.

31. Is there any research evidence that motivational speakers like Anthony Robbins produce long-term changes in people's behavior?

32. Most drive reduction theories propose that we're motivated to maintain a given level of psychological _____.

33. The _____ law describes an inverted U-shaped relation between arousal on the one hand and performance and mood on the other.

34. _____ theories propose that we're often motivated by positive goals.

35. Using Maslow's Hierarchy of Needs, insert the appropriate need at each level of the pyramid in the path to achieving self-actualization.

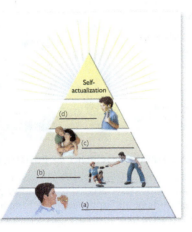

8 DESCRIBE THE DETERMINANTS OF HUNGER, WEIGHT GAIN, AND OBESITY.

The lateral hypothalamus has been called a "feeding center" and the ventromedial hypothalamus a "satiety center," although these descriptions oversimplify scientific reality. Hunger is also associated with hormones (ghrelin), low glucose levels, neurotransmitters (leptin, serotonin), a genetically programmed set point for body fat and muscle mass, specific genes (melanocortin-4 receptor gene, leptin gene), and sensitivity to food cues and expectations.

36. According to _____ theory, when our blood glucose levels drop, hunger creates a drive to eat to restore the proper level of glucose.

37. Each of us may have a genetically programmed _____ _____ that establishes a range of body and muscle mass we tend to maintain.

9 IDENTIFY THE SYMPTOMS OF BULIMIA AND ANOREXIA.

Bulimia nervosa is marked by recurrent binge eating, followed by attempts to minimize weight gain. Anorexia nervosa is characterized by a refusal to eat, resulting in a significantly low body weight expected for age and height.

38. _____ is the most common eating disorder, and 95 percent of the people with this diagnosis are women.

10 DESCRIBE THE HUMAN SEXUAL RESPONSE CYCLE AND FACTORS THAT INFLUENCE SEXUAL ACTIVITY.

Masters and Johnson described four stages of the sexual response cycle: excitement, plateau, orgasm, and resolution.

Frequency of sexual activity decreases with age, but sexual satisfaction doesn't. Expression of sexual desire is shaped by social norms and culture.

39. Masters and Johnson reported in their pioneering investigation that the basic sexual arousal cycle is (the same/different) for men and women.

11 IDENTIFY COMMON MISCONCEPTIONS ABOUT AND POTENTIAL INFLUENCES ON SEXUAL ORIENTATION.

Common myths include the notions that gay individuals (a) typically adopt a masculine or feminine role, (b) are especially likely to sexually abuse children and adolescents, and (c) are usually inadequate parents. Potential influences on sexual orientation are an inherited tendency toward childhood gender nonconformity, sex hormones, prenatal influences, and brain differences.

40. According to one theory of influences on sexual orientation, girls exposed to excessive testosterone in the womb develop _____ brains, and boys exposed to too little testosterone develop _____ brains.

Attraction, Love, and Hate: The Greatest Mysteries of Them All

12 IDENTIFY PRINCIPLES AND FACTORS THAT GUIDE ATTRACTION AND RELATIONSHIP FORMATION.

Factors guiding attraction and relationship formation are proximity (physical closeness), similarity (like attracts like), reciprocity (give what we get), physical attractiveness (more important to men than to women), evolutionary influences, social roles, and preference for "average" faces.

41. Physical nearness, or _____, affords the opportunity for relationship formation.

42. We're often attracted to people with whom we have high levels of _____, or things in common.

43. For a relationship to move to deeper levels, the rule of give and take, or _____, is often crucial.

44. According to Buss, across cultures, (men/women) attach more importance to physical attractiveness?

45. Across vastly different cultures, men and women tend to (agree/disagree) on whom they find physically attractive.

46. Average faces are rated as (less/more) attractive than distinctive or exotic faces?

13 DESCRIBE THE MAJOR TYPES OF LOVE AND THE ELEMENTS OF LOVE AND HATE.

The major love types are passionate and companionate. According to Sternberg's model of love, the major love elements are intimacy, passion, and commitment. The major hate elements are negation of intimacy, passion, and commitment.

47. _____ love can be a mix of delirious happiness when we're near the object of our desire and misery when separated from it.

48. A relationship marked by a sense of deep friendship and fondness for our partner is called _____.

49. Using Sternberg's triangular theory of love, complete this figure by identifying the three major elements of love (forming the points of the triangle) illustrated. According to Sternberg, which is the ultimate form of love (box d)?

50. Teaching individuals to overcome their _____ _____ toward perceiving only negative attributions of groups they dislike may be an essential first step in unlearning hate.

Apply Your Scientific Thinking Skills

Use your scientific thinking skills to answer the following questions, referencing specific scientific thinking principles and common errors in reasoning whenever possible.

1. Research three books or training programs designed to enhance self-esteem. How do they connect self-esteem to happiness and success in life? Do they confuse correlation with causation? Have they considered rival hypotheses for how people become happy or successful in life? If so, which ones?

2. The popular media is filled with examples of body language experts claiming to identify which celebrity couples are truly in love and which are headed for a breakup. Find a few examples of Internet sites devoted to interpreting body language. Are their claims about their ability to interpret nonverbal communication extraordinary? Are there more parsimonious explanations for these claims?

3. Select a recent debate surrounding sexual orientation, such as the "the issue of civil unions and gay marriage," and examine at least two scientific arguments on both sides of the issue. What assumptions does each side make regarding the role of genetic and environmental influences in sexual orientation? Has either side misrepresented the scientific research or neglected to consider alternative interpretations? Explain.

Further Your Understanding

EXTEND YOUR KNOWLEDGE WITH THE MYPSYCHLAB VIDEO SERIES

Watch these videos in MyPsychLab. Follow the "Video Series" link.

The Basics: Theories of Emotion and Motivation Compare popular motivation and emotion theories and learn about intrinsic and extrinsic motivation.

Special Topics: Detecting Lies Find out what lie detector tests scientifically measure and whether it's possible for a person to improve lying—and lying detection—techniques.

Thinking Like a Psychologist: Predicting Future Emotion and Desire Learn about affective forecasting, duration bias, impact bias, and focalism as you analyze a relationship breakup.

In the Real World: Eating Disorders Learn about eating disorders, their causes, and the treatments available.

Thinking Like a Psychologist: Sexual Orientation Learn about sexual and gender orientation and discover how we categorize the person to whom we are romantically and sexually attracted.

What's In It for Me?: The Dating Game Find out about the purpose of evolutionary psychology and the relationship between evolution and modern-day mate selection and learn why conflict between men and women arises so often.

EXPERIENCE PSYCHOLOGICAL RESEARCH WITH MYPSYCHLAB SIMULATIONS

Access these simulations in MyPsychLab. Follow the "Simulations" link.

How to Deal with Your Emotions Participate in a survey to define trends in how, why, and to whom you express your emotions.

What Motivates You? Participate in a survey to discover what motivates you and why.

Implicit Association Test: Sexuality Sort images and words into categories to identify your implicit preferences and prejudices toward representations of heterosexual and homosexual people.

APPLY YOUR CRITICAL THINKING SKILLS WITH MYPSYCHLAB WRITING ASSESSMENTS

Complete these writing assignments in MyPsychLab.

Imagine you are walking alone late at night and hear footsteps behind you. Think about your emotional reaction to this situation. Consider the major theories of emotion: James–Lange theory, Cannon–Bard theory, and Schachter–Singer theory. From the perspective of these major theories of emotion, describe how each of them predicts the sequence of events that would occur as you experience a reaction to this situation.

Answer Key

THEORIES OF EMOTION: WHAT CAUSES OUR FEELINGS?

1. discrete emotions
2. Charles Darwin
3. the Duchenne smile
4. cognitive
5. James-Lange
6. do
7. simultaneously
8. We first experience arousal after an emotion-provoking event and then look to the situation to determine the cause of that arousal. The emotional label we attach to our arousal based on our interpretation of the situation is the emotion we experience.
9. more
10. facial features

NONVERBAL EXPRESSION OF EMOTION: THE EYES, BODIES, AND CULTURES HAVE IT

11. nonverbal leakage
12. Because email messages are devoid of nonverbal cues, people have developed a variety of emoticons to convey various emotions that might not be obvious over email or instant messaging.
13. illustrators
14. manipulators
15. emblems
16. low
17. Controlled Question Test (CQT)
18. false positives
19. The Pinocchio response is a perfect physiological or behavioral indicator of lying. Like Pinocchio's nose, people's bodily reactions supposedly give them away whenever they lie.
20. integrity

HAPPINESS AND SELF-ESTEEM: SCIENCE CONFRONTS POP PSYCHOLOGY

21. The king plans to boost GNH in Bhutan by preserving the beauty of its natural environment, promoting cultural values, and giving citizens more of a voice in government decisions. This is beneficial because happiness often breeds both health and success in work, family, and love life.
22. broaden and build
23. can't
24. positivity
25. affective forecasting
26. durability bias
27. Probably because silver medal winners compare their outcome with what "might have been."
28. positive illusions
29. character strengths; virtues
30. Defensive pessimism

MOTIVATION: OUR WANTS AND NEEDS

31. No
32. homeostasis
33. Yerkes-Dodson
34. Incentive
35. a) physiological needs; b) safety needs; c) belonging needs; d) esteem needs
36. glucostatic
37. set point
38. Bulimia
39. the same
40. masculinized; feminized

ATTRACTION, LOVE, AND HATE: THE GREATEST MYSTERIES OF THEM ALL

41. proximity
42. similarity
43. reciprocity
44. men
45. agree
46. more
47. Passionate
48. companionate
49. a) Intimacy; b) Passion; c) Commitment; d) Consummate love
50. confirmation bias

References

Acevedo, B. P, & Aron, A. (2009). Does a long-term relationship kill romantic love? *Review of General Psychology, 13,* 59–65.

Adelmann, P. K., & Zajonc, R. B. (1989). Facial efference and the experience of emotion. *Annual Review of Psychology, 40,* 249–280.

Agosta, S., Pezzoli, P., & Sartori, G. (2013). How to detect deception in everyday life and the reasons underlying it. *Applied Cognitive Psychology.*

Anand, B. K., & Brobeck, J. R. (1951). Hypothalamic control of food intake in rats and cats. *Yale Journal of Biological Medicine, 24,* 123.

Anderson, K. J., Revelle, W., & Lynch, M. J. (1989). Caffeine, impulsivity, and memory scanning: A comparison of two explanations for the Yerkes-Dodson effect. *Motivation and Emotion, 13,* 1–20.

Angier, N. (2006, January 3). The cute factor. *New York Times.* Retrieved from http://www.nytimes.com/2006/01/03/science/03cute.html?ex=1293944400&en=9942fdaf51f1211c&ei=5090&partner=rssuserland&emc=rss

Archer, D. (1997). *A world of differences: Understanding cross-cultural communication* [Video]. Berkeley, CA: University of California, Extension Center for Media and Independent Learning.

Aronoff, J., Barclay, A. M., & Stevenson, L. A. (1988) The recognition of threatening facial stimuli. *Journal of Personality and Social Psychology, 54,* 647–655.

Ax, A. F. (1953). The physiological differentiation between fear and anger in humans. *Psychosomatic Medicine, 55,* 433–442.

Axtell, R. E. (1997). *Do's and taboos of body language around the world.* New York, NY: Wiley.

Babyak, M. A., Blumenthal, J. A., Herman, S., Khatri, P., Doraiswamy, P. M., Moore, K. A.,... Ranga Krishnan, K. (2000). Exercise treatment for major depression: Maintenance of therapeutic benefit at 10 months. *Psychosomatic Medicine, 62,* 633–638.

Badman, M. K., & Flier, J. S. (2005). The gut and energy balance: Visceral allies in the obesity wars. *Science, 307,* 1909–1914.

Bagemihl, B. (1999). *Biological exuberance, animal homosexuality and natural diversity.* London, England: Profile Books.

Bailey, J. M., Dunne, M. P., & Martin, N. G. (2000). Genetic and environmental influences on sexual orientation and its correlates in an Australian twin sample. *Journal of Personality and Social Psychology, 78,* 524–536.

Bailey, J. M., Pillard, R. C., Neale, M. C., & Agyei, Y. (1993). Heritable factors influence sexual orientation in women. *Archives of General Psychiatry, 50,* 217–223.

Bailey, J. M., & Zucker, K. J. (1995). Childhood sex-typed behavior and sexual orientation: A conceptual analysis and quantitative review. *Developmental Psychology, 31,* 43–55.

Baker, W. E. (1999). When can affective conditioning and mere exposure directly influence brand choice? *Journal of Advertising, 28,* 31–47.

Bard, P. (1942). Neural mechanisms in emotional and sexual behavior. *Psychosomatic Medicine, 4,* 171–172.

Bargh, J. A., & Chartrand, T. L. (1999). The unbearable automaticity of being. *American Psychologist, 54,* 462–479.

Bargh, J. A., & Ferguson, M. L. (2000). Beyond behaviorism: On the automaticity of higher mental processes. *Psychological Bulletin, 126,* 925–945.

Barnett, R. C., & Rivers, C. (2004, October 13). The persistence of gender myths in math. *Education Week, 24*(7), 39.

Bartlett, T. (2013). Power of suggestion. *Chronicle Review.* Retrieved from http://chronicle.com/article/Power-of-Suggestion/136907

Bartoli, E., & Gillem, A. R. (2008). Continuing to depolarize the debate on sexual orientation and religious identity and the therapeutic process. *Professional Psychology: Research and Practice, 39,* 202–209.

Bashore, T. T., & Rapp, P. E. (1993). Are there alternatives to traditional polygraph procedures? *Psychological Bulletin, 113,* 2–22.

Baumeister, R. F., Campbell, J. D., Krueger, J. I., & Vohs, K. D. (2003). Does high self-esteem cause better performance, interpersonal success, happiness, or healthier lifestyles? *Psychological Science in the Public Interest, 4,* 1–44.

Baumeister, R. F., Catanese, K. R., & Vohs, K. D. (2001). Is there a gender difference in strength of sex drive? Theoretical views, conceptual distinctions, and a review of relevant evidence. *Personality and Social Psychology Review, 5,* 242–273.

Bayer, R., & Spitzer, R. L. (1985). Neurosis, psychodynamics, and DSM-III: A history of the controversy. *Archives of General Psychiatry, 42,* 187–196.

Becker, A. E., Burwell, R. A., Gilman, S. E., Herzog, D. B., & Hamburg, P. (2002). Eating behaviors and attitudes following prolonged television exposure among ethnic Fijian adolescent girls. *British Journal of Psychiatry, 180,* 509–514.

Becker, S. W., & Eagly, A. H. (2004). The heroism of women and men. *American Psychologist, 59,* 163–178.

Bell, A. P., Weinberg, M. S., & Hammersmith, S. K. (1981). *Sexual preference: Its development in men and women.* Bloomington, IN: Indiana University Press.

Bell, A., P., & Weinberg, M. S. (1978). *Homosexualities: A study of diversity among men and women.* New York, NY: Simon & Schuster.

Belliveau, F., & Richter, L. (1970). *Understanding human sexual inadequacy.* New York, NY: Bantam.

Bem, D. J. (1996). Exotic becomes erotic: A developmental theory of sexual orientation. *Psychological Review, 103,* 320–335.

Bem, D. J. (2000). Exotic becomes erotic: Interpreting the biological correlates of sexual orientation. *Archives of Sexual Behavior, 29,* 531–548.

Ben-Shakhar, G. (2011). *Countermeasures in Memory Detection: Theory and Application of the Concealed Information Test, 200.*

Ben-Shakhar, G., & Elaad, E. (2003). The validity of psychophysiological detection of information with the Guilty Knowledge Test: A meta-analytic review. *Journal of Applied Psychology, 88,* 131–151.

Benson, E. (2006, June). All that's gold doesn't glitter: How the Golden Fleece tarnished psychological science. *APS Observer*. Retrieved from http://www.psychologicalscience.org/index.php/publications/observer

Berg, J. H., & Archer, R. L. (1980). Disclosure or concern: A second look at liking for the norm breaker. *Journal of Personality, 48*, 245–257.

Berlyne, D. E. (1960). *Conflict, arousal, and curiosity.* New York, NY: McGraw-Hill.

Berry, C. M., Sackett, P. R., & Wiemann, S. A. (2007). A review of recent developments in integrity test research. *Personnel Psychology, 60*, 270–301.

Berscheid, E., & Reis, H. T. (1998). Attraction and close relationships. In D. Gilbert, S. Fiske, & G. Lindzey (Eds.), *The handbook of social psychology* (Vol. 2, 4th ed., pp. 193–281). New York, NY: McGraw-Hill.

Biernbaum, M. A., & Ruscio, M. (2004). Differences between matched heterosexual and non-heterosexual college students on measures of defense mechanisms and psychopathological symptoms. *Journal of Homosexuality, 48*, 125–141.

Birch, S. A. J., & Bloom, P. (2003). Children are cursed: An asymmetric bias in mental state attribution. *Psychological Science, 14*, 283–286.

Birmingham, C. L., Su, J., Hlynsky, J. A., Goldner, E. M., & Gao, M. (2005). The mortality rate from anorexia nervosa. *International Journal of Eating Disorders, 38*, 143–146.

Birnbaum, G., Glaubman, H., & Mikulincer, M. (2001). Women's experience of heterosexual intercourse—Scale construction, factor structure, and relations to orgasmic disorder. *Journal of Sex Research, 38*, 191–204.

Blanchard, R. (2008). Review and theory of handedness, birth order, and homosexuality in men. *Laterality: Asymmetries of Body, Brain, and Cognition, 13*, 51–70.

Blanchard, R., & Bogaert, A. F. (1996). Homosexuality in men and number of older brothers. *American Journal of Psychiatry, 153*, 27–31.

Bloom, P. (2004). *Descartes' baby: How the science of child development explains what makes us human.* New York, NY: Basic Books.

Bogartz, R. S. (1965). The criterion method: Some analyses and remarks. *Psychological Bulletin, 64*, 1–14.

Bonanno, G. A., Field, N. P., Kovacevic, A., & Kaltman, S. (2002). Self-enhancement as a buffer against extreme adversity: Civil war in Bosnia and traumatic loss in the United States. *Personality and Social Psychology Bulletin, 28*, 184–196.

Bonanno, G. A., & Keltner, D. (1997). Facial expressions of emotion and the course of conjugal bereavement. *Journal of Abnormal Psychology, 106*, 126–137.

Bond, C. F. (2006). A world of lies. *Journal of Cross-Cultural Psychology, 30*, 60–74.

Bond, C. F., Jr., & DePaulo, B. M. (2006). Accuracy of deception judgments. *Personality and Social Psychology Review, 10*, 214–234.

Bornstein, R. F. (1989). Exposure and affect: Overview and meta-analysis of research, 1968–1987. *Psychological Bulletin, 106*, 265–289.

Borrell, B. (2008). What is truth serum? *Scientific American.* Retrieved from http://www.scientificamerican.com/article.cfm?id=what-is-truth-serum

Bos, H. M. W., van Balen, F., & van den Boom, D. C. (2007). Child adjustment and parenting in planned lesbian-parent families. *American Journal of Orthopsychiatry, 77*, 38–48.

Bosson, J. K., Johnson, A. B., Niederhoffer, K., & Swann, W. B., Jr. (2006). Interpersonal chemistry through negativity: Bonding by sharing negative attitudes about others. *Personal Relationships, 13*, 135–150.

Branden, N. (1994). *Six pillars of self-esteem.* New York, NY: Bantam.

Bray G. A. (1985). Complications of obesity. *Journal of the American Medical Association, 240*, 1607–1634.

Brehm, S. S., Miller, R. S., Perlman, D., & Campbell, S. M. (2002). *Intimate relationships* (3rd ed.). New York, NY: McGraw-Hill.

Brickman, P., & Campbell, D. T. (1971). Hedonic relativism and planning the good society. In M. H. Appley (Ed.), *Adaptation level theory: A symposium* (pp. 287–305). New York, NY: Academic Press.

Brickman, P., Coates, D., & Janoff-Bulman, R. (1978). Lottery winners and accident victims: Is happiness relative? *Journal of Personality and Social Psychology, 36*, 917–927.

Brodsky, S. L., Hooper, N., Tipper, D., and Yates, B. (1999). Attorney invasion of witness space. *Law and Psychology Review, 23*, 49–69.

Brody, & Weiss, P. (2011). Simultaneous penile-vaginal intercourse orgasm is associated with satisfaction (sexual, life, partnership, and mental health). *The Journal of Sexual Medicine, 8*(3), 734–741.

Brown, D. (2006, November 20). Some believe "truth serums" will come back. *Washington Post*, A08.

Bruckert, L., Bestelmeyer, P., Latinus, M., Rouger, J., Charest, I., Rousselet, G. A.,... Belin, P. (2010). Vocal attractiveness increases by averaging. *Current Biology, 20*, 116–120.

Bulik, C. M., Sullivan, P. F., & Kendler, K. S. (1998). Heritability of binge-eating and broadly defined bulimia nervosa. *Biological Psychiatry, 44*, 1210–1218.

Burns, G. L., & Farina, A. (1992). The role of physical attractiveness in adjustment. *Genetic, Social, and General Psychology Monographs, 118*, 157–194.

Bushman, B. J., & Baumeister, R. F. (1998). Threatened egotism, narcissism, self-esteem, and direct and displaced aggression: Does self-love or self-hate lead to violence? *Journal of Personality and Social Psychology, 75*, 219–229.

Buss, D. M. (1989). Sex differences in human mate preferences: Evolutionary hypotheses tested in 37 cultures. *Behavioral and Brain Sciences, 12*, 1–14.

Buss, D. M. (1994). *The evolution of desire: Strategies of human mating.* New York, NY: Basic Books.

Buss, D. M., & Schmitt, D. P. (1993). Sexual strategies theory: An evolutionary perspective on human mating. *Psychological Review, 100*, 204–232.

Buss, D. M., Shackelford, T. K., Kirkpatrick, L. A., & Larsen, R. J. (2001). A half-century of mate preferences: The cultural evolution of values. *Journal of Marriage and Families, 63*, 492–503.

Buunk, B. P., Dijkstra, P., Fetchenhauer, D., & Kenrick, D. (2002). Age and gender differences in mate selection criteria for various involvement levels. *Personal Relationships, 9*, 271–278.

Byrne, D. (1971). *The attraction paradigm.* New York, NY: Academic Press.

Cacioppo, J. T., Berntson, G. G., Klein, D. J., & Poehlmann, K. M. (1997). The psychophysiology of emotion across the lifespan. *Annual Review of Gerontology and Geriatrics, 17*, 27–74.

Cacioppo, J. T., Tassinary, L. G., & Berntson, G. G. (2000). *Handbook of psychophysiology.* Cambridge, England: Cambridge University Press.

Cale, E. M., & Lilienfeld, S. O. (2006). Psychopath factors and risk for aggressive behavior: A test of the "threatened egotism" hypothesis. *Law and Human Behavior, 30*, 51–74.

Call, V., Sprecher, S., & Schwartz, P. (1995). The incidence and frequency of marital sex in a national sample. *Journal of Marriage and the Family, 57*, 639–652.

Cameron, J., & Pierce, W. D. (1994). Reinforcement, reward, and intrinsic motivation: A meta-analysis. *Review of Educational Research, 64*, 363–423.

Campfield, L. A., Smith, F. J., Rosenbaum, M., & Hirsch, J. (1996). Human eating: Evidence for a physiological basis using a modified paradigm. *Neuroscience Biobehavioral Review, 20*, 133–137.

Canetti, L., Bachar, E., & Berry, E. M. (2002). Food and emotion. *Behavioural Processes, 60*, 157–164.

Cannon, W. B. (1929). *Bodily changes in pain, hunger, fear and rage.* New York, NY: D. Appleton.

Cannon, W. B., & Washburn, A. L. (1912). An explanation of hunger. *American Journal of Physiology, 29*, 441–454.

Capaldi, E. D. (1996). Conditioned food preferences. In E. D. Capaldi (Ed.), *Why we eat what we eat: The psychology of eating* (pp. 53–80). Washington, DC: American Psychological Association.

Carlson, J. G., & Hatfield, E. (1992). *Psychology of emotion.* New York, NY: Harcourt, Brace, Jovanovich.

Carlson, W., & Rose, A. J. (2007). The role of reciprocity in romantic relationships in middle childhood and early adolescence. *Merrill-Palmer Quarterly, 53*, 262–290.

Carstensen, L. L., & Lockenhoff, C. E. (2003). Aging, emotion, and evolution. *Annals of the New York Academy of Science, 1000*, 152–179.

Carton, J. S. (1996). The differential effects of tangible rewards and praise on intrinsic motivation: A comparison of cognitive evaluation theory and operant theory. *The Behavior Analyst, 19*, 237–255.

Charles, S. T., Mather, M., & Carstensen, L. L. (2003). Aging and emotional memory: The forgettable nature of negative images for older adults. *Journal of Experimental Psychology: General, 132*, 310–324.

Chivers, M. L., & Bailey, J. M. (2005). A sex difference in features that elicit genital response. *Biological Psychology, 70*, 115–120.

Choquet, H., & Meyre, D. (2011). Molecular basis of obesity: Current status and future prospects. *Current Genomics, 12*, 154–168.

Chwalisz, K., Diener, E., & Gallagher, D. (1988). Autonomic arousal feedback and emotional experience: Evidence from the spinal cord injured. *Journal of Personality and Social Psychology, 54*, 820–828.

Ciarella, G., Ciarella, M., Graziani, P., & Mirante, M. (1991). Changes in food consumption of obese patients induced by dietary treatment combined with dexfenfluramine. *International Journal of Obesity, 15*, 69.

Coppari, R., Ichinose, M., Lee, C. E., Pullen, A. E., Kenny, C. D., McGovern, R. A., ... Elmquist, J. K. (2005). The hypothalamic arcuate nucleus: A key site for mediating leptin's effects on glucose homeostasis and locomotor activity. *Cell Metabolism, 1*, 63–72.

Cornelius, R. R. (2001). Crying and catharsis. In A. J. M. Vingerhoets & R. R. Cornelius (Eds.), *Adult crying: A biopsychosocial approach* (pp. 199–211). Hove, United Kingdom: Brunner-Routledge.

Craighead, L. W. (2002). Obesity and eating disorders. In M. M. Antony & D. H. Barlow (Eds.), *A guide to treatments that work* (2nd ed., pp. 245–262). New York, NY: Oxford.

Crespi, L. P. (1942). Quantitative variation of incentive and performance in the white rat. *American Journal of Psychology, 55*, 467–517.

Csikszentmihalyi, M. (1990). *Flow, the psychology of optimal experience.* New York, NY: Harper & Row.

Cullen, M. J., & Sackett, P. R. (2004). Integrity testing in the workplace. In J. C. Thomas & M. Hersen (Eds.), *Comprehensive handbook of psychological assessment, Volume 4: Industrial and organizational psychology* (pp. 149–165). Hoboken, NJ: Wiley.

Cunningham, M. R., Roberts, A. R., Wu, H., Barbee, A. P., & Bruen, P. B. (1995). Their ideas of beauty are, on the whole, the same as ours: Consistency and variability in the cross-cultural perception of female physical attractiveness. *Journal of Personality and Social Psychology, 68*, 261–279.

Curran, J. P., & Lippold, S. (1975). The effects of physical attraction and attitude similarity on attraction in dating dyads. *Journal of Personality, 43*, 528–539.

Curtis, R. C., & Miller, K. (1986). Believing another likes or dislikes you: Behavior making the beliefs come true. *Journal of Personality and Social Psychology, 51,* 284–290.

Damasio, A. (1994). *Descartes' error.* New York, NY: G. P. Putnam's Sons.

Danner, D. D., Snowdon, D. A., & Friesen, W. V. (2001). Positive emotions in early life and longevity: Findings from the nun study. *Journal of Personality and Social Psychology, 80,* 804–813.

Darwin, C. R. (1872). *The expression of the emotions in man and animals.* London, England: John Murray.

Davis, J. I., Senghas, A., Brandt, F., & Ochsner, K. N. (2010). The effects of BOTOX injections on emotional experience. *Emotion, 10,* 433–440.

Dawes, R. M. (1994). *House of cards: Psychology and psychotherapy built on myth.* New York, NY: Free Press.

Deci, E. L. (1971). Effects of externally mediated rewards on intrinsic motivation. *Journal of Personality and Social Psychology, 18,* 105–115.

Deci, E. L., Koestner, R., & Ryan, R. M. (1999). A meta-analytic review of experiments examining the effects of extrinsic rewards on intrinsic motivation. *Psychological Bulletin, 125,* 627–668.

Delgado, J. M. R., & Anand, B. K. (1952). Increase of food intake induced by electrical stimulation of the lateral hypothalamus. *American Journal of Physiology, 172,* 162–168.

DePaulo, B. M., Kashy, D. A., Kirkendol, S. E., Wyer, M. M., & Epstein, J. A. (1996). Lying in everyday life. *Journal of Personality and Social Psychology, 70,* 979–995.

DePaulo, B. M., Lindsay, J. J., Malone, B. E., Muhlenbruck, L., Charlton, K., & Cooper, H. (2003). Cues to deception. *Psychological Bulletin, 129,* 74–118.

DePaulo, B. M., & Pfeifer, R. L. (1986). On-the-job experience and skill at detecting deception. *Journal of Applied Social Psychology, 16,* 249–267.

de Waal, F. B. M. (2009). *The age of empathy: Nature's lessons for a kinder society.* New York, NY: Random House.

Diamond, L. M. (2003). What does sexual orientation orient? A biobehavioral model distinguishing romantic love and sexual desire. *Psychological Review, 110,* 173–192.

Diamond, L. M. (2004). Emerging perspectives on distinctions between romantic love and sexual desire. *Current Directions in Psychological Science, 13,* 116–119.

Diener, E., & Biswas-Diener, R. (2008). *Happiness: Unlocking the mysteries of psychological wealth.* Malden, MA: Blackwell.

Diener, E., Gohm, C. L., Suh, E., & Oishi, S. (2000). Similarity of the relations between marital status and subjective well-being across cultures. *Journal of Cross-Cultural Psychology, 31,* 419–436.

Diener, E., Kesebir, P., & Tov, W. (2012). Happiness. In M. Leary & R.H Hoyle (Eds.), *Handbook of individual differences in social behavior* (pp. 147–160). New York, NY: Guilford Press.

Diener, E., Lucas, R., & Scollon, C. N. (2006). Beyond the hedonic treadmill: Revising the adaptation theory of well-being. *American Psychologist, 61,* 305–314.

Diener, E., & Seligman, M. E. P. (2002). Very happy people. *Psychological Science, 13,* 81–84.

Dimberg, U., Thunberg, M., & Elmehed, K. (2000). Unconscious facial reactions to emotional facial expressions. *Psychological Science, 11,* 86–89.

Dion, K., Berscheid, E., & Walster, E. (1972). What is beautiful is good. *Journal of Personality and Social Psychology, 24,* 285–290.

Dollard, J., & Miller, N. (1950). *Personality and psychotherapy: An analysis in terms of learning, thinking and culture.* New York, NY: McGraw-Hill.

Donnellan, M. B., Trzesniewski, K. H., Robins, R. W., Moffitt, T. E., & Caspi, A. (2005). Exploring the link between self-esteem and externalizing behaviors: Low self-esteem is related to antisocial behavior, conduct disorder, and delinquency. *Psychological Science, 16,* 328–335.

Driscoll, R., Davis, K. E., & Lipetz, M. E. (1972). Parental interference and romantic love: The Romeo and Juliet effect. *Journal of Personality and Social Structure, 24,* 1–10.

Duclos, S., Laird, J., Schneider, E., Sexter, M., Stern, L., & van Lighten, O. (1989). Emotion-specific effects of facial expressions and postures on emotional experience. *Journal of Personality and Social Psychology, 57,* 100–108.

Duenwald, M. (2002, May 7). Religion and health: New research revives an old debate. *New York Times,* D5.

Dunn, E. W., Aknin, L., & Norton, M. I. (2008). Spending money on others promotes happiness. *Science, 319,* 1687–1688.

Dutton, D. G., & Aron, A. (1974). Some evidence for heightened sexual attraction under conditions of high anxiety. *Journal of Personality and Social Psychology, 30,* 510–517.

Dysken, M. W., Kooser, J. A., Haraszti, J. S., & Davis, J. M. (1979). Clinical usefulness of sodium amobarbitol interviewing. *Archives of General Psychiatry, 36,* 789–794.

Eagly, A. H., & Wood, W. (1999). The origins of sex differences in human behavior: Evolved dispositions versus social roles. *American Psychologist, 54,* 408–423.

Eagly, A. H., Wood, W., & Johannesen-Schmidt, M. C. (2004). Social role theory of sex differences and similarities: Implications for the partner preferences of women and men. In A. H. Eagly, A. Beall, & R. S. Sternberg (Eds.), *The psychology of gender* (2nd ed., pp. 269–295). New York, NY: Guilford Press.

Eastwick, P. W., & Finkel, E. J. (2008). The attachment system in fledgling relationships: An activating role for attachment anxiety. *Journal of Personality and Social Psychology, 95,* 628–647.

Ehrenreich, B. (2009). *Bright sided: How positive thinking is undermining America.* New York, NY: Picador.

Eibl-Eibesfeldt, I. (1973). The expressive behaviour of the deaf-and-blind-born. In M. von Cranach & I. Vine (Eds.), *Social communication and movement* (pp. 163–194). London, England: Academic Press.

Eisenberger, R., & Cameron, J. (1996). Detrimental effects of reward: Reality or myth? *American Psychologist, 51,* 1153–1166.

Ekman, P. (1994). Strong evidence for universals in facial expressions: A reply to Russell's mistaken critique. *Psychological Bulletin, 115,* 268–287.

Ekman, P. (1999). Facial expressions. In T. Dalgleish & M. J. Power (Eds.), *Handbook of cognition and emotion* (pp. 301–320). New York, NY: Wiley.

Ekman, P. (2001). *Telling lies: Clues to deceit in the marketplace, politics, and marriage.* New York, NY: Norton.

Ekman, P., Davidson, R. J., & Friesen, W. V. (1990). Duchenne's smile: Emotional expression and brain physiology II. *Journal of Personality and Social Psychology, 58,* 342–353.

Ekman, P., & Friesen, W. V. (1971). Constants across cultures in the face and emotion. *Journal of Personality and Social Psychology, 17,* 124–129.

Ekman, P., & Friesen, W. V. (1975). *Unmasking the face: A guide to recognizing emotions from facial clues.* Englewood Cliffs, NJ: Prentice Hall.

Ekman, P., & Friesen, W. V. (1986). A new pancultural facial expression of emotion. *Motivation and Emotion, 10,* 159–168.

Ekman, P., Levenson, R. W., & Friesen, W. V. (1983). Autonomic nervous system activity distinguishes between emotions. *Science, 221,* 1208–1210.

Ekman, P., & O'Sullivan, M. (1991). Who can catch a liar? *American Psychologist, 46,* 913–920.

Ekman, P., O'Sullivan, M., & Frank, M. G. (1999). A few can catch a liar. *Psychological Science, 10,* 263–266.

Elfenbein H. A. (2013). Nonverbal dialects and accents in facial expressions of emotion. *Emotion Review, 5,* 90–96.

Elfenbein, H. A., & Ambady, N. (2002). On the universality and cultural specificity of emotion recognition: A meta-analysis. *Psychological Bulletin, 128,* 203–235.

Ellis, L., & Ames, M. A. (1987). Neurohormonal functioning and sexual orientation: A theory of homosexuality-heterosexuality. *Psychological Bulletin, 101,* 233–258.

Emmons, R. A., & McCullough, M. E. (2003). Counting blessings versus burdens: An experimental investigation of gratitude and subjective well-being in daily life. *Journal of Personality and Social Psychology, 84,* 377–389.

Engelberg, N. (2012). Self-help books sometimes send wrong message. *Teller County News.* Retrieved from http://www.ourcoloradonews.com/tellercounty/opinion/self-help-books-sometimes-send-wrong-message/article_0e35f87c-3db7-11e2-b299-0019bb2963f4.html

Eslinger, P. J., & Damasio, A. R. (1985). Severe disturbance of higher cognition after bilateral frontal lobe ablation. Patient EVR. *Neurology, 35,* 1731–1741.

Fairburn, C. G., Cooper, Z., & Shafran, R. (2003). Cognitive behaviour therapy for eating disorders: A "transdiagnostic" theory and treatment. *Behaviour Research and Therapy, 41,* 509–528.

Fang, X., Singh, S., & AhluWalia, R. (2007). An examination of different explanations for the mere exposure effect. *Journal of Consumer Research, 34,* 97–103.

Farwell, L. A., & Donchin, E. (1991). The truth will out: Interrogative polygraphy ("lie detection") with event-related brain potentials. *Psychophysiology, 28,* 531–547.

Farwell, L. A., & Smith, S. S. (2001). Using brain MERMER testing to detect knowledge despite efforts to conceal. *Journal of Forensic Science, 46,* 135–143.

Fehr, B. (2008). Friendship formation. In S. Sprecher, A. Wenzel, & J. Harvey (Eds.), *Handbook of relationship formation* (pp. 29–55). New York, NY: Psychology Press.

Feingold, A. (1992). Good-looking people are not what we think. *Psychological Bulletin, 111,* 304–341.

Feinman, S. (1978). The blind as "ordinary people." *Journal of Visual Impairment and Blindness, 72,* 231–238.

Feldman Barrett, L., & Bliss-Moreau, E. (2009). She's emotional. He's having a bad day: Attributional explanations for emotion stereotypes. *Emotion, 9,* 649–658.

Feldman Barrett, L., Lindquist, K., Bliss-Moreau, E., Duncan, S., Gendron, M., Mize, J., & Brennan, L. (2007). Of mice and men: Natural kinds of emotion in the mammalian brain? *Perspectives on Psychological Science, 2,* 297–312.

Feldman Barrett, L., & Russell, J. A. (1999). Structure of current affect. *Current Directions in Psychological Science, 8,* 10–14.

Ferguson, D. M., Horwood, L. J., & Beautrais, A. L. (1999). Is sexual orientation related to mental health problems and suicidality in young people? *Archives of General Psychiatry, 56,* 876–880.

Festinger, L., Schachter, S., & Back, K. (1950). *Social pressures in informal groups.* New York, NY: Harper.

Finkel, E. J., Eastwick, P. W., Karney, B. R., Reis, H. T., & Sprecher, S. (2012). Online dating: A critical analysis from the perspective of psychological science. *Psychological Science in the Public Interest, 13*(1), 3–66. http://dx.doi.org/10.1177/1529100612436522

Finzi, E., & Wasserman, E. (2006). Treatment of depression with botulinum toxin A: A case series. *Dermatologic Surgery, 32,* 645–650.

Fisher, T. D. (2009). The impact of socially conveyed norms on the reporting of sexual behavior and attitudes by men and women. *Journal of Experimental Social Psychology, 45,* 567–572.

Fok, H. K., Hui, C. M., Bond, M. H., Matsumoto, D., & Yoo, S. H. (2008). Integrating personality, context, relationship, and emotion type into a model of display rules. *Journal of Research in Personality, 42,* 133–150.

Ford, C. S., & Beach, F. (1951). *Patterns of sexual behavior.* New York, NY: Harper.

Frederick, S., & Loewenstein, G. (1999). Hedonic adaptation. In D. Kahneman, E. Diener, & N. Schwarz (Eds.), *Well-being: The foundations of hedonic psychology* (pp. 302–329). New York, NY: Russell Sage Foundation.

Fredrickson, B. L. (2001). The role of positive emotions in positive psychology: The broaden-and-build theory of positive emotions. *American Psychologist, 56,* 218–226.

Freedman, D. G. (1964). Smiling in blind infants and the issue of innate versus acquired. *Journal of Child Psychology and Psychiatry, 5,* 171–184.

Freund, K., Watson, R., & Rienzo, D. (1989). Heterosexuality, homosexuality, and erotic age preference. *The Journal of Sex Research, 26,* 107–117.

Frey, W. H. (1985). *Crying: The mystery of tears.* Minneapolis, MN: Winston Press.

Friesen, W. V. (1972). *Cultural differences in facial expressions in a social situation: An experimental test of the concept of display rules.* Unpublished doctoral dissertation, University of California, San Francisco, CA.

Frijda, N. H. (1986). *The emotions.* Cambridge, England: Cambridge University.

Furnham, A., & Cheng, H. (2000). Perceived parental behavior, self-esteem and happiness. *Social Psychiatry and Psychiatric Epidemiology, 35,* 463–470.

Furnham, A., Petrides, K. V., & Constantinides, A. (2005). The effects of body mass index and waist-to-hip ratio on ratings of female attractiveness, fecundity, and health. *Personality and Individual Differences, 38,* 1823–1834.

Galton, F. (1878). Composite portraits made by combining those of many different persons into a single resultant figure. *Journal of the Anthropological Institute of Great Britain and Ireland, 8,* 132.

Gamer, M., Rill, H. G., Vossel, G., & Gädert, H. W. (2006). Psychophysiological and vocal measures in the detection of guilty knowledge. *International Journal of Psychophysiology, 60,* 76–87.

Gangestad, S., & Scheyd, G. J. (2005). The evolution of human physical attractiveness. *Annual Review of Anthropology, 34,* 523–548.

Geier, A. B., Rozin, P., & Doros, G. (2006). Unit bias: a new heuristic that helps explain the effect of portion size on food intake. *Psychological Science, 17,* 521–525.

Gilbert, D. T. (2006). *Stumbling on happiness.* New York, NY: Knopf.

Gilbert, D. T., Pinel, E. C., Wilson, T. D., Blumberg, S. J., & Wheatley, T. (1998). Immune neglect: A source of durability bias in affective forecasting. *Journal of Personality and Social Psychology, 75,* 617–638.

Glassgold, J. M., Beckstead, L., Drescher, J., Greene, B., Miller, R. L., & Worthington, R. L. (2009). *Report of the American Psychological Association Task Force on the appropriate therapeutic responses to sexual orientation.* Washington, DC: American Psychological Association.

Golden, N., & Sacker, I. M. (1984). An overview of the etiology, diagnosis, and management of anorexia nervosa. *Clinical Pediatrics, 23,* 209–214.

Goldman, A. I., & de Vignemont, F. (2009). Is social cognition embodied? *Trends in Cognitive Sciences, 13,* 154–159.

Gonzaga, G. C., Turner, R. A., Keltner, D., Campos, B., & Altemus, M. (2006). Romantic love and sexual desire in close relationships. *Emotion, 6,* 163–179.

Gottdiener, J. S., Gross, H. A., Henry, W. L., Borer, J. S., & Ebert, M. H. (1978). Effects of self-induced starvation on cardiac size and function in anorexia nervosa. *Circulation, 58,* 425–433.

Gouldner, A. W. (1960). The norm of reciprocity: A preliminary statement. *American Sociological Review, 25,* 161–178.

Gray, J. (1992). *Men are from mars, women are from venus.* New York, NY: HarperCollins.

Gray, J. A. (1982). *The neuropsychology of anxiety: An enquiry into the functions of the septo-hippocampal system.* Oxford, England: Oxford University Press.

Greely H. T., & Illes, J. (2007). Neuroscience-based lie detection: The urgent need for regulation. *American Journal of Law & Medicine, 33,* 377–431.

Green, R. (1987). *The "sissy boy syndrome" and the development of homosexuality.* New Haven, CT: Yale University Press.

Greene, J. D., & Paxton, J. M. (2009). Patterns of neural activity associated with honest and dishonest moral decisions. *Proceedings of the National Academy of Sciences, 106,* 12506–12511.

Griffiths, P. E. (1997). *What emotions really are: The problem of psychological categories.* Chicago, IL: Chicago University Press.

Grill, H. J., & Kaplan, J. M. (2002). The neuroanatomical axis for control of energy balance. *Frontiers in Neuroendocrinology, 21,* 2–40.

Grill, H. J., Schwartz, M. W., Kaplan, J. M., Foxhall, J. S., Breininger, J., & Baskin, D. G. (2002). Evidence that the caudal brainstem is a target for the inhibitory effect of leptin on food intake. *Endocrinology, 143,* 239–246.

Haidt, J. (2012). *The righteous mind: Why good people are divided by politics and religion.* New York, NY: Vintage Books.

Halberstadt, J., & Rhodes, G. (2003). It's not just the average face that's attractive: The attractiveness of averageness of computer-manipulated birds, fish, and automobiles. *Psychonomic Bulletin and Review, 10,* 149–156.

Hall, A. (2009). "I screamed, but there was nothing to hear": Man trapped in 23-year "coma" reveals horror of being unable to tell doctors he was conscious. *Mail Online.* Retrieved from http://www.dailymail.co.uk/news/article-1230092/Rom-Houben-Patient-trapped-23-year-coma-conscious-along.html

Hall, E. T. (1966). *The hidden dimension.* New York, NY: Anchor Books.

Hall, E. T. (1976). *Beyond culture.* New York, NY: Doubleday.

Hall, J. A. Y., & Kimura, D. (1994). Dermatoglyphic asymmetry and sexual orientation in men. *Behavioral Neuroscience, 108,* 1203–1206.

Hamann, A., & Matthaei, S. (1996). Regulation of energy balance by leptin. *Experimental Clinical Endocrinology Diabetes, 104,* 293–300.

Harker, L., & Keltner, D. (2001). Expressions of positive emotion in women's college yearbook pictures and their relationship to personality and life outcomes across adulthood. *Journal of Personality and Social Psychology, 80,* 112–124.

Harmon-Jones, E., & Allen, J. J. B. (2001). The role of affect in the mere exposure effect: Evidence from psychophysiological and individual differences approaches. *Personality and Social Psychology Bulletin, 27,* 889–898.

Harmon-Jones, E., & Peterson, C. K. (2009). Supine body position reduces neural response to anger evocation. *Psychological Science, 20,* 1209–1210.

Harrington, E. R. (2004). The social psychology of hatred. *Journal of Hate Studies, 3,* 49–82.

Hatfield, E., Aronson, V., Abrahams, D., & Rottman, L. (1966). The importance of physical attractiveness in dating behavior. *Journal of Personality and Social Psychology, 4,* 508–516.

Hatfield, E., & Rapson, R. (1996). *Love and sex: Cross-cultural perspectives.* Boston, MA: Allyn & Bacon.

Hatfield, E., & Walster, G. W. (1978). *A new look at love.* Reading, MA: Addison-Wesley.

Hayduk, L. (1983). Personal space: Where we now stand. *Psychological Bulletin, 94,* 293–335.

Heider, F. (1958). *The psychology of interpersonal relations.* New York, NY: Wiley.

Heims, H. C., Critchley, H. D., Dolan, R., Mathias, C. J., & Cipolotti, L. (2004). Social and motivational functioning is not critically dependent on feedback of autonomic responses: Neuropsychological evidence from patients with pure autonomic failure. *Neuropsychologia, 42,* 1979–1988.

Held, B. (2004). The negative side of positive psychology. *Journal of Humanistic Psychology, 44,* 9–46.

Helliwell, J. F., & Putnam, R. D. (2004). The social context of well-being. *Philosophical Transactions of the Royal Society (London) Series B, 359,* 1435–1446.

Helson, H. (1948). Adaptation-level as a basis for a quantitative theory of frames of reference. *Psychological Review, 55,* 297–313.

Henig, R. M. (2006, February 5). Looking for the lie. *New York Times Magazine,* 46–53, 76, 83.

Herbert, W. (2011). *On second thought: Outsmarting your mind's hard-wired habits.* New York, NY: Broadway.

Hertwig, R., Herzog, S. M., Schooler, L. J., & Reimer, T. (2008). Fluency heuristic: A model of how the mind exploits a by-product of information retrieval. *Journal of Experimental Psychology: Learning, Memory, and Cognition, 34,* 1191–1206.

Hetherington, A. W., & Ranson, S. W. (1940). Hypothalamic lesions and adiposity in the rat. *Anatomical Record, 78,* 149–158.

Hill, C., Rubin, Z., & Peplau, L. A. (1976). Breakups before marriage: The end of 103 affairs. *Journal of Social Issues, 32,* 147–168.

Hiller, J. (2005). Gender differences in sexual motivation. *Journal of Men's Health and Gender, 2,* 339–345.

Himes, S. M., & Thompson, J. K. (2007). Fat stigmatization in television shows and movies: A content analysis. *Obesity, 15,* 712–718.

Hines, M. (2010). Sex-related variation in human behavior and the brain. *Trends in Cognitive Sciences, 14(10),* 448–456.

Hohmann, G. W. (1966). Some effects of spinal cord lesions on experienced emotional feelings. *Psychophysiology, 3,* 143–156.

Honts, C. R., Raskin, D. C., & Kircher, J. C. (1994). Mental and physical countermeasures reduce the accuracy of polygraph tests. *Journal of Applied Psychology, 79,* 252–259.

Hoppa, H., & Hallstrom, T. (1981). Weight gain in adulthood in relation to socioeconomic factors, mental illness, and personality traits: A prospective study of middle-aged men. *Journal of Psychosomatic Research, 25,* 83–89.

Houle, T. T., Dhingra, L. K., Remble, T. A., Rokicki, L. A., & Penzien, D. B. (2006). Not tonight, I have a headache? *Headache: The Journal of Head and Face Pain, 46,* 983–990.

Hudson, D. B., Elek, S., & Campbell-Grossman, C. (2000). Depression, self-esteem, loneliness, and social support among adolescent mothers participating in the new parents project. *Adolescence, 35,* 445–453.

Hull, C. L. (1943). *Principles of behavior.* New York, NY: Appleton-Century-Crofts.

Iacono, W. G. (2001). Forensic "lie detection": Procedures without scientific basis. *Journal of Forensic Psychology Practice, 1,* 75–86.

Iacono, W. G. (2009). Psychophysiological detection of deception and guilty knowledge. In J. L. Skeem, K. S. Douglas, & S. O. Lilienfeld (Eds.), *Psychological science in the courtroom: Consensus and controversy* (pp. 224–241). New York, NY: Guilford Press.

Isen, A. M., Rosenzweig, A. S., & Young, M. J. (1991). The influence of positive affect on clinical problem solving. *Medical Decision Making, 11*, 221–227.

Izard, C. E. (1971). *The face of emotion.* New York, NY: Appleton-Century-Crofts.

Izard, C. E. (1994). Innate and universal facial expressions: Evidence from developmental and cross-country research. *Psychological Bulletin, 115*, 288–299.

Jack, R. E., Garrod, O. G. B., Yu, H., Caldara, R., & Schyns, P. G. (2012). Facial expressions of emotion are not culturally universal. *Proceedings of the National Academy of Sciences*, awaiting page numbers.

James, W. (1890). *The principles of psychology.* Cambridge, MA: Harvard University Press.

Jay, K., & Young, A. (1979). *Out of the closets: Voices of gay liberation.* New York, NY: BJ Publishing Group.

Johnson, C. L., Tobin, D. L., & Steinberg, S. L. (1989). Etiological, developmental and treatment considerations for bulimia. Special issue: The bulimic college student: Evaluation, treatment and prevention. *Journal of College Student Psychotherapy, 3*, 57–73.

Johnson, F., & Wardle, J. (2005). Dietary restraint, body dissatisfaction, and psychological distress: A prospective analysis. *Journal of Abnormal Psychology, 114*, 119–125.

Jones, A. (1969). Stimulus-seeking behavior. In J. Zubek (Ed.), *Sensory deprivation: Fifteen years of research* (pp. 167–206). New York, NY: Appleton-Century-Crofts.

Jones, S. E. (1979). Integrating etic and emic approaches in the study of intercultural communication. In M. Asante, E. Newmark, & C. A. Blake (Eds.), *Handbook of intercultural communication.* Beverly Hills, CA: Sage.

Jordan, H. A. (1969). Voluntary intragastric feeding: Oral and gastric contributions to food intake and hunger in man. *Journal of Comparative and Physiological Psychology, 68*, 498–506.

Kahneman, D., & Deaton, A. (2010). High income improves evaluation of life but not emotional well-being. *Proceedings of the National Academy of Sciences, 107*, 16489–16493.

Kahneman, D., Krueger, A., Schkade, D., Schwarz, N., & Stone, A. (2006). Would you be happier if you were richer? A focusing illusion. *Science, 312*, 1908–1910.

Kahneman, D., Krueger, A. B., Schkade, D. A. Schwarz, N., & Stone, A. A. (2004). A survey method for characterizing daily life experience: The day reconstruction method. *Science, 306*, 1776–1780.

Kaplan, H. S. (1977). Hypoactive sexual desire. *Journal of Sex and Marital Therapy, 3*, 3–9.

Kassin, S. M., & Gudjonsson, G. H. (2004). The psychology of confession: A review of the literature and issues. *Psychological Science in the Public Interest, 5*, 33–67.

Katzman, D. K. (2005). Medical complications in adolescents with anorexia nervosa: A review of the literature. *International Journal of Eating Disorders, 37*(Suppl.), S52–S59.

Keel, P. K., & Klump, K. L. (2003). Are eating disorders culture-bound syndromes? Implications for conceptualizing their etiology. *Psychological Bulletin, 129*, 747–769.

Keen, S. (1986). *Faces of the enemy: Reflections of the hostile imagination.* San Francisco, CA: Harper & Row.

Kennedy, K. (2009). Sleep starved: Too little sleep could be more dangerous than you may think. *Army Times.* Retrieved from http://www.armytimes.com/offduty/health/offduty_sleep_051906

Kenrick, D. T., Griskevicius, V., Neuberg, S. L., & Schaller, M. (2010). Renovating the pyramid of needs: Contemporary extensions built upon ancient foundations. *Perspectives on Psychological Science, 5*, 292–314.

Kenrick, D. T., Neuberg, S. L., & Cialdini, R. B. (2005). *Social psychology: Unraveling the mystery* (3rd ed.). Boston, MA: Allyn & Bacon.

Kesebir, P., & Diener, E. D. (2008). In pursuit of happiness: Empirical answers to philosophical questions. *Perspectives on Psychological Science, 3*, 117–125.

Keski-Rahkonen, A., Hoek, H. W., Linna, M. S., Raevuori, A., Sihvola, E., Bulik, C. M.,...Kaprio, J. (2008). Incidence and outcomes of bulimia nervosa: A nation-wide population-based study. *Psychological Medicine, 8*, 1–9.

Keyes, C. L. M., Fredrickson, B. L., & Park, N. (2012). Positive psychology and the quality of life. In K. Land (Ed.), *Handbook of social indicators and quality of life studies* (pp. 99–112). New York, NY: Springer.

Keyes, C. L. M., & Haidt, J. (Eds.). (2003). *Flourishing: Positive psychology and the life well lived.* Washington, DC: American Psychological Association.

Keys, A., Brozek, J., Henschel, A., Mickelsen, O., & Taylor, H. L. (1950). *The biology of human starvation* (2 vols.). Minneapolis, MN: University of Minnesota Press.

King, B. (2006). The rise, fall, and resurrection of the ventromedial hypothalamus in the regulation of feeding behavior and body weight. *Physiology & Behavior, 87*, 221–224.

Kircher, J. C., Horowitz, S. W., & Raskin, D. C. (1988). Meta-analysis of mock crime studies of the control question polygraph technique. *Law and Human Behavior, 12*, 79–90.

Kirsch, I., & Lynn, S. J. (1999). Automaticity in clinical psychology. *American Psychologist, 54*, 504–515.

Kistner, J. A., David-Ferdon, C. F., Repper, K. K., & Joiner, T. E., Jr. (2006). Bias and accuracy of children's perceptions of peer acceptance: Prospective associations with depressive symptoms. *Journal of Abnormal Child Psychology, 34*, 349–361.

Klusmann, D. (2002). Sexual motivation and the duration of partnership. *Archives of Sexual Behavior, 31*, 275–287.

Knecht, S., Ellger, T., & Levine, J. A. (2007). Obesity in neurobiology. *Progress in Neurobiology, 84*, 85–103.

Knox, D., Zusman, M., & Nieves, W. (1997). College students' homogamous preferences for a date and mate. *College Student Journal, 31*, 445–448.

Koerner, B. I. (2002, November 1). Lie detector roulette. *Mother Jones.* Retrieved from http://www.newamerica.net/publications/articles/2002/lie_detector_roulette

Kohn, A. (1993). *Punished by rewards: The trouble with gold stars, incentive plans, A's, praise and other bribes.* Boston, MA: Houghton Mifflin.

Komori, M., Kawamura, S., & Ishihara, S. (2009). Averageness or symmetry: Which is more important for facial attractiveness? *Acta Psychologica, 131*, 136–142.

Konner, M. (2003). *The tangled wing: Biological constraints on the human spirit.* New York, NY: Henry Holt.

Kraft, T. L., & Pressman, S. D. (2012). Grin and bear it: The influence of manipulated facial expression on the stress response. *Psychological Science*, 1372–1378.

Kraut, R. E., & Poe, D. (1980). Behavioral roots of person perception: The deception judgments of customs inspectors and laymen. *Journal of Personality and Social Psychology, 39*, 784–798.

Kruger, J., Epley, N., Parker, J., & Ng, Z. (2005). Egocentrism over email: Can we communicate as well as we think? *Journal of Personality and Social Psychology, 89*, 925–936.

Kunst-Wilson, W. R., & Zajonc, R. B. (1980). Affective discrimination of stimuli that cannot be recognized. *Science, 207*, 557–558.

Kurzban, R., & Weeden, J. (2005). HurryDate: Mate preferences in action. *Evolution and Human Behavior, 26*, 227–244.

Lalumière, M. L., Blanchard, R., & Zucker, K. L. (2000). Sexual orientation and handedness in men and women: A meta-analysis. *Psychological Bulletin, 126*, 575–592.

Langleben, D. D. (2008). Detection of deception with fMRI: Are we there yet? *Legal and Criminological Psychology, 13*, 1–9.

Langleben, D. D., & Moriarty, J. C. (2012). Using brain imaging for lie detection: Where science, law and research policy collide. *Psychology, Public Policy, and Law*, awaiting page numbers.

Langlois, J. H., Kalakanis, L., Rubenstein, A. J., Larson, A., Hallam, M., & Smoot, M. (2000). Maxims or myths of beauty? A meta-analytic and theoretical review. *Psychological Bulletin, 126*, 390–423.

Langlois, J. H., & Roggman, L. A. (1990). Attractive faces are only average. *Psychological Science, 1*, 115–121.

Laumann, E. O., Gagnon, J. H., Michael, R. T., & Michaels, S. (1994). *The social organization of sexuality: Sexual practices in the United States.* Chicago, IL: University of Chicago Press.

Laumann, E. O., Glasser, D. B., Neves, R. C. S., & Moreira, E. D. (2009). A population-based survey of sexual activity, sexual problems and associated help-seeking behavior patterns in mature adults in the United States of America. *International Journal of Impotence Research, 21*(3), 171–178.

Lazarus, R. S. (1984). On the primacy of cognition. *American Psychologist, 39*, 124–129.

Lazarus, R. S. (2003). Does the positive psychology movement have legs? *Psychological Inquiry, 14*, 93–109.

Lazarus, R. S., & Folkman, S. (1984). *Stress, appraisal, and coping.* New York, NY: Springer.

Leitenberg, H., & Henning, K. (1995). Sexual fantasy. *Psychological Bulletin, 117*, 469–496.

Lepper, M. R., Greene, D., & Nisbett, R. E. (1973). Undermining children's intrinsic interest with extrinsic rewards: A test of the "overjustification" hypothesis. *Journal of Personality and Social Psychology, 28*, 129–137.

Levenson, R. (2005, April). Desperately seeking Phil. *APS Observer.* Retrieved from https://www.psychologicalscience.org/index.php/uncategorized/desperately-seeking-phil.html

Lever, J. (1995, August 22). The 1995 Advocate survey of sexuality and relationship: The women. *Advocate*, 212–230.

Levin, B. E., Dunn-Meynell, A. A., & Routh, V. H. (1999). Regulatory, integrative, and comparative physiology. *American Journal of Physiology, 276*, 1223–1231.

Levine, D. S. (1998). *Explorations in common sense and common nonsense.* Retrieved from http://dspace.uta.edu/handle/10106/5039

Levine, D. W. (2005). Do dogs resemble their owners? A reanalysis of Roy and Christenfeld. *Psychological Science, 16*, 83–84.

Levitsky, D. A., Obarzanek, E., Mrdjenovic, G., & Strupp, B. J. (2005). Imprecise control of energy intake: Absence of a reduction in food intake following overfeeding in young adults. *Physiology and Behavior, 84*, 669–675.

Lewin, K. (1935). *A dynamic theory of personality.* New York, NY: McGraw-Hill.

Lewis, M., Haviland-Jones, J. M., & Barrett, L. F. (2008). *Handbook of Emotions.* New York, NY: Guilford Press.

Lilienfeld, S. O., Alliger, G. M., & Mitchell, K. E. (1995). Why integrity testing remains controversial. *American Psychologist, 50*, 457–458.

Lilienfeld, S. O., Lynn, S. J., Ruscio, J., & Beyerstein, B. (2009). *50 great myths in psychology: shattering widespread misconceptions about human behavior.* Malden, MA: Wiley-Blackwell.

Linder, K. (2013). *Your killer emotions*. Austin Texas: Greenleaf Book Press.

Lindquist, K. A., Wager, T. D., Kober, H., Bliss-Moreau, E., & Feldman Barrett, L. (2012). The brain basis of emotion: A meta-analytic review. *Behavioral and Brain Sciences, 35*, 121–143.

Lippa, R. A. (2006). Is high sex drive associated with increased sexual attraction to both sexes? It depends on whether you are male or female. *Psychological Science, 17*, 46–52.

Lippa, R. A. (2009). Sex differences in sex drive, sociosexuality, and height across 53 nations: Testing evolutionary and social structural theories. *Archives of Sexual Behavior, 38*, 631–651.

Long, G. T., & Krall, V. L. (1990). The measurement of stress by voice analysis. *Journal of Social Behavior and Personality, 5*, 723–731.

Lorenz, K. (1971). *Studies in animal and human behavior* (Vol. 2). Cambridge, MA: Harvard University Press.

Lowe, M. R., & Levine, A. S. (2005). Eating motives and the controversy over dieting: Eating less than needed versus less than wanted. *Obesity Research, 13*, 797–806.

Lucas, R. E., Clark, A. E., Georgellis, Y., & Diener, E. (2003). Reexamining adaptation and the set point model of happiness: Reactions to changes in marital status. *Journal of Personality and Social Psychology, 84*, 527–539.

Luhmann, M., Lucas, R. E., Eid, M., & Diener, E. (2012). The prospective effect of life satisfaction on life events. *Social Psychological and Personality Science*. Advanced online publication. http://dx.doi.org/10.1177/1948550612440105

Luo, S., & Klohnen, E. C. (2005). Assortative mating and marital quality in newlyweds: A couple-centered approach. *Journal of Personality and Social Psychology, 88*, 304–325.

Lykken, D. T. (1959). The GSR in the detection of guilt. *Journal of Applied Psychology, 43*, 385–388.

Lykken, D. T. (1978). The psychopath and the lie detector. *Psychophysiology, 15*, 137–142.

Lykken, D. T. (1998). *A tremor in the blood: Uses and abuses of the lie detector* (2nd ed.). Reading, MA: Perseus.

Lykken, D. T., & Tellegen, A. (1996). Happiness is a stochastic phenomenon. *Psychological Science, 7*, 186–189.

Lynn, S. J. (1978). Three theories of self-disclosure exchange. *Journal of Experimental Social Psychology, 14*, 466–479.

Lynn, S. J., Matthews, A., Williams, J. C., Hallquist, M. N., & Lilienfeld, S. O. (2007). Some forms of psychopathology are partly socially constructed. In S. O. Lilienfeld & W. T. O'Donohue (Eds.), *The great ideas of clinical science: 17 principles that every mental health professional should know* (pp. 347–374). New York, NY: Routledge.

Lyubomirsky, S., King, L. A., & Diener, E. (2005). The benefits of frequent positive affect: Does happiness lead to success? *Psychological Bulletin, 131*, 803–855.

Maia, T. V., & McClelland, J. L. (2004). A re-examination of the evidence for the somatic marker hypothesis: What participants know in the Iowa gambling task. *Proceedings of the National Academy of Sciences, 101*, 16075–16080.

Mandler, G., Nakamura, Y., & Shebo-Van Zandt, B. J. (1987). Nonspecific effects of exposure on stimuli that cannot be recognized. *Journal of Experimental Psychology: Learning, Memory, & Cognition, 13*, 646–648.

Mann, J. (1969). The use of sodium amobarbital in psychiatry. *Ohio State Medical Journal, 65*, 700–702.

Marsh, A., Elfenbein, H. A., & Ambady, N. (2003). Nonverbal "accents": Cultural differences in facial expressions of emotion. *Psychological Science, 14*, 373–376.

Marsh, A. A., Adams, R. B., Jr., & Kleck, R. E. (2005). Why do fear and anger look the way they do? Form and social function in facial expressions. *Personality and Social Psychology Bulletin, 31*, 73–86.

Marsh, H. W., & Craven, R. G. (2006). Reciprocal effects of self-concept and performance from a multidimensional perspective: Beyond seductive pleasure and unidimensional perspectives. *Perspectives on Psychological Science, 1*, 133–163.

Marshall, G. D., & Zimbardo, P. G. (1979). Affective consequences of inadequately explained arousal. *Journal of Personality and Social Psychology, 37*, 970–988.

Marston, W. M. (1938). *The lie detector test*. New York, NY: Richard R. Smith.

Martin, D. (2006, November 20). The truth about happiness may surprise you. CNN.com. Retrieved from http://www.cnn.com/2006/HEALTH/conditions/11/10/happiness.overview/index.html

Maslach, C. (1979). Negative and emotional biasing of unexplained arousal. *Journal of Personality and Social Psychology, 37*, 953–969.

Mastekaasa, A. (1994). The subjective well-being of the previously married: The importance of unmarried cohabitation and time since widowhood or divorce. *Social Forces, 73*, 665–692.

Masters, W. H., & Johnson, V. E. (1966). *Human sexual response*. Boston, MA: Little, Brown.

Mather, M., Canli, T., English, T., Whitfield, S., Wais, P., Ochsner, K.,... Carstensen, L. L. (2004). Amygdala responses to emotionally valenced stimuli in older and younger adults. *Psychological Science, 15*, 259–263.

Matsumoto, D., & Ekman, P. (2004). The relationship between expressions, labels, and descriptions of contempt. *Journal of Personality and Social Psychology, 87*, 529–540.

Matsumoto, D., & Willingham, B. (2006). The thrill of victory and the agony of defeat: Spontaneous expressions of medal winners of the 2004 Athens Olympic Games. *Journal of Personality and Social Psychology, 91*, 568–581.

Matsumoto, D., Yoo, S. H., Hirayama, S., & Petrova, G. (2005). Development and validation of a measure of display rule knowledge: The Display Rule Assessment Inventory. *Emotion, 5*, 23–40.

Mattes, R. D., Hollis, J., Hayes, D., & Stunkard, A. J. (2005). Appetite measurement and manipulation misgivings. *Journal of the American Dietetic Association, 105*, 87–97.

Max, D. T. (2007, January 7). Happiness 101. *New York Times*. Retrieved from http://www.nytimes.com/2007/01/07/magazine/07happiness.t.html?ex=1183608000&en=946a9bb65d8be3b7&ei=5070

McClelland, D. C., Atkinson, J. W., Clark, R. A., & Lowell, E. L. (1953). *The achievement motive*. New York, NY: Century Psychology Series.

McClelland, D. C., Atkinson, J. W., Clark, R. A., & Lowell, E. L. (1958). A scoring manual for the achievement motive. In J. W. Atkinson (Ed.), *Motives in fantasy, action, and society* (pp. 179–204). Princeton, NJ: Van Nostrand.

Medvec, V. H., Madey, S., & Gilovich, T. (1995). When less is more: Counterfactual thinking and satisfaction among Olympic medal winners. *Journal of Personality and Social Psychology, 69*, 603–610.

Mehler, P. S. (2003). Bulimia nervosa. *New England Journal of Medicine, 349*, 875–881.

Meston, C. M. (1997). Aging and sexuality. *Western Journal of Medicine, 167*, 285–290.

Meston, C. M., & Frohlich, P. F. (2003). Love at first fright: Partner salience moderates roller coaster–induced excitation transfer. *Archives of Sexual Behavior, 32*, 537–544.

Meyer, J. P., & Pepper, S. (1977). Need compatibility and marital adjustment in young married couples. *Journal of Personality and Social Psychology, 35*, 331–342.

Mita, T. H., Dermer, M., & Knight, J. (1977). Reversed facial images and the mere-exposure hypothesis. *Journal of Personality & Social Psychology, 13*, 89–111.

Montoya, R. M., Horton, R. S., & Kirchner, J. (2008). Is actual similarity necessary for attraction? A meta-analysis of actual and perceived similarity. *Journal of Social and Personal Relationships, 25*, 889–992.

Moons, W. G., & Mackie, D. M. (2007). Thinking straight while seeing red: The influence of anger on information processing. *Personality and Social Psychology Bulletin, 33*, 706–720.

Moreland, R. L., & Beach, S. R. (1992). Exposure effects in the classroom: The development of affinity among students. *Journal of Experimental Social Psychology, 28*, 255–276.

Morgenstern, M., Isensee, B., & Hanewinkel, R. (2013). Seeing and liking cigarette advertisements: Is there a 'mere exposure' effect? *European Addiction Research, 19*, 42–46.

Morton, E. W. (1977). On the occurrence and significance of motivation-structural roles in some bird and mammal sounds. *American Naturalist, 111*, 855–869.

Mroczek, D. K., & Kolarz, C. M. (1998). The effect of age on positive and negative affect: A developmental perspective on happiness. *Journal of Personality and Social Psychology, 75*, 1333–1349.

Mroczek, D. K., & Spiro, A. (2005). Change in life satisfaction during adulthood: Findings from the Veteran Affairs normative aging study. *Journal of Personality and Social Psychology, 88*, 189–192.

Mrosovsky, N., & Powley, T. L. (1977). Set points for body weight and fat. *Behavioral Biology, 20*, 205–223.

Murphy, F. C., Nimmo-Smith, I., & Lawrence, A. D. (2003). Functional neuroanatomy of emotion: A meta-analysis. *Cognitive, Affective, & Behavioral Neuroscience, 3*, 207–233.

Murray, H. A. (1938). *Explorations in personality*. New York, NY: Oxford University Press.

Murray, S. H., & Milhausen, R. R. (2012). Sexual desire and relationship duration in young men and women. *Journal of Sex & Marital Therapy, 38*, 28–40.

Murray, S. L., Holmes, J. G., & Griffin, D. W. (1996). The self-fulfilling nature of positive illusions in romantic relationships: Love is not blind but prescient. *Journal of Personality and Social Psychology, 71*, 1155–1180.

Murstein, B. I. (1977). The stimulus-value-role (SVR) theory of dyadic relationship. In S. Duck (Ed.), *Theory and practice in interpersonal attraction* (pp. 105–127). New York, NY: Academic Press.

Myers D. G. (2000). The funds, friends, and faith of happy people. *American Psychologist, 55*, 56–67.

Myers, D. G. (1993b). *The pursuit of happiness*. London, England: Aquarian.

Myers, D. G., & Diener, E. (1996). The pursuit of happiness. *Scientific American*, 70–72.

Nahemow, L., & Lawton, M. P. (1975). Similarity and propinquity in friendship formation. *Journal of Personality and Social Psychology, 32*, 205–213.

National Opinion Research Center (2003). *General social surveys, 1972–2002: Cumulative codebook*. Chicago, IL: Author.

National Research Council. (2003). *The polygraph and lie detection*. Committee to review the scientific evidence on the polygraph. Washington, DC: National Academies Press.

Nettle, D. (2005). *Happiness: The science behind your smile*. Oxford, England: Oxford University Press.

Niedenthal, P. M. (2007). Embodying emotion. *Science, 316*, 1002–1005.

Nisbett, R. E. (1972). Hunger, obesity, and the ventromedial hypothalamus. *Psychological Review, 79*, 433–453.

Norem, J. K. (2001). *The positive power of negative thinking*. New York, NY: Basic Books.

Norem, J. K., & Cantor, N. (1986). Defensive pessimism: "Harnessing" anxiety as motivation. *Journal of Personality and Social Psychology, 52,* 1208–1217.

Norem, J. K., & Chang, E. C. (2002). The positive psychology of negative thinking. *Journal of Clinical Psychology, 37,* 1204–1238.

Office of Technology Assessment. (1990). *The use of integrity tests for pre-employment screening*. Washington, DC: U.S. Congress Office of Technology Assessment.

Oishi, S., Diener, E., & Lucas, R. E. (2007). The optimal level of well-being: Can we be too happy? *Perspectives on Psychological Science, 2,* 346–360.

Olds, J. (1959). Studies of neuropharmacologicals by electrical and chemical manipulation of the brain in animals with chronically implanted electrodes. In P. B. Bradley, P. Deniker, and C. Radouco-Thomas (Eds.), *Neuro-Psychopharmacology* (pp. 20–32). Amsterdam: Elsevier.

O'Leary, K. D., Acevedo, B. P., Aron, A., Huddy, L., & Mashek, D. (2012). Is long-term love more than a rare phenomenon? If so, what are it's correlates? *Social Psychological and Personality Science, 3,* 241–249.

Oliver, M. B., & Hyde, J. S. (1993). Gender differences in sexuality: A meta-analysis. *Psychological Bulletin, 114,* 29–51.

Ones, D. S., Viswesvaran, C., & Schmidt, F. L. (1993). Comprehensive meta-analysis of integrity test validities. *Journal of Applied Psychology, 78,* 679–703.

Ortony, A., & Turner, T. J. (1990). What's basic about basic emotions? *Psychological Review, 97,* 315–331.

Ostwald, P. (1972). The sounds of infancy. *Developmental Medicine and Child Neurology, 14,* 350–361.

Panksepp, J. (2005). Beyond a joke: From animal laughter to human joy? *Science, 208,* 62–63.

Panksepp, J. (2007). Neurologizing the psychology of affects: How appraisal-based constructivism and basic emotion theory can coexist. *Perspectives in Psychological Science, 2,* 281–296.

Park, N., Peterson, C., & Seligman, M. E. P. (2004). Strengths of character and well-being. *Journal of Social and Clinical Psychology, 23,* 603–619.

Patrick, C. J. (Ed.). (2006). *Handbook of psychopathy*. New York, NY: Guilford Press.

Patrick, C. J., & Iacono, W. G. (1989). Psychopathy, threat, and polygraph test accuracy. *Journal of Applied Psychology, 74,* 347–355.

Patterson, C. J. (1992). Children of lesbian and gay parents. *Child Development, 63,* 1025–1042.

Pazhoohi, F., & Liddle, J. R. (2012). Identifying feminine and masculine ranges for waist-to-hip ratio. *Journal of Social, Evolutionary, and Cultural Psychology, 6,* 227–232.

Pew Research Center. (2006, February 13). Are we happy yet? Retrieved from http://pewresearch.org/pubs/301/are-we-happy-yet

Phillips, M. L., Young, A. W., Senior, C., Brammer, M., Andrew, C., Calder, A. J.,... David, A. S. (1997). A specific neural substrate for perceiving facial expressions of disgust. *Nature, 389,* 495–498.

Piper, A. (1993). "Truth serum" and "recovered memories" of sexual abuse: A review of the evidence. *Journal of Psychiatry & Law, 21,* 447–471.

Pittas, A. G., Hariharan, R., Stark, P. C., Hajduk, C. L., Greenberg, A. S., & Roberts, S. B. (2005). Interstitial glucose level is a significant predictor of energy intake in free-living women with healthy body weight. *Journal of Nutrition, 135,* 1070–1074.

Plutchik, R. (2000). *Emotions in the practice of psychotherapy: Clinical implications of affect theories*. Washington, DC: American Psychological Association.

Plutchik, R. (2003). *Emotions and life: Perspectives from psychology, biology, and evolution*. Washington, DC: American Psychological Association.

Plutchik, R., & Kellerman, H. (Eds.). (1986). *Emotion: Theory, research, and experience: Biological foundations of emotion*. New York, NY: Academic Press.

Post, J. M. (2010). The electronic revolution and the virtual communities of cooperation and hatred. Presentation at International Society of Political Psychology. Retrieved from http://www.ispp.org/meetings/abstract/the-electronic-revolution-and-the-virtual-communities-of-cooperation-and-ha

Prinz, J. J. (2004). *Gut reactions: A perceptual theory of emotion*. New York, NY: Oxford University Press.

Provine, R. R. (2000). *Laughter: A scientific investigation*. New York, NY: Viking Press.

Provine, R.R. (2012). *Curious behavior: Yawning, laughing, hiccupping, and beyond*. Cambridge, MA: Belknap Press.

Rainville, P., Bechara, A., Naqvi, N., & Damasio, A. R. (2006). Basic emotions are associated with distinct patterns of cardiorespiratory activity. *International Journal of Psychophysiology, 61,* 5–18.

Reasoner, R. (2000). *Self-esteem and youth: What research has to say about it*. Port Ludlow, WA: International Council for Self-Esteem.

Reed, A. E., & Carstensen, L. L. (2012). The theory behind the age-related positivity effect. *Frontiers in Psychology, 3,* 339. http://dx.doi.org/10.3389/fpsyg.2012.00339

Regan, P. C., & Berscheid, E. (1999). *Lust: What we know about human sexual desire*. Thousand Oaks, CA: Sage.

Reimann, M., & Bechara, A. (2010). The somatic marker framework as a neurological theory of decision-making: Review, conceptual comparisons, and future neuroeconomics research. *Journal of Economic Psychology, 31,* 767–776.

Reisenzein, R. (1983). The Schachter theory of emotion: Two decades later. *Psychological Bulletin, 94,* 239–264.

Resnick, A. G., & Ithman, M. H. (2009). The human sexual response cycle: Psychotropic side effects and treatment strategies. *Psychiatric Annals, 38,* 267–280.

Revelle, W., Humphreys, M. S., Simon, L., & Gilliland, K. (1980). The interactive effect of personality, time of day, and caffeine: A test of the arousal model. *Journal of Experimental Psychology: General, 109,* 1–31.

Rhodes, G., Halberstadt, J., & Brajkovich, G. (2001). Generalization of mere exposure effects to averaged composite faces. *Social Cognition, 19,* 57–70.

Root, T. L., Thornton, L., Lindroos, A. K., Stunkard, A. J., Lichtenstein, P., Pedersen, N. L.,... Bulik, C. M. (2010). Shared and unique genetic and environmental influences on binge eating and night eating: A Swedish twin study. *Eating Behaviors, 11*(2), 92.

Rosenblum, D., & Lewis, M. (1999). The relations among body image, physical attractiveness, and body mass in adolescence. *Child Development, 70,* 50–64.

Rosenfeld, J. P. (2005). "Brain fingerprinting": A critical analysis. *Scientific Review of Mental Health Practice, 4,* 20–37.

Rotenberg, K. J., & Mann, L. (1986). The development of the norm of the reciprocity of self-disclosure and its function in children's attraction to peers. *Child Development, 57,* 1349–1357.

Rottenberg, J., Bylsma, L. M., & Vingerhoets, A. J. J. M. (2008). Is crying beneficial? *Current Directions in Psychological Science, 17,* 400–404.

Rowan, J. (1998). Maslow amended. *Journal of Humanistic Psychology, 38,* 81–92.

Roy, M. M., & Christenfeld, N. J. S. (2004). Do dogs resemble their owners? *Psychological Science, 15,* 361–363.

Rozanski, A. (2012). Exercise as a medical treatment for depression. *Journal of the American College of Cardiology, 60,* 1064–1066.

Rudd, M., Vohs, K. D., & Aaker, J. (2013). Awe expands people's perception of time, alters decision making, and enhances well-being. *Psychological Science,* awaiting page numbers.

Rule, N. O., & Ambady, N. (2008). Brief exposures: Male sexual orientation is accurately perceived at 50 ms. *Journal of Experimental Social Psychology, 44,* 1100–1105.

Ruscio, J. (2005). Exploring controversies in the art and science of polygraph testing. *Skeptical Inquirer, 29,* 34–39.

Russell, J. A. (1994). Is there universal recognition of emotion from facial expression? A review of cross-cultural studies. *Psychological Bulletin, 115,* 102–141.

Sackett, P. R., & Decker, P. J. (1979). Detection of deception in the employment context: A review and critical analysis. *Personnel Psychology, 32,* 487–506.

Sackett, P. R., & Wanek, J. E. E. (1996). New developments in the use of measures of honesty, integrity, conscientiousness, dependability, trustworthiness, and reliability for personnel selection. *Personnel Psychology, 49,* 787–829.

Salmon, P. (2001). Effects of physical exercise on anxiety, depression, and sensitivity to stress: A unifying theory. *Clinical Psychology Review, 21,* 33–61.

Satel, S., & Lilienfeld, S.O. (2013). *Brainwashed: How we are seduced by mindless neuroscience*. New York, NY: Basic Books.

Saxe, L. (1991). Lying: Thoughts of an applied social psychologist. *American Psychologist, 46,* 409–415.

Saxe, L., & Ben-Shakhar, G. (1999). Admissibility of polygraph tests: The application of scientific standards post-Daubert. *Psychology, Public Policy, and Law, 5,* 203–223.

Schachter, S. (1968). Obesity and eating. *Science, 161,* 751–761.

Schachter, S., & Gross, L. (1968). Manipulated time and eating behavior. *Journal of Personality and Social Psychology, 10,* 98–106.

Schachter, S., & Singer, J. E. (1962). Cognitive, social and physiological determinants of emotional state. *Psychological Review, 69,* 379–399.

Scherer, K. R. (1988). Criteria for emotion-antecedent appraisal: A review. In V. Hamilton, G. H. Bower, & N. H. Frijda (Eds.), *Cognitive perspectives on emotion and motivation* (pp. 89–126). Dordrecht: Nijhoff.

Schienle, A., Stark, R., Walter, B., Blecker, C., Ott, U., Kirsch, P.,... Vaitl, D. (2002). The insula is not specifically involved in disgust processing: An fMRI study. *Neuroreport, 13,* 2023–2026.

Schkade, D. A., & Kahneman, D. (1998). Does living in California make people happy? A focusing illusion in judgments of life satisfaction. *Psychological Science, 9,* 340–346.

Schwartz, N. W., Woods, S. C., Porte, D., Seeley, R. J., & Baskin, D. G. (2000). Central nervous system control of food intake. *Nature, 404,* 661–671.

Scott, V., McDade, D. M., & Luckman, S. M. (2007). Rapid changes in the sensitivity of the arcuate nucleus neurons to central ghrelin in relation to feeding status. *Physiology and Behavior, 90,* 180–185.

Segal, M. W. (1974). Alphabet and attraction: An unobtrusive measure of the effect of propinquity in a field setting. *Journal of Personality and Social Psychology, 30,* 654–657.

Segerstrom, S. C. (2005). Optimism and immunity: Do positive thoughts always lead to positive effects? *Brain, Behavior, and Immunity, 19,* 195–200.

Seligman, M. E. P., & Csikszentmihalyi, M. (2000). Positive psychology: An introduction. *American Psychologist, 55,* 5–14.

Seligman, M. E. P., & Pawelski, J. O. (2003). Positive psychology: FAQs. *Psychological Inquiry, 14,* 159–163.

Sevdalis, N., & Harvey, N. (2007) Biased forecasting of postdecisional affect. *Psychological Science, 18,* 678–681.

Sheldon, K. M., & King, L. (2001). Why positive psychology is necessary. *American Psychologist, 56*, 216–217.

Sheldon, K. M., & Lyubomirsky, S. (2006). How to increase and sustain positive emotion: The effects of expressing gratitude and visualizing best possible selves. *The Journal of Positive Psychology, 1*, 73–82.

Shiota, M. N., Keltner, D., & Mossman, A. (2007). The nature of awe: Elicitors, appraisals, and effects on self-concept. *Cognition and Emotion, 21*, 944–963.

Shoemaker, G. E., & Fagen, J. W. (1984). Stimulus preference and its effect on visual habituation and dishabituation in four-month-old infants. *Genetic Psychology Monographs, 109*, 3–18.

Sieff, E. M., Dawes, R. M., & Loewenstein, G. (1999). Anticipated versus actual reaction to HIV test results. *American Journal of Psychology, 112*, 297–311.

Singh, D. (1993). Adaptive significance of female physical attractiveness: Role of waist-to-hip ratio. *Journal of Personality and Social Psychology, 65*, 293–307.

Singh, D. (1995). Female judgment of male attractiveness and desirability for relationships: Role of waist-to-hip ratio and financial status. *Journal of Personality and Social Psychology, 69*, 1089–1101.

Smith, G. P. (1996). The direct and indirect controls of meal size. *Neuroscience Biobehavioral Review, 20*, 40–46.

Smith, G. T., Spillane, N. S., & Annus, A. M. (2006). Implications of an emerging integration of universal and culturally-specific psychologies. *Perspectives on Psychological Science, 1*, 211–233.

Sommers, C. H., & Satel, S. (2005). *One nation under therapy: How the helping culture is eroding self-reliance.* New York, NY: St. Martin's Press.

Soper, B., Milford, G., & Rosenthal, G. (1995). Belief when evidence does not support theory. *Psychology & Marketing, 12*, 415–422.

Spitzer, R. (2003). Can some gay men and lesbians change their sexual orientation? 200 participants reporting a change from homosexual to heterosexual orientation. *Archives of Sexual Behavior, 32*, 403–417.

Spitzer, R. L. (2012). Spitzer reassesses his 2003 study of reparative therapy of homosexuality. *Archives of Sexual Behavior*, 1–2.

Sprecher, S. (1998). Insider's perspectives on reasons for attraction to a close other. *Social Psychology Quarterly, 61*, 287–300.

Sprecher, S., Barbee, A., & Schwartz, P. (1995). "Was it good for you, too?": Gender differences in first sexual experiences. *Journal of Sex Research, 32*, 3–15.

Stathopoulou, G., Powers, M. B., Berry, A. C., Smits, J. A. J., & Otto, M. W. (2006). Exercise interventions for mental health: A quantitative and qualitative review. *Clinical Psychology: Science and Practice, 13*, 179–193.

Sternberg, R. J. (1986). A triangular theory of love. *Psychological Review, 93*, 119–135.

Sternberg, R. J. (2003a). A duplex theory of hate: Development and application to terrorism, massacres, and genocide. *Review of General Psychology, 7*, 299–328.

Sternberg, R. J. (2004). *Psychology* (4th ed.). Belmont, CA: Wadsworth.

Stice, E., Cameron, R., Killen, J. D., Hayward, C., & Taylor, C. B. (1999). Naturalistic weight reduction efforts prospectively predict growth in relative weight and onset of obesity among female adolescents. *Journal of Consulting and Clinical Psychology, 67*, 967–974.

Stice, E., Presnell, K., Shaw, H., & Rhode, P. (2005). Psychological and behavioral risk factors for obesity onset in adolescent girls: A prospective study. *Journal of Consulting and Clinical Psychology, 73*, 195–202.

Stix, G. (2008). Can fMRI really tell if you're lying? *Scientific American.* Retrieved from http://www.scientificamerican.com/article.cfm?id=new-lie-detector

Strack, F., Martin, L., & Stepper, S. (1988). Inhibiting and facilitating conditions of the human smile: A nonobtrusive test of the facial feedback hypothesis. *Journal of Personality and Social Psychology, 54*, 768–777.

Stunkard, A. (1975). Satiety is a conditioned reflex. *Journal of Psychosomatic Medicine, 37*, 383–387.

Sullivan, P. F. (1995). Mortality of anorexia nervosa. *American Journal of Psychiatry, 152*, 1073–1074.

Swami, V., & Furnham, A. (2008). *The body beautiful: Evolutionary and socio-cultural perspectives.* Basingstoke, England: Palgrave Macmillan.

Swann, W. B., Jr., Chang-Schneider, C., & McClarty, K. (2007). Do our self-views matter? Self-concept and self-esteem in everyday life. *American Psychologist, 62*, 84–94.

Swann, W. B., Jr., & Pelham, B. W. (2002). Who wants out when the going gets good? Psychological investment and preference for self-verifying college roommates. *Journal of Self and Identity, 1*, 219–233.

Symons, D. (1979). *The evolution of human sexuality.* New York, NY: Oxford University Press.

Szczucka, K. (2012). Attraction at first fright? What Dutton & Aron really demonstrated almost 40 years ago. *Polish Psychological Bulletin, 43*, 191–198.

Tassinary, L. G., & Hansen, K. A. (1998). A critical test of the waist-to-hip ratio hypothesis of female physical attractiveness. *Psychological Science, 9*, 150–155.

Teitelbaum, P., & Epstein, A. N. (1962). The lateral hypothalamic syndrome: Recovery of feeding and drinking after lateral hypothalamic lesions. *Psychological Review, 69*, 74–90.

Tennison, M. N., & Moreno, J. D. (2012). Neuroscience, ethics, and national security: The state of the art. *PLoS Biology, 10*(3), e1001289.

Tennov, D. (1979). *Love and limerence: The experience of being in love.* New York, NY: Stein & Day.

Thompson, J. K., Heinberg, L. J., Altabe, M. N., & Tantleff-Dunn, S. (2004). *Exacting beauty: Theory, assessment, and treatment of body image disturbance.* Washington, DC: American Psychological Association.

Tiggemann, M., & Pickering, A. S. (1996). Role of television in adolescent women's body dissatisfaction and drive for thinness. *International Journal of Eating Disorders, 20*, 199–203.

Todorovic, A., & Haskell-Luevano, C. (2005). A review of melanocortin receptor small molecule ligands. *Peptides, 26*, 2026–2036.

Tomkins, S. S. (1962). *Affect, imagery, consciousness: Vol. 1: The positive affects.* New York, NY: Springer.

Tomkins, S. S., & McCarter, R. (1964). What and where are the primary affects? Some evidence for a theory. *Perceptual and Motor Skills, 18*, 119–158.

Tracy, J. L., & Robins, R. W. (2007). Emerging insights into the nature and function of pride. *Current Directions in Psychological Science, 16*, 147–150.

Trimble, M. (2012). *Why humans like to cry: The evolutionary origins of tragedy.* New York, NY: Oxford University Press.

Vaillancourt, T. (2012). Students aggress against professors in reaction to receiving poor grades: An effect moderated by student narcissism and self-esteem. *Aggressive Behavior.* http://dx.doi.org/10.1002/ab.21450

Valentine, T., Darling, S., & Donnelly, M. (2004). Why are average faces attractive? The effect of view and averageness on the attractiveness of female faces. *Psychonomic Bulletin & Review, 11*, 482–487.

Van Ijzendoorn, M. H., & Bakermans-Kranenburg, M. J. (2012). Differential susceptibility experiments: Going beyond correlational evidence. *Developmental Psychology, 48*, 769–774.

Van Litalie, T. B. (1990). The glucostatic theory 1953–1988: Roots and branches. *International Journal of Obesity, 14*, 1–10.

Veenhoven, R. (2012). World database of happiness. Retrieved from http://www1.eur.nl/fsw/happiness

Verr̈ier, D. B. (2012). Evidence for the influence of the mere-exposure effect on voting in the Eurovision Song Contest. *Judgment and Decision Making, 7*, 639–643.

Vohs, K. D., Mead, N. L., & Goode, M. R. (2006). The psychological consequences of money. *Science, 314*, 1154–1156.

Vrij, A. (2008). Nonverbal dominance versus verbal accuracy: A plea to change police practice. *Criminal Justice and Behavior, 35*, 1323–1335.

Vrij, A., Granhag, P. A., & Porter, S. B. (2010). Pitfalls and opportunities in nonverbal and verbal lie detection. *Psychological Science in the Public Interest, 11*, 89–121.

Vrught, A., & Kerkstra, A. (1984). Sex differences in nonverbal communication. *Semiotica, 50*, 141.

Vytal, K., and Hamann, S. (2010). Neuroimaging support for discrete neural correlates of basic emotions: A voxel-based meta-analysis, *Journal of Cognitive Neuroscience, 12*, 2864–2885.

Waid, W. M., & Orne, M. T. (1982). The physiological detection of deception. *American Scientist, 70*, 402–409.

Walsh, B. T. (1993). Binge eating in bulimia nervosa. In C. G. Fairburn & G. T. Wilson (Eds.), *Binge eating: Nature, assessment, and treatment* (pp. 37–49). New York, NY: Guilford Press.

Walsh, B. T., Hadigan, C. M., Kissileff, H. R., & LaChaussee, J. L. (1992). Bulimia nervosa: A syndrome of feast and famine. In G. H. Anderson & S. H. Kennedy (Eds.), *The biology of feast and famine.* New York, NY: Academic Press.

Walster, E., Berscheid, E., & Walster, G. W. (1973). New directions in equity theory and research. *Journal of Personality and Social Psychology, 25*, 151–176.

Walter, C. (2006). Why do we cry? *Scientific American Mind, 17*(6), 44.

Wansink, B. (2009). *Mindless eating: Why we eat more than we think.* New York, NY: Bantam.

Wansink, B., Painter, J. E., & North, J. (2005). Bottomless bowls: Why visual cues of portion size may influence intake. *Obesity Research, 13*, 93–100.

Warren, G., Schertler, E., & Bull, P. (2009). Detecting deception from emotional and emotional cues. *Journal of Nonverbal Behavior, 33*, 59–69.

Watson, D., & Clark, L. A. (1984). Negative affectivity: The disposition to experience negative emotional states. *Psychological Bulletin, 96*, 465–490.

Wegner, D. M. (2002). *The illusion of conscious will.* Cambridge, MA: MIT Press.

White, A. (2006). [Map]. *A global projection of subjective well-being: The first published map of world happiness.* Retrieved from http://news.bbc.co.uk/2/shared/bsp/hi/pdfs/28_07_06_happiness_map.pdf

Widmer, E. D., Treas, J., & Newcomb, R. (1998). Attitudes toward nonmarital sex in 24 countries. *Journal of Sex Research, 35*, 349–357.

Williams, K. W., Scott, M. M., & Elmquist, J. K. (2009). From observation to experimentation: Leptin action in the mediobasal hypothalamus. *The American Journal of Clinical Nutrition, 89*(3), 985S–990S.

Williams, T. J., Pepitone, M. E., Christensen, S. E., Cooke, B. M., Huberman, A. D., Breedlove, N. J.,... Breedlove, S. M. (2000). Finger length patterns and human sexual orientation. *Nature, 404*, 455–456.

Williamson, D. A., Womble, L. G., Smeets, M. A. M., Netemeyer, R. G., Thaw, J. M., Kutlesic, V., Gleaves, D. H. (2002). Latent structure of eating disorder symptoms: A factor analytic and taxometric investigation. *American Journal of Psychiatry, 159*, 412–418.

Wilson, N. (2003). Commercializing mental health issues: Entertainment, advertising, and psychological advice. In S. O. Lilienfeld, S. J. Lynn, & J. M. Lohr (Eds.), *Science and pseudoscience in clinical psychology* (pp. 425–459). New York, NY: Guilford Press.

Wilson, T. D. (2002). *Strangers to ourselves: Discovering the adaptive unconscious.* Cambridge, MA: Harvard University Press.

Winter, A. (2005). The making of "truth serum." *Bulletin of the History of Medicine, 79,* 500–533.

Winton, W. M. (1987). Do introductory textbooks present the Yerkes-Dodson law correctly? *American Psychologist, 42,* 202–203.

Witelson, S. F., Kigar, D. L., Scamvougeras, A., Kideckel, D. M., Buck, B., Stanchev, P. L.,... Black, S. (2008). Corpus callosum anatomy in right-handed homosexual and heterosexual men. *Archives of Sexual Behavior, 37,* 857–863.

Wojciszke, B. (2002). From the first sight to the last breath: A six-stage model of love. *Polish Psychological Bulletin, 33,* 15–25.

Woods, S. C., Seeley, R. J., Porte, D., & Schwartz, N. W. (1998). Signals that regulate food intake and energy homeostasis. *Science, 280,* 1378–1383.

Wooldridge, T., & Pauline "Polly" Lytle. (2012). An overview of anorexia nervosa in males. *Eating Disorders, 20*(5), 368–378.

Yerkes, R. M., & Dodson, J. D. (1908). The relation of strength of stimulus to rapidity of habit-formation. *Journal of Comparative Neurology and Psychology, 18,* 459–482.

Young, L., & Nestle, M. (2002). The contribution of expanding portion sizes to the US obesity epidemic. *American Journal of Public Health, 92,* 246–249.

Young, M., Denny, G., Young, T., & Luquis, R. (2000). Sexual satisfaction among married women. *American Journal of Health Studies, 16,* 73–84.

Young, S. M., & Pinsky, D. (2006). Narcissism and celebrity. *Journal of Research in Personality, 40,* 463–471.

Zajonc, R. B. (1968). Attitudinal effects of mere exposure. *Journal of Personality and Social Psychology Monographs, 9,* 1–27.

Zajonc, R. B. (1984). On the primacy of affect. *American Psychologist, 39,* 117–123.

Zajonc, R. B. (2001). Mere exposure: A gateway to the subliminal. *Current Directions in Psychological Science, 10,* 225–228.

Zajonc, R. B., Murphy, S. T., & Inglehart, M. (1989). Feeling and facial efference: Implications for the vascular theory of emotion. *Psychological Review, 96,* 395–416.

Zaslow, J. (2007). The most-praised generation goes to work. *Wall Street Journal.* Retrieved from http://online.wsj.com/article/SB117702894815776259-search.html

Zautra, A. J. (2003). *Emotions, stress, and health.* New York, NY: Oxford University Press.

Zietsch, B. P., Verweij, K. J. H., Heath, A. C., Madden, P. A. F., Martin, N. G., Nelson, E. C., & Lynskey, M. T. (2012). Do shared etiological factors contribute to the relationship between sexual orientation and depression? *Psychological Medicine, 1*(1), 1–12.

Zion, I. B., Tessler, R., Cohen, L., Lerer, E., Raz, Y., Bachner-Melman, R.,... Ebstein, R. (2006). Polymorphisms in the dopamine D4 receptor gene (DRD4) contribute to individual differences in human sexual behavior: Desire, arousal and sexual function. *Journal for Molecular Psychiatry, 11,* 782–786.

Zuckerman, M., DePaulo, B. M., & Rosenthal, R. (1981). Verbal and non-verbal communication of deception. In L. Berkowitz (Ed.), *Advances in experimental and social psychology* (Vol. 14, pp. 1–59). New York, NY: Academic Press.

Zuckerman, M., & Hopkins, J. (1966). Hallucinations or dreams: A study of arousal levels and reported visual sensations during sensory deprivation. *Perceptual and Motor Skills, 22,* 447–459.

Zuger, B. (1988). Is early effeminate behavior in boys early homosexuality. *Comprehensive Psychiatry, 29,* 509–519.

Zullow, H. M., Oettingen, G., Peterson, C., & Seligman, M. E. P. (1988). Pessimistic explanatory style in the historical record. *American Psychologist, 43,* 673–682.

Credits

Credits listed in order of appearance.

Text: Linder, K. (2013). Your killer emotions. Austin Texas: Greenleaf Book Press. **Figure 1:** From Aronoff, J., Barclay, A. M., & Stevenson, L. A. (1988) The recognition of threatening facial stimuli. Journal of Personality and Social Psychology, 1988, April 54 (4), 647–655. **Figure 3:** Nick Epley, 2006 Pairs of polygons used in the mere exposure research of Robert Zajonc from Laboratory Manual—Cognitive Science in Context Laboratory—Spring 2006. (Cornell Univerisity). http://www.csic.cornell.edu/201/subliminal/#appB. Printed with permission from Nick Epley. **Text:** Yogi Berra. **Figure 4:** 2010 Microsoft Corp. Used by permission. **Figure 5:** Ekman, P., O'Sullivan, M., & Frank, M. G. (1999). A few can catch a liar. Psychological Science, 10, 263–266. **Figure 6:** Based on Ekman, P., O'Sullivan, M., & Frank, M. G. (1999). A few can catch a liar. Psychological Science, 10, 263–266. **Text:** Martin, D. (2006, November 20). The truth about happiness may surprise you.

Retrieved from www.cnn.com/2006/HEALTH/conditions/11/10/happiness.overview/index.html. **Figure 11:** Adapted from "Are We Happy Yet?" Pew Research Center, Washington, D.C. (February 13, 2006). http://www.pewsocialtrends.org/2006/02/13/are-we-happy-yet/. **Figure 14:** Rathsum Spencer A.; Nevid, Jeffrey S.; Fichner-Rathus, Lois, Human Sexuality in a World of Diversity, 7th Ed., © 2008, p.149. Reprinted and electronically reproduced by permission of Pearson Education, Inc. Upper Saddle River, New Jersey. **Text:** Ford, C. S., & Beach, F. (1951). Patterns of sexual behavior. New York: Harper and Row. **Text:** Hatfield, E., & Walster, G. W. (1978). A new look at love. Reading, MA: Addison-Wesley. **Text:** Symons, D. (1979). The evolution of human sexuality. New York: Oxford University Press. **Text:** Elizabeth Barrett Browning.

Photo Credits

Photo Credits listed in order of appearance.

Stress, Coping, and Health

Stress, Coping, and Health

THE MIND–BODY INTERCONNECTION

Think About It

Do most people who encounter highly aversive events develop posttraumatic stress disorder?

Are some people more prone to heart attacks than other people are?

Are crash diets that promise quick and enduring weight loss effective?

Are acupuncture and other alternative medical treatments more effective than traditional medical procedures?

Can placebos affect brain activity?

Firefighters and police officers who merely witness traumatic events often experience high levels of stress.

Stress, Coping, and Health

🔊 **Listen** in **MyPsychLab** to chapter audio

Tuesday, September 11, 2001, is a day few Americans will forget. Across the country, people were glued to their television sets watching in horror as two loaded passenger planes flew into the Twin Towers of the World Trade Center (WTC) in New York City. In the worst terrorist attack in American history, more than 2,700 people were killed at the WTC alone. Hundreds more were killed when terrorists crashed two other planes—one into the Pentagon and one into a field in rural Pennsylvania, where passengers had attempted to regain control of the plane.

In the aftermath of this tragedy, inspiring stories emerged of courageous first responders—firefighters, paramedics, police, and emergency service workers—who risked their lives to save others. Nearly 400 people who participated in rescue operations died on 9/11. Many others survived to tell their stories. The following accounts by first responders at the WTC (McNally, 2001) are a sample of reactions to some of the most stressful circumstances imaginable—and some unimaginable.

- Juana Lomi, a paramedic, raced to the WTC and survived the collapse of the towers. "It was an overwhelming feeling of fear, horror—and not being able to do more. There were hundreds of people that needed to be treated. I was at risk of losing my life, but I had to stay and help other people."

- Louie Cacchioli, a firefighter, saved the lives of many people. "I stepped outside after bringing about 40 or 50 people down a stairway. I looked around. It was crazy. Somebody yelled, 'Look out! The tower's coming down!' I started running. I tossed my air mask away to make myself lighter. Next thing I know, there's a big black ball of smoke. I threw myself on my knees, and I'm crying. I said to myself, 'Oh, my God, I'm going to die.' I was crawling. Then—the biggest miracle thing in the world. My hands came onto an air mask. It still had air. Another 15 seconds, I wouldn't have made it."

- Mike Hanson, a member of the Emergency Services Unit of the New York Police Department, used a torch to cut through steel to rescue people. "Emotionally, it's taken a toll. Just like I work in small sectors of massive destruction, I have to take it in little pieces mentally. That's the only way I can manage it."

These stories raise fascinating questions that are crucial to the study of stress, coping, and health. What happens after we experience a traumatic event? How do people like Louie Cacchioli fare following a close brush with death? Do the effects reverberate long afterward, producing lasting psychological or physical illnesses? Or can many people manage to cope, even thrive, in the aftermath of harrowing circumstances?

In this chapter, we'll explore the myriad ways in which people cope with stressful circumstances, ranging from the annoyance of a computer crash to the terror of surviving a plane crash. We'll also examine the complex interplay between stress and physical health. Ronald Kessler and his colleagues (Kessler et al., 1995) studied nearly 6,000 men and women in the general population and found that most (60–90 percent) had experienced at least one potentially traumatic event, such as a sexual or physical assault or car accident. So it's actually the unusual person who doesn't experience severe stress in his or her lifetime (de Vries & Olff, 2009; Ozer et al., 2003). Groups at especially high risk for stressful events include the young and unmarried, African Americans, and people of low socioeconomic status (Kessler et al., 1994; Miranda & Green, 1999; Turner, Wheaton, & Lloyd, 1995). Women are more likely than men to experience sexual assault and child abuse, but less likely to experience nonsexual assaults, accidents, disasters, fires, or wartime combat (Tolin & Foa, 2006). Many people assume that individuals who live in rural areas or nonindustrialized countries experience minimal stress compared with residents of urban and more developed areas. Yet scientists have discovered little support for this popular belief: Stress-producing events are widespread among all sectors of society (Bigbee, 1990).

Fortunately, exposure to events like Hurricane Katrina, frontline combat in Afghanistan, the 2010 earthquake in Haiti—or even the horrific 2012 school shooting in Newtown, Connecticut—doesn't guarantee that people will be traumatized for life. Herein lies another case in which scientific research contradicts popular psychology. Many self-help books inform us that most people require psychological help in the face of stressful circumstances (Sommers & Satel, 2005). Some companies dispense squadrons of grief counselors to help people cope with the upshot of stressful events; these companies often assume that without psychological help, most witnesses to trauma are doomed to serious psychological problems. In 2007, grief counselors arrived at the scene to help traumatized college students deal with the horrific shootings at Virginia Tech, and in 1998, they even traveled to the Boston Public Library to help librarians deal with their feelings of loss following the destruction of books in a flood.

Yet we'll discover in this chapter that even in the face of horrific circumstances like shootings and natural disasters, most of us are surprisingly resilient (Bonanno, 2004; Bonanno, Westphal, & Mancini, 2011). Even most victims of child sexual abuse turn out to be psychologically healthy adults, although there are certainly exceptions (Rind, Tromovitch, & Bauserman, 1998). Because practicing psychologists tend to see only those people who react emotionally to stress—after all, the healthy people don't come for help—they probably overestimate most people's fragility and underestimate their resilience, an error sometimes called the *clinician's illusion* (Cohen & Cohen, 1984).

Before we discuss why some people thrive and others nosedive when confronted with stressful life events, we'll consider the fundamental question of what stress is. We'll then explore competing views of stress, the mind–body link responsible for stress-related disorders, how we cope with stressful situations, and the rapidly growing fields of health psychology and alternative medicine.

What Is Stress?

1   Explain how stress is defined and approached in different ways.
2   Identify different approaches to measuring stress.

Before we proceed further, it's important to distinguish two terms—*stress* and *trauma*—that are commonly confused. **Stress**—a type of response—consists of the tension, discomfort, or physical symptoms that arise when a situation, called a *stressor*—a type of stimulus—strains our ability to cope effectively. A *traumatic* event is a stressor that's so severe that it can produce long-term psychological or health consequences.

The field's thinking about stress has evolved over the years (Cooper & Dewe, 2004). Before the 1940s, scientists rarely used the term *stress* outside the engineering profession (Hayward, 1960), where it referred to stresses on materials and building structures. A building was said to withstand stress if it didn't collapse under intense pressure. It wasn't until 1944 that the term *stress* found its way into the psychological literature (Jones & Bright, 2001). This engineering analogy highlights the notion that "if the body were like a machine and machines are subject to wear and tear then so too would be the body" (Doublet, 2000, p. 48). But just as two buildings can withstand different amounts of stress before weakening and collapsing, people differ widely in their personal resources, the significance they attach to stressful events, and their ability to grapple with them.

Stress in the Eye of the Beholder: Three Approaches

Researchers have approached the study of stress in three different, yet interrelated and complementary ways (Kessler, Price, & Wortman, 1985). Each approach has yielded valuable insights and, when considered together, illuminate the big and small events that generate distress and the ways we perceive and respond to stressful situations.

STRESSORS AS STIMULI. The *stressors as stimuli* approach focuses on identifying different types of stressful events, ranging from job loss to combat. This approach has pinpointed categories of events that most of us find dangerous and unpredictable (Collins et al., 2003; Costa & McCrae, 1990). For example, pregnancy is often a joyous yet stressful event, fraught with uncertainties, including concerns about the child's health. Women who are highly anxious or experience negative life events during pregnancy are more likely to

Some researchers call the psychological and physical response to a stressor "strain," much as a material can be said to be strained when under stress.

The stress of unemployment includes not only the frustration and despair of looking for a new job, but also the economic hardship of living on a sharply reduced income.

 Simulate in **MyPsychLab** the **Experiment:** Stress and Health

stress
the tension, discomfort, or physical symptoms that arise when a situation, called a stressor—a type of stimulus—strains our ability to cope effectively

In 2012, Hurricane Sandy cut a wide swath of devastation across the east coast of the United States, killing at least 106 people, destroying the homes of thousands, and uprooting families.

Emotion-focused coping may encourage people who've divorced to begin dating again.

Explore in **MyPsychLab** the **Concept:**
The Effect of Cognitive Appraisal on Responses to Stressors

corticosteroid
stress hormone that activates the body and prepares us to respond to stressful circumstances

primary appraisal
initial decision regarding whether an event is harmful

secondary appraisal
perceptions regarding our ability to cope with an event that follows primary appraisal

problem-focused coping
coping strategy by which we problem-solve and tackle life's challenges head-on

emotion-focused coping
coping strategy that features a positive outlook on feelings or situations accompanied by behaviors that reduce painful emotions

deliver their babies early—3–5 weeks before normal gestation of 40–42 weeks—compared with women who experience more typical worries (Dunkel-Schetter, 2009). When people retire, the combination of low income and physical disability can make matters worse, suggesting that stressful situations can produce cumulative effects (Smith et al., 2005). The stressors as stimuli approach also identifies the people who are most susceptible to stress following different events. For example, college freshmen show a greater response to such negative life events as the breakup of a relationship compared with older men or women (Jackson & Finney, 2002).

STRESS AS A RESPONSE. Stress researchers also study *stress as a response*—they assess people's psychological and physical reactions to stressful circumstances. Typically, scientists expose participants to stress-producing stimuli in the laboratory; in other cases, they study people who've encountered real-life stressors. Then they measure a host of outcome variables: stress-related feelings such as depression, hopelessness, hostility, and physiological responses such as increases in heart rate and the release of stress hormones called **corticosteroids**. These hormones activate the body and prepare us for stressful circumstances.

Highly stressful life events such as disasters can exert positive as well as negative effects on people and communities. For example, disasters can unify communities and bring out the best in us, as our examples of first responders underscores. Christopher Peterson and Martin Seligman (2003) conducted a survey of character strengths of 4,817 Americans before the 9/11 terrorist attacks and within two months afterward. After the attacks, kindness, teamwork, leadership, gratitude, hope, love, and spirituality increased. One team of researchers performed a linguistic analysis on the diaries of 1,084 users of an online journaling service two months before and two months after the 9/11 attacks. Forty-five percent of the entries after the attack dealt with a larger social group, such as the community and nation, in contrast with none of the entries before the attack (Cohen, Mehl, & Pennebaker, 2004). These findings suggest that stressful circumstances that touch the lives of an entire community can increase social awareness, cement interpersonal bonds, and enhance a variety of positive personal characteristics. Yet the effects of highly aversive events, for good or ill, are often temporary, with the most negative aftereffects seen in people with preexisting psychological problems or prior trauma exposure (Bonanno et al., 2010).

STRESS AS A TRANSACTION. Stress is a subjective experience; not all people react to the same stressful events in the same way. Some people are devastated by the breakup of a meaningful relationship, whereas others are optimistic about the opportunity to start afresh. Researchers who study *stress as a transaction* between people and their environments examine the interaction between potentially stressful life events and how people interpret and cope with them (Coyne & Holroyd, 1982; Lazarus & Folkman, 1984). Richard Lazarus and his coworkers contended that a critical factor influencing whether we experience an event as stressful is our appraisal, that is, evaluation, of the event. When we encounter a potentially threatening event, we initially engage in **primary appraisal**. That is, we first decide whether the event is harmful before making a **secondary appraisal** about how well we can cope with it (Lazarus & Folkman, 1984).

When we believe we can't cope, we're more likely to experience a full-blown stress reaction than when we believe we can (Lazarus, 1999). When we're optimistic and think we can achieve our goals, we're especially likely to engage in **problem-focused coping**, a strategy in which we tackle life's challenges head-on (Carver & Scheier, 1999; Lazarus & Folkman, 1984). When we earn a disappointing grade on a test, we may analyze why we fell short and devise a workable plan to improve our performance on the next test. When situations arise that we can't avoid or control, we're more likely to adopt **emotion-focused coping**, a strategy in which we try to place a positive spin on our feelings or predicaments and engage in behaviors to reduce painful emotions (Carver, Scheier, & Weintraub, 1989; Lazarus & Folkman, 1984). After the breakup of a relationship, we may remind ourselves that we were unhappy months before it occurred and reenter the dating arena.

No Two Stresses Are Created Equal: Measuring Stress

Measuring stress is a tricky business, largely because what's exceedingly stressful for one person, such as an argument with a boss, may be a mere annoyance for another. Two scales—the Social Readjustment Rating Scale and the Hassles Scale—endeavor to gauge the nature and impact of different stressful events.

MAJOR LIFE EVENTS. Adopting the view that stressors are stimuli, David Holmes and his colleagues developed the Social Readjustment Rating Scale (SRRS), the first of many efforts to measure life events systematically. The SRRS is based on 43 life events such as "jail term" and "personal injury or illness," ranked in terms of their stressfulness (Holmes & Rahe, 1967; Miller & Rahe, 1997). Studies using the SRRS and related measures indicate that the number of stressful events people report over the previous year or so is associated with a variety of physical disorders (Dohrenwend & Dohrenwend, 1974; Holmes & Masuda, 1974) and psychological disorders like depression (Coyne, 1992; Holahan & Moos, 1991; Schmidt et al., 2004).

Nevertheless, the sheer number of stressful life events is far from a perfect predictor of who'll become physically or psychologically ill (Coyne & Racioppo, 2000). That's because this approach to measuring stressors doesn't consider other crucial factors, including people's interpretation of events, coping behaviors and resources, and difficulty recalling events accurately (Coyne & Racioppo, 2000; Lazarus, 1999). In addition, it neglects to take into account some of the more "chronic," or ongoing, stressors that many individuals experience. Even subtle forms of discrimination or differential treatment based on race, gender, sexual orientation, or religion, for example, can be a significant source of stress even though they rarely are prompted by or lead to a single stressful event we can check off a list. This approach also neglects the fact that some stressful life events, like divorce and troubles with the boss, can be *consequences* rather than *causes* of people's psychological problems (Depue & Monroe, 1986). That's because people's psychological difficulties, such as severe depression and anxiety, can create a host of interpersonal problems, such as difficult interactions with loved ones and coworkers.

HASSLES: DON'T SWEAT THE SMALL STUFF. We've all had days when just about everything goes wrong and everybody seems to get on our nerves: Our daily lives are often loaded with **hassles**, minor nuisances that strain our ability to cope. But can lots of hassles add up to be as taxing as the monumental events that shake the foundations of our world?

Researchers developed the Hassles Scale to measure how stressful events, ranging from small annoyances to major daily pressures, impact our adjustment (DeLongis, Folkman, & Lazarus, 1988; Kanner et al., 1981). Both major life events and hassles are associated with poor general health, but the frequency and perceived severity of hassles are actually better predictors of physical health, depression, and anxiety than are major life events (Fernandez & Sheffield, 1996; Kanner et al., 1981).

Researchers have questioned whether some items on the Hassles Scale, such as difficulties with relaxing and insomnia, may reflect symptoms of psychological disorders such as depression or anxiety, rather than hassles themselves (Monroe, 1983). To address this question, the scale developers (DeLongis et al., 1988) revised the scale by removing all words related to psychological symptoms and found that hassles were still associated with health outcomes.

Another possibility researchers have considered is that major, not minor, stressful events are the real culprits because they set us off when we already feel hassled or create hassles with which we then need to cope. To test this alternative hypothesis, researchers have used statistical procedures to show that even when the influence of major life events is subtracted from the mix, hassles still predict psychological adjustment (Forshaw, 2002; Kanner et al., 1981). These findings suggest that everyday hassles do indeed contribute to stress.

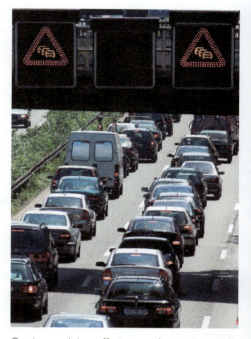

Getting stuck in traffic is one of many "hassles" we encounter in our daily lives. Research suggests that such hassles can be quite stressful over the long haul.

◄ **CORRELATION VS. CAUSATION**
Can we be sure that A causes B?

hassle
minor annoyance or nuisance that strains our ability to cope

◄ **RULING OUT RIVAL HYPOTHESES**
Have important alternative explanations for the findings been excluded?

◄ **RULING OUT RIVAL HYPOTHESES**
Have important alternative explanations for the findings been excluded?

Simulate in **MyPsychLab** the **Experiment:** How Stressed Are You?

Study and **Review** in **MyPsychLab**

We've learned that measuring stress is no easy feat. In response to this challenge, researchers have devised interview-based methods, which provide a more in-depth picture of life stress than self-report measures. Interviewers can identify the positive and negative events that people experience as stressful, distinguish ongoing from "one-shot" stressors, and consider how events interact to produce physical and psychological problems (Dohrenwend, 2006; Monroe, 2008). Still, in assessing stress, researchers must balance the rich information yield from interviews with the ease of administration and efficiency of questionnaires.

Assess Your Knowledge   FACT or FICTION?

1. Most people at one time or another will experience an extremely stressful event.
    True / False

2. The effects of stressors can be cumulative.   **True / False**

3. Natural disasters may sometimes result in stronger community bonds.   **True / False**

4. According to the stress as a transaction viewpoint, almost all people respond to stressful events in the same way.   **True / False**

5. Major life events have a greater effect on adjustment than do everyday hassles.
    True / False

Answers: 1. T; 2. T; 3. T; 4. F; 5. F

How We Adapt to Stress: Change and Challenge

3   Describe Selye's general adaptation syndrome.

4   Describe the diversity of stress responses.

As any of us who's had to confront a harrowing event, like a car accident or high-pressure interview for a big job, knows, adapting to stress isn't easy. Yet natural selection has endowed us with a set of responses for coping with anxiety-provoking circumstances.

The Mechanics of Stress: Selye's General Adaptation Syndrome

In 1956, Canadian physician Hans Selye ignited the field of modern-day stress research by publishing *The Stress of Life*, a landmark book that unveiled his decades of study on the effects of prolonged stress on the body. Selye's genius was to recognize a connection between the stress response of animals, including stomach ulcers and increases in the size of the adrenal gland, which produces stress hormones, and that of physically ill patients, who showed a consistent pattern of stress-related responses. Dovetailing with the engineering analogy we've already discussed, Selye believed that too much stress leads to breakdowns. He argued that we're equipped with a sensitive physiology that responds to stressful circumstances by kicking us into high gear. He called the pattern of responding to stress the **general adaptation syndrome (GAS)**. According to Selye, all prolonged stressors take us through three stages of adaptation: *alarm*, *resistance*, and *exhaustion* (see **FIGURE 1**). To illustrate key aspects of the GAS and the extent to which our appraisals determine our reactions to stress, let's consider the experience of a hypothetical person, named Mark, who's terrified of flying.

THE ALARM REACTION. Selye's first stage, the *alarm reaction*, involves excitation of the autonomic nervous system, the discharge of the stress hormone adrenaline, and physical symptoms of anxiety. Joseph LeDoux (1996) and others have identified the seat of anxiety within the limbic system—sometimes dubbed the *emotional brain*—that includes the amygdala, hypothalamus, and hippocampus. Once in flight, Mark feels the plane moving through pockets of turbulence and his cold, clammy hands clutch the shaking seat. His mouth is dry. His heart pounds. His breathing is rapid and shallow. He feels lightheaded

FIGURE 1 Selye's General Adaptation Syndrome. According to Selye's general adaptation syndrome, our level of resistance to stress drops during the alarm phase, increases during the resistance phase, and drops again during the exhaustion phase.

Simulate in **MyPsychLab** the **Experiment:** Stress and Selye's General Adaptation Syndrome

general adaptation syndrome (GAS)
stress-response pattern proposed by Hans Selye that consists of three stages: alarm, resistance, and exhaustion

and dizzy. Images of plane crashes he's seen on television pop uncontrollably into his mind. Mark's swift emotional reaction to the turbulence is tripped largely by his amygdala, where vital emotional memories are stored and create gut feelings of a possible crash.

The hypothalamus sits atop a mind–body link known as the *hypothalamus-pituitary-adrenal* (HPA) axis, shown in **FIGURE 2**. When the hypothalamus (H) receives signals of fear, the sympathetic nervous system activates the adrenal gland (A), which secretes the stress hormones epinephrine (adrenaline) and norepinephrine (noradrenalin). In a matter of moments, Mark's blood pressure rises, his pupils dilate, and his heart pumps blood to vital organs, readying Mark for the **fight-or-flight response**. This response, first described by Walter Cannon in 1915, is a set of physiological and psychological reactions that mobilize us either to confront or leave a threatening situation. Cannon noted that when animals, including humans, face a threat, they have two options: *fight* (actively attack the threat or cope in the immediate situation) or *flee* (escape). Of course, Mark can't flee, so his fear escalates. The hypothalamus and pituitary gland (P) orchestrate the adrenal gland's release of another stress hormone, cortisol, which floods Mark with energy, while his hippocampus retrieves terrifying images from news stories of planes going down in flames.

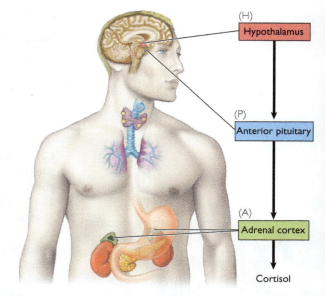

FIGURE 2 The Hypothalamus-Pituitary-Adrenal (HPA) Axis.

RESISTANCE. After the initial rush of stress hormones, Mark enters Selye's second stage of the GAS: *resistance*. He adapts to the stressor and finds ways to cope with it. The instant Mark's hippocampus detected danger from the first apparent jolt of rough air, it opened up a gateway to portions of his cerebral cortex, which neuroscientist Joseph LeDoux (1996) called the "thinking brain." At one point, Mark experiences a sudden impulse to bolt from his seat, but his basal ganglia, linked to the frontal cortex of his thinking brain, wisely leads him to think better of it. Mark slowly but surely gets a handle on his fears. He reminds himself that flying is statistically much safer than driving and that he's flown through choppy air in the past without being injured. He looks around and notices that most of the other passengers look calm. He reminds himself to breathe slowly, and with each breath his relaxation replaces tension.

EXHAUSTION. Mark calms down and is able to get through his flight without panicking. But what happens when a stressor, such as wartime combat lasting months, is more prolonged and uncontrollable? Here's when the third stage of Selye's GAS—*exhaustion*—sets in. If our personal resources are limited and we lack good coping measures, our resistance may ultimately break down, causing our levels of activation to bottom out. The results can range from damage to an organ system, to depression and anxiety, to a breakdown in the immune system (which we'll discuss later in the chapter).

The Diversity of Stress Responses

Not all of us react to stressors with a fight-or-flight response. Our reactions vary from one stressor to another, and these reactions are shaped by gender.

FIGHT OR FLIGHT OR TEND AND BEFRIEND? Shelley Taylor and her colleagues coined the catchy phrase **tend and befriend** to describe a common pattern of reacting to stress among women (Taylor et al., 2000; Taylor, 2006), although some men display it, too. The researchers observed that in times of stress, women generally rely on their social contacts and nurturing abilities—they *tend* to those around them and to themselves—more than men do. When stressed out, women typically *befriend*, or turn to others for support.

That's not to say that women lack a self-preservation instinct or that they don't experience a fight-or-flight pattern when endangered. They certainly don't shirk from defending themselves and their children or from attempting to escape when physically threatened. Nevertheless, compared with men, women generally have more to lose—especially when they're pregnant, nursing, or caring for children—if they're injured or

In stressful times, women often rely on friendships for support and comfort, a pattern that psychologist Shelley Taylor called "tend and befriend."

fight-or-flight response
physical and psychological reaction that mobilizes people and animals to either defend themselves (fight) or escape (flee) a threatening situation

tend and befriend
reaction that mobilizes people to nurture (tend) or seek social support (befriend) under stress

539

killed when fighting or fleeing. Therefore, over the course of evolutionary history, they've developed a tend-and-befriend response to threat which, along with the fight-or-flight response, boosts the odds of their and their offspring's survival. Oxytocin, a hormone that plays key roles in love and emotional bonding, further counters stress and promotes the tend-and-befriend response (Kosfeld et al., 2005; Taylor & Master, 2011). Researchers discovered that women with high levels of oxytocin during pregnancy and in the first month after giving birth are more likely to touch their children affectionately, sing special songs to them, and bathe and feed them in special ways (Feldman et al., 2007).

LONG-LASTING STRESS REACTIONS. Bad things happen to all of us. For most of us, life goes on. But others of us experience long-lasting psychological repercussions, including posttraumatic stress disorder (Comijs et al., 2008; Meichenbaum, 1994). On April 16, 2007, 23-year-old Cho Seung-Hui, a student at Virginia Tech, went on a shooting rampage, killing 31 classmates and professors before taking his own life. When Marjorie Lindholm, 24, heard the news of the massacre, she immediately relived the terror she experienced as a student at Columbine High School on April 20, 1999. On that day, two students, Eric Harris and Dylan Klebold, shot 12 of her classmates and a teacher before turning the guns on themselves. In a television interview, she said, "I started crying, then shaking. I remembered everything I saw at Columbine. I got physically ill. There is no way I'm going to forget that day" (Stepp, 2007).

Marjorie displays some of the hallmark symptoms of *posttraumatic stress disorder* (PTSD), a condition that sometimes follows extremely stressful life events. Its telltale symptoms include vivid memories, feelings, and images of traumatic experiences, known commonly as *flashbacks*. Other symptoms of PTSD include efforts to avoid reminders of the trauma; feelings of detachment or estrangement from others; and symptoms of increased arousal, such as difficulty sleeping and startling easily. The severity, duration, and nearness to the stressor all affect people's likelihood of developing PTSD (American Psychiatric Association, 2013; Ozer et al., 2003).

The horrific 2007 shooting spree at Virginia Tech left some survivors with symptoms of posttraumatic stress disorder.

psychomythology

ARE ALMOST ALL PEOPLE TRAUMATIZED BY HIGHLY AVERSIVE EVENTS?

A widespread view in popular psychology is that most people exposed to trauma develop posttraumatic stress disorder (PTSD) or other serious psychological disorders. Immediately following the 9/11 attacks, for example, many mental health professionals predicted an epidemic of PTSD across the United States (Sommers & Satel, 2005). Were they right?

George Bonanno and his colleagues conducted a study that underscores the remarkable resilience of survivors of extremely aversive events (Bonanno et al., 2006). Using a random-digit dialing procedure, the researchers sampled 2,752 adults in the New York City area about six months after the 9/11 attacks. They conducted their assessments using a computer-assisted telephone interview system. People were judged to be resilient if they reported zero or one PTSD symptoms during the first six months after the attack. Bonanno's results offered surprising evidence for psychological adjustment: 65.1 percent of the sample was resilient. A quarter of the people who were in the World Trade Center at the time of the attack developed probable PTSD, although more than half of the people in this category were resilient. Other research indicates that although most Americans were profoundly upset for several days following the 9/11 attacks, nearly all quickly regained their equilibrium and returned to their previous level of functioning (McNally, 2003). So when it comes to responses to trauma, resilience is the rule rather than the exception.

People who cope well in the aftermath of a serious stressor tend to display relatively high levels of functioning before the event (Bonanno et al., 2005). Yet resilience isn't limited to a few particularly well-adjusted, brave, or tough-minded people, nor to a single type or class of events. Instead, it's the most common response to traumatic events. Most people who take care of a partner dying of AIDS, suffer the death of a spouse, experience divorce, become unemployed, suffer a spinal cord injury, or survive a physical or sexual assault report few long-term psychological symptoms (Bonanno, 2004; Bonanno et al., 2012a; Galatzer-Levy, Bonanno, & Mancini, 2010).

Resilience is the rule rather than the exception even among children, who are commonly regarded as fragile and vulnerable to stress (Sommers & Satel, 2005). William Copeland and his associates interviewed 1,420 children aged 9, 11, and 13 and reinterviewed them every year through 16 years of age. More than two-thirds of the children had been exposed to at least one potentially traumatic event such as abuse, a serious accident, or the violent death of a loved one. Nevertheless, only a tiny fraction of the children (fewer than .5 percent) met criteria for PTSD, and few children showed signs of any traumatic reaction at all (Copeland et al., 2007).

Although at some time most of us will experience a potentially traumatic stressor, the lifetime prevalence of PTSD is only 5 percent in men and 10 percent in women (Keane, Marshall, & Taft, 2006; Kessler et al., 1995). Even among military personnel who served in support of the wars in Iraq and Afghanistan, the rate of long-term posttraumatic reactions reported in the best-controlled studies hovers around 7 percent (Bonanno et al., 2012b). These percentages again remind us that most of us are resilient, even in the face of extremely disturbing events.

Watch in **MyPsychLab** the **Video:** Sara Post-Traumatic Stress Disorder

Study and **Review** in **MyPsychLab**

Assess Your Knowledge   FACT or FICTION?

1. People's first reaction to an extreme stressor involves activation of the autonomic nervous system.   **True / False**

2. Physical illness can be a reaction to a prolonged stressor.   **True / False**

3. Men and women are equally likely to exhibit a tend-and-befriend response.   **True / False**

4. The likelihood of developing PTSD is unrelated to the severity or duration of the stressor. **True / False**

5. Few people are resilient in the face of extreme stress.   **True / False**

Answers: 1. T; 2. T; 3. F; 4. F; 5. F

How Stress Impacts Our Health

5   Describe how the immune system is affected by stress.

6   Identify how physical disorders such as ulcers are related to stress.

7   Describe the role of personality, everyday experiences, and socioeconomic factors in coronary heart disease.

In 1962, two Japanese physicians conducted a study demonstrating the intimate connection between brain and body. Their study, which researchers today might find difficult to carry out for ethical reasons, showed how hypnotic and direct suggestions from a respected authority figure could produce dramatic skin reactions. The researchers selected 13 boys and divided them into two groups. The first group consisted of five boys who received a hypnotic induction with suggestions for relaxation and drowsiness. The second group was made up of eight boys who received no prior hypnotic induction—just suggestions for relaxation administered while they were awake and alert.

In the first phase of the study, all of the boys sat with their eyes closed while a respected physician told them he was touching them with the leaves of a plant similar to poison ivy. In fact, he was touching them with leaves from a harmless plant. The reactions were remarkable. All of the boys—the hypnotic participants and the suggestion-alone participants—showed significant skin disturbance after believing they had been touched by the poison ivy–type leaves. As is so often the case in psychology, beliefs can create reality, in this case a *nocebo effect*.

Suggestion alone can produce an uncomfortable rash much like that of poison ivy in people who are highly sensitive to leaves of a tree with effects similar to those of poison ivy.

541

In the second phase of the study, the researchers reversed the conditions: They rubbed the boys' arms with the poison–ivy type leaves, but told them the leaves were harmless. Four of the five hypnotic participants and seven of the eight suggestion-alone participants didn't show any skin reactions to the leaves. Interestingly, all had developed skin reactions to the leaves *prior* to the study (Ikemi & Nakagawa, 1962).

This study demonstrates how psychological factors, in this case the stressful idea of contracting an itchy rash, can influence physical processes. Indeed, much of what we call a "psychological" response to events manifests itself in physiological reactions. In this chapter, we'll see that stress can spill over into multiple domains of life, creating physical difficulties that disrupt our sleep and sexual functioning. But can stress seep into our cells and weaken our body's defenses against infections? A number of fascinating studies tell us that the answer is yes.

The Immune System

Ordinarily (and thankfully!), we don't have to think about the billions of viruses, fungi, protozoa, and bacteria that share our environment or inhabit our body. That's because our **immune system** neutralizes or destroys them. The immune system is our body's defense against invading bacteria, viruses, and other potentially illness-producing organisms and substances. Our first shield from these foreign invaders is the skin, which blocks the entry of many disease-producing organisms. When we cough or sneeze, our lungs expel harmful bacteria and viruses. Saliva, urine, tears, perspiration, and stomach acid also rid our body of these troublemakers.

Some viruses and bacteria penetrate these defenses, but our immune system is wily and has other means of safeguarding us. Three types of white blood cells—phagocytes, T cells, and B cells—play prominent roles in the night-and-day battle to keep us healthy. *Phagocytes* are first at the scene of an infection and engulf the invader. Substances called cytokines signal natural killer T cells to move through the body and attach to proteins on the surface of virus- and cancer-infected cells, popping them like balloons. B cells produce proteins called *antibodies*, which stick to the surface of invaders, slow their progress, and attract other proteins that destroy the foreign organisms. Longer-lived phagocytes wander through the body as scavengers and conduct mop-up operations, destroying remaining viruses, bacteria, and dead tissue.

Under ordinary circumstances, the immune system is remarkably effective. But it's not a perfect barrier against infection. For example, many early-stage forms of breast cancer and other cancers vanish or get smaller without treatment (Esserman, Shieh, & Thompson, 2009), yet some cancer cells can suppress an effective immune response, multiply, and wreak havoc in the body. Serious disorders of the immune system, such as **acquired immune deficiency syndrome (AIDS)**, are life threatening. AIDS is a currently incurable yet often treatable condition in which the human immunodeficiency virus (HIV) attacks and damages the immune system. When the immune system is overactive, it can launch an attack on various organs of the body, causing *autoimmune diseases* like arthritis, in which the immune system causes swelling and pain at the joints, and multiple sclerosis, in which the immune system attacks the protective myelin sheath surrounding neurons.

Psychoneuroimmunology: Our Bodies, Our Environments, and Our Health

The study of the relationship between the immune system and central nervous system—which consists of the brain and spinal cord, the seats of our reactions to the environment —goes by a mouthful of a name: **psychoneuroimmunology** (Cohen & Herbert, 1996). When evaluating psychoneuroimmunology, we must be careful not to fall prey to exaggerated claims. For example, physical diseases aren't the result of negative thinking, nor can positive thinking reverse serious illnesses like cancer (Hines, 2003;

People from all walks of life can contract the HIV virus and develop AIDS.

Simulate in MyPsychLab the **Experiment:** Stress and the Immune System

immune system
our body's defense system against invading bacteria, viruses, and other potentially illness-producing organisms and substances

acquired immune deficiency syndrome (AIDS)
a life-threatening, incurable, and yet treatable condition in which the human immunodeficiency virus (HIV) attacks and damages the immune system

psychoneuroimmunology
study of the relationship between the immune system and central nervous system

EXTRAORDINARY CLAIMS ▶
Is the evidence as strong as the claim?

Lilienfeld et al., 2010)—despite assertions by immensely popular alternative medical practitioners like Andrew Weil (2000) and Deepak Chopra (1989). Nor, despite early and widely publicized claims (Fawzy et al., 1993; Spiegel et al., 1989), does psychotherapy appear to prolong the survival of women with breast cancer (Coyne, Stefanek, & Palmer, 2007). These cautions aside, researchers using rigorous designs have discovered fascinating links between our life circumstances and our ability to fend off illnesses.

Dr. Andrew Weil (*left*) and Dr. Deepak Chopra (*right*) have popularized the idea that the "mind" can cure serious illnesses. Yet most of their optimistic claims aren't supported by scientific evidence.

STRESS AND COLDS. Many people believe they're more likely to get a cold when they're really stressed out—and they're right. Sheldon Cohen and his associates discovered that significant stressors, such as unemployment and interpersonal difficulties lasting at least a month, predicted which volunteers, who were deliberately exposed to a cold virus in the laboratory, developed a cold (Cohen et al., 1998). A decrease in desirable events and an increase in hassles four days prior to a cold are also associated with the onset of a cold (Evans & Edgerton, 2011). But a network of friends and relatives and close ties to the community seems to afford protection against colds (Cohen et al., 1997; Cohen et al., 2003).

— more stress = worse cold.

It's possible that stress affects health-related behaviors but has no direct impact on the immune system. For instance, our susceptibility to a cold may increase because when we're under stress, we tend to sleep poorly, eat non-nutritious foods, and smoke and drink alcohol excessively, all of which depress the immune system. Cohen and his colleagues (Cohen et al., 2009) found that people who slept an average of only seven hours a night before they were exposed to a cold virus were almost three times more likely to catch a cold than were people who slept for eight hours or more. Still, the investigators found that even when they controlled for sleep quality and other health-related behaviors, the relation between stress and colds remained.

◀ **RULING OUT RIVAL HYPOTHESES**
Have important alternative explanations for the findings been excluded?

STRESS AND IMMUNE FUNCTION: BEYOND THE COMMON COLD. Janice Kiecolt-Glaser and her associates found that caring for a family member with Alzheimer's disease, a severe form of dementia, can be exceedingly stressful and cause long-term disruption of the immune system. They demonstrated that a small wound (standardized for size) took 24 percent longer to heal in Alzheimer's caregivers compared with a group of people who weren't taking care of a relative with Alzheimer's (Kiecolt-Glaser et al., 1995). The kinds of stressors that can lead to disruptions in the immune system include the following (Kiecolt-Glaser et al., 2002):

- Taking an important test
- Death of a spouse
- Unemployment
- Marital conflict
- Living near a damaged nuclear reactor
- Natural disasters

The good news is that positive emotions and social support, which we'll consider later in the chapter, can strengthen our immune systems (Esterling, Kiecolt-Glaser, & Glaser, 1996; Kennedy, Kiecolt-Glaser, & Glaser, 1990).

Stress-Related Illnesses: A Biopsychosocial View

Not long ago, a common myth of popular psychology was that beliefs and mental states were the root causes of many physical ailments. Certain illnesses or disorders were once called *psychosomatic*, because psychologists believed that deep-seated conflicts and emotional reactions were the culprits. For example, Franz Alexander (1950) argued that stomach ulcers—an inflamed area in the gastrointestinal tract that can

Caretakers of people with Alzheimer's disease experience high levels of stress, are at heightened risk of developing depression, and even show decreases in their blood's ability to clot (associated with having a stroke) in response to stressful life events (von Känel et al., 2001). For reasons that are unknown, the negative psychological effects of such caretaking seem to be lower among African Americans than Caucasians (Janevic & Connell, 2001).

543

Contrary to popular belief, stress isn't the major cause of ulcers. Instead, the bacterium *Helicobacter pylori* is the prime culprit.

CORRELATION VS. CAUSATION ▶
Can we be sure that A causes B?

cause pain, nausea, and loss of appetite—are linked to infantile cravings to be fed and feelings of dependency. Even today, many people believe that ulcers are produced by stress (Lilienfeld et al., 2010).

Yet we now know that ulcers aren't caused by dependency or stress or by eating spicy foods like salsa and hot chicken wings. Rather, *Helicobacter pylori* (*H. pylori*)—an unusual bacterium that thrives in stomach acid—is the cause of as many as 90 percent of stomach ulcers. Still, stress may play an indirect role in contributing to ulcers—perhaps by reducing the efficiency of the immune system and increasing vulnerability to the bacterium.

Psychologists use the term **psychophysiological** to describe authentic illnesses like ulcers in which emotions and stress contribute to, maintain, or aggravate physical conditions. Scientists widely acknowledge that emotions and stress are associated with physical disorders, including coronary heart disease, asthma, headaches, and AIDS. For example, changes in stress levels appear to be an influential predictor of headaches in children aged 8–17 years (Connelly & Bickel, 2011). In the case of asthma, in which people experience tightness in the chest, cough, and wheeze, physical responses to stress or responses, such as crying, laughing, and coughing, can trigger attacks in some asthma patients (Purcell, 1963).

The causal arrow goes both ways: physical disorders can also create stress. Not surprisingly, being diagnosed with a potentially fatal illness that has an uncertain outcome, such as cancer or AIDS, can be unimaginably stressful and pose innumerable challenges. Conversely, when the treatment for severe illnesses is successful, the transition from poor to dramatically improved health can introduce new and difficult decisions, such as whether to return to work or to begin or end relationships (Catz & Kelly, 2001).

Most psychologists have adopted a **biopsychosocial perspective**, which proposes that most medical conditions are neither all physical nor all psychological. Numerous physical illnesses depend on the complex interplay of genes, lifestyle, immunity, social support, everyday stressors, and self-perceptions (Engel, 1977; Fava & Sonino, 2008; Turk, 1996). In the next section on coronary heart disease, we'll provide a more in-depth example of how multiple risk factors contribute to illness.

psychophysiological
illnesses such as asthma and ulcers in which emotions and stress contribute to, maintain, or aggravate the physical condition

biopsychosocial perspective
the view that an illness or a medical condition is the product of the interplay of biological, psychological, and social factors

from inquiry to understanding

MORGELLONS DISEASE: HOW CAN HEALTHY PEOPLE BECOME CONVINCED THEY ARE SERIOUSLY ILL?

Morgellons disease is one of the most mysterious afflictions to light up the Internet in recent years. In 2001, the story goes, Mary Leitao inspected several irritated areas under the lip of her 2-year-old son, who complained that he felt itching and said the word *bugs*. In rubbing his lips with cream, she discovered what appeared to be fibers erupting from the boy's skin sores, which she later examined under a microscope and described as white, red, black, and blue. Puzzled and disturbed by her son's strange condition, for which there appeared to be no medical explanation, she established a website and a foundation; she also coined the term Morgellons for his condition, after an account of similar symptoms published in 1674. News of this fascinating ailment spread quickly over the Internet and became the darling disease of the media, after which people came forward in droves with reports of hairs embedded in their skin, accompanied by crawling, itching, and stinging sensations, often with muscle and joint pain, fatigue, and depression.

A mailing campaign organized by the foundation gained the attention of members of Congress. In response to mounting concerns, the Centers For Disease Control and Prevention (CDC) conducted a rigorous scientific inquiry, finding no evidence for infection by foreign organisms such as bacteria, fungi, or parasites, based on the examination of over 100 Morgellons sufferers (Pearson et al., 2012).

Researchers at the Mayo Clinic in Minnesota were quick to replicate the CDC findings (Hylwa et al., 2011). They studied all people treated at their clinic between 2001 and 2007 with Morgellons-like symptoms or beliefs they were infested with parasites. Twenty-two percent of the patients reported fibers; 7 percent, "specks"; and 4 percent, either "triangles" or gravel or grain-like materials in the skin. After a thorough evaluation, in only one case did the scientists identify a true parasite (lice) and in another case a tick, but neither could account for the stress-producing symptoms. Most of the patients, however, did suffer from dermatitis (skin irritation), a common condition that produces itching, and almost half had skin sores. A study of 148 patients drawn from four European countries replicated these findings and determined that the specimens people brought in as proof of infestation were mostly hair and skin particles (Freudenmann et al., 2012).

The scientists at the Mayo Clinic and the European study group called the condition "delusional infestation." Reviewing medical records, the Mayo Clinic researchers found that 81 percent of the patients had prior psychiatric conditions (Foster et al., 2012) and many people were deeply troubled by their symptoms. Morgellons underscores the fact that regardless of whether physical symptoms have a medical basis or are the product of a fervent imagination, they can be stressful to the point that they interfere with everyday life.

CORONARY HEART DISEASE. Scientists have learned that psychological factors, including stress and personality traits, are key risk factors for **coronary heart disease (CHD)**. CHD is the complete or partial blockage of the arteries that provide oxygen to the heart and is the number one cause of death and disability in the United States (Kung et al., 2008). CHD develops when deposits of *cholesterol*—a waxy, fatty substance that travels in the bloodstream—collect in the walls of arteries, narrowing and blocking the coronary arteries, creating a condition called *atherosclerosis*. If this condition worsens, it can lead to chest pain and the deterioration and death of heart tissue, otherwise known as a heart attack (see **FIGURE 3**).

The Role of Stress in CHD. Many risk factors are associated with CHD, including a history of smoking, high cholesterol, and high blood pressure (Clarke et al., 2009). A family history of CHD, diabetes, and low levels of vitamin D—the "sunshine vitamin"—can also boost the risk of heart disease (Wang et al., 2008).

Stress deserves a prominent place on the list of CHD risk factors. Stressful life events predict recurrences of heart attacks, high blood pressure, and enlargement of the heart (Repetti, Taylor, & Seeman, 2002; Schnall et al., 1990; Troxel et al., 2003). Although only correlational, these data are consistent with this hypothesis that stressors may sometimes produce negative physiological effects. Moreover, high levels of stress hormones triggered by extreme stress can lead to disruptions in normal heart rhythm and even sudden death, as well as to atherosclerosis in people who are highly reactive to everyday stressors (Carney, Freedland, & Veith, 2005; Sarafino, 2006). People with CHD also show signs of a hyped-up autonomic nervous system, with elevated heart rates and extreme responses to physical stressors (Carney et al., 2005). Even though stress may exert a direct effect on CHD, stress is also associated with behavioral risk factors for CHD, including poor diet and inadequate exercise (Chandola et al., 2008). So at least some of the effects of stress on CHD may actually be due to the overlap between stress and these risk factors.

◄ REPLICABILITY
Can the results be duplicated in other studies?

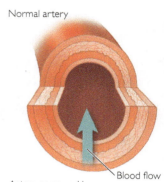

Normal artery

Blood flow

Artery narrowed by atherosclerosis

Plaque

FIGURE 3 Atherosclerosis. Cholesterol deposits in the large arteries form plaque, restricting the flow of blood. This condition, called *atherosclerosis*, can result in stroke, heart attack, and serious chest pain.

◄ CORRELATION VS. CAUSATION
Can we be sure that A causes B?

The pioneering Framingham Study, which began in 1948, is one of most influential investigations of health in America. This longitudinal study has provided a treasure trove of data on risk factors for CHD and continues to examine the health of over 5,000 men and women in Framingham, Massachusetts.

coronary heart disease (CHD)
damage to the heart from the complete or partial blockage of the arteries that provide oxygen to the heart

◄ RULING OUT RIVAL HYPOTHESES
Have important alternative explanations for the findings been excluded?

The Role of Personality in CHD. In addition to stress, researchers have suggested that long-standing behavior patterns contribute to risk for CHD. Two cardiologists, Meyer Friedman and Ray Rosenman (1959), coined the term **Type A personality**, now widely popularized in the media, to describe a curious behavior pattern they observed among CHD patients. They noticed that the chairs in their hospital waiting room were rapidly becoming worn out around the edges. Many of their CHD patients were literally sitting and bouncing on the edge of their seats because of restlessness. Later, Friedman and Rosenman (1974) identified additional characteristics that clustered under the Type A description: perfectionistic, prone to hostility, stubborn, opinionated, cynical, controlling, and concerned with deadlines. Although early studies revealed high rates of CHD among extreme Type A individuals, later studies yielded many negative results (Gatchel & Oordt, 2003). Accordingly, scientists began to wonder whether certain Type A traits are more associated with heightened risk than other traits.

Of all Type A traits researchers have studied, hostility turned out to be most predictive of heart disease (Matthews et al., 2004; Myrtek, 2001; Nabi et al., 2008; Smith & Gallo, 2001). Hostility is associated with well-documented risk factors for CHD, such as alcohol consumption, smoking, and weight gain (Bunde & Suls, 2006), so an alternative hypothesis is that its effects on CHD are indirect. Nevertheless, in a study of older white men, hostility surpassed these traditional risk factors in predicting CHD (Niaura et al., 2002). Luckily, there's a silver lining to this gray cloud: tamping down hostility and practicing forgiveness of others helps to reduce CHD risk (McCullough et al., 2009).

CHD, EVERYDAY EXPERIENCES, AND SOCIOECONOMIC FACTORS. Hostility and other negative emotions don't always arise from enduring personality traits. Negative emotions can stem from the many pressures and demands we confront in our fast-paced, competitive society. Even one significant drop in income produces a 30 percent increase in risk of dying from any cause (Duncan, 1996), and CHD is associated with substantial job stress and dissatisfaction (Quick et al, 1997). In addition, African-American women who report discrimination, unfair treatment, and high stress levels have more narrowing and blockage of their arteries than do other African-American women (Troxel et al., 2003). However, it's possible that the causal arrow is reversed: Perhaps CHD causes job stress in some people, a possibility that scientists have yet to examine in depth. Another hypothesis is that a third variable, such as personality makeup, attitudes toward others, or early experiences with trauma, contribute to both job stress and CHD.

Although researchers have established a strong correlation between poverty and poor health (Antonovsky, 1967; Repetti, Taylor, & Seeman, 2002), we still need to ask, "What's responsible for this association?" According to Linda Gallo and Karen Matthews (2003) life can prove immensely challenging for people who have little education, struggle in a bad job with a nasty supervisor, and barely make enough money to make ends meet. These drains on personal resources decrease the ability to cope with stressors and with depression, and engender hopelessness, feelings of loss of control, and hostility, which increase the risk of poor health and CHD (Williams et al., 2011). To make matters worse, negative thoughts and feelings can promote unhealthy habits like smoking, drinking, and lack of exercise, which further increase the risk of physical problems (Gallo & Matthews, 2003). It's important to consider the role of a host of factors, including personality, genes, everyday experiences, coping ability, behavioral risk factors, and socioeconomic conditions, in explaining how psychophysiological disorders like CHD develop.

REPLICABILITY ▶
Can the results be duplicated in other studies?

RULING OUT RIVAL HYPOTHESES ▶
Have important alternative explanations for the findings been excluded?

👁 **Watch** in **MyPsychLab** the **Video:**
Thinking Like a Psychologist: Personality and Health

Type A personality
personality type that describes people who are competitive, driven, hostile, and ambitious

CORRELATION VS. CAUSATION ▶
Can we be sure that A causes B?

RULING OUT RIVAL HYPOTHESES ▶
Have important alternative explanations for the findings been excluded?

 Why can chronic anger be bad for our health? (See answer upside down below.)

Answer: Research indicates that the anger component of the Type A personality can be deadly, increasing our risk for coronary heart disease.

Assess Your Knowledge — FACT or FICTION?

Study and **Review** in **MyPsychLab**

1. Overactivity of the immune system sometimes leads to disease. **True / False**

2. One major cause of ulcers is eating hot, spicy foods late at night. **True / False**

3. Most psychologists adopt a biopsychosocial perspective, which proposes that most medical conditions are neither all physical nor all psychological. **True / False**

4. The number one cause of death and disability in the United States is coronary heart disease. **True / False**

5. Social and economic factors are largely or entirely unrelated to risk for physical diseases. **True / False**

Answers: 1. T; 2. F; 3. T; 4. T; 5. F

Coping With Stress

8 Describe the role of social support and different types of control in coping with stress.

9 Explain how our attitudes, beliefs, and personality may influence our responses to stress.

Clearly, some of us adapt better in the face of challenge and change than others. Why is this so, and what can we do to reduce stress, manage our lives, and stay healthy? We'll next take stock of how we can use social support and coping strategies to deal with stressful circumstances.

Social Support

Imagine that you survived the 9/11 World Trade Center attack or a terrifying mass shooting. What would be helpful? When we ask our students this question, many say that the support of family, friends, neighbors, teachers, coworkers, and clergy would be invaluable. **Social support** encompasses interpersonal relations with people, groups, and the larger community. Social support can provide us with emotional comfort; financial assistance; and information to make decisions, solve problems, and contend with stressful situations (Schaefer, Coyne, & Lazarus, 1981; Stroebe, 2000; Wills & Fegan, 2001). Lisa Berkman and Leonard Syme (1979) conducted a landmark study of the hypothesis that social support buffers us against the adverse effects of stress on health. They analyzed data from nearly 5,000 men and women in Alameda County, California, over a nine-year period. They honed in on four kinds of social ties: marriage, contact with friends, church membership, and formal and informal group associations. They then created a social network index reflecting the number of social connections and social supports available to each person.

During the nine-year period, Berkman and Syme found a strong relationship between the number of social connections and the probability of dying. But do these findings mean that isolation increases our chances of dying? A rival hypothesis is that poor health results in few social bonds, rather than the other way around. To rule out this possibility, the researchers surveyed participants when they started the study. People with high and low levels of support reported a comparable illness history, suggesting that poor initial health can't explain why people with the least social support are later more likely to die.

Still, people aren't necessarily accurate when they judge their health. To address this concern, James House, Cynthia Robbins, and Helen Metzner (1982) ensured that their 2,700 participants received a medical examination *before* their study got under way. This exam provided a more objective assessment of health status. The researchers replicated Berkman and Syme's (1979) findings: Even when they took initial health status into account, people with less social support had higher mortality rates.

Support and comfort from others can buffer the effects of highly aversive situations.

◄ **RULING OUT RIVAL HYPOTHESES**
Have important alternative explanations for the findings been excluded?

social support
relationships with people and groups that can provide us with emotional comfort and personal and financial resources

◄ **REPLICABILITY**
Can the results be duplicated in other studies?

STRESS
MANAGEMENT
TECHNIQUES
1. _____
2. _____
3. _____
4. _____

— GLASBERGEN

"Howl at an ambulance or fire siren every chance you get. Run around the room in circles with a sock in your mouth. Eat a messy meal without using your hands or utensils. Ask a friend to scratch your belly..."

(Copyright 2003 by Randy Glasbergen. www.glasbergen.com)

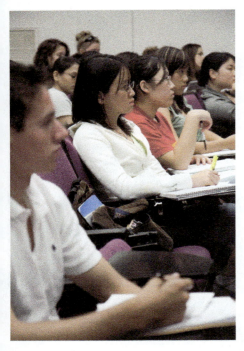

GRE preparation classes can be one useful source of informational control.

Fortunately, the positive influence of social support isn't limited to health outcomes. Supportive and caring relationships can help us cope with short-term crises and life transitions and protect against depression, even when we encounter major stressors (Alloway & Bebbington, 1987; Gotlib & Hammen, 1992; Ibarra-Rovillard & Kuiper, 2011). But the breakup of close relationships through separation, divorce, discrimination, or bereavement ranks among the most stressful events we can experience (Gardner, Gabriel, & Deikman, 2000).

Gaining Control

As mentioned earlier, we can also relieve stress by acquiring control of situations. Next, we'll discuss five types of control we can use, either alone or in combination, in different situations (Sarafino, 2006).

BEHAVIORAL CONTROL. Behavioral control is the ability to step up and do something to reduce the impact of a stressful situation or prevent its recurrence. As you may recall, this type of active coping is *problem-focused* and is generally more effective in relieving stress than is *avoidance-oriented coping*—avoiding action to solve our problems or giving up hope (Lazarus & Folkman, 1984; Roth & Cohen, 1986). Research in the United States and Iceland shows that the more high school and college students use problem-focused coping techniques, the less likely they are to develop drinking problems (Rafnsson, Jonsson, & Windle, 2006). In another study, researchers followed patients with dementia and their caregivers for up to six years. The progression of dementia in patients was slower when their caregivers used problem-focused coping (Tschanz et al., 2012).

COGNITIVE CONTROL. Cognitive control is the ability to *think differently about* negative emotions that arise in response to stress-provoking events (Higgins & Endler, 1995; Lazarus & Folkman, 1984; Skinner et al., 2003). This type of control includes *emotion-focused coping,* which we introduced earlier, a strategy that comes in handy when adjusting to uncertain situations or aversive events we can't control or change. In a novel study, Thomas Strentz and Stephen Auerbach (1988) exposed airline pilots and flight attendants to a simulated hijacking attempt and four days of captivity. Participants who had received instructions to use emotion-focused coping strategies before the hijacking reported less distress during captivity compared with those who had received instructions to use problem-focused coping.

DECISIONAL CONTROL. Decisional control is the ability to choose among alternative courses of action (Sarafino, 2006). For example, we can gain control over the often stressful college experience by consulting with trusted friends about which classes to take and which professors to avoid, and we can gain control over our health by making decisions about which surgeon to consult to perform a high-stakes operation.

INFORMATIONAL CONTROL. Informational control is the ability to acquire information about a stressful event. Knowing what types of questions are on the SAT or GRE can help us prepare for them, as can knowing something about the person we're "fixed up with" on an upcoming date. We engage in **proactive coping** when we anticipate stressful situations and take steps to prevent or minimize difficulties before they arise (Greenglass, 2002; Karasek & Theorell, 1990; Schwarzer & Taubert, 2002). People who engage in proactive coping tend to perceive stressful circumstances as opportunities for growth (Greenglass, 2002).

EMOTIONAL CONTROL. Emotional control is the ability to suppress and express emotions. Writing in a diary, for example, can facilitate emotional control and has a host of long-lasting benefits (Pennebaker, 1997). In a now classic study,

proactive coping
anticipation of problems and stressful situations that promotes effective coping

James Pennebaker and his colleagues (Pennebaker, Kiecolt-Glaser, & Glaser, 1988) asked one group of college students to write for four consecutive days for 20 minutes a day about their deepest thoughts and feelings about past traumas. They asked another group of students to write about superficial topics. Six weeks after the study, students who "opened up" about their traumatic experiences made fewer visits to the health center and showed signs of improved immune functioning compared with the students who wrote about trivial topics. Replications in laboratories around the world have confirmed that writing about traumatic events can influence a variety of academic, social, and cognitive variables and improve the health and well-being of people ranging from arthritis sufferers to maximum security prisoners (Campbell & Pennebaker, 2003; Pennebaker & Graybeal, 2001; Smyth et al., 1999), although scientific debate regarding the size of these effects continues (Frisina, Borod, & Lepore, 2004).

The work of James Pennebaker suggests that writing about our stressors can ward off physical illness, although this effect is only modest.

Still, there may be times when it's best to conceal our emotions, such as cloaking our fears when we're giving a speech and suppressing our anger, at least for the moment, when trying to resolve a problem with a coworker (Bonanno et al., 2004; Gross & Muñoz, 1995). As the old saying goes, "There's a time and a place for everything."

IS CATHARSIS A GOOD THING? Contrary to the popular notion that expressing what we feel is always beneficial, disclosing painful feelings, called *catharsis*, is a double-edged sword. When it involves problem solving and constructive efforts to make troubling situations "right," it can be beneficial. But when catharsis reinforces a sense of helplessness, as when we voice our rage about something we can't or won't change, catharsis can actually be harmful (Littrell, 1998). This finding is worrisome, because a slew of popular psychotherapies rely on catharsis, encouraging clients to "get it out of your system," "get things off your chest," or "let it all hang out." Some of these therapies instruct clients to yell, punch pillows, or throw balls against a wall when they become upset (Bushman, Baumeister, & Phillips, 2001; Lewis & Bucher, 1992; Lohr et al., 2007). Yet research shows that these activities rarely reduce our long-term stress, although they may make us feel slightly better for a few moments. In other cases, they actually seem to heighten our anger or anxiety in the long run (Tavris, 1989), perhaps because emotional upset often generates a vicious cycle: we can become distressed about the fact that we're distressed.

◀ REPLICABILITY
Can the results be duplicated in other studies?

? According to research on the expression of anger, how will this girl feel after punching this pillow repeatedly?
(See answer upside down at bottom of page.)

DOES CRISIS DEBRIEFING HELP? Some therapists—especially those employed by fire, police, or other emergency services—administer a popular treatment called *crisis debriefing*, which is designed to ward off PTSD among people exposed to trauma. Several thousand crisis debriefers descended on lower Manhattan in the wake of the 9/11 attacks in a well-meaning effort to help traumatized witnesses of the attacks. Crisis debriefing is a single-session procedure, typically conducted in groups, that usually lasts three to four hours. Most often, therapists conduct this procedure within one or two days of a traumatic event such as a terrible accident. It proceeds according to standardized steps, including strongly encouraging group members to discuss and "process" their negative emotions, listing the posttraumatic symptoms that group members are likely to experience, and discouraging group members from discontinuing participation once the session has started.

Crisis debriefing sessions, in which people discuss their reactions to a traumatic event in a group, may actually increase PTSD risk.

Recent studies indicate that crisis debriefing isn't effective for trauma reactions. What's worse, several studies suggest that it may actually increase the risk of PTSD among people exposed to trauma, perhaps because it gets in the way of people's natural coping strategies (Lilienfeld, 2007; Litz et al., 2002; McNally, Bryant, & Ehlers, 2003).

Answer: Although many psychotherapies encourage this cathartic release of anger, research shows that it actually heightens long-term stress.

Nor is there much evidence that merely talking about our problems when we're upset is helpful. A systematic review of 61 studies (Meads & Nouwen, 2005) revealed no overall benefits for emotional disclosure, compared with nondisclosure, on a variety of measures of physical and psychological health. None of this implies that we should never discuss our feelings with others when we're upset. But it does mean that doing so is most likely to be beneficial when it allows us to think about and work through our problems in a more constructive light.

Individual Differences in Coping: Attitudes, Beliefs, and Personality

Some people survive almost unimaginably horrific circumstances with few or no visible psychological scars, whereas others view the world through the dark lens of pessimism and crumble when the little things in life don't go their way. Our attitudes, personality, and socialization shape our reactions—for better and worse—to potential stressors.

HARDINESS: CHALLENGE, COMMITMENT, AND CONTROL. More than three decades ago, Salvatore Maddi and his colleagues (Kobasa, Hilker, & Maddi, 1979) initiated a study of the qualities of stress-resistant people. They found that resilient people possess a set of attitudes they called **hardiness**. Hardy people view change as a challenge rather than a threat, are committed to their life and work, and believe they can control events (Maddi, 2004).

Suzanne Kobasa and Maddi asked 670 managers at a public utility to report their stressful experiences on a checklist. From this group, they selected participants who scored high on both stress and illness, as well as participants who scored equally high on stress but reported below-average levels of illness. Managers who showed high stress but low levels of illness were more oriented to challenge, higher in their sense of control over events, and felt a deep sense of involvement in their work and social lives.

When we're physically ill, we don't usually feel especially hardy. So we can appreciate the fact that another explanation for Kobasa and Maddi's findings is that illness creates negative attitudes, rather than the other way around. To address the question of causal direction, Maddi and Kobasa (1984) conducted a longitudinal study of changes in health and attitudes over time. At the end of two years, people whose attitudes toward life reflected high levels of control, commitment, and challenge remained healthier than those whose attitudes didn't. Hardiness also can boost stress resistance among nurses in hospice settings, immigrants adjusting to life in the United States, and military personnel who survive life-threatening stressors (Atri, Sharma, & Cottrell, 2006; Bartone, 1999; Maddi, 2002). Still, because hardiness is closely associated with low levels of anxiety-proneness, it's not clear whether hardiness itself—as opposed to a general tendency to react calmly to life stressors—is the major predictor of successful coping (Coifman et al., 2007; Sinclair & Tetrick, 2000; Smeets et al., 2010).

OPTIMISM. We know them when we meet them. Optimistic people have a rosy outlook and don't dwell on the dark side of life. Even on a cloudy day, we can bask in their sunshine. And there are some distinct advantages to being optimistic. Compared with pessimists, optimistic people are more productive, focused, persistent, and better at handling frustration (Peterson, 2000; Seligman, 1990). Optimism is also associated with a lower mortality rate (Stern, Dhanda, & Hazuda, 2001), a more vigorous immune response (Segerstrom et al., 1998), lower distress in infertile women trying to have a child (Abbey, Halman, & Andrews, 1992), improved perceptions of health among cardiac patients (Karademas et al., 2013), better surgical outcomes (Scheier et al., 1989), and fewer physical complaints (Scheier & Carver, 1992).

SPIRITUALITY AND RELIGIOUS INVOLVEMENT. **Spirituality** is the search for the sacred, which may or may not extend to belief in God. Spiritual and religious beliefs play vital roles in many of our lives. According to a Harris Poll (Taylor, 2009), 82 percent of Americans

Optimists—who proverbially see the glass as "half full" rather than "half empty"—are more likely than pessimists to view change as a challenge.

hardiness
set of attitudes marked by a sense of control over events, commitment to life and work, and courage and motivation to confront stressful events

spirituality
search for the sacred, which may or may not extend to belief in God

CORRELATION VS. CAUSATION ▶
Can we be sure that A causes B?

RULING OUT RIVAL HYPOTHESES ▶
Have important alternative explanations for the findings been excluded?

Factoid

People who are self-centered and who think highly of themselves cope successfully under stress. Such people are called self-enhancers and are able to shrug off many of the ill effects of stressful events such as the premature death of a spouse, combat exposure, and potentially traumatic events during college (Bonanno et al., 2002; Gupta & Bonanno, 2010).

believe in God. Compared with nonreligious people, individuals who describe themselves as religious (who say they believe in God) have lower mortality rates, improved immune system functioning, lower blood pressure, and a greater ability to recover from illnesses (Koenig, McCullough, & Larson, 2001; Levin, 2001; Matthews, Larson, & Barry, 1993). One explanation for these findings is that religious involvements activate a healing energy that scientists can't measure (Ellison & Levin, 1998). As we'll see in our discussion of energy medicines, however, explanations that depend on an undetectable force or energy can't be falsified and therefore lie outside the boundaries of science.

The correlation between religiosity and physical health isn't easy to interpret. Some authors have measured religiosity by counting how often people attend church or other religious services and found that such attendance is associated with better physical health. But this correlation is potentially attributable to a confound: people who are sick are less likely to attend religious services than are healthy people, so the causal arrow may be reversed (Sloan et al., 1999).

Research on the links between spirituality and religious involvement, on the one hand, and health, on the other hand, is limited (Powell, Shahabi, & Thoresen, 2003). But until more definitive evidence is available, let's consider several potential reasons why spirituality and religious involvements may be a boon to many people.

- Many religions foster self-control and prohibit risky health behaviors, including alcohol, drugs, and unsafe sexual practices (McCullough & Willoughby, 2009).

- Religious engagement, such as attendance at services, often boosts social support and increases marital satisfaction (Orathinkal & Vansteenwegen, 2006).

- A sense of meaning and purpose, control over life, positive emotions, and positive appraisals of stressful situations associated with prayer and religious activities may enhance coping (Potts, 2004).

Flexible Coping

The ability to adjust coping strategies as the situation demands is critical to contending with many stressful situations (Bonanno & Kaltman, 2001; Cheng, 2003; Westphal & Bonanno, 2004). George Bonanno and his colleagues studied students who'd just started college in New York City when terrorists destroyed the World Trade Center in 2001 (Bonanno et al., 2004). They predicted that students who had difficulties with managing their emotions would find the transition to college life particularly difficult. Participants completed a checklist of psychological symptoms at the start of the study and two years later. Those who were better at flexibly controlling their emotions by suppressing or expressing them on demand on a laboratory task reported less distress at the two-year follow-up.

Expending a great deal of effort to suppress and avoid emotions can distract us from problem solving and lead to an unintended consequence: The emotions may return in full or greater force. In fact, the attempt to suppress negative emotions and thoughts associated with aversive events tends to backfire and increase the very negative experiences we're struggling so hard to avoid (Beck et al., 2006; Richards, Butler, & Gross, 2003; Wegner, 2005). Accepting circumstances and feelings we can't change—and finding positive ways of thinking about our problems—can be a potent means of contending with stressful situations (Skinner et al., 2003).

RUMINATION: RECYCLING THE MENTAL GARBAGE. So far we've considered adaptive ways of coping with taxing circumstances without becoming unhinged. But some ways of reacting to stressful situations are clearly counterproductive. Susan Nolen-Hoeksema (1987) suggested that recycling negative events in our minds can lead us to become depressed. More specifically, some of us spend a great deal of time *ruminating*—focusing on how bad we feel and endlessly analyzing the causes and consequences of our problems.

◄ **FALSIFIABILITY**
Can the claim be disproved?

◄ **CORRELATION VS. CAUSATION**
Can we be sure that A causes B?

Watch in **MyPsychLab** the **Video:**
Religion and Longevity

Research suggests that instructing someone *not* to think of something, like a white bear, often results in increases in the very thought the person is trying to suppress (Wegner et al., 1987).

Men may be more likely than women to play sports, which often decreases the tendency to ruminate when stressed out.

 Study and **Review** in **MyPsychLab**

"I'm learning how to relax, doctor —
but I want to relax *better* and *faster!*
I want to be on the cutting edge of relaxation!"

(Randy Glasbergen, www.glasbergen.com. Used by permission.)

Watch in **MyPsychLab** the **Video:** The Big Picture Health Psychology

---

health psychology
field of psychology, also called behavioral medicine, that integrates the behavioral sciences with the practice of medicine

Nolen-Hoeksema (2000, 2003) contended that women have much higher rates and more frequent bouts of depression compared with men because they tend to ruminate more than men do. In contrast, when stressed out, men are more likely to focus on pleasurable or distracting activities such as working, watching football games, or drinking copious amounts of alcohol (which we don't recommend). They also adopt a more direct approach to solving their problems than do women (Nolen-Hoeksema, 2002). Early socialization may in part pave the way for these different reactions (Nolen-Hoeksema & Girgus, 1994). Although parents encourage girls to analyze and talk about their problems, they often actively discourage boys from expressing their feelings and instead encourage them to take action or tough it out. Still, men and women alike can benefit from cutting down on rumination and, instead, confronting their problems head-on.

Assess Your Knowledge — FACT or FICTION?

1. During a nine-year study, researchers found a strong connection between social support and people's chance of dying.   **True / False**

2. Optimistic people are especially skilled at tolerating frustration.   **True / False**

3. Participation in religious activities can increase social support.   **True / False**

4. One general coping strategy tends to work for all situations.   **True / False**

5. Rumination is usually an adaptive strategy for dealing with anxiety and depression.   **True / False**

Answers: 1. T; 2. T; 3. T; 4. F; 5. F

Promoting Good Health—and Less Stress!

10   Identify four behaviors that contribute to a healthy lifestyle.

11   Identify why it is difficult to change our lifestyle.

12   Describe different alternative and complementary medical approaches and compare their effectiveness with placebos.

If we could all reduce or eliminate stress in our lives, the public health consequences would be enormous. Stress is a risk factor for many behaviors, such as smoking and alcohol abuse, which are themselves risk factors for many illnesses. What can we do to decrease stress-related diseases and modify our health-destructive habits? **Health psychology**, also called *behavioral medicine*, is a rapidly growing field that has contributed to our understanding of the influences of stress and other psychological factors on physical disorders.

Health psychologists integrate behavioral sciences with the practice of medicine (Gatchel & Baum, 1983). They also combine educational and psychological interventions to promote and maintain health and to prevent and treat illness (France et al., 2008; Leventhal et al. 2006; Matarazzo, 1980). Health psychologists work in hospitals, rehabilitation centers, medical schools, industry, government agencies, and academic and research settings. Interventions developed within health psychology include teaching patients stress management skills and pain reduction techniques and helping people to mobilize social support, comply with medical regimens, and pursue healthy lifestyles.

Toward a Healthy Lifestyle

Health psychologists help patients break the grip of unhealthy habits. Smoking, excessive drinking, and overeating can be triggered by stress and can be maintained when these activities reduce stress (Polivy, Schueneman, & Carlson, 1976; Young, Oei, & Knight, 1990). Women who are sexual assault survivors are at risk for alcoholism because they may drink to reduce their distress (Ullman et al., 2005). Smokers are four times more likely to suffer from clinical depression compared with nonsmokers and may smoke in part to relieve distress (Breslau, Kilbey & Andreski, 1993; Flensborg-Madsen et al., 2011). According to a survey of more than 2,000 adults (American Psychological Association, 2006), one in four Americans uses food to relieve stress and cope with problems. Unfortunately, when we engage in unhealthy behaviors that reduce stress in the short run, we place ourselves at risk for health and stress-related problems in the long run. We'll next examine four behaviors that can counteract these negative cycles and promote health.

HEALTHY BEHAVIOR #1: STOP SMOKING. Smoking ranks as the leading cause of preventable disease and death in the United States (Centers for Disease Control and Prevention, 2005). In America, about 21 percent of men and 18 percent of women smoke cigarettes (Schiller et al., 2012). These statistics are alarming given that one in five regular smokers dies of a smoking-related disease (Centers for Disease Control and Prevention, 2008). A 30- to 40-year-old male cigarette smoker with a two-pack-a-day habit loses about eight years of his life on average (Green, 2000). Smoking doubles our chances of dying from either CHD or stroke (McBride, 1992) and is responsible for one-third of all cancer deaths (Haxby, 1995). Smoking is also the primary cause of lung disease among men and women (Woloshin et al., 2002).

About two-thirds to three-quarters of people who stop smoking do so on their own (Chapman & MacKenzie, 2010). Still, only about 5 percent of the approximately 40 percent of U.S. smokers who try to stop each year unaided succeed (American Psychiatric Association, 2000; Schoenborn et al., 2004). Mark Twain captured in his famous quote the challenges that smokers face: "Giving up smoking is the easiest thing in the world. I know because I've done it thousands of times."

Health psychologists make smoking treatment and prevention a high priority. Stop-smoking approaches typically educate people about the health consequences of smoking and teach smokers to manage stress. They also help smokers to pinpoint and avoid high-risk situations associated with past smoking, such as parties and bars (Marlatt & Gordon, 1985; Miller & Rollnick, 2002). These strategies are effective with 25–35 percent of long-term smokers and are also helpful for people who eat or drink excessively.

Each time people try to stop smoking, their chances of succeeding improve (Lynn & Kirsch, 2006). People who stop smoking live longer than those who don't, and women who stop smoking during the first few months of pregnancy reduce their risk of problem pregnancies (such as low-birth-weight babies) to that of women who've never smoked. After 10 to 15 years of nonsmoking, an ex-smoker's risk of premature death approaches that of someone who's never smoked (National Cancer Institute, 2000). So if you're a smoker, don't quit your attempts to quit!

HEALTHY BEHAVIOR #2: CURB ALCOHOL CONSUMPTION. According to a recent survey, more than 65 percent of adults reported having drunk alcohol in the past year (Schiller et al., 2012). Repeated bouts of heavy drinking, especially *heavy episodic drinking* (formerly called binge drinking)—defined as drinking five or more drinks on one occasion for men and four or more drinks on one occasion for women—is associated with increases in many types of cancer, serious and sometimes fatal liver problems, pregnancy complications, and brain shrinkage and other neurological problems (Bagnardi et al., 2001).

Several controversial studies (French & Zavala, 2007; Mukamal et al., 2003, 2005) suggest that light to moderate drinking—defined as two drinks per day for men and one drink per day for women—lessen the risk of heart disease and stroke. Nevertheless, a rival explanation for these findings is that people who drink only moderate amounts of alcohol, such as wine, also may have higher incomes and healthier lifestyles compared with people who either abstain from drinking or drink more than two drinks at a sitting (Lieber, 2003; Saarni et al., 2008).

Another hypothesis is that people who abstain are in poorer health to begin with than are light or moderate drinkers. Nevertheless, systematic reviews of studies comparing drinkers with nondrinkers who abstained because they chose to do so (not because of poor health, disability, or weakness) found no health differences between drinkers and teetotalers (Fillmore et al., 2006).

Health psychologists use a variety of educational and behavioral interventions to promote and maintain health and to assist people in coping with serious illnesses.

Factoid

The severity of hangovers, with nasty symptoms of headache, nausea, vomiting, sweating, thirst, and diarrhea, is related to the level of toxic substances called *congeners* in alcoholic drinks. Researchers discovered that people who consume bourbon, a dark-colored drink with high congener levels, experience more severe hangovers compared with people who consume vodka, a clear drink with low congener levels (Rosenhow et al., 2010). Still, drinking excessive amounts of any type of alcohol will produce a hangover.

Evidence is clear that heavy drinking can produce long-term physical problems.

◀ **RULING OUT RIVAL HYPOTHESES**
Have important alternative explanations for the findings been excluded?

◀ **RULING OUT RIVAL HYPOTHESES**
Have important alternative explanations for the findings been excluded?

Calculate BMI by dividing weight in pounds (lbs) by height in inches (in) squared and multiplying by a conversion factor of 703.

Example: Weight = 155 lbs, height = 5'9" (69")
Calculation: [155 ÷ (69)^2] × 703 = 22.89

BMI	Weight Status
Below 18.5	Underweight
18.5 to 24.9	Normal
25.0 to 29.9	Overweight
30.0 and above	Obese

Height	Weight Range	BMI	Weight Status
	124 lbs or less	Below 18.5	Underweight
5'9"	125 lbs to 168 lbs	18.5 to 24.9	Normal
	169 lbs to 202 lbs	25.0 to 29.9	Overweight
	203 lbs or more	30 or higher	Obese

FIGURE 4 Body Mass Index (BMI) and Weight Status. (*Data Source:* Centers for Disease Control and Prevention, 2007a, Division of Nutrition and Physical Activity National Center for Chronic Disease Prevention and Health Promotion).

CORRELATION VS. CAUSATION ▶
Can we be sure that A causes B?

Factoid

Reservatol, a substance found in red wine, may have beneficial health effects. Reservatol may explain why the French, whose diet is rich in fat, have a normal life expectancy. Recent studies with human volunteers mirror the findings from animal studies indicating that reservatol increases muscle efficiency, reduces blood sugar, and lowers blood pressure (Timmers et al., 2011). But we should keep in mind that the amount of reservatol provided in pill form to participants in the study was the equivalent of about two gallons of red wine a day.

RULING OUT RIVAL HYPOTHESES ▶
Have important alternative explanations for the findings been excluded?

At this time, we can't be sure that any amount of alcohol is safe, much less good for our health. One thing's reasonably certain, however: drinking heavily is associated with a heightened risk of cardiovascular disease (Bagnardi et al., 2001). In addition, drinking three or more drinks a week may increase a woman's risk for breast cancer (Chen et al, 2011). Fortunately, many of the negative effects of alcohol, including changes in the brain, can be reversed or minimized when we abstain from drinking (Tyas, 2001).

HEALTHY BEHAVIOR #3: ACHIEVE A HEALTHY WEIGHT. The statistics tell the grim story. As of 2010, 34 percent of adult Americans were overweight, and another 28 percent of Americans were obese, as indicated by a statistic known as the *body mass index (BMI)* (see **FIGURE 4**) (Schiller et al., 2012). The number of obese children and adolescents has tripled over the past decade or so, signaling an ominous trend (Ogden et al., 2006). According to some researchers, our society faces an "obesity epidemic" of enormous proportions, due in large measure to decreases in our physical activity (Heini & Weinsier, 1997; Wing & Polley, 2001; see **TABLE 1**).

People who are obese are at heightened risk of heart disease, injuries from falls, stroke, high blood pressure, arthritis, some types of cancer, respiratory problems, and diabetes (Himes & Reynolds, 2012; Klein et al., 2004; Kurth et al., 2003). Yet if obese people don't suffer from complications commonly associated with obesity, such as high blood pressure or diabetes, they live just as long as do lean individuals (Kuk et al., 2011). Still, if an obese person, say a 300-pound man, sheds even 10 percent of his weight, his health is likely to improve (Wing & Polley, 2001). Exercise is one of the best means of shedding that annoying fat around the belly and of losing weight over the long haul (Pronk & Wing, 1994). The more inactive we are and the more time we spend watching television, the more likely we are to be obese (Ching et al., 1996; Gortmaker et al., 1993). Of course, these findings are only correlational; it's also possible that people who are obese are weaker and less energetic and become couch potatoes as a result. Indeed, there's considerable controversy over how much of the negative association between obesity and physical health is due to obesity itself as opposed to the behaviors that often go along with it, such as inactivity and poor nutrition (Campos, 2004; Johnson, 2005).

Overweight individuals suffer from a variety of social and emotional problems, too. Many obese children are subject to teasing (Thompson et al., 2005). When they become adolescents and adults, they often experience discrimination in the social arena and workplace (Crandall, 1994; Schwartz, et al., 2006). In one study of 9,125 adults, obese people were 25 percent more likely to suffer from depression or an anxiety disorder compared with people of normal weight (Simon et al., 2006). It's not clear whether depression triggers obesity or whether obesity sets the stage for depression. Yet the positive association between obesity and depression counters the popular stereotype of the obese person as cheerful or "jolly" (Roberts et al., 2002). Our negative attitudes toward obesity run so deep that 46 percent of people say they'd rather give up at least a year of their lives than be obese, and 30 percent would rather be divorced than obese (Schwartz et al., 2006).

Clearly, overweight people suffer in many respects. Researchers followed a group of people aged 16–24 for seven years (Gortmaker et al., 1993). At the end of the study, individuals who were overweight were less wealthy, didn't progress as far in school, and were less likely to be married. These changes occurred independently of intelligence and financial status at the start of the study, bolstering the claim that prejudice and discrimination account for the plight of overweight people.

Tips for Achieving a Healthy Weight. Given the many social and medical reasons for losing weight, it's no wonder people have tried all manner of products and diets touted as effective for weight loss. The fad treatments include appetite-suppressing eyeglasses, magic weight-loss earrings, electrical muscle stimulators, and "magnet diet pills" to flush

TABLE 1 Reasons for Obesity in America Aside From Diet and Lack of Exercise.

- Lack of adequate sleep, which directly causes weight gain.

- Endocrine disruptors in foods that modify fats in the body.

- Comfortable temperatures as a result of heating/air conditioning that decrease calories burned from sweating and shivering.

- Use of medicines that contribute to weight gain.

- Increases in certain segments of the population, including Hispanics and middle-aged people, who have higher rates of obesity.

- Increase in mothers who give birth at older ages, which is associated with heavier children.

- Genetic influences during pregnancy.

- Moderately overweight people may have an evolutionary advantage over very thin people and be more likely to survive: Darwinian natural selection.

- People tend to marry people with a similar body type, a phenomenon called *assortative mating*. When heavy people reproduce, they're likely to give birth to relatively heavy children.

Being overweight or obese increases the risk of various physical health problems and is associated with depression and other adjustment difficulties.

fat out of the body—all of which are entirely devoid of scientific support (Corbett, 2006). Many fad diets offer conflicting and confusing recommendations based on little more than someone's pet theory rather than careful research that's been replicated. Some of our favorite fad diets include the "cabbage soup" diet, in which you feast on little more than—guess what?—cabbage soup (sounds yummy, doesn't it?), the popcorn diet (ideal for compulsive movie-goers), and the grapefruit diet (Danbrot, 2004; Herskowitz, 1987; Thompson & Ahrens, 2004). Some people on these diets may experience dramatic short-term weight loss, but this loss is almost always followed by a gradual return of the initial weight (Brownell & Rodin, 1994), resulting in the well-known "yo-yo effect" that often accompanies dieting. What seems to count more in dieting than the particular foods people eat is the total amount of calories they consume (Bray et al., 2012). However, *crash diets*—diets in which people severely restrict calories (often down to 1,000 calories per day for several weeks)—aren't likely to result in long-term weight loss and are unhealthy (Shade et al., 2004). Importantly, after one year, people on most or all diets begin to regain their weight and stray from their diet plans. Yet about one-fifth of people can lose at least

◀ **REPLICABILITY**
Can the results be duplicated in other studies?

The huge number of diet books published each year can be bewildering to people who are trying to lose weight. How many of these books are based on adequate science?

Factoid

People who carry their fat around the abdomen (so-called spare tires) are at greater risk for health problems than people whose fat is distributed elsewhere. Scientists sampled the blood of extremely obese patients who underwent stomach bypass surgery and found that the fat in the abdomen was secreting high levels of interleukin-6, a molecule associated with inflammation linked to high blood pressure, diabetes, atherosclerosis, cancer, and possibly aging (Fontana et al., 2007).

10 percent of their body weight and keep it off for at least a year (Nicklas et al., 2011; Wing & Hill, 2001).

One variable that affects our dieting success is our genes. Perhaps as much as half of the differences in people's tendency to become overweight is genetically influenced (Bouchard, 1995; Wing & Polley, 2001). Researchers have pinpointed specific genes associated with obesity, which appear related to appetite and energy use (Bouchard et al., 2004; Campfield, Smith, & Burn, 1996). These discoveries suggest that it might one day be possible to develop drugs that switch genes on and off to control weight. But while we're waiting, there's much we can do to achieve a stable, healthy weight, regardless of our genetic heritage.

Here's some basic yet scientifically supported advice to follow for controlling your weight and eating a healthy diet:

1. Exercise regularly, stop smoking and drinking excessively, sleep at least eight hours a night, and cut down on television time—unless you're watching it while exercising, of course (Mozaffarian et al., 2011).

2. Monitor total calories and body weight (Wing & Hill, 2001).

3. Eat foods with "good fats," such as olive oil and fish oil, to protect against and even lower heart disease risk (Estruch et al., 2013); lower your salt and caffeine intake to reduce blood pressure; and eat high-fiber foods to lower the risk of CHD and diabetes (Cook, 2008; Covas, Konstantinidou, & Fito, 2009; Vuksan et al., 2009).

4. Limit your intake of potato chips, sugar-sweetened beverages, unprocessed red meats, and processed meats, and eat more whole grains, nuts, yogurt, and fruits (Mozaffarian et al., 2011).

5. Get help from your social network to support your efforts to lose weight (Wing & Jeffrey, 1999).

6. Control portion size. By all means, don't make a habit of "supersizing" your cheeseburgers and fries.

HEALTHY BEHAVIOR #4: EXERCISE. Help for some psychological ailments may be as close as our running shoes. Jogging, swimming, bicycling, and other regular **aerobic exercises**, which promote the use of oxygen in the body, can lower blood pressure and risk for CHD, improve lung function, relieve the symptoms of arthritis, decrease diabetes risk, and cut the risk of breast and colon cancer (Barbour, Houle, & Dubbert, 2003; Wei et al., 1999). Running, lifting weights, and practicing yoga for eight weeks or longer can also improve cardiovascular recovery and relieve both depression and anxiety (Chafin, Christenfeld & Gerin, 2008; Phillips, Kiernan, & King, 2001; Stathopoulou et al., 2006).

Contrary to the popular "no pain, no gain" belief that exercise must be vigorous and sustained to do any good, 30 minutes of activity on most days of the week, including gardening and cleaning our rooms, can lead to improved fitness and health (Blair et al., 1992; Pate et al., 1995). In a study in Finland (Paffenbarger et al., 1986), middle-aged men who didn't get much physical activity on the job but who burned off 2,000 calories (the equivalent of about four Big Macs) a week in their spare time lived two-and-a-half years longer on average than did men who were less active in their leisure hours. Of course, people who are less active may be less physically fit to begin with, so the causal arrow may run in both directions. Although even moderate exercise—at about the level of a brisk walk—can reap health benefits, including improved cognitive functioning in older adults and perhaps even the growth of neurons (Erickson & Kramer, 2009; Middleton et al., 2011), more sustained and vigorous exercise is typically needed to reach our fitness potential.

BUT CHANGING LIFESTYLES IS EASIER SAID THAN DONE. Why do we have difficulty changing our lifestyles, even when we know that bad habits can endanger our health? As many as 30 to 70 percent of patients don't take their physician's medical advice

Aerobic exercise, including rowing, swimming, and biking, is an excellent way to lose weight, stay fit, and maintain or even improve cardiovascular health.

CORRELATION VS. CAUSATION ▶
Can we be sure that A causes B?

aerobic exercise
exercise that promotes the use of oxygen in the body

(National Heart, Lung, and Blood Institute, 1998), and as many as 80 percent don't follow their physician's recommendations to exercise, stop smoking, change their diet, or take prescribed medications (Berlant & Pruitt, 2003). The extent of some medical noncompliance is truly staggering. Paula Vincent (1971) found that 58 percent of patients with glaucoma, a serious eye disease, didn't take their prescribed eye drops, even though they knew that their failure to do so could make them go blind!

Personal Inertia. One reason for noncompliance is that it's difficult to overcome personal inertia—our reluctance to try something new. Many self-destructive habits relieve stress and don't create an imminent health threat, so it's easy for us to "let things be." Eating a heaping portion of ice cream doesn't seem terribly dangerous when we view heart disease as a distant and uncertain catastrophe. John Norcross and his colleagues found that only 19 percent of people who made a New Year's resolution to change a problem behavior, including changing their diet or exercising more, maintained the change when followed up two years later (Norcross, Ratzin, & Payne, 1989; Norcross & Vangarelli, 1989).

Misestimating Risk. Another reason we maintain the status quo is that we underestimate certain risks to our health and overestimate others. To illustrate this point, try answering the following three questions before reading on:

In the United States, which causes more deaths?

1. All types of accidents combined or strokes
2. All motor vehicle (car, truck, bus, and motorcycle) accidents combined or digestive cancer
3. Diabetes or homicide?

If we told you that four fully loaded jumbo jets were crashing every day in the United States, you'd be outraged. Yet the equivalent of that number—about 1,200 people—die each day in America from smoking-related causes (Centers for Disease Control and Prevention, 2005). How likely is it we'll actually die in a plane crash? Not likely at all. We'd need to fly in commercial airliners for about 10,000 years straight—that is, around the clock without any breaks—before the odds of our dying in a plane crash exceed 50 percent. But because plane crashes make big news, we overestimate their frequency.

 Watch in **MyPsychLab** the **Video:** What's in It for Me?: The Challenge of Quitting Bad Health Habits

Answers are located at the end of the text.

STRESS REDUCTION AND RELAXATION TECHNIQUES   evaluating CLAIMS

We all have stress in our lives, whether it comes from our course work, jobs, families, or all three. The Internet offers a wide array of techniques for reducing stress, but it's often difficult to identify which techniques are supported by sound science. Let's evaluate some of these claims, which are modeled after actual stress-reduction websites.

"Here are some helpful tips for reducing stress. Remember, there is no 'one size fits all' solution and all of these methods require that you change the way you approach and deal with potential stressors in your life."

This site avoids exaggerated claims by acknowledging that there's no miracle cure for stress. The methods of stress reduction and relief differ for every person and require us to make changes in our lives.

"Our all-natural pills allow you to wipe away all the stress in your life—instantly and naturally."

What's wrong with this advertiser's claim that the pills offer an "all-natural" approach to stress reduction? Does the promise to eliminate all forms of stress in your life seem plausible? Why or why not?

"Top experts agree that Trans-Cortex space-dimensional music CDs can relax up to 90% of overstressed listeners!"

How much weight should we give to statements that appeal to the authority of unnamed "top experts" who endorse a product with a fancy-sounding, made-up name? What might be the problem with statistics that claim a success rate of "up to 90%"?

Factoid

Some people may find it difficult to lose weight because they find eating fatty foods to be comforting. Researchers who delivered either fatty acids or a nonfat saline solution directly into the stomachs of normal weight volunteers found that the fatty acids decreased negative moods in response to sad facial expressions and sad music, compared with the saline solution. Accompanying differences in neural activity were also observed in brain scans (Van Oudenhove et al., 2011).

The answers are (1) strokes (by about twofold), (2) digestive cancer (by about threefold), and (3) diabetes (by about fourfold). If you got one or more of these questions wrong (and most people do), the odds are that you relied on the *availability heuristic* —the mental shortcut by which we judge the likelihood of an event by the ease with which it comes to mind (Hertwig, Pachur, & Kurzenhauser, 2005; Tversky & Kahneman, 1974). Because the news media provide far more coverage of dramatic accidents and homicides than strokes, digestive cancer, or diabetes, we overestimate the probability of accidents and homicides and underestimate the probability of many diseases. And because the media feature so many emotional and memorable stories of famous women who've developed breast cancer, we're likely to think of breast cancer as a more frequent and deadly illness compared with heart disease (Ruscio, 2000). Heart disease is less newsworthy precisely because it's more commonplace, and perhaps less terrifying, than cancer is with its troubling treatment-related side effects, including very obvious hair loss.

In general, we underestimate the frequency of the most common causes of death, and overestimate the frequency of the least common causes of death (Lichtenstein et al., 1978). These errors in judgment can be costly: if women believe that heart disease isn't a threat, they may not change their lifestyle.

Many people are well aware of health risks but don't take them to "heart," pun intended. Smokers greatly overestimate their chances of living to the age of 75 (Schoenbaum, 1997). Other people rationalize their lifestyle choices by telling themselves, "Something's going to kill me anyway, so I might as well enjoy my life and do whatever I want."

Feeling Powerless. Still other people feel powerless to change, perhaps because their habits are so deeply ingrained. Consider a person who's smoked a pack of cigarettes a day for the last 15 years. She's inhaled cigarette smoke over a million times. It's no wonder she feels helpless to change her habit.

PREVENTION PROGRAMS. Because modifying such deeply entrenched behaviors can be so difficult, we're best off not developing them in the first place. Prevention efforts should begin by adolescence, if not earlier, because the earlier in life we develop unhealthy habits, the more likely they'll create problems, like alcohol abuse, for us later in life (Hingson, Heeren, & Winter, 2006). Health psychologists have developed prevention programs that contain the following elements:

- Educating young people about the risks and negative consequences of obesity, smoking, and excessive drinking, as well as positive health behaviors such as good nutrition and the importance of exercise
- Teaching young people to recognize and resist peer pressure to engage in unhealthy behaviors
- Exposing young people to positive role models who don't drink or smoke
- Teaching effective coping skills for daily living and dealing with stressful life events

But not all prevention efforts are successful. The Drug Abuse Resistance Education, or DARE, program is used in schools nationwide to teach students how to avoid getting into drugs, gangs, and violent activities (Ringwalt & Greene, 1993). The program uses uniformed police officers and targets fifth- and sixth-graders. It emphasizes the negative aspects of excessive drinking and substance abuse and the positive aspects of self-esteem and healthy life choices. The program is popular with school administrators and parents; there's a good chance you've seen DARE bumper stickers on cars in your neighborhood. Nevertheless, researchers have repeatedly found that the program doesn't produce positive long-term effects on substance abuse or boost self-esteem (Lynam et al., 1999). A few researchers have even found that it may occasionally backfire to produce increases in mild forms of substance abuse (Lilienfeld, 2007; Werch & Owen, 2002). Programs that focus on using coping skills and managing stress generally show better treatment and prevention outcomes (MacKillop & Gray, in press). These findings remind us that we need to evaluate programs carefully before they're widely promoted based on their intuitive appeal alone (Wilson, 2011).

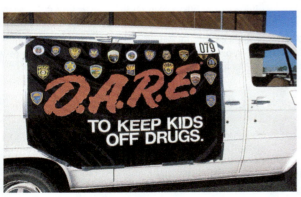

Despite its popularity, the DARE program isn't effective for preventing substance abuse or enhancing self-esteem.

Complementary and Alternative Medicine

What do the following three practices have in common?

1. Consuming supplements of *gracinia cambogia*, a substance derived from the tamarind rind, to lose weight

2. Placing thin needles in the external ear to relieve nausea following an operation

3. Manipulating the spine to treat pain and prevent disease

The answer: each is an alternative or nonstandard treatment that falls outside the mainstream of modern medicine. **Alternative medicine** refers to health care practices and products used *in place of* conventional medicine, that is, medicine for which there's solid evidence of safety and effectiveness. **Complementary medicine**, in contrast, refers to products and practices that are used *together with* conventional medicine (National Center for Complementary and Alternative Medicine, 2002). Together, both forms of medicine are known as CAM (complementary and alternative medicine). What unites them is that they've not yet been shown to be safe and effective using scientific standards (Bausell, 2007; Singh & Ernst, 2008).

Each year, Americans fork out about $34 billion to CAM practitioners and to purchase CAM products (Nahin et al., 2009). In a national survey, 38 percent of adults and 12 percent of children reported using some form of CAM over the preceding year (Barnes, Bloom, & Nahin, 2008). We can examine various CAM therapies in **TABLE 2**.

BIOLOGICALLY BASED THERAPIES: VITAMINS, HERBS, AND FOOD SUPPLEMENTS. Americans shell out more than $22 billion each year for herbal treatments of uncertain effectiveness (Gupta, 2007; Walach & Kirsch, 2003). Yet many herbal and natural preparations that some once viewed as promising have been found to be no more effective than a placebo (Bausell, 2007). Contrary to popular belief, scientific findings suggest that

- the herb St. John's wort does not alleviate the symptoms of moderate to severe depression (Davidson et al., 2002).

- shark cartilage cannot cure cancer (Loprinzi et al., 2005).

- the widely used supplements glucosamine and chondroitin do not relieve mild arthritis pain (Reichenbach et al., 2007).

- acai berries do not improve sexual performance, increase energy, or aid in digestion or weight loss (Bender, 2008; Cassileth, Heitzer, & Wesa, 2009).

- an extract from the leaves of the ginkgo biloba tree does not slow cognitive decline in aging adults, prevent Alzheimer's disease, or reduce heart attacks or strokes (DeKosky et al., 2008; Kuller et al., 2010).

TABLE 2 Use of CAM Therapies Among American Adults During the Previous Year.

TYPE OF THERAPY	PERCENTAGE OF USERS DURING THE PREVIOUS YEAR
Natural Products	17.7%
Deep Breathing	12.7%
Meditation	9.4%
Chiropractic and Related Methods	8.6%
Massage	8.3%
Yoga	6.1%
Diet-Based Therapies	3.6%
Progressive Relaxation	2.9%
Guided Imagery	2.2%
Homeopathy	1.8%
Acupuncture	1.4%
Biofeedback	0.2%

Statistics taken from 2007 National Health Interview Survey (Barnes et al., 2008).

Factoid

One alternative medical treatment, chelation therapy, can be dangerous. This treatment, which practitioners use occasionally to treat autism, attempts to remove heavy metals (including mercury, which some people claim can trigger autism) from the body by injecting patients with a chemical that binds to these metals. Three deaths have been associated with chelation, which were caused by low calcium levels that led to heart failure (Centers for Disease Control and Prevention, 2006). There's no controlled evidence that chelation therapy is effective for autism or any other psychological disorder (DeNoon, 2005).

alternative medicine
health care practices and products used in place of conventional medicine

complementary medicine
health care practices and products used together with conventional medicine

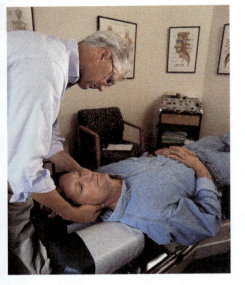

Chiropractors typically manipulate the spine and muscles to treat a variety of health problems. But there's little evidence that their approaches are more effective than those derived from traditional medicine.

In 2007, meditation was practiced by nearly 10 percent of people in the United States, reflecting increased perceptions of the possible benefits of meditation by the general public and the scientific community (Barnes et al., 2008).

biofeedback
feedback by a device that provides almost an immediate output of a biological function, such as heart rate or skin temperature

meditation
a variety of practices that train attention and awareness

Many vitamins and dietary supplements haven't fared well, either. Dietary supplementation with calcium doesn't prevent much bone loss in women (Jackson et al., 2006), vitamin C doesn't markedly decrease the severity or duration of colds (Douglas et al., 2004), iron supplementation is associated with a greater risk of death among older women (Mursu et al., 2011), and high doses of vitamin E may actually increase the risk of death from prostate cancer (Klein et al., 2011). Vitamin deficiencies can cause serious health problems, but there isn't much benefit in taking "mega doses" of vitamins or minerals far in excess of recommended amounts.

The U.S. Food and Drug Administration (FDA) carefully regulates most medicines. But because of controversial congressional legislation passed in 1999, it no longer monitors the safety, purity, or effectiveness of herbs, vitamins, or dietary supplements. So if we go to our local drugstore and purchase a bottle of St. John's wort or ginkgo, we're gambling with our safety. Some impure herbal preparations contain dangerous amounts of lead and even the poison arsenic (Ernst, 2002); other natural products can interfere with the actions of conventional medicines. Just because something is natural doesn't mean that it's necessarily safe or healthy for us (this false belief is called the *natural commonplace*). Finally, because the FDA doesn't monitor these products, there's no guarantee they even contain what they claim to contain.

MANIPULATIVE AND BODY-BASED METHODS: THE EXAMPLE OF CHIROPRACTIC MEDICINE. Chief among body-based methods is *chiropractic manipulation*, which is, not surprisingly, practiced by chiropractors. Chiropractors manipulate the spine to treat a wide range of pain-related conditions and injuries and often provide nutrition and lifestyle counseling. Nearly 20 percent of Americans report having visited a chiropractor (Barnes et al., 2004). Unlike medical doctors, chiropractors can't perform surgeries or prescribe medications. Historically, chiropractic medicine was based on the now discredited idea that irregularities in the alignment of the spine prevent the nervous and immune systems from functioning properly. Although chiropractic procedures may sometimes be helpful, they're no better than standard approaches, including exercise, general practitioner care, pain relievers, and physical therapy (Assendelft et al., 2003; Astin & Ernst, 2002). More important, there's no evidence that these procedures can treat diseases, such as cancer, that aren't associated with back problems, even though they're frequently used for those purposes. Still, some people may benefit from the attention, support, and advice they receive from chiropractors, which may relieve stress and create a strong placebo effect.

MIND-BODY MEDICINE: BIOFEEDBACK AND MEDITATION. **Biofeedback** is feedback by a device that provides almost an immediate output of a biological function, such as heart rate or skin temperature (Miller, 1978). Over time, some patients can learn to use this feedback to change their physiological responses associated with stress or illness. Compared with its heyday in the 1970s, the popularity of biofeedback has waned somewhat, probably because training in altering physiological responses can be time-consuming for patients and because biofeedback requires special training (Andrasik, 2012). Moreover, health psychologists have raised questions about whether biofeedback yields beneficial effects beyond the relaxation associated with sitting quietly. In fact, relaxation training and biofeedback are about equally effective in reducing stress and treating anxiety, insomnia, and the side effects associated with cancer chemotherapy (Gatchel, 2001). Still, there are indications that biofeedback is more effective than relaxation in treating headaches and that the combination of biofeedback with relaxation produces the best results with respect to certain headaches (Nestoriuc et al., 2008).

Meditation refers to a variety of practices that train attention and awareness and assist in the control of emotions (Hölzel et al., 2012; Shapiro & Walsh, 2003). Meditative practices are embedded in many world religions and integrated into the lives of people of all races and creeds. In Western countries, people typically practice meditation to achieve stress reduction, whereas in non-Western countries, people typically practice meditation to achieve insight and spiritual growth. Contrary to stereotypes, there's no one "right" way to meditate. Meditation can include focusing attention on the breath, a flame, feelings of compassion toward all living things, or whatever comes to mind (Hofmann, Grossman, & Hinton, 2011).

For centuries, meditation fell well outside the scientific mainstream. Yet in the 1960s, scientists began to take a serious look at its possible benefits. Since then, they've identified a wide range of positive effects, including heightened creativity, empathy, alertness, and self-esteem (Haimerl & Valentine, 2001; So & Orme-Johnson, 2001), along with decreases in anxiety, interpersonal problems (Tloczynski & Tantriella, 1998), and recurrences of depression (Segal, Williams, & Teasdale, 2012). Clinicians have added meditative techniques to a variety of psychotherapies and have used them with some success in treating pain and numerous medical conditions (Baer, 2003; Kabat-Zinn, 2003). Meditation can also enhance blood flow in the brain (Newberg et al., 2001; Wang et al., 2011) and immune function (Davidson et al, 2003; Jacobs et al., 2011).

Many people seem to benefit from meditation, although it's not clear why: Its positive effects may derive from a greater acceptance of our troubling thoughts and feelings (Kabat-Zinn, 2003). They may also derive not from meditation itself, but from sitting quietly, resting, and relaxing with eyes closed (Farthing, 1992; Holmes, 1987). People's positive attitudes and expectancies about meditation may also account for why it's beneficial. Few studies have followed meditators for long periods of time, so we don't know whether positive effects persist, generalize to different situations, or apply to large numbers of meditators. When researchers find differences between experienced meditators and nonmeditators, they need to be careful about how they interpret the results. Meditation might create specific changes in brain wave activity, but people who show certain brain wave patterns may be especially attracted to meditation in the first place (Lutz et al., 2004). Therefore, the direction of the causal arrow is difficult to determine.

ENERGY MEDICINE: THE CASE OF ACUPUNCTURE. *Energy medicines* are increasingly popular (refer to Table 2) and are based on the idea that disruptions in our body's energy field can be mapped and treated. Chinese physicians first developed and practiced **acupuncture** at least 2,000 years ago. In acupuncture, practitioners insert thin needles into specific points in the body. More than 4 percent of Americans (Barnes et al., 2004) have consulted acupuncturists at some point. These practitioners place the needles on specific spots called *meridians*, which they believe channel a subtle energy or life force called *qi* (pronounced "chee"). Acupuncturists claim to relieve blockages of qi by applying needles or electrical, laser, or heat stimulation to one or more of 2,000 points on the body.

Acupuncture can help to relieve nausea following surgical operations and treat pain-related conditions (Berman & Straus, 2004). Still, there's no reason to believe that any of its positive effects are due to energy changes (Posner & Sampson, 1999). The acupuncture points were mapped long before the rise of modern science. Even today, scientists haven't been able to measure, much less identify, the energy associated with specific illnesses. If a concept can't be measured and isn't falsifiable—in this case, it's impossible to disprove that "qi" is the effective mechanism—then it's not scientific.

WHOLE MEDICAL SYSTEMS: THE EXAMPLE OF HOMEOPATHY. Entire medical systems have developed apart from conventional medicine for thousands of years in China and India. A more recent example of such a system is **homeopathic medicine**, practiced in the United States since the early 1800s. Nearly 4 percent of Americans report having used one or more homeopathic remedies in their lifetime (Barnes et al., 2004). These remedies are based on the premise that consuming an extremely diluted dose of a substance known to produce an illness in a healthy person will alleviate that illness. To understand how homeopathy supposedly works, we should recall the joke about the patient who forgot to take his homeopathic remedy and died of an underdose. The principle behind homeopathy is that "like cures like." This is a good example of the *representativeness heuristic*, a mental shortcut with which we judge the similarity between two things by gauging the extent to which they resemble each other ("like goes with like").

Biofeedback of forehead muscle tension can provide substantial control of this tension, thereby offering relief from muscle contraction headaches. But biofeedback may often be no more effective than relaxation.

◄ **CORRELATION VS. CAUSATION**
Can we be sure that A causes B?

Acupuncture needles are thin and can be inserted virtually any place on the skin.

◄ **FALSIFIABILITY**
Can the claim be disproved?

acupuncture
ancient Chinese practice of inserting thin needles into one or more of 2,000 points in the body to alter energy forces believed to run through the body

homeopathic medicine
remedies that feature a small dose of an illness-inducing substance to activate the body's own natural defenses

When we rely too heavily on the representativeness heuristic, we can make errors in judgment. In this case, we might assume that the treatment for a disorder must resemble its cause—so if a disorder is caused by too much of chemical A, we should treat it by presenting the patient with as little of chemical A as possible. Nevertheless, homeopaths often dilute remedies to the point that not even a single molecule of the original substance remains. Homeopaths' belief that the "memory" of the substance is enough to stimulate the body's defenses is an extraordinary claim that makes utterly no sense from a scientific perspective. Medicine that contains no medicine isn't medicine. Not surprisingly, homeopathic remedies haven't been shown to be effective for any medical condition (Giles, 2007).

PLACEBOS AND CAM. R. Barker Bausell (2007), a former advocate of CAM, reviewed research on acupuncture and other CAM treatments and concluded that, for the most part, they've failed to demonstrate that they're more effective than placebos or "sham" (fake) treatment. For example, patients with low back pain (Brinkhaus et al., 2006) and migraine headaches (Diener, Kronfeld, & Boewing, 2006) benefit from sham acupuncture treatment in which researchers place needles at locations that don't match the acupuncture points or in which needles don't actually penetrate the skin. Indeed, most research suggests that sham acupuncture relieves symptoms as much as standard acupuncture does (Hall, 2008; Hines, 2003). The placebo effect is a simpler explanation that better accounts for the data than the hypothesis that an undetectable energy field is responsible for acupuncture's effects.

Indeed, placebo effects are often impressive in their own right and exert a measurable impact on brain chemistry and activity (Kirsch, 2010). Placebos and acupuncture both stimulate the release of endorphins, although many activities, including eating hot chili, laughing, running vigorously, and hitting one's finger with a hammer, do too (Cabyoglu, Ergene, & Tan, 2006; Hall, 2008; Pert, 1997). Pain, often the target of CAM treatments, is notoriously responsive to placebos. Tor Wager and his colleagues told patients that a cream would reduce the pain of heat or electric shock (Wager et al., 2004). After the scientists applied the placebo cream to patients' skin, patients reported less pain, and brain imaging (fMRI) detected less activity in brain areas that register pain.

Doctors may be able to harness the power of placebos—by increasing patients' hope and positive expectancies to alleviate some physical symptoms and enhance the effects of available treatments. Researchers, in turn, need to carefully control for placebo effects in evaluating any new medical treatment, be it CAM or conventional, to rule out the possibility that they account for the treatment's effectiveness (Bausell, 2007).

Many CAM treatments have little or no scientific support, yet they remain popular. Why is this so? In addition to placebo effects, here are four probable reasons for the apparent effectiveness of unsupported CAM treatment, including homeopathy (Bausell, 2007; Beyerstein, 1997):

1. People may assume that natural products like herbs and megavitamins improve their health because they perceive no adverse effects to counter this belief.

2. The symptoms of many physical disorders come and go, so consumers may attribute symptom relief to the treatment, rather than to changes in the natural course of the illness.

3. When CAM treatments accompany conventional treatments, people may attribute their improvement to the CAM treatment, rather than to the less dramatic or interesting conventional treatment.

4. The problem may be misdiagnosed in the first place, so the condition isn't as severe as was initially believed.

EXTRAORDINARY CLAIMS ▶
Is the evidence as strong as the claim?

? Reiki is a Japanese energy therapy and spiritual healing practice in which practitioners first suggest that patients relax and then place their hands on or above them to rebalance and focus reiki energy (qi) on different body parts. Researchers have found no evidence that reiki is helpful in treating medical or stress-related conditions (Lee, Pittler, Ernst, 2008). What explanation, other than energy transfer, could account for reports of stress reduction or symptom improvement following reiki treatment? (See answer upside down at bottom of page.)

OCCAM'S RAZOR ▶
Does a simpler explanation fit the data just as well?

RULING OUT RIVAL HYPOTHESES ▶
Have important alternative explanations for the findings been excluded?

RULING OUT RIVAL HYPOTHESES ▶
Have important alternative explanations for the findings been excluded?

Factoid

According to some historical accounts, acupuncture was discovered on ancient Chinese battlefields when soldiers pierced by arrows and sharp stones reported relief from their other ailments (Gori & Firenzuoli, 2007).

Answer: Alternative explanations include the placebo effect, relaxation, and naturally occurring changes in the course of an illness.

CAM TREATMENTS: TO USE OR NOT TO USE, THAT IS THE QUESTION. Choosing scientifically unsupported alternative treatments over well-established traditional ones can be hazardous to our health. The popular media often serves up misinformation about CAM with potentially far-reaching public health consequences. For example, in numerous talk show appearances and a best-selling book, former sitcom actress Suzanne Somers (2009) has rejected the use of standard—and often highly effective—chemotherapy for breast and prostate cancer and touted alternative treatments and vitamin supplements that research has shown to be worthless or even dangerous.

Should we uncritically accept medical opinion and advice we encounter in the media or elsewhere? By now, you should be able to guess our answer: no! Conversely, should we conclude that all CAM treatments are worthless? Not at all. It's essential that we keep an open mind and not dismiss new treatments out of hand. Many drugs derive from plant and natural products, and many effective medicines surely remain to be discovered. Every year, drug companies screen thousands of natural products for disease-fighting properties, and a few prove worthy of further testing. For example, *taxol*, derived from the Pacific yew tree, has been shown to be effective as an anticancer drug. Although St. John's wort isn't especially effective for severe depression, some evidence suggests that it is somewhat helpful for mild depression (Kasper et al., 2007; Wallach & Kirsch, 2003). Nevertheless, not all researchers have replicated these positive findings (Rapaport et al., 2011), so caution is needed, especially because St. John's wort can interfere with the effectiveness of certain medications. At the same time, St. John's wort and other herbal medicines may eventually become part of mainstream treatment if they turn out to be safe and effective.

The same is true of psychological practices. Meditation, once regarded as an alternative approach, now appears to be an effective means of reducing stress and has increasingly blended into the spectrum of conventional approaches.

Barry Beyerstein (1997) recommended that we ask the following two questions before trying an alternative approach:

1. Does it lack a scientific rationale or contradict well-accepted scientific laws or principles?

2. Do carefully done studies show that the product or treatment is less effective than conventional approaches?

If the answer to both questions is "yes," we should be especially skeptical. When in doubt, it's wise to consult a physician about a CAM treatment. Doing so will give us confidence that the treatment we select, regardless of whether it's conventional, is genuinely a "good alternative."

"Now that you're fully recovered, Mr. Dawkins, we can tell you the truth. The 12-hour operation, the intravenous meals, the three weeks of bed rest ... all were part of an elaborate placebo effect."

◄ **REPLICABILITY**

Can the results be duplicated in other studies?

? Some celebrities have expressed strong opinions against conventional medical practices. For example, Bill Maher has voiced strong opposition to the swine flu vaccine despite the medical establishment's call for preventive vaccination. **What might be a public health consequence of Maher's opinion about vaccination?** (See answer upside down at bottom of page.)

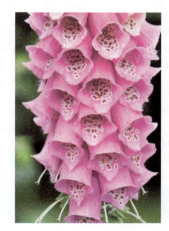

Since the late 1700s, physicians have known that digitalis, a drug that comes from the purple foxglove plant, can control heart rate and treat heart disease. Some, but by no means all, natural plants are effective medicines.

Answer: People will heed his "advice," not get vaccinated, and become ill with the flu. In turn, they may place others at risk for the flu.

Assess Your Knowledge   FACT or FICTION?

1. Most smokers who want to stop smoking each year succeed without professional help. **True / False**

2. Obese people tend to be "jollier" than non-obese people. **True / False**

3. Women tend to overestimate their risk of dying from breast cancer as opposed to heart disease. **True / False**

4. The fact that a health product is "natural" means it's likely to be safe. **True / False**

5. The effects of acupuncture appear to be due to the redistribution of energy in the body. **True / False**

Answers: 1. F; 2. F; 3. T; 4. F; 5. F

✓ **Study** and **Review** in **MyPsychLab**

Your Complete Review System

✓ **Study** and **Review** in **MyPsychLab**

((• **Listen** in **MyPsychLab** to chapter audio

What Is Stress?

1 EXPLAIN HOW STRESS IS DEFINED AND APPROACHED IN DIFFERENT WAYS.

Stress is a part of daily life. Most people experience one or more extremely stressful events in their lifetime. People experience stress when they feel physically threatened, unsafe, or unable to meet the perceived demands of life. Stress can be viewed as a stimulus, a response, or a transaction with the environment. Identifying specific categories of stressful events (unemployment, natural disasters) is the focus of stressors as stimuli view of stress, whereas reactions to stressful events and their consequences are important in studying the response aspects of stress. The stress as a transaction view holds that the experience of stress depends on both primary appraisal (the decision regarding whether the event is harmful) and secondary appraisal (perceptions of our ability to cope with the event) of the potentially stressful event.

1. The tension, discomfort, or physical symptoms that arise when a situation strains our ability to cope is called _____.

2. People who are recently divorced might be of particular interest to researchers who study stress from which viewpoint?

3. People's varied reactions to the same event suggest that we can view stress as a(n) _____ between people and their environments.

4. When we encounter a potentially threatening event, we initially engage in _____ _____ to decide whether the event is harmful.

5. We make a(n) _____ _____ to determine how well we can cope with a harmful event.

6. _____ _____ is a coping strategy people use to tackle life's challenges head-on.

7. When we try to put a positive spin on our feelings or predicaments and engage in behaviors to reduce painful emotions, we are engaging in _____ _____.

2 IDENTIFY DIFFERENT APPROACHES TO MEASURING STRESS.

Psychologists often assess life events that require major adaptations and adjustments, such as illness and unemployment. They also assess hassles—annoying, frustrating daily events that may be more related to adverse psychological and health outcomes than major stressors. Interview-based methods provide a more in-depth picture of life stress than do questionnaires.

8. The _____ _____ _____ Scale is based on 43 life events ranked in terms of stressfulness.

9. How can daily hassles such as getting stuck in traffic, dealing with a difficult boss, or getting the wrong order at a drive-through restaurant affect our health?

10. The frequency and perceived severity of hassles are (better/ worse) predictors of physical health than are major life events.

How We Adapt to Stress: Change and Challenge

3 DESCRIBE SELYE'S GENERAL ADAPTATION SYNDROME.

The GAS consists of three stages: (1) alarm: the autonomic nervous system is activated; (2) resistance: adaptation and coping occurs; and (3) exhaustion: resources and coping abilities are depleted, which can damage organs and contribute to depression and posttraumatic stress disorder (PTSD).

11. Identify the brain and body components activated in the alarm reaction proposed by Selye's GAS, depicted here.

12. The _____ response is a set of physiological or psychological reactions that mobilize us either to confront or escape a threatening situation.

13. During the _____ stage of the GAS, we adapt to the stressor and try to find a way to cope with it.

14. During the _____ stage of the GAS, resources and coping abilities are limited and stress can damage organs and engender depression and posttraumatic stress disorder.

4 DESCRIBE THE DIVERSITY OF STRESS RESPONSES.

Our stress reactions vary from one stressor to another and may be shaped by gender. The tend-and-befriend response is more common in women than in men. In times of stress, women often rely more on their social contacts, nurture others, and befriend or turn to others for support. About 5 percent (men) to 10 percent (women) of people experience PTSD in the face of a potentially traumatic stressor. Yet as many as two-thirds of people are resilient in the face of powerful stressors.

15. What are the similarities and differences between Shelley Taylor's tend-and-befriend response and the fight-or-flight response?

16. The hormone _____ further counters stress and promotes the tend-and-befriend response.

17. In a survey of NYC area residents after 9/11, researchers found that (25 percent/65 percent) of the sample were resilient.

18. People who cope well in the aftermath of a stressor tend to display relatively (high/low) levels of functioning before the event.

19. The severity, duration, and nearness to the stressor affect people's likelihood of developing _____ _____ _____.

20. The telltale symptoms of PTSD include vivid memories; feelings; and images of traumatic experiences, known commonly as _____.

How Stress Impacts Our Health

5 DESCRIBE HOW THE IMMUNE SYSTEM IS AFFECTED BY STRESS.

The immune system is the body's defensive barrier against disease. Phagocytes and lymphocytes neutralize viruses and bacteria and produce proteins called antibodies that fight infection. Diseases of the immune system include AIDS and autoimmune diseases in which the immune system is overactive. Stress can decrease resistance to illness, delay healing, and impair the immune system.

21. AIDS is a life-threatening, incurable, yet treatable condition in which the _____ _____ _____ attacks and damages the immune system.

22. An example of an autoimmune disease in which the immune system is overactive is (arthritis/alcoholism).

23. Psychoneuroimmunology is the study of the relationship between the immune system and the _____ _____ system.

24. Research has shown that stress (can/can't) decrease resistance to the cold virus.

6 IDENTIFY HOW PHYSICAL DISORDERS SUCH AS ULCERS ARE RELATED TO STRESS.

Psychologists use the term *psychophysiological* to describe illnesses like ulcers in which emotions and stress contribute to, maintain, or aggravate physical conditions. Ulcers, which appear to be caused by the *H. pylori* bacterium and exacerbated by stress, can be understood in terms of a biopsychosocial perspective, which considers both physical and psychological factors.

25. Ulcers (are/are not) caused by hot, spicy foods.

26. A biopsychosocial perspective proposes that most medical conditions are neither all physical nor all _____.

7 DESCRIBE THE ROLE OF PERSONALITY, EVERYDAY EXPERIENCES, AND SOCIOECONOMIC FACTORS IN CORONARY HEART DISEASE.

For many years, the Type A personality was thought to promote risk of CHD, but more recent work points to chronic hostility as a more central risk factor. Socioeconomic factors and everyday life experience can set the stage for many physical problems, including coronary heart disease.

27. Scientists have learned that psychological factors, including stress and personality traits, are key risk factors for _____ _____ _____.

28. What are the characteristics of a Type A personality, and what health risks are associated with such a personality?

29. Although job stress is correlated with CHD, it may not _____ it in all circumstances.

30. Researchers have established a (weak/strong) correlation between poverty and poor health.

Coping With Stress

8 DESCRIBE THE ROLE OF SOCIAL SUPPORT AND DIFFERENT TYPES OF CONTROL IN COPING WITH STRESS.

Social support and the following types of stress control are important: (1) behavioral control (taking action to reduce stress), (2) cognitive control (reappraising stressful events that can't be avoided), (3) decisional control (choosing among alternatives), (4) informational control (acquiring information about a stressor), and (5) emotional control (suppressing and expressing emotions at will). Flexible coping (adjusting coping strategies to specific situations) is also helpful.

31. _____ _____ encompasses our relationships with people and groups that provide emotional and financial assistance as we contend with important decisions or stressful situations.

32. What are the benefits of a strong social network when an individual is undergoing stressful or challenging life events?

33. The ability to step up and take action to reduce the impact of a stressful situation is an example of _____ _____.

34. _____ _____ is the ability to think differently about negative emotions that arise in response to stress-provoking events.

35. We engage in _____ _____ when we anticipate stressful situations and take steps to prevent or minimize difficulties before they arise.

36. What is crisis debriefing, and how effective is it for people who have experienced a traumatic event?

9 EXPLAIN HOW OUR ATTITUDES, BELIEFS, AND PERSONALITY MAY INFLUENCE OUR RESPONSES TO STRESS.

Hardy people view change as challenge, have a deep sense of commitment to their life and work, and believe they can control events. Optimism and spirituality boost stress resistance, whereas rumination is not an adaptive way of coping with stressful circumstances.

37. _____ is a set of attitudes, marked by a sense of control over events, commitment to life and work, and motivation and courage to confront stressful events.

38. Optimistic people are (better/worse) at handling frustration than pessimists are.

39. _____ is the search for the sacred, which may or may not extend to belief in God.

40. Spending a good deal of time ruminating is a (productive/counterproductive) way of reacting to a stressful situation.

Promoting Good Health—and Less Stress!

10 IDENTIFY FOUR BEHAVIORS THAT CONTRIBUTE TO A HEALTHY LIFESTYLE.

Behaviors that can promote health include not smoking, curbing alcohol consumption, maintaining a healthy weight, and exercising.

41. The field of psychology that integrates the behavioral sciences with the practice of medicine is called _____ _____.

42. Health psychologists make the treatment and prevention of _____ a high priority, because it's the leading cause of preventable disease and deaths in the United States.

43. Research has shown that heavy _____ is associated with significant increases in many different types of cancer, serious and sometimes fatal liver problems, and brain shrinkage and other neurological problems.

44. Follow the formula below to calculate your BMI and determine your weight status from the categories listed.

45. Genes (play/do not play) a role in people's tendency to become overweight.

Calculate BMI by dividing weight in pounds (lbs) by height in inches (in) squared and multiplying by a conversion factor of 703.

Example: Weight = 155 lbs, height = 5'9" (69")
Calculation: $[155 \div (69)^2] \times 703 = 22.89$

BMI	Weight Status
Below 18.5	Underweight
18.5 to 24.9	Normal
25.0 to 29.9	Overweight
30.0 and above	Obese

11 IDENTIFY WHY IT IS DIFFICULT TO CHANGE OUR LIFESTYLE.

Reasons it's difficult to change our lifestyle include personal inertia, tendency to misestimate risk, and feelings of powerlessness.

46. Because of the _____ heuristic, we tend to underestimate certain risks to our health and overestimate others.

12 DESCRIBE DIFFERENT ALTERNATIVE AND COMPLEMENTARY MEDICAL APPROACHES AND COMPARE THEIR EFFECTIVENESS WITH PLACEBOS.

Alternative medicine approaches include biologically based therapies (vitamins, herbs, and food supplements), manipulative and body-based methods (chiropractic medicine), mind–body medicine (biofeedback and meditation), energy medicine (acupuncture), and whole medical systems (homeopathy). Many alternative approaches are no more effective than placebos. Alternative medical products and procedures can become part of conventional medicine when demonstrated to be safe and effective.

47. _____ _____ refers to health care practices and products that are used in place of conventional medicine.

48. Herbs, vitamins, and dietary supplements (are/are not) regulated by the FDA for safety, purity, and effectiveness.

49. List some of the positive effects of meditation and possible explanations for each.

50. _____ _____ is based on the premise that consuming an extremely diluted dose of an illness-inducing substance will activate the body's own natural defenses against it.

Apply Your Scientific Thinking Skills

Use your scientific thinking skills to answer the following questions, referencing specific scientific thinking principles and common errors in reasoning whenever possible.

1. People can attend a wide variety of support groups, both in person and online. Research at least two of them and describe the types of social support that each offers. What scientifically supported methods do they use to help individuals gain control over their problems?

2. An estimated 21 percent of American men and 18 percent of American women smoke cigarettes, despite scientific research that shows the negative impact that smoking has on their health. Compare the approaches used by three different anti-smoking programs (such as those using behavior modification, hypnosis, or drugs in a patch or gum). Are their methods and claims about success rates supported by research? Explain your answer.

3. Many websites advertise products or methods designed to enhance people's ability to cope with stress. Identify three such ads and evaluate the scientific support for each of the techniques or approaches recommended. Then, create a brief ad for a product or approach that's well supported by scientific evidence.

Further Your Understanding

EXTEND YOUR KNOWLEDGE WITH THE MYPSYCHLAB VIDEO SERIES

Watch these videos in MyPsychLab. Follow the "Video Series" link.

The Big Picture: Health Psychology   Look back at the history of heart disease and learn how our current understanding of the mind-body connection has opened up new possibilities for heart disease prevention and treatment.

The Basics: Stress and Your Health   See how stress affects our memory and physiological health and how our bodies recover after periods of stress.

Special Topics: Health Disparities   Find out what is preventing people from establishing a "medical home."

Thinking Like a Psychologist: Personality and Health   Learn how stress affects the body, what strategies people use to cope, and how coping strategies can differ among cultures.

In the Real World: Reducing Stress, Improving Health   See why yoga and meditation have become popular in recent years as treatments for stress and other health problems.

What's In It For Me?: The Challenge of Quitting Bad Health Habits   Learn how habits form, the most effective ways to change behaviors, and the characteristics that make a good health education program.

EXPERIENCE PSYCHOLOGICAL RESEARCH WITH MYPSYCHLAB SIMULATIONS

Access these simulations in MyPsychLab. Follow the "Simulations" link.

Will This Survey Stress You Out?   Participate in a survey to learn about how and why stress affects your life.

APPLY YOUR CRITICAL THINKING SKILLS WITH MYPSYCHLAB WRITING ASSESSMENTS

Complete these writing assignments in MyPsychLab.

Imagine a friend just lost his or her job, which helped your friend cover tuition costs. Applying Lazarus and Folkman's cognitive theory of stress, describe your friend's potential reactions to this job loss. In your answer, be sure to describe the following: Stressful Event, Primary Appraisal, Secondary Appraisal, and Stress Response.

Answer Key

WHAT IS STRESS?

1. stress
2. stressors as stimuli approach
3. transaction
4. primary appraisal
5. secondary appraisal
6. Problem-focused coping
7. emotion-focused coping
8. Social Readjustment Rating
9. Daily hassles and minor annoyances can add up and strain our ability to cope.
10. better

HOW WE ADAPT TO STRESS: CHANGE AND CHALLENGE

11. The alarm reaction involves the excitation of the autonomic nervous system, the discharge of the stress hormone adrenaline, and physical symptoms of anxiety.
12. fight-or-flight
13. resistance
14. exhaustion
15. Both responses refer to ways of coping with stressors. During the fight-or-flight responses, a person is physically and psychologically mobilized either to fight the enemy or flee from the situation. In contrast, during times of stress, women often rely on their social supports and nurturing abilities (the tend-and-befriend response) to help them cope with stressful situations.
16. oxytocin
17. 65 percent
18. high
19. posttraumatic stress disorder (PTSD)
20. flashbacks

HOW STRESS IMPACTS OUR HEALTH

21. human immunodeficiency virus
22. arthritis
23. central nervous
24. can
25. are not
26. psychological
27. coronary heart disease
28. Type A personality describes people who are competitive, driven, hostile, ambitious, and impatient.

Research indicates that the anger component of the Type A personality can be deadly, increasing the risk for coronary heart disease.

29. cause
30. strong

COPING WITH STRESS

31. Social support
32. Social support can provide emotional comfort; financial assistance; and information to make decisions, solve problems, and contend with stressful situations.
33. behavioral control
34. Cognitive control
35. proactive coping
36. Crisis debriefing sessions, in which a facilitator structures a group discussion of people's reactions to a shared traumatic event, may actually increase PTSD risk.
37. Hardiness
38. better
39. Spirituality
40. counterproductive

PROMOTING GOOD HEALTH—AND LESS STRESS!

41. health psychology
42. smoking
43. drinking
44. Answers will vary based on weight/height.
45. play
46. availability
47. Alternative medicine
48. are not
49. Positive effects include increases in creativity, empathy, alertness, and self-esteem, as well as decreases in anxiety, interpersonal problems, and recurrence of depression. It can also enhance blood flow in the brain and immune function. Its positive effects may derive from a greater acceptance of our troubling thoughts and feelings. The effects may not be due to meditation itself, but from sitting quietly, resting, and relaxing with eyes closed. Positive attitudes, beliefs, and expectancies about meditation may also explain why it's beneficial.
50. Homeopathic medicine

References

Abbey, A., Halman, L., & Andrews, F. (1992). Psychosocial, treatment and demographic predictors of the stress associated with infertility. *Fertility and Sterility, 57*, 122–127.

Alexander, F. (1950). *Psychosomatic medicine: Its principles and applications.* New York, NY: Norton.

Alloway, R., & Bebbington, P. (1987). The buffer theory of social support: A review of the literature. *Psychological Medicine, 17*, 91–108.

American Psychological Association. (2006). Americans engage in unhealthy behaviors to manage stress. *APA Practice Media Room.* Retrieved from http://www.apa.org/news/press/releases/2006/01/stress-management.aspx

Andrasik, F. (2012). Behavioral treatment of headaches: Extending the reach. *Neurological Sciences, 33*, 127–130.

Antonovsky, A. (1967). Social class, life expectancy and overall mortality. *Milbank Memorial Fund Quarterly, 45*, 31–73.

Assendelft, W. J. J., Morton, S. C., Yu, E. I., Suttorp, M. J., & Shekelle, P. G. (2003). Spinal manipulative therapy for low back pain: A meta-analysis of effectiveness relative to other therapies. *Annals of Internal Medicine, 138*, 871–881.

Astin, J. A., & Ernst, E. (2002). The effectiveness of spinal manipulation for the treatment of headache disorders: A systematic review of randomized clinical trials. *Cephalalgia, 22*, 617–623.

Atri, A., Sharma, M., & Cottrell, R. (2006). Role of social support, hardiness, and acculturation as predictors of mental health among international students of Asian Indian origin. *International Quarterly of Community Health Education, 27*, 59–73.

Baer, R. A. (2003). Mindfulness training as a clinical intervention: A conceptual and an empirical review. *Clinical Psychology: Science and Practice, 10*, 125–143.

Bagnardi, V., Blangiardo, M., LaVecchia, C. L., & Corrado, G. (2001). *Alcohol consumption and the risk of cancer: A meta-analysis.* Bethesda, MD: National Institute on Alcohol Abuse and Alcoholism.

Barbour, K. A., Houle, T. T., & Dubbert, P. M. (2003). Physical inactivity as a risk factor for chronic disease. In L. M. Cohen, D. E. McCargie, & F. L. Collins (Eds.), *The health psychology handbook* (pp. 146–168). Thousand Oaks, CA: Sage.

Barnes, P. M., Bloom, B., & Nahin, R. (2008). CDC National Health Statistics Report #12. *Complementary and alternative medicine use among adults and children: United States, 2007.* Retrieved from http://www.ncbi.nlm.nih.gov/pubmed/19361005

Barnes, P. M., Powell-Griner, E., McFann, K., & Nahin, R. L. (2004). *Complementary and alternative medicine use among adults: United States, 2002.* CDC Advance Data Report #343.

Bartone, P. T. (1999). Hardiness protects against war-related stress in army reserve forces. *Consulting Psychology Journal, 51*, 72–82.

Bausell, R. B. (2007). *The truth about complementary and alternative medicine.* Oxford, England: Oxford University Press.

Beck, J. G., Gudmundsdottir, B., Palyo, S. A., Miller, L. M., & Grant, D. M. (2006). Rebound effects following deliberate thought suppression: Does PTSD make a difference? *Behavior Therapy, 37*, 170–180.

Bender, D. A. (2008). What we don't know that we need to know. *Healthwatch. Newsletter, 71*, 4–5.

Berkman, L. F., & Syme, S. L. (1979). Social networks, host resistance, and mortality: A nine year follow-up study of Alameda County residents. *American Journal of Epidemiology, 109*, 186–204.

Berlant, N. E., & Pruitt, S. D. (2003). Adherence to medical recommendations. In L. M. Cohen, D. E. McChargue, & F. L. Collins (Eds.), *The health psychology handbook* (pp. 208–224). Thousand Oaks, CA: Sage Publications.

Berman, J. D., & Straus, S. E. (2004). Implementing a research agenda for complementary and alternative medicine. *Annual Review of Medicine, 55*, 239–254.

Beyerstein, B. L. (1997, September/October). Why bogus therapies seem to work. *Skeptical Inquirer, 21*, 29–34.

Bigbee, J. (1990). Stressful life events and illness occurrence in rural versus urban women. *Journal of Community Health Nursing, 7*, 105–113.

Blair, S. N., Kohl, H. W., Gordon, N. F., & Paffenberger, R. S. (1992). How much physical activity is good for health? *Annual Review of Public Health, 13*, 99–126.

Bonanno, G. A., Galea, S., Bucciarelli, A., & Vlahov, D. (2006). Psychological resilience after disaster: New York City in the aftermath of the September 11th terrorist attack. *Psychological Science, 17*, 181–186.

Bonanno, G. A., & Kaltman, S. (2001). The varieties of grief experience. *Clinical Psychology Review, 21*, 705–734.

Bonanno, G. A., Kennedy, P., Galatzer-Levy, I. R., Lude, P., & Elfström, M. L. (2012a). Trajectories of resilience, depression, and anxiety following spinal cord injury. *Rehabilitation Psychology, 57*(3), 236–247. http://dx.doi.org/10.1037/a0029256

Bonanno, G. A., Moskowitz, J. T., Papa, A., & Folkman, S. (2005). Resilience to loss in bereaved spouses, bereaved parents, and bereaved gay men. *Journal of Personality and Social Psychology, 88*, 827–843.

Bonanno, G. A., Papa, A., Lalande, K., Westphal, M., & Coifman, K. (2004). The importance of being flexible: The ability to enhance and suppress emotional expression predicts long-term adjustment. *Psychological Science, 157*, 482–487.

Bonanno, G. A., Westphal, M., & Mancini, A. D. (2011). Resilience to loss and potential trauma. *Annual Review of Clinical Psychology, 7*, 511–535.

Bouchard, C. (1995). Genetics and the metabolic syndrome. *International Journal of Obesity, 19*, 552–559.

Bouchard, L., Drapeau, V., Provencher, V., Lemieux, S., Chagnon, Y., Rice, T., . . . Pérusse, L. (2004). Neuromedin β: A strong candidate gene linking eating behaviors and susceptibility to obesity. *The American Journal of Clinical Nutrition, 80*(6), 1478–1486.

Bray, G. A., Smith, S. R., de Jonge, L., Xie, H., Rood, J., Martin, C. K., . . . Redman, L. M. (2012). Effect of dietary protein content on weight gain, energy expenditure, and body composition during overeating. *Journal of the American Medical Association, 307*(1), 47–55.

Breslau, N., Kilbey, K. M., & Andreski, P. (1993). Nicotine dependence and major depression. *Archives of General Psychiatry, 50*, 31–35.

Brinkhaus, B., Witt, C. M., Jena, S., Linde, K., Streng, A., Wagenpfeil, S., . . . Willich, S. N. (2006). Acupuncture in patients with chronic low back pain: A randomized controlled trial. *Archives of Internal Medicine, 166*, 450–457.

Brownell, K. D., & Rodin, J. (1994). The dieting maelstrom: Is it possible and advisable to lose weight? *American Psychologist, 49*, 781–791.

Bunde, J., & Suls, J. (2006). A quantitative analysis of the relationship between the Cook-Medley Hostility Scale and traditional coronary artery disease risk factors. *Health Psychology, 25*, 493–500.

Bushman, B. J., Baumeister, R. F., & Phillips, C. M. (2001). Do people aggress to improve their mood? Catharsis beliefs, affect regulation opportunity, and aggressive responding. *Journal of Personality and Social Psychology, 81*, 17–32.

Cabyoglu, M. T., Ergene, N., & Tan, U. (2006). The mechanism of acupuncture and clinical applications. *International Journal of Neuroscience, 116*, 115–125.

Campbell, R. S., & Pennebaker, J. (2003). The secret life of pronouns: Flexibility in writing style and physical health. *Psychological Science, 14*, 60–65.

Campfield, L. A., Smith, F. J., & Burn, P. (1996). The OB protein (leptin) pathway—A link between adipose tissue mass and central neural networks. *Hormone and Metabolic Research, 28*, 619–632.

Campos, P. (2004). The obesity myth: *Why America's obsession with weight is hazardous to your health.* New York, NY: Gotham Books.

Carney, R. M., Freedland, K. E., & Veith, R. C. (2005). Depression, the autonomic nervous system, and coronary heart disease. *Psychosomatic Medicine, 67*, 29–33.

Carver, C. S., & Scheier, M. F. (1999). Themes and issues in the self-regulation of behavior. In R. S. Wyer, Jr. (Ed.), *Advances in social cognition* (Vol. 12). Mahwah, NJ: Erlbaum.

Carver, C. S., Scheier, M. F., & Weintraub, J. K. (1989). Assessing coping strategies: A theoretically based approach. *Journal of Personality and Social Psychology, 56*, 267–283.

Cassileth, B. R., Heitzer, M., & Wesa, K. (2009). The public health impact of herbs and nutritional supplements. *Pharmaceutical Biology, 47*, 761–767.

Catz, S. L., & Kelly, J. A. (2001). Living with HIV disease. In A. Baum, T. A. Revenson, & J. E. Singer (Eds.), *Handbook of health psychology* (pp. 841–849). Mahwah, NJ: Lawrence Erlbaum.

Centers for Disease Control and Prevention (2006). Deaths associated with hypocalcemia from chelation therapy—Texas, Pennsylvania, and Oregon, 2003–2005. *Morbidity and Mortality Weekly Report, 55*(08), 204–207.

Centers for Disease Control and Prevention (2008). *Behavioral Risk Factor Surveillance System prevalence data.* Atlanta, GA: Centers for Disease Control and Prevention. Retrieved from http://www.cdc.gov/brfss

Chafin, S., Christenfeld, N., & Gerin, W. (2008). Improving cardiovascular recovery from stress with brief post-stress exercise. *Health Psychology, 27*, 64–72.

Chandola, T., Britton, A., Brunner, E., Hemingway, H., Malik, M., Kumari, M., . . . Marmot, M. (2008). Work stress and coronary heart disease: What are the mechanisms? *European Heart Journal, 29*, 640–648.

Chapman, S., & MacKenzie, R. (2010). The global research neglect of unassisted smoking cessation: Causes and consequences. *PLoS Medicine, 7*(2), e1000216.

Chen, W. Y., Rosner, B., Hankinson, S. E., Colditz, G. A., & Willett, W. C. (2011). Moderate alcohol consumption during adult life, drinking patterns, and breast cancer risk. *Journal of the American Medical Association, 306*(17), 1884–1890.

Cheng, C. (2003). Cognitive and motivational processes underlying coping flexibility: A dual-process model. *Journal of Personality and Social Psychology, 84*, 425–438.

Ching, P. I., Willett, W. C., Rimm, E. B., Colditz, G. A., Gortmaker, S. L., & Stampfer, M. J. (1996). Activity level and risk of overweight in male health professionals. *American Journal of Public Health, 86*, 25–30.

Chopra, D. (1989). *Quantum healing: Exploring the frontiers of mind/body medicine.* New York, NY: Bantam.

Christakis, N. A., & Fowler, J. H. (2007). The spread of obesity in a large social network over 32 years. *New England Journal of Medicine, 357*, 370–379.

Clarke, R., Emberson, J., Fletcher, A., Breeze, E., Marmot, M., & Shipley, M. J. (2009). Life expectancy in relation to cardiovascular risk factors: 38 year follow-up of 19,000 men in the Whitehall study. *British Medical Journal, 339*, b3513.

Cohen, M. A., Mehl, M. R., & Pennebaker, J. W. (2004). Linguistic markers of psychological change surrounding September 11, 2001. *Psychological Science, 15*, 687–693.

Cohen, P., & Cohen, J. (1984). The clinician's illusion. *Archives of General Psychiatry, 41*, 1178–1182.

Cohen, S., Doyle, W. J., Alper, C. M., Janicki-Deverts, D., & Turner, R. B. (2009). Sleep habits and susceptibility to the common cold. *Archives of Internal Medicine, 169*, 62–67.

Cohen, S., Doyle, W. J., Skoner, D. P., Rabin, B. S., & Gwaltney, J. M. (1997). Social ties and susceptibility to the common cold. *Journal of the American Medical Association, 277*, 1940–1944.

Cohen, S., Doyle, W. J., Turner, R. B., Alper, C. M., & Skoner, D. P. (2003). Emotional style and susceptibility to the common cold. *Psychosomatic Medicine, 65*, 652–657.

Cohen, S., Frank, E., Doyle, B. J., Skoner, D. P., Rabin, B. S., & Gwaltney, J. M. (1998). Types of stressors that increase susceptibility to the common cold. *Health Psychology, 17*, 214–223.

Cohen, S., & Herbert, T. B. (1996). Health psychology: Psychological factors and physical disease from the perspective of human psychoneuroimmunology. *Annual Review of Psychology, 47*, 113–142.

Coifman, K. G., Bonanno, G. A., Ray, R. D., & Gross, J. J. (2007). Does repressive coping promote resilience? Affective-autonomic response discrepancy during bereavement. *Journal of Personality and Social Psychology, 92*, 745–758.

Collins, F. L., Sorocco, K. H., Haala, K. R., Miller, B. I., & Lovallo, W. R. (2003). Stress and health. In L. M. Cohen, D. E. McChargue, & F. L. Collins (Eds.), *The health psychology handbook: Practical issues for the behavioral medicine specialist* (pp. 169–186). London, England: Sage Publications.

Comijs, H., Beekman, A., Smits, F., Bremmer, M., Tilburg, T., & Deeg, D. (2008). Childhood adversity, recent life events, and depression in later life. *Journal of Affective Disorders, 103*, 243–246.

Connelly, M., & Bickel, J. (2011). An electronic daily diary process study of stress and health behavior triggers of primary headaches in children. *Journal of Pediatric Psychology, 36*(8), 852–862.

Cook, N. R. (2008). Salt intake, blood pressure, and clinical outcomes. *Current Opinion in Nephrology and Hypertension, 17*, 310–314.

Cooper, C. L., & Dewe, P. (2004). *Stress: A brief history.* Malden, MA: Blackwell.

Copeland, W. E., Keeler, G., Angold, A., & Costello, E. J. (2007). Traumatic events and posttraumatic stress in childhood. *Archives of General Psychiatry, 64*, 577–584.

Corbett, T. (2006). The facts about weight loss products and programs. Federal Trade Commission, Food and Drug Administration. Retrieved from http://weightnomoreohio.com/pdfs/DHHSPublication_92-1189.pdf

Costa, P. T., Jr., & McCrae, R. R. (1990). Personality disorders and the five-factor model of personality. *Journal of Personality Disorders, 4*, 362–371.

Covas, M. I., Konstantinidou, V., & Fito, M. (2009). Olive oil and cardiovascular health. *Journal of Cardiovascular Pharmacology, 54*, 477–482.

Coyne, J. C. (1992). Cognition in depression: A paradigm in crisis. *Psychological Inquiry, 3*, 232–235.

Coyne, J. C., & Holroyd, K. (1982). Stress, coping, and illness: A transactional perspective. In T. Millon, C. Green, & R. Meachem (Eds.), *Handbook of clinical health psychology* (pp. 103–127). New York, NY: Plenum Press.

Coyne, J. C., & Racioppo, M. W. (2000). Never the twain shall meet? Closing the gap between coping research and clinical intervention research. *American Psychologist, 55*, 655–664.

Coyne, J. C., Stefanek, M., & Palmer, S. C. (2007). Psychotherapy and survival in cancer: The conflict between hope and evidence. *Psychological Bulletin, 133*, 367–394.

Crandall, C. S. (1994). Prejudice against fat people: Ideology and self-interest. *Journal of Personality and Social Psychology, 66*, 882–894.

Danbrot, M. (2004). *The new cabbage soup diet.* New York, NY: St. Martin's Press.

Davidson, J. R., Gadde, K. M., Fairbank, J. A., Krishnan, R. R., Califf, R. M., Binanay, C., . . . Weisler, R. H. (2002). Hypericum Depression Trial Study Group. Effect of Hypericum perforatum (St. John's wort) in major depressive disorder: A randomized, controlled trial. *Journal of the American Medical Association, 287*, 1807–1814.

Davidson, R. J., Kabat-Zinn, J., Schumacher, J., Rosenkranz, M., Muller, D., Santorelli, S. F., . . . Sheridan, J. F. (2003). Alternations in brain and immune function produced by mindfulness meditation. *Psychosomatic Medicine, 65*, 564–570.

DeLongis, A., Folkman, S., & Lazarus, R. (1988). The impact of daily stress on health and mood psychological and social resources as mediators. *Journal of Personality and Social Psychology, 54*, 486–495.

DeNoon, D. (2005): Experts: Autism therapy not worth the risk. Fox News. Retrieved from http://www.foxnews.com/story/0,2933,167195,00.html

Depue, R. A., & Monroe, S. M. (1986). Conceptualization and measurement of human disorder in life stress research—The problem of chronic disturbance. *Psychological Bulletin, 99*, 36–51.

de Vries, G. J., & Olff, M. (2009). The lifetime prevalence of traumatic events and posttraumatic stress disorder in the Netherlands. *Journal of Traumatic Stress, 22*, 259–267.

Diener, H. C., Kronfeld, K., & Boewing, G. (2006). Efficacy of acupuncture for the prophylaxis of migraine: A multi-center randomized controlled trial. *The Lancet Neurology,* Online, March 2.

Dohrenwend, B. P. (2006). Inventorying stressful life events as risk factors for psychopathology: Toward resolution of the problem of intracategory variability. *Psychological Bulletin, 132*, 477–495.

Dohrenwend, B. S., & Dohrenwend, B. P. (Eds.) (1974). *Stressful life events: Their nature and effects* (pp. 245–258). New York, NY: Wiley.

Doublet, S. (2000). *The stress myth.* Freemans Reach, New South Wales, Australia: Ipsilon.

Douglas, R. M., Hemilä, H., D'Souza, R., Chalker, E. B., & Treacy, B. (2004). Vitamin C for preventing and treating the common cold. *Cochrane Database System Review, 4*, CD000980.

Duncan, G. (1996). Income dynamics and health. *International Journal of Health Services, 26*, 419–444.

Dunkel-Schetter, C. (2009). Stress processes in pregnancy and preterm birth. *Current Directions in Psychological Science, 18*, 205–209.

Ellison, C. G., & Levin, S. L. (1998). The religion-health connection: Evidence, theory, and future directions. *Health Education and Behavior, 25*, 700–720.

Engel, G. L. (1977). The need for a new medical model: A challenge for biomedicine. *Science, 196*, 129–136.

Erickson, K. I., & Kramer, A. F. (2009). Aerobic exercise effects on cognitive and neural plasticity in older adults. *British Journal of Sports Medicine, 43*, 22–24.

Ernst, E. (2002). Heavy metals in traditional Indian remedies. *European Journal of Clinical Pharmacology, 57*, 891–896.

Esserman, L., Shieh, Y., & Thompson, I. (2009). Rethinking screening for breast cancer and prostate cancer. *Journal of the American Medical Association, 302*(15), 1685–1692.

Esterling, B. A., Kiecolt-Glaser, J. K., & Glaser, R. (1996). Psychosocial modulation of cytokine-induced natural killer cell activity in older adults. *Psychosomatic Medicine, 58*, 264–272.

Estruch, R., Ros, E., Salas-Salvadó, J., Covas, M. I., Pharm, D., Corella, D.,... Martínez-González, M. A. (2013). Primary prevention of cardiovascular disease with a Mediterranean diet. *New England Journal of Medicine.* http://dx.doi.org/10.1056/NEJMoa1200303

Evans, P. D., & Edgerton, N. (2011). Life-events and mood as predictors of the common cold. *British Journal of Medical Psychology, 64*(1), 35–44.

Farthing, G. W. (1992). *The psychology of consciousness*. Englewood Cliffs, NJ: Prentice Hall.

Fava, G., & Sonino, N. (2008). The biopsychosocial model thirty years later. *Psychotherapy and Psychosomatics, 77*, 1–2.

Fawzy, F. I., Fawzy, N. W., Hyun, C. S., Elashoff, R., Guthrie, D., Fahey, J. L., & Morton, D. L. (1993). Malignant melanoma. Effects of an early structured psychiatric intervention, coping, and affective state on recurrence and survival 6 years later. *Archives of General Psychiatry, 50*, 681–689.

Feldman, R., Weller, A., Zagoory-Sharon, O., & Levine, A. (2007). Evidence for a neuroendocrinological foundation of human affiliation: Plasma oxytocin levels across pregnancy and the postpartum period predict mother–infant bonding. *Psychological Science, 18*, 965–970.

Fernandez, E., & Sheffield, J. (1996). Relative contributions of life events versus daily hassles to the frequency and intensity of headaches. *Headache, 36*, 595–602.

Fillmore, K. M., Kerr, W. C., Stockwell, T., Chikritzhs, T., & Bostrom, A. (2006). Moderate alcohol use and reduced mortality risk: Systematic error in prospective studies. *Addiction Research and Theory, 14*, 101–132.

Flensborg-Madsen, T., Bay von Scholten, M., Flachs, E. M., Mortensen, E. L., Prescott, E., & Tolstrup, J. S. (2011). Tobacco smoking as a risk factor for depression. A 26-year population-based follow-up study. *Journal of Psychiatric Research, 45*(2), 143–149.

Fontana, L., Eagon, J. C., Trujilio, M. E., Scherer, P. E., & Klein, S. (2007). Visceral fat adipokine secretion is associated with systemic inflammation in obese humans. *Diabetes, 56*, 1010–1013.

Forshaw, M. (2002). *Essential health psychology*. New York, NY: Oxford University Press.

Foster, A. A., Hylwa, S. A., Bury, J. E., Davis, M. D., Pittelkow, M. R., & Bostwick, J. M. (2012). Delusional infestation: Clinical presentation in 147 patients seen at Mayo Clinic. *Journal of the American Academy of Dermatology, 67*(4), 673.e1–10. 10.1016/j.jaad.2011.12.012.

France, C. R., Masters, K. S., Belar, C. D., Kerns, R. D., Klonoff, E. A., Larkin, K.,... Thorn, B. E. (2008). Application of the competency model to clinical health psychology. *Professional Psychology: Research and Practice, 39*, 573–580.

French, M. T., & Zavala, S. K. (2007). The health benefits of moderate drinking revisited: Alcohol use and self-reported health status. *American Journal of Health Promotion, 21*, 484–491.

Freudenmann, R. W., Lepping, P., Huber, M., Dieckmann, S., Bauer-Dubau, K., Ignatius, R.,... Bewley, A. P. (2012). Delusional infestation and the specimen sign: A European multicentre study in 148 consecutive cases. *British Journal of Dermatology, 167*(2), 247–251.

Friedman, M., & Rosenman, R. H. (1959). Association of a specific overt behavior pattern with increases in blood cholesterol, blood clotting time, incidence of arcus senilis and clinical coronary artery disease. *Journal of the American Medical Association, 169*, 1286–1296.

Friedman, M., & Rosenman, R. H. (1974). *Type A behavior and your heart*. New York, NY: Alfred A. Knopf.

Frisina, P. G., Borod, J. C., & Lepore, S. J. (2004). A meta-analysis of the effects of written disclosure on the health outcomes of clinical populations. *Journal of Nervous and Mental Disease, 192*, 629–634.

Galatzer-Levy, I. R., Bonanno, G. A., & Mancini, A. D. (2010). From marianthal to latent growth mixture modeling: A return to the exploration of individual differences in response to unemployment. *Journal of Neuroscience, Psychology, and Economics, 3*(2), 116–125.

Gallo, L. C., & Matthews, K. A. (2003). Understanding the association between socioeconomic status and physical health: Do negative emotions play a role? *Psychological Bulletin, 129*, 10–51.

Gardner, W. L., Gabriel, S., & Diekman, A. B. (2000). Interpersonal processes. In J. T. Cacioppo, L. G. Tassinary, & G. G. Berntson (Eds.), *Handbook of psychophysiology* (2nd ed., pp. 643–664). New York, NY: Cambridge University Press.

Gatchel, R. J. (2001). Biofeedback and self-regulation of physiological activity: A major adjunctive treatment modality in health psychology. In A. Baum, T. A. Revenson, & J. E. Singer (Eds.), *Handbook of health psychology* (pp. 95–103). Mahwah, NJ: Erlbaum.

Gatchel, R. J., & Baum, A. (1983). *An introduction to health psychology*. Reading, MA: Addison-Wesley.

Gatchel, R. J., & Oordt, M. S. (2003). *Clinical psychology and primary health care*. Washington, DC: American Psychological Association.

Giles, J. (2007). Degrees in homeopathy slated as unscientific. *Nature, 446*, 352–352.

Gori, L., & Firenzuoli, F. (2007). Ear acupuncture in European traditional medicine. *Evidence-Based Complementary and Alternative Medicine, 4*, 13–16.

Gortmaker, S. L., Must, A., Perrin, J. M., Sobol, A. M., & Dietz, W. H. (1993). Social and economic consequences of overweight in adolescence and young adulthood. *New England Journal of Medicine, 329*, 1009–1012.

Gotlib, I. H., & Hammen, C. (1992). *Psychological aspects of depression: Toward a cognitive-interpersonal integration*. New York, NY: Wiley.

Green, J. P. (2000). Treating women who smoke: The benefits of using hypnosis. In L. Hornyak & J. P. Green (Eds.), *Healing from within: The use of hypnosis in women's health care* (pp. 91–118). Washington, DC: American Psychological Association.

Greenglass, E. (2002). Proactive coping. In E. Frydenberg (Ed.), *Beyond coping: Meeting goals, vision, and challenges* (pp. 37–62). London, England: Oxford University Press.

Gross, J. J., & Muñoz, R. F. (1995). Emotional regulation and mental health. *Clinical Psychology: Science & Practice, 2*, 151–164.

Gupta, S. (2007, May 24). Herbal remedies' potential dangers. *Time.* Retrieved from http://www.time.com/time/magazine/article/0,9171,1625175,00.html

Gupta, S., & Bonanno, G. A. (2010). Trait self-enhancement as a buffer against potentially traumatic events: A prospective study. *Psychological Trauma: Theory, Research, Practice, and Policy, 2*(2), 83.

Haimerl, C. J., & Valentine, E. (2001). The effect of contemplative practice on intrapersonal, interpersonal, and transpersonal dimensions of the self-concept. *Journal of Transpersonal Psychology, 33*, 37–52.

Hall, H. (2008). Puncturing the acupuncture myth. *Skeptic, 14*, 5.

Haxby, D. G. (1995). Treatment of nicotine dependence. *American Journal of Health-System Pharmacy, 52*, 265–281.

Hayward, L. R. C. (1960). The subjective meaning of stress. *British Journal of Psychology, 33*, 185–194.

Heini, A. F., & Weinsier, R. L. (1997). Divergent trends in obesity and fat intake patterns: The American paradox. *American Journal of Medicine, 102*, 259–264.

Herskowitz, J. (1987). *The popcorn diet plus*. New Delhi, India: Pharos Books.

Higgins, J. E., & Endler, N. (1995). Coping, life stress, and psychological and somatic distress. *European Journal of Personality, 9*, 253–270.

Himes, C. L., & Reynolds, S. L. (2012). Effect of obesity on falls, injury, and disability. *Journal of the American Geriatrics Society, 60*(1), 124–129.

Hingson, R., Heeren, T., & Winter, M. R. (2006). Drinking onset and alcohol dependence: Age at onset, duration, and severity. *Archives of Pediatrics and Adolescent Medicine, 160*, 739–746.

Hofmann, S. G., Grossman, P., & Hinton, D. E. (2011). Loving-kindness and compassion meditation: Potential for psychological interventions. *Clinical Psychology Review, 31*(7), 1126–1132.

Holahan, C., & Moos, R. H. (1991). Life stressors, personal and social resources and depression: A four-year structural model. *Journal of Abnormal Psychology, 100*, 31–38.

Holmes, D. S. (1987). The influence of meditation versus rest on physiological arousal. In M. West (Ed.), *The psychology of meditation* (pp. 81–103). Oxford, England: Clarendon Press.

Holmes, E. A., James, E. E., Coode-Bate, T., & Deeprose, C. (2009). Can playing the computer game "Tetris" reduce the build-up of flashbacks for trauma? A proposal from cognitive science. *PLoS One, 4*, e4153.

Holmes, T. H., & Masuda, M. (1974). Life change and illness susceptibility. In B. S. Dohrenwend & P. P. Dohrenwend (Eds.), *Stressful life events: Their nature and effects* (pp. 45–72). New York, NY: Wiley.

Holmes, T. H., & Rahe, R. H. (1967). The Social Readjustment Scale. *Journal of Psychosomatic Research, 11*, 213–218.

Hölzel, B. K., Lazar, S. W., Gard, T., Schuman-Olivier, Z., Vago, D. R., & Ott, U. (2011). How does mindfulness meditation work? Proposing mechanisms of action from a conceptual and neural perspective. *Perspectives on Psychological Science, 6*(6), 537–559.

House, J. S., Robbins, C., & Metzner, H. L. (1982). The association of social relationships and activities with mortality: Prospective evidence from the Tecumseh Community Health Study. *American Journal of Epidemiology, 116*, 123–140.

Hylwa, S. A., Bury, J. E., Davis, M. D., Pittelkow, M., & Bostwick, J. M. (2011). Delusional infestation, including delusions of parasitosis: Results of histologic examination of skin biopsy and patient-provided skin specimens. *Archives of Dermatology, 147*(9), 1041.

Ibarra-Rovillard, M., & Kuiper, N. A. (2011). Social support and social negativity findings in depression: Perceived responsiveness to basic psychological needs. *Clinical Psychology Review, 31*(3), 342–352.

Ikemi, Y., & Nakagawa, S. (1962). A psychosomatic study of contagious dermatitis. *Kyushu Journal of Medical Science, 13*, 335–350.

Jackson, P. B., & Finney, M. (2002). Negative life events and psychological distress among young adults. *Social Psychology Quarterly, 65*, 186–201.

Jackson, R. D., LaCroix, A. Z., Gass, M., Wallace, R. B., Robbins, J., Lewis, C. E.,... Barad, D. (2006). Calcium plus vitamin D supplementation and risk of fractures. *New England Journal of Medicine, 354*, 669–683.

Jacobs, T. L., Epel, E. S., Lin, J., Blackburn, E. H., Wolkowitz, O. M., Bridwell, D. A., . . . Saron, C. D. (2011). Intensive meditation training, immune cell telomerase activity, and psychological mediators. *Psychoneuroendocrinology, 36*(5), 664–681.

Janevic, M. R., & Connell, C. M. (2001). Racial, ethnic, and cultural differences in the dementia caregiving experience. *The Gerontologist, 41*, 334–347.

Johnson, P. (2005). Obesity: Epidemic or myth? *Skeptical Inquirer, 29*, 25–29.

Jones, F., & Bright, J. (2001). *Stress: Myth, theory, and research.* Harlow, England: Prentice Hall.

Kabat-Zinn, J. (2003). Mindfulness-based interventions in context: Past, present, and future. *Clinical Psychology: Science & Practice, 10*, 144–156.

Kanner, A. D., Coyne, J. C., Schaefer, C., & Lazarus, R. S. (1981). Comparison of two modes of stress measurement: Daily hassles and uplifts versus major life events. *Journal of Behavioral Medicine, 4*, 1–39.

Karademas, E. C., Frokkai, E. F., Tsotra, E., & Papazachariou, R. (2013). The relation of optimism to cardiac patients' subjective health through illness representations: Does the level of optimism matter? *A Positive Psychology Perspective on Quality of Life*, 175–188.

Karasek, R., & Theorell, T. (1990). *Health work: Stress, productivity and the reconstruction of life.* New York, NY: Basic Books.

Kasper, S., Gastpar, M., Müller, W. E., Volz, H. P., Dienel, A., Kieser, M., & Möller, H. J. (2007). Efficacy of St. John's wort extract WS 5570 in acute treatment of mild depression. *European Archives of Psychiatry and Clinical Neuroscience, 258*, 59–63.

Keane, T., Marshall, A. D., & Taft, C. T. (2006). Posttraumatic stress disorder: Etiology, epidemiology, and treatment outcome. *Annual Review of Clinical Psychology, 2*, 161–197.

Kennedy, S., Kiecolt-Glaser, J. K., & Glaser, R. (1990). Social support, stress, and the immune system. In B. R. Sarason, I. G. Sarason, & G. R. Pierce (Eds.), *Social support: An interactional view* (pp. 253–266). New York, NY: Wiley.

Kessler, R. C., McGonagle, K. A., Zhao, S., Nelson, C. B., Hughes, M., Eshleman, S.,... Kendler, K. S. (1994). Lifetime and 12-month prevalence of DSM-III-R psychiatric disorders in the United States: Results from the National Comorbidity Survey. *Archives of General Psychiatry, 51*, 8–19.

Kessler, R. C., Price, R. H., & Wortman, C. B. (1985). Social factors in psychopathology: Stress, social support and coping processes. *Annual Review of Psychology, 36*, 351–372.

Kessler, R. C., Sonnega, A., Bromet, E., Hughes, M., & Nelson, C. B. (1995). Post-traumatic stress disorder in the National Comorbidity Survey. *Archives of General Psychiatry, 52*, 1048–1060.

Kiecolt-Glaser, J. K., Marucha, P. T., Malarkey, W. B., Mercado, A. M., & Glaser, R. (1995). Slowing of wound healing by psychological stress. *Lancet, 346*, 1194–1196.

Kiecolt-Glaser, J. K., McGuire, L., Robles, T. F., & Glaser, R. (2002). Psychoneuroimmunology: Psychological influences on immune function and health. *Journal of Consulting and Clinical Psychology, 70*, 537–547.

Kirsch, I. (2010). *The emperor's new drugs.* New York, NY: Basic Books.

Klein, E. A., Thompson, I. M., Jr., Tangen, C. M., Crowley, J. J., Lucia, M. S., Goodman, P. J.,... Baker, L. H. (2011). Vitamin E and the risk of prostate cancer. *Journal of the American Medical Association, 306*(14), 1549–1556.

Klein, S., Burke, L. E., Bray, G. A., Blair, S., Allison, D. B., Pi-Sunyer, X.,... Eckel, R. H. (2004). AHA scientific statement: Clinical implications of obesity with specific focus on cardiovascular disease. *Circulation, 1110*, 2952–2967.

Kobasa, S. C., Hilker, R. R., & Maddi, S. R. (1979). Who stays healthy under stress? *Journal of Occupational Medicine, 21*, 595–598.

Koenig, H. G., McCullough, M. E., & Larson, D. B. (2001). *Handbook of religion and health.* New York, NY: Oxford University Press.

Kosfeld, M., Heinrichs, M., Zaks, P., Fischbacher, U., & Fehr, E. (2005). Oxytocin increases trust in humans. *Nature, 435*, 673–676.

Kuk, J. L., Ardern, C. I., Church, T. S., Sharma, A. M., Padwa, R., Sui, X, & Blair, S. N. (2011). Edmonton Obesity Staging System: Association with weight history and mortality risk *Applied Physiology and Nutritional Metabolism, 6*(4), 570–576.

Kuller, L. H., Ives, D. G., Fitzpatrick, A. L., Carlson, M. C., Mercado, C., Lopez, O. L., . . . DeKosky, S. T. (2010). Does Ginkgo biloba reduce the risk of cardiovascular events? *Circulation: Cardiovascular Quality and Outcomes, 3*, 41–71.

Kung, H. C., Hoyert, D. L., Xu, J., & Murphy, S. L. (2008). Deaths: Final data for 2005. *National Vital Statistics Reports, 56*, 1–120.

Kurth, T., Gaziano, J. M., Berger, K., Kase, C. S., Rexrode, K. M., Cook, N. R.,... Manson, J. E. (2003). Body mass index and the risk of stroke in men. *Archives of Internal Medicine, 163*, 2557–2662.

Lazarus, R. S. (1999). *Stress and emotion: A new synthesis.* New York, NY: Springer.

LeDoux, J. (1996). *The emotional brain: The mysterious underpinnings of emotional life.* New York, NY: Simon & Schuster.

Lee, M. S., Pittler, M. H., & Ernst, E. (2008). Effects of Reiki in clinical practice: A systematic review of randomised clinical trials. *The International Journal of Clinical Practice, 62*, 947–954.

Leventhal, H., Weinman, J., Leventhal, E. A., & Phillips, L. A. (2006). Health psychology: The search for pathways between behavior and health. *Annual Review of Psychology, 59*, 477–505.

Levin, J. (2001). *God, faith, and health: Exploring the spirituality-healing connection.* New York, NY: Wiley.

Lewis, W. A., & Bucher, A. M. (1992). Anger, catharsis, the reformulated frustration-aggression hypothesis, and health consequences. *Psychotherapy, 29*, 385–392.

Lieber, C. M. (2003). Alcohol and health: A drink a day won't keep the doctor away. *Cleveland Clinic Journal of Medicine, 70*, 945–953.

Lilienfeld, S. O. (2007). Psychological treatments that cause harm. *Perspectives on Psychological Science, 2*(1), 53–70. http://dx.doi.org/10.1111/j.1745-6916.2007.00029.x

Littrell, J. (1998). Is the experience of painful emotion therapeutic? *Clinical Psychology Review, 18*, 71–102.

Litz, B. T., Gray, M. J., Bryant, R., & Adler, A. B. (2002). Early intervention for trauma: Current status and future directions. *Clinical Psychology: Science and Practice, 9*, 112–134.

Lohr, J. M., Olatunji, B. O., Baumeister, R. F., & Bushman, B. J. (2007). The pseudopsychology of anger venting and empirically supported alternatives that do no harm. *Scientific Review of Mental Health Practice, 5*, 54–65.

Loprinzi, C. L., Levitt, R., Barton, E. L., Sloan, J. A., Atherton, P. J., Smith, D. J.,... Kim, G. P. (2005). Evaluation of shark cartilage in patients with advanced cancer: A North Central Center Cancer Treatment Group trial. *Cancer, 104*, 176–182.

Lutz, A., Greischar, L. L., Rawlings, N. B., Ricard, M., & Davidson, R. J. (2004). Long-term meditators self-induce high-amplitude gamma synchrony during mental practice. *Proceedings of the National Academy of Sciences, 101*, 16369–16373.

Lynam, D. R., Milich, R., Zimmerman, R., Novak, S. P., Logan, T. K., Martin, C.,... Clayton, R. (1999). Project DARE: No effects at 10-year follow-up. *Journal of Consulting and Clinical Psychology, 67*, 590–593.

Lynn, S. J., & Kirsch, I. (2006). *Essentials of clinical hypnosis: An evidence-based approach.* Washington, DC: American Psychological Association.

MacKillop, J., & Gray, J. (in press). Controversial treatments for alcohol use disorders. In S.O. Lilienfeld, S. Lynn, & J. Lohr (Eds.), *Science and pseudosicence in clinical psychology* (2nd ed.). New York, NY: Guilford Press.

Maddi, S. R. (2002). The story of hardiness: Twenty years of theorizing, research, and practice. *Consulting Psychology Journal, 54*, 173–185.

Maddi, S. R. (2004). On hardiness and other pathways to resilience. *American Psychologist, 60*, 261–262.

Maddi, S. R., & Kobasa, S. C. (1984). *The hardy executive: Health under stress.* Homewood, IL: Dow Jones-Irwin.

Marlatt, G. A., & Gordon, J. R. (Eds.). (1985). *Relapse prevention: Maintenance strategies in the treatment of addictive behaviors.* New York, NY: Guilford Press.

Marlatt, G. A., & Rosenhow, D. J. (1980). Cognitive processes in alcohol use: Expectancy and balanced placebo design. In N. K. Mello (Ed.), *Advances in substance abuse: Behavioral and biological research* (pp. 159–199). Greenwich, CT: JAI Press.

Matarazzo, J. D. (1980). Behavioral health and behavioral medicine: Frontiers for a new health psychology. *American Psychologist, 35*, 807–817.

Matthews, D. A., Larson, D. B., & Barry, C. P. (1993). *The faith factor: An annotated bibliography of clinical research on spiritual subjects* (Vol. 1). Rockville, MD: National Institute for Mental Healthcare Research.

Matthews, K. A., Gump, B. B., Harris, K. F., Haney, T. L., & Barefoot, J. C. (2004). Hostile behaviors predict cardiovascular mortality among men enrolled in the Multiple Risk Factor Intervention Trial. *Circulation, 109*, 66–70.

McBride, P. E. (1992). The health consequences of smoking: Cardiovascular diseases. *Medical Clinics of North America, 76*, 333–353.

McCullough, M. E., Root, L. M., Tabka, B., & Witviliet, C. V. O. (2009). Forgiveness. In S. J. Lopez (Ed.), *Handbook of positive psychology* (2nd ed., pp. 427–435). New York, NY: Oxford.

McCullough, M. E., & Willoughby, B. L. B. (2009). Religion, self-regulation, and self-control: Associations, explanations, and implications. *Psychological Bulletin, 135*, 69–93.

McNally, J. (2001). Faces of ground zero. Joe McNally photography. Retrieved from http://www.facesofgroundzero.com/index.php#mi=2&pt=1&pi=10000&s=0&p=0&a=0&at=0

McNally, R. J., Bryant, R. A., & Ehlers, A. (2003). Does early psychological intervention promote recovery from posttraumatic stress? *Psychological Science in the Public Interest, 4*, 45–79.

Meads, C., & Nouwen, A. (2005). Does emotional disclosure have any effects? A systematic review of the literature with meta-analyses. *International Journal of Technology Assessment in Health Care, 21*, 153–164.

Meichenbaum, D. (1994). *A clinical handbook/practical therapist manual for assessing and treating adults with post-traumatic stress disorder* (PTSD). Clearwater, FL: Institute Press.

Middleton, L. E., Manini, T. M., Simonsick, E. M., Harris, T. B., Barnes, D. E., Tylavsky, F.,... Yaffe, K. (2011). Activity energy expenditure and incident cognitive impairment in older adults. *Archives of InternalMedicine, 171*(14), 1251.

Miller, M. A., & Rahe, R. H. (1997). Life changes scaling for the 1990s. *Journal of Psychosomatic Research, 43*, 279–292.

Miller, N. E. (1978). Biofeedback and visceral learning. *Annual Review of Psychology* (Vol. 29). Palo Alto, CA: Annual Reviews.

Miller, W. R., & Rollnick, S. (2002). *Motivational interviewing: Preparing people for change.* New York, NY: Guilford Press.

Miranda, J., & Green, B. L. (1999). The need for mental health services research focusing on poor young women. *Journal of Mental Health Policy and Economics, 2*, 73–89.

Monroe, S. M. (1983). Major and minor events as predictors of psychological distress: Further issues and findings. *Journal of Behavioral Medicine, 6*, 189–205.

Monroe, S. M. (2008). Modern approaches to conceptualizing and measuring human life stress. In S. Nolen-Hoeksema, T. D. Cannon, & T. Widiger (Eds.), *Annual review of clinical psychology* (pp. 37–52). Palo Alto, CA: Annual Reviews.

Mozaffarian, D., Hao, T., Rimm, E. B., Willett, W. C., & Hu, F. B. (2011). Changes in diet and lifestyle and long-term weight gain in women and men. *New England Journal of Medicine, 364*(25), 2392–2404.

Mukamal, K. J., Chung, H., Jenny, N. S., Kuller, L. H., Longstreth, W. T., Jr., Mittleman, M. A.,... Siscovick, D. S. (2005). Alcohol use and risk of ischemic stroke among older adults: The cardiovascular health study. *Stroke, 36*, 1830–1834.

Mursu, J., Robien, K., Harnack, L. J., Park, K., & Jacobs, D. R., Jr. (2011). Dietary supplements and mortality rate in older women: The Iowa Women's Health Study. *Archives of Internal Medicine, 171*(18), 1625.

Myrtek, M. (2001). Meta-analyses of prospective studies on coronary heart disease, type A personality, and hostility. *International Journal of Cardiology, 79*, 245–251.

Nabi, H., Kivimäki, M., Zins, M., Elovainio, M., Consoli, S. M., Cordier, S., . . . Singh-Manoux, A. (2008). Does personality predict mortality? Results from the GAZEL French prospective cohort study. *International Journal of Epidemiology, 37*, 386–396.

Nahin, R. L., Barnes, P. M., Stussman, B. J., & Bloom, B. (2009). Costs of complementary and alternative medicine (CAM) and frequency of visits to CAM practitioners: United States, 2007. *National Health Statistics Report*, No. 18. Hyattsville, MD: National Center for Health Statistics.

National Cancer Institute. (2000, December 12). Harms of smoking and health benefits of quitting. Retrieved from http://www.cancer.gov/cancertopics/factsheet/tobacco/cessation

National Center for Complementary and Alternative Medicine. (2002). *What is complementary and alternative medicine?* (Publication No. D156). Gaithersburg, MD: NCCAM.

National Heart, Lung, and Blood Institute. (1998). *Behavioral research in cardiovascular, lung, and blood health and disease.* Washington, DC: U.S. Department of Health and Human Services.

Nestoriuc, Y., Martin, A., Rief, W., & Andrasik, F. (2008). Biofeedback treatment for headache disorders: A comprehensive efficacy review. *Applied Psychophysiology and Biofeedback, 33*(3), 125–140.

Newberg, A., Alavi, A., Baime, M., Pourdehnad, M., Santanna, J., & d'Aquili, E. (2001). The measurement of regional cerebral blood flow during the complex cognitive task of meditation: A preliminary psychiatry research study. *Neuroimaging, 106*, 113–122.

Niaura, R., Todaro, J. F., Stroud, L., Spiro, A., Ward, K. D., & Weiss, S. (2002). Hostility, the metabolic syndrome, and incident coronary heart disease. *Health Psychology, 21*, 588–593.

Nicklas, B. J., Gaukstern, J. E., Legault, C., Leng, I., & Rejeski, J. (2011). Intervening on spontaneous physical activity to prevent weight regain in older adults: Design of a randomized, clinical trial. *Contemporary Clinical Trials, 33*(2), 450–455.

Nolen-Hoeksema, S. (1987). Sex differences in unipolar depression: Evidence and theory. *Psychological Bulletin, 101*, 259–282.

Nolen-Hoeksema, S. (2000). The role of rumination in depressive disorders and mixed anxiety/depressive symptoms. *Journal of Abnormal Psychology, 109*, 504–511.

Nolen-Hoeksema, S. (2002). Gender differences in depression. In I. H. Gotlib & C. L. Hammen (Eds.), *Handbook of depression* (pp. 492–509). New York, NY: Guilford Press.

Nolen-Hoeksema, S., & Girgus, J. S. (1994). The emergence of gender differences in depression during adolescence. *Psychological Bulletin, 115*, 424–443.

Norcross, J. C., Ratzin, A. C., & Payne, D. (1989). Ringing in the new year: The change processes and reported outcomes of resolutions. *Addictive Behaviors, 14*, 205–212.

Norcross, J. C., & Vangarelli, D. J. (1989). The resolution solution: Longitudinal examination of New Year's change attempts. *Journal of Substance Abuse, 1*, 127–134.

Ogden, C., Carroll, M., Curtin, L., McDowell, M., Tabak, C., & Flegal, K. (2006). Prevalence of overweight and obesity in the Unites States, 1999–2004. *Journal of the American Medical Association, 295*, 1549–1555.

Orathinkal, J., & Vansteenwegen, A. (2006). Religiosity and marital satisfaction. *Contemporary Family Therapy, 28*, 497–504.

Ozer, E. J., Best, S. R., Lipsey, T. L., & Weiss, D. S. (2003). Predictors of post-traumatic stress disorder symptoms in adults: A meta-analysis. *Psychological Bulletin, 129*, 52–73.

Paffenbarger, R. S., Hyde, R. T., Wing, A. L., & Hsieh, C. C. (1986). Physical activity, all-cause mortality, and longevity of college alumni. *New England Journal of Medicine, 314*, 605–613.

Pate, R. R., Pratt, M., Blair, S. N., Haskell, W. L., Macera, C. A., Bouchard, C.,... Wilmore, J. H. (1995). Physical activity and public health: A recommendation from the Centers for Disease Control and the American College of Sports Medicine. *Journal of the American Medical Association, 273*, 402–407.

Pearson, M. L., Selby, J. V., Katz, K. A., Cantrell, V., Braden, C. R., Parise, M. E.,... Eberhard, M. L. (2012). Clinical, epidemiologic, histopathologic and molecular features of an unexplained dermopathy. *PLoS One, 7*(1), e29908.

Pennebaker, J. W. (1997). Writing about emotional experiences as a therapeutic process. *Psychological Science, 8*, 162–166.

Pennebaker, J. W., & Graybeal, A. (2001). Patterns of natural language use: Disclosure, personality, and social integration. *Current Directions, 10*, 90–93.

Pennebaker, J. W., Kiecolt-Glaser, J., & Glaser, R. (1988). Disclosure of traumas and immune function: Health implications for psychotherapy. *Journal of Consulting and Clinical Psychology, 56*, 239–245.

Pert, C. (1997). *Molecules of emotion.* New York, NY: Simon & Schuster.

Peterson, C. (2000). The future of optimism. *American Psychologist, 55*, 44–55.

Peterson, C., & Seligman, M. E. P. (2003). *Character strengths and virtues: A handbook and classification.* New York, NY: Oxford University Press.

Phillips, K. T., Kiernan, M., & King, A. C. (2001). The effects of physical activity on physical and psychological health. In A. Baum, T. A. Revenson, & J. E. Singer (Eds.), *Handbook of health psychology* (pp. 627–660). Mahwah, NJ: Erlbaum.

Polivy, J., Schueneman, A. L., & Carlson, K. (1976). Alcohol and tension reduction: Cognitive and physiological effects. *Journal of Abnormal Psychology, 85*, 595–600.

Posner, G. P., & Sampson, W. (1999, Fall/Winter). Chinese acupuncture for heart surgery anesthesia. *The Scientific Review of Alternative Medicine, 3*, 15–19.

Potts, R. G. (2004). Spirituality, religion, and the experience of illness. In P. Camic & S. Knight (Eds.), *Clinical handbook of health psychology: A practical guide to effective interventions* (pp. 297–314). Cambridge, MA: Hogrefe & Huber.

Powell, L. H., Shahabi, L., & Thoresen, C. E. (2003). Religion and spirituality: Linkages to physical health. *American Psychologist, 58*, 36–52.

Pronk, N. P., & Wing, R. R. (1994). Physical activity and long-term maintenance of weight loss. *Obesity Research, 2*, 587–599.

Purcell, K. (1963). Distinctions between subgroups of asthmatic children. *Pediatrics, 31*(3), 486–494.

Quick, J. C., Quick, J. D., Nelson, D. L., & Hurrell, J. J. (1997). *Preventive stress management in organizations.* Washington, DC: American Psychological Association.

Rafnsson, F. D., Jonsson, F. H., & Windle, M. (2006). Coping strategies, stressful life events, problem behaviors, and depressed affect. *Anxiety, Stress, & Coping, 19*, 241–257.

Rapaport M. H., Nierenberg, A. A., Howland, R., Dording, C., Schettler, P. J., & Mischoulon, D. (2011). The treatment of minor depression with St. John's Wort or citalopram: Failure to show benefit over placebo. *Journal of Psychiatric Research, 45*, 931–941.

Reichenbach, S., Sterchi, R., Scherer, M., Trelle, S., Bürgi, E., Bürgi, U.,... Jüni, P. (2007). Meta-analysis: Chondroitin for osteoarthritis of the knee or hip. *Annals of Internal Medicine, 146*, 580–590.

Repetti, R., Taylor, S., & Seeman, T. (2002). Risky families: Family social environments and the mental and physical health of offspring. *Psychological Bulletin, 128*, 330–366.

Richards, J. M., Butler, E. A., & Gross, J. J. (2003). Emotion regulation in romantic relationships: The cognitive consequences of concealing feelings. *Journal of Social and Personal Relationships, 20*, 599–620.

Ringwalt, C. L., & Greene, J. M. (1993, March). *Results of school districts' drug prevention coordinators survey.* Paper presented at the Alcohol, Tobacco, and Other Drugs Conference on Evaluating School-Linked Prevention Strategies, San Diego, CA.

Roberts, R. E., Strawbridge, W. J., Deleger, S., & Kaplan, G. A. (2002). Are the fat more jolly? *Annals of Behavioral Medicine, 24*, 169–180.

Roth, S., & Cohen, L. J. (1986). Approach, avoidance, and coping with stress. *American Psychologist, 41*, 813–819.

Saarni, S. I., Parmanne, P., & Halila, R. (2008). Alcohol consumption, abstaining, health utility, and quality of life: A general population survey in Finland. *Alcohol and Alcoholism, 43*, 376–386.

Sarafino, E. P. (2006). *Health psychology: Biopsychosocial interactions* (5th ed.). Hoboken, NJ: Wiley.

Schaefer, C., Coyne, J. C., & Lazarus R. S. (1981). The health-related functions of social support. *Journal of Behavioral Medicine, 4*, 381–406.

Scheier, M. F., & Carver, C. S. (1992). Effects of optimism on psychological and physical well-being: Theoretical overview and empirical update. *Cognitive Therapy and Research, 16*, 201–228.

Scheier, M. F., Matthews, K. A., Owens, J. F., Magovern, G. J., Lefebvre, R. C., Abbott, R. A., & Carver, C. A. (1989). Dispositional optimism and recovery from coronary artery bypass surgery: The beneficial effects on physical and psychological well-being. *Journal of Personality and Social Psychology, 57*, 1024–1040.

Schiller J. S., Lucas J. W., Ward B. W., & Peregoy J. A. (2012). Summary health statistics for U.S. adults: National Health Interview Survey, 2010. *National Center for Health Statistics. Vital Health Statistics*, 10(252).

Schmidt, P. J., Murphy, J. H., Haq, N., Rubinow, D. R., & Danaceau, M. A. (2004). Stressful life events, personal losses, and perimenopause-related depression. *Archives of Women's Mental Health, 7*, 19–26.

Schnall, P. L., Pieper, C., Schwartz, J. E., Karasek, R. A., Schlussel, Y., Devereux, R. B.,... Pickering, T. G. (1990). The relationship between "job strain," workplace diastolic blood pressure, and left ventricular mass index: Results of a case-control study. *Journal of the American Medical Association, 263*, 1929–1935.

Schoenbaum, M. (1997). Do smokers understand the mortality effects of smoking? Evidence from the health and retirement survey. *American Journal of Public Health, 87*, 755–759.

Schoenborn, C. A., Adams, P. F., Barnes, P. M., Vickerie, J. L., & Schiller, J. S. (2004). Health behaviors of adults: United States, 1999–2001. National Center for Health Statistics, *Vital Health Statistics, 10*, 219.

Schwartz, M. B., Vartanian, L. R., Nosek, B. A., & Brownell, K. D. (2006). The influence of one's own body weight on implicit and explicit anti-fat bias. *Obesity, 14*, 440–447.

Schwarzer, R., & Taubert, S. (2002). Tenacious goal pursuits and striving toward personal growth: Proactive coping. In E. Fydenberg (Ed.), *Beyond coping: Meeting goals, visions and challenges* (pp. 19–35). London, England: Oxford University Press.

Segal, Z. V., Williams, J. M. G., & Teasdale, J. D. (2012). *Mindfulness-based cognitive therapy for depression*. New York, NY: Guilford Press.

Segerstrom, S. C., Taylor, S. E., Kemeny, M. E., & Fahey, J. L. (1998). Optimism is associated with mood, coping, and immune change in response to stress. *Journal of Personality and Social Psychology, 74*, 1646–1655.

Seligman, M. E. P. (1990). *Learned optimism*. New York, NY: Knopf.

Shade, E. D., Ulrich, C. M., Wener, M. H., Wood, B., Yasui, Y., Lacroix, K.,... McTiernan, A. (2004). Frequent intentional weight loss is associated with lower natural killer cell cytotoxicity in postmenopausal women: Possible long-term immune effects. *Journal of the American Dietetic Association, 104*, 903–912.

Shapiro, S. L., & Walsh, R. (2003). An analysis of recent meditation research and suggestions for future directions. *The Humanistic Psychologist, 31*, 86–113.

Simon, G., von Korff, M., Saunders, K., Miglioretti, D. L., Crane, K., Van Belle, K., & Kessler, R. (2006). Association between obesity and psychiatric disorders in the U.S. population. *Archives of General Psychiatry, 63*, 824–830.

Sinclair, R. R., & Tetrick, L. E. (2000). Implications of item wording for hardiness structure, relation with neuroticism, and stress buffering. *Journal of Research in Personality, 34*, 1–25.

Singh, S., & Ernst, E. (2008). *Trick or treatment: Alternative medicine on trial*. New York, NY: Bantam.

Skinner, E., Edge, K., Altman, J., & Sherwood, H. (2003). Searching for the structure of coping: A review and critique of category systems for classifying ways of coping. *Psychological Bulletin, 129*, 216–219.

Sloan, R. P., Bagiella, E., & Powell, T. (1999). Religion, spirituality, and medicine. *Lancet, 353*, 644–647.

Smeets, T., Giesbrecht, T., Raymaekers, L., Shaw, J., & Merckelbach, H. (2010). Autobiographical integration of trauma memories and repressive coping predict post-traumatic stress symptoms in undergraduate students. *Clinical Psychology and Psychotherapy, 17*, 211–218.

Smith, D. M., Langa, K. M., Kabeto, M. U., & Ubel, P. A. (2005). Health, wealth, and happiness: Financial resources buffer subjective well-being after the onset of a disability. *Psychological Science, 16*, 663–666.

Smith, T. W., & Gallo, L. C. (2001). Personality traits as risk factors for physical illness. In A. Baum, T. A. Revenson, & J. Singer (Eds.), *Handbook of health psychology* (pp. 139–173). Mahwah, NJ: Erlbaum.

Smyth, J. M., Stonr, A. A., Hurewitz, A., & Kaell, A. (1999). Effects of writing about stressful experiences on symptom reduction in patients with asthma or rheumatoid arthritis: A randomized trial. *Journal of the American Medical Association, 281*, 1304–1309.

So, K., & Orme-Johnson, D. (2001). Three randomized experiments on the longitudinal effects of the transcendental meditation technique on cognition. *Intelligence, 29*, 419–440.

Somers, S. (2009). *Knockout: Interviews with doctors who are curing cancer: And how to prevent getting it in the first place*. New York, NY: Crown.

Spiegel, D., Bloom, J. R., Kramer, H. C., & Gottheil, E. (1989). Effect of psychosocial treatment on survival of patients with metastatic breast cancer. *Lancet, 2*, 888–891.

Stepp, L. S. (2007, April 24). For Virginia Tech survivors, memories will be powerful. Washingtonpost.com. Retrieved from http://www.washingtonpost.com/wp-dyn/content/article/2007/04/20/AR2007042001790.html

Stern, S. L., Dhanda, R., & Hazuda, H. P. (2001). Hopelessness predicts mortality in older Mexican and European Americans. *Psychosomatic Medicine, 63*, 344–351.

Strentz, T., & Auerbach, S. M. (1988). Adjustment to the stress of simulated captivity: Effects of emotion-focused versus problem-focused preparation on hostages differing in locus of control. *Journal of Personality and Social Psychology, 55*, 652–660.

Stroebe, W. (2000). *Social psychology and health* (2nd ed.). Buckingham, England: Open University Press.

Tavris, C. (1989). *Anger: The misunderstood emotion*. New York, NY: Touchstone.

Taylor, H. (2009). *The religious and other beliefs of Americans 2009*. The Harris Poll #140, December 15, 2009. Rochester, NY: Harris Interactive.

Taylor, S. E. (2006). Tend and befriend: Biobehavioral bases of affiliation under stress. *Current Directions in Psychological Science, 15*(6), 273–277.

Taylor, S. E., Klein, L. C., Lewis, B. P., Gruenewald, T. L., Gurung, R. A., & Updegraff, J. A. (2000). Biobehavioral responses to stress in females: Tend-and-befriend, not fight-or-flight. *Psychological Review, 107*(3), 411.

Taylor, S. E., & Master, S. L. (2011). Social responses to stress: The tend-and-befriend model. In R. J. Contrada & A. Baum (Eds.), *The handbook of stress science: Biology, psychology, and health* (pp. 101–109). New York, NY: Springer.

Thompson, D. L., & Ahrens, M. J. (2004). *The grapefruit solution: Lower your cholesterol, lose weight, and achieve optimal health with nature's wonderful fruit*. [Brochure]. Linx Corporation.

Thompson, J. K., Herbozo, S. M., Himes, S. M., & Yamamiya, Y. (2005) Weight-related teasing in adults. In K. D. Brownell, L. Rudd, R. M. Puhl, & M. B. Schwartz (Eds.), *Weight bias: Nature, consequences and remedies* (pp. 137–149). New York, NY: Guilford Press.

Timmers, S., Konings, E., Bilet, L., Houtkooper, R. H., van de Weijer, T., Goossens, G. H.,... Schrauwen, P. (2011). Calorie restriction-like effects of 30 days of resveratrol supplementation on energy metabolism and metabolic profile in obese humans. *Cell Metabolism, 14*(5), 612–622.

Tloczynski, J., & Tantriella, M. (1998). A comparison of the effects of Zen breath meditation or relaxation on college adjustment. *Psychologia: An International Journal of Psychology in the Orient, 41*, 32–43.

Tolin, D. F., & Foa, E. B. (2006). Sex differences in trauma and posttraumatic stress disorder: A quantitative review of 25 years of research. *Psychological Bulletin, 132*, 959–992.

Troxel, W. M., Matthews, K. A., Bromberger, J. T., & Sutton-Tyrell, K. (2003). Chronic stress burden, discrimination, and subclinical carotid artery disease in African American and Caucasian women. *Health Psychology, 22*, 300–309.

Tschanz, J. T., Piercy, K., Corcoran, C. D., Fauth, E., Norton, M. C., Rabins, P. V.,... Lyketsos, C. G. (2012, August). Caregiver coping strategies predict cognitive and functional decline in dementia: The Cache County Dementia Progression Study. *American Journal of Geriatric Psychiatry.*

Turk, D. C. (1996). Psychological aspects of pain and disability. *Journal of Musculoskeletal Pain, 4*, 145–154.

Turner, R. J., Wheaton, B., & Lloyd, D. A. (1995). The epidemiology of stress. *American Sociological Review, 60*, 104–125.

Tyas, S. L. (2001). Alcohol use and the risk of developing Alzheimer's disease. *Alcohol Research and Health, 25*, 299–306.

Ullman, S. E., Filipas, H. H., Townsend, S. M., & Starzynski, L. L. (2005). Trauma exposure, posttraumatic stress disorder and problem drinking in sexual assault survivors. *Journal of Studies of Alcohol, 66*, 610–619.

Van Oudenhove, L., McKie, S., Lassman, D., Uddin, B., Paine, P., Coen, S.,... Aziz, Q. (2011). Fatty acid–induced gut-brain signaling attenuates neural and behavioral effects of sad emotion in humans. *The Journal of Clinical Investigation, 121*(8), 3094–3099.

Vincent, P. (1971). Factors influencing patient noncompliance: A theoretical approach. *Nursing Research, 20*, 509–516.

von Känel, R., Dimsdale, J. E., Ziegler, M. G., Mills, P. J., Patterson, T. L., Lee, S. K., & Grant, I. (2001). Effect of acute psychological stress on the hypercoagulable state in subjects (spousal caregivers of patients with Alzheimer's disease) with coronary or cerebrovascular disease and/or systemic hypertension. *The American Journal of Cardiology, 87*(12), 1405–1408.

Vuksan, V., Rogovik, A. L., Jovanovski, E., & Jenkins, A. L. (2009). Fiber facts: Benefits and recommendations for individuals with type 2 diabetes. *Current Diabetes Reports, 9*, 405–411.

Wager, T. D., Rilling, J. K., Smith, E. E., Sokolik, A., Casey, K. L., Davidson, R. J., ... Cohen, J. D. (2004). Placebo-induced changes in fMRI in anticipation and experience of pain. *Science, 303*, 1162–1167.

Walach, H., & Kirsch, I. (2003). Herbal treatments and antidepressant medication: Similar data, divergent conclusions. In S. O. Lilienfeld, S. J. Lynn, & J. M. Lohr (Eds.), *Science and pseudoscience in clinical psychology* (pp. 306–330). New York, NY: Guilford Press.

Wallach, H., & Kirsch, I. (2003). Herbal treatments and antidepressant medication: Similar data, divergent conclusions. In S. O. Lilienfeld, S. J. Lynn, & J. M. Lohr (Eds.), *Science and pseudoscience in clinical psychology* (pp. 306–332). New York, NY: Guilford Press.

Wang, D. J., Rao, H., Korczykowski, M., Wintering, N., Pluta, J., Khalsa, D. S., & Newberg, A. B. (2011). Cerebral blood flow changes associated with different meditation practices and perceived depth of meditation. *Psychiatry Research: Neuroimaging, 191*(1), 60–67.

Wang, P. S., Gruber, M. J., Powers, R. E., Schoenbaum, M., Speier, A., Wells, K. B., & Kessler, R. C. (2008). Disruption of existing mental health treatments and failure to initiate new treatment after hurricane Katrina. *American Journal of Psychiatry, 165*, 34–41.

Wegner, D. M. (2005). The illusion of conscious will. *Behavioral and Brain Sciences, 27*, 649–692.

Wegner, D. M., Schneider, D. J., Carter, S. R., & White, T. L. (1987). Paradoxical effects of thought supression. *Journal of Personality and Social Psychology, 53*, 5–13.

Wei, M., Kampert, J. B., Barlow, C. E., Nichaman, M. Z., Gibbons, L. W., Paffenbarger, R. S., Jr., & Blair, S. N. (1999). Relationship between low cardiorespiratory fitness and mortality in normal weight, overweight, and obese men. *Journal of the American Medical Association, 282*, 1547–1553.

Weil, A. (2000). *Spontaneous healing: How to discover and embrace your body's natural ability to maintain and heal itself.* New York, NY: Ballantine Books.

Werch, C. E., & Owen, D. (2002). Iatrogenic effects of alcohol and drug prevention programs. *Journal of Studies on Alcohol, 63*, 581–590.

Westphal, M., & Bonanno, G. A. (2004). Emotional self-regulation. In M. Beauregard (Ed.), *Consciousness, emotional self-regulation, and the brain* (pp. 1–34). Philadelphia, PA: Benjamins.

Williams, L., O'Connor, R. C., Grubb, N. R., & O'Carroll, R. E. (2011). Type D personality and illness perceptions in myocardial infarction patients. *Journal of Psychosomatic Research, 70*(2), 141–144.

Wills, T. A., & Fegan, M. F. (2001). Social networks and social support. In A. S. Baum, T. A. Revenson, & J. E. Singer (Eds.), *Handbook of health psychology* (pp. 209–234). Mahwah, NJ: Erlbaum.

Wilson, T. D. (2011). *Redirect: The surprising new science of psychological change.* Boston, MA: Little, Brown.

Wing, R. R., & Hill, J. O. (2001). Successful weight loss maintenance. *Annual Review of Nutrition, 21*, 323–341.

Wing, R. R., & Jeffrey, R. W. (1999). Benefit of recruiting participants with friends and increasing social support for weight loss and maintenance. *Journal of Consulting and Clinical Psychology, 67*, 132–138.

Wing, R. R., & Polley, B. A. (2001). Obesity. In A. Baum, T. A. Revenson, & J. E. Singer (Eds.), *Handbook of health psychology* (pp. 263–279). Mahwah, NJ: Erlbaum.

Woloshin, S., Schwartz, L. M., & Welch, H. G. (2002). Risk charts: Putting cancer in context. *Journal of the National Cancer Institute, 94*, 799–804.

Young, R. M., Oei, T. P. S., & Knight, R. G. (1990). The tension reduction hypothesis revisited: An alcohol expectancy perspective. *British Journal of Addiction, 85*, 31–40.

Credits

Credits listed in order of appearance.

Photo Credits

Photo Credits listed in order of appearance.

Social Psychology

From Chapter 13 of *Psychology: From Inquiry to Understanding*, Third Edition. Scott O. Lilienfeld, Steven Jay Lynn, Laura L. Namy, Nancy J. Woolf. Copyright © 2014 by Pearson Education, Inc. All rights reserved.

Social Psychology

HOW OTHERS AFFECT US

Think About It

What causes mass hysteria over rumors about things like Martian landings?

How do cults persuade people to become fanatics?

Were the Nazis particularly evil, or would we have done the same thing in their boots?

How can a woman be raped in plain view of many people without anyone coming to her aid?

What's the best way to persuade others to do something for us?

RULING OUT RIVAL HYPOTHESES ▶
Have important alternative explanations for the findings been excluded?

FALSIFIABILITY ▶
Can the claim be disproved?

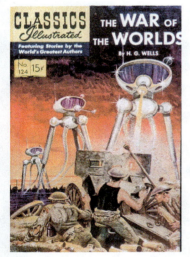

Orson Welles created mass panic in 1938 when he persuaded tens of thousands of Americans of the existence of a widespread Martian invasion.

social psychology
study of how people influence others' behavior, beliefs, and attitudes

On October 30, 1938—a few hours before Halloween—large parts of the United States temporarily lost their grip on reality. That night, 6 million Americans tuned in to a popular radio show hosted by 23-year-old Hollywood sensation Orson Welles. The program featured an adaptation of H. G. Wells's science fiction classic *The War of the Worlds,* which vividly describes the invasion of Earth by a race of enormous Martians. To make *The War of the Worlds* more entertaining—and to play a good-natured pre-Halloween trick on his listeners—Welles presented the story in the form of a phony news broadcast. Anyone listening carefully to the program would have recognized it as a clever hoax, as Welles informed his audience no fewer than four times that the show was merely an adaptation of a science fiction story.

As the broadcast unfolded over the next hour, a newscaster periodically interrupted live orchestral music with increasingly alarming news bulletins that reported a series of explosions on the surface of Mars and later the landing of a mysterious metal capsule on a farm in Grover's Mill, New Jersey, 50 miles from New York City. Against the backdrop of screaming witnesses, a terrified reporter described a large alien with tentacles emerging from a hatch in the capsule. By the program's end, the newscaster informed listeners that an army of giant Martians was launching a full-scale invasion of New York City.

The War of the Worlds triggered a mass panic (Bartholomew, 1998). Hundreds of frightened listeners fled into the streets, and others hid in their basements. Still others called the police or loaded their guns. Some wrapped their heads in towels in preparation for a Martian chemical attack (Cantril, 1947). Although most listeners didn't panic, at least tens of thousands did (Bainbridge, 1987). Surprisingly, many listeners apparently never bothered to consider alternative explanations for the program or to seek out evidence that could have falsified claims of a massive alien invasion. Had they tuned their radios to a different station, they would have heard no coverage of this presumably momentous event in human history. Instead, many listeners fell prey to confirmation bias, focusing on only one hypothesis—that the news bulletins were real—at the expense of others.

Welles had pulled off the most successful Halloween prank of all time. How did he do it? One thing's for certain: Welles had never taken an introductory psychology course, so he didn't rely on formal scientific research. Yet he understood the power of social influence, although even he was caught off guard by just how potent it was.

What Is Social Psychology?

1. Identify the ways in which social situations influence the behavior of individuals.
2. Explain how the fundamental attribution error can cause us to misjudge others' behaviors.

Social psychology helps us to understand not only why *The War of the Worlds* hoax succeeded, but also why many forms of interpersonal influence are so powerful. **Social psychology** is the study of how people influence others' behavior, beliefs, and attitudes—for both good and bad (Lewin, 1951). Social psychology helps us understand not only why we sometimes act helpfully and even heroically in the presence of others, but also why we occasionally show our worst sides, caving in to group pressure or standing by idly while others suffer. It also sheds light on why we're prone to accept blindly irrational, even pseudoscientific, beliefs. There's a catch here, however. Research shows that we tend to believe that others are vulnerable to social influence, but we don't believe that we are (Pronin, 2008). So we may initially resist some social psychological findings because they seem to apply to everyone else but us. In reality, they're relevant to us, too.

In this chapter, we'll begin by examining the social animals we call human beings (Aronson, 2012) and discuss how and why we often underestimate the impact of social influence on others' behavior. We'll move on to examine two especially potent social influences—conformity and obedience—and then address the question of why we help people at some times and harm them at others. Then, we'll discuss our attitudes and how social pressure shapes them. We'll conclude by exploring the troubling question of how prejudice toward others arises and, more optimistically, how we can combat or least compensate for it.

Humans as a Social Species

Social psychology is important for one reason: we humans are a highly social species. Most evidence suggests that as early hominids in Africa hundreds of thousands of years ago, we evolved in relatively small and tight social bands (Barchas, 1986). Even as modern-day humans, most of us gravitate to small groups. In forming cliques, or groups that include some people—in-group members—we by extension exclude others—out-group members.

GRAVITATING TO EACH OTHER—TO A POINT. Anthropologist Robin Dunbar (1993) has become famous for a number: 150. This number is the approximate size of most human social groups, from the hunter-gatherers of days of yore to today's scientists working in a specialized research area (Gladwell, 2005). Research suggests that 150 is also close to the average number of people that each of us knows reasonably well. Interestingly, the median number of "friends" in people's Facebook profiles is a bit over 100, not far from Dunbar's number (Backstrom, 2011). Dunbar argued that the size of our cortex relative to the rest of our brain places limits on how many people with whom we can closely associate. For animals with smaller cortices relative to the rest of their brains, such as chimpanzees and dolphins, the number of relations may be smaller (Dunbar, 1993; Marino, 2005). Whether 150 is the universal "magic number," Dunbar is probably right that our highly social brains are predisposed to forming intimate interpersonal networks that are large—but only so large.

THE NEED TO BELONG: WHY WE FORM GROUPS. When we're deprived of social contact for a considerable length of time, we usually become lonely. According to Roy Baumeister and Mark Leary's (1995) *need-to-belong theory,* we humans have a biologically based need for interpersonal connections. Stanley Schacter (1959) discovered the power of this social need in a small pilot study. He asked five male volunteers to live alone in separate rooms for an extended time period. All five were miserable. One participant with an especially low tolerance for isolation bailed out after only 20 minutes and three lasted only two days. The lone holdout, who reported feeling extremely anxious, made it to eight days. Research on inmates placed in solitary confinement suggests that they experience more psychological symptoms, especially mood and anxiety problems, than do other inmates (Andersen et al., 2000; Grassian, 2006), although because the former inmates may be more emotionally maladjusted to begin with, this finding is difficult to interpret.

More systematic research shows that the threat of social isolation can lead us to behave in self-destructive ways and even impair our mental functioning. In a series of experiments, Jean Twenge and her colleagues asked undergraduates to complete a personality measure and gave them bogus feedback based on their test results: they told some of the participants "You're the type who will end up alone later in life" and others "You're likely to be accident prone later in life." The students who received feedback that they'd be isolated toward the end of their lives were significantly more likely than those in the other group to engage in unhealthy behaviors like eating a fattening snack and procrastinating on an assignment (Twenge, Catanese, & Baumeister, 2002). The same negative feedback is so upsetting that it may even impair students' performance on IQ tests (Baumeister, Twenge, & Nuss, 2002).

Brain imaging research goes a step further, shedding light on the commonplace observation that being cut off from social contact "hurts," literally and figuratively. Kip Williams and his coworkers placed participants in an fMRI scanner as they played a computerized ball tossing game with other players whom they were led to believe were real (in fact, these players didn't exist). The researchers rigged the game so that participants were eventually excluded from the game; as the game progressed, the other (nonexistent) players began to toss the ball only to each other, ignoring the actual participant. Upon experiencing the sting of social rejection, participants displayed pronounced activation in the cingulate cortex, a brain region that becomes active during physical pain. So that "ouch" we feel after being thrown out of a group may bear more than a coincidental similarity to the pain we feel after stubbing our toe (Eisenberger, 2012; Eisenberger, Lieberman, & Williams, 2003). Recent research using the ball tossing game even suggests

◄ **RULING OUT RIVAL HYPOTHESES**
Have important alternative explanations for the findings been excluded?

579

that the pain-killer Tylenol—compared with a placebo—blunts the activity of the cingulate cortex in response to social rejection (DeWall et al., 2010).

Work by John Cacioppo and his colleagues further suggests that long-term loneliness can exert negative, at times devastating, effects on our psychological adjustment (Cacioppo & Patrick, 2009). Although 80 percent of teenagers and 40 percent of adults 65 years or older report occasional loneliness, for some people—between 15 and 30 percent depending on how loneliness is defined—loneliness is a way of life (Hawkley & Cacioppo, 2010). Increases in loneliness are tied to heightened rates of depression a year later (Cacioppo et al., 2006). Although these data are correlational and don't conclusively demonstrate a cause-and-effect relation, increases in depression don't predict increases in loneliness (Cacioppo, Hawkley, & Thisted, 2010), suggesting that loneliness may contribute to depression, rather than vice-versa. Moreover, loneliness predicts cognitive decline and perhaps even heightened risk for Alzheimer's disease (Hawkley & Cacioppo, 2010), although it's unclear whether this link is causal.

CORRELATION VS. CAUSATION ▶
Can we be sure that A causes B?

HOW WE CAME TO BE THIS WAY: EVOLUTION AND SOCIAL BEHAVIOR. Because we'll soon be examining many unhealthy forms of social influence, such as how unquestioning acceptance of authority figures can lead us to do foolish things, we might be tempted to conclude that almost all social influence is negative. That would be a serious mistake. Virtually all of the social influence processes we'll discuss are adaptive under most circumstances and help to regulate cultural practices. From the perspective of an evolutionary approach to social behavior, many social influence processes have been naturally selected, because they've generally served us well over the course of evolution (Buss & Kenrick, 1998; Tybur & Griskevicius, 2013). Even if we're skeptical of this view, we can still accept a core premise: social influence processes work for us well most of the time, but they can occasionally backfire on us if we're not careful.

An evolutionary perspective on social behavior leads us to one crucial conclusion: *conformity, obedience, and many other forms of social influence become maladaptive only when they're blind or unquestioning.* From this standpoint, irrational group behavior—like the disastrous obedience of thousands of German citizens during the nazi regime of the 1930s and 1940s and the massive genocide in Sudan in the late twentieth and early twenty-first centuries—are by-products of basically adaptive processes that have gone terribly wrong. There's nothing wrong with looking to a persuasive leader for guidance, as long as we don't stop asking questions. Once we accept social influence without evaluating it critically, though, we place ourselves at the mercy of powerful others.

Although the data are only correlational, mounting evidence suggests that loneliness is associated with a heightened risk for later depression—a link that may be causal.

SOCIAL COMPARISON: WHERE DO I STAND? One reason others affect us is that they often serve as a mirror of sorts, providing us with helpful information about ourselves (Cooley, 1902; Schrauger & Schoeneman, 1979). According to Leon Festinger's (1954) social comparison theory, we evaluate our abilities and beliefs by comparing them with those of others. Doing so helps us to understand ourselves and our social worlds better. If you want to find out if you're a good psychology student, it's only natural to compare your exam performance with that of your classmates (Kruglanski & Mayseless, 1990). Doing so gives you a better sense of how you stack up relative to them and can spur you on to make needed improvements in your study habits.

Orderly evacuation of a building in an emergency highlights how conformity and obedience can be constructive.

Social comparison comes in two different "flavors." In *upward social comparison,* we compare ourselves with people who seem superior to us in some way, as when a new member of the basketball team compares herself with the team's top two superstars. In *downward social comparison,* we compare ourselves with others who seem inferior to us in some way, as when the same basketball player compares herself with her clumsy friends who keep bouncing basketballs off of their feet.

Despite their differences, both upward and downward social comparison can boost our self-concepts (Buunk et al., 1990; Suls, Martin, & Wheeler, 2002). When we engage in upward social comparison, especially with people who aren't too different from us, we may feel better because we conclude that "If he can achieve that, I bet I can, too." When we

social comparison theory
theory that we seek to evaluate our abilities and beliefs by comparing them with those of others

580

engage in downward social comparison, we often end up feeling superior to our peers who are less competent than us in an important domain of life. Downward social comparison probably accounts in part for the popularity of televised reality shows, which often feature the daily lives of people who are unsuccessful in their romantic relationships or friendships. Interestingly, even when social comparison makes us look inferior relative to someone else, we may buffer our self-concepts by persuading ourselves that it's only because the other person is exceptionally talented (Alicke et al., 1997). In one study, participants learned—falsely—that another person had outperformed them on a test of intelligence. Relative to observers, these participants markedly overestimated that person's intelligence. By concluding that "the person who outperformed me is a genius", participants salvaged their self-esteem: "It's not that I'm dumb, it's that he's incredibly smart."

SOCIAL CONTAGION. Just as we often turn to others to better understand ourselves, we often look to them when a situation is ambiguous and we're not sure what to do. That's only natural, and it's often a pretty good idea. When we experience severe turbulence on an airplane, we often look to the faces of other passengers as cues for how to react. If they appear calm, we'll generally relax; if they appear nervous or panicked, we'll probably start looking around for the nearest emergency exit. But what if others are thinking and behaving irrationally? Then, we may do the same, because social behavior is often contagious. *The War of the Worlds* might seem like an isolated case of human irrationality, but that's far from the truth.

Mass Hysteria: Irrationality at a Group Level. **Mass hysteria** is a contagious outbreak of irrational behavior that spreads much like a flu epidemic. Because we're most likely to engage in social comparison when a situation is ambiguous, many of us are prone to mass hysteria under certain circumstances. In some cases, episodes of mass hysteria lead to *collective delusions*, in which many people simultaneously come to be convinced of bizarre things that are false. Consider how the frequency of unidentified flying object (UFO) sightings shot up at times when societal consciousness of space travel was heightened (see **FIGURE 1**).

This trend started on June 24, 1947, when pilot Kenneth Arnold spotted nine mysterious shiny objects while flying over the ocean near Mount Rainier in Washington State. Interestingly, Arnold told reporters that these objects were shaped like *sausages*. Nevertheless, he also made the offhand observation that they'd "skipped over the water like saucers."

Within days, the phrase *flying saucers* appeared in over 150 newspapers across the United States (Bartholomew & Goode, 2000). Within only a few years, thousands of people were claiming to see saucer-shaped objects in the sky. Had the newspapers been more accurate in their coverage of Arnold's words, we might today be hearing UFO reports of flying sausages rather than flying saucers. But once the media introduced the term *flying saucers*, the now familiar circular shape of UFOs took hold in the American consciousness and never let go.

Another collective delusion occurred in the spring of 1954, when the city of Seattle, Washington, experienced an epidemic of "windshield pitting." Thousands of residents became alarmed by tiny indentations, or pits, in their car windshields that they suspected were the result of secret nuclear tests performed by the federal government. (Bartholomew & Goode, 2000). Although the residents of Seattle hadn't realized it, the windshield pits had been there all along, as they are on most cars. The windshield-pitting epidemic offers another illustration of how shared societal beliefs can influence our interpretations of reality. When confronted with two explanations for the pitting—a secret nuclear explosion or the impact of dirt particles hitting the windshield—Seattle residents would have been better off picking the simpler one.

Urban Legends. Another demonstration of the power of social contagion comes from *urban legends*: false stories repeated so many times that people believe them to be true (Brunvand, 1999). As Gordon Allport and Leo Postman (1945) noted over six decades ago, rumors tend to grow less accurate with repeated retellings, often becoming oversimplified to make for a good story. With the increasing popularity of the Internet, YouTube,

FIGURE 1 Graph of UFO Sightings. In the 1950s and 1960s, the number of UFO sightings shot up dramatically following the launches of *Sputnik I* and *II* (the Russian satellites that were the first objects launched into space) and following the U.S. launch of the space probe *Mariner 4*. Although these data don't permit definite cause-and-effect conclusions, they're consistent with the possibility that UFO sightings are of social origin. (*Source:* Hartmann, 1992)

◄ **OCCAM'S RAZOR**
Does a simpler explanation fit the data just as well?

mass hysteria
outbreak of irrational behavior that is spread by social contagion

581

and social media, urban legends and other erroneous rumors can now spread "virally," becoming virtual overnight sensations in the absence of any objective evidence (Fernback, 2003; Sunstein, 2009). How many of the urban legends in **FIGURE 2** have you heard?

All of the stories in Figure 2 are false, yet scores of people believe them. Urban legends are convincing in part because they're surprising, yet plausible (Gilovich, 1991). They also make for good stories because they tug on our emotions, especially negative ones (Heath & Heath, 2007; Rosnow, 1980). Research shows that the most popular urban legends contain a heavy dose of material relevant to the emotion of disgust, perhaps because they arouse our perverse sense of curiosity. As a result, they often spread like wildfire. It's perhaps not coincidental that many feature rats and other animals that we don't find especially appealing (Heath, Bell, & Sternberg, 2001).

SOCIAL FACILITATION: FROM BICYCLISTS TO COCKROACHES. Because we're social creatures, even the mere presence of others can enhance our performance in certain situations, a phenomenon that Robert Zajonc called **social facilitation**. In the world's first social psychological study, Norman Triplett (1897) found that bicycle racers obtained faster speeds when racing along with other bicyclists than when racing against

A woman heated her poodle in a microwave oven in a well-meaning attempt to dry it off following a rainstorm. It exploded.

While still alive, Walt Disney arranged to have his body frozen after his death so that it could be unfrozen at a future date when advanced technology will permit him to live again.

Outside her home, a woman found a stray Chihuahua. She cared for the pet for several weeks and eventually brought it to a veterinarian, who informed her that her cute little "dog" was actually a giant rat.

Many gang members drive around late at night without their car lights on and then shoot people who flash their lights at them.

A woman on a transatlantic flight was trapped in the bathroom for over 2 hours after flushing the toilet created a vacuum, binding her to the seat.

FIGURE 2 Urban Legend? Some popular urban legends: all are widely known, yet all are false. Incidentally, if you ever want to find out whether a remarkable rumor from the Internet or media is true, check the high-quality website www.snopes.com, which continually tracks the accuracy of urban legends.

Psychological research bears out our everyday observation that yawning is contagious.

social facilitation
enhancement of performance brought about by the presence of others

from inquiry to understanding

WHY ARE YAWNS CONTAGIOUS?

One vivid illustration of the power of social influence comes from the phenomenon of contagious yawning. Both everyday observation and systematic research bear out the fact that once someone in a group starts yawning, others do, too (Provine, 2012). Yawning doesn't spread merely from person to person; it even spreads from written material to people (Platek et al., 2003; Provine, 2005). Indeed, as you're reading this paragraph, you may find yourself starting to yawn (hopefully not because you're bored!). Between 40 and 60 percent of adults yawn soon after seeing another person yawn, and many yawn even after reading the word *yawn* (Platek, Mohamed, & Gallup, 2005). Yet the psychological and physiological functions of yawning, and contagious yawning in particular, remain mysterious.

Although yawning emerges in fetuses as early as 3 months following conception, contagious yawning doesn't typically emerge until about age 4 (Helt et al., 2010). This developmental trend may reflect the emergence of empathy and theory of mind in children; as we become better able to identify with others' mental states, we become more likely to mimic their actions. Interestingly, individuals with autism spectrum disorder, who tend to exhibit theory of mind deficits, are less likely than other individuals to engage in contagious yawns (Helt et al., 2010). People prone to schizophrenia may exhibit the same absence of contagious yawning (Haker & Rossler, 2009). Recent research has also examined the existence of contagious yawning in animals. Although most species don't display contagious yawning, chimpanzees do (Anderson, Myowa-Yamokowshi, & Matsozawa, 2004). Interestingly, chimpanzees exhibit contagious yawning more to members of their own groups than to other chimpanzees, again suggesting a tie to empathy (Campbell & de Waal, 2011). In some studies, dogs, who've co-evolved closely with humans for thousands of years and have grown highly attuned to our social signals (Hare & Woods, 2013), have been found to yawn in response to other people's yawns (Provine, 2012).

Still, none of this tells us why yawning is contagious. The truth is that psychologists don't know. Some psychologists argue that contagious yawning promotes the social bonding of individuals within groups. Because people often yawn when they're drowsy or underaroused (Guggisberg et al., 2010), contagious yawning may have evolved to foster alertness within a group (Gallup, 2011), which might in turn protect group members against threats. Of course, it's also possible that contagious yawning has no actual function itself. It may merely be an indirect consequence of the fact that natural selection has shaped us to become social beings who are exquisitely attuned to the behaviors of others.

only the clock. The difference—8.6 miles per hour on average—was substantial. Zajonc (1965) reported that social facilitation applies to birds, fish, and even insects. In what's surely one of the most creative studies in the history of psychology, Zajonc and two colleagues randomly assigned cockroaches to two conditions: one in which they ran a maze alone and another in which they ran a maze while being observed by an audience of fellow cockroaches from a "spectator box." Compared with the lone cockroaches, cockroaches in the second condition ran the maze significantly faster and committed fewer errors (Zajonc, Heingartner, & Herman, 1969).

Yet the impact of others on our behavior isn't always positive (Bond & Titus, 1983). Social facilitation occurs only on tasks we find easy, whereas *social disruption*—a worsening of performance in the presence of others—occurs on tasks we find difficult. You've probably happened upon this effect if you've ever "choked" in the company of others while singing a difficult song or telling a joke with a complicated punch line. One team of five researchers watched people playing pool (Michaels et al., 1982). The experienced pool players did better in the presence of others, but the inexperienced pool players did worse. So the effects of social influence can be positive or negative depending on the situation. We're especially likely to "choke" on a difficult task when we're distracted—such as by the knowledge that others are watching us—which can limit the working memory we can devote to solving the problem (Beilock, 2008; Beilock & Carr, 2005).

The Fundamental Attribution Error: The Great Lesson of Social Psychology

When we try to figure out why people, ourselves included, did something, we're forming **attributions**, or assigning causes to behavior. Some attributions are internal (inside the person), such as when we conclude that Joe Smith robbed a bank because he's impulsive. Other attributions are external (outside the person), such as when we conclude that Bill Jones robbed a bank because his family was broke (Kelley, 1973). We can explain a great deal of our everyday behavior by situational factors that are external to us, such as social pressure.

When we read about the frenzied behavior of some Americans during *The War of the Worlds*, we may laugh and pat ourselves on the back with the confident reassurance that we would never have acted this way. Yet if the field of social psychology imparts one lesson that we should take with us for the rest of our lives (Myers, 1993a), it's that we attribute too much of people's behavior to who they are. This mistake is known as the **fundamental attribution error**. Coined by Lee Ross (1977), this term refers to the tendency to overestimate the impact of *dispositional influences* on others' behavior. By dispositional influences, we mean enduring characteristics, such as personality traits, attitudes, and intelligence.

Because of the fundamental attribution error, we also tend to underestimate the impact of *situational influences* on others' behavior, meaning that we attribute too little of their behavior to what's going on around them. For instance, we may assume incorrectly that a boss in a failing company who fired several of his loyal employees to save money must be callous, when in fact he was under enormous pressure to spare the jobs of hundreds of other loyal employees. Similarly, we may assume that we'd never have panicked during *The War of the Worlds* hoax, even though we might well have.

No one knows for sure why we commit the fundamental attribution error, but one likely culprit is the fact that we're rarely aware of all of the situational factors impinging on others' behavior at a given moment (Gilbert & Malone, 1995; Pronin, 2008). When we witness a senator caving into political influence on a vote, we may think to ourselves, "What a coward!" because we may not recognize—or appreciate—the intense social pressure he was experiencing. Interestingly, we're less likely to commit the fundamental attribution error if we've been in the same situation ourselves (Balcetis & Dunning, 2008) or have been encouraged to feel empathic toward those we're observing (Regan & Totten, 1975). Perhaps taking a walk in others' shoes helps us grasp what they have to contend with. This explanation dovetails with a curious finding. We tend to commit the fundamental attribution error only when explaining *others'* behavior; when explaining the causes of our *own* behavior, we're a

The presence of others enhances our performance on simple or familiar tasks. These cyclists will probably ride faster together than either would alone.

The 1960s television show *Candid Camera*, which placed ordinary people in absurd situations, illustrates the *fundamental attribution error* (Maas & Toivanen, 1978). Viewers laugh at people's often silly reactions, underestimating how likely most of us are to fall victim to situational influences—in this case, group pressure. In one classic episode (shown here), an unsuspecting person enters an elevator filled with *Candid Camera* staff (a and b). Suddenly and for no reason, all of the staff turn to the right (c). Sure enough, the bewildered person turns to the right also (d).

attribution
process of assigning causes to behavior

fundamental attribution error
tendency to overestimate the impact of dispositional influences on other people's behavior

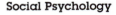

Social Psychology

bit more likely to invoke situational influences, probably because we're well aware of all of the situational factors affecting us (Jones & Nisbett, 1972). For example, if we ask you why your best friend in college chose to attend this school, you'll most likely mention dispositional factors: "She's a really motivated person and likes to work hard." In contrast, if we ask *you* why you chose to attend this school, you'll most likely mention situational factors: "When I visited the college, I really liked the campus and was impressed by what I heard about the professors." Still, this difference isn't large in size and usually holds only when we're describing people we know well (Malle, 2006).

EVIDENCE FOR THE FUNDAMENTAL ATTRIBUTION ERROR. Edward E. Jones and Victor Harris (1967) conducted the first study to demonstrate the fundamental attribution error. They asked undergraduates to serve as "debaters" in a discussion of U.S. attitudes toward Cuba and its controversial leader Fidel Castro. In full view of the other debaters, they randomly assigned students to read aloud debate speeches that adopted either a pro-Castro or an anti-Castro position.

After hearing these speeches, the researchers asked the other debaters to evaluate each debater's *true* attitudes toward Castro. That is, putting aside the speech he or she read, what do you think each debater *really* believes about Castro? Students fell prey to the fundamental attribution error; they assumed that what debaters said reflected their true position regarding Castro *even though they knew that the assignment to conditions was entirely random* (see **FIGURE 3**). They forgot to take the situation—namely, the random assignment of participants to the experimental condition—into account when evaluating debaters' attitudes (Ross, Amabile, & Steinmetz, 1977).

THE FUNDAMENTAL ATTRIBUTION ERROR: CULTURAL INFLUENCES. Like many psychological phenomena, the fundamental attribution error is influenced by culture. Although almost everyone is prone to this error, Japanese and Chinese people seem to be less so (Mason & Morris, 2010; Nisbett, 2003). That may be because they're more likely than people in Western cultures to view behaviors in context. As a result, they may be more prone to seeing others' behavior as a complex stew of both dispositional and situational influences.

For example, after reading newspaper descriptions of mass murderers, Chinese participants are less likely to invoke dispositional explanations for their behavior ("He must be an evil person") and more likely to invoke situational explanations ("He must have been under terrible stress in his life"). In contrast, U.S. participants show the opposite pattern (Morris & Peng, 1994). This cultural difference even extends to inanimate objects. When shown a circle moving in various directions, Chinese students are more likely to say that the circle's movement is due to situational factors ("Something is pushing on the circle") than to dispositional factors ("The circle wants to move to the right"). We again find the opposite pattern among U.S. students (Nisbett, 2003).

Explore in **MyPsychLab** the **Concept:** Fundamental Attribution Error

FIGURE 3 Participants' Performance in Jones & Harris (1967) Castro Study. Participants inferred that debaters' pro-Castro positions reflected their actual attitudes even though debaters couldn't choose which position to adopt—an example of the fundamental attribution error. (Figure is based on data from Jones & Harris, 1967.)

Study and **Review** in **MyPsychLab**

Assess Your Knowledge   FACT or FICTION?

1. From the standpoint of an evolutionary approach to social behavior, conformity and obedience are inherently maladaptive.   **True / False**

2. Social comparison almost always involves comparing ourselves with people who are worse off than we are.   **True / False**

3. The presence of other people always enhances our performance.   **True / False**

4. The fundamental attribution error reminds us that we tend to attribute others' behavior primarily to their personality traits and attitudes.   **True / False**

Answers: 1. F; 2. F; 3. F; 4. T

Social Influence: Conformity and Obedience

3 Determine the factors that influence when we conform to others.

4 Recognize the dangers of group decision making and identify ways to avoid mistakes common in group decisions.

5 Identify the factors that maximize or minimize obedience to authority.

Think of an organization or group to which you've belonged, like a club, school committee, fraternity, or sorority. Have you ever just gone along with one of the group's ideas even though you knew it was bad, perhaps even unethical? If so, you're in good company. **Conformity** refers to the tendency of people to alter their behavior as a result of group pressure (Kiesler & Kiesler, 1969; Pronin, Berger, & Molouki, 2007; Sherif, 1936). We all conform to social pressure from time to time. Yet as we'll soon see, we occasionally take this tendency too far.

👁 **Watch** in **MyPsychLab** the **Video:** Conformity and Influence in Groups

Conformity: The Asch Studies

Solomon Asch conducted the classic study of conformity in the 1950s. Asch's (1955) research design was as straightforward as it was elegant. In some social psychological studies such as Asch's, participants are lured in by a cover story that conceals the study's true goal. Often, other "participants" in the study are actually *confederates*, or undercover agents of the researcher. But the actual participants are not aware of that deception.

In this chapter, we'll ask you to imagine yourself as a participant in several classic social psychological studies. Let's begin with Asch's.

The Setup: Asch invites participants to a "study of perceptual judgments" that asks eight participants—including you—to compare a standard line with three comparison lines: 1, 2, and 3. Unbeknownst to you, the other "participants" are actually confederates. A researcher explains that your job is to say aloud which of three comparison lines matches the standard line. The researcher starts with a person across the table, so you're always the fifth to be called.

The Study: On the first trial (figure not shown), the correct answer is clearly "1." You listen intently as the first few participants call out their answers. Participant 1: "1." Participant 2: "1." Participant 3: "1." Participant 4: "1." As Participant 5, you simply follow, and say "1." The three participants following you give the same answer: 1. "This study's going to be a breeze," you say to yourself.

The second trial displays a similar problem, just as easy to answer, in which the correct answer is clearly "2" (see **FIGURE 4a**). Again, you listen while the participants call out their answers. Participant 1: "3." Participant 2: "3." Participant 3: "3." Participant 4: "3."

You can hardly believe your eyes (see **FIGURE 4b**). It seems obvious that "2" is the correct answer, but everyone is calling "3." What on Earth is going on? Are your eyes deceiving you? What are you going to do?

The Results: If you're like 75 percent of participants in the original Asch study, you'd conform to the incorrect norm on at least one of 12 trials. Across all 12 trials in the Asch study,

---

conformity
tendency of people to alter their behavior as a result of group pressure

FIGURE 4 Asch's Conformity Study. (a) Which of the "comparison lines" is the same length as the "standard line"? If several other participants said it was line 3, would you go along with them? (b) Here we see the lone actual participant (middle), barely believing his eyes, straining to look at the stimulus cards after the confederates gave the wrong answer. This participant was one of only 25 percent of Asch's participants who stuck to his guns and gave the correct answer in all 12 trials. After the study, he insisted, "I have to call them as I see them." (c) In Asch's studies, conformity increased as the size of the majority increased—but only up to about five or six confederates. (*Source:* Asch, 1955)

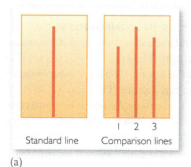

Standard line   Comparison lines
                  1 2 3

(a)

(b)

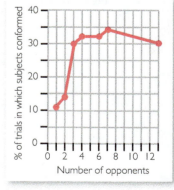

% of trials in which subjects conformed

Number of opponents

(c)

Social Psychology

participants conformed to the wrong answer 37 percent of the time. Some conformed even when the comparison line differed from the standard line by more than 6 inches! Understandably, participants reported being confused and even distressed because they experienced a sharp conflict between their perceptions and what they believed to be others' perceptions.

SOCIAL INFLUENCES ON CONFORMITY. Asch (1955) and later researchers went on to pinpoint some of the social factors that influence how likely we are to conform. They concluded that conformity was influenced by the following independent variables:

- **Uniformity of Agreement:** If all confederates gave the wrong answer, the participant was more likely to conform. Nevertheless, if one confederate gave the correct response, the level of conformity plummeted by three-fourths.
- **Difference in the Wrong Answer:** Knowing that someone else in the group differed from the majority—*even if that person held a different view from that of the participant*—made the participant less likely to conform.
- **Size:** The size of the majority made a difference, but only up to about five or six confederates. People were no more likely to conform in a group of ten than in a group of five (see **FIGURE 4c**).

RULING OUT RIVAL HYPOTHESES ▶
Have important alternative explanations for the findings been excluded?

Asch also tried to rule out alternative hypotheses for his findings. To determine whether group norms affected participants' *perceptions* of the lines, he repeated his original study but asked participants to write, rather than call out, their responses. In this condition, their answers were right more than 99 percent of the time.

IMAGING STUDIES: PROBING FURTHER INFLUENCES. Nevertheless, brain imaging data raise the possibility that social pressure sometimes influences perception. Gregory Berns and his colleagues (Berns et al., 2005) placed participants in an fMRI scanner and showed them two figures. They asked participants to determine whether the figures were the same or different. To do so, they had to mentally rotate one or both of them. The researchers led participants to believe that four other people were making the same judgments along with them; in fact, these judgments were preprogrammed into a computer.

On some trials, the other "participants" gave unanimously correct answers; on others, they gave unanimously incorrect answers. Like Asch, Berns and his collaborators found high levels of conformity: Participants went along with others' wrong answers 41 percent of the time. Their conforming behavior was associated with activity in the amygdala, which triggers anxiety in response to danger cues. This finding suggests that conformity may come with a price tag of negative emotions, particularly anxiety. Berns and his colleagues also found that conformity was associated with activity in the parietal and occipital lobes, the areas of the brain responsible for visual perception. This finding suggests that social pressure might sometimes affect how we perceive reality, although activity in these brain areas may have instead reflected participants' tendency to doubt and then recheck their initial perceptions.

RULING OUT RIVAL HYPOTHESES ▶
Have important alternative explanations for the findings been excluded?

INDIVIDUAL, CULTURAL, AND GENDER DIFFERENCES IN CONFORMITY. People's responses to social pressure are also associated with individual and cultural differences. People with low self-esteem are especially prone to conformity (Hardy, 1957). Asians are also more likely to conform compared with Americans (Bond & Smith, 1996), probably because most Asian cultures are more collectivist than is American culture (Oyserman, Coon, & Kemmelmeier, 2002). This greater collectivism probably leads many Asians to be more concerned about peer opinion than are Americans. In addition, people in individualistic cultures like the United States generally prefer to stand out from the crowd, whereas those in collectivist cultures prefer to blend in. In one study, researchers presented American and Asian participants with a bunch of orange and green pens that had a majority of one color and a minority of the other. Americans tended to pick the minority-colored pens, whereas Asians tended to pick the majority-colored pens (Kim & Markus, 1999).

In contrast, gender doesn't seem to matter much when it comes to conformity. Early studies suggested that women were more likely to conform than men are (Eagly & Carli, 1981). But because the experimenters were all male, this difference may have been due to an alternative explanation: perhaps male experimenters had unknowingly provoked submissive behavior in female participants. When later studies were conducted by female experimenters, the sex difference in conformity largely vanished (Feldman-Summers et al., 1980; Javornisky, 1979).

◀ **RULING OUT RIVAL HYPOTHESES**
Have important alternative explanations for the findings been excluded?

Deindividuation: Losing Our Typical Identities

One process that can make us more vulnerable to conformity is **deindividuation**: the tendency of people to engage in atypical behavior when stripped of their usual identities (Festinger, Pepitone, & Newcomb, 1952). Several factors contribute to deindividuation, but the most prominent are a feeling of anonymity and a lack of personal responsibility (Dipboye, 1977; Postmes & Spears, 1998). When we're deindividuated, we become more vulnerable to social influences, including the impact of social roles.

The advent of email, text messaging, and other largely impersonal forms of communication may contribute to deindividuation, in turn leading to a heightened risk of "flaming"—sending insulting messages to others (Kato, Kato, & Akahori, 2007). Indeed, once people start posting nasty anonymous online comments on YouTube videos, others quickly join in (Moor, Heuvelman, & Verleur, 2010).

The face painting of warriors and the masks donned by the Ku Klux Klan may also fuel deindividuation by fostering anonymity (Watson, 1973). In one study, children asked to wear masks were more likely than other children to help themselves to forbidden Halloween candy (Miller & Rowold, 1979).

? Research on deindividuation suggests that irresponsible behavior would probably be more likely to occur in which of these two settings. Why? (See answer upside down on bottom of page.)

Every day, we play multiple social roles: student, son or daughter, roommate, and club member, to name but a few. What happens when we temporarily lose our typical social identities and are forced to adopt different ones?

STANFORD PRISON STUDY: CHAOS IN PALO ALTO. Philip Zimbardo and his colleagues first approached this question four decades ago (Haney, Banks, & Zimbardo, 1973). Zimbardo knew about the dehumanizing conditions in many prisons and wondered whether they stemmed from peoples' personalities or from the roles they're required to adopt. The roles of prisoner and guard, which are inherently antagonistic, may carry such powerful expectations that they generate self-fulfilling prophecies. What would happen if ordinary people played the roles of prisoner and guard? Would they begin to assume the identities assigned to them?

Setup: Zimbardo and his colleagues advertised for volunteers for a two-week "psychological study of prison life." Using a coin toss, they randomly assigned 24 male undergraduates, prescreened for normal adjustment using personality tests, to be either prisoners or guards.

The Study: Zimbardo and his collaborators transformed the basement of the Stanford psychology department in Palo Alto, California, into a simulated prison, complete with jail cells. To add to the realism, actual Palo Alto police officers arrested the would-be prisoners at their homes and transported them to the simulated prison. The prisoners and guards were forced to dress in clothes befitting their assigned roles. Zimbardo, who acted as the prison "superintendent," instructed guards to refer to prisoners only by numbers, not by names.

The Results: The first day passed without incident, but something soon went horribly wrong. Guards began to treat prisoners cruelly and to subject them to harsh punishments. Guards forced prisoners to perform humiliating lineups, do push-ups, sing, strip naked, and clean filthy toilets with their bare hands. In some cases, they even placed bags over prisoners' heads.

👁 **Watch** in **MyPsychLab** the **Video:** The Stanford Prison Experiment: Phil Zimbardo

deindividuation
tendency of people to engage in uncharacteristic behavior when they are stripped of their usual identities

Answer: Situation on right, because (1) people aren't wearing name tags and aren't easily identifiable and (2) the room is dark and may foster greater anonymity.

REPLICABILITY ▶
Can the results be duplicated in other studies?

By day 2, the prisoners mounted a rebellion, which the guards quickly quashed. Things went steadily downhill from there. The guards became increasingly sadistic, using fire extinguishers on the prisoners and forcing them to simulate sodomy. Soon, many prisoners began to display signs of emotional disturbance, including depression, hopelessness, and anger. Zimbardo released two prisoners from the study because they appeared to be on the verge of a psychological breakdown. One prisoner went on a hunger strike in protest.

At day 6, Zimbardo—after some prodding from one of his former graduate students, Christina Maslach—ended the study eight days early. Although the prisoners were relieved at the news, some guards were disappointed (Haney et al., 1973). Perhaps Zimbardo was right; once prisoners and guards had been assigned roles that deemphasized their individuality, they adopted their designated roles more easily than anyone might have imagined. Yet because of the fundamental attribution error, which leads us to underestimate the power of the situation, most of us find the results of the Stanford Prison Study startling (Haney & Zimbardo, 2009).

Nevertheless, Zimbardo's study wasn't carefully controlled: in many respects, it was more of a demonstration than an experiment. In particular, his prisoners and guards may have experienced demand characteristics to behave in accord with their assigned roles. Among other things, they may have assumed that the investigators wanted them to play the parts of prisoners and guards and obliged. Moreover, at least one attempt to replicate the Stanford prison study was unsuccessful, suggesting that the effects of deindividuation may not be inevitable (Reicher & Haslam, 2006).

THE REAL WORLD: CHAOS IN ABU GHRAIB. The Stanford prison study wasn't an isolated event (Zimbardo, 2007). In 2004, the world witnessed disturbingly similar images in the now-infamous Iraqi prison of Abu Ghraib. There, we saw guards—this time, U.S. soldiers—placing bags over Iraqi prisoners' heads, leading them around with dog leashes, pointing mockingly at their exposed genitals, and arranging them in human pyramids for the soldiers' amusement. These similarities weren't lost on Zimbardo (2004b, 2007), who maintained that the Abu Ghraib fiasco was a product of situational forces. According to Zimbardo, the dehumanization of prisoners and prison guards made it likely they'd lose themselves in the social roles to which superiors assigned them.

That said, the overwhelming majority of U.S. prison guards during the Iraqi War didn't engage in abuse, so the reasons for such abuse don't lie entirely in the situation. As research using Asch's studies reminds us, individual differences in personality play a key role in conformity. Indeed, several guards who perpetrated the Abu Ghraib abuses had a long history of irresponsible behavior (Saletan, 2004).

Furthermore, deindividuation doesn't necessarily make us behave badly; it makes us more likely to conform to whatever norms are present in the situation (Postmes & Spears, 1998). A loss of identity actually makes people more likely to engage in prosocial, or helping, behavior when others are helping out (Johnson & Downing, 1979). Moreover, being anonymous sometimes makes us more, not less, likely to assist others. For example, when people can't be identified, they're especially likely to help strangers by pointing out fashion gaffes that could embarrass them, such as the fact that their zippers are open (Hirsch, Galinsky, & Zhong, 2011). For good, bad, and often both, deindividuation makes us behave more like a member of the group and less like an individual.

CROWDS: MOB PSYCHOLOGY IN ACTION. Deindividuation helps explain why crowd behavior is so unpredictable: the actions of people in crowds depend largely on whether others are acting prosocially or antisocially (against others). A myth that's endured for centuries is that crowds are always more aggressive than individuals. In the late nineteenth century, sociologist Gustav Le Bon (1895) argued that crowds are a recipe for irrational and even destructive behavior. According to Le Bon, people in crowds are more anonymous and therefore more likely to act on their impulses than are individuals.

In some cases, Le Bon was right. In November 2008, a Long Island, New York, Wal-Mart employee was trampled to death by a stampeding crowd of over 200 people after the doors opened for post-Thanksgiving shopping. Four other people, including a pregnant woman, were injured. Some shoppers, eager to get good deals on discounted products, ran over emergency workers assisting the victims. Yet in other cases, crowds are less aggressive than individuals (de Waal, 1989; de Waal, Aureli, & Judge, 2000). Depending on prevailing social norms, deindividuation can make us either more or less aggressive. Moreover, people in crowds typically limit their social interactions to minimize conflict (Baum, 1987). For example, people on crowded buses and elevators generally avoid staring at one another. This behavior is probably adaptive, because people are less likely to say or do something that could offend others.

Groupthink

Closely related to conformity is a phenomenon that Irving Janis (1972) termed **groupthink**: an emphasis on group unanimity at the expense of critical thinking. Groups sometimes become so intent on ensuring that everyone agrees with everyone else that they lose their capacity to evaluate issues objectively. To be sure, groups, including juries and presidential cabinets, often make good decisions, especially when group members are free to contribute opinions that aren't influenced—and potentially contaminated—by peer pressure (Surowiecki, 2004). Yet groups sometimes make poor decisions, especially when members' judgments aren't independent of each other. When groups combine information from members, they typically rely on "common knowledge"—information that group members share—rather than unique knowledge, resulting in no net gain in new information (Stasser & Titus, 2003). But widely held knowledge isn't always incorrect knowledge.

To some observers, some of the behaviors documented at Abu Ghraib prison in Iraq (photos at right) are eerily similar to those of Zimbardo's prison study (photos at left). Were the same processes of deindividuation at work?

GROUPTHINK IN THE REAL WORLD. Janis arrived at the concept of groupthink after studying the reasoning processes behind the failed 1961 invasion of the Bay of Pigs in Cuba. Following lengthy discussions with cabinet members, President John F. Kennedy recruited 1,400 Cuban immigrants to invade Cuba and overthrow its dictator, Fidel Castro. But the invasion was ineptly planned, and nearly all of the invaders were captured or killed.

   Although the members of Kennedy's cabinet were uncommonly brilliant, their actions were astonishingly foolish. After the failed invasion, Kennedy asked, "How could I have been so stupid?" (Dallek, 2003). The Bay of Pigs invasion wasn't the last time groupthink led intelligent people to make catastrophic decisions. In 1986, the space shuttle *Challenger* exploded, killing the seven astronauts aboard a mere 73 seconds after takeoff. Following group discussions, project managers of the *Challenger* agreed to launch it after a series of bitterly cold days in January, despite warnings from NASA engineers that the shuttle might explode because rubber rings on the rocket booster could fail in freezing temperatures (Esser & Lindoerfer, 1989).

   TABLE I depicts some of the "symptoms" identified by Janis (1972) that render groups vulnerable to groupthink. Nevertheless, some psychologists have pointed out that Janis's descriptions of groupthink derived from anecdotal observations, which we've learned are often flawed as sources of evidence. Moreover, groupthink doesn't always lead to bad decisions, just overconfident ones (Tyson, 1987). Seeking group consensus isn't always a bad idea, but doing so before all of the evidence is available is (Longley & Pruitt, 1980).

   Janis (1972) noted that the best way to avoid groupthink is to encourage dissent within an organization. He recommended that all groups appoint a "devil's advocate"—a person whose role is to voice doubts about the wisdom of the group's decisions. Studies show

 Watch in **MyPsychLab** the **Video:**
IT Video: Group Thinking

Although crowds *sometimes* engage in irrational, even violent, behavior, research suggests that compared with individuals, crowds aren't necessarily more aggressive. The January 2013 inauguration of President Barack Obama, shown here, was marked by only one reported arrest despite an estimated crowd size of over 1 million people.

groupthink
emphasis on group unanimity at the expense of critical thinking

TABLE I Symptoms of Groupthink.

SYMPTOM	EXAMPLE
An illusion of the group's invulnerability	"We can't possibly fail!"
An illusion of the group's unanimity	"Obviously, we all agree."
An unquestioned belief in the group's moral correctness	"We know we're on the right side."
Conformity pressure—pressure on group members to go along with everyone else	"Don't rock the boat!"
Stereotyping of the out-group—a caricaturing of the enemy	"They're all morons."
Self-censorship—the tendency of group members to keep their mouths shut even when they have doubts	"I suspect the group leader's idea is stupid, but I'd better not say anything."
Mindguards—self-appointed individuals whose job it is to stifle disagreement	"Oh, you think you know better than the rest of us?"

"All those in favor say 'Aye.'"
"Aye."   "Aye."   "Aye."   "Aye."   "Aye."

? What symptom of groupthink does this cartoon illustrate? (See answer upside down at bottom of page.) (© *The New Yorker Collection 1979 Henry Martin from cartoonbank.com. All Rights Reserved.*)

group polarization
tendency of group discussion to strengthen the dominant positions held by individual group members

cult
group of individuals who exhibit intense and unquestioning devotion to a single cause

that including a devil's advocate in groups tends to reduce groupthink and to result in better decisions (Schwenk, 1989). In addition, Janis suggested having independent experts on hand to evaluate whether the group's decisions make sense. Holding a follow-up meeting to evaluate whether the decision reached in the first meeting still seems reasonable can serve as a helpful check against errors in reasoning. Although not explicitly recommended by Janis, research suggests that increasing racial diversity within groups can result in better decisions, partly because it may lead to consideration of alternative perspectives. For example, in studies of jury decision making, including at least two African-Americans in predominantly white juries is associated with fewer factual mistakes on the part of jurors, more detailed consideration of the facts of the case, and fairer verdicts (Sommers, 2006).

GROUP POLARIZATION: GOING TO EXTREMES. Related to groupthink is **group polarization**, which occurs when group discussion strengthens the dominant position held by individual group members (Isenberg, 1986; Myers & Lamm, 1976). In one study, a group of students who were slightly unprejudiced became less prejudiced after discussing racial issues, whereas a group that was slightly prejudiced became *more* prejudiced after discussing racial issues (Myers & Bishop, 1970). Group polarization can be helpful if it leads to efficient decisions. Yet in other cases, it can be destructive, as when juries rush to unanimous decisions before they've considered all the evidence (Daftary-Kapur, Dumas, & Penrod, 2010; Myers & Kaplan, 1976).

There's evidence that the American electorate is becoming increasingly polarized, with left-leaning citizens becoming more liberal, and right-leaning citizens becoming more conservative (Abramowitz & Saunders, 2008). At least some of this polarization may be due to the increasing accessibility of Internet blogs, radio talk shows, and cable television, which provide political partisans on both sides with a steady diet of information that supports their views—and fuels their confirmation bias (Jamieson & Cappella, 2007; Lilienfeld, Ammirati, & Landfield, 2009; Sunstein, 2002). Moreover, research on book-buying habits shows that liberals read almost exclusively liberal books and conservatives read almost exclusively conservative books (Eakin, 2004). Few people on either end of the political spectrum expose themselves to information that challenges their views, probably generating further polarization.

CULTS AND BRAINWASHING. In extreme forms, groupthink can lead to **cults**: groups that exhibit intense and unquestioning devotion to a single cause. Although most cults aren't dangerous (Bridgstock, 2009), they can occasionally have disastrous consequences. Consider Heaven's Gate, a southern California–based group founded in 1975 by Marshall

Cult membership involves following the cult's practices without question. Reverend Sun Yung Moon of the Unification Church has united thousands of total strangers in mass wedding ceremonies. The couples are determined by pairing photos of prospective brides and grooms. They meet for the first time during the week leading up to the wedding day, often on the day of the ceremony itself.

Applewhite, a former psychiatric patient. Cult members believed that Applewhite was a reincarnated version of Jesus Christ. Applewhite, they were convinced, would take them to a starship in their afterlives. In 1997, a major comet approached Earth, and several false reports circulated in the media that a spaceship was tailing it. The Heaven's Gate members believed this was their calling. Virtually all of the cult members—39 of them—committed suicide by drinking a poisoned cocktail.

Because cults are secretive and difficult to study, we know relatively little about them. But evidence suggests that cults promote groupthink in four major ways (Lalich, 2004): having a persuasive leader who fosters loyalty; disconnecting group members from the outside world; discouraging questioning of the group's assumptions; and establishing training practices that gradually indoctrinate members (Galanter, 1980).

Despite what many people believe, most cult members are psychologically normal (Aronoff, Lynn, & Malinowski, 2000; Lalich, 2004), although many cult *leaders* probably suffer from serious mental illness. This erroneous belief probably stems from the fundamental attribution error. In trying to explain why people join cults, we overestimate the role of personality traits and underestimate the role of social influences.

One widespread misconception is that all cult members are *brainwashed,* or transformed by group leaders into unthinking zombies. Although some psychologists have argued that many cults use brainwashing techniques (Singer, 1979), the existence of brainwashing is scientifically controversial. There's not much evidence that brainwashing permanently alters victims' beliefs (Melton, 1999). Moreover, there's reason to doubt whether brainwashing is a unique means of changing people's behavior. Instead, the persuasive techniques of brainwashing probably aren't all that different from those used by effective political leaders and salespeople (Zimbardo, 1997).

How can we best resist the indoctrination that leads to cults? Here, the psychological research is clear, although counterintuitive: First expose people to information consistent with cult beliefs and then debunk it. In his work on the **inoculation effect**, William McGuire (1964) demonstrated that the best way of immunizing people against an undesirable belief is to gently introduce them to reasons this belief seems to be correct, which gives them the chance to generate their own counterarguments against those reasons. In this way, they'll be more resistant to arguments for this belief—and more open to arguments against it—in the future (Compton & Pfau, 2005). This approach works much like a vaccine, which inoculates people against a virus by presenting them with a small dose of it, thereby activating the body's defenses (McGuire, 1964; McGuire &

Factoid

Most suicide bombers in the Middle East, including the September 11 hijackers and many Al Qaeda members, aren't mentally disordered (Gordon, 2002); in this respect, they appear to be similar to most cult members. Moreover, most suicide bombers are relatively well off and well educated (Sageman, 2004).

inoculation effect
approach to convincing people to change their minds about something by first introducing reasons why the perspective might be correct and then debunking them

591

Papageorgis, 1961). For example, if we want to persuade someone to purchase a used car, we might list all of the reasons buying this car seems like a bad idea and then point out why these reasons aren't as convincing as they seem.

Obedience: The Psychology of Following Orders

In the case of conformity, we go along to get along. The transmission is "horizontal"—the group influence originates from our peers. In the case of **obedience**, we take our marching orders from people above us in the hierarchy of authority, such as a teacher, parent, or boss. Here the transmission is "vertical"—the group influence springs not from our peers, but from our leaders (Loevinger, 1987). Many groups, such as cults, acquire their influence from a potent combination of both conformity and obedience.

OBEDIENCE: A DOUBLE-EDGED SWORD. Obedience is a necessary, even essential, ingredient in our daily lives. Without it, society couldn't run smoothly. You're reading this text in part because your professor told you to, and you'll obey the traffic lights and stop signs on your next trip to school because you know you're expected to. Yet like conformity, obedience can produce troubling consequences when people stop asking questions about *why* they're behaving as others want them to. As British writer C. P. Snow wrote, "When you look at the dark and gloomy history of man, you will find that more hideous crimes have been committed in the name of obedience than have ever been committed in the name of rebellion." Let's look at one infamous example.

During the Vietnam War, U.S. Lieutenant William Calley commanded a platoon of a division named Charlie Company that had encountered heavy arms fire for weeks. Understandably, the members of Charlie Company were on edge during the morning of March 16, 1968, as they entered the village of My Lai (pronounced "Me Lie"), expecting to find a hideout for North Vietnamese soldiers. Although the platoon located no enemy soldiers in My Lai, Calley ordered soldiers to open fire on villagers, none of whom had initiated combat. They bludgeoned several old men to death with the butts of their rifles and shot praying children and women in the head. When all was said and done, the American platoon had brutally slaughtered about 500 innocent Vietnamese ranging in age from 1 to 82.

Calley insisted that he was merely taking orders from his superiors and bore no direct responsibility for the massacre: "I was ordered to go in there and destroy the enemy. That was my job that day. That was the mission I was given" (Calley, 1971). In turn, the soldiers in Calley's platoon claimed they were merely taking orders from Calley. In 1971, Calley was convicted of murder and sentenced to life in military prison, but President Richard Nixon reduced his sentence.

In sharp contrast to Calley's behavior, Officer Hugh Thompson, Jr., attempted to halt the massacre by landing his U.S. Army helicopter between Calley's troops and the innocent villagers. Risking their lives, Thompson and his two crewmen ordered the troops to stop shooting, saving scores of innocent lives.

As inexplicable as the My Lai massacre seems, it's only one instance of the perils of unthinking obedience. How can we make sense of this behavior?

STANLEY MILGRAM: SOURCES OF DESTRUCTIVE OBEDIENCE. Stanley Milgram was a graduate student of Solomon Asch's who sought to understand the principles underlying irrational group behavior. The child of Jewish parents who grew up during World War II, Milgram was preoccupied with the profoundly troubling question of how the Holocaust could have occurred. The prevailing wisdom in the late 1940s and 1950s was that the Holocaust was primarily the product of twisted minds that had perpetuated dastardly deeds. Yet Milgram suspected that the truth was subtler, and in some ways more frightening, as he came to believe that the psychological processes that give rise to destructive obedience are surprisingly commonplace.

Two sides of the coin of obedience: Lt. William Calley (*left*) was charged with murder by the Army for ordering his platoon to massacre unarmed civilians in the My Lai massacre in 1968. Calley was the only one in the platoon to be charged with a crime. Hugh Thompson (*right*) and his fellow crew members landed their helicopter between their fellow Army platoon and the civilians in the My Lai massacre in an effort to save the lives of the unarmed villagers. Thompson and crew were awarded the Soldier's Medal for bravery.

obedience
adherence to instructions from those of higher authority

THE MILGRAM PARADIGM. In the early 1960s, Milgram began to tinker with a laboratory paradigm (a model experiment) that could provide a window into the causes of obedience (Blass, 2004). After a few years of pilot testing, Milgram finally hit on the paradigm he wanted, not knowing that it would become one of the most influential in the history of psychology (Cialdini & Goldstein, 2004; Slater, 2004).

The Setup: You spot an advertisement in a local New Haven, Connecticut, newspaper, asking for volunteers for a study of memory. The ad notes that participants will be paid $4.50, a hefty chunk of change in the 1960s. You arrive at the laboratory at Yale University, where a tall and imposing man in a white lab coat, Mr. Williams, greets you. You also meet another friendly, middle-aged participant, Mr. Wallace, who unbeknownst to you is actually a confederate. The cover story is that you and Mr. Wallace will be participating in a study of the effects of "punishment on learning," with one of you being the teacher and the other the learner. Drawing lots to see who'll play which role, you get the piece of paper that says "teacher" (in fact, the lots are rigged). From here on, Mr. Williams refers to you as the "teacher" and to Mr. Wallace as the "learner."

As the teacher, Mr. Williams explains, you'll present Mr. Wallace with what psychologists call a *paired-associate task*. In this task, you'll read a long list of word pairs, like *strong–arm* and *black–curtain*. Then you'll present the learner with the first word in each pair (such as *strong*) and ask him to select the second word (*arm*) from a list of four words. Now here's the surprise: To evaluate the effects of punishment on learning, you'll be delivering a series of painful electric shocks to the learner. With each wrong answer, you'll move up one step on a shock generator. The shocks range from 15–450 volts and are accompanied by labels ranging from "Slight Shock" and "Moderate Shock" to "Danger: Severe Shock" and, finally and most ominously, "XXX."

The Study: You watch as Mr. Williams brings the learner into a room and straps his arm to a shock plate. The learner, Mr. Williams explains, will push a button corresponding to his answer to the first word in each pair. His answer will light up in an adjoining room where you sit. For a correct answer, you'll do nothing. But for an incorrect answer, you'll give the learner an electric shock, with the intensity increasing with each mistake. At this point, the learner mentions to Mr. Williams that he has "a slight heart condition" and asks anxiously how powerful the shocks will be. Mr. Williams responds curtly that although the shocks will be painful, they "will cause no permanent tissue damage."

You're led into the adjoining room and seated in front of the shock generator. Following Milgram's plan, the learner makes a few correct responses, but soon begins to make errors. If at any time you turn to Mr. Williams to ask if you should continue, he responds with a set of prearranged prompts that urge you to go on ("Please go on." or "The experiment requires that you continue." or "You have no other choice; you *must* go on."). Milgram standardized the verbal statements of the learner, which also unbeknownst to you, have been prerecorded on audiotape (Milgram, 1974). At 75 volts, the learner grunts "Ugh!" and by 330 volts, he frantically yells "Let me out of here!" repeatedly and complains of chest pain. From 345 volts onward, there's nothing—only silence. The learner stops responding to your items, and Mr. Williams instructs you to treat these nonresponses as incorrect answers and to keep administering increasingly intense shocks.

The Results: When Milgram first designed this study, he asked 40 psychiatrists at Yale University to forecast the outcome. Most participants, they predicted, would break off at 150 volts. Only .1 percent (that's 1 in 1,000), representing a "pathological fringe" (Milgram, 1974), would go all the way to 450 volts, they guessed. Before reading on, you may want to ask yourself what you would have done had you been a participant in Milgram's study. Would you have delivered any shocks? If so, how far would you have gone?

In fact, in the original Milgram study, *all* participants administered at least some shocks. Most went up to at least 150 volts, and a remarkable 62 percent displayed complete compliance, going all the way up 450 volts (see **FIGURE 5**). This means that the Yale psychiatrists were off by a factor of several hundred.

These results were, well, shocking. Milgram himself was startled by them (Blass, 2004). Before Milgram's study, most psychologists assumed that the overwhelming

Four panels from Milgram's obedience study:

The shock generator.

The "learner" Mr. Wallace, being strapped to the shock plate by Mr. Williams and an assistant.

Mr. Williams delivering instructions to the "teacher," the actual participant.

The "teacher" breaking off the study after refusing to comply with Mr. Williams' orders.

majority of normal people would disobey what were obviously cruel and outrageous orders. But like the Yale psychiatrists, they committed the fundamental attribution error: they underestimated the impact of the situation on participants' behaviors.

There were other surprises. Many participants showed uncontrollable tics and fits of nervous laughter. Yet few appeared to be sadistic. Even those who complied until the bitter end seemed reluctant to deliver shocks, asking or begging the experimenter to allow them to stop. Yet most participants still followed Mr. Williams' orders despite these pleas, often assuming no responsibility for their actions. One person's responses were illustrative; after the study was over he claimed, "I stopped, but he [the experimenter] made me go on" (Milgram, 1974).

Milgram Themes and Variations. Like his mentor Solomon Asch, Milgram conducted a variety of follow-up studies to pinpoint the situational factors that affected obedience and to rule out alternative explanations for his findings. These studies provide an elegant demonstration of social psychological research at its best. In addition, they afford a powerful test of the replicability of Milgram's paradigm and its generalizability across situations.

We've summarized the major variations Milgram conducted on his original paradigm in **TABLE 2**. As we can see, the level of participants' obedience varied substantially depending on a number of independent variables, including the amount of feedback and proximity from the learner to the teacher, and the physical proximity and prestige of the experimenter. Although this table displays numerous variations, two key themes emerge. First, the greater the "psychological distance" between teacher (the actual participant) and experimenter, the *less* the obedience. As the experimenter became more psychologically distant, as when he gave instructions by telephone, compliance plummeted. Second, the greater the psychological distance between teacher and learner, the *more* the obedience. For example, when Milgram increased the psychological distance between teacher and learner by having the teacher direct someone else to administer the shocks, there was virtually complete compliance. Like Lieutenant Calley, whose defense during the My Lai massacre was that he was "just taking orders," participants in this condition probably felt relieved of personal responsibility.

Individual, Gender, and Cultural Differences. When evaluating Milgram's findings, it's only natural to focus on the sizable proportion of participants who followed orders. Yet many of his participants didn't go along with the experimenter's commands despite intense pressure to do so. Recall that at My Lai, some American soldiers disobeyed Calley's orders by ordering his soldiers to stop firing. Moreover, during the Holocaust, thousands of European families risked their lives to offer safe haven to Jewish civilians in clear defiance of Nazi laws (Wilson, 1993). So despite powerful situational pressures, some people disobey authority figures who give unethical orders.

Surprisingly, Milgram (1974) found that obedient and disobedient participants were similar on most personality variables. For example, he found no evidence that obedient participants were more sadistic than disobedient participants, suggesting that participants didn't follow orders because they enjoyed doing so (Aronson, 1998).

Nevertheless, researchers have identified a few predictors of obedience in Milgram's paradigm. For example, more morally advanced participants are more willing to defy the experimenter (Kohlberg, 1965; Milgram, 1974). Especially moral people may sometimes be more willing to violate rules than less moral people, especially if they view the rules as unreasonable. Another researcher found that people with high levels of a personality trait called

In the "touch proximity" condition (see Table 2), participants were instructed to hold the "learner's" hand on a shock plate. Here the level of obedience plummeted. This condition illustrates the point that decreasing the psychological distance between teacher and learner leads to decreased obedience.

FIGURE 5 Milgram's Obedience Study: The Shocking Findings. This graph displays the percentage of participants in Milgram's obedience study who complied with the experimenter's commands at different shock levels. As we can see, about two-thirds of participants obeyed until the bitter end.

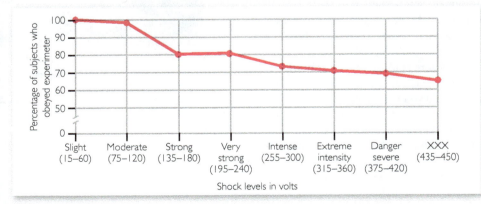

TABLE 2 The Milgram Paradigm: Themes and Variations.

VARIATION/CONDITION	DESCRIPTION	PERCENTAGE WHO COMPLIED TO 450 VOLTS
Remote feedback condition (initial study)	No verbal feedback from the learner; teacher hears only the learner pounding the wall in protest after being shocked.	65%
Voice feedback condition	Teacher hears the learner's screams of pain and complaints.	62%
Proximity condition	Learner is in the same room as the teacher so that teacher not only hears, but also observes the learner's agony.	40%
Touch proximity condition	Teacher is required to hold the learner's hand on a shock plate; whenever the learner's hand flies off the shock plate, the teacher must jam it back down to ensure electrical contact.	30%
Telephone condition	Experimenter gives instructions by telephone from a separate room (*Note*: Some participants "cheated" by giving less intense shocks than what the experimenter directed).	30%
Second experimenter condition	A second experimenter is present and begins disagreeing with the first experimenter about whether to carry on with the session.	0%
Less prestigious setting for study	Study is conducted (voice feedback condition is replicated) in a run-down office building in nearby Bridgeport, Connecticut, removing all affiliation with Yale University.	48%
Ask teacher to direct a different participant to administer shock	Teacher is asked to give orders to another "participant" (actually a confederate), who then delivers the shocks. In this condition, teachers can reassure themselves, "I'm not actually giving any shocks; I'm just telling him to do it."	93%

authoritarianism are more likely to obey the experimenters' demands (Elms & Milgram, 1966). People with high levels of authoritarianism see the world as a big hierarchy of power. For them, authority figures are to be respected, not questioned (Adorno et al., 1950; Dillehay, 1978).

Milgram found no consistent sex differences in obedience; this finding has held up in later studies using his paradigm (Blass, 1999). Milgram's findings have also been replicated in many countries. The overall rates of obedience among Americans don't differ significantly from those of non-Americans (Blass, 2004), including people in Italy (Ancona & Pareyson, 1968), South Africa (Edwards et al., 1969), Spain (Miranda et al., 1981), Germany (Mantell, 1971), Australia (Kilham & Mann, 1974), and Jordan (Shanab & Yahya, 1977).

Milgram's Studies: Lessons. Milgram's work teaches us that the power of authority figures is greater than almost anyone had imagined and that obedience doesn't typically result from sadism. Milgram's research also reminds us of the power of the fundamental attribution error. Most people, even psychiatrists, underestimate situational influences on behavior (Bierbrauer, 1973; Sabini & Silver, 1983).

Psychologists continue to debate whether Milgram's study offers an adequate model of what happened during the Holocaust and My Lai. Milgram's critics correctly note that in contrast to Milgram's participants, some concentration camp guards actively enjoyed torturing innocent people (Cialdini & Goldstein, 2004). These critics further argue that destructive obedience on a grand scale probably requires not only an authority figure bearing an official stamp of approval, but also a core group of genuinely wicked people. They may well be right. Still others have questioned whether Milgram's participants—and others who engage in destructive obedience—are truly mindless, blind followers. Perhaps the obedient participants believe that authority figures are doing the right thing (such as pursuing an important research question) and are actively choosing to help them (Reicher, Haslam, & Smith, 2012).

These controversies aside, there's no doubt that Stanley Milgram has forever changed how we think about ourselves and others. He made us more keenly aware of the fact that good people can do bad things and that rational people can behave irrationally (Aronson, 1998). By warning us of these perils, Milgram may have steered us toward guarding against them.

◀ **REPLICABILITY**
Can the results be duplicated in other studies?

Factoid

In a disturbing study, a research team told 32 undergraduates to deliver electric shocks to a small male dog (Larsen et al., 1974). Only two refused, and the average voltage level delivered was slightly over 100 volts.

Rosa Parks (1913–2005) became a role model for "civil disobedience" during the 1950s and 1960s when she refused to give up her seat on a bus to a white man as was required by law. Morality, for her, overrode law.

Assess Your Knowledge   FACT or FICTION?

1. Asch's studies demonstrated that several allies are required to counteract the effects of conformity on an individual.   True / False

2. Deindividuation can make people more likely to engage in prosocial, as well as antisocial, behavior.   True / False

3. Groups almost always make less extreme decisions than do individuals.   True / False

4. Obedience is by itself maladaptive and unhealthy.   True / False

Answers: 1. F; 2. T; 3. F; 4. F

This remarkable photo by primate researcher Frans de Waal shows a male chimpanzee (*left*) extending a hand of appeasement to another chimpanzee after a fight. Many psychologists have argued that our tendency toward prosocial behavior has deep roots in our primate heritage.

Helping and Harming Others: Prosocial Behavior and Aggression

6 Explain which aspects of a situation increase or decrease the likelihood of bystander intervention.

7 Describe the social and individual difference variables that contribute to human aggression.

For centuries, philosophers have debated the question of whether human nature is good or bad. Yet scientific truth rarely falls neatly into one of two extremes. Indeed, mounting evidence suggests that human nature is a blend of both socially constructive and destructive tendencies.

Primate researcher Frans de Waal (1982, 1996) argues that our two closest animal relatives, the bonobo and the chimpanzee, display the seeds of both prosocial and antisocial behavior. Because we share more than 98 percent of our DNA with both species, they offer a slightly fuzzy evolutionary window into our own nature. Although these species overlap in their social behaviors, the bonobo is more of a model for *prosocial behavior*—behavior intended to help others—and the chimpanzee is more of a model for antisocial behavior, including aggressive acts. Bonobos are veritable experts at reconciling after arguments, often making peace by making love—literally. They also engage in helping behaviors that we ordinarily associate with humans. de Waal described a remarkable event at the San Diego Zoo, where bonobo caretakers

were filling up the water moat. The juveniles of the [bonobo] group were playing in the empty moat, and the caretakers had not noticed. When they went to the kitchen to turn on the water, all of a sudden in front of the window they saw Kakowet, the old male of the group, and he was waving and screaming at them to draw their attention. [The caretakers] looked at the moat and saw the juveniles and then got them out of there, before the moat filled up.

Chimpanzees engage in prosocial behavior, too, like making up after fights. Yet they're far more prone to aggression than are bonobos. In the 1970s, Jane Goodall (1990) stunned the scientific world by reporting that chimpanzees occasionally wage all-out wars against other chimpanzee groups, replete with brutal murders, infanticide, and cannibalism.

To which species are we more similar, the peace-loving bonobo or the belligerent chimpanzee? In reality, we're a bit of both. de Waal (2006) is fond of calling the human species "the bipolar ape," because our social behavior is a blend of that of our closest ape relatives.

In the next section, we'll examine the roots of prosocial and antisocial actions, with a particular emphasis on situational factors that contribute to both behaviors. We'll begin by examining why we fail to help in some situations but help in others. We'll then explore why we occasionally act aggressively toward members of our species. As we've seen, Milgram's obedience research sheds light on the social influences that can lead us to harm others. But we'll soon discover that obedience to authority is only part of the story.

Factoid

One familiar example of pluralistic ignorance is the "silent classroom scenario," which often occurs after a professor has delivered a lecture that has left everyone in the class thoroughly confused. Following the lecture, the professor asks "Are there are any questions?" and no one responds. Each student in the class looks nervously at the other students, all of whom are sitting quietly, and assumes mistakenly that he or she is the only one who didn't understand the lecture (Wardell, 1999).

Safety in Numbers or Danger in Numbers? Bystander Nonintervention

You've probably heard the saying, "There's safety in numbers." Popular wisdom teaches us that when we find ourselves in danger, it's best to be in the company of others. Is that true? Let's look at two real-life examples.

TWO TRAGIC STORIES OF BYSTANDER NONINTERVENTION.

- On March 13, 1964, at 3 a.m., 28-year-old Catherine (Kitty) Genovese was returning to her apartment in New York City, having just gotten off work. Suddenly, a man appeared and began stabbing her. He came and left no fewer than three times over a 35-minute time span. Kitty repeatedly screamed and pleaded for help as the lights from nearby apartments flipped on. Although the precise facts remain in dispute and some early reports appear to have been exaggerated (Manning, Levine, & Collins, 2007), most of the evidence suggests that at least half a dozen—and perhaps many more—of her 30 or so neighbors heard the events but failed to come to her aid. Most didn't even bother to call the police. By the end of the gruesome attack, Kitty Genovese was dead (see **FIGURE 6**).

- On October 23, 2009, as many as 20 bystanders stood and watched while a 16-year-old girl was brutally gang-raped for over two hours outside a school dance in Richmond, California. According to reports, no one called the police, even though many of the onlookers had cellphones.

CAUSES OF BYSTANDER NONINTERVENTION: WHY WE DON'T HELP. Like most anecdotes, these real-world stories are useful for illustrating concepts, but they don't allow for scientific generalizations. For years, many psychologists assumed that the nonresponsiveness of bystanders was due simply to a lack of caring; some even referred to the phenomenon as "bystander apathy." But psychologists John Darley and Bibb Latané suspected that the *bystander effect* was less a consequence of apathy than of "psychological paralysis." According to Darley and Latané (1968a), bystanders in emergencies typically want to intervene but often find themselves frozen, seemingly helpless to help. Darley and Latané also suspected that popular psychology was wrong—that there's actually danger rather than safety in numbers. Bucking conventional wisdom, they hypothesized that the presence of others makes people *less*, not more, likely to help in emergencies. Why?

Pluralistic Ignorance: It Must Just Be Me. Darley and Latané maintained that two major factors explain bystander nonintervention. The first is **pluralistic ignorance**: the error of assuming that no one in the group perceives things as we do. To intervene in an emergency, we first need to recognize that the situation is really an emergency. Imagine that on your way to class tomorrow you see a student in dirty clothing slumped across a bench. As you stroll by, thoughts whiz through your mind: Is he asleep? Is he drunk? Could he be seriously ill, even dead? Could my psychology professor be conducting a study to examine my responses to emergencies? Here's where pluralistic ignorance comes into play. We look around, notice that nobody is responding, and assume—perhaps mistakenly—that the situation isn't an emergency. We assume we're the only one who thinks the situation might be an emergency. Reassured that the coast is clear and there's nothing to worry about, we continue on our merry way.

So pluralistic ignorance is relevant when we're trying to figure out whether an ambiguous situation is really an emergency. But it doesn't fully explain the behavior of bystanders in the Kitty Genovese or Richmond, California, gang rape tragedies, because those situations were clearly emergencies. Even once we've recognized that the situation is an emergency, the presence of others still tends to inhibit helping.

Diffusion of Responsibility: Passing the Buck. A second step is required for us to intervene in an emergency. We need to feel a burden of responsibility for the consequences of *not* intervening. Here's the catch: the more people present at an emergency, *the less each person feels responsible for the negative consequences of not helping*. Darley and Latané called

FIGURE 6 The Murder of Kitty Genovese. Place in Kew Gardens, New York, where Kitty Genovese was murdered on March 13, 1964, at 3:20 a.m. She drove into the parking lot at the Kew Gardens train station and parked her car at spot **1**. Noticing a man in the lot, she became nervous and headed toward a police telephone box. The man caught her and attacked her with a knife at spot **2**. She managed to get away, but he attacked her again at spot **3** and again at spot **4**.

 Watch in **MyPsychLab** the **Video:** The Basics: Under the Influence of Others

pluralistic ignorance
error of assuming that no one in a group perceives things as we do

597

? What social psychological principles help explain why these people don't stop to help the man lying on the ground? (See answer upside down on bottom of page.)

REPLICABILITY ▶
Can the results be duplicated in other studies?

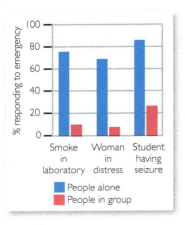

FIGURE 7 Bystander Intervention. Across three classic experiments on bystander intervention, the percentage of people helping when in groups was markedly lower than the percentage of people helping when alone.

✳ **Explore** in **MyPsychLab** the **Concept:** Bystander Intervention

diffusion of responsibility
reduction in feelings of personal responsibility in the presence of others
social loafing
phenomenon whereby individuals become less productive in groups

Answer: Pluralistic ignorance (people walking by may assume the man is drunk or asleep rather than injured) and diffusion of responsibility (the presence of numerous people present makes each person feel less responsible for the consequences of not helping)

598

this phenomenon **diffusion of responsibility**: the presence of others makes each person feel less responsible for the outcome. If you don't assist someone in a crowded park who's having a heart attack and that person dies, you can always say to yourself, "Well, that's a terrible tragedy, but it wasn't really *my* fault. After all, plenty of other people could have helped, too." The participants in Milgram's study who complied with the experimenter's commands when instructing someone else to deliver shocks probably experienced diffusion of responsibility: they could reassure themselves "Well, I wasn't the only one who did it."

So we can experience pluralistic ignorance, which prevents us from interpreting a situation as an emergency, *and* we can experience diffusion of responsibility, which discourages us from offering assistance in an emergency. From this perspective, it's perhaps surprising that any of us helps in emergencies, because the obstacles to intervening are considerable.

Studies of Bystander Nonintervention. To get at the psychological roots of the bystander effect, Darley, Latané, and their colleagues tested the effect of bystanders on participants' willingness to (1) report that smoke was filling a room (Darley & Latané, 1968b); (2) react to what sounded like a woman falling off a ladder and injuring herself (Latané & Rodin, 1969); and (3) respond to what sounded like another student experiencing an epileptic seizure (Darley & Latané, 1968a). In all of these studies, participants were significantly more likely to seek or offer help when they were alone than in a group (see **FIGURE 7**).

Researchers have replicated these findings many times using slightly different designs. In an analysis of almost 50 studies of bystander intervention involving close to 6,000 participants, Bibb Latané and Steve Nida (1981) found that people were more likely to help when alone than in groups about 90 percent of the time. That's an impressive degree of replicability. Even *thinking* about being in a large group makes us less likely to help in an emergency (Garcia et al., 2002). Still, there's some room for optimism. Research suggests that when an emergency is physically dangerous for victims, bystanders may be somewhat more likely to intervene than when it's not especially dangerous (Fischer et al., 2011). Of course, the tragic stories of Kitty Genovese and many others remind us, however, that even in genuine emergencies, many people sometimes stand by idly, waiting for others to help.

Social Loafing: With a Little Too Much Help From My Friends

Have you ever been a member of a group that got virtually nothing accomplished? (All of your textbook authors regularly attend meetings of university faculty members, so we're particular experts on this topic.) If so, you may have been a victim of **social loafing**, a phenomenon in which people slack off when they are in groups (Latané, Williams, & Harkins, 1979; North, Linley, & Hargreaves, 2000). As a consequence of social loafing, the whole is less than the sum of its parts.

Some psychologists believe that social loafing is a variant of bystander nonintervention. That's because social loafing appears to be due in part to diffusion of responsibility: people working in groups typically feel less responsible for the outcome of a project than they do when working alone. As a result, they don't invest as much effort.

Psychologists have demonstrated social loafing in numerous experiments (Ohlert & Kleinert, 2012). In one, a researcher placed blindfolds and headphones on six participants and asked them to clap or yell as loudly as possible. When participants thought they were making noise as part of a group, they were less loud than when they thought they were making noise alone (Williams, Harkins, & Latané, 1981). Cheerleaders also cheer less loudly when they believe they're part of a group than when they believe they're alone (Hardy & Latané, 1986). Investigators have also identified social loafing effects in studies of rope-pulling (tug-of-war), navigating mazes, identifying radar signals, and evaluating job candidates (Karau & Williams, 1995). Like many other social psychological phenomena, social loafing may be influenced by cultural factors. People in individualistic countries like the United States are more prone to social loafing than are people in collectivist countries like China, probably because people in the latter countries feel more responsible for the outcomes of group successes or failures (Earley, 1989).

IS BRAINSTORMING IN GROUPS A GOOD WAY TO GENERATE IDEAS?

Imagine that you've been hired by an advertising firm to cook up a new marketing campaign for Mrs. Yummy's Chicken Noodle Soup. The soup hasn't been selling well of late, and your job is to come up with an advertising jingle that will instill in every American an uncontrollable urge to reach for the nearest cup of chicken noodle soup.

Although you initially plan to come up with slogans on your own, your boss walks into your cubicle and informs you that you'll be participating in a "group brainstorming" meeting later that afternoon in the executive suite. There, you and 12 other firm members will let your imaginations run wild, saying whatever comes to mind in the hopes of hitting on a winning chicken noodle soup advertising formula. Indeed, companies across the world regularly use group brainstorming as a means of generating novel ideas. They assume that several heads that generate a flurry of ideas are better than one. In a book entitled *Applied Imagination*, which influenced many companies to adopt brainstorming, Alex Osborn (1957) argued that "the average person can think up twice as many ideas when working with a group than when working alone".

Although the idea behind group brainstorming is intuitively appealing, it turns out to be wrong. Numerous studies demonstrate that group brainstorming is less effective than individual brainstorming (Brown & Paulus, 2002; Byron, 2012; Diehl & Stroebe, 1987). When brainstorming, groups tend to come up with fewer ideas, and often fewer good ones, than do individuals (Paulus, 2004; Putman & Paulus, 2009). Group brainstorming also generally results in ideas that are less creative than those generated by individual brainstorming. Making matters worse, groups often overestimate how successful they are at producing new ideas, which may help to explain brainstorming's popularity (Paulus, Larey, & Ortega, 1995).

There are at least two reasons group brainstorming is less effective than individual brainstorming. One is that group members may be anxious about being evaluated by others, leading them to hold back potentially good ideas. The second is social loafing. When brainstorming in groups, people frequently engage in what's called "free riding": They sit back and let others do the hard work (Diehl & Stroebe, 1987). Whatever the reason, research suggests that when it comes to brainstorming, one brain may be better than two—or many more—at least when the brains can communicate with each other.

One of the best antidotes to social loafing is to ensure that each person in the group is identifiable, for example, by guaranteeing that managers and bosses can evaluate each individual's performance. By doing so, we can help "diffuse" the diffusion of responsibility that often arises in groups.

Prosocial Behavior and Altruism

Even though there's usually danger rather than safety in numbers when it comes to others helping us, many of us do help in emergencies even when others are around (Fischer et al., 2006). In the Kitty Genovese tragedy, at least one person apparently did call police (Manning et al., 2007). Indeed, there's good evidence that many of us engage in **altruism**, that is, helping others for unselfish reasons (Batson, 1987; Dovidio et al., 2006; Penner et al., 2005).

ALTRUISM: HELPING SELFLESSLY. Over the years, some scientists have argued that we help others entirely for egoistic (self-centered) reasons, like relieving our own distress, experiencing the joy of others we've helped (Hoffman, 1981), or anticipating that people we've helped will be more likely to reciprocate by helping us later (Gintis et al., 2003). From this perspective, we help others only to benefit ourselves. Yet in a series of experiments, Daniel Batson

Studies of social loafing demonstrate that in large groups, individuals often work (or in this case, pull) less hard than they do when alone.

altruism
helping others for unselfish reasons

Psychological research suggests that we sometimes engage in genuine altruism—helping largely out of empathy.

and his colleagues showed that we sometimes engage in genuine altruism. That is, in some cases, we help others in discomfort primarily because we feel empathic toward them; that is, we sympathize with their feelings (Batson et al., 1991; Batson & Shaw, 1991; Fischer et al., 2006). In some studies, they exposed participants to a female victim (actually a confederate) who was receiving painful electric shocks and gave them the option of either (a) taking her place and receiving shocks themselves or (b) turning away and not watching her receive shocks. When participants were made to feel empathic toward the victim (for example, by learning that their values and interests were similar to hers), they generally offered to take her place and receive shocks rather than turn away (Batson et al., 1981). In some cases, we seem to help not only to relieve our distress, but also to relieve the distress of others.

Along with empathy, a number of psychological variables increase the odds of helping. Let's look at some of the most crucial ones.

HELPING: SITUATIONAL INFLUENCES. People are more likely to help in some situations than in others. They're more likely to help others when they can't easily escape the situation—for example, by running away, driving away, or as in the case of the Kitty Genovese murder, turning off their lights and drifting back to sleep. They're also more likely to help someone who collapses on a crowded subway than on the sidewalk. Characteristics of the victim also matter. In one study, bystanders helped a person with a cane 95 percent of the time, but helped an obviously drunk person only 50 percent of the time (Piliavin, Rodin, & Piliavin, 1969). Being in a good mood also makes us more likely to help (Isen, Clark, & Schwartz, 1976). So does exposure to role models who help others (Bryan & Test, 1967; Rushton & Campbell, 1977).

One striking study examined seminary students who were on their way across campus to deliver a sermon on the Biblical story of the Good Samaritan, which describes the moral importance of assisting injured people (Darley & Batson, 1973). The investigators led some students to believe that they needed to rush over to give the lecture; others believed they had some extra time. While walking across campus, the students came across a man (actually a confederate) who was slumped over in a doorway and who twice coughed and moaned loudly. The seminary students were significantly less likely to offer assistance to the man if they were in a hurry (only 10 percent) than if they had time to spare (63 percent). Some of the students simply stepped over him on their way to the lecture. So much for the Good Samaritan!

If there's a silver lining to the gray cloud of bystander nonintervention, it's that exposure to research on bystander effects may increase the chances of intervening in emergencies. This is an example of what Kenneth Gergen (1973) called an **enlightenment effect**: learning about psychological research can change real-world behavior for the better (Katzev & Brownstein, 1989). A group of investigators (Beaman et al., 1978) presented the research literature on bystander intervention effects to one psychology class—containing much of the same information you've just read—but didn't present this literature to a very similar psychology class. Two weeks later, the students, accompanied by a confederate, came upon a person slumped over on a park bench. Compared with 25 percent of students who hadn't received the lecture on bystander intervention, 43 percent of students who'd received the lecture intervened to help. This study worked, probably because it imparted new knowledge about bystander intervention and perhaps also because it made people more aware of the importance of helping. So the very act of reading this chapter may have made you more likely to become a responsive bystander.

Helping: Individual and Gender Differences. Individual differences in personality also influence the likelihood of helping. Participants who are less concerned about social approval are more likely to go against the grain and intervene in emergencies even when others are present (Latané & Darley, 1970). Extraverted people are also more prone to help others than are introverted people (Krueger, Hicks, & McGue, 2001). Not surprisingly, even when they're off duty, people with lifesaving skills, such as trained medical workers, are more likely to offer assistance to others in emergencies than are other people (Huston et al., 1981). Some people may not help on certain occasions simply because they don't know what to do.

Some researchers have reported a slight tendency for men to help more than women (Eagly & Crowley, 1986). This difference isn't especially consistent across studies (Becker & Eagly, 2004), and it seems to be accounted for by an alternative explanation, namely, the

---

enlightenment effect
learning about psychological research can change real-world behavior for the better

---

RULING OUT RIVAL HYPOTHESES ▶
Have important alternative explanations for the findings been excluded?

tendency of men to help more than women only in situations involving physical or social risk. Moreover, men are especially likely to help women rather than other men, especially if the women are physically attractive (Eagly & Crowley, 1986).

Aggression: Why We Hurt Others

Like our primate cousins, the chimpanzees, we occasionally engage in violence toward others. And like them, we're a war-waging species; as we write this chapter, there are at least nine full-scale wars, often defined as conflicts that kill more than 1,000 people per year, raging across the globe. The good news, if there is any, is that the world today is probably safer than it's ever been. For example, the proportion of people killed in wars, as high as it is, is lower now that it's been in the past several centuries (Pinker, 2011). Yet, even with this caveat in mind, large pockets of the world remain terribly violent places.

Psychologists define **aggression** as behavior intended to harm others, either verbally or physically. To account for aggressive behavior on both large and small scales, we need to examine the role of both situational and dispositional factors.

SITUATIONAL INFLUENCES ON AGGRESSION. Using both laboratory and naturalistic designs, psychologists have pinpointed a host of situational influences—some short-term, others long-term—on human aggression. Here are some of the best-replicated findings.

- **Interpersonal Provocation:** Not surprisingly, we're especially likely to strike out aggressively against those who have provoked us, say, by insulting, threatening, or hitting us (Geen, 2001).

- **Frustration:** We're especially likely to behave aggressively when frustrated, that is, thwarted from reaching a goal (Anderson & Bushman, 2002b; Berkowitz, 1989). In one study, a research assistant asked participants to perform a difficult paper-folding (origami) task at an unreasonably rapid rate and either apologized for moving participants along too quickly or told them to pick up the pace ("I would like to hurry and get this over with"). Frustrated participants—those in the second condition—were more likely to give the assistant a low job-related evaluation (Dill & Anderson, 1995).

- **Media Influences:** An impressive body of laboratory and naturalistic evidence points to the conclusion that watching media violence increases the odds of violence through observational learning (Anderson et al., 2003; Bandura, 1973). Numerous laboratory experiments suggest that playing violent video games also boosts the odds of violence in both Western and Asian cultures (Anderson et al., 2010; Gentile & Anderson, 2003). Still, some critics have argued that the link between video games and violence is overhyped and have questioned how well these laboratory findings generalize to the real world (Ferguson, 2009; Ferguson & Kilburn, 2010; Freedman, 2002). For example, even if exposure to violent video games leads to greater aggression in few minutes or hours, it's not clear that it contributes to heightened aggression months or years later (Ferguson et al., 2013).

- **Aggressive Cues:** External cues associated with violence, such as guns and knives, can serve as discriminative stimuli for aggression, making us more likely to act violently in response to provocation (Carlson, Marcus-Newhall, & Miller, 1990). Leonard Berkowitz and Anthony LePage (1967) found that the mere presence of a gun—as opposed to a badminton racket—on a table triggered more aggression in participants who'd been provoked by mild electric shocks for supposed poor performance on a task.

- **Arousal:** When our autonomic nervous system is hyped up, we may mistakenly attribute this arousal to anger, leading us to act aggressively (Zillman, 1988). Dolf Zillmann and his colleagues found that participants who pedaled an exercise bicycle delivered more intense electric shocks to someone who'd annoyed them than did participants who sat still (Zillmann, Katcher, & Milavsky, 1972).

◄ **REPLICABILITY**
Can the results be duplicated in other studies?

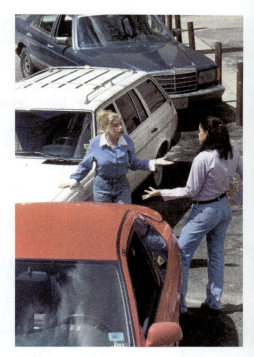

Both interpersonal provocation and frustration from being stuck in traffic probably contribute to "road rage."

aggression
behavior intended to harm others, either verbally or physically

- **Alcohol and Other Drugs:** Certain substances can disinhibit our brain's prefrontal cortex, lowering our inhibitions toward behaving violently (Bègue & Subra, 2008; Kelly et al., 1988). After being provoked with electric shocks by an "opponent" (who was actually fictitious) during a competitive game, participants chose more intense electric shocks after consuming alcohol or benzodiazepines such as Valium, than after consuming a placebo (Taylor, 1993). Alcohol is likely to trigger aggression when the target of our aggression occupies the focus of our attention, as when someone is threatening us directly (Giancola & Corman, 2007). In addition, the effects of alcohol on aggression are especially pronounced in participants who are already impulsive to begin with (Birkley, Giancola, & Lance, 2012).

- **Temperature:** Rates of violent crime in different regions of the United States mirror the average temperatures in the regions (Anderson, Bushman, & Groom, 1997). Because warm temperatures increase irritability, they may make people more likely to lose their tempers when provoked or frustrated (Anderson & Bushman, 2002b; Gamble & Hess, 2012). Nevertheless, because extremely warm temperatures are more common in the southern United States, in which violent crime rates are especially high (see the Cultural Differences section, which follows), investigators have had to rule out the rival hypothesis that this "heat effect" is due to geographical region. They've generally succeeded in doing so by demonstrating that even within the same geographical region, warmer temperatures are associated with higher rates of violence (Anderson & Anderson, 1996; see **FIGURE 8**). Even getting people to think about words associated with heat (like *sunburn*)—compared with words associated with cold or neutral words—makes them more likely to act aggressively (DeWall & Bushman, 2009).

RULING OUT RIVAL HYPOTHESES ▶
Have important alternative explanations for the findings been excluded?

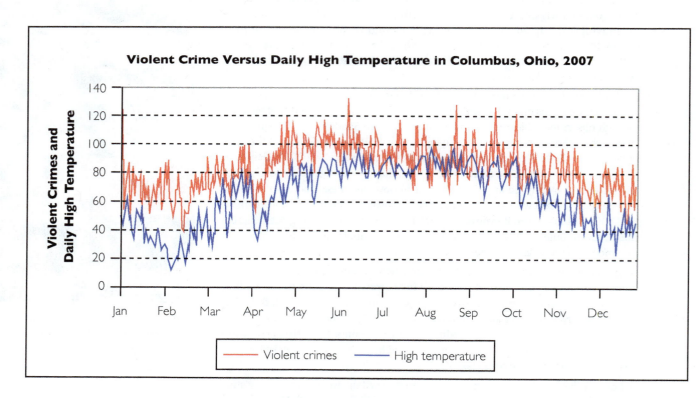

FIGURE 8 Violent Crime Versus Daily High Temperature in Columbus, Ohio, 2007. Research demonstrates that violent crime rates coincide with outdoor temperatures. How might we determine whether this correlation indicates a causal effect? (*Source:* Fox, 2010)

AGGRESSION: INDIVIDUAL, GENDER, AND CULTURAL DIFFERENCES. On a typical day in the United States, there are between 40 and 45 murders; that's one about every half hour. There are also about 230 reported rapes, or one about every five or six minutes (Federal Bureau of Investigation, 2005). These statistics paint a grim picture. Yet the substantial majority of people are generally law-abiding, and only a tiny percentage ever engage in serious physical aggression toward others. Across a wide swath of societies that scientists have studied, only a small percentage of people—perhaps 5 or 6 percent—account for half or more of all crimes, including violent crimes (Wilson & Herrnstein, 1985). Why?

Personality Traits. When confronted with the same situation, like an insult, people differ in their tendencies to behave aggressively. Certain personality traits can combine to create a dangerous cocktail of aggression proneness. People with high levels of negative emotions (such as irritability and mistrust), impulsivity, and a lack of closeness to others are especially prone to violence (Gvion & Apter, 2011; Krueger et al., 1994).

Sex Differences. One of the best replicated sex differences in humans (and across the animal kingdom for that matter) is the higher level of physical aggressiveness among males than females (Eagly & Steffen, 1986; Maccoby & Jacklin, 1980; Storch et al., 2004). At least some of this difference may be due to the fact that when angered, men are more likely than women to want to exact revenge against people who've offended them (Wilkowski et al., 2012). In conjunction with biological sex, age plays a role: the rates of crime, including violent crime, would drop by two-thirds if all males between the ages of 12 and 28 were magically placed in a state of temporary hibernation (Lykken, 1995).

The reasons for the sex difference in aggression are unknown, although some researchers tie it to higher levels of the hormone testosterone in males (Dabbs, 2001). Nevertheless, the correlation between testosterone and aggression is controversial, because aggression may cause higher testosterone rather than the other way around (Sapolsky, 1998). One of the precious few exceptions to the sex difference in aggression is the spotted hyena (or "laughing hyena"), in which females are more aggressive than males. This exception may prove the rule, because the female spotted hyena has unusually high levels of a hormone closely related to testosterone (Glickman et al., 1987). Social factors almost surely play a role, too, at least in humans: parents and teachers pay more attention to boys when they engage in aggression and to girls when they engage in dependent behaviors like clinginess (Eagly, Wood, & Diekman, 2000; Serbin & O'Leary, 1975).

Yet the well-replicated male predominance in aggression may apply only to direct aggression like physical violence and bullying, not indirect aggression—which is typically marked by "stabbing others in the back." Nicki Crick (1995) discovered that girls tend to be higher than boys in **relational aggression**, a form of indirect aggression marked by spreading rumors, gossiping, social exclusion, and using nonverbal putdowns (like giving other girls "the silent treatment") for purposes of interpersonal manipulation. Crick's findings dovetail with results suggesting that females are just as likely as males, if not more so, to express anger in subtle ways (Archer, 2004; Eagly & Steffen, 1986; Frieze et al., 1978). In contrast, boys have much higher rates of bullying compared with girls (Espelage, Mebane, & Swearer, 2004; Olweus, 1993).

Cultural Differences. Culture also shapes aggression. Physical aggression and violent crime are less prevalent among Asian individuals such as Japanese and Chinese than among Americans and Europeans (Wilson & Herrnstein, 1985; Zhang & Snowden, 1999). Richard Nisbett, Dov Cohen, and colleagues have also found that people from the southern regions of the United States are more likely than those from other regions of the country to adhere to a *culture of honor*, a social norm of defending one's reputation in the face of perceived insults (Nisbett & Cohen, 1996; Vandello, Cohen, & Ransom, 2008). The culture of honor may help explain why rates of violence are higher in the South than in other parts of the United States (Barnes, Brown, & Tamborski, 2012). Interestingly, these rates are higher only for violence that arises in the context of disputes, not in robberies, burglaries, or other crimes (Cohen & Nisbett, 1994). The culture of honor even shows itself in the relatively safe confines of the laboratory. In three experiments,

◀ **REPLICABILITY**
Can the results be duplicated in other studies?

◀ **CORRELATION VS. CAUSATION**
Can we be sure that A causes B?

relational aggression
form of indirect aggression prevalent in girls, involving spreading rumors, gossiping, and using nonverbal putdowns for the purpose of social manipulation

◀ **REPLICABILITY**
Can the results be duplicated in other studies?

Research suggests although males tend to be more physically aggressive compared with females, girls are more likely than boys to engage in relational aggression, which includes gossiping and making fun of others behind their backs.

a male confederate bumped into a male college student in a narrow hallway, muttering a profanity about him before storming away. Students from southern states were more likely than students from other states to react with a boost in testosterone and to display aggressive behavior against another confederate (Cohen et al., 1996).

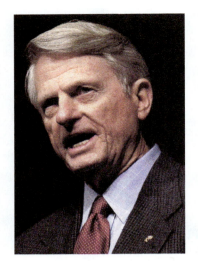

In a heated television interview in 2004 with host Chris Matthews, former Georgia governor Zell Miller stunned viewers by saying that he wished he could challenge Matthews to a duel. Yet social psychologists familiar with the "culture of honor" could not have been surprised, as Southern gentlemen of days past frequently settled challenges to their reputation in this manner.

✔ **Study** and **Review** in **MyPsychLab**

Assess Your Knowledge   FACT or FICTION?

1. Research suggests that the old saying "there's safety in numbers" is wrong.
   True / False

2. The primary reason for bystander nonintervention is the apathy of onlookers.
   True / False

3. Most people tend to work especially hard in groups.   **True / False**

4. People who have lifesaving skills are more likely to help than those without the skills.   **True / False**

5. Drinking can calm us down, lowering our risk for aggression.   **True / False**

6. The "culture of honor" may contribute to lower levels of violent crime in the U.S. South.   **True / False**

Answers: 1. T; 2. F; 3. F; 4. T; 5. F; 6. F

Attitudes and Persuasion: Changing Minds

8 Describe how attitudes relate to behavior.

9 Evaluate theoretical accounts of how and when we alter our attitudes.

10 Identify common and effective persuasion techniques and how they're exploited by pseudoscientists.

First, answer the following question: Do you think the death penalty is an effective deterrent against murder? Second, answer this question: How do you feel about the death penalty?

Having gone through this exercise, you can now grasp the difference between beliefs and attitudes. The first question assessed your *beliefs* about the death penalty; the second question assessed your *attitudes* toward the death penalty. A belief is a conclusion regarding factual evidence, whereas an **attitude** is a belief that includes an emotional component. Attitudes reflect how we feel about an issue or a person. For that reason, they're an important part of our social worlds.

Attitudes and Behavior

A prevalent misconception is that attitudes are good predictors of behavior. For example, most people believe that how we feel about a political candidate predicts with a high level of certainty whether we'll vote toward or against the candidate. It doesn't (Wicker, 1969). In part, this finding explains why even carefully conducted political polls are rarely foolproof.

WHEN ATTITUDES DON'T PREDICT BEHAVIOR. In a study conducted over 70 years ago, Robert LaPiere surveyed 128 American hotel and restaurant owners to find out whether they'd be willing to serve guests who were Chinese, who at the time were widely discriminated against. Over 90 percent of LaPiere's participants said no. Yet when LaPiere had previously toured the country with a Chinese couple, 127 of 128 owners of the same establishments had already served them (LaPiere, 1934). To be sure, LaPiere's study was imperfect; for example, there's no way to know if the people who filled out the survey were the same people who'd served them (Dockery & Bedeian, 1989).

Still, his conclusion has generally stood the test of time. Indeed, a review of 88 studies revealed that the average correlation between attitudes and behavior is about .38 (Kraus, 1995), which is only a moderate association. So although attitudes forecast behavior at better-than-chance levels, they're far from powerful predictors (Friedkin, 2010).

People's expressed voting preferences to pollsters don't always predict their actual voting behavior.

---

attitude
belief that includes an emotional component

This finding probably reflects the fact that our behaviors are the outcome of many factors, only one of which is our attitudes. For example, LaPiere's prejudiced participants may not have been especially fond of the idea of serving Chinese guests. Yet when they met these guests in person, they may have found them more likable than they expected. Or when push came to shove, they may have been reluctant to pass up the chance for good business.

WHEN ATTITUDES DO PREDICT BEHAVIOR. Occasionally, though, our attitudes predict our behaviors reasonably well. Attitudes that are highly *accessible*—which come to mind easily—tend to be strongly predictive of our behavior (Fazio, 1995). Imagine that we asked you two questions: (1) How do you feel about the idea of buying a new brand of yogurt that's been scientifically demonstrated to decrease levels of low-density cholesterol? (2) How do you feel about the idea of buying chocolate ice cream? If you're like most people, you'll find the second question easier to answer than the first question, because you've thought more about it. If so, your attitude toward chocolate ice cream is more likely to predict your purchasing behavior than your attitude toward the new-fangled yogurt. Perhaps not surprisingly, attitudes also tend to predict behavior when they're firmly held and stable over time (Conner et al., 2000; Kraus, 1995).

Attitudes also predict behavior well for a group of people called low *self-monitors* (Kraus, 1995). **Self-monitoring** is a trait that assesses the extent to which people's behaviors reflect their true feelings and attitudes (Gangestad & Snyder, 2000; Oh et al., 2013; Snyder, 1974). Low self-monitors tend to be straight shooters, whereas high self-monitors tend to be social chameleons. We can more often trust low self-monitors' actions to mirror their attitudes.

Still, the fact that attitudes are correlated with behaviors doesn't mean they cause them. Other explanations are possible; for example, our behaviors may sometimes cause our attitudes. Imagine that we start out with a negative attitude toward homeless persons. If a friend persuades us to volunteer to help the homeless for three hours a week and we end up enjoying this type of work, our attitudes toward homeless people may improve.

◄ **CORRELATION VS. CAUSATION**
Can we be sure that A causes B?

Origins of Attitudes

Our attitudes stem from a variety of sources, including our prior experience and personalities. Here, we'll review some of the key influences on our attitudes.

RECOGNITION. Our experiences shape our attitudes. The *recognition heuristic* makes us more likely to believe something we've heard many times (Arkes, 1993). Like most heuristics (mental shortcuts or rules of thumb), the recognition heuristic generally serves us well, because things we hear many times from many different people often *are* true. Moreover, this heuristic can help us make snap judgments that are surprisingly accurate. For example, when asking people who'll win a big tennis match, many of them pick the player they've heard of; more often than not, this simple approach is effective (Goldstein & Gigerenzer, 2011).

But when a story is persuasive or interesting, the recognition heuristic can get us into trouble. It can lead us to fall for stories that are too good to be true, like some urban legends, or buy products that seem familiar just because we've heard their names repeatedly. All good advertisers make use of this heuristic by cooking up catchy, easily repeated jingles. The *band-wagon fallacy* says that we shouldn't believe—or buy—something merely because most people do. Moreover, hearing one person express an opinion ten times ("Grandma Sally's spaghetti tastes delicious!") can lead us to conclude falsely that this view is as widely held as hearing ten people express it only once (Weaver et al., 2007).

ATTITUDES AND PERSONALITY. Our attitudes are associated in important ways with our personality traits. Although we may persuade ourselves that our political attitudes derive from completely objective analyses of social issues, these attitudes are often affected by our personalities.

In an article that stirred up more than its share of controversy, one team of researchers (Jost et al., 2003) reported that across many studies, political conservatives tend to be more fearful, more sensitive to threat, and less tolerant of uncertainty than do political liberals. They and others have suggested that these personality traits are the "psychological glue" that binds conservatives' political attitudes toward the death penalty, abortion, gun control,

self-monitoring
personality trait that assesses the extent to which people's behavior reflects their true feelings and attitudes

school prayer, national defense, and a host of seemingly unrelated issues (Haidt, 2012). Other research shows that conservatives display a higher skin conductance response—a measure of arousal—than do liberals following threatening stimuli like sudden loud noises or pictures of large spiders or badly wounded people (Oxley et al., 2008). Compared with liberals, conservatives even tend to have larger volume in the amygdala, a brain region linked to threat (Jost & Amodio, 2012). Nevertheless, some researchers have questioned whether findings comparing conservatives and liberals are due to an alternative hypothesis: they might reflect political extremism in general rather than right-wing conservatism specifically (Greenberg & Jonas, 2003). According to them, left-wing extremists are just as likely to be fearful, dogmatic, and the like as right-wing extremists are. Because there are few studies of left-wing extremists, we don't know who's right.

Our personalities even relate to, and perhaps influence, our attitudes toward religion. The specific religion we adopt is largely a function of our religious exposure while growing up and is mostly independent of our personality. Nevertheless, our *religiosity*—the depth of our religious convictions—is linked to certain personality traits. Adolescents with high levels of conscientiousness are especially likely to become deeply religious adults (Issazadegan, 2012; McCullough, Tsang, & Brion, 2003).

Attitude Change: Wait, Wait, I Just Changed My Mind

Many of us are surprised to discover that our attitudes on many topics, like the death penalty and abortion, change over the years. We tend to perceive ourselves as more consistent over time in our attitudes than we really are (Bem & McConnell, 1970; Goethals & Reckman, 1973; Ross, 1989), perhaps in part because we don't like to think of ourselves as weak-willed flip-floppers. Yet this point raises a question that psychologists have long struggled to answer: Why and how do our attitudes change?

COGNITIVE DISSONANCE THEORY. In the 1950s, Leon Festinger developed *cognitive dissonance theory,* an influential model of attitude change. According to this theory, we alter our attitudes because we experience an unpleasant state of tension—**cognitive dissonance**—between two or more conflicting thoughts (cognitions). Because we dislike this state of tension, we're motivated to reduce or eliminate it. If we hold an attitude or a belief (cognition A) that's inconsistent with another attitude or belief (cognition B), we can reduce the anxiety resulting from this inconsistency in three major ways: change cognition A; change cognition B; or introduce a new cognition, C, that resolves the inconsistency between A and B (see **FIGURE 9**).

Let's move from *A*s, *B*s, and *C*s to a real-world example. Imagine you believe that your new friend, Sandy, is a nice person. You learn from another friend, Chris, that Sandy recently stole a wallet from a fellow classmate. According to Festinger, this news should produce cognitive dissonance, because it creates a conflict between cognition A (Sandy is a nice person) and cognition B (Sandy stole money from someone and therefore isn't such a nice person after all). To resolve this nagging sense of tension, you can change cognition A and decide that Sandy actually isn't such a nice person. Or you can change cognition B, perhaps by deciding that the news that Sandy stole money must be a false rumor spread by her enemies. Or you can instead introduce a new thought, cognition C, that resolves the discrepancy between cognitions A and B. For example, you could persuade yourself that Sandy is still a nice person but that she took her classmate's wallet because she was starving and in desperate need of a short-term infusion of cash ("I'm sure she'll return the wallet and all of the money in a day or two once she's grabbed something to eat," you reassure yourself).

Festinger, along with J. Merrill Carlsmith, conducted the first systematic test of cognitive dissonance theory in the late 1950s (Festinger & Carlsmith, 1959).

The Setup: You sign up for a two-hour study of "Measures of Performance." At the lab, an experimenter provides you with instructions for some manual tasks—all mind-numbingly boring, like inserting 12 spools into a tray, emptying the tray,

RULING OUT RIVAL HYPOTHESES ▶

Have important alternative explanations for the findings been excluded?

? How would cognitive dissonance theory explain why some fraternities ask their members to perform bizarre and embarrassing hazing rituals before joining? If you're curious, one classic study investigated this issue (Aronson & Mills, 1959). (See answer upside down on bottom of page.)

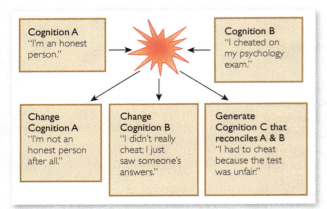

FIGURE 9 Cognitive Dissonance Theory. According to cognitive dissonance theory, we can reduce the conflict between two cognitions (beliefs) in multiple ways—by changing the first cognition, changing the second cognition, or introducing a third cognition that resolves the conflict.

cognitive dissonance
unpleasant mental experience of tension resulting from two conflicting thoughts or beliefs

Answer: People who willingly undergo a severe initiation to a group feel a need to justify this action and thereby convince themselves that the group must be worthwhile.

refilling the tray, and so on, for half an hour. Now here's the twist: The experimenter explains that a research assistant normally informs the next participant waiting in the hallway about the study and, to help recruit this participant, he tells him or her how interesting and enjoyable the study was. Unfortunately, the research assistant couldn't make it to the lab today. So, the experimenter wonders, would you be kind enough to substitute for him and tell the next participant how interesting the study was?

The Study: Festinger and Carlsmith randomly assigned some participants to receive $1 to perform this favor and others to receive $20. Afterward, they asked participants how much they enjoyed performing the tasks. From the perspective of learning theory, especially operant conditioning, we might expect participants paid $20 to say they enjoyed the task more. Yet cognitive dissonance theory makes the counterintuitive prediction that participants paid $1 should say that they enjoyed the task more.

Why? Because all participants should experience cognitive dissonance: they performed an incredibly boring task but told the next participant it was fun. Yet participants given $20 had a good *external justification* for telling this little fib, namely, that the experimenter bribed them to do it. In contrast, participants given $1 had almost no external justification. As a result, the only easy way to resolve their cognitive dissonance was to persuade themselves that they must have enjoyed the task after all. They deceived themselves.

The Results: The results supported this surprising prediction. Participants given less money reported enjoying the task more, presumably because they needed to justify their lies to themselves. Their behaviors had changed their attitudes. Since Festinger and Carlsmith's study, hundreds of experiments have yielded results broadly consistent with cognitive dissonance theory (Cooper, 2007; Harmon-Jones & Mills, 1999). Interestingly, individuals with psychopathic personality traits, who experience minimal guilt when lying, display little or no attitude change in the Festinger and Carlsmith dissonance paradigm (Murray, Wood, & Lilienfeld, 2012).

ALTERNATIVES TO COGNITIVE DISSONANCE THEORY. Cognitive dissonance theory is alive and well, although researchers continue to debate whether alternative processes account for attitude change. Some scholars contend that it's not dissonance itself that's responsible for shifting our attitudes, but rather threats to our self-concept (Aronson, 1992; Wood, 2000). In Festinger and Carlsmith's (1959) study, perhaps what motivated participants in the $1 condition to change their attitudes was a discrepancy between who they believed they were (a decent person) and what they did (lie to another participant). From this perspective, only certain conflicts between attitudes produce cognitive dissonance, namely, those that challenge our views of who we are.

There are at least two other explanations for cognitive dissonance effects. The first, **self-perception theory**, proposes that we acquire our attitudes by observing our behaviors (Bem, 1967). According to this model, Festinger and Carlsmith's participants in the $1 condition looked at their behavior and said to themselves, "I told the other participant that I liked the task, and I got paid only one lousy buck to do so. So I guess I must have really liked the task." The second, **impression management theory** (Goffman, 1959), proposes that we don't really change our attitudes in cognitive dissonance studies; we only tell the experimenters we have. We do so because we don't want to appear inconsistent (Tedeschi, Schlenker, & Bonoma, 1971). According to this model, Festinger and Carlsmith's participants in the $1 condition didn't want to look like hypocrites. So they told the experimenter they enjoyed the task even though they didn't. As is often the case in psychology, there may be some truth to each explanation. Some participants may exhibit attitude change because of cognitive dissonance; others, because of self-perception; and still others, because of impression management (Bem & Funder, 1978).

Persuasion: Humans as Salespeople

Whether or not we realize it, we encounter attempts at persuasion every day. If you're like the average student entering college, you've already watched 360,000 commercials; that number will reach a staggering 2 million by the time you turn 65. Each time you walk into a store or supermarket, you see hundreds of products that marketers have carefully crafted to make you more likely to purchase them.

Factoid

In one creative study of cognitive dissonance theory, researchers asked participants to taste fried grasshoppers (Zimbardo et al., 1965). They randomly assigned some participants to receive this bizarre request from a friendly person and others to receive it from an unfriendly person. The latter participants reported liking the fried grasshoppers more than the former participants did. Participants who tasted the grasshoppers at the behest of the friendly person had a good external justification ("I did it to help out a nice person"), but the other participants didn't. So the latter participants resolved their dissonance by changing their attitudes— hmmm, those little critters were delicious.

◄ **REPLICABILITY**
Can the results be duplicated in other studies?

Simulate in **MyPsychLab** the **Experiment:** Cognitive Dissonance

◄ **RULING OUT RIVAL HYPOTHESES**
Have important alternative explanations for the findings been excluded?

Factoid

Even monkeys may display a primitive form of cognitive dissonance. When researchers gave capuchin monkeys a choice between two different-colored candies, their preference for the candy they didn't pick decreased (Egan, Santos, & Bloom, 2007). This effect, called *post-decision dissonance*, is familiar to all of us who've found that our positive feelings toward a product we were thinking of buying decrease immediately after we decide to buy a slightly different product. By decreasing our liking of what we didn't select, we reduce our cognitive dissonance.

self-perception theory
theory that we acquire our attitudes by observing our behaviors

impression management theory
theory that we don't really change our attitudes, but report that we have so that our behaviors appear consistent with our attitudes

ROUTES TO PERSUASION. According to *dual process models* of persuasion, there are two alternative pathways to persuading others (Petty & Cacioppo, 1986; Petty & Wegener, 1999). One, the *central* route, leads us to evaluate the merits of persuasive arguments carefully and thoughtfully. Here, we focus on the *informational content* of the arguments: Do they hold up under close scrutiny? We're especially likely to take this route when we're motivated and able to evaluate information carefully, as when we're deciding between two colleges we like and have plenty of time and relevant information. The attitudes we acquire via this route tend to be strongly held and relatively enduring.

The other, the *peripheral* route, leads us to respond to persuasive arguments on the basis of snap judgments. Here, we focus on *surface aspects* of the arguments: For example, how appealing or interesting are they? We're especially likely to take this route when we're not motivated to weigh information carefully and don't have the ability to do so, as when we're distracted while watching a commercial. Although the attitudes we acquire via this route tend to be weaker and relatively unstable, they can affect our short-term choices in powerful ways. The danger of persuasive messages that travel through the peripheral route is that we can be easily fooled by superficial factors, such as how physically attractive, famous, or likable the communicator is or how many times we've heard the message (Hemsley & Doob, 1978; Hovland, Janis, & Kelly, 1953; Kenrick, Neuberg, & Cialdini, 2005).

PERSUASION TECHNIQUES. Drawing on the research literature concerning attitudes and attitude change, psychologists have identified a host of effective techniques for persuading others. Many of these methods operate by means of the peripheral persuasion route, largely bypassing our scientific thinking capacities. Interestingly, successful businesspeople have used many of these techniques for decades (Cialdini, 2001). Let's look at four of them.

- **Foot-in-the-door technique:** Following on the heels of cognitive dissonance theory (Freedman & Fraser, 1966; Gorassini & Olson, 1995), the **foot-in-the-door technique** suggests that we start with a small request before making a bigger one. If we want to get our classmate to volunteer five hours a week for the "Helping a Starving Psychologist" charity organization, we can ask her to volunteer one hour a week. Once we've gotten her to agree to that request, we have our "foot in the door," because from the perspective of cognitive dissonance theory, she'll feel a need to justify her initial commitment (Dolinski, 2012). As a consequence, she'll probably end up with a positive attitude toward the organization, boosting the odds that she'll volunteer even more of her time.

- **Door-in-the-face technique:** Alternatively, we can start with a large request, like asking for a $100 donation to our charity, before asking for a small one, like a $10 donation (Cialdini et al., 1975; O'Keefe & Hale, 2001). One reason this **door-in-the-face technique** works may be that the initial large request often induces guilt in recipients (O'Keefe & Figge, 1997). But if the initial request is so outrageous that it appears insincere or unreasonable, this method can backfire (Cialdini & Goldstein, 2004). Research suggests that the foot-in-the-door and door-in-the-face techniques are effective for getting people to agree to requests (Feeley, Anker, & Aloe, 2012) and work about equally well (Pascual & Guéguen, 2005).

- **Low-ball technique:** In the **low-ball technique**, the seller of a product starts by quoting a price well below the actual sales price (Burger & Petty, 1981; Cialdini, 2001). Once the buyer agrees to purchase the product, the seller mentions all of the desirable or needed add-ons that come along with the product. By the time the deal is done, the buyer may end up paying twice as much as he or she had initially agreed to pay. We can even use this technique to obtain favors from friends. In one study, a confederate asked strangers to look after his dog while he visited a friend in the hospital. In some cases, he first got the stranger to agree to the request and only then told him that he'd be gone for half an hour; in other cases, he told the stranger up front that he'd be gone for half an hour. The first tactic worked better (Guéguen, Pascual, & Dagot, 2002).

When asking for a raise, one approach is for a person to request a much larger raise than he or she expects in the hope the boss will offer a raise close to what the person wants. **What do psychologists call this technique?** (See answer upside down on bottom of page.)

This car salesperson begins the deal by quoting the base price, and then once the customer has agreed to purchase the car, he mentions all of the added features that cost more. **What persuasion technique is he using?** (See answer upside down at bottom of page.)

foot-in-the-door technique
persuasive technique involving making a small request before making a bigger one

door-in-the-face technique
persuasive technique involving making an unreasonably large request before making the small request we're hoping to have granted

low-ball technique
persuasive technique in which the seller of a product starts by quoting a low sales price and then mentions all of the add-on costs once the customer has agreed to purchase the product

"but you are free" technique
persuasive technique in which we convince someone to perform a favor for us by telling them that they are free not to do it

- **"But you are free" technique:** One easy but powerful means of getting people to agree to requests is giving them the sense that they're free to choose whether to perform the act ("We'd like you to send 50 cents to the poor authors of this introductory psychology textbook, but you are free to say no"; Guéguen & Pascual, 2000). Research suggests that this **"but you are free" technique** doubles the odds of compliance to a request (Carpenter, 2013; Wilson, 2011), probably because people given a free choice can convince themselves that they made the choice on their own and weren't pressured by the person making the request.

CHARACTERISTICS OF THE MESSENGER. Research demonstrates that we're more likely to swallow a persuasive message if famous or attractive people deliver it—whether or not they'd logically know something about the product they're hawking.

Fortunately, we can safeguard consumers against this error by teaching them to distinguish legitimate from illegitimate authorities (Cialdini & Sagarin, 2005). We're also more likely to believe messages when the source possesses high credibility, such as presumed expertise (Heesacker, Petty, & Cacioppo, 1983; Hovland et al., 1953; Pornpitakpan, 2004). That's almost surely why so many drug commercials feature physicians dressed in white lab coats and why so many product advertisements assure that us "Four out of five doctors recommend...." (Briñol & Petty, 2009).

In addition, messages are especially persuasive if the messenger seems similar to us. In one study, researchers asked students to read a description of the bizarre and not especially likable Russian mystic Grigory Rasputin. Some students were randomly assigned a description of Rasputin that featured his birth date (December 16), whereas others were randomly assigned a description of Rasputin that featured the student's birth date. Students who believed they shared a birth date with Rasputin thought more positively of him compared with students who didn't share a birth date (Finch & Cialdini, 1989).

Researchers have now reported this *implicit egotism* effect—the finding that we're more positively disposed toward people, places, or things that resemble us—across a number of domains (Pelham, Carvallo, & Jones, 2005). In matters of love and friendship, we may be more likely than chance to select people whose names contain the first letter of our first or last name. All things being equal, Johns tend to be fond of Jessicas, Roberts of Ronalds, and so on. Nevertheless, most people are unaware of this *name-letter effect* (Nuttin, 1985). People even seem to gravitate to places that are similar to their names. One group of researchers found a higher than expected number of Louises living in Louisiana, Virginias in Virginia, Georgias in Georgia, and Florences in Florida (Pelham, Mirenberg, & Jones, 2002; see **FIGURE 10**). Nevertheless, these findings are subject to an alternative explanation, namely, that parents tended to name their children after the state in which they were born. Investigators have tried to rule out this rival hypothesis by demonstrating that adults tend to move into states with names similar to their own, but the findings are mixed (Dyjas et al., 2012).

THE MARKETING OF PSEUDOSCIENCE. Many proponents of pseudoscience make good use of persuasion tactics, although they may sometimes do so with the best of intentions. The appeal of these tactics helps to explain why so many intelligent people fall prey to pseudoscientific claims. To resist these tactics, we must first be able to recognize them. Anthony Pratkanis (1995) identified a variety of persuasion tactics to watch for when evaluating unsubstantiated claims. **TABLE 3** lists seven of them; we should bear in mind that people can use these tactics to persuade us of a variety of claims of both the pseudoscientific and everyday variety.

As we can see, several of these tactics make use of heuristics—mental shortcuts that are appealing and seductive, but occasionally misleading. Many also take the peripheral route to persuasion, rendering it less likely we'll evaluate these claims scientifically. For example, by using vivid testimonials, advertisers exploit the availability heuristic.

Endorsements from attractive celebrities like Brad Pitt can lead us to prefer some products over others for irrational reasons.

◀ **RULING OUT RIVAL HYPOTHESES**
Have important alternative explanations for the findings been excluded?

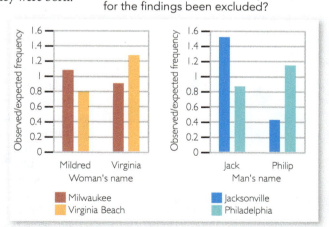

FIGURE 10 Graph Illustrating Implicit Egotism Effect. Research suggests a tendency for us to choose to live in areas with names similar to ours. (Based on data from Pelham, Mirenberg, & Jones, 2002)

TABLE 3 Pseudoscience Marketing Techniques.

PSEUDOSCIENCE TACTIC	CONCEPT	EXAMPLE	PROBLEM
Creation of a "phantom" goal	Capitalize on desire to accomplish unrealistic objectives	"Master the complete works of Shakespeare while sleeping!"	Extreme claims are usually impossible to achieve
Vivid testimonials	Learn about someone else's personal experience	"Sandra Sadness was severely depressed for five years until she underwent rebirthing therapy!"	A single person's perspective is virtually worthless as scientific evidence but can be extremely persuasive
Manufacturing source credibility	We're more likely to believe sources that we judge to be trustworthy or legitimate	"Dr. Jonathan Nobel from Princeton endorses this subliminal tape to build self-esteem."	Advertisers may present source in a deceptive fashion
Scarcity heuristic	Something that's rare must be especially valuable	"Call before midnight to get your copy of Dr. Genius's Improvement Program; it's going to sell out fast!"	Scarcity may be false or a result of low production because of low anticipated demand
Consensus heuristic	If most people believe that something works, it must work	"Thousands of psychologists use the Rorschach Inkblot Test, so it must be valid."	Common "knowledge" is often wrong
The natural commonplace	A widely held belief that things that are natural are good	"Mrs. Candy Cure's new over-the-counter antianxiety medication is made from all-natural ingredients!"	*Natural* doesn't mean healthy—just look at poisonous mushrooms
The goddess-within commonplace	A widely held belief that we all possess a hidden mystical side that traditional Western science neglects or denies	"The Magical Mind ESP Enhancement program allows you to get in touch with your unrecognized psychic potential!"	Carefully controlled tests fail to support supernatural ability or potential

As a result, one dramatic case report of a person's psychological improvement following an herbal remedy can be more compelling than 20 carefully controlled studies showing that this remedy is worthless. Or by manufacturing source credibility, advertisers can fool consumers into believing that a source is more trustworthy than it is. For example, a commercial for a weight-loss plan might present a person who received a certificate at a weekend workshop ("Robert Smith, Officially Certified Dietary Trainer") as a scientific expert.

CORRECTING MISINFORMATION. As we've learned in this text, many intelligent and well-educated people hold false beliefs regarding a host of topics. For example, 29 percent of Americans believe that vaccines contribute to autism despite the lack of compelling scientific evidence for this claim (Chabris & Simons, 2010). How can we best persuade people not to adopt erroneous beliefs? Psychological research yields intriguing insights.

We might assume that merely debunking a falsehood over and over again ("Evidence shows that vaccines don't cause autism") would be sufficient to reduce misinformation. Yet this approach is typically ineffective. In fact, debunking a myth many times can occasionally backfire, leading people to become even more likely to believe it (Lewandowski et al., 2012). That's probably because the myth begins to sound familiar ("Gee, I've been hearing something about vaccines and autism lately—maybe it's about vaccines causing autism"), and as we've learned in this chapter from research on the recognition heuristic, claims that are familiar often seem correct.

Research demonstrates that to persuade people that their beliefs are false, one should ideally provide listeners with an alternative explanation for these beliefs. For example, in addition to telling people that vaccines don't cause autism, it may be helpful to tell them that because there's a strong genetic basis for autism (Anderson, 2012), it's unlikely that vaccines play a major role in causing the condition. In addition, when dispelling false beliefs, it can be important to emphasize truths as least as much as myths so that the truths begin to sound familiar (Lewandowski et al., 2012). In many respects, this advice parallels the approach we've tried to adopt in this text: to rebut widespread psychological misinformation by countering it with accurate psychological information.

RULING OUT RIVAL HYPOTHESES ▶
Have important alternative explanations for the findings been excluded?

Answers are located at the end of the text.

WORK-FROM-HOME JOBS

evaluating CLAIMS

The Internet is chock-full of advertisements for jobs that offer us the chance to earn huge sums of money from the comfort of our own home. Many of these ads use social psychological persuasion techniques to persuade us that we can achieve instant wealth, typically with little more than a phone or Internet connection. Let's evaluate some of these claims, which are modeled after actual ads for home business opportunities.

"Download our guide to starting your own business now *before they run out.*"

Just because there are limited copies of this guide doesn't mean it must be valuable—perhaps the manufacturer printed only a small quantity of the guides in the first place. What marketing tactic does this claim employ? (See Table 3 for a hint.)

"I started out with almost no savings and now *make $5,000–$6,000 every month* working from home."

Beware of claims that rely heavily on anecdotal evidence. It would be hard to verify that this person makes $70,000 per year working from home. This person's sales results may also be unrepresentative of most people, who could earn far less (or even lose money) working from home.

"Want to use the power of the Internet to become rich? Now you can with this report *developed by a well-known sales executive.*"

What would you want to know about the background and success of this sales executive? Should the fact that an expert created this report make you more likely to trust it? What logical fallacy does this claim commit?

Assess Your Knowledge

FACT or FICTION?

1. People's attitudes often don't predict their behaviors especially well.   True / False

2. We're less likely to believe something we've heard many times.   True / False

3. The best way to change people's minds on an issue is to pay them a large sum of money for doing so.   True / False

4. Using the door-in-the-face technique, we begin with a small request before making a larger one.   True / False

Answers: 1. T; 2. F; 3. F; 4. F

✓ **Study** and **Review** in **MyPsychLab**

Prejudice and Discrimination

11 Distinguish prejudice and stereotypes as beliefs from discrimination as a behavior.

12 Identify some of the causes of prejudice and describe methods for combating it.

The term **prejudice** means to prejudge something negatively—to arrive at an unfavorable conclusion before we've evaluated all of the evidence. If we're prejudiced toward a specific class of persons, whether they be women, gays, Norwegians, or hair stylists, it means we've jumped to a premature and negative conclusion about them.

Stereotypes

To understand prejudice, we need to begin with stereotypes. A **stereotype** is a belief—positive or negative—about a group's characteristics that we apply to most members of that group. Like many mental shortcuts, stereotypes typically stem from adaptive psychological processes. We humans are *cognitive misers*—we

prejudice
the drawing of negative conclusions about a person, group of people, or situation prior to evaluating the evidence

stereotype
a belief, positive or negative, about the characteristics of members of a group that is applied generally to most members of the group

FIGURE 11 The Danger of Stereotypes. Gordon Allport and Leo Postman (1956) used a drawing similar to this one to show how negative stereotypes can distort the transmission of information across people. They asked one white participant to look at the drawing—which clearly depicts a white man wielding a razor at an African-American man—and then relay the scene to a string of five or six other white participants in a "game of telephone." As the story was passed from participant to participant, it became progressively warped—with over half of the retellings of the story describing the African American man as holding the razor.

strive to save mental energy by simplifying reality. By lumping enormous numbers of people who share a single characteristic, like skin color, sexual orientation, nationality, or religion, into a single category, stereotypes help us make sense of our often confusing social world (Macrae & Bodenhausen, 2000). In this regard, they're like other schemas in that they help us to process information.

Yet stereotypes can be the seeds from which prejudice grows. They can mislead us when we paint them with too broad a brush, as when we assume that *all* members of a group share a given characteristic. They can also mislead us when we cling to them too rigidly and are unwilling to modify them in light of disconfirming evidence. In such cases, stereotypes fuel confirmation bias about people who differ from us. Stereotypes, like other schemas, can also lead us to spread erroneous negative information about members of other groups, as the classic study described in **FIGURE 11** demonstrates.

Stereotypes can even affect our split-second interpretations of ambiguous stimuli. One line of research demonstrating this point was inspired by a real-life tragedy. In 1999, Western African immigrant Amadou Diallo was shot 41 times by four New York City police officers who believed mistakenly that he was reaching for a gun. In fact, he was reaching for his wallet, presumably in a desperate attempt to display his identification to the officers. As displayed in **FIGURE 12**, Joshua Correll and his colleagues brought the Diallo incident into the laboratory by showing participants a video of a man—in some cases white, in other cases African American—reaching for a cell phone, a wallet, or a handgun. Participants had less than a second to decide whether to "shoot" the man in a simulated computer game. Participants were more likely to shoot unarmed African American than unarmed white men; this finding held true even for African-American participants (Correll et al., 2002).

Many stereotypes contain a kernel of truth, and still others are largely accurate. For instance, laypersons' estimates of the magnitude of sex differences on various psychological traits, such as aggression, helpfulness, talkativeness, and conformity, correspond closely to the actual magnitude of these differences found by researchers (Swim, 1994).

Nevertheless, some stereotypes are massive overgeneralizations. These stereotypes reflect the presence of *illusory correlation*, because they indicate the perception of an erroneous association between a minority group and a given characteristic (Hamilton & Rose, 1980). For example, although most people believe that there's a powerful correlation between mental illness and violence, studies indicate that the risk of violence is markedly elevated only among a small subset of mentally ill individuals, particularly those with paranoid beliefs or substance misuse (Douglas, Guy, & Hart, 2009; Monahan, 1984). Similarly, surveys demonstrate that most Americans believe that lesbian women are at especially high risk for HIV infection, even though lesbian women actually have lower rates of HIV infection than heterosexuals of both sexes and homosexual men (Aronson, 1992).

Stereotypes can also result in what Thomas Pettigrew (1979) called the **ultimate attribution error**: the mistake of attributing the negative behavior of entire groups—like women, gay males, Christians, or African Americans—to their dispositions ("All people of race X are unsuccessful because they're lazy"). When we commit this error, we also tend to attribute any positive behaviors of disliked groups to luck ("Unlike other members of race Y, she was successful because she was fortunate to be raised by extremely supportive parents") or to rare exceptions that prove the rule ("He's not greedy like all of the other members of race Z"). Like the fundamental attribution error, after which it's named, the ultimate attribution error leads us to underestimate the impact of situational factors on people's behavior (Hewstone, 1990). For example, Caucasian students are more likely to interpret a shove as intentionally aggressive, as opposed to accidental, when it originates from an African American than from another Caucasian (Duncan, 1976).

Once we've learned them, stereotypes come to us naturally. Research suggests that overcoming stereotypes takes mental work. The key difference between prejudiced and nonprejudiced people isn't that the former hold stereotypes of minority groups and the latter don't, because both groups harbor such stereotypes. Instead, it's that prejudiced people don't try hard to resist their stereotypes, but nonprejudiced people do (Devine, 1989; Devine et al., 1991).

ultimate attribution error
assumption that behaviors among individual members of a group are due to their internal dispositions

Indeed, neuroimaging research shows that presenting white participants with extremely quick (30 milliseconds, or about one-thirtieth of a second) images of African Americans triggers activation in the amygdala, a region linked to the perception of threat (Cunningham et al., 2004). Yet presenting whites with these images for a longer duration (525 milliseconds, or about half a second) results in lower amygdala activation, as well as higher levels of activation in the frontal lobes, which inhibit the amygdala (Ochsner et al., 2002). This provocative finding suggests that many whites experience an automatic negative reaction to black faces, which they suppress moments later. Moreover, many of us default to prejudiced beliefs when our self-control is weakened. In one study, heterosexual undergraduates drank lemonade sweetened with glucose (the experimental condition) or Splenda (the control condition) and then wrote an essay describing a day in the life of a gay male named Sam. Glucose is the brain's gasoline, so when our brains receive it, we're better at inhibiting our impulses. Interestingly, students who drank lemonade sweetened with glucose wrote essays that contained fewer gay-related stereotypes and negative statements about Sam than did students in the control group. These findings again suggest that many of us hold stereotyped beliefs regarding sexual orientation but that we can inhibit them with mental effort (Gailliot et al., 2009).

The Nature of Prejudice

It's safe to say that we all hold at least some prejudices against certain groups of people (Aronson, 2000). Some have argued that a tendency toward prejudice is deeply rooted in the human species. From the standpoint of natural selection, organisms benefit from forging close alliances with insiders and mistrusting outsiders (Cottrell & Neuberg, 2005). This is part of a broader evolutionary principle called **adaptive conservatism** (Henderson, 1985; Mineka, 1992): better safe than sorry. Indeed, members of one race tend to show large skin conductance responses to fear-inducing stimuli—such as a snake and a spider—that have been paired repeatedly with faces of a different race (Olsson et al., 2005). We quite easily, and perhaps quite naturally, associate scary things with people from other races.

Still, notice that we wrote *tendency* and *tend* in the previous paragraph. Even if there's an evolutionary predisposition toward fearing or mistrusting outsiders, that doesn't mean prejudice is inevitable. Two major biases are associated with our tendency to forge alliances with people similar to us.

The first is **in-group bias**, the tendency to favor individuals inside our group relative to members outside our group (Van Bavel, Packer, & Cunningham, 2008). If you've ever watched a sporting event, you've observed in-group bias. There, you'll witness thousands of red-faced fans (the word *fan*, incidentally, is short for *fanatic*) cheering their home team wildly and booing the visiting team with equal gusto, even though most of these fans have no financial stake in the game's outcome—and have never met a single player on either team. Yet the home team is their "tribe," and they'll happily spend several hours out of their day to cheer them on.

In-group bias may be reinforced by our tendency to "turn off" our compassion toward out-group members. In one study, researchers using functional magnetic resonance imaging (fMRI) imaged the brains of liberal college students while they pondered the description of someone similar to themselves—a liberal person—and then someone dissimilar from themselves—a Christian conservative. The medial prefrontal cortex, which tends to become active when we feel empathy toward others, became more active when participants thought about the liberal. But it became less active when they thought about the Christian conservative (Mitchell, Macrae, & Banaji, 2006).

The second bias is **out-group homogeneity**, the tendency to view all people outside our group as highly similar (Park & Rothbart, 1982). Out-group homogeneity makes it easy for us to dismiss members of other groups, such as different races, in one fell swoop, because we can simply tell ourselves that they all share at least one undesirable characteristic—like greediness or laziness ("All people of Race X act the same way," "All gay males look similar"). In this way, we don't need to bother getting to know them.

FIGURE 12 Leaping to Mistaken Conclusions. Quick—Is this man armed or unarmed? In a computer study by Correll et al. (2002), participants asked to make a split-second decision after viewing ambiguous photos such as this one were more likely to incorrectly judge an African-American man than a white man as holding a gun—and to shoot at him. The man in the photograph above, by the way, is holding a cell phone.

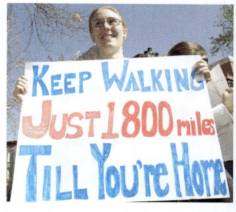

Demonizing an outgroup (such as all immigrants) is a frequent manifestation of in-group bias.

adaptive conservatism
evolutionary principle that creates a predisposition toward distrusting anything or anyone unfamiliar or different

in-group bias
tendency to favor individuals within our group over those from outside our group

out-group homogeneity
tendency to view all individuals outside our group as highly similar

613

Thanks largely to psychological research, most U.S. orchestras now use blind auditions as a safeguard against sex bias and discrimination.

Discrimination

Just as stereotypes can lead to prejudice, prejudice in turn can lead to discrimination, a term with which it's often confused. **Discrimination** is the act of treating members of out-groups differently from members of in-groups. *Whereas prejudice refers to negative attitudes toward others, discrimination refers to negative behaviors toward others.* We can be prejudiced against people without discriminating against them.

CONSEQUENCES OF DISCRIMINATION. Discrimination has significant real-world consequences. For example, far fewer women than men are members of major American orchestras. To find out why, one research team examined how music judges evaluated female musicians during auditions. In some cases, judges could see the musicians; in others, the musicians played behind a screen. When judges were blind to musicians' sex, women were 50 percent more likely to pass auditions (Goldin & Rouse, 2000). For this reason, most major American orchestras today use blind auditions (Gladwell, 2005).

In another study, investigators (Word, Zanna, & Cooper, 1974) observed Caucasian undergraduates as they interviewed both Caucasian and African-American applicants (who were actually confederates) for a job. When interviewing African-American applicants, interviewers sat farther away from the interviewee, made more speech errors, and ended the interview sooner.

These findings, which focused on interviewer behavior, didn't demonstrate whether the different treatment affected the applicants' behavior. So the researchers trained Caucasian interviewers to treat Caucasian job applicants the same way they'd treated African-American applicants. Independent evaluators blind to the behavior of the interviewers coded the behavior of applicants from videotaped interviews. The results were striking. The evaluators rated job applicants who received the "African-American treatment" as significantly more nervous and less qualified for the job than job applicants who received the "Caucasian treatment." This study shows how subtle discriminatory behaviors can adversely affect the quality of interpersonal interactions. Discrimination can be subtle, yet powerful.

CREATING DISCRIMINATION: DON'T TRY THIS AT HOME. It's remarkably easy to cook up discrimination. The recipe? Just create two groups that differ on any characteristic, no matter how trivial. To demonstrate this point, Henry Tajfel (1982) developed the *minimal intergroup paradigm,* a laboratory method for creating groups based on arbitrary differences. In one study, Tajfel and colleagues flashed groups of dots on a screen and asked participants to estimate how many dots they saw. In reality, the researchers ignored participants' answers, randomly classifying some as "dot overestimators" and others as "dot underestimators." They then gave participants the opportunity to distribute money and resources to other participants. People within each group allotted more goodies to people inside than outside their dot estimator group (Tajfel et al., 1971).

Iowa schoolteacher Jane Elliott created similarly random discrimination in her third-grade classroom in 1969. The day after civil rights leader Reverend Martin Luther King, Jr., was assassinated, she divided her class into favored and disfavored groups based solely on their eye color (Monteith & Winters, 2002). Informing her pupils that brown-eyed children are superior because of excess melanin in their eyes, Elliott deprived blue-eyed children of basic rights, such as having second helpings at lunch or drinking from the water fountain. She also insulted blue-eyed children, calling them lazy, dumb, and dishonest. According to Elliott, the results were dramatic; most brown-eyed children quickly become arrogant and condescending, and most blue-eyed children became submissive and insecure.

Teachers across the United States used the now-famous blue eyes–brown eyes demonstration in the late 1960s and 1970s to teach students about the dangers of discrimination (the first author of your textbook was a participant in one of these demonstrations as an elementary school student in New York City). One follow-up study investigating the effects of this demonstration suggests that Caucasian students who experience it report less prejudice toward minorities than do Caucasian students in a control group (Stewart et al., 2003). Nevertheless, because students who underwent this demonstration may have felt demand characteristics to report less prejudice, additional studies are needed to rule out this alternative explanation.

Jane Elliott's classic blue eyes–brown eyes demonstration highlighted the negative interpersonal effects of discrimination.

discrimination
negative behavior toward members of out-groups

RULING OUT RIVAL HYPOTHESES ▶
Have important alternative explanations for the findings been excluded?

Roots of Prejudice: A Tangled Web

The roots of prejudice are complex and multifaceted. Nevertheless, psychologists have honed in on several crucial factors that may contribute to prejudice. We'll examine a few of the prime culprits.

SCAPEGOAT HYPOTHESIS. According to the **scapegoat hypothesis**, prejudice arises from a need to blame other groups for our misfortunes. It can also stem from competition over scarce resources (Jackson, 1993). For example, data show that as unemployment rates in European countries increase, hatred toward immigrants also increases (Cochrane & Nevitte, 2012). This finding suggests that Europeans may blame immigrants for poor economic conditions, although we don't know this for certain. For example, perhaps higher employment rates are tied to greater prejudice against many members of society, not just immigrants. Nevertheless, there's more direct research support for the scapegoat hypothesis. In an experiment disguised as a study of learning, Caucasian students administered more intense electric shocks to an African-American student than to a Caucasian student, but only when the African-American student was unfriendly (Rogers & Prentice-Dunn, 1981). This finding is consistent with the possibility that frustration can trigger aggression, which people then displace onto minority groups.

JUST-WORLD HYPOTHESIS. Melvin Lerner's (1980) **just-world hypothesis** implies that many of us have a deep-seated need to perceive the world as fair—to believe that all things happen for a reason. Ironically, this need for a sense of fair play, especially if powerful, may foster prejudice. That's because it can lead us to place blame on groups that are already in a one-down position, including women who are discriminated against by men (Choma et al., 2012). Many people with a strong belief in a just world are likely to believe that victims of serious illnesses, including cancer and AIDS, are responsible for their plights (Hafer & Begue, 2005). Sociologists and psychologists refer to this phenomenon as "blaming the victim" (Ryan, 1976).

CONFORMITY. Some prejudiced attitudes and behaviors probably stem from conformity to social norms. A study conducted in South Africa half a century ago revealed that Caucasians with a high need for conformity were especially likely to be prejudiced against blacks (Pettigrew, 1958). Such conformity may stem from a need for social approval. In a study of college fraternities and sororities, researchers found that established members of Greek organizations were about equally likely to express negative views of out-groups (other fraternities and sororities) regardless of whether their opinions were public or private. In contrast, new pledges were more likely to express negative views of out-groups when their opinions were public (Noel, Wann, & Branscombe, 1995). Presumably, the pledges wanted to be liked by in-group members and went out of their way to voice their dislike of "outsiders."

INDIVIDUAL DIFFERENCES IN PREJUDICE. Some people exhibit high levels of prejudice against a wide variety of out-groups. For example, people with authoritarian personality traits (which we discussed earlier), are prone to high levels of prejudice against many groups, including Native Americans and gay individuals (Altemeyer, 2004; Whitley & Lee, 2000), as are people with a strong need to "pigeonhole" people into distinct categories (Schaller et al., 1995). In addition, people with high levels of *extrinsic religiosity*, who view religion as a means to an end, such as obtaining friends or social support, tend to have high levels of prejudice (Batson & Ventis, 1982). In contrast, people with high levels of *intrinsic religiosity*—for whom religion is a deeply ingrained part of their belief system—tend to have equal or lower levels of prejudice than do nonreligious people (Gorsuch, 1988; Pontón & Gorsuch, 1988).

Prejudice "Behind the Scenes"

Surveys demonstrate that interracial prejudice has declined substantially in the United States over the past four to five decades (Schuman et al., 1997). Nevertheless, some scholars contend that much prejudice, particularly that of Caucasians toward African

Explore in **MyPsychLab** the **Concept:** Prejudice vs. Discrimination

◀ **RULING OUT RIVAL HYPOTHESES**
Have important alternative explanations for the findings been excluded?

Factoid

People with high levels of prejudice toward multiple ethnic groups may display prejudice toward entirely fictitious groups of people (Bishop, Oldendick, & Tuchfarber, 1986). In a classic study, a researcher found that people who were prejudiced against Jews and African Americans also expressed dislike of the Pireneans, Danireans, and Wallonians—all of which are nonexistent ethnic groups (Hartley, 1946).

scapegoat hypothesis
claim that prejudice arises from a need to blame other groups for our misfortunes

just-world hypothesis
claim that our attributions and behaviors are shaped by a deep-seated assumption that the world is fair and all things happen for a reason

Set 1:

Press left key if | | | Press right key if

Photo of a Black person **or** Positive word | Photo of a White person **or** Negative word

JOY | ANGRY

Set 2:

Press left key if | | | Press right key if

Photo of a Black person **or** Negative word | Photo of a White person **or** Positive word

KNIFE | SMILE

FIGURE 13 The Implicit Association Test.
The Implicit Association Test (IAT) is the most widely researched measure of implicit or unconscious prejudice. This is a rendered example: Most white participants associate negative words more readily with African-American than white faces, and many African-American participants display the same effect. But does the test really measure unconscious prejudice, or does it measure something else?

explicit prejudice
unfounded negative belief of which we're aware regarding the characteristics of an out-group

implicit prejudice
unfounded negative belief of which we're unaware regarding the characteristics of an out-group

FALSIFIABILITY ▶
Can the claim be disproved?

Beginning with the classic Robber's Cave study, research shows that campers from diverse groups who work together toward shared goals will end up with lower levels of prejudice.

Americans, has merely "gone underground"—that is, become subtler (Dovidio et al., 1997; Fiske, 2002; Hackney, 2005; Sue et al., 2007). One approach to studying subtle prejudice is to measure implicit (unconscious) prejudice (Fazio & Olson, 2003; Vanman et al., 2004). In contrast to **explicit prejudices**, of which we're aware, **implicit prejudices** are those of which we're unaware. For example, one research team asked whites to cooperate with blacks on a task. Although white participants claimed to like their black partners, sensitive measures of their facial activity implied otherwise: their forehead muscles involved in frowning became active (Vanman et al., 1997).

An implicit prejudice technique that's received substantial attention in recent years is the Implicit Association Test (IAT) developed by Anthony Greenwald and Mahzarin Banaji. As shown in **FIGURE 13**, researchers might ask a participant to press a key on the computer keyboard with his left hand if he sees a photograph of an African American or a positive word (like *joy*) and to press a different key with his right hand if he sees a photograph of a Caucasian or a negative word (like *bad*). After performing this task for a number of trials, researchers ask participants to again press the left and right keys, but this time for the reverse pairing (that is, to press the left key for a photograph of either an African American or a negative word and the right key for a photograph of either a Caucasian or a positive word) (Greenwald, McGhee, & Schwartz, 1998). Many studies demonstrate that most Caucasian participants respond more quickly to pairings in which African-American faces are paired with negative words and Caucasian faces are paired with positive words (Banaji, 2001; De Houwer et al., 2009). According to proponents of the IAT, this finding suggests that many whites hold implicit (unconscious) prejudice against African Americans (Gladwell, 2005; Greenwald & Nosek, 2001). About 40 percent of African Americans display the same bias on the IAT (Banaji & Greenwald, 2013), suggesting that even some African Americans might harbor subtle biases against members of their own race. Investigators have expanded the IAT to detect a variety of forms of subtle prejudice, including racism, sexism, homophobia, religious discrimination, and ageism (prejudice against older individuals). If you want to try out the IAT, check out the website https://implicit.harvard.edu/implicit/demo.

Nevertheless, things may not be quite that simple (De Houwer et al., 2009). For one thing, the IAT often doesn't correlate significantly with explicit measures of prejudice, such as questionnaire measures of racist attitudes (Arkes & Tetlock, 2004). Proponents of the IAT argue that this absence of a correlation actually supports the IAT's validity, because the IAT supposedly measures unconscious rather than conscious racial attitudes. Yet this reasoning raises questions regarding the falsifiability of the IAT because IAT proponents could presumably interpret a positive or zero correlation as evidence for the IAT's validity. Moreover, it's unclear whether the IAT measures prejudice as much as *awareness* of, or familiarity with, stereotypes (Kaufman, 2011). Unprejudiced persons may correctly perceive that much of mainstream American society links Muslims, for example, with many negative characteristics and Christians with many positive characteristics, yet they may reject these associations as biased (Arkes & Tetlock, 2004; Levitin, 2013; Redding, 2004).

Another problem is that at least some positive findings linking the IAT to real-world racism may stem from only a handful of participants with extreme scores; as a result, the IAT may not measure implicit prejudice for the substantial majority of people (Blanton et al., 2009). So scholars continue to debate whether the IAT and similar measures genuinely measure prejudice (Blanton & Jaccard, 2008; De Houwer et al., 2009; Gawronski, LeBel, & Peters, 2007).

Combating Prejudice: Some Remedies

Having traversed some pretty depressing ground—blind conformity, destructive obedience, bystander nonintervention, social loafing, and now prejudice—we're pleased to close our chapter with a piece of good news: We can overcome prejudice, at least to some extent (Aboud et al., 2012). But how?

ROBBERS CAVE STUDY. We can find some clues in a study that Muzafer Sherif and his colleagues conducted in Robbers Cave, Oklahoma (so named because robbers once used these caves to hide from law enforcement authorities). Sherif split 22 well-adjusted fifth grade students into two groups, the Eagles and the Rattlers, and sent them packing to summer camp. After giving the boys within each group the chance to form strong bonds, Sherif introduced the groups to each other and engaged them in a four-day sports and games tournament. When he did, pandemonium ensued. The Eagles and Rattlers displayed intense animosity toward one another, eventually manifesting in name-calling, food throwing, and fistfights.

Sherif next wanted to find out whether he could "cure" the prejudice he'd helped to create. His treatment was simple: engage the groups in activities that required them to cooperate to achieve an overarching goal. For example, he rigged a series of mishaps, such as a breakdown of a truck carrying food supplies, which forced the Eagles and Rattlers to work together. Sure enough, such cooperation toward a shared goal produced a dramatic decrease in hostility between the groups (Sherif et al., 1961). The Robbers Cave study imparts a valuable lesson: one means of reducing prejudice is to encourage people to work toward a shared higher purpose. By doing so, they can believe they're no longer members of completely separate groups, but part of a larger and more inclusive group: "We're all in this together" (Fiske, 2000).

JIGSAW CLASSROOMS. Elliott Aronson (Aronson et al., 1978) incorporated the lessons of the Robbers Cave study into his educational work on **jigsaw classrooms**, in which teachers assign children separate tasks that all need to be fitted together to complete a project. A teacher might give each student in a class a different piece of history to investigate regarding the U.S. Civil War. One might present on Virginia's role, another on New York's, another on Georgia's, and so on. The students then cooperate to assemble the pieces into an integrated lesson. Numerous studies reveal that jigsaw classrooms result in significant decreases in racial prejudice (Aronson, 2004; Slavin & Cooper, 1999).

The Robbers Cave study and Aronson's work on jigsaw classrooms underscore a lesson confirmed by many other social psychology studies: *increased contact between racial groups alone is rarely sufficient to reduce prejudice*. Indeed, during the early Civil Rights era in the United States, many attempts to reduce prejudice by means of desegregation may have backfired, resulting in increases in racial tension (Stephan, 1978). The advocates of these well-intended efforts assumed mistakenly that contact by itself could heal the deep wounds of prejudice. Although inter-group contact is sometimes helpful in reducing prejudice against individuals of different races (Pettigrew & Tropp, 2008) and different sexual orientations (Smith, Axelton, & Saucier, 2009), we now know that interventions are most likely to reduce prejudice only if they satisfy several conditions (see **TABLE 4**). These conditions lead to an optimistic conclusion: prejudice is neither inevitable nor irreversible.

In jigsaw classrooms, children cooperate on a multipart project, with each child assuming a small but essential role.

TABLE 4 Ideal Conditions for Reducing Prejudice.

- The groups should cooperate toward shared goals.
- The contact between groups should be enjoyable.
- The groups should be of roughly equal status.
- Group members should disconfirm the other group's negative stereotypes.
- Group members should have the potential to become friends.

(Based on Kenrick et al., 2005; Pettigrew, 1998)

Assess Your Knowledge — FACT or FICTION?

1. Prejudice refers to negative behavior against out-group members. **True / False**

2. By definition, all stereotypes are inaccurate. **True / False**

3. Research demonstrates that nonprejudiced people lack stereotypes of other groups. **True / False**

4. Cooperation toward shared goals is a key ingredient in reducing prejudice. **True / False**

5. Research suggests that increased contact between groups is sufficient to reduce prejudice. **True / False**

Answers: 1. F; 2. F; 3. F; 4. T; 5. F

✓ **Study** and **Review** in **MyPsychLab**

jigsaw classroom
educational approach designed to minimize prejudice by requiring all children to make independent contributions to a shared project

Your Complete Review System

✔ **Study** and **Review** in **MyPsychLab**

((•)) **Listen** in **MyPsychLab** to chapter audio

What Is Social Psychology?

1 IDENTIFY THE WAYS IN WHICH SOCIAL SITUATIONS INFLUENCE THE BEHAVIOR OF INDIVIDUALS.

The need-to-belong theory proposes that humans have a biological need for interpersonal connections. According to social comparison theory, we're motivated to evaluate our beliefs, attitudes, and reactions by comparing them with the beliefs, attitudes, and reactions of others. Mass hysteria and urban legends reflect outbreaks of irrational behavior spread largely by social contagion. Social facilitation refers to the presence of others enhancing our performance in certain situations.

1. Social psychologists study how people influence others' _____, _____, and _____, for both good and bad.

2. The idea that we have a biologically based need for interpersonal connections is known as the _____ theory.

3. According to Festinger's _____ _____ theory, we evaluate our abilities and beliefs largely by judging how we rank relative to others.

4. The flying saucer craze is arguably one of the most widespread cases of what phenomenon?

5. What factors contribute to the rise and spread of urban legends?

6. A worsened performance in the presence of others is explained by _____ _____.

7. Researchers have found that our performance in front of others is influenced by our level of _____ in that performance area.

2 EXPLAIN HOW THE FUNDAMENTAL ATTRIBUTION ERROR CAN CAUSE US TO MISJUDGE OTHERS' BEHAVIORS.

Attributions refer to our efforts to explain behavior. Some attributions are internal; others, external. The great lesson of social psychology is the fundamental attribution error—the tendency to overestimate the impact of dispositions on others' behavior. As a result of this error, we also tend to underestimate the impact of situations on others' behavior.

8. We tend to form _____ in our desire to assign causes to other people's behavior.

9. The tendency to overestimate the impact of _____ _____ on others' behavior is called the fundamental attribution error.

10. The fundamental attribution error (does/doesn't) apply to people's attributions about themselves.

Social Influence: Conformity and Obedience

3 DETERMINE THE FACTORS THAT INFLUENCE WHEN WE CONFORM TO OTHERS.

Conformity refers to the tendency of people to change their behavior as a result of group pressure. Asch's conformity studies underscore the power of social pressure, although there are individual and cultural differences in conformity. Deindividuation refers to the tendency of people to engage in atypical behavior when stripped of their usual identities. The Stanford prison study is a powerful demonstration of the effects of deindividuation on behavior.

11. Changing your personal style, habits, or behavior to fit into a social or peer group is an example of _____.

12. Under what circumstances discussed in the text would you identify line 3 as equal in length to the standard line?

Standard line	Comparison lines

13. According to research by Berns and his colleagues, conformity is associated with activity in the _____ and _____ lobes of the brain.

14. People with (high/low) self-esteem are especially prone to conformity.

15. Researchers like Phil Zimbardo found that two prominent factors that contribute to deindividuation are a feeling of _____ and a lack of _____ _____.

16. The Stanford prison study results have been compared with the prison guard atrocities at _____ _____ in Iraq.

4 RECOGNIZE THE DANGERS OF GROUP DECISION MAKING AND IDENTIFY WAYS TO AVOID MISTAKES COMMON IN GROUP DECISIONS.

Groupthink is a preoccupation with group unanimity that impairs critical thinking. It can be "treated" by interventions that encourage dissent within the group. Group polarization refers to the tendency of group discussion to strengthen the dominant positions of individual group members. Cults are groups of individuals who exhibit extreme groupthink marked by intense and unquestioning devotion to a single individual.

17. NASA's decision to launch the 1986 *Challenger* shuttle despite warnings of potential problems from engineers may have resulted from _____.

18. The best way to resist the indoctrination that leads to cults is through the _____ _____, which involves first introducing reasons why the perspective might be correct, then debunking them.

5 IDENTIFY THE FACTORS THAT MAXIMIZE OR MINIMIZE OBEDIENCE TO AUTHORITY.

Milgram's classic work on authority demonstrates the power of destructive obedience to authority and helps to clarify the situational factors that both foster and impede obedience.

19. Milgram's study testing the effects of "punishment on learning" was, in reality, designed to measure _____.

20. What factors in the Milgram study increased the likelihood that participants would refuse to comply with orders to shock the "learner"?

Helping and Harming Others: Prosocial Behavior and Aggression

6 EXPLAIN WHICH ASPECTS OF A SITUATION INCREASE OR DECREASE THE LIKELIHOOD OF BYSTANDER INTERVENTION.

Although common wisdom suggests that there's "safety in numbers," research suggests otherwise. Bystander nonintervention results from two major factors: pluralistic ignorance and diffusion of responsibility. The first affects whether we recognize ambiguous situations as emergencies, and the second affects how we respond once we've identified situations as emergencies. People are more likely to help when they're unable to escape from a situation, have adequate time to intervene, are in a good mood, and have been exposed to research on bystander intervention.

21. What phenomenon did primate researcher Frans de Waal capture in this photo of two chimpanzees?

22. The presence of others tends to make people (less/more) likely to help someone in need.

23. What steps could you take to improve your chances of obtaining help if you were badly hurt or seriously ill in a public place?

24. As diffusion of responsibility occurs, each individual feels (more/less) accountable for helping someone in need.

25. The phenomenon in which people exert less effort on a task when in a group than when alone is known as _____ _____.

26. Prior exposure to psychological research (can/can't) change an individual's real-world behavior for the better.

27. Extraverted people tend to be (more/less) prone to help others than introverted people.

7 DESCRIBE THE SOCIAL AND INDIVIDUAL DIFFERENCE VARIABLES THAT CONTRIBUTE TO HUMAN AGGRESSION.

A variety of situational variables, including provocation, frustration, aggressive cues, media influences, arousal, and temperature, increase the likelihood of aggression. Men tend to be more physically aggressive compared with women, although girls are more relationally aggressive compared with boys. The southern "culture of honor" may help to explain why murder rates are higher in the southern United States than in other regions of the country.

28. Aggressive behavior, both at the individual and group levels, is influenced by _____ and _____ factors.

29. Because warm temperatures increase _____, they may make people more likely to lose their temper when provoked or frustrated.

30. _____ aggression is a form of indirect aggression that involves spreading rumors, gossiping, and using nonverbal putdowns for the purpose of social manipulation.

Attitudes and Persuasion: Changing Minds

8 DESCRIBE HOW ATTITUDES RELATE TO BEHAVIOR.

Attitudes aren't typically good predictors of behavior, although attitudes predict behavior relatively well when they're highly accessible, firmly held, and stable over time.

31. The major distinction between a belief and an attitude is that an attitude involves a(n) _____ component.

32. LaPiere's research suggested that people's stated attitudes (did/didn't) accurately predict their situational behavior.

33. The behavior of someone who is a (low/high) self-monitor is likely to reflect his or her true feelings and attitudes.

34. The _____ _____, which makes us more likely to believe something we've heard many times, generally reflects accurate information.

9 EVALUATE THEORETICAL ACCOUNTS OF HOW AND WHEN WE ALTER OUR ATTITUDES.

According to cognitive dissonance theory, a discrepancy between two beliefs leads to an unpleasant state of tension that we're motivated to reduce. In some cases, we reduce this state by altering our attitudes. Two alternative views are self-perception theory, which proposes that we infer our attitudes from observing our behaviors, and impression management theory, which proposes that we don't really change our attitudes but report that we have so that we appear consistent.

35. Using your knowledge of cognitive dissonance, complete the bottom set of boxes with statements geared toward resolving the stated conflict.

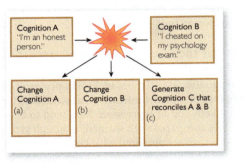

36. In Festinger and Carlsmith's test of cognitive dissonance theory, participants given less money reported enjoying the task (more/less).

10 IDENTIFY COMMON AND EFFECTIVE PERSUASION TECHNIQUES AND HOW THEY'RE EXPLOITED BY PSEUDOSCIENTISTS.

According to dual process models of persuasion, there are two routes to persuasion: a central route that involves careful evaluation of arguments and a peripheral route that relies on superficial cues. Effective persuasion techniques include the foot-in-the-door technique, the door-in-the-face technique, and the low-ball technique. Many techniques designed to market pseudoscientific products largely make use of the peripheral route to persuasion.

37. Match up the technique to the definition.

_____	Foot-in-the-door technique	1. Making an unreasonably large request with the goal of getting someone to agree to a lesser request
_____	Door-in-the-face technique	2. "Adding on" costs hidden until an agreement to buy the item at lower cost is reached
_____	Low-ball technique	3. Asking someone to do something for you while informing them that they can refuse
_____	"But you are free" technique	4. Making a small request of someone followed by a bigger request

38. Once a friend has agreed to help you select paint colors for your dorm room, asking her to help you paint the room is an example of the _____ technique.

39. Messages are especially persuasive if the messenger seems (similar to/different from) us.

40. By manufacturing _____ _____, advertisers can fool consumers into believing that a source is more trustworthy than it is.

Prejudice and Discrimination

11 DISTINGUISH PREJUDICE AND STEREOTYPES AS BELIEFS FROM DISCRIMINATION AS A BEHAVIOR.

Prejudice is coming to a negative conclusion before we've evaluated all the evidence. Prejudice is accompanied by several other biases, including in-group bias and out-group homogeneity. Stereotypes are beliefs about a group's characteristics that we apply to most members of that group. They can be either positive or negative. Discrimination is the act of treating out-group members differently from in-group members.

41. Concluding that all Americans are loud, materialistic, and arrogant without ever having spent time with any of them is an example of _____.

42. A belief that all cheerleaders are ditzy, flirty, and interested only in dating is a(n) _____.

43. Our tendency to view all people outside of our group as highly similar is known as (in-group bias/out-group homogeneity).

44. Believing—without firsthand knowledge—that teens with nose piercings who frequent the local mall are all troublemakers is a form of _____, and refusing to serve them in your mall restaurant is a form of _____.

45. How did one school teacher use her pupils' eye color to demonstrate how discrimination arises?

12 IDENTIFY SOME OF THE CAUSES OF PREJUDICE AND DESCRIBE METHODS FOR COMBATING IT.

There's evidence for various explanations of prejudice, including scapegoating, belief in a just world, and conformity. One of the most effective means of combating prejudice is to make members of different groups work together toward achieving shared overarching goals.

46. According to the _____ _____, prejudice arises from a need to blame other groups for our misfortunes.

47. The idea that our behaviors and attributions are based on the assumption that all things happen for a reason supports the _____ hypothesis.

48. The _____ _____ _____ is a technique that measures implicit prejudice.

49. How do Aronson's jigsaw classrooms work to reduce prejudice?

50. One condition for reducing prejudice is to (encourage group members to become/discourage group members from becoming) friends.

Apply Your Scientific Thinking Skills

Use your scientific thinking skills to answer the following questions, referencing specific scientific thinking principles and common errors in reasoning whenever possible.

1. Although we like to think of ourselves as individuals, we all belong to groups that require some form of conformity. List a few of the groups to which you belong (such as religious institutions, college clubs, and fraternities or sororities) and describe the advantages and disadvantages of being a part of each group. How does each group promote conformity?

2. Sadly, we read or hear about acts of violence in the news every day. Select an aggressive act (like a high-profile murder or bombing) that has been in the headlines recently and read at least two articles about it. What situational influences does each article list as possible causes of the act? Have the articles considered rival hypotheses for the aggressive actions, such as individual, gender, or cultural differences? If so, which hypotheses did the article present?

3. Visit three or four websites that promote a political candidate or party. What persuasive techniques do they use to attempt to gain your support (including your donation, volunteering, or your vote)? How effective are these techniques in each case?

Further Your Understanding

EXTEND YOUR KNOWLEDGE WITH THE MYPSYCHLAB VIDEO SERIES

Watch these videos in MyPsychLab. Follow the "Video Series" link.

The Big Picture: The Social World Learn about the types of things social psychologists study and how our social relationships influence how we behave, think, and feel.

The Basics: Under the Influence of Others See why our actions depend on social situations, how individual identity merges with group identity, and what recent research tells us about group behavior.

Special Topics: Mental Shortcuts in a Social Context Learn about our tendency to use heuristics in our daily judgments and decision making, learn why we use them, and see some specific examples of commonly used heuristics.

Thinking Like a Psychologist: Changing Attitudes and Behaviors Understand how we relieve the discomfort of cognitive dissonance and the significance of culture when aiming to changing a person's attitude.

In the Real World: Are Stereotypes and Prejudices Inevitable? Learn to distinguish between stereotype and prejudice and gain a better understanding of how they come about.

What's In It for Me?: Persuasion Learn how the brain processes persuasive messages and discover a variety of persuasion techniques commonly used by salespeople.

EXPERIENCE PSYCHOLOGICAL RESEARCH WITH MYPSYCHLAB SIMULATIONS

Access these simulations in MyPsychLab. Follow the "Simulations" link.

Implicit Association Test: Prejudice Sort images and words into categories to identify your implicit associations between race and weapons.

Could You Be a Hero? Participate in a survey to discover if you have what it takes to be a hero.

Answer Key

WHAT IS SOCIAL PSYCHOLOGY?

1. behavior; beliefs; attitudes
2. need-to-belong
3. social comparison
4. collective delusion
5. Urban legends are convincing in part because they fit our preconceptions. They make good stories because they tug on our emotions, especially negative ones (such as disgust).
6. social disruption
7. experience
8. attributions
9. dispositional influences
10. doesn't

SOCIAL INFLUENCE: CONFORMITY AND OBEDIENCE

11. conformity
12. If others responding before you all consistently supplied this same (obviously incorrect) answer, you'd be extremely likely to provide the same wrong answer as well.
13. parietal; occipital
14. low
15. anonymity; individual responsibility

16. Abu Ghraib
17. groupthink
18. inoculation effect
19. obedience
20. The greater the psychological distance between the teacher and experimenter, the less the obedience. For instance, obedience plummeted when the experimenter gave instructions by telephone. Obedience also varied depending on the psychological distance between the teacher and learner. For example, if the teacher was in the same room with the learner, obedience decreased, but if the teacher was instructed to have a third person administer the shock, obedience increased.

HELPING AND HARMING OTHERS: PROSOCIAL BEHAVIOR AND AGGRESSION

21. prosocial behavior
22. less
23. Address a specific person ("Man in the blue shirt, please help me!") to decrease the chances of bystander nonintervention.

24. less
25. social loafing
26. can
27. more
28. situational; dispositional
29. irritability
30. Relational

ATTITUDES AND PERSUASION: CHANGING MINDS

31. emotional
32. didn't
33. low
34. recognition heuristic
35. a) "I'm not an honest person after all"; b) "I didn't really cheat; I just saw someone's answers"; c) "I had to cheat because the test was unfair"
36. more
37. 4) foot-in-the-door; 1) door-in-the-face; 2) low-ball; 3) "but you are free"
38. foot-in-the-door
39. similar to
40. source credibility

PREJUDICE AND DISCRIMINATION

41. prejudice
42. stereotype
43. out-group homogeneity
44. prejudice; discrimination
45. Jane Elliott divided her class into favored and disfavored groups based solely on their eye color, informing her students that children with brown eyes are superior because of excess melanin in their eyes. The results were dramatic: the brown-eyed children quickly became arrogant and condescending, and the blue-eyed children became submissive and insecure.
46. scapegoat hypothesis
47. just-world
48. Implicit Association Test (IAT)
49. In jigsaw classrooms, children cooperate on a multipart project, with each child assuming a small but essential role.
50. encourage group members to become

References

Aboud, F. E., Tredoux, C., Tropp, L. R., Brown, C. S., Niens, U., & Noor, N. M. (2012). Interventions to reduce prejudice and enhance inclusion and respect for ethnic differences in early childhood: A systematic review. *Developmental Review, 32*, 307–336.

Abramowitz, A. I., & Saunders, K. L. (2008). Is polarization a myth? *Journal of Politics, 70*, 542–555.

Adorno, T. W., Frenkel-Brunswik, E., Levinson, D., & Sanford, R. N. (1950). *The authoritarian personality.* New York, NY: Harper.

Alicke, M. D., LoSchiavo, F. M., Zerbst, J. I., & Zhang, S. (1997). The person who outperforms me is a genius: Esteem maintenance in upward social comparison. *Journal of Personality and Social Psychology, 73*, 781–789.

Allport, G. W., & Postman, L. J. (1945). The basic psychology of rumor. *Transactions of the New York Academy of Sciences; Transactions of the New York Academy of Sciences.*

Allport, G. W., & Postman, L. J. (1956). The basic psychology of rumor. *Journal of Abnormal and Social Psychology, 53*, 27–33.

Altemeyer, B. (2004). Highly dominating, highly authoritarian personalities. *Journal of Social Psychology, 14*, 421–427.

Ancona, L., & Pareyson, R. (1968). Contributo allo studio della aggressione: La dinamica della obbedienza distruttiva [Contribution to the study of aggression: The dynamics of destructive obedience]. *Archivio di Psicologia, Neurologia, e Psichiatria, 29*, 340–372.

Andersen, H. S., Sestoft, D., Lillebaek, T., Gabrielsen, G., Hemmingsen, R., & Kramp, P. (2000). A longitudinal study of prisoners on remand: Psychiatric prevalence, incidence and psychopathology in solitary vs. non-solitary confinement. *Acta Psychiatrica Scandinavica, 102*, 19–25.

Anderson, A. K., Christoff, K., Stappen, I., Panitz, D., Ghahremani, D. G., Glover, G.,... Sobel, N. (2003). Dissociated neural representations of intensity and valence in human olfaction. *Nature Neuroscience, 6*, 196–202.

Anderson, C. A., & Anderson, K. B. (1996). Violent crime rate studies in philosophical context: A destructive testing approach to heat and southern culture of violence effects. *Journal of Personality and Social Psychology, 70*, 740–756.

Anderson, C. A., & Bushman, B. J. (2002b). Human aggression. *Annual Review of Psychology, 53*, 27–51.

Anderson, C. A., Bushman, B. J., & Groom, R. W. (1997). Hot years and serious and deadly assault: Empirical tests of the heat hypothesis. *Journal of Personality and Social Psychology, 73*, 1213–1223.

Anderson, C. A., Shibuya, A., Ihiri, N., Swing, E. L., Bushman, B. J., Sakamoto, A., . . . Saleem, M. (2010). Violent video game effects on aggression, empathy, and prosocial behavior in Eastern and Western countries. *Psychological Bulletin, 136*, 151–173.

Anderson, G. M. (2012). Twin studies in autism: What they might say about genetic and environmental influences. *Journal of Autism and Developmental Disorders, 42*, 1526–1527.

Anderson, J. R., Myowa-Yamakoshi, M., & Matsuzawa, T. (2004). Contagious yawning in chimpanzees. *Proceedings of the Royal Society B: Biological Sciences, 271*, S468.

Archer, J. (2004). Sex differences in aggression in real-world settings: A meta-analytic review. *Review of General Psychology, 8*(4), 291–322.

Arkes, H. R. (1993). Some practical judgment and decision-making research. In N. J. Castellan (Ed.), *Individual and group decision making: Current issues* (pp. 3–19). Hillsdale, NJ: Erlbaum.

Arkes, H. R., & Tetlock, P. E. (2004). Attributions of implicit prejudice or "Would Jesse Jackson 'fail' the Implicit Association Test?" *Psychological Inquiry, 15*, 257–278.

Aronoff, J., Lynn, S. J., & Malinowski, P. (2000). Are cultic environments psychologically harmful? *Clinical Psychology Review, 20*, 91–111.

Aronson, E. (2000) The jigsaw strategy: Reducing prejudice in the classroom. *Psychology Review, 7*, 2–5.

Aronson, E. (2004). Reducing hostility and building compassion: Lessons from the jigsaw classroom. In A. G. Miller (Ed.), *The social psychology of good and evil* (pp. 469–488). New York, NY: Guilford Press.

Aronson, E. (2012). *The social animal* (11th ed.). New York, NY: Worth.

Aronson, E., Blaney, N., Stephan, C., Sikes, J., & Snapp, M. (1978). *The jigsaw classroom.* Beverly Hills, CA: Sage.

Aronson, E., & Mills, J. (1959). The effect of severity of initiation on liking for a group. *Journal of Abnormal and Social Psychology, 59*, 177–181.

Asch, S. E. (1955). Opinions and social pressure. *Scientific American, 193*, 31–35.

Backstrom, L. (2011, November 2). *Anatomy of Facebook.* Retrieved from http://www.facebook.com/notes/facebook-data-team/anatomy-of-facebook/10150388519243859

Bainbridge, W. S. (1987). Collective behavior and social movements. In R. Stark (Ed.), *Sociology* (pp. 544–576). Belmont, CA: Wadsworth.

Balcetis, E., & Dunning, D. A. (2008). A mile in moccasins: How situational experience diminishes dispositionism in social inference. *Personality and Social Psychology Bulletin, 34*, 102–144.

Banaji, M. R. (2001). Implicit attitudes can be measured. In H. D. Roediger, III, J. S. Naime, I. Neath, & A. Surprenant (Eds.), *The nature of remembering: Essays* in honor of Robert G. Crowder (pp. 117–150). Washington, DC: American Psychological Association.

Banaji, M. R., & Greenwald, A. G. (2013). *Blindspot: Hidden biases of good people.* New York, NY: Delacorte Press.

Bandura, A. (1973). *Aggression: A social learning analysis.* Oxford, England: Prentice Hall.

Barchas, P. (1986). A sociophysiological orientation to small groups. In E. Lawler (Ed.), *Advances in group processes* (Vol. 3, pp. 209–246). Greenwich, CT: JAI Press.

Barnes, C. D., Brown, R. P., & Tamborski, M. (2012). Living dangerously: Culture of honor, risk-taking, and the non-randomness of 'accidental' deaths. *Social Psychological and Personality Science, 3*, 100–107.

Bartholomew, R. E. (1998). The Martian panic sixty years later: What have we learned? *Skeptical Inquirer, 22*(6), 40–43.

Bartholomew, R. E., & Goode, E. (2000). Mass delusions and hysterias: Highlights from the past millennium. *Skeptical Inquirer, 24*, 20–28.

Batson, C. D. (1987). Prosocial motivation: Is it ever truly altruistic? In L. Berkowitz (Ed.), *Advances in experimental social psychology* (Vol. 20, pp. 65–122). New York, NY: Academic Press.

Batson, C. D., Batson, J., Singlsby, J., Harrell, K., Peekna, H., & Todd, R. (1991). Empathic joy and the empathy-altruism hypothesis. *Journal of Personality and Social Psychology, 61*, 413–426.

Batson, C. D., Duncan, B. D., Ackerman, P., Buckley, T., & Birch, K. (1981). Is empathic emotion a source of altruistic motivation? *Journal of Personality and Social Psychology, 40*, 290–302.

Batson, C. D., & Shaw, L. (1991). Evidence for altruism: Toward a pluralism of prosocial motives. *Psychological Inquiry, 2*, 107–122.

Batson, C. D., & Ventis, W. L. (1982). *The religious experience: A social psychological perspective.* New York, NY: Oxford University Press.

Baum, H. S. (1987). *The invisible bureaucracy.* Oxford, England: Oxford University Press.

Baumeister, R. F., & Leary, M. R. (1995). The need to belong: Desire for interpersonal attachments as a fundamental human motivation. *Psychological Bulletin, 117*, 497–529.

Baumeister, R. F., Twenge, J. M., & Nuss, C. (2002). Effects of social exclusion on cognitive processes: Anticipated aloneness reduces intelligent thought. *Journal of Personality and Social Psychology, 83*, 817–827.

Beaman, A., Barnes, P., Klentz, B., & McQuirk, B. (1978). Increasing helping rates through information dissemination: Teaching pays. *Personality and Social Psychology Bulletin, 4*, 406–411.

Bègue, L., & Subra, B. (2008). Alcohol and aggression: Perspectives on controlled and uncontrolled social information processing. *Social and Personality Psychology Compass, 2*, 511–538.

Beilock, S. L. (2008). Math performance in stressful situations. *Current Directions in Psychological Science, 17*, 339–343.

Beilock, S. L., & Carr, T. H. (2005). When high-powered people fail: Working memory and "choking under pressure" in math. *Psychological Science, 16*, 101–105.

Bem, D. J. (1967). Self-perception: An alternative interpretation of cognitive dissonance phenomena. *Psychological Review, 74*, 183–200.

Bem, D. J., & Funder, D. C. (1978). Predicting more of the people more of the time: Assessing the personality of situations. *Psychological Review, 85*, 485–500.

Bem, D. J., & McConnell, H. K. (1970). Testing the self-perception explanation of dissonance phenomena: On the salience of premanipulation attitudes. *Journal of Personality and Social Psychology, 14*, 23–31.

Berkowitz, L. (1989). Frustration-aggression hypothesis: Examination and reformulation. *Psychological Bulletin, 106*, 59–73.

Berkowitz, L., & LePage, A. (1967). Weapons as aggression-eliciting stimuli. *Journal of Personality and Social Psychology, 7*, 202–207.

Berns, G. S., Chappelow, J., Zink, C. F., Pagnoni, G., Martin-Skurski, M. E., & Richards, J. (2005). Neurobiological correlates of social conformity and independence during mental rotation. *Biological Psychiatry, 58*, 245–253.

Bierbrauer, G. (1973). *Effect of set, perspective, and temporal factors in attribution.* Unpublished doctoral dissertation, Stanford University, Palo Alto, CA.

Birkley, E. L., Giancola, P. R., & Lance, C. E. (2012). Psychopathy and the prediction of alcohol-related physical aggression: The roles of impulsive antisociality and fearless dominance. *Drug and Alcohol Dependence, 128*, 58–63.

Bishop, G. F., Oldendick, R. W., & Tuchfarber, A. J. (1986). Opinions on fictitious issues: The pressure to answer survey questions. *Public Opinion Quarterly, 50*, 240–250.

Blanton, H., & Jaccard, J. (2008). Representing versus generalizing: Two approaches to external validity and their implications for the study of prejudice. *Psychological Inquiry, 19*, 99–105.

Blanton, H., Klick, J., Mitchell, G., Jaccard, J., Mellers, B., & Tetlock, P. E. (2009). Strong claims and weak evidence: Reassessing the predictive validity of the IAT. *Journal of Applied Psychology, 94*(3), 567–582.

Blass, T. (1999). The Milgram paradigm after 35 years. *Journal of Applied Social Psychology, 29*, 955–978.

Blass, T. (2004). *The man who shocked the world: The life and legacy of Stanley Milgram.* New York, NY: Perseus.

Bond, R., & Smith, R. P. (1996). Culture and conformity: A meta-analysis of studies using Asch's line judgment task. *Psychological Bulletin, 119*, 111–137.

Bond, R., & Titus, L. J. (1983). Social facilitation: A meta-analysis of 241 studies. *Psychological Bulletin, 94*, 265–292.

Bridgestock, M. (2009). *Beyond belief: Skepticism, science and the paranormal.* Cambridge: Cambridge University Press.

Briñol, P., & Petty, R. E. (2009). Persuasion: Insights from the self-validation hypothesis. In M. P. Zanna (Ed.), *Advances in experimental social psychology* (Vol. 41, pp. 69–118). New York, NY: Academic Press.

Brown, V. R., & Paulus, P. B. (2002). Making group brainstorming more effective: Recommendations from an associative memory perspective. *Current Directions in Psychological Science, 11*, 208–212.

Brunvand, J. H. (1999). *Too good to be true: The colossal book of urban legends.* New York, NY: Norton.

Bryan, J. H., & Test, M. A. (1967). Models and helping: Naturalistic studies in aiding behavior. *Journal of Personality and Social Psychology, 6*, 400–407.

Burger, J. M., & Petty, R. E. (1981). The low-ball compliance technique: Task or person commitment? *Journal of Personality and Social Psychology, 40*, 492–500.

Buss, D. M., & Kenrick, D. T. (1998). Evolutionary social psychology. In D. T. Gilbert, S. T. Fiske, & G. Lindzey (Eds.), *The handbook of social psychology* (4th ed., Vol. 1, pp. 982–1026). Boston, MA: McGraw-Hill.

Buunk, B. P., Collins, R. L., Taylor, S. E., VanYperen, N. C., & Dakof, G. A. (1990). The affective consequences of social comparison: Either direction has its ups and downs. *Journal of Personality and Social Psychology, 59*, 1238–1249.

Byron, K. C. (2012). Creative reflections on brainstorming. *London Review of Education, 10*, 201–213.

Cacioppo, J. T., Hawkley, L. C., Ernst, J. M., Burleson, M. H., Berntson, G. G., Nouriani, B., & Spiegel, D. (2006). Loneliness within a nomological net: An evolutionary perspective. *Journal of Research in Personality, 40*, 1054–1085.

Cacioppo, J. T., Hawkley, L. C., & Thisted, R. A. (2010). Perceived social isolation makes me sad: Five year cross-lagged analyses of loneliness and depressive symptomatology in the Chicago Health, Aging, and Social Relations Study. *Psychology and Aging, 25*, 453–463.

Cacioppo, J. T., & Patrick, W. (2009). *Loneliness: Human nature and the need for social connection.* New York, NY: Norton.

Calley, W. (1971). William Calley Court-Martial: 1970—Some Refused Orders. Retrieved from http://law.jrank.org/pages/3208/William-Calley-Court-Martial-1970.html

Campbell, M. W., & de Waal, F. B. (2011) Ingroup-outgroup bias in contagious yawning by chimpanzees supports link to empathy. *PLoS One, 6*(4), e18283.

Cantril, H. (1947). *The invasion from Mars.* Princeton, NJ: Princeton University Press.

Cappella, J. N., & Jamieson, K. H. (1997). *Spiral of cynicism: The press and the public good.* Oxford, England: Oxford University Press.

Carlson, M., Marcus-Newhall, A., & Miller, N. (1990). The effects of situational aggression cues: A quantitative review. *Journal of Personality and Social Psychology, 58*, 622–633.

Carnahan, T., & McFarland, S. G. (2007). Revisiting the Stanford Prison Experiment: Could participant self-selection have led to the cruelty? *Personality and Social Psychology Bulletin, 33*, 603–614.

Carpenter, C. D. (2013). A meta-analysis of the effectiveness of the "but you are free" compliance-gaining technique, *Communication Studies, 64*, 6–17.

Choma, B., Hafer, C., Crosby, F., & Foster, M. (2012). Perceptions of personal sex discrimination: The role of belief in a just world and situational ambiguity. *Journal of Social Psychology, 152*, 568–585.

Cialdini, R. B. (2001). *Influence: Science and practice* (4th ed.). Boston. MA: Allyn & Bacon.

Cialdini, R. B., & Goldstein, N. J. (2004). Social influence: Compliance and conformity. *Annual Review of Psychology, 55*, 591–621.

Cialdini, R. B., & Sagarin, B. J. (2005). Interpersonal influence. In T. Brock & M. Green (Eds.), *Persuasion: Psychological insights and perspectives* (pp. 143–169). Newbury Park, CA: Sage Press.

Cialdini, R. B., Vincent, J. E., Lewis, S. K., Catalan, J., Wheeler, D., & Darby, B. L. (1975). Reciprocal concessions procedure for inducing compliance: The door-in-the-face technique. *Journal of Personality and Social Psychology, 31*, 206–215.

Cochrane, C., & Nevitte, N. (2012). Scapegoating: Unemployment, far-right parties and anti-immigrant sentiment. *Comparative European Politics*, awaiting page numbers.

Cohen, D., & Nisbett, R. E. (1994). Self-protection and the culture of honor: Explaining Southern violence. *Personality and Social Psychology Bulletin, 20*, 551–567.

Cohen, D., Nisbett, R. E., Bowdle, B. F., & Schwarz, N. (1996). Insult, aggression, and the southern culture of honor: An experimental ethnography. *Journal of Personality and Social Psychology, 70*, 945–960.

Compton, J. A., & Pfau, M. (2005). Inoculation theory of resistance to influence at maturity: Recent progress in theory development and application and suggestions for future research. *Communication Yearbook, 29*, 97–145.

Conner, M., Sheeran, P., Norman, P., & Armitage, C. J. (2000). Temporal stability as a moderator of relationships in the Theory of Planned Behaviour. *British Journal of Social Psychology, 39*, 469–493.

Cooley, C. H. (1902). *Human nature and the social order.* New York, NY: Scribner.

Cooper, J. (2007). *Cognitive dissonance: Fifty years of a classic theory.* New York, NY: Sage.

Correll, J., Park, B., Judd, C. M., & Wittenbrink, B. (2002). The police officer's dilemma: Using ethnicity to disambiguate potentially threatening individuals. *Journal of Personality and Social Psychology, 83*, 1314–1329.

Cottrell, C. A., & Neuberg, S. L. (2005). Different emotional reactions to different groups: A sociofunctional threat-based approach to "prejudice." *Journal of Personality and Social Psychology, 88*, 770–789.

Crick, N. (1995). Relational aggression: The role of intent attributions, feelings of distress, and provocation type. *Development and Psychopathology, 7*, 313–322.

Cunningham, W. A., Nezlek, J. B., & Banaji, M. R. (2004). Implicit and explicit ethnocentrism: Revisiting the ideologies of prejudice. *Personality and Social Psychology, 30*, 1332–1346.

Dabbs, J. M., Jr., & Dabbs, M. G. (2000) *Heroes, rogues, and lovers: Testosterone and behavior.* New York, NY: McGraw-Hill.

Daftary-Kapur, T., Dumas, R., & Penrod, S. D. (2010). Jury decision-making biases and methods to counter them. *Legal and Criminological Psychology, 15*, 133–154.

Dallek, R. (2003). *An unfinished life: John F. Kennedy, 1917–1963.* Boston, MA: Little, Brown.

Darley, J. M., & Batson, D. (1973). From Jerusalem to Jericho: A study of situational and dispositional variables in helping behavior. *Journal of Personality and Social Psychology, 27*, 100–108.

Darley, J. M., & Latané, B. (1968a). Bystander intervention in emergencies: Diffusion of responsibility. *Journal of Personality and Social Psychology, 8*, 377–383.

Darley, J. M., & Latané, B. (1968b). When will people help in a crisis? *Psychology Today, 2*, 54–57, 70–71.

De Houwer, J., Teige-Mocigemba, S., Spruyt, A., & Moors, A. (2009). Implicit measures: A normative analysis and review. *Psychological Bulletin, 135*, 347–368

Devine, P. G. (1989). Stereotypes and prejudice: Their automatic and controlled components. *Journal of Personality and Social Psychology, 56*, 5–18.

Devine, P. G., Monteith, M. J., Zuwerink, J. R., & Elliot, A. J. (1991). Prejudice with and without compunction. *Journal of Personality and Social Psychology, 60*, 817–830.

de Waal, F. B. M. (1982). *Chimpanzee politics: Power and sex among apes.* Baltimore, MD: Johns Hopkins University Press.

de Waal, F. B. M. (2002). Evolutionary psychology: The wheat and the chaff. *Current Directions in Psychological Science, 11*, 187–191.

de Waal, F. B. M. (2006). *Primates and philosophers: How morality evolved.* S. Macedo & J. Ober (Eds.). Princeton, NJ: Princeton University Press.

DeWall, C. N., & Bushman, B. J. (2009). Hot under the collar in a lukewarm environment: Words associated with hot temperature increase aggressive thoughts and hostile perceptions. *Journal of Experimental Social Psychology, 45*, 1045–1047.

DeWall C. N., MacDonald, G., Webster, G. D., Masten, C. L., Baumeister, R. F., Powell, C.,... Eisenberger, N. I. (2010). Acetaminophen reduces social pain: Behavioral and neural evidence. *Psychological Science, 21*, 1–7

Diehl, M., & Stroebe, W. (1987). Productivity loss in brainstorming groups: Toward the solution of a riddle. *Journal of Personality and Social Psychology, 53*, 497–509.

Dill, J. C., & Anderson, C. A. (1995). Effects of frustration justification on hostile aggression. *Aggressive Behavior, 21*, 359–369.

Dillehay, R. C. (1978). Authoritarianism. In H. London & J. E. Exner (Eds.), *Dimensions of personality* (pp. 85–127). New York, NY: Wiley.

Dipboye, R. L. (1977). Alternative approaches to deindividuation. *Psychological Bulletin, 85*, 1057–1075.

Dockery, T. M., & Bedeian, A. G. (1989). Attitudes versus actions: LaPiere (1934) classic study revisited. *Social Behavior and Personality, 17*, 9–16.

Dolinski, D. (2012). The nature of the first small request as a decisive factor in the effectiveness of the foot-in-the-door technique. *Applied Psychology, 61*, 437–453.

Douglas, K. S., Guy, L. S., & Hart, S. D. (2009). Psychosis as a risk factor for violence to others: A meta-analysis. *Psychological Bulletin, 135*, 679–706.

Dovidio, J., Kawakami, K., Johnson, C., Johnson, B., & Howard, A. (1997). On the nature of prejudice: Automatic and controlled processes. *Journal of Experimental Social Psychology, 33*, 510–540.

Dovidio, J., Piliavin, J., Schroeder, D., & Penner, L. (2006). *The social psychology of prosocial behavior.* Mahwah, NJ: Erlbaum.

Dunbar, R. (1993). Coevolution of neocortical size, group size, and language in humans. *Behavioral and Brain Sciences, 16*, 681–735.

Duncan, B. (1976). Differential social perception and attribution of intergroup violence. *Journal of Personality and Social Psychology, 34*, 590–598.

Dyjas, O., Grasman, R. P. P. P., Wetzels, R., van der Maas, H. L. J., & Wagenmakers, E. J. (2012). What's in a name: A Bayesian hierarchical Analysis of the name-letter effect. *Frontiers in Psychology, 3*, 334.

Eagly, A. H., & Carli, L. L. (1981). Sex of researchers and sex-typed communications as determinants of sex differences in influenceability: A meta-analysis of social influence studies. *Psychological Bulletin, 90*, 1–20.

Eagly, A. H., & Crowley, M. (1986). Gender differences in helping behavior: A meta-analytic review of the social psychological literature. *Psychological Bulletin, 100*, 283–308.

Eagly, A. H., & Steffen, V. J. (1986). Gender and aggressive behavior: A meta-analytic review of the social psychological literature. *Psychological Bulletin, 100*, 309–330.

Eagly, A. H., Wood, W., & Diekman, A. B. (2000). Social role theory of sex differences and similarities: A current appraisal. In T. Eckes & H. M. Trauntner (Eds.), *The developmental social psychology of gender* (pp. 123–174). London, England: Erlbaum.

Eakin, P. J. (2004). What are we reading when we read autobiography? *Narrative, 12*, 121–132.

Earley, P. C. (1989). Social loafing and collectivism: A comparison of the United States and the People's Republic of China. *Administrative Science Quarterly, 34*, 565–581.

Edwards, D. M., Franks, P., Friedgood, D., Lobban, G., & Mackay, H. C. G. (1969). *An experiment on obedience.* Unpublished student report, University of the Witwatersrand, Johannesburg, South Africa.

Egan, L. C., Santos, L. R., & Bloom, P. (2007). The origins of cognitive dissonance: Evidence from children and monkeys. *Psychological Science, 18*, 978–983.

Eisenberger, N. (2012). Broken hearts and broken bones: A neural perspective on the similarities between social and physical pain. *Current Directions in Psychological Science, 21*, 42–47.

Eisenberger, N. I., Lieberman, M. D., & Williams, K. D. (2003). Does rejection hurt? An fMRI study of social exclusion. *Science, 302*, 290–292.

Elms, A., & Milgram, S. (1966). Personality characteristics associated with obedience and defiance toward authoritative commands. *Journal of Experimental Research in Personality, 2*, 292–289.

Espelage, D. L., Mebane, S. E., & Swearer, S. M. (2004). Gender differences in bullying: Moving beyond mean level differences. In D. L. Espelage & S. M. Swearer (Eds.), *Bullying in American Schools: A social-ecological perspective on prevention and intervention* (pp. 15–35). Mahwah, NJ: Erlbaum.

Esser, J. K., & Lindoerfer, J. L. (1989), Groupthink and the Space Shuttle Challenger accident: Toward a quantitative case analysis. *Journal of Behavioral Decision Making, 2*, 167–177.

Fazio, R. H. (1995). Attitudes as object-evaluation associations: Determinants, consequences, and correlates of attitude accessibility. In R. E. Petty & J. A. Krosnick (Eds.), *Attitude strength: Antecedents and consequences* (pp. 247–283). Mahwah, NJ: Erlbaum.

Fazio, R. H., & Olson, M. A. (2003). Implicit measures in social cognition: Their meaning and use. *Annual Review of Psychology, 54*, 297–327.

Federal Bureau of Investigation. (2005). *Crime in the United States.* Washington, DC: Author.

Feeley, T. H., Anker, A. E., & Aloe, A. (2012). The door-in-the-face persuasive message strategy: A meta-analysis of the first 35 years. *Communication Monographs, 79*, 316–343.

Feldman-Summers, S., Montano, D. E., Kasprzyk, D., & Wagner, B. (1980). Influence attempts when competing views are gender-related: Sex as credibility. *Psychology of Women Quarterly, 5*, 311–320.

Ferguson, C. J. (2009) Violent video games: Dogma, fear, and pseudoscience. *Skeptical Inquirer, 33*(5), 38–54.

Ferguson, C. J., & Kilburn, J. (2010). Much ado about nothing: The misestimation and overinterpretation of violent video game effects in Eastern and Western nations: Comment on Anderson et al. (2010). *Psychological Bulletin, 136*, 174–178.

Fernback, J. (2003). Legends on the net: An examination of computer-mediated communication as a locus of oral culture. *New Media & Society, 5*, 29–45.

Festinger, L. (1954). A theory of social comparison processes. *Human Relations, 7*, 117–140.

Festinger, L., & Carlsmith, J. M. (1959). Cognitive consequences of forced compliance. *Journal of Abnormal and Social Psychology, 58*, 202–210.

Festinger, L., Pepitone, A., & Newcomb, T. (1952). Some consequences of deindividuation in a group. *Journal of Abnormal and Social Psychology, 47*, 382–389.

Finch, J. F., & Cialdini, R. B. (1989). Another indirect tactic of (self-)image management: Boosting. *Personality and Social Psychology Bulletin, 15*, 222–232.

Fischer, P., Greitemeyer, T., Pollozek, F., & Frey, D. (2006). The unresponsive bystander: Are bystanders more responsive in dangerous emergencies? *European Journal of Social Psychology, 36*, 267–278.

Fischer, P., Krueger, J. I., Greitemeyer, T., Vogrincic, C., Kastenm, I. A.,... Kainbacher, M. (2011). The bystander-effect: A meta-analytic review on bystander intervention in dangerous and non-dangerous emergencies, *Psychological Bulletin, 137*, 517–537.

Fiske, S. T. (2000). Stereotying, prejudice, and discrimination at the seam between the centuries: Evolution, culture, mind, and brain. *European Journal of Social Psychology, 30*, 299–322.

Fiske, S. T. (2002). What we know about bias and intergroup conflict, problem of the century. *Current Directions in Psychological Science, 11*, 123–128.

Fox, J. A. 2010. Heat wave has chilling effect on violent crime. Boston.com. Retrieved from http://boston.com/community/blogs/crime_punishment/2010/07/heat_wave_has_chilling_effect.html

Freedman, J. L. (2002). *Media violence and its effects on aggression: Assessing the scientific evidence.* Toronto, Ontario, Canada: University of Toronto Press.

Freedman, J. L., & Fraser, S. C. (1966). Compliance without pressure: The foot-in-the-door technique. *Journal of Personality and Social Psychology, 4*, 195–203.

Friedkin, N. E. (2010). The attitude-behavior linkage in behavioral cascades. *Social Psychology Quarterly, 73*, 196–213.

Frieze, I. H., Peterson, J. E., Johnson, P. B., Ruble, D. N., & Zellman, G. (1978). *Women and sex roles: A social psychological perspective*. New York, NY: Norton.

Gailliot, M. T., Peruche, B. M., Plant., E. A., & Baumeister, R. F. (2009). Stereotypes and prejudice in the blood: Sucrose drinks reduce prejudice and stereotyping. *Journal of Experimental Social Psychology, 45*, 288–290.

Galanter, M. (1980). Psychological induction into the large group: Findings from a modern religious sect. *American Journal of Psychiatry, 137*, 1574–1579.

Gallup A. C. (2011). Why do we yawn? Primitive versus derived features. *Neuroscience and Biobehavioral Reviews, 35*, 765–769.

Gamble, J. L., & Hess, J. J. (2012). Temperature and violent crime in Dallas, Texas: Relationships and implications of climate change. *Western Journal of Emergency Medicine, 13*, 239–246.

Gangestad, S. W., & Snyder, M. (2000). Self-monitoring: Appraisal and reappraisal. *Psychological Bulletin, 126*, 530–555.

Garcia, S. M., Weaver, K., Moskowitz, G. B., & Darley, J. M. (2002). Crowded minds: The implicit bystander effect. *Journal of Personality and Social Psychology, 83*, 843–853.

Gawronski, B., LeBel, E. P., & Peters, K. R. (2007). What do implicit measures tell us? Scrutinizing the validity of three common assumptions. *Perspectives on Psychological Science, 2*, 181–193.

Geen, R. G. (2001). *Human aggression* (2nd ed.). New York, NY: Taylor & Francis.

Gentile, D. A., & Anderson, C. A. (2003). Violent video games: The newest media violence hazard. In D. A. Gentile (Ed.), *Media violence and children* (pp. 131–152). Westport, CT: Praeger.

Gergen, K. J. (1973). Social psychology as history. *Journal of Personality and Social Psychology, 26*, 309–320.

Giancola, P. R., & Corman, M. D. (2007). Alcohol and aggression: A test of the attention-allocation model. *Psychological Science, 18*, 649–655.

Gilbert, D. T., & Malone, P. S. (1995). The correspondence bias. *Psychological Bulletin, 117*, 21–38.

Gintis, H., Bowles, S., Boyd, R., & Fehr, E. (2003). Explaining altruistic behavior in humans. *Evolution and Human Behavior, 24*, 153–172.

Glickman, S. E., Frank, L. G., Davidson, J. M., Smith, E. R., & Siiteri, P. K. (1987). Androstenedione may organize or activate sex-reversed traits in female spotted hyenas. *Proceedings of the National Academy of Sciences, 84*, 3444–3447.

Goethals, G. R., & Reckman, R. F. (1973). The perception of consistency in attitudes. *Journal of Experimental Social Psychology, 9*, 491–501.

Goffman, E. (1959). *The presentation of self in everyday life*. London, England: Penguin.

Goldin, C., & Rouse, C. (2000). Orchestrating impartiality. *American Economic Review, 90*, 715–741.

Goldstein, D. G., & Gigerenzer, G. (2011). Models of ecological rationality: The recognition heuristic. In G. Gigerenzer, R. Hertwig, & T. Pachur (Eds.), *Heuristics: The foundations of adaptive behavior* (pp. 60–81). New York, NY: Oxford University Press.

Goodall, J. (1990). *Through a window*. Boston, MA: Houghton Mifflin.

Gorassini, D., & Olson, J. (1995). Does self-perception change explain the foot-in-the-door effect? *Journal of Personality and Social Psychology, 69*, 91–105.

Gordon, H. (2002). The suicide bomber: Is it a psychiatric phenomenon? *Psychiatric Bulletin, 26*, 285–287.

Gorsuch, R. L. (1988). Psychology of religion. *Annual Review of Psychology, 39*, 201–221.

Grassian, S. (2006). Psychiatric effects of solitary confinement. *Washington University Journal of Law & Policy, 22*, 325.

Greenberg, J., & Jonas, E. (2003). Psychological motives and political orientation: The left, the right, and the rigid: Comment on Jost et al. (2003). *Psychological Bulletin, 129*, 376–382.

Greenwald, A. G., & Nosek, B. A. (2001). Health of the Implicit Association Test at age 3. *Zeitschrift für Experimentelle Psychologie, 48*, 85–93.

Greenwald, A. G., McGhee, D. E., & Schwartz, J. L. K. (1998). Measuring individual differences in implicit cognition: The implicit association test. *Journal of Personality and Social Psychology, 74*, 1464–1480.

Guéguen, N., & Pascual, A. (2000). Evocation of freedom and compliance: The "but you are free of" technique. *Current Research in Social Psychology, 5*, 264–270.

Guéguen, N., Pascual, A., & Dagot, L. (2002). The low-ball technique: An application in a field setting, *Psychological Reports, 91*, 81–84.

Guggisberg, A. G., Mathis, J., Schnider, A., & Hess, C. W. (2010). Why do we yawn? *Neuroscience and Biobehavioral Reviews, 34*, 1267–1276.

Gvion, Y., & Apter, A. (2011). Aggression, impulsivity, and suicide behavior: A review of the literature. *Archives of Suicide Research, 15*, 93–112.

Hackney, A. (2005). Teaching students about stereotypes, prejudice, and discrimination: An interview with Susan Fiske. *Teaching of Psychology, 32*, 196–199.

Hafer, C. L., & Begue, L. (2005). Experimental research on just-world theory: Problems, developments, and future challenges. *Psychological Bulletin, 131*, 128–167.

Haker, H., & Rössler, W. (2009). Empathy in schizophrenia: Impaired resonance. *European Archives of Psychiatry and Clinical Neuroscience, 259*, 352–361.

Hamilton, D. L., & Rose, T. L. (1980). Illusory correlation and the maintenance of stereotypic beliefs. *Journal of Personality and Social Psychology, 39*, 832–845.

Haney, C., Banks, W. C., & Zimbardo, P. G. (1973). Interpersonal dynamics in a simulated prison. *International Journal of Criminology & Penology, 1*, 69–97.

Haney, C., & Zimbardo, P. G. (2009). Persistent dispositionalism ininteractionist clothing: Fundamental attribution error in explaining prison abuse. *Personality and Social Psychology Bulletin, 25*, 807–814.

Hardy, C., & Latane, B. (1986). Social loafing on a cheering task. *Social Science, 71*, 165–172.

Hardy, K. R. (1957). Determinants of conformity and attitude change. *Journal of Abnormal and Social Psychology, 4*, 289–294.

Hare, B., & Woods, V. (2013). *The genius of dogs: How dogs are smarter than you think*. New York, NY: Dutton Adult.

Harmon-Jones, E., & Mills, J. (Eds.). (1999). *Cognitive dissonance: Progress on a pivotal theory in social psychology*. Washington, DC: American Psychological Association.

Hartley, E. (1946). *Problems in prejudice*. New York, NY: King's Crown Press.

Hartmann, W. K. (1992). *Astronomy: The cosmic journey*. Belmont, CA: Wadsworth.

Hawkley, L. C., & Cacioppo, J. T. (2010). Loneliness matters: A theoretical and empirical review of consequences and mechanisms. *Annals of Behavioral Medicine, 40*, 218–227.

Heath, C., & Heath, D. (2007). *Made to stick: Why some ideas survive and others die*. New York, NY: Random House.

Heath, C. B., Bell, C., & Sternberg, E. (2001). Emotional selection in memes: The case of urban legends. *Journal of Personality and Social Psychology, 81*, 1028–1041.

Heesacker, M., Petty, R. E., & Cacioppo, J. T. (1983). Field dependence and attitude change: Source credibility can alter persuasion by affecting message-relevant thinking. *Journal of Personality, 51*, 653–666.

Helt M. S., Eigsti I. M., Snyder P. J., & Fein, D. A. (2010). Contagious yawning in autistic and typical development. *Child Development, 81*, 1620–1631.

Hemsley, G. D., & Doob, A. N. (1978). The effect of looking behavior on perceptions of a communicator's credibility. *Journal of Applied Social Psychology, 8*, 136–144.

Henderson, R. W. (1985). Fearful memories: The motivational significance of forgetting. In F. R. Brush & J. B. Overmier (Eds.), *Affect, conditioning, and cognition: Essays on the determinants of behavior* (pp. 43–53). Hillsdale, NJ: Erlbaum.

Hewstone, M. (1990). The "ultimate attribution error"? A review of the literature on intergroup causal attribution. *European Journal of Social Psychology, 20*, 311–335.

Hirsch, J. B., Galinsky, A. D., & Zhong, C.-B. (2011). Drunk, powerful, and in the dark: How general processes of disinhibition produce both prosocial and antisocial behavior. *Perspectives on Psychological Science, 6*, 415–427.

Hoffman, M. L. (1981). Is altruism part of human nature? *Journal of Personality and Social Psychology, 40*, 121–137.

Hovland, C. I., Janis, I. L., & Kelley, H. H. (1953). *Communication and persuasion: Psychological studies of opinion change*. New Haven, CT: Yale University Press.

Huston, T. L., Ruggiero, M., Conner, R., & Geis, G. (1981). Bystander intervention into crime: A study based on naturally-occurring episodes. *Social Psychology Quarterly, 44*, 14–23.

Isen, A. M., Clark, M., & Schwartz, M. F. (1976). Duration of the effect of good mood on helping: Footprints in the sand of time. *Journal of Personality & Social Psychology, 34*, 385–393.

Isenberg, D. J. (1986). Group polarization: A critical review and meta-analysis. *Journal of Personality and Social Psychology, 50*, 1141–1151.

Issazadegan, A. (2012). Religiosity orientations and personality traits with death obsession. *International Journal of Psychological Studies, 4*, 150–157.

Jackson, J. W. (1993) Realistic group conflict theory: A review and evaluation of the theoretical and empirical literature. *Psychological Record, 43*, 395–414.

Janis, I. L. (1972). *Victims of groupthink*. Boston, MA: Houghton Mifflin.

Javornisky, G. (1979). Task content and sex differences in conformity. *Journal of Psychology, 108*, 213–220.

Johnson, R. D., & Downing, L. L. (1979). Deindividuation and valence of cues: Effects on prosocial and anti-social behavior. *Journal of Personality and Social Psychology, 37*, 1532–1538.

Jones, E. E., & Harris, V. A. (1967). The attribution of attitudes. *Journal of Experimental Social Psychology, 3*, 1–24.

Jones, E. E., & Nisbett, R. E. (1972). The actor and the observer: Divergent perceptions of the causes of the behavior. In E. E. Jones, D. E. Kanouse, H. H. Kelley, R. E. Nisbett, S. Valins, & B. Weiner (Eds.), *Attribution: Perceiving the causes of behavior* (pp. 79–94). Morristown, NJ: General Learning Press.

Jost, J. T., & Amodio, D. M. (2012). Political ideology as motivated social cognition: Behavioral and neuroscientific evidence. *Motivation and Emotion, 36*, 55–64.

Jost, J. T., Glaser, J., Kruglanski, A. W., & Sulloway, F., (2003). Political conservatism as motivated social cognition. *Psychological Bulletin, 129*, 339–375.

Karau, S. J., & Williams, K. D. (1995). Social loafing—Research findings, implications, and future directions. *Current Directions in Psychological Science, 4*, 134–140.

Kato, Y., Kato, S., & Akahori, K. (2007). Effects of emotional cues transmitted in e-mail communication on the emotions experienced by senders and receivers. *Computers in Human Behavior, 23*, 1894–1905.

Katzev, R., & Brownstein, R. (1989). The influence of enlightenment on compliance. *Journal of Social Psychology, 129*, 335–347.

Kaufman, S. B. (2011). Does the Implicit Association Test (IAT) really measure racial prejudice? Probably not. *Psychology Today Blog*. Retrieved from http://www.psychologytoday.com/blog/beautiful-minds/201101/does-the-implicit-association-test-iat-really-measure-racial-prejudice-p

Kelley, H. H. (1973). Processes of causal attribution. *American Psychologist, 28*, 107–128.

Kelly, T. H., Cherek, D. R., Steinberg, J. L., & Robinson, D. (1988). Effects of provocation and alcohol on human aggressive behavior. *Drug and Alcohol Dependence, 21*, 105–112.

Kiesler, C. A., & Kiesler, S. B. (1969). *Conformity*. Menlo Park, CA: Addison-Wesley.

Kilham, W., & Mann, L. (1974). Level of destructive obedience as a function of transmitter and executant roles in the Milgram obedience paradigm. *Journal of Personality and Social Psychology, 29*, 696–702.

Kim, H., & Markus, H. R. (1999). Deviance or uniqueness, harmony or conformity? A cultural analysis. *Journal of Personality and Social Psychology, 77*, 785–800.

Kohlberg, L. (1965, March 26). *Relationships between the development of moral judgment and moral conduct*. Paper presented at the Annual Meeting of the Society for Research in Child Development, Minneapolis, MN.

Kraus, S. J. (1995). Attitudes and the prediction of behaviour: A meta-analysis of the empirical literature. *Personality and Social Psychology Bulletin, 21*, 58–75.

Krueger, R. F., Hicks, B. M., & McGue, M. (2001). Altruism and antisocial behavior: Independent tendencies, unique personality correlates, distinct etiologies. *Psychological Science, 12*, 397–402.

Krueger, R. F., Schmutte, P. S., Caspi, A., Moffitt, T. E., Campbell, K., & Silva P. A. (1994). Personality traits are linked to crime among men and women: Evidence from a birth cohort. *Journal of Abnormal Psychology, 103*, 328–338.

Kruglanski, A. W., & Mayseless, O. (1990). Classic and current social comparison research: Expanding the perspective. *Psychological Bulletin, 108*, 195–208.

Lalich, J. (2004). *Bounded choice: True believers and charismatic cults*. Berkeley, CA: University of California Press.

LaPiere, R. T. (1934). Attitudes vs. action. *Social Forces, 13*, 230–237.

Larsen, K. S., Ashlock, J., Carroll, C., Foote, S., Feeler, J., Keller, E.,... Watkins, D. (1974). Laboratory aggression where the victim is a small dog. *Social Behavior and Personality, 2*, 174–176.

Latané, B., & Darley, J. M. (1970). *The unresponsive bystander: Why doesn't he help?* New York, NY: Appleton-Century-Crofts.

Latané, B., & Nida, S. (1981). Ten years of research on group size and helping. *Psychological Bulletin, 89*, 308–324.

Latané, B., & Rodin, J. (1969). A lady in distress: Inhibiting effects of friends and strangers on bystander intervention. *Journal of Experimental Social Psychology, 5*, 189–302.

Latané, B., Williams, K., & Harkins, S. (1979). Many hands make light the work: The causes and consequences of social loafing. *Journal of Personality and Social Psychology, 37*, 822–832.

Le Bon, G. (1895). *Psychology of the crowd*. New York, NY: Viking Press.

Lerner, M. J. (1980). *The belief in a just world: A fundamental delusion*. New York, NY: Plenum Press.

Levitin, D. J. (2013, February 8). What you might be missing. *Wall Street Journal*. Retrieved from http://online.wsj.com/article/SB10001424127887323829504578272241035441214.html

Lewandowski, S., Ecker, U. K., Seifert, C., Schwarz, N., & Cook, J. (2012). Misinformation and its correction: Continued influence and successful debiasing. *Psychological Science in the Public Interest, 13*, 106–131.

Lewin, K. (1951). *Field theory in social science: Selected theoretical papers*. D. Cartwright (Ed.). New York, NY: Harper.

Longley, J., & Pruitt, D. G. (1980). Groupthink: A critique of Janis's theory. In L. Wheeler (Ed.), *Review of personality and social psychology* (Vol. I, pp. 74–93). Beverly Hills, CA: Sage.

Maas, J., & Toivanen, K. (1978). *Candid Camera* and the behavioral sciences. *Teaching of Psychology, 5*, 226–228.

Maccoby, E. E., & Jacklin, C. N. (1980). Sex differences in aggression: A rejoinder. *Child Development, 51*, 964–980.

Malle, B. F. (2006). The actor-observer asymmetry in attribution: A (surprising) meta-analysis. *Psychological Bulletin, 132*, 895–919.

Manning, R., Levine, M., & Collins, A. (2007). The Kitty Genovese murder and the social psychology of helping: The parable of the 38 witnesses. *American Psychologist, 62*, 555–562.

Mantell, D. M. (1971). The potential for violence in Germany. *Journal of Social Issues, 27*, 101–112.

Marino, L. (2005). Big brains matter in novel environments. *Proceedings of the National Academy of Sciences, 102*, 5306–5307.

Mason, M. F., & Morris, M.W. (2010). Culture, attribution and automaticity: A social cognitive neuroscience view. *Social Cognitive and Affective Neuroscience, 5*, 292–306.

McCullough, M. E., Tsang, J., & Brion, S. (2003). Personality traits in adolescence as predictors of religiousness in early adulthood: Findings from the Terman longitudinal study. *Personality and Social Psychology Bulletin, 29*, 980–991.

McGuire, W. J. (1964). Inducing resistance to persuasion: Some contemporary approaches. In L. Berkowitz (Ed.), *Advances in experimental social psychology* (Vol. 1, pp. 191–229). San Diego, CA: Academic Press.

McGuire, W. J., & Papageorgis, D. (1961). The relative efficacy of various types of prior belief-defense in producing immunity against persuasion. *Journal of Abnormal and Social Psychology, 62*, 327–337.

Melton, G. J. (1999). *Brainwashing and the cults: The rise and fall of a theory*. Retrieved from http://www.cesnur.org/testi/melton.htm

Michaels, J. W., Blommel, J. W., Brocato, R. M., Linkous, R. A., & Rowe, J. S. (1982). Social facilitation and inhibition in a natural setting. *Replications in Social Psychology, 2*, 21–24.

Milgram, S. (1974). *Obedience to authority: An experimental view*. New York, NY: Harper & Row.

Miller, F. G., & Rowold, K. L. (1979). Halloween masks and deindividuation. *Psychological Reports, 44*, 422.

Mineka, S. (1992). Evolutionary memories, emotional processing, and the emotional disorders. In D. Medin (Ed.), *The psychology of learning and motivation* (Vol. 28, pp. 161–206). San Diego, CA: Academic.

Miranda, F. S. B., Caballero, R. B., Gomez, M. N. G., & Zamorano, M. A. M. (1981). Obediencia a la authoridad [Obedience to authority]. *Psiquis, 2*, 212–221.

Mitchell, J. P., Macrae, C. N., & Banaji, M. R. (2006). Dissociable medial prefrontal contributions to judgments of similar and dissimilar others. *Neuron, 50*, 655–663.

Monahan, J. (1984). The prediction of violent behavior: Toward a second generation of theory and policy. *American Psychologist, 141*, 10–15.

Monteith, M., & Winters, J. (2002). Why we hate. *Psychology Today, 35*(3), 44–52.

Moor, P. J., Heuvelman, A., & Verleur, R. (2010). Flaming on YouTube. *Computers in Human Behavior, 26*, 1536–1546.

Morris, M. W., & Peng, K. (1994). Culture and cause: American and Chinese attributions for social and physical events. *Journal of Personality and Social Psychology, 67*, 949–971.

Murray, A. A., Wood, J. M., & Lilienfeld, S. O. (2012). Psychopathic personality traits and cognitive dissonance: Individual differences in attitude change. *Journal of Research in Personality, 46*, 525–536.

Myers, D. G. (1993a). *Social psychology*. New York, NY: McGraw-Hill.

Myers, D. G., & Bishop, G. D. (1970). Discussion effects on racial attitudes. *Science, 169*, 778–789.

Myers, D. G., & Kaplan, M. F. (1976). Group-induced polarization in simulated juries. *Personality and Social Psychology Bulletin, 2*, 63–66.

Myers, D. G., & Lamm, H. (1976). The group polarization phenomenon. *Psychological Bulletin, 83*, 602–627.

Nisbett, R. E. (2003). *The geography of thought: How Asians and Westerners think differently... and why*. New York, NY: Free Press.

Nisbett, R. E., & Cohen, D. (1996). *Culture of honor: The psychology of violence in the South*. Boulder, CO: Westview.

Noel, J. G., Wann, D. L., & Branscombe, N. R. (1995). Peripheral ingroup membership status and public negativity toward outgroups. *Journal of Personality and Social Psychology, 68*, 127–137.

North, A. C., Linley, P. A., & Hargreaves, D. J. (2000). Social loafing in a co-operative classroom task. *Educational Psychology, 20*, 389–392.

Nuttin, J. M. (1985). Narcissism beyond Gestalt and awareness: The name letter effect. *European Journal of Social Psychology, 15*, 353–361.

Ochsner, K. N., Bunge, S. A., Gross, J. J., & Gabieli, J. D. E. (2002). Rethinking feelings: An fMRI study of the cognitive regulation of emotion. *Journal of Cognitive Neuroscience, 14*, 1215–1229.

Ohlert, J., & Kleinert, J. (2012). Social loafing during preparation for performance situations. *Social Psychology, 11*, 1–7.

O'Keefe, D. J., & Figge, M. (1997). A guilt-based explanation of the door-in-the-face influence strategy. *Human Communication Research, 24*, 64–81.

O'Keefe, D. J., & Hale, S. L. (2001). An odds-ratio-based meta-analysis of research on the door-in-the-face influence strategy. *Communication Reports, 14*, 31–38.

Olsson, A., Ebert, J. P., Banaji, M. R., & Phelps, E. A. (2005). The role of social groups in the persistence of learned fear. *Science, 309*, 785–787.

Olweus, D. (1993). *Bullying at school: What we know and what we can do*. Oxford, England: Blackwell.

Osborn, A. F. (1957). Applied imagination: Principles and procedures of creative problem solving (Rev. ed.). New York, NY: Scribner.

Oxley, D. R., Smith, K. B., Alford, J. R., Hibbing, M. V., Miller, J. L., Scalora, M.,... Hibbing, J. R. (2008). Political attitudes vary with physiological traits. *Science, 321*, 1667–1670.

Oyserman, D., Coon, H. M., & Kemmelmeier, M. (2002). Rethinking individualism and collectivism: Evaluation of theoretical assumptions and meta-analyses. *Psychological Bulletin, 128*, 3–72.

Park, B., & Rothbart, M. (1982). Perception of out-group homogeneity and levels of social categorization: Memory for the subordinate attributes of in-group and out-group members. *Journal of Personality and Social Psychology, 42*, 1051–1068.

Pascual, A., & Guéguen, N. (2005). Foot-in-the-door and door-in-the-face: A comparative meta-analytic study. *Psychological Reports, 96*, 122–128.

Paulus, P. B., Larey, T. S., & Ortega, A. H. (1995). Performance and perceptions of brainstormers in an organizational setting. *Basic and Applied Social Psychology, 17*, 249–265.

Paulus, T. M. (2004). Collaboration or cooperation? Small group interactions in a synchronous educational environment. In T. S. Roberts (Ed.), *Computer-supported collaborative learning in higher education* (pp. 100–124). Hershey, PA: Idea Group.

Pelham, B. W., Carvallo, M., & Jones, J. T. (2005). Implicit egotism. *Current Directions in Psychological Science, 14*, 106–110.

Pelham, B. W., Mirenberg, M. C., & Jones, J. T. (2002). Why Susie sells seashells by the seashore: Implicit egotism and major life decisions. *Journal of Personality and Social Psychology, 82*, 469–487.

Penner, L. A., Dovidio, J. F., Schroeder, D. A., & Piliavin, J. A. (2005). Prosocial behavior: Multilevel perspectives. *Annual Review of Psychology, 56*, 365–392.

Pettigrew, T. F. (1958). Personality and sociocultural factors in intergroup attitudes: A cross-national comparison. *Journal of Conflict Resolution, 2*, 29–42.

Pettigrew, T. F. (1979). The ultimate attribution error: Extending Allport's cognitive analysis of prejudice. *Personality and Social Psychology Bulletin, 5*, 461–476.

Pettigrew, T. F. (1998). Intergroup contact theory. *Annual Review of Psychology, 49*, 65–85.

Pettigrew, T. F., & Tropp, L. R. (2008) How does intergroup contact reduce prejudice? Meta-analytic tests of three mediators. *European Journal of Social Psychology, 38*, 922–934.

Petty, R. E., & Cacioppo, J. T. (1986). *Communication and persuasion: Central and peripheral routes to attitude change.* New York, NY: Springer Verlag.

Petty, R. E., & Wegener, D. T. (1999). The elaboration likelihood model: Current status and controversies. Dual-process theories in social psychology. In S. Chaiken & Y. Trope (Eds.), *Dual-process theories in social psychology* (pp. 37–72). New York, NY: Guilford Press.

Piliavin, I. M., Rodin, J., & Piliavin, J. A. (1969). Good samaritanism: An underground phenomenon? *Journal of Personality and Social Psychology, 13*, 289–299.

Pinker, S. (2011). *The better angels of our nature: Why violence has declined.* New York, NY: Viking Press, 15–17.

Platek, S. M., Critton, S. R., Myers, T. E., & Gallup, G. G. (2003). Contagious yawning: The role of self-awareness and mental state attribution. *Cognitive Brain Research, 17*, 223–227.

Platek, S. M., Mohamed, F. B., & Gallup, G. G. (2005). Contagious yawning and the brain. *Cognitive Brain Research, 23*, 448–452.

Pontón, M. O., & Gorsuch, R. L. (1988). Prejudice and religion revisited: A cross-cultural investigation with a Venezuelan sample. *Journal for the Scientific Study of Religion, 27*, 260–271.

Pornpitakpan, C. (2004). The persuasiveness of source credibility: A critical review of five decades' evidence. *Journal of Applied Social Psychology, 34*, 243–281.

Postmes, T., & Spears, R. (1998). Deindividuation and antinormative behavior: A meta-analysis. *Psychological Bulletin, 123*, 238–259.

Pratkanis, A. R. (1995, July/August). How to sell a pseudoscience. *Skeptical Inquirer, 19*, 19–25.

Pronin, E. (2008). How we see ourselves and how we see others. *Science, 320*, 1177–1180.

Pronin, E., Berger, J., & Molouki, S. (2007). Alone in a crowd of sheep: Asymmetric perceptions of conformity and their roots in an introspective illusion. *Journal of Personality and Social Psychology, 92*, 585–595.

Provine, R. R. (2005). Yawning. *American Scientist, 93*, 532–539.

Putman, V. L., & Paulus, P. B. (2009). Brainstorming, brainstorming rules, and decision making. *Journal of Creative Behavior, 42*, 23–29.

Redding, R. E. (2004). Bias or prejudice? The politics of research on racial prejudice. *Psychological Inquiry, 15*, 289–293.

Regan, D. T., & Totten, J. (1975). Empathy and attribution: Turning observers into actors. *Journal of Personality and Social Psychology, 32*, 850–856.

Reicher, S. D., & Haslam, S. A. (2006). Rethinking the social psychology of tyranny: The BBC Prison Study. *British Journal of Social Psychology, 45*, 1–40.

Reicher, S. D., Haslam, A., & Smith, J. (2012). Working toward the experimenter: Reconceptualizing obedience within the Milgram paradigm as identification-based followership. *Perspectives on Psychological Science, 7*, 315–324.

Rogers, R. W., & Prentice-Dunn, S. (1981). Deindividuation and anger-mediated interracial aggression: Unmasking regressive racism. *Journal of Personality and Social Psychology, 41*, 63–73.

Rosnow, R. L. (1980). Psychology of rumor reconsidered. *Psychological Bulletin, 87*, 578–591.

Ross, L., Amabile, T. M., & Steinmetz, J. L. (1977). Social roles, social control and biases in social perception. *Journal of Personality and Social Psychology, 35*, 485–494.

Rushton, J. P., & Campbell, A. C. (1977). Modelling, vicarious reinforcement, and extraversion on blood donating in adults: Immediate and long term effects. *European Journal of Social Psychology, 7*, 297–306.

Ryan, R. (1976). *Blaming the victim.* New York, NY: Vintage Books.

Sabini, J., & Silver, M. (1983). Dispositional vs. situational interpretations of Milgram obedience experiments: The fundamental attributional error. *Journal for the Theory of Social Behavior, 13*, 147–154.

Sageman, M. (2004). *Understanding terror networks.* Philadelphia, PA: University of Pennsylvania Press.

Saletan, W. (2004, May 12). The Stanford Prison Experiment doesn't explain Abu Ghraib. *Slate.* Retrieved from http://slate.msn.com/id/2100419

Sapolsky, R. M. (1998). Molecular neurobiology: The stress of Gulf War syndrome. *Nature, 393*, 308–309.

Schacter, S. (1959). *The psychology of affiliation: Experimental studies of the sources of gregariousness.* Stanford, CA: Stanford University Press.

Schaller, M., Boyd, C., Yohannes, J., & O'Brien. (1995). The prejudiced personality revisited: Personal need for structure and formation of erroneous group stereotypes. *Journal of Personality and Social Psychology, 68*, 544–555.

Schuman, H., Steeh, C., Bobo, L., & Krysan, M. (1997). *Racial attitudes in America: Trends and interpretations* (Rev. ed.). Cambridge, MA: Harvard University Press.

Schwenk, C. R. (1989). A meta-analysis on the comparative effectiveness of devil's advocacy and dialectical inquiry. *Strategic Management Journal, 10*, 303–306.

Shanab, M. E., & Yahya, K. A. (1977). A behavioral study of obedience in children. *Journal of Personality and Social Psychology, 35*, 530–536.

Sherif, M. (1936). *The psychology of social norms.* New York, NY: Harper.

Sherif, M., Harvey, O. J., White, B. J., Hood, W. R., & Sherif, C. W. (1961). *The Robbers Cave experiment: Intergroup conflict and cooperation.* Middletown, CT: Wesleyan University Press.

Shrauger, J. S., & Schoeneman, T. J. (1979). Symbolic interactionist view of self-concept: Through the looking glass darkly. *Psychological Bulletin, 86*, 549–573.

Singer, M. (1979, January). Coming out of the cults. *Psychology Today*, 72–82.

Slater, L. (2004). *Opening Skinner's box: Great psychological experiments of the 20th century.* New York, NY: Norton.

Slavin, R. E., & Cooper, R. (1999). Improving intergroup relations: Lessons learned from cooperative learning programs. *Journal of Social Issues, 55*, 647–663.

Smith, S. J., Axelton, A. M., & Saucier, D. A. (2009). The effects of contact on sexual prejudice: A meta-analysis. *Sex Roles, 61*, 178–191.

Snyder, M. (1974). Self monitoring of expressive behavior. *Journal of Personality and Social Psychology, 30*, 526–537.

Sommers, S. R. (2006). On racial diversity and group decision-making: Identifying multiple effects of racial composition on jury deliberations. *Journal of Personality and Social Psychology, 90*, 597–612.

Stasser, G., & Titus, W. (2003). Hidden profiles: A brief history. *Psychological Inquiry, 14*, 304–313.

Stephan, W. G. (1978). School desegregation: An evaluation of predictions made in *Brown v. Board of Education. Psychological Bulletin, 85*, 217–238.

Stewart, T. L., LaDuke, J. R., Bracht, C., Sweet, B. A. M., & Gamarel, K. E. (2003). Do the "eyes" have it? A program evaluation of Jane Elliott's "Blue-Eyes/Brown-Eyes" diversity training exercise. *Journal of Applied Social Psychology, 33*, 1898–1921.

Storch, E., Bagner, D., Geffken, G., & Baumeister, A. (2004). Association between overt and relational aggression and psychosocial adjustment in undergraduate college students. *Violence and Victims, 19*, 689–700.

Sue, D. W., Capodilupo, C. M., Torino, G. C., Bucceri, J. M., Holder, A. M. B., Nadal, K. L., & Esquilin, M. (2007). Racial microaggressions in everyday life: Implications for clinical practice. *American Psychologist, 62*, 271–286.

Suls, J., Martin, R., & Wheeler, L. (2002). Social comparison: Why, with whom and with what effect? *Current Directions in Psychological Science, 11*, 159–163.

Sunstein, C. R. (2002). *Republic.com.* Princeton, NJ: Princeton University Press.

Sunstein, C. R. (2009). On rumors: How falsehoods spread, why we believe them, and what can be done. New York, NY: Farrar, Straus and Giroux.

Surowiecki, J. (2004). Mass intelligence. *Forbes, 173*(11), 48.

Swim, J. K. (1994). Perceived versus meta-analytic effect sizes: An assessment of the accuracy of gender stereotypes. *Journal of Personality and Social Psychology, 66*, 21–36.

Tajfel, H. (1982). *Social identity and intergroup relations.* Cambridge, England: Cambridge University Press.

Tajfelt, H., Billig, M., Bundy, R., & Flament, C. L. (1971). Social categorization and intergroup behavior. *European Journal of Social Psychology, 1*, 149–177.

Taylor, S. P. (1993). Experimental investigation of alcohol-induced aggression in humans. *Alcohol Health and Research World, 17*, 108–112.

Tedeschi, J. T., Schlenker, B. R., & Bonoma, T. V. (1971). Cognitive dissonance: Private ratiocination or public spectacle? *American Psychologist, 26*, 680–695.

Triplett, N. (1897). The dynamogenic factors in pacemaking and competition. *American Journal of Psychology, 9*, 507–533.

Twenge, J. M., Catanese, K. R., & Baumeister, R. F. (2002). Social exclusion causes self-defeating behavior. *Journal of Personality and Social Psychology, 83*, 606–615.

Tybur, J. M., & Griskevicius, V. (2013). Evolutionary psychology: A fresh perspective for understanding and changing problematic behavior. *Public Administration Review, 73*, 12–22.

Tyson, G. A. (1987). *Introduction to psychology.* Johannesburg, South Africa: Westro Educational Books.

Van Bavel, J. J., Packer, D. J., & Cunningham, W. A. (2008). The neural subtrates of in-group bias: A function magnetic resonance imaging investigation. *Psychological Science, 19*, 1131–1139.

Vandello, J. A., Cohen, D., & Ransom, S. (2008). U.S. southern and northern differences in perceptions of norms about aggression: Mechanisms for the perpetuation of a culture of honor. *Journal of Cross-Cultural Psychology, 39*, 162–177.

Vanman, E. J., Paul, B. Y., Ito, T. A., & Miller, N. (1997). The modern face of prejudice and structural features that moderate the effect of cooperation on affect. *Journal of Personality and Social Psychology, 73*, 941–959.

Vanman, E. J., Saltz, J. L., Nathan, L. R., & Warren, J. A. (2004). Racial discrimination by low-prejudiced whites: Facial movements as implicit measures of attitudes related to behavior. *Psychological Science, 15*, 711–714.

Wardell, D. (1999). Children in difficulty: A guide to understanding and helping. *Contemporary Psychology, 44*, 514–515.

Watson, R. I. (1973). Investigation into deindividuation using a cross-cultural survey technique. *Journal of Personality and Social Psychology, 25*, 342–345.

Weaver, K., Garcia, S. M., Schwarz, N., & Miller, D. T. (2007). Inferring the popularity of an opinion from its familiarity: A repetitive voice can sound like a chorus. *Journal of Personality and Social Psychology, 92*, 821–833.

Whitley, B. E., & Lee, S. E. (2000). The relationship of authoritarianism and related constructs to attitudes towards homosexuality. *Journal of Applied Social Psychology, 30*, 144–170.

Wicker, A. W. (1969). Attitudes versus actions: The relationship of verbal and overt behavioral responses to attitude objects. *Journal of Social Issues, 25*, 41–78.

Wilkowski, B., Hartung, C., Crowe, S., & Chai, C. (2012). Men don't just get mad; they get even: Revenge but not anger mediates gender differences in physical aggression. *Journal of Research in Personality, 46*, 546–555.

Williams, K., Harkins, S. G., & Latané, B. (1981). Identifiability as a deterrent to social loafing: Two cheering experiments. *Journal of Personality and Social Psychology, 40*, 303–311.

Wilson, J. Q. (1993). *The moral sense.* New York, NY: Free Press.

Wood, W. (2000). Attitude change: Persuasion and social influence. *Annual Review of Psychology, 51*, 539–570.

Word, C. O., Zanna, M. P., & Cooper, J. (1974). Nonverbal mediation of self-fulfilling prophecies in interracial interaction. *Journal of Experimental Social Psychology, 10*, 109–120.

Zajonc, R. B. (1965). Social facilitation. *Science, 149*, 169–274.

Zajonc, R. B., Heingartner, A., & Herman, E. M. (1969). Social enhancement and impairment of performance in the cockroach. *Journal of Personality and Social Psychology, 13*, 83–92.

Zhang, A. Y., & Snowden, L. R. (1999). Ethnic characteristics of mental disorders in five U.S. communities. *Cultural Diversity and Ethnic Minority Psychology, 5*, 134–136.

Zhong, C., Bohns, V. K., & Gino, F. (2010). A good lamp is the best police: Darkness increases self-interested behavior and dishonesty. *Psychological Science, 21*, 311–314.

Zillmann, D. (1988). Cognition-excitation interdependencies in aggressive behavior. *Aggressive Behavior, 14*, 51–64.

Zillmann, D., Katcher, A. H., & Milavsky, B. (1972). Excitation transfer from physical exercise to subsequent aggressive behavior. *Journal of Experimental Social Psychology, 8*, 247–259.

Zimbardo, P. G. (1997, May). What messages are behind today's cults? *American Psychological Association Monitor, 28*(5), 14.

Zimbardo, P. G. (2004b, May 9). Power turns good soldiers into "bad apples." *Boston Globe.* Retrieved from http://www.boston.com/news/globe/editorial_opinion/oped/articles/2004/05/09/power_turns_good_soldiers_into_bad_apples

Zimbardo, P. G. (2007). *The Lucifer effect: How good people turn evil.* New York, NY: Random House.

Zimbardo, P. G., Weisenberg, M., Firestone, I., & Levy, M. (1965). Communicator effectiveness in producing public conformity and private attitude change. *Journal of Personality, 33*, 233–255.

Credits

Credits listed in order of appearance.

Text: Twenge, Catanese, & Baumeister, 2002. **Figure 1:** Reprinted with permission from William K. Hartmann. Hartmann, W. K. (1992). Astronomy: The cosmic journey. Belmont, CA: Wadsworth. **Text:** Alicke et al., 1997. **Figure 3:** Jones, E. E., & Harris, V. A. (1967). The attribution of attitudes. Journal of Experimental Social Psychology, 3, 1–24. **Figure 4:** Source: Asch, S. E. (1955). Opinions and social pressure. Scientific American, 193, 31–35. **Text:** President Kennedy (Dallek, 2003). **Text:** From William Calley: Court Martial. Retrieved October 29, 2007, from http://law.jrank.org/pages/3208/William-Calley-Court-Martial-1970.html. **Text:** C.P. Snow. **Text:** Milgram, 1974. **Text:** Interview conducted at the Columbus Zoo on September 29, 2005 by Sue Western. **Figure 9:** Heat wave has chilling effect on violent crime. Boston.com. Retrieved February 18, 2013. http://boston.com/community/blogs/crime_punishment/2010/07/heat_wave_has_chilling_effect.html. Permission granted by James Alan Fox, Northeastern University. **Text:** Brinol & Petty, 2009. **Figure 10:** Based on data from Pelham, B. W., Mirenberg, M. C., & Jones, J. T. (2002). Why Susie sells seashells by the seashore: Implicit egotism and major life decisions. Journal of Personality and Social Psychology, 82, 469–487. © 2002 by the American Psychological Association. **Table 4:** Based on Kenrick et al., 2005; Pettigrew, 1998.

Photo Credits

Photo Credits listed in order of appearance.

Masterfile; Tischenko Irina/Shutterstock; **(bottom left):** Fortean/Topham/The Image Works; **(center left):** Yuri Arcurs/Fotolia; **(bottom right):** Tony Freeman/PhotoEdit; **(center right):** Sarah2/Shutterstock; **(top right):** SuperStock; **(center right):** Dave King/Dorling Kindersley/Pearson Education; **(bottom left):** Arquiplay77/Fotolia; **(bottom right):** Jordan Polizzi/Shutterstock; **(bottom left):** Stephan Hoerold/E+/Getty Images; **(top right):** Tim DeFrisco/BlueMoon Stock/Alamy; **(bottom center):** Reproduced with permission. Copyright 1955 Scientific American, Inc. All rights reserved.; **(center left):** Daniel Allan/Digital Vision/Getty Images; **(center right):** Ryan McVay/Photodisc/Getty Images; **(top left):** Philip G. Zimbardo; **(center right):** Philip G. Zimbardo; **(top right):** AP Images; **(center right):** DSK/EPA/Newscom; **(bottom right):** Fang Zhe/Xinhua/Photoshot; **(center left):** Copyright The New Yorker Collection 1979 Henry Martin from cartoonbank.com. All Rights Reserved.; **(top left):** Ahn Young-joon/AP Images; **(center left):** Joe HollowayJr/AP Images; **(center right):** AP Images; **(top right):** Archives of the History of American Psychology; **(top right):** Courtesy of Alexandra Milgram; **(center):** Courtesy of Alexandra Milgram; **(bottom):** Courtesy of Alexandra Milgram; **(center left):** Courtesy of Alexandra Milgram; **(center left):** Courtesy of Alexandra Milgram; **(bottom):** Khue Bui/AP Photos; **(bottom left):** Frans B.M. de Waal, Ph.D.; **(top right):** The New York Times/Redux; **(top):** Justin Guariglia/National Geographic/Getty Images; **(bottom right):** David Young-Wolff/PhotoEdit; **(top left):** Keith Brofsky/Digital Vision/Getty Images; **(bottom right):** Bob Daemmrich/The Image Works; **(bottom):** oliveromg/Shutterstock; **(top):** Ben DeVries/The Daily Nonpareil/AP Images; **(bottom left):** Bob Daemmrich/PhotoEdit; **(top):** Everett Collection; **(top):** Ryan McVay/The Image Bank/Getty Images; **(center left):** Barry Austin Photography/Photodisc/Getty Images; **(top right):** infusny-236/Walter McBride/INFphoto/Newscom; **(top):** Scantaur/Shutterstock; **(top right):** PBNJ Productions/Blend Images/Alamy; **(center right):** Mannie Garcia/AP Images; **(top left):** Sanjay Deva/Fotolia; **(top left):** Anton Zabielskyi/Fotolia; **(top left):** Erik Isakson/Blend Images/Alamy; **(top left):** Pio3/Fotolia; **(bottom left):** Bob Daemmrich/PhotoEdit; **(top):** fstop123/E+/Getty Images; **(top left):** SuperStock; **(center):** Tim DeFrisco/BlueMoon Stock/Alamy; **(top):** Courtesy of Alexandra Milgram; **(bottom):** Frans B.M. de Waal, Ph.D.; **(bottom):** Fstop123/E+/Getty Images.

Personality

From Chapter 14 of *Psychology: From Inquiry to Understanding*, Third Edition. Scott O. Lilienfeld, Steven Jay Lynn, Laura L. Namy, Nancy J. Woolf.

Personality

WHO WE ARE

Think About It

Does a similar upbringing lead to similarities in children's personalities?

Can we reduce the enormous variation in people's personalities to a mere handful of underlying factors?

How consistent is our behavior across situations?

Can we use responses to inkblots to infer people's personality traits?

Is criminal profiling scientific?

Personality
Listen in **MyPsychLab** to chapter audio

Born in 1933, Jack and Oskar are alike in two crucial ways. The first is obvious when you meet them: They're identical twins, genetic clones of each other. In contrast to most identical twins, though, they didn't grow up together. Instead, along with several dozen twin pairs studied by Thomas Bouchard and his colleagues at the University of Minnesota during the 1980s and 1990s, Jack and Oskar were separated almost immediately after birth and reunited decades later (Begley & Kasindorf, 1979). In addition to their looks, there's another similarity: Despite not having known each other for 40 years (they met once only briefly in 1954), Jack and Oskar have nearly identical personalities. Their scores on the Minnesota Multiphasic Personality Inventory, a personality questionnaire that we'll learn about later in the chapter, are about as similar as those of the same person taking the test twice.

That's where the similarities end. Jack was raised by a Jewish family in the Caribbean until age 17, when he moved to Israel and joined a kibbutz. Oskar was raised by his maternal grandmother in a region of the former Czechoslovakia that was under Hitler's control during World War II. Although Jack's and Oskar's personalities are similar, their political attitudes are as different as night and day. Jack is a devoutly religious Jew who once enjoyed war movies that portrayed Germans in a bad light. While in Israel, he worked to help build the Jewish state. In stark contrast, Oskar was once an ardent Nazi and anti-Semite who became a dedicated member of the Hitler Youth movement as World War II drew to a close. So although Jack and Oskar have similar personalities—intense, loyal, and politically engaged—they have manifested these personalities in dramatically different ways.

The case of Jack and Oskar is just that—a case. And case studies have their limitations. For one thing, it's hard to know how far we can generalize the Jack and Oskar story to other twins, let alone to other people. Yet like some case studies, Jack and Oskar's story raises a host of fascinating questions that psychologists can examine using rigorous research designs. How can identical twins like Jack and Oskar be so similar in personality despite having had no contact with each other for decades? How can two people with such similar personalities end up with such dissimilar political attitudes? How do environmental influences shape the expression of our personalities?

The answers to those questions, we'll soon learn, aren't simple. Although most of us believe we can explain why people act as they do, we're wrong at least as often as we're right (Hamilton, 1980; Nisbett & Wilson, 1977).

Few are more confident in their abilities to explain behavior than radio and television "advice experts," many of whom liberally sprinkle their shows with off-the-cuff psychological accounts for people's behavior (Heaton & Wilson, 1995; Williams & Ceci, 1998). Consider the following statements typical of those offered by talk show psychologists: "He murdered all of those people because he had an unhappy childhood." "She overeats because she has low self-esteem." Intuitively appealing as those explanations are, we must beware of *single-cause explanations* of human behavior. When trying to uncover the root causes of people's actions, we must keep in mind that personality is multiply determined. Indeed, personality is the unimaginably complicated outcome of hundreds of causal factors: genetic, prenatal, parenting, peer influences, life stressors, and plain old luck, both good and bad.

Personality: What Is It and How Can We Study It?

I Describe how twin and adoption studies shed light on genetic and environmental influences on personality.

Our social context can influence our behavior in profound ways. The *fundamental attribution error* is the tendency to attribute too much of others' behavior to their dispositions, including their personalities, and not enough to the situations they confront.

Radio and talk show personalities such as Dr. Phil McGraw ("Dr. Phil") often provide single-cause explanations for complex, multiply determined psychological problems.

Even bearing this error in mind, most psychologists agree that there *is* such a thing as **personality**—people's typical ways of thinking, feeling, and behaving. We aren't exclusively a product of the social factors that affect us at any given moment, although we're certainly influenced by them. Most also agree with the American psychologist Gordon Allport's (1966) definition of personality as consisting of relatively enduring predispositions that influence our behavior across many situations (Funder, 1991; John, Robins, & Pervin, 2008; Tellegen, 1991). These predispositions, also called **traits**—like introversion, aggressiveness, and conscientiousness—account in part for consistencies in our behavior across both time and situations.

There are two major approaches to studying personality (Scurich, Monahan, & John, 2012). A **nomothetic approach** strives to understand personality by identifying general laws that govern the behavior of all individuals. Most modern personality research, including most of the research we'll examine in this chapter, is nomothetic because it aims to derive principles that explain the thinking, emotions, and behaviors of all people. This approach typically allows for generalization across individuals, but limited insight into the unique patterning of attributes within one person.

In contrast, an **idiographic approach** (think of the word *idiosyncratic*) strives to understand personality by identifying the unique configuration of characteristics and life history experiences within a person. Most case studies are idiographic. Gordon Allport (1965) presented a classic example of the idiographic approach in his book *Letters from Jenny*, which features an analysis of 301 letters written by one woman over 12 years. In these letters, Allport uncovered themes that characterized Jenny's attitudes toward her son, Ross. When Jenny wrote about Ross in positive terms, themes of her early life often emerged; when she wrote about him in negative terms, themes of her unappreciated sacrifices for him often emerged. The idiographic approach reveals the richly detailed tapestry of one person's life, but allows for limited generalizability to other people. Moreover, it generates hypotheses that are often difficult to falsify, because these hypotheses are frequently *post hoc* ("after the fact") explanations about events that have already occurred.

How do personality traits originate? We'll first approach this question from the vantage point of behavior-genetic studies of personality and move on to specific theories of personality, including Freudian, behavioral, and humanistic models, that offer competing answers to this question. As we'll discover, all of these theories aim to explain *both commonalities and differences* among people in their personalities. For example, they try to account for not only how we develop a conscience, but also why some of us have a stronger conscience than others.

Behavior-genetic methods help psychologists disentangle the following three broad sets of influences on personality:

- *Genetic* factors.
- *Shared environmental* factors—experiences that make individuals within the same family more alike. If parents try to make all of their children more outgoing by reinforcing them with attention and succeed in doing so, their parenting in this case is a shared environmental factor.
- *Nonshared environmental* factors—experiences that make individuals within the same family less alike. If a parent treats one child more affectionately than another and as a consequence this child ends up with higher self-esteem than the other child, the parenting in this case is a nonshared environmental factor.

Investigating the Causes of Personality: Overview of Twin and Adoption Studies

To distinguish among these three sets of influences, behavior geneticists have applied twin studies and adoption studies to personality. Because identical (monozygotic) twins are more similar genetically than are fraternal (dizygotic) twins, a higher correlation of a trait among identical than fraternal twins—assuming that the environmental influences on

Watch in **MyPsychLab** the **Video:** The Big Picture: What Is Personality?

◀ **FALSIFIABILITY**
Can the claim be disproved?

personality
people's typical ways of thinking, feeling, and behaving

trait
relatively enduring predisposition that influences our behavior across many situations

nomothetic approach
approach to personality that focuses on identifying general laws that govern the behavior of all individuals

idiographic approach
approach to personality that focuses on identifying the unique configuration of characteristics and life history experiences within a person

TABLE 1 Comparison of Correlations of Twins Reared Together and Apart for Selected Personality Traits.

	TWINS REARED TOGETHER		TWINS REARED APART	
	IDENTICAL TWIN CORRELATION	FRATERNAL TWIN CORRELATION	IDENTICAL TWIN CORRELATION	FRATERNAL TWIN CORRELATION
Anxiety proneness	.52	.24	.61	.27
Aggression	.43	.14	.46	.06
Alienation	.55	.38	.55	.38
Impulse control	.41	.06	.50	.03
Emotional well-being	.58	.23	.48	.18
Traditionalism	.50	.47	.53	.39
Achievement orientation	.36	.07	.36	.07

(*Source:* Based on data from Tellegen et al., 1988)

both sets of twins are comparable—suggests a genetic influence. In contrast, identical twin correlations that are equal to or less than fraternal twin correlations suggest the absence of a genetic component and instead point to nonshared environmental influences—those that make people within a family (including twins) different.

REARED-TOGETHER TWINS: GENES OR ENVIRONMENT? From the findings of one landmark twin study of personality, we can see that numerous personality traits—including anxiety proneness, impulse control, and traditionalism (the extent to which people believe in well-established social values, such as the importance of obeying one's parents and teachers)—are influenced substantially by genetic factors (see the left side of **TABLE 1**). This study examined identical twin pairs raised together and fraternal twins who were either both male or both female (Tellegen et al., 1988). A number of researchers have replicated these findings in twin samples from intact families (Kendler et al., 2009; Loehlin, 1992; Plomin, 2004).

The results in Table 1 impart another lesson. What do the identical twin correlations have in common? The answer is so self-evident that we can easily overlook it: All are substantially less than 1.0. This finding demonstrates that nonshared environment, environmental influences that differ within families, plays an important role in personality (Krueger, 2000; Plomin & Daniels, 1987; Turkheimer, 2000). If heritability were 1.0 (that is, 100 percent), the identical twin correlations would also be 1.0. Because they're considerably less than 1.0, nonshared environmental influences must play a key role in personality. Regrettably, these twin findings don't tell us what these nonshared environmental influences are.

REARED-APART TWINS: SHINING A SPOTLIGHT ON GENES. Table 1 might tempt us to conclude that the similarities between identical twins are primarily a result of their similar upbringing rather than their shared genes. But this explanation is refuted by studies of identical and fraternal twins raised apart.

In an extraordinary investigation, researchers at the University of Minnesota spent more than two decades accumulating the largest ever sample of identical and fraternal twins reared apart—about 130 in total (Bouchard et al., 1990). Many had been separated almost immediately after birth, raised in different states and sometimes different countries, and reunited for the first time decades later in the Minneapolis–St. Paul airport. Jack and Oskar, whom we met at the outset of this chapter, were among those in the "Minnesota Twins" study, as it affectionately came to be known.

Before psychologists conducted these studies, some prominent social scientists predicted confidently that identical twins reared apart would barely resemble each other in personality (Mischel, 1981). Were they right? The right side of Table 1 displays

Watch in **MyPsychLab** the **Video:** Special Topics: Twins and Personality

REPLICABILITY ▶
Can the results be duplicated in other studies?

FALSIFIABILITY ▶
Can the claim be disproved?

some of the principal findings from the Minnesota Twins study. Two findings in the right side of this table stand out. First, identical twins reared apart tend to be strikingly similar in their personality traits. They're also far more similar than fraternal twins who are reared apart (Tellegen et al., 1988). A more convincing case for the role of genetic influences on personality would be hard to come by.

These identical twin brothers, Gerald Levey and Mark Newman, were separated at birth. Remarkably, both became firefighters despite being unaware of each other's existence (one in New Jersey and the other in Queens, New York).

Second, when comparing the results in the left and right sides of Table 1, it's evident that identical twins reared apart are about as similar as identical twins reared together. This remarkable finding suggests that shared environment, the sum total of environmental influences shared by members of the same family, plays little or no role in the causes of adult personality. Behavior-genetic researchers have replicated this result in other twin samples (Loehlin, 1992; Pedersen et al., 1988; Vernon et al., 2008).

This finding is sufficiently surprising that it bears repeating: *Shared environment plays little or no role in adult personality.* In many respects, this may be the most stunning finding in recent personality psychology, although it's yet to exert a substantial impact on popular psychology (Harris, 2006; Pinker, 2002; Rowe, 1994). For much of the twentieth century, most psychologists put their money on shared environmental influences as causal factors, as they believed that the most important environmental influences are transmitted from parents to children (Harris, 1994). But these and other results suggest that they were mistaken (Lilienfeld et al., 2010).

Admittedly, shared environment generally plays some role in childhood personality, but this impact generally dissipates as we grow older. By the time we reach adulthood, the impact of shared environment on our personalities is weak at best (Beauchaine & Gatzke-Kopp, 2012; Plomin & McClearn, 1993; Torgersen et al., 2008). This finding suggests that if parents try to make all of their children outgoing, for example, by exposing them to friendly children and encouraging them to attend parties, they're likely to fail in the long run.

ADOPTION STUDIES: FURTHER SEPARATING GENES AND ENVIRONMENT. *Adoption studies* permit investigators to separate the effects of genes and environment by examining children who were separated at an early age from their biological families. The finding that an adopted child's personality is similar to that of his or her biological parents points to genetic influence; in contrast, the finding that an adopted child's personality is similar to that of his or her adoptive parents points to shared environmental influence.

In one adoption study conducted in Texas, investigators examined several personality traits as measured by the California Psychological Inventory, which we'll encounter later in the chapter. In **TABLE 2**, we'll focus on one such trait: *sociability*, or the extent to which people enjoy being with others.

As we can see in Table 2, the correlations between biological parents and their adopted-away children in their sociability levels are slightly higher than the correlations between adoptive parents and their adopted children *even though the biological parents had essentially no environmental contact with their children after birth* (Loehlin & Horn, 2010). Most researchers have obtained similar findings for other personality traits (Bezdjian, Baker, & Tuvblad, 2011; Loehlin, 1992; Scarr et al., 1981). These results again run counter to the intuitively plausible hypothesis that shared environment is influential in personality: Being raised together doesn't lead to much similarity in personality between parents and offspring.

◀ **REPLICABILITY**
Can the results be duplicated in other studies?

Factoid

One pair of identical twins separated at birth in the Minnesota Twins study (both named "Jim" by their adoptive parents) both constructed similar-looking tree houses in their backyards, named their dogs "Toy," and were married twice, both to women named Linda and Betty. Another pair of separated adult identical twins in that study—in this case, female—both attempted to conquer their fear of the ocean by entering the water backward up to their ankles and then turning around (Segal, 1999). Yet because these are anecdotes and could reflect chance coincidences (Wyatt et al., 1984), we need to turn to systematic analyses of twins reared apart.

TABLE 2 Correlations Among Various Relatives in an Adoption Study of Sociability.

CORRELATION	
Biological mother and child	.15
Adoptive mother and child	.01
Biological father and child	.20
Adoptive father and child	.08
(*Source:* Based on data from Loehlin & Horn, 2010)	

◀ **REPLICABILITY**
Can the results be duplicated in other studies?

WHERE IS THE ENVIRONMENTAL INFLUENCE ON PERSONALITY?

As we've seen, nonshared environmental influences—those that make people within a family different from each other—play a key role in personality. Yet when psychologists have searched for specific nonshared environmental influences, they've generally come up empty-handed. For example, the extent to which parents treat their children differently or differences in the kinds of peers to which children interact don't seem to account for much, if any, of the differences in their personalities as adults (Turkheimer & Waldron, 2000).

Even in the domain of psychopathology, the search for nonshared environmental influences has been disappointing. Some investigators have examined monozygotic (identical) twin pairs *discordant* for mental disorders such as schizophrenia (Dempster et al., 2011). In such pairs, one twin has the disorder, but the other doesn't. This design cleverly controls for genetic factors, because monozygotic twins share all of their genes, so any differences between them must be due to nonshared environment. Yet in the case of schizophrenia, investigators have found few, if any, differences in nonshared environment that could account for the difference between the twins (Wahl, 1976). For example, differences in how the twins were raised as children don't consistently predict which one later developed the disorder.

Another long-time candidate for a nonshared environmental factor is birth order. Many popular books, such as *Birth Order: What Your Position in the Family Really Tells You about Your Character* (Blair, 2013) claim that firstborns tend toward achievement; middle-borns, toward diplomacy; and later-borns, toward risk taking. Yet in fact, most researchers have failed to uncover consistent associations between birth order and personality (Ernst & Angst, 1983; Dunkel, Harbke, & Papini, 2009; Jefferson, Herbst, & McCrae, 1998).

Nevertheless, popular claims regarding the importance of birth order received a boost from the work of science historian Frank Sulloway (1996). He examined the association between birth order and attitudes toward revolutionary scientific theories such as Copernicus' theory of the sun-centered universe and Darwin's theory of natural selection. Sulloway asked panels of historians to evaluate how 4,000 scientists reacted to scientific controversies when their developers proposed them. He found that later-borns were 3.1 times more likely than firstborns to favor revolutionary ideas; for extremely radical ideas, this ratio increased to 4.7. In contrast, firstborns usually supported the status quo. Sulloway's findings raise the possibility that birth order is an important nonshared environmental influence, but it's not clear how much we can generalize his findings to nonscientific disciplines. Moreover, critics have noted that when rating whether scientists were revolutionaries, Sulloway's panel of historians may not have been blind to their birth order (Harris, 1998). In addition, some scientists haven't replicated Sulloway's finding that later-borns are more rebellious than firstborns (Freese, Powell, & Steelman, 1999).

There's one final possibility we haven't considered. Perhaps the principal nonshared environmental influence on personality is simply luck—both good and bad (Meehl, 1978; Turkheimer & Waldron, 2000). Some of us encounter positive events in our lives, whereas others encounter negative events, and these largely random events may shape us in powerful ways. If so, nomothetic approaches may never be sufficient to understand personality; we may need to complement them with idiographic approaches, which capture the full complexity of each person's life history.

REPLICABILITY ▶
Can the results be duplicated in other studies?

Behavior-Genetic Studies: A Note of Caution

Researchers using twin and adoption studies have found that genes influence a variety of behaviors that are often associated with personality traits. These behaviors include divorce (McGue & Lykken, 1992), religiosity (Waller et al., 1990), political views (Hatemi & McDermott, 2012), and even the tendency to watch television (Plomin et al., 1990). Perhaps surprisingly, many social attitudes, including those concerning the death penalty and nudist colonies, are moderately heritable (Martin et al., 1986). For each of these characteristics, identical twin correlations are considerably higher than fraternal twin correlations.

Do these findings mean, as the popular press often implies, that there are specific genes for divorce, religiosity, political preferences, death penalty attitudes, and the like? Don't bet on it. Genes code for proteins, not specific behaviors or attitudes, and therefore affect most psychological characteristics in a highly indirect fashion (N. Block, 1995). As we learned from Jack and Oskar, genes probably exert an indirect influence on certain personality traits—like a tendency to experience deep emotions—but the environment influences how these traits play out in our lives, such as becoming an observant Jew or a passionate anti-Semite. The pathways from genes to behavior are lengthy and circuitous. So when we hear media reports of a "gay gene," "alcoholism gene," "conservative gene," or "divorce gene," we should be skeptical. Although there are probably genetic influences on political views, homosexuality, and even divorce, it's exceedingly unlikely that a single gene codes directly for these or other multifaceted behaviors (Kendler, 2005; Nigg & Goldsmith, 1994).

Although twin and adoption studies provide remarkably useful information concerning the heritability of personality traits, they tell us little about *which* genes are related to personality. In an attempt to answer this question, researchers have turned to **molecular genetic studies**, which may allow them to pinpoint those genes associated with specific personality traits (Canli, 2008; Plomin et al., 1997). These studies rest on two premises:

1. Genes code for proteins that in turn often influence the functioning of neurotransmitters like dopamine and serotonin.

2. The functioning of many neurotransmitters is associated with certain personality traits (Cloninger, 1987; Gardini, Cloninger, & Venneri, 2009). For example, people with low levels of serotonin activity tend to be more impulsive and aggressive than other persons are (Carver & Miller, 2006; Dolan, Anderson, & Deakin, 2001).

Although the methodology of molecular genetic studies is complicated, most of these designs work by examining the linkage between specific genes and known genetic markers on each chromosome. At this point, however, there have been relatively few consistently replicated associations between specific genes and personality traits.

One notable exception is the connection between *novelty seeking*—a trait that refers to the tendency to search out and enjoy new experiences (Cloninger, 1987)—and genetic markers of the dopamine system, which is intimately involved in reward seeking. Several researchers have reported significant associations between measures of novelty seeking and various genes influencing the activity of the neurotransmitter dopamine (Epstein et al., 1996; Munafo et al., 2008). In addition, some investigators have reported a linkage between symptoms of attention-deficit/hyperactivity disorder, a childhood disorder associated with novelty seeking, and genes influencing the dopamine system (Waldman & Gizer, 2006). Nevertheless, findings linking dopamine-related genes to novelty seeking haven't always been consistently replicated (Pogue-Geile et al., 1998; Waldman & Gizer, 2006) and tend to be weak in magnitude, so we should view them with a bit of caution. It's possible that we'll see more progress linking specific genes, such as those of the serotonin system (Lesch et al., 1996; Wang & Saudino, 2012), to specific personality traits in the coming decade.

Twin studies demonstrate that religiosity has a substantial genetic component. But does that finding mean there are specific genes for religiosity?

◄ **REPLICABILITY**
Can the results be duplicated in other studies?

◄ **REPLICABILITY**
Can the results be duplicated in other studies?

✓ **Study** and **Review** in **MyPsychLab**

Assess Your Knowledge   FACT or FICTION?

1. Identical twins reared together tend to be about as similar in their personality traits as identical twins reared apart.   **True / False**

2. Environmental factors shared among members of the same family play an important role in the causes of most personality traits in adulthood.   **True / False**

3. Birth order is weakly related to most personality traits.   **True / False**

4. We shouldn't trust the findings from molecular genetic studies of personality until independent investigators have replicated them.   **True / False**

Answers: 1. T; 2. F; 3. T; 4. T

molecular genetic study
investigation that allows researchers to pinpoint genes associated with specific personality traits

Psychoanalytic Theory: The Controversial Legacy of Sigmund Freud and His Followers

2 Describe the core assumptions of psychoanalytic theory.

3 Describe key criticisms of psychoanalytic theory and the central features of neo-Freudian theories.

Long before researchers stepped in to conduct controlled studies of the causes of personality, psychologists, psychiatrists, and many other thinkers had generated theoretical models that sought to explain the development and workings of personality. These models address three key questions:

1. How do our personalities develop?
2. What are the core driving forces in our personalities, or more informally, what makes us tick?
3. What accounts for individual differences in personality?

We'll examine and evaluate four influential models of personality, starting with the granddaddy of them all: Sigmund Freud's psychoanalytic theory.

To most nonpsychologists, psychoanalytic theory—indeed, much of personality theory itself—is virtually synonymous with the writings of a Viennese physician named Sigmund Freud (1856–1939), who is undeniably one of the most influential figures in all of psychology. Yet ironically, Freud's training wasn't in psychology or psychiatry—specialties that scarcely existed in his day—but in neurology. Largely as a consequence of his neurological background, Freud initially believed that mental disorders were physiologically caused. Yet his views changed dramatically in 1885, when he spent a year in Paris studying under neurologist Jean-Martin Charcot. Charcot had been treating patients, most of them women, who had a condition then known as "grande hysteria." They exhibited an assortment of spectacular physical symptoms: paralyses of the arms and legs, fainting spells, and seizures. Careful investigation failed to turn up any physical causes of these symptoms, some of which made little or no physiological sense. For example, some of Charcot's patients exhibited *glove anesthesia*, a loss of sensation in the hand alone, with no accompanying loss of sensation in the arm. Glove anesthesia defies standard neurological principles because the sensory pathways extending to the hand run through the arm. If the hand lacks sensation, the arm should, too.

This and related observations led Freud to conclude that many mental disorders were produced by psychological rather than physiological factors. He developed a theoretical model to explain these disorders, traditionally called *psychoanalytic theory*, and an accompanying treatment called *psychoanalysis*.

Freud's Psychoanalytic Theory of Personality

Psychoanalytic theory rests on three core assumptions (Brenner, 1973; Loevinger, 1987). These assumptions, especially the second and third, set this theory apart from most other personality theories.

- *Psychic Determinism.* Freudians believe in **psychic determinism**: the assumption that all psychological events have a cause. We aren't free to choose our actions, Freudians claim, because we're at the mercy of powerful inner forces that lie outside our awareness (Custer & Aarts, 2010). Dreams, neurotic symptoms, and "Freudian slips" of the tongue are all reflections of deep psychological conflict bubbling up to the surface (see **TABLE 3**). Moreover, for Freudians, many key influences on adult personality stem from early childhood experiences, especially parenting.

Sigmund Freud, the founder of psychoanalysis, is simultaneously the most worshipped and most criticized figure in personality psychology.

Listen in **MyPsychLab** the **Podcast:**
Freud's View of the Human Mind

TABLE 3 Examples of "Freudian Slips" From Notes by Freud.

"A member of the House of Commons referred to another as the honorable member for Central Hell instead of Central Hull."
"A soldier said to a friend that 'I wish there were a thousand men mortified on that hill' instead of 'fortified on that hill.'"
"A lady, attempting to compliment another, says that 'I am sure that you must have thrown this delightful hat together' instead of 'sewn it together,' thereby betraying her thought that the hat was poorly made."
"A lady states that few gentlemen know how to value the 'ineffectual' qualities in a woman, as opposed to 'intellectual.'"

(*Source:* Freud, 1901)

psychic determinism
the assumption that all psychological events have a cause

- *Symbolic Meaning.* For Freudians, no action, no matter how trivial it may seem, is meaningless. All are attributable to preceding mental causes, even if we can't figure out what they are. If while teaching a class your male professor manages to crack a long piece of chalk in two, some might be inclined to ignore this behavior. Freudians, in contrast, would be likely to argue that this piece of chalk is *symbolic* of something else, most likely something sexual in nature. Yet even strict Freudians agree that not all behaviors are symbolic. In response to a questioner who asked Freud why he enjoyed smoking cigars, Freud supposedly responded that "a cigar is sometimes just a cigar" (although some scholars argue that this quotation is an urban legend).

- *Unconscious Motivation.* According to Freud (1933), we rarely understand why we do what we do, although we quite readily cook up explanations for our actions after the fact. Some authors have likened the Freudian view of the mind (Freud, 1923) to an iceberg, with the unconscious—the part of personality of which we're entirely unaware—being the vast and largely uncharted area of the psyche submerged entirely underwater (see **FIGURE 1**). The conscious component of the mind, the part of personality of which we're aware, is merely the "tip of the iceberg," barely visible above the water's surface. For Freud, the unconscious is of immensely greater importance in the causes of our personality than the conscious.

(© ScienceCartoonsPlus.com)

The Id, Ego, and Superego: The Structure of Personality

Freud (1933, 1935) hypothesized that the human psyche consists of three *agencies* or components: id, ego, and superego. For Freud, the interplay among these three agencies gives rise to our personalities, and differences in the strength of these agencies account largely for individual differences in personality.

THE ID: BASIC INSTINCTS. The **id**, according to Freud, is the reservoir of our most primitive

Conscious
Contact with
outside world

EGO

SUPEREGO

Unconscious
Difficult to retrieve
material; well below
the surface of
awareness

ID

FIGURE 1 Freud's Model of Personality Structure. According to some authors, Freud's conception of personality is analogous to an iceberg, with the conscious mind being the tip barely visible above the surface and the unconscious being the vast submerged area entirely underwater. Nevertheless, we shouldn't take the iceberg metaphor too literally (indeed, Freud himself apparently never used it), because according to Freud, different aspects of personality are in constant interaction.

impulses, a seething cauldron of desires that provides the driving force for much of our behavior. The id is entirely unconscious; it's the part of the iceberg submerged underwater. It contains a variety of drives, particularly the sexual drive, or *libido*, and aggressive drive. According to Freud, the id operates by means of the **pleasure principle**. The pleasure principle strives for immediate gratification: The word *no* isn't in the id's vocabulary.

THE EGO: THE BOSS. The **ego** is the boss of the personality, its principal decision maker. The ego's primary tasks are interacting with the real world and finding ways to resolve the competing demands of the other two psychic agencies. We shouldn't confuse the Freudian ego with the concept of the ego that's crept into everyday language, meaning an inflated sense of self-worth ("Wow, that athlete has a big ego").

In contrast to the id, the ego is governed by the **reality principle**. The reality principle strives to delay gratification until it can find an appropriate outlet. If you find

id
reservoir of our most primitive impulses, including sex and aggression

pleasure principle
tendency of the id to strive for immediate gratification

ego
psyche's executive and principal decision maker

reality principle
tendency of the ego to postpone gratification until it can find an appropriate outlet

639

FIGURE 2 Id, Ego, and Superego. Many works of art portray an individual trying to make a difficult moral decision with a devil on one shoulder—urging immoral behavior—and an angel—urging moral behavior—on the other. Freudians would say that such artwork captures the distinction among ego (the person trying to make the decision), id (demon), and superego (angel).

Explore in **MyPsychLab** the **Concept:**
Freud: Id, Ego, and Superego

Most dream dictionaries available in bookstores imply that there are universal meanings for dream symbols. Even most psychoanalysts reject this claim.

superego
our sense of morality

defense mechanisms
unconscious maneuvers intended to minimize anxiety

today's introductory psychology lecture to be inordinately frustrating, your id may want to satisfy your aggressive impulses by screaming aloud in class. This is the pleasure principle rearing its ugly head. But the ego's reality principle requires that you delay this gratification until you can find a socially appropriate outlet for your aggression, such as throwing darts at a dartboard—perhaps one featuring your professor's face as the bull's-eye—when you get home from class.

THE SUPEREGO: MORAL STANDARDS. The **superego** is our sense of morality. The term literally means "above ego," and Freud conceptualized this agency much like a judgmental parent looking down upon the ego. The superego contains the sense of right and wrong we've internalized from our interactions with society, particularly our parents. According to Freudians, people with overly developed superegos are guilt-prone; guilt-free people in particular have underdeveloped superegos and are at risk for developing psychopathic personality.

HOW THE PSYCHIC AGENCIES INTERACT. Much of the time, id, ego, and superego interact harmoniously, much like a chamber music trio playing in perfect synchrony. Yet the agendas of these agencies sometimes collide (see **FIGURE 2**). Indeed, Freud (1935) hypothesized that psychological distress results from conflict among these three agencies. If you're attracted to your best friend's partner, your id is at odds with your ego and (hopefully) your superego. You might fantasize about a romantic fling with this person (id), but feel frightened about what would happen to you (ego) and stricken with pangs of guilt about hurting your friend's feelings (superego) if you were foolish enough to act on your impulses.

For an intimate view of the three psychic agencies in action, we have only to look to the third of our lives we spend asleep. Dreams, Freud (1900) suggested, are the "royal road to the unconscious mind" because they not only reveal the inner workings of our id in action, but also illustrate how ego and superego cooperate to keep the id's wishes in check. According to Freud, all dreams are *wish fulfillments,* that is, expressions of the id's impulses. Yet they don't always seem that way on the surface, said Freud, because these wishes are disguised. When the superego perceives the id's desires to be threatening, it "commands" the ego to plaster over these wishes with symbols. But popular psychology books notwithstanding, most Freudians don't regard dream symbols as universal. If we peruse the section of our local bookstores devoted to dreams, we'll find several dictionaries of dream symbols. One such dictionary (Schoenewolf, 1997) offers the following rules for interpreting dream symbols: a duck, an icicle, a spear, an umbrella, or a tie symbolizes the penis; a pocket, tunnel, jug, or gate symbolizes the vagina; and a kangaroo symbolizes sexual vitality (please don't ask us to explain that one). These and other dream dictionaries (Ackroyd, 1993; Lennox, 2011) vastly oversimplify psychoanalytic theory, because Freudians believe that different symbols can mean different things to different dreamers.

ANXIETY AND THE DEFENSE MECHANISMS. A principal function of the ego, according to Freud, is to contend with threats from the outside world. When danger arises, the ego experiences anxiety, signaling it to undertake corrective actions. Sometimes these actions are straightforward, like jumping out of the way of an oncoming car. In other cases, though, we can't do much to correct the situation, so we must change our *perception* of it.

In these cases, the ego engages in **defense mechanisms**: unconscious maneuvers intended to minimize anxiety. Freud and his daughter, Anna, who became a prominent psychoanalyst in her own right, outlined the principal defense mechanisms (A. Freud, 1937). We'll present a brief discussion of some of the most important ones here, bearing in mind that many psychologists today don't subscribe to the Freudian view of them (see **TABLE 4** for a list of these and other defense mechanisms).

TABLE 4 Major Freudian Defense Mechanisms and an Example of Each.

DEFENSE MECHANISM	DEFINITION	EXAMPLE
Repression	Motivated forgetting of emotionally threatening memories or impulses	A person who witnesses a traumatic combat scene finds himself unable to remember it.
Denial	Motivated forgetting of distressing experiences	A mother who loses a child in a car accident insists her child is alive.
Regression	Returning psychologically to a younger and safer time	A college student starts sucking his thumb during a difficult exam.
Reaction-formation	Transforming an anxiety-producing experience into its opposite	A married woman who's sexually attracted to a coworker experiences hatred and revulsion toward him.
Projection	Unconscious attribution of our negative qualities onto others	A married man with powerful unconscious sexual impulses toward females complains that other women are always "after him."
Displacement	Directing an impulse from a socially unacceptable target onto a more acceptable one	A golfer angrily throws his club into the woods after missing an easy putt.
Rationalization	Providing reasonable-sounding explanations for unreasonable behaviors or failures	A political candidate who loses an election convinces herself that she didn't really want the position after all.
Intellectualization	Avoiding the emotions associated with anxiety-provoking experiences by focusing on abstract and impersonal thoughts	A woman whose husband cheats on her reassures herself that "according to evolutionary psychologists, men are naturally sexually promiscuous, so there's nothing to worry about."
Identification with the aggressor	Adopting the psychological characteristics of people we find threatening	A college basketball player who initially fears his tyrannical coach comes to admire him and adopts his dictatorial qualities.
Sublimation	Transforming a socially unacceptable impulse into an admired and socially valued goal	A boy who enjoys beating up on other children grows up to become a successful professional boxer.

- **Repression**, the most critical defense mechanism in psychoanalytic theory, is the *motivated forgetting* of emotionally threatening memories or impulses. Unlike other types of forgetting, repression is presumably triggered by anxiety: We forget because we want to forget. According to Freud, we repress unhappy memories of early childhood to avoid the pain they produce. This repression leads us to experience *infantile amnesia*, the inability to remember anything prior to about age 3 (Fivush & Hudson, 1990). Early childhood, Freud contended, is too anxiety-provoking for us to remember fully. We now know this explanation is unlikely, because investigators have identified infantile amnesia in other animals, including mice and rats (Berk, Vigorito, & Miller, 1979; Richardson, Riccio, & Axiotis, 1986). A committed Freudian could presumably argue that mice and other rodents also repress traumatic memories of early childhood (perhaps memories of seeing too many cats?), but Occam's razor renders this explanation implausible.

- Whereas repression deals with past events, **denial** is the refusal to acknowledge current events in our lives, such as a serious problem in our marriage. We most often observe denial in people with psychotic disorders such as schizophrenia although individuals undergoing extreme stress occasionally engage in denial, too. It's not uncommon, for example, for the relatives of individuals who have recently died in a tragic accident to insist that their loved ones must somehow, somewhere, be alive.

- **Regression** is the act of returning psychologically to a younger age, typically early childhood, when life was simpler and safer. Older children who've long since stopped sucking their thumbs sometimes suddenly resume thumb sucking under stress.

◄ **OCCAM'S RAZOR**
Does a simpler explanation fit the data just as well?

repression
motivated forgetting of emotionally threatening memories or impulses

denial
refusal to acknowledge current events in our lives

regression
the act of returning psychologically to a younger, and typically simpler and safer, age

- **Reaction-formation** is the transformation of an anxiety-provoking emotion into its opposite. The observable emotion we see actually reflects the opposite emotion the person feels unconsciously. Freud contended that we can infer the presence of reaction-formation by the intensity with which the person expresses the emotion, as this emotion displays an exaggerated or "phony" quality.

  In a remarkable study, Henry Adams and his colleagues found that males with high levels of *homophobia*—a dislike (not technically a fear, as the word implies) of homosexuals—showed significantly *greater* increases in penile circumference than did males with low levels of homophobia in response to sexually explicit videotapes of homosexual stimuli, such as men engaging in sex with other men (Adams, Wright, & Lohr, 1996). This finding is tantalizingly consistent with the Freudian concept of reaction-formation; some homophobics may harbor unconscious homosexual impulses they find unacceptable and transform them into a conscious dislike of homosexuals. Still, there's an alternative explanation: Anxiety can increase sexual arousal and perhaps trigger penile erections (Barlow, Sakheim, & Beck, 1983). So future investigators will need to rule out this rival hypothesis.

- **Projection** is the unconscious attribution of our negative characteristics to others. According to psychoanalysts, people with paranoia are projecting their unconscious hostility onto others. Deep down they want to harm others, but because they can't accept these impulses, they perceive others as wanting to harm them.

- Closely related to projection is **displacement**, in which we direct an impulse from a socially unacceptable target onto a safer and more socially acceptable target. After a frustrating day at work, we may pound our fist against the punching bag at the gym rather than into the faces of our annoying coworkers.

- **Rationalization** provides a reasonable-sounding explanation for our unreasonable behaviors or for failures. Some people who receive *posthypnotic suggestions* to perform bizarre actions engage in rationalizations to explain these actions. A participant given a posthypnotic suggestion to bark like a dog after emerging from hypnosis may do so. When the hypnotist asks him why he barked, he may rationalize his behavior: "Hmmm... I was just thinking about how much I missed my dog, so I felt like barking" (see **FIGURE 3**). A related defense mechanism, *intellectualization*, allows us to avoid anxiety by thinking about abstract and interpersonal ideas (refer to Table 4).

- **Sublimation** transforms a socially unacceptable impulse into an admired goal. George Vaillant's (1977) book *Adaptation to Life,* which is a 40-year longitudinal study of Harvard University graduates, features several striking examples of sublimation. Among them is the story of a man who set fires in childhood and went on to become chief of his local fire department.

Stages of Psychosexual Development

No aspect of Freud's theory is more controversial than his model of psychosexual development. Nor has any aspect of his theory been more widely criticized as pseudoscientific (Cioffi, 1998). According to Freud, personality development proceeds through a series of stages. He termed these stages *psychosexual* because each focuses on a different sexually arousing zone of the body. Although we're accustomed to thinking of our genitals as our primary sexual organs, Freud believed that other bodily areas are

RULING OUT RIVAL HYPOTHESES ▶
Have important alternative explanations for the findings been excluded?

? In this photograph from a 2008 game, frustrated player Prince Fielder throws his bat to the ground after popping out. Freudians would say that Fielder is engaging in which defense mechanism? (See answer upside down at bottom of page.)

reaction-formation
transformation of an anxiety-provoking emotion into its opposite

projection
unconscious attribution of our negative characteristics to others

Answer: Displacement

sources of sexual gratification in early development. Contrary to prevailing wisdom at the time, Freud insisted that sexuality begins in infancy. He maintained that the extent to which we resolve each stage successfully bears crucial implications for later personality development (see **TABLE 5**). He further believed that individuals can become *fixated*, or "stuck," in an early stage of development. Fixations can occur because children were deprived of sexual gratification they were supposed to receive during that stage or were excessively gratified during that stage. In either case, they experience difficulty moving ahead to the next stage. Let's examine the five psychosexual stages as Freud conceptualized them, again bearing in mind that many modern critics don't share his views.

THE ORAL STAGE. The first stage of psychosexual development, the **oral stage**, which generally lasts from birth to 12–18 months, focuses on the mouth. During this stage, infants obtain sexual pleasure primarily by sucking and drinking. Freud believed that adults who are orally fixated tend to react to stress by becoming intensely dependent on others for reassurance—a form of regression, according to Freud—just as infants depend on their mother's breast as a source of satisfaction. These adults also are prone to unhealthy "oral" behaviors like overeating, drinking excessively, or smoking.

THE ANAL STAGE. At the **anal stage**, which lasts from about 18 months to three years, children first come face-to-face with psychological conflict. During this stage, children want to alleviate tension and experience pleasure by moving their bowels, but soon discover they can't do so whenever nature calls. Instead, they must learn to inhibit their urges and wait to move their bowels in a socially appropriate place—ideally, the toilet. If children's toilet training is either too harsh or too lenient, they'll become fixated and prone to regressing to this stage during anxiety-provoking circumstances. Freudians believe that anally fixated individuals—*anal personalities*—tend toward excessive neatness, stinginess, and stubbornness in adulthood.

THE PHALLIC STAGE. The **phallic stage**, which lasts from approximately three to six years, is of paramount importance to Freudians in explaining personality. During this stage, the penis (for boys) and clitoris (for girls) become the primary sexual zone for pleasure. Simultaneously, children enter into a love triangle involving their parents. According to Freud, whether we resolve this love triangle successfully bears enormous implications for our later personality development. In boys, the phallic stage is termed the **Oedipus complex**, after the tragic Greek character who unknowingly killed his father and married his mother (in girls it's sometimes called the *Electra complex*). In girls, the phallic stage supposedly takes the form of *penis envy*, in which the girl desires to possess a penis, just like Daddy has. For reasons that Freud never clearly explained, girls believe themselves inferior to boys because of their "missing" organ, an inferiority that persists beyond childhood for years or even decades. Penis envy is probably Freud's most ridiculed concept—and with good reason, largely because there's no research support for it.

FIGURE 3 "Sour Grapes." According to psychoanalysts, rationalization often involves a psychological minimization of previously desired outcomes. This etching from Aesop's fables illustrates one example of rationalization, namely, the famous "sour grapes" phenomenon: The fox, who can't reach the previously desired grapes, tells himself, "These grapes are much too green and sour. Even if I could reach them, I would not eat them."

displacement
directing an impulse from a socially unacceptable target onto a safer and more socially acceptable target

rationalization
providing a reasonable-sounding explanation for unreasonable behaviors or for failures

sublimation
transforming a socially unacceptable impulse into an admired goal

oral stage
psychosexual stage that focuses on the mouth

anal stage
psychosexual stage that focuses on toilet training

phallic stage
psychosexual stage that focuses on the genitals

Oedipus complex
conflict during phallic stage in which boys supposedly love their mothers romantically and want to eliminate their fathers as rivals

TABLE 5 Freud's Stages of Psychosexual Development.

STAGE	APPROXIMATE AGE	PRIMARY SOURCE OF SEXUAL PLEASURE
Oral	Birth to 12–18 months	Sucking and drinking
Anal	18 months to 3 years	Alleviating tension by expelling feces
Phallic*	3 years to 6 years	Genitals (penis or clitoris)
Latency	6 years to 12 years	Dormant sexual stage
Genital	12 years and beyond	Renewed sexual impulses; emergence of mature romantic relationships

*Includes Oedipus and Electra complexes.

During the Oedipus complex, the child wants the opposite-sex parent all for himself or herself and wants to eliminate the same-sex parent as a rival. Ultimately, though, reality sets in, leading children to abandon their love for the opposite-sex parent. The children then identify with their same-sex parent and adopt that parent's characteristics: Like father, like son; like mother, like daughter. Nevertheless, if children don't fully resolve the Oedipus complex, claimed Freud, the stage is set for psychological problems later in life.

THE LATENCY AND GENITAL STAGES. The fourth psychosexual stage, the **latency stage**, is a period of calm following the stormy phallic stage. During the latency stage, which lasts from about 6 to 12 years, sexual impulses are submerged into the unconscious. Consistent with this belief, most boys and girls during this stage find members of the opposite sex to be "yucky" and utterly unappealing.

During the fifth and final psychosexual stage, the **genital stage**—which generally begins at around age 12—sexual impulses reawaken. If development up to this point has proceeded without major glitches, this stage witnesses the emergence of mature romantic relationships. In contrast, if serious problems weren't resolved at earlier stages, difficulties with establishing intimate love attachments are likely.

Psychoanalytic Theory Evaluated Scientifically

Freud's psychoanalytic theory has greatly influenced our thinking about personality, and for that reason alone, his ideas merit careful examination (Kramer, 2007). Even Freud's most vocal detractors acknowledge that he was an ingenious thinker. But ingenuity shouldn't be confused with scientific support, and many authors have raised troubling questions concerning the scientific status of psychoanalytic theory. Here we'll examine five major criticisms.

FALSIFIABILITY ▶
Can the claim be disproved?

UNFALSIFIABILITY. Critics have noted that many hypotheses derived from Freudian theory are difficult or impossible to refute (Shermer, 2011). To take just one example, the concept of the defense mechanism of reaction-formation offers a convenient escape hatch that allows many psychoanalytic hypotheses to evade falsification. If we were to find evidence that most 5-year-old boys report being sexually repulsed by their mothers, would this observation refute the existence of the Oedipus complex? Superficially, the answer would seem to be yes, but Freudians could respond that these boys are engaging in reaction-formation and are attracted to their mothers at an unconscious level.

Indeed, Freud often used *ad hoc maneuvers* to protect his pet hypotheses from refutation (Cioffi, 1998). One of Freud's patients intensely disliked her mother-in-law and took pains to ensure that she wouldn't spend a summer vacation with her. Yet while in therapy with Freud, she dreamt of spending a summer vacation with her mother-in-law. This dream seemingly falsifies Freud's theory that all dreams are wish fulfillments. Yet Freud argued that her dream *supported* his theory because her underlying wish was to prove Freud incorrect (Dolnick, 1998). Although we might marvel at Freud's ingenuity, this "heads I win, tails you lose" reasoning renders psychoanalytic theory difficult to falsify.

FAILED PREDICTIONS. Although much of Freudian theory is difficult to falsify, those portions of the theory that can be falsified often have been (Grunbaum, 1984). For example, Freud claimed that children exposed to overly harsh toilet training would grow up to be rigid and perfectionistic. Yet most investigators have found no association between toilet training practices and adult personality (Fisher & Greenberg, 1996). Similarly, there's little scientific support for many Freudian defense mechanisms, including repression (McNally, 2003). In particular, laboratory research shows that

latency stage
psychosexual stage in which sexual impulses are submerged into the unconscious

genital stage
psychosexual stage in which sexual impulses awaken and typically begin to mature into romantic attraction toward others

people are no more likely to forget negative life experiences than equally arousing but positive life experiences (Holmes, 1974, 1990).

QUESTIONABLE CONCEPTION OF THE UNCONSCIOUS. There's increasing reason to doubt the existence of the unconscious as Freud conceived of it. It's true that we're often unaware of why we do things. Richard Nisbett and Timothy Wilson (1977) reviewed a broad range of studies demonstrating that we often convince ourselves that we behave for reasons that are plausible but incorrect. For example, in the context of a memory study, investigators randomly exposed some participants but not others to the word pair *ocean–moon* embedded in a list of word pairs. When later asked to name their favorite laundry detergent, the former participants were significantly more likely than the latter to name "Tide." Yet when asked the reasons for their choice, none came up with the correct explanation, namely, that the words *ocean* and *moon* triggered an association to *tide*. Instead, participants came up with presumably false but plausible explanations (such as "I recently saw a Tide commercial on television").

Some recent evidence suggests that subliminally presented stimuli, that is, stimuli presented below the threshold for awareness, can affect our behavior in subtle ways (Mlodinow, 2012). Other controversial evidence derives from priming paradigms, in which researchers observe the effects of subtle stimuli on people's behavior. In one study, researchers primed some participants but not others with words relevant to old age (like *Florida* and *wrinkle*) in the context of a language task. Remarkably, after the study was over, primed participants walked down the hallway more slowly than did unprimed participants (Bargh & Chartrand, 1999). Nevertheless, several research teams have recently failed to replicate this and similar priming findings (Doyen et al., 2012; LeBel & Paunonen, 2011), so a bit of caution is needed.

The positive results we've described may seem to support Freudian theory because they suggest that factors of which we're unaware influence our behavior (Westen, 1998). Yet they don't provide evidence for *the* unconscious: a massive reservoir of impulses and memories submerged beneath awareness (Wilson, 2002). Freud viewed the unconscious as a "place" where sexual and aggressive energies, along with repressed memories, are housed. Research doesn't support the existence of this place, let alone tell us where it's located (Kihlstrom, 1987).

RELIANCE ON UNREPRESENTATIVE SAMPLES. Many authors have charged that Freud based his theories on atypical samples and generalized them to the rest of humanity. Most of Freud's patients were upper-class neurotic Viennese women, a far cry from the average Nigerian man or Malaysian woman. Freud's theories may therefore possess limited *external validity*, that is, generalizability, for people from other cultural backgrounds. Moreover, although Freud's methods of inquiry were idiographic, his theory was nomothetic: He studied a relatively small number of individuals in depth, but applied his theories to virtually all of humanity.

FLAWED ASSUMPTION OF SHARED ENVIRONMENTAL INFLUENCE. Many Freudian hypotheses presume that shared environment plays a key role in molding personality. For example, Freudians claim that the child emerging from the phallic stage assumes the personality characteristics of the same-sex parent. Nevertheless, as behavior-genetic studies have shown, shared environment plays scant role in adult personality (Loehlin, 2011), contradicting a key proposition of Freudian theory.

In summary, Freudian theory has had a profound influence on modern conceptions of the mind, but much of it is problematic from a scientific standpoint. The one insight of Freud that's best stood the test of time is that we're often unaware of why we do what we do. But this insight wasn't original to Freud (Crews, 1998), and as we'll learn later in the chapter, it's consistent with other models of personality, including behaviorism.

◀ **REPLICABILITY**
Can the results be duplicated in other studies?

One of Freud's best-known patients, known as "Anna O.," was Bertha Pappenheim, who later became the founder of social work in Germany (she was even honored with her own postage stamp). Because many of Freud's patients, like Pappenheim, were relatively wealthy Viennese women, critics have questioned the generalizability of his conclusions to other cultures.

Freud's Followers: The Neo-Freudians

Largely in reaction to criticisms of Freudian theory, a number of theorists—many of them Freud's own students—broke from their mentor to forge their own models of personality. Because these thinkers modified Freud's views in significant ways, they're typically referred to as neo-Freudians.

NEO-FREUDIAN THEORIES: CORE FEATURES. Most neo-Freudian theories share with Freudian theory an emphasis on (a) unconscious influences and (b) the importance of early experience in shaping personality. Nevertheless, **neo-Freudian theories** differ from Freudian theory in two key ways:

1. Compared with Freudian theory, Neo-Freudian theories place less emphasis on sexuality as a driving force in personality and more emphasis on social drives, such as the need for approval.
2. Compared with Freudian theory, most neo-Freudian theories are more optimistic concerning the prospects for personality growth throughout the life span. Freud was notoriously pessimistic about the possibility of personality change after childhood; he once wrote that the goal of psychoanalysis was to turn neurotic misery into ordinary, everyday unhappiness (Breuer & Freud, 1895).

ALFRED ADLER: THE STRIVING FOR SUPERIORITY. The first major follower of Freud to defect from the fold was Viennese psychiatrist Alfred Adler (1870–1937). According to Adler (1931), the principal motive in human personality is not sex or aggression, but the *striving for superiority*. Our overriding goal in life, said Adler, is to be better than others. We aim to accomplish this goal by crafting our distinctive **style of life**, or long-standing pattern of achieving superiority over our peers. People may try to satisfy their superiority strivings by becoming famous entertainers, great athletes, or outstanding parents.

Adler (1922) maintained that neurotic difficulties stem from early childhood; children who are either pampered or neglected by their parents are at later risk for an **inferiority complex**, a popular term inspired by Adler. People with an inferiority complex are prone to low self-esteem and tend to overcompensate for this feeling. As a result, they often attempt to demonstrate their superiority to others at all costs, even if it means dominating them. For Adler, most forms of mental illness are unhealthy attempts to overcompensate for the inferiority complex.

Adler's hypotheses, like Freud's, are difficult to falsify (Popper, 1965). Critics once asked Adler to explain how someone's decision to become a homeless person with alcoholism supported his theory that people always try to attain superiority over others. He responded that such a person has selected a lifestyle that affords a convenient excuse for being unable to achieve greatness. In effect, he can tell himself or herself, "If only I didn't drink, I would have become successful." As we can see, with a little creativity, we can cook up an Adlerian explanation after the fact for almost any behavior.

CARL JUNG: THE COLLECTIVE UNCONSCIOUS. Another pupil of Freud who parted ways with his mentor was Swiss psychiatrist Carl Gustav Jung (1875–1961). Although Freud originally anointed Jung to be the standard-bearer of the next generation of psychoanalysts, Jung became disenchanted with Freud's overemphasis on sexuality. Jung's views have become enormously influential in popular psychology, and Jung is something of a cult figure in pop psychology circles.

Factoid

Some psychotherapists use *Jungian sandplay therapy* (Steinhardt, 1998) to uncover children's deep-seated conflicts. These practitioners try to infer the existence of archetypes on the basis of shapes that children draw in sand and use them as a springboard for therapy. Nevertheless, there's no evidence that Jungian sandplay therapy is effective (Lilienfeld, 1999b), even though it's probably a lot of fun for children, not to mention therapists.

Jung believed that the collective unconscious is our shared storehouse of ancestral memories. He even claimed that episodes of synchronicity, which involve the simultaneous occurrence of thoughts and events, reflect the actions of the collective unconscious. Is this claim falsifiable? (© ScienceCartoonPlus.com)

FALSIFIABILITY ▶
Can the claim be disproved?

neo-Freudian theories
theories derived from Freud's model, but with less emphasis on sexuality as a driving force in personality and more optimism regarding the prospects for long-term personality growth

style of life
according to Adler, each person's distinctive way of achieving superiority

inferiority complex
feelings of low self-esteem that can lead to overcompensation for such feelings

Jung (1936) argued that in addition to Freud's version of the unconscious—which Jung termed the *personal unconscious*—there's also a **collective unconscious**. For Jung, the collective unconscious comprises the memories that ancestors have passed down to us across the generations. It's our shared storehouse of ancestral memories that accounts for cultural similarities in myths and legends. We recognize our mothers immediately after birth, Jung argued, because the memories of thousands of generations of individuals who've seen their mothers after birth have been passed down to us genetically.

Jung further believed that the collective unconscious contains numerous **archetypes**, or cross-culturally universal symbols, which explain the similarities among people in their emotional reactions to many features of the world. Archetypes include the mother, the goddess, the hero, and the mandala (circle), which Jung believed symbolized a desire for wholeness or unity (Campbell, 1988; Jung, 1950). Jung (1958) even speculated that the modern epidemic of flying saucer reports stems from an unconscious desire to achieve a sense of unity with the universe, because flying saucers are shaped like mandalas.

Provocative as it is, Jung's theory suffers from some of the same shortcomings as those of Freud and Adler. It's difficult to falsify, as it generates few clear-cut predictions (Gallo, 1994; Monte, 1995). For example, it's hard to imagine what evidence could falsify Jung's claim that flying saucer sightings stem from an underlying wish for wholeness with the universe. In addition, although Jung hypothesized that archetypes are transmitted to us from our ancestral past, he may not have sufficiently considered a rival explanation. Perhaps archetypes are cross-culturally universal because they reflect crucial elements of the environment—mothers, wise elders, the sun, and the moon (the sun and moon are, after all, shaped like mandalas)—that people across all cultures experience. Shared experiences rather than shared genes may account for commonalities in archetypes across the world (McGowan, 1994).

KAREN HORNEY: FEMINIST PSYCHOLOGY. German physician Karen Horney (1885–1952) was the first major feminist personality theorist. Although not departing drastically from Freud's core assumptions, Horney (1939) took aim at those aspects of his theory that she saw as gender biased. She viewed Freud's concept of penis envy as especially misguided. Horney maintained that women's sense of inferiority stems not from their anatomy, but from their excessive dependency on men, which society has ingrained in them from an early age. She similarly objected to the Oedipus complex on the grounds that it's neither inevitable nor universal. This complex, she maintained, is a *symptom* rather than a cause of psychological problems, because it arises only when the opposite-sex parent is overly protective and the same-sex parent is overly critical.

FREUD'S FOLLOWERS EVALUATED SCIENTIFICALLY. Many neo-Freudian theorists tempered some of the excesses of Freudian theory. They pointed out that anatomy isn't always destiny when it comes to the psychological differences between the sexes, and they argued that social influences must be reckoned with in the development of personality. Nevertheless, as we've seen, falsifiability remains a serious concern for neo-Freudian theories, especially those of Adler and Jung. As a consequence, their scientific standing remains almost as controversial as that of Freudian theory.

Jung believed that the mandala *(left)* was an archetype, or cross-culturally universal symbol. Jung might have taken the notion too far, neglecting to consider the fact that many other archetypes are also circular.

Karen Horney, the first major feminist psychological theorist, believed that Freud greatly underemphasized social factors as causes of inferiority feelings in many women.

◄ **FALSIFIABILITY**
Can the claim be disproved?

◄ **RULING OUT RIVAL HYPOTHESES**
Have important alternative explanations for the findings been excluded?

> **collective unconscious**
> according to Jung, our shared storehouse of memories that ancestors have passed down to us across generations
>
> **archetype**
> cross-culturally universal symbols

◄ **FALSIFIABILITY**
Can the claim be disproved?

Personality

Assess Your Knowledge — FACT or FICTION?

1. Freud believed that sex is the only important drive in personality.   True / False

2. Freudians would say that most persons with very high opinions of themselves have overdeveloped egos.   True / False

3. According to Freudians, a given dream symbol such as a snake doesn't have the same underlying meaning for every dreamer.   True / False

4. According to Freud, a person who is orally fixated would be likely to drink excessively.   True / False

5. One strength of Freudian theory is that many of its predictions are hard to disprove.   True / False

6. Most neo-Freudian theorists, like Adler, placed less emphasis than did Freud on social influences on personality development.   True / False

Answers: 1. F; 2. F; 3. T; 4. T; 5. F; 6. F

Behavioral and Social Learning Theories of Personality

4 Identify the core assumptions of behavioral and social learning theories of personality.

5 Describe key criticisms of behavioral and social learning approaches.

So why are we again crossing paths with behaviorism? After all, behaviorism is a theory of learning rather than a theory of personality, isn't it?

Actually, behaviorism is both a theory of learning *and* a theory of personality. Radical behaviorists like B. F. Skinner believe that differences in our personalities stem largely from differences in our learning histories. Unlike Freudians, radical behaviorists reject the notion that the first few years of life are especially critical in personality development. Childhood certainly matters, but our learning histories continue to mold our personalities throughout the life span.

For radical behaviorists, our personalities are bundles of habits acquired by classical and operant conditioning. In contrast to other personality theorists, radical behaviorists don't believe that personality *causes* behavior. For them, personality *consists of* behaviors. These behaviors are both overt (observable) and covert (unobservable), such as thoughts and feelings. A radical behaviorist wouldn't have much trouble accepting the idea that some people are extraverted or that extraverted people tend to have many friends and attend many parties. But a radical behaviorist would strongly dispute the conclusion that certain people have many friends and attend many parties *because* they're extraverted.

Behavioral Views of the Causes of Personality

Radical behaviorists view personality as under the control of two major influences: (a) genetic factors and (b) *contingencies* in the environment, that is, reinforcers and punishers. Together, these influences explain why our personalities differ.

BEHAVIORAL VIEWS OF DETERMINISM. Like psychoanalysts, radical behaviorists are determinists: They believe all of our actions are products of preexisting causal influences. This is one of the precious few issues on which Freud and Skinner would likely have agreed if we could magically bring them back to life for a debate, one that most modern psychologists would probably pay a sizable chunk of their life savings to witness. For radical

Although this person may perceive her decision to eat or not eat a piece of candy as under her control, radical behaviorists would regard her perception as an illusion.

behaviorists, free will is an illusion. We may believe we're free to continue reading this sentence or to stop to grab a long-awaited bowl of ice cream, but we're fooling ourselves. We're convinced that we're free to select our behaviors only because we're usually oblivious to the situational factors that trigger them (Skinner, 1974).

BEHAVIORAL VIEWS OF UNCONSCIOUS PROCESSING. Both Freudians and Skinnerians agree that we often don't understand the reasons for their behavior (Overskeid, 2007), but their views of why this is the case differ sharply. For Skinner, we're "unconscious" of many things because we're often unaware of immediate situational influences on our behavior (Skinner, 1974). We may have had the experience of suddenly humming a song to ourselves and wondering why we were doing so, until we realized that this song had been playing softly on a distant radio. According to Skinner, we were initially unaware of the external cause of this behavior, in this case, the song in the background.

Yet such unawareness is a far cry from the Freudian unconscious, which is a vast storehouse of inaccessible thoughts, memories, and impulses. For radical behaviorists, there's no such storehouse because the unconscious variables that play a role in causing behavior lie *outside*, not inside, us.

Social Learning Theories of Personality: The Causal Role of Thinking Resurrected

Although influenced by radical behaviorists, **social learning theorists** (also sometimes called social cognitive theorists) believed that Skinner had gone too far in his wholesale rejection of the influence of thoughts on behavior. Spurred on by Edward Chase Tolman and others who believed that learning depends on our plans and goals, these theorists emphasized thinking as a cause of personality. How we interpret our environments affects how we react to them; if we perceive others as threatening, we'll typically be hostile and suspicious in return. According to social learning theorists, classical conditioning and operant conditioning are not automatic or reflexive processes; they are the products of cognition. That is, as we acquire information in classical and operant conditioning, we're actively thinking about and interpreting what this information means. For example, in classical conditioning, the organism is gradually building up expectancies regarding the relation between conditioned and unconditioned stimuli (Mischel, 1973).

SOCIAL LEARNING VIEWS OF DETERMINISM. Most social learning theorists hold a more complex view of determinism than do radical behaviorists. Albert Bandura (1986) made a compelling case for **reciprocal determinism**, a form of causation whereby personality and cognitive factors, behavior, and environmental variables mutually influence one another. Our high levels of extraversion may motivate us to introduce ourselves to our introductory psychology classmates and thereby make new friends. In turn, our newfound friends may reinforce our extraversion, encouraging us to attend parties we'd otherwise skip. Attending these parties may result in our acquiring additional friends who further reinforce our extraversion, and so on.

OBSERVATIONAL LEARNING AND PERSONALITY. Social learning theorists proposed that much of learning occurs by watching others. *Observational learning* appears to be a key form of learning neglected by traditional behaviorists (Bandura, 1965; Nadel et al., 2011). Observational learning greatly expands the range of stimuli from which we can benefit. It also means that our parents and teachers can play significant roles in shaping our personalities, because we acquire both good and bad habits by watching and later emulating them. For example, through observational learning, we can learn to behave altruistically by seeing our parents donate money to charities.

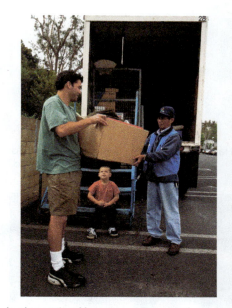

In observational learning, parents, teachers, and other adults play significant roles in shaping children's personalities: Children learn good and bad habits by watching and later emulating adults. This child may learn early that charitable giving is a worthy endeavor.

social learning theorists
theorists who emphasize thinking as a cause of personality

reciprocal determinism
tendency for people to mutually influence each other's behavior

SENSE OF PERCEIVED CONTROL. Social learning theorists emphasized individuals' sense of control over life events. Julian Rotter (1966) introduced the concept of **locus of control** to describe the extent to which we believe that reinforcers and punishers lie inside or outside our control. People with an internal locus of control ("internals") believe that life events are due largely to their own efforts and personal characteristics. In contrast, people with an external locus of control ("externals") believe that life events are largely a product of chance and fate. For example, an "internal" would be likely to respond "true" to a statement such as *If I set my mind to it, I can accomplish just about anything I want*, whereas an "external" would be likely to respond "false."

Rotter hypothesized that internals are less prone than externals to emotional upset following life stressors, because they're more likely to believe they can remedy problems on their own. Indeed, almost all forms of psychological distress, including depression and anxiety, are associated with an external locus of control (Benassi, Sweeney, & Dufour, 1988; Carton & Nowicki, 1996; Coyne & Thompson, 2011). It's not clear, though, whether these correlational findings reflect a causal relationship between external locus of control and mental disorders, as Rotter believed. Perhaps once people develop depression or anxiety, they begin to feel their lives are spiraling out of control. Or perhaps people who doubt their abilities are prone to an external locus of control, on the one hand, and depression and anxiety, on the other.

When people in difficult circumstances obtain a measure of control over their lives, their adjustment improves. Ellen Langer and Judith Rodin (1976) gave residents on one floor of a nursing home control over several aspects of their environment. Residents on that floor had more freedom in arranging their rooms, lodging complaints, and attending films, whereas residents on a different floor had minimal control over those matters. Langer and Rodin found that residents afforded greater control showed better emotional adjustment than did other residents. Remarkably, one year later, fewer residents in the former condition had died. Although these results seem to suggest that a heightened sense of control enhances psychological and physical health, they're a bit difficult to interpret. Perhaps residents given more control actually took advantage of it by sprucing up their rooms or voicing concerns to staff. So it may not be the amount of perceived control as much as the amount of *actual* control that matters.

Behavioral and Social Learning Theories Evaluated Scientifically

B. F. Skinner and his fellow radical behaviorists agreed with Freud that our behavior is determined, but they maintained that the primary causes of our behavior—contingencies—lie outside rather than inside us. Even critics of radical behaviorism acknowledge that Skinner and his followers placed the field of psychology on firmer scientific footing. Many of them charged, however, that the claim of radical behaviorists that our thoughts play no causal role in our behavior is implausible from an evolutionary perspective. Natural selection has endowed us with an enormous cerebral cortex, which is specialized for problem solving, planning, reasoning, and other high-level cognitive processes. It seems difficult to comprehend why our huge cortexes would have evolved if our thoughts were merely by-products of contingencies.

Social learning theorists rekindled psychologists' interests in thinking and argued that observational learning is a crucial form of learning in addition to classical and operant conditioning. Nevertheless, social learning theory isn't immune to criticism. In particular, the claim that observational learning exerts a powerful influence over our personalities implies an important causal role of shared environment. After all, if we learn largely by modeling the behaviors of our parents and other relatives, we should become like them. Yet as we've learned, behavior-genetic studies have shown that the effects of shared environment on adult personality are weak or nonexistent (Harris, 1998).

Although social learning theorists believe that learning processes depend on cognition (thinking), scientists have observed these processes in animals with tiny cerebral cortexes and even with no cortexes at all. For example, they've documented classical

---

CORRELATION VS. CAUSATION ▶
Can we be sure that A causes B?

RULING OUT RIVAL HYPOTHESES ▶
Have important alternative explanations for the findings been excluded?

How much of the daughter's personality and mannerisms are due to social learning from her mother? The scientific jury is still out.

locus of control
extent to which people believe that reinforcers and punishers lie inside or outside their control

conditioning in honeybees (Alcock, 1999) and starfish (McClintock & Lawrence, 1985). There's even evidence that classical conditioning occurs in such microscopic organisms as protozoa (Bergstrom, 1968) and hydra (Tanaka, 1966), although not all researchers have replicated these findings (Applewhite et al., 1971). There have also been reports of observational learning in the octopus (Fiorito & Scotto, 1993), although these findings are controversial.

The fact that learning occurs in relatively simple animals implies any one of three things. First, perhaps social learning theorists are wrong that basic forms of learning depend on cognition. Second, perhaps the thinking processes involved in these forms of learning are primitive in certain cases, although we might justifiably question whether a starfish, let alone a protozoan, is capable of genuine "thought." Third, the learning processes of simple animals may rely on different mechanisms from those of humans. At this point, the scientific evidence doesn't permit a clear answer.

◀ **REPLICABILITY**
Can the results be duplicated in other studies?

 Explore in **MyPsychLab** the **Concept:** Behavioral versus Social Learning Theories of Personality

 Study and **Review** in **MyPsychLab**

Assess Your Knowledge — FACT or FICTION?

1. For radical behaviorists, our personalities are bundles of habits influenced by learning.   **True / False**

2. Radical behaviorists argue that we're sometimes "unconscious" of the true causes of our behavior.   **True / False**

3. Social learning theorists believe that observational learning is a key form of learning in addition to classical and operant conditioning.   **True / False**

4. According to social learning theorists, individuals with an internal locus of control are more prone to depression than individuals with an external locus of control.   **True / False**

Answers: 1. T ; 2. T ; 3. T ; 4. F

Humanistic Models of Personality: The Third Force

6 Explain the concept of self-actualization and its role in humanistic models.

7 Describe key criticisms of humanistic approaches.

Psychoanalytic theory, along with behavioral and social learning models, dominated personality psychology throughout the first half of the twentieth century. In the 1950s and 1960s, however, *humanistic models* emerged as a "third force" in personality psychology. Humanistic psychologists rejected the strict determinism of psychoanalysts and behaviorists and embraced the notion of free will. We're perfectly free, they maintained, to choose either socially constructive or destructive paths in life.

Most humanistic psychologists propose that the core motive in personality is **self-actualization**: the drive to develop our innate potential to the fullest possible extent. Freudians would say that self-actualization would be disastrous for society because our innate drives, housed in the id, are selfish and potentially harmful if not controlled. For Freudians, a society of self-actualized people would result in sheer pandemonium, with citizens expressing their sexual and aggressive urges with reckless abandon. Humanistic theorists, in contrast, view human nature as inherently constructive, so they see self-actualization as a worthy goal.

Carl Rogers, pioneer of humanistic psychology, held an optimistic view of human nature, although some critics have accused him of being naive in minimizing the dark side of human nature.

Rogers and Maslow: Self-Actualization Realized and Unrealized

The best-known humanistic theorist was Carl Rogers (1902–1987), who used his personality theory as a point of departure for an influential form of psychotherapy. Ever the optimist, Rogers believed that we could all achieve our full potential for emotional fulfillment if only society allowed it.

self-actualization
drive to develop our innate potential to the fullest possible extent

ROGERS'S MODEL OF PERSONALITY. According to Rogers (1947), our personalities consist of three major components: organism, self, and conditions of worth.

1. The *organism* is our innate—and substantially genetically influenced—blueprint. In this regard, it's like the Freudian id, except that Rogers viewed the organism as inherently positive and helpful toward others. Rogers wasn't terribly specific, however, about the makeup of the organism.

2. The *self* is our self-concept, the set of beliefs about who we are.

3. **Conditions of worth** are the expectations we place on ourselves for appropriate and inappropriate behavior. Like the Freudian superego, they emanate from our parents and society, and eventually we internalize them. Conditions of worth arise—typically in childhood—when others make their acceptance of us conditional (that is, dependent) on certain behaviors but not others. As a result, we accept ourselves only if we act in certain ways. A child who enjoys writing poetry may develop conditions of worth if taunted by peers. "When I'm teased for writing poetry, I'm not worthwhile. When I stop, I'm not teased; so I become worthwhile." For Rogers, individual differences in personality stem largely from differences in the conditions of worth that others impose on us. Although in his idealistic moments Rogers envisioned a world in which conditions of worth no longer existed, he reluctantly acknowledged that in modern society, even the best adjusted among us inevitably harbor certain conditions of worth. Conditions of worth result in **incongruence** between self and organism. Incongruence means that our personalities are inconsistent with our innate dispositions: We're no longer our genuine selves, because we're acting in ways that are inconsistent with our genuine potentialities.

MASLOW: THE CHARACTERISTICS OF SELF-ACTUALIZED PEOPLE. Whereas Rogers focused largely on individuals whose tendencies toward self-actualization were thwarted and therefore ended up with psychological problems, Abraham Maslow (1908–1970) focused on individuals who were self-actualized, especially historical figures. He regarded full self-actualization as a rare feat, one accomplished by only about 2 percent of people. Among those whom Maslow considered self-actualized were Thomas Jefferson; Abraham Lincoln; Martin Luther King, Jr.; Helen Keller; and Mahatma Gandhi.

According to Maslow (1971), self-actualized people tend to be creative, spontaneous, and accepting of themselves and others. They're self-confident but not self-centered. They focus on real-world and intellectual problems and have a few deep friendships rather than many superficial ones. Contrary to what we might expect, self-actualized individuals typically crave privacy and can come off as aloof or even difficult to deal with, because they've outgrown the need to be popular. As a consequence, they're not afraid to "rock the boat" when necessary or express unpopular opinions. They're also prone to **peak experiences**—transcendent moments of intense excitement and tranquility marked by a profound sense of connection to the world.

Humanistic Models Evaluated Scientifically

Humanistic models of personality boldly proclaimed the importance of free will and personal choice, and appealed to a generation of young people disenchanted with the determinism of psychoanalysis and behaviorism. Yet investigators in *comparative psychology*, the branch of psychology that compares behavior across species, have challenged Rogers's claim that human nature is entirely positive. Their research suggests that the capacity for aggression is inherent in our close primate cousins, the chimpanzees (Goodall & van Lawick, 1971; Wrangham & Glowacki, 2012). There's also compelling evidence from twin studies that aggression is part of humans' genetic heritage (Anholt, 2012; Krueger, Hicks, & McGue, 2001). Therefore, actualization of our full genetic potential is

Mahatma Gandhi is one of the historical figures whom Abraham Maslow considered to be self-actualized.

conditions of worth
according to Rogers, expectations we place on ourselves for appropriate and inappropriate behavior

incongruence
inconsistency between our personalities and innate dispositions

peak experience
transcendent moment of intense excitement and tranquility marked by a profound sense of connection to the world

unlikely to bring about the state of eternal bliss that Rogers imagined. At the same time, research suggests that the capacity for altruism is intrinsic to both chimpanzees and humans (de Waal, 1990, 2009; Wilson, 1993). Human nature, it seems, is a complex mix of selfish and selfless motives.

Rogers's research demonstrated that the discrepancy between people's descriptions of their actual versus ideal selves is greater for emotionally disturbed than for emotionally healthy individuals. This difference decreases over the course of psychotherapy (Rogers & Dymond, 1954). Rogers interpreted this finding as reflecting a lessening of conditions of worth. Yet these results are hard to interpret, because the people who showed decreases in incongruence following therapy weren't the same people who improved (Loevinger, 1987).

Maslow's research on the characteristics of self-actualized individuals paved the way for today's "positive psychology" movement. Indeed, although he rarely receives credit for it, Maslow (1954) was the first person to use this term. Yet his work is problematic on methodological grounds. In beginning with the assumption that self-actualized individuals tend to be creative and spontaneous, Maslow may have limited his search to historical figures who displayed these traits. As such, he may have fallen prey to confirmation bias (Aronson, 2011): Because he wasn't blind to his hypothesis concerning the personality features of self-actualized individuals, he had no good way of guarding against this bias.

Humanistic models are also difficult to falsify. If a study of the general population showed that many people were self-actualized, humanistic psychologists could interpret this finding as evidence that self-actualization is a key influence on personality. But if this study showed that virtually no one was self-actualized, humanistic psychologists could explain away this finding by saying that most individuals' drives toward self-actualization had been stifled. Although the claim that self-actualization is the central motive in personality may not be testable scientifically, the principle that we should develop our potential to the fullest may have considerable value as a philosophy of life.

◀ **FALSIFIABILITY**
Can the claim be disproved?

✔ **Study** and **Review** in **MyPsychLab**

Assess Your Knowledge — FACT or FICTION?

1. According to Rogers, human nature is inherently positive. True / False

2. Rogers believed that only severely disturbed individuals acquire conditions of worth. True / False

3. Maslow argued that almost all self-actualized individuals are sociable and easy to get along with. True / False

4. Many claims of humanistic models are difficult to falsify. True / False

Answers: 1. T; 2. F; 3. F; 4. T

Trait Models of Personality: Consistencies in Our Behavior

8 Describe trait models of personality, including the Big Five.

9 Identify key criticisms of trait models.

In contrast to most personality theorists we've reviewed, proponents of trait models are interested primarily in describing and understanding the *structure* of personality. That is, they examine the question of what makes up our personality, rather than the question of what causes it. Much like early chemists who strove to identify the elements of the periodic table, trait theorists aim to pinpoint the major traits of personality, which, as we've learned, are relatively enduring dispositions that affect our behaviors across situations.

Factoid

Individuals' handshakes can tell us something about their Big Five personality traits. Research demonstrates that people with firm handshakes tend to be somewhat higher in extraversion and openness to experience, and lower in neuroticism, than people with limp handshakes (Chaplin et al., 2000).

factor analysis
statistical technique that analyzes the correlations among responses on personality inventories and other measures

Big Five
five traits that have surfaced repeatedly in factor analyses of personality measures

Identifying Traits: Factor Analysis

Invoking personality traits as causes of behavior has its challenges. To start with, we must avoid the *circular reasoning fallacy*. We might conclude that a child who kicks others on the playground is aggressive. But in asking how we know that the child is aggressive, we might respond "because he kicks other children on the playground." Note that this answer merely restates the same evidence we used to infer that the child was aggressive in the first place. To avoid this error in logic, we need to demonstrate that personality traits predict behaviors in novel situations or correlate with biological or laboratory measures.

From there, we need to narrow down the pool of possible traits. As Gordon Allport observed, there are over 17,000 terms in the English language referring to personality traits: shy, stubborn, impulsive, greedy, cheerful, and on and on (Allport & Odbert, 1936). To reduce this enormous diversity of traits to a much smaller number of underlying traits, trait theorists use a statistical technique called **factor analysis**. This method analyzes the correlations among responses on personality measures to identify the underlying "factors" that give rise to these correlations.

TABLE 6 presents the correlations among six different variables—sociability, popularity, liveliness, risk-taking, sensation seeking, and impulsivity—in a hypothetical correlation matrix: a table of correlations. As we look over this correlation matrix, we'll notice that only some of the cells contain numbers; that's because correlation matrixes present each correlation only once. (That's why, for example, the matrix displays the correlation between variables 1 and 4 only once.) We can see that variables 1 through 3 are highly correlated, as are variables 4 through 6. But these two sets of variables aren't correlated much with one another, so the correlation matrix suggests the presence of two factors. We might call the factor comprising variables 1 through 3 (in blue) "extraversion," and we might call the factor comprising variables 4 through 6 (in green) "fearlessness." The formal technique of factor analysis uses more rigorous statistical criteria to accomplish the same goal as the "eyeball method" we just walked you through.

The Big Five Model of Personality: The Geography of the Psyche

Although there's no universal consensus among trait theorists regarding the most scientifically supported model of personality structure, one model has amassed an impressive body of research evidence. This model, the **Big Five**, consists of five traits that have surfaced repeatedly in factor analyses of personality measures.

The Big Five were uncovered using a **lexical approach** to personality, which proposes that the most crucial features of human personality are embedded in our language (Goldberg, 1993; Lynam, 2012). The logic here is straightforward. If a personality trait is important in our daily lives, it's likely that we talk a lot about it. The Big Five emerged

TABLE 6 An "Eyeball" Factor Analysis of Six Variables. Follow along as we describe this correlation matrix of six personality measures (the 1.00s on the diagonal represent the correlation of each variable with itself, which is a perfect correlation).

	MEASURES					
	VARIABLE 1 SOCIABILITY	**VARIABLE 2 POPULARITY**	**VARIABLE 3 LIVELINESS**	**VARIABLE 4 RISK-TAKING**	**VARIABLE 5 SENSATION SEEKING**	**VARIABLE 6 IMPULSIVITY**
Variable 1	1.00	.78	.82	.12	.07	−.03
Variable 2		1.00	.70	.08	.02	.11
Variable 3			1.00	.05	.11	.18
Variable 4				1.00	.69	.85
Variable 5					1.00	.72
Variable 6						1.00

from factor analyses of trait terms in dictionaries and works of literature. According to Paul Costa, Robert McCrae, and their collaborators (Costa & McCrae, 1992; Miller, 2012; Widiger, 2001), these five dimensions (listed roughly in order of their consistency of appearance across studies) are:

- *Extraversion*—extraverted people tend to be social and lively.
- *Neuroticism*—neurotic people tend to be tense and moody.
- *Agreeableness*—agreeable people tend to be sociable and easy to get along with.
- *Conscientiousness*—conscientious people tend to be careful and responsible.
- *Openness to Experience*, sometimes just called "Openness"—open people tend to be intellectually curious and unconventional in their interests and outlook on the world.

We can use either of two waterlogged acronyms—OCEAN or CANOE—as a handy mnemonic for remembering the Big Five. According to Big Five advocates, we can use these factors to describe *all* people, including those with psychological disorders (Widiger & Costa, 2012). Each of us occupies some location on each of these dimensions, with most of us falling roughly in the middle of the distributions of these traits. In contrast, people with psychological disorders tend to receive more extreme scores. A severely depressed person, for example, may be low in Extraversion, high in Neuroticism, and about average on the other three dimensions.

The Big Five appear in people's ratings of personality even when researchers ask participants to describe people they've only seen, not met (Passini & Norman, 1966). This finding suggests that we harbor *implicit personality theories*, that is, intuitive ideas concerning personality traits and their associations with behavior. The popular dating website eHarmony.com uses the Big Five to match prospective partners, although the research evidence for its success is minimal (Finkel et al., 2012). The work of Samuel Gosling and others suggests that the Big Five, in addition to a sixth trait of dominance, also emerge in studies of chimpanzee personality (Gosling, 2001, 2008; King & Figueredo, 1997), although it's difficult to exclude the possibility that raters in these studies are *anthropomorphizing*— that is, unintentionally imposing their implicit personality theories on chimpanzees.

THE BIG FIVE AND BEHAVIOR. The Big Five predict many important real-world behaviors. High Conscientiousness, low Neuroticism, and perhaps high Agreeableness are associated with successful job performance (Barrick & Mount, 1991; Tett, Jackson, & Rothstein, 1991) and good grades in school (Conard, 2006; Heaven, Ciarrochi, & Vialle, 2007). In some but not all studies, Extraversion is positively correlated with successful performance among salespersons (Furnham & Fudge, 2008). Conscientiousness is positively associated with physical health and even life span (Martin & Friedman, 2000), probably in part because conscientious people are more likely than others to engage in healthy behaviors like exercising regularly and not smoking (Bogg & Roberts, 2004; Hill & Roberts, 2011) and because they may be especially likely to consult with their physicians. Three researchers (Rubenzer, Fashingbauer, & Ones, 2000) asked presidential biographers to rate the U.S. presidents from George Washington through George W. Bush. Scores on Conscientiousness and Openness to Experience were correlated positively with independently assessed ratings of presidents' historical greatness. Interestingly, Agreeableness was (slightly) *negatively* correlated with historical greatness, suggesting that the best presidents often aren't always the easiest to get along with.

CULTURE AND THE BIG FIVE. In seeking to address enduring questions concerning the cross-cultural relevance of personality, researchers have discovered that the Big Five are identifiable in China, Japan, Italy, Hungary, and Turkey (De Raad et al., 1998; McCrae & Costa, 1997; Triandis & Suh, 2002; Trull, 2012). Nevertheless, there may be limits to the Big

 Research shows that the Big Five trait of openness to experience predicts art preferences (Feist & Brady, 2004). **Which painting above would a person high in openness to experience be most likely to prefer? Why?** (See answer upside down on bottom of page.)

✳ **Explore** in **MyPsychLab** the **Concept:** The Big Five

lexical approach
approach proposing that the most crucial features of personality are embedded in our language

Answer: Painting on the top. Openness to experience is correlated with preference for abstract art, probably because this trait is related to unconventionality and tolerance for ambiguity.

Five's cross-cultural universality. Openness to experience doesn't emerge clearly in all cultures (Church, 2008; De Raad & Perugini, 2002), and some investigators have found dimensions in addition to the Big Five. For example, personality studies in China have revealed an additional "Chinese tradition" factor that encompasses aspects of personality distinctive to Chinese culture, including an emphasis on group harmony and on saving face to avoid embarrassment (Cheung & Leung, 1998). Moreover, studies in Germany, Finland, and several other countries sometimes suggest the presence of a factor comprising honesty and humility in addition to the Big Five (Lee & Ashton, 2004; Weller & Thulin, 2012).

Are you a dog person or a cat person? Recent research suggests that scores on the Big Five can help predict the answer: Dog people tend to have somewhat higher scores than do cat people on extraversion, agreeableness, and conscientiousness, whereas cat people tend to have somewhat higher scores than do dog people on neuroticism and openness to experience (Gosling, Sandy, & Potter, 2010).

Individualism-Collectivism and Personality. Cross-cultural researchers have devoted considerable attention to a key dimension relevant to personality: *individualism-collectivism*. People from largely individualistic cultures like the United States tend to focus on themselves and their personal goals, whereas people from largely collectivist cultures, primarily in Asia, tend to focus on their relations with others (Triandis, 1989). People from individualistic cultures usually report higher self-esteem than those from collectivist cultures (Heine et al., 1999). In addition, personality traits may be less predictive of behavior in collectivist than individualistic cultures, probably because people's behavior in collectivist cultures is more influenced by social norms (Church & Katigbak, 2002).

Still, we shouldn't oversimplify the distinction between individualistic and collectivist cultures. Only about 60 percent of people in individualist cultures possess individualist personalities, and only about 60 percent of people in collectivist cultures possess collectivist personalities (Triandis & Suh, 2002). Furthermore, Asian countries differ markedly in their levels of collectivism, reminding us of the perils of stereotyping and overgeneralizing. For example, although Chinese are generally more collectivist compared with Americans, Japanese and Koreans aren't (Oyserman, Coon, & Kemmelmeier, 2002).

ALTERNATIVES TO THE BIG FIVE. The Big Five is a useful system for organizing individual differences in personality. Nevertheless, there's reason to question the lexical approach, as people may not be consciously aware of all important features of personality (J. Block, 1995). As a consequence, our language may not adequately reflect these features. In addition, there's no Big Five factor corresponding to morality (Loevinger, 1993), despite the centrality of this variable to many theories of personality, including those of Freud and his followers. Still other psychologists like Hans Eysenck (1991), Auke Tellegen (1982; Tellegen & Waller, 2008), and C. Robert Cloninger (1987; Cloninger & Svrakic, 2009) maintain that three dimensions rather than five offer the most accurate model of personality structure. According to them, the Big Five dimensions of Agreeableness, Conscientiousness, and (low) Openness to Experience combine to form one larger dimension of impulse control or fearfulness along with the dimensions of Extraversion and Neuroticism (Church, 1994). The "Big Three" model of personality structure is a worthy alternative to the Big Five (Harkness, 2007).

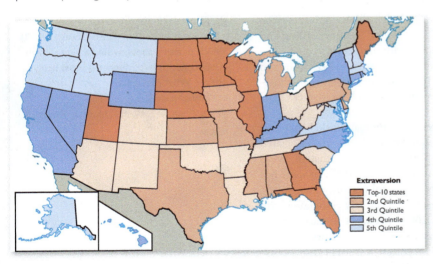

Extraversion
- Top-10 states
- 2nd Quintile
- 3rd Quintile
- 4th Quintile
- 5th Quintile

Research by Peter Rentfrow, Samuel Gosling, and Jeff Potter (2008) shows that the Big Five traits differ across geographical regions. Here, for example, is a map of the levels of extraversion across the 50 U.S. states. This research raises intriguing questions: For example, does living in relatively isolated states like Idaho or Alaska make a person introverted, or are introverted people drawn to living in isolated states?

Basic Tendencies versus Characteristic Adaptations

Personality traits don't tell the whole story of why we differ from each other. The story of Jack and Oskar underscores the distinction between *basic tendencies* and *characteristic adaptations* (Harkness & Lilienfeld, 1997; McCrae & Costa, 1995; Terracciano & McCrae, 2012). Basic tendencies are underlying personality traits, whereas characteristic adaptations are their behavioral manifestations. The key point is that people can express their personality traits in dramatically different ways. In Jack and Oskar's case, the same basic tendencies—intense loyalty and devotion to social causes—were expressed in markedly different characteristic adaptations: Jack's Judaism and profound dislike of Germans and Oskar's Nazism and profound dislike of Jews.

Sensation seeking (Zuckerman, 1979), or the tendency to seek out new and exciting stimuli, offers another example of this distinction. High sensation seekers enjoy parachuting from airplanes, sampling spicy foods, and living life in the fast lane. In contrast, low sensation seekers dislike risk, adventure, and novelty; when they go out to eat, they go to the same restaurant and always order chicken parmigiana (or whatever their favorite dish might be). Interestingly, the average sensation-seeking scores of firefighters and prisoners are essentially identical, but significantly higher than those of average college students (Harkness & Lilienfeld, 1997; Zuckerman, 1994). Apparently, people can express tendencies toward risk taking and danger seeking in either socially constructive (firefighting) or destructive (crime) outlets. Why some sensation seekers end up in firehouses and others in prisons remains a mystery (Dutton, 2012).

Can Personality Traits Change?

Longitudinal studies demonstrate that prior to age 30, personality traits sometimes change over time. Openness, extraversion, and neuroticism tend to decline a bit from the late teens to early thirties, whereas conscientiousness and agreeableness tend to increase a bit (Costa & McCrae, 1992; Srivastava et al., 2003). Yet studies also show that the levels of most traits don't change much after age 30 and change even less after about age 50 (McCrae & Costa, 1994; Roberts & DelVecchio, 2000). We don't know whether psychotherapy can change personality, although many psychologists today are even less optimistic about this prospect than they were in Freud's day.

The last two decades have witnessed a good deal of discussion about whether medication can change personality traits (Jylha et al., 2012; Kramer, 1993). There's anecdotal evidence that certain mood-altering medications like Prozac, Paxil, and Zoloft produce calmness and decreased shyness, even among people without mental illness (Concar, 1994), perhaps suggesting that these drugs may allow us to become "better than well." Although the evidence is preliminary, the results of one study demonstrate that well-adjusted people who ingest Paxil experience less hostility and more interest in socializing than those who ingested a placebo (Knutson et al., 1988). In a more recent studies, among people with clinical depression (Dunlop et al., 2011; Tang et al., 2009), Paxil and Zoloft—compared with a placebo—increased levels of such traits as extraversion and fearlessness and decreased levels of such traits as neuroticism and impulsivity.

These findings raise intriguing scientific, practical, and ethical questions. On the scientific side, might our personalities, which we think of as being an intrinsic part of ourselves, be easier to modify than we might have supposed? On the practical and ethical sides, could the use of medication to change personality have any important disadvantages? Eevolutionary psychologists argue that many emotions serve essential adaptive functions. Anxiety, for example, may be a crucial warning signal of potential danger. If we reduced most people's anxiety levels, could we produce a civilization of passive citizens unconcerned about impending disaster? The questions don't lend themselves to simple answers, but they're important for us to consider as a society.

Personality research reveals that prisoners and firefighters tend to receive equally high scores on measures of sensation seeking, suggesting that they may have channeled their basic tendencies into dramatically different characteristic adaptations.

Watch in **MyPsychLab** the **Video:** Personality Not Set in Stone

Personality

Trait Models Evaluated Scientifically

Trait theory was highly influential through the early and mid-twentieth century. Then in his bombshell 1968 book *Personality and Assessment*, Walter Mischel called the very notion of personality traits into question, embroiling the field of trait psychology in heated controversy for well over a decade.

WALTER MISCHEL'S ARGUMENT: BEHAVIORAL INCONSISTENCY. As noted earlier, psychologists had long assumed that traits influence behavior across many situations. But in his review of the literature, Mischel found low correlations among different behaviors presumed to reflect the same trait. For example, a study by Hugh Hartshorne and Mark May (1928) had examined the correlations among behavioral indicators of honesty among children. Hartshorne and May concocted situations that allowed children to behave honestly or dishonestly, giving them the opportunity to steal a dime, change answers on an exam, and lie. Surprisingly, the correlations among children's behavior across these situations were low, with none exceeding .30. So children who steal, for example, aren't much more likely than other children to cheat. Numerous researchers have reported similar findings in adults for such traits as dependency, friendliness, and conscientiousness (Bem & Allen, 1974; Diener & Larsen, 1984; Mischel, 1968). People, it seems, aren't nearly as consistent across situations as most of us believe.

Mischel concluded that measures of personality aren't especially helpful for what they were designed to do—forecast behavior. Some psychologists later tried to explain our persistent belief in the predictive power of personality traits in terms of our cognitive biases, especially the fundamental attribution error. For them, we "see" people's personalities all around us because we mistake situational influences on their behavior, such as peer pressure, for personality influences (Bem & Allen, 1974; Ross & Nisbett, 1991).

PERSONALITY TRAITS REBORN: PSYCHOLOGISTS RESPOND TO MISCHEL. Were Mischel's criticisms valid? Yes and no. As Seymour Epstein (1979) noted, Mischel was correct that personality traits aren't highly predictive of isolated behaviors, such as lying or cheating, in a single situation. Nevertheless, in several studies, Epstein showed that personality traits are often highly predictive of *aggregated* behaviors, that is, composites of behavior averaged across many situations. If we use a measure of extraversion to predict whether our friend will attend a party next Saturday night, we'll probably do only slightly better than chance. In contrast, if we use this measure to predict our friend's behavior across an average of many situations—attendance at parties, friendliness in small seminars, and willingness to engage in conversations with strangers—we'll probably do rather well. Contrary to Mischel's initial conclusions, personality traits can be useful for predicting overall behavioral trends—such as whether someone will be a responsible employee or a difficult marital partner (Kenrick & Funder, 1988; Rushton, Brainerd, & Presley, 1983; Roberts, 2009; Tellegen, 1991).

In contrast to other personality theories we've reviewed, trait models are primarily efforts to *describe* individual differences in personality rather than to *explain* their causes. This emphasis on description is both a strength and a weakness. On the one hand, these models have advanced our understanding of personality structure and helped psychologists predict performance in jobs, even the job of leader of the world's largest superpower. On the other hand, some trait models don't provide much insight into the causes of personality. Although the Big Five, for example, do a decent job of capturing personality differences among people, they don't shed much light on the origins of these differences.

Some researchers, like Hans Eysenck, have tried to remedy this shortcoming. For example, according to Eysenck (1973), the personality dimension of extraversion–introversion is produced by differences in the threshold of arousal of the reticular activating system (RAS). The RAS controls alertness and is responsible for keeping us awake. If your RAS is still functioning at this late point in the chapter, you might be wondering how RAS activity is related to extraversion and introversion. Although the following hypothesis is paradoxical, Eysenck argued that extraverts have an *underactive*

Explore in **MyPsychLab** the **Concept:** Mischel's Theory of Personality

RAS: They're habitually underaroused and bored. So they seek out stimulation, including other people, to jack up their arousal. In contrast, introverts tend to have an overactive RAS: They're habitually overaroused and try to minimize or shut out stimulation, again including other people (Campbell et al., 2011). Interestingly, extraverts, unlike introverts, prefer loud to soft music (Geen, 1984; Kageyama, 1999). Although the evidence for Eysenck's hypothesis isn't entirely consistent (Gray, 1981; Matthews & Gilliland, 1999), his theorizing demonstrates that trait theories can generate fruitful hypotheses concerning the relations between personality traits and biological variables.

Assess Your Knowledge — FACT or FICTION?

1. One limitation of the Big Five model is that researchers have identified these traits only in American culture.   **True / False**

2. Research demonstrates that after late childhood, the levels of most personality traits virtually never change over the life span.   **True / False**

3. Personality traits typically predict behavior in a single situation with high levels of accuracy.   **True / False**

4. According to Eysenck, extraverts tend to be less aroused than introverts.   **True / False**

Answers: 1. F; 2. F; 3. F; 4. T

Study and **Review** in **MyPsychLab**

Personality Assessment: Measuring and Mismeasuring the Psyche

10 Describe structured personality tests such as the MMPI-2 and their methods of construction.

11 Describe projective tests, particularly the Rorschach, and their strengths and weaknesses.

12 Identify common pitfalls in personality assessment.

Personality wouldn't be helpful to psychologists if they had no way of measuring it. That's where personality assessment enters into the picture: It offers us the promise of detecting individual differences in personality in a scientifically rigorous fashion. But developing accurate tools to measure personality is easier said than done.

Famous—and Infamous—Errors in Personality Assessment

Indeed, personality psychology has long been plagued by a parade of dubious assessment methods. Phrenology purported to detect people's personality traits by measuring the patterns of bumps on their heads. Related to phrenology was *physiognomy*, popular in the eighteenth and nineteenth centuries, which claimed to detect people's personality traits from their facial characteristics (Collins, 1999). The term *lowbrow*, which today refers to someone who's uncultured, derives from the old belief that most nonintellectual people have protruding foreheads and a low brow line. This claim, like virtually all other claims of physiognomy, has been falsified. Still, physiognomy may contain a tiny kernel of truth (Quist et al., 2011). Research suggests that women do better than chance at figuring out which men are most interested in children merely by looking at still photographs of their faces (Roney et al., 2006), although it's not clear to which features of men's faces observers based these judgments. In another study, observers accurately gauged men's tendencies toward physical aggressiveness by glancing briefly at their faces (Carre, McCormick, & Mondloch, 2009). Interestingly, these estimates were highly correlated with the ratio of the width to the length of men's faces

Traditional beliefs persist that people with protruding foreheads and low brow lines are less intelligent or cultured than other people. (© Clive Goddard/www.CartoonStock.com)

Simulate in **MyPsychLab** the **Experiment:** IPIP Neo Personality Inventory

◄ **FALSIFIABILITY**
Can the claim be disproved?

FIGURE 4 Sheldon's Body Types. According to William Sheldon, three major body types are associated with different personality traits. Yet research hasn't borne out most of Sheldon's claims. Because Sheldon wasn't blind to body type when rating people's personality traits, his findings may have been due largely to confirmation bias.

Ectomorph   Mesomorph   Endomorph

Factoid

Mark Twain (1835–1910), often considered America's greatest humorist, once underwent a phrenology reading from Lorenzo Fowler, probably the foremost U.S. exponent of phrenology. Fowler, who was then unaware of Twain's identity, informed Twain that the pattern of bumps on his skull indicated that he had an entirely unremarkable personality with one exception: He lacked a sense of humor. When Twain returned three months later and identified himself, Fowler "discovered" a large skull bump corresponding to humor (Lopez, 2002).

structured personality test
paper-and-pencil test consisting of questions that respondents answer in one of a few fixed ways

Minnesota Multiphasic Personality Inventory (MMPI)
widely used structured personality test designed to assess symptoms of mental disorders

(with faces that are wider than longer reflecting more aggressiveness) perhaps because this ratio reflects the influence of hormones secreted during puberty that also affect aggressiveness.

In the vein of physiognomy, psychologist William Sheldon believed that he could draw inferences about people's personalities from their body types (see **FIGURE 4**). Highly muscular people (mesomorphs), he thought, tend to be assertive and bold, whereas lean and skinny people (ectomorphs) tend to be introverted and intellectual (Sheldon, 1971). Yet Sheldon failed to consider an alternative explanation: He wasn't blind to people's body types when he judged their personality traits and may have fallen prey to confirmation bias. Perhaps not surprisingly, well-controlled studies later found the correlations between Sheldon's body types and personality traits to be weak or nonexistent (Deabler, Hartl, & Willis, 1973; Lester, Kaminsky, & McGovern, 1993).

With these errors of the past in mind, how can we distinguish scientific from unscientific or even pseudoscientific personality assessment methods? Two key criteria for evaluating all tests, including personality tests, are reliability and validity. *Reliability* refers to consistency of measurement and *validity* to the extent to which a test measures what it purports to measure. We'll keep these dual criteria in mind as we survey the two major types of personality tests: structured and projective.

Structured Personality Tests

The best-known personality instruments are **structured personality tests**. These are typically paper-and-pencil tests consisting of questions that respondents answer in one of a few fixed ways. By fixed ways, we mean choosing between true and false answers or by selecting options on a scale with, for example, 1 being "always true," 2 being "somewhat true," and so on, until 5, which is "always false" (these numerical scales are called *Likert* formats). Structured personality tests have several advantages: They're typically easy to administer and score, and they allow researchers to collect data from many participants simultaneously.

MMPI AND MMPI-2: DETECTING ABNORMAL PERSONALITY. The **Minnesota Multiphasic Personality Inventory (MMPI)** (Hathaway & McKinley, 1940) is the most extensively researched of all structured personality tests. Psychologists across the world use the MMPI to detect symptoms of mental disorders. Developed in the early 1940s by psychologist Starke Hathaway and neurologist J. Charnley McKinley of the University of Minnesota, the MMPI was revised in the 1980s by James Butcher and his colleagues (Butcher et al., 1989). This revised test, the MMPI-2, consists of 567 true-false items.

MMPI and MMPI-2: Construction and Content. The MMPI-2, like its predecessor, consists of ten *basic* scales, eight of which assess mental disorders such as paranoia, depression, and schizophrenia. Hathaway and McKinley developed these scales by means of an **empirical method of test construction**. Using an empirical (or data-based) approach, researchers begin with two or more criterion groups, such as a group of people with a specific psychological disorder and a group of people with no psychological disorder, and examine which items best distinguish these groups. For example, the items on the MMPI depression scale are those that best differentiate persons with clinical depression from those with no diagnosed mental disorder.

One consequence of the empirical method of test construction is that many MMPI and MMPI-2 items possess low **face validity**. Face validity is the extent to which respondents can tell what the items are measuring. In a face-valid test, we can take the items on "face value": They assess what they seem to assess. Face validity is actually a misnomer, because it isn't really a form of validity at all. Because Hathaway and McKinley were concerned only with *whether*, not *why*, the MMPI items differentiated among criterion groups, they ended up with many items that bear little obvious connection with the disorder they supposedly assess. As an example of an item with low face validity from another structured personality test, can you guess which personality trait the following item assesses: "I think newborn babies look very much like little monkeys"? The answer is nurturance, that is, a tendency to care for others—with a "True" answer reflecting low nurturance and a "False" answer reflecting high nurturance—although few test-takers can figure that out (Jackson, 1971, p. 238).

Researchers don't agree on whether low face validity is an overall advantage or disadvantage. Some believe that items with low face validity assess key aspects of personality that are subtle or lie outside respondents' awareness (Meehl, 1945). Moreover, such items have the advantage of being difficult for respondents to fake. In contrast, other researchers believe that these items don't add to the MMPI's diagnostic capacity (Jackson, 1971; Weed, Ben-Porath, & Butcher, 1990).

The MMPI-2 contains three major *validity* scales. These scales detect various *response sets*, which are tendencies to distort responses to items. Response sets, which can diminish the validity of psychological tests, include *impression management*—making ourselves look better than we really are—and *malingering*—making ourselves appear psychologically disturbed. The MMPI *L* (Lie) Scale consists of items assessing the denial of trivial faults (such as "I occasionally become angry"). If you deny a large number of such faults, it's likely that you're either (a) engaging in impression management or (b) a promising candidate for sainthood. Given that (a) is more likely than (b), psychologists typically use scores on the *L* scale to detect a dishonest approach to test-taking. The *F* (Frequency) Scale consists of items that people in the general population rarely endorse (such as "I have a cough most of the time"). High scores on *F* can indicate malingering, although they can also reflect serious psychological disturbance or carelessness in responding to items. The *K* (Correction) Scale consists of items that are similar to, although subtler than, those on the *L* scale; this scale measures defensive or guarded responding (Graham, 2011).

As we can see in **FIGURE 5**, psychologists plot the ten basic scales and three validity scales of the MMPI-2 in profile form, which displays the pattern of each person's scale scores. Although many clinicians enjoy interpreting MMPI-2 profiles, research demonstrates that simple statistical formulas that can be programmed into a computer yield interpretations that are equally, if not more, valid than those of experienced clinicians (Garb, 1998; Goldberg, 1969). Nevertheless, these findings, which hold not only for the MMPI-2, but also for most or even all personality tests, haven't exerted an appreciable impact on clinical practice (Dawes, Faust, & Meehl, 1989; Vrieze & Grove, 2009).

The MMPI and MMPI-2 Evaluated Scientifically. Extensive research supports the reliability of most MMPI-2 scales, as well as their validity for differentiating among mental disorders (Graham, 2011; Greene, 2000; Nichols, 2011). For example, the MMPI-2 schizophrenia scale distinguishes individuals with schizophrenia from those with other severe disorders, like clinical depression (Walters & Greene, 1988).

empirical method of test construction
approach to building tests in which researchers begin with two or more criterion groups and examine which items best distinguish them

face validity
extent to which respondents can tell what the items are measuring

FIGURE 5 An MMPI-2 Profile. MMPI-2 scores of 50 are average, and scores of 65 or above are abnormally high. This individual received elevated scores on several MMPI-2 clinical scales, namely, Hs (Hypochondriasis), D (Depression), Hy (Hysteria), Pt (Psychasthenia—Anxiety), and Sc (Schizophrenia), suggesting high levels of physical and mental anxiety, sad mood, and disturbed thinking. (*Source:* Adapted from the *MMPI®-2 (Minnesota Multiphasic Personality Inventory®-2) Manual for Administration, Scoring, and Interpretation,* Revised Edition. Copyright © 2001 by the Regents of the University of Minnesota. Used by permission of the University of Minnesota Press. All rights reserved. "MMPI-2" and "Minnesota Multiphasic Personality Inventory-2" are trademarks owned by the Regents of the University of Minnesota.)

Nevertheless, the MMPI-2 is problematic in several respects. Many of its scales are correlated highly and are therefore largely redundant with each other (Helmes & Reddon, 1993), probably because they are all contaminated with a broad dimension of emotional maladjustment. In an effort to minimize this problem, some researchers have recently developed a briefer version of the MMPI-2 that contains scales that are more independent of this dimension (Ben-Porath & Tellegen, 2008), although it's still too early to tell whether this new MMPI-2 version will be an improvement over the existing version. In addition, psychologists can't use MMPI-2 scales by themselves to make formal diagnoses of mental disorders such as schizophrenia or clinical depression because high scores on these scales aren't specific to a single disorder. Nevertheless, clinicians sometimes misuse these scales for this purpose (Graham, 2011).

CPI: DESCENDENT OF THE MMPI. An offspring of the MMPI is the California Psychological Inventory (CPI; Gough, 1957), sometimes called the "common person's MMPI." Like the MMPI, the CPI was constructed empirically. Unlike the MMPI, the CPI is designed primarily for assessing personality traits in the normal range, such as dominance, flexibility, and sociability, making it a popular measure in college counseling centers and industry. Most CPI scales are reasonably reliable over time and are valid for assessing personality traits; for example, people's CPI scores tend to correlate moderately with how their roommates view them (Ashton & Goldberg, 1973). Nevertheless, the CPI inherited some of its parent's shortcomings. In particular, many of the CPI scales are highly correlated and largely redundant with each other (Megargee, 1972).

RATIONALLY/THEORETICALLY CONSTRUCTED TESTS. Psychologists have also developed many structured personality measures using a **rational/theoretical method of test construction**. In contrast to an empirical approach, this approach requires test developers to begin with a clear-cut conceptualization of a trait and write items to assess that conceptualization. Paul Costa and Robert McCrae (1992) used a rational-theoretical approach to develop the NEO Personality Inventory-Revised (NEO-PI-R), a widely used measure of the Big Five. The NEO-PI-R has demonstrated impressive validity in a large number of studies (Gaughan, Miller, & Lynam, 2012). For example, scores on the NEO-PI-R Conscientiousness scale are negatively correlated with measures of risk taking, and scores on the NEO-PI-R Agreeableness scale are negatively correlated with measures of physical aggressiveness (Trull et al., 1995).

But not all rational/theoretical tests boast a strong track record of validity. The Myers-Briggs Type Indicator (MBTI) is probably the most widely administered personality

rational/theoretical method of test construction

approach to building tests that requires test developers to begin with a clear-cut conceptualization of a trait and then write items to assess that conceptualization test in the world. Given several million times a year, it's used by thousands of companies in the United States alone, including 89 of the Fortune 100 (Paul, 2004). Even Harry Potter was assigned to his mythical school after taking a variant of the MBTI. Based loosely on Jung's theory of personality, the MBTI sorts respondents into one of four categories—introversion-extraversion, sensing-intuiting, thinking-feeling, and judging-perceiving—yielding a total of 16 personality types. Although some claim that the MBTI is helpful for predicting job performance and satisfaction, research raises serious doubts about its reliability and validity. Most respondents don't obtain the same MBTI personality type on retesting only a few months later, indicating that the test has low test-retest reliability. In addition, MBTI scores don't relate in especially consistent ways to either the Big Five or measures of job preferences, suggesting that the test has questionable validity (Costa & McCrae, 1998; Hunsley, Lee, & Wood, 2003).

Projective Tests

Projective tests ask examinees to interpret or make sense of ambiguous stimuli such as inkblots, drawings of social situations, or incomplete sentences. If you've ever looked for shapes in clouds in the sky, you have a sense of what it's like to take a projective test.

Influenced by psychoanalytic views of personality (Westen, Feit, & Zittel, 1999), especially Freud's notion of projection, these techniques rest on a crucial premise: the **projective hypothesis** (Frank, 1948). This hypothesis assumes that in the process of interpreting ambiguous stimuli, people inevitably project aspects of their personality onto these stimuli. Test interpreters can then work in reverse by examining people's answers for clues concerning their personality traits. In contrast to structured personality measures, projective techniques permit respondents considerable latitude in their answers.

Proponents of projective tests view them as the "stealth weapons" of the psychologist's arsenal. By circumventing respondents' defense mechanisms, they presumably offer valuable information concerning unconscious conflicts (Dosajh, 1996). Projective tests are among the most controversial of all psychological instruments, because their reliability and validity remain in dispute (Hunsley & Bailey, 1999; Lilienfeld, 1999b; Lilienfeld, Wood, & Garb, 2001).

RORSCHACH INKBLOT TEST: WHAT MIGHT THIS BE? The best-known projective measure is the **Rorschach Inkblot Test**, developed by Swiss psychiatrist Hermann Rorschach in the early 1920s. The Rorschach, as it's commonly known, consists of ten symmetrical inkblots, five in black and white and five containing color (see **FIGURE 6**). The Rorschach is one of the most commonly used personality measures (Watkins et al., 1995): It's administered to about 6 million people every year (Sutherland, 1992; Wood et al., 2000).

The Rorschach: Scoring and Interpretation. Rorschach examiners ask respondents to look at each inkblot and say what it resembles. Examiners then score respondents' answers for numerous characteristics supposedly associated with personality traits. For example, people who focus on tiny details in the inkblots presumably have many obsessive-compulsive tendencies, people who respond to color in the inkblots are presumably emotional; and people who see reflections in the blots tend to be narcissistic (self-centered) (see **TABLE 7**). Many of these interpretations have a certain surface plausibility, which may account partly for the Rorschach's popularity.

The Rorschach Evaluated Scientifically. Despite its widespread use, the Rorschach is scientifically controversial. The test-retest reliabilities of many of its scores are unknown, and their interrater reliabilities are often problematic (Lilienfeld et al., 2001; Sultan et al., 2006; Wood & Lilienfeld, 1999). Moreover, although psychologists commonly use the Rorschach to assist them in making psychiatric diagnoses (Weiner, 1997), there's little evidence that it validly detects the features of most mental disorders (Wood et al., 2000) or predicts criminal traits or behaviors (Wood et al., 2010). Specifically, with the exception of schizophrenia, bipolar disorder, and a few other conditions marked by abnormal thinking,

We can find variants of the Myers-Briggs Type Indicator on the Internet—personality inventories that claim to tell us which characters from books, TV shows, and movies we most closely resemble.

Anatomically detailed dolls (also known as "anatomically correct" dolls) are one popular type of projective device. Many investigators and social workers try to infer whether children have been sexually abused based on observation of the children playing freely with the dolls. Nevertheless, conclusions derived from these devices have led to numerous false identifications, because many nonabused children engage in sexualized doll play (Hunsley, Lee, & Wood, 2003).

projective test
test consisting of ambiguous stimuli that examinees must interpret or make sense of

projective hypothesis
hypothesis that in the process of interpreting ambiguous stimuli, examinees project aspects of their personality onto the stimulus

Rorschach Inkblot Test
projective test consisting of ten symmetrical inkblots

FIGURE 6 An Inkblot Similar to That on the Rorschach Inkblot Test. Although widely used, the Rorschach appears not to possess the magical powers often attributed to it by its most enthusiastic proponents.

TABLE 7 Four Widely Used Rorschach Scores and Their Interpretation and Sample Responses That Reflect Them. These sample responses are based on the Rorschach-like inkblot in Figure 6.

RORSCHACH SCORE	SAMPLE RESPONSE	TYPICAL INTERPRETATION
Pair response	"I see two dogs looking at each other."	Self-centeredness
Unusual detail response	"On the very top of the blot, I see a little heart-shaped thing."	Obsessive-compulsive tendencies
Space response	"That white area in the lower middle sort of looks like the head of an alien."	Rebelliousness, anger
Human movement response	"The right upper part of the blot looks like a man bending his head forward."	Impulse control, inhibition

REPLICABILITY ▶

Can the results be duplicated in other studies?

there are relatively few replicated associations between Rorschach scores and mental illnesses (Mihura et al., 2012). Nor are there consistent associations between Rorschach scores and most personality traits like impulsivity and anxiety-proneness (Wood, Nezworski, & Stejskal, 1996). There's also evidence that respondents can successfully fake schizophrenia, depression, and perhaps other disorders on the Rorschach (Schretlen, 1997). This is a particular problem, because in contrast to the MMPI-2, the Rorschach doesn't contain scales to detect malingering.

Perhaps the greatest shortcoming of the Rorschach is the lack of evidence for its incremental validity. **Incremental validity** is the extent to which a test contributes information beyond other more easily collected measures (Sechrest, 1963). Given that the Rorschach takes a long time to administer (typically about 45 minutes) and even longer to interpret (one-and-a-half to two hours) (Ball, Archer, & Imhoff, 1994), we'd hope that it yields information we couldn't glean from more efficient measures. Yet with only a few exceptions, there's no evidence that the Rorschach exhibits incremental validity beyond more easily collected data such as life history information or the MMPI (Lilienfeld et al., 2001). In fact, adding the Rorschach to other measures sometimes *decreases* the validity of clinicians' diagnostic judgments (Garb, 1984; Garb et al. 2005), probably because some clinicians attend too heavily to invalid Rorschach information at the expense of more valid information.

FIGURE 7 Thematic Apperception Test (TAT) Sample Item. One of the 31 cards of the TAT.

TAT: TELL A TALE. The second most frequently administered projective test is the **Thematic Apperception Test (TAT)**, developed by Henry Murray and his student Christiana Morgan (Morgan & Murray, 1935). The TAT consists of 31 cards depicting ambiguous situations, most of them interpersonal in nature (see **FIGURE 7**). One of these cards is the epitome of ambiguity: It's entirely blank. As a mnemonic device, we can think of the TAT as the "Tell a Tale" test, because examinees construct a story based on each card. Most clinicians interpret the TAT on an "impressionistic" basis, meaning that they inspect the content of the examinee's stories and analyze them using clinical intuition alone (Vane, 1981).

Some authors' claims to the contrary (Karon, 2000), there's little evidence that impressionistic TAT interpretations generate scores with adequate reliability or validity (Ryan, 1985). Scores derived from the TAT have often failed to distinguish psychiatric patients, such as people with clinical depression, from nonpatients or to correlate in predicted directions with personality traits (Lilienfeld, 1999b). Nor is there much evidence that TAT scores possess incremental validity beyond other sources of information such as the MMPI (Garb, 1984; Lilienfeld et al., 2001).

incremental validity
extent to which a test contributes information beyond other more easily collected measures

Thematic Apperception Test (TAT)
projective test requiring examinees to tell a story in response to ambiguous pictures

One promising scoring system for the TAT uses cards similar to those on the TAT to assess needs for achievement (McClelland et al., 1953). Using this system, psychologists score responses to the cards based on the extent to which respondents' stories emphasize achievement-oriented themes such as academic or career success. In contrast to most TAT scoring schemes, TAT measures of achievement possess at least some validity: They correlate positively with occupational success and income, although these associations are low in magnitude (Spangler, 1992). The TAT is also moderately valid for assessing what psychologists call *object relations*—perceptions of others, such as whether people see others as helpful or harmful (Ackerman et al., 2001; Westen, 1991).

HUMAN FIGURE DRAWINGS. Another popular group of projective tests is *human figure drawings* such as the Draw-A-Person test (DAP; Machover, 1949). The DAP, for instance, requires respondents to draw a person (or persons) in any way they wish (Malchiodi, 2012). Many clinicians who administer these measures interpret them on the basis of specific drawing "signs" (Chapman & Chapman, 1967; Smith & Dumont, 1995). For example, large eyes in drawings presumably reflect suspiciousness, while large genitalia in drawings presumably reflect concerns about sexuality.

Nevertheless, the correlations between human figure drawing signs and personality traits are low to nonexistent (Kahill, 1984; Motta, Little, & Tobin, 1993; Swenson, 1968). Moreover, because people often produce markedly different drawing characteristics on different occasions, the test-retest reliabilities of these signs are frequently poor (Thomas & Jolley, 1998). Perhaps most problematically, scores derived from human figure drawings are confounded with artistic ability: Research suggests that people may be diagnosed as psychologically disturbed merely because they draw poorly (Cressen, 1975; Lilienfeld et al., 2000).

GRAPHOLOGY. A final widely used projective technique is **graphology**: the psychological interpretation of handwriting (see **FIGURE 8**). Many firms in the United States and abroad use graphology to detect potential employees who are prone to dishonest behavior (Beyerstein & Beyerstein, 1992). Proponents of "graphotherapeutics" even claim to cure psychological disorders by altering people's handwriting (Beyerstein, 1996).

Looking for Mr. Write
The hidden clues in the signatures of Barack Obama and Mitt Romney, analyzed by Sylvia Tooker, a Dallas-area handwriting expert and business consultant, and Ruth Holmes, president of a Michigan-based firm that specializes in personality assessment, jury consulting and forensic handwriting examination:

The capital B, larger than the O of his last name, indicates he wants to be recognized for his personal accomplishments, instead of family connections or external influence.

The extra round shapes of those two letters means he "dreams big and is open to possibilities." — Tooker

The garland and points in the capital M show he's "quick to understand when he must adjust."

The dotted I signals that he's "loyal and attentive to details." -- Holmes

FIGURE 8 Handwriting Sample. Graphologists often rely substantially on the representativeness heuristic. These graphologists analyzed the handwriting of the two major candidates in the 2012 presidential election and concluded, for example, that Barack Obama's large open letters reflect his tendency to dream about big possibilities and that Mitt Romney's dotting of the *i* in his first name reflects his attention to details.

graphology
psychological interpretation of handwriting

Many of the handwriting signs used by graphologists rely heavily on the *representativeness heuristic*: Because certain handwriting features bear a superficial resemblance to certain traits, graphologists assume that they go together. For example, some graphologists maintain that individuals who cross their *t*s with lines resembling little whips are sadistic (Carroll, 2003).

Nevertheless, graphological interpretations have low reliability. Lewis Goldberg (1986) presented professional graphologists with one person's handwriting but told them it was produced by different people over time. The graphologists' interpretations of the handwriting changed whenever they believed it was generated by a different person. Other carefully conducted studies have found almost no correlation between handwriting signs and either personality traits or job performance (Ben-Shakhar et al., 1986; Klimoski, 1992). A few investigations (Drory, 1986) suggested that certain handwriting indicators are valid predictors of job success, but these studies were flawed because researchers asked participants to write brief autobiographies. As a consequence, graphologists may have based their interpretations on the *content* of participants' autobiographies—which could yield clues to their personalities—rather than on participants' handwriting (Hines, 2003). To exclude this confound, investigators have asked participants to write identical passages. When they've done so, the validities of graphological interpretations have plummeted to about zero.

Common Pitfalls in Personality Assessment

Imagine that as part of a research requirement for your introductory psychology class you've just completed a structured personality test like the MMPI-2. You look on with anxious anticipation as the research assistant inputs your data into a computer, which then spits out the following personality description:

> Some of your hopes and dreams are pretty unrealistic. You have a great deal of unused potential that you have not yet turned to your advantage. Although you sometimes enjoy being around others, you value your privacy. You prize your independence and dislike being hemmed in by rules and restrictions. You are an independent thinker and do not accept others' opinions without strong evidence. You sometimes have serious doubts about whether you have made the right decision or done the right thing. Despite these doubts, you are a strong person whom others can count on in times of trouble.

After reading this description, you turn to the research assistant with a mixture of amazement and awe and exclaim, "This description fits me perfectly. You've hit the nail on the head!"

But there's a catch. This description, the research assistant informs you, wasn't based on your test results at all. Instead, this description is identical to one that all 100 previous participants received. You've been the victim of a devilish hoax. This example illustrates what Paul Meehl (1956) termed the *P. T. Barnum effect,* after the circus entrepreneur who said, "I try to give a little something to everyone."

THE P. T. BARNUM EFFECT: THE PERILS OF PERSONAL VALIDATION. The **P. T. Barnum effect** is the tendency of people to accept descriptions that apply to almost everyone as applying specifically to them. This effect demonstrates that *personal validation*—the use of subjective judgments of accuracy (Forer, 1949)—is a flawed method of evaluating a test's validity. We may be convinced that the results of a personality test fit us to a T, but that doesn't mean the test is valid.

The P. T. Barnum effect probably accounts largely for the popularity of astrological horoscopes; palmistry; and crystal ball, tea leaf, and tarot card readings. Despite the widespread use of all of these methods, there's no evidence for their validity (Hines, 2003; Park, 1982). People are especially likely to accept P. T. Barnum descriptions they believe are tailored specifically to them (Snyder, Shenkel, & Lowery, 1977). This finding probably helps to explain why horoscopes—which specify the precise year, month, day, and occasionally time of the person's birth—are often so convincing.

RULING OUT RIVAL HYPOTHESES ►
Have important alternative explanations for the findings been excluded?

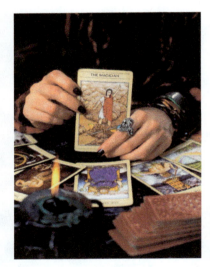

The popularity of tarot card readings, crystal ball readings, palmistry, and other similar techniques probably stems largely from the P. T. Barnum effect.

👁 **Watch** in **MyPsychLab** the **Video:** In the Real World: Putting Popular Personality Assessments to the Test

P. T. Barnum effect
tendency of people to accept descriptions that apply to almost everyone as applying specifically to them

In an illustration of the P. T. Barnum effect, Susan Blackmore (1983) found that clients couldn't pick out their own tarot card readings from nine other readings at better-than-chance levels. Yet when tarot card readers gave their readings to clients on a face-to-face basis, clients found them extremely accurate. Because each reading contained general statements that apply to everyone, clients who heard only one reading found it believable.

The same principle applies to astrology. People can't pick out their horoscope from others at better-than-chance levels (Dean, 1987). Nevertheless, when people read their horoscope in the newspaper, they're often certain it applies to them. One probable reason for this curious discrepancy is that people tend to read only the horoscope for their own sign but not for others. If they didn't fall prey to confirmation bias and forced themselves to read all 12 horoscopes, they'd probably realize that most or even all of the horoscopes fit them equally well. Although astrology makes extraordinary claims, namely, that it can divine people's personality traits with nearly perfect accuracy, the evidence for these claims is virtually nonexistent.

The P. T. Barnum effect can also fool psychologists into believing that certain traits describe specific groups of people even when they don't (Lilienfeld, Garb, & Wood, 2012). Many pop psychologists claim that adult children of alcoholics (ACOAs) display a distinctive constellation of personality traits. ACOAs are supposedly perfectionistic, concerned about others' approval, overly protective of others, and prone to hiding their feelings. But when three researchers (Logue, Sher, & Frensch, 1992) administered a questionnaire consisting of presumed ACOA characteristics (such as "You sometimes project a front, hiding your own true feelings") to both ACOAs and non-ACOAs, they found no significant differences between the groups. Both groups found the supposed ACOA statements to fit them well and just about as well as a set of P. T. Barnum statements. Because these traits are so widespread in the general population, the commonly accepted personality profile of the ACOA is probably attributable to the P. T. Barnum effect.

PERSONALITY ASSESSMENT EVALUATED SCIENTIFICALLY. Personality assessment has contributed to psychologists' ability to detect personality traits, both normal and abnormal, and has helped them predict significant real-world behaviors. Moreover, psychologists have succeeded in developing numerous personality measures, especially structured personality tests, with adequate reliability and validity. Research also indicates that a few projective techniques can achieve satisfactory reliability and validity. For instance, scores on certain *sentence completion tests*, which ask respondents to complete a sentence stem (for example, "My father was …"), are associated with delinquency, moral development, and other important characteristics (Cohn & Westenberg, 2004; Loevinger, 1987).

Given the scientific progress that psychologists have made in assessing personality, however, why do many continue to use measures with weak scientific support (Lilienfeld et al., 2001)? In particular, why do some clinicians still rely on scores derived from the Myers-Briggs and several projective tests like the Rorschach, TAT, and human figure drawings that possess questionable reliability and validity?

◀ **EXTRAORDINARY CLAIMS**
Is the evidence as strong as the claim?

psychomythology

HOW ACCURATE IS CRIMINAL PROFILING?

Another practice whose popularity may derive in part from the P. T. Barnum effect is *criminal profiling*, a technique depicted in the 1991 movie *The Silence of the Lambs* and once popular television shows such as *Criminal Minds* and *Law and Order*. Criminal profilers at the FBI and other law enforcement agencies claim to draw detailed inferences about perpetrators' personality traits and motives from the pattern of crimes committed.

It's true that we can often guess certain characteristics of criminals at better-than-chance levels. If we're investigating a homicide, we'll do better than flipping a coin by guessing that the murderer was a male (most murders are committed by men) between the ages of 15 and 25 (most murders are committed by adolescents and young adults) who suffers from psychological problems (most murderers suffer from psychological problems). But criminal profilers purport to go

Hit shows such as *CSI: New York* have stimulated Americans' interest in criminal profiling. Nevertheless, research suggests that criminal profiling is more art than science.

Personality

considerably beyond such widely available statistics. They typically claim to possess unique expertise and to be able to harness their years of accumulated experience to outperform statistical formulas.

Nevertheless, their assessments sometimes echo P. T. Barnum. In the fall of 2002, when the Washington, D.C., area was paralyzed by random sniper shootings at gas stations and in parking lots, one former FBI profiler predicted that the sniper would turn out to be someone who is "self-centered" and "angry" at others (Kleinfield & Goode, 2002)—both obvious guesses that most laypersons could make.

Indeed, research demonstrates that police officers can't distinguish genuine criminal profiles from bogus criminal profiles consisting of vague and general personality characteristics (such as "he has deep-seated problems with hostility"). This finding suggests the parsimonious hypothesis that profilers often base their conclusions about criminals on little more than P. T. Barnum statements (Alison, Smith, & Morgan, 2003; Gladwell, 2007). Moreover, although some researchers have found that profilers sometimes perform better than do untrained individuals in identifying criminal suspects, other researchers have found that professional profilers are no more accurate in gauging the personality features of murderers than are college students with no training in criminology (Homant & Kennedy, 1998; Snook et al., 2008). In one study, chemistry majors actually produced more accurate profiles of a murderer than did experienced homicide detectives and police officers (Kocsis, Hayes, & Irwin, 2002). Perhaps most important, there's no persuasive evidence that criminal profilers do better than statistical formulas that take into account the psychological traits of known murderers.

Criminal profiling may therefore be more of an urban legend than a scientifically demonstrated ability. Yet tradition dies hard, and the FBI and other crime organizations remain in the full-time business of training criminal profilers (Jackson, Wilson, & Kaur-Rana, 2011).

OCCAM'S RAZOR ▶
Does a simpler explanation fit the data just as well?

The answer is that they're prone to the same errors in thinking as the rest of us (Lilienfeld, Wood, & Garb, 2007). One such error is *illusory correlation*, the perception of nonexistent statistical associations between variables (Eder, Fiedler, & Hamm-Eder, 2011). An illusory correlation is a mirage that leads us to see something, namely, a relationship between two variables, that isn't there.

Loren and Jean Chapman (1967) showed college students a series of concocted human figure drawings containing certain physical features (such as large eyes and large genitals) along with a description of the personality traits of the person of who supposedly produced each drawing (such as paranoid and overly concerned about sexuality). They then asked participants to estimate the extent to which these physical features and personality traits co-occurred in the drawings. Unbeknownst to participants, there was *no* correlation between the drawing features and personality traits, because the researchers had paired these two sets of variables randomly.

Yet students consistently saw certain drawing features as associated with certain personality traits. Interestingly, these were the same drawing features that experienced clinicians tend to believe are related to these traits—and that research has shown to be invalid (Kahill, 1984). For example, students reported incorrectly that people who produced drawings with large eyes tended to be paranoid and that people who produced drawings with large genitals tended to be overly concerned with sexuality.

Like graphologists, the students in the Chapmans' study probably relied on the representativeness heuristic: Like goes with like (Kahneman, 2011). As a result, they were fooled, because things that seem similar on the surface don't always go together in real life. These students probably also relied on availability heuristic, recalling the cases in which drawing signs correspond to personality traits and forgetting the cases in which they don't. Clinicians, being mere mortals like the rest of us, can easily fall victim to these heuristics too, which may explain why some of them are convinced that certain personality tests are more valid than the scientific evidence indicates.

These commonplace errors in thinking remind us of a theme we've underscored throughout this text: Personal experience, although useful in generating hypotheses, can be misleading when it comes to testing them. But there's good news here too.

Scientific methods, which are essential safeguards against human error, can allow us to determine whether we should trust our personal experience or disregard it in favor of evidence to the contrary. In this way, these methods can help us reduce the risk of error and help us to better measure and understand personality.

Answers are located at the end of the text.

ONLINE PERSONALITY TESTS

evaluating **CLAIMS**

The Internet offers a wide array of personality tests, including ones that claim to identify your personality based on your facial features, color preferences, or responses to word-association tests. Some even claim to "diagnose" your personality based on your preferences for movies, fictional characters, or animals. Let's evaluate some of these claims, which are modeled after actual personality tests found online.

"This color test has been used for decades and given to thousands of people worldwide."

Does the fact that a test has been used by many people for many years tell us anything about its validity? What two logical fallacies does this claim commit?

"Over 70% of people who take this test rate it as very accurate."

What's the danger of asking people who take the test to determine its accuracy? What other methods should we use when evaluating personality assessment methods?

"Results: You are *confident, self-reliant, prudent, and have strong instincts* in life."

This test's results include descriptors typical of the P. T. Barnum effect. Who doesn't like to think of themselves as "confident," "self-reliant," "prudent," and having "strong instincts"?

"The self-scoring inventories on this site allow you to approximate your MBTI Type preferences, but *have not met commonly accepted psychometric standards for reliability and validity. Therefore, they should not be used as a substitute for taking an MBTI®.*"

This site includes an appropriate disclaimer that reminds those taking the tests of the importance of reliability and validity.

Assess Your Knowledge   FACT or FICTION?

 Study and **Review** in **MyPsychLab**

1. Items with low face validity tend to be especially easy for respondents to fake.
    True / False

2. Simple formulas that can be programmed into computers yield MMPI-2 interpretations that are equal or superior to those of experienced clinicians.   **True / False**

3. Adding the Rorschach Inkblot Test to other measures in a test battery sometimes produces decreases in validity.   **True / False**

4. The more detailed and specific an astrological horoscope is about someone's personality traits, the more likely that person will perceive it as accurate.
    True / False

5. Research suggests that although students sometimes fall victim to illusory correlation, experienced psychologists don't.   **True / False**

Answers: 1. F; 2. T; 3. T; 4. T; 5. F

Personality: What Is It and How Can We Study It?

1 DESCRIBE HOW TWIN AND ADOPTION STUDIES SHED LIGHT ON GENETIC AND ENVIRONMENTAL INFLUENCES ON PERSONALITY.

Twin and adoption studies suggest that many personality traits are heritable and point to a key role for nonshared environment but not shared environment for adult personality.

1. Name the major influences (factors) on personality discussed by behavior geneticists.

   1. _____
   2. _____
   3. _____

2. _____ _____ influences make individuals within the same family less alike.

3. To distinguish the effects of genes from the effects of environment, behavior geneticists have conducted _____ studies and _____ studies of personality.

4. If the heritability of personality were 1.0 (that is, 100 percent), then correlations of personality traits in identical twins would be _____.

5. The Minnesota Twins study found that identical twins reared apart tend to be strikingly (similar/dissimilar) in their personality traits.

6. According to the Minnesota Twins study, _____ environment plays little to no role in adult personality.

7. Adoption studies permit investigators to separate the effects of _____ and _____ by comparing adopted children's similarities to their adoptive versus biological parents.

8. In one adoption study of sociability conducted in Texas, the correlations between biological parents and their adopted-away children were slightly (lower/higher) than the correlations between adoptive parents and their adopted children.

9. How would you challenge the notion that a specific gene exists for divorce, religiosity, or political attitudes?

10. In an attempt to identify which genes are associated with specific personality traits, some researchers have turned to _____ _____ studies, but the findings of these studies often have not been replicated.

Psychoanalytic Theory: The Controversial Legacy of Sigmund Freud and His Followers

2 DESCRIBE THE CORE ASSUMPTIONS OF PSYCHOANALYTIC THEORY.

Freud's psychoanalytic theory rests on three core assumptions: psychic determinism, symbolic meaning, and unconscious

motivation. According to Freud, personality results from the interactions among id, ego, and superego. The ego copes with threat by deploying defense mechanisms. Freud's five psychosexual stages are oral, anal, phallic, latency, and genital.

11. Freudians believe in _____ _____, the assumption that all psychological events have a cause.

12. The _____, according to Freud, is the reservoir of our most primitive impulses (like sex and aggression), whereas the _____ is the psyche's executive and principal decision maker.

13. Freud hypothesized that _____ _____ results from conflicts among the id, ego, and superego.

14. Freud believed that the ego maintains psychological health by engaging in _____ _____, unconscious maneuvers intended to minimize anxiety.

15. Complete the table by indicating the approximate age ranges for each of Freud's psychosexual stages of development.

STAGE	APPROXIMATE AGE
Oral	_____
Anal	_____
Phallic*	_____
Latency	_____
Genital	_____

*Includes Oedipus (male) and Electra (female) complexes

16. The conflict during Freud's phallic stage in which children supposedly love their opposite-sex parents romantically and want to eliminate their same-sex parents as rivals is termed the _____ _____.

3 DESCRIBE KEY CRITICISMS OF PSYCHOANALYTIC THEORY AND THE CENTRAL FEATURES OF NEO-FREUDIAN THEORIES.

Psychoanalytic theory has been criticized for unfalsifiability, failed predictions, questionable conception of the unconscious, lack of evidence, and a flawed assumption of shared environmental influence. Neo-Freudians shared with Freud an emphasis on unconscious influences and the importance of early experience, but placed less emphasis on sexuality as a driving force in personality.

17. Recent research has shown that many aspects of Freud's psychoanalytic theory (are/aren't) supported when scientific standards such as falsifiability are applied.

18. There's increasing reason to doubt the existence of the _____ as Freud conceived of it, namely as a "place" where sexual and aggressive energies, along with repressed memories, are housed.

19. According to Alfred Adler, the principal motive in human personality is not sex or aggression, but the _____ _____ _____.

20. Describe Jung's theory of archetypes and the collective unconscious and identify a possible shortcoming in this theory.

Behavioral and Social Learning Theories of Personality

4 **IDENTIFY THE CORE ASSUMPTIONS OF BEHAVIORAL AND SOCIAL LEARNING THEORIES OF PERSONALITY.**

Radical behaviorists view personality as under the control of two major influences: genetic factors and contingencies in the environment. Radical behaviorists, like psychoanalysts, are determinists and believe in unconscious processing, but deny the existence of "the" unconscious. In contrast to radical behaviorists, social learning theorists accord a central role to thinking in the causes of personality and argue that observational learning and a sense of personal control play key roles in personality.

21. Radical behaviorists like Skinner believe that our personalities stem largely from differences in our learning _____.

22. Radical behaviorists believe that personality (causes/consists of) behaviors.

23. One of the few things on which Freud and Skinner would have agreed is the concept of _____, the belief that all our actions are products of preexisting causal influences.

24. Unlike Skinner, social learning theorists emphasize _____ as a cause of personality.

25. Albert Bandura made a compelling case for _____ _____, a form of causation whereby personality and cognitive factors, behavior, and environmental variables mutually influence one another.

26. Summarize the role of observational learning in shaping children's personalities.

27. Rotter introduced the concept of _____ _____ _____ to describe the extent to which individuals believe that reinforcers and punishers lie inside or outside their control.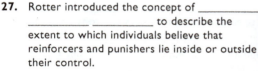

28. Based on what you have learned in the chapter, identify whether each response indicates an internal or external locus of control.

SAMPLE ITEM	INTERNAL OR EXTERNAL LOCUS OF CONTROL
(1) Many people live miserable lives because of their parents.	_____
(2) If you set realistic goals, you can succeed no matter what.	_____
(3) One can climb the professional ladder just by being around at the right time.	_____
(4) If I study hard enough, I can pass any exam.	_____

29. Someone with an internal locus of control is (more/less) prone than someone with an external locus of control to emotional upset following life stressors.

5 **DESCRIBE KEY CRITICISMS OF BEHAVIORAL AND SOCIAL LEARNING APPROACHES.**

Critics have accused radical behaviorists of going too far in their exclusion of thinking as a cause of personality. The social learning theory claim that observational learning plays a crucial role in personality runs counter to findings that shared environmental influence on adult personality is minimal.

30. Social learning theorists' claim that observational learning plays a powerful role in adult personality is subject to criticism because it implies that _____ _____ plays a causal role.

Humanistic Models of Personality: The Third Force

6 **EXPLAIN THE CONCEPT OF SELF-ACTUALIZATION AND ITS ROLE IN HUMANISTIC MODELS.**

Most humanistic psychologists argue that the core motive in personality is self-actualization. According to Carl Rogers, unhealthy behavior results from the imposition of conditions of worth, which block drives toward self-actualization. According to Abraham Maslow, self-actualized individuals are creative, spontaneous, accepting, and prone to peak experiences.

31. Humanistic psychologists rejected the determinism of psychoanalysts and behaviorists and embraced the notion of _____ _____.

32. Freudians would say that self-actualization would be (disastrous/helpful) for society.

33. Carl Rogers, pioneer of humanistic psychology, held a(n) (optimistic/pessimistic) view of human nature.

34. Complete the table by listing and describing the three major components of personality according to Rogers's model.

MAJOR COMPONENT OF PERSONALITY	DESCRIPTION
1. _____	_____
2. _____	_____
3. _____	_____

35. _____ occurs when our personalities are inconsistent with our innate dispositions.

36. Maslow studied self-actualized people and found that they were prone to _____ _____, transcendent moments of intense excitement.

37. Followers of Maslow would probably argue that Mahatma Gandhi is a good example of a self-actualized person. Name three to five traits of self-actualized people.

7 DESCRIBE KEY CRITICISMS OF HUMANISTIC APPROACHES.

Critics have attacked humanistic models for being naive about human nature and for advancing theories that are difficult to falsify.

38. Investigators in _____ _____, the branch of psychology that compares behavior across species, have challenged Rogers's claim that human nature is entirely positive.

39. Critics argue that actualization of our full genetic potential is (likely/unlikely) to bring about the state of bliss that Rogers imagined.

40. Maslow may have fallen prey to _____ _____ because he limited his study to individuals who displayed the traits he hypothesized were associated with self-actualized people.

Trait Models of Personality: Consistencies in Our Behavior

8 DESCRIBE TRAIT MODELS OF PERSONALITY, INCLUDING THE BIG FIVE.

Trait theories use factor analysis to identify groups of personality features that tend to correlate with each other. These groupings often correspond to broader traits such as extraversion and agreeableness. One influential model of personality is the Big Five, which predicts many important aspects of real-world behavior, including job performance. Nevertheless, the Big Five may be limited as a model of personality structure because people may not have conscious access to all important features of personality.

41. Trait theorists are interested primarily in describing and understanding the _____ of personality.

42. Claiming that a child is "aggressive" merely because he or she engages in aggressive behavior gives us no new information and is an example of circular reasoning. What must personality traits do to be meaningful?

43. A statistical technique called _____ _____ analyzes the correlations among responses on personality inventories.

44. A group of traits that have surfaced repeatedly in factor analyses of personality measures is known as the _____ _____.

45. Using the acronym OCEAN as a mnemonic device, the traits in this group are _____ _____, _____, _____, _____, and _____.

46. Match the appropriate personality trait and description using the Big Five measure.

___ Extraversion	a. tendency to be careful and responsible
___ Neuroticism	b. tendency to be intellectually curious and unconventional
___ Conscientiousness	c. tendency to be friendly and easy to get along with
___ Agreeableness	d. tendency to be sociable and lively
___ Openness to Experience	e. tendency to be tense and moody

47. In studying cultural influences on personality, researchers have found that _____ _____ _____ doesn't emerge clearly in all cultures.

9 IDENTIFY KEY CRITICISMS OF TRAIT MODELS.

In the late 1960s, Walter Mischel pointed out that personality traits rarely predict isolated behaviors with high levels of accuracy; later research vindicated his claim, but demonstrated that personality traits are often helpful in predicting long-term behavioral trends. Some models of personality structure, including the Big Five, are more descriptive than explanatory.

48. Mischel's review suggested that people's behaviors (are/aren't) very consistent across different situations.

49. Personality traits can be useful predictors of real-world behaviors, but only when they're _____ across different situations.

50. Although the Big Five do a decent job of capturing personality differences among people, they don't shed much light on the _____ of these differences.

Personality Assessment: Measuring and Mismeasuring the Psyche

10 DESCRIBE STRUCTURED PERSONALITY TESTS SUCH AS THE MMPI-2 AND THEIR METHODS OF CONSTRUCTION.

Structured personality tests consist of questions that people can answer in only one of a few fixed ways. Some, like the MMPI-2 and CPI, are developed empirically; others, like the NEO-PI-R, are developed rationally/theoretically.

51. The _____ _____ _____ _____ is widely used to assess mental disorders and consists of ten basic scales.

52. Hathaway and McKinley developed these scales using a(n) _____ method of test construction.

53. Many MMPI and MMPI-2 items possess low _____ _____, which refers to the extent to which respondents can tell what the items are measuring.

54. Extensive research (supports/doesn't support) the reliability of most MMPI-2 scales as well as their validity for differentiating among mental disorders.

55. The _____ method of test construction requires test developers to begin with a clear-cut conceptualization of a trait and then write items to assess that conceptualization.

11 DESCRIBE PROJECTIVE TESTS, PARTICULARLY THE RORSCHACH, AND THEIR STRENGTHS AND WEAKNESSES.

Projective tests consist of ambiguous stimuli that the examinee must interpret. Many of these tests lack adequate levels of reliability, validity, and incremental validity.

56. The _____ hypothesis assumes that in the process of interpreting ambiguous stimuli, examinees inevitably project aspects of their personality onto the stimulus.

57. In what situations might investigators or social workers use these dolls? What are the pitfalls of this technique?

58. The widely used _____ _____ test consists of ten symmetrical inkblots and remains scientifically controversial.

59. From which projective test of personality does this item derive?

12 IDENTIFY COMMON PITFALLS IN PERSONALITY ASSESSMENT.

Two common pitfalls in personality assessment are the P. T. Barnum effect and illusory correlation, which highlight the need for scientific methods as safeguards against human error.

60. The tendency of people to endorse high base rate descriptions—descriptions that apply to almost everyone—is called the _____ _____ _____.

Apply Your Scientific Thinking Skills

Use your scientific thinking skills to answer the following questions, referencing specific scientific thinking principles and common errors in reasoning whenever possible.

1. Consult two or three books or websites designed to help parents identify and understand their child's personality. What emphasis do these sources place on genetic factors, shared environmental factors, and nonshared environmental factors in shaping personality? To what extent are their claims consistent with evidence from behavior-genetic studies? Have they considered alternative explanations and avoided confusing correlation with causation? Explain.

2. As we've learned in this chapter, Freud's writings have exerted an enormous impact on popular culture, although many modern psychologists have questioned their scientific basis. Find two or three recent articles in the popular press that refer to Freudian theory in explaining the causes or treatment of a psychological disorder. To what extent is the press coverage consistent with contemporary scientific evidence regarding Freudian theory?

3. Studies show that people can't pick out their horoscope from others at better-than-chance levels (Dean, 1987), yet are often certain their horoscope applies to them. Look up the astrology section in at least three different newspapers or websites and read the horoscopes for all 12 astrological signs. What commonalities do you see across the horoscopes (both across signs and across the sources that you consulted)? How accurately do the horoscopes for your sign describe your personality? Now think of other people who share your birthday or astrological sign. Does the horoscope apply equally well to their personalities?

Further Your Understanding

EXTEND YOUR KNOWLEDGE WITH THE MYPSYCHLAB VIDEO SERIES

Watch these videos in MyPsychLab. Follow the "Video Series" link.

The Big Picture: What Is Personality? Watch a series of interviews to see how comfortable people are with sharing different aspects of their personalities.

The Basics: Personality Theories Learn about the four main personality theories and their theorists and see how they compare.

Special Topics: The Plastic Brain Twins and Personality See how the two types of twins are formed at conception and how research on twins is helping us understand how genes and the environment influence individual development.

Thinking Like a Psychologist: Measuring Personality Learn the criteria for a valid personality test and characteristics of the MMPI-2, the TAT, and the Rorschach.

In the Real World: Putting Popular Personality Assessments to the Test Take a closer look at the Big Five model and discuss why this personality test is considered scientifically valid and how it could be useful in finding a mate.

EXPERIENCE PSYCHOLOGICAL RESEARCH WITH MYPSYCHLAB SIMULATIONS

Access these simulations in MyPsychLab. Follow the "Simulations" link.

IPIP-Neo Personality Inventory Answer selected questions from the IPIP-NEO inventory to measure your Big Five personality traits.

What Has Shaped Your Personality? Participate in a survey to discover what types of events and factors have shaped your personality.

APPLY YOUR CRITICAL THINKING SKILLS WITH MYPSYCHLAB WRITING ASSESSMENTS

Complete these writing assignments in MyPsychLab.

Describe the four major theories of personality (psychodynamic, trait or five-factor model, humanistic, and social-cognitive) and identify advantages and disadvantages of each theory.

Answer Key

PERSONALITY: WHAT IS IT AND HOW CAN WE STUDY IT?

1. 1) genetic factors; 2) shared environmental factors; 3) nonshared environmental factors
2. Nonshared environmental
3. twin; adoption
4. 1.0
5. similar
6. shared
7. genes; environment
8. higher
9. Genes code for proteins, not specific behaviors or attitudes. It's far more likely that genes influence behaviors and attitudes in a highly indirect fashion.
10. molecular genetic

PSYCHOANALYTIC THEORY: THE CONTROVERSIAL LEGACY OF SIGMUND FREUD AND HIS FOLLOWERS

11. psychic determinism
12. id; ego
13. psychological distress
14. defense mechanisms
15. Oral: birth to 12–18 months; Anal: 18 months to 3 years; Phallic: 3–6 years; Latency: 6–12 years; Genital: 12 years and beyond
16. Oedipus complex
17. aren't
18. unconscious
19. striving for superiority
20. Jung argued that in addition to

Freud's version of the unconscious, there's also a collective unconscious that comprises all of the memories that ancestors have passed down to us across the generations. Jung believed that the collective unconscious contains numerous archetypes, or cross-culturally universal emotional symbols, which explain the similarities among people in their emotional reactions to many features of the world. Jung's theory is difficult to falsify and does not rule out rival hypotheses.

BEHAVIORAL AND SOCIAL LEARNING THEORIES OF PERSONALITY

21. histories
22. consists of
23. determinism
24. thinking
25. reciprocal determinism
26. In observational learning, parents, teachers, and others play significant roles in shaping children's personalities: Children learn good and bad habits by watching and later emulating adults. A child may learn early that charitable giving is a worthy endeavor.
27. locus of control
28. 1) external; 2) internal; 3) external; 4) internal
29. less
30. shared environment

HUMANISTIC MODELS OF PERSONALITY: THE THIRD FORCE

31. free will
32. disastrous
33. optimistic
34. 1) organism/our innate blueprint; 2) self/our self-concept, the set of beliefs about who we are; 3) conditions of worth/expectations we place on ourselves for appropriate and inappropriate behavior
35. Incongruence
36. peak experiences
37. Self-actualized people tend to be creative, spontaneous, and accepting of themselves and others. They're self-confident (but not self-centered) and focus on real-world and intellectual problems and have a few deep friendships rather than many superficial ones. They typically crave privacy and can come off as introverted or aloof.
38. comparative psychology
39. unlikely
40. confirmation bias

TRAIT MODELS OF PERSONALITY: CONSISTENCIES IN OUR BEHAVIOR

41. structure
42. Personality traits must do more than merely describe behaviors we've already observed—they must predict behaviors in novel situations or correlate with biological or laboratory measures.

43. factor analysis
44. Big Five
45. openness to experience, conscientiousness, extraversion, agreeableness, neuroticism
46. d: Extraversion; e: Neuroticism; a: Conscientiousness; c: Agreeableness; b: Openness to Experience
47. openness to experience
48. aren't
49. aggregated
50. origins

PERSONALITY ASSESSMENT: MEASURING AND MISMEASURING THE PSYCHE

51. Minnesota Multiphasic Personality Inventory
52. empirical
53. face validity
54. supports
55. rational/theoretical
56. projective
57. Investigators and social workers allow children to play freely with anatomically detailed dolls to try to infer whether the children have been sexually abused. This projective test has led to numerous false accusations, because many nonabused children engage in sexualized doll play.
58. Rorschach Inkblot
59. Thematic Apperception Test (TAT)
60. P. T. Barnum effect

References

Ackerman, S. J., Hilsenroth, M. J., Clemence, A. J., Weatherill, R., & Fowler J. C. (2001). Convergent validity of Rorschach and TAT scales of object relations. *Journal of Personality Assessment, 77*, 295–306.

Ackroyd, E. (1993). *A dictionary of dream symbols*. London, England: Blanford.

Adams, H. E., Wright, L. E., & Lohr, B. A. (1996). Is homophobia associated with homosexual arousal? *Journal of Abnormal Psychology, 105*, 440–445.

Adler, A. (1922). *Practice and theory of individual psychology*. London, England: Routledge.

Adler, A. (1931). *What life should mean to you*. Boston, MA: Little, Brown.

Alcock, J. (1999) The nesting behaviour of Dawson's burrowing bee Amegilla dawsoni (Hymenoptera: Anthophorini) and the production of offspring of different sizes. *Journal of Insect Behavior, 12*, 363–384.

Alison, L. J., Smith, M. D., & Morgan, K. (2003). Interpreting the accuracy of offender profiles. *Psychology, Crime & Law, 9*, 185–195.

Allport, G. W. (1965). *Letters from Jenny*. New York, NY: Harcourt, Brace, & World.

Allport, G. W. (1966). Traits revisited. *American Psychologist, 21*, 1–10.

Allport, G. W., & Odbert, H. S. (1936). Trait names, a psycholexical study. *Psychological Monographs, 47* (1, Whole No. 211).

Anholt, R. R. (2012). Genetics of aggression. *Annual Review of Genetics, 46*, 145–164.

Applewhite, P. B., Gardner, F., Foley, D., & Clendenin, M. (1971). Failure to condition tetrahymena. *Scandinavian Journal of Psychology, 12*, 65–67.

Aronson, E. (2011). *Not by chance alone: My life as a social psychologist*. New York, NY: Basic Books.

Ashton, S. G., & Goldberg, L. W. (1973). In response to Jackson's challenge: The comparative validity of personality scales constructed by the external (empirical) strategy and scales developed intuitively by experts, novices, and laymen. *Journal of Research in Personality, 7*, 1–20.

Ball, J. D., Archer, R. P., & Imhoff, E. A. (1994). Time requirements of psychological testing: A survey of practitioners. *Journal of Personality Assessment, 63*, 239–249.

Bandura, A. (1965). Vicarious processes: A case of no-trial learning. In L. Berkowitz (Ed.), *Advances in experimental social psychology* (Vol. 2, pp. 3–55). New York, NY: Academic Press.

Bandura, A. (1986). *Social foundations of thought and action: A social-cognitive theory*. Englewood, Cliffs, NJ: Prentice Hall.

Barlow, D. M., Sakheim, D. K., and Beck, J. G. (1983). Anxiety increases sexual arousal. *Journal of Abnormal Psychology, 92*, 49–54.

Barrick, M. R., & Mount, M. K. (1991). The Big Five personality dimensions and job performance: A meta-analysis. *Personnel Psychology, 44*, 1–26.

Beauchaine, T. P., & Gatzke-Kopp, L. M. (2012). Instantiating the multiple levels of analysis perspective in a program of study on externalizing behavior. *Development and Psychopathology, 24*, 1003–1018. http://dx.doi.org/10.1017/S0954579412000508

Begley, S., & Kasindorf, M. (1979, December 3). Twins: Nazi and Jew. *Newsweek*, 139.

Bem, D. J., & Allen, A. (1974). On predicting some of the people some of the time: The search for cross-situational consistencies in behavior. *Psychological Review, 81*, 506–520.

Benassi, V. A., Sweeney, P. D., & Dufour, C. L. (1988). Is there a relation between locus of control orientation and depression? *Journal of Abnormal Psychology, 8*, 357–367.

Ben-Porath, Y., & Tellegen, A. (2008). Empirical correlates of the MMPI-2 restructured clinical (RC) scales in mental health, forensic, and nonclinical settings: An introduction. *Journal of Personality Assessment, 90*, 119–121. http://dx.doi.org/10.1080/00223890701845120

Ben-Shakhar, G., Bar-Hillel, M., Bilu, Y., Ben-Abba, E., & Flug, A. (1986). Can graphology predict occupational success? Two empirical studies and some methodological ruminations. *Journal of Applied Psychology, 71*, 645–653.

Bergstrom, S. R. (1968). Acquisition of an avoidance reaction to the light in the protozoa tetrahymena. *Scandinavian Journal of Psychology, 9*, 220–224.

Berk, A. M., Vigorito, M., & Miller, R. R. (1979). Retroactive stimulus interference with conditioned emotional response retention in infant and adult rats: Implications for infantile amnesia. *Journal of Experimental Psychology: Animal Behavior Processes, 3*, 284–299.

Beyerstein, B. (1996). Graphology. In G. Stein (Ed.), *The encyclopedia of the paranormal* (pp. 309–324). Buffalo, NY: Prometheus.

Beyerstein, B. L., & Beyerstein, D. F. (1992). *The write stuff: Evaluations of graphology—The study of handwriting analysis.* Buffalo, NY: Prometheus.

Bezdjian, S., Baker, L. A., & Tuvblad, C. (2011). Genetic and environmental influences on impulsivity: A meta-analysis of twin, family and adoption studies. *Clinical Psychology Review, 31*, 1209–1223. http://dx.doi.org/10.1016/j.cpr.2011.07.005

Blackmore, S. (1984). Accounting for out-of-body experiences. *Bulletin of the British Psychological Society, 37*, A53.

Blair, L. (2013). *Birth order: What your position in the family really tells you about your character* (2nd ed.). London, England: Piatkus Books.

Block, J. (1995). A contrarian view of the five-factor approach to personality description. *Psychological Bulletin, 117*, 187–215.

Block, N. (1995). How heritability misleads about race. *Cognition, 56*, 99–128.

Bogg, T., & Roberts, B. W. (2004). Conscientiousness and health behaviors: A meta-analysis. *Psychological Bulletin, 130*, 887–919.

Brenner, C. (1973). *An elementary textbook of psychoanalysis.* New York, NY: International Universities Press.

Breuer, J., & Freud, S. (1895). Studies on hysteria. In J. Strachey (Trans. and Ed.), *The standard edition of the complete psychological works of Sigmund Freud (1953–74)* (Vol. 2). London, England: Hogarth.

Butcher, J. N., Dahlstrom, W. G., Graham, J. R., Tellegen, A., & Kaemmer, B. (1989). *MMPI-2: Manual for administration and scoring.* Minneapolis, MN: University of Minnesota Press.

Campbell, A. M., Davalos, D. B., McCabe, D. P., & Troup, L. J. (2011). Executive functions and extraversion. *Personality and Individual Differences, 51*, 720–725. http://dx.doi.org/10.1016/j.paid.2011.06.018

Campbell, J. (1988). *The power of myth.* New York, NY: Doubleday.

Canli, T. (2008, March/April). The character code. *Scientific American Mind, 19*, 52–57.

Carre, J. M., McCormick, C. M., & Mondloch, C. J. (2009). Facial structure is a reliable cue of aggressive behavior. *Psychological Science, 20*, 1194–1198.

Carton, J. S., & Nowicki, S., Jr. (1996). Origins of generalized control expectancies: Reported child stress and observed maternal control and warmth. *Journal of Social Psychology, 136*, 753–760.

Carver, C. S., & Miller, C. J. (2006). Relations of serotonin function to personality: Current views and a key methodological issue. *Psychiatry Research, 144*, 1–15.

Chaplin, W. F., Phillips, J. B., Brown, J. D., Clanton, N. R., & Stein, J. L. (2000). Handshaking, gender, personality, and first impressions. *Journal of Personality and Social Psychology, 79*, 110–117.

Chapman, L. J., & Chapman, J. P. (1967). Genesis of popular but erroneous diagnostic observations. *Journal of Abnormal Psychology, 72*, 193–204.

Cheung, F. M., & Leung, K. (1998). Indigenous personality measures: Chinese examples. *Journal of Cross-Cultural Psychology, 29*, 233–248.

Church, A. T. (1994). Relating the Tellegen and five-factor models of personality structure. *Journal of Personality and Social Psychology, 67*, 898–909. http://dx.doi.org/10.1037/0022-3514.67.5.898

Church, A. T. (2008). Current controversies in the study of personality across cultures. *Social and Personality Psychology Compass, 2*, 1930–1951. http://dx.doi.org/10.1111/j.1751-9004.2008.00132.x

Church, A. T., & Katigbak, M. S. (2002). The five-factor model in the Philippines: Investigating trait structure and levels across cultures. In R. R. McCrae & J. Allik (Eds.), *The five-factor model across cultures* (pp. 129–154). New York, NY: Kluwer Academic/Plenum.

Cioffi, F. (1998). *Freud and the question of pseudoscience.* Chicago, IL: Open Court.

Cloninger, C. R. (1987). A systematic method for clinical description and classification of personality variants: A proposal. *Archives of General Psychiatry, 44*, 573–588. http://dx.doi.org/10.1001/archpsyc.1987.01800180093014

Cloninger, C. R., & Svrakic, D. M. (2009). Personality disorders. In J. Sadock & V.A. Sadock (Eds.), *Kaplan & Sadock's comprehensive textbook of psychiatry* (9th ed., pp. 2197–2240). Philadelphia, PA: Lippincott Williams & Wilkins.

Cohn, L. D., & Westenberg P. M. (2004). Intelligence and maturity: Meta-analytic evidence for the incremental and discriminant validity of Loevinger's measure of ego development. *Journal of Personality and Social Psychology, 86*, 760–772.

Collins, A. F. (1999). The enduring appeal of physiognomy: Physical appearance as a sign of temperament, character, and intelligence. *History of Psychology, 2*, 251–276.

Conard, M. A. (2006). Aptitude is not enough: How personality and behavior predict academic performance. *Journal of Research in Personality, 40*, 339–346.

Concar, D. (1994). Design your own personality. *New Scientist, 141*, 22–26.

Costa, P. T., & McCrae, R. R. (1992). 4 ways 5 factors are basic. *Personality and Individual Differences, 13*, 653–665.

Costa, P. T., & McCrae, R. R. (1998). Trait theories of personality. In D. F. Barone, M. Hersen, & V. B. Van Hasselt (Eds.), *Advanced Personality* (pp. 103–121). New York, NY: Plenum.

Coyne, L. W., & Thompson, A. D. (2011). Maternal depression, locus of control, and emotion regulatory strategy as predictors of preschoolers' internalizing problems. *Journal of Child and Family Studies, 20*, 873–883. http://dx.doi.org/10.1007/s10826-011-9455-2

Cressen, R. (1975). Artistic quality of drawings and judges' evaluations of the DAP. *Journal of Personality Assessment, 39*, 132–137.

Crews, F. C. (Ed.). (1998). *Unauthorized Freud: Doubters confront a legend.* New York, NY: Viking Press.

Custer, R., & Aarts, H. (2010). The unconscious will: How the pursuit of goals operates outside of conscious awareness. *Science, 329*, 47–50.

Deabler, H. L., Hartl, E. M., & Willis, C. A. (1973). Physique and personality: Somatotype and the 16PF. *Perceptual and Motor Skills, 36*, 927–933.

Dean, G. (1987). Does astrology need to be true? Part 2: The answer is no. *Skeptical Inquirer, 11*, 257–273.

Dempster, E. L., Pisdley, R., Schalkwyk, L. C., Owens, S., & Mill, J. (2011). Disease-associated epigenetic changes in monozygotic twins discordant for schizophrenia and bipolar disorder. *Human Molecular Genetics, 20*, 4786–4796.

De Raad, B., & Perugini, M. (2002). *Big Five assessment.* Ashland, OH: Hogrefe & Huber.

De Raad, B., Perugini, M., Hrebickova, M., & Szarota, P. (1998). The lingua franca of personality: Taxonomies and structure. *Journal of Cross Cultural Psychology, 29*, 212–232.

de Waal, F. B. M. (1990). *Peacemaking among primates.* Cambridge, MA: Harvard University Press.

Diener, E., & Larsen, R. J. (1984). Temporal stability and cross-situational consistency of affective, cognitive, and behavioral responses. *Journal of Personality and Social Psychology, 47*, 871–883.

Dolan, M., Anderson, I. M., & Deakin, J. F. (2001). Relationship between 5-HT function and impulsivity and aggression in male offenders with personality disorders. *British Journal of Psychiatry, 178*, 352–359.

Dolnick, E. (1998). *Madness on the couch: Blaming the victim in the heyday of psychoanalysis.* New York, NY: Simon & Schuster.

Dosajh, N. L. (1996). Projective techniques with particular reference to inkblot tests. *Journal of Projective Psychology and Mental Health, 3*, 59–68.

Doyen, S., Klein, O., Pichon, C. L., & Cleeremans, A. (2012). Behavioral priming: It's all in the mind, but whose mind? *PLoS One, 7*(1), e29081.

Drory, A. (1986). Graphology and job performance: A validation study. In B. Nevo (Ed.), *Scientific aspects of graphology* (pp. 165–173). Springfield, IL: Charles C. Thomas.

Dunkel, C. S., Harbke, C. R., & Papini, D. R. (2009). Direct and indirect effects of birth order on personality and identity: Support for the null hypothesis. *The Journal of Genetic Psychology: Research and Theory on Human Development, 170*, 159–175. http://dx.doi.org/10.3200/GNTP.170.2.159-175

Dunlop, B. W., DeFife, J. A., Marx, L., Garlow, S. J., Nemeroff, C. B., & Lilienfeld, S. O. (2011). The effects of sertraline on psychopathic traits. *International Clinical Psychopharmacology, 26*, 329–337.

Dutton, K. (2012). *The wisdom of psychopaths: What saints, spies, and serial killers can teach us about success.* New York, NY: Scientific American /Farrar, Straus and Giroux.

Eder, A. B., Fiedler, K., & Hamm-Eder, S. (2011). Illusory correlations revisited: The role of pseudocontingencies and working-memory capacity. *The Quarterly Journal of Experimental Psychology, 64*, 517–532. http://dx.doi.org/10.1080/17470218.2010.509917

Epstein, S. (1979). The stability of behavior: I. On predicting more of the people more of the time. *Journal of Personality and Social Psychology, 37*, 1097–1126.

Ernst, C., & Angst, J. (1983). *Birth order.* Berlin, Germany: Springer-Verlag.

Eysenck, H. J. (1973). *Eysenck on extraversion.* New York, NY: Wiley.

Eysenck, H. J. (1991). Dimensions of personality: 16, 5, or 3?—Criteria for a taxonomic paradigm. *Personality and Individual Differences, 12*, 773–790.

Feist, G. J., & Brady, T. R. (2004). Openness to experience, non-conformity, and the preference for abstract art. *Empirical Studies of the Arts, 22*, 77–89.

Fiorito, G., & Scotto, P. (1993). Observational learning in *Octopus vulgaris. Science, 256*, 545–546.

Fisher, S., & Greenberg, R. (1996). *Freud scientifically appraised.* New York, NY: Wiley.

Forer, B. R. (1949). The fallacy of personal validation. *Journal of Abnormal and Social Psychology, 44*, 118–123.

Frank, L. K. (1948). *Projective methods.* Springfield, IL: Charles C Thomas.

Freese, J., Powell, B., & Steelman, L. C. (1999). Rebel without a cause or effect: Birth order and social attitudes. *American Sociological Review, 64*, 207–231.

Freud, A. (1937). *The ego and the mechanisms of defense.* London, England: Hogarth.

Freud, S. (1900). *The interpretation of dreams* (J. Crick, Trans.). London, England: Oxford University Press.

Freud, S. (1923). *The ego and the id. Standard Edition, 19*, 3–66.

Freud, S. (1933). *New introductory lectures on psychoanalysis.* New York, NY: Carleton House.

Freud, S. (1935). *A general introduction to psychoanalysis.* New York, NY: Washington Square Press.

Funder, D. C. (1991). Global traits: A neo-Allportian approach to personality. *Psychological Science, 2*, 31–39.

Furnham, A., & Fudge, C. (2008). The Five Factor model of personality and sales performance. *Journal of Individual Differences, 29*, 11–16.

Gallo, E. (1994). Synchronicity and the archetypes: The imprecision of C. G. Jung's language and concepts. *Skeptical Inquirer, 18*, 376–403.

Garb, H. N. (1984). The incremental validity of information used in personality assessment. *Clinical Psychology Review, 4*, 641–655.

Garb, H. N. (1998). *Studying the clinician: Judgment, research, and psychological assessment.* Washington, DC: American Psychological Association.

Garb, H. N., Wood, J. M., Lilienfeld, S. O., & Nezworski, T. (2005). Roots of the Rorschach controversy. *Clinical Psychology Review, 25*, 97–118.

Gardini, S., Cloninger, C. R., & Venneri, A. (2009). Individual differences in personality traits reflect structural variance in specific brain regions. *Brain Research Bulletin, 79*, 265–270.

Gaughan, E. T., Miller, J. D., & Lynam, D. R. (2012). Examining the utility of general models of personality in the study of psychopathy: A comparison of the HEXACO-PI-R and NEO PI-R. *Journal of Personality Disorders, 26*, 513–523. http://dx.doi.org/10.1521/pedi.2012.26.4.513

Geen, R. G., (1984). Preferred stimulation levels in introverts and extroverts: Effects on arousal and performance. *Journal of Personality and Social Psychology, 46*, 1303–1312.

Gladwell, M. (2007, November 12). Dangerous minds: Criminal profiling made easy. *New Yorker.* Retrieved from http://www.newyorker.com/reporting/2007/11/12/071112fa_fact_gladwell

Goldberg, L. (1986). Some informal explorations and ruminations about graphology. In B. Nevo (Ed.), *Scientific aspects of graphology* (pp. 281–293). Springfield, IL: Charles C. Thomas.

Goldberg, L. R. (1969). The search for configural relationships in personality assessment: The diagnosis of psychosis vs. neurosis from the MMPI. *Multivariate Behavioral Research, 4*, 523–536.

Goodall, J., & van Lawick, H. (1971). *In the shadow of man.* Boston, MA: Houghton-Mifflin.

Gosling, S. D. (2001). From mice to men: What can we learn about personality from animal research? *Psychological Bulletin, 127*, 45–86.

Gosling, S. D., Sandy, C. J., & Potter, J. (2010). Personalities of self-identified dog people and cat people. *Anthrozoos: A Multidisciplinary Journal of The Interactions of People & Animals, 23*, 213–222.

Gough, H. G. (1957). *California Psychological Inventory manual.* Palo Alto, CA: Consulting Psychologists Press.

Graham, J. R. (2011). *MMPI-2: Assessing personality and psychopathology.* New York, NY: Oxford University Press.

Gray, J. (1981). A critique of Eysenck's theory of personality. In H. J. Eysenck (Ed.), *A model for personality* (pp. 246–276). New York, NY: Springer.

Greene, R. L. (2000). *The MMPI-2: An interpretive manual* (2nd ed.). Boston, MA: Allyn & Bacon.

Grunbaum, A. (1984). *The foundations of psychoanalysis: A philosophical critique.* Berkeley, CA: University of California Press.

Hamilton, V. L. (1980). Intuitive psychologist or intuitive lawyer? Alternative models of the attribution process. *Journal of Personality and Social Psychology, 39*, 767–772. http://dx.doi.org/10.1037/0022-3514.39.5.767

Harkness, A. R. (2007). Personality traits are essential for a complete clinical science. In S. O. Lilienfeld and W. O'Donohue (Eds.), *The great ideas of clinical science: 17 concepts that every mental health professional should understand* (pp. 263–290). New York, NY: Routledge.

Harkness, A. R., & Lilienfeld, S. O. (1997). Individual differences science for treatment planning: Personality traits. *Psychological Assessment, 9*, 349–360. http://dx.doi.org/10.1037/1040-3590.9.4.349

Harris, P. L. (1994). The child's understanding of emotion: Developmental change and the family environment. *Journal of Child Psychology and Psychiatry and Allied Disciplines, 35*, 3–28.

Hartshorne, H., & May, M. A. (1928). *Studies in the nature of character: Vol. 1. Studies in deceit.* New York, NY: Macmillan.

Hatemi, P. K., & McDermott, R. (2012). The political psychology of biology, genetics, and behavior. *Political Psychology, 33*, 307–312. http://dx.doi.org/10.1111/j.1467-9221.2012.00901.x

Hathaway, S. R., & McKinley, J. C. (1940). A multiphasic personality schedule (Minnesota): I. Construction of the schedule. *Journal of Psychology, 14*, 73–84.

Heaton, J. A., & Wilson, N. L. (1995). *Tuning in trouble: Talk TV's destructive impact on mental health.* San Francisco, CA: Jossey-Bass.

Heaven, P. C. L., Ciarrochi, J., & Vialle, W. (2007). Conscientiousness and Eysenckian psychoticism as predictors of school grades: A one-year longitudinal study. *Personality and Individual Differences, 42*, 535–546.

Heine, S. J., Lehman, D. R., Markus, H. R., & Kitayama, S. (1999). Is there a universal need for positive self-regard? *Psychological Review, 106*, 766–794.

Helmes, E., & Reddon, J. R. (1993). A perspective on developments in assessing psychopathology: A critical review of the MMPI and MMPI-2. *Psychological Bulletin, 113*, 453–471.

Hill, P. L., & Roberts, B. W. (2011). The role of adherence in the relationship between conscientiousness and perceived health. *Health Psychology, 30*, 797–804. http://dx.doi.org/10.1037/a0023860

Holmes, C., Wurtz, P., Waln, R., Dungan, D., & Joseph, C. (1984). Relationship between the Luscher Color Test and the MMPI. *Journal of Clinical Psychology, 40*, 126–128.

Holmes, D. S. (1974). Investigation of repression: Differential recall of material experimentally or naturally associated with ego threat. *Psychological Bulletin, 81*, 632–653.

Homant, R. J., & Kennedy, D. B. (1998). Psychological aspects of crime scene profiling. *Criminal Justice and Behavior, 25*, 319–343.

Horney, K. (1939). *New ways in psychoanalysis.* New York, NY: Norton.

Hunsley, J., & Bailey, J. M. (1999). The clinical utility of the Rorschach: Unfulfilled promises and an uncertain future. *Psychological Assessment, 11*, 266–277.

Hunsley, J., Lee, C. M., & Wood, J. (2003). Controversial and questionable assessment techniques. In S. O. Lilienfeld, J. M. Lohr, & S. J. Lynn (Eds.), *Science and pseudoscience in contemporary clinical psychology* (pp. 39–76). New York, NY: Guilford Press.

Jackson C. A., Wilson, D., & Kaur-Rana, B. (2011). The usefulness of criminal profiling. *Criminal Justice Matters, 84*, 6–7.

Jackson, D. N. (1971). The dynamics of structured personality tests: 1971. *Psychological Review, 78*, 229–248.

Jefferson, T., Herbst, J. H., & McCrae, R. R. (1998). Associations between birth order and personality traits: Evidence from self-reports and observer ratings. *Journal of Research in Personality, 32*, 498–509.

John, O. P., Robins, R. W., & Pervin, L. A. (2008). *Handbook of personality: Theory and research* (3rd ed.). New York, NY: Guilford Press.

Jung, C. G. (1936). *Archetypes and the collective unconscious.* Princeton, NJ: Princeton University Press.

Jung, C. G. (1950). On mandalas. In *The collected works of C. G. Jung* (Vol. 9ii). Princeton, NJ: Princeton University Press.

Jung, C. G. (1958). Flying saucers: A modern myth of things seen in the skies. In *The collected works of C. G. Jung* (Vol. 14). Princeton, NJ: Princeton University Press.

Jylhä, P., Ketokivi, M., Mantere, O., Melartin, T., Holma, M., Rytsälä, H., & Isometsä, E. (2012). Do antidepressants change personality?—A five-year observational study. *Journal of Affective Disorders, 142*, 200–207. http://dx.doi.org/10.1016/j.jad.2012.04.026

Kageyama, T. (1999). Loudness in listening to music with portable headphone stereos. *Perceptual and Motor Skills, 88*, 423.

Kahill, S. (1984). Human figure drawing in adults: An update of the empirical evidence, 1967–1982. *Canadian Psychology, 25*, 395–410.

Karon, B. P. (2000). A clinical interpretation of the Thematic Apperception Test, Rorschach, and other clinical data: A reexamination of statistical versus clinical prediction. *Professional Psychology: Research and Practice, 31*, 230–233.

Kendler, K. S. (2005). Toward a philosophical structure for psychiatry. *American Journal of Psychiatry, 162*, 433–440.

Kendler, K. S., Myers, J., Potter, J., & Opaleskyl, J. (2009). A web-based study of personality, psychopathology and substance use in twin, other relative and relationship pairs. *Twin Research and Human Genetics, 12*, 137–141. http://dx.doi.org/10.1375/twin.12.2.137

Kenrick, D. T., & Funder, D. C. (1988). Profiting from controversy: Lessons from the person-situation debate. *American Psychologist, 43*, 23–34.

Kihlstrom, J. F. (1987). The cognitive unconscious. *Science, 237*, 1445–1452.

King, J. E., & Figueredo, A. J. (1997). The five-factor model plus dominance in chimpanzee personality. *Journal of Research in Personality, 31*, 257–271.

Kleinfield, N. R., & Goode, E. (2002, October 28). Retracing a trail: The sniper suspects. *New York Times.* Retrieved from http://www.nytimes.com/2002/10/28/us/retracing-trail-sniper-suspects-serial-killing-s-squarest-pegs-not-solo-white.html?pagewanted=1

Klimoski, R. (1992). Graphology in personnel selection. In B. L. Beyerstein & D. F. Beyerstein (Eds.), *The write stuff: Evaluations of graphology—The study of handwriting analysis* (pp. 232–268). Buffalo, NY: Prometheus.

Knutson, B., Wolkowitz, O. M., Cole, S. W., Chan, T., Moore, E. A., Johnson, R. C., . . . Reus, V. I. (1988). Selective alteration of personality and social behavior by serotonergic intervention. *American Journal of Psychiatry, 155*, 373–379.

Kocsis, R. N., Hayes, A. F., & Irwin, H. J. (2002). Investigative experience and accuracy in psychological profiling of a violent crime. *Journal of Interpersonal Violence, 17*, 811–823.

Kramer, P. (1993). *Listening to Prozac.* New York, NY: Penguin Press.

Kramer, P. (2006). *Freud: Inventor of the modern mind.* New York, NY: HarperCollins.

Krueger, R. F. (2000). Phenotypic, genetic, and nonshared environmental parallels in the structure of personality: A view from the Multidimensional Personality Questionnaire. *Journal of Personality and Social Psychology, 79*, 1057–1067.

Langer, E. J., & Rodin, J. (1976). The effects of choice and enhanced personal responsibility for the aged: A field experiment in an institutional setting. *Journal of Personality and Social Psychology, 34*, 191–198.

LeBel, E. P., & Paunonen, S. V. (2011). Sexy but often unreliable: The impact of unreliability on the replicability of experimental findings with implicit measures. *Personality and Social Psychology Bulletin, 37*, 570–583. http://dx.doi.org/10.1177/0146167211400619

Lee, K., & Ashton, M. C. (2004). Psychometric properties of the HEXACO personality inventory. *Multivariate Behavioral Research, 39*, 329–358.

Lennox, M. (2011). *Dream sight: A dictionary and guide for interpreting any dream.* Portland, Oregon: Llewellyn Publications.

Lesch, K. P., Bengel, D., Heils, A., Sabol, S., Greenberg, B. D., Petri, S., . . . Murphy, D. L. (1996). Association of anxiety-related traits with a polymorphism in the serotonin transporter gene regulatory region. *Science, 274,* 1527–1531.

Lester, D., Kaminsky, S., & McGovern, M. (1993). Sheldon's theory of personality in young children. *Perceptual and Motor Skills, 77,* 1330.

Levenberg, S. B. (1975). Professional training, psychodiagnostic skill, and kinetic family drawings. *Journal of Personality Assessment, 39*(4), 389–393. http://dx.doi.org/10.1207/s15327752jpa3904_11

Lilienfeld, S. O. (1999b). Projective measures of personality and psychopathology: How well do they work? *Skeptical Inquirer, 23,* 32–39.

Lilienfeld, S. O., Garb, H. N., & Wood, J. M. (2012). Unresolved questions concerning the effectiveness of psychological assessment as a therapeutic intervention: Comment on Poston and Hanson (2010). *Psychological Assessment, 23,* 47–55.

Lilienfeld, S. O., Wood, J. M., & Garb, H. N. (2000). The scientific status of projective techniques. *Psychological Science in the Public Interest, 1*(2), 27–66. http://dx.doi.org/10.1111/1529-1006.002

Lilienfeld, S. O., Wood, J. M., & Garb, H. N. (2001). The scientific status of projective techniques. *Psychological Science in the Public Interest, 1,* 27–66.

Lilienfeld, S. O., Wood, J. M., & Garb, H. N. (2007). Why questionable psychological tests remain popular. *Scientific Review of Alternative Medicine and Aberrant Medical Practices, 10,* 6–15.

Loehlin, J. C. (1992). *Genes and environment in personality development.* Newbury Park, CA: Sage.

Loehlin, J. C. (2011). Genetic and environmental structures of personality: A cluster-analysis approach. *Personality and Individual Differences, 51,* 662–666. http://dx.doi.org/10.1016/j.paid.2011.06.005

Loehlin, J. C., & Horn, J. M. (2010). *Personality and intelligence in adoptive families.* New York, NY: Sage.

Loevinger, J. (1993). Conformity and conscientiousness: One factor or two stages? In D. C. Funder, R. D. Parke, C. Tomlinson-Keasey, & K. Widaman (Eds.), *Studying lives through time: Personality and development* (pp. 189–205). Washington, DC: American Psychological Association.

Logue, M. B., Sher, K. J., & Frensch, P. A. (1992). Purported characteristics of adult children of alcoholics: A possible "Barnum effect." *Professional Psychology: Research and Practice, 23,* 226–232.

Lopez, D. J. (2002). Snaring the Fowler: Mark Twain debunks phrenology. *Skeptical Inquirer, 26* (1), 33–36.

Luscher, M., & Scott, I. (1969) *The Luscher Color Test.* New York, NY: Random House.

Lynam, D. R. (2012). Assessment of maladaptive variants of five-factor model traits. *Journal of Personality, 80,* 1593–1613.

Machover, K. (1949). *Personality projection in the drawing of the human figure.* Springfield, IL: Charles C. Thomas.

Malchiodi, C. (2012). *Art therapy and health care.* New York, NY: Guilford Press.

Martin, L. R., & Friedman, H. S. (2000). Comparing personality scales across time: An illustrative study of validity and consistency in life-span archival data. *Journal of Personality, 68,* 85–110.

Martin, N. G., Eaves, L. J., Heath, A. C., Jardine, R., Feingold, L. M., & Eysenck, H. J. (1986). Transmission of social attitudes. *Proceedings of the National Academy of Sciences, 83,* 4364–4368.

Maslow, A. H. (1954). *Motivation and personality.* New York, NY: Harper.

Maslow, A. H. (1971). *The farther reaches of human nature.* New York, NY: Viking Press.

Matthews, G., & Gilliland, K. (1999). The personality theories of H. J. Eysenck and J. A. Gray: A comparative review. *Personality and Individual Differences, 26,* 583–626.

McClintock, J. B., & Lawrence, J. M. (1985). Characteristics of foraging in the soft-bottom benthic starfish *Luidia clathrata* (Echinodermata: Asteroidea): Prey selectivity, switching behavior, functional responses and movement patterns. *Oecologia, 66,* 291–298.

McCrae, R. R., & Costa, P. T. (1994). The stability of personality: Observation and evaluations. *Current Directions in Psychological Science, 3,* 173–175.

McCrae, R. R., & Costa, P. T. (1995). Trait explanations in personality psychology. *European Journal of Personality, 9,* 231–252.

McCrae, R. R., & Costa, P. T. (1997). Personality trait structure as a human universal. *American Psychologist, 52,* 509–516.

McDaniel, M. A., Whetzel, D. L., Schmidt, F. L., & Maurer, S. D. (1994). The validity of employment interviews: A comprehensive review and meta-analysis. *Journal of Applied Psychology, 79,* 599–616.

McGowan, D. (1994). *What is wrong with Jung.* Buffalo, NY: Prometheus.

McGue, M., & Lykken, D. T. (1992). Genetic influence on risk of divorce. *Psychological Science, 3,* 368–373.

Meehl, P. E. (1945). The dynamics of "structured" personality tests. *Journal of Clinical Psychology, 1,* 296–303.

Meehl, P. E. (1956). Wanted: A good cookbook. *American Psychologist, 11,* 263–272.

Meehl, P. E. (1978). Theoretical risks and tabular asterisks: Sir Karl, Sir Ronald, and the slow progress of soft psychology. *Journal of Consulting and Clinical Psychology, 46,* 806–834. http://dx.doi.org/10.1037/0022-006X.46.4.806

Megargee, E. I. (1972). *The California Psychological Inventory handbook.* San Francisco, CA: Jossey-Bass.

Mihura, J. L., Meyer, G. J., Dumitrascu, N., & Bombel, G. (2012). The validity of individual Rorschach variables: Systematic reviews and meta-analyses of the comprehensive system. *Psychological Bulletin.* http://dx.doi.org/10.1037/a0029406

Miller, J. D. (2012). Five-factor model personality disorder prototypes: A review of their development, validity, and comparison to alternative approaches. *Journal of Personality, 80,* 1565–1591.

Mischel, W. (1968). *Personality and assessment.* New York, NY: Wiley.

Mischel, W. (1973). Toward a cognitive social learning reconceptualization of personality. *Psychological Review, 80,* 252–283. http://dx.doi.org/10.1037/h0035002

Mischel, W. (1981). *Introduction to personality* (3rd ed.). New York, NY: Holt, Rinehart and Winston.

Mlodinow, L. (2012). *Subliminal: How your unconscious mind rules your behavior.* New York, NY: Pantheon.

Monte, C. F. (1995). *Beneath the mask: An introduction to theories of personality.* Fort Worth, TX: Harcourt Brace.

Morgan, C. D., & Murray, H. A. (1935). A method for investigating fantasies. *Archives of Neurology and Psychiatry, 34,* 289–304.

Motta, R. W., Little, S. G., & Tobin, M. I. (1993). The use and abuse of human figure drawings. *School Psychology Quarterly, 8,* 162–169.

Munafo, M. R., Yalcin, B., Willis-Owen, S. A., & Flint, J. (2008). Association of the dopamine D4 receptor (DRD4) gene and approach-related personality traits: Meta-analysis and new data. *Biological Psychiatry, 63,* 197–206.

Nadel, J., Aouka, N., Coulon, N., Gras-Vincendon, A., Fagard, J., & Bursztejn, C. (2011). Yes, they can! An approach to observational learning in low-functioning children with autism. *Autism, 15,* 421–435.

Nichols, D. S. (2011). *Essentials of MMPI-2 assessment.* Hoboken, NJ: Wiley.

Nigg, J. T., & Goldsmith, H. H. (1994). Genetics of personality disorders: Perspectives from personality and psychopathology research. *Psychological Bulletin, 115,* 346–380.

Nisbett, R. E., & Wilson, T. D. (1977). Telling more than we can know: Verbal reports on mental processes. *Psychological Review, 84,* 231–259.

Overskeid, G. (2007). Looking for Skinner and finding Freud. *American Psychologist, 65,* 590–595.

Park, M. A. (1982). Palmistry: Science or hand jive? *Skeptical Inquirer, 5,* 198–208.

Passini, F. T., & Norman, W. T. (1966). A universal conception of personality structure? *Journal of Personality and Social Psychology, 4,* 44–49.

Paul, A. M. (2004). *The cult of personality: How personality tests are leading us to miseducate our children, mismanage our companies, and misunderstand ourselves.* New York, NY: Free Press.

Pedersen, N. L., Plomin, R., McClearn, G. E., & Friberg, L. (1988). Neuroticism, extraversion, and related traits in adult twins reared apart and reared together. *Journal of Personality and Social Psychology, 55,* 950–957.

Pinker, S. (2002). *The blank slate: The modern denial of human nature.* New York, NY: Penguin Press.

Plomin, R. (2004). Genetics and developmental psychology. *Merrill-Palmer Quarterly Journal of Developmental Psychology, 50,* 341–352.

Plomin, R., Corley, R., DeFries, J. C., & Fulker, D. W. (1990). Individual differences in television viewing in early childhood: Nature as well as nurture. *Psychological Science, 1,* 371–377.

Plomin, R., & Daniels, D. (1987). Why are children in the same family so different from one another? *Behavioral and Brain Sciences, 10,* 1–16.

Plomin, R., DeFries, J. C., McClearn, G. E., & Rutter, M. (1997). *Behavioral genetics* (3rd ed.). New York, NY: W. H. Freeman.

Plomin, R., & McClearn, G. E. (1993). *Nature, nurture, and psychology.* Washington, DC: American Psychological Association.

Pogue-Geile, M., Ferrell, R., Deka, R., Debski, T., & Manuck, S. (1998). Human novelty-seeking personality traits and dopamine D4 receptor polymorphisms: A twin and genetic association study. *American Journal of Medical Genetics, 81,* 44–48.

Popper, K. R. (1965). *The logic of scientific discovery.* New York, NY: Harper & Row.

Quist, M. C., Watkins, C. D., Smith, F. G., DeBruine, L. M., & Jones, B. C. (2011). Facial masculinity is a cue to women's dominance. *Personality and Individual Differences, 50,* 1089–1093. http://dx.doi.org/10.1016/j.paid.2011.01.032

Rentfrow, P. J., Gosling, S. D., & Potter, J. (2008). A theory of the emergence, persistence, and expression of geographic variation in psychological characteristics. *Perspectives on Psychological Science, 3*(5), 339–369.

Richardson, R., Riccio, C., & Axiotis, R. (1986). Alleviation of infantile amnesia in rats by internal and external contextual cues. *Developmental Psychobiology, 19,* 453–462.

Roberts, B. W. (2009). Back to the future: *Personality and Assessment* and personality development. *Journal of Research in Personality, 43,* 137–145.

Roberts, B. W., & DelVecchio, W. F. (2000). The rank-order consistency of personality traits from childhood to old age: Review of longitudinal studies. *Psychological Bulletin, 126,* 3–25.

Rogers, C. R. (1947). Some observations on the organization of personality. *American Psychologist, 2,* 358–368.

Rogers, C. R., & Dymond, R. (1954). *Psychotherapy and personality change.* Chicago, IL: University of Chicago Press.

Roney, J. R., Hanson, K. N., Durante, K. M., & Maestripieri, D. (2006). Reading men's faces: Women's mate attractiveness judgments track men's testosterone and interest in infants. *Proceedings of the Royal Society of London B, 273,* 2169–2175.

Ross, L., & Nisbett, L. E. (1991). *The person and the situation: Essential contributions of social psychology.* New York, NY: McGraw-Hill.

Rotter, J. B. (1966). Generalized expectancies for internal versus external control of reinforcement. *Psychological Monographs* (1, Whole No. 609).

Rowe, D. C. (1994). *The limits of family influence: Genes, experience, and behavior.* New York, NY: Guilford Press.

Rubenzer, S. J., Faschingbauer, T. R., & Ones, D. S. (2000, August). *Assessing the U.S. presidents using the Revised NEO Personality Inventory.* Paper presented at the Annual Convention of the American Psychological Association, Washington, DC.

Rushton, J. P., Brainerd, C. J., & Presley, M. (1983). Behavioral development and construct validity: The principle of aggregation. *Psychological Bulletin, 94,* 18–38.

Ryan, R. M. (1985). Thematic Apperception Test. In D. J. Keyser & R. C. Swetland (Eds.), *Test critiques* (Vol. 2, pp. 799–814). Kansas City, MO: Test Corporation of America.

Scarr, S., Webber, P. L., Weinberg, R. A., & Wittig, M. A. (1981). Personality resemblance among adolescents and their parents in biologically related and adoptive families. *Journal of Personality and Social Psychology, 40,* 885–898.

Schoenewolf, G. (1997). *The dictionary of dream interpretation, including a glossary of dream symbols.* Northvale, NJ: Jason Aronson.

Schretlen, D. J. (1997). Dissimulation on the Rorschach and other projective measures. In R. Rogers (Ed.), *Clinical assessment of malingering and deception* (2nd ed., pp. 208–222). New York, NY: Guilford Press.

Scurich, N., Monahan, J., & John, R. S. (2012). Innumeracy and unpacking: Bridging the nomothetic/idiographic divide in violence risk assessment. *Law and Human Behavior, 36,* 548–554. http://dx.doi.org/10.1037/h0093994

Sechrest, L. (1963). Incremental validity: A recommendation. *Educational and Psychological Measurement, 12,* 153–158.

Segal, N. (1999). *Twins and what they tell us about human behavior.* New York, NY: Dutton.

Sheldon, W. (1971). The New York study of physical constitution and psychotic pattern. *Journal of the History of the Behavioral Sciences, 7,* 115–126.

Shermer, M. (2011). *The believing brain: From ghosts to Gods to politics and conspiracies—How we construct beliefs and reinforce them as truths.* New York, NY: Times Books.

Skinner, B. F. (1974). *About behaviorism.* New York, NY: Vintage Books.

Smith, D., & Dumont, F. (1995). A cautionary study: Unwarranted interpretations of the Draw-A-Person Test. *Professional Psychology: Research and Practice, 26,* 298–303.

Snook, B., Cullen, R. M., Bennell, C., Taylor, P. J., & Gendreau, P. (2008). The criminal profiling illusion: What's behind the smoke and mirrors? *Criminal Justice and Behavior, 35,* 1257–1276.

Snyder, C. R., Shenkel, R. J., & Lowery, C. R. (1977). Acceptance of personality interpretations: The "Barnum effect" and beyond. *Journal of Consulting and Clinical Psychology, 45,* 104–114.

Spangler, W. D. (1992). Validity of questionnaire and TAT measures of need for achievement: Two meta-analyses. *Psychological Bulletin, 112,* 140–154.

Srivastava, S., John, O. P., Gosling, S. D., & Potter, J. (2003). Development of personality in early and middle adulthood: Set like plaster or persistent change? *Journal of Personality and Social Psychology, 84,* 1041–1053.

Steinhardt, L. (1998). Sand, water, and universal form in sandplay and art therapy. *Art Therapy, 15,* 252–260.

Sulloway, F. J. (1996). *Born to rebel: Birth order, family dynamics and creative lives.* New York, NY: Pantheon Books.

Sultan, S., Andronikof, A., Reveillere, C., & Lemmel, G. (2006). A Rorschach stability study in a nonpatient adult sample. *Journal of Personality Assessment, 87,* 330–348.

Sutherland, S. (1992). *Irrationality: Why we don't think straight!* New Brunswick, NJ: Rutgers University Press.

Swenson, C. (1968). Empirical evaluations of human figure drawings: 1957–1966. *Psychological Bulletin, 70,* 20–44.

Tanaka, T. (1966). A study of conditioned response in hydra. *Annual of Animal Psychology, 16,* 37–41.

Tang, T., DeRubeis, R., Hollon, S., Amsterdam, J., Shelton, R., & Schalet, B. (2009). Personality change during depression treatment: A placebo-controlled trial. *Archives of General Psychiatry, 66,* 1322–1330.

Tellegen, A. (1982). *Brief manual for the Multidimensional Personality Questionnaire.* Unpublished manuscript, University of Minnesota, Minneapolis, MN. (Original work created 1978)

Tellegen, A. (1991). Personality traits: Issues of definition, evidence, and assessment. In D. Cicchetti & W. M. Grove (Eds.), *Thinking clearly about psychology: Essays in honor of Paul Everett Meehl* (pp. 10–35). Minneapolis, MN: University of Minnesota Press.

Tellegen, A., Lykken, D. T., Bouchard, T. J., Wilcox, K. J., Segal, N. L., & Rich, S. (1988). Personality similarity in twins reared apart and together. *Journal of Personality and Social Psychology, 54,* 1031–1039.

Tellegen, A., & Waller, N. G. (2008). Exploring personality through test construction: Development of the Multidimensional Personality Questionnaire. In G. J. Boyle, G. Matthews, & D. H. Saklofske (Eds.), *The Sage handbook of personality theory and assessment: Vol. II. Personality measurement and testing* (pp. 261–292). London, England: Sage.

Terracciano, A., & McCrae, R. R. (2012). Why do (some) birds flock? Causality and the structure of characteristic adaptations. *European Journal of Personality, 26,* 449–450. http://dx.doi.org/10.1002/per.1878

Tett, R. P., Jackson, D. N., & Rothstein, M. (1991). Personality measures as predictors of job performance: A meta-analytic review. *Personnel Psychology, 44,* 703–742.

Thomas, G. V., & Jolley, R. P. (1998). Drawing conclusions: A re-examination of empirical and conceptual bases for psychological evaluation of children from their drawings. *British Journal of Clinical Psychology, 37,* 127–139.

Torgersen, S., Czajkowski, N., Jacobson, K., Reichborn-Kjennerud, T., Røysamb, E., Neale, M. C., & Kendler, K. S. (2008). Dimensional representations of DSM-IV cluster B personality disorders in a population-based sample of Norwegian twins: A multivariate study. *Psychological Medicine, 38,* 1–9.

Triandis, H. C. (1989). The self and social behavior in differing cultural contexts. *Psychological Review, 96,* 506–520.

Trull, T. J. (2012). The five-factor model of personality disorder and DSM-5. *Journal of Personality Disorder, 80,* 1697–1720.

Trull, T. J., Useda, J. D., Costa, P. T., & McCrae, R. R. (1995). Comparison of the MMPI-2 Personality Psychopathology Five (PSY-5), the NEO-PI, and the NEOPI-R. *Psychological Assessment, 7,* 508–516.

Turkheimer, E. (2000). Three laws of behavior genetics and what they mean. *Current Directions in Psychological Science, 9,* 160–163.

Turkheimer, E., & Waldron, M. (2000). Nonshared environment: A theoretical, methodological, and quantitative review. *Psychological Bulletin, 126,* 78–108.

Vaillant, G. E. (1977). *Adaptation to life.* Boston, MA: Little, Brown.

Vane, J. R. (1981). The Thematic Apperception Test: A review. *Clinical Psychology Review, 1,* 319–336.

Vernon, P. A., Villani, V. C., Vickers, L. C., & Harris, J. A. (2008). A behavioral genetic investigation of the Dark Triad and the Big 5. *Personality and Individual Differences, 44,* 445–452.

Vrieze, S., & Grove, W. G. (2009). Survey on the use of clinical and mechanical prediction methods in clinical psychology. *Professional Psychology: Research and Practice, 40,* 525–531.

Wahl, O. F. (1976). Monozygotic twins discordant for schizophrenia: A review. *Psychological Bulletin, 83,* 91–106.

Waldman, I. D., & Gizer, I. R. (2006). The genetics of attention deficit hyperactivity disorder. *Clinical Psychology Review, 26,* 396–432.

Waller, N. G., Kojetin, B. A., Bouchard, T. J., Lykken, D. T., & Tellegen, A. (1990). Genetic and environmental influences on religious interests, attitudes, and values: A study of twins reared apart and together. *Psychological Science, 1,* 1–5.

Walters, G. D., & Greene, R. L. (1988). Differentiating between schizophrenia and manic inpatients by means of the MMPI. *Journal of Personality Assessment, 52,* 91–95.

Wang, M., & Saudino, K. J. (2012). Genetic and environmental contributions to stability and change of sleep problems in toddlerhood. *Journal of Pediatric Psychology, 37,* 697–706. http://dx.doi.org/10.1093/jpepsy/jss048

Weed, N. C., Ben-Porath, Y. S., & Butcher, J. N. (1990). Failure of Weiner and Harmon MMPI subtle scales as personality descriptors and as validity indicators. *Psychological Assessment, 2,* 281–285.

Weiner, I. B. (1997). Current status of the Rorschach Inkblot Method. *Journal of Personality Assessment, 68,* 5–19.

Weisner, W., & Cronshaw, S. (1988). A meta-analytic investigation of interview format and degree of structure on the validity of the employment interview. *Journal of Occupational Psychology, 61,* 275–290.

Weller, J. A., & Thulin, E. W. (2012). Do honest people take fewer risks? Personality correlates of risk-taking to achieve gains and avoid losses in HEXACO space. *Personality and Individual Differences, 53,* 923–926. http://dx.doi.org/10.1016/j.paid.2012.06.010

Westen, D. (1991). Clinical assessment of object relations using the TAT. *Journal of Personality Assessment, 56,* 56–74.

Westen, D. (1998). The scientific legacy of Sigmund Freud: Toward a psychodynamically informed psychological science. *Psychological Bulletin, 124,* 333–371.

Westen, D., Feit, A., & Zittel, C. (1999). Methodological issues in research using projective methods. In P. C. Kendall & J. N. Butcher (Eds.), *Handbook of research methods in clinical psychology* (2nd ed., pp. 224–240). New York, NY: Wiley.

Widiger, T. A. (2001). The best and the worst of us? *Clinical Psychology: Science and Practice, 8,* 374–377.

Widiger, T. A., & Costa P. T. (2012). Integrating normal and abnormal personality structure: The five-factor model. *Journal of Personality, 80,* 1471–1506.

Williams, W. M., & Ceci, S. J. (1998). *Escaping the advice trap.* Kansas City, MO: Andrews McMeel.

Wood, J. M., & Lilienfeld, S. O. (1999). The Rorschach Inkblot Test: A case of overstatement? *Assessment, 6,* 341–351.

Wood, J. M., Lilienfeld, S. O., Garb, H. N., & Nezworski, M. T. (2000). The Rorschach test in clinical diagnosis: A critical review, with a backward look at Garfield (1947). *Journal of Clinical Psychology, 56*, 395–430.

Wood, J. M., Lilienfeld, S. O., Garb, H. N., & Nezworski, M. T. (2010). The validity of the Rorschach Inkblot Test for discriminating psychopaths from non-psychopaths in forensic populations: A meta-analysis. *Psychological Assessment, 22*, 336–349.

Wood, J. M., Nezworski, M. T., & Stejskal, W. J. (1996). The comprehensive system for the Rorschach: A critical examination. *Psychological Science, 7*, 3–10.

Wrangham, R. W., & Glowacki, L. (2012). Intergroup aggression in chimpanzees and war in nomadic hunter-gatherers. *Human Nature, 23*, 5–29. http://dx.doi.org/10.1007/s12110-012-9132-1

Wyatt, W., Posey, A., Welker, W., & Seamonds, C. (1984). Natural levels of similarities between identical twins and between unrelated people. *Skeptical Inquirer, 9*, 62–66.

Zuckerman, M. (1979). *Sensation seeking: Beyond the optimal level of arousal.* Hillsdale, NJ: Erlbaum.

Zuckerman, M. (1994). *Behavioral expressions and biosocial bases of sensation seeking.* New York, NY: Cambridge University Press.

Credits

Credits listed in order of appearance.

Photo Credits

Photo Credits listed in order of appearance.

Psychological Disorders

From Chapter 15 of *Psychology: From Inquiry to Understanding,* Third Edition. Scott O. Lilienfeld, Steven Jay Lynn, Laura L. Namy, Nancy J. Woolf. Copyright © 2014 by Pearson Education, Inc. All rights reserved.

Psychological Disorders

WHEN ADAPTATION BREAKS DOWN

Think About It

Are psychiatric diagnoses meaningful, or are they just labels for undesirable behaviors?

Is the insanity defense successful most of the time?

Does everyone who attempts suicide want to die?

Is schizophrenia the same as split personality?

Are all people with psychopathic personalities violent?

Psychological Disorders
Listen in **MyPsychLab** to chapter audio

Below are descriptions of five actual patients (with names changed to safeguard their identity) drawn from the clinical experiences of two of your text's authors. Read each description and ask yourself what these people have in common.

Ida, 43 years old, was strolling around a shopping mall by herself. Suddenly and out of the blue, she experienced a burst of incredibly intense anxiety that left her feeling terrified, faint, and nauseated. She thought she was having a heart attack and took a taxi to the nearest emergency room. The doctors found nothing wrong with her heart and told her the problem was "all in her head." Ida has since refused to leave her house or go anywhere without her husband. She's scared to drive or take a bus. Ida's diagnosis: *panic disorder (with agoraphobia)*.

Bill, 45 years old, hasn't shaved or showered in over ten years. His beard is several feet long. Bill doesn't want to shave or shower because he's terrified that tiny "metal slivers" from the water will find their way into his skin. As much as possible, Bill avoids talking on the telephone or walking through doorways because he's petrified of acquiring germs. Whenever he experiences a thought he feels he shouldn't be having—such as a desire to kiss a married woman—he counts backward from 100 by sevens to relieve his anxiety. Bill recognizes these behaviors as irrational, but he hasn't been able to change them despite two decades of treatment. Bill's diagnosis: *obsessive-compulsive disorder*.

A few days after having a baby at age 30, Ann became incredibly giddy. She felt on top of the world, barely needed any sleep, and for the first time began sleeping with men she'd just met. Ann also became convinced she'd turned into a clown—literally. She was even persuaded that she had a bright red round nose, even though her nose was entirely normal. Ann's diagnosis: *bipolar disorder*.

Terrell, 28 years old, has just been released from the intensive care unit of a city hospital. He had shot himself in the stomach after becoming convinced that fish were swimming inside it. He suspects these fish are part of a government conspiracy to make him physically ill. Terrell's diagnosis: *schizophrenia*.

Johnny is 19 years old. He's charming, articulate, and fun-loving; he's especially popular among young women. Yet he's furious that he's been committed to the inpatient unit of a psychiatric hospital, and he blames his parents, teachers, and former friends for his problems. Johnny is well aware that his actions, like cursing at employers, holding live cats under water until they drown, and attempting to blow up his school with stolen dynamite, aren't exactly popular among his peers. Yet he sees nothing especially wrong with these behaviors and admits he's never felt guilty about anything. Johnny's diagnosis: *antisocial personality disorder*.

Conceptions of Mental Illness: Yesterday and Today

1   Identify criteria for defining mental disorders.

2   Describe conceptions of diagnoses across history and cultures.

3   Identify common misconceptions about psychiatric diagnoses, and the strengths and limitations of the current diagnostic system.

These brief sketches don't do justice to the extraordinarily rich and complex lives of these five people, but they give us some sense of the broad scope of *psychopathology*, or mental illness. In almost all mental disorders, we witness a striking failure of adaptation to the environment. In one way or another, people with mental disorders aren't adjusting well to the demands of daily life. Many psychopathology researchers adopt a *failure analysis approach* to mental disorders (Harkness, 2007). Just as engineers use accidents, such as plane crashes, to help them understand how mechanical systems work properly, psychopathology researchers examine breakdowns in adaptation to help them understand healthy functioning.

But what do Ida, Bill, Ann, Terrell, and Johnny have in common? Putting it differently, what distinguishes psychological abnormality from normality?

Watch in **MyPsychLab** the **Video:** The Big Picture: What Does it Mean to Have a Mental Disorder?

What Is Mental Illness? A Deceptively Complex Question

The answer to this question isn't as simple as we might assume, because the concept of *mental disorder* doesn't lend itself to a clear-cut dictionary definition (McNally, 2011). Instead, psychologists and psychiatrists have proposed a host of criteria for what mental disorder is. We'll review five of them here. Each criterion captures something important about mental disorder, but each has its shortcomings (Gorenstein, 1984; Wakefield, 1992).

STATISTICAL RARITY. Many mental disorders like schizophrenia—Terrell's condition—are uncommon in the population. Yet we can't rely on statistical rarity to define mental disorder, because not all infrequent conditions—such as extraordinary creativity—are pathological, and many mental illnesses—such as mild depression—are quite common (Kendell, 1975).

SUBJECTIVE DISTRESS. Most mental disorders, including mood and anxiety disorders, produce emotional pain for individuals afflicted with them. But not all psychological disorders generate distress. For example, during the manic phases of bipolar disorder, which Ann experienced, people frequently feel better than normal and perceive nothing wrong with their behaviors. Similarly, many adults with antisocial personality disorder, like Johnny, experience less distress than the typical person.

IMPAIRMENT. Most mental disorders interfere with people's ability to function in everyday life. These disorders can destroy marriages, friendships, and jobs. Yet the presence of impairment by itself can't define mental illness, because some conditions, such as laziness, can produce impairment but aren't mental disorders.

SOCIETAL DISAPPROVAL. Nearly 50 years ago, the late psychiatrist Thomas Szasz (1960) argued famously that "mental illness is a myth" and that "mental disorders" are nothing more than conditions that society dislikes. He even proposed that psychologists and psychiatrists use diagnoses as weapons of control: by attaching negative labels to people whose behaviors they find objectionable, they're putting these people "in their place." Szasz was both right and wrong. He was right that our negative attitudes toward those with serious mental illnesses are often deep-seated and widespread. Szasz was also right that societal attitudes shape our views of abnormality.

Psychiatric diagnoses have often mirrored the views of the times. For centuries, some psychiatrists invoked the diagnosis of *masturbational insanity* to describe individuals whose compulsive masturbation supposedly drove them mad (Hare, 1962). Homosexuality was classified as a mental illness until members of the American Psychiatric Association voted to remove it from their list of disorders in 1973 (Bayer, 1981). As society became more accepting of homosexuality, mental health professionals came to reject the view that such behavior is indicative of psychological disorder.

But Szasz was wrong that society regards all disapproved conditions as mental disorders (Wakefield, 1992). To take just one example, racism is justifiably deplored by society, but isn't considered a mental disorder by either laypersons or mental health professionals (Yamey & Shaw, 2002). Neither is messiness nor rudeness even though they're both considered undesirable by society.

BIOLOGICAL DYSFUNCTION. Many mental disorders probably result from breakdowns or failures of physiological systems. For example, we'll learn that schizophrenia is often marked by an underactivity in the brain's frontal lobes. In contrast, some mental disorders, like specific phobias, which as we'll soon learn are intense and irrational fears, appear to be acquired largely through learning experiences and often require only a weak genetic predisposition to trigger them.

In fact, it's unlikely that any one criterion distinguishes mental disorders from normality, which explains why mental disorder is difficult or impossible to define (McNally, 2011; Stein et al., 2010). As a consequence, some authors have argued for

Psychiatric diagnoses are often shaped by the views—and biases—of the historical period. In the mid-1800s, some psychiatrists applied the diagnosis of *drapetomania* to describe the "disorder" of slaves who attempted repeatedly to escape from their masters. In a journal article, a physician even prescribed whipping and toe amputation as "treatments" for this condition (Cartwright, 1851).

Brothers and sisters share a family resemblance; they look like each other but don't have all features in common. The broad category of "mental disorders" may be similar. Different mental disorders aren't exactly alike, but they share a number of features.

The infamous "dunking test" for witches, popular during the witch scares of the sixteenth and seventeenth centuries. According to the dunking test, if a woman drowned, it meant she wasn't a witch. In contrast, if she floated to the top of the water, it meant she was a witch and needed to be executed. Either way, she died.

RULING OUT RIVAL HYPOTHESES ▶
Have important alternative explanations for the findings been excluded?

demonic model
view of mental illness in which behaving oddly, hearing voices, or talking to oneself was attributed to evil spirits infesting the body

medical model
view of mental illness as due to a physical disorder requiring medical treatment

asylum
institution for people with mental illnesses created in the fifteenth century

a *family resemblance view* of mental disorder (Kirmayer & Young, 1999; Lilienfeld & Marino, 1995; Rosenhan & Seligman, 1989). According to this perspective, mental disorders don't all have one thing in common. Just as brothers and sisters within a family look similar but don't all possess the same eyes, ears, or noses, mental disorders share a loose set of features. These features include those we've described—statistical rarity, subjective distress, impairment, societal disapproval, and biological dysfunction—as well as others, such as a need for treatment, irrationality, and loss of control over one's behavior (Bergner, 1997). So Ida, Bill, Ann, Terrell, and Johnny aren't alike in precisely the same way. Yet they overlap enough in their features that we recognize each of them as having a mental disorder.

Historical Conceptions of Mental Illness: From Demons to Asylums

Throughout history, people have recognized certain behaviors as abnormal. Yet their explanations and treatments for these behaviors have shifted in tune with prevailing cultural conceptions. The history of society's evolving views of mental illness tells the fascinating story of a bumpy road from nonscience to science.

THE DEMONIC AND MEDICAL MODELS. During the Middle Ages, many people in Europe and later in America viewed mental illnesses through the lens of a **demonic model**. They attributed hearing voices, talking to oneself, and behaving oddly to the actions of evil spirits infesting the body (Hunter & Macalpine, 1963). The often bizarre "treatments" of the day, including exorcisms, flowed directly from the demonic model. Yet the legacy of the demonic model lives on today in the thousands of exorcisms still performed in Italy, Mexico, and other countries (Harrington, 2005).

As the Middle Ages faded and the Renaissance took hold, views of those with mental illness became more enlightened. Over time, more people came to perceive mental illness primarily as a physical disorder requiring medical treatment—a view that some scholars refer to as the **medical model** (Blaney, 1975). Beginning in the fifteenth century and especially in later centuries, European governments began to house these individuals in **asylums**—institutions for those with mental illness (Gottesman, 1991).

Yet the medical treatments of that era were scarcely more scientific than those of the demonic era, and several were equally barbaric. Treatments included "bloodletting" (the draining of "excessive" blood, then believed to cause mental illness) and frightening patients "out of their diseases" by tossing them into a snake pit, hence the term *snake pit* as a synonym for an insane asylum (Szasz, 2006).

Not surprisingly, most patients of this era deteriorated, and in the case of bloodletting, some died. Even those who improved in the short term may have merely been responding to the *placebo effect*—improvement resulting from the expectation of improvement (Horowitz, 2012). Yet few physicians of the day considered the placebo effect as a rival explanation for these treatments' seeming effectiveness. Although most of these treatments seem preposterous to us today, it's crucial to recognize that psychological and medical treatments are products of the times. Society's beliefs about the causes of mental illness shape its interventions.

Fortunately, reform was on the way. Thanks to the heroic efforts of Phillippe Pinel (1745–1826) in France and Dorothea Dix (1802–1887) in America, an approach called **moral treatment** gained a foothold in Europe and America. Advocates of moral treatment insisted that those with mental illness be treated with dignity, kindness, and respect. Prior to moral treatment, patients in asylums were often bound in chains; following moral treatment, they were free to roam the halls of hospitals, get fresh air, and interact freely with staff and other patients. Still, effective treatments for mental illnesses were virtually nonexistent, so many people continued to suffer for years with no hope of relief.

THE MODERN ERA OF PSYCHIATRIC TREATMENT. It wasn't until the early 1950s that a dramatic change in society's treatment of individuals with mental illness arrived on the scene. It was then that psychiatrists introduced a medication imported from France called *chlorpromazine* (its brand name is Thorazine) into mental hospitals. Chlorpromazine wasn't a miracle cure, but it offered a modestly effective treatment for some symptoms of schizophrenia and similar disorders marked by a loss of contact with reality. Many patients with these conditions became able to function independently, and some returned to their families and jobs.

By the 1960s and 1970s, the advent of chlorpromazine and similar medications became the primary impetus for a governmental policy called **deinstitutionalization**, which allowed the release of hospitalized psychiatric patients into the community and contributed to the closure of many mental hospitals (Torrey, 1997). Following deinstitutionalization, the number of hospitalized psychiatric patients plummeted through the beginning of the twenty-first century (see **FIGURE 1**). But deinstitutionalization was a mixed blessing. Some patients returned to a semblance of a regular life, but tens of thousands of others spilled into cities and rural areas without adequate follow-up care. Many went off their medications and wandered the streets aimlessly. Some of the homeless people we can see today on the streets of major American cities are a tragic legacy of deinstitutionalization (Leeper, 1988). Today, psychologists, social workers, and other mental health professionals are working to improve the quality and availability of community care for severely affected psychiatric patients. Among the consequences of these efforts are *community mental health centers* and *halfway houses,* free or low-cost care facilities in which people can obtain treatment.

Thankfully, our understanding of mental illness and its treatment today is considerably more sophisticated than it was centuries ago. Still, precious few of today's treatments are genuine cures.

Psychiatric Diagnoses Across Cultures

Psychiatric diagnoses are shaped not only by history, but also by culture (Chentsova-Dutton & Tsai, 2007; Watters, 2010). Psychologists have increasingly recognized that certain conditions are *culture-bound*— specific to one or more societies—although most of these conditions remain insufficiently researched (see **TABLE 1** on page 590) (Kleinman, 1988; Simons & Hughes, 1986).

CULTURE-BOUND SYNDROMES. For example, some parts of Malaysia and several other Asian countries, including China and India, have witnessed periodic outbreaks of a strange condition known as *koro* (Crozier, 2012). The victims of *koro,* most of whom are male, typically believe that their penis and testicles are disappearing and receding into their abdomen (female victims of *koro* sometimes believe that their breasts are disappearing). *Koro* is spread largely by social contagion. Once one man begins to experience its symptoms, others often follow suit, triggering widespread panic. In one region of India in 1982, the *koro* epidemic spun so out of control that the local government took to the streets with loudspeakers to reassure terrified civilians that their genitals weren't vanishing. Government officials even measured male residents' penises with rulers in an attempt to prove their fears unfounded (Bartholomew, 1994).

Another disorder specific to Malaysia, the Philippines, and some African countries is *amok.* This condition is marked by episodes of intense sadness and brooding followed by uncontrolled behavior and unprovoked attacks on people or animals (American Psychiatric Association, 2000). This condition gave rise to the popular phrase *running amok,* meaning "going wild." More recently, in Japan, a growing number of

Dorothea Dix was a Massachusetts schoolteacher whose lobbying efforts resulted in the establishment of more humane psychiatric facilities in the 1800s.

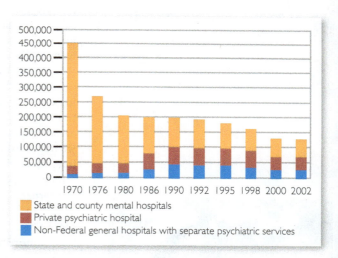

Legend:
- State and county mental hospitals
- Private psychiatric hospital
- Non-Federal general hospitals with separate psychiatric services

(x-axis years: 1970 1976 1980 1986 1990 1992 1995 1998 2000 2002; y-axis: 0 to 500,000)

FIGURE 1 Decline in Psychiatric Inpatients. Over the past several decades, the number of hospitalized psychiatric patients has gradually declined. (*Source:* www.ahrq.gov/legacy/about/annualconf09/vandivort_mark_owens/slide4.jpg)

moral treatment
approach to mental illness calling for dignity, kindness, and respect for those with mental illness

deinstitutionalization
1960s and 1970s governmental policy that focused on releasing hospitalized psychiatric patients into the community and closing mental hospitals

TABLE I A Sampling of Common Culture-Bound Syndromes Not Discussed in the Text.

SYNDROME	REGION/POPULATION AFFECTED	DESCRIPTION
Arctic Hysteria	Alaska Natives (Inuit)	Abrupt episode accompanied by extreme excitement and frequently followed by convulsive seizures and coma.
Ataque de Nervios	Latin America	Symptoms include uncontrollable shouting, attacks of crying, trembling, heat in the chest rising to the head, and verbal or physical aggression.
Brain Fog	West Africa	Symptoms include difficulties in concentrating, remembering, and thinking.
Latah	Malaysia and Southeast Asia	Found mostly among women; marked by an extreme startle reaction, followed by a loss of control, cursing, and mimicking of others' actions and speech.
Mal de Ojo (Evil Eye)	Spain and Latin America	A common term to describe the cause of disease, misfortune, and social disruption.
Windigo	Native Americans Central and Northeastern Canada	Morbid state of anxiety with fears of becoming a cannibal.

(*Source:* Based on Simons, 2001)

Mal de ojo, or the "evil eye," is a culture-bound syndrome common in many Mediterranean and Latin countries. Believed by its victims to be brought on by the glance of a malicious person, *mal de ojo* is marked by insomnia, nervousness, crying for no reason, and vomiting. Here, customers in Egypt select pendants for warding off the evil eye.

men appear to have developed a condition known as "2-D love," which is characterized by an attraction to two-dimensional imaginary characters such as cartoon women; one man with the disorder has collected over 150 pillow covers featuring drawings of young women (Katayama, 2009).

Other culture-bound syndromes seem to be variants of conditions in Western culture. In Japan, for example, social anxiety is typically expressed as a fear of offending others (called *taijin kyofushu*), such as by saying something offensive or giving off a terrible body odor (Kleinknecht et al. 1994; Vriends et al., 2013). But in the United States, social anxiety is more commonly generated by fear of public embarrassment, such as what we might experience when giving a speech. Culture may influence how people express interpersonal anxiety. Because Japanese culture is more collectivistic compared with Western culture, Japanese tend to be more concerned about their impact on others than are Westerners.

In contrast, Western culture is more individualistic, so people tend to worry more about what may happen to them as individuals. European-Canadian patients report more psychological symptoms than do their Chinese counterparts, perhaps suggesting a tendency to "psychologize" symptoms of distress. Because Chinese patients frequently focus their thoughts "externally," as opposed to "internally" on their emotional states, they may be more likely to notice somatic symptoms like aches and pains when distressed (Ryder et al., 2008). The focus on the self in individualistic societies may also contribute to certain culture-bound disorders in Western countries. Some eating disorders are largely specific to the United States and Europe, where the media bombard viewers with images of thin models, probably making already self-conscious women even more self-conscious (Keel & Klump, 2003; McCarthy, 1990).

CULTURAL UNIVERSALITY. Despite the cultural differences we've noted, we shouldn't exaggerate the cultural relativity of mental disorders. Many mental disorders, especially those that are severe, appear to exist in most and perhaps all cultures. Jane Murphy (1976) conducted a classic study of two isolated societies—a group of Yorubas in Nigeria and a group of Inuit Eskimos near the Bering Strait—that had experienced essentially no contact with Western culture. These cultures possessed terms for disorders that are strikingly similar to schizophrenia, alcoholism, and *psychopathic personality*. For example, in Inuit, *kunlangeta* describes a person who lies, cheats, steals, is unfaithful to women, and doesn't obey elders—a description that fits almost perfectly the Western concept of psychopathic personality. When Murphy asked one of the Inuit how they dealt with such individuals, he replied that "somebody would have pushed him off the ice when no one was looking." Apparently, Inuit aren't much fonder of psychopaths than we are.

Special Considerations in Psychiatric Classification and Diagnosis

Because there are so many ways in which psychological adaptation can go awry, we'd be hopelessly lost without some system of diagnostic classification. Psychiatric diagnoses serve at least two crucial functions. *First,* they help us pinpoint the psychological problem a person is experiencing. Once we've identified this problem, it's often easier to select a treatment. *Second,* psychiatric diagnoses make it easier for mental health professionals to communicate. When a psychologist diagnoses a patient with schizophrenia, he or she can be reasonably certain that other psychologists know the patient's principal symptoms. Diagnoses operate as forms of mental shorthand, simplifying complex descriptions of problematic behaviors into convenient summary phrases.

Still, there are a host of misconceptions regarding psychiatric diagnosis. Before turning to our present system of psychiatric classification, we'll examine four prevalent misunderstandings, along with the facts that rebut them:

Misconception 1: *Psychiatric diagnosis is nothing more than pigeonholing, that is, sorting people into different "boxes."* According to this criticism, when we diagnose people with a mental disorder, we deprive them of their uniqueness: we imply that all people within the same diagnostic category are alike in all important respects.

Reality: To the contrary, a diagnosis implies only that all people with a particular diagnosis are alike in at least *one* important respect (Lilienfeld, Smith, & Watts, in press). Psychologists recognize that even within a diagnostic category like schizophrenia or bipolar disorder, people differ dramatically in their other psychological difficulties, race and cultural background, personality traits, interests, and cognitive skills. People are far more than their disorders.

Misconception 2: *Psychiatric diagnoses are unreliable. Reliability* refers to consistency of measurement. In the case of psychiatric diagnoses, the form of reliability that matters most is *interrater reliability:* the extent to which different raters (such as different psychologists) agree on patients' diagnoses.

Reality: In fact, for major mental disorders like schizophrenia, mood disorders, anxiety disorders, and alcoholism, interrater reliabilities are typically about as high—correlations between raters of .8 or above out of a maximum of 1.0—as for most medical disorders (Matarazzo, 1983). Still, the picture isn't entirely rosy. For many personality disorders, a class of disorders we'll discuss later, interrater reliabilities tend to be lower (Freedman et al., 2013; Zimmerman, 1994).

Misconception 3: *Psychiatric diagnoses are invalid.* From the standpoint of Thomas Szasz (1960) and other critics, psychiatric diagnoses are largely useless because they don't provide us with much, if any, new information. They're merely descriptive labels for behaviors we don't like.

Reality: When it comes to some pop psychology labels, Szasz probably has a point. Consider the explosion of diagnostic labels that are devoid of scientific support, such as codependency, sexual addiction, Internet addiction, road rage disorder, and compulsive shopping disorder (Granello & Beamish, 1998; Kessler et al., 2006; Koran et al., 2006; McCann, Shindler, & Hammond, 2003). Although frequently used in talk shows, television programs, movies, and self-help books, these labels aren't recognized as formal psychiatric diagnoses.

Trials involving "dueling expert witnesses" may contribute to the erroneous public perception that psychologists can't agree on the diagnoses of individuals with suspected mental disorders.

Actor David Duchovny and golfer Tiger Woods are among the many celebrities who've reportedly sought treatment for "sexual addiction," which is not an official psychiatric diagnosis. Is sexual addiction a genuine condition, or is it merely a descriptive label for problematic behavior? Many psychologists argue the latter.

labeling theorists
scholars who argue that psychiatric diagnoses exert powerful negative effects on people's perceptions and behaviors

Yet there's now considerable evidence that many psychiatric diagnoses *do* tell us something new about the person. In a classic paper, psychiatrists Eli Robins and Samuel Guze (1970) outlined several criteria for determining whether a psychiatric diagnosis is valid. According to Robins and Guze, a valid diagnosis

1. distinguishes that diagnosis from other similar diagnoses.
2. predicts diagnosed individuals' performance on laboratory tests, including personality measures, neurotransmitter levels, and brain imaging findings (Andreasen, 1995).
3. predicts diagnosed individuals' family history of psychiatric disorders.
4. predicts diagnosed individuals' *natural history*—that is, what tends to happen to them over time.

In addition, some authors have argued that a valid diagnosis ideally

5. predicts diagnosed individuals' response to treatment (Waldman, Lilienfeld, & Lahey, 1995).

There's good evidence that unlike most pop psychology labels, many mental disorders fulfill Robins and Guze's criteria for validity. **TABLE 2** illustrates these criteria using the example of *attention-deficit/hyperactivity disorder (ADHD)*, a disorder we'll encounter later in the chapter that's characterized by inattention, impulsivity, and overactivity.

Misconception 4: *Psychiatric diagnoses stigmatize people.* According to **labeling theorists**, psychiatric diagnoses exert powerful negative effects on people's perceptions and behaviors (Scheff, 1984; Slater, 2004). Labeling theorists argue that once a mental health professional diagnoses us, others perceive us differently. Suddenly, we're "weird," "strange," even "crazy." This diagnosis leads others to treat us differently, in turn often leading us to behave in weird, strange, or crazy ways. The diagnosis thereby becomes a self-fulfilling prophecy.

Reality: In a sensational study, David Rosenhan (1973) asked eight individuals with no symptoms of mental illness (himself included) to pose as fake patients in 12 psychiatric hospitals. These "pseudopatients" (fake patients) presented themselves to admitting psychiatrists with a single complaint: they were hearing a voice saying "empty, hollow, and thud." In all 12 cases, the psychiatrists admitted these pseudopatients to the hospital, almost always with diagnoses of schizophrenia (one received a diagnosis of manic depression, or what would today be called bipolar disorder). Remarkably, they remained there for an average of three weeks despite displaying no further symptoms of mental illness. The diagnosis of schizophrenia, Rosenhan concluded, became a

TABLE 2 Criteria for Validity: The Case of ADHD. Although controversial in many respects, the diagnosis of attention-deficit/hyperactivity disorder (ADHD) largely satisfies the Robins and Guze criteria for validity.

ROBINS AND GUZE CRITERIA	FINDINGS CONCERNING THE ADHD DIAGNOSIS
1. Distinguishes a particular diagnosis from other similar diagnoses	The child's symptoms can't be accounted for by other diagnoses, such as substance abuse and anxiety disorders.
2. Predicts performance on laboratory tests (personality measures, neurotransmitter levels, brain imaging findings)	The child is likely to perform poorly on laboratory measures of concentration.
3. Predicts family history of psychiatric disorders	The child has a higher probability than the average child of having biological relatives with ADHD.
4. Predicts what happens to the individual over time	The child is likely to show continued difficulties with inattention in adulthood, but improvements in impulsivity and overactivity in adulthood.
5. Predicts response to treatment	The child has a good chance of responding positively to stimulant medications like Ritalin.

self-fulfilling prophecy, leading doctors and nursing staff to view these individuals as disturbed. For example, the nursing staff interpreted one pseudopatient's note taking as "abnormal writing behavior."

It's true that there's still stigma attached to some psychiatric diagnoses. If someone tells us that a person has schizophrenia, for instance, we may be wary of the individual at first or misinterpret his or her behavior as consistent with the diagnosis. Yet the negative effects of labels last only so long. Even in Rosenhan's study, all pseudopatients were released from the hospital with diagnoses of either schizophrenia or manic depression "in remission" ("in remission" means without any symptoms) (Spitzer, 1975). These discharge diagnoses tell us that psychiatrists eventually recognized that these individuals were behaving normally. Overall, there's not much evidence that most psychiatric diagnoses themselves generate long-term negative effects (Ruscio, 2003).

Psychiatric Diagnosis Today: DSM-5

The official system for classifying individuals with mental disorders is the ***Diagnostic and Statistical Manual of Mental Disorders*** (DSM), which originated in 1952 and is now in its fifth edition, called DSM-5 (APA, 2013). There are 18 different classes of disorders in the DSM-5, several of which we'll be discussing in the pages to come.

DIAGNOSTIC CRITERIA AND DECISION RULES. The DSM-5 provides psychologists and psychiatrists with a list of diagnostic criteria for each condition and a set of decision rules for deciding how many of these criteria need to be met. For example, to diagnose a person with major depressive disorder, DSM-5 requires the person to exhibit at least five of nine symptoms, including fatigue, insomnia, problems concentrating, and significant weight loss over a two-week period, with the requirement that the person experience either depressed mood, diminished interest or pleasure in everyday activities, or both.

"THINKING ORGANIC." DSM-5 warns diagnosticians about physical—or "organic," that is, medically induced—conditions that can simulate certain psychological disorders (Morrison, 1997). DSM-5 notes that certain substance use or medical disorders can mimic the clinical picture of depression. For example, it informs readers that *hypothyroidism,* a disorder marked by underactivity of the thyroid gland (in our lower necks), can produce depressive symptoms (Tallis, 2011). If a patient's depression appears due to hypothyroidism, the psychologist shouldn't diagnose major depression. It's essential to "think organic," or to first rule out medical causes of a disorder, when diagnosing psychological conditions.

THE DSM-5: OTHER FEATURES. DSM-5 is more than a tool for diagnosing mental disorders; it's a valuable source of information concerning the characteristics, such as the **prevalence**, of many mental disorders. Prevalence refers to the percentage of people in the population with a disorder. In the case of major depression, the lifetime prevalence is at least 10 percent among women and at least 5 percent among men (some estimates are even higher). That means that for a woman, the odds are at least 1 in 10 she'll experience an episode of major depression at some point in her life; for a man, the odds are at least 1 in 20 (APA, 2013).

DSM-5 also recognizes that there's more to people than their disorders. The manual adopts a *biopsychosocial approach,* which acknowledges the interplay of biological (like hormonal abnormalities), psychological (like irrational thoughts), and social (interpersonal interactions) influences. Specifically, it reminds diagnosticians to attend carefully to patients' ongoing life stressors, past and present medical conditions, and overall level of functioning when evaluating their psychological status.

Finally, DSM-5 acknowledges that we live in a diverse world filled with people from different ethnic, socioeconomic, and cultural backgrounds. Some of them embrace unconventional beliefs, sexual identities, and behaviors that are "abnormal" from the vantage point of our contemporary society. DSM-5 provides information about how differing cultural backgrounds can affect the content and expression of symptoms.

Diagnostic and Statistical Manual of Mental Disorders **(DSM)**
diagnostic system containing the American Psychiatric Association (APA) criteria for mental disorders

prevalence
percentage of people within a population who have a specific mental disorder

A clinical psychologist would probably perceive cutting oneself as pathological, but DSM-5 reminds clinicians that in some cultures, such practices are used to produce tribal scars and should be regarded as normal.

Like some psychological disorders, blood pressure better fits a dimensional than a categorical model, as there's no sharp dividing line between normal and high blood pressure.

comorbidity
co-occurrence of two or more diagnoses within the same person

categorical model
model in which a mental disorder differs from normal functioning in kind rather than degree

dimensional model
model in which a mental disorder differs from normal functioning in degree rather than kind

This information is vital to ensuring that diagnosticians do not incorrectly label someone from a different culture with a mental disorder merely because that person is exhibiting behaviors that those of us in Western culture might find unusual or unfamiliar.

THE DSM-5: CRITICISMS. There's little dispute that DSM-5 is a helpful system for slicing up the enormous pie of psychopathology into more meaningful and manageable pieces. Yet DSM-5 and previous versions of the manual have received more than their share of criticism—and sometimes for good reason (Frances & Widiger, 2012; Widiger & Clark, 2000).

There are well over 300 diagnoses in DSM-5, not all of which meet the Robins and Guze criteria for validity. To take only one example, the DSM-5 diagnosis of "Mathematics Disorder" describes little more than difficulties with performing arithmetic or math reasoning problems. It seems to be more of a label for learning problems than a diagnosis that tells us something new about the person. In addition, although the diagnostic criteria and decision rules for many DSM-5 disorders are based primarily on scientific findings, others are based largely on subjective committee decisions. Another problem with DSM-5 is the high level of **comorbidity** among many of its diagnoses (Angold, 1999; Cramer et al., 2010; Lilienfeld, Waldman, & Israel, 1994), meaning that individuals with one diagnosis frequently have one or more additional diagnoses. For example, it's extremely common for people with a major depression diagnosis to meet criteria for one or more anxiety disorders. This extensive comorbidity raises the troubling question of whether DSM-5 is diagnosing genuinely independent conditions as opposed to slightly different variations of one underlying condition (Cramer et al., 2010).

Another criticism of DSM-5 is its substantial reliance on a **categorical model** of psychopathology (Trull & Durett, 2005). In a categorical model, a mental disorder—such as major depression—is either present or absent, with no in between. Categories differ from each other in kind, not degree. Pregnancy fits a categorical model, because a woman is either pregnant or she's not. Yet scientific evidence suggests that many and perhaps most disorders in DSM-5 better fit a **dimensional model**, meaning they differ from normal functioning in degree, not kind (Haslam, Holland, & Kuppens, 2012; Krueger & Piasecki, 2002). Height fits a dimensional model, because although people differ in height, these differences aren't all or none. The same may be true of many forms of depression and anxiety, which most research suggests lie on a continuum with normality (Kollman et al., 2006; Slade & Andrews, 2005). These findings square with our everyday experience, because we all feel at least a bit depressed and anxious from time to time.

Some authors have proposed that the Big Five, a system of personality dimensions, may better capture the true "state of nature" than many of the categories in DSM-5 (Widiger & Clark, 2000; Wright et al., in press). For example, depression is typically characterized by high levels of neuroticism and introversion. Indeed, DSM-5 initially planned to include a system of personality dimensions similar to the Big Five in the main text of the manual (Krueger et al., 2007), but this dimensional system was eventually placed in a secondary section of the manual dedicated to future research. Indeed, many psychologists and psychiatrists have resisted a dimensional model, perhaps because they, like the rest of us, are *cognitive misers*; they strive to simplify the world. Most of us find it easier to think of the world in terms of simple black or white categories than complex shades of gray (Lilienfeld & Waldman, 2004; Macrae & Bodenhausen, 2000).

A particular concern voiced regarding DSM-5 is its tendency to "medicalize normality," that is, to classify relatively mild psychological disturbances as pathological (Frances & Widiger, 2012). For example, in a sharp break from previous versions of the DSM, DSM-5 now allows individuals to be diagnosed with Major Depressive Disorder following the loss of a loved one (assuming they meet the pertinent DSM-5 criteria), including the death of a spouse. Although this change may be justified by research (Pies, 2012), critics worry that it will open the floodgates to diagnosing many people with relatively normal grief reactions as disordered (Wakefield & First, 2012).

Like virtually all documents crafted by human beings, DSM-5 is vulnerable to political influences (Kirk & Kutchins, 1992). For example, some researchers have lobbied successfully for the inclusion of their "favorite" disorder or area of specialty. But like all scientific endeavors, the system of psychiatric classification tends to be self-correcting.

Just as homosexuality was stricken from the DSM in the 1970s, science will continue to weed out invalid disorders, ensuring that future editions of the DSM will be based on better evidence.

Watch in **MyPsychLab** the **Video:** Special Topics Diagnosing Mental Disorders

NORMALITY AND ABNORMALITY: A SPECTRUM OF SEVERITY. As you read case histories or descriptions in this chapter, you may wonder, "Is my behavior abnormal?" or "Maybe my problems are more serious than I thought." At times like this, it's useful to be aware of *medical students' syndrome* (Howes & Salkovskis, 1998). As medical students first become familiar with the symptoms of specific diseases, they often begin to focus on their bodily processes. Soon they find it hard to stop wondering whether a slight twinge in their chest might be an early warning of heart trouble or a mild headache the first sign of a brain tumor. Similarly, as we learn about psychological disorders, it's only natural to "see ourselves" in some patterns of behavior, largely because in meeting the complex demands of daily life, we all experience disturbing impulses, thoughts, and fears from time to time. So don't become alarmed as you learn about these conditions, as many are probably extremes of psychological difficulties we all experience on occasion.

But at some point in your life, you may experience a psychological problem that's so disturbing and persistent that you'll want to talk with someone about it. If so, you'll probably find it worthwhile to consult with a family member, friend, physician, dormitory counselor, clergy person, or mental health professional such as a social worker, psychologist, or psychiatrist.

MENTAL ILLNESS AND THE LAW: A CONTROVERSIAL INTERFACE. Psychological problems not only affect our mental functioning, but also can place us at risk for legal problems. There are few topics about which the general public is certain it knows more, yet actually knows less, than the controversial interface between mental illness and the law. The last few years have witnessed horrific acts of mass violence perpetrated by individuals who apparently suffer from severe mental illness, including the 2011 shooting of Congresswoman Gabrielle Giffords and 12 others near Tucson, Arizona (Giffords survived,

Answers are located at the end of the text.

ONLINE TESTS FOR MENTAL DISORDERS

evaluating **CLAIMS**

We're all familiar with medical websites that allow us to type in our symptoms ("itchy throat, headache, no fever") and receive a free, instant diagnosis of our physical ailments. But did you know that similar sites exist for the diagnosis of mental illnesses, including attention-deficit/hyperactivity disorder? Let's evaluate some claims and statements that are modeled after information on actual sites devoted to the self-diagnosis of adult ADHD.

"This 20 question self-test is *the most valid and reliable* screening measure for adult ADHD available on the Internet!"

Be suspicious of claims like "most valid and reliable" put forward with no supportive evidence. Because information on the Internet is vast and constantly subject to change, it's difficult to evaluate this extraordinary claim. Moreover, most online diagnostic tests have never been evaluated in peer-reviewed studies.

"*High scores on the self-test may result from* depression, anxiety, and bipolar disorder, so *it's important to rule out these conditions* before a diagnosis of ADHD can be made with confidence."

The site states accurately that ADHD symptoms often overlap with those of other disorders and that it may be challenging to distinguish the symptoms of ADHD, anxiety, depression, and bipolar disorder.

"Keep in mind that this is a screening test. Remember, it's *only the first step in arriving at an accurate diagnosis* of ADHD."

This statement rightly cautions against arriving at an ADHD diagnosis based on information contained in a brief questionnaire: It's often necessary to consider historical information and current behaviors and performance in different settings (such as school, workplace, and home), as well as tests of attention and input from different professionals (such as physicians, teachers, and family members).

but six people died), the 2012 theater shooting in Aurora, Colorado, and the 2012 Sandy Hook school shooting in Newtown, Connecticut. These tragic events raise complex questions regarding how, if at all, DSM-5 disorders relate to violence and how society should deal with mentally ill people who've committed violence.

Mental Illness and Violence. One of the most pervasive myths in psychology is that people with mental illness are at greatly heightened risk for violence (Link et al., 1999). In fact, the overwhelming majority of people with schizophrenia and other psychotic disorders aren't physically aggressive toward others; moreover, people with these conditions are much more likely to be victims than perpetrators of violence (Friedman, 2006; Steadman et al., 1998; Teplin, 1985). One might have hoped that the seemingly endless parade of "real crime" shows on television would have helped to combat this misconception, but it's probably done the opposite. Although only a few percent of people with mental disorders commit aggressive acts, about 75 percent of televised characters with mental illness are violent (Wahl, 1997).

Still, like many misconceptions, this one contains a kernel of truth. Although most people with mental illness aren't at increased risk for violence, a subset—especially those who are convinced they are being persecuted (by the government, for example) and those with substance abuse—is (Douglas, Guy, & Hart, 2009; Monahan, 1992; Steadman et al., 1998).

The horrific school shooting in Newtown, Connecticut, in 2012 brought public attention to the complex link between serious mental illness and violence. Research shows that this association is weaker and more limited than most people believe.

*psycho*mythology

THE INSANITY DEFENSE: FREE WILL VERSUS DETERMINISM

In courts of law, mental illnesses and the law occasionally collide head-on, often with unpredictable consequences. The best-known example of this clash is the **insanity defense**, which is premised on the idea that we shouldn't hold people legally responsible for their crimes if they weren't of "sound mind" when they committed them. The insanity defense comes in many forms, which differ across state and federal courts. As of 2013, 46 U.S. states use some version of this defense, with four—Utah, Montana, Idaho, and Kansas—opting out of it.

Most contemporary forms of this defense are based loosely on the *M'Naghten rule,* formulated during an 1843 British trial. This rule requires that to be declared insane, persons must either have (1) not known what they were doing at the time of the crime or (2) not known that what they were doing was wrong (Melton et al., 1997). A defendant (accused person) who was so disoriented during an epileptic seizure that he didn't realize he was attacking a police officer might fulfill the first prong of M'Naghten; a defendant who believed he was actually murdering Adolf Hitler when he shot his next-door neighbor might fulfill the second. Several other versions of the insanity defense strive to determine whether defendants were incapable of controlling their impulses at the moment of the crime. Because this judgment is exceedingly difficult (how can we know whether a man who murdered his wife in the heat of overwhelming anger *could* have controlled his temper had he really tried?), some courts ignore it.

The insanity defense is controversial, to put it mildly. To its proponents, this defense is necessary for defendants whose mental state is so deranged that it impairs their freedom to decide whether to commit a crime (Sadoff, 1992; Stone, 1982). To its critics, this defense is nothing more than a legal cop-out that excuses criminals of responsibility (Lykken, 1982; Szasz, 1991). These divergent perspectives reflect a more deep-seated disagreement about free will versus determinism. The legal system assumes that our actions are freely chosen, whereas scientific psychology assumes that our actions are completely determined by prior variables, including our genetic makeup and learning history. So lawyers and judges tend to view the insanity defense as a needed exception for the small minority of defendants who lack free will. In contrast, many psychologists view this defense as illogical, because they see all crimes, including those committed by people with severe mental disorders, as equally "determined."

There are numerous misconceptions regarding the insanity verdict (Daftary-Kapur et al., 2011; see **TABLE 3**). For example, although most people believe that a sizable proportion, perhaps 15–20 percent, of criminals are acquitted (found innocent) on the basis of the insanity verdict, the actual percentage is less than 1 percent (Silver, Cirincione, & Steadman, 1994). This erroneous belief probably stems from the *availability heuristic*: Because we hear a great deal about a few widely publicized cases of defendants acquitted on the grounds of insanity, we over-estimate this verdict's prevalence (Butler, 2006). A better appreciation of the facts surrounding the insanity defense may help to dispel unwarranted public views regarding its use.

TABLE 3 Misconceptions—and Realities—Regarding the Insanity Defense.

MYTH	REALITY
Insanity is a psychological or psychiatric term.	Insanity is a purely legal term that refers only to whether the person was responsible for the crime, not to the nature of his or her psychiatric disorder.
The determination of insanity rests on a careful evaluation of the person's current mental state.	The determination of insanity rests on a determination of the person's mental state at the time of the crime.
The insanity defense requires a judgment of the defendant's incompetence to stand trial.	Competence to stand trial bears on defendant's ability to assist in his or her own defense.
A large proportion of criminals escape criminal responsibility by using the insanity defense.	The insanity defense is raised in only about 1 percent of criminal trials and is successful only about one-fourth of the time.
Most people acquitted on the basis of an insanity defense quickly go free.	The average insanity acquittee spends close to three years in a psychiatric hospital, often longer than the length of a criminal sentence for the same crime.
Insanity defenses are complicated and frequently fool juries as a result.	Most successful insanity verdicts are delivered by judges, not juries.
Most people who use the insanity defense are faking mental illness.	The rate of faking mental illness among insanity defendants appears to be low.

(Based on Butler, 2006; Grisso, 2003; McCutcheon & McCutcheon, 1994; Pasewark & Pantle, 1979; Phillips, Wolf, & Coons, 1998; Silver et al., 1994)

Diagnosed with postpartum depression, Andrea Yates drowned her five young children in the bathtub, apparently following orders from Satan. In 2006, Yates was acquitted on the basis of an insanity verdict. The intense publicity surrounding this and several other trials involving the insanity verdict has probably contributed to public misperceptions regarding the verdict's prevalence.

Involuntary Commitment. We're all familiar with *criminal commitment,* which is just a fancy term for putting someone in jail or prison. Yet society possesses another mechanism for committing individuals against their will. Known as **involuntary commitment** or *civil commitment,* it's a procedure for protecting us from certain people with mental disorders and protecting them from themselves. Most U.S. states specify that individuals with mental illness can be committed against their will only if they (1) pose a clear and present threat to themselves or others or (2) are so psychologically impaired that they can't care for themselves (Appelbaum, 1997; Werth, 2001). Although psychiatrists (but not psychologists) can recommend involuntary commitment to a hospital, only a judge can formally approve it following a hearing. Nevertheless, in most states, two psychiatrists or other physicians can place an emergency "hold" on patients to hospitalize them involuntarily for a brief period of time, typically three days. When that period expires, the patient is legally entitled to a judicial hearing.

Involuntary commitment raises difficult ethical questions. Advocates of this procedure contend that the government has the right to assume the role of "parent" over individuals with mental illness who are dangerous and don't possess sufficient insight to appreciate the impact of their actions (Chodoff, 1976; Satel, 1999). In contrast, critics argue that by involuntarily institutionalizing people who haven't committed crimes, the government is depriving them of their civil liberties (Schaler, 2004; Szasz, 1978). Critics of involuntary commitment also point to research demonstrating that mental health professionals typically do a poor job of forecasting violence (Monahan, 1992; Mossman, 2013), often predicting that patients

involuntary commitment
procedure of placing some people with mental illnesses in a psychiatric hospital or another facility based on their potential danger to themselves or others or their inability to care for themselves

Psychological Disorders

will commit violence when they won't. African-American psychiatric patients are especially likely to be misclassified as potentially violent (Garb, 1998). Still, mental health professionals can predict violence at better-than-chance levels, especially when patients have very recently engaged in or are immediately threatening violence (Kramer, Wolbransky, & Heilbrun, 2007; Lidz, Mulvey, & Gardner, 1993; Monahan et al., 2000).

Study and **Review** in **MyPsychLab**

Assess Your Knowledge — FACT or FICTION?

1. According to a family resemblance view, no one criterion distinguishes mental disorder from normality. **True / False**

2. Once the medical model began to take hold in the Renaissance, treatments for mental disorders came to be based on strong scientific evidence. **True / False**

3. Almost all deinstitutionalized patients returned successfully to their families and communities. **True / False**

4. Some mental disorders appear to be present in most, if not all, cultures. **True / False**

5. Virtually all psychiatric diagnoses are unreliable. **True / False**

6. Most individuals with severe mental illness are not prone to violence. **True / False**

Answers: 1. T; 2. F; 3. F; 4. T; 5. F; 6. T

Many anxiety disorders, including phobias, frequently have an initial onset in childhood.

somatic symptom disorder
condition marked by excessive anxiety about physical symptoms with a medical or purely psychological origin

illness anxiety disorder
condition marked by intense preoccupation with the possibility of a serious undiagnosed illness

generalized anxiety disorder (GAD)
continual feelings of worry, anxiety, physical tension, and irritability across many areas of life functioning

panic attack
brief, intense episode of extreme fear characterized by sweating, dizziness, light-headedness, racing heartbeat, and feelings of impending death or going crazy

696

Anxiety-Related Disorders: The Many Faces of Worry and Fear

4 Describe the many ways people experience anxiety.

We'll begin our tour of psychological disorders with problems stemming from anxiety. Fortunately, most everyday anxieties generally don't last long or feel especially uncomfortable. Anxiety in small doses can even be adaptive. It can permit a lightning-quick response to danger, steer us away from harmful behaviors, and inspire us to solve festering problems. Yet sometimes anxiety spins out of control, becoming excessive and inappropriate. It may even feel life-threatening (Mendelowicz & Stein, 2000).

Anxiety disorders are among the most prevalent of all mental disorders; 31 percent of us will meet the diagnostic criteria for one or more such disorders at some point in our lives (Kessler et al., 2007). The average age of onset for anxiety disorders (11 years) is earlier than for most other disorders, including substance use disorders (20 years) and mood disorders (30 years; Kessler et al., 2005). **FIGURE 2** displays the lifetime prevalence of anxiety disorders, along with many other disorders we'll consider in this chapter.

Yet anxiety isn't limited to anxiety disorders. Anxiety can seep into numerous aspects of our functioning, including concerns regarding our physical health. In a controversial condition called **somatic symptom disorder**, new to DSM-5, anxieties about physical symptoms—that are either medically verified or purely psychological in origin—can become so intense and "over the top" that they interfere with daily living. In cases of **illness anxiety disorder** (another new diagnosis that is similar to what was previously called hypochondriasis), people become so preoccupied with the idea that they're suffering from a serious undiagnosed illness, that no amount of reassurance can relieve their anxiety. Much like radar operators who stay on their toes for signs of incoming planes, people with illness anxiety disorder seem continually on the alert for signs of physical illness, constantly checking the Internet, for example, for information about symptoms and signs of diseases. Despite repeated medical reassurance and physical examinations they may insist that their mild aches, pains, and twinges are signs of serious diseases like cancer, AIDS, or heart disease.

Generalized Anxiety Disorder: Perpetual Worry

We all get caught up with worry from time to time. Yet for the 3 percent of us who have **generalized anxiety disorder (GAD)**, worry is a way of life. People with GAD spend an average of 60 percent of each day worrying, compared with 18 percent for the rest of the general population (Craske et al., 1989). Many describe themselves as "worry warts." They tend to think anxious thoughts, feel irritable and on edge, have trouble sleeping, and experience considerable bodily tension and fatigue (Andrews et al., 2010; Barlow, Chorpita, & Turovsky, 1996). Often they worry too much about the small things in life, like an upcoming meeting at work or social event. One-third of those with GAD develop it following a major stressful event—like a wedding, an illness, physical abuse, the death of a relative—or as the result of lifestyle changes, such as completing school and embarking on a career (Mellinger & Lynn, 2003; Hazlett-Stevens, Pruitt, & Collins, 2008). People with GAD are more likely to be female than male—as is the case with most anxiety disorders—as well as middle-aged, widowed or divorced, poor, and prone to "self medication" with alcohol and drugs to relieve symptoms (Grant et al., 2005; Noyes, 2001). Asians, Hispanics, and African Americans are at relatively low risk for GAD (Grant et al., 2005). GAD may be the core anxiety disorder out of which all others develop (Barlow, 2002). Indeed, people with GAD often experience other anxiety disorders, including phobias and panic disorder, which we'll consider next.

Panic Disorder: Terror That Comes Out of the Blue

The Greek god Pan was a mischievous spirit who popped out of the bushes to scare the living daylights out of travelers. Pan lent his name to **panic attacks**, which occur when nervous feelings gather momentum and escalate into intense bouts of fear, even terror. Panic attacks can occur only rarely, or they can occur on a daily basis for weeks, months, or even years at a time. People are diagnosed with **panic disorder** when they experience panic attacks that are repeated and unexpected and when they either experience persistent concerns about panicking or change their behavior to avoid future attacks (for example, change jobs) (APA, 2013). Panic attacks typically peak within ten minutes and can include sweating, dizziness, light-headedness, a racing or pounding heart, shortness of breath, feelings of unreality, and fears of going crazy or dying (Craske et al., 2010). Because many patients experiencing their initial panic attack believe they're having a heart attack, many first go to the emergency room, only to be sent home and—like Ida, whom we met at the outset of the chapter—told "it's all in your head." Some panic attacks are associated with specific situations, such as riding in elevators or shopping in supermarkets, whereas others come entirely out of the blue, that is, without warning, often generating fears of the situations in which they occur.

Panic attacks can occur in every anxiety disorder, as well as in mood and eating disorders. Even high-functioning people can experience panic attacks in anticipation of stressful events (Cox & Taylor, 1998): about 20–25 percent of college students report at least one panic attack in a one-year period, with about half that number reporting unexpected attacks (Lilienfeld, 1997). Panic disorder often develops in early adulthood (Kessler et al., 2007) and is associated with a history of fears of separation from a parent during childhood (Lewinsohn et al., 2008). It's unclear, though, whether this correlation means that separation fears predispose to later panic disorder or whether such fears are merely an early reflection of the same underlying condition that gives rise to panic disorder.

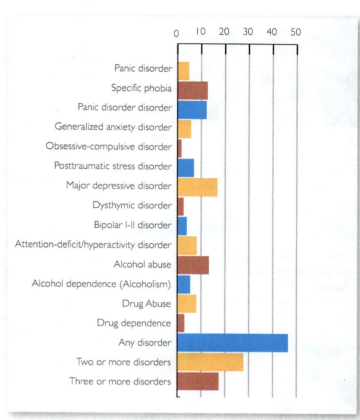

FIGURE 2 Lifetime Prevalence Estimates of Disorders (in percent). (*Source:* Based on data from Merikangas et al., 2007; Kessler et al., 2005)

First-Person Account:
PANIC DISORDER

"For me, a panic attack is almost a violent experience. I feel disconnected from reality. I feel like I'm losing control in a very extreme way. My heart pounds really hard, I feel like I can't get my breath, and there's an overwhelming feeling that things are crashing in on me."

(Dickey, 1994)

 Watch in **MyPsychLab** the **Video:** the Animation The Vicious Cycle of Panic Attacks

panic disorder repeated and unexpected panic attacks, along with either persistent concerns about future attacks or a change in personal behavior in an attempt to avoid them

◄ **CORRELATION VS. CAUSATION** Can we be sure that A causes B?

Symptoms of a panic attack include a pounding or racing heart, shortness of breath, and faintness or dizziness. This can lead people to believe they are having a heart attack.

Factoid

Although many people believe that people with agoraphobia are typically housebound, being unable or afraid to leave the house occurs only in severe cases of agoraphobia.

Some of the most common fears involve insects and animals such as spiders and snakes.

....

First-Person Account:
SOCIAL ANXIETY DISORDER

"When I would walk into a room full of people, I'd turn red and it would feel like everybody's eyes were on me. I was embarrassed to stand off in a corner by myself, but I couldn't think of anything to say to anybody. It was humiliating. I felt so clumsy, I couldn't wait to get out."

(Dickey, 1994)

....

phobia
intense fear of an object or a situation that's greatly out of proportion to its actual threat

agoraphobia
fear of being in a place or situation from which escape is difficult or embarrassing or in which help is unavailable in the event of a panic attack

social anxiety disorder
intense fear of negative evaluation in social situations

Phobias: Irrational Fears

A **phobia** is an intense fear of an object or a situation that's greatly out of proportion to its actual threat. Many of us have mild fears—of things like spiders and snakes—that aren't severe enough to be phobias. For a fear to be diagnosed as a phobia, it must restrict our life, create considerable distress, or do both.

Phobias are the most common of all anxiety disorders. One in nine of us has a phobia of an animal, blood or injury, or a situation like a thunderstorm. Social fears are just as common (Kessler et al., 1994). Agoraphobia, which we'll examine next, is the most debilitating of the phobias and occurs in about 1 in 20 of us (Keller & Craske, 2008; Kessler et al., 2006).

AGORAPHOBIA. Some 2,700 years ago in the city-states of ancient Greece, agoraphobia acquired its name as a condition in which certain fearful citizens couldn't pass through the central city's open-air markets (*agoras*). A common misconception is that agoraphobia is a fear of crowds or public places. But **agoraphobia** actually refers to a fear of being in a place or situation in which escape is difficult or embarrassing or in which help is unavailable in the event of a panic attack (APA, 2013).

Agoraphobia typically emerges in the midteens and is often a direct outgrowth of panic disorder. In fact, most people with panic disorder develop agoraphobia (Cox & Taylor, 1998; Sanderson & Dublin, 2010) and become apprehensive in a host of settings outside the home, such as stores, movie theaters, lines of people, public transportation, crowds, bridges, and wide-open spaces. The expression of agoraphobia seems to differ across cultures. For example, some Eskimos in Greenland suffer from a condition called "kayak angst," marked by a pronounced fear of going out to sea by oneself in a kayak (Barlow, 2000; Gusow, 1963).

In some cases, agoraphobia reaches extreme proportions. Two clinicians saw a 62-year-old woman with agoraphobia who hadn't left her house—even once—for 25 years (Jensvold & Turner, 1988). Having experienced severe panic attacks and terrified by the prospect of still more, she spent almost all of her waking hours locked away in her bedroom with curtains drawn. The therapists attempted to treat her agoraphobia by encouraging her to take short trips out of her house, but she repeatedly refused to walk even a few steps past her front door.

SPECIFIC PHOBIA AND SOCIAL ANXIETY DISORDER. Phobias of objects, places, or situations—called *specific phobias*—commonly arise in response to animals, insects, thunderstorms, water, elevators, and darkness. Many of these fears, especially of animals, are widespread in childhood but disappear with age (APA, 2013).

Surveys show that most people rank public speaking as a greater fear than dying (Wallechinsky, Wallace, & Wallace, 1977). Given that statistic, imagine how people with **social anxiety disorder**—formerly called social phobia in DSM-IV—must feel. They experience an intense fear of negative evaluation in social situations, such as while eating, giving a speech, conversing with others, and performing in public. Their social fears can even extend to swimming, swallowing, and signing their checks in the presence of others (Mellinger & Lynn, 2003). Their anxiety goes well beyond the stage fright that most of us feel occasionally (Heimberg & Juster, 1995).

Posttraumatic Stress Disorder: The Enduring Effects of Experiencing Horror

One of the most significant changes in DSM-5 is that posttraumatic stress disorder and obsessive-compulsive disorders, which were formerly included in the category of anxiety disorders, now are positioned in their own separate diagnostic categories. Yet because both disorders are associated with significant anxiety, we consider them under the heading of anxiety-related disorders.

When people experience or witness a traumatic event such as front-line combat, an earthquake, or sexual assault, they may develop **posttraumatic stress disorder (PTSD)**. In the DSM-5, PTSD is in a new class of "trauma and stressor-related disorders" in which the definition of a traumatic event is broad. It includes direct exposure to a traumatic event, such as a rape, wartime combat, or a natural disaster. Nevertheless, it also includes situations in which people learn about an event from a friend or relative who experienced threatened or actual death or in which people are exposed repeatedly to distressing details of a traumatic event, such as the sexual abuse of an elderly person.

Flashbacks are among the hallmarks of PTSD. The terror of war can return decades after the original trauma and be reactivated by everyday stressful experiences (Foa & Kozak, 1986). In recounting his war experiences, Vietnam veteran Tim O'Brien (1990) commented: "The hardest part, by far, is to make the bad pictures go away. In war time, the world is one big long horror movie, image after image, and if it's anything like Vietnam, I'm in for a lifetime of wee-hour creeps".

Other symptoms include efforts to avoid thoughts, feelings, places, objects, and conversations that remind the person of the event; recurrent dreams of the trauma; and increased arousal reflected in difficulty sleeping and startling easily (APA, 2013). Reminders of the incident can trigger full-blown panic attacks, as in the case of a Vietnam veteran who hid under his bed whenever he heard a city helicopter in the distance—over 20 years after the war ended (Baum, Cohen, & Hall, 1993; Foa & Rothbaum, 1998; Jones & Barlow, 1990). PTSD isn't easy to diagnose. Some of its symptoms, such as anxiety and difficulty sleeping, may have been present *before* the stressful event and commonly occur in other disorders. Moreover, some people *malinger* (fake) PTSD to obtain government benefits, so diagnosticians must rule out this possibility (Rosen, 2006).

Posttraumatic stress disorder involves a constellation of symptoms that can be quite debilitating. Combat veterans are at high risk for developing this disorder.

◀ **RULING OUT RIVAL HYPOTHESES**
Have important alternative explanations for the findings been excluded?

Obsessive-Compulsive and Related Disorders: Trapped in One's Thoughts and Behaviors

The hallmarks of obsessive-compulsive and related disorders are repetitive and distressing thoughts and behaviors (Hollander et al., 2011). The most common of these disorders are obsessive-compulsive disorder, body dysmorphic disorder, and Tourette's Disorder.

Just about all of us have had a thought or even a silly jingle that we just couldn't get out of our head. Patients with **obsessive-compulsive disorder (OCD)** know all too well what this experience is like, except that their symptoms are more severe. Like Bill from the chapter opening, they typically suffer from **obsessions**: persistent ideas, thoughts, or urges that are unwanted and inappropriate and cause marked distress. Unlike typical worries, obsessions aren't extreme responses to everyday stressors. They usually center around "unacceptable" thoughts about such topics as contamination, sex, aggression, or religion (Franklin & Foa, 2008). For example, individuals with OCD may be consumed with fears of being dirty or thoughts of killing others. Unlike ordinary worriers, people with OCD typically are disturbed by their thoughts and usually see them as irrational or nonsensical (Fullana et al., 2009). They may even label themselves "crazy" or dangerous. Despite their best efforts, people with OCD can't find a way to make these thoughts stop.

Most OCD patients also experience symptoms linked closely to obsessions, namely, **compulsions**: repetitive behaviors or mental acts that they undertake to reduce or prevent distress or to relieve shame and guilt (Abramowitz, Taylor, & McKay, 2009). In most cases, patients feel driven to perform the action that accompanies an obsession, to prevent some

Some dogs suffer from a condition called canine lick acral dermatitis, in which they lick themselves compulsively, resulting in severe skin damage (Derr, 2010). Some scientists believe that this condition may be an animal variant of obsessive-compulsive disorder; interestingly, this condition sometimes responds to the same medications used to treat human obsessive-compulsive disorder.

posttraumatic stress disorder (PTSD)
marked emotional disturbance after experiencing or witnessing a severely stressful event

obsessive-compulsive disorder (OCD)
condition marked by repeated and lengthy (at least one hour per day) immersion in obsessions, compulsions, or both

obsession
persistent idea, thought, or urge that is unwanted, causing marked distress

compulsion
repetitive behavior or mental act performed to reduce or prevent stress

David Beckham, the famous British soccer player, has reported that he feels compelled to count his clothes and cans of cola and to arrange magazines in straight lines (Dolan, 2006).

Factoid

Have you ever been unable to get a song or a snatch of a tune out of your head? Psychologists have a term for this phenomenon; it's called an "earworm." A recent study revealed that 98 percent of students have experienced earworms, with the jingle "It's a small world after all" being one of the most frequent (Kellaris, 2003).

First-Person Account:
OBSESSIVE-COMPULSIVE DISORDER

"I couldn't do anything without rituals. They transcended every aspect of my life. Counting was big for me. When I set my alarm at night, I had to set it to a number that wouldn't add up to a 'bad' number. I would wash my hair three times as opposed to once because three was a good-luck number and one wasn't. It took me longer to read because I'd count the lines in a paragraph. If I was writing a term paper, I couldn't have a certain number of words on a line if it added up to a bad number. I was always worried that if I didn't do something, my parents were going to die."

(Dickey, 1994)

RULING OUT RIVAL HYPOTHESES ▶
Have important alternative explanations for the findings been excluded?

 Simulate in **MyPsychLab** the **Experiment:** The Obsessive Compulsive Test

dreaded event, or to "make things right." A patient treated by one of your text's authors awoke early each morning to wash the hood of his car until it was spotless and felt compelled to repeat this ritual as soon as he arrived home at the end of the workday. Common OCD rituals include the following:

- Repeatedly checking door locks, windows, electronic controls, and ovens
- Performing tasks in set ways, like putting on one's shoes in a fixed pattern
- Repeatedly arranging and rearranging objects
- Washing and cleaning repeatedly and unnecessarily
- Counting the number of dots on a wall or touching or tapping objects

Many people without OCD occasionally engage in one or more of these activities (Mataix-Cols, Rosario-Campos, & Lackman, 2005). Nevertheless, individuals with OCD spend an hour or more a day immersed in obsessions, compulsions, or both; one patient spent 15–18 hours per day washing his hands, showering, getting dressed, and cleaning money. Still, many individuals with OCD lead remarkably successful lives. Several celebrities have spoken publicly about their struggles with the disorder. For example, Cameron Diaz avoids touching doorknobs by opening doors with her elbows, Leonardo DiCaprio sidestepped cracks in sidewalks as a child, and Megan Fox is fearful of using restaurant silverware because of concerns about contamination with bacteria (Fisher, Marikar, & Shaw, 2013).

People with the related condition of body dysmorphic disorder (BDD) become preoccupied with imagined or slight defects in their appearance, such as lips that are perceived to be "too thin" or ears that are "too big." One patient with BDD treated by one of your text's authors was so preoccupied with tiny moles on his forehead that he spent hours every day thinking about them, checking mirrors, and wearing hats in attempt to cover them up. One-third of patients with BDD also suffer from OCD (Phillips et al., 2005). Some individuals with BDD undergo repeated cosmetic surgeries to correct their perceived body imperfections, yet they receive little comfort from these procedures because their underlying obsession about their appearance remains untreated. Celebrities may be particularly prone to body dysmorphic disorder because our culture places a high premium on physical attractiveness; Michael Jackson and Heidi Montag underwent numerous cosmetic surgeries and may have exhibited features of this condition.

Tourette's Disorder is a condition marked by repeated automatic behaviors—motor tics like twitching and facial grimacing and vocal tics like grunting and throat clearing. A common myth about the disorder is that most individuals with Tourette's Disorder engage in frequent cursing, a symptom known as *coprolalia*. However, 70 percent or more of patients with Tourette's Disorder do not curse (Goldenberg, Brown, & Weiner, 2004).

Nearly 30 percent of individuals with OCD suffer from a tic disorder (Richter et al., 2003). Some researchers suggest that OCD and Tourette's Disorder share biological roots (Mell, Davis, & Owens, 2005). A number of children develop OCD or Tourette's Disorder after experiencing strep throat or scarlet fever infections caused by streptococcal (strep) bacteria. Scientists are seeking to determine whether strep triggers an immune system response that affects the brain and brings about OCD symptoms or whether the relationship between strep and OCD symptoms is coincidental (Gause et al., 2009; Kurlan & Kaplan, 2004; Nicholson et al., 2012). Another possibility is that children with strep feel irritable and uncomfortable, which worsens OCD symptoms.

The Roots of Pathological Anxiety, Fear, and Repetitive Thoughts and Behaviors

How do anxiety disorders arise? Different theories propose explanations focusing on the environment, catastrophic thinking, and biological influences.

from inquiry to understanding

MORE THAN A PACK RAT: WHY DO PEOPLE HOARD?

Mark is an art dealer, and he's also a hoarder. Financially well off, he built an add-on room to his home to store his clutter. From floor to ceiling, the room is filled with books, catalogues, newspapers, and comic books, with a tiny footpath (often called a "goat path") cleared to enter and exit. In the last six months, the clutter has spilled over into his living room, dining room, and bedroom. The mere thought of which items to discard paralyzes him with indecision and intense anxiety. He dares not invite a woman he recently met on the art circuit to his home for fear she'd be turned off by the mess. His bed is so covered with "stuff" that he's slept in a hotel for the past week. Instead of doing a major cleanup, he approached a realtor about buying a second home so that he could "store his stuff" in his current home and "start fresh."

Mark is a composite of several patients treated by one of your authors. Mark's hoarding behavior meets all of the DSM-5 criteria for the new disorder of hoarding, which is distinct from its close cousin, OCD. Hoarders often experience a strong urge to acquire possessions, often with little or no actual value, and become convinced that they can't part with them. Some hoarders harbor large numbers of animals, such as cats and dogs, that they're unable to care for. Compulsive buying or collecting free items can severely limit livable space and pose a serious fire hazard.

Hoarding disorder and OCD differ in key respects. Only a minority of hoarders—probably less than 20 percent—meet diagnostic criteria for OCD (Frost et al., 2006). Moreover, hoarders don't perform rituals related to their possessions and typically become anxious only when they encounter a situation in which they feel pressured to discard items they've accumulated. In addition, many hoarders have limited insight and rarely acknowledge that they have a problem unless they're confronted by family members, friends, or employers or, like Mark, become concerned about how others view them (Pertusa et al., 2010).

Hoarding is a curious combination of impulsiveness, reflected in the urge to accumulate, compulsive acquisition of possessions, and anxiety-related avoidance of parting with what's hoarded. Hoarding is associated with indecisiveness, leading hoarders to question whether they might need the item in the future, whether it is valuable, or whether they'll regret throwing it away for sentimental reasons (Frost & Gross, 1993).

Researchers still aren't sure why people hoard. Brain imaging studies reveal that hoarders show impairments in brain circuits associated with judgment, decision making, and emotional regulation (Pertusa et al., 2010). In addition, research on animal models suggests that some primates, including monkeys and apes, as well some rodents, including rats, engage in hoarding behaviors, and that such behaviors may be associated with similar brain abnormalities as in humans (Andrews-McClymont, Lilienfeld, & Duke, in press). Perhaps hoarding is a case of a basically adaptive behavior gone terribly awry. In some cases, it makes perfect sense to store up food and possessions, especially when they're important for our survival and we're running short of them. But when this drive becomes rigid and overpowering, pathological hoarding may result.

LEARNING MODELS OF ANXIETY: ANXIOUS RESPONSES AS ACQUIRED HABITS.
According to learning theories, fears are—you guessed it—learned. John B. Watson and Rosalie Rayner's (1920) famous demonstration of classical conditioning of the fear of a small furry animal powerfully conveys how people learn fears.

Operant conditioning, which relies on reinforcements and punishments offers another account of how fears are maintained. If a socially awkward girl repeatedly experiences rejection when she asks boys to go to movies, she may become shy around them. If this pattern of rejection continues, she could develop a full-blown social anxiety disorder. Paradoxically, her avoidance of boys provides negative reinforcement, because it allows her to escape the unpleasant consequences of social interaction. This sense of relief perpetuates her avoidance, and ultimately her anxiety.

Factoid

Following birth, perhaps as many as 2–3 percent of new mothers experience a condition called postpartum obsessive-compulsive disorder. In some cases, the infant becomes the focus of the mother's bizarre thoughts and compulsive behaviors. These symptoms can include repeatedly checking the child to ensure his or her safety, hiding knives for fear of stabbing the child, and excessive cleaning. Some mothers become so fearful of what they might do to their children that they're reluctant to take care of them (Arnold, 1999). Fortunately, such women almost never harm their children, and effective treatments are available.

TABLE 4 Anxiety and Interpretation of Ambiguity.

| SELECTED HOMOPHONES ||
THREATENING MEANING/ SPELLING	NONTHREATENING MEANING/ SPELLING
Bury	Berry
Die	Dye
Patients	Patience
Bruise	Brews
Flu	Flew
Sword	Soared
Bore	Boar

Learning theorists (Rachman, 1977) believe that fears can arise in two additional ways. First, we can acquire fears by observing others engage in fearful behaviors (Mineka & Cook, 1993). A father's fear of dogs might instill the same in his child. Second, fears can stem from information or misinformation from others. If a mother tells her children that riding in elevators is dangerous, they may end up taking the stairs.

CATASTROPHIZING, AMBIGUITY, AND ANXIETY SENSITIVITY. People with social anxiety disorder predict that many social encounters will be interpersonal disasters, and some people with specific phobia who are afraid of lightning are so fearful that they seek the shelter of a basement when mild thunderstorms are detected on radar 50 miles away (Voncken, Bogels, & deVries, 2003). As these examples illustrate, *catastrophizing* is a core feature of anxious thinking (Beck, 1976; Ellis, 1962; Ellis & Dryden, 1997). People catastrophize when they predict terrible events—such as contracting a life-threatening illness from turning a doorknob—despite their low probability (A. T. Beck, 1964; J. Beck, 1995).

One reason anxious people catastrophize is because they tend to interpret ambiguous situations in a negative light (Matthews & MacLeod, 2005; see **TABLE 4**). Researchers have asked anxious and nonanxious participants to listen to *hompophones*—words that sound the same but have two different meanings and spellings—and to write down the word they heard. In these studies, they've used homophone pairs in which one meaning (and spelling) is threatening and the other is nonthreatening. Compared with non-anxious participants, anxious participants are more likely to write down the version of the homophone that's threatening, such as *bury* as opposed to *berry* (Blanchette & Richards, 2003; Mathews, Richard, & Eysenck, 1989).

Many people with anxiety disorders harbor high levels of **anxiety sensitivity**, a fear of anxiety-related sensations (Reiss & McNally, 1985; Stein, Jang, & Livesley, 1999). Think of the times you felt a bit dizzy when you stood up quickly or your heart raced after you climbed a flight of stairs. You probably dismissed these physical symptoms as harmless. Yet people with high anxiety sensitivity tend to misinterpret them as dangerous—perhaps as early signs of a heart attack or stroke—and react with intense worry (Clark, 1986; Lilienfeld, 1997; McNally & Eke, 1996). As a result, their barely noticeable physical sensations or minor anxiety can spiral into full-blown panic attacks (Schmidt, Zvolensky, & Maner, 2006; Zavos, Gregory, & Eley, 2012).

ANXIETY: BIOLOGICAL INFLUENCES. Twin studies show that many anxiety-related disorders, including panic disorder, phobias, PTSD, and OCD, are genetically influenced (Afifi et al., 2010; Roy et al., 1995; Samuels et al., 2011; Van Grootheest et al., 2007). In particular, genes influence people's levels of neuroticism—a tendency to be high-strung, guilt-prone, and irritable —which can set the stage for excessive worry (Anderson, Taylor, & McLean, 1996; Zinbarg & Barlow, 1996). On a genetic basis, people who experience GAD are virtually indistinguishable from those who experience major depression, which is also associated with elevated neuroticism (Kendler & Karkowski-Shuman, 1997). This finding suggests a shared genetic pathway for these disorders.

Studies that have attempted to identify a single gene associated with OCD have provided mixed results at best, although evidence is accumulating that genes that transport serotonin and glutamate probably play some role in the development of OCD (Samuels et al., 2011). Much like a car that's stuck in gear, people with OCD experience problems with shifting thoughts and behaviors (Schwartz & Bayette, 1996). Brain scans reveal abnormalities in white matter and increased activity in portions of the frontal lobes where information is filtered, prioritized, and organized (Zohar et al., 2012). Under these circumstances, people can't seem to get troubling thoughts out of their minds or inhibit repeated rituals.

anxiety sensitivity
fear of anxiety-related sensations

Assess Your Knowledge   FACT or FICTION?

1. According to some theorists, GAD is the core anxiety disorder out of which others develop. **True / False**

2. Panic attacks typically peak in ten minutes or less. **True / False**

3. Because PTSD is characterized by dramatic symptoms, it's typically an easy disorder to diagnose. **True / False**

4. Catastrophizing is a core feature of anxious thinking. **True / False**

5. Genes exert little influence on obsessive-compulsive disorder. **True / False**

Answers: 1. T; 2. T; 3. F; 4. T; 5. F

Mood Disorders and Suicide

5 Identify the characteristics of different mood disorders.

6 Describe major explanations for depression and how life events can interact with characteristics of the individual to produce depression symptoms.

7 Identify common myths and misconceptions about suicide.

Imagine we're therapists interviewing someone who's come to us for help. As the client begins to talk about his life, it becomes clear that even the simplest activities, like dressing and driving to work, have become enormous acts of will. He reports difficulty sleeping and unaccountably wakes up before dawn each day. He refuses to answer the telephone. He lies listlessly for hours staring at the television. His mood is downcast, and occasionally tears well up in his eyes. He recently lost a fair amount of weight. His world is gray, a void. Toward the end of the interview, he tells us he's begun to contemplate suicide.

We've just interviewed a person with a *mood disorder,* so called because his difficulties center on his bleak mood, which colors all aspects of his existence. His symptoms meet the criteria for a **major depressive episode**, a key feature of major depressive disorder, which we encountered earlier in our discussion of psychiatric diagnosis. We'll soon encounter another mood disorder, *bipolar disorder,* in which people's mood is often the mirror image of depression. We focus on these two disorders because they represent the extremes of a spectrum of mood disorders, ranging from major depressive disorder on one end to bipolar disorder on the other (Angst et al., 2010).

Major Depressive Disorder: Common, But Not the Common Cold

Over the course of a lifetime, more than 20 percent of us will experience a mood disorder. Major depression alone darkens the lives of more than 16 percent of Americans (Kessler et al., 2005). Due to its frequency, some have dubbed depression the "common cold" of psychological disorders (Seligman, 1975). Yet we'll soon see that this description doesn't begin to capture the profound depths of suffering that people with this condition experience. Depressive disorders can begin at any age, but are most likely to strike people in their thirties. Contrary to popular misconception, they're less common in elderly adults than in younger people (Kessler et al., 2010; Klerman, 1986).

As we mentioned earlier, women are about twice as likely to experience depression as men are. This gender difference may be associated with women's tendency to ruminate more than men (Nolen-Hoeksema, 2002, 2003). Yet it may also be associated with differences between men and women in economic power, sex hormones, social support, and history of physical or sexual abuse (Howland & Thase, 1998). The sex difference in depression is widespread but not universal. In some cultures, such as certain Mediterranean populations, Orthodox Jews, and the Amish, this sex difference is largely absent (Piccinelli & Wilkinson, 2000). But researchers don't know why. One possibility is

In most cultures, women are generally at greater risk for developing depression than men are. Nevertheless, the reasons for this difference aren't fully understood.

major depressive episode
state in which a person experiences a lingering depressed mood or diminished interest in pleasurable activities, along with symptoms that include weight loss and sleep difficulties

703

that the differences in the rates of depression across genders in Western cultures reflect an underdiagnosis of depression in men. In the United States, compared with men, who are socialized to "act tough" (Kilmartin, 2006), women are more willing to admit to depression and seek psychological services. The symptoms of depression may develop gradually over days or weeks; in other cases, they may surface rather suddenly.

Depression, like the common cold, is recurrent. The average person with major depression experiences five or six episodes over the course of a lifetime. Most episodes last from six months to a year. But in as many as a fourth or more of cases, depression is *persistent* and can be present for as long as decades with no relief (Murphy & Byrne, 2012; Satyanarayana et al., 2009). Generally, the earlier depression strikes the first time, the more likely it will persist or recur (Coryell et al., 2009). In sharp contrast to the common cold, depression can produce severe impairment. In extreme cases, people may fail to feed or clothe themselves or take care of basic health needs like brushing their teeth or showering.

Watch in **MyPsychLab** the **Video:** Depression

Explanations for Major Depressive Disorder: A Tangled Web

Depression illustrates how multiple factors can combine to produce psychological symptoms. Let's reconsider the depressed man we imagined interviewing at the beginning of this section. From his severely depressed father and perpetually anxious mother, he may have inherited a tendency to respond to stressful situations with negative emotions (neuroticism). Each day he wasted hours ruminating about losing his job and became convinced that a competitive colleague was trying to undermine his authority. The quality of his work nose-dived. He withdrew socially and began to refuse invitations to go golfing with his buddies. His friends tried to cheer him up, but the black cloud that hung over his head wouldn't budge. Feeling rebuffed, his friends stopped inviting him to do anything. His once-bright social world became a black void, and he moped around doing virtually nothing. He felt helpless. Eventually, his dark thoughts turned to suicide.

This example highlights a key point. To fully understand depression, we must appreciate the complex interplay of all of the following: inborn tendencies, stressful events, interpersonal relationships, loss of reinforcers in everyday life, negative thoughts, and feelings of helplessness (Akiskal & McKinney, 1973; Ilardi & Feldman, 2001).

DEPRESSION AND LIFE EVENTS. Sigmund Freud (1917) suggested that early loss can render us vulnerable to depression later in life. He may have been on to something because stressful life events that represent loss or threat of separation are especially tied to depression (Brugha, 1995; Mazure, 1998; Paykel, 2003). But a crucial determinant of whether we'll become depressed is whether we've lost or are about to lose something we value dearly, like someone we love, financial support, or self-esteem (Beck, 1983; Blatt, 1974; Prince et al., 1997; Zuroff, Mongrain, & Santor, 2004). Recall that in DSM-5, people who become depressed following the loss of a loved one can be formally diagnosed with depression, whereas this was not the case in previous editions of the manual.

CORRELATION VS. CAUSATION ▶
Can we be sure that A causes B?

Pessimism and other symptoms of depression can set the stage for negative life circumstances, like getting fired from a job or losing a close relationship (Hammen, 1991; Harkness & Luther, 2001). The causal arrow of this association thus points in both directions. Negative life events set us up to bring us down, but depression can create problems in living.

INTERPERSONAL MODEL: DEPRESSION AS A SOCIAL DISORDER. James Coyne hypothesized that depression creates interpersonal problems (Coyne, 1976; Joiner & Coyne, 1999; Rudolf, 2009). When people become depressed, he argued, they seek excessive reassurance, which in turn leads others to dislike and reject them. Coyne (1976) asked female undergraduates to talk on the telephone for 20 minutes with patients with depression, patients without depression, or nondepressed women drawn from the community. He didn't inform students they'd be interacting with patients with depression. Yet following the interaction, students who spoke with these patients became more depressed, anxious, and hostile than those who had interacted with patients and nonpatients without depression. Moreover, participants were more rejecting of patients with depression and expressed much less interest in interacting with them in the future. For Coyne, depression is a vicious cycle. People with depression often elicit hostility and rejection from others, which in turn maintains or worsens their depression.

Many, but not all, studies have replicated Coyne's findings that people with depression seek excessive reassurance and tend to stir up negative feelings in others (Burns et al., 2006; Hames, Hagen, & Joiner, 2013; Starr & Davilla, 2008). Constant worrying, mistrust, fears of rejection and abandonment, and socially inappropriate behaviors can also be a social turnoff to many people (Wei et al., 2005; Zborowski & Garske, 1993).

BEHAVIORAL MODEL: DEPRESSION AS A LOSS OF REINFORCEMENT.
Peter Lewinsohn's (1974) *behavioral model* proposes that depression results from a low rate of response-contingent positive reinforcement. Put in simpler terms, when people with depression try different things and receive no payoff for them, they eventually give up. They stop participating in many pleasant activities, affording them little opportunity to obtain reinforcement from others. In time, their personal and social worlds shrink, as depression seeps into virtually every nook and cranny of their lives. Lewinsohn later observed that some people with depression lack social skills (Segrin, 2000; Youngren & Lewinsohn, 1980), making it harder for them to obtain reinforcement from people they value. To make matters worse, if others respond to individuals with depression with sympathy and concern, they may reinforce and maintain their withdrawal. This view implies a straightforward recipe for breaking the grip of depression: pushing ourselves to engage in pleasant activities. Sometimes merely getting out of bed can be the first step toward conquering depression (Dimidjian et al., 2006).

COGNITIVE MODEL: DEPRESSION AS A DISORDER OF THINKING.
In contrast, Aaron Beck's influential **cognitive model of depression** holds that depression is caused by negative beliefs and expectations (Beck, 1967, 1987). Beck focused on the *cognitive triad,* three components of depressed thinking: negative views of oneself, the world, and the future. These habitual thought patterns, called *negative schemas,* presumably originate in early experiences of loss, failure, and rejection. Activated by stressful events in later life, these schemas reinforce people with depression's negative experiences (Scher, Ingram, & Segal, 2005).

A depressed person's view of the world is bleak because they put a decidedly negative mental spin on their experiences, and they are biased to recall negative, rather than positive, events. They also suffer from *cognitive distortions,* which are skewed ways of thinking. One example is selective abstraction, in which people come to a negative conclusion based on only an isolated aspect of a situation. A man might consistently single out a trivial error he committed in a softball game and blame himself completely for the loss. It's as though people with depression are wearing glasses that filter out all of life's positive experiences and bring all of life's negative experiences into sharper focus. Moreover, inaccurate perceptions may lead to depression, and depressed feelings may contribute to inaccurate perceptions, bringing about a downward spiral of depression (Kistner et al., 2006).

There's considerable support for Beck's idea that people with depression hold negative views of themselves, the future, and the world (Haaga, Dyck, & Ernst, 1991; Disner et al., 2011). But the evidence for the role of cognitive distortions in nonhospitalized, or not seriously depressed, individuals isn't as strong (Haack et al., 1996). In fact, a review of research suggests that compared with people without depression, individuals with mild depression actually have a slightly *more* accurate view of circumstances, a phenomenon called *depressive realism* (Moore & Fresco, 2012).

LEARNED HELPLESSNESS: DEPRESSION AS A CONSEQUENCE OF UNCONTROLLABLE EVENTS.
Martin Seligman (1975; Seligman & Maier, 1967) accidentally stumbled across an unusual finding related to depression in his work with dogs. He was testing dogs in a shuttle box, depicted in **FIGURE 3**; one side of the box was electrified, and the other side,

◄ **REPLICABILITY**
Can the results be duplicated in other studies?

According to James Coyne's interpersonal model of depression, depression can trigger rejection from others, in turn contributing to further depression.

Most people have an illusion of control; for example, they mistakenly believe that they're more likely to win a gamble if they toss the dice than if someone else does. Interestingly, people who have mild depression are less likely to fall prey to this thinking error compared with nondepressed people (Golin, Terrell, & Johnson, 1977), suggesting they may actually be more realistic than people without depression under certain circumstances.

cognitive model of depression
theory that depression is caused by negative beliefs and expectations

FIGURE 3 The Shuttle Box. Using an apparatus like this, Martin Seligman found that dogs who were first prevented from escaping the shock gave up trying to escape electric shocks even when they were free to do so. He called this phenomenon "learned helplessness."

CORRELATION VS. CAUSATION ▶
Can we be sure that A causes B?

separated by a low barrier, wasn't. Ordinarily, dogs avoid painful shocks by jumping over the barrier to the nonelectrified side of the box. Yet Seligman found something surprising. Dogs first restrained in a hammock and exposed to shocks they couldn't escape later often made no attempt to escape shocks in the shuttle box, even when they could easily get away from them. Some of the dogs just sat there, whimpering and crying, passively accepting the shocks as though they were inescapable. They'd learned to become helpless.

Bruce Overmier and Seligman (1967) described **learned helplessness** as the tendency to feel helpless in the face of events we can't control and argued that it offers an animal model of depression. Seligman noted striking parallels between the effects of learned helplessness and depressive symptoms: passivity, appetite and weight loss, and difficulty learning that one can change circumstances for the better. But we must be cautious in drawing conclusions from animal studies because many psychological conditions, including depression, may differ in animals and humans (Raulin & Lilienfeld, 2008).

Provocative as it is, Seligman's model can't account for all aspects of depression. It doesn't explain why people with depression make internal attributions (explanations) for failure. In fact, the tendency to assume personal responsibility for failure contradicts the notion that people with depression regard negative events as beyond their control. The original model also doesn't acknowledge that the mere expectation of uncontrollability isn't sufficient to induce depression. After all, people don't become sad when they receive large amounts of money in a lottery, even though they have no control over that event (Abramson, Seligman, & Teasdale, 1978).

When data don't fit a model, good scientists revise it. Seligman and his colleagues (Abramson et al., 1978) altered the learned helplessness model to account for the attributions people make to explain their worlds. They argued that persons prone to depression attribute failure to *internal* as opposed to external factors and success to *external* as opposed to internal factors. A person with depression might blame a poor test grade on a lack of ability, an internal factor, and a good score on the ease of the exam, an external factor. The researchers also observed that depression-prone persons make attributions that are *global* and *stable*: they tend to see their failures as general and fixed aspects of their personalities. Still, internal, global, and stable attributions may be more a consequence than a cause of depression (Harvey & Weary, 1984). The depression brought on by undesirable life events may skew our thinking, leading us to make negative attributions, a tendency that may be evident as early as the primary grades (Fincham, Diener, & Hokoda, 2011; Gibb & Alloy, 2006).

Whether we develop depression depends not only on our attributions of outcomes, but also on the difference between how we feel—our actual affect—and how we want to feel—our ideal affect (Tsai, 2007). Jeanne Tsai and her colleagues found that cultural factors influence people's ideal affect (Tsai, Knutson, & Fung, 2006). Compared with Hong Kong Chinese, European Americans and Asian Americans value excitement, whereas compared with European Americans, Hong Kong Chinese and Asian Americans value calm. Yet across all three cultural groups, the size of the gap between ideal and actual affect predicts depression.

DEPRESSION: THE ROLE OF BIOLOGY. Twin studies indicate that genes exert a moderate effect on the risk of major depression (Kendler et al., 1993). Some researchers have suggested that specific variations in the serotonin transporter gene (which affects the rate of reuptake of serotonin) play a role in depression, especially in conjunction with life experiences. Scientists first reported that people who inherit two copies of this stress-sensitive gene are two and a half times more likely to develop depression following four stressful events than people with another version of the gene that isn't sensitive to stress (Caspi et al., 2003). The stress-sensitive gene appears to affect people's ability to dampen negative emotions in the face of stress (Kendler, Gardner, & Prescott, 2003). Nevertheless, researchers who reviewed all the available evidence concluded that there was no basis for a link between the gene and stressful life events, on the one hand, and depression, on the other (Risch et al., 2009). In response, other scientists challenged how these authors analyzed previous findings (Rutter, 2009), and an even more recent review, which included studies with substantial,

learned helplessness
tendency to feel helpless in the face of events we can't control

specific stressors, claimed to find strong and consistent evidence for the important part genes play in determining the relationship between negative emotions and stress (Karg et al., 2011). To resolve questions regarding the role of gene-life events interactions in depression, researchers will need to conduct well-designed studies in which stressful life events are carefully defined to determine whether the positive findings are replicable. The hope is that these studies will clarify whether any genetic irregularities that surface are specific to depression; they may be associated with anxiety, too (Hariri et al., 2002).

Depression also appears linked to low levels of the neurotransmitter norepinephrine (Leonard, 1997; Robinson, 2007) and diminished neurogenesis (growth of new neurons), which brings about reduced hippocampal volume (Pittinger & Duman, 2008; Videbech & Ravnkilde, 2004). Many patients with depression have problems in the brain's reward and stress-response systems (Depue & Iacono, 1989; Forbes, Shaw, & Dahl, 2007) and decreased levels of dopamine, the neurotransmitter most closely tied to reward (Martinot et al., 2001). This finding may help to explain why depression is often associated with an inability to experience pleasure.

Bipolar Disorder: When Mood Goes to Extremes

Ann, the giddy patient with bipolar disorder whom we met at the beginning of the chapter, experienced many classic symptoms of a **manic episode**. These episodes are typically marked by dramatically elevated mood (feeling "on top of the world"), decreased need for sleep, greatly heightened energy and activity, inflated self-esteem, increased talkativeness, and irresponsible behavior. People in a manic episode often display "pressured speech," as though they can't get their words out quickly enough, and are difficult to interrupt (Goodwin & Jamison, 1990). Their ideas often race through their heads quickly, which may account for the heightened rate of creative accomplishments in some individuals with bipolar disorder. Symptoms of a manic episode typically begin with a rapid increase over only a few days. People usually experience their first manic episode after their early twenties (Kessler et al., 2005).

Bipolar disorder, formerly called manic-depressive disorder, is diagnosed when there's a history of at least one manic episode (APA, 2013). In contrast to major depression, bipolar disorder is equally common in men and women. In the great majority of cases—upward of 90 percent—people who've had one manic episode experience at least one more (Alda, 1997). Some have episodes separated by many years and then have a series of episodes, one rapidly following the other. More than half the time, a major depressive episode precedes or follows a manic episode (Solomon et al., 2010). Manic episodes often produce serious problems in social and occupational functioning, such as substance abuse and unrestrained sexual behavior. Because their judgment is so impaired, people in the midst of manic episodes may go on wild spending sprees or drive while intoxicated. One of your book's authors treated a manic patient who passed himself off to a financial company as his own father, gained access to his father's savings for retirement, and gambled away his entire family fortune. Another frittered away most of his life's savings by purchasing more than 100 bowling balls, none of which he needed. The negative effects of a manic episode, including loss of employment, family conflicts, and divorce, can persist for many years (Coryell et al., 1993).

Bipolar disorder is among the most genetically influenced of all mental disorders (Miklowitz & Johnson, 2006). Twin studies suggest that its heritability ranges from about 60 percent to as high as 85 percent (Alda, 1997; Lichtenstein et al., 2009; McGuffin et al., 2003). Scientists believe that genes that increase the sensitivity of the dopamine receptors (Willner, 1995) and decrease the sensitivity of serotonin receptors may boost the risk of bipolar disorder (Ogden et al., 2004). Many genes appear to be culprits in increasing the risk of bipolar disorder, and there is at least some genetic overlap between psychotic symptoms in bipolar disorder and schizophrenia (Craddock, O'Donovan, & Owen, 2005; Lichtenstein et al., 2009; Purcell et al., 2009).

◀ **REPLICABILITY**
Can the results be duplicated in other studies?

People in the midst of manic episodes frequently go on uncontrolled spending sprees and may "max out" multiple credit cards in the process.

First-Person Account:
BIPOLAR DISORDER

"When I start going into a high, I no longer feel like an ordinary housewife. Instead I feel organized and accomplished and I begin to feel I am my most creative self. I can write poetry easily ... melodies without effort ... paint ... I feel a sense of euphoria or elation.... I don't seem to need much sleep ... I've just bought six new dresses ... I feel sexy and men stare at me. Maybe I'll have an affair, or perhaps several.... However, when I go beyond this state, I become manic.... I begin to see things in my mind that aren't real.... One night I created an entire movie.... I also experienced complete terror ... when I knew that an assassination scene was about to take place.... I went into a manic psychosis at that point. My screams awakened my husband.... I was admitted to the hospital the next day."

(Fieve, 1975, p. 17)

manic episode
experience marked by dramatically elevated mood, decreased need for sleep, increased energy, inflated self-esteem, increased talkativeness, and irresponsible behavior

bipolar disorder
condition marked by a history of at least one manic episode

Brain imaging studies suggest that people with bipolar disorder experience increased activity in structures related to emotion, including the amygdala (Chang et al., 2004; Yergelun-Todd et al., 2000), and decreased activity in structures associated with planning, such as the prefrontal cortex (Kruger et al., 2003). Still, the cause–effect relationship between physiological findings and mood disorders isn't clear. For example, the high levels of norepinephrine and differences in brain activity observed in people with bipolar disorder may be an effect rather than a cause of the disorder (Thase, Jindal, & Howland, 2002).

CORRELATION VS. CAUSATION ▶
Can we be sure that A causes B?

Bipolar disorder is influenced by more than biological factors. Stressful life events are associated with an increased risk of manic episodes, more frequent relapse, and a longer recovery from manic episodes (Johnson & Miller, 1997; Yan-Meier et al., 2011). Interestingly, some manic episodes appear to be triggered by *positive* life events associated with striving for and achieving goals, such as job promotions or winning poetry contests (Johnson et al., 2000; Johnson et al., 2008). Once again, we can see that psychological disorders arise from the intersection of biological, psychological, and sociocultural forces.

Suicide: Facts and Fictions

Major depression and bipolar disorder are associated with a higher risk of suicide than are most other disorders (Miklowitz & Johnson, 2006; Wolfsdorf et al., 2003). Estimates suggest that more than a third of people with bipolar disorder have attempted suicide and that the suicide rate of people with bipolar disorder is about 15 times higher than that of the general population (Harris & Barraclough, 1997; Novick, Swartz, & Frank, 2010). Some anxiety disorders, like panic disorder, social anxiety disorder, and substance abuse are also associated with heightened suicide risk (Spirito & Esposito-Smythers, 2006). In 2008, scientists ranked suicide as the eleventh leading cause of death in the United States (Heron, 2012).

Typically, more than 30,000 people commit suicide in the United States each year, a number that surely underestimates the problem because relatives report many suicides as accidents. For each completed suicide, there are an estimated 8 to 25 attempts. Contrary to what many believe, most people are more of a threat to themselves than others. For every two people who are victims of homicide, three take their own lives (NIMH, 2004). In **TABLE 5**, we present a number of other common myths and misconceptions about suicide, along with correct information in each case. It's essential to try to predict suicide attempts because most people are acutely suicidal for only a short window of time (Schneidman, Farberow, & Litman, 1970; Simon, 2006), and intervention during that time can be critical. Unfortunately,

TABLE 5 Common Myths and Misconceptions About Suicide.

MYTH	REALITY
Talking to persons with depression about suicide often makes them more likely to commit the act.	Talking to persons with depression about suicide makes them more likely to obtain help.
Suicide is almost always completed with no warning.	Many or most individuals who commit suicide communicate their intent to others, which gives us an opportunity to seek help for a suicidal person.
As a severe depression lifts, people's suicide risk decreases.	As a severe depression lifts, the risk of suicide may actually increase, in part because individuals possess more energy to attempt the act.
Most people who threaten suicide are seeking attention.	Although attention seeking motivates some suicidal behaviors, most suicidal acts stem from severe depression and hopelessness.
People who talk a lot about suicide almost never commit it.	Talking about suicide is associated with a considerably greater risk of suicide.

Psychological Disorders

the prediction of suicide poses serious practical problems. First, we can't easily conduct longitudinal studies to determine which people will attempt suicide. It would be unethical to allow people believed to be at high suicide risk to go through with attempts to allow us to pinpoint predictors of suicide. Second, it's difficult to study the psychological states associated with suicide because the period of high risk for a suicide attempt is often brief. Third, the low prevalence of suicide makes predicting it difficult (Finn & Kamphuis, 1995; Meehl & Rosen, 1955). Most estimates put the rate of completed suicide at 12 or 13 out of 100,000 people in the general population. So if only about one-hundredth of 1 percent of the population completes a suicide, our best guess—with about 99.9 percent accuracy—is that no one will commit suicide. Nevertheless, the social costs of failing to predict a suicide are so great that efforts to accurately predict suicide attempts continue (see **FIGURE 4**).

Fortunately, research has taught us a great deal about risk factors for suicide. The single best predictor of suicide is a previous attempt, because 30–40 percent of all people who kill themselves have made at least one prior attempt (Maris, 1992; Pelkonen & Marttunen, 2003). About three times as many men as women commit suicide, but nearly three times as many women try it (NIMH, 2004). Interestingly, compared with depressed mood, hopelessness may be an even better predictor of suicide (Beck et al., 1990; Goldston et al., 2001), because people are most likely to try to kill themselves when they see no escape from their pain. Intense agitation is also a powerful predictor of suicide risk (Fawcett, 1997). A list of risk factors for suicide appears in **TABLE 6**.

TABLE 6 Major Suicide Risk Factors.

1. Depression
2. Hopelessness
3. Substance abuse
4. Schizophrenia
5. Homosexuality, probably because of social stigma
6. Unemployment
7. Chronic, painful, or disfiguring physical illness
8. Recent loss of a loved one; being divorced, separated, or widowed
9. Family history of suicide
10. Personality disorders, such as borderline personality disorder (see later discussion)
11. Anxiety disorders, such as panic disorder and social anxiety disorder
12. Old age, especially in men
13. Recent discharge from a hospital

East ← → West

San Francisco tower

The number of suicides at this spot continues to grow

Marin tower

Marin County

FIGURE 4 Suicides by Location. The famed Golden Gate Bridge in San Francisco has been the site of well over 1,200 suicides. One inch on each of the blue lines equates to about 20 suicides. (*Source:* SFGate.com)

Study and Review in MyPsychLab

Assess Your Knowledge   FACT or FICTION?

1. Men and women are equally likely to suffer from major depression.   True / False

2. Depression is associated with stressful life events.   True / False

3. According to Lewinsohn, depression is caused by a low rate of response-contingent positive reinforcement.   True / False

4. According to Seligman, depression-prone people make specific and unstable attributions for negative life events.   True / False

5. Depressed mood is a better predictor of suicide than is hopelessness.   True / False

Answers: 1. F; 2. T; 3. T; 4. F; 5. F

Personality and Dissociative Disorders: The Disrupted and Divided Self

8 Identify the characteristics of borderline and psychopathic personality disorders.

9 Explain the controversies surrounding dissociative disorders, especially dissociative identity disorder.

Most of us are accustomed to thinking of ourselves as one coherent unified identity. But some individuals—especially those with personality and dissociative disorders—experience a serious disruption in their thoughts or behaviors that prevents them from experiencing a healthy, consistent identity. Identifying personality disorders isn't easy because we all have some variations in personality and sense of self.

Personality Disorders

Of all psychological conditions, personality disorders are historically among the least reliably diagnosed (Fowler, O'Donohue & Lilienfeld, 2007; Perry, 1984; Zimmerman, 1994). That's because clinicians sometime disagree about whether a given patient exhibits certain personality disturbances, such as excessive impulsivity or identity problems. DSM-5 states that we should diagnose a **personality disorder** only when personality traits first appear by adolescence; are inflexible, stable, and expressed in a wide variety of situations; and lead to distress or impairment (APA, 2013). But more than most patterns of behavior we've described, whether we perceive someone with a personality disorder as abnormal depends on the context in which their behavior occurs (Price & Bouffard, 1974). The suspiciousness of a person with a paranoid personality disorder may be a liability in a cooperative work group, but an asset in a private investigator.

Although the ten personality disorders in DSM-5 are distinguishable from each other, they often exhibit substantial comorbidity with each other and with other mental disorders, such as major depression and generalized anxiety disorder (Lenzenweger et al., 2007), leading some to question whether they are truly distinct from one another and from other psychological conditions (Harkness & Lilienfeld, 1997). Only a handful of these disorders have been the focus of extensive and systematic research (Blashfield & Intoccia, 2000); as a consequence, in this section we'll consider in detail the two most widely investigated personality disorders—borderline personality disorder and psychopathic personality. In many respects, the fascinating issues raised by these extensively studied disorders highlight the complexities involved in diagnosing and understanding personality disorders in general.

BORDERLINE PERSONALITY DISORDER: STABLE INSTABILITY. Estimates suggest that between 2 and 6 percent of adults, most of them women (Swartz et al., 1990; Zanarini et al., 2011), develop **borderline personality disorder**, a condition marked by instability in mood, identity, and impulse control. Individuals with borderline personality disorder tend to be extremely impulsive and unpredictable, although many are married and hold down good jobs. They are often unsure of who they are, and their interests and life goals frequently shift dramatically from year to year. Their relationships frequently alternate from extremes of worshipping partners one day to hating them the next. Some scholars have aptly described this disorder as a pattern of "stable instability" (Grinker & Werble, 1977). The name *borderline personality* stems from the now outmoded belief that this condition lies on the border between psychotic and "neurotic"—relatively normal, yet mildly disabled—functioning (Stern, 1938).

Borderline Personality: A Volatile Blend of Traits. Persons with borderline personality's impulsivity and rapidly fluctuating emotions often have a self-destructive quality: many engage in drug abuse; sexual promiscuity; overeating; and even self-mutilation, like cutting themselves when upset (Salsman & Linehan, 2012). They may threaten suicide to manipulate others, reflecting the chaotic nature of their relationships (Leichsenring et al., 2011). Because many experience intense feelings of abandonment when alone, they may jump frantically from one unhealthy relationship to another.

At least in mild doses, features of some personality disorders may be adaptive in certain occupations. For example, the traits of obsessive-compulsive personality disorder, which include attention to detail and perfectionism, may come in handy for accountants.

Watch in **MyPsychLab** the **Video:**
Speaking Out: Liz: Borderline Personality Disorder

personality disorder
condition in which personality traits, appearing first in adolescence, are inflexible, stable, expressed in a wide variety of situations, and lead to distress or impairment

borderline personality disorder
condition marked by extreme instability in mood, identity, and impulse control

Explanations of Borderline Personality Disorder. Psychoanalyst Otto Kernberg (1967, 1973) traced the roots of borderline personality to childhood problems with developing a sense of self and bonding emotionally to others. According to Kernberg, individuals with borderline personality disorder can't integrate differing perceptions of people, themselves included. This defect supposedly arises from an inborn tendency to experience intense anger and frustration from living with a cold, unempathetic mother. Kernberg argued that borderline individuals experience the world and themselves as unstable because they tend to "split" people and experiences into either all good or all bad. Although influential, Kernberg's model of borderline personality remains inadequately researched.

According to Marsha Linehan's (1993) sociobiological model, individuals with borderline personality disorder inherit a tendency to overreact to stress and experience lifelong difficulties with regulating their emotions (Crowell, Beauchaine, & Linehan, 2009). Indeed, twin studies suggest that borderline personality traits are substantially heritable (Carpenter et al., 2013; Torgersen et al., 2000). Difficulties in controlling emotions may be responsible for the rejection many individuals with borderline personality disorder encounter, as well as their excessive concerns about being validated, loved, and accepted.

Edward Selby and Thomas Joiner's emotional cascade model holds that intense rumination about negative events or emotional experiences may result in uncontrolled "emotional cascades," which prompt self-injurious actions like cutting. Although these impulsive and desperate actions succeed in providing brief distraction from rumination, they often fuel further bouts of rumination, creating a vicious cycle of problems with regulating emotions (Selby et al., 2009; Selby & Joiner, 2009).

For many years, psychologists believed that borderline personality was a lifelong condition that was highly resistant to treatment. Yet according to a recent study of treatment-seeking patients with BPD, 85 percent improved with treatment over a ten-year period, and only 12 percent relapsed (Gunderson et al, 2011). The patients with borderline personality actually showed a lower relapse rate compared with patients with major depression and other personality disorders.

PSYCHOPATHIC PERSONALITY: DON'T JUDGE A BOOK BY ITS COVER. We don't intend to alarm you. Yet the odds are high that in your life, you've met—perhaps even dated—at least one person whom psychologists describe as a **psychopathic personality**, which used to be known informally as a *psychopath* or *sociopath*.

Psychopathic personality is not formally a psychological disorder and is not listed in DSM-5. Nevertheless, it overlaps moderately to highly with the DSM-5 diagnosis of **antisocial personality disorder (ASPD)**. In contrast to ASPD, which is marked by a lengthy history of illegal and irresponsible actions, psychopathic personality is marked by a distinctive set of personality traits (Lilienfeld, 1994). Because much more psychological research has concentrated on psychopathic personality than on ASPD (Hare, 2003; Patrick, 2006), we focus on psychopathy here, as the latter condition is far better understood.

Psychopathic Personality: A Dangerous Mixture of Traits. Those with psychopathic personality—most of them male—are guiltless, dishonest, manipulative, callous, and self-centered (Cleckley, 1941/1988; Lykken, 1995). Because of these distinctly unpleasant personality traits, one might assume we'd all go out of our way to avoid individuals with this disorder—and we'd probably be better off if we did. However, many of us seek out people with psychopathic personality as friends and even romantic partners because they tend to be charming, personable, and engaging (Dutton, 2012; Hare, 1993). This was certainly the case with Johnny, whom we'll recall from the beginning of the chapter. Like Johnny, many people with this condition have a history of *conduct disorder*, marked by lying, cheating, and stealing in childhood and adolescence.

If the traits we've described fit someone you know to a T, there's no need to panic. Despite popular conception, most people with psychopathic personality aren't physically aggressive. Nevertheless, they are at somewhat heightened risk for crime compared with the average person, and a handful—probably a few percent—are habitually violent (Leistico et al., 2008). Mass murderer Ted Bundy almost certainly met the criteria for psychopathic

Psychologist Marsha Linehan of the University of Washington is the world's leading expert on the treatment of borderline personality disorder. In 2011, she surprised many people by acknowledging publicly that she had been diagnosed with the condition earlier in life. Linehan's courageous admission may help to dispel some of the unjustified stigma surrounding this personality disorder.

First-Person Account:
PSYCHOPATHIC PERSONALITY

"In my lifetime I have murdered 21 human beings. I have committed thousands of burglaries, robberies, larcenys, arsons and last but not least I have committed sodomy on more than 1,000 male human beings. For all of these things I am not the least bit sorry. I have no conscience so that does not worry me." (King, 1997, p. 169).

Quote from Carl Panzram, a serial killer, burglar, and arsonist.

Factoid

Although the view that individuals with psychopathic personality are "hopeless cases" who can't be rehabilitated is widely accepted, recent evidence suggests that at least some people with this disorder may improve as a consequence of psychotherapy (Salekin, 2002; Skeem, Monahan, & Mulvey, 2002). This may be especially true when treatment is prolonged and intensive (Caldwell, 2011).

psychopathic personality
condition marked by superficial charm, dishonesty, manipulativeness, self-centeredness, and risk taking

antisocial personality disorder (ASPD)
condition marked by a lengthy history of irresponsible and/or illegal actions

personality disorder, as do about 25 percent of prison inmates (Hare, 2003). Also, despite scores of movie portrayals of crazed serial killers, people with this disorder typically aren't psychotic. To the contrary, most are entirely rational. They know full well that their irresponsible actions are morally wrong; they just don't care (Cima, Tonnaer, & Hauser, 2010).

There's reason to suspect that people with this condition populate not only much of the criminal justice system, but also positions of leadership in corporations and politics (Babiak & Hare, 2006). For example, among the U.S. presidents, higher estimated levels of a constellation of traits called fearless dominance, which assess the boldness and adventurousness often found in psychopaths, are linked to superior leadership as rated by expert historians (Lilienfeld et al., 2012). Indeed, some psychopathic traits, such as interpersonal skills, superficial likability, ruthlessness, and risk taking, may give people with this disorder a leg up for getting ahead of the rest of the pack. Still, there's surprisingly little research on "successful psychopaths"—people with high levels of psychopathic traits who function well in society (Hall & Benning, 2006; Widom, 1977).

Causes of Psychopathic Personality. Despite nearly six decades of research, the causes of psychopathic personality remain largely unknown (Skeem et al., 2011). Classic research shows that individuals with this disorder don't show much classical conditioning to unpleasant unconditioned stimuli like electric shocks (Lykken, 1957). Similarly, when asked to sit patiently in a chair for an impending electric shock or a loud blast of noise, their levels of skin conductance—an indicator of arousal—increase only about one-fifth as much as those without psychopathic personality (Hare, 1978; Lorber, 2004). These abnormalities probably stem from a deficit in fear, which may give rise to some of the key features of the disorder (Fowles & Dindo, 2009; Lykken, 1995; Patrick, 2006). Perhaps partly as a consequence of this dearth of fear, people with psychopathic personality aren't motivated to learn from punishment and tend to repeat the same mistakes in life (Newman & Kosson, 1986; Zeier et al., 2012).

An alternative explanation is that individuals with this disorder are underaroused. The *Yerkes–Dodson law* describes a well-established psychological principle: an inverted U-shaped relationship between arousal, on the one hand, and mood and performance, on the other. As this law reminds us, people who are habitually underaroused experience *stimulus hunger*: they're bored and seek out excitement. The underarousal hypothesis may help to explain why those with psychopathic personality tend to be risk takers (Zuckerman, 1989), as well as why they frequently get in trouble with the law and abuse all manner of substances (Taylor & Lang, 2006). Nevertheless, the causal arrow between underarousal and psychopathy may run in the opposite direction: if people with psychopathic traits are fearless, they may experience little arousal in response to stimuli (Lykken, 1995).

Dissociative Disorders

When speaking about ourselves, we use the words *me* and *I* without giving it a second thought. That's not the case in most **dissociative disorders**, which involve disruptions in consciousness, memory, identity, or perception (APA, 2013). The idea that one person can have more than one identity—let alone more than a hundred—is an extraordinary claim. So it's no wonder that dissociative identity disorder (DID) is one of the most controversial of all diagnoses. Before we consider the debate that swirls around this condition, we'll consider several other dissociative disorders.

DEPERSONALIZATION/DEREALIZATION DISORDER. If you've ever felt detached from yourself, as though you're living in a movie or dream or observing your body from the perspective of an outsider, you've experienced *depersonalization*. More than half of adults have experienced one brief episode of depersonalization, and such experiences are especially common among adolescents and college students (APA, 2000; Simeon et al., 1997). Derealization, the sense that the external world is strange or unreal, often accompanies both depersonalization and panic attacks. Only if people experience multiple episodes of depersonalization, derealization, or both, do they qualify for a diagnosis of **depersonalization/derealization disorder**.

In rare cases, violent individuals with psychopathic personality are women (Arrigo & Griffin, 2004). Aileen Wuornos (pictured above), a serial killer called the Damsel of Death, was executed for the murders of six men she lured into helping her by posing as a stranded driver. Wuornos's life was dramatized in the movie *Monster*.

RULING OUT RIVAL HYPOTHESES ▶
Have important alternative explanations for the findings been excluded?

CORRELATION VS. CAUSATION ▶
Can we be sure that A causes B?

EXTRAORDINARY CLAIMS ▶
Is the evidence as strong as the claim?

dissociative disorder
condition involving disruptions in consciousness, memory, identity, or perception

depersonalization/derealization disorder
condition marked by multiple episodes of depersonalization, derealization, or both

DISSOCIATIVE AMNESIA. In **dissociative amnesia**, people can't recall important personal information—most often following a stressful experience—that isn't due to ordinary forgetting. Their memory loss is extensive and can include suicide attempts or violent outbursts (Sar et al., 2007). More commonly, psychologists diagnose dissociative amnesia when adults report gaps in their memories for child abuse.

This diagnosis has proven controversial for several reasons. First, memory gaps regarding nontraumatic events are common in healthy individuals and aren't necessarily stress-related or indicative of dissociation (Belli et al., 1998). Second, most people may not be especially motivated to recall child abuse or other upsetting events. As Richard McNally (2003) pointed out, not thinking about something isn't the same as being *unable* to remember it, which is amnesia. Third, careful studies have turned up no convincing cases of amnesia that can't be explained by other factors, like disease, brain injury, normal forgetting, or an unwillingness to think about disturbing events (Kihlstrom, 2005; Pope et al., 2007). Fourth, individuals with high levels of dissociation are *less* likely to forget supposedly threatening (sexual) words, which experimenters direct them to forget (Elzinga et al., 2000).

At times, we've all felt like running away from our troubles. In **dissociative fugue**, a type of dissociative amnesia, people not only forget significant events in their lives, but also flee their stressful circumstances (*fugue* is Latin for "flight"). In some cases, they move to another city or another country, assuming a new identity. Fugues can last for hours or, in unusual cases, years. Dissociative fugue is rare, occurring in about 2 of every 1,000 people (APA, 2000), with more prolonged fugue states even rarer (Karlin & Orne, 1996).

In 2006, a 57-year-old husband, father, and Boy Scout leader from New York was found living under a new name in a homeless shelter in Chicago after he left his garage near his office and disappeared. When a tip to *America's Most Wanted* uncovered his true identity six months later, his family contacted him, but he claimed to have no memory of who they were (Brody, 2007).

In this and other fugue cases, it's essential to find out whether the fugue resulted from a head injury, a stroke, or another neurological cause. Moreover, some people merely claim amnesia to avoid responsibilities or stressful circumstances, relocate to a different area, and get a fresh start in life. Even when fugues occur shortly after a traumatic event, it's difficult to know whether the trauma caused the amnesia. Scientists don't fully understand the role trauma, psychological factors, and neurological conditions play in fugue states (Kihlstrom, 2005).

DISSOCIATIVE IDENTITY DISORDER: MULTIPLE PERSONALITIES, MULTIPLE CONTROVERSIES. **Dissociative identity disorder (DID)** is characterized by the presence of two or more distinct personality states (the term "identities" was deleted in DSM-5) that markedly disrupt the person's usual sense of identity and may be observed by others or reported by the individual. These personality states or "alters," as they're sometimes called, are often very different from the primary or "host" personality and may be of different names, ages, genders, and even races. In some cases, these features are the opposite of those exhibited by the host personality. For example, if the host personality is shy and retiring, one or more alters may be outgoing or flamboyant. Psychologists have reported the number of alters to range from one (the so-called split personality) to hundreds or even thousands, with one reported case of 4,500 personalities (Acocella, 1999). In general, women are more likely to receive a DID diagnosis and report more alters than men (APA, 2000).

Researchers have identified intriguing differences among alters in their respiration rates (Bahnson & Smith, 1975), brain wave activity (EEG; Ludwig et al., 1972), eyeglass prescriptions (Miller, 1989), handedness (Savitz et al., 2004), skin conductance responses (Brende, 1984), voice patterns, and handwriting (Lilienfeld & Lynn, 2003). Fascinating as these findings are, they don't provide conclusive evidence for the existence of alters. These differences could stem from changes in mood or thoughts over time or to bodily changes, such as muscle tension, that people can produce on a voluntary basis (Allen & Movius, 2000; Merckelbach, Devilly, & Rassin, 2002). Moreover, scientists have falsified claims that alters are truly distinct. When psychologists have used objective measures of memory, they've typically found that information presented to one alter is available to the other, providing no evidence for amnesia across alters (Allen & Moravius, 2000; Huntjens et al., 2012).

◄ **RULING OUT RIVAL HYPOTHESES**
Have important alternative explanations for the findings been excluded?

Factoid

Sleep disturbances may play a prominent role in symptoms of dissociation such as depersonalization. When people are deprived of sleep for 24 hours, they report more dissociative-like symptoms, and when they're taught sleep hygiene techniques to improve their sleep, they report fewer dissociative symptoms (van der Kloet et al., 2012b). Some researchers propose that a disturbed sleep-wake cycle produces dreamlike thoughts during the daytime that cause or at least fuel dissociative experiences.

◄ **CORRELATION VS. CAUSATION**
Can we be sure that A causes B?

dissociative amnesia
inability to recall important personal information—most often related to a stressful experience—that can't be explained by ordinary forgetfulness

dissociative fugue
sudden, unexpected travel away from home or the workplace, accompanied by amnesia for significant life events

dissociative identity disorder (DID)
condition characterized by the presence of two or more distinct personality states that recurrently take control of the person's behavior

 Watch in **MyPsychLab** the **Video:**
Dissociative Identity Disorder:
Dr. Holliday Milby

◄ **RULING OUT RIVAL HYPOTHESES**
Have important alternative explanations for the findings been excluded?

◄ **FALSIFIABILITY**
Can the claim be disproved?

Psychological Disorders

Jeffrey Ingram, aged 40, experienced a dissociative fugue in which he claimed for over a month that he couldn't remember anything about his life. He was reunited with his fiancée in 2006 only after he appeared on television shows asking the public to identify him.

EXTRAORDINARY CLAIMS ▶
Is the evidence as strong as the claim?

RULING OUT RIVAL HYPOTHESES ▶
Have important alternative explanations for the findings been excluded?

"I HAVE 25 PATIENTS IN MY COUNSELING GROUP--MRS. SHERMAN, MR. MARTIN, AND MR. MARTIN'S 23 OTHER PERSONALITIES."

(*Source:* Dan Rosandich, www.CartoonStock.com)

The primary controversy surrounding DID revolves around one question: is DID a response to early trauma, or is it a consequence of social and cultural factors (Merskey, 1992)? According to the *posttraumatic model* (Gleaves, May, & Cardeña, 2001; Ross, 1997), DID arises from a history of severe abuse—physical, sexual, or both—during childhood. This abuse leads individuals to "compartmentalize" their identity into distinct alters as a means of coping with intense emotional pain. In this way, the person can feel as though the abuse happened to someone else.

Advocates of the posttraumatic model claim that 90 percent or more of individuals with DID were severely abused in childhood (Gleaves, 1996). Nevertheless, many studies that reported this association didn't check the accuracy of abuse claims against objective information such as court records of abuse (Coons, Bowman, & Milstein, 1988). Moreover, researchers haven't shown that early abuse is specific to DID, as it's present in many other disorders (Pope & Hudson, 1992). These considerations don't exclude a role for early trauma in DID, but they suggest that researchers must conduct further controlled studies before drawing strong conclusions (Gleaves, 1996; Gleaves et al., 2001).

According to advocates of the competing *sociocognitive model*, the claim that some people have hundreds of personalities is extraordinary, but the evidence for it is unconvincing (Giesbrecht et al., 2008; Lilienfeld et al., 1999; McHugh, 1993; Merskey, 1992; Spanos, 1994, 1996). According to this model, people's expectancies and beliefs—shaped by certain psychotherapeutic procedures and cultural influences and a tendency to fantasize and misremember events, rather than early traumas—account for the origin and maintenance of DID. Advocates of this model claim that some therapists use procedures like hypnosis and repeated prompting of alters that suggest to patients that their puzzling symptoms are the products of indwelling identities (Lilienfeld & Lynn, 2003; Lilienfeld et al., 1999). The following observations and findings support this hypothesis:

- Many or most DID patients show few or no clear-cut signs of this condition, such as alters, prior to psychotherapy (Kluft, 1984).
- Mainstream treatment techniques for DID reinforce the idea that the person possesses multiple identities. These techniques include using hypnosis to "bring forth" hidden alters, communicating with alters and giving them different names, and encouraging patients to recover repressed memories supposedly housed in dissociated selves (Spanos, 1994, 1996).
- The number of alters per DID individual tends to increase substantially when therapists use these techniques (Piper, 1997).
- Researchers have reported a link between dissociation and the tendency to fantasize in everyday life (Giesbrecht et al., 2008), which may be related to the production of false memories, although the interpretation of these findings has proven controversial (Dalenberg et al., 2011).

As of 1970, there were 79 documented cases of DID in the world literature. As of 1986, the number of DID cases had mushroomed to approximately 6,000 (Lilienfeld et al., 1999), and some estimates in the early twenty-first century are in the hundreds of thousands. The sociocognitive model holds that the popular media have played a pivotal role in the DID epidemic (Elzinga et al., 1998). Indeed, much of the dramatic increase in DID's prevalence followed closely on the release of the best-selling book *Sybil* (Schreiber, 1973) in the mid-1970s, later made into an Emmy Award–winning television movie starring Sally Field. The book and later film told the heartbreaking story of a young woman with 16 personalities who reported a history of sadistic child abuse. Interestingly, subsequently released audiotapes of Sybil's therapy sessions suggested that she had no alters or memories of child abuse prior to treatment and that her therapist had urged her to behave differently on different occasions (Rieber, 1999).

Over the past two decades, media coverage of DID has skyrocketed (Showalter, 1997; Spanos, 1996; Wilson, 2003), with some celebrities, like comedian Roseanne Barr and football star Hershel Walker, claiming to suffer from the disorder. Although DID is virtually nonexistent in Japan and India, it is now diagnosed with considerable frequency in some countries, such as Holland, in which it has recently received more publicity

(Lilienfeld et al., 1999). In summary, there's considerable support for the sociocognitive model and the claim that therapists, along with the media, are creating alters rather than discovering them. The dissociative disorders provide a powerful, although troubling, example of how social and cultural forces can shape psychological disorders.

✔ **Study** and **Review** in **MyPsychLab**

Sheri Storm was diagnosed with dissociative identity disorder, but later became convinced that a therapist had inadvertently implanted her alter personalities using suggestive techniques. This painting—completed by Storm during therapy—depicts the seemingly endless parade of her alters emerging in treatment.

Assess Your Knowledge   FACT or FICTION?

1. Personality disorders are almost always reliably diagnosed.   **True / False**
2. Borderline personality is among the most unstable of the personality disorders. **True / False**
3. Most people with psychopathic personality disorder are not habitually violent. **True / False**
4. Child abuse clearly causes DID.   **True / False**
5. The media have played little role in the recent increase in DID diagnoses.   **True / False**

Answers: 1. F; 2. T; 3. T; 4. F; 5. F

The Enigma of Schizophrenia

10 Recognize the characteristic symptoms of schizophrenia.

11 Explain how psychosocial, neural, biochemical, and genetic influences create the vulnerability to schizophrenia.

Psychiatrist Daniel Weinberger has called **schizophrenia** the "cancer" of mental illness: it's perhaps the most severe of all disorders—and the most mysterious (Levy-Reiner, 1996). As we'll discover, it's a devastating disorder of thought and emotion associated with a loss of contact with reality.

Symptoms of Schizophrenia: The Shattered Mind

Even today, many people confuse schizophrenia with DID (Wahl, 1997). Swiss psychiatrist Eugen Bleuler gave us the modern term *schizophrenia* in 1911. The term literally means "split mind," which no doubt contributed to the popular myth that the symptoms of schizophrenia stem from a split personality. You may have even heard people refer to a "schizophrenic attitude" when explaining that they're "of two minds" regarding an issue. Don't be misled. As Bleuler recognized, the difficulties of individuals with schizophrenia arise from disturbances in attention, thinking, language, emotion, and relationships with others. In contrast to DID, which is supposedly characterized by multiple intact personalities, schizophrenia is characterized by one personality that's shattered.

Schizophrenia causes most of its sufferers' levels of functioning to plunge. More than half suffer from serious disabilities, such as an inability to hold a job and maintain close relationships (Harvey, Reichenberg, & Bowie, 2006). Indeed, more than 10 percent of homeless people, with some estimates ranging as high as 45 percent, qualify for a diagnosis of schizophrenia (Folsom & Jeste, 2008). Individuals who experience schizophrenia comprise less than 1 percent of the population, with most estimates ranging from .4–.7 percent (Saha et al., 2005). Yet they make up half of the approximately 100,000 patients in state and county mental institutions in the United States (Grob, 1997). But there's some good news. Today, more than ever, people with schizophrenia can function in society, even though they may need to return periodically to hospitals for treatment (Lamb & Bachrach, 2001; Mueser & McGurk, 2004).

Researchers have struggled with the problem of describing schizophrenia since the eighteenth century, when Emil Kraepelin first outlined the features of patients with *dementia praecox,* meaning psychological deterioration in youth. But Kraepelin didn't get it quite right. Even though the typical onset of schizophrenia is in the mid-twenties for men and the late twenties for women, schizophrenia can also strike after age 45 (APA, 2000).

The Daily News, June 1 2013   Page 1

Study Shows American Public Has Schizophrenic Views on Taxes

Staff writer, Caroline Beimford

A recently published study shows that Americans are very divided on the issue of taxes. While some are opposed to any tax increases, others see the necessity of

? What's wrong with the headline of this newspaper story, which refers to American's divided views on taxes?

(See answer upside down on bottom of page.)

👁 **Watch** in **MyPsychLab** the **Video:**
Schizophrenia: The Case of Georgina

schizophrenia
severe disorder of thought and emotion associated with a loss of contact with reality

Answer: It confuses schizophrenia with split personality.

First-Person Account:
SCHIZOPHRENIA

"The reflection in the store window—it's me, isn't it? I know it is, but it's hard to tell. Glassy shadows, polished pastels, a jigsaw puzzle of my body, face, and clothes, with pieces disappearing whenever I move… Schizophrenia is painful, and it is craziness when I hear voices, when I believe people are following me, wanting to snatch my very soul. I am frightened, too, when every whisper, every laugh is about me; when newspapers suddenly contain cures, four-letter words shouting at me; when sparkles of light are demon eyes."

(McGrath, 1984)

Factoid

One of the more unusual delusions is *folie a deux* (French for the "folly of two"), known technically as "shared psychotic disorder" in DSM-5. In *folie a deux*, one person in a close relationship, often a marriage, induces the same delusion in his or her partner. For example, both partners may end up convinced that the government is poisoning their food (Silveira & Seeman, 1995). Rare cases of *folie a deux* in identical twins, *folie a trois* (involving three people) and *folie a famille* (involving an entire family) have also been reported.

? In the 2001 film *A Beautiful Mind*, actor Russell Crowe (*left*) portrays Nobel Prize–winning mathematician John Nash, who was diagnosed with schizophrenia. In this scene, Nash is shown talking to a friend whom he sees—but does not exist. **What's scientifically unrealistic about this scene?** (See answer upside down on bottom of page.)

delusion
strongly held fixed belief that has no basis in reality

psychotic symptom
psychological problem reflecting serious distortions in reality

hallucination
sensory perception that occurs in the absence of an external stimulus

Answer: Extremely vivid or detailed visual hallucinations are very rare in schizophrenia.

DELUSIONS: FIXED FALSE BELIEFS. Among the hallmark symptoms of schizophrenia are **delusions**—strongly held fixed beliefs that have no basis in reality. Delusions are called **psychotic symptoms** because they represent a serious distortion of reality. Terrell, whom we met at the beginning of the chapter, experienced delusions that led to a suicide attempt.

Delusions commonly involve themes of persecution. One of your book's authors treated a man who believed that coworkers tapped his phone and conspired to get him fired. Another was convinced that a helicopter in the distance beamed the Beatles song "All You Need Is Love" into his head to make him feel jealous and inadequate. The authors of your book have also treated patients who reported delusions of grandeur (greatness), including one who believed that she'd discovered the cure for cancer even though she had no medical training. Other delusions center on the body and may include a belief that one is dead (so-called Cotard's syndrome). Still others involve elaborate themes of sexuality or romance. John Hinckley, the man who nearly assassinated then–President Ronald Reagan in 1981, was convinced that murdering the president would gain him the affection of actress Jodie Foster.

HALLUCINATIONS: FALSE PERCEPTIONS. Among the other serious symptoms of schizophrenia are **hallucinations**: sensory perceptions that occur in the absence of an external stimulus. They can be auditory (involving hearing), olfactory (involving smell), gustatory (involving taste), tactile (involving the sense of feeling), or visual. Most hallucinations in schizophrenia are auditory, usually consisting of voices. In some patients, hallucinated voices express disapproval or carry on a running commentary about the person's thoughts or actions. *Command hallucinations,* which tell patients what to do ("Go over to that man and tell him to shut up!"), may be associated with a heightened risk of violence toward others (McNiel, Eisner, & Binder, 2000). Incidentally, extremely vivid or detailed visual hallucinations—especially in the absence of auditory hallucinations—are usually signs of an organic (medical) disorder or substance abuse rather than schizophrenia (Shea, 1998).

Do your thoughts sound like voices in your head? Many people experience their thoughts as inner speech, which is entirely normal. Some researchers suggest that auditory hallucinations occur when people with schizophrenia believe mistakenly that their inner speech arises from a source outside themselves (Bentall, 2000; Frith, 1992; Thomas, 1997). Brain scans reveal that when people experience auditory hallucinations, brain areas associated with speech perception and production become activated (Jardri et al., 2011; McGuire, Shah, & Murray, 1993).

DISORGANIZED SPEECH. Consider this example of the speech of a patient with schizophrenia: "It was shockingly not of the best quality I have known all such evildoers coming out of doors with the best of intentions" (Grinnell, 2008). We can see that this patient skips from topic to topic in a disjointed way. Most researchers believe that this peculiar language results from thought disorder (Meehl, 1962; Stirk et al., 2008). The usual associations that we forge between two words, such as *mother–child*, are considerably weakened or highly unusual for individuals with schizophrenia (for example, *mother–rug*) (Kuperberg et al., 2006). In severe forms, the resulting speech is so jumbled it's almost impossible to understand, leading psychologists to describe it as *word salad*. Language problems, like thought disorder, point to fundamental impairments in schizophrenia in the ability to shift and maintain attention, which influence virtually every aspect of affected individuals' daily lives (Cornblatt & Keilp, 1994; Fuller et al., 2006).

GROSSLY DISORGANIZED BEHAVIOR AND CATATONIA. When people develop schizophrenia, self-care, personal hygiene, and motivation often deteriorate. They may avoid conversation; laugh, cry, or swear inappropriately; or wear a warm coat on a sweltering summer day.

Catatonic symptoms involve motor (movement) problems, including holding the body in bizarre or rigid postures, curling up in a fetal position, resisting simple suggestions to move or speak, and pacing aimlessly. Catatonic individuals may also repeat a phrase in conversation in a parrotlike manner, a symptom called *echolalia*. At the opposite extreme, they may occasionally engage in bouts of frenzied, purposeless motor activity.

Catatonic individuals, like the one shown here, may permit their limbs to be moved to any position and maintain this posture for lengthy periods of time, a condition called *waxy flexibility*.

Explanations for Schizophrenia: The Roots of a Shattered Mind

Today, virtually all scientists believe that psychosocial factors play some role in schizophrenia. Nevertheless, they also agree that these factors probably trigger the disorder only in people with a genetic vulnerability.

THE FAMILY AND EXPRESSED EMOTION. Early theories of schizophrenia mistakenly laid the blame for the condition on mothers, with so-called *schizophrenogenic* (schizophrenia-producing) mothers being the prime culprits. Based on informal observations of families of children with schizophrenia, some authors described such mothers as overprotective, smothering, rejecting, and controlling (Arieti, 1959; Lidz, 1973). Other theorists pointed the finger of blame at the interactions among all family members (Dolnick, 1998).

But as important as clinical experience can be in generating hypotheses, it doesn't provide an adequate arena for testing them. Indeed, these early studies were severely flawed, largely because they lacked control groups of people without schizophrenia. A now widely accepted rival hypothesis is that family members' responses aren't the cause of schizophrenia, but instead are typically a response to the stressful experience of living with a severely disturbed person.

It's widely acknowledged that parents and family members don't "cause" schizophrenia (Gottesman, 1991; Walker et al., 2004). Still, families may influence whether patients with the disorder relapse. After leaving hospitals, patients experience more than twice the likelihood of relapse (50–60 percent) when their relatives display high *expressed emotion* (EE)—that is, criticism, hostility, and overinvolvement (Brown et al., 1962; Butzlaff & Hooley, 1998; Kuipers, 2011). Criticism is especially predictive of relapse (Halweg et al., 1989; McCarty et al., 2004), even over 20 years, and may result in part from relatives' frustrations in living with a person with schizophrenia who displays disruptive behaviors (Cechnicki et al., 2012). Indeed, EE may reflect family members' reactions to their loved one's schizophrenia as much as contribute to their loved one's relapse (King, 2000).

The apparent effects of EE vary across ethnic groups. Critical comments from family members may undermine recovering patients' confidence and sense of independence, which are valued in Caucasian-American culture (Chentsova-Dutton & Tsai, 2007). In contrast, in Mexican-American culture, independence isn't as highly valued, so criticism doesn't predict relapse. Nevertheless, a lack of family warmth, which is prized in Mexican-American families, does predict relapse (Lopez et al., 2004). Moreover, in African-American families, high levels of EE predict *better* outcomes among individuals with schizophrenia, perhaps because family members perceive EE as an expression of openness, honesty, and caring (Rosenfarb, Bellack, & Aziz, 2006). Although EE often predicts relapse, well-controlled studies don't support the hypothesis that child rearing directly *causes* schizophrenia, any more than does extreme poverty, childhood trauma, or parental conflict, all of which are correlated with schizophrenia (Cornblatt, Green, & Walker, 1999; Schofield & Balian, 1959).

Factoid

As many as one-half to two-thirds of people with schizophrenia improve significantly, although not completely, and a small percentage recover completely after a single episode (Harrow et al., 2005; Robinson et al., 2004). Researchers found that 20 high-functioning people with schizophrenia—which included doctors, an attorney, and a chief executive—used such strategies as taking medication, getting exercise and adequate sleep, avoiding alcohol and crowds, and seeking social support to manage their illness successfully (Marder et al., 2008).

◄ **RULING OUT RIVAL HYPOTHESES**
Have important alternative explanations for the findings been excluded?

◄ **CORRELATION VS. CAUSATION**
Can we be sure that A causes B?

catatonic symptom
motor problem, including holding the body in bizarre or rigid postures, curling up in a fetal position, and resisting simple suggestions to move

◄ **CORRELATION VS. CAUSATION**
Can we be sure that A causes B?

In one identical twin with schizophrenia, the fluid-filled ventricles of the brain (see *red arrows*) are enlarged relative to his or her co-twin without schizophrenia. Such enlargement probably reflects a deterioration in brain tissue surrounding the ventricles, which expand to fill the missing space.

CORRELATION VS. CAUSATION ▶
Can we be sure that A causes B?
RULING OUT RIVAL HYPOTHESES ▶
Have important alternative explanations for the findings been excluded?

CORRELATION VS. CAUSATION ▶
Can we be sure that A causes B?

RULING OUT RIVAL HYPOTHESES ▶
Have important alternative explanations for the findings been excluded?

SCHIZOPHRENIA: BRAIN, BIOCHEMICAL, AND GENETIC FINDINGS. Research using a variety of technologies has uncovered intriguing biological clues to the causes of schizophrenia. We'll focus on three such clues: brain abnormalities, neurotransmitter differences, and genetic influences.

Brain Abnormalities. Research indicates that one or more of four fluid-filled structures called *ventricles*, which cushion and nourish the brain, are typically enlarged in individuals with schizophrenia. This finding is important for two reasons. First, these brain areas frequently expand when others shrink (Barta et al., 1990; Raz & Raz, 1990), suggesting that schizophrenia is a disorder of brain deterioration. Second, deterioration in these areas is associated with thought disorder (Vita et al., 1995).

Other brain abnormalities in schizophrenia include increases in the size of the *sulci*, or spaces between the ridges of the brain (Cannon, Mednick, & Parnas, 1989), and decreases in (a) the size of the temporal lobes (Boos et al., 2007; Job et al., 2005), (b) activation of the amygdala and hippocampus (Hempel et al., 2003), and (c) the symmetry of the brain's hemispheres (Luchins, Weinberger, & Wyatt, 1982; Zivotofsky et al., 2007). Functional brain imaging studies show that the frontal lobes of people with schizophrenia are less active than those of nonpatients when engaged in demanding mental tasks (Andreasen et al., 1992; Knyazeva et al., 2008), a phenomenon called *hypofrontality*. Still, it's not clear whether these findings are causes or consequences of the disorder. For example, hypofrontality could be due to the tendency of patients with schizophrenia to concentrate less on tasks compared with other individuals. Researchers also need to rule out alternative explanations for brain underactivity that could arise from patients' diet, drinking and smoking habits, and medication use (Hanson & Gottesman, 2005).

Some studies have suggested that marijuana use in adolescence can bring about schizophrenia and other psychotic disorders in genetically vulnerable individuals (Compton et al., 2009; Degenhardt et al., 2009; Degenhardt & Hall, 2006). Nevertheless, it's difficult to pin down a causal relationship between marijuana use and schizophrenia for three reasons: (1) people who use marijuana are likely to use a variety of other drugs, which they may be reluctant to report on surveys; (2) individuals with schizophrenia may be more likely to use marijuana, so the causal arrow may be reversed; and (3) the rates of schizophrenia remained stable between 1970–2005 in the United Kingdom, although marijuana use increased over this period (Frisher et al., 2009). Still, people with a personal or family history of psychotic disorders, including schizophrenia, would be particularly ill advised to use marijuana.

Neurotransmitter Differences. The biochemistry of the brain is one of the keys to unlocking the mystery of schizophrenia. One early explanation was the *dopamine hypothesis* (Carlsson, 1995; Keith et al., 1976; Nicol & Gottesman, 1983). The evidence for the role of dopamine in schizophrenia is mostly indirect. First, most antischizophrenic drugs block dopamine receptor sites. To put it crudely, the drugs "slow down" nerve impulses by partially blocking the action of dopamine. Second, amphetamine, a stimulant that blocks the reuptake of dopamine, tends to worsen the symptoms of schizophrenia (Lieberman & Koreen, 1993; Snyder, 1975).

Nevertheless, the hypothesis that a simple excess of dopamine creates the symptoms of schizophrenia doesn't seem to fit the data. A better-supported rival hypothesis is that abnormalities in dopamine *receptors* produce these symptoms. Receptor sites in the brain appear to be highly specific for dopamine transmission. These sites respond uniquely to drugs designed to reduce psychotic symptoms and are associated with difficulties in attention, memory, and motivation (Busatto et al., 1995; Keefe & Henry, 1994; Reis et al., 2004).

These findings provide evidence for a direct tie between dopamine pathways and symptoms of schizophrenia, such as paranoia. As we've seen, some symptoms of schizophrenia represent excesses of normal functions and include hallucinations, delusions, and disorganized speech and behavior. We can contrast these *positive symptoms* with *negative symptoms*, which reflect decreases or losses of normal functions. These symptoms include social withdrawal and diminished motivations, decreased expression of emotions, and brief and limited speech (Andreasen et al., 1995). People with schizophrenia are less impaired when their symptoms are predominantly positive rather than negative (Harvey, Reichenberg, & Bowie, 2006). There's evidence that positive symptoms result from dopamine excesses in some brain regions and negative symptoms from dopamine deficits in other brain regions (Davis et al., 1991). However, the causes of negative symptoms are difficult to pinpoint, because they may arise from prolonged institutionalization and medication side effects. Dopamine is probably only one of several neurotransmitters that play a role in schizophrenia; other likely candidates are norepinephrine, glutamate, and serotonin (Cornblatt, Green, & Walker, 1999; Grace, 1991).

Genetic Influences. Still unresolved is the question of which biological deficits are present prior to schizophrenia and which appear after the disorder begins (Seidman et al., 2003). The seeds of schizophrenia are often sown well before birth and lie partly in individuals' genetic endowment. As we can see in **FIGURE 5**, being the offspring of someone diagnosed with schizophrenia greatly increases one's odds of developing the disorder. If we have a sibling with schizophrenia, we have about a 1 in 10 chance of developing the disorder; these odds are about 10 times higher than those of the average person. As genetic similarity increases, so does the risk of schizophrenia.

Still, it's possible the environment accounts for these findings because siblings not only share genes, but also grow up in the same family. To eliminate this ambiguity, researchers have conducted twin studies, which provide convincing support for a genetic influence on schizophrenia. If we have an identical twin with schizophrenia, our risk rises to about 50 percent. An identical twin of a person with schizophrenia is about 3 times as likely as a fraternal twin of a person with schizophrenia to develop the disorder and about 50 times as likely as an average person (Gottesman & Shields, 1972; Kendler & Diehl, 1993; Meehl, 1962). Adoption data also point to a genetic influence. Even when children who have a biological parent with schizophrenia are adopted by parents with no hint of the disorder, their risk of schizophrenia is greater than that of a person with no biological relative with schizophrenia (Gottesman, 1991). Interestingly, scientists have identified structural brain abnormalities, like ventricular enlargement and decreases in brain volume, in the healthy close relatives of patients with schizophrenia, further suggesting that genetic influences produce a vulnerability to schizophrenia (Staal et al., 2000).

VULNERABILITY TO SCHIZOPHRENIA: DIATHESIS-STRESS MODELS. Diathesis-stress models incorporate much of what we know about schizophrenia. Such models propose that schizophrenia, along with many other mental disorders, is a joint product of a genetic vulnerability, called a *diathesis,* and stressors that trigger this vulnerability (Meehl, 1962; Walker & DiForio, 1997; Zubin & Spring, 1977).

Paul Meehl (1990) suggested that approximately 10 percent of the population has a genetic predisposition to schizophrenia. What are people with this predisposition like? During adolescence and adulthood, they may strike us as "odd ducks." They may seem socially uncomfortable, and their speech, thought processes, and perceptions may impress us as unusual. They're likely to endorse items on psychological tests such as "Occasionally, I have felt as though my body did not exist" (Chapman, Chapman, & Raulin, 1978). Such individuals display symptoms of psychosis-proneness or *schizotypal personality disorder.* Most people with schizotypal personality disorder don't develop full-blown schizophrenia, perhaps because they have a weaker genetic vulnerability or because they've experienced fewer stressors.

Well before people experience symptoms of schizophrenia, we can identify "early warning signs" or markers of vulnerability to this condition. People with schizotypal personality disorder display some of these markers, which include social withdrawal, thought and movement abnormalities (Mittal et al., 2007; Walker, Baum, & DiForio, 1998), learning and memory deficits (Volgmaier et al., 2000), elevated neuroticism (Lonnqvist et al., 2009), temporal lobe abnormalities (Siever & Davis, 2004), impaired attention (Keefe et al., 1997), and eye movement disturbances when tracking moving objects (Iacono, 1985; Lenzenweger, McLachlan, & Rubin, 2007). Their difficulties begin early in life. Elaine Walker and Richard

◄ **CORRELATION VS. CAUSATION**
Can we be sure that A causes B?

👁 **Watch** in **MyPsychLab** the **Video:**
Genetics Research in Schizophrenia

◄ **RULING OUT RIVAL HYPOTHESES**
Have important alternative explanations for the findings been excluded?

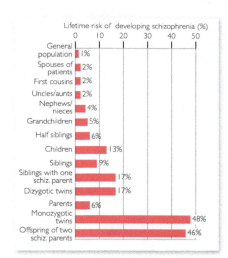

FIGURE 5 Schizophrenia Risk and the Family. The lifetime risk of developing schizophrenia is largely a function of how closely an individual is genetically related to a person with schizophrenia. (*Source:* Feldman, 1991)

diathesis-stress model
perspective proposing that mental disorders are a joint product of a genetic vulnerability, called a diathesis, and stressors that trigger this vulnerability

Many people with schizotypal personality disorder are prone to "magical thinking"—the belief that their thoughts can influence actions through supernatural or otherwise mysterious processes. For example, they may believe that stepping on a crack in the sidewalk will create misfortune.

Factoid

Data show that more people with schizophrenia are born in the winter and spring than at other times of the year (Davies et al., 2003; Torrey et al., 1997). The reason for this strange finding doesn't appear to lie in astrology: certain viral infections that affect pregnant women and that may trigger schizophrenia in vulnerable fetuses are most common in winter months.

Watch in **MyPsychLab** the **Video:**
Autism: Dr. Kathy Pratt

autism spectrum disorder
DSM-5 category that includes Autistic Disorder and Asperger's Disorder

Lewine (1990) found that people who viewed home movies of siblings interacting could identify which children later developed schizophrenia at better-than-chance levels. Even at an early age, vulnerable children's lack of emotions and decreased eye contact and social responsiveness tipped off observers. This design is valuable because it gets around the retrospective bias introduced by asking adults to report on their childhood experiences.

But most people with a vulnerability to schizophrenia don't develop it. Whether someone ends up with the disorder depends, in part, on the impact of events that interfere with normal development. Children of women who had the flu during their second trimester of pregnancy (Brown et al., 2004; Mednick et al., 1988), suffered starvation early in pregnancy (Susser & Lin, 1992), or experienced complications while giving birth (Weinberger, 1987) are at a somewhat heightened risk of schizophrenia. Viral infections in the uterus may also play a key role in triggering certain cases of schizophrenia (Walker & DiForio, 1997). But the great majority of people exposed to infection or trauma before birth never show signs of schizophrenia. So these events probably create problems only for people who are genetically vulnerable to begin with (Cornblatt, Green, & Walker, 1999; Verdoux, 2004).

✔ **Study** and **Review** in **MyPsychLab**

Assess Your Knowledge   FACT or FICTION?

1. Delusions are rare in schizophrenia.   **True / False**
2. Most hallucinations in schizophrenia are visual.   **True / False**
3. Schizophrenogenic mothers often cause schizophrenia.   **True / False**
4. The evidence for the dopamine hypothesis is mostly indirect.   **True / False**
5. There's little support for the genetic transmission of schizophrenia.   **True / False**

Answers: 1. F; 2. F; 3. F; 4. T; 5. F

Childhood Disorders: Recent Controversies

12   Describe the symptoms and debate surrounding disorders diagnosed in childhood.

Although in this chapter we've focused primarily on disorders of adulthood, we'll now close with a few words about childhood disorders, especially those that have been front and center in the public eye. Each of the disorders we'll consider—autism spectrum disorders, attention-deficit/hyperactivity disorder, and early onset bipolar disorder—have garnered their share of controversy in the popular media and the scientific community.

Autistim Spectrum Disorders

One in 88. According to the Centers for Disease Control (CDC, 2013) that's the proportion of individuals with **autism spectrum disorder (ASD)**, a category in DSM-5 that includes Autistic Disorder (better known as autism) and Asperger's Disorder, a less severe form of autism. DSM-5 contends that the symptoms of autism can best be described as on a continuum of severity, rather than in categorical terms, with many children with Asperger's disorder being able to function effectively in a school or occupational setting.

Although the proportion of people with ASD may not seem all that high, it's remarkably high compared with the figure of 1 in 2,000 to 2,500, which researchers had until recently accepted for many years (Wing & Potter, 2002). Across a mere ten-year period—from 1993 to 2003—statistics from the U.S. Department of Education revealed a 657 percent increase in the rates of autism (technically called infantile autism) across the country (see **FIGURE 6**). In Wisconsin, the increase was a staggering 15,117 percent (Rust, 2006). These dramatic upsurges in the prevalence of autism have led many researchers and educators, and even some politicians, to speak of an autism "epidemic" (Kippes & Garrison, 2006). But is the epidemic real?

Individuals with autism are marked by persistent deficits in language, social bonding, and imagination, sometimes accompanied by intellectual impairment (APA, 2013). The DSM-5 breaks down the symptoms of autism spectrum disorders into social impairments and repetitive or restrictive behaviors, which can include repetitive speech or movements, resistance to change, and highly specialized and limited interests and preoccupation with certain foods or unusual objects such as lightbulbs. The

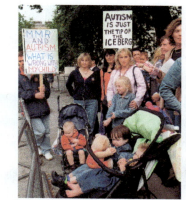

FIGURE 6 The Autism Epidemic in America from 1992 to 2008. The fact that autism diagnoses have been skyrocketing isn't controversial—but the reasons for the increase are.

causes of autism remain mysterious, although twin studies suggest that genetic influences play a prominent role (Hallmayer et al., 2011; Rutter, 2000). The children of both the youngest and oldest parents of twins studied in Sweden were at highest risk of developing ASD, but the genetic mechanisms underlying this association between parental age and ASD remain unknown (Lundström et al., 2010). Still, genetic influences alone can't easily account for an astronomical rise in a disorder's prevalence over the span of a decade. It's therefore not surprising that researchers have looked to environmental variables to explain this bewildering increase. In particular, some investigators have pointed their fingers squarely at one potential culprit: vaccines (Rimland, 2004).

Much of the hype surrounding the vaccine–autism link was fueled by a study of only 12 children in the late 1990s (Wakefield et al., 1998) demonstrating an apparent linkage between autistic symptoms and the MMR vaccine, the vaccine for mumps, measles, and rubella, also known as German measles (the journal *Lancet*, which published the study, officially retracted it in 2010, saying that Wakefield never received ethical clearance for the investigation and that the article contained false claims about participant recruitment). The symptoms of autism usually become most apparent shortly after the age of 2, not long after infants have received MMR and other vaccinations for a host of diseases. Indeed, tens of thousands of parents insist that their children developed autism following the MMR vaccine or following vaccines containing a preservative known as *thimerosol*, which is present in many mercury-bearing vaccines.

Nevertheless, studies in the United States, Europe, and Japan failed to replicate the association between the MMR vaccine and autism, strongly suggesting that the seeming correlation between vaccinations and autism was a mirage (Offit, 2008). The results of several large American, European, and Japanese studies show that even as the rate of MMR vaccinations remained constant or declined, the rate of autism diagnoses continued to soar (Herbert, Sharp, & Gaudiano, 2002; Honda, Shimizu, & Rutter, 2005). Moreover, even after the Danish government stopped administering thimerosol-containing vaccines, the prevalence of autism still skyrocketed (Madsen et al., 2002).

Many parents of children with autism probably fell prey to *illusory correlation*; they'd "seen" a statistical association that didn't exist. Their error was entirely understandable. Given that their children had received vaccines and developed autistic symptoms at around the same time, it was only natural to perceive an association between the two events.

Making matters more complex, recent research calls into question the very existence of the autism epidemic (Grinker, 2007; Wilson, 2005). Most previous investigators had neglected to take into account an alternative explanation—changes in diagnostic practices over time, which have expanded the autism diagnosis to include more mildly affected children, including those with *Asperger's Disorder* (which appears to be a mild form of autism). Evidence suggests that more liberal diagnostic criteria rather than vaccines can account for most, if not all, of the reported autism epidemic (Gernsbacher, Dawson, & Goldsmith, 2005; Lilienfeld & Arkowitz, 2007). In addition, the Americans with Disabilities Act and Individuals with Disabilities Education Act, both passed in the 1990s, indirectly encouraged school districts to classify more children as having autism and other developmental disabilities, as these children could now receive more extensive educational accommodations.

Tens of thousands of parents remain convinced that vaccines trigger autism, despite scientific evidence to the contrary.

◄ REPLICABILITY
Can the results be duplicated in other studies?

 Watch in **MyPsychLab** the **Video:** Speaking Out: Xavier: Autism

◄ RULING OUT RIVAL HYPOTHESES
Have important alternative explanations for the findings been excluded?

Of course, at least a small part of the epidemic might be genuine, and some still unidentified environmental cause could account for the increase. But in evaluating the evidence, we should ask ourselves a critical question. Which is more parsimonious as an explanation of a 657 percent increase within one decade, a vaccine that's yet to be shown to produce any increase in the symptoms of autism or a simple change in diagnostic practices?

Many children have problems concentrating. There can be a fine line between children who have trouble paying attention in class and children who are diagnosed with ADHD.

Factoid

Although attentional problems are a key component of ADHD, many children with the condition can concentrate when sufficiently motivated. Sit with a child with ADHD playing his or her favorite computer game, and you'll probably be impressed with the child's intense concentration. This curious phenomenon occurs because children with ADHD can sometimes "hyperfocus" when something captures their attention; however, they experience difficulty shifting their attention to focus on tasks that *aren't* attention-grabbing, like homework and chores (Barkley, 1997).

Watch in **MyPsychLab** the **Video:**
Attention Deficit Hyperactivity Disorder (ADHD): Dr. Raun Mel

attention-deficit/hyperactivity disorder (ADHD)
childhood condition marked by excessive inattention, impulsivity, and activity

Attention-Deficit/Hyperactivity Disorder and Early-Onset Bipolar Disorder

Even the best-adjusted children often appear overactive, energetic, and restless. But children with **attention-deficit/hyperactivity disorder (ADHD)** often behave like caricatures of the exuberant child. You probably know or have known someone with ADHD: 3–7 percent of school-age children satisfy the diagnostic criteria for the disorder (Barkley, 2006; Bird, 2002). The male-to-female ratio of ADHD ranges from 3.4 to 1 across studies, and between 30 and 80 percent of children with ADHD continue to display ADHD symptoms into adolescence and adulthood (Barkley, 2006; Monastra, 2008). The ADHD diagnosis subsumes two subtypes: (1) with hyperactivity and (2) without hyperactivity, in which inattention is predominant (APA, 2013).

SYMPTOMS OF ADHD. The first signs of ADHD may be evident as early as infancy. Parents often report that children with ADHD are fussy, cry incessantly, and frequently move and shift their position in the crib (Wolke, Rizzo, & Woods, 2002). By 3 years of age, they're constantly walking or climbing and are restless and prone to emotional outbursts. But it's not until elementary school that their behavior patterns are likely to be labeled "hyperactive" and a treatment referral made. Teachers complain that such children won't remain in their seats, follow directions, or pay attention and that they display temper tantrums with little provocation. Such children often struggle with learning disabilities, difficulties with processing verbal information, and poor balance and coordination (Jerome, 2000; Mangeot et al., 2001). By middle childhood, academic problems and disruptive behavior are frequently evident.

A high level of physical activity often diminishes as children with ADHD mature and approach adolescence. Nevertheless, by adolescence, impulsiveness, restlessness, inattention, problems with peers, delinquency, and academic difficulties comprise a patchwork of adjustment problems (Barkley, 2006; Hoza, 2007; Kelly, 2009). Alcohol and substance abuse are frequent (Molina & Pelham, 2003), and many adolescents with ADHD appear in juvenile court as a result of running away from home, skipping school, and stealing (Foley, Carlton, & Howell, 1996). Adults with ADHD are at increased risk for accidents and injuries (Woodward, Fergusson, & Horwood, 2000), divorce (Wymbs et al., 2008), unemployment, and contact with the legal system (Hinshaw, 2002).

ADHD appears to be genetically influenced in many cases, with estimates of its heritability as high as .80 (Swanson & Castellanos, 2002). What may be inherited are abnormalities in genes that influence (a) serotonin, dopamine, and norepinephrine; (b) a smaller brain volume; and (c) decreased activation in the frontal areas of the brain (Monastra, 2008).

People with ADHD can be treated successfully with stimulant medications. Nevertheless, these medications occasionally have serious side effects, making accurate diagnosis a serious public health issue. Yet an accurate diagnosis of ADHD can be dicey. A host of conditions that can cause problems in attention and behavioral control, including traumatic brain injuries, diabetes, thyroid problems, vitamin deficiencies, anxiety, and depression, must first be ruled out (Monastra, 2008). In addition, there's sometimes a fine line between highly energetic children and children with mild ADHD. As a consequence, some scholars have expressed concerns that ADHD is overdiagnosed in some settings (LeFever, Arcona, & Antonuccio, 2003), although others point to evidence that some children with ADHD are actually overlooked by many diagnosticians (Sciutto & Eisenberg, 2007).

THE CONTROVERSY OVER EARLY-ONSET BIPOLAR DISORDER. Perhaps the most controversial diagnostic challenge is distinguishing children with ADHD from children with bipolar disorder (Meyer & Carlson, 2008). The diagnosis of early-onset bipolar disorder was once rare, but ballooned from only.42 percent of cases of outpatient mental health visits in the early 1990s to 6.67 percent of such visits in 2003 (Moreno et al., 2007), raising concerns about its overdiagnosis. Children are particularly likely to receive a diagnosis of early-onset bipolar disorder when they show rapid mood changes, reckless behavior, irritability, and aggression (McClellan, Kowatch, & Findling, 2007). Popular books like *The Bipolar Child* (Papolos & Papolos, 2007), which list these and other symptoms, catch the eye of many parents with troubled children and raise concerns about bipolar disorder. Yet a moment's reflection suggests that many children fit this description, and surely many children with ADHD can be so characterized. Because 60–90 percent of children with bipolar disorder share an ADHD diagnosis, a hypothesis to consider is that many children diagnosed with bipolar disorder are merely those with severe symptoms of ADHD, such as extreme temper outbursts and mood swings (Geller et al., 2002; Kim & Miklowitz, 2002). To address concerns about the overdiagnosis of bipolar disorder in children, DSM-5 developed a new category of *disruptive mood dysregulation disorder* to diagnose children with persistent irritability and frequent behavior outbursts (APA, 2013). Nevertheless, the validity of this condition remains controversial, and some experts have expressed concerns that it may result in labeling children with repeated temper tantrums as pathological (Frances, 2012). A thorough evaluation involving parents, teachers, and mental health professionals is essential to an accurate diagnosis of early-onset bipolar disorder, as well as ADHD.

◀ **RULING OUT RIVAL HYPOTHESES**
Have important alternative explanations for the findings been excluded?

✔ **Study** and **Review** in **MyPsychLab**

Assess Your Knowledge   FACT or FICTION?

1. The rates of diagnosed autism have sharply declined in recent years.   True / False

2. Most cases of autism are caused by vaccines.   True / False

3. More boys than girls are diagnosed with ADHD.   True / False

4. Parents first notice their children's attention problems in elementary school.   True / False

5. Children with bipolar disorder are likely also to be diagnosed with ADHD.   True / False

Answers: 1. F; 2. F; 3. T; 4. F; 5. T

Your Complete Review System

 Study and **Review** in **MyPsychLab**

Conceptions of Mental Illness: Yesterday and Today

1 IDENTIFY CRITERIA FOR DEFINING MENTAL DISORDERS.

The concept of mental disorder is difficult to define. Nevertheless, criteria for mental disorders include statistical rarity, subjective distress, impairment, societal disapproval, and biological dysfunction. Some scholars argue that mental illness is best captured by a family resemblance view.

1. Describe the family resemblance view of mental disorder.

2 DESCRIBE CONCEPTIONS OF DIAGNOSES ACROSS HISTORY AND CULTURES.

The demonic model of mental illness was followed by the medical model of the Renaissance. In the early 1950s, medications to treat schizophrenia led to deinstitutionalization. Some psychological conditions are culture-specific. Still, many mental disorders, such as schizophrenia, can be found in most or all cultures.

2. During the Middle Ages, _____ was often used to treat mental illness.

3. Institutions for the mentally ill created in the fifteenth century were known as _____.

4. In America in the nineteenth century, Dorothea Dix advocated for _____ _____, an approach calling for dignity, kindness, and respect for those with mental illness.

5. In the early 1950s, medications that treated schizophrenia, like chlorpromazine, led to a government policy called _____.

6. Some eating disorders are examples of a(n) _____ disorder specific to Western cultures.

3 IDENTIFY COMMON MISCONCEPTIONS ABOUT PSYCHIATRIC DIAGNOSES, AND THE STRENGTHS AND LIMITATIONS OF THE CURRENT DIAGNOSTIC SYSTEM.

Misconceptions include the ideas that a diagnosis is nothing more than pigeonholing and that diagnoses are unreliable, invalid, and stigmatizing. The *Diagnostic and Statistical Manual of Mental Disorders* (DSM-5) is a valuable tool, but its limitations include high levels of comorbidity and an assumption of a categorical model in the absence of compelling evidence.

7. What misconception regarding psychiatric diagnosis is fueled by high-profile media coverage of "dueling expert witnesses" in criminal trials?

 Listen in **MyPsychLab** to chapter audio

8. _____ refers to the percentage of people in the population with a disorder.

9. The diagnostic criteria used to classify individuals with mental disorders in DSM-5 (are/are not) based completely on scientific evidence.

10. One of the problems with DSM-5 is the high level of _____ among many of its diagnoses.

Anxiety-Related Disorders: The Many Faces of Worry and Fear

4 DESCRIBE THE MANY WAYS PEOPLE EXPERIENCE ANXIETY.

Panic attacks involve intense yet brief rushes of fear that are greatly out of proportion to the actual threat. People with generalized anxiety disorder spend much of their day worrying. In phobias, fears are intense and highly focused. In posttraumatic stress disorder, extremely stressful events produce enduring anxiety. Obsessive-compulsive and related disorders are marked by repetitive and distressing thoughts and behaviors. Learning theory proposes that fears can be learned via classical and operant conditioning and observation. Anxious people tend to catastrophize or exaggerate the likelihood of negative events. Many anxiety disorders are genetically influenced.

11. People with _____ _____ _____ spend an average of 60 percent of each day worrying.

12. People suffer from _____ _____ when they experience panic attacks that are repeated and unexpected and when they change their behavior in an attempt to avoid panic attacks.

13. A(n) _____ is an intense fear of an object or a situation that's greatly out of proportion to its actual threat.

14. What are the symptoms of PTSD? Who is at high risk for developing this disorder?

15. Persistent ideas, thoughts, or impulses that are unwanted and inappropriate and cause distress are called

_____.

16. Repetitive behaviors or mental acts initiated to reduce or prevent stress are called

_____.

17. Name some well-known people who suffer from obsessive-compulsive disorder.

18. People _____ when they predict terrible events, despite the low probability of their actual occurrence.

19. Anxious people tend to interpret ambiguous situations in a (negative/positive) light.

20. Many people with anxiety disorders harbor high levels of _____ _____, a fear of anxiety-related sensations.

Mood Disorders and Suicide

5 IDENTIFY THE CHARACTERISTICS OF DIFFERENT MOOD DISORDERS.

The sad mood of major depression is the mirror image of the expansive mood associated with a manic episode, seen in bipolar disorder. Depression can be recurrent or, more rarely, chronic. Manic episodes are often preceded or followed by bouts of depression. Bipolar disorder is among the most genetically influenced of all mental disorders.

21. The state in which a person experiences a lingering depressed mood or diminished interest in pleasurable activities is called a(n) _____ _____ _____.

22. Over the course of a lifetime, more than _____ percent of us will experience a mood disorder.

6 DESCRIBE MAJOR EXPLANATIONS FOR DEPRESSION AND HOW LIFE EVENTS CAN INTERACT WITH CHARACTERISTICS OF THE INDIVIDUAL TO PRODUCE DEPRESSION SYMPTOMS.

Stressful life events are linked to depression. Depressed people may face social rejection, which can amplify depression. According to Lewinsohn's behavioral model, depression results from a low rate of response-contingent positive reinforcement. Aaron Beck's cognitive model holds that negative schemas play an important role in depression, whereas Martin Seligman's model emphasizes learned helplessness. Genes exert a moderate effect on the risk of developing depression.

23. Describe James Coyne's interpersonal model of depression.

24. Lewinsohn's behavioral model assumes that depression

results from a (low/high) rate of response-contingent positive reinforcement.

25. Aaron Beck's cognitive model focused on three components of depressed thinking: negative views of _____, the _____, and the _____.

26. Identify and describe the theory Martin Seligman proposed based

on his shuttle box research.

Light dims, warning of impending shock

Grid floor—shocks can be administered

Dog will be safe from shock on this side

Bars on this side will be electrified

27. Bipolar disorder is (equally common/more common) in women compared with men.

28. Twin studies suggest that the _____ of bipolar disorder may be as high as 85 percent.

7 IDENTIFY COMMON MYTHS AND MISCONCEPTIONS ABOUT SUICIDE.

Myths about suicide include the misconception that talking to depressed people about suicide makes them more likely to commit the act, suicide is almost always completed with no warning, suicide risk decreases as severe depression lifts, most people who threaten suicide are seeking attention, and people who talk a lot about suicide almost never commit it.

29. _____ _____ and _____ _____ are associated with a higher risk of suicide than are most other disorders.

30. Many or most individuals who commit suicide (communicate/do not communicate) their intent to others.

Personality and Dissociative Disorders: The Disrupted and Divided Self

8 IDENTIFY THE CHARACTERISTICS OF BORDERLINE AND PSYCHOPATHIC PERSONALITY DISORDERS.

Borderline personality disorder is marked by instability in mood, identity, and impulse control. People with psychopathic personality are guiltless, dishonest, callous, and self-centered.

31. Of all psychiatric conditions, personality disorders are historically (least/most) reliably diagnosed.

32. Persons with borderline personality disorder's impulsivity and rapidly fluctuating emotions often have a(n) _____ quality.

33. A diagnosis of _____ personality disorder is characterized by a lengthy history of illegal and irresponsible actions.

34. Most people with psychopathic personalities (are/are not) physically aggressive.

35. From a psychological perspective, what's rare about the case of serial killer Aileen Wuornos?

9 EXPLAIN THE CONTROVERSIES SURROUNDING DISSOCIATIVE DISORDERS, ESPECIALLY DISSOCIATIVE IDENTITY DISORDER.

Dissociative disorders involve disruptions in consciousness, memory, identity, or perception. The role of severe child abuse in DID is controversial. The sociocognitive model holds that social influences, including the media and suggestive procedures in psychotherapy, shape symptoms of DID.

36. In DID, the alternate personality states are often very (similar to/different from) the primary personality.

37. The intriguing differences that researchers have identified among alters in their respiration rates, brain wave activity, eyeglass prescription, handedness, skin conductance responses, voice patterns, and handwriting (do/don't) provide conclusive evidence for the existence of different alters.

38. According to the _____ model, DID arises from a history of severe abuse during childhood.

39. According to the sociocognitive model, how might a therapist contribute to the origin and maintenance of DID, as the artist of this painting claimed?

40. Some psychologists hold that the _____ _____ have played a pivotal role in the DID epidemic.

The Enigma of Schizophrenia

10 RECOGNIZE THE CHARACTERISTIC SYMPTOMS OF SCHIZOPHRENIA.

The symptoms of schizophrenia include delusions, hallucinations, disorganized speech, and grossly disorganized behavior or catatonia.

41. Despite the origin of the term *schizophrenia*, it shouldn't be confused with _____ _____ _____.

42. Strongly held fixed beliefs that have no basis in reality are called _____.

43. _____ symptoms represent serious reality distortions.

44. Most _____ in schizophrenia are auditory, usually consisting of voices.

45. People with schizophrenia can exhibit _____ _____, in which their language becomes severely jumbled and skips from topic to topic in a disjointed way.

46. _____ symptoms involve experiencing motor problems, being extremely resistant to complying with simple suggestions, holding the body in rigid postures, and refusing to speak or move.

11 EXPLAIN HOW PSYCHOSOCIAL, NEURAL, BIOCHEMICAL, AND GENETIC INFLUENCES CREATE THE VULNERABILITY TO SCHIZOPHRENIA.

Scientists have discovered brain abnormalities in patients with schizophrenia. Individuals with schizophrenia are prone to relapse when their relatives display high expressed emotion (criticism, hostility, and overinvolvement).

47. It is widely acknowledged today that parents and family members (cause/don't cause) schizophrenia.

48. Research indicates that one or more of four fluid-filled structures called ventricles, which cushion and nourish the brain, are typically (enlarged/diminished) in individuals with schizophrenia.

49. As illustrated in this figure, the lifetime risk of developing schizophrenia is largely a function of what?

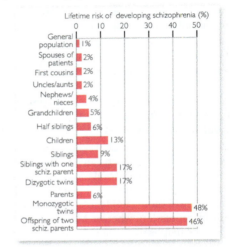

50. A(n) _____ model proposes that schizophrenia, along with many other mental disorders, is a product of genetic vulnerability and stressors that trigger this vulnerability.

Childhood Disorders: Recent Controversies

12 DESCRIBE THE SYMPTOMS AND DEBATE SURROUNDING DISORDERS DIAGNOSED IN CHILDHOOD.

Individuals with Autistic Disorder suffer from severe deficits in language, social bonding, and imagination, usually accompanied by mental retardation. Aspberger's Disorder is a less severe form of autism on the autism spectrum. Children with ADHD experience problems with inattention, impulsivity, and hyperactivity and often struggle with learning disabilities, difficulties processing verbal information, and poor balance and coordination. Some scholars have expressed concerns that ADHD is overdiagnosed in some settings, although others point to evidence that some children with ADHD are actually overlooked by many diagnosticians. One of the most controversial diagnostic challenges is distinguishing children with ADHD from children with bipolar disorder.

Answers are located at the end of the text.

51. Genetic influences alone (can/can't) easily account for an astronomical rise in autism's prevalence over the span of a decade.

52. Research studies have (failed/succeeded) in replicating the association between the MMR vaccine and autism.

53. Many parents of children with Autistic Disorder probably fall prey to _____ _____; they "see" a statistical association that didn't exist.

54. What really accounts for most of the reported autism epidemic, despite many parents' conviction that vaccines trigger the disorder?

55. The diagnosis of ADHD subsumes two subtypes: (1) with _____ and (2) without, in which _____ is predominant.

56. The first signs of hyperactivity may be evident in _____.

57. Although a high level of physical activity often diminishes as children with ADHD mature and approach adolescence, adjustment problems such as _____ and _____ _____ are frequent.

58. ADHD is associated with (increased/decreased) activation in the frontal areas of the brain.

59. List at least three conditions that must be ruled out before an accurate diagnosis of ADHD can be made.

   1. _____

   2. _____

   3. _____

60. Because _____ to _____ percent of children with bipolar disorder share an ADHD diagnosis, a hypothesis to consider is that many children diagnosed with bipolar disorder are merely those with more severe symptoms of ADHD.

Apply Your Scientific Thinking Skills

Use your scientific thinking skills to answer the following questions, referencing specific scientific thinking principles and common errors in reasoning whenever possible.

1. The popular media use many diagnostic labels, such as codependency and sexual or Internet addiction, that have minimal scientific support. Go online or to your local bookstore and locate at least three examples of these labels. How is each disorder or addiction diagnosed? Do the disorders fulfill the criteria for validity outlined by Robins and Guze (refer to Table 2)? Why or why not?

2. As the text notes, the insanity defense is the subject of many popular misconceptions. Locate two popular articles that discuss the use of this defense in a recent legal case. To what extent was the coverage of the insanity defense factually accurate? Did it fall prey to any of the myths described in the chapter? Explain.

3. Locate two or three articles or websites that argue for a connection between childhood vaccinations and the increase in autism rates. What evidence do they provide to support a link between vaccines and autism? Have the sources considered alternative explanations for the increase in autism rates? If so, what explanations did they provide?

Further Your Understanding

EXTEND YOUR KNOWLEDGE WITH THE MYPSYCHLAB VIDEO SERIES

Watch these videos in MyPsychLab. Follow the "Video Series" link.

The Big Picture: What Does It Mean to Have a Mental Disorder? Learn the definition of a mental disorder and the differences between what is considered normal and abnormal behavior.

The Basics: Living with a Disorder Watch an overview of the four important categories of psychological disorders: depression, anxiety, schizophrenia, and autism spectrum disorder.

Special Topics: Diagnosing Mental Disorders See how the DSM's development and refinement has led it to become the most important, if not controversial, guideline for psychologists in diagnosing and treating psychological disorders today.

EXPERIENCE PSYCHOLOGICAL RESEARCH WITH MYPSYCHLAB SIMULATIONS

Access these simulations in MyPsychLab. Follow the "Simulations" link.

Are You Normal? Participate in a survey to see how experiences and traumas affect your view of what's normal.

APPLY YOUR CRITICAL THINKING SKILLS WITH MYPSYCHLAB WRITING ASSESSMENTS

Complete these writing assignments in MyPsychLab.

Why do most researchers consider schizophrenia a brain disorder? What evidence suggests that schizophrenia could begin in the womb?

Answer Key

CONCEPTIONS OF MENTAL ILLNESS: YESTERDAY AND TODAY

1. Brothers and sisters share a family resemblance; they look like each other but don't have any one feature in common. The broad category of "mental disorders" may be similar. Different mental disorders aren't exactly alike, but they share a number of features.
2. exorcism
3. asylums
4. moral treatment
5. deinstitutionalization
6. culture-bound
7. Trials involving dueling expert witnesses may contribute to the erroneous public perception that psychologists can't agree on the diagnoses of individuals with suspected mental disorders.
8. Prevalence
9. are not
10. comorbidity

ANXIETY-RELATED DISORDERS: THE MANY FACES OF WORRY AND FEAR

11. generalized anxiety disorder
12. panic disorder
13. phobia
14. PTSD is marked by emotional disturbance after experiencing or witnessing a severely stressful event. Symptoms include flashbacks to the event; efforts to avoid thoughts, feelings, places, and conversations

associated with the trauma; recurrent dreams of the trauma; and increased arousal reflected in difficulty sleeping and startling easily. Combat veterans and those who have experienced a natural disaster or sexual assault are at high risk.
15. obsessions
16. compulsions
17. Cameron Diaz, Leonardo DiCaprio, Megan Fox, David Beckham
18. catastrophize
19. negative
20. anxiety sensitivity

MOOD DISORDERS AND SUICIDE

21. major depressive episode
22. 20
23. According to this model, depression can trigger rejection from others, in turn contributing to further depression.
24. low
25. oneself; world; future
26. Using the shuttle box, Seligman found that dogs that were first prevented from escaping the shock gave up trying to escape electric shocks even when they were free to do so. He called this phenomenon "learned helplessness" and hypothesized that this might be one way that depression develops in humans.
27. equally common

28. heritability
29. Major depression; bipolar disorder
30. communicate

PERSONALITY AND DISSOCIATIVE DISORDERS: THE DISRUPTED AND DIVIDED SELF

31. least
32. self-destructive
33. antisocial
34. are not
35. She's a woman—individuals with psychopathic personality disorder are usually men.
36. different from
37. don't
38. posttraumatic
39. Mainstream treatment techniques for DID reinforce the idea that the person possesses multiple identities. These techniques include using hypnosis to "bring forth" hidden alters, communicating with alters and giving them different names, and encouraging patients to recover repressed memories supposedly housed in dissociated selves.
40. popular media

THE ENIGMA OF SCHIZOPHRENIA

41. dissociative identity disorder
42. delusions
43. Psychotic
44. hallucinations
45. word salad

46. Catatonic
47. don't cause
48. enlarged
49. It is a function of how closely an individual is genetically related to a person with schizophrenia.
50. diathesis-stress

CHILDHOOD DISORDERS: RECENT CONTROVERSIES

51. can't
52. failed
53. illusory correlation
54. Evidence suggests that more liberal diagnostic criteria rather than vaccines can account for most, if not all, of the reported autism epidemic. In addition, the Americans with Disabilities Act and Individuals with Disabilities Education Act both passed in the 1990s, indirectly encouraging school districts to classify more children as having autism and other developmental disabilities, as these children could now receive more extensive educational accommodations.
55. hyperactivity; inattention
56. infancy
57. alcohol, substance abuse
58. decreased
59. Possible answers: traumatic brain injuries, diabetes, thyroid problems, vitamin deficiencies, anxiety, bipolar disorder, and depression
60. 60, 90

References

Abramowitz, J. S., Taylor, S., & McKay, D. (2009). Obsessive-compulsive disorder. *Lancet, 374,* 491–499.

Abramson, L. Y., Seligman, M. E. P., & Teasdale, J. D. (1978). Learned helplessness in humans: Critique and reformulation. *Journal of Abnormal Psychology, 87,* 49–74.

Acocella, J. (1999). *Creating hysteria: Women and multiple personality disorder.* San Francisco, CA: Jossey-Bass.

Afifi, T. O., Asmundson, G. J., Taylor, S., & Jang, K. L. (2010). The role of genes and environment on trauma exposure and posttraumatic stress disorder symptoms: A review of twin studies. *Clinical Psychology Review, 30*(1), 101–112.

Akiskal, H. S., & McKinney, W. T. (1973). Depressive disorders: Toward a unified hypothesis. *Science, 182,* 20–29.

Alda, M. (1997). Bipolar disorder: From families to genes. *Canadian Journal of Psychiatry, 42,* 378–387.

Allen, J. J. B., & Movius, H. L. (2000). The objective assessment of amnesia in dissociative identity disorder using event-related potentials. *International Journal of Psychophysiology, 38,* 21–41.

American Psychiatric Association. (2000). *Diagnostic and statistical manual of mental disorders: DSM-IV-TR* (4th ed.). Washington, DC: Author.

American Psychiatric Association. (2013). *Diagnostic and statistical manual of mental disorders* (5th ed.). Washington, DC: Author.

Anderson, K. W., Taylor, S., & McLean, P. (1996). Panic disorder associated with blood-injury-reactivity: The necessity of establishing functional relationships among maladaptive behaviors. *Behavior Therapy, 27,* 463–472.

Andreasen, N. C. (1995). The validation of psychiatric-diagnosis: New models and approaches. *American Journal of Psychiatry, 152,* 161–162.

Andreasen, N. C., Rezai, K., Alliger, R., Swayze, V. W. II, Flaum, M., Kirchner, P.,... O'Leary D. S., (1992). Hypofrontality in neuroleptic-naive patients and in patients with chronic schizophrenia: Assessment with xenon 133 single-photon emission computed tomography and the Tower of London. *Archives of General Psychiatry, 49,* 943–958.

Andrews, G., Hobbs, M. J., Borkovec, T. D., Beesdo, K., Craske, M. G., Heimberg, R. G.,... Stanley, M. A. (2010). Generalized worry disorder: A review of DSM-IV generalized anxiety disorder and options for DSM-V. *Depression and Anxiety, 27*(2), 134–147.

Andrews-McClymont, J., Lilienfeld, S. O., & Duke, M. P. (in press). Evaluating an animal model of compulsive hoarding in humans. *Review of General Psychology.*

Angold, A. (1999). Comorbidity. *Journal of Child Psychology and Psychiatry, 40,* 57–87.

Angst, J., Cui, L., Swendsen, J. J., Rothen, S., Cravchik, A., Kessler, R., & Merikangas, K. (2010). Major depressive disorder with sub-threshold bipolarity in the National Comorbidity Survey Replication. *The American Journal of Psychiatry, 167*(10), 1194.

Appelbaum, P. S. (1997). Almost a revolution: An international perspective on the law of involuntary commitment. *Journal of the American Academy of Psychiatry and Law, 25,* 135–147.

Arieti, S. (1959). Manic-depressive psychosis. In S. Arieti (Ed.), *American handbook of psychiatry* (pp. 439–444). New York, NY: Basic Books.

Arkowitz, H., & Lilienfeld, S. O. (2007). A pill to fix your ills? *Scientific American Mind, 18,* 80–81.

Arnold, L. M. (1999). A case series of women with postpartum-onset obsessive-compulsive disorder. *Primary Care Companion Journal of Clinical Psychiatry, 1,* 103–108.

Arrigo, B., & Griffin, A. (2004). Serial murder and the case of Aileen Wuornos: Attachment theory, psychopathy, and predatory aggression. *Behavioral Sciences and the Law, 22,* 375–393.

Babiak, P., & Hare, R. D. (2006). *Snakes in suits: When psychopaths go to work.* New York, NY: Regan Books.

Bahnson, C. B., & Smith, K. (1975). Autonomic changes in a multiple personality. *Psychosomatic Medicine, 37,* 85–86.

Barkley, R. A. (1997). *ADHD and the nature of self-control.* New York, NY: Guilford Press.

Barkley, R. A. (2006). *Attention-deficit-hyperactivity disorder: A handbook for diagnosis and treatment*. New York, NY: Guilford Press.

Barlow, D. H. (2000). Unraveling the mysteries of anxiety and its disorders from the perspective of emotion theory. *American Psychologist, 55*, 1247–1263.

Barlow, D. H. (2002). *Anxiety and its disorders: The nature and treatment of anxiety and panic*. New York, NY: Guilford Press.

Barlow, D. H., Chorpita, B. F., & Turovsky, J. (1996). Fear, panic, anxiety, and disorders of emotion. In D. A. Hope (Ed.), *Perspectives on anxiety, panic, and fear* (The 43rd Annual Nebraska Symposium on Motivation) (pp. 251–328). Lincoln, NB: University of Nebraska Press.

Barta, P. E., Pearlson, G. D., Powers, R. E., Richards, S. S., & Tune, L. E. (1990). Auditory hallucinations and smaller superior temporal gyral volume in schizophrenia. *American Journal of Psychiatry, 147*, 1457–1462.

Bartholomew, R. E. (1994). The social psychology of "epidemic" koro. *International Journal of Social Psychiatry, 40*, 46–60.

Baum, A., Cohen, L., & Hall, M. (1993). Control and intrusive memories as possible determinants of chronic stress. *Psychosomatic Medicine, 55*, 274–286.

Bayer, R. (1981). *Homosexuality and American psychiatry: The politics of diagnosis*. Princeton, NJ: Princeton University Press.

Beck, A. T., (1964). Thinking and depression: 2. Theory and therapy. *Archives of General Psychiatry, 10*, 561–571.

Beck, A. T. (1967). *Depression: Clinical, experimental, and theoretical aspects* (Vol. 32). Philadelphia, PA: University of Pennsylvania Press.

Beck, A. T. (1976). *Cognitive therapy and the emotional disorders*. New York, NY: International Universities Press.

Beck, A. T. (1983). Treatment of depression. *New York Times Book Review, 88*(10), 35.

Beck, A. T., Brown, G., Berchick, R. J., Stewart, B. L., & Steer, R. A. (1990). Relationship between hopelessness and ultimate suicide: A replication with psychiatric outpatients. *American Journal of Psychiatry, 147*, 190–195.

Beck, J. S. (1995). *Cognitive therapy: Basics and beyond*. New York, NY: Guilford Press.

Belli, R. F., Winkielman, P., Read, J. D., Schwarz, N., & Lynn, S. J. (1998). Recalling more childhood events leads to judgments of poorer memory: Implications for the recovered/false memory debate. *Psychonomic Bulletin & Review, 5*, 318–323.

Bentall, R. P. (2000). Hallucinatory experiences. In E. Cardeña, S. J. Lynn, & S. Krippner (Eds.), *Varieties of anomalous experience: Examining the scientific evidence* (pp. 85–120). Washington, DC: American Psychological Association.

Bergner, R. M. (1997). What is psychopathology? And so what? *Clinical Psychology: Science and Practice, 4*, 235–248.

Bird, H. R. (2002). The diagnostic classification, epidemiology, and cross-cultural validity of ADHD. In P. S. Jensen & J. R. Cooper (Eds.) *Attention Deficit Hyperactivity Disorder: State of the science, best practices* (pp. 212–216). Kingston, NJ: Civil Research Institute.

Blanchette, I., & Richards, A. (2003). Anxiety and the interpretation of ambiguous stimuli: Beyond the emotion-congruent effect. *Journal of Experimental Psychology: General, 13*, 294–309.

Blaney, P. H. (1975). Implications of the medical model and its alternatives. *American Journal of Psychiatry, 132*, 911–914.

Blashfield, R. K., & Intoccia, V. (2000). Growth of the literature on the topic of personality disorders. *American Journal of Psychiatry, 157*(3), 472–473.

Blatt, S. J. (1974). Levels of object representation in anaclitic and introjective depression. *Psychoanalytic Studies of the Child, 29*, 107–157.

Boos, H. B. M., Aleman, A., Pol, H. H., Cahn, W., & Kahn, R. (2007). Brain volumes in relatives of patients with schizophrenia: A meta-analysis. *Schizophrenia Bulletin, 33*, 329.

Brende, J. O. (1984). The psychophysiologic manifestations of dissociation: Electrodermal responses in a multiple personality patient. *Psychiatry Clinics of North America, 7*, 41–50.

Brody, J. (2007, April 17). When a brain forgets where memory is. *New York Times*. Retrieved from http://www.nytimes.com/2007/04/17/health/psychology/17brody.html

Brown, A. S., Begg, M. D., Gravenstein, S., Schaefer, C. A., Wyatt, W. J., Bresnahan, M.,... Susser, E. S. (2004). Serologic evidence for prenatal influenza in the etiology of schizophrenia. *Archives of General Psychiatry, 61*, 774–780.

Brown, G. W., Monck, E. M., Carstairs, G. M., & Wing, J. K. (1962). Influence of family life on the course of schizophrenic illness. *British Journal of Preventive and Social Medicine, 16*, 55–68.

Brugha, T. S. (Ed.). (1995). *Social support and psychiatric disorder research findings and guidelines for clinical practice*. Cambridge, England: Cambridge University Press.

Burns, A. B., Brown, J. S., Plant, A., Sachs-Ericsson, N., & Joiner, T. E. (2006). On the specific depressotypic nature of excessive reassurance-seeking. *Personality and Individual Differences, 40*, 135–145.

Busatto, G. F., Pilowsky, L. S., Costa, D. C., Ell, P. J., Lingford-Hughes, A., & Kerwin, R. W. (1995). In vivo imaging of GABAA receptors using sequential whole-volume iodine-123 iomazenil single-photon emission tomography. *European Journal of Nuclear Medicine, 22*, 1–26.

Butler, B. (2006). NGRI revisited: Venirepersons' attitudes toward the insanity defense. *Journal of Applied Social Psychology, 36*, 1833–1847.

Butzlaff, R. L., & Hooley, J. M. (1998). Expressed emotion and psychiatric relapse: A meta-analysis. *Archives of General Psychiatry, 55*, 547–552.

Caldwell, M. F. (2011). Treatment-related changes in behavioral outcomes of psychopathy facets in adolescent offenders. *Law and Human Behavior, 35*(4), 275–287.

Cannon, T. D., Mednick, S. A., & Parnas, J. (1989). Genetic and perinatal determinants of structural brain deficits in schizophrenia. *Archives of General Psychiatry, 46*, 883–889.

Carlsson, A. (1995). Towards a new understanding of dopamine receptors. Symposium: Dopamine receptor subtypes in neurological and psychiatric diseases. *Clinical Neuropharmacology, 18*(Suppl.), 65–135.

Carpenter, R. W., Tomko, R. L., Trull, T. J., & Boomsma, D. I. (2013). Gene-environment studies and borderline personality disorder: A review. *Current Psychiatry Reports, 15*(1), 1–7.

Cartwright, S. A. (1851, May). Report on the diseases and physical peculiarities of the Negro race. *The New Orleans Medical and Surgical Journal*, 691–715.

Caspi, A., Sugden, K., Moffitt, T. E., Taylor, A., Craig, I., Harrington, H. L.,... Poulton, R. (2003). Influence of life stress on depression: Moderation by a polymorphism in the 5-HTT gene. *Science, 301*, 386–389.

Cechnicki, A., Bielańska, A., Hanuszkiewicz, I., & Daren, A. (2012). The predictive validity of Expressed Emotions (EE) in schizophrenia. A 20-year prospective study. *Journal of Psychiatric Research, 47*(2), 208–214.

Centers for Disease Control and Prevention (2013). Autism spectrum disorders: Data & Statistics. Retrieved from http://www.cdc.gov/ncbddd/autism/data.html

Chang, K., Adleman, N. E., Dienes, K., Simeonova, D. I., Menon, V., & Reiss, A. (2004). Anomalous prefrontal-subcortical activation in familial pediatric bipolar disorder—A functional magnetic resonance imaging investigation. *Archives of General Psychiatry, 61*, 781–792.

Chapman, L. J., Chapman J. P., & Raulin M. L. (1978). Body-image aberration in schizophrenia. *Journal of Abnormal Psychology, 87*, 399–407.

Chentsova-Dutton, Y. E., & Tsai, J. L. (2007). Cultural factors influence the expression of psychopathology. In S. O. Lilienfeld & W. O'Donohue (Eds.), *The great ideas of clinical science: 17 principles that every mental health professional should understand* (pp. 375–396). New York, NY: Brunner-Taylor.

Chodoff, P. (1976). The case for involuntary hospitalization of the mentally ill. *American Journal of Psychiatry, 133*, 396–501.

Cima, M., Tonnaer, F., & Hauser, M. D. (2010). Psychopaths know right from wrong but don't care. *Social Cognitive and Affective Neuroscience, 5*(1), 59–67. http://dx.doi.org/10.1093/scan/nsp051

Clark, D. M. (1986). A cognitive approach to panic. *Behaviour Research and Therapy, 24*, 156–163.

Cleckley, H. (1941/1988). *The mask of sanity*. St. Louis, MO: Mosby.

Compton, M. T., Kelley, M. E., Ramsay, C. E., Pringle, M., Goulding, S. M., Esterberg, M. L.,... Walker, E. F. (2009). Association of pre-onset cannabis, alcohol, and tobacco use with age at onset of prodrome and age at onset of psychosis in first-episode patients. *American Journal of Psychiatry, 166*, 1251–1257.

Coons, P. M., Bowman, E. S., & Milstein, V. (1988). Multiple personality disorder: A clinical investigation of 50 cases. *Journal of Nervous and Mental Disease, 176*, 519–527.

Cornblatt, B. A., Green, M. F., & Walker, E. F. (1999). Schizophrenia: Etiology and neurocognition. In T. Millon, P. H. Blaney, & R. D. Davis (Eds.), *Oxford textbook of psychopathology* (pp. 227–310). New York, NY: Oxford University Press.

Cornblatt, B. A., & Keilp, J. G. (1994). Impaired attention, genetics, and the pathophysiology of schizophrenia. *Schizophrenia Bulletin, 20*, 31–46.

Coryell, W., Scheftner, W., Keller, M., Endicott, J., Maser, J., & Klerman, G. L. (1993). The enduring psychosocial consequences of mania and depression. *American Journal of Psychiatry, 150*, 720–727.

Coryell, W., Solomon, S., Leon, A., Fiedorowicz, J. G., Schettler, P., Judd, L., & Keller, M. (2009). Does major depressive disorder change with age? *Psychological Medicine, 39*, 1689–1695.

Cox, B. J., & Taylor, S. (1998). Anxiety disorders: Panic and phobias. In T. Millon, P. H. Blaney, & R. D. Davis (Eds.), *Oxford textbook of psychopathology* (pp. 81–113). New York, NY: Oxford University Press.

Coyne, J. C. (1976). Depression and the response of others. *Journal of Abnormal Psychology, 85*, 186–193.

Craddock, N., O'Donovan, M. C., & Owen, M. J. (2005). The genetics of schizophrenia and bipolar disorder: Dissecting psychosis. *Journal of Medical Genetics, 42*(3), 193–204.

Cramer, A. O., Waldorp, L. J., van der Maas, H. L., & Borsboom, D. (2010). Comorbidity: A network perspective. *Behavioral and Brain Sciences, 33*(2-3), 137–150.

Craske, M. G., Kircanski, K., Epstein, A., Wittchen, H. U., Pine, D. S., Lewis-Fernández, R., & Hinton, D. (2010). Panic disorder: A review of DSM-IV panic disorder and proposals for DSM-V. *Depression and Anxiety, 27*(2), 93–112.

Craske, M. G., Rapee, R. M., Jackel, L., & Barlow, D. H. (1989). Qualitative dimensions of worry in DSM-III-R generalized anxiety disorder subjects and non-anxious controls. *Behaviour Research and Therapy, 27*, 397–402.

Crowell, S. E., Beauchaine, T. P., & Linehan, M. M. (2009). A biosocial developmental model of borderline personality disorder: Elaborating and extending Linehan's theory. *Psychological Bulletin, 135*, 495–510.

Crozier, I. (2012). Making up koro: Multiplicity, psychiatry, culture, and penis-shrinking anxieties. *Journal of the History of Medicine and Allied Sciences, 67*(1), 36–70.

Daftary-Kapur, T., Groscup, J. L., O'Connor, M., Coffaro, F., & Galietta, M. (2011). Measuring knowledge of the insanity defense: Scale construction and validation. *Behavioral Sciences & the Law, 29*(1), 40–63.

Dalenberg, C. J., Brand, B. L., Gleaves, D. H., Dorahy, M. J., Loewenstein, R. J., Cardeña, E.,... Spiegel, D. (2012). Evaluation of the evidence for the trauma and fantasy models of dissociation. *Psychological Bulletin, 138*(3), 550–588.

Davies, G., Welham, J., Chant, D., Torrey, E. F., & McGrath, J. (2003). A systematic review and meta-analysis of northern hemisphere season of birth in schizophrenia. *Schizophrenia Research, 29,* 587–593.

Davis, K. L., Kahn, R. S., Ko, G., & Davidson, M. (1991). Dopamine in schizophrenia: Review and reconceptualization. *American Journal of Psychiatry, 148,* 1474–1486.

Degenhardt, L., & Hall, W. (2006). Is cannabis a contributory cause of psychosis? *Canadian Journal of Psychiatry, 51,* 556–565.

Degenhardt, L., Hall, W. D., Lynskey, M., McGrath, J. M., McLaren, J., Calabria, B., ... Vos, T. (2009). Should burden of disease estimates include cannabis use as a risk factor for psychosis? *PLoS Medicine, 6*(9).

Depue, R. A., & Iacono, W. G. (1989). Neurobehavioral aspects of affective disorders. *Annual Review of Psychology, 40,* 457–492.

Derr, M. (2010, January 18). Study finds a shared gene in dogs with compulsive behavior. *New York Times.* Retrieved from http://www.nytimes.com/2010/01/19/science/19dogs.html

Dickey, M. (1994). *Anxiety disorders.* National Institute of Mental Health. Washington, DC: U.S. Government Printing Office.

Dimidjian, S., Hollon, S. D., Dobson, K. S., Schmaling, K. B., Kohlenberg, R. J., Addis, M. E.,... Jacobson, N. S. (2006). Randomized trial of behavioral activation, cognitive therapy and antidepressant medication in the acute treatment of adults with mild depression. *Journal of Consulting and Clinical Psychology, 74*(4), 658–670.

Disner, S. G., Beevers, C. G., Haigh, E. A., & Beck, A. T. (2011). Neural mechanisms of the cognitive model of depression. *Nature Reviews Neuroscience, 12*(8), 467–477.

Dolan, A. (2006). *The obsessive disorder that haunts my life.* Mail Online. Retrieved from http://www.dailymail.co.uk/tvshowbiz/article-381802/The-obsessive-disorder-haunts-life.html

Dolnick, E. (1998). *Madness on the couch: Blaming the victim in the heyday of psychoanalysis.* New York, NY: Simon & Schuster.

Douglas, K. S., Guy, L. S., & Hart, S. D. (2009). Psychosis as a risk factor for violence to others: A meta-analysis. *Psychological Bulletin, 135,* 679–706.

Dutton, K. (2012). *The wisdom of psychopaths: What saints, spies, and serial killers can teach us about success.* New York, NY: Scientific American /Farrar, Straus and Giroux.

Ellis, A. (1962). *Reason and emotion in psychotherapy.* New York, NY: Lyle Stuart.

Ellis, A., & Dryden, W. (1997). *The practice of rational-emotive behavior therapy.* New York, NY: Springer.

Elzinga, B. M., de Beurs, E., Sergeant, J. A., Van Dyck, R., & Phaf, R. H. (2000). Dissociative style and directed forgetting. *Cognitive Therapy and Research, 24,* 279–295.

Elzinga, B. M., van Dyck, R., & Spinhoven, P. (1998). Three controversies about dissociative identity disorder. *Clinical Psychology and Psychotherapy, 5,* 13–23.

Fawcett, J. (1997). The detection and consequences of anxiety in clinical depression. *Journal of Clinical Psychiatry, 58,* 35–40.

Feldman, E. (1991). Identifying the genes for diabetes and schizophrenia. *British Medical Journal, 303*(6794), 124.

Fincham, F. D., Diener, C. I., & Hokoda, A. (2011). Attributional style and learned helplessness: Relationship to the use of causal schemata and depressive symptoms in children. *British Journal of Social Psychology, 26*(1), 1–7.

Finn, S. E., & Kamphuis, J. H. (1995). What a clinician needs to know about base rates. In J. N. Butcher (Ed.), *Clinical personality assessment: Practical approaches* (pp. 224–235). New York, NY: Oxford University Press.

First, M. B. (2004) Desire for amputation of a limb: Paraphilia, psychosis, or a new type of identity disorder. *Psychological Medicine, 35,* 919–928.

Fisher, L., Marikar, S., & Shaw, A. (2013). Leana Dunham and 9 more stars with OCD. ABC News. Retrieved from http://abcnews.go.com/Entertainment/lena-dunham-stars-obsessive-compulsive-disorder/story?id=18513623#3

Foa, E. B., & Kozak, M. J. (1986). Emotional processing of fear: Exposure to corrective information. *Psychological Bulletin, 99,* 20–35.

Foa, E. B., & Rothbaum, B. O. (1998). *Treating the trauma of rape: Cognitive behavioral therapy for PTSD.* New York, NY: Guilford Press.

Foley, H. A., Carlton, C. O., & Howell, R. J. (1996). The relationship of attention deficit hyperactivity disorder and conduct disorder to juvenile delinquency: Legal implications. *Bulletin of the American Academy of Psychiatry and the Law, 24,* 333–345.

Folsom, D., & Jeste, D. V. (2008). Schizophrenia in homeless persons: A systematic review of the literature. *Acta Psychiatrica Scandinavica, 105*(6), 404–413.

Forbes, E. E., Shaw, D. S., & Dahl, R. E. (2007). Alterations in reward-related decision making in boys with recent and future depression. *Biological Psychiatry, 61,* 633–639.

Fowler, K. A., O'Donohue, W. T., & Lilienfeld, S. O. (2007). Personality disorders in perspective. In W. T. O'Donohue, K. A. Fowler, & S. O. Lilienfeld (Eds.), *Personality disorders: Toward the DSM-V* (pp. 1–19). Los Angeles, CA: Sage.

Fowles, D. C., & Dindo, L. (2009). Temperament and psychopathy: A dual-pathway model. *Current Directions in Psychological Science, 18,* 179–183.

Frances, A. (2012, December 03). DSM-5 is a guide, not a bible: Simply ignore its 10 worst changes. *Huffington Post.* Retrieved from http://www.huffingtonpost.com/allen-frances/dsm-5_b_2227626.html

Frances, A. J., & Widiger, T. (2012). Psychiatric diagnosis: Lessons from the DSM-IV past and cautions for the DSM-5 future. *Annual Review of Clinical Psychology, 8,* 109–130.

Franklin, M. E., & Foa, E. B. (2008). Obsessive compulsive disorder. In D. Barlow (Ed.), *Clinical handbook of psychological disorders: A step-by-step treatment manual* (pp. 164–215). New York, NY: Guilford Press.

Freedman, R., Lewis, D. A., Michels, R., Pine, D. S., Schultz, S. K., Tamminga, C. A.,... Yager, J. (2013). The initial field trials of DSM-5: New blooms and old thorns. *American Journal of Psychiatry, 170*(1), 1–5.

Freud, S. (1917/1953). "Mourning and Melancholia" in *The Standard Edition of the Complete Psychological Works of Sigmund Freud* (Vol. 14, pp. 239–258). (J. Strachey, Trans. and Ed.). London, England: Hogarth Press.

Friedman, R. A. (2006). Mental illness and violence: How strong is the link? *New England Journal of Medicine, 355,* 2064–2066.

Frisher M., Crome, I., Martino, O., & Croft, P. (2009). Assessing the impact of cannabis use on trends in diagnosed schizophrenia in the United Kingdom from 1996 to 2005. *Schizophrenia Research, 113,* 123–128.

Frith, C. D. (1992). *The cognitive neuropsychology of schizophrenia.* Hillsdale, NJ: Erlbaum.

Frost, R., Steketee, G., Tolin, D., & Brown, T. (2006). Diagnostic issues in compulsive hoarding. Paris: Paper presented at the European Association of Behavioural and Cognitive Therapies.

Frost, R. O., & Gross, R.C. (1993). The hoarding of possessions. *Behavioural Research and Therapy, 31*(4), 367–381.

Fullana, M. A., Mataix-Cols, D., Caspi, A., Harrington, H., Grisham, J. R., Moffitt, T. E., & Poulton, R. (2009). Obsessions and compulsions in the community: Prevalence, interference, help seeking, developmental stability, and co-occurring psychiatric conditions. *The American Journal of Psychiatry, 166,* 329–336.

Fuller, R. L., Luck, S. J., Braun, E. L., Robinson, B. M., McMahon, R. P., & Gold, J. M. (2006). Impaired control of visual attention in schizophrenia. *Journal of Abnormal Psychology, 115,* 266–275.

Garb, H. N. (1998). *Studying the clinician: Judgment, research, and psychological assessment.* Washington, DC: American Psychological Association.

Gause, C., Morris, C., Vernekar, S., Pardo-Villamizar, C., Grados, M. A., & Singer, H. S. (2009). Antineuronal antibodies in OCD: Comparisons in children with OCD-only, OCD+chronic tics and OCD+PANDAS. *Journal of Neuroimmunology, 214,* 118–124.

Geller, B., Zimmerman, B., Williams, M., DelBello, M. P., Bolhofner, K., Craney, J. L.,... Nickelsburg, M. J. (2002). DSM-IV mania symptoms in a prepubertal and early adolescent bipolar disorder phenotype compared to attention deficit hyperactive and normal controls. *Journal of the American Academy of Child and Adolescent Psychopharmacology, 12,* 11–25.

Gernsbacher, M. A., Dawson, M., & Goldsmith, H. H. (2005). Three reasons not to believe in an autism epidemic. *Current Directions in Psychological Science, 14,* 55–58.

Gibb, B. E., & Alloy, L. B. (2006). A prospective test of the hopelessness theory of depression in children. *Journal of Clinical Child and Adolescent Psychology, 35,* 264–274.

Giesbrecht, T., Lynn, S. J., Lilienfeld, S. O., & Merckelbach, H. (2008). Cognitive processes in dissociation: An analysis of core theoretical assumptions. *Psychological Bulletin, 134,* 617–647.

Gleaves, D. H. (1996). The sociocognitive model of dissociative identity disorder: A reexamination of the evidence. *Psychological Bulletin, 120,* 42–59.

Gleaves, D. H., May, M. C., & Cardeña, E. (2001). An examination of the diagnostic validity of dissociative identity disorder. *Clinical Psychology Review, 21,* 577–608.

Goldenberg, J. N., Brown, S. B., & Weiner, W. J. (2004). Coprolalia in younger patients with Gilles de la Tourette syndrome. *Movement Disorders, 9,* 622–625.

Goldston, D. B., Daniel, S. S., Reboussin, B., Reboussin, D., Frazier, P. H., & Harris, A. (2001). Cognitive risk factors and suicide attempts among formerly hospitalized adolescents: A prospective naturalistic study. *Journal of the American Academy of Child and Adolescent Psychiatry, 40,* 155–162.

Golin, S., Terrell, T., & Johnson, B. (1977). Depression and the illusion of control. *Journal of Abnormal Psychology, 86,* 440–442.

Goodwin, F. K., & Jamison K. R. (1990), *Manic-depressive illness.* New York, NY: Oxford University Press.

Gorenstein, E. E. (1984). Debating mental illness: Implications for science, medicine, and social policy. *American Psychologist, 39,* 50–56.

Gottesman, I. I. (1991). *Schizophrenia genesis: The origins of madness.* New York, NY: W. H. Freeman.

Gottesman, I. I., & Shields, J. (1972). *Schizophrenia and genetics: A twin study vantage point.* New York, NY: Academic Press.

Grace, A. A. (1991). The cortical regulation of dopamine system responsivity—A hypothesis regarding its role in the etiology of schizophrenia. *Schizophrenia Research, 4,* 345.

Granello, D. H., & Beamish, P. M. (1998). Reconceptualizing codependency in women: A sense of connectedness, not pathology. *Journal of Mental Health Counseling, 20,* 344–358.

Grant, B. F., Hansin, D. S., Stinson, F. S., Dawson D. A., June Ruan, W., Goldstein, R. B.,... Huang, B. (2005). Prevalence, correlates, co-morbidity, and comparative disability of DSM-IV generalized anxiety disorder in the USA: Results from the National Epidemiologic Survey on alcohol and related conditions. *Psychological Medicine, 35,* 1747–1759.

Grinker, R. R. (2007). *Unstrange minds: Remapping the world of autism.* New York, NY: Basic Books.

Grinker, R. R., & Werble, B. (1977). *The borderline patient.* New York, NY: Jason Aronson.

Grinnell, R. (2008). Word salad. In J. M. Grohol, *Encyclopedia of psychology.* Retrieved from http://psychcentral.com/encyclopedia

Grisso, T. (2003). *Evaluating competencies: Forensic assessments and instruments* (2nd ed). New York, NY: Kluwer.

Grob, G. N. (1997). Deinstitutionalization: The illusion of policy. *Journal of Policy History, 9*, 48–73.

Gunderson, J. G., Stout, R. L., McGlashan, T. H., Shea, M. T., Morey, L. C., Grilo, C. M.,... Skodol, A. E. (2011). Ten-year course of borderline personality disorder: Psychopathology and function from the Collaborative Longitudinal Personality Disorders Study. *Archives of General Psychiatry, 68*(8), 827–837.

Gusow, W. (1963). A preliminary report of kayak-angst among the Eskimo of West Greenland: A study in sensory deprivation. *International Journal of Social Psychiatry, 9*, 18–26.

Haack, L. J., Metalsky, G. I., Dykman, B. M., & Abramson, L. Y. (1996). Use of current situational information and causal inference: Do dysphoric individuals make "unwarranted" causal inferences? *Cognitive Therapy and Research, 20*, 309–331.

Haaga, D. A., Dyck, M. J., & Ernst, D. (1991). Empirical status of cognitive theory of depression. *Psychological Bulletin, 110*, 215–236.

Hall, J. R., & Benning, S. D. (2006). The "successful" psychopath: Adaptive and subclinical manifestations of psychopathy in the general population. In C. J. Patrick (Ed.), *Handbook of psychopathy* (pp. 459–478). New York, NY: Guilford Press.

Halweg, K., Goldstein, M. J., Nuechterlein, K. H., Magaña, A. B., Mintz, J., Doane, J. A.,... Snyder, K. S. (1989). Expressed emotion and patient-relative interaction in families of recent onset schizophrenics. *Journal of Consulting and Clinical Psychology, 57*, 11–18.

Hames, J. L., Hagan, C. R., & Joiner, T. E. (2013). Interpersonal processes in depression. *Annual Review of Clinical Psychology, 9*(1).

Hammen, C. (1991). Generation of stress in the course of unipolar depression. *Journal of Abnormal Psychology, 100*, 555–561.

Hanson, D. R., & Gottesman, I. I. (2005). Theories of schizophrenia: A genetic-inflammatory-vascular synthesis. *Biomed Central Medical Genetics, 6*, 7. http://dx.doi.org/10.1186/1471-2350-6-7

Hare, E. H. (1962). Masturbatory insanity: The history of an idea. *Journal of Mental Science, 108*, 2–25.

Hare, R. D. (1978). Electrodermal and cardiovascular correlates of psychopathy. In R. D. Hare & D. Schalling (Eds.), *Psychopathic behavior: Approaches to research* (pp. 107–144). Chichester, England: Wiley.

Hare, R. D. (1993). *Without conscience: The disturbing world of the psychopaths among us.* New York, NY: Simon & Schuster.

Hare, R. D. (2003). *The Hare Psychopathy Checklist—Revised.* Toronto, Ontario, Canada: Multi-Health Systems.

Hariri, A. R., Mattay, V. S., Tessitore, A., Kolachana, B., Fera, F., Goldman, D.,... Weinberger, D. R. (2002). Serotonin transporter genetic variation and the response of the human amygdala. *Science, 297*, 400–403.

Harkness, A. R. (2007). Personality traits are essential for a complete clinical science. In S. O. Lilienfeld and W. O'Donohue (Eds.), *The great ideas of clinical science: 17 concepts that every mental health professional should understand* (pp. 263–290). New York, NY: Routledge.

Harkness, A. R., & Lilienfeld, S. O. (1997). Individual differences science for treatment planning: Personality traits. *Psychological Assessment, 9*, 349–360. http://dx.doi.org/10.1037/1040-3590.9.4.349

Harkness, K. L., & Luther, J. (2001). Clinical risk factors for the generation of life events in major depression. *Journal of Abnormal Psychology, 110*, 564–572.

Harrington, P. (2005, December). Exorcisms rise in Mexico, keeping Father Mendoza, healers busy. *Bloomberg News.* Retrieved from http://www.banderasnews.com/0512/nr-mexorcisms.htm

Harris, E. C., & Barraclough, B. (1997). Suicide as an outcome for mental disorders—A meta-analysis. *British Journal of Psychiatry, 170*, 205–228.

Harrow, M., Grossman, L. S., Jobe, T. H., & Herbener, E. S. (2005) Do patients with schizophrenia ever show periods of recovery? A 15-year multi-follow-up study. *Schizophrenia Bulletin, 31*, 723–734.

Harvey, J. H., & Weary, G. (1984). Current issues in attribution theory and research. *Annual Review of Psychology, 35*, 427–460.

Harvey, P. D., Reichenberg, A., & Bowie, C. R. (2006). Cognition and aging in psychopathology: Focus on schizophrenia and depression. In S. Nolen-Hoeksema, T. D. Cannon, & T. Widiger (Eds.), *Annual Review of Clinical Psychology* (Vol. 2, pp. 389–409). Palo Alto, CA: Annual Reviews.

Haslam, N., Holland, E., & Kuppens, P. (2012). Categories versus dimensions in personality and psychopathology: A quantitative review of taxometric research. *Psychological Medicine, 1*(1), 1–18.

Hazlett-Stevens, H., Pruitt, L. D., & Collins, A. (2008). Phenomenology of generalized anxiety disorder. In M. M. Anthony & M. B. Stein (Eds.), *Oxford handbook of anxiety and related disorders* (pp. 47–64). New York, NY: Oxford University Press.

Heimberg, R. G., & Juster, H. R. (1995). Cognitive-behavioral treatments: Literature review. In R. G. Heimberg, M. R. Liebowitz, D. A. Hope, & F. R. Schneier (Eds.), *Social phobia: Diagnosis, assessment, and treatment.* New York, NY: Guilford Press.

Hempel, A., Hempel, E., Schänknecht, P., Stippich, C., & Schräder, J. (2003). Impairment in basal limbic function in schizophrenia during affect recognition. *Psychiatry Research, 122*, 115–124.

Herbert, J. D., Sharp, I. R., & Gaudiano, B. A. (2002). Separating fact from fiction in the etiology and treatment of autism: A scientific review of the evidence. *Scientific Review of Mental Health Practice, 1*, 25–45.

Heron, M. (2012). Deaths: Leading causes for 2008. *National vital statistics reports: From the Centers for Disease Control and Prevention, National Center for Health Statistics, National Vital Statistics System, 60*(6), 1.

Hinshaw, S. P. (2002). Is ADHD an impairing condition in childhood and adolescence? In P. S. Jensen & J. R. Cooper (Eds.), *Attention deficit hyperactivity disorder: State of the science • Best practices* (pp. 515–521). Kingston, NJ: Civic Research Institute.

Hollander, E., Zohar, J., Sirovatka, M. S., & Regier, D. A. (2011). *Obsessive-compulsive spectrum disorders: Refining the research agenda for DSM-V.* Washington, DC: American Psychiatric Publishing.

Hallmayer, J., Cleveland, S., Torres, A., Phillips, J., Cohen, B., Torigoe, T.,... Risch, N. (2011). Genetic heritability and shared environmental factors among twin pairs with autism. *Archives of General Psychiatry, 68*(11), 1095.

Honda, H., Shimizu, Y., & Rutter, M. (2005). No effect of MMR withdrawal on the incidence of autism: A total population study. *Journal of Child Psychology and Psychiatry, 46*, 572–579.

Horowitz, S. (2012). New perspectives on the placebo effect: Implications for research and clinical practice. *Alternative and Complementary Therapies, 18*(3), 130–135.

Howes, O. D., & Salkovskis, P. M. (1998). Health anxiety in medical students. *Lancet, 351*, 1332.

Howland, R. H., & Thase, M. E. (1998). Cyclothymic disorder. In T. A. Widiger (Ed.), *DSM-IV Sourcebook* (pp. 37–51). Washington, DC: American Psychiatric Association.

Hoza, B. (2007). Peer functioning in children with ADHD. *Journal of Pediatric Psychology, 32*, 665–663.

Hunter, R. A., & Macalpine, I. (1963). *Three hundred years of psychiatry: 1535–1860.* London, England: Oxford University Press.

Huntjens, R. J., Verschuere, B., & McNally, R. J. (2012). Inter-identity autobiographical amnesia in patients with dissociative identity disorder. *PLoS One, 7*(7), e40580.

Iacono, W. G. (1985). Psychophysiologic markers of psychopathology: A review. *Canadian Psychology, 26*, 96–112.

Ilardi, S. S., & Feldman, D. (2001). The cognitive neuroscience paradigm: A unifying meta-theoretical framework for the science and practice of clinical psychology. *Journal of Clinical Psychology, 57*, 1067–1088.

Jardri, R., Pouchet, A., Pins, D., & Thomas, P. (2011). Cortical activations during auditory verbal hallucinations in schizophrenia: A coordinate-based meta-analysis. *The American Journal of Psychiatry, 168*, 73–81.

Jensvold, M. F., & Turner, S. M. (1988). The woman who hadn't been out of her house in 25 years. In J. A. Talbott & A. Z. A. Manevitz (Eds.), *Psychiatric house calls* (pp. 161–167). Washington, DC: American Psychiatric Association Press.

Jerome, L. (2000). Central auditory processing disorder and ADHD. *Journal of the American Academy of Child & Adolescent Psychiatry, 39*, 399–400.

Job, D., Whalley, H. C., Johnstone, E. C., & Lawrie, S. M. (2005). Grey matter changes over time in high risk subjects developing schizophrenia. *NeuroImage, 25*, 1023–1030.

Johnson, S. L., & Miller, I. (1997). Negative life events and time to recovery from episodes of bipolar disorder. *Journal of Abnormal Psychology, 106*, 449–457.

Johnson, S. L., Sandrow, D., Meyer, B., Winters, R., Miller, I., Solomon D., & Keitner, G. (2000). Increases in manic symptoms after life events involving goal attainment. *Journal of Abnormal Psychology, 109*, 721–727.

Joiner, T. E., & Coyne, J. C. (1999). *The interactional nature of depression: Advances in interpersonal approaches.* Washington, DC: American Psychological Association.

Jones, J. C., & Barlow, D. H. (1990). The etiology of posttraumatic stress disorder. *Clinical Psychology Review, 10*, 299–328.

Karg, K., Burmeister, M., Shedden, K., & Sen, S. (2011). The serotonin transporter promoter variant (5-HTTLPR), stress, and depression meta-analysis revisited: Evidence of genetic moderation. *Archives of General Psychiatry, 68*(5), 444.

Karlin, R. A., & Orne, M. T. (1996). Commentary on *Borawick v. Shay*: Hypnosis, social influence, incestuous child abuse, and satanic ritual abuse: The iatrogenic creation of horrific memories for the remote past. *Cultic Studies Journal, 13*, 42–94.

Katayama, L. (2009). Love in 2-D. *New York Times.* Retrieved from http://www.nytimes.com/2009/07/26/magazine/26FOB-2DLove-t.html

Keefe, R., & Henry, P. S. (1994). Understanding schizophrenia: A guide to the new research on causes and treatment. New York, NY: Free Press.

Keefe, R. S., Silverman, J. M., Mohs, R. C., Siever, L. J., Harvery, P. D., Friedman, L.,... Davis, K. L. (1997). Eye tracking, attention, and schizotypal symptoms in nonpsychotic relatives of patients with schizophrenia. *Archives of General Psychiatry, 54*, 169–176.

Keel, P. K., & Klump, K. L. (2003). Are eating disorders culture-bound syndromes? Implications for conceptualizing their etiology. *Psychological Bulletin, 129*, 747–769.

Keith, S. J., Gunderson, J. G., Reifman, A., Buchsbaum, S., & Mosher, L. R. (1976). Special report: Schizophrenia, 1976. *Schizophrenia Bulletin, 2*, 510–565.

Kellaris, J. J. (2003). *Dissecting earworms: Further evidence on the song-stuck-in-your-head phenomenon.* Paper presented at the the Society for Consumer Psychology Winter 2003 Conference, New Orleans, LA.

Keller, M. L., & Craske, M. G. (2008). Panic disorder and agoraphobia. In J. Hunsley & E. J. Mash (Eds.), *A guide to assessments that work* (pp. 229–253). New York, NY: Oxford University Press.

Kelly, E. (2009). *Encyclopedia of attention deficit hyperactivity disorder.* New York, NY: Greenwood.

Kendell, R. E. (1975). The concept of disease and its implications for psychiatry. *British Journal of Psychiatry, 127*, 305–315.

Kendler, K. S., & Diehl, S. R. (1993). The genetics of schizophrenia: A current, genetic-epidemiologic perspective. *Schizophrenia Bulletin, 19*, 261–285.

Kendler, K. S., Gardner, C. O., & Prescott, C. A. (2003). Personality and the experience of environmental adversity. *Psychological Medicine, 33*, 1193–1202.

Kendler, K. S., & Karkowski-Shuman, L. (1997). Stressful life events and genetic liability to major depression: Genetic control of exposure to the environment? *Psychological Medicine, 27*, 539–547.

Kendler, K. S., Neale, M. C., Kessler, R. C., Heath, A. C., & Eaves, L. J. (1993). A test of the equal-environment assumption in twin studies of psychiatric illness. *Behavior Genetics, 23*, 21–27.

Kernberg, O. F. (1967). Borderline personality organization. *Journal of the American Psychoanalytic Association, 15*, 641–685.

Kessler, R. C., Angermeyer, M., Anthony, J. C., de Graff, R. O. N., Demyttenaere, K., Gasquet, I.,... Üstün, T. B. (2007). Lifetime prevalence and age-of-onset distributions of mental disorders in the World Health Organization's World Mental Health Survey Initiative. *World Psychiatry, 6*(3), 168–176.

Kessler, R. C., Berglund, P., Demler, O., Jin, R., & Walters, E. E. (2005). Lifetime prevalence and age-of-onset distributions of DSM-IV disorders in the National Comorbidity Survey Replication. *Archives of General Psychiatry, 62*, 593–602.

Kessler, R. C., Birnbaum, H., Bromet, E., Hwang, I., Sampson, N., & Shahly, V. (2010). Age differences in major depression: Results from the National Comorbidity Survey Replication (NCS-R). *Psychological Medicine, 12*(2), 225.

Kessler, R. C., Chiu, W. T., Jin, R., Ruscio, A. M., Shear, K., & Walters, E. E. (2006). The epidemiology of panic attacks, panic disorder, and agoraphobia in the National Comorbidity Survey Replication. *Archives of General Psychiatry, 63*, 415–424.

Kessler, R. C., McGonagle, K. A., Zhao, S., Nelson, C. B., Hughes, M., Eshleman, S.,... Kendler, K. S. (1994). Lifetime and 12-month prevalence of DSM-III-R psychiatric disorders in the United States: Results from the National Comorbidity Survey. *Archives of General Psychiatry, 51*, 8–19.

Kihlstrom, J. F. (2005). Dissociative disorders. In S. Nolen-Hoeksema, T. D. Cannon, & T. Widiger (Eds.), *Annual Review of Clinical Psychology, 1*, 227–254.

Kilmartin, C. (2006). Depression in men: Communication, diagnosis and therapy. *The Journal of Men's Health & Gender, 2*, 95–99.

Kim, E. Y., & Miklowitz, D. J. (2002). Childhood mania, attention deficit hyperactivity disorder and conduct disorder: A critical review of diagnostic dilemmas. *Bipolar Disorders, 4*(4), 215–225.

King, J. (2000) Treatment of schizophrenia—What in fact is schizophrenia? *British Medical Journal, 320*, 800.

Kippes, C., & Garrison, C. B. (2006). Are we in the midst of an autism epidemic? A review of prevalence data. *Missouri Medicine, 103*, 65–68.

Kirk, S. A., & Kutchins, H. (1992). *The selling of DSM: The rhetoric of science in psychiatry.* Hawthorne, NY: Aldine de Gruyter.

Kirmayer, L. J., & Young, A. (1999). Culture and context in the evolutionary concept of mental disorder. *Journal of Abnormal Psychology, 108*, 446–452.

Kistner, J. A., David-Ferdon, C. F., Repper, K. K., & Joiner, T. E., Jr. (2006). Bias and accuracy of children's perceptions of peer acceptance: Prospective associations with depressive symptoms. *Journal of Abnormal Child Psychology, 34*, 349–361.

Kleinknecht, R. A., Dinnel, D. L., Tanouye-Wilson, S., & Lonner, W. J. (1994). Cultural variation in social anxiety and phobia: A study of Taijin Kyofusho. *The Behavior Therapist, 17*, 175–178.

Kleinman, A. (1988). *Rethinking psychiatry: From cultural category to personal experience.* New York, NY: Free Press.

Klerman, G. L. (1986). The National Institute of Mental Health—Epidemiologic Catchment Area (NIMH-ECA) Program—Background, preliminary findings and implications. *Social Psychiatry, 21*, 159–166.

Kluft, R. P. (1984). Multiple personality in childhood. *Psychiatric Clinics of North America, 7*, 121–134.

Knyazeva, M. G., Jalili, M., Meuli, R., Hasler, M., DeFeo, Ol, & Do, K. Q. (2008). Alpha rhythm and hypofrontality in schizophrenia. *Acta Psychiatrica Scandinavica, 118*, 188–199.

Kollman, D. M., Brown, T. A., Liverant, G. I., & Hofmann, S. G. (2006). A taxometric investigation of the latent structure of social anxiety disorder in outpatients with anxiety and mood disorders. *Depression and Anxiety, 23*, 190–199.

Koran, L. M., Faber, R. J., Aboujaoude, E., Large, M. D., & Serpe, R. T. (2006). Estimated prevalence of compulsive buying behavior in the United States. *American Journal of Psychiatry, 163*, 1806–1812.

Kramer, G. M., Wolbransky, M., & Heilbrun, K. (2007) Plea bargaining recommendations by criminal defense attorneys: Evidence strength, potential sentence, and defendant preference. *Behavioral Sciences & the Law, 25*, 573–585.

Krueger, R., & Piasecki, T., M. (2002). Toward a dimensional and psychometrically-informed approach to conceptualizing psychopathology. *Behaviour Research and Therapy, 40*, 485–499.

Krueger, R. F., Skodol, A. E., Livesley, W. J., Shrout, P. E., & Huang, Y. (2007). Synthesizing dimensional and categorical approaches to personality disorders: Refining the research agenda for DSM-V Axis II. *International Journal of Methods in Psychiatric Research, 16*(S1), S65–S73.

Kruger, S., Seminowicz, D., Goldapple, K., Kennedy, S. H., & Mayberg, H. S. (2003). State and trait influences on mood regulation in bipolar disorder: Blood flow differences with an acute mood challenge. *Biological Psychiatry, 54*, 1274–1283.

Kuipers, L. (2011). Expressed emotion: A review. *British Journal of Social and Clinical Psychology, 18*(2), 237–243.

Kuperberg, G. R., Sitnikova, T., Goff, D., & Holcomb, P. J. (2006). Making sense of sentences in schizophrenia: Electrophysiological evidence for abnormal interactions between semantic and syntactic processing. *Journal of Abnormal Psychology, 115*, 251–265.

Kurlan, R., & Kaplan, E. L. (2004). The pediatric autoimmune neuropsychiatric disorders associated with streptococcal infection (PANDAS) etiology for tics and obsessive-compulsive symptoms: Hypothesis or entity. Practical considerations for the clinician. *Pediatrics, 112*, 884–886.

Lamb, H. R., & Bachrach, L. L. (2001). Some perspectives on deinstitutionalization. *Psychiatric Services, 52*, 1039–1045.

Leeper, P. (1988). Having a place to live is vital to good health. *News Report, 38*, 5–8.

LeFever, G. B., Arcona, A. P., & Antonuccio, D. O. (2003). ADHD among American schoolchildren: Evidence of overdiagnosis and overuse of medication. *Scientific Review of Mental Health Practice, 2*, 49–60.

Leichsenring, F., Leibing, E., Kruse, J., New, A. S., & Leweke, F. (2011). Borderline personality disorder. *Lancet, 377*(9759), 74–84.

Leistico, A. M. R., Salekin, R. T., DeCoster, J., & Rogers, R. (2008). A large-scale meta-analysis relating the Hare measures of psychopathy to antisocial conduct. *Law and Human Behavior, 32*(1), 28–45.

Lenzenweger, M. F., McLachlan, G., & Rubin, D. B. (2007). Resolving the latent structure of schizophrenia endophenotypes using expectation-maximization-based finite mixture modeling. *Journal of Abnormal Psychology, 116*, 16–29.

Leonard, B. E. (1997). The role of noradrenaline in depression: A review. *Journal of Psychopharmacology, 11*, S39–S47.

Levy-Reiner, S. (1996). The decade of the brain: Library and NIMH hold symposia on mental illness. *Library of Congress Information Bulletin, 55*, 326–327.

Lewinsohn, P. M. (1974). A behavioral approach to depression. In R. J. Friedman & M. M. Katz (Eds.), *Psychology of depression: Contemporary theory and research* (pp. 157–158). Oxford, England: Wiley.

Lewinsohn, P. M., Holm-Denoma, J. M., Small, J. W., Seeley, J. R., & Joiner, T. E. (2008). Separation in childhood as a risk factor for future mental illness. *Journal of the American Academy for Child and Adolescent Psychiatry, 47*(5), 548–555.

Lichtenstein, P., Yip, B. H., Björk, C., Pawitan, Y., Cannon, T. D., Sullivan, P. F., & Hultman, C. M. (2009). Common genetic determinants of schizophrenia and bipolar disorder in Swedish families: A population-based study. *Lancet, 373*(9659), 234–239.

Lidz, C. W., Mulvey, E. P., & Gardner, W. (1993). The accuracy of predictions of violence to others. *Journal of the American Medical Association, 269*, 1007–1111.

Lidz, T. (1973). *The origin and treatment of schizophrenic disorders.* New York, NY: Basic Books.

Lieberman, J. A., & Koreen, A. R. (1993). Neurochemistry and neuroendocrinology of schizophrenia: A selective review. *Schizophrenia Bulletin, 2*, 371–428.

Lilienfeld, S. O. (1994). Conceptual problems in the assessment of psychopathy. *Clinical Psychology Review, 14*, 17–38.

Lilienfeld, S. O. (1997). The relation of anxiety sensitivity to higher and lower order personality dimensions: Implications for the etiology of panic attacks. *Journal of Abnormal Psychology, 106*, 539–544.

Lilienfeld, S. O. (2012). Public skepticism of psychology: Why many people perceive the study of human behavior as unscientific. *American Psychologist, 67*, 111–129.

Lilienfeld, S. O., & Lynn, S. J. (2003). Dissociative identity disorder: Multiple personalities, multiple controversies. In S. O. Lilienfeld, S. J. Lynn, & J. M. Lohr (Eds.), *Science and pseudoscience in clinical psychology* (pp. 109–143). New York, NY: Guilford Press.

Lilienfeld, S. O., Lynn, S. J., Kirsch, I., Chaves, J. F., Sarbin, T. R., Ganaway, G. K., & Powell, R. A. (1999). Dissociative identity disorder and the sociocognitive model: Recalling the lessons of the past. *Psychological Bulletin, 125*, 507–523.

Lilienfeld, S. O., & Marino, L. (1995). Mental disorder as a Roschian concept: A critique of Wakefield's "harmful dysfunction" analysis. *Journal of Abnormal Psychology, 104*, 411–420.

Lilienfeld, S. O., Smith, S. F., & Watts, A. L. (in press). Issues in diagnosis: Conceptual issues and controversies. In E. W. Craighead, D. J. Miklowitz, & L. W. Craighead (Eds.), *Psychpathology: History, diagnosis, and empirical foundations.* New York, NY: Wiley.

Lilienfeld, S. O., & Waldman, I. D. (2004). Comorbidity and Chairman Mao. *World Psychiatry, 3*, 26–27.

Lilienfeld, S. O., Waldman, I. D., & Israel, A. C. (1994). A critical examination of the use of the term "comorbidity" in psychopathology research. *Clinical Psychology: Science and Practice, 1*, 71–83.

Linehan, M. M. (1993). *Cognitive behavioral treatment of borderline personality disorder.* New York, NY: Guilford Press.

Link, B. G., Phelan, J. C., Bresnahan, M., Stueve, A., & Pescosolido, B. A. (1999). Public conceptions of mental illness: Labels, causes, dangerousness and social distance. *American Journal of Public Health, 89*, 1328–1333.

Littlewood, R. (2004). Unusual psychiatric syndromes: An introduction. *Psychiatry, 3*, 1–3.

Lönnqvist, J. E., Verkasalo, M., Haukka, J., Nyman, K., Tihonen, J., Laaksonen, I.,... Henriksson, M. (2009). Premorbid personality factors in schizophrenia and bipolar disorder: Results from a large cohort study of male conscripts. *Journal of Abnormal Psychology, 118*, 418–423.

López, S. R., Nelson Hipke, K., Polo, A. J., Jenkins, J. H., Karno, M., Vaughn, C., & Snyder, K. S. (2004). Ethnicity, expressed emotion, attributions, and course of schizophrenia: Family warmth matters. *Journal of Abnormal Psychology, 113*, 428–439.

Lorber, M. F. (2004). Autonomic psychophysiology of aggression, psychopathy, and conduct problems: A meta-analysis. *Psychological Bulletin, 130*, 531–552.

Luchins, D. J., Weinberger, D. R., & Wyatt, R. J. (1982). Schizophrenia and cerebral asymmetry detected by computed tomography. *American Journal of Psychiatry, 139*, 753–757.

Ludwig, A. M., Brandsma, J. M., Wilbur, C. B., Bendfeldt, F., & Jameson, D. H. (1972). The objective study of a multiple personality: Or, are four heads better than one? *Archives of General Psychiatry, 26*, 298–310.

Lundström, S., Haworth, C., Carlström, E., Gillberg, C., Mill, J., Råstam, M.,... Reichenberg, A. (2010). Trajectories leading to autism spectrum disorders are affected by paternal age: Findings from two nationally representative twin studies. *Journal of Child Psychology and Psychiatry, 51*(7), 850–856.

Lykken, D. T. (1957). A study of anxiety in the sociopathic personality. *Journal of Abnormal and Social Psychology, 55*, 6–10.

Lykken, D. T. (1982). If a man be mad. *The Sciences, 22*, 11–13.

Lykken, D. T. (1995). *The antisocial personalities.* Mahwah, NJ: Erlbaum.

Macrae, C. N., & Bodenhausen, G. V. (2000). Social cognition: Thinking categorically about others. *Annual Review of Psychology, 51*, 93–120.

Madsen, K. M., Hviid, A., Vestergaard, M., Schendel, D., Wohlfart, J., Thorsen, P.,... Melbye, M. (2002). A population-based study of measles, mumps and rubella vaccination and autism. *New England Journal of Medicine, 347*, 1477–1482.

Mangeot, S. D., Miller, L. J., McIntosh, D. N., McGrath-Clarke, J., Simon, J., Hagerman, R. J., & Goldson, E. (2001). Sensory modulation dysfunction in children with attention-deficit-hyperactivity disorder. *Developmental Medicine & Child Neurology, 43*, 399–406.

Marder, S., Cohen, A., Hamilton, A., Saks, E., Glynn, S., Hollan, D., & Brekke, J. (2008). Characteristics of high-functioning people with schizophrenia. *Schizophrenia Research, 102*(1), 232–232.

Maris, R. W. (1992). The relationship of nonfatal suicide attempts to completed suicides. In R. W. Maris, A. L. Berman, J. T. Maltsberger, & R. I. Yufit (Eds.), *Assessment and prediction of suicide* (pp. 362–380). New York, NY: Guilford Press.

Martinot, M. L., Bragulat, V., Artiges, E., Dollé, F., Hinnen, F., Jouvent, R., & Martinot, J. (2001). Decreased presynaptic dopamine function in the left caudate of depressed patients with affective flattening and psychomotor retardation. *American Journal of Psychiatry, 158*, 314–316.

Mataix-Cols, D., Rosario-Campos, M. C., & Lackman, J. F. (2005). A multidimensional model of obsessive-compulsive disorder. *American Journal of Psychiatry, 162*, 228–238.

Matarazzo, J. D. (1983). The reliability of psychiatric and psychological diagnosis. *Clinical Psychology Review, 3*, 103–145.

Mathews, A., Richards, A., & Eysenck, M. W. (1989). Interpretation of homophones related to threat in anxiety states. *Journal of Abnormal Psychology, 98*, 31–34.

Matthews, A., & MacLeod, C. (2005). Cognitive vulnerability to emotional disorders. In S. Nolen-Hoeksema, T. D. Cannon, & T. Widiger (Eds.), *Annual Review of Clinical Psychology* (Vol. 1, pp. 167–196). Palo Alto, CA: Annual Reviews.

Mazure, C. M. (1998). Life stressors as risk factors in depression. *Clinical Psychology: Science and Practice, 5*, 291–313.

McCann, J. T., Shindler, K. L., & Hammond, T. R. (2003). The science and pseudoscience of expert testimony. In S. O. Lilienfeld, S. J. Lynn, & J. M. Lohr (Eds.), *Science and pseudoscience in clinical psychology* (pp. 77–108). New York, NY: Guilford Press.

McCarthy, M. (1990). The thin ideal, depression and eating disorders in women. *Behaviour Research and Therapy, 28*, 205–215.

McCarty, C. A., Lau, A. S., Valeri, S. M., & Weisz, J. R. (2004). Parent-child interactions proxy for behavior. *Journal of Abnormal Child Psychology, 32*, 83–93.

McClellan, J., Kowatch, R. A., & Findling, R. L. (2007). Practice parameters for the assessment and treatment of children and adolescents with bipolar disorder. *Journal of the American Academy of Child and Adolescent Psychiatry, 46*, 107–125.

McCutcheon, L. E., & McCutcheon, L. E. (1994). Not guilty by reason of insanity: Getting it right or perpetuating the myths? *Psychological Reports, 74*, 764–766.

McGrath, M. E. (1984). 1st-person account—Where did I go? *Schizophrenia Bulletin, 10*, 638–640.

McGuffin, P., Rijsdijk, F., Andrew, M., Sham, P., Katz, R., & Cardino, A. (2003). The heritability of bipolar affective disorder and the genetic relationship to unipolar depression. *Archives of General Psychiatry, 60*, 497–502.

McGuire, P. K., Shah, G. M. S., & Murray, R. M. (1993). Increased blood flow in Broca's area during auditory hallucinations. *Lancet, 342*, 703–706.

McHugh, P. R. (1993). Multiple personality disorder. *Harvard Mental Health Newsletter, 10*(3), 4–6.

McNally, R. J. (2003). *Remembering trauma.* Cambridge, MA: Belknap Press.

McNally, R. J. (2011). *What is mental illness?* Cambridge, MA: Harvard University Press.

McNally, R. M., & Eke, M. (1996). Anxiety sensitivity, suffocation fear, and breath-holding duration as predictors of response to carbon dioxide challenge. *Journal of Abnormal Psychology, 105*, 146–149.

McNiel, D. E., Eisner, J. P., & Binder, R. L. (2000). The relationship between command hallucinations and violence. *Psychiatric Services, 51*, 1288–1292.

Mednick, S. A., Machon, R. A., Huttunen, M. O., & Bonett, D. (1988). Adult schizophrenia following prenatal exposure to an influenza epidemic. *Archives of General Psychiatry, 45*, 189–192.

Meehl, P. E. (1962). Schizotaxia, schizotypy, and schizophrenia. *American Psychologist, 17*, 827–838.

Meehl, P. E. (1990). Toward an integrated theory of schizotaxia, schizotypy, and schizophrenia. *Journal of Personality Disorders, 4*, 1–99.

Meehl, P. E., & Rosen, A. (1955). Antecedent probability and the efficiency of psychometric signs, patterns, or cutting scores. *Psychological Bulletin, 52*, 194–216.

Mell, L. K., Davis, R. L., & Owens, D. (2005). Association between streptococcal infection and obsessive-compulsive disorder, Tourette's syndrome, and tic disorder. *Pediatrics, 116*, 56–60.

Mellinger, D. M., & Lynn, S. J. (2003). *The monster in the cave: How to face your fear and anxiety and live your life.* New York, NY: Berkeley.

Melton, G. B., Petrilla, J., Poythress, N. G., & Slobogin, L. A. (1997). *Psychological evaluations for the courts: A handbook for mental health professionals and lawyers* (2nd ed.). New York, NY: Guilford Press.

Mendelowicz, M. V., & Stein, M. B. (2000). Quality of life in individuals with anxiety disorders. *American Journal of Psychiatry, 157*, 669–682.

Merikangas, K. R., Akiskal, H. S., Angst, J., Greenberg, P. E., Hirschfeld, R., Petukhova, M., & Kessler, R. C. (2007). Lifetime and 12-month prevalence of bipolar spectrum disorder in the National Comorbidity Survey replication. *Archives of General Psychiatry, 64*(5), 543–552.

Merskey, H. (1992). The manufacture of personalities: The production of multiple personality disorder. *British Journal of Psychiatry, 160*, 327–340.

Meyer, S. E., & Carlson, G. A. (2008). Early-onset bipolar disorder. *Focus: The Journal of Lifelong Learning in Psychiatry, 6*, 271–283.

Miklowitz, D. J., & Johnson, S. L. (2006). The psychopathology and treatment of bipolar disorder. *Annual Review of Clinical Psychology, 2*, 199–235.

Miller, S. D. (1989). Optical differences in cases of multiple personality disorder. *Journal of Nervous and Mental Disease, 177*, 480–486.

Mineka, S., & Cook, M. (1993). Mechanisms involved in the observational conditioning of fear. *Journal of Experimental Psychology: General, 122*, 23–38.

Mittal, V. A., Tessner, K. D., Trotman, H. D., Esterberg, M., Dhrub, S. H., Simenova, D. I.,... Walker, E. F. (2007). Movement abnormalities and the progression of prodromal symptomatology in adolescents at risk for psychotic disorders. *Journal of Abnormal Psychology, 116*, 260–267.

Molina, B., & Pelham, W. (2003). Childhood predictors of adolescent substance use in a longitudinal study of children with ADHD. *Journal of Abnormal Psychology, 112*, 497–507.

Monahan, J. (1992). Mental disorder and violent behavior: Perceptions and evidence. *American Psychologist, 47*, 511–521.

Monahan, J., Steadman, H. J., Appelbaum, P. S., Robbins, P. C., Mulvey, E. P., Silver, E.,... Grisso, T. (2000). Developing a clinically useful actuarial tool for assessing violence risk. *British Journal of Psychiatry, 176*, 312–319.

Monastra, V. J. (2008). *Unlocking the potential of patients with ADHD.* Washington, DC: American Psychological Association.

Moore, M. T., & Fresco, D. M. (2012). Depressive realism: A meta-analytic review. *Clinical Psychology Review, 32*(6), 496–509.

Moreno, C., Laje, G., Blanco, C., Jiang, H., Schmidt, A. B., & Olfson, M. (2007). National trends in the outpatient diagnosis and treatment of bipolar disorder in youth. *Archives of General Psychiatry, 64*, 1032–1039.

Morrison, J. (1997). *When psychological problems mask medical disorders: A guide for psychotherapists.* New York, NY: Guilford Press.

Mossman, D. (2013). Evaluating risk assessments using receiver operating characteristic analysis: Rationale, advantages, insights, and limitations. *Behavioral Sciences & the Law, 31*, 23–39.

Mueser, K. T., & McGurk, S. R. (2004). Schizophrenia. *Lancet, 363*, 2063–2072.

Murphy, J. A., & Byrne, G. J. (2012). Prevalence and correlates of the proposed DSM-5 diagnosis of Chronic Depressive Disorder. *Journal of Affective Disorders, 139*(2), 172–180.

Murphy, J. B. (1976). Psychiatric labeling in cross-cultural perspective: Similar kinds of disturbed behavior appear to be labeled abnormal in diverse cultures. *Science, 191*, 1019–1028.

National Institute of Mental Health (2013). *Statistics in the U.S.: Statistics and prevention.* http://www.nimh.nih.gov/health/publications/suicide-in-the-us-statistics-and-prevention/index.shtml

Newman, J. P., & Kosson, D. S. (1986). Passive avoidance learning in psychopathic and nonpsychopathic offenders. *Journal of Abnormal Psychology, 95*, 252–256.

Nicholson, T. R., Ferdinando, S., Krishnaiah, R. B., Anhoury, S., Lennox, B. R., Mataix-Cols, D.,... Heyman, I. (2012). Prevalence of anti-basal ganglia antibodies in adult obsessive–compulsive disorder: Cross-sectional study. *The British Journal of Psychiatry, 200*(5), 381–386.

Nicol, S. E., & Gottesman, I. I. (1983). Clues to the genetics and neurobiology of schizophrenia. *American Scientist, 71*, 398–404.

Nolen-Hoeksema, S. (2002). Gender differences in depression. In I. H. Gotlib & C. L. Hammen (Eds.), *Handbook of depression* (pp. 492–509). New York, NY: Guilford Press.

Novick, D. M., Swartz, H. A., & Frank, E. (2010). Suicide attempts in bipolar I and bipolar II disorder: A review and meta-analysis of the evidence. *Bipolar Disorders, 12*(1), 1–9.

Noyes, R., Jr. (2001). Comorbidity in generalized anxiety disorder. *Psychiatric Clinics of North America, 24*, 41–55.

O'Brien, T. (1990). *The things they carried.* New York, NY: Broadway.

Offit, P. A. (2008). Vaccines and autism revisited: The Hanna Poling case. *New England Journal of Medicine, 358*, 2089–2091.

Ogden, C. A., Rich, M. E., Schork, N. J., Paulus, M. P., Geyer, M. A., Lohr, J. B., . . . Niculescu, A. B. (2004). Candidate genes, pathways and mechanisms for bipolar (manic-depressive) and related disorders: An expanded convergent functional genomics approach. *Molecular Psychiatry, 9*, 1007–1029.

Overmier, J. B., & Seligman, M. E. P. (1967). Effects of inescapable shock upon subsequent escape and avoidance responding. *Journal of Comparative and Physiological Psychology, 63*, 28–33.

Papolos, D., & Papolos, J. (2007). *The bipolar child: The definitive and reassuring guide to childhood's most misunderstood disorder* (3rd ed.). New York, NY: Broadway.

Pasewark, R. A., & Pantle, M. L. (1979). Insanity plea: Legislator's view. *American Journal of Psychiatry, 136*, 222–223.

Patrick, C. J. (Ed.). (2006). *Handbook of psychopathy.* New York, NY: Guilford Press.

Paykel, E. S. (2003). Life events and affective disorders. *Acta Psychiatrica Scandinavia Supplement, 108*, 61–66.

Pelkonnen, M., & Marttunen, M. (2003). Child and adolescent suicide: Epidemiology, risk factors, and approaches to prevention. *Psychiatric Drugs, 5*, 243–265.

Perry, J. C. (1984). *The borderline personality disorder scale: Reliability and validity.* Unpublished manuscript, Department of Psychiatry, Harvard Medical School at the Cambridge Hospital, Cambridge, MA.

Phillips, K. A., Menard, W., Fay, C., & Weisberg, R. (2005). Demographic characteristics, phenomenology, comorbidity, and family history in 200 individuals with body dysmorphic disorder. *Psychosomatics, 46*, 317–325.

Phillips, M. R., Wolf, A. S., & Coons, D. J. (1988). Psychiatry and the criminal justice system: Testing the myths. *American Journal of Psychiatry, 145*, 605–610.

Piccinelli, M., & Wilkinson, G. (2000). Gender differences in depression—Critical review. *British Journal of Psychiatry, 177*, 486–492.

Pies, R. (2012). Bereavement, complicated grief, and the rationale for diagnosis in psychiatry. *Dialogues in Clinical Neuroscience, 14*(2), 111–113.

Piper, A. (1997). *Hoax and reality: The bizarre world of multiple personality disorder.* Northvale, NJ: Jason Aronson.

Pittinger, C, & Duman, R. S. (2008). Stress, depression, and neuroplasticity: A convergence of mechanisms. *Neuropsychopharmacology Reviews, 33*, 88–109.

Pope, H. G., Jr., & Hudson, J. I. (1992). Is childhood sexual abuse a risk factor for bulimia nervosa? *American Journal of Psychiatry, 149*, 455–463.

Pope, H. G., Jr., Poliakoff, M. B., Parker, M. P., Boynes, M., & Hudson, J. I. (2007). Is dissociative amnesia a culture-bound syndrome? Findings from a survey of historical literature. *Psychological Medicine, 37*, 225–233.

Price, R. H., & Bouffard, D. L. (1974). Behavioral appropriateness and situational constraint as dimensions of social behavior. *Journal of Personality and Social Psychology, 30*, 579–586.

Prince, M. J., Harwood, R. H., Blizard, R. A., Thomas, A., & Mann, A. H. (1997). Social support deficits, loneliness and life events as risk factors for depression in old age. The Gospel Oak Project VI. *Psychological Medicine, 27*, 323–332.

Purcell, S. M., Wray, N. R., Stone, J. L., Visscher, P. M., O'Donovan, M. C., Sullivan, P. F.,... Fraser, G. (2009). Common polygenic variation contributes to risk of schizophrenia and bipolar disorder. *Nature, 460*(7256), 748–752.

Rachman, S. (1977). The conditioning theory of fear-acquisition: A critical examination. *Behaviour Research and Therapy, 15*, 375–387.

Raulin, M. L., & Lilienfeld, S. O. (2008). Research paradigms in the study of psychopathology. In P. H. Blaney & T. Milton (Eds.), *Oxford textbook of psychopathology.* (2nd ed., pp. 86–115). New York, NY: Oxford University Press.

Raz, S., & Raz, N. (1990). Structural brain abnormalities in the major psychoses: A quantitative review of the evidence from computerized imaging. *Psychological Bulletin, 108*, 93–108.

Reis, F. L., Masson, S., deOliveira, A. R., & Brandao, M. L. (2004). Dopaminergic mechanisms in the conditioned and unconditioned fear as assessed by the two-way avoidance and light switch-off tests. *Pharmacology, Biochemistry and Behavior, 79*, 359–365.

Reiss, S., & McNally, R. J. (1985). The expectancy model of fear. In S. Reiss & R. R. Bootzin (Eds.), *Theoretical issues in behavior therapy* (pp. 107–121). New York, NY: Academic Press.

Richter, M. A., Summerfeldt, L. J., Antony, M. M., & Swinson, R. P. (2003). Obsessive-compulsive spectrum conditions in obsessive-compulsive disorder and other anxiety disorders. *Depression and Anxiety, 18*, 118–127.

Rieber, R. W. (1999). Hypnosis, false memory, and multiple personality: A trinity of affinity. *History of Psychiatry, 10*, 3–11.

Rimland, B. (2004). Association between thimerosol-containing vaccine and autism. *Journal of the American Medical Association, 291*, 180.

Risch, N., Herrell, R., Lehner, T., Liang, K. Y., Eaves, L., Hoh, J.,... Merikangas, K. R. (2009). The interaction between the serotonin transporter gene (5-HTTLPR), stressful life events, and risk of depression: A meta-analysis. *Journal of the American Medical Association, 301*, 2462–2471.

Robins, E., & Guze, S. B. (1970). Establishment of diagnostic validity in psychiatric illness: Its application to schizophrenia. *American Journal of Psychiatry, 126*, 983–987.

Robinson, D. G., Woerner, M. G., McMeniman, M., Mendelowitz, A., & Bilder, R. M. (2004). Systematic and functional recovery from a first episode of schizophrenia or schizoaffective disorder. *American Journal of Psychiatry, 161*, 473–479.

Robinson, D. S. (2007). The role of dopamine and norepinephrine in depression. *Primary Psychiatry, 14*, 21–23.

Rosen, G. M. (2006). DSM's cautionary guideline to rule out malingering can protect the PTSD data base. *Journal of Anxiety Disorders, 20*, 530–535.

Rosenfarb, I. S., Bellack, A. S., & Aziz, N. (2006). Family interactions and the course of schizophrenia in African-American and white patients. *Journal of Abnormal Psychology, 115*, 112–120.

Rosenhan, D. L. (1973). On being sane in insane places. *Science, 179*, 250–258.

Rosenhan, D. L., & Seligman, M. E. P. (1989). *Abnormal psychology.* New York, NY: Norton.

Ross, C. A. (1997). *Dissociative identity disorder: Diagnosis, clinical features, and treatment of multiple personality.* New York, NY: Wiley.

Roy, M., McNeale, M. C., Pedersen, N. L., Mathe, A. A., & Kendler, K. S. (1995). A twin study of generalized anxiety disorder and major depression. *Psychological Medicine, 25*, 1037–1049.

Rudolf, K. (2009). The interpersonal context of adolescent depression. In S. Nolen Hoeksema & L. M. Hilt (Eds.), *Handbook of depression in adolescents* (pp. 378–412). New York, NY: Routledge.

Ruscio, J. (2003). Diagnoses and the behaviors they denote: A critical evaluation of the labeling theory of mental illness. *Scientific Review of Mental Health Practice, 3*, 5–22.

Rust, S. (2006, April 3). Autism epidemic doubted. *Milwaukee Sentinel.* Retrieved from http://www.highbeam.com/doc/1G1-143988354.html

Rutter, M. (2000). Genetic studies of autism: From the 1970s into the millennium. *Journal of Abnormal Child Psychology, 28*, 3–14.

Rutter, M. (2009). Gene-environment interactions: Biologically valid pathway or artifact. *Archives of General Psychiatry, 66*, 1287–1289.

Ryder, A. G., Yang, J., Zhu, X., Yao, S., Yi, J., Heine, S., & Bagby, R. M. (2008). The cultural shaping of depression: Somatic symptoms in China, psychological symptoms in North America. *Journal of Abnormal Psychology, 117*, 300–313.

Sadoff, R. L. (1992) In defense of the insanity defense. *Psychiatric Annals, 22*, 556–560.

Saha, S., Chant, D., Welham, J., & McGrath, J. (2005). A systematic review of the prevalence of schizophrenia. *PLoS Medicine, 2*, e141. http://dx.doi.org/10.1371/journal.pmed.0020141

Salekin, R. T. (2002). Psychopathy and therapeutic pessimism: Clinical lore or clinical reality? *Clinical Psychology Review, 22*, 79–112.

Salsman, N. L., & Linehan, M. M. (2012). An investigation of the relationships among negative affect, difficulties in emotion regulation, and features of borderline personality disorder. *Journal of Psychopathology and Behavioral Assessment*, 1–8.

Samuels, J. F., Grados, M. A., Planalp, E., & Bienvenu, O. J. (2011). 6 Genetic Understanding of OCD and Spectrum Disorders. *The Oxford handbook of obsessive compulsive and spectrum disorders*, 111–127.

Sanderson, W. C., & Dublin, R. A. (2010). Panic disorder. *Corsini Encyclopedia of Psychology.* Wiley Online Library.

Satel, S. L. (1999). *Drug treatment: The case for coercion.* Washington, DC: American Enterprise Institute Press.

Satyanarayana, S., Enns, M. W., Cox, B. J., & Sareen, J. (2009). Prevalence and correlates of chronic depression in the Canadian community health survey: Mental health and well-being. *Canadian Journal of Psychiatry. Revue Canadienne de Psychiatrie, 54*(6), 389.

Savitz, J., Solms, M., Pietersen, E., Ramesar, R., & Flor-Henry, P. (2004). Dissociative identity disorder associated with mania and change in handedness. *Cognitive and Behavioral Neurology, 17*, 233–237.

Schaler, J. (2004). *Addiction is a choice.* La Salle, IL: Open Court.

Scheff, T. J. (1984). *Being mentally ill: A sociological theory.* New York, NY: Aldine.

Scher, C. D., Ingram, R. E., & Segal, Z. V. (2005). Cognitive reactivity and vulnerability: Empirical evaluation of construct activation and cognitive diatheses in unipolar depression. *Clinical Psychology Review, 25*, 487–510.

Schmidt, N. B., Zvolensky, M. J., & Maner, J. (2006). Anxiety sensitivity: Prospective prediction of panic attacks and Axis I pathology. *Journal of Psychiatric Research, 40*, 691–699.

Schneidman, E. S., Farberow, N. L., & Litman, R. E. (1970). *The psychology of suicide.* New York, NY: Science House.

Schofield, W., & Balian, L. (1959). A comparative study of the personal histories of schizophrenics and non-psychiatric patients. *Journal of Abnormal and Social Psychology, 59*, 216–225.

Schreiber, F. R. (1973). *Sybil*. New York, NY: Warner.

Schwartz, J. M., & Bayette, B. (1996). *Brain lock: Free yourself from obsessive-compulsive behavior: A four-step self-treatment method to change your brain chemistry*. New York, NY: HarperCollins.

Sciutto, M. J., & Eisenberg, M. (2007). Evaluating the evidence for and against the overdiagnosis of ADHD. *Journal of Attention Disorders, 11*, 106–113.

Segrin, C. (2000). Social skill deficits associated with depression. *Clinical Psychology Review, 20*, 379–403.

Seidman, L. J., Pantelis, C., Keshavan, M., Faraone, S., Goldstein, J., Horton, N. J.,... Tsuang, M. T. (2003). A review and new report of medial temporal lobe dysfunction as a vulnerability indicator for schizophrenia: A magnetic resonance imaging morphometric family study of the parahippocampal gyrus. *Schizophrenia Bulletin, 29*, 803–830.

Selby, E. A, Anestis, M. D., Bender, T. W., & Joiner, T. E., Jr. (2009). An exploration of the emotional cascade model in borderline personality disorder. *Journal of Abnormal Psychology, 118* (2), 375–387.

Selby, E. A., & Joiner, T. E., Jr. (2009). Cascades of emotion: The emergence of borderline personality disorder from emotional and behavioral dysregulation. *Review of General Psychology, 12*(3), 219–229.

Seligman, M. E. P. (1975). *Helplessness: On depression, development, and death*. San Francisco, CA: W. H. Freeman.

Seligman, M. E. P., & Maier, S. F. (1967). Failure to escape traumatic shock. *Journal of Experimental Psychology, 74*, 1–9.

Shea, S. C. (1998). *Psychiatric interviewing: The art of understanding* (2nd ed). Philadelphia, PA: W. B. Saunders.

Showalter, E. (1997). *Hystories: Hysterical epidemics and modern culture*. New York, NY: Columbia University Press.

Siever, L. J., & Davis, K. L. (2004). The pathophysiology of schizophrenia disorders: Perspectives from the spectrum. *American Journal of Psychiatry, 161*, 398–413.

Silveira, J. M., & Seeman, M. V. (1995). Shared psychotic disorder: A critical review of the literature. *Canadian Journal of Psychiatry, 40*, 389–395.

Silver, E., Cirincione, C., & Steadman, H. J. (1994). Demythologizing inaccurate perceptions of the insanity defense. *Law and Human Behavior, 18*, 63–70.

Simeon, D., Gross, S., Guralnik, O., Stein, D. J., Schmeidler, J., & Hollander, E. (1997). Feeling unreal: 30 Cases of DSM-III-R depersonalization. *American Journal of Psychiatry, 154*, 1107–1113.

Simon, R. I. (2006). Imminent suicide: The illusion of short-term prediction. *Suicide and Life-Threatening Behavior, 36*, 296–301.

Simons, R. C., & Hughes, C. C. (1986). *The culture-bound syndromes: Folk illnesses of psychiatric and anthropological interest*. Boston, MA: D. Reidel.

Skeem, J. L., Monahan, J., & Mulvey, E. P. (2002). Psychopathy, treatment involvement, and subsequent violence among civil psychiatric patients. *Law and Human Behavior, 26*, 577–603.

Skeem, J. L., Polaschek, D. L., Patrick, C. J., & Lilienfeld, S. O. (2011). Psychopathic personality bridging the gap between scientific evidence and public policy. *Psychological Science in the Public Interest, 12*(3), 95–162.

Slade, T., & Andrews, G. (2005). Latent structure of depression in a community sample: A taxometric analysis. *Psychological Medicine, 35*, 489–497.

Slater, L. (2004). *Opening Skinner's box: Great psychological experiments of the 20th century*. New York, NY: Norton.

Snyder, S. H. (1975). *Madness and the brain*. New York, NY: McGraw-Hill.

Solomon, D. A., Leon, A. C., Coryell, W. H., Endicott, J., Li, C., Fiedorowicz, J. G.,... Keller, M. B. (2010). Longitudinal course of bipolar I disorder: Duration of mood episodes. *Archives of General Psychiatry, 67*(4), 339–347.

Spanos, N. P. (1994). Multiple identity enactments and multiple personality disorder: A sociocognitive perspective. *Psychological Bulletin, 116*, 143–165.

Spanos, N. P. (1996). *Multiple identities and false memories: A sociocognitive perspective*. Washington, DC: American Psychological Association.

Spirito, A., & Esposito-Smythers, C. (2006). Attempted and completed suicide in adolescence. *Annual Review of Clinical Psychology, 2*, 237–266.

Spitzer, R. L. (1975). On pseudoscience, science, logic in remission, and psychiatric diagnosis: A critique of Rosenhan's "On being sane in insane places." *Journal of Abnormal Psychology, 84*, 442–452.

Staal, W. G., Pol, H.E. H., Schnack, H. G., Mechteld, L. C., Hoogendoorn, M. S. Jellema, K., & Kahn, R. S. (2000). Structural brain abnormalities in patients with schizophrenia and their healthy siblings. *American Journal of Psychiatry, 157*, 416–421.

Starr, L. R., & Davila, J. (2008). Excessive reassurance seeking, depression, and interpersonal rejection: A meta-analytic review. *Journal of Abnormal Psychology, 117*, 762–765.

Steadman, H. J., Mulvey, E. P., Monahan, J., Robbins, P. C., Appelbaum, P., Grisso, T.,... Silver, E. (1998). Violence by people discharged from acute psychiatric inpatient facilities and by others in the same neighborhoods. *Archives of General Psychiatry, 55*, 1–9.

Stein, D. J., Phillips, K. A., Bolton, D., Fulford, K. W. M., Sadler, J. Z., & Kendler, K. S. (2010). What is a mental/psychiatric disorder? From DSM-IV to DSM-V. *Psychological Medicine, 40*(11), 1759–1765.

Stein, M. B., Jang, K. L., & Livesley, W. J. (1999). Heritability of anxiety sensitivity: A twin study. *American Journal of Psychiatry, 156*, 246–251.

Stern, A. (1938). Psychoanalytic investigation of and therapy in the borderline group of neuroses. *Psychoanalytical Quarterly, 7*, 467–489.

Stirk, W., Dierks, T., Hubl, D., & Horn, H. (2008). Hallucinations, thought disorders, and the language domain in schizophrenia. *Clinical EEG and Neuroscience, 39*(2), 91–94.

Stone, A. A. (1982). The insanity defense on trial. *Hospital and Community Psychiatry, 33*, 636–640.

Susser, E. S., & Lin, S. P. (1992). Schizophrenia after prenatal exposure to the Dutch Hunger Winter of 1944–1945. *Archives of General Psychiatry, 49*, 983–988.

Swanson, J. M., & Castellanos, F. X. (2002). Biological bases of ADHD—Neuroanatomy, genetics, and pathophysiology. In P. S. Jensen & J. R. Cooper (Eds.), *Attention deficit hyperactivity disorder: State of the science—best practices*. Kingston, NJ: Civic Research Institute.

Swartz, M., Blazer, D., George, L., & Winfield, I. (1990). Estimating the prevalence of borderline personality disorder in the community. *Journal of Personality Disorders, 4*, 257–272.

Szasz, T. S. (1960). The myth of mental illness. *American Psychologist, 15*, 113–118.

Szasz, T. S. (1978). Should psychiatric patients ever be hospitalized involuntarily? Under any circumstances—No. In J. P. Brady & H. K. H. Brodie (Eds.), *Controversy in psychiatry* (pp. 965–977). Philadelphia, PA: W. B. Saunders.

Szasz, T. S. (1991). *Insanity*. Chichester, England: Wiley.

Szasz, T. S. (2006). *Mental illness as a brain disease: A brief history lesson*. Cybercenter for Liberty and Responsibility. Retrieved from http://www.szasz.com/freeman13.html

Tallis, F. (2011). Primary hypothyroidism: A case for vigilance in the psychological treatment of depression. *British Journal of Clinical Psychology, 32*(3), 261–270.

Taylor, J., & Lang, A. R. (2006). Psychopathy and substance use disorders. In C. J. Patrick (Ed.), *Handbook of psychopathy* (pp. 495–511). New York, NY: Guilford Press.

Teplin, L. A. (1985) The criminality of the mentally ill: A dangerous misconception. *American Journal of Psychiatry, 142*, 593–599.

Thase, M. E., Jindal, R., & Howland, R. H. (2002). Biological aspects of depression. In I. H. Gotlib & C. L. Hammen (Eds.), *Handbook of depression* (pp. 192–218). New York, NY: Guilford Press.

Thomas, P. (1997). *The dialectics of schizophrenia*. Bristol, England: Free Association Books.

Torgersen, S., Lygren, S., Oien, P. A., Skre, I., Onstad, S., Edvardsen, J.,... Kringlen, E. (2000). A twin study of personality disorders. *Comprehensive Psychiatry, 41*, 416–425.

Torrey, E. F. (1997). *Out of the shadows: Confronting America's mental illness crisis*. New York, NY: Wiley.

Torrey, E. G., Miller, J., Rawlings, R., & Yolken, R. H. (1997). Seasonality of births in schizophrenia and bipolar disorder: A review of the literature. *Schizophrenia Research, 28*, 1–38.

Trull, T. J., & Durett, C. A. (2005). Categorical and dimensional models of personality disorder. *Annual Review of Clinical Psychology, 1*, 355–380.

Tsai, J. L. (2007). Ideal affect: Cultural causes and behavioral consequences. *Perspectives on Psychological Science, 3*, 242–259.

Tsai, J. L., Knutson, B., & Fung, H. H. (2006). Cultural variation in affect valuation. *Journal of Personality and Social Psychology, 90*, 288–307.

Van der Kloet, D., Giesbrecht, T., Lynn, S.J., Merckelbach, H., & de Zutter, A. (2012b). Sleep normalization and decreases in dissociative experiences: Evaluation in an inpatient sample. *Journal of Abnormal Psychology, 121*, 140–150.

Van Grootheest, D. S., Cath, D. C., Beekman, A. T., & Boomsma, D. I. (2007). *Psychological Medicine, 37*, 1635–1644.

Verdoux, H. (2004). Perinatal risk factors for schizophrenia: How specific are they? *Current Psychiatry Reports, 6*, 162–167.

Videbech, P., & Ravnkilde, B. (2004): Hippocampal volume and depression. A meta-analysis of MRI studies. *American Journal of Psychiatry, 161*, 1957–1966.

Vita, A., Dieci, G., Giobbio, A., Caputo, L., Ghiringhelli, M., & Comazzi, M.,... Invernizzi, G. (1995). Language and thought disorder in schizophrenia: Brain morphological correlates. *Schizophrenia Research, 15*, 243–251.

Volgmaier, M. M., Seidman, L. J., Niznikiewicz, M. A., Dickey, C. C., Shenton, M. E., & McCarley, R. W. (2000). Verbal and nonverbal neuropsychological test performance in subjects with schizotypal personality disorder. *American Journal of Psychiatry, 157*, 787–797.

Voncken, M. J., Bogels, S. M., & deVries, K. (2003). Interpretation and judgmental biases in social phobias. *Behavior Research and Therapy, 41*, 1481–1488.

Vriends, N., Pfaltz, M. C., Novianti, P., & Hadiyono, J. (2013). Taijin Kyofusho and social anxiety and their clinical relevance in Indonesia and Switzerland. *Frontiers in Psychology, 4*.

Wahl, O. (1997). *Consumer experience with stigma: Results of a national survey*. Alexandria, VA: NAMI.

Wakefield, A. J., Murch, S., Anthony, A., Linnell, J., Casson, D. M., Malik, M.,... Walker-Smith, J. A. (1998). Ileal lymphoid nodular hyperplasia, non-specific colitis, and regressive developmental disorder in children. *Lancet, 351*, 637–641.

Wakefield, J. C. (1992). The concept of mental disorder: On the boundary between biological facts and social values. *American Psychologist, 47*, 373–388.

Wakefield, J. C., & First, M. B. (2012). Placing symptoms in context: The role of contextual criteria in reducing false positives in Diagnostic and Statistical Manual of Mental Disorders Diagnoses. *Comprehensive Psychiatry, 53*(2), 130–139.

Waldman, I. D., Lilienfeld, S. O., & Lahey, B. B. (1995). Toward construct validity in the childhood disruptive behavior disorders: Classification and diagnosis in DSM-IV and beyond. In T. H. Ollendick & R. J. Prinz (Eds.), *Advances in clinical child psychology* (Vol. 17, pp. 323–363). New York, NY: Plenum Press.

Walker, E. F., Baum, K., & Diforio, D. (1998). Developmental changes in the behavioral expression of vulnerability for schizophrenia. In M. Lenzenweger & B. Dworkin (Eds.), *Experimental psychopathology and pathogenesis of schizophrenia* (pp. 469–492). Washington, DC: American Psychological Association.

Walker, E. F., & DiForio, D. (1997). Schizophrenia: A neural-diathesis stress model. *Psychological Review, 104*, 1–19.

Walker, E. F., Kestler, L., Bollini, A., & Hochman, K. (2004). Schizophrenia: Etiology and course. *Annual Review of Psychology, 55*, 401–430.

Walker, E. F., & Lewine, R. J. (1990). Prediction of adult-onset schizophrenia from childhood home movies of the patients. *American Journal of Psychiatry, 147*, 1052–1056.

Wallechinsky, D., Wallace, D., & Wallace, H. (1977). *The book of lists.* New York, NY: Bantam.

Watson, J. B., & Rayner, R. (1920). Conditioned emotional reactions. *Journal of Experimental Psychology, 3*, 1–14.

Watters, E. (2010). Crazy like us: The globalization of the American psyche. New York, NY: Free Press.

Wei, M., Mallinckrodt, B., Larson, L. M., & Zakalik, R. A. (2005). Adult attachment, depressive symptoms, and validation from self versus others. *Journal of Counseling Psychology, 52*, 368–377.

Weinberger, D. R. (1987). Implications of normal brain development for the pathogenesis of schizophrenia. *Archives of General Psychiatry, 44*, 660–669.

Werth, J. L. (2001). U.S. involuntary mental health commitment statutes: Requirements for persons perceived to be a potential harm to self. *Suicide and Life-Threatening Behavior, 31*, 348–357.

Widiger, T. A., & Clark, L. A. (2000). Toward DSM-V and the classification of psychopathology. *Psychological Bulletin, 126*, 946–963.

Widom, C. S. (1977). A methodology for studying noninstitutionalized psychopaths. *Journal of Consulting and Clinical Psychology, 45*, 674–683.

Willner, P. (1995). Animal models of depression—Validity and applications. *Depression and Mania, 49*, 19–41.

Wilson, C. (2005). What is autism? *New Scientist, 187*, 39.

Wilson, N. (2003). Commercializing mental health issues: Entertainment, advertising, and psychological advice. In S. O. Lilienfeld, S. J. Lynn, & J. M. Lohr (Eds.), *Science and pseudoscience in clinical psychology* (pp. 425–459). New York, NY: Guilford Press.

Wing, L., & Potter, D. (2002). The epidemiology of autistic spectrum disorders: Is the prevalence rising? *Mental Retardation and Developmental Disabilities Research Reviews, 8*, 151–161.

Wolfsdorf, B. A., Freeman, J., D'Eramo, K., Overholser, J., & Spirito, A. (2003). Mood states: Depression, anger, and anxiety. In A. Spirito & J. Overholser (Eds.), *Evaluating and treating adolescent suicide attempters: From research to practice* (pp. 53–88). New York, NY: Academic Press.

Wolke, D., Rizzo, P., & Woods, S. (2002). Persistent infant crying and hyperactivity problems in middle childhood. *Pediatrics, 109*, 1054–1060.

Woodward, L. J., Fergusson, D. M., & Horwood, L. J. (2000). Driving outcomes of young people with attentional difficulties in adolescence. *Journal of the American Academy of Child and Adolescent Psychiatry, 39*, 627–634.

Wright, A. G., Krueger, R. F., Hobbs, M. J., Markon, K. E., Eaton, N. R., & Slade, T. (in press). The structure of psychopathology: Toward an expanded quantitative empirical model. *Journal of Abnormal Psychology*.

Wymbs, B. T., Pelham, W. E., Jr., Moline, B. S. B., Gnagy, E. M., Wilson, T. K., & Greenhouse, J. B. (2008). Rate and predictors of divorce among parents of youths with ADHD. *Journal of Consulting and Clinical Psychology, 76*, 735–744.

Yamey, G., & Shaw, P. (2002). Is extreme racism a mental illness? No. *Western Journal of Medicine, 176*, 5.

Yan-Meier, L., Eberhart, N. K., Hammen, C. L., Gitlin, M., Sokolski, K., & Altshuler, L. (2011). Stressful life events predict delayed functional recovery following treatment for mania in bipolar disorder. *Psychiatry Research, 186*(2), 267–271.

Youngren, M. A., & Lewinsohn, P. M. (1980). The functional relationship between depressed and problematic interpersonal behavior. *Journal of Abnormal Psychology, 89*, 333–341.

Yurgelun-Todd, D. A., Gruber, S. A., Kanayama, G., Killgore, W. D. S., Baird, A. A., & Young, A. D. (2000). fMRI during affect discrimination in bipolar affective disorder. *Bipolar Disorders, 2*(3), 237–248.

Zanarini, M. C., Horwood, J., Wolke, D., Waylen, A., Fitzmaurice, G., & Grant, B. F. (2011). Prevalence of DSM-IV borderline personality disorder in two community samples: 6,330 English 11-year-olds and 34,653 American adults. *Journal of Personality Disorders, 25*(5), 607–619.

Zavos, H., Gregory, A. M., & Eley, T. C. (2012). Longitudinal genetic analysis of anxiety sensitivity. *Developmental Psychology, 48*, awaiting page numbers.

Zborowski, M. J., & Garske, J. P. (1993). Interpersonal deviance and consequent social impact in hypothetically schizophrenia-prone men. *Journal of Abnormal Psychology, 102*, 482–489.

Zeier, J. D., Baskin-Sommers, A. R., Hiatt Racer, K. D., & Newman, J. P. (2012). Cognitive control deficits associated with antisocial personality disorder and psychopathy. *Personality Disorders: Theory, Research, and Treatment, 3*(3), 283–293.

Zimmerman, M. (1994). Diagnosing personality disorders: A review of issues and research methods. *Archives of General Psychiatry, 51*, 225–245.

Zinbarg, R. E., & Barlow, D. H. (1996). The structure of anxiety and the anxiety disorders: A hierarchical model. *Journal of Abnormal Psychology, 105*, 81–193.

Zivotofsky, A. Z., Edelman, S., Green, T., Fostick, L., & Strous, R. D. (2007). Hemisphere asymmetry in schizophrenia as revealed through line bisection, line trisection, and letter cancellation. *Brain Research, 1142*, 70–79.

Zohar, J., Greenberg, B., & Denys, D. (2012). Obsessive-compulsive disorder. *Neurobiology of Psychiatric Disorders E-Book: Handbook of Clinical Neurology (Series Editors: Aminoff, Boller and Swaab), 106*, 375–392.

Zubin, J., & Spring, B. (1977). Vulnerability: A new view of schizophrenia. *Journal of Abnormal Psychology, 86*, 103–126.

Zuckerman, M. (1989). Personality in the third dimension: A psychobiological approach. *Personality and Individual Differences, 10*, 391–418.

Zuroff, D. C., Mongrain, M., & Santor, D. A. (2004). Investing in the personality vulnerability research program: Current dividends and future growth: Rejoinder to Coyne, Thompson, and Whiffen. *Psychological Bulletin, 130*, 518–522.

Credits

Credits listed in order of appearance.

Photo Credits

Photo Credits listed in order of appearance.

Psychological and Biological Treatments

From Chapter 16 of *Psychology: From Inquiry to Understanding*, Third Edition. Scott O. Lilienfeld, Steven Jay Lynn, Laura L. Namy, Nancy J. Woolf.

Psychological and Biological Treatments

HELPING PEOPLE CHANGE

Are more experienced therapists better than inexperienced therapists?

Do all psychotherapies require people to achieve insight to improve?

Is Alcoholics Anonymous better than other types of treatment for alcoholism?

Are some psychotherapies harmful?

Does electroshock treatment produce long-term brain damage?

Popular portrayals of psychotherapy have a long history in the media. (© CartoonBank.com)

psychotherapy
psychological intervention designed to help people resolve emotional, behavioral, and interpersonal problems and improve the quality of their lives

Psychological and Biological Treatments

Listen in **MyPsychLab** to chapter audio

Before reading on, picture a typical psychotherapy session. What's the person in therapy—often called the "client"—doing? How about the therapist? What does the room look like? Perhaps your first thought is of the proverbial client on a couch, with the therapist sitting behind him or her, pen and pad in hand, intent on unearthing long-forgotten memories, analyzing dreams, and encouraging the client to vent painful feelings.

If this scenario comes to mind, it's no wonder. From the early days of psychotherapy (often simply called "therapy"), these images have been etched into our cultural consciousness. But we'll discover that this picture doesn't begin to tell the story of the vast array of psychotherapeutic approaches that encompass individual therapy; treatments conducted in groups and with families; and even art, dance, and music therapy. Nor does the scenario capture the powerful biological treatments that have transformed the lives of people with psychological disorders by directly targeting the brain's functioning. In this chapter, we'll examine a broad spectrum of therapies, both psychological and biological, that are designed to alleviate emotional suffering.

Like many concepts in psychology, *psychotherapy* isn't easy to define. Over a half century ago, one pioneer in psychotherapy wrote, half-jokingly, "Psychotherapy is an undefined technique applied to unspecified problems with unpredictable outcomes. For this technique, we recommend rigorous training" (Raimy, 1950, p. 63). Some might contend that things haven't changed much since then. Still, for our purposes, we can define **psychotherapy** as a psychological intervention designed to help people resolve emotional, behavioral, and interpersonal problems and improve the quality of their lives (Engler & Goleman, 1992). Although the popular media often speak of therapy as though it were one thing, there are well over 500 "brands" of psychotherapy (Eisner, 2000), about three times as many as there were in the 1970s. As we'll learn, research demonstrates that many of these therapies are effective, but scores of others haven't been tested. In the pages to come, we'll offer critical thinking tools to help us distinguish scientifically supported psychological and biomedical therapies from therapies that are either ineffective or promising but scientifically unsupported.

Psychotherapy: Clients and Practitioners

1   Describe who seeks treatment, who benefits from psychotherapy, and who practices psychotherapy.
2   Distinguish between professionals and paraprofessionals and describe what it takes to be an effective therapist.

We'll begin by considering several questions: who seeks and benefits from psychotherapy? How is psychotherapy practiced? What makes a psychotherapist effective?

Who Seeks and Benefits from Treatment?

The most recent survey of the U.S. public—a 2006 *Newsweek* poll—found that about 20 percent of Americans have received psychological treatment at some point and that about 4 percent are currently in psychotherapy. People grapple with specific problems in psychotherapy, but they also contend frequently with generalized feelings of helplessness, social isolation, and a sense of failure (Garfield, 1978; Lambert, 2003). Still others turn to therapy to expand their self-awareness, learn better ways of relating to others, and consider lifestyle changes.

GENDER, ETHNIC, AND CULTURAL DIFFERENCES IN ENTERING TREATMENT. Some people are more likely to enter psychological treatment than others. Women are more likely to seek treatment than men are (Addis & Mahalik, 2003; DuBrin & Zastowny, 1988), although both sexes benefit equally from psychotherapy (Petry, Tennen, & Affleck, 2000). Members of many racial and ethnic minority groups, particularly Asian Americans and Hispanic Americans, are less likely to seek mental health services than are Caucasian Americans (Sue & Lam, 2002), perhaps because of the lingering stigma surrounding psychotherapy in these groups. Socioeconomic factors also predict who seeks therapy. Therapy can be very costly for those without health insurance or whose health plans don't include mental health coverage (Wang et al., 2008). Nevertheless, when individuals hailing from diverse cultural and ethnic backgrounds obtain psychotherapy, they're likely to benefit from it (Navarro, 1993; Prochaska & Norcross, 2007).

Culturally sensitive psychotherapists maximize their effectiveness by tuning their interventions to clients' cultural values and the difficulties they encounter in adapting to a dominant culture that may differ vastly from their own (Benish et al., 2011; Norcross & Wampold, 2011a; Sue & Sue, 2003). Although ethnic minorities prefer therapists with a similar ethnic background (Coleman, Wampold, & Casali, 1995), there's no consistent evidence that client–therapist ethnic (Shin et al., 2005) or gender (Bowman et al., 2001) matches enhance therapy outcome. Still, when clients are relative newcomers to a culture and not well acquainted with its traditions, therapist–client ethnic match may play a greater role in therapy's effectiveness (Sue, 1998). The good news is that people can be helped by therapists who differ from them in significant ways, including ethnicity and gender (Cardemil, 2010; Whaley & Davis, 2007).

REAPING BENEFITS FROM TREATMENT. The effectiveness of therapy depends on a host of individual differences. Clients who are most likely to improve are better adjusted to begin with, realize they may be contributing to their problems, and are motivated to work on those problems (Prochaska & DiClemente, 1982; Prochaska & Norcross, 2002). Clients who experience some anxiety do better in psychotherapy than do other clients—probably because their distress fuels their motivation to make life changes (Frank, 1974; Miller et al., 1995)—as do clients with temporary or situational problems, such as relationship upheavals (Gasperini et al., 1993; Steinmetz, Lewinsohn, & Antonuccio, 1983).

The ideal client? A 1964 study (Schofield, 1964) found that many therapists preferred to treat people who were relatively young, attractive, verbal, intelligent, and successful (YAVIS clients). Nevertheless, therapists have recently become more aware of the importance of assisting a broad clientele of all ages and cultural backgrounds.

Who Practices Psychotherapy?

Licensed professionals, especially clinical psychologists, psychiatrists, mental health counselors, and clinical social workers, are the mainstays of the mental health profession (see **TABLE 1**). But unlicensed religious, vocational, and rehabilitation counselors, as well as art and music therapists also provide psychological services.

TABLE 1 Occupations, Degrees, Roles, and Work Settings of Mental Health Professionals. Not all therapists are the same: mental health consumers are often unaware of the substantial differences in education, training, and roles of different psychotherapists. This table provides some guidance.

OCCUPATION	DEGREE/LICENSE	SETTINGS/ROLE
Clinical Psychologist	Ph.D./Psy.D., M.A., M.S.	Private practice, hospitals, schools, community agencies, medical settings, academic, other
Psychiatrist	M.D. or D.O.	Physicians, private practice, hospitals, medical centers, schools, academic, other
Counseling Psychologist	Ph.D., Ed.D., M.A., M.S., M.C.	University clinics, mental health centers; treat people with less severe psychological problems
School Psychologist	Ph.D., Psy.D., Ed.D., Ed.S., M.A., M.S., M.Ed.	In-school interventions, assessment, prevention programs; work with teachers, students, parents
Clinical Social Worker	Training varies widely; B.S.W., M.S.W., D.S.W., L.C.S.W.	Private practice following supervised experience, psychiatric facilities, hospitals/community agencies, schools, case managers; help with social and health problems
Mental Health Counselor	M.S.W., M.S., M.C.	Private practice, community agencies, hospitals, other; career counseling, marriage issues, substance abuse
Psychiatric Nurse	Training varies widely; associate degree, B.S.N., M.S.N., D.N.P., Ph.D.	Hospitals, community health centers, primary care facilities, outpatient mental health clinics; manage medications; with advanced degrees can diagnose, treat mental patients
Pastoral Counselor	Training varies; from bachelor's degree to more advanced degrees	Counseling, support in spiritual context, wellness programs; group, family, and couples therapy

Degree Key: B.S.N., bachelor of science in nursing; B.S.W., bachelor of social work; D.N.P., doctorate nurse practitioner; D.O., doctor of osteopathy; D.S.W., doctor of social work; Ed.D., doctor of education; Ed.S., specialist in education; L.C.S.W., licensed clinical social worker; M.A., master of arts; M.C., master of counseling; M.D., doctor of medicine; M.Ed., master of education; M.S., master of science; M.S.N., master of science in nursing; M.S.W., master of social work; Ph.D., doctor of philosophy; Psy.D., doctor of psychology.

Factoid

During the first month of treatment, many clients improve considerably. In fact, 40–66 percent of clients report improvement even before attending their first session (Howard et al., 1986). The act of seeking help—doing something about one's problems—apparently inspires hope and breeds confidence (Kirsch, 1990).

? In the HBO television series *In Treatment*, Laura (played by Melissa George) develops sexual feelings for her therapist, Paul (played by Gabriel Byrne). Paul doesn't have a sexual relationship with her, because he experiences a panic attack. A sexual relationship with a client is highly unethical. **Which of the following behaviors is also unethical?** (A) Revealing a client's plan to commit suicide to a family member to prevent the suicide. (B) Revealing a client's plan to assault another person to prevent the assault. (C) Informing a client's elderly father that she harbors hateful feelings toward him. (See answer upside down at bottom of page.)

paraprofessional
person with no professional training who provides mental health services

Answer: (C) With few exceptions, therapists keep all information confidential. However, therapists can share information without the client's written permission when the client is at serious risk for suicide or endangering others.

PROFESSIONALS VERSUS PARAPROFESSIONALS. Contrary to the myth that all psychotherapists have advanced degrees in mental health, volunteers and **paraprofessionals**, helpers who have no formal professional training, often provide psychological services in such settings as crisis intervention centers and other social service agencies. In most states, the term *therapist* isn't legally protected, so virtually anyone can hang up a shingle and offer treatment. Many paraprofessionals obtain agency-specific training and attend workshops that enhance their educational backgrounds. They may also be trained to recognize situations that require consultation with professionals with greater expertise. Paraprofessionals help to compensate for the sizable gap between the high demand for and meager supply of licensed practitioners (den Boer et al., 2005).

Again, contrary to popular belief, therapists don't need to be professionally trained or have many years of experience to be effective (Berman & Norton, 1985; Blatt et al., 1996; Christensen & Jacobson, 1994). Indeed, most studies reveal few or no differences in effectiveness between more and less experienced therapists (Dawes, 1994; McFall, 2006). Why is this so? As psychiatrist Jerome Frank (1961) noted, regardless of level of professional training, people who fulfill the role of therapist may provide clients with hope, empathy, advice, support, and opportunities for new learning experiences (Frank & Frank, 1991; Lambert & Ogles, 2004).

Even if there are few or no differences in therapy outcome as a function of professional training, there are several clear advantages to consulting with a professional. Professional helpers (1) understand how to operate effectively within the mental health system; (2) appreciate complex ethical, professional, and personal issues; and (3) can select treatments of demonstrated effectiveness (Garske & Anderson, 2003).

WHAT DOES IT TAKE TO BE AN EFFECTIVE PSYCHOTHERAPIST? Given that training and years of experience aren't critical determinants of what makes a good therapist, what does make a good therapist? Effective therapists are likely to be warm and direct, establish a positive working relationship with clients, and tend not to contradict clients (Friedlander, 1984; Garske & Anderson, 2003; Kazdin, Marciano, & Whitley, 2005; Luborsky et al., 1997; Westerman, Foote, & Winston, 1995). Effective therapists also select important topics on which to focus in sessions (Goldfried, Raue, & Castonguay, 1998), match their treatments to the needs and characteristics of clients (Beutler & Harwood, 2002), and collect feedback from their clients (Norcross & Wampold, 2011b). Still, sizable differences in therapist characteristics and abilities may overshadow the relatively small differences in the effectiveness of the types of treatments they provide (Ahn & Wampold, 2001; Luborsky et al., 1986). So when it comes to the success of psychotherapy, the choice of *therapist* is every bit as important as the choice of *therapy* (Blow, Sprenkle, & Davis, 2007).

What makes a good therapist from the client's point of view? The composite view of the "good" therapist is that of an expert who's warm, respectful, caring, and engaged (Littauer, Sexton, & Wyan, 2005; Strupp, Fox, & Lessler, 1969). In **TABLE 2**, we present some tips for both selecting good therapists and avoiding bad ones.

TABLE 2 What Should I Look for in a Therapist, and What Type of Therapist Should I Avoid? Tens of thousands of people call themselves therapists, and it's often hard to know what kind of therapist to seek out or avoid. This checklist may help you, your friends, or your loved ones to select a good therapist—and to steer clear of a bad one.

1. I can talk freely and openly with my therapist.
2. My therapist listens carefully to what I say and understands my feelings.
3. My therapist is warm, direct, and provides useful feedback.
4. My therapist explains up front what he or she will be doing and why and is willing to answer questions about his or her qualifications and training, my diagnosis, and our treatment plan.
5. My therapist encourages me to confront challenges and solve problems.
6. My therapist uses scientifically based approaches and discusses the pros and cons of other approaches.
7. My therapist regularly monitors how I'm doing and is willing to change course when treatment isn't going well.

(Continued)

TABLE 2 What Should I Look for in a Therapist, and What Type of Therapist Should I Avoid? (Continued)

If your answer is yes to one or more of the following statements, the therapist may *not* be in a good position to help you and even may be harmful.

1. My therapist gets defensive and angry when challenged.
2. My therapist has a "one size fits all" approach to all problems.
3. My therapist spends considerable time each session making "small talk," telling me exactly what to do, and sharing personal anecdotes.
4. My therapist isn't clear about what is expected of me in the treatment plan, and our discussions lack any focus and direction.
5. My therapist doesn't seem willing to discuss the scientific support for what he or she is doing.
6. There are no clear professional boundaries in my relationship with my therapist; for example, my therapist talks a lot about his or her personal life or asks me for personal favors.

Assess Your Knowledge   FACT or FICTION?

 Study and **Review** in **MyPsychLab**

1. Asian Americans are more likely to seek psychotherapy than are Caucasian Americans. **True / False**

2. Clients who are poorly adjusted to begin with are most likely to improve with therapy. **True / False**

3. All people who practice therapy have advanced degrees in mental health. **True / False**

4. Professional training is necessary to produce good therapy outcomes. **True / False**

5. The choice of a therapist is as important as the choice of therapy. **True / False**

Answers: 1. F; 2. F; 3. F; 4. F; 5. T

Insight Therapies: Acquiring Understanding

3 Describe the core beliefs and criticisms of psychodynamic therapies.

4 Describe and evaluate the effectiveness of humanistic therapies.

In much of the chapter that lies ahead, we'll examine some of the more prominent therapeutic approaches and evaluate their scientific status. We'll begin with **insight therapies**, which aim to cultivate insight, that is, expanded self-awareness and knowledge. The psychodynamic and humanistic therapies we'll review are two prominent schools of insight therapy.

Psychodynamic therapies are treatments inspired by classical psychoanalysis and influenced by Freud's techniques. Compared with psychoanalysis, which tends to be expensive and lengthy (often lasting years or even decades) and often involves meeting most days of the week, psychodynamic therapy is typically less costly, is briefer—weeks or months or open-ended—and involves meeting only once or twice a week (Shedler, 2010). After we examine Freud's techniques, we'll consider a group of therapists called *neo-Freudians*, who adopted Freud's psychodynamic perspective but modified his approach in distinctive ways.

Under the umbrella of **humanistic therapies**, we can find a variety of approaches rooted in the humanistic perspective on personality. Therapies within this orientation share an emphasis on insight, self-actualization, and the belief that human nature is basically positive (Maslow, 1954; Rogers, 1961; Shlien & Levant, 1984). Humanistic therapists reject the interpretive techniques of psychoanalysis. Instead, they strive to understand clients' inner worlds through empathy and focus on clients' thoughts and feelings in the present moment.

Psychoanalytic and Psychodynamic Therapies: Freud's Legacy

Psychodynamic therapists share the following three approaches and beliefs, which form the core of their approach (Blagys & Hilsenroth, 2000; Shedler, 2010):

1. They believe the causes of abnormal behaviors, including unconscious conflicts, wishes, and impulses, stem from traumatic or other adverse childhood experiences.

insight therapies
psychotherapies, including psychodynamic, humanistic, and group approaches, with the goal of expanding awareness or insight

humanistic therapies
therapies that emphasize the development of human potential and the belief that human nature is basically positive

743

Before Freud developed the technique of free association, he brought forth associations in a very different way. He told his clients to close their eyes and concentrate while he pressed his hand on their forehead. He then suggested that their repressed memories would return to consciousness (Ellenberger, 1970). Today, many therapists would probably regard this procedure as carrying a risk of generating false memories.

The Freudian concept of free association is a bit like a magician pulling kerchiefs out of a hat, with one thought leading to the next, in turn leading to the next, and so on.

free association
technique in which clients express themselves without censorship of any sort

resistance
attempts to avoid confrontation and anxiety associated with uncovering previously repressed thoughts, emotions, and impulses

transference
act of projecting intense, unrealistic feelings and expectations from the past onto the therapist

interpersonal therapy (IPT)
treatment that strengthens social skills and targets interpersonal problems, conflicts, and life transitions

RULING OUT RIVAL HYPOTHESES ►
Have important alternative explanations for the findings been excluded?

2. They strive to analyze (a) distressing thoughts and feelings clients avoid, (b) wishes and fantasies, (c) recurring themes and life patterns, (d) significant past events, and (e) the therapeutic relationship.

3. They believe that when clients achieve insight into previously unconscious material, the causes and the significance of symptoms will become evident, often causing symptoms to disappear.

PSYCHOANALYSIS: KEY INGREDIENTS. Freud's psychoanalysis was one of the first forms of psychotherapy. According to Freud, the goal of psychoanalysis is to decrease guilt and frustration and *make the unconscious conscious* by bringing to awareness previously repressed impulses, conflicts, and memories (Bornstein, 2001; Mellinger & Lynn, 2003). Psychoanalytic therapists, sometimes called "analysts," attempt to fill this tall order using six primary approaches.

(1) Free Association. As clients lie on a couch in a comfortable position, therapists instruct them to say whatever thoughts come to mind, no matter how meaningless or nonsensical they might seem. This process is called **free association**, because clients are permitted to express themselves without censorship.

(2) Interpretation. From the client's string of free associations, analysts form hypotheses regarding the origin of the client's difficulties and share them with him or her as the therapeutic relationship evolves. Therapists also formulate *interpretations—* explanations—of the unconscious bases of a client's dreams, emotions, and behaviors. They point out the supposedly disguised expression of a repressed idea, impulse, or wish, as in the following interpretation of a client's repeated "accidents" resulting in injury: "Having these accidents perhaps served an unconscious purpose; they assured you of getting the attention you felt you could not get otherwise." As in comedy, timing is everything: if the therapist offers the interpretation before the client is ready to accept it, psychoanalysts maintain, anxiety may derail the flow of new associations.

(3) Dream Analysis. According to Freud, dreams express unconscious themes that influence the client's conscious life. The therapist's task is to interpret the relation of the dream to the client's waking life and the dream's symbolic significance. The therapist might interpret the appearance of an ogre in a dream—the manifest (observable) content—as representing a hated and feared parent—the latent (hidden) content.

(4) Resistance. As treatment progresses and people become aware of previously unconscious and often feared aspects of themselves, they often experience **resistance**: they try to avoid further confrontation. Clients express resistance in many ways, including skipping therapy sessions or drawing a blank when the therapist asks a question about painful moments in their past, but all forms of resistance can stall their progress. To minimize resistance, psychoanalysts attempt to make clients aware that they're unconsciously blocking therapeutic efforts and make clear *how* and *what* they're resisting (Anderson & Stewart, 1983).

(5) Transference. As analysis continues, clients begin to experience **transference**: they project intense, unrealistic feelings and expectations from their past onto the therapist. The ambiguous figure of the analyst supposedly becomes the focus of emotions once directed at significant persons from the client's childhood. In one example, a client brought a gun into treatment and pointed it at the therapist. The therapist replied: "This is what I meant about your murderous feelings toward your father (Laughs). Do you see it now?" (Monroe, 1955). Freud believed that transference provides a vehicle for clients to understand their irrational expectations and demands of others, including the therapist.

Research suggests that we indeed often react to people in our present life in ways similar to people in our past (Berk & Andersen, 2000; Luborsky, et al., 1985). These findings may suggest that Freud was right about the transference; alternatively, they may mean that our stable personality traits lead us to react to people in similar ways over time. These lingering questions aside, therapists' interpretations of the transference may be helpful for some clients (Ogrodniczuk & Piper, 1999).

(6) Working Through. In the final stage of psychoanalysis, therapists help clients *work through,* or process, their problems. The insight gained in treatment is a helpful starting point, but it's not sufficient. As a consequence, therapists must repeatedly address conflicts and resistance to achieving healthy behavior patterns and help clients confront old and ineffective coping responses as they reemerge in everyday life (Menninger, 1958; Wachtel, 1997).

DEVELOPMENTS IN PSYCHOANALYSIS: THE NEO-FREUDIAN TRADITION. Freud's ideas spawned new therapeutic approaches in the psychodynamic tradition (Ellis, Abrams, & Abrams, 2008). In contrast to Freudian therapists, neo-Freudian therapists are more concerned with conscious aspects of the client's functioning. For example, according to neo-Freudian Carl Jung, the goal of psychotherapy is *individuation*—the integration of opposing aspects of the personality, like passive versus aggressive tendencies, into a harmonious "whole," namely, the self. To help clients achieve individuation, Jung considered their future goals as well as past experiences. Neo-Freudians also emphasize the impact of cultural and interpersonal influences, such as close friendships and loving relationships, on behavior across the lifespan (Adler, 1938; Mitchell & Black, 1995). Beyond Freud's emphasis on sexuality and aggression, neo-Freudians acknowledge the impact of other needs, including love, dependence, power, and status. They're also more optimistic than was Freud regarding people's prospects for achieving healthy functioning.

The emphasis on interpersonal relationships is the hallmark of Harry Stack Sullivan's *interpersonal psychotherapy.* According to Sullivan (1954), psychotherapy is a collaborative undertaking between client and therapist. Sullivan contended that the analyst's proper role is that of *participant observer.* Through ongoing observations, the analyst discovers and communicates to clients their unrealistic attitudes and behaviors in everyday life.

Sullivan's work influenced the contemporary approach of **interpersonal therapy (IPT)**. Originally a treatment for depression (Klerman et al., 1984; Santor & Kusumakar, 2001), IPT is a short-term intervention (12–16 sessions) designed to strengthen people's social skills and assist them in coping with interpersonal problems, conflicts (such as disputes with family members), and life transitions (such as childbirth and retirement). In addition to effectively treating depression (Klerman et al., 1984; Hinrichsen, 2008), IPT has demonstrated success in treating substance abuse and eating disorders comparable with that of cognitive-behavioral therapies (Klerman & Weissman, 1993; Murphy et al., 2012).

Is Insight Necessary? As we've seen, psychodynamic therapies rely heavily on insight. Many Hollywood films, such as *Good Will Hunting* (1997) and *Analyze This* (1999), reinforce the impression that insight—especially into the childhood origins of problems—is the crucial ingredient in therapeutic change. Yet extensive research demonstrates that understanding our emotional history, however deep and gratifying, isn't required to relieve psychological distress (Weisz et al., 1995). To improve, clients typically need to practice new and more adaptive behaviors in everyday life—that is, to engage in *working through* (Wachtel, 1977).

Some psychodynamic concepts, including therapeutic interpretations, are difficult to falsify. How can we demonstrate that a person's dream of his father scowling at him, for example, points to repressed memories of child abuse, as a therapist might infer? A client might respond, "Aha, that's it!" but this reaction could reflect transference or an attempt to please the therapist. If the client improves, the therapist might conclude that the interpretation is accurate, but the timing could be coincidental rather than causal (Grunbaum, 1984).

The failure to rule out rival hypotheses may lead both therapist and client to mistakenly attribute progress to insight and interpretation when other influences, like placebo effects, are responsible (Meyer, 1981). Research supports this caution. In one long-term study of psychoanalytic treatment (Bachrach et al., 1991), half of 42 clients improved but failed to show insight into their "core conflicts." Yet patients attributed improvement more to the support the therapist provided than to insight.

Are Traumatic Memories Repressed? Although many psychodynamic therapists believe that current difficulties often stem from the repression of traumatic events such as childhood abuse (Frederickson, 1992; Levis, 1995), research doesn't bear out this claim

? This client began crying after her therapist gently suggested that she take more risks in life. "That's exactly what my father used to tell me as a child," she said, and "now I feel criticized by you the same way I felt criticized by my father." According to psychoanalysts, the client is experiencing what phenomenon? (See answer upside down on bottom of page.)

Factoid

One of the strangest psychotherapies of all time is surely "direct analysis," developed by psychiatrist John Rosen as a treatment for schizophrenia. Called direct analysis because Rosen claimed to speak directly to clients' unconscious minds, this method required therapists to yell at clients, call them crazy, and threaten to slice them into pieces. In some cases, Rosen even enlisted psychiatric aides to dress up as FBI agents to question clients about their fantasies. Although once highly influential—Rosen received the 1971 American Academy of Psychotherapy "Man of the Year" award—direct analysis is no longer accepted in the therapeutic community (Dolnick, 1998). The science of psychotherapy, like other domains of science, is self-correcting.

◄ **FALSIFIABILITY**
Can the claim be disproved?

◄ **RULING OUT RIVAL HYPOTHESES**
Have important alternative explanations for the findings been excluded?

◄ **RULING OUT RIVAL HYPOTHESES**
Have important alternative explanations for the findings been excluded?

It's always the same dream. I'm in therapy, analyzing my recurring dream.

REPLICABILITY ▶

Can the results be duplicated in other studies?

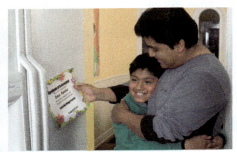

? According to Rogers, if a father gives his child love only when he receives a good grade, but not when he receives a poor grade, is the father expressing conditional regard or unconditional regard? (See answer upside down at bottom of page.)

person-centered therapy
therapy centering on the client's goals and ways of solving problems

Answer: Conditional regard

(Lynn et al., 2004; McHugh, 2008). Try this thought experiment. Which event would you be more likely to forget: an instance when your peers ridiculed you and beat you up in third grade for being the class know-it-all or a time when the teacher praised you in class for your participation? Odds are you thought you'd be better able to recall the unsettling event, and you'd be right. Disturbing events are actually *more* memorable and *less* subject to being forgotten than are everyday occurrences (Loftus, 1993; Porter & Peace, 2007;. After reviewing the research evidence, Richard McNally (2003) concluded that the scientific support for repressed memories is weak and that many memories, especially those that stretch to the distant past, are often subject to distortion. Nevertheless, the issue remains controversial (Anderson & Green, 2001; Erdelyi, 2006).

Psychodynamic Therapies Evaluated Scientifically. Valuable as they've been, classical psychodynamic therapies are questionable from a scientific standpoint. Freud and Jung based their therapeutic observations largely on small samples of wealthy, intelligent, and successful people, rendering their external validity unclear. Their clinical sessions weren't observed by others or conducted on a systematic basis that permitted replication by others, as would be the case with rigorously controlled research.

The concerns we've raised aside, research indicates that interpersonal therapies have generally, but not consistently, fared well in comparisons with scientifically supported treatments such as cognitive-behavioral therapy (Luty et al., 2010; Murphy et al., 2012; Vos et al., 2012). Brief versions of psychodynamic therapy are better than no treatment (Leichsenring, Rabung, & Leibing, 2004; Shedler, 2010), although they may be somewhat less effective than or comparable with cognitive-behavioral therapies, which don't emphasize insight (Grawe, Donati, & Bernauer, 1998; Shapiro & Shapiro, 1982; Watzke et al., 2012). Moreover, psychodynamic therapy isn't especially effective for psychotic disorders like schizophrenia, even though some practitioners continue to use it for this purpose (Karon, 1994).

Humanistic Therapies: Achieving Our Potential

Humanistic therapists share a desire to help people overcome the sense of alienation so prevalent in our culture; to develop their sensory and emotional awareness; and to express their creativity and help them become loving, responsible, and authentic. Humanistic therapists stress the importance of assuming responsibility for decisions, not attributing our problems to the past, and living fully and finding meaning in the present.

PERSON-CENTERED THERAPY: ATTAINING ACCEPTANCE. No therapist better exemplifies the practice of humanistic therapy than Carl Rogers. Rogers developed a therapy called **person-centered therapy** (formerly called client-centered therapy) in which therapists don't tell clients how to solve their problems and clients can use the therapy hour however they choose (Rogers, 1942). Person-centered therapy is *nondirective* because therapists encourage clients to direct the course of therapy and don't define or diagnose clients' problems or try to get at the root cause of their difficulties. To ensure a positive outcome, the therapist must satisfy three conditions:

1. The therapist must be an authentic, genuine person who reveals his or her own reactions to what the client is communicating.

   Client: I think I'm beyond help.
   Therapist: Huh? Feel as though you're beyond help. I know. You feel just completely hopeless about yourself. I can understand that. I don't feel hopeless, but I realize you do (Meador & Rogers, 1979, p. 157).

2. The therapist must express *unconditional positive regard,* that is, a nonjudgmental acceptance of all feelings the client expresses. Rogers was convinced that unconditional positive regard elicits a more positive self-concept. He maintained that it allows clients to reclaim aspects of their "true selves" that they disowned earlier in life due to others placing conditions of worth on them.

3. The therapist must relate to clients with empathic understanding. In Rogers's words: "To sense the patient's world as if it were our own, but without ever losing the 'as if' quality. This is empathy" (Rogers, 1957, p. 98).

One way to communicate empathy is by way of *reflection,* that is, mirroring back the client's feelings—a technique for which Rogers was famous. Here's an example.

> **Client:**   I was small and I envied people who were large. I was—well, I took beatings by boys and I couldn't strike back....
> **Therapist:**   You've had plenty of experience in being the underdog.
> (Rogers, 1942, pp. 145–146)

With increased awareness and heightened self-acceptance, people hopefully come to think more realistically, become more tolerant of others, and engage in more adaptive behaviors (Rogers, 1961). Some researchers have developed computer programs that attempt to simulate Rogers's person-centered therapy, especially Rogers's method of reflection (see **TABLE 3**).

Person-centered interviewing techniques, including showing warmth, empathy, and unconditional acceptance; using reflective listening; and avoiding confrontation, lie at the heart of *motivational interviewing* (Miller & Rollnick, 2002; Miller & Rose, 2009). This one- to two-session procedure recognizes that many clients are ambivalent about changing long-standing behaviors and is geared toward clarifying and bringing forth their reasons for changing—and not changing—their lives. Motivational interviewing, initially shown to be helpful in treating alcohol-related problems (Project MATCH Research Group, 1997), has been successful in modifying a variety of health-related behaviors, including exercising, dieting, and complying with medical therapies (Burke, Arkowitz, & Dunn, 2002; Burke, Arkowitz, & Menchola, 2003; Olsen et al., 2012).

GESTALT THERAPY: BECOMING WHOLE. Fritz Perls, the flamboyant founder of **Gestalt therapy**, was trained as a psychodynamic therapist, but imported some concepts from Gestalt psychology into a new brand of therapy. The word *gestalt* (configuration) means an organized whole. Gestalt therapists believe that people with psychological difficulties are "incomplete gestalts" because they've excluded from their awareness experiences and aspects of their personalities that trigger anxiety. As a consequence, Gestalt therapists aim to integrate different and sometimes opposing aspects of clients' personalities into a unified sense of self.

For Gestalt therapists, the key to personal growth is accepting responsibility for one's feelings and maintaining contact with the here and now. Gestalt therapy was the first of many therapies that recognize the importance of awareness, acceptance, and expression of feelings. In the *two-chair technique,* Gestalt therapists ask clients to move from chair to chair, creating a dialogue with two conflicting aspects of their personalities (see **FIGURE 1**). The "good boy" versus the "spoiled brat" may serve as the focal point for such an interchange. Gestalt therapists believe this procedure allows a synthesis of the opposing sides to emerge. For example, the good boy, always eager to please others, may learn from a conversation with the spoiled brat that it's acceptable in certain instances to be assertive, even demanding. Thus, the "good brat" may be more effective and authentic than either personality aspect alone.

HUMANISTIC THERAPIES EVALUATED SCIENTIFICALLY. The core concepts of humanistic therapies, such as meaning and self-actualization, are difficult to measure and falsify. For example, at exactly what point can we say a person is self-aware and authentic?

To his credit, however, Rogers specified three conditions for effective psychotherapy that could be falsified. Research has shown that he was largely on the mark when it comes to the therapeutic relationship. Establishing a strong alliance is helpful to the ultimate success of therapy (Horvath et al., 2011; Wampold, 2001). In fact, the therapeutic relationship is typically a stronger predictor of success in therapy than the use of specific techniques

TABLE 3 Simulated Conversation between Client and Computer Therapist, Eliza. Some researchers have developed computer programs that attempt to simulate Rogers's person-centered therapy, especially Rogers's method of reflection. Here, we can read excerpts from a conversation between a client and the computer therapist, Eliza, developed by computer scientist Joseph Weizenbaum. Would Eliza make a good therapist?

> **Eliza:** Hi, I am Eliza.
> **Client:** Hi Eliza.
> **Eliza:** How are you today....What would you like to discuss?
> **Client:** My girlfriend.
> **Eliza:** Tell me more…
> **Client:** I don't know how I feel about her.
> **Eliza:** Why don't you know how you feel about her?
> **Client:** Sometimes she is nice, other times she is not.
> **Eliza:** What does that suggest to you?
> **Client:** She has psychological problems.
> **Eliza:** Come come, elucidate your thoughts.
> **Client:** She changes all the time.
> **Eliza:** I see.
> **Client:** She can be very mean.
> **Eliza:** I see.
> **Client:** But I still love her.
> **Eliza:** I'm not sure I understand you fully.
> **Client:** I don't understand myself.
> **Eliza:** Does that trouble you?

Watch in **MyPsychLab** the **Video:** Classic Footage of Carl Rogers on the Role of a Therapist

◄ **FALSIFIABILITY**
Can the claim be disproved?

Gestalt therapy
therapy that aims to integrate different and sometimes opposing aspects of personality into a unified sense of self

(Bohart et al., 2002). But Rogers was wrong in one key respect: the three core conditions he specified aren't "necessary and sufficient" for improvement (Bohart, 2003; Norcross & Beutler, 1997). Although he overstated their impact, empathy (Bohart, Elliott, & Greenberg, 2002) and positive regard (Farber & Lane, 2002) are modestly related to therapy outcome (Orlinsky & Howard, 1986). Some studies have revealed a positive relation between genuineness and therapeutic outcome, but others haven't (Klein et al., 2002; Orlinsky, Grawe, & Parks, 1994). As we'll learn later, some people can derive considerable benefits from self-help programs that don't even involve therapists (Gould & Clum, 1993), so the therapeutic relationship isn't necessary for improvement. Moreover, research suggests that the causal direction of the relation between the therapeutic alliance and improvement may often be the reverse of what Rogers proposed: clients may first improve and then develop a stronger emotional bond with the therapist as a result (DeRubeis & Feeley, 1990; Kazdin, 2007).

Person-centered therapy is more effective than no treatment (Greenberg, Elliot, & Lietaer, 1994). But findings concerning the effectiveness of person-centered therapy are inconsistent, with some suggesting it may not help much more than a placebo treatment such as merely chatting for the same amount of time with a nonprofessional (Smith, Glass, & Miller, 1980). In contrast, other studies suggest that person-centered therapies often result in substantial improvement and may be comparable in effectiveness to the cognitive-behavioral therapies we'll encounter later (Elliott, 2002; Greenberg & Watson, 1998).

CORRELATION VS. CAUSATION ▶
Can we be sure that A causes B?

FIGURE I The Two-Chair Technique. Gestalt therapy's two-chair technique aims to integrate opposing aspects of the client's personality, such as the "good boy" and the "spoiled brat."

✔ **Study** and **Review** in **MyPsychLab**

Assess Your Knowledge — FACT or FICTION?

1. The first Freudian analysts were called neo-Freudian therapists.   **True / False**

2. Insight is a necesssary and sufficient condition for change to occur in psychotherapy.   **True / False**

3. An important criticism of psychoanalytic therapy is that many of its key concepts aren't falsifiable.   **True / False**

4. Humanistic psychotherapists place an emphasis on exploring past issues and conflicts.   **True / False**

5. Reflection is a central component of person-centered therapy.   **True / False**

Answers: 1. F; 2. F; 3. T; 4. F; 5. T

Group Therapies: The More the Merrier

5. List the advantages of group methods.

6. Describe the research evidence concerning the effectiveness of Alcoholics Anonymous.

7. Identify different approaches to treating the dysfunctional family system.

Since the early 1920s, when Viennese psychiatrist Jacob Moreno introduced the term **group therapy**, helping professionals have appreciated the value of treating more than one person at a time. The popularity of group approaches has paralleled the increased demand for psychological services in the general population. Group therapies, which typically range in size from 3 to as many as 20 clients, are efficient, time-saving, and less costly than individual treatments and span all major schools of psychotherapy (Levine, 1979). In a safe group environment, participants can provide and receive support, exchange information and feedback, model effective behaviors and practice new skills, and recognize that they're not alone in struggling with adjustment problems (Yalom, 1985).

Today, psychologists conduct group sessions in a variety of settings, including homes, hospitals, inpatient and residential settings, community agencies, and professional offices. They reach people who are divorced, experiencing marital problems, struggling with gender identity, and experiencing problems with alcoholism and eating disorders, among many other problems in living (Dies, 2003; Lynn & Frauman, 1985). The most recent trend is for self-help groups to form over the Internet, especially for people with problems that may be embarrassing to share in face-to-face encounters (Davison, Pennebaker, & Dickerson, 2000; Golkaramnay

Group therapy procedures are efficient, time-saving, and less costly than many individual treatment methods.

group therapy
therapy that treats more than one person at a time

748

et al., 2007). Research suggests that group procedures are effective for a wide range of problems and about as helpful as individual treatments (McEvoy, 2007; Fuhriman & Burlingame, 1994).

Alcoholics Anonymous

Self-help groups are composed of peers who share a similar problem; often they don't include a professional mental illness specialist. Over the past several decades, these groups, of which **Alcoholics Anonymous** (AA) is the best known, have become remarkably popular. AA was founded in 1935 and is now the largest organization for treating people with alcoholism, with more than 2.1 million members and an estimated 114,000 groups worldwide (Galanter, Dermatis, & Santucci, 2012; MacKillop & Gray, in press). At AA meetings, people share their struggles with alcohol, and new members are "sponsored" or mentored by more senior members, who've often achieved years of sobriety.

The program is organized around the famous "Twelve Steps" toward sobriety and is based on the assumptions that alcoholism is a physical disease and "once an alcoholic, always an alcoholic," which require that members never drink another drop after entering treatment. Several of the Twelve Steps ask members to place their trust in a "higher power" and to acknowledge their powerlessness over alcohol. AA also offers a powerful social support network (Vaillant & Milofsky, 1982). Groups based on the Twelve-Step model have been established for drug users (Narcotics Anonymous), gamblers, overeaters, spouses and children of alcoholics, "shopaholics" (compulsive shoppers), sexual addicts, and scores of others experiencing problems with impulse control. Nevertheless, there's virtually no research on the effectiveness of these other Twelve-Step approaches.

Although AA appears to be helpful for some people, many claims regarding its success aren't supported by data. People who attend AA meetings or receive treatment based on the Twelve Steps fare about as well as, but no better than, people who receive other treatments, including cognitive-behavioral therapy (Brandsma, Maultsby, & Welsh, 1980; Ferri, Amoto, & Davoli, 2006; Project MATCH Research Group, 1997). Moreover, AA members who end up in studies are usually the most active participants and have received prior professional help, resulting in an overestimate of how well AA works. Also, as many as 68 percent of participants drop out within three months of joining AA (Emrick, 1987), and those who remain in treatment are probably those who've improved (MacKillop et al., 2003). A study that followed AA members for 16 years found that attendance in the first and third years each predicted abstinence and fewer drinking problems (Moos & Moos, 2006). A key factor in who improves in AA is the ability to participate in an adaptive social network (Kelly et al., 2012). Clearly, for some people with alcoholism, participation in AA may lead to positive outcomes (MacKillop & Gray, in press).

Controlled Drinking and Relapse Prevention

Contrary to the AA philosophy, the behavioral view assumes that excessive drinking is a learned behavior that therapists can modify and control without total abstinence (Marlatt, 1983). There's bitter controversy about whether *controlled drinking,* that is, drinking in moderation, is even an appropriate treatment goal. Nevertheless, there's considerable evidence that treatment programs that encourage people with alcoholism to set limits, drink moderately, and reinforce their progress can be effective for many clients (MacKillop, et al., 2003; Miller & Hester, 1980; Sobell & Sobell, 1973, 1976). Programs that teach people skills to cope with stressful life circumstances and tolerate negative emotions (Monti, Gulliver, & Myers, 1994) are at least as effective as Twelve-Step programs (Project MATCH Research Group, 1997).

Bucking the popular belief, sometimes repeated in the AA community, of "one drink, one drunk," *relapse prevention* (RP) treatment assumes that many people with alcoholism will at some point experience a lapse, or slip, and resume drinking (Larimer, Palmer, & Marlatt, 1999; Marlatt & Gordon, 1985). RP teaches people not to feel ashamed, guilty, or discouraged when they lapse. Negative feelings about a slip can lead to continued drinking, called the *abstinence violation effect* (Marlatt & Gordon, 1985; Polivy & Herman, 2002). Once someone slips up, he or she figures, "Well, I guess I'm back to drinking again" and goes back to drinking at high levels. RP therapists teach people to rebound after a lapse and avoid

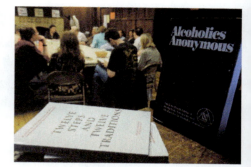

Alcoholics Anonymous has been in existence since the 1930s and provides self-help to people of all ages and backgrounds.

Alcoholics Anonymous
Twelve-Step self-help program that provides social support for achieving sobriety

FIGURE 2 Where's the Problem? According to the strategic family therapy approach, families often single out one family member as "the problem" when the problem is actually rooted in the interactional patterns of all family members.

In structural family therapy, the therapist immerses himself or herself in the family's everyday activities. Having observed what goes on in the family, the therapist can then advocate for changes in how the family arranges and organizes its interactions.

 Study and **Review** in **MyPsychLab**

strategic family intervention
family therapy approach designed to remove barriers to effective communication

structural family therapy
treatment in which therapists deeply involve themselves in family activities to change how family members arrange and organize interactions

situations in which they're tempted to drink. Thus, they learn that a *lapse* doesn't mean a *relapse*. Research suggests that relapse prevention programs are often effective (Irvin et al., 1999). Still, total abstinence is probably the best goal for people with severe dependence on alcohol or for whom controlled drinking has failed (Rosenberg, 1993).

Family Therapies: Treating the Dysfunctional Family System

Family therapists see most psychological problems as rooted in a dysfunctional family system. For them, treatment must focus on the family context out of which conflicts presumably arise. In *family therapy*, the "patient"—the focus of treatment—isn't one person with the most obvious problems, but rather the family unit itself. Family therapists therefore focus on interactions among family members.

STRATEGIC FAMILY THERAPY. Strategic family interventions are designed to remove barriers to effective communication. According to strategic therapists, including Virginia Satir (1964), Jay Haley (1976), and Paul Watzlawick (Watzlawick, Weakland, & Fisch, 1974), the real source of psychological problems of one or more family members often lies in the dysfunctional ways in which they communicate, solve problems, and relate to one another (see **FIGURE 2**).

Strategic therapists invite family members to carry out planned tasks known as *directives,* which shift how family members solve problems and interact. They often involve *paradoxical requests,* which many of us associate with the concept of "reverse psychology." Some researchers (Beutler, Clarkin, & Bongar, 2000) have found that therapists often achieve success when they command their "resistant" or uncooperative clients to intentionally produce the thought, feeling, or behavior that troubled them.

Consider a therapist who "reframed" (cast in a positive light) a couple's arguments by interpreting them as a sign of their emotional closeness. The therapist gave the couple the paradoxical directive to *increase* their arguing to learn more about their love for each other. To show the therapist they were "not in love," they stopped arguing, which was, of course, the therapist's goal in the first place. Once their arguments ceased, their relationship improved (Watzlawick, Beavin, & Jackson, 1967).

STRUCTURAL FAMILY THERAPY. In **structural family therapy** (Minuchin, 1974), the therapist actively immerses himself or herself in the everyday activities of the family to make changes in how they arrange and organize interactions. Salvatore Minuchin and his colleagues successfully treated a 14-year-old girl named Laura who obtained her father's attention by refusing to eat. Eventually, Laura could express in words the message that her refusal to eat conveyed indirectly, and she no longer refused to eat to attain affection (Aponte & Hoffman, 1973). Research indicates that family therapy is more effective than no treatment (Hazelrigg, Cooper, & Borduin, 1987; Vetere, 2001) and at least as effective as individual therapy (Foster & Gurman, 1985; Shadish, 1995).

Assess Your Knowledge — FACT or FICTION?

1. Group psychotherapies are generally as effective as individual psychotherapies. **True / False**
2. Self-help groups are often assisted by a professional therapist. **True / False**
3. Alcoholics Anonymous is no more effective than many other alcohol abuse treatments. **True / False**
4. Family therapies focus on the one person in the family with the most problems. **True / False**
5. Planned tasks for family members suggested by strategic family therapists are called directives. **True / False**

Answers: 1. T; 2. F; 3. T; 4. F; 5. T

Behavioral and Cognitive-Behavioral Approaches: Changing Maladaptive Actions and Thoughts

8 Describe the characteristics of behavior therapy and identify different behavioral approaches.

9 Describe the features of cognitive-behavioral therapies (CBT) and third wave therapies.

In sharp contrast to psychotherapists who hold that insight is the key to improvement, **behavior therapists** are so named because they focus on the specific behaviors that lead the client to seek therapy and address the current variables that maintain problematic thoughts, feelings, and behaviors (Antony & Roemer, 2003). Behavior therapists assume that behavior change results from the operation of basic principles of learning, especially classical conditioning, operant conditioning, and observational learning. For example, a client with a dog phobia may reinforce his problematic behaviors by crossing the street whenever he sees a dog. Avoiding the dog helps him obtain negative reinforcement—in this case, escaping anxiety—although he is probably unaware of this function.

Behavior therapists use a wide variety of *behavioral assessment* techniques to pinpoint environmental causes of the person's problem, establish specific and measurable treatment goals, and devise therapeutic procedures. Behavior therapists may use direct observations of current and specific behaviors, verbal descriptions of the nature and dimensions of the problem, scores on paper-and-pencil tests, standardized interviews (First et al., 1996), and physiological measures (Yartz & Hawk, 2001) to plan treatment and monitor its progress. A complete assessment considers clients' gender, race, socioeconomic class, culture, sexual orientation, and ethnic factors (Hays, 2009; Ivey, Ivey, & Simek-Morgan, 1993), as well as information about their interpersonal relationships and drug use (Lazarus, 2003). Evaluation of treatment effectiveness is integrated seamlessly into all phases of therapy, and therapists encourage clients to apply their newly acquired coping skills to everyday life. Let's now examine the nuts and bolts of several behavioral approaches.

Systematic Desensitization and Exposure Therapies: Learning Principles in Action

Systematic desensitization is an excellent example of how behavior therapists apply learning principles to treatment. Psychiatrist Joseph Wolpe developed systematic desensitization (SD) in 1958 to help clients manage phobias. SD gradually exposes clients to anxiety-producing situations through the use of imagined scenes. This technique was the earliest **exposure therapy**, a class of procedures that aims to reduce clients' fears by confronting them directly with the source of their fears.

HOW DESENSITIZATION WORKS: ONE STEP AT A TIME. SD is based on the principle of *reciprocal inhibition,* which says that clients can't experience two conflicting responses simultaneously. If a client is relaxed, he or she can't be anxious at the same time. Wolpe described his technique as a form of classical conditioning and called it *counterconditioning.* By pairing an incompatible relaxation response with anxiety, we condition a more adaptive response to anxiety-arousing stimuli.

A therapist begins SD by teaching the client how to relax by alternately tensing and relaxing his or her muscles (Bernstein, Borkovec, & Hazlett-Stevens, 2000; Jacobson, 1938). Next, the therapist helps the client to construct an *anxiety hierarchy*—a "ladder" of situations that climbs from least to most anxiety provoking. We can find a hierarchy used to treat a person with a phobia of dogs in **TABLE 4**. The therapy proceeds in a stepwise manner. The therapist asks the client to relax and imagine the first scene, moving to the next, more anxiety-producing scene only after the client reports feeling relaxed while imagining the first scene.

Consider the following example of how a client moves stepwise up the anxiety hierarchy, from the least to most anxiety-producing scene.

A behavior therapist treating a bad habit, like nail biting, would try to determine the situations in which nail biting occurs, as well as the consequences of nail biting for the person—such as distraction from anxiety.

Factoid

Because behavior therapies focus only on observable problems rather than their "root cause," many psychoanalysts once predicted that they would result in *symptom substitution*. That is, following behavior therapy, the client's underlying conflict, such as early aggression toward parents, would merely manifest itself as a different symptom. Yet data show that behavior therapies rarely, if ever, produce symptom substitution (Kazdin & Hersen, 1980; Tryon, 2008). For example, clients whose phobias are eliminated with behavioral therapy don't tend to develop other problems, like depression.

behavior therapist
therapist who focuses on specific problem behaviors and current variables that maintain problematic thoughts, feelings, and behaviors

systematic desensitization
clients are taught to relax as they are gradually exposed to what they fear in a stepwise manner

exposure therapy
therapy that confronts clients with what they fear with the goal of reducing the fear

In vivo desensitization: clients gradually approach and handle any fears, as these clients are doing as they overcome their fear of flying.

TABLE 4 A Systematic Desensitization Hierarchy of a Person With a Fear of Dogs.

1. You are looking at pictures of dogs in magazines.
2. You are looking at a video of a dog playing with another dog.
3. You are looking at a video of a dog playing with a person.
4. From 100 feet away, you are watching an Irish Setter playing with the therapist.
5. You are approaching the dog and observing the interaction with the therapist from a distance of 50, 25, 10, and 5 feet in successive trials.
6. You are petting the dog.
7. You are playing with the dog.
8. You are allowing the dog to lick you.

Therapist: "Soon I shall ask you to imagine a scene. After you hear a description of the situation, please imagine it as vividly as you can, through your own eyes, as if you were actually there. Try to include all the details in the scene. While you're visualizing the situation, you may continue feeling as relaxed as you are now. . . After 5, 10, or 15 seconds, I'll ask you to stop imagining the scene... and to just relax. But if you begin to feel even the slightest increase in anxiety or tension, please signal this to me by raising your left forefinger. . . I'll step in and ask you to stop imagining the situation and then will help you get relaxed once more" (Goldfried & Davison, 1976, pp. 124–125).

If the client reports anxiety at any point, the therapist interrupts the process and helps him or her relax again. Then, the therapist reintroduces the scene that preceded the one that caused anxiety. This process continues until the client can confront the most frightening scenes without anxiety.

Desensitization can also occur *in vivo,* that is, in "real life." In vivo SD involves gradual exposure to what the client actually fears, rather than imagining the anxiety-provoking situation. SD is effective for a wide range of phobias, insomnia, speech disorders, asthma attacks, nightmares, and some cases of problem drinking (Spiegler & Guevremont, 2003).

The Effectiveness of Systematic Desensitization. Behavior therapists strive to discover not only what works, but also why it works. Researchers can evaluate many therapeutic procedures by isolating the effects of each component and comparing these effects with that of the full treatment package (Wilson & O' Leary, 1980). This approach is called **dismantling,** because it enables researchers to examine the effectiveness of isolated components of a broader treatment. Dismantling helps rule out rival hypotheses about the effective mechanisms of SD and other treatments.

Dismantling studies show that no single component of desensitization (relaxation, imagery, an anxiety hierarchy) is essential: we can eliminate each without affecting treatment outcome. Therefore, the door is open to diverse interpretations for the treatment's success (Kazdin & Wilcoxon, 1976; Lohr, DeMaio, & McGlynn, 2003). One possibility is that the credibility of the treatment creates a strong placebo effect (Mineka & Thomas, 1999). Interestingly, desensitization may fare no better than a placebo procedure designed to arouse an equivalent degree of positive expectations (Lick, 1975). Alternatively, when therapists expose clients to what they fear, clients may realize that their fears are irrational, or their fear response may extinguish following repeated uneventful contact with the feared stimulus (Casey, Oei, & Newcombe, 2004; Rachman, 1994; Zinbarg, 1993).

FLOODING AND VIRTUAL REALITY EXPOSURE. Flooding therapies provide a vivid contrast to SD. Flooding therapists jump right to the top of the anxiety hierarchy and expose clients to images of the stimuli they fear the most for prolonged periods, often for an hour or even several hours. Flooding therapies are based on the idea that fears are maintained by avoidance. For example, because individuals with a height phobia continually avoid high places, they never learn that the disastrous consequences they envision won't occur. Ironically, their avoidance only perpetuates their fears by means of negative reinforcement. The flooding therapist repeatedly provokes anxiety in the absence of actual negative consequences so that extinction of the fear can proceed.

RULING OUT RIVAL HYPOTHESES ▶
Have important alternative explanations for the findings been excluded?

RULING OUT RIVAL HYPOTHESES ▶
Have important alternative explanations for the findings been excluded?

dismantling
research procedure for examining the effectiveness of isolated components of a larger treatment

Like SD, flooding can be conducted in vivo. To paraphrase the Nike slogan ("Just do it"): "If you're afraid to do it, do it!" During the first session, a therapist who practices in vivo flooding might accompany a person with a height phobia to the top of a skyscraper and look down for an hour—or however long it takes for anxiety to dissipate. Remarkably, many people with specific phobias—including those who were in psychodynamic therapy for decades with no relief—have been essentially cured of their fears after only a single session (Antony & Barlow, 2002; Williams, Turner, & Peer, 1985). Therapists have successfully used flooding with numerous anxiety disorders, including obsessive-compulsive disorder (OCD), social phobia, posttraumatic stress disorder, and agoraphobia.

A crucial component of flooding is **response prevention** (more recently called "ritual prevention" in the case of obsessive-compulsive disorder), in which therapists prevent clients from performing their typical avoidance behaviors (Spiegler, 1983). A therapist may treat a person with a hand-washing compulsion by exposing her to dirt and preventing her from washing her hands (Franklin & Foa, 2002). Research demonstrates that this treatment is effective for OCD and closely related conditions (Chambless & Ollendick, 2001; Gillihan et al., 2012).

Virtual reality exposure therapy is the "new kid on the block" of exposure therapies. With high-tech equipment, which provides a "virtually lifelike" experience of fear-provoking situations, therapists can treat many anxiety-related conditions, including height phobia (Emmelkamp et al., 2001), thunderstorm phobia (Botella et al., 2006), flying phobia (Emmelkamp et al., 2002), and posttraumatic stress disorder (Reger et al., 2011; Rothbaum et al., 2001). Virtual reality exposure not only rivals the effectiveness of traditional in vivo exposure, but also provides repeated exposure to situations that often aren't feasible in real life, like flying in airplanes.

In 2005, researchers discovered that the antibiotic D-cycloserine, used for many years to treat tuberculosis, facilitates long-term extinction of fear of heights when administered several hours before people undergo exposure riding in a "virtual glass elevator" (Davis et al., 2005). D-cycloserine works by boosting the functioning of a receptor in the brain that enhances fear-extinction learning in both animals and humans. Today, D-cycloserine is recognized as a promising adjunct to treatments for anxiety-related conditions, including obsessive-compulsive disorder (Norberg, Krystal, & Tolin, 2008) and possibly posttraumatic stress disorder (Kleine et al., 2012). Still, D-cyclocerine does not consistently outperform placebos (Litz et al., 2012), so the verdict regarding its specific effects on various psychological disorders is not settled.

EXPOSURE: FRINGE AND FAD TECHNIQUES. Traditionally, behavior therapists have been careful not to exaggerate claims of the effectiveness of exposure therapies and promote them to the public as cure-alls. We can contrast this cautious approach with that of recent proponents of fringe therapeutic techniques, some of who've made extraordinary claims that don't stack up well against the evidence.

Roger Callahan, who developed *Thought Field Therapy* (TFT), claimed that his procedure could cure phobias in as little as five minutes (Callahan, 1995, 2001) and cure not only human fears, but also fears of horses and dogs. In TFT, the client thinks of a distressing problem while the therapist taps specific points on the client's body in a predetermined order. Meanwhile, the client hums parts of "The Star Spangled Banner," rolls her eyes, or counts (how TFT therapists accomplish these feats with animals is unknown). These decidedly strange procedures supposedly remove invisible "energy blocks" associated with a specific fear. There's no research evidence for the assertion that the technique cures anxiety by manipulating energy fields, which have never been shown to exist, or for the implausible claim of virtually instantaneous cures for the vast majority of phobia sufferers (Lohr et al., 2003; Pignotti & Thyler, 2009). Because the "energy blocks" of TFT aren't measurable, the theoretical claims of TFT are unfalsifiable.

Some other exposure-based therapies feature numerous "bells and whistles" that provide them with the superficial veneer of science. Take *eye movement desensitization and reprocessing* (EMDR), which has been marketed widely as a "breakthrough" treatment for

Thought Field Therapists claim that touching body parts in a set order can play a role in treating long-standing phobias resistant to treatment by other means.

In EMDR, the client focuses on the therapist's fingers as they move back and forth. Nevertheless, studies indicate that such eye movements play no useful role in EMDR's effectiveness.

◀ **EXTRAORDINARY CLAIMS**
Is the evidence as strong as the claim?

response prevention
technique in which therapists prevent clients from performing their typical avoidance behaviors

◀ **FALSIFIABILITY**
Can the claim be disproved?

anxiety disorders (Shapiro, 1995; Shapiro & Forrest, 1997). As of 2010, more than 80,000 therapists have been trained in EMDR. EMDR proponents claim that clients' lateral eye movements, made while they imagine a past traumatic event, enhance their processing of painful memories. Yet systematic reviews of research demonstrate that the eye movements of EMDR play no role in this treatment's effectiveness. Moreover, EMDR is no more effective than standard exposure treatments (Davidson & Parker, 2001; Lohr, Tolin, & Lilienfeld, 1998; Rubin, 2003). Accordingly, a parsimonious hypothesis is that the active ingredient of EMDR isn't the eye movements for which it's named, but rather the exposure the technique provides.

OCCAM'S RAZOR ▶
Does a simpler explanation fit the data just as well?

Modeling in Therapy: Learning by Watching

Clients can learn many things by observing therapists model positive behaviors. Modeling is one form of *observational or vicarious learning*. Albert Bandura (1971, 1977) has long advocated **participant modeling**, a technique in which the therapist models a calm encounter with the client's feared object or situation and then guides the client through the steps of the encounter until he or she can cope unassisted.

ASSERTION TRAINING. Modeling is an important component of assertion and social skills training programs designed to help clients with social anxiety. The primary goals of assertion training are to facilitate the expression of thoughts and feelings in a forthright and socially appropriate manner and to ensure that clients aren't taken advantage of, ignored, or denied their legitimate rights (Alberti & Emmons, 2001). In assertion training, therapists teach clients to avoid extreme reactions to others' unreasonable demands, such as submissiveness, on the one hand, and aggressiveness, on the other. Assertiveness, the middle ground between these extremes, is the goal.

BEHAVIORAL REHEARSAL. Therapies commonly use behavioral rehearsal in assertion training and other participant modeling techniques. In behavioral rehearsal, the client engages in role-playing with a therapist to learn and practice new skills. The therapist plays the role of a relevant person such as a spouse, parent, or boss. The client reacts to the character enacted by the therapist, and in turn, the therapist offers coaching and feedback. To give the client an opportunity to model assertive behaviors, therapist and client reverse roles, with the therapist playing the client's role. By doing so, the therapist models not only what the client might say, but also how the client might say it.

To transfer what clients learn to everyday life, therapists encourage them to practice their newfound skills outside therapy sessions. Modeling and social skills training can make valuable contributions to treating (although not curing) schizophrenia, autism, depression, attention-deficit/hyperactivity disorder (ADHD), and social anxiety (Antony & Roemer, 2003; Scattone, 2007; Monastra, 2008).

Operant and Classical Conditioning Procedures

Psychologists have used operant conditioning procedures to good effect among children with autism and a host of other childhood disorders. Operant conditioning is learning in which behavior is modified by its consequences. An example of an operant procedure is the **token economy**, widely used in treatment programs in institutional and residential settings, as well as the home. In token economies, certain behaviors, like helping others, are consistently rewarded with tokens that clients can later exchange for more tangible rewards, whereas other behaviors, like screaming at hospital staff, are ignored or punished. In this way, such programs shape, maintain, or alter behaviors by the consistent application of operant conditioning principles (Boerke & Reitman, 2011; Kazdin, 1978). Critics of token economies argue that the benefits don't necessarily generalize to other settings and that they're difficult and impractical to administer (Corrigan, 1995). Nevertheless, token economies have shown some

participant modeling
technique in which the therapist first models a problematic situation and then guides the client through steps to cope with it unassisted

token economy
method in which desirable behaviors are rewarded with tokens that clients can exchange for tangible rewards

success in the classroom (Boniecki & Moore, 2003), in treating children with ADHD at home and at school (Mueser & Liberman, 1995), and in treating clients with schizophrenia who require long-term hospitalization (Dixon et al., 2010; Paul & Lentz, 1977).

Aversion therapies are based primarily on classical conditioning and pair undesirable behaviors with stimuli that most people experience as painful, unpleasant, or even revolting. For example, therapists have used medications such as disulfiram—better known as Antabuse—to make people vomit after drinking alcohol (Brewer, 1992), electric shocks to treat psychologically triggered recurrent sneezing (Kushner, 1968), and verbal descriptions of feeling nauseated while people imagine smoking cigarettes (Cautela, 1971).

Research provides, at best, mixed support for the effectiveness of aversive procedures (Spiegler & Guevremont, 2003). For example, people with alcoholism often simply stop taking Antabuse rather than stop drinking (MacKillop & Gray, in press). In general, therapists attempt minimally unpleasant techniques before moving on to more aversive measures. The decision to implement aversion therapies should be made only after carefully weighing their costs and benefits relative to alternative approaches.

Cognitive-Behavioral and Third Wave Therapies: Learning to Think and Act Differently

Advocates of **cognitive-behavioral therapies** hold that beliefs play the central role in our feelings and behaviors. These therapies share three core assumptions: (1) Cognitions are identifiable and measureable; (2) cognitions are the key players in both healthy and unhealthy psychological functioning; and (3) irrational beliefs or catastrophic thinking such as "I'm worthless and will never succeed at anything" can be replaced with more rational and adaptive cognitions, or viewed in a more accepting light.

THE ABCS OF RATIONAL EMOTIVE BEHAVIOR THERAPY. Beginning in the mid-1950s, pioneering therapist Albert Ellis (Ellis, 1958, 1962) advocated *rational emotive therapy* (RET), later renamed *rational emotive behavior therapy* (REBT). In many respects, REBT is a prime example of a cognitive-behavioral approach. It is cognitive in its emphasis on changing how we think (that's the "cognitive" part), but it also focuses on changing how we act (that's the "behavioral" part).

Ellis argued that we respond to an unpleasant activating (internal or external) event (A) with a range of emotional and behavioral consequences (C). As we all know, people often respond very differently to the same objective event; some students respond to a 75 on an exam by celebrating, whereas others respond by berating themselves for not getting a 90 or even a 100. For Ellis, the differences in how we respond to the same event stem largely from differences in (B)—our belief systems (see **FIGURE 3**). The ABCs Ellis identified lie at the heart of most, if not all, cognitive-behavior therapies.

Some beliefs are rational: they are flexible, are logical, and promote self-acceptance. In contrast, others are irrational: they're associated with unrealistic demands about the self ("I must be perfect"), others ("I must become worried about other people's problems"), and life conditions ("I must be worried about things I can't control."). Ellis also maintained that psychologically unhealthy people frequently "awfulize," that is, engage in catastrophic thinking about their problems ("If I don't get this job, it would be the worst thing that ever happened to me"). We can find examples of 12 irrational beliefs outlined by Ellis in **TABLE 5**. According to Ellis, our vulnerability to psychological disturbance is a product of the frequency and strength of our irrational beliefs (David, Lynn, & Ellis, 2010).

To his ABC scheme, Ellis added a (D) and (E) component to describe how therapists treat clients. REBT therapists encourage clients to actively dispute (D) their irrational beliefs and adopt more effective (E) and rational beliefs to increase adaptive responses. To modify clients' irrational beliefs, the therapist forcefully encourages them to rethink their assumptions and personal philosophy. REBT therapists often assign "homework" designed to falsify clients' maladaptive beliefs. For example, they may give shy clients an assignment to talk to an attractive man or woman to falsify their belief that "If I'm rejected by someone I like, it will be absolutely terrible."

aversion therapy
treatment that uses punishment to decrease the frequency of undesirable behaviors

cognitive-behavioral therapies
treatments that attempt to replace irrational cognitions and maladaptive behaviors with more rational cognitions and adaptive behaviors

◀ **FALSIFIABILITY**
Can the claim be disproved?

FIGURE 3 The ABCs of Rational Emotive Behavior Therapy. How someone feels about an event is determined by his or her beliefs about the event.

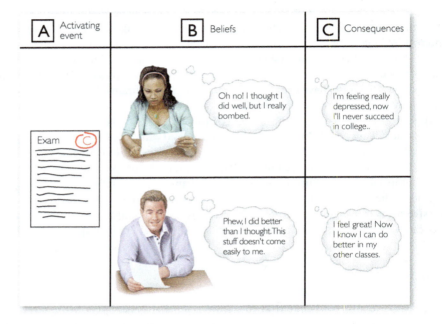

A Activating event	B Beliefs	C Consequences
Exam	Oh no! I thought I did well, but I really bombed.	I'm feeling really depressed, now I'll never succeed in college..
	Phew, I did better than I thought. This stuff doesn't come easily to me.	I feel great! Now I know I can do better in my other classes.

There's some evidence that therapists' theoretical orientation is correlated with their personality traits. Several, although not all, studies suggest that compared with other therapists, psychoanalytic therapists tend to be especially insecure and serious, behavior therapists tend to be especially assertive and self-confident, and cognitive-behavioral therapists tend to be especially rational (Keinan, Almagor, & Ben-Porath, 1989; Walton, 1978).

TABLE 5 Irrational Beliefs: "The Dirty Dozen." Albert Ellis identified 12 irrational ideas ("The Dirty Dozen") that are widespread in our culture. You may find it interesting to see which of these beliefs you've entertained at some point in your life. Because these ideas are so much a part of many people's thinking, don't be surprised if you hold a number of them.

1. You must have nearly constant love and approval from everyone who is important to you.
2. You must prove yourself highly adequate and successful, or at least extremely competent or talented at some valued activity.
3. People who hurt you or treat you poorly are bad, evil, and blameworthy, and deserve to be punished harshly for their actions.
4. When things don't go your way, it's an awful, horrible, or terrible catastrophe.
5. External factors, such as life events, are responsible for your misery; you have little ability to control or eliminate your negative feelings, including sadness and anger.
6. You must become upset and preoccupied with frightening or dangerous situations or people.
7. It's easier to avoid confronting many of life's challenges and responsibilities than it is to become self-disciplined.
8. The past must continue to dominate your feelings and behavior because previous experiences once exerted a strong impact on you.
9. If you can't cope with or resolve everyday hassles quickly, it's terrible; things and relationships should work out better than they do.
10. Being passive with no commitment to accomplish anything other than "enjoying oneself" is a good way to achieve happiness.
11. To feel comfortable, you must be highly organized or certain about how things will turn out.
12. Your worth and acceptance depend on your performance and how others rate you. Rather than evaluate your performance in specific areas of functioning, you should give yourself a global rating ("I'm good," "I'm bad," and so on).

(Based on: Ellis, 1977)

Two pioneers of cognitive-behavioral therapy, Aaron Beck (*left*; 1921–) and Albert Ellis (1913–2007).

OTHER COGNITIVE-BEHAVIORAL APPROACHES. Cognitive-behavioral therapists differ in the extent to which they incorporate behavioral methods. Aaron Beck's enormously popular *cognitive therapy*, which many credit as playing an instrumental role in creating the field of cognitive-behavioral therapy (Smith, 2009), emphasizes identifying and modifying distorted thoughts and long-held negative core beliefs ("I'm unlovable") (Beck et al., 1979; J. Beck, 1995). Nevertheless, cognitive therapy places somewhat greater weight on behavioral procedures than does Ellis's REBT (Stricker & Gold, 2003). Researchers have found Beck's approach helpful for people with depression; anxiety disorders; and perhaps even bipolar disorder, schizophrenia, and certain personality disorders such as borderline personality disorder (A. T. Beck, 2005; A.T. Beck & Dozois, 2011; Hollon, Thase, & Markowitz, 2002).

In Donald Meichenbaum's (1985) *stress inoculation training,* therapists teach clients to prepare for and cope with future stressful life events. In this approach, therapists "inoculate" clients against an upcoming stressor by getting them to anticipate it and develop cognitive skills to minimize its harm, much as we receive a vaccine (inoculation) containing a small amount of a virus to ward off illness. Therapists modify clients' *self-statements,* that is, their ongoing mental dialogue (Meichenbaum, 1985). Clients fearful of giving a speech may learn to say things to themselves, like "Even though it's scary, the outcome probably won't be as bad as I fear." Therapists have applied stress inoculation successfully to children and adults facing medical and surgical procedures, public speaking, and exams (Meichenbaum, 1996), as well as to clients with anger problems (Cahill et al., 2003; Novaco, 1994).

ACCEPTANCE: THE THIRD WAVE OF COGNITIVE-BEHAVIORAL THERAPY. The past few decades have witnessed a surge of interest in so-called *third wave therapies* that represent a shift from both the first (behavioral) and second (cognitive) waves of the cognitive-behavioral tradition (Hayes, 2004). Instead of trying to change maladaptive behaviors and negative thoughts, third wave therapies embrace a different goal: to assist clients with accepting and being mindful of and attuned to all aspects of their experience, including thoughts, feelings, memories, and physical sensations. Consistent with this goal, research suggests that avoiding and suppressing disturbing experiences, rather than accepting or confronting them, often backfires, creating even greater emotional turmoil (Amir et al., 2001; Teasdale, Segal, & Williams, 2003).

Steven Hayes and colleagues' (Hayes, Follette, & Linehan, 2004; Hayes, Strosahl, & Wilson, 1999) acceptance and commitment therapy (ACT) stands at the vanguard of such approaches. ACT practitioners teach clients that negative thoughts such as "I'm worthless" are merely thoughts, not "facts," while encouraging them to accept and tolerate the full range of their feelings and to act in keeping with their goals and values.

ACT and a growing number of third wave therapies often train clients in mindfulness practices such as meditation, which may involve nothing more than paying attention to the inflow and outflow of the breath while allowing thoughts and feelings to come and go without judgment (Kabat-Zinn, 2003). Mindfulness-based cognitive therapy (Segal, Williams, & Teasdale, 2012), which combines mindfulness with cognitive therapy, produces reductions in the average rate of relapse in depression on the order of 50 percent (Hofmann et al., 2010; Piet & Hougaard, 2011) and substantially reduces anxiety in adults and children (Kim et al., 2010; Semple & Lee, 2011).

Marsha Linehan's (Linehan 1993) dialectical behavior therapy (DBT), another third wave therapy used frequently in the treatment of clients with borderline personality disorder, addresses the *dialectic*—the apparent contradiction between opposing tendencies—of changing problematic behavior and accepting it. Linehan encourages clients to accept their intense emotions while actively attempting to cope with these emotions by making changes in their lives. Research supports the effectiveness of DBT for a number of symptoms of borderline personality disorder, including self-harm behaviors (McMain et al., 2012).

It remains to be seen whether these new techniques are more effective than standard behavioral and cognitive-behavioral therapies. Critics have raised concerns that new wave therapies have been overhyped in the absence of convincing scientific evidence and have questioned whether they represent a significant departure from more traditional cognitive-behavioral therapies (Hofmann & Asmundson, 2008; Ost, 2008). Perhaps a better analogy to these recent developments in psychotherapy is not a wave, but a tree, which represents cognitive-behavioral therapy, with many branches, one of them being third wave approaches (Hofmann, 2010). After all, cognitive-behavioral techniques represent a broad swath of approaches, and asking people to perceive their

PERSONAL   110(

About 9 months ago I began to notice a man wearing sunglasses who was watching me from a parking lot across the street. I thought he was suspicious and eventually concluded that he and his colleagues were following me everywhere I went. Even when I went on vacation to California 3000 miles away, I noticed that the same man and his colleagues were not far behind. After several weeks of careful investigation, I decided to leave home and travel to Europe in an attempt to escape him. Even while in Paris, I felt his eyes on me and was quite sure that I even saw him on television one night. I fear he has already contacted my employer and possibly some of my friends, because they all seem more distant from me lately. I want you all to know that everything he says about me is a lie.

 Each of the three statements below—provided by therapists in response to the person who placed the personal ad—is typical of a different psychotherapy. **Match each statement with the therapy (A. client-centered, B. Freudian, C. REBT) it best represents.** (See answer upside down on bottom of page.)

1. You're being irrational and jumping to conclusions. Even if someone were following you, why conclude that he's contacted your friends just because they're more distant?

2. You've told me that during childhood, your father constantly judged you and that when he stared at you, it brought about tremendous guilt. Perhaps this man you can't escape symbolizes your father?

3. Starting nine months ago, you became suspicious of a man you're now pretty sure will damage relationships you prize. How terrible it must feel to think he's telling lies about you!

Watch in **MyPsychLab** the **Video:** Cognitive Behavioral Therapy for Schizophrenia

Answers: 1-C, 2-B, 3-A

TABLE 6 Primary Theoretical Orientations of Practicing Clinical Psychologists in the United States. As we can see, the largest proportion of clinical psychologists calls themselves eclectic/integrative.

ORIENTATION	% CLINICAL PSYCHOLOGISTS
Eclectic/Integrative	29
Cognitive	28
Psychodynamic	12
Behavioral	10
Other	7
Interpersonal	4
Psychoanalytic	3
Family Systems	3
Existential-Humanistic	2
Person-Centered	1

(*Sources:* Prochaska & Norcross, 2007; derived from Bechtold et al., 2001; Norcross, Karpiak, & Santoro, 2005; Norcross, Strausser, & Missar, 1988)

RULING OUT RIVAL HYPOTHESES ▶
Have important alternative explanations for the findings been excluded?

✔ **Study** and **Review** in **MyPsychLab**

negative thoughts as nothing more than thoughts, as is done in ACT and mindfulness approaches, can be viewed as yet another way of modifying disturbing cognitions, or at least how one thinks about such cognitions.

Many third wave therapies fall in line with the current trend in psychotherapy for therapists to create individually tailored *eclectic* approaches—treatments that integrate techniques and theories from more than one existing approach (Lazarus, 2006; Stricker & Gold, 2003; Wachtel, 1997). For example, ACT and DBT therapists adopt behavioral techniques and meditation practices from a Buddhist tradition and borrow from humanistic psychology's emphasis on awareness and emotional expression. As we can see in **TABLE 6**, the largest percentage of practicing clinical psychologists describe their theoretical orientation as eclectic/integrative (Norcross, 2005; Prochaska & Norcross, 2007).

Only recently have psychologists come to learn which specific therapeutic components contribute to treatment success. For example, *behavioral activation*—getting clients, such as those who are depressed, to participate in reinforcing activities—is a key component of many third wave and cognitive-behavioral approaches and is emerging as a key element of successful psychotherapy (Dimidjian et al., 2006; Hopko, Robertson, & Lejuez, 2006; Ritschel et al., 2011). Intentional or incidental exposure to negative thoughts and feelings is another component of treatment that is probably associated with the success of numerous psychotherapies (Carey, 2011; Kazdin, 2009). Still, the more ingredients that are tossed into the therapeutic mix, the more challenging it becomes to dismantle integrative approaches and evaluate rival hypotheses regarding which ingredients matter.

CBT AND THIRD WAVE APPROACHES EVALUATED SCIENTIFICALLY. Research allows us to draw the following conclusions about the effectiveness of behavioral and cognitive-behavioral therapies:

1. They're more effective than no treatment or placebo treatment (Bowers & Clum, 1988; Smith, Glass, & Miller, 1980).

2. They're at least as effective (Sloane et al., 1975; Smith & Glass, 1977)—and in some cases more effective—than psychodynamic and person-centered therapies (Grawe, Donati, & Bernauer, 1998).

3. They're at least as effective as drug therapies for depression (Elkin, 1994).

4. In general, CBT and behavioral treatments are about equally effective for most problems (Feske & Chambless, 1995; Jacobson et al., 1996).

5. Third wave approaches have scored successes in treating a variety of disorders, including depression and alcoholism (Marlatt, 2002; Segal, Williams, & Teasdale, 2012), and CBT and ACT achieve comparable outcomes in treating depression and anxiety (Forman et al., 2007).

Assess Your Knowledge   FACT or FICTION?

1. Behavior therapies place a great deal of importance on insight.   True / False

2. One commonly used assertion training technique is behavioral rehearsal.
   True / False

3. Token economy programs are based on operant conditioning principles.
   True / False

4. According to Albert Ellis, feelings create irrational beliefs.   True / False

5. Acceptance and commitment therapy borrows techniques from a Buddhist tradition.   True / False

Answers: 1. F; 2. T; 3. T; 4. F; 5. T

Is Psychotherapy Effective?

10 Evaluate the claim that all psychotherapies are equally effective.

11 Explain how ineffective therapies can sometimes appear to be effective.

In Lewis Carroll's book *Alice in Wonderland,* the Dodo bird proclaimed after a race, "Everybody has won, and all must have prizes." Seventy years ago, Saul Rosenzweig (1936) delivered the same verdict regarding the effectiveness of different psychotherapies. That is, all appear to be helpful, but are roughly equivalent in their outcomes (see **FIGURE 4**).

The Dodo Bird Verdict: Alive or Extinct?

Before the mid-1970s, there was considerable controversy regarding whether psychotherapy was effective at all. Some investigators concluded that it was virtually worthless (Eysenck, 1952), whereas others concluded the opposite.

Beginning in the late 1970s, a scientific consensus emerged that psychotherapy works in alleviating human suffering (Landman & Dawes, 1982; Smith & Glass, 1977)—a consensus that holds to this day. This conclusion derived from studies using a technique called *meta-analysis.* A **meta-analysis**, meaning "analysis of analysis," is a statistical method that helps researchers interpret large bodies of psychological literature. By pooling the results of many studies as though they were one big study, meta-analysis allows researchers to seek patterns across large numbers of studies and to draw general conclusions that hold up across independent laboratories (Hunt, 1997; Rosenthal & DiMatteo, 2001).

Today, some researchers using meta-analysis have claimed to support the Dodo bird verdict. Their results suggest that a wide range of psychotherapies are about equal in their effects (Duncan, 2010; Wampold et al., 1997, 2002; Wampold, 2010). Studies with experienced therapists who've practiced behavioral, psychodynamic, and person-centered approaches have found that all are more successful in helping clients compared with no treatment, but are no different from each other in their effects (DiLoretto, 1971; Sloane et al., 1975).

Other researchers aren't convinced. They contend that the Dodo bird verdict, like the real Dodo bird, is extinct. Although most forms of psychotherapy work well and many are about equal in their effects, there are notable exceptions (Beutler, 2002; Hunsley & DiGuilio, 2002). For example, behavioral and cognitive-behavioral treatments are clearly more effective compared with other treatments for children and adolescents with behavior problems (Garske & Anderson, 2003; Weisz et al., 1995). Moreover, behavioral and cognitive-behavioral therapies consistently outperform most other therapies for anxiety disorders, including phobias, panic disorder, and obsessive-compulsive disorder (Addis et al., 2004; Chambless & Ollendick, 2001; Tolin, 2010).

Also calling into question the Dodo bird verdict are findings that some psychotherapies can make people worse (Barlow, 2010; Dimidjian & Hollon, 2010; Lilienfeld, 2007). Although we might assume that doing something is always better than doing nothing for psychological distress, research suggests otherwise. A nontrivial proportion of clients, perhaps 5–10 percent, become worse following psychotherapy, and some may become worse *because of* psychotherapy (Castonguay et al., 2010; Rhule, 2005; Strupp, Hadley, & Gomez-Schwartz, 1978). For example, several researchers have found that crisis debriefing can sometimes increase the risk of posttraumatic stress symptoms in people exposed to trauma. The same appears to be true of Scared Straight interventions, which try to "scare away" at-risk adolescents from a life a life of crime by introducing them to actual prisoners (Petrosino, Turpin-Petrosino, & Buehler, 2003). We can see a number of other potentially harmful therapies in **TABLE 7**.

The bottom line? Many therapies are effective, and many do about equally well. Yet there are clear-cut exceptions to the Dodo bird verdict. Moreover, because at least some therapies are harmful, we shouldn't assume that we'll always be safe randomly picking a therapist out of the telephone book.

In Lewis Carroll's book *Alice in Wonderland*, the Dodo bird declared after a race, "Everybody has won, and all must have prizes." Psychotherapy researchers use the term *Dodo bird verdict* to refer to the conclusion that all therapies are equivalent in their effects. Not all investigators accept this verdict.

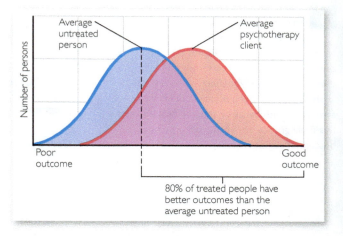

FIGURE 4 The Effectiveness of Psychotherapy. This graph shows two normal distributions derived from nearly 500 studies of psychotherapy outcomes. The distribution on the left shows people who haven't received psychotherapy, and the distribution on the right shows people who have received psychotherapy. As we can see, across a variety of treatments and samples, 80 percent of people who receive therapy do better than people who don't. (Based on Smith, Glass, & Miller, 1980)

Simulate in **MyPsychLab** the **Experiment:** Ineffective Therapies

meta-analysis
statistical method that helps researchers interpret large bodies of psychological literature

759

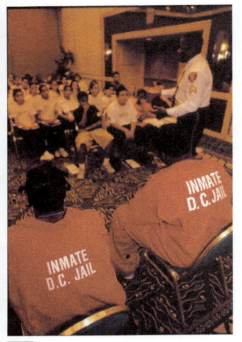

Scared Straight programs expose adolescents to prisoners and prison life in an effort to "scare them" away from criminal careers. Despite the popularity of these programs, research suggests that they are not merely ineffective, but harmful in some cases. Which principle of learning associated with behavior therapy best explains this finding? (See answer upside down at bottom of page.)

TABLE 7 List of Potentially Harmful Therapies. Research suggests that some psychotherapies are potentially harmful for certain individuals.

THERAPY	INTERVENTION	POTENTIAL HARM
Facilitated communication	A facilitator holds the hands of children with autism or other developmental disabilities as they type messages on a keyboard.	False accusations of child abuse against family members
Scared Straight programs	At-risk adolescents are exposed to the harsh realities of prison life to frighten them away from a life of future crime.	Worsening of conduct problems
Recovered-memory techniques	Therapists use methods to recover memories, including prompting of memories, leading questions, hypnosis, and guided imagery.	Production of false memories of trauma
Dissociative identity disorder (DID)–oriented psychotherapy	Therapists use techniques that imply to clients that they harbor "alter" personalities. Therapists attempt to summon and interact with alters.	Production of alters, creation of serious identity problems
Critical incident stress (crisis) debriefing	Shortly after a traumatic event, therapists urge group members to "process" their negative emotions, describe posttraumatic stress disorder symptoms that members are likely to experience, and discourage members from discontinuing participation.	Heightened risk for posttraumatic stress symptoms
DARE (Drug Abuse and Resistance Education) programs	Police officers teach schoolchildren about the risks of drug use and about social skills to resist peer pressure to try drugs.	Increased intake of alcohol and other substances (such as cigarettes)
Coercive restraint therapies	Therapists physically restrain children who have difficulty forming attachments to their parents. These therapies include rebirthing and holding therapy, in which the therapist holds children down until they stop resisting or begin to show eye contact.	Physical injuries, suffocation, death

(*Source:* Based on data from Lilienfeld, 2007)

Answer: Modeling

How Different Groups of People Respond to Psychotherapy

A void exists in our knowledge of how certain segments of the population respond to psychotherapy (Brown, 2006; Olkin & Taliaferro, 2005; U.S. Surgeon General, 2001). Research suggests that socioeconomic status (SES), gender, race, ethnicity, and age typically have little or no bearing on the outcome of therapy (Beutler, Machado, & Neufeldt, 1994; Cruz et al., 2007; Petry, Tennen, & Affleck, 2000; Rabinowitz & Renert, 1997; Schmidt & Hancey, 1979). Still, we must be tentative in our conclusions because researchers haven't studied these variables in depth. Many controlled studies of psychotherapy don't report participants' race, ethnicity, disability status, or sexual orientation, nor do they analyze whether the effectiveness of psychotherapy depends on these variables (Cardemil, 2010; Sue & Zane, 2006). So we can't be completely confident that therapies effective for Caucasians are equally effective for other populations.

Common Factors

One probable reason many therapies are comparable in effectiveness is that certain *common factors*—those that cut across many or most therapies—are responsible for improvement across diverse treatments. As Jerome Frank (1961) noted in his classic book *Persuasion and Healing*, these common factors include listening with empathy, instilling hope, establishing a strong emotional bond with clients, providing a clear theoretical rationale for treatment, and implementing techniques that offer new ways of thinking, feeling, and behaving (Del Re et al., 2012; Lambert & Ogles, 2004; Miller, Duncan, & Hubble, 2005). Frank observed that these common factors are also shared by many forms of faith healing, religious conversion, and interpersonal persuasion over the centuries and that they extend across most, if not all, cultures. Additional common factors include the therapist assisting the client in making sense of the world, exerting influence and mastery through social means and connecting with others, and developing positive treatment expectancies (Wampold, 2007, 2012). Although we might be tempted to dismiss common factors as "placebos," this would miss the crucial point that they're essential in instilling in clients the motivation to change. Indeed, studies show that common factors typically account for a hefty chunk of improvement in therapy (Cuijpers et al., 2008; Sparks, Duncan, & Miller, 2008).

In contrast, *specific factors* characterize only certain therapies: they include meditating, challenging irrational beliefs, and social skills training. In some cases, specific factors may be key ingredients in psychotherapeutic change; in other cases, they may not enhance treatment effectiveness beyond common factors (Stevens, Hynan, & Allen, 2000). Psychologists are divided about the extent to which common versus specific factors influence the outcome of psychotherapy (Craighead, Sheets, & Bjornsson, 2005; DeRubeis, Brotman, & Gibbons, 2005; Kazdin, 2005), although most agree that both matter.

Some therapists claim that contact with dolphins can treat a variety of psychological problems, including autism. However, research does not support the idea that dolphin therapy is effective for any problem or disorder (Marino & Lilienfeld, 1998; 2007).

Positive life events that occur outside therapy sessions, like major job promotions, can help to explain spontaneous remissions of some psychological problems, such as depression. As neo-Freudian theorist Karen Horney observed, "Life itself still remains a very effective therapist" (Horney, 1945, p. 240).

from inquiry to understanding

WHY CAN INEFFECTIVE THERAPIES APPEAR TO BE HELPFUL? HOW WE CAN BE FOOLED

Effective psychotherapy empowers people to contend with the most challenging problems in living. Yet some therapists have successfully marketed a wide variety of interventions that lack research support and rest on questionable premises (Lilienfeld et al., 2003; Norcross, Garofalo, & Koocher, 2006; Singer & Nievod, 2003). They include treatments as seemingly bizarre as dolphin therapy; laughter therapy; primal scream therapy; treatment for the trauma of abduction by aliens (Appelle, Lynn, & Newman, 2000); Neurolinguistic Programming (NLP), in which therapists match clients' nonverbal behaviors such as tone of voice to influence them; and even treatment for resolving problems due to presumed traumas in a past life (Mills & Lynn, 2000).

How might clients and therapists alike come to believe that treatments that are ineffective are helpful? The following five reasons can help us understand why bogus therapies gain a dedicated public following (Arkowitz & Lilienfeld, 2006; Beyerstein, 1997).

1. **Spontaneous remission.** The client's recovery may have nothing at all to do with the treatment. All of us have our "ups and downs." Similarly, many psychological problems are self-limiting or cyclical and improve without intervention. A breakup with our latest "crush" may depress us for a while, but most of us will improve even without professional help. This phenomenon, known as *spontaneous remission*, occasionally occurs even in serious medical conditions, including cancer (Silverman, 1987).

Spontaneous remission is surprisingly common in psychotherapy. In the first formal review of psychotherapy outcomes, Hans Eysenck (1952) reported the findings of two uncontrolled studies of neurotic (mildly disturbed) clients who received no formal therapy.

Psychological and Biological Treatments

The rate of spontaneous remission in these studies was a staggering 72 percent! Admittedly, the studies Eysenck selected may have had unusually high rates of spontaneous remission because the individuals he claimed were "untreated" received reassurance and suggestion. Still, there's no question that many people with psychological problems like depression often improve without treatment. Only if people who are treated improve at a rate that exceeds that of untreated people or those on a wait list can we rule out the effects of spontaneous remission.

RULING OUT RIVAL HYPOTHESES ▶
Have important alternative explanations for the findings been excluded?

2. **The placebo effect.** The pesky placebo effect can lead to significant symptom relief. Virtually any credible treatment can be helpful in alleviating our demoralization.

3. **Self-serving biases.** Even when they don't improve, clients who are strongly invested in psychotherapy and have shelled out a lot of money in the pursuit of well-being can persuade themselves they've been helped. Because it would be too troubling to admit to oneself (or others) that it's all been a waste of time, energy, and effort, there's often a strong psychological pull to find value in a treatment (Axsom & Cooper, 1985) while ignoring, downplaying, or explaining away failures as a means of maintaining self-esteem (Beyerstein & Hadaway, 1991).

4. **Retrospective rewriting of the past.** In some cases, we may believe we've improved even when we haven't because we misremember our initial (pretreatment) level of adjustment as worse than it was. We *expect* to change after treatment and may adjust our memories to fit this expectation. In one study, investigators randomly assigned college students either to take a study skills course or serve in a wait-list control group. On objective measures of grades, the course proved worthless. Yet students who took the course thought they'd improved. (Students in the control group did not.) Why? They mistakenly recalled their initial study skills as worse than they actually were (Conway & Ross, 1984). The same phenomenon may sometimes occur in psychotherapy.

5. **Regression to the mean.** It's a statistical fact of life that extreme scores tend to become less extreme on retesting, a phenomenon known as *regression to the mean*. If you receive a zero on your first psychology exam, there's a silver lining to this gray cloud: you'll almost surely do better on your second exam! Conversely, if you receive a 100 on your first exam, odds are also high you won't do as well the second time around. Scores on measures of psychopathology are no different. If a client comes into treatment extremely depressed, the chances are high that he or she will be less depressed in a few weeks. Regression to the mean can fool therapists and clients into believing that a useless treatment is effective. It's an especially tricky problem in evaluating whether psychotherapy is effective, because most clients enter psychotherapy when their symptoms are most extreme.

Factoid

Many "jinxes" probably stem from a failure to consider regression to the mean (Kruger, Savitsky, & Gilovich, 1999). If we've been doing far better than we had expected in a sports tournament and a friend says "Wow, you're doing great," we may fear that our friend has jinxed us. In fact, we *are* likely to do worse after our friend says that, but because of regression to the mean, not because of a jinx. The post hoc fallacy states that because A comes before B doesn't mean that A causes B.

Good psychotherapists keep up with the current state of the research literature, staying informed about which therapies do and don't have strong scientific support.

REPLICABILITY ▶
Can the results be duplicated in other studies?

empirically supported treatment (EST)
intervention for specific disorders supported by high-quality scientific evidence

Empirically Supported Treatments

Because we can be fooled into thinking a therapy is effective when it's not, it may come as a surprise that psychologists are split on the extent to which they should base their treatments on subjective experience and intuition as opposed to carefully controlled research. The *scientist-practitioner gap* (Fox, 1996; Lilienfeld et al., in press b; Tavris, 2003) refers to the sharp cleft between psychologists who view psychotherapy as more an art than a science and those who believe that clinical practice should primarily reflect well-replicated scientific findings (Dawes, 1994; Lilienfeld et al., 2003; Baker, McFall, & Shoham, 2009). Clearly, subjective judgment plays a crucial role in therapy, but such judgment should be informed by scientific evidence. But what kind of evidence should therapists consider? Over the past 15 years or so, researchers have responded to this question by putting forth lists of **empirically supported treatments (ESTs)**, now sometimes called "research supported treatments"—interventions for specific disorders backed by high-quality scientific evidence derived from controlled studies (Chambless et al., 1996; Lebow, 2010).

Behavior therapy and cognitive-behavioral therapy have emerged as ESTs for depression, anxiety disorders, obesity, marital problems, sexual dysfunction, and alcohol problems. Interpersonal therapy has considerable support for depression and bulimia, as do acceptance-based approaches for borderline personality disorder. Still, we shouldn't conclude that a treatment that's not on the EST list isn't effective. The fact that a treatment isn't on the list may mean only that investigators haven't yet conducted research to demonstrate its effectiveness (Arkowitz & Lilienfeld, 2006).

The movement to develop lists of ESTs is controversial. Critics of this movement contend that the research literature isn't sufficiently well developed to conclude that certain treatments are clearly superior to others for certain disorders, so why not base one's treatment on subjective feelings and intuition about "what works" (Levant, 2004; Westen, Novotny, & Thompson-Brenner, 2004)? In response, proponents of this movement argue that the best scientific evidence available should inform clinical practice (Baker et al., 2009). Because current data suggest that at least some treatments are superior to others for some disorders, such as exposure therapy for anxiety disorders, they contend, practitioners have an ethical obligation to rely on ESTs unless there's a compelling reason not to (Chambless & Ollendick, 2001; Crits-Christoph, Wilson, & Hollon, 2005; Hunsley & DiGuilio, 2002). The authors of your text find the latter argument more compelling, because the burden of proof for selecting and administering a treatment should always fall on therapists. Therefore, if there's reasonable evidence that certain treatments are better than others for certain disorders, therapists should be guided by that evidence.

Factoid

Survey data suggest that only a minority of therapists use empirically supported treatments (Baker et al., 2009; Freiheit et al., 2004). For example, a survey of practitioners who treat clients with eating disorders (especially anorexia and bulimia) indicated that most of them don't regularly administer either cognitive-behavioral or interpersonal therapies, the primary interventions found to be helpful for these conditions (Lilienfeld et al., in press a; Pederson et al., 2000).

Answers are located at the end of the text.

PSYCHOTHERAPIES — evaluating **CLAIMS**

There are over 500 different therapies on the market, yet only a small percentage of them are empirically supported. How can you identify which therapies might be helpful, which aren't, and which might even be harmful? Let's evaluate some of these claims, which are modeled after actual advertisements for therapies found online.

"Our breakthrough energy therapy is far superior to any short-term therapy available for anxiety."

What types of control groups would be especially important to include in research evaluating this claim?

"Our debriefing process allows those involved in the incident to process the event and vent their fears and anger associated with it."

What does scientific research tell us about crisis debriefing? Is the "venting" of fears and anger always a good thing?

"Cognitive-behavioral therapy may not be effective in all cases, but studies have shown that CBT is equally as effective in the treatment of depression as anti-depressant medication."

This claim avoids exaggerating the benefits of cognitive-behavioral therapy (CBT) by noting that it may not be effective in all cases. The ad notes correctly that CBT is about as effective as antidepressant medication for clinical depression.

ARE SELF-HELP BOOKS ALWAYS HELPFUL?

Each year Americans can choose from about 3,500 newly published self-help books that promise everything from achieving everlasting bliss and expanded consciousness to freedom from virtually every human failing and foible imaginable. Self-help books are only one piece of the massive quilt of the self-improvement industry that extends to Internet sites; magazines; radio and television shows; CDs; DVDs; lectures; workshops; advice columns; and, most recently, smartphone applications and computerized delivery of evidence-based treatments (Abroms et al., 2011; Craske et al., 2011).

It's no mystery why self-help books are so popular that Americans spend $650 million a year on them, and at least 80 percent of therapists recommend them to their clients (Arkowitz & Lilienfeld, 2007). Researchers have studied the effects of reading self-help books, known in psychology lingo as "bibliotherapy." The relatively small number of studies conducted on self-help books suggests that bibliotherapy and psychotherapy often lead to comparable improvements in depression, anxiety, and other problems (Gould & Clum, 1993).

Still, we should bear in mind three points. First, we can't generalize the limited findings to all of the books on the shelves of our local bookstore, because the overwhelming majority of self-help books are untested (Rosen et al., in press). Second, people who volunteer for research on self-help books may be more motivated to read the entire book and benefit from it compared with the curious person who purchases the book under more casual circumstances. Third, many self-help books address relatively minor problems, like everyday worries and public speaking. When researchers (Menchola, Arkowitz, & Burke, 2007) have examined more serious problems, like major depression and panic disorder, psychotherapy has fared better than bibliotherapy, although both do better than no treatment.

Some people don't respond at all to self-help books (Febbraro et al., 1999), and many self-help books promise far more than they can deliver. Readers who fall short of how the promotional information on the cover assures them they'll respond may feel like failures and be less likely to seek professional help or make changes on their own. Bearing this possibility in mind, Hal Arkowitz and Scott Lilienfeld (2007) offered the following recommendations about selecting self-help books.

- Use books that have research support and are based on valid psychological principles of change (Gambrill, 1992). Make sure the author refers to published research that supports the claims made. Books that have shown positive effects in studies include *Feeling Good* by David Burns, *Mind Over Mood* by Dennis Greenberger and Christine Padesky, and *Coping with Panic* by George Clum.
- Evaluate the author's credentials. Does he or she have the professional training and expertise to write on the topic at hand?
- Be wary of books that make far-fetched promises, such as curing a phobia in five minutes. The 2007 blockbuster best seller *The Secret* (Byrne, 2007), popularized by Oprah Winfrey, informs readers that positive thinking alone can cure cancer, help one become a millionaire, or achieve just about any goal one wants. Yet there's not a shred of research evidence that this kind of wishful thinking is helpful (Smythe, 2007).
- Beware of books that rely on a "one size fits all" approach. A book that tells us to always express anger to our relationship partner fails to take into account the complexity and specifics of the relationship.
- Serious problems like clinical depression, obsessive-compulsive disorder, and schizophrenia warrant professional help rather than self-help alone.

The "secret" to the 2007 best seller *The Secret* by Rhonda Byrne is the so-called *law of attraction*—good thoughts attract good things, and bad thoughts attract bad things. Yet there's no evidence that merely wishing for something good to happen without taking concrete steps to accomplish it is effective. We should be skeptical of self-help books that promise simple answers to complex problems.

Biomedical Treatments: Medications, Electrical Stimulation, and Surgery

12 Recognize different types of drugs and cautions associated with drug treatment.

13 Outline key considerations in drug treatment.

14 Identify misconceptions about biomedical treatments.

Biomedical treatments—including medications, electrical stimulation techniques, and brain surgery—directly alter the brain's chemistry or physiology. Just as the number of psychotherapy approaches has more than tripled since the 1970s, antidepressant prescriptions have quadrupled from 1988–1994 through 2005–2008. Today, antidepressants are the most frequently prescribed medication for adults aged 18–44 years (Pratt et al., 2011). Many people are surprised to learn that about 10 percent of inpatients with major depression still receive electroconvulsive therapy (ECT)—informally called "shock therapy"—which delivers small electric shocks to people's brains to lift their mood (Olfson et al., 1998; Pagnin et al., 2008). By the 1950s, as many as 50,000 patients received psychosurgery, in which the frontal lobes or other brain regions were damaged or removed in an effort to control serious psychological disorders (Tooth & Newton, 1961; Valenstein, 1973). Today, surgeons rarely perform such operations, reflecting the controversies surrounding psychosurgery, and the fact that less risky and more effective treatments are available. As we consider the pros and cons of various biomedical treatments, we'll see that each approach has attracted ardent critics and defenders.

Psychopharmacotherapy: Targeting Brain Chemistry

We'll begin our tour of biomedical treatments with **psychopharmacotherapy**—the use of medications to treat psychological problems. For virtually every psychological disorder treated with psychotherapy, there's an available medication. In 1954, the widespread marketing of the drug Thorazine (chlorpromazine) ushered in the "pharmacological revolution" in the treatment of serious psychological disorders. For the first time, professionals could prescribe powerful medications to ease the symptoms of schizophrenia and related conditions. By 1970, it was unusual for any patient with schizophrenia not to be treated with Thorazine or other "major tranquilizers," as they came to be known.

Pharmaceutical companies soon sensed the promise of medicines to treat a broad spectrum of patients, and their efforts paid off handsomely. Researchers discovered that the emotional storms that torment people with bipolar disorder could be tamed with Lithium, Tegretol, and a new generation of mood stabilizer drugs. Medications are now available for people with more common conditions, ranging from anxiety about public speaking to the harsh realities of stressful circumstances. We can attribute the staggering number of prescriptions for depression largely to the phenomenal popularity of the selective serotonin reuptake inhibitor (SSRI) antidepressants, including Prozac, Zoloft, and Paxil, which boost levels of the neurotransmitter serotonin.

In **TABLE 8**, we present commonly used drugs and their presumed mechanisms of action to treat anxiety disorders (anxiolytics or *antianxiety drugs*), depression

psychopharmacotherapy
use of medications to treat psychological problems

Psychological and Biological Treatments

(*antidepressants*), bipolar disorders (*mood stabilizers*), psychotic conditions (neuroleptics/ *antipsychotics* or major tranquilizers, along with atypical (second generation) antipsychotics, with often fewer yet variable side effects), and attention problems (*psychostimulants*, which stimulate the nervous system yet paradoxically treat symptoms of attention-deficit/ hyperactivity disorder). As we can see from the table, many of these medications ease the symptoms of multiple psychological conditions.

Explore in **MyPsychLab** the **Concept:** Drugs Commonly Used to Treat Psychiatric Disorders

TABLE 8 Commonly Used Medications for Psychological Disorders, Mechanisms of Action, and Other Uses.

	MEDICATION	EXAMPLES	ACTION	OTHER USES
Antianxiety Medications	Benzodiazepines	Diazepam (Valium), alprazolam (Xanax), clonazepam (Klonopin), lorazepam (Ativan)	Increase efficiency of GABA binding to receptor sites	Use with antipsychotic medications, treat medication side effects, alcohol detox
	Buspirone (Buspar)		Stabilizes serotonin levels	Depressive and anxiety states; sometimes used with antipsychotics; aggression in people with brain injuries and dementia
	Beta blockers	Atenolol (Tenormin), propranolol (Inderal)	Compete with norepinephrine at receptor sites that control heart and muscle function; reduce rapid heartbeat, muscle tension	Control blood pressure, regulate heartbeat
Antidepressants	Monoamine oxidase (MAO) inhibitors	Isocarboxazid (Marplan), phenelzine (Nardil), tranylcypromine (Parnate)	Inhibit action of enzymes that metabolize norepinephrine and serotonin; inhibit dopamine	Panic and other anxiety disorders
	Cyclic (including tryclic) antidepressants	Amitriptyline (Elavil), imipramine (Tofranil), desipramine (Norpramine), nortriptyline (Pamelor)	Inhibit reuptake of norepinephrine and serotonin	Panic and other anxiety disorders, pain relief
	SSRIs (selective serotonin reuptake inhibitors)	Fluoxetine (Prozac), citalopram (Celexa), sertraline (Zoloft)	Selectively inhibit reuptake of serotonin	Eating disorders (especially bulimia), obsessive-compulsive disorder, social phobia
Mood Stabilizers	Mineral salts	Lithium carbonate (Lithium)	Decrease noradrenaline, increase serotonin	
	Anticonvulsant medications	Carbamazepine (Tegretol), lamotrigine (Lamictal), divalproex sodium (Depakote)	Increase levels of neurotransmitter GABA, inhibit norepinephrine reuptake (Tegretol)	Bipolar disorder
Antipsychotics	First generation antipsychotics	Chlorpromazine (Thorazine), haloperidol (Haldol)	Block postsynaptic dopamine receptors	Tourette syndrome (Haldol), bipolar disorder with the exception of Clozaril
	Serotonin-dopamine antagonists (atypical antipsychotics/ second generation antipsychotics)	Clozapine (Clozaril), risperidone (Risperdal), olanzapine (Zyprexa), ziprasidone (Geodon), quetiapine (Seroquel)	Block activity of serotonin and/or dopamine; also affect norepinephrine, acetylcholine	Schizophrenia, bipolar disorder, sometimes autism off-label
		aripiprazole (Abilify)	Moderates/stabilizes dopamine and serotonin receptors	Schizophrenia, bipolar disorder, clinical depression, and autism
Psychostimulants and Other Medications for Attentional Problems	Psychostimulants	Methylphenidate (Ritalin, Concerta), amphetamine (Adderall), dexmethylphenidate (Focalin)	Release or reuptake of norepinephrine, dopamine, serotonin in frontal regions of the brain, where attention and behavior are regulated	Narcolepsy (Ritalin), Investigated for treatment of major depressive disorder, binge eating disorder, cognitive impairment with schizophrenia, daytime sleepiness (Vyvanse)
		Lisdexamfetamine (Vyvanse)		
	Non-stimulant medications	Atomoxetine (Strattera)	Selectively inhibit reuptake of norepinephrine	Some patients also report reduction in depression

Nevertheless, we should bear in mind that we don't know for sure how most of these medications work. Although drug company advertisements, including those we've seen on television, often claim that medications—especially antidepressants—correct a "chemical imbalance" in the brain, this notion is almost surely oversimplified (Kirsch, 2010). For one thing, most medications probably work on multiple neurotransmitter systems. Moreover, there's no scientific evidence for an "optimal" level of serotonin or other neurotransmitters in the brain (Lacasse & Leo, 2005). Finally, many medications, including antidepressants, may exert their effects largely by affecting the sensitivity of neuron receptors rather than the levels of neurotransmitters.

Today, psychologists often refer patients to psychiatrists and other professionals who can prescribe medications and consult with prescribers to plan treatment. Until recently, only psychiatrists and a few other mental health professionals, like psychiatric nurse practitioners, could prescribe medications. But beginning in 1999, psychologists in the U.S. territory of Guam were granted legal permission to prescribe medications followed by two U.S. states (New Mexico in 2002 and Louisiana in 2004). Before being allowed to prescribe, these psychologists must complete a curriculum of course work on physiology, anatomy, and psychopharmacology (the study of medications that affect psychological functioning). Nevertheless, the growing movement to allow psychologists to prescribe medications has been controversial, in part because many critics charge that psychologists don't possess sufficient knowledge of the anatomy and physiology of the human body to adequately evaluate the intended effects and side effects of medications (Fox et al., 2009; Stuart & Heiby, 2007).

CAUTIONS TO CONSIDER: DOSAGE AND SIDE EFFECTS. Psychopharmacotherapy isn't a cure-all. Virtually all medications have side effects that practitioners must weigh against the potential benefits. Most adverse reactions, including nausea, drowsiness, weakness, fatigue, and impaired sexual performance, are reversible when medications are discontinued or when their dosage is lowered. Nevertheless, this isn't the case with *tardive dyskinesia* (TD), a serious side effect of some older antipsychotic medications, those used to treat schizophrenia and other psychoses. The symptoms of TD include grotesque involuntary movements of the facial muscles and mouth and twitching of the neck, arms, and legs. Most often, the disorder begins after several years of high-dosage treatment (*tardive,* like *tardy,* means late-appearing), but it occasionally begins after only a few months of therapy at low dosages (Simpson & Kline, 1976). Newer antipsychotic medicines such as Risperdal, which treat the negative as well as positive symptoms of schizophrenia, generally produce fewer serious adverse effects. But they too occasionally produce serious side effects, including sudden cardiac deaths, and the verdict is out regarding whether they're more effective compared with earlier and less costly medications (Correll & Schenk, 2008; Lieberman et al., 2005; Schneeweiss & Avorn, 2009).

One Dose Doesn't "Fit All": Differences in Responses to Medication. People don't all respond equally to the same dose of medication. Weight, age, and even racial differences often affect drug response. African Americans tend to require lower doses of certain antianxiety and antidepressant drugs and have a faster response than do Caucasians, and Asians metabolize (break down) these medications more slowly than do Caucasians (Baker & Bell, 1999; Campinha-Bacote, 2002; Strickland et al., 1997). Because some people become physically and psychologically dependent on medications such as the widely prescribed antianxiety medications Valium and Xanax (known as benzodiazepines), physicians must proceed with caution and determine the lowest dose possible to achieve positive results and minimize unpleasant side effects (Wigal et al., 2006). Discontinuation of certain drugs, such as those for anxiety and depression, should be performed gradually to minimize withdrawal reactions, including anxiety and agitation (Lejoyeux & Ades, 1997).

Most modern medications for depression, like fluoxetine (whose brand name is Prozac), appear to work by increasing the amount of serotonin in the brain. Yet this medication for depression, tianeptine (whose brand name is Stablon), appears to work by *decreasing* the amount of serotonin. The fact that medications can treat depression by either raising or lowering serotonin levels suggests that popular "chemical imbalance" theories of depression are oversimplified.

Parenting a child with attention-deficit/ hyperactivity disorder (ADHD) can be challenging and often requires support from teachers and medical professionals.

Polypharmacy—the practice of prescribing multiple medications at the same time—can increase the risk of infrequent yet serious side effects produced by interactions among drugs. The tragic death of actor Heath Ledger in 2008 highlights the possibility of overdose by taking multiple medications that aren't carefully monitored by medical professionals.

Medications on Trial: Harmful and Overprescribed? Some psychologists have raised serious questions about the effectiveness of the SSRIs, especially among children and adolescents (Healy, 2004; Kendall, Pilling, & Whittington, 2005). There also are widely publicized indications that SSRIs increase the risk of suicidal thoughts in people younger than 18 years of age, although there's no clear evidence that they increase the risk of *completed* suicide (Goldstein & Ruscio, 2009). For this reason, the U.S. Food and Drug Administration (FDA) now requires drug manufacturers to include warnings on the labels of SSRIs of possible suicide risk. Following these "black box" warnings (so called because they're enclosed in a box with black borders on the medication label), antidepressant prescriptions dropped by nearly 20 percent (Nemeroff et al., 2007; Gibbons et al., 2010).

Scientists don't understand why antidepressants increase suicidal thoughts in some children and adolescents. These drugs sometimes produce agitation, so they may make already depressed people even more distressed and possibly suicidal (Brambilla et al., 2005). Yet the risk of suicide attempts and completions among people prescribed SSRIs remains very low.

Another area of public concern is overprescription. Parents, teachers, and helping professionals have expressed particular alarm that psychostimulants for attention-deficit/ hyperactivity disorder (ADHD), such as Ritalin (methylphenidate), are overprescribed and may substitute for teaching effective coping strategies for focusing attention (LeFever, Arcona, & Antonuccio, 2003; Safer, 2000). Since the early 1990s, the number of prescriptions for ADHD has increased fourfold. Although little is known about the long-term safety of Ritalin with children under 6, the number of prescriptions for children ages 2 (!) to 4 nearly tripled between 1991 and 1995 alone (Bentley & Walsh, 2006).

Critics of psychostimulants have pointed to their potential for abuse. Moreover, their adverse effects include decreased appetite, gastrointestinal pain, headache, insomnia, irritability, heart-related complications, and stunted growth (Aagaard & Hansen, 2011). A recent survey indicated that only a fifth of children with ADHD received stimulants for the disorder (Merikangas et al., 2013), suggesting that these medications aren't generally overprescribed. Nevertheless, stimulant overprescription clearly occurs in some cases (Smith & Farah, 2011). Children should be diagnosed with ADHD and placed on stimulants only after they've been evaluated with input from parents and teachers. The good news is that 70–80 percent of children with ADHD can be treated effectively with stimulants (Steele et al., 2006), which can sometimes be combined to good advantage with behavior therapy (Jensen et al., 2005). Moreover, more recently developed nonstimulant medications for ADHD, such as Strattera, hold promise for improving concentration and attention.

Fad treatments and diets are poor alternatives to medications and psychological treatments of ADHD. For example, there's no convincing scientific evidence that reducing the amount of sugar in the diet improves symptoms of ADHD. Other dietary changes, like eliminating artificial food colors or flavors, also have little or no impact on ADHD symptoms (Waschbusch & Hill, 2003).

A final area of concern is *polypharmacy:* prescribing many medications—sometimes five or more—at the same time. This practice can be hazardous if not carefully monitored, because certain medications may interfere with the effects of others or interact with them in dangerous ways. Polypharmacy is a particular problem among the elderly, who tend to be especially susceptible to drug side effects (Fulton & Allen, 2005).

EVALUATING PSYCHOPHARMACOTHERAPY. To medicate or not to medicate, that is the question. In many instances, psychotherapy, with no added medications, can successfully treat people with many disorders. CBT is at least as effective as antidepressants, even for severe depression, and perhaps more effective than antidepressants are in preventing relapse (DeRubeis, Brotman, & Gibbons, 2005; Hollon, Thase, & Markowitz, 2002). Psychotherapy alone is also effective for a variety of anxiety disorders, mild and moderate depression, bulimia, and insomnia (Otto, Smits, & Reese, 2005; Thase, 2000).

Scientists are finding that when patients benefit from psychotherapy, this change is reflected in the workings of their brain. In some cases, psychotherapy and medication produce similar brain changes, suggesting that different routes to improvement share similar mechanisms (Kumari, 2006) and reminding us that "mind" and "brain" describe the same phenomena at different levels of explanation. Yet although medication and psychotherapy may both normalize brain function, they may also do so in different ways. In a review of 63 studies investigating psychotherapy or pharmacotherapy effects in patients with anxiety and major depressive disorders, medications decreased activity in the limbic system, the seat of emotion and reaction to threat. In contrast, psychotherapy produced changes mostly in the frontal areas of the brain, perhaps reflecting its success at transforming maladaptive to adaptive thoughts (Quidé et al, 2012).

This research cautions us against a widespread logical error, namely, inferring a disorder's optimal treatment from its cause (Ross & Pam, 1995). Many people believe mistakenly that a condition that's largely biological in its causes, like schizophrenia, should be treated with medication and that a condition that's largely environmental in its causes, such as a specific phobia, should be treated with psychotherapy. Yet the research we've reviewed shows that this logic is erroneous, because psychological treatments affect our biology, just as biomedical treatments affect our psychology.

Critics of pharmacotherapy claim that medications are of little value in helping patients learn social skills, modify self-defeating behaviors, or cope with conflict. For example, when patients with anxiety disorders discontinue their medications, half or more may relapse (Marks et. al., 1993). Over the long haul, psychotherapy may be much less expensive than medications, so it often makes sense to try psychotherapy first (Arkowitz & Lilienfeld, 2007).

Still, there are often clear advantages of combining medication with psychotherapy (Thase, 2000). If people's symptoms interfere greatly with their functioning or if psychotherapy alone hasn't worked for a two-month period, adding medication is frequently justified. Generally, research suggests that combining medication with psychotherapy is warranted for schizophrenia, bipolar disorder, long-term major depression, and major depression with psychotic symptoms (Otto, Smits, & Reese, 2005; Thase, 2000). As of 2007, 61 percent of physicians prescribed medications to patients while the patients participated in psychotherapy, reflecting a national trend toward combining medical and psychological treatments (Olfson & Marcus, 2010).

It's a logical error to infer a disorder's cause from its treatment, or vice versa. Headaches can be treated with aspirin, but that doesn't imply that headaches are due to a deficiency of aspirin in the body.

 Watch in **MyPsychLab** the **Video:** Recent Trends in Treatment: Sue Mineka

Electrical Stimulation: Conceptions and Misconceptions

Consider the following account of **electroconvulsive therapy (ECT)**, which we introduced at the outset of our discussion of biomedical treatments:

> They brought me into the ECT room with the electrodes dangling from the side of a gray machine. The friendly nurse placed them on me and then gave me an injection to "put me out," apparently so I wouldn't be conscious to feel the jolt of electricity. Then suddenly I was awake, but, no matter how hard I tried, I couldn't remember anything. There was a curtain cloaking my memories that I couldn't peer behind, no matter how hard I tried. What exactly happened? How long did it take? Did they do anything to me, after all? But the doctor seemed to be pleased, and the nurse was smiling, so I concluded, it must be over and done with.

ELECTROCONVULSIVE THERAPY: FACT AND FICTION. What happened here? As in other cases of modern ECT, medical personnel injected a muscle relaxant and anesthetic and then administered brief electrical pulses to the patient's brain to relieve severe depression that hadn't responded to other treatments. This patient, like others receiving ECT, experienced a full-blown seizure lasting about a minute, much like that experienced by patients with epilepsy. Physicians typically recommend ECT for individuals with serious depression, bipolar disorder, schizophrenia, and severe catatonia and only then as a last resort when all other treatments have failed. A typical course of ECT is six to ten treatments, given three times a week.

Misconceptions about ECT abound, including the erroneous beliefs that ECT is painful or dangerous and that it invariably produces long-term memory loss, personality changes, and even brain damage (Dowman, Patel, & Rajput, 2005; Malcom, 1989; Santa

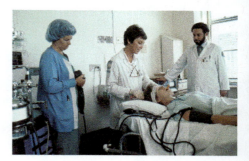

A team of professionals administer electroconvulsive therapy.

electroconvulsive therapy (ECT)
treatment for serious psychological problems in which patients receive brief electrical pulses to the brain that produce a seizure

769

Maria, Baumeister, & Gouvier, 1999). Media characterizations of ECT, such as in the Academy Award–winning 1975 film *One Flew Over the Cuckoo's Nest*, promote the mistaken idea that ECT is little more than a brutal means of punishment or behavioral control with no redeeming value. Not surprisingly, most Americans hold negative attitudes about ECT (McDonald & Walter, 2004).

Nevertheless, the picture looks quite different when researchers study individuals who've undergone ECT (Chakrabarti, Grover, & Rajagopal, 2010). In one study of 24 patients, 91 percent reported being happy to have received ECT (Goodman et al., 1999). In another study, 98 percent of patients said they'd seek ECT again if their depression returned, and 62 percent said that the treatment was less frightening than a visit to the dentist (Pettinati et al., 1994). More important, researchers report improvement rates as high as 80–90 percent following ECT for severe depression (APA, 2001).

Although harsh public perceptions about ECT may be unwarranted, we should note a few cautions. About 50 percent of people with an initially positive response relapse within six months or so (Bourgon & Kellner, 2000), so ECT isn't a cure-all. In addition, people who experience ECT may be motivated to convince themselves that the treatment helped. Although many patients report feeling better after ECT, they don't always show parallel changes on objective measures of depression and mental functioning (Scovern & Kilmann, 1980). ECT may be helpful because it increases the levels of serotonin in the brain (Rasmussen, Sampson, & Rummans, 2002) and stimulates growth of brain cells in the hippocampus (Bolwig, 2009). A rival hypothesis is that ECT induces strong expectations of improvement and serves as an "electrical placebo." But studies showing that ECT works better than "sham" (fake) ECT render this explanation less likely (Carney et al., 2003).

In prescribing ECT, the physician's challenge is to determine whether the therapeutic gains outweigh the potential adverse effects. As the case we read suggests, ECT can create short-term confusion and cloud memory. In most cases, memory loss is restricted to events that occur right before the treatment and generally subsides within a few weeks (Sackeim, 1986). However, memory and attention problems persist in some patients for six months after treatment (Sackeim et al., 2007). When psychiatrists use ECT, it's crucial that patients and their family members understand the procedure, as well as its potential benefits and risks.

VAGUS NERVE AND TRANSCRANIAL STIMULATION. In a recent development, surgeons can implant a small electrical device under the skin near the breastbone to stimulate the *vagus nerve* to treat severe depression. The vagus nerve projects to many brain areas, and electrical pulses to this nerve may stimulate serotonin and increase brain blood flow (George et al., 2000). The FDA has approved this procedure, as well as repeated transcranial magnetic stimulation (TMS), for depression that hasn't responded to other treatments. Although recent research indicates that repeated TMS is slightly less effective compared with ECT in treating major depression, it produces fewer negative effects on cognition compared with ECT, implying that TMS should be considered as a treatment option (Hansen et al., 2011). Still, well-controlled, large-scale studies on these procedures are mostly lacking. Studies comparing these methods with devices that don't provide any stimulation suggest that improvement may be due to placebo effects (Herwig et al., 2007; Rush et al., 2005).

Researchers have recently experimented with deep brain stimulation (DBS) of regions of the frontal cortex and other brain structures with treatment-resistant depressed patients, but it's too early to draw firm conclusions about this procedure's value (Mayberg et al., 2005). A recent study of DBS with treatment-resistant depressed patients followed after three to six years found that at the last follow-up visit, about two-thirds of patients improved, with no adverse events during the follow-up (Kennedy et al., 2011). However, two patients died by suicide when their depression relapsed. Clearly, the risks and benefits of each procedure we reviewed must be weighed carefully.

RULING OUT RIVAL HYPOTHESES ▶
Have important alternative explanations for the findings been excluded?

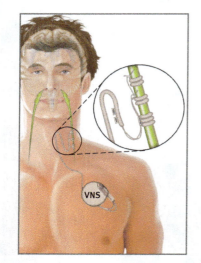

A small vagus nerve stimulator can be implanted under the breastbone in cases of serious treatment-resistant depression.

RULING OUT RIVAL HYPOTHESES ▶
Have important alternative explanations for the findings been excluded?

Psychosurgery: An Absolute Last Resort

One reason deep brain stimulation may be a tough sell for patients and physicians is that it conjures up disturbing memories of the dangers of psychosurgery (Johnson, 2009). **Psychosurgery**, or brain surgery to treat psychological disorders, is the most radical and controversial of all biomedical treatments. As is often the case with new treatments, psychosurgery was hailed as a promising innovation not long after it was introduced. Most of the early psychosurgical operations were prefrontal lobotomies. Psychosurgery remained popular until the mid-1950s, when the tide of enthusiasm receded in the face of reports of scores of "dehumanized zombies" and the availability of medicines as alternatives to surgery (Mashour, Walker, & Matura, 2005; Valenstein, 1973). To most critics, the benefits of psychosurgery rarely, if ever, outweighed the costs of impairing memory, diminishing emotion and creativity, and the risks of brain surgery (Neville, 1978).

Critics also noted that the motives for conducting psychosurgery weren't always benign (Valenstein, 1973). Social goals such as the control of behavior of violent sexual criminals, homosexual child abusers, and prison inmates who received lobotomies were occasionally confused with therapeutic goals (Mashour et al., 2005).

In the 1960s, surgeons ushered new forms of psychosurgery to the forefront. Surgeons replaced primitive procedures with ultrasound, electricity, freezing of tissues, and implants of radioactive materials. Automated surgical devices added precision to delicate brain surgery. With the advent of modern psychosurgical techniques, negative physical side effects became less frequent.

Today, surgeons sometimes perform psychosurgery as a last resort for patients with a handful of conditions, such as severe OCD, major depression, and bipolar disorder. There are few well-controlled long-term studies of psychosurgery and an absence of data about which patients respond best. Even when psychosurgery appears successful, we can generate alternative explanations, including placebo effects and self-serving biases, to account for apparent treatment gains (Dawes, 1994).

Recognizing the need to protect patient interests, institutional review boards (IRBs) in hospitals where surgeons perform psychosurgery must approve each operation. IRBs help ensure that (1) there's a clear rationale for the operation, (2) the patient has received an appropriate preoperative and postoperative evaluation, (3) the patient has consented to the operation, and (4) the surgeon is competent to conduct the procedure (Mashour et al., 2005). Scientific research may one day lead to more effective forms of psychosurgery, but the scientific and ethical debates surrounding such surgery are likely to endure.

Before sophisticated surgical techniques were developed, surgeons used tools like these to perform early lobotomies.

psychosurgery
brain surgery to treat psychological problems

◀ **RULING OUT RIVAL HYPOTHESES**
Have important alternative explanations for the findings been excluded?

Psychosurgery has a long history, as this photo of a 2,000-plus-year-old skull from Peru shows. As we can see, this skull contains a huge hole produced by a procedure called "trephining." Scientists believe that trephining may have been performed in an effort to heal mental disorders or to relieve brain diseases like epilepsy and tumors (Alt et al., 1997).

☑ **Study** and **Review** in **MyPsychLab**

Assess Your Knowledge | FACT or FICTION?

1. The first major drug for psychological conditions was developed to treat bipolar disorder.   **True / False**

2. One serious side effect of antipsychotic medications is tardive dyskinesia. **True / False**

3. People of different races and cultures respond similarly to the same dose of medication.   **True / False**

4. Most people experience long-lasting brain damage after a course of ECT. **True / False**

5. Most early psychosurgery operations were prefrontal lobotomies.   **True / False**

Answers: 1. F; 2. T; 3. F; 4. F; 5. T

Your Complete Review System

Psychotherapy: Clients and Practitioners

I DESCRIBE WHO SEEKS TREATMENT, WHO BENEFITS FROM PSYCHOTHERAPY, AND WHO PRACTICES PSYCHOTHERAPY.

Therapists treat people of all ages and social, cultural, and ethnic backgrounds. Individuals with anxiety and those with minor and temporary problems are most likely to benefit from therapy. Socioeconomic status, gender, and ethnicity predict who will seek psychotherapy.

1. _____ can be defined as a psychological intervention designed to help people resolve emotional, behavioral, and interpersonal problems and improve the quality of their lives.

2. In general, (women/men) are more likely to seek psychotherapy.

3. Hispanic Americans are (less/more) likely than non–Hispanic Americans to seek mental health services.

4. People (can/can't) be helped by therapists who differ from them in significant ways.

5. Individuals who experience some anxiety or minor temporary problems are (not likely/likely) to benefit from therapy.

6. What was the ideal client like, according to a 1964 study of people in therapy? Has that view changed today?

2 DISTINGUISH BETWEEN PROFESSIONALS AND PARAPROFESSIONALS AND DESCRIBE WHAT IT TAKES TO BE AN EFFECTIVE THERAPIST.

Unlicensed paraprofessionals with no formal training, as well as licensed professionals, can be equally effective as trained therapists. Showing warmth, selecting important topics to discuss, not contradicting clients, and establishing a positive relationship are more important determinants of a therapist's effectiveness than is being formally trained or being licensed.

7. A person with no professional training who provides mental health services is called a(n) _____.

8. In most states, the term *therapist* (is/isn't) legally protected.

9. How ethical was the client–therapist relationship in the television drama *In Treatment*?

10. A therapist who talks a lot about his/her personal life is likely to be (effective/ineffective).

Insight Therapies: Acquiring Understanding

3 DESCRIBE THE CORE BELIEFS AND CRITICISMS OF PSYCHODYNAMIC THERAPIES.

The core beliefs of psychodynamic therapies are the importance of (a) analyzing unconscious conflicts, wishes, fantasies, impulses, and life patterns; (b) childhood experiences, including traumatic and adverse life events; (c) the therapeutic relationship; and (d) acquiring insight. Evidence for psychodynamic therapies is based largely on small and highly select patient samples, anecdotal studies, and the questionable curative value of insight, although controlled studies suggest that these therapies may be helpful in some cases.

11. In the technique of _____ _____, clients are allowed to express themselves without censorship of any sort.

12. Neo-Freudians placed (more/less) emphasis on the unconscious than did Freudians.

13. Acccording to Jung, _____ is the integration of opposing aspects of the patient's personality into a harmonious "whole," namely, the self.

14. Critics of psychodynamic therapies assert that understanding our emotional history (is/isn't) required to relieve psychological distress.

15. Psychodynamic therapy (is/isn't) especially effective for psychotic disorders like schizophrenia.

4 DESCRIBE AND EVALUATE THE EFFECTIVENESS OF HUMANISTIC THERAPIES.

Humanistic therapies hold that self-actualization is a universal human drive and adopt an experience-based approach in which clients work to fulfill their potential. Research suggests that genuineness, unconditional positive regard, and empathic understanding are related to improvement but not necessary and sufficient conditions for effective psychotherapy.

16. In Rogers's _____ therapy, the therapist uses reflection to communicate empathy to the client.

17. Rogers believed that therapists must express ____ _____ ____, a nonjudgmental acceptance of all feelings, thoughts, and behaviors the client expresses.

18. Explain the two-chair technique used by Gestalt therapists.

19. Research indicates that the therapeutic _____ is often a stronger predictor of success in therapy than the use of specific techniques.

20. Although person-centered therapy is more effective than no treatment, some studies suggest that it may not help much more than a(n) _____ treatment.

Group Therapies: The More the Merrier

5 **LIST THE ADVANTAGES OF GROUP METHODS.**

Group methods span all schools of psychotherapy and are efficient, time-saving, and less costly than individual methods. Participants learn from others' experiences, benefit from feedback and modeling others, and discover that problems and suffering are widespread.

21. Group therapies are (less helpful than/as helpful as) individual treatments.

22. It is (rare/common) for self-help groups to form on the Internet.

6 **DESCRIBE THE RESEARCH EVIDENCE CONCERNING THE EFFECTIVENESS OF ALCOHOLICS ANONYMOUS.**

AA is helpful for some clients, but it appears to be no more effective than other treatments, including CBT. Research suggests that controlled drinking approaches can be effective with some people with alcoholism.

23. AA's famous "Twelve Steps" is based on the assumption that alcoholism is a _____ that requires members never to drink another drop after entering treatment.

24. People who attend AA meetings or receive treatment based on the Twelve Steps typically fare (better than/no better than) people who receive other treatments.

25. A key factor in who improves in AA is the ability to participate in a(n) ____ _____ ___.

26. The relapse prevention approach teaches people to not feel ashamed or discouraged when they lapse, in an effort to avoid the _____ _____ effect.

7 **IDENTIFY DIFFERENT APPROACHES TO TREATING THE DYSFUNCTIONAL FAMILY SYSTEM.**

Family therapies treat problems in the family system. Strategic family therapists remove barriers to effective communication, whereas structural family therapists plan changes in the way family interactions are structured.

27. Family therapists focus on _____ among family members rather than on the person with the most obvious problems.

28. _____ _____ _____ are designed to remove barriers to effective communication.

29. In _____ family therapy, the therapist is actively involved in the everyday activities of the family to change the structure of their interactions.

30. Research suggests that family therapy is (more effective than/about the same as) no treatment.

Behavioral and Cognitive-Behavioral Approaches: Changing Maladaptive Actions and Thoughts

8 **DESCRIBE THE CHARACTERISTICS OF BEHAVIOR THERAPY AND IDENTIFY DIFFERENT BEHAVIORAL APPROACHES.**

Behavior therapy is grounded in the scientific method and based on learning principles. Exposure therapies confront people with their fears. Exposure can be gradual and stepwise or start with the most frightening scenes imaginable. Modeling techniques, based on observational learning principles, include behavioral rehearsal and role-playing to foster assertiveness. Token economies and aversion therapies are based on operant conditioning and classical conditioning principles, respectively.

31. A class of procedures that confronts patients with what they fear with the goal of reducing this fear is called _____ _____.

32. During _____ _____, clients are taught to relax as they are gradually exposed to what they fear in a stepwise manner.

33. What is in vivo exposure therapy? How can it help people with a fear of flying?

34. During _____, for prolonged periods, patients are exposed right away to images of stimuli they fear the most.

35. A crucial component of flooding is _____ _____, in which the therapist blocks clients from performing their typical avoidance behaviors.

36. What is EMDR therapy? What role do eye movements play in treatment outcome?

37. During _____ _____, the therapist first models a problematic situation and then guides the client through steps to cope with it.

38. In _____ _____ programs, desirable behaviors are rewarded through the consistent application of operant conditioning principles.

9 **DESCRIBE THE FEATURES OF COGNITIVE-BEHAVIORAL THERAPIES (CBT) AND THIRD WAVE THERAPIES.**

Cognitive-behavioral therapists modify irrational and negative beliefs and distorted thoughts that contribute to unhealthy feelings and behaviors. Ellis's rational emotive behavior therapy, Beck's cognitive therapy, and Meichenbaum's stress inoculation training are influential variations of CBT. So-called third wave CBT approaches include mindfulness and acceptance-based psychotherapies.

39. Ellis's rational emotive-behavior therapy (REBT) emphasizes that our _____ systems play a key role in how we function psychologically.

40. In Meichenbaum's (1985) _____ _____ _____, therapists teach clients to prepare for and cope with future stressful life events.

Is Psychotherapy Effective?

10 EVALUATE THE CLAIM THAT ALL PSYCHOTHERAPIES ARE EQUALLY EFFECTIVE.

Many therapies are effective. Nevertheless, some therapies, including behavioral and cognitive-behavioral treatments, are more effective than other treatments for specific problems such as anxiety disorders. Still other treatments, like crisis debriefing, appear to be harmful in some cases.

41. The Dodo bird verdict suggests that all types of psychotherapies are equally _____.

42. Among researchers, there is (strong consensus/no consensus) that the Dodo bird verdict is correct.

43. Research shows that behavioral and cognitive behavioral therapies are (more/less) effective than other treatments for children and adolescents with behavioral problems.

44. Most studies show that (20 percent/ 80 percent) of people who receive psychotherapy do better than the average person who does not receive psychotherapy.

45. What does the research suggest about the effectiveness of Scared Straight programs?

46. What kind of effect can positive life events, like major job promotions, have on psychological problems?

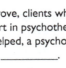

11 EXPLAIN HOW INEFFECTIVE THERAPIES CAN SOMETIMES APPEAR TO BE EFFECTIVE.

Ineffective therapies can appear to be helpful because of spontaneous remission, the placebo effect, self-serving biases, regression to the mean, and retrospective rewriting of the past.

47. Even when they don't improve, clients who have invested time, money, and emotional effort in psychotherapy may convince themselves they've been helped, a psychological phenomenon known as the _____ _____.

48. According to the regression to the mean phenomenon, if a client comes into treatment extremely depressed, the chances are (high/low) that he or she will be less depressed in a few weeks.

49. _____ _____ _____ are treatments for specific disorders that are supported by high-quality scientific evidence.

50. Americans spend $650 million a year on _____ _____ that promise self-improvement.

Biomedical Treatments: Medications, Electrical Stimulation, and Surgery

12 RECOGNIZE DIFFERENT TYPES OF DRUGS AND CAUTIONS ASSOCIATED WITH DRUG TREATMENT.

Medications are available to treat psychotic conditions (neuroleptics/antispsychotics or major tranquilizers), bipolar disorder (mood stabilizers), depression (antidepressants), anxiety (anxiolytics), and attentional problems (psychostimulants).

51. The use of medications to treat psychological problems is called _____.

52. The first major drug for a psychological disorder, Thorazine, was used to treat _____.

53. Prozac and Zoloft are among the best-known _____ _____ _____ inhibitors.

54. There (is/is not) scientific evidence for an "optimal level" of serotonin or other neurotransmitters in the brain.

13 OUTLINE KEY CONSIDERATIONS IN DRUG TREATMENT.

People who prescribe drugs must be aware of side effects, must not overprescribe medications, and must carefully monitor the effects of multiple medications (polypharmacy).

55. People of different races and cultures (do/do not) respond equally to the same dose of medication.

56. The safety and effectiveness of SSRIs when prescribed to _____ and _____ have been called into question because of increased risk of suicidal thoughts.

57. The drug Ritalin, used to treat ADHD, is an example of a medication that many believe has been _____ and may substitute for effective coping strategies for focusing attention.

14 IDENTIFY MISCONCEPTIONS ABOUT BIOMEDICAL TREATMENTS.

Contrary to popular belief, electroconvulsive therapy (ECT) is not painful or dangerous and doesn't invariably produce memory loss, personality changes, or brain damage. Psychosurgery may be useful as a treatment of absolute last resort.

58. During _____ _____, patients receive brief electrical pulses to the brain that produce a seizure to treat serious psychological problems.

59. How does electrical stimulation to the vagus nerve work? Has research shown it to be an effective treatment?

60. Define psychosurgery and explain its potential side effects.

Apply Your Scientific Thinking Skills

Use your scientific thinking skills to answer the following questions, referencing specific scientific thinking principles and common errors in reasoning whenever possible.

1. There's been a lot of media coverage recently on the overprescription of drugs, particularly to younger children with ADHD. Read articles on both sides of this issue and summarize their arguments. What scientific evidence does each side offer? Has each interpreted the research correctly? Explain.

2. Browse through some of the self-help books at your local bookstore or online and select three or four of them (ideally, select books on a wide variety of issues). What scientific research does each book use to support its claims? Do any of the books make extraordinary claims or rely on a "one size fits all" approach to psychological problems? What professional training or expertise, if any, do the authors have?

3. Research one of the potentially harmful therapies in Table 7. To what do the proponents of this therapy attribute their success? What, if any, alternative hypotheses have they considered? Do they discuss any of the potentially negative effects of the therapy on their websites or in articles?

Further Your Understanding

EXTEND YOUR KNOWLEDGE WITH THE MYPSYCHLAB VIDEO SERIES

Watch these videos in MyPsychLab. Follow the "Video Series" link.

The Basics: Therapies in Action Learn about the history and application of psychoanalytic, humanistic, behavior, and cognitive behavioral approaches to therapy.

Thinking Like a Psychologist: Assessing Treatment Effectiveness Find out about the incredible advancements in psychological and drug therapies since the Middle Ages, particularly over the last 40 years.

In the Real World: Cognitive Behavioral Therapy Learn how cognitive behavioral therapy works and how it is used to treat patients with anxiety disorders.

What's In It for Me?: Finding a Therapist If You Need One Find out how students can get in touch with a good therapist for very little cost and the four criteria that psychologists consider when deciding whether a person needs professional help.

EXPERIENCE PSYCHOLOGICAL RESEARCH WITH MYPSYCHLAB SIMULATIONS

Access these simulations in MyPsychLab. Follow the "Simulations" link.

 How Do You Take Care of Your Mental Health? Participate in a survey to discover how you and others manage personal mental health.

APPLY YOUR CRITICAL THINKING SKILLS WITH MYPSYCHLAB WRITING ASSESSMENTS

Complete these writing assignments in MyPsychLab.

Compare and contrast the following forms of psychotherapy: cognitive, humanistic, and behavioral. Identify the focus of each approach as well as areas in which they are the same and in which they are different.

Answer Key

PSYCHOTHERAPY: CLIENTS AND PRACTITIONERS

1. Psychotherapy
2. women
3. less
4. can
5. likely
6. A 1964 study found that many therapists preferred to treat people who were relatively young, attractive, verbal, intelligent, and successful. Therapists have recently become more aware of the importance of assisting a broad clientele of all ages and cultural backgrounds.
7. paraprofessional
8. isn't
9. In this show, the character Laura develops sexual feelings for her therapist, Paul. Paul almost follows through with a sexual relationship with her, but doesn't because he experiences a panic attack. Clearly, had he done so, such behavior would have been unethical.
10. ineffective

INSIGHT THERAPIES: ACQUIRING UNDERSTANDING

11. free association
12. less
13. individuation
14. isn't
15. isn't
16. person-centered
17. unconditional positive regard
18. Gestalt therapy's two-chair technique aims to integrate opposing aspects of the client's personality, such as the "good boy" and the "spoiled brat."
19. relationship
20. placebo

GROUP THERAPIES: THE MORE THE MERRIER

21. as helpful as
22. common
23. physical disease
24. no better than
25. adaptive social network
26. abstinence violation
27. interactions
28. Strategic family interventions
29. structural
30. more effective than

BEHAVIORAL AND COGNITIVE-BEHAVIORAL APPROACHES: CHANGING MALADAPTIVE ACTIONS AND THOUGHTS

31. exposure therapy
32. systematic desensitization
33. Clients gradually approach and handle any fears, as these clients are doing as they overcome their fear of flying. In vivo desensitization involves real-life gradual exposure to what the patient actually fears, rather than imagining the anxiety-provoking situation.
34. flooding
35. response prevention
36. In EMDR, while reliving a traumatic memory, the patient focuses on the therapist's fingers as they move back and forth. Studies indicate that such eye movements play no useful role in EMDR's effectiveness.
37. participant modeling
38. token economy
39. belief
40. stress inoculation training

IS PSYCHOTHERAPY EFFECTIVE?

41. effective
42. no consensus
43. more
44. 80 percent
45. Scared Straight programs expose adolescents to prisoners and prison life in an effort to scare them away from criminal careers. Despite their popularity, research suggests that such programs are not merely ineffective, but can actually increase the rate of problem behaviors in teens.
46. Positive life events can help to explain spontaneous remission, the phenomenon of a psychological problem improving without any intervention.
47. self-serving bias
48. high
49. Empirically supported treatments
50. self-help books

BIOMEDICAL TREATMENTS: MEDICATIONS, ELECTRICAL STIMULATION, AND SURGERY

51. psychopharmacotherapy
52. schizophrenia
53. selective serotonin reuptake
54. is not
55. do not
56. children; adolescents
57. overprescribed
58. electroconvulsive therapy
59. A small electrical device is implanted under the skin near the breastbone to stimulate the vagus nerve (which projects into many brain areas) and is believed to stimulate serotonin release. It is used to treat severe depression. Well-controlled, large-scale studies are mostly lacking.
60. Psychosurgery is brain surgery used to treat psychological problems. Psychosurgery once involved destruction of significant portions of the brain, resulting in impaired memory, diminished emotion and creativity, and personality change. Psychosurgery today is more sophisticated and is associated with significantly milder side effects. Nonetheless, the stigma surrounding psychosurgery remains.

References

Addis, M. E., Hatgis, C., Krasnow, A. D., Jacob, K., Bourne, L., & Mansfield, A. (2004). Effectiveness of cognitive-behavioral treatment for panic disorder versus treatment as usual in a managed care setting. *Journal of Consulting and Clinical Psychology, 72*, 625–635.

Addis, M. E., & Mahalik, J. R. (2003). Men, masculinity, and the contexts of help seeking. *American Psychologist, 58*, 5–14.

Adler, A. (1938). *Social interest: A challenge of mankind*. London, England: Faber & Faber.

Ahn, H., & Wampold, B. E. (2001). Where oh where are the specific ingredients? A meta-analysis of component studies in counseling and psychotherapy. *Journal of Counseling Psychology, 48*, 251–257.

Alberti, R. E., & Emmons, M. L. (2001). *Your perfect right: Assertiveness and equality in your life and relationships* (8th ed.). New York, NY: Impact.

Alt, K. W., Jeunesse, C., Buitrago-Téllez, C. H., Wächter, R., Boes, E., & Pichler, S. L. (1997). Evidence for Stone Age cranial surgery. *Nature, 387*, 360.

Amir, N., Coles, M. E., Brigidi, B., & Foa, E. B. (2001). The effect of practice on recall of emotional information in individuals with generalized social phobia. *Journal of Abnormal Psychology, 110*, 76–78.

Anderson, C. M., & Stewart, S. (1983). *Mastering resistance*. New York, NY: Guilford Press.

Anderson, M. C., & Green, C. (2001). Suppressing unwanted memories by executive control. *Nature, 410*, 366–369.

Antony, M. A., & Barlow, D. H. (2002). Specific phobia. In D. H. Barlow (Ed.), *Anxiety and its disorders: The nature and treatment of anxiety and panic* (2nd ed., pp. 380–417). New York, NY: Guilford Press.

Antony, M. A., & Roemer, L. (2003). Behavior therapy. In A. S. Gurman & S. B. Messer (Eds.), *Essential psychotherapies: Theory and practice* (2nd ed., pp. 182–223). New York, NY: Guilford Press.

Aponte, H., & Hoffman, L. (1973). The open door: A structural approach to a family with an anorectic child. *Family Process, 12*, 1–44.

Appelle, S., Lynn, S. J., & Newman, L. (2000). The alien abduction experience: Theoretical and empirical issues. In E. Cardeña, S. J. Lynn, & S. Krippner (Eds.), *The varieties of anomalous experience: Examining the scientific evidence* (pp. 253–283). Washington, DC: American Psychological Association.

Arkowitz, H., & Lilienfeld, S. O. (2006). Psychotherapy on trial. *Scientific American Mind, 3*, 42–49.

Axsom, D., & Cooper, J. (1985). Cognitive dissonance and psychotherapy: The role of effort justification in inducing weight loss. *Journal of Experimental Social Psychology, 21*, 149–160.

Bachrach, H., Galatzer-Levy, R., Skolnikoff, A., & Waldron, S. (1991). On the efficacy of psychoanalysis. *Journal of the American Psychoanalytic Association, 39*, 871–916.

Baker, F. M., & Bell, C. C. (1999). Issues in the psychiatric treatment of African Americans. *Psychiatry Services, 50*, 362–368.

Baker, T. B., McFall, R. M., & Shoham, V. (2009). Current status and future prospects of clinical psychology toward a scientifically principled approach to mental and behavioral health care. *Perspectives on Psychological Science, 9*, 67–103.

Bandura, A. (1971). *Psychological modeling*. Chicago, IL: Aldine-Atherton.

Barlow, D. H. (2010). Negative effects from psychological treatment: A perspective. *American Psychologist, 65*, 13–20.

Beck, A. T., Rush, A. J., Shaw, B. F., & Emery, G. (1979). *Cognitive therapy of depression*. New York, NY: Guilford Press.

Beck, J. S. (1995). *Cognitive therapy: Basics and beyond*. New York, NY: Guilford Press.

Benish, S. G., Quintana, S., & Wampold, B. E. (2011). Culturally adapted psychotherapy and the legitimacy of myth: A direct-comparison meta-analysis. *Journal of Counseling Psychology, 58*(3), 279–289.

Bentley, K. J., & Walsh, J. (2006). *The social worker and psychotropic medication: Toward effective collaboration with mental health clients, families, and providers* (3rd ed.). Belmont, CA: Thompson.

Berk, M. S., & Andersen, S. M. (2000). The impact of past relationships on interpersonal behavior: Behavioral confirmation in the social-cognitive process of transference. *Journal of Personality and Social Psychology, 79*, 546–562.

Berman, J. S., & Norton, N. C. (1985). Does professional training make a therapist more effective? *Psychological Bulletin, 98*, 401–406.

Bernstein, D. A., Borkovec, T. D., & Hazlett-Stevens, H. (2000). *New directions in progressive relaxation training: A guidebook for helping professionals.* Westport, CT: Praeger.

Beutler, L. E. (2002). The dodo bird is extinct. *Clinical Psychology: Science and Practice, 9,* 30–34.

Beutler, L. E., Clarkin, J. F., & Bongar, B. (2000). *Guidelines for the systematic treatment of the depressed person.* Oxford, England: Oxford University Press.

Beutler, L. E., & Harwood, T. M. (2002). What is and can be attributed to the therapeutic relationship. *Journal of Contemporary Psychotherapy, 32,* 25–33.

Beutler, L. E., Machado, P. P., & Neufeldt, S. A. (1994). Therapist variables. In A. E. Bergin & S. L. Garfield (Eds.), *Handbook of psychotherapy and behavior change* (4th ed., pp. 259–260). New York, NY: Wiley.

Beyerstein, B. L. (1997, September/October). Why bogus therapies seem to work. *Skeptical Inquirer, 21,* 29–34.

Beyerstein, B., & Hadaway, P. (1991). On avoiding folly. *Journal of Drug Issues, 20,* 689–700.

Blagys, M. D., & Hilsenroth, M. J. (2000). Distinctive features of short-term psychodynamic-interpersonal psychotherapy: A review of the comparative psychotherapy process literature. *Clinical Psychology-Science and Practice, 7,* 167–188.

Blatt, S. J., Sanislow, C. A., Zuroff, D. C., & Pilkonis, P. A. (1996). Characteristics of effective therapists: Further analyses of data from the NIMH. *TDCRP, Journal of Consulting and Clinical Psychology, 64,* 1276–1284.

Blow, A. J., Sprenkle, D. H., & Davis, S. D. (2007). Is who delivers the treatment more important than the treatment itself? The role of the therapist in common factors. *Journal of Marital and Family Therapy, 33,* 298–317.

Boerke, K. W., & Reitman, D. (2011). Token Economies. In W. W. Fisher, C.C. Piazza, & H. S. RoAne (Eds.), *Handbook of Applied Behavior Analysis* (pp. 370–381). New York: Guilford Press.

Bohart, A., Elliott, R., Greenberg, L. S., & Watson, J. C. (2002). Empathy redux. In J. Norcross & M. Lambert (Eds.), *Psychotherapy relationships that work* (pp. 89–109). Oxford, England: Oxford University Press.

Bohart, A. C. (2003). Person-centered psychotherapy and related experiential approaches. In A. S. Gurman & S. B. Messer (Eds.), *Essential psychotherapies: Theory and practice* (2nd ed., pp. 107–148). New York, NY: Guilford Press.

Bolwig, T. (2009). Electroconvulsive therapy: The role of hippocampal neurogenesis. *European Psychiatry, 24,* Supplement 1, S75.

Boniecki, K. A., & Moore, S. (2003). Breaking the silence: Using a token economy to reinforce classroom participation. *Teaching of Psychology, 30,* 224–227.

Bornstein, R. F. (2001). The impending death of psychoanalysis. *Psychoanalytic Psychology, 18,* 3–20.

Botella, C., Banos, R. M., Guerrero, B., Garcia-Palacio, A., Quero, S., & Alcaniz, M. (2006). Using a flexible virtual environment for treating a storm phobia. *PsychNology, 4,* 129–144.

Bourgon, L. N., & Kellner, C. H. (2000). Relapse of depression after ECT: A review. *Journal of ECT, 16,* 19–31.

Bowers, T., & Clum, G. A. (1988). Specific and nonspecific treatment effects in controlled psychotherapy research. *Psychological Bulletin, 103,* 315–323.

Bowman, D., Scogin, F., Floyd, M., & McKendree-Smith, N. (2001). Psychotherapy length of stay and outcome: A meta-analysis of the effect of therapist sex. *Psychotherapy, 38,* 142–150.

Brambilla, P., Cipriani, A., Hotopf, M., & Barbui, C. (2005). Side-effect profile of fluoxetine in comparison with other SSRIs, tricyclic, and newer antidepressants: A meta-analysis of clinical trial data. *Pharmacopsychiatry, 38,* 69–77.

Brandsma, J. M., Maultsby, M. C., & Welsh, R. J. (1980). Alcoholics Anonymous: An empirical outcome study. *Addictive Behaviors, 5,* 359–370.

Brewer, C. (1992). Controlled trials of Antabuse in alcoholism: The importance of supervision and adequate dosage. *Acta Psychiatrica Scandinavica, 86,* 51–58.

Brown, D. (2006, November 20). Some believe "truth serums" will come back. *Washington Post,* A08.

Burke, B. L., Arkowitz, H., & Dunn, C. (2002). The efficacy of motivational interviewing. In W. R. Miller & S. Rollnick (Eds.), *Motivational interviewing: Preparing people for change* (2nd ed., pp. 217–250). New York, NY: Guilford Press.

Burke, B. L., Arkowitz, H., & Menchola, M. (2003). The efficacy of motivational interviewing: A meta-analysis of controlled clinical trials. *Journal of Consulting and Clinical Psychology, 71,* 843–861.

Byrne, R. (2007). *The secret.* New York, NY: Atria Books.

Cahill, S. P., Rauch, S. A. M., Hembree, E. A., & Foa, E. B. (2003). Effectiveness of cognitive behavioral treatments for PTSD on anger. *Journal of Cognitive Psychotherapy, 17*(2), 113–131.

Callahan, R. J. (1995, August). *A thought field therapy (TFT) algorithm for trauma: A reproducible experiment in psychotherapy.* Paper presented at the 105th Annual Convention of the American Psychological Association, Chicago, IL.

Campinha-Bacote, J. (2002). *Resources in transcultural care and mental health* (13th ed.). Cincinnati, OH: Transcultural Care Associated.

Cardemil, E. V. (2010). Cultural adaptations to empirically supported treatments: A research agenda. *Scientific Review of Mental Health Practice, 7*(2), 8–21.

Carey, T. A. (2011). Exposure and reorganization: The what and how of effective psychotherapy. *Clinical Psychology Review, 31*(2), 236–248.

Carney, S., Cowen, P., Geddes, J., Goodwin, G., Rogers, R., Dearness, K.,... Scott, A. (2003). Efficacy and safety of electroconvulsive therapy in depressive disorders: A systematic review and meta-analysis. *Lancet, 361,* 799–808.

Casey, L. M., Oei, T. P. S., & Newcombe, P. A. (2004). An integrated cognitive model of panic disorder: The role of positive and negative cognitions. *Clinical Psychology Review, 24,* 529–555.

Castonguay, L. G., Boswell, J. F., Constantino, M. J., Goldfried, M. R., & Hill, C. E. (2010). Training implications of harmful effects of psychological treatments. *American Psychologist, 65,* 34–49.

Cautela, J. R. (1971). Covert conditioning. In A. Jacobs & L. B. Sachs (Eds.), *The psychology of private events: Perspectives on covert response systems.* New York, NY: Academic Press.

Chakrabarti, S., Grover, S., & Rajagopal, R. (2010). Electroconvulsive therapy: A review of knowledge, experience and attitudes of patients concerning the treatment. *World Journal of Biological Psychiatry, 11*(3), 525–537.

Chambless, D. L., & Ollendick, T. H. (2001). Empirically supported psychological interventions: Controversies and evidence. *Annual Review of Psychology, 52,* 685–716.

Chambless, D. L., Sanderson, W. C., Shoham, V., Bennett Johnson, S., Pope, K. S., Crits-Christoph, P.,... McCurry, S. (1996). An update on empirically validated therapies. *The Clinical Psychologist, 49,* 5–18.

Christensen, A., & Jacobson, N. S. (1994). Who (or what) can do psychotherapy: The status and challenge of nonprofessional therapies. *Psychological Science, 5,* 8–14.

Coleman, H. L. K., Wampold, B. E., & Casali, S. L. (1995). Ethnic minorities' ratings of ethnically similar and European American counselors: A meta-analysis. *Journal of Counseling Psychology, 42,* 55–64.

Conway, M., & Ross, M. (1984). Getting what you want by revising what you had. *Journal of Personality and Social Psychology, 47,* 783–748.

Correll, C. U., & Schenk, E. M. (2008). Tardive dyskinesia and new antipsychotics. *Current Opinion in Psychiatry, 21,* 151–156.

Corrigan, P. W. (1995). Use of a token-economy with seriously mentally-ill patients: Criticisms and misconceptions. *Psychiatric Services, 46,* 1258–1263.

Craighead, E., Sheets, E. S., & Bjornsson, A. S. (2005). Specificity and non-specificity in psychotherapy. *Clinical Psychology: Science and Practice, 12,* 189–193.

Crits-Christoph, P., Wilson, G. T., & Hollon, S. D. (2005). Empirically supported psychotherapies: Comment on Westen, Novotny, and Thompson-Brenner (2004). *Psychological Bulletin, 131,* 412–417.

Cruz, M., Scott, J., Houck, P., Reynolds, C. F., Frank, E., & Shear, M. K. (2007). Clinical presentation and treatment outcome of African Americans with complicated grief. *Psychiatric Services, 58,* 700–702.

Cuijpers, P., Vanstraten, A., Warmerdam, L., & Smits, N. (2008). Characteristics of effective psychological treatments of depression: A metaregression analysis. *Psychothreapy Research, 18,* 225–236.

David, D., Lynn, S. J., & Ellis, A. (2010). *Rational and irrational beliefs.* New York, NY: Oxford University Press.

Davidson, P. R., & Parker, K. C. (2001). Eye movement desensitization and reprocessing (EMDR): A meta-analysis. *Journal of Consulting and Clinical Psychology, 69,* 305–316.

Davis, S. R., Davison, S. L., Donath, S., & Bell, R. J. (2005). Circulating androgen levels and self-reported sexual function in women. *Journal of the American Medical Association, 294,* 91–96.

Davison, K. P., Pennebaker, J. W., & Dickerson, S. S. (2000). Who talks? The social psychology of illness support groups. *American Psychologist, 55,* 205–217.

Dawes, R. M. (1994). *House of cards: Psychology and psychotherapy built on myth.* New York, NY: Free Press.

den Boer, P. C. A. M., Wiersma, D., Russo, S., & van den Bosch, R. J. (2005). Paraprofessionals for anxiety and depressive disorders: A meta-analysis. *The Cochrane Database of Systematic Reviews,* Issue 2. Art No: CD004688.

DeRubeis, R. J., Brotman, M. A., & Gibbons, C. J. (2005). A conceptual and methodological analysis of the nonspecifics argument. *Clinical Psychology: Science & Practice, 12,* 174–183.

DeRubeis, R. J., & Feeley, M. (1990). Determinants of change in cognitive therapy for depression. *Cognitive Therapy and Research, 14,* 469–482.

Dies, R. R. (2003). Group psychotherapies. In A. S. Gurman & S. B. Messer (Eds.), *Essential psychotherapies:* Theory and practice (2nd ed., pp. 515–550). New York, NY: Guilford Press.

DiLoretto, A. O. (1971). *Comparative psychotherapy: An experimental analysis.* Chicago, IL: Aldine-Atherton.

Dimidjian, S., & Hollon, S. D. (2010). How would we know if psychotherapy were harmful? *American Psychologist, 65,* 21–33.

Dimidjian, S., Hollon, S. D., Dobson, K. S., Schmaling, K. B., Kohlenberg, R. J., Addis, M. E.,... Jacobson, N. S. (2006). Randomized trial of behavioral activation, cognitive therapy and antidepressant medication in the acute treatment of adults with mild depression. *Journal of Consulting and Clinical Psychology, 74*(4), 658–670.

Dixon, L. B., Dickerson, F., Bellack, A. S., Bennett, M., Dickinson, D., Goldberg, R. W.,... Kreyenbuhl, J. (2010). The 2009 Schizophrenia PORT psychosocial treatment recommendations and summary statements. *Schizophrenia Bulletin, 36,* 48–70.

Dolnick, E. (1998). *Madness on the couch: Blaming the victim in the heyday of psychoanalysis*. New York, NY: Simon & Schuster.

Dowman, J., Patel, A., & Rajput, K. (2005). Electroconvulsive therapy: Attitudes and misconceptions. *Journal of ECT, 21*, 84–87.

DuBrin, J. R., & Zastowny, T. R. (1988). Predicting early attrition from psychotherapy: An analysis of a large private practice cohort. *Psychotherapy, 25*, 393–498.

Eisner, D. A. (2000). *The death of psychotherapy: From Freud to alien abductions*. Westport, CT: Praeger.

Elkin, I. (1994). The NIMH Treatment of Depression Collaborative Research Program: Where we began and where we are now. In A. E. Bergin & S. L. Garfield (Eds.), *Handbook of psychotherapy and behavior change* (4th ed., pp. 114–135). New York, NY: Wiley.

Ellenberger, H. F. (1970). *The discovery of the unconscious: The history and evolution of dynamic psychiatry*. New York, NY: Basic Books.

Elliott, R. (2002). The effectiveness of humanistic therapies: A meta-analysis. In D. J. Cain & J. Seeman (Eds.), *Humanistic psychotherapies: Handbook of research and practice* (pp. 57–81). Washington, DC: American Psychological Association.

Ellis, A. (1958). *Sex without guilt*. New York, NY: Lyle Stuart.

Ellis, A., Abrams, M., & Abrams, L. D. (2008). *Personality theories: Critical perspectives*. New York, NY: Sage.

Emmelkamp, P. M. G., Bruynzeel, M., Drost, L., & van der Mast, C. A. P. G. (2001). Virtual reality treatment in acrophobia: A comparison with exposure in vivo. *CyberPsychology & Behavior, 4*, 335–339.

Emmelkamp, P. M. G., Krijn, M., Hulsbosch, A. M., de Vries, S., Schuemie, M. J., & Van der Mast, C. A. P. G. (2002). Virtual reality treatment versus exposure in vivo: A comparative evaluation in acrophobia. *Behaviour Research and Therapy, 40*, 509–516.

Emrick, C. D. (1987). Alcoholics Anonymous: Affiliation processes and effectiveness as treatment. *Alcoholism: Clinical and Experimental Research, 11*, 416–423.

Engler, J., & Goleman, D. (1992). *A consumer's guide to psychotherapy*. New York, NY: Simon & Schuster.

Erdelyi, M. H. (2006). The unified theory of repression. *Behavioral and Brain Sciences, 29*, 499–551.

Eysenck, H. J. (1952). The effects of psychotherapy: An evaluation. *Journal of Consulting Psychology, 16*, 319–324.

Farber, B. A., & Lane, J. S. (2002). Effective elements of the therapy relationship: Positive regard and support. In J. Norcross (Ed.), *Psychotherapy relationships that work: Therapists' relational contributions to effective psychotherapy* (pp. 175–194). New York, NY: Oxford.

Febbraro, G. A. R., Clum, G. A., Roodman, A. A., & Wright, J. H. (1999). The limits of bibliotherapy: A study of the differential effectiveness of self-administered interventions in individuals with panic attacks. *Behavior Therapy, 30*, 209–222.

Ferri, M., Amoto, L., & Davoli, M. (2006). Alcoholics Anonymous and other 12-step programmes for alcohol dependence. *The Cochrane Review*. Art. No: CD005032. http://dx.doi.org/10.1002/14651858.CD005032.pub2

Feske, U., & Chambless, D. L. (1995). Cognitive behavioral versus exposure only treatment for social phobia: A meta-analysis. *Behavior Therapy, 26*, 695–720.

First, M. B., Spitzer, R. L., Gibbon, M., & Williams, J. B. W. (1996). *Structured clinical interview for DSM-IV Axis I disorders—Patient Edition (SCID-I/P, Version 2.0)*. New York, NY: Biometrics Research Department, New York State Psychiatric Institute.

Forman, E. M., Herbert, J. D., Moltra, E., Yeomans, P. D., & Geller, P. A. (2007). A randomized controlled effectiveness trial of acceptance and commitment therapy and cognitive therapy for anxiety and depression. *Behavior Modification, 31*, 772–799.

Foster, S., & Gurman, A. (1985). Family therapies. In S. Lynn & J. P. Garske (Eds.), *Contemporary psychotherapies: Models and methods* (pp. 377–418). Columbus, OH: Charles E. Merrill.

Fox, R. E. (1996). Charlatanism, scientism, and psychology's social contract. *American Psychologist, 51*, 777–784.

Frank, J. D. (1961). *Persuasion and healing: A comparative study of psychotherapy* (2nd ed.). Baltimore, MD: Johns Hopkins University Press.

Frank, J. D. (1974). Common features of psychotherapies and their patients. *Psychotherapy and Psychosomatics, 24*, 368–371.

Frank, J. D., & Frank, J. B. (1991). *Persuasion and healing: A comparative study of psychotherapy* (3rd ed.). Baltimore, MD: Johns Hopkins University Press.

Franklin, M. E., & Foa, E. B. (2002). Cognitive behavioral treatment of obsessive-compulsive disorder. In P. Nathan & J. Gorman (Eds.), *A guide to treatments that work* (2nd ed., pp. 367–386). Oxford, England: Oxford University Press.

Frederickson, R. (1992). *Repressed memories*. New York, NY: Fireside/Parkside.

Freiheit, S. R., Vye, D., Swan, R., & Cady, M. (2004). Cognitive-behavioral therapy for anxiety: Is dissemination working? *The Behavior Therapist, 27*, 25–32.

Friedlander, M. L. (1984). Psychotherapy talk as social control. *Psychotherapy, 21*, 335–341.

Fuhriman, A., & Burlingame, G. M. (1994). Group psychotherapy: Research and practice. In A. Fuhriman & G. M. Burlingame (Eds.), *Handbook of group psychotherapy: An empirical and clinical synthesis* (pp. 3–40). New York, NY: Wiley.

Fulton, M. M., & Allen, E. R. (2005). Polypharmacy in the elderly: A literature review. *Journal of the American Academy of Nurse Practitioners, 17*, 123–132.

Galanter, M., Dermatis, H., & Santucci, C. (2012). Young people in Alcoholics Anonymous: The role of spiritual orientation and AA member affiliation. *Journal of Addictive Diseases, 31*(2), 173–182.

Gambrill, E. D. (1992). Self-help books: Pseudoscience in the guise of science? *Skeptical Inquirer, 16*(4), 389–399.

Garfield, S. L. (1978). Research on client variables. In S. Garfield & A. Bergin (Eds.), *Handbook of psychotherapy and behavior change* (pp. 191–232). New York, NY: Wiley.

Garske, J. P., & Anderson, T. (2003). Toward a science of psychotherapy research: Present status and evaluation. In S. O. Lilienfeld, S. J. Lynn, & J. M. Lohr (Eds.), *Science and pseudoscience in clinical psychology* (pp. 145–175). New York, NY: Guilford Press.

Gasperini, M., Scherillo, P., Manfredonia, M. G., Franchini, L., & Smeraldi, E. (1993). A study of relapse in subjects with mood disorder on lithium treatment. *European Neuropsychopharmacology, 3*, 103–110.

George, M. S., Sackeim, H., Rush, A. J., Marangell, L. B., Nahas, Z., Husain, M. M., . . . Ballenger, J. C. (2000). Vagus nerve stimulation: A new tool for treatment-resistant depression. *Biological Psychiatry, 47*, 287–295.

Goldfried, M. R., & Davison, G. C. (1976). *Clinical behavior therapy*. New York, NY: Holt, Rinehart, & Winston.

Goldfried, M. R., Raue, P. J., & Castonguay, L. G. (1998). The therapeutic focus in significant sessions of master therapists: A comparison of cognitive-behavioral and psychodynamic-interpersonal interventions. *Journal of Consulting and Clinical Psychology, 66*, 803–810.

Goldstein, L., & Ruscio, J. (2009). Thinking outside the Black Box: The relative risk of suicide with antidepressant use. *Scientific Review of Mental Health Practice, 7*, 3–16.

Golkaramnay, V., Bauer, S., Haug, S., Wolf, M., & Kordy, H. (2007). The exploration of the effectiveness of group therapy through an Internet chat as aftercare: A controlled naturalistic study. *Psychotherapy and Psychosomatics, 76*, 219–225.

Goodman, J. A., Krahn, L. E., Smith, G. G., Rummans, T. A., & Pileggi, T. S. (1999). Patient satisfaction with electroconvulsive therapy. *Mayo Clinic Proceedings, 74*, 967–971.

Gould, R. A., & Clum, G. A. (1993). A meta-analysis of self-help treatment approaches. *Clinical Psychology Review, 13*, 169–186.

Grawe, K., Donati, R., & Bernauer, F. (1998). *Psychotherapy in transition*. Seattle, WA: Hogrefe & Huber.

Greenberg, L. S., Elliot, R., & Lietaer, G. (1994). Research on humanistic and experiential psychotherapies. In A. E. Bergin & L. S. Garfield (Eds.), *Handbook of psychotherapy and behavior change* (4th ed., pp. 509–539). New York, NY: Wiley.

Greenberg, L. S., & Watson, J. C. (1998). Experiential therapy of depression: Differential effects of client-centered relationship conditions and process experiential interventions. *Psychotherapy Research, 8*, 210–224.

Grunbaum, A. (1984). *The foundations of psychoanalysis: A philosophical critique*. Berkeley, CA: University of California Press.

Haley, J. (1976). *Problem-solving therapy*. San Francisco, CA: Jossey-Bass.

Hansen, P. E. B., Ravnkilde, B., Videbech, P., Clemmensen, K., Sturlason, R., Reiner, M.,... Vestergaard, P. (2011). Low-frequency repetitive transcranial magnetic stimulation inferior to electroconvulsive therapy in treating depression. *Journal of ECT, 27*(1), 26–32.

Hayes, S. C. (2004). Acceptance and commitment therapy, relational frame theory, and the third wave of behavioral and cognitive therapies. *Behavior Therapy, 35*(4), 639–665.

Hayes, S. C., Strosahl, K., & Wilson, K. G. (1999). *Acceptance and commitment therapy*. New York, NY: Guilford Press.

Hazelrigg, M. D., Cooper, H. M., & Borduin, C. M. (1987). Evaluating the effectiveness of family therapies: An integrative review and analysis. *Psychological Bulletin, 101*, 428–442.

Healy, D. (2004). SSRI and suicide? Reply. *Psychotherapy and Psychosomatics, 73*, 262.

Herwig, U., Fallgatter, A. J., Höppner, J., Eschweiler, G. W., Kron, M., Hajak, G.,... Schönfeldt-Lecuona, C. (2007). Antidepressant effects of augmentative transcranial magnetic stimulation. A randomized multicenter trial. *British Journal of Psychiatry, 191*, 441–448.

Hinrichsen, G. A. (2008). Interpersonal psychotherapy for late life depression: Current status and new applications. *Journal of Rational-Emotive & Cognitive-Behavior Therapy, 26*, 263–275.

Hofmann, S. G., & Asmundson, G. J. G. (2008). Acceptance and mindfulness-based therapy: New wave or old hat? *Clinical Psychology Review, 28*, 1–16.

Hofmann, S. G., Sawyer, A. T., Witt, A. A., & Oh, D. (2010). The effect of mindfulness-based therapy on anxiety and depression: A meta-analytic review. *Journal of Consulting and Clinical Psychology, 78*(2), 169–183.

Hollon, S. D., Thase, M. E., & Markowitz, J. C. (2002). Treatment and prevention of depression. *Psychological Science in the Public Interest, 3*, 2002.

Hopko, D. R., Robertson, S. M. C., & Lejuez, C. W. (2006). Behavioral activation for anxiety disorders. *The Behavior Analyst Today, 7*, 212–224.

Horney, K. (1945). *Our inner conflicts: A constructive theory of neurosis*. New York, NY: Summit Books.

Horvath, A. O., Del Re, A. C., Flückiger, C., & Symonds, D. (2011). Alliance in individual psychotherapy. *Psychotherapy, 48*(1), 9.

Howard, K. I., Kopta, S. M., Krause, M. S., & Orlinsky, D. E. (1986). The dose-effect relationship in psychotherapy. *American Psychologist, 41*, 159–164.

Hunsley, J., & DiGuilio, G. (2002). Dodo bird, phoenix, or urban legend? *Scientific Review of Mental Health Practice, 1*, 11–22.

Hunt, M. (1997). *How science takes stock: The story of meta-analysis*. New York, NY: Russell Sage Foundation.

Irvin, J. E., Bowers, C. A., Dunn, M. E., & Wang, M. C. (1999). Efficacy of relapse prevention: A meta-analytic review. *Journal of Consulting and Clinical Psychology, 67*, 563–570.

Ivey, A. E., Ivey, M. B., & Simek-Morgan, L. (1993). *Counseling and psychotherapy: A multi-cultural perspective* (3rd ed.). Boston, MA: Allyn & Bacon.

Jacobson, E. (1938). *Progressive relaxation*. Chicago, IL: University of Chicago Press.

Jacobson, N. S., Dobson, K. S., Truax, P. A., Addis, M. E., Koerner, K., Gollan, J. K.,... Prince, S. E. (1996). A component analysis of cognitive-behavioral treatment for depression. *Journal of Consulting and Clinical Psychology, 64*, 295–304.

Jensen, P. S., Garcia, J. A., Glied, S., Crow, M., Foster, M., Schlander, M.,... Wells, K. (2005). Cost-effectiveness of ADHD treatments: Findings from the multi-modal treatment study of children with ADHD. *American Journal of Psychiatry, 162*, 1628–1636.

Johnson, J. (2009). A dark history: Memories of lobotomy in the new era of psychosurgery. *Medicine Studies, 1*(4), 367–378.

Kabat-Zinn, J. (2003). Mindfulness-based interventions in context: Past, present, and future. *Clinical Psychology: Science & Practice, 10*, 144–156.

Karon, B. P. (1994). *Effective psychoanalytic therapy of schizophrenia and other severe disorders* (APA Videotape Series). Washington, DC: American Psychological Association.

Kazdin, A. E. (1978). The application of operant techniques in treatment, rehabilitation, and education. In S. L. Garfield & A. E. Bergin (Eds.), *Handbook of psychotherapy and behavior change* (2nd ed.). New York, NY: Wiley.

Kazdin, A. E. (2005). Treatment outcomes, common factors, and continued neglect of mechanisms of change. *Clinical Psychology: Science and Practice, 12*, 184–188.

Kazdin, A. E. (2007). Mediators and mechanisms of change in psychotherapy research. *Annual Review of Clinical Psychology, 3*, 1–27.

Kazdin, A. E., & Hersen, M. (1980). The current status of behavior therapy. *Behavior Modification, 4*, 283–302.

Kazdin, A. E., Marciano, P. L., & Whitley, M. K. (2005). The therapeutic alliance in cognitive-behavioral treatment of children referred for oppositional, aggressive, and antisocial behavior. *Journal of Consulting and Clinical Psychology, 73*, 725–730.

Kazdin, A. E., & Wilcoxon, L. A. (1976). Systematic desensitization and non-specific treatment effects: A methodological evaluation. *Psychological Bulletin, 83*, 729–758.

Keinan, G., Almagor, M., & Ben-Porath, Y. S. (1989). A reevaluation of the relationships between psychotherapeutic orientation and perceived personality characteristics. *Psychotherapy, 26*, 218–226.

Kelly, J. F., Hoeppner, B., Stout, R. L., & Pagano, M. (2012). Determining the relative importance of the mechanisms of behavior change within Alcoholics Anonymous: A multiple mediator analysis. *Addiction, 107*(2), 289–299. http://dx.doi.org/10.1111/j.1360-0443.2011.03593.x

Kendall, T., Pilling, S., & Whittington, C. J. (2005). Are the SSRIs and atypical antidepressants safe and effective for children and adolescents? *Current Opinion in Psychiatry, 18*, 21–25.

Kim, B., Lee, S., Kim, Y. W., Choi, T. K., Yook, K., Suh, S. Y., &Yook, K. (2010). Effectiveness of a mindfulness-based cognitive therapy program as an adjunct to pharmacotherapy in patients with panic disorder. *Journal of Anxiety Disorders, 24*(6), 590–595. http://dx.doi.org/10.1016/j.janxdis.2010.03.019

Kirsch, I. (1990). *Changing expectations: A key to effective psychotherapy*. Pacific Grove, CA: Brooks/Cole.

Kirsch, I. (2010). *The emperor's new drugs*. New York, NY: Basic Books.

Klein, M. H., Kolden, G. G., Michels, J., & Chisholm-Stockard, S. (2002). Effective elements of the therapy relationship: Congruence/genuineness. In J. C. Norcross (Ed.), *Psychotherapy relationships that work: Therapists' relational contributions to effective psychotherapy* (pp. 195–215). London, England: Oxford University Press.

Klerman, G. L., & Weissman, M. M. (Eds.). (1993). *New applications of interpersonal psychotherapy*. Washington, DC: American Psychiatric Press.

Klerman, G. L., Weissman, M. M., Rounsaville, B. J., & Chevron, E. S. (1984). *Interpersonal psychotherapy of depression*. New York, NY: Basic Books.

Kruger, J., Savitsky, K., & Gilovich, T. (1999). Superstition and the regression effect. *Skeptical Inquirer, 23*, 24–29.

Kumari, V. (2006). Do psychotherapies produce neurobiological effects? *Acta Neuropsychiatrica, 18*, 61–70.

Kushner, M. (1968). The operant control of intractable sneezing. In C. D. Spielberger, R. Fox, & B. Masterson (Eds.), *Contributions to general psychology: Selected readings for introductory psychology*. New York, NY: Roland Press.

Lacasse, J. R., & Leo, J. (2005). Serotonin and depression: A disconnect between the advertisements and the scientific literature. *PLoS Medicine, 2*, 101–106.

Lambert, K. G. (2003). The life and career of Paul MacLean: A journey toward social and neurobiological harmony. *Physiology & Behavior, 79*, 373–381.

Lambert, M. J., & Ogles, B. M. (2004). The efficacy and effectiveness of psychotherapy. In M. J. Lambert (Ed.), *Bergin and Garfield's handbook of psychotherapy and behavior change* (5th ed., pp. 139–193). New York, NY: Wiley.

Landman, J. T., & Dawes, R. M. (1982). Psychotherapy outcome: Smith and Glass conclusions stand up under scrutiny. *American Psychologist, 37*, 504–516.

Larimer, M. E., Palmer, R. S., & Marlatt, G. A. (1999). Relapse prevention: An overview of Marlatt's cognitive-behavioural model. *Alcohol Research and Health, 23*, 151–160.

Lazarus, A. A. (2006). *Brief but comprehensive psychotherapy: The multimodal way*. New York, NY: Springer.

Lazarus, R. S. (2003). Does the positive psychology movement have legs? *Psychological Inquiry, 14*, 93–109.

Lebow, J. L. (2010). The effective treatment of personality disorders: Easily within our grasp. *Professional Psychology: Research and Practice, 41*, 73–74.

LeFever, G. B., Arcona, A. P., & Antonuccio, D. O. (2003). ADHD among American schoolchildren: Evidence of overdiagnosis and overuse of medication. *Scientific Review of Mental Health Practice, 2*, 49–60.

Lejoyeux, M., & Ades, J. (1997). Antidepressant discontinuation: A review of the literature. *Journal of Clinical Psychiatry, 58*(Suppl. 7), 11–15.

Levant, R. F. (2004). The empirically validated treatments movement: A practitioner/educator perspective. *Clinical Psychology: Science and Practice, 11*, 219–224.

Levine, B. (1979). *Group psychotherapy: Practice and development*. Englewood Cliffs, NJ: Prentice Hall.

Levis, D. J. (1995). Decoding traumatic memory: Implosive theory of psychopathology. In W. O. Donohue & L. Kranser (Eds.), *Theories in behavior therapy* (pp. 173–207). Washington, DC: American Psychological Association.

Lick, J. (1975). Expectancy, false galvanic skin response feedback, and systematic desensitization in the modification of phobic behavior. *Journal of Consulting and Clinical Psychology, 43*, 557–557.

Lieberman, J. A., Stroup, T. S., McEvoy, J. P., Swartz, M. S., Rosenheck, R. A., Perkins, D. O.,... Hsiao, J. K. (2005). Effectiveness of antipsychotic drugs in patients with chronic schizophrenia. *New England Journal of Medicine, 353*(12), 1209–1223.

Lilienfeld, S. O. (2007). Psychological treatments that cause harm. *Perspectives on Psychological Science, 2*(1), 53–70. http://dx.doi.org/10.1111/j.1745-6916.2007.00029.x

Lilienfeld, S. O., & Arkowitz, H. (2007). Autism: An epidemic? *Scientific American Mind, 18*(2), 82–83.

Lilienfeld, S. O., & Lynn, S. J. (2003). Dissociative identity disorder: Multiple personalities, multiple controversies. In S. O. Lilienfeld, S. J. Lynn, & J. M. Lohr (Eds.), *Science and pseudoscience in clinical psychology* (pp. 109–143). New York, NY: Guilford Press.

Lilienfeld, S. O., Ritschel, L. A., Lynn, S. J., Brown, A. P., Cautin, R. M., & Latzman, R. L. (in press a). The research-practice gap: Bridging the schism between eating disorder researchers and practitioners. *International Journal of Eating Disorders*.

Lilienfeld, S. O., Ritschel, L. A., Lynn, S. J., Cautin, R. L., & Latzman, R. D. (in press b). Why many clinical psychologists are resistant to evidence-based practice: Root causes and constructive remedies. *Clinical Psychology Review*.

Linehan, M. M. (1993). *Cognitive behavioral treatment of borderline personality disorder*. New York, NY: Guilford Press.

Littauer, H., Sexton, H., & Wynn, R. (2005). Qualities clients wish for in their therapists. *Scandanavian Journal of Caring Science, 19*, 28–31.

Loftus, E. F. (1993). The reality of repressed memories. *American Psychologist, 48*, 518–537.

Lohr, J. M., DeMaio, C., & McGlynn, F. D. (2003). Specific and nonspecific treatment factors in the experimental analysis of behavioral treatment efficacy. *Behavior Modification, 27*, 322–368.

Lohr, J. M., Hooke, W., Gist, R., & Tolin, D. F. (2003). Novel and controversial treatments for trauma-related disorders. In S. O. Lilienfeld, S. J. Lynn, & J. M. Lohr (Eds.), *Science and pseudoscience in clinical psychology* (pp. 243–272). New York, NY: Guilford Press.

Lohr, J. M., Tolin, D. F., & Lilienfeld, S. O. (1998). Efficacy of eye movement desensitization and reprocessing. *Behavior Therapy, 29*, 123–156.

Luborsky, L., Crits-Christoph, P., McLellan, T., Woody, G., Piper, W., Imber, S., & Liberman, B. (1986). Do therapists vary much in their success? Findings from four outcome studies. *American Journal of Orthopsychiatry, 56*, 501–512.

Luborsky, L., McLellan, A. T., Diguer, L., Woody, G., & Seligman, D. A. (1997). The psychotherapist matters: Comparison of outcomes across twenty-two therapists and seven patient samples. *Clinical Psychology: Science and Practice, 4*(1), 53–65.

Luborsky, L., Mellon, J., van Ravenswaay, P., Childress, A. R., Colen, K., Hole, A.,... Alexander, K. (1985). A verification of Freud's grandest clinical hypothesis: The transference. *Clinical Psychology Review, 5*, 231–246.

Luty, S. E., Carter, J. D., McKenzie, J. M., Rae, A. M., Frampton, C., Mulder, R. T., & Joyce, P. R. (2010). Randomised controlled trial of interpersonal psychotherapy and cognitive-behavioural therapy for depression. *Focus, 8*(1), 110.

Lynn, S. J., & Frauman, D. (1985). Group psychotherapy. In S. J. Lynn, & J. P. Garske (Eds.), *Contemporary psychotherapies: Models and methods* (pp. 419–458). Columbus, OH: Charles E. Merrill.

Lynn, S. J., Knox, J. A., Fassler, O., Lilienfeld, S. O., & Loftus, E. F. (2004). Memory, trauma, and dissociation. In G. M. Rosen (Ed.), *Posttraumatic stress disorder: Issues and controversies* (pp. 163–186). New York, NY: Wiley.

MacKillop, J., & Gray, J. (in press). Controversial treatments for alcohol use disorders. In S.O. Lilienfeld, S. Lynn, & J. Lohr (Eds.), *Science and pseudosicence in clinical psychology* (2nd ed.). New York, NY: Guilford Press.

MacKillop, J., Lisman, S. A., Weinstein, A., & Rosenbaum, D. (2003). Controversial treatments for alcoholism. In S. O. Lilienfeld, S. J. Lynn, & J. W. Lohr (Eds.), *Science and pseudoscience in clinical psychology* (pp. 273–306). New York, NY: Guilford Press.

Malcom, K. (1989). Patients' perceptions and knowledge of electroconvulsive therapy. *Psychiatric Bulletin, 13*, 161–165.

Marino, L., & Lilienfeld, S. O. (1998). Dolphin-assisted therapy: Flawed data, flawed conclusions. *Anthrozoos, 11*, 194–200.

Marks, R. P., Swinson, M., Basoglu, K., & Kuch, H. (1993). Alpraxolam and exposure alone and combined in panic disorder with agoraphobia. *British Journal of Psychiatry, 162*, 788–799.

Marlatt, G. A. (1983). The controlled-drinking controversy: A commentary. *American Psychologist, 10*, 1097–1110.

Marlatt, G. A. (2002). Buddhist philosophy and the treatment of addictive behavior. *Cognitive and Behavioral Practice, 9*, 44–47.

Marlatt, G. A., & Gordon, J. R. (Eds.). (1985). *Relapse prevention: Maintenance strategies in the treatment of addictive behaviors.* New York, NY: Guilford Press.

Mashour, G. A., Walker, E. E., & Martuza, R. L. (2005). Psychosurgery: Past, present, and future. *Brain Research Reviews, 48*, 409–419.

Maslow, A. H. (1954). *Motivation and personality.* New York, NY: Harper.

Mayberg, H. S., Lozano, A. M., Voon, V., McNeely, H. E., Seminowicz, D., Hamani, C.,... Kennedy, S. H. (2005). Deep brain stimulation for treatment-resistant depression. *Neuron, 45*, 651–660.

McDonald, A., & Walter, G. (2004). The portrayal of ECT in American movies. *Journal of ECT, 20*, 230–236.

McEvoy, P. M. (2007). Effectiveness of cognitive behavioural group therapy for social phobia in a community clinic: A benchmarking study. *Behaviour Research and Therapy, 45*, 3030–3040.

McFall, R. M. (2006). Doctoral training in clinical psychology. *Annual Review of Clinical Psychology, 2*, 21–49.

McHugh P. R. (2008). *Try to remember: Psychiatry's clash over meaning, memory, and mind.* New York, NY: Dana Press.

Meador, B. D., & Rogers, C. R. (1979). Person centered therapy. In J. R. Corsini (Ed.), *Current psychotherapies.* Itasca, IL: F. E. Peacock.

Meichenbaum, D. (1985). Cognitive-behavioral therapies. In S. J. Lynn, & J. P. Garske (Eds.), *Contemporary psychotherapies: Models and methods* (pp. 261–286). Columbus, OH: Charles E. Merrill.

Meichenbaum, D. (1996). Stress inoculation training for coping with stressors. *The Clinical Psychologist, 49*, 4–10.

Mellinger, D. M., & Lynn, S. J. (2003). *The monster in the cave: How to face your fear and anxiety and live your life.* New York, NY: Berkeley.

Menchola, B. L., Arkowitz, H., & Burke, B. L. (2007). Efficacy of self-administered treatments for depression and anxiety: A meta-analysis. *Professional Psychology: Research and Practice, 38*, 421–429.

Menninger, K. (1958). *Theory of psychoanalytic technique.* New York, NY: Basic Books.

Meyer, A. (Ed.). (1981). The Hamburg Short Psychotherapy Comparison Experiment. *Psychotherapy and Psychosomatics, 35*, 81–207.

Miller, S. D., Duncan, B. L., & Hubble, M. A. (2005). Outcome-informed clinical work. In J. C. Norcross & M. R. Goldfried (Eds.), *Handbook of psychotherapy integration* (2nd ed., pp. 84–102). New York, NY: Oxford.

Miller, W. R., Brown, J. M., Simpson, T. L., Handmaker, N. S., Bien, T. H., Luckie, L. F.,... Tonigan, J. S. (1995). What works? A methodological analysis of the alcohol treatment outcome literature. In R. K. Hester (Ed.), *Handbook of alcoholism treatment approaches: Effective alternatives* (2nd ed., pp. 12–44). Boston, MA: Allyn & Bacon.

Miller, W. R., & Hester, R. K. (1980). Treating the problem drinker: Modern approaches. In W. R. Miller (Ed.), *The addictive behaviors: Treatment of alcoholism, drug abuse, smoking, and obesity* (pp. 11–141). Oxford, England: Pergamon Press.

Miller, W. R., & Rollnick, S. (2002). *Motivational interviewing: Preparing people for change.* New York, NY: Guilford Press.

Miller, W. R., & Rose, G. S. (2009). Toward a theory of motivational interviewing. *American Psychologist; American Psychologist, 64*(6), 527–537.

Mills, A., & Lynn, S. J. (2000). Past-life experiences. In E. Cardeña, S. J. Lynn, & S. Krippner (Eds.), *The varieties of anomalous experience.* New York, NY: Guilford Press.

Mineka, S., & Thomas, C. (1999). Mechanisms of change in exposure therapy for anxiety disorders. In T. Dalgleish & M. J. Power (Eds.), *Handbook of cognition and emotion* (pp. 747–764). Chichester, England: Wiley.

Minuchin, S. (1974). *Families and family therapy.* Cambridge, MA: Harvard University Press.

Mitchell, S. A., & Black, M. J. (1995). *Freud and beyond: A history of modern psychoanalytic thought.* New York, NY: Basic Books.

Monastra, V. J. (2008). *Unlocking the potential of patients with ADHD.* Washington, DC: American Psychological Association.

Monroe, R. (1955). *Schools of psychoanalytic thought.* New York, NY: Dryden.

Monti, P. M., Gulliver, S. B., & Myers, M. G. (1994). Social skills training for alcoholics: Assessment and treatment. *Alcohol and Alcoholism, 29*, 627–637.

Moos, R. H., & Moos, B. S. (2006). Participation in treatment and Alcoholics Anonymous: A 16-year follow-up of initially untreated individuals. *Journal of Clinical Psychology, 62*(6), 735–750. http://dx.doi.org/10.1002/jclp.20259

Mueser, K. T., & Liberman, R. P. (1995). Behavior therapy in practice. In B. Bongar & L. E. Beutler (Eds.), *Comprehensive textbook of psychotherapy: Theory and practice* (pp. 84–110). New York, NY: Oxford University Press.

Murphy, R., Straebler, S., Basden, S., Cooper, Z., & Fairburn, C. G. (2012). Interpersonal psychotherapy for eating disorders. *Clinical Psychology & Psychotherapy, 19*, 150–158.

Navarro, A. M. (1993). Effectiveness of psychotherapy with Latinos in the United States: A revised meta-analysis. *Interamerican Journal of Psychology, 27*, 131–146.

Nemeroff, C. B., Kalali, A., Keller, M. B., Charney, D. S., Lenderts, S. E., Cascade, E. F.,... Schatzberg, A. F. (2007). Impact of publicity concerning pediatric suicidality data on physician practice patterns in the United States. *Archives of General Psychiatry, 64*, 397.

Neville, R. (1978). Psychosurgery. In W. Reich (Ed.), *Encyclopedia of bioethics, Vol. 3* (pp. 1387–1391). New York, NY: Macmillan-Free Press.

Norcross, J. C. (2005). A primer on psychotherapy integration. In J. C. Norcross & M. R. Goldfried (Eds.), *Handbook of psychotherapy integration* (2nd ed., pp. 3–23). New York, NY: Oxford University Press.

Norcross, J. C., & Beutler, L. (1997). Determining the relationship of choice in brief therapy. In J. N. Butcher (Ed.), *Personality assessment in managed health care* (pp. 42–60). New York, NY: Oxford University Press.

Norcross, J. C., Garofalo, A., & Koocher, G. (2006). Discredited psychological treatments and tests: A Delphi poll. *Professional Psychology: Research and Practice, 137*, 515–522.

Norcross, J. C., & Wampold, B. E. (2011a). What works for whom: Tailoring psychotherapy to the person. *Journal of Clinical Psychology, 67*(2), 127–132.

Norcross, J. C., & Wampold, B. E. (2011b). Evidence-based therapy relationships: Research conclusions and clinical practices. *Psychotherapy, 48*(1), 98–102.

Novaco, R. W. (1994). Clinical problems of anger and its assessment and regulation through a stress coping skills approach. In W. O'Donohue & L. Krasner (Eds.), *Handbook of skills training* (pp. 320–338). New York, NY: Pergamon Press.

Ogrodniczuk, J. S., & Piper, W. E. (1999). Use of transference interpretations in dynamically oriented individual psychotherapy for patients with personality disorders. *Journal of Personality Disorders, 13*, 297–311.

Olfson, M., Marcus, S., Sackheim, H. A., Thompson, J., & Pincus, H. A. (1998). Use of ECT for the inpatient treatment of recurrent major depression. *American Journal of Psychiatry, 155*, 22–29.

Olkin, R., & Taliaferro, G. (2005). Evidence-based practices have ignored people with disabilities. In J. C. Norcross, L. E. Beutler, & R. F. Levant (Eds.), *Evidence-based practices in mental health* (pp. 353–358). Washington, DC: American Psychological Association.

Olsen, S., Smith, S. S., Oei, T. P., & Douglas, J. (2012). Motivational interviewing (MINT) improves continuous positive airway pressure (CPAP) acceptance and adherence: A randomized controlled trial. *Journal of Consulting and Clinical Psychology, 80*(1), 151.

Orlinsky, D. E., Grawe, K., & Parks, B. K. (1994). Process and outcome in psychotherapy—Noch einmal. In A. E. Bergin & S. L. Garfield (Eds.), *Handbook of psychotherapy and behavior change* (4th ed., pp. 270–376). New York, NY: Wiley.

Orlinksy, D. E., & Howard, K. I. (1986). Process and outcome in psychotherapy. In S. L. Garfield & A. E. Bergin (Eds.), *Handbook of psychotherapy and behavior change* (3rd ed., pp. 311–384). New York, NY: Wiley.

Ost, L. G. (2008). Efficacy of the third wave of behavioral therapies: A systematic review and meta-analysis. *Behaviour Research and Therapy, 46*, 296–321.

Otto, M. W., Smits, J. A. J., & Reese, H. E. (2005). Combined psychotherapy and pharmacotherapy for mood and anxiety disorders in adults: Review and analysis. *Clinical Psychology: Science & Practice, 12*, 72–86.

Pagnin, D., de Queiroz, V., Pini, S., & Cassano, G. B. (2008, Winter). Efficacy of ECT in depression: A meta-analytic review. *Focus, 6*, 155–162.

Paul, G., & Lentz, R. J. (1977). *Psychosocial treatment of chronic mental patients: Milieu versus social-learning programs.* Cambridge, MA: Harvard University Press.

Pederson Mussell, M., Crosby, R. D., Crow, S. J., Knopke, A. J., Peterson, C. B., Wonderlich, S. A., & Mitchell, J. E. (2000). Utilization of empirically supported psychotherapy treatments for individuals with eating disorders: A survey of psychologists. *International Journal of Eating Disorders, 27*, 230–237.

Petrosino. A., Turpin-Petrosino, C., & Buehler, J. (2003, November). "'Scared Straight' and other juvenile awareness programs for preventing juvenile delinquency. Campbell Review Update I." In *The Campbell Collaboration*

Psychological and Biological Treatments

Reviews of Intervention and Policy Evaluations (C2-RIPE). Philadelphia, PA: Campbell Collaboration. Retrieved from http://web.archive.org/web/20070927013116/http://www.campbellcollaboration.org/doc-pdf/ssrupdt.pdf

Petry, N. M., Tennen, H., & Affleck, G. (2000). Stalking the elusive client variable in psychotherapy research. In C. R. Snyder & R. Ingram (Eds.), *Handbook of psychological change: Psychotherapy processes and practices for the 21st century* (pp. 88–108). New York, NY: Wiley.

Pettinati, H. M., Tamburello, T. A., Ruetsch, C. R., & Kaplan, F. N. (1994). Patient attitudes toward electroconvulsive therapy. *Psychopharmacological Bulletin, 30,* 471–475.

Polivy, J., & Herman, C. P. (2002). If you first don't succeed. False hopes of self-change. *American Psychologist, 57,* 677–689.

Porter, S., & Peace, K. A. (2007). The scars of memory: A prospective longitudinal investigation of the consistency of traumatic and positive emotional memories in adulthood. *Psychological Science, 18,* 435–441.

Prochaska, J. O., & DiClemente, C. C. (1982). Transtheoretical therapy: Toward a more integrative model of change. *Psychotherapy: Theory, Research, and Practice, 20,* 161–173.

Prochaska, J. O., & Norcross, J. C. (2002). Stages of change. In J. C. Norcross (Ed.), *Psychotherapy relationships that work.* New York, NY: Oxford University Press.

Prochaska, J. O., & Norcross, J. C. (2007). *Systems of psychotherapy: A transtheoretical approach* (6th ed.). Pacific Grove, CA: Brooks/Cole.

Project MATCH Research Group. (1997). Matching alcoholism treatments to client heterogeneity: Project MATCH posttreatment drinking outcomes. *Journal of Studies on Alcohol, 58,* 7–29.

Rabinowitz, J., & Renert, N. (1997). Clinicians' predictions of length of psychotherapy. *Psychiatric Services, 48,* 97–99.

Rachman, S. (1994). Psychological treatment of panic: Mechanisms. In B. E. Wolfe & J. D. Maser (Eds.), *Treatment of panic disorder: A consensus development conference* (pp. 133–148). Washington, DC: American Psychiatric Press.

Raimy, V. C. (Ed.). (1950). *Training in clinical psychology (Boulder Conference).* New York, NY: Prentice Hall.

Rasmussen, K., Sampson, S. M., & Rummans, T. A. (2002). Electroconvulsive therapy and newer modalities for the treatment of medication-refractory mental illness. *Mayo Clinic Proceedings, 77,* 552–556.

Rhule, D. M. (2005). Take care to do no harm: Harmful interventions for youth problem behavior. *Professional Psychology: Research and Practice, 36,* 618–625.

Rogers, C. R. (1942). *Counseling and psychotherapy.* New York, NY: Houghton Mifflin.

Rogers, C. R. (1957). The necessary and sufficient conditions of therapeutic personality change. *Journal of Consulting Psychology, 21,* 95–103.

Rogers, C. R. (1961). *On becoming a person.* Boston, MA: Houghton Mifflin.

Rosenberg, H. (1993). Prediction of controlled drinking by alcoholics and problem drinkers. *Psychological Bulletin, 113,* 129–139.

Rosenthal, R., & DiMatteo, M. R. (2001). Meta-analysis: Recent developments in quantitative methods for literature reviews. *Annual Review of Psychology, 52,* 59–82.

Rosenzweig, S. (1936). Some implicit common factors in diverse methods in psychotherapy. *American Journal of Orthopsychiatry, 6,* 412–415.

Ross, C. A., & Pam, A. (1995). *Pseudoscience in biological psychiatry: Blaming the body.* New York, NY: Wiley.

Rothbaum, B. O., Hodges, L., Ready, D., Graap, K., & Alarcon, R. D. (2001). Virtual reality exposure therapy for Vietnam veterans with posttraumatic stress disorder. *Journal of Clinical Psychiatry, 62,* 617–622.

Rubin, A. (2003). Unanswered questions about the empirical support for EMDR in the treatment of PTSD: A review of research. *Traumatology, 9*(1), 4–30.

Rush, A. J., Marangell, L. B., Sackeim, H. A., George, M. S., Brannan, S. K., Davis, S. M.,... Cooke, R. G. (2005). Vagus nerve stimulation for treatment-resistant depression: A randomized, controlled acute phase trial. *Biological Psychiatry, 58,* 347–354.

Sackeim, H. A. (1986). The efficacy of electroconvulsive therapy. *Annals of the New York Academy of Sciences, 462,* 70–75.

Sackeim, H. A., Prudic, J., Fuller, R., Keilp, J., Lavori, P. W., & Olfson, M. (2007). The cognitive effects of electroconvulsive therapy in community settings. *Neuropsychopharmacology, 32,* 244–254.

Safer, D. J. (2000). Are stimulants overprescribed for youths with ADHD? *Annals of Clinical Psychiatry, 12,* 55–62.

Santa Maria, M. P., Baumeister, A. A., & Gouvier, W. D. (1999). Public knowledge and misconceptions about electroconvulsive therapy: A demographically stratified investigation. *International Journal of Rehabilitation and Health, 4,* 111–116.

Santor, D. A., & Kusumakar, V. (2001). Open trial of interpersonal therapy in adolescents with moderate to severe major depression: Effectiveness of novice IPT therapists. *Journal of the American Academy of Child and Adolescent Psychiatry, 40,* 236–240.

Satir, V. (1964). *Conjoint family therapy.* New York, NY: Science and Behavior Books.

Scattone, D. (2007). Social skills interventions for children with autism. *Psychology in the Schools, 44,* 717–726.

Schmidt, J. P., & Hancey, R. (1979). Social class and psychiatric treatment: Application of a decision-making model to use patterns in a cost-free clinic. *Journal of Consulting and Clinical Psychology, 47,* 771–772.

Schneeweiss, S., & Avorn, J. (2009). Antipsychotic agents and sudden cardiac death—How should we manage the risk. *New England Journal of Medicine, 360,* 294–296.

Schofield, W. (1964). *Psychotherapy: The purchase of friendship.* Englewood Cliffs, NJ: Prentice Hall.

Scovern, A. W., & Kilmann, P. R. (1980). Status of electroconvulsive therapy: Review of the outcome literature. *Psychological Bulletin, 87,* 260–295.

Segal, Z. V., Williams, J. M. G., & Teasdale, J. D. (2012). *Mindfulness-based cognitive therapy for depression.* New York, NY: Guilford Press.

Shadish, W. R. (1995). The logic of generalization: Five principles common to experiments and ethnographies. *American Journal of Community Psychology, 23,* 419–428.

Shapiro, D. A., & Shapiro, D. (1982). Meta-analysis of comparative therapy outcome studies: A replication and refinement. *Psychological Bulletin, 92,* 581–604.

Shapiro, F. (1995). *Eye movement desensitization and reprocessing: Basic principles, protocols, and procedures.* New York, NY: Guilford Press.

Shapiro, F., & Forrest, M. S. (1997). *EMDR: The breakthrough therapy for overcoming anxiety, stress, and trauma.* New York, NY: Basic Books.

Shedler, J. (2010). The efficacy of psychodynamic psychotherapy. *American Psychologist, 65,* 98–109.

Shin, S. M., Chow, C., Camacho-Gonsalves, T., Levy, R. J., Allen, E., & Leff, S. H. (2005). A meta-analytic review of racial-ethnic matching for African American and Caucasian American clients and clinicians. *Journal of Counseling Psychology, 52,* 45–56.

Shlien, J., & Levant, R. (1984). Introduction. In R. Levant & J. Shlien (Eds.), *Client-centered therapy and the person-centered approach: New directions in theory, research and practice* (pp. 1–16). New York, NY: Praeger.

Silverman, S. (1987, July). Medical "miracles": Still mysterious despite claims of believers. *Newsletter of the Sacramento Skeptics Society,* Sacramento, CA, pp. 2–7.

Simpson, G. M., & Kline, N. S. (1976). Tardive dyskinesias: Manifestations, etiology, and treatment. In M. D. Yahr (Ed.), *The basal ganglia* (pp. 167–183). New York, NY: Raven Press.

Singer, M. T., & Nievod, A. (2003). New age therapies. In S. O. Lilienfeld, S. J. Lynn, & J. M. Lohr (Eds.), *Science and pseudoscience in clinical psychology* (pp. 176–204). New York, NY: Guilford Press.

Sloane, R. B., Staples, F., Cristol, A., Yorkston, N., & Whipple, K. (1975). *Psychotherapy versus behavior therapy.* Cambridge, MA: Harvard University Press.

Smith, J. (2009). *Pseudoscience and extraordinary claims of the paranormal.* New York, NY: Wiley.

Smith, M. E., & Farah, M. J. (2011). Are prescription stimulants "smart pills"? The epidemiology and cognitive neuroscience of prescription stimulant use by normal healthy individuals. *Psychological Bulletin, 137,* 717–741.

Smith, M. L., & Glass, G. V. (1977). Meta-analysis of psychotherapy outcome studies. *American Psychologist, 32,* 752–760.

Smith, M. L., Glass, G. V., & Miller, T. I. (1980). *The benefits of psychotherapy.* Baltimore, MD: Johns Hopkins University Press.

Smythe, I. H. (2007). The secret behind "The Secret": What is attracting millions to the "Law of Attraction"? *Skeptic, 13*(2), 8–11.

Sobell, M. B., & Sobell, L. C. (1973). Alcoholics treated by individualized behavior therapy: One year treatment outcome. *Behaviour Research and Therapy, 11,* 599–618.

Sparks, J. A., Duncan, B. L., & Miller, S. D. (2008). Common factors in psychotherapy. In J. L. Lebow (Ed.), *Twenty-first century psychotherapies: Contemporary approaches to theory and practice* (pp. 453–497). Hoboken, NJ: Wiley.

Spiegler, M. (1983). *Contemporary behavior therapy.* Palo Alto, CA: Mayfield.

Spiegler, M. D., & Guevremont, D. C. (2003). *Contemporary behavior therapy* (4th ed). Belmont, CA: Wadsworth/Thompson Learning.

Steele, M., Weiss, M., Swanson, J., Wang, J., Prinzo, R., & Binder, C. (2006). A randomized, controlled effectiveness trial of OROS-methylphenidate compared to usual care with immediate release methylphenidate in ADHD. *Canadian Journal of Clinical Pharmacology, 14,* 50–62.

Steinmetz, J. L., Lewinsohn, P. M., & Antonuccio, D. O. (1983). Prediction of individual outcome in a group intervention for depression. *Journal of Consulting and Clinical Psychology, 51,* 331–337.

Stevens, S. E., Hynan, M. T., & Allen, M. (2000). A meta-analysis of common factor and specific treatment effects across the outcome domains of the phase model of psychotherapy. *Clinical Psychology: Science and Practice, 7,* 273–290.

Stricker, G., & Gold, J. (2003). Integrative approaches to psychotherapy. In A. S. Gurman & S. B. Messer (Eds.), *Essential psychotherapies: Theory and practic* (2nd ed., pp. 317–349). New York, NY: Guilford Press.

Strickland, T. L., Stein, R., Lin, K. M., Risby, E., & Fong, R. (1997). The pharmacologic treatment of anxiety and depression in African Americans: Considerations for the general practitioner. *Archives of Family Medicine, 6,* 371–375.

Strupp, H. H., Fox, R. E., & Lessler, K. (1969). *Patients view their therapy*. Baltimore, MD: Johns Hopkins University Press.

Strupp, H. H., Hadley, S. W., & Gomez-Schwartz, B. (1978). *Psychotherapy for better or worse: An analysis of the problem of negative effects*. New York, NY: Jason Aronson.

Stuart, R. B., & Heiby, E. M. (2007). To prescribe or not prescribe: Eleven exploratory questions. *Scientific Review of Mental Health Practice, 5*, 4–32.

Sue, D. W., & Sue, D. (2003). *Counseling the culturally diverse: Theory and practice* (4th ed.). New York, NY: Wiley.

Sue, S. (1998). In search of cultural competence in psychotherapy and counseling. *American Psychologist, 53*, 440–448.

Sue, S., & Lam, A. G. (2002). Cultural and demographic diversity. In J. C. Norcross (Ed.), *Psychotherapy relationships that work* (pp. 401–421). New York, NY: Oxford University Press.

Sue, S., & Zane, N. (2006). Ethnic minority populations have been neglected by evidence-based practices. In J. C. Norcross, L. E. Beutler, & R. F. Levant (Eds.), *Evidence-based practices in mental health* (pp. 329–337). Washington, DC: American Psychological Association.

Sullivan, H. S. (1954). *The psychiatric interview*. New York, NY: Norton.

Tavris, C. (2003, September 28). Mind games: Warfare between therapists and scientists. *Chronicle Review, 45*(29), B7.

Teasdale, J. D., Segal, Z. V., & Williams, J. M. G. (2003). Mindfulness training and problem formulation. *Clinical Psychology: Science and Practice, 10*, 157–160.

Thase, M. E. (2000). Psychopharmacology in conjunction with psychotherapy. In C. R. Snyder & R. E. Ingram (Eds.), *Handbook of psychological change* (pp. 474–498). New York, NY: Wiley.

Tooth, G. C., & Newton, M. P. (1961). *Leukotomy in England and Wales 1942–1954*. London, Engalnd: Her Majesty's Stationary Office.

Tryon, W. W. (2008). Whatever happened to symptom substitution? *Clinical Psychology Review, 28*, 963–968.

U.S. Surgeon General. (2001). *Mental health: Culture, race, and ethnicity—A supplement to mental health: A report of the Surgeon General*. Rockville, MD: U.S. Department of Health and Human Services.

Vaillant, G. E., & Milofsky, E. S. (1982). Natural history of male alcoholism IV: Paths to recovery. *Archives of General Psychiatry, 39*, 127–133.

Valenstein, E. S. (1973). *Brain control*. New York, NY: Wiley.

Vetere, A. (2001). Structural family therapy. *Child Psychology and Psychiatry Review, 6*, 133–139.

Vos, S. P. F., Huibers, M. J. H., Diels, L., & Arntz, A. (2012). A randomized clinical trial of cognitive behavioral therapy and interpersonal psychotherapy for panic disorder with agoraphobia. *Psychological Medicine, 1*(1), 1–12.

Wachtel, P. L. (1977). *Psychoanalysis and behavior therapy: Toward an integration*. New York, NY: Basic Books.

Wachtel, P. L. (1997). *Psychoanalysis, behavior therapy, and the relational world*. Washington, DC: American Psychological Association.

Walton, D. E. (1978). An exploratory study: Personality factors and theoretical orientations of therapists. *Psychotherapy: Theory, Research, and Practice, 15*, 390–395.

Wampold, B. E. (2001). *The great psychotherapy debate: Models, methods, and findings*. Mahwah, NJ: Erlbaum.

Wampold, B. E. (2010). The research evidence for the common factors models: A historically situated perspective. In B. M. Duncan, S. D. Miller, M. A. Hubble & B. E. Wampold, (Eds). *The Heart and Soul of Therapy*. (2nd ed., 49–82). Washington, DC: American Psychological Association.

Wampold, B. E. (2012). Humanism as a common factor in psychotherapy. *Psychotherapy Theory Research Practice Training, 49*(4), 445–449.

Wang, P. S., Gruber, M. J., Powers, R. E., Schoenbaum, M., Speier, A., Wells, K. B., & Kessler, R. C. (2008). Disruption of existing mental health treatments and failure to initiate new treatment after hurricane Katrina. *American Journal of Psychiatry, 165*, 34–41.

Waschbusch, D. A., & Hill, G. P. (2003). Empirically supported, promising, and unsupported treatments for children with attention-deficit/hyperactivity disorder. In S. O. Lilienfeld, S. J. Lynn, & J. M. Lohr (Eds.), *Science and pseudoscience in clinical psychology* (pp. 333–362). New York, NY: Guilford Press.

Watzlawick, P., Beavin, J., & Jackson, D. D. (1967). *Pragmatics of human communication: A study of interactional patterns, pathologies, and paradoxes*. New York, NY: Norton.

Watzlawick, P., Weakland, J. H., & Fisch, R. (1974). *Change: Principles of problem formation and problem resolution*. New York, NY: Norton.

Weisz, J. R., Weiss, B., Han, S. S., Granger, D. A., & Morton, T. (1995). Effects of psychotherapy with children and adolescents revisited: A meta-analysis of treatment outcome studies. *Psychological Bulletin, 117*, 450–468.

Westen, D., Novotny, C. M., & Thompson-Brenner, H. (2004). The empirical status of empirically supported psychotherapies: Assumptions, findings, and reporting in controlled clinical trials. *Psychological Bulletin, 130*, 631–663.

Westerman, M. A., Foote, J. P., & Winston, A. (1995). Change in coordination across phases of psychotherapy and outcome: Two mechanisms for the role played by patients' contribution to the alliance. *Journal of Consulting and Clinical Psychology, 63*, 672–675.

Whaley, A. L., & Davis, K. E. (2007). Cultural competence and evidence-based practice in mental health services: A complementary perspective. *American Psychologist, 62*, 563–574.

Wigal, T., Greenhill, L., Chuang, S., McGough, J., Vitiello, B., Skrobala, A.,... Stehli, A. (2006). Safety and tolerability of methylphenidate in preschool children with ADHD. *Journal of the American Academy of Adolescent Psychiatry, 45*, 1294.

Williams, S. L., Turner, S. M., & Peer, D. F. (1985). Guided mastery and performance desensitization treatments for severe acrophobia. *Journal of Consulting and Clinical Psychology, 53*, 234–247.

Wilson, G. T., & O'Leary, K. D. (1980). *Principles of behavior therapy*. Englewood Cliffs, NJ: Prentice Hall.

Yalom, I. (1985). *The theory and practice of group psychotherapy*. New York, NY: Basic Books.

Yartz, A. R., & Hawk, L. W., Jr. (2001). Psychophysiological assessment of anxiety: Tales from the heart. In M. M. Antony, S. M. Orsillo, & L. Roemer (Eds.), *Practitioner's guide to empirically-based measures of anxiety* (pp. 25–30). New York, NY: Kluwer Academic/Plenum.

Zinbarg, R. (1993). Information processing and classical conditioning: Implications for exposure therapy and the integration of cognitive therapy and behavior therapy. *Journal of Behavior Therapy and Experimental Psychiatry, 24*, 129–139.

Credits

Credits listed in order of appearance.

Text: Raimy, V. C. (ed.). (1950). Training in clinical psychology (Boulder Conference). New York: Prentice-Hall. **Text:** Monroe, R. (1955). Schools of psychoanalytic thought. New York: Dryden. **Text:** Meador, B. D., & Rogers, C. R. (1979). Person centered therapy. In J. R. Corsini (ed.), Current psychotherapies. Itasca, IL: F. E. Peacock Publishers. **Text:** Rogers, C. R. (1957). The necessary and sufficient conditions of therapeutic personality change. Journal of Consulting Psychology, 21, 95–103. **Text:** Rogers, C. R. (1942). Counseling and psychotherapy. New York: Houghton Mifflin. **Figure 4:** Based on Smith, M. L., Glass, G. V., & Miller, T. I. (1980). The benefits of psychotherapy. Baltimore: Johns Hopkins University Press. **Text:** Goldfried, M. R., & Davison, G. C. (1976). Clinical behavior therapy. New York: Holt, Rinehart, & Winston. **Table 6:** Prochaska & Norcross, 2007; derived from Bechtold et al., 2001; Norcross, Karpiak, & Santoro, 2005; Norcross, Strausser, & Missar, 1988. **Text:** Lewis Carroll, Alice in Wonderland. **Table 7:** Based on data from Lilienfeld, 2007.

Photo Credits

Photo Credits listed in order of appearance.

Psychology As A Major At Portland State University

What comes to mind when you think of psychology? A lot of people think therapist, psychiatrist or social worker. However, psychology is a diverse science as well as a helping profession. Psychology is a broadly defined field. The psychology major at PSU has been designed to allow students to explore its breadth, as well as focus in on specific areas that interest them. Having a broad education in psychology is important no matter what field of psychology you plan to work in and the major at PSU aims to offer that diversity in its curriculum.

What types of psychology can I explore at PSU? Portland State offers a variety of classes to help students learn more about research and theory as well as the practice of psychology. Courses reflect areas of psychology which include:

Industrial/Organizational Psychology applies psychological concepts and methods to the study of employees, workplaces, and organizations and works towards improving the performance and well-being of the people involved in these settings. Some popular classes offered include: Motivation; Organizational Psychology; and Industrial Psychology.

Developmental Psychology focuses on the development of the mind throughout an individual's lifetime beginning at birth and studying changes as we age. Popular classes include: Human Development; Infant Development; and Child Psychology.

Cognitive Psychology focuses on the mental processes underlying psychology which involve perception, memory, learning, and emotion. Some examples of classes offered at PSU include: Perception; Cognition; and Learning.

Social Psychology focuses on how we human beings think about and relate to each other. It delves into how we influence each other, our beliefs and stereotypes of others and individuals' behavior as a result of these attitudes, beliefs, and perceptions towards others. Some examples of classes offered include: Personality; Self Attitudes and Social Influence; and Applied Social Psychology.

Community Psychology focuses on relationships between individuals and their communities (and in some cases society as a whole). Community psychologists aim to understand and appreciate the attitudes of individuals and their quality of life through their relationship with the community. PSU offers classes that are specific to this branch of psychology as well as classes that overlap with social psychology, for instance: Community Psychology; Group Process; Social Relationships and Groups, and Preventing Sexual Violence.

Clinical/Counseling Psychology focuses on understanding individuals' psychopathogy, strengths, and mental health difficulties as well as the structure, strengths, and dysfunction of couples and families. This area also explores effective therapeutic solutions geared toward individuals and families. Courses offered in the department include: Psychopathology; Counseling; Human Sexuality; Marriage and Family Therapy; and Family Dynamics Through Film.

Other Department Courses: Evolutionary Psychology, Neuroscience, Health Psychology, Sports Psychology, and Research Methods are some of the other options available for students taking classes in the psychology department.

Introductory Psychology As A Foundation For The Psychology Major

The PSU Introductory Psychology course sequence is composed of Psy 200 and Psy 204, two four credit courses that are required for the major. These courses provide a rich overview of the breadth of areas that compose the field of Psychology. Psy 200 and 204 do not need to be taken in a particular order and they are recommended as courses early on in your work within the psychology major. These courses are also helpful surveys of the field for psychology minors, students in related fields, and those interested in better understanding human behavior. A description of the two courses follows below:

PSY 200 PSY AS NATURAL SCIENCE
Covers the scientific foundations of human behavior in areas such as physiological and biological psychology, cognitive, moral, and emotional development, sensation and perception, consciousness, learning, thinking and memory. Also focuses on issues in experimental design and teaches students how to critically evaluate psychological research.

PSY 204 PSY AS A SOCIAL SCIENCE
Explores human individuality and the social context of behavior. Topics include intelligence, personality, motivation, social psychology, coping with stress, and psychological disorders. Describes theories and research findings in the context of social issues and introduces students to challenges of psychological measurement.

Psychology Major Requirements*
Portland State University
College of Liberal Arts & Sciences

All courses taken to satisfy the requirements for a major in psychology, including the mandatory statistics courses, must be passed with a grade of C- or above. Courses taken under the undifferentiated grading option (pass/no pass) will not be accepted toward fulfilling departmental major requirements. In addition to meeting the general university degree requirements, students majoring in psychology must meet the following requirements in the Department of Psychology:

Classes	Credits Required
Stat 243 (Non-Business)	4

Stat 244 (Non-Business)	4	
Psy 200	4	
Psy 204	4	
Psy 321	4	
Psy Electives 410-498	16	
Psy Electives 300/400	20	(excluding courses numbered 399-409)

Total (catalog year before fall 2010)   **56**
Total (catalog year 2010 and after)   **60**

*See the Psychology Department Website for additional details and requirements regarding the Psychology major (at www.pdx.edu/psy/psu-department-of-psychology).

Index